SETTLERS BY THE LONG GREY TRAIL

Harrison

PLATES BY LANMAN ENGRAVING CO.,
WASHINGTON, D. C.

A Contribution to The History and Genealogy of Colonial Families of Rockingham County, Virginia

SETTLERS BY THE LONG GREY TRAIL

Some Pioneers to Old Augusta County, Virginia, and Their Descendants, of the Family of

HARRISON

and Allied Lines

BY

J. HOUSTON HARRISON

GENEALOGICAL PUBLISHING CO., INC.
Baltimore 1984

Originally Published
Dayton, Virginia
1935

Reprinted
Genealogical Publishing Co., Inc.
Baltimore, 1975, 1984

Library of Congress Catalogue Card Number 75-636
International Standard Book Number 0-8063-0664-5

Reprinted from a volume in
the George Peabody Branch,
Enoch Pratt Free Library,
Baltimore, Maryland
1975

Made in the United States of America

FOREWORD

To an appreciable extent this study might be entitled Sidelights on the History of Rockingham County, Virginia, and the Shenandoah Valley. While the theme of the work, so to speak, is strung on the thread of genealogy, much of an historical nature is included.

The title chosen was suggested by a poem I have much admired, descriptive of the route of the old Valley Turnpike which traverses the Virginia region considered. The poem appeared some years ago in one of Dr. John Walter Wayland's guides to the Valley. The author kindly consenting I have taken the liberty to quote several of the verses in the course of these pages. On or near the old trail many of the early Valley of Virginia settlers noticed herein located, and from this region their descendants have scattered throughout the Republic.

As these early pioneers were so closely related with the development of this region, it has been deemed appropriate to sketch something of the beginnings of the Valley settlements in general, more especially of that part of Augusta County that was later formed into Rockingham.

The history of our country is after all the history of her people, and the history of her people is of the same warp and woof as the history of her families. The old pioneers suffered innumerable hardships to build for their children and their "children's children" a free Nation, and regardless of how minor a part any of them may have played in the annals of their time, their names deserve to be remembered, and their records preserved.

There was perhaps no family more intimately associated with the early history of Rockingham County, Virginia, than the Harrisons, and their connections. The county seat itself was named for one of them. Their history affords a typical instance in the study of the great currents of migration that have figured so largely in the development of our country. The trail has been followed with much difficulty.

Much that has been written regarding them has been found erroneous, and it has been necessary to refer continually to original sources, many of which are here cited in full.

As a family these Harrisons seem to have been unnecessarily careless in regard to preserving their records. The early branches widely scattered as the settlement of the great region to the West went forward, and correspondingly all traces of the parent stems have in many instances become lost. For this reason it appears all the more desirable to preserve so far as possible for posterity what traces of connections may yet exist, and be found.

The scope of this work has been widened to include some account of the origin of many of the early Harrison families of Colonial times. Also many English lines have been touched on. It is believed in this connection that more references have been cited as to different families of the name, of separate origins, than has heretofore been included in one volume. Most of the works referred to in the Bibliography at the end of this book contain Harrison references.

In tracing the Augusta or Rockingham family the maternal lines have been handled as fully as the paternal ones. No attempt has been made to confine the work to strictly Harrison families. Many genealogies are involved. Among the lines traced other than Harrisons, in more or less detail, may be named; Bears, Bowmans, Browns, Burkholders, Byrds, Campbells, Chrismans, Conrads, Cravens, Creeds, Davises, Davisons, Deckers, Ewings, Gaines, Gordons, Hannas, Henkels, Hentons, Herrings, Hemphills, Hinkles, Hites, Hollingsworths, Hoppers, Houstons, Howards, Jordans, Keezells, Kennerlys, Koontzs, Lincolns, Logans, McWilliams, Martzs, Mauzys, Monroes, Moores, Newmans, Otts, Pickerings, Prices, Smiths, Watsons, Williamses, Williamsons, Woodleys, and Yanceys, to refer to some of them only; approximately 1,000 families being embraced all told, and 2,000 family names. About 7,200 names borne by individuals other than Harrisons are included.

This work has been entirely a labor of love, pursued at odd times, as circumstances permitted, over a number of years. Some of the lines traced are handled more fully than others owing to more material regarding them coming to hand. In many instances matters of a biographical nature have been included.

Much of the research work was conducted at the Library of Congress, supplemented by studies at the New York Public Library, the Pennsylvania Historical Society Library, the Virginia State Library, the University of Virginia Library, and the Carnegie Library of Atlanta, Georgia, and by personal investigations of the original records at Oyster Bay, Long Island, New York; Trenton and Salem, New Jersey; Georgetown, Delaware; the Virginia State Land Office, at Richmond, Virginia; Orange, Staunton, Harrisonburg, and Winchester, Virginia, and at Lexington and Georgetown, Kentucky.

Through correspondence some investigations of English records were also made at London and Chester, England, and at Dublin, Ireland.

I am deeply grateful for the valuable aid I have received from others, and under "Acknowledgments" I have attempted to convey my thanks.

It is hoped that through these pages some contribution may be made to the fostering of a more lively interest among the rising generation of the descendants of Old Virginia in the history of her Colonial times. To the posterity of Isaiah Harrison, Sr., I commit this work, and entrust it to your keeping.

—J. H. H.

"Rosemont," Alexandria, Virginia.
April 26, 1934.

CONTENTS

See also Historical Contents, Page References to; and "A Word of Explanation" as to the Plan of the Genealogy, pages 123, and 291.

ILLUSTRATIONS

Historical Contents

PAGE REFERENCES TO

* * * * *

* * * * *

* * * * *

HARRISON FAMILIES

English

COLONIAL

EARLY LONG ISLAND FAMILIES

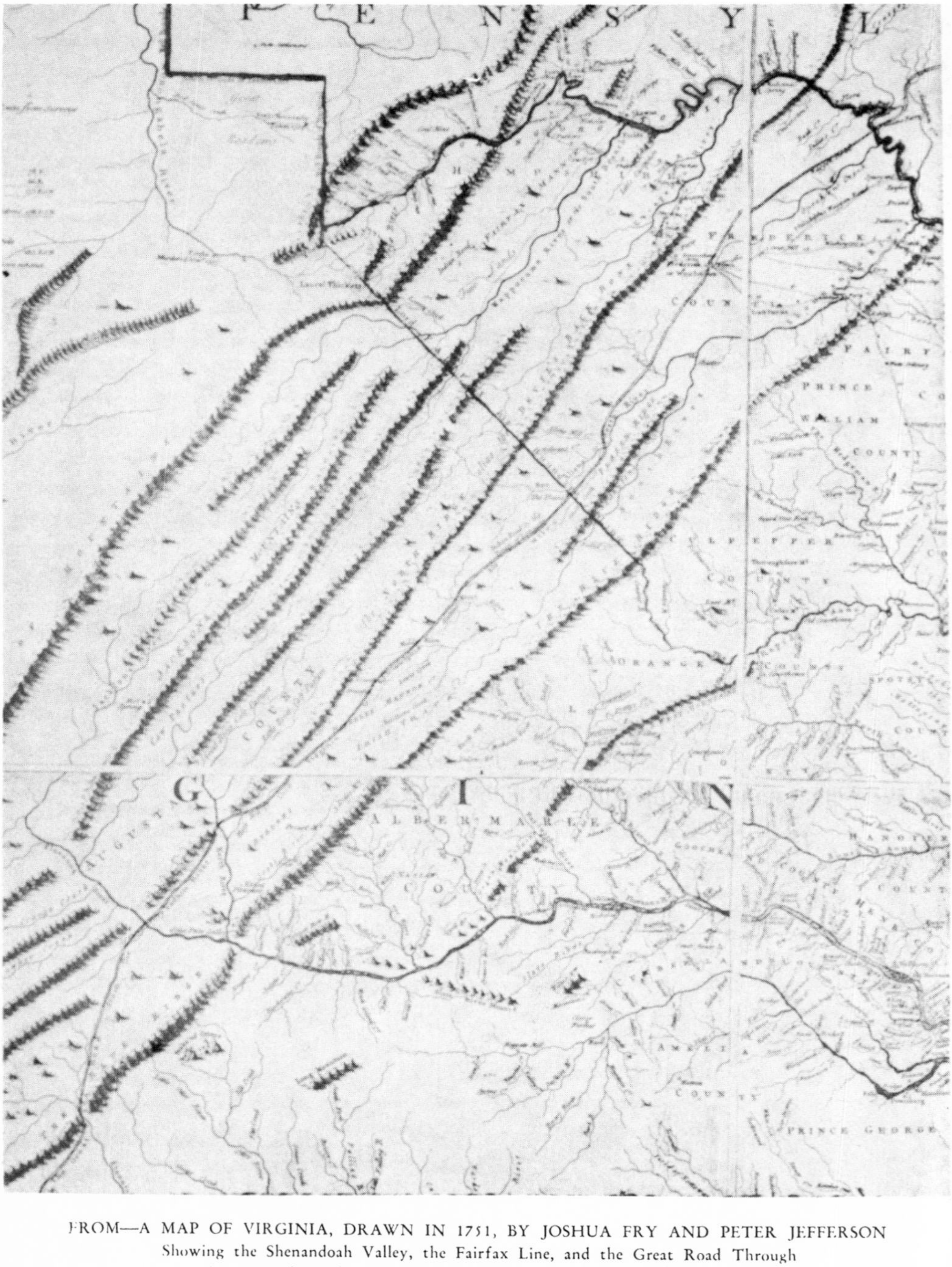

FROM—A MAP OF VIRGINIA, DRAWN IN 1751, BY JOSHUA FRY AND PETER JEFFERSON
Showing the Shenandoah Valley, the Fairfax Line, and the Great Road Through Virginia, the early route now traversed by THE LONG GREY TRAIL.

SETTLERS BY THE LONG GREY TRAIL

CHAPTER I

"O my Valley! Beauteous Valley!
You have seen and you have heard
More than I can feel or utter,
More than lies in human word;
You have watched and you have listened;
And though voice and song should fail,
You'll still cheer and you'll still shelter
All that pass the long grey trail."

—WAYLAND.

THE LONG GREY TRAIL dates back to the period of earliest history of the Valley of Virginia. The pioneers followed it as an old Indian trail. According to traditon, it was first merely a beaten path of the buffalo. As the earliest settlers were mostly from the northern Provinces they passed along this route on their way to their pioneer homes. It crossed the Cohongoroota—now known as the Potomac—at what was first called Pack Horse Ford, later Mecklenburg, and finally Shepherdstown. The old trail when first cleared by these early settlers was called the Indian Road, later they called it the Great Road, and at times, a little later still—before the Revolution—the King's Highway. After the Revolution it is found referred to as the Big Road. Finally the old highway was resurveyed, various details of its route changed here and there, and the roadbed thoroughly modernized by the reduction of grades, and a McAdam surface. This was done by the Valley Turnpike Company, which was authorized by the General Assembly, March 24, 1838. Among other things the preamble to the petition for the turnpike to the Assembly recited, "that the proposed route for the Pike would take the general course of a great Stage Road running from Winchester via Staunton to the Tennessee Roads. This Big Road having been the travel way for a great many years for the wagon line of commerce from Baltimore to Knoxville and other points in Tennessee." In more recent years—1918—the state of Virginia has taken over the turnpike and further improved it, making of it a splendid asphalt driveway from Winchester to Staunton, through the heart of the Valley of the Shenandoah.

The old Indian trail was used by the northern tribes of savages in passing through the Valley on their way to the Carolinas. For a long time prior to the first settlements the northern tribes of Indians—Algonquins and others—had made incessant war on the southern Catawbas, but shortly before the first settlements of the white man these tribes had ceased warring and had established a truce. This truce was observed for a number of years; thus for some time the first settlers were left unmolested.

Governor Spotswood, and his Knights of the Golden Horseshoe, in their discovery of the Valley, and first organized effort to explore it, found the country peacefully sleeping in the warm autumn sunshine, as they looked down on it from the top of the Blue Ridge that memorable afternoon of September 5, 1716. The wild echoes awakened by the sound of the silver trumpet resounded across the hills without any answering war cry of the savage. The resourceful Governor no doubt at once saw the great advantage of speedily inducing settlers to locate in the beautiful region his eyes surveyed. This would mightily help to protect his colony from the encroachments of the French as well as from the treacherous savage. To this end he was instrumental in bringing about later the treaty of five nations of Indians at Albany in 1722. This treaty forbade the northern tribes of Indians from passing through the Colony of Virginia on the eastern side of the Great Mountains without a passport from the Governor of New York. The Virginia Indians engaged not to pass over the Potomac or go westward of the mountains without a passport from the Governor of Virginia. The Valley region became a neutral hunting ground for the northern and southern tribes, and the truce established was shortly followed by explorations, and then by the tide of settlers that began to rise with the coming of Lewis and Hite in 1732.

As the settlements grew, the need for a road increased. The first order for the opening up of a road up the Valley was made by the Orange Court, March 30, 1745. Waddell, in his *Annals of Augusta County,* (page 48) mentions this order, but states that he did not see any futher reference to it revealing when the road was laid out. The futher reference and order is to be found in the Orange County Court Order Book for the years 1743 to 1746, page 331. This shows the route of the old Indian Road as it passed through what was then known as Augusta County. This and Frederick County were taken from Orange, November 1, 1738, but the first court of Augusta was not held until December 9, 1745. The old Order reads as follows:

> "Friday May 24, 1745. James Patton and John Buchanon Gents having viewed the way from Frederick County Line Through that Part of this County Called Augusta according to the order made at Last March Court, made their Report in these words
>
> Pursuant to an Order of Orange Court dated the Thirtieth day of March 1745 We the Subscribers have viewed laid off and Marked the said road mentioned in the said Order as followeth Viz.,
>
> To begin at Thom's Brook at Frederick County line and to go from thence to Benjamin Allen's Ford and Robert Colnells Path and that Henry Fulkinburg Jonas Danton, and Charles Buck and Abraham Strickler be overseers of that Part and that they have for their gang all the Inhabitants between the mountains from Frederick County Line up to Colnell's Path and that the said Road be continued
>
> from Colnells Path Cross Beards Ford on The North River and Alexander Thompson's Ford on the Middle River and that John Harrison and Capt. Daniel Harrison, Robert Cravens, Samuel Stuart, William Thompson and John Stenson be Overseers of the Same and have for their Gangs all the Inhabitants Between the Mountains above Colnell's Path to Thompson's Ford, and that the said Road Continue
>
> from Thompson's Ford to the Tinklin Spring and that James Cathy and James Carr be overseers of that Part and that all the Inhabitants between the Mountains above Thompson's Ford to Tinklin Spring do Clear the Same and that the said Road Continue
>
> from Tinklin Spring to Beverly Manner line and that Patk. Campbell, John Buchanon and William Henderson be Overseers and that all the Inhabitants above Tinklin Spring to Beverly Manner line do clear the same and the said Road Continue
>
> from Beverly Manner Line to Gilbert Campbell's Ford on the north branch of James River and that Capt. Benjamin Borden, Capt. William Evins and Capt. Joseph Culton be Overseers of the same and that the Gangs to Clear the

Same be all of the Inhabitants above Beverly Manner line to the said Gilbert Campbell's ford and that the Road Continue

from Gilbert Campbell's ford to a ford in the Cherry tree Bottom James River and that Richard Wood, Gilbert Campbell, Joseph Sapley and Joseph Long be overseers and that the Inhabitants betwixt the said Rivers Clear the same and that the said Road Continue

from the said Cherry tree Bottom to Adam Harmon's on the New or Woods River and that Capt. George Robinson and James Campbell and Mark Evans and James Davison be Overseers of the same and that all the Inhabitants between James River and Woods River Clear the Same and that

A Distinct Order be given Every Gang to Clear the Same and that it be Cleared as it is already Blazed and laid off with Two notches and a Cross.

Given under our hands this 8th. Day of April 1745. James Patton, John Buchannon.

Whereupon it is Ordered that the said way be from henceforth established a Publick Road and that the Persons mentioned in the said Report are hereby Appointed Surveyors of the Several Districts therein also mentioned and it is Ordered that they Cause the said Road to be Cleared and that all the male Tithables mentioned in the Said Report do attend and Obey the Respective Overseers in Clearing the Same as it is already Blazed and laid off with two knotches and a Cross and when cleared to keep the same in repair and it is further Ordered that the said Several Overseers do Set up points of Direction if Necessary according to law."

Same Order Book page 441. "Sept. 28, 1745. Ordered that the inhabitants of the county on the South River from Frederick County Line to the upper Hawksbill Mountain including John Maggot Between the Sherando Mountains and the Blue Ridge be excepted from working on the Road through Augusta called the Indian Road."

This shows that the first name given to the old highway was the Indian Road. Besides giving the names of a number of the early settlers along the old trail the Order identifies part of the first boundary between Frederick and Augusta counties as Tom's Brook. A graphic picture of the days of the first travellers and settlers along the old trail is given by Charles Campbell in his History of Virginia. In referring to the early history of the Valley region, he says;

"One who would become acquainted with these matters must travel back a century or more; he must witness the early adventures leaving the abodes of civilization, and singly or in families, or in groups composed of several families, like pioneers on a forlorn hope, entering the dark, dreary, trackless forest, which had been for ages the nursery of wild beasts and the pathway of the Indian. After traversing this inhospitable solitude for days or weeks, and having become weary of their pilgrimage, they determined to separate, and each family taking its own course in quest of a place where they may rest, they find a spot such as choice, chance, or necessity points out; here they sit down; this they call their home—a cheerless, houseless home. If they have a tent, they stretch it, and in it they all nestle; otherwise the umbrage of a wide-spreading oak, or mayhap the canopy of heaven, is their only covering.

"In this new found home, while they are not exempt from the common frailties and ills of humanity, many peculiar to their present condition thicken around them. Here they must endure excessive labor, fatigue, and exposure to inclement seasons; here innumerable perils and privations await them; here they are exposed to the alarms from wild beasts and from Indians. Sometimes driven from home, they take shelter in the brakes and recesses of the mountains, where they continue for a time in a state of anxious suspense; venturing at length to reconnoitre their home, they perhaps find it in a heap of ruins, the whole of their little peculium destroyed. This frequently happened. The inhabitants of the country being few, and in most cases widely separated from each other, each group, fully occupied with its own difficulties and distresses, seldom could have the consolation of hoping for the advice, assistance, or even sympathy of each other. Many of them, worn out by hardships inseparable from their new condition found premature graves; many hundreds, probably thousands, were massacred by the hands of the Indians; and peace and tranquility, if they came at all, came at a late day to the few survivors.

"Here we have stated in a few items the first cost of this country, but the half has not been told, nor can we calculate in money the worth of the sufferings of these people, especially we cannot estimate in dollars and cents the value of the lives that were lost."

The Indian road as laid out "to begin at Tom's Brook at Frederick County line" joined there a continuation of the trail ordered opened through Frederick County in 1743. This county having established its court November 11, 1743, had jurisdiction of the settlements north of Tom's Brook at the time of the Orange court order; hence the beginning at this line.

The old order for the road appears remarkable in point of distance covered as very nearly one hundred and seventy-five miles were ordered opened at one time. In general, the route approximated that of the present Valley Pike from Tom's Brook to Staunton, and of the Lee Highway from Staunton to Buchanan, (Looney's Ferry, in Cherry Tree Bottom, 1751), and apparently of the same highway from Buchanan to Shawsville, continuing from there by way of Blacksburg , (Draper's Meadows, 1748), to New River, on the route to Eggleston Springs, (near which Adam Harmon is found a settler about 1750).

As the Valley Pike and the Lee Highway are one and the same road from New Market to Staunton, the old road may be said to have followed the general route of the present Lee Highway from New Market to a short distance west of Shawsville. In the long section between Cherry Tree Bottom and New River no stations are mentioned in the order, thus the route in this region is drawn very sketchily. An alternate route from Cherry Tree Bottoms to Draper's Meadow (or near the latter) by way of present Fincastle, was later a part of the Wilderness Road, Fincastle being a station on the trail, and while it may be that the old road of the court order, as first laid out, led this way, it is certain that by 1751 the "Great Road" ran approximately via the present Lee Highway from Buchanan to a point about eight miles north of Roanoke, where it led off to Carolina.

For the section of the Indian Road traversing the Shenandoah Valley the name was changed to the Great Road before 1751. The route of the Great Road is shown on Fry and Jefferson's map of Virginia of 1755 (drawn in 1751), whereon it is described as "The Great Road from the Yadkin River thro Virginia to Philadelphia distant 435 Miles," with a further notation along its route, in the region west of the Massanutten "Indian Road by the Treaty of Lancaster."

The road began at a point known as Unitas, about present Winston-Salem, and after crossing the North Carolina-Virginia state line at or near the junction of what are now Rockingham and Stokes counties (N. C.), crossed the Blue Ridge mountain where the Staunton (now Roanoke) river pierces it. Leaving the mountain the road skirted the course of the river and Tinker Creek, to the above mentioned Highway.

Following along this closely to the James, it crossed the river at "Looney's Ferry," and bearing somewhat to the west of the highway at the Natural Bridge, and to the west of the course of the North River (a branch of the James) from the region of what is now Lexington, crossed the North River a small distance west of Hays (Mill) Creek, near present Rockbridge Baths. A few miles further north it crossed the creek, following its waters to today's Middlebrook neighborhood. From here it led directly to "Staunton Courthouse," where it again joined the route of the highway, and continued on down the Valley, varying little at any point from the line of the Valley Pike, to "Frederick Town or Winchester."

From Winchester it paralleled the waters of the Opequon to the Potomac River, crossing the latter at "Williams Ferry," now Williamsport, Maryland. A second route from Winchester (styled Philadelphia Waggon Road) led via present Shepherdstown, and after crossing the river at this point turned northward along "Audetum Creek" (Antietam Creek) to join the above route. From the creek, at about present Hagerstown, the road led east over the Blue Ridge (crossing this on or near the Maryland-Pennsylvania state line) to York, Pennsylvania, a short distance beyond which it crossed the "Susquesahanock," at about present Wrightstown, and from there continued through Lancaster to Philadelphia.

Such was the route of one of the most important early highways that contributed to the building of the nation; and over it travelled, from the days of Daniel Boone onward, a great host of pioneers to the South and West. Volumes have been written, and many more may be written regarding the famous characters of history who have passed by this old route through the Valley of the Shenandoah, and yet the story of their lives will ever remain new. Truly, the early settlers of the Orange court order built greater than their dreams when with their "Gangs" they cleared the link between Thom's Brook and the waters of the James, and directed "that the said way be from henceforth established a Public Road."

The first station after Tom's Brook mentioned in the order is Benjamin Allen's Ford and Robert Colnell's Path. The ford was just south of present Mt. Jackson, and crossed the North Fork of the Shenandoah, which on the old map is called "Ben Allens or North River." Before crossing the river the road crossed "Allens Mill Creek," and after crossing the river continued over Smiths Creek. The first and second named streams are now crossed in this region by bridges, the present route eliminating the crossing of Smiths Creek, along which Colnell's Path apparently ran.

A mile or so south of what is now New Market the old road crossed "Lord Fairfax his Boundary Line," (now the line between Rockingham and Shenandoah counties), and as shown by Thomas Lewis' Journal of the survey of this famous line in 1746—in which he notes the distance of the Indian Road from Smiths Creek—the road crossed the line at the same point as the Valley Pike today. Other points along the road between New Market and Harrisonburg may be identified by old deeds yet in existence, and by traces of the old roadbed, (see later mention), showing that there was little variation, when any, of the Great Road from today's line of the Pike in this region.

After Colnell's Path the next points named in the court order are Beard's Ford on the North River and Alexander Thompson's Ford on the Middle River. Beard and Thompson were settlers residing in the present neighborhood of Mt. Meridian, where the two rivers (branches of the South Fork of the Shenandoah) join. The year following the order Thompson sold a part of his land to Beard, mentioning the ford, and Cave Hill nearby. From Middle River the road led to Tinkling Spring, near today's Fishersville, in the region to the east of Staunton.

In the territory now between Harrisonburg and Staunton the Indian Road thus ran somewhat to the east of the Great Road shown on the early map. The latter crossed the North River between Muddy and Naked Creeks (see land patent to David Frame, 136 acres, 12th May, 1759, mentioned in Deed Book 14, page 135, Augusta County), and the Middle River to the west of Lewis' Creek, keeping about on line of the present Pike, while the Indian Road traversed the Cross Keys, Mt. Meridian, New Hope, and Tinkling Spring neighborhoods of today, a few miles to the east of the Pike.

From Tinkling Spring to Beverly Manor line, the next station, was the shortest link named in the court order. This line crossed today's Pike near Greenville, in which region the old road of the court order also crossed the Manor line, and apparently a little futher to the southwest joined the route of the Great Road, to follow this to the neighborhood now between Brownsburg and Back Creek, (Rockbridge County). Here it seems to have left this route and continued to Timber Ridge, from which point it led about on the line of the present highway to North River, crossing this at Gilbert Campbell's Ford.

The ford was at what is now the town of Lexington. Campbell bought his land of Benjamin Borden through a deed recorded at Orange, July 26, 1742, (Deed Book 8, page 184), the land being located on the south side of the river at the juncture with Wood's Creek (now Wood's Run), and bounded on the north by the river, and on the east, for a short distance back from the river, by the creek. The tract consisted of 389 acres, which following his death in 1750, was sold in two tracts, the first by his widow Prudence and his son George, in 1765, the second by his son Charles, in 1769, to Andrew McClure, and Joseph Walker, respectively. His executor was Andrew Hays, who resided on Hays' Creek, several miles further up the river.

At or near the ford the old road was again in the region of the Great Road, which route it evidently joined to follow this to the James, as before traced. The shifting of the crossing of the Great Road over the river from that of the Indian Road, to the point shown on the map, was doubtless due to the early growth of settlements, and to the rise of the milling industry in the region to the west of Campbell's Ford; and too, to the access given to the settlers on the Calf Pasture to market and court. That the route of the Indian Road along Mill Creek, to the north of present Lexington, was also known as the Great Road, is shown by a road petition of 1751, the year of the map, wherein a plea was made for a road from Joseph Long's Mill, to James Young's Mill, and to Wm. Hall's on North River, and into the "great road" on James Thompson's plantation. (See—Morton's *History of Rockbridge County*, page 162). Thompson was located on Mill Creek as early as 1748, and was one of the witnesses to Campbell's will, 29th August, 1750.

After the organization of Augusta County, and the fixing of the site for the court house, it became highly desirable that the county seat be on the route of the main highway; thus the variation of the line of the Great Road from that of the Indian Road in the Staunton community. Upon the organization of Rockbridge County in later years a further modification seems to have occurred in the region to the north of Lexington, whereby a more direct route between the two towns was afforded, incidently returning to the original crossing of the river. The spreading fame of the Natural Bridge no doubt played its part in deflecting the line somewhat also in the region to the south of the town.

Numerous orders following the establishment of Augusta court are found mentioning the Indian Road in relation to other roads. Among these, one of the earliest appears in Order Book No. 1, page 68, under date of 20th June, 1746, appointing

"Alexander Herron overseer from Robert Cravens to Samuel Wilkins, and Thomas and Jeremiah Harrison from Cravens to the Indian Road, Capt Scholl to lay off the precints." The road embraced in this order ran from the "Court House" to the Indian Road, and was manifestly the section of the Great Road that connected the present cities of Harrisonburg and Staunton. This is shown by a court order of August 20, 1747,—same order book, page 225—"Robert Cravens and Samuel Wilkins appointed overseers from the Court House to the Indian Road near said Cravens vice Alexander Herron, Thomas Harrison, Jeremiah Harrison."

Robert Cravens was one of the number of the first "Gentleman Justices" appointed by Governor Gooch in issuing his Commission of the Peace, October 30, 1745, establishing Augusta court. He was a neighbor of "Thomas Harrison's."

That "Thomas Harrison's" was an early point of juncture of the county roads with the Great Road, and that Harrison was located on the old trail, is revealed by a record of January 2, 1761. On this date various settlers presented a "petition for a road from Adam Reader's Mines to Isaac Robertson's, from thence to Widow Wright's Mill, from thence to Thomas Harrison's in the Great Road to the Court House." The road thus petitioned for was authorized in 1767—see Order Book XI, page 65.

A little later is found under the date of November 23, 1767—Order Book XI, page 432,—another order in regard to the old trail reading as follows—"Andrew Greer appointed surveyor of (the) highway from John Harrison's at (the) Big Spring to the County Line." By this time the need for a further improvement of the road was evidently felt.

The Big Spring referred to is now known as Lacey Spring, and here occured another juncture of the early county roads with the Great Road. On June 20, 1769, Thomas Moore was appointed overseer of this section "vice Andrew Greer, from County Line to Fork of Road by John Harrison's,"—See Order Book XIII, page 212. The county line mentioned was that between Frederick and Augusta counties; by this time the line was the same as the dividing line between "his Majesty (King George II) and Lord Fairfax," now the Rockingham-Shenandoah county line.

In the original order of 1745 establishing the Indian Road, the section "from (Robert) Colnell's Path Crossing Beard's Ford on the North River and Alexander Thompson's Ford on the Middle River," crossed the present county of Rockingham. For this territory "John Harrison and Captain Daniel Harrison, Robert Cravens, Samuel Stuart, William Thompson and John Stenson" were appointed surveyors and overseers to "Cause the said Road to be cleared" and to "have for their Gangs all the Inhabitants (male Tithables) Between the Mountains above Colnell's Path to Thompson's Ford." Thomas and Jeremiah Harrison, and Alexander Herron, are mentioned, as previously noted, in orders of 1746 and 1747, and at least John Harrison, Thomas Harrison, and Robert Cravens have been shown to have been living along the old trail at this time.

John, Daniel, Thomas, and Jeremiah Harrison, were brothers, and the four were brothers-in-law of Robert Cravens and Alexander Herron. All were pioneers, and all settled in that part of Augusta which at the time of the Revolution was erected into Rockingham County.

CHAPTER II

The Origin of the Harrison Family of Rockingham

SEVERAL WRITERS have given different accounts as to the origin of the Harrison family of Augusta and Rockingham. Waddell, the historian of Augusta, states that "the Harrisons of Rockingham were intimately connected with the Smiths, but the early history of the former family is involved in much obscurity. They are said to have come from Connecticut, and to have been descendants of Thomas Harrison, one of the judges who condemned King Charles I, to death." Boogher, in his Gleanings of Virginia History—which has been widely quoted—in speaking of the founder of Harrisonburg, with whom he heads the family says; "The publisher is of the opinion that Thomas Harrison descended from one of the early Maryland immigrants, some of whom are known to have settled in Virginia, in what was then Stafford County, about 1700; after 1730 Prince William County, which at this date embraced the counties of Fairfax, Loudoun, and Fauquier; this territory being the natural route to Augusta County where about 1743-4 he removed and settled on Cook's Creek." According to Peyton's *History of Augusta County*, "Thomas Harrison is claimed by some of his descendants to belong to the James River Harrisons. Some writers claim that he was an emigrant direct from Chester County, Pennsylvania, as there is no proof of his being a James River Harrison. Moved first to what is now Loudoun County, then Augusta County, near Leesburg. This being the natural route to Augusta where he moved to in 1743-4 and settled on Cook's Creek."

Augusta County was largely settled by the Scotch Irish who began to arrive in great numbers early in 1740, or shortly before. These immigrants were from the province of Ulster in Ireland, and many records of such settlers proving their importation are preserved at Orange court. No such records are found however at Orange in regard to the Harrisons, Cravens, or Herrons. The Smith family, mentioned as being intimately connected with the Harrisons, was a distinguished one founded by Capt. John Smith who proved his importation at Orange on the 26th of June, 1740, he having come from Ireland through Philadelphia with his wife Margaret and their sons Abraham, Henry, Daniel, John and Joseph, together with Robert McDowell. Capt. Smith settled first in Chester County, Pennsylvania, from which he removed to Augusta. This no doubt accounts for Peyton's statement in regard to Thomas Harrison, as above. Boogher, in speaking of Robert Cravens, says, "He is believed to have first immigrated into Orange County (later Augusta) with the Smiths and McDowells, about 1740."

The Augusta court records throw scarcely any more light on the origin of the Harrison family than those of Orange court. Chalkley, in his Abstracts from the Records of Augusta County, (on page 475, Vol. I), under Judgments Suffered, November, 1764, gives an abstract in regard to a lawsuit, as follows: "Herron vs. Harrison (Samuel Harrison vs. Alexander Herron) Alexander Herron's answer says; That complainant removed from the province of —— at the time and for the purpose mentioned in his bill, and moved to Virginia and settled on Linville's Creek, where he took up 400 acres. Sometime afterwards defendant came to Virginia, and hearing of complainant, proceeded to that settlement, thinking that as they were acquainted in the government from which they removed, complainant could direct him to a convenient tract of land. Complainant allowed him to take up an entry of his own of 200 acres, adjoining his own land. At that time the best lands on the creek could be purchased for three pounds per hundred acres. That at the time of Braddock's defeat complainant took it into his head to remove to Carolina. Robert Harrison was complainant's nephew."

An exhaustive effort was made to find the original papers in this case with the hope that the name of the blank province could be supplied, but unfortunately these papers could not be found. The abstract shows that Samuel Harrison and Alexander Herron came from the same province to Virginia. The Robert Harrison mentioned was a son of Daniel; thus Daniel and Samuel are identified as brothers.

In one branch of the Rockingham family an old tradition in regard to the origin of the Harrisons has been handed down from generation to generation. Recently there has come to light, as a partial copy of a letter written during one of the administrations of President Benjamin Harrison, a version of this tradition, which is given by the writer, Miss Elizabeth Harrison, 1841-1902, as follows;

> "Our ancestors came from England and settled on Long Island (but I do not know the date, I think they must have come to Virginia about 1700.) Tradition says there were fourteen brothers [who] came over together, and it is I think very likely that some settled in Connecticut.
>
> "There were three brothers [who] came to the Valley; their father started with them and died on the way in Page County and was buried there near the Shenandoah River. I do not know that he was one of the original fourteen, but I suppose he was of the same family [that] settled on the James River in Eastern Virginia, and [there was] one I think who went south.
>
> "Of the three that came to the Valley, one settled where Harrisonburg now is and from whom it was named. I think his name was Thomas. One settled at what is now known as Linville, a village on the Valley Branch of the B. & O. R. R. The other one, Reuben, my great great grand-father settled near here at a place called Lacey Spring, a very large spring. His son Reuben, my great grand-father, took up some land near there, built a cabin, had a bear skin door &c. &c.
>
> "It seems that he was engaged to be married to a lady on Long Island but knowing that she had been brought up in a more luxurious home than he was able to offer, he concluded not to go back after her, but went down to the Potomac River and married his first cousin, Lydia Harrison, so there must have been some of the same family settled there."

The writer goes on to state that she believes that the first Harrisons of Rockingham were Presbyterians, and mentions Benjamin Harrison, the signer of the Declaration of Independence, and "the present President." Her letter was in answer to an enquiry of some one located apparently in New Jersey. It may be noted here in passing, that the name of her great great grand-father should have been given as John instead of Reuben, and it is likely that the number of the original brothers had by her time been magnified from four to fourteen.

In an interview a few years before his death, a brother of the above, the late William C. Harrison, kindly furnished some additional details of the old tradition as obtained from his father, whose father in turn was born only four years after John Harrison, the above pioneer, died; these are substantially as follows;

The immigrants landed on either Rhode Island or Long Island on their arrival from England. Five brothers are said to have come to Virginia together, one of whom "stopped off east of the Blue Ridge," and settled there. Their route to the Valley lay from what is now Alexandria, Virginia, through Thornton's Gap. There were sixteen in the party that crossed the Ridge, brothers and half brothers with their families, and among them they brought over the mountain the first wheeled vehicle, a cart, that is said to have appeared in the Valley. At first they camped a while along the Shenandoah River near where the "White House" in Page County now stands, but the climate proving malarious they either went around the Massanutten mountain or crossed over it into the section of the Valley now known as Rockingham County. Here the party divided up and camped at the various springs where they finally settled. Of the four brothers, one settled at the Big Spring, now Lacey Spring, one at Krotzer's Spring, now Linville, one at the head spring of Cook's Creek, now Harrisonburg, and one at what is now the town of Dayton; all settling at very large springs.

Some versions of this account locate the fourth brother at Flook's Spring. Of the Harrisons previously noted, John, Thomas, Daniel and Samuel, it has been observed that the first settled at the Big Spring, and that the second located at the present town of Harrisonburg, which is at the head spring of Cook's Creek, both of these points being on the old Indian trail, the later Great Road. Captain Daniel settled a short distance southwest of Thomas on the head spring of a branch of Cook's Creek where the town of Dayton now stands, and Samuel, the last mentioned, located on the head waters of Linville's Creek, a few miles north of Daniel. Thus the four brothers of the tradition are identified.

John Harrison, the oldest of these brothers, signed his will July 30, 1769, and died in 1771, his will being proved at Augusta court, May 21st, of this year. The key to the origin of the Rockingham family is given in one short paragraph near the end of his will; this paragraph reads as follows—

> "and I furthermore ordain my said Executors that they provide a Baptist Minister if they can so do with Conveniency to Preach my Funeral Sarment if noon of them is to be had that then they Provide some other Christian Minister for it as Proposed [and] for that Service to pay him twenty Shillings."

This shows that undoubtedly the testator was a member of the Baptist church. The Big Spring at which he settled is a head spring of Smiths Creek, and at an early date a Baptist church was organized on Linville's Creek several miles to the west, composed of members from families settled in this neighborhood and on Smiths Creek. This church was called the Smith and Linville's Creek church. This was the first Baptist church organized in Augusta County and the second one gathered west of the Blue Ridge. An account of this church is given in Robert Semple's *History of the Rise and Progress of the Baptists in Virginia,* published in 1810, and also in *A General History of the Baptist Denomination in America,* by David Benedict, which was published at Boston in 1813. According to the latter authority, Volume II, page 28; "The Smiths and Linville's Creek church, afterwards called Smith's Creek, is said to have been constituted also in 1756. There were some Baptist families in this place as early as 1745, eleven years before the church was organized, but from what church they emigrated, we are not informed, only it is stated that one John Harrison, wishing to be baptized, went as far as Oyster Bay on Long Island, in the State of New York, to obtain an administrator. As there were Baptist churches and ministers much nearer, the presumption is, that he, if no others, had removed from that place."

Semple's history indicates that the Smiths and Linville's Creek church kept a journal of its meetings. After several years of patient search the old journal or session book of the church was finally located, and from this many interesting items are gleaned.

The book is in an excellent state of preservation, but time has turned the leaves yellow and worn away the edges in places. A brown limp sheepskin back was used for the binding, and the first part of the book is in an excellent handwriting, no doubt that of John Lincoln, the clerk of the church, who was appointed to copy the record from an older book in 1788. Frequent reference to this journal will be made in carrying on this work.

This pioneer church was organized, according to the old church book, "this sixth Day of August in the Year of our Lord one Thousand, seven Hundred, and Fifty-six, To join together in a Gospel Church Relation." The book begins with an introduction and prayer, and then follows a lengthy "Covenant", closing with the last paragraph as follows;

"We therefore hoping and relying upon Almighty God, for Grace, Wisdom and Spiritual Understanding, Guidance, and Ability, to adorn this our Profession, and covenant Promises; and to perform our Duties, each to the other; and to bless us with Grace, suitable to our Privileges, that he in his Goodness & Mercy hath bestoneed upon us in his House; through Jesus Christ our Lord. To whom be Glory in the Church, throughout all Ages, World without End. Amen . . .

Subscribed on the Day aforesaid,

John Alderson.
Samuel Newman.
John Harrison.
William Castle Berry.

Jane Alderson.
Martha Newman.
Margaret Castle Berry.

. . . .

"Which sd. Persons were all that were incorporated in the Church at its first Constitution; but John Thomas having been baptized before the sd. Constitution, and his brother James Thomas, the Day after Constitution; the next Day being appointed for the celebration of the Lords Supper, the sd. Persons came under the solemn Ordinance of Laying on of Hands, and were received into full Communion and Fellowship in the Church; whose Body was then composed of nine Members; and our first Communion consisted but of Eleven Brethren and Sisters. Rees Thomas & Mary States, belonging to other Churches in Pennsylvania, craved thransient Communion, and were admitted. Immediately after constitution, the Church gave her Call to Samuel Newman to officiate in the Office of a Deacon, which he was to act in upon Trial; which Call he accordingly accepted of. They then called him to be Clerk of the Church, and diligently to keep the Church Register by her Order; and then appointed the second Sabbath, in each Month, to be the Day of Communion, and the Seventh Day of the Week before it, to be the Day of carrying on Church Business. And, likewise Ordered that there should be a Register taken of Gods Mercy towards us, in sending Means here to raise a Church, which is as followeth viz.

"SAMUEL NEWMAN and his WIFE, being Members of Montgomery Church, in the county of Philadelphia, was the first Members of any Baptist Church that Settled here. But in some small Time after he was settled, John Harrison senior, being convinced of his Duty, to come to the holy Ordinance of Baptism, went for it somewhere towards New York, to a Place called Oyster-Bay; but was received then a member of no particular Church: But by a Certificate of his Baptism, was recommended to be received, or associated into any Church of that Order, where God in his Providence should shew most convenient for him. In all this While, there was no Minister of that

Denomination came here. The next family of that Denomination, (whereof the Head was a Member,) was Rees Thomas, and he settled on Linvilles Creek.

"The next Member was a Sister viz. Mary Newman the Wife of Jonathan Newman, belonging to the Church of Christ in Southhampton, in the County of Bucks; as Rees Thomas belonged to the Church of the same Order in Cumry Township, Lancaster County. About this time Mr. Samuel Eaton, (the first Baptist Minister in Orders,) visited these parts, and preached at old Mr. Harrisons, the only Disciple he knew to be in the Place. The next in Order was Mr. Benjamin Griffith, who came on purpose to visit the aforesaid Brother Samuel Newman. The next after him was our Reverened Brother whom God at last was pleased to send as his Instrument, to settle this Church.

"Then God was pleased to visit the Inhabitants of Smiths Creek, Linvilles Creek, and North River of Shenandoah, (the Places where now the Church is built,) by Mr. John Gano, (a faithful servant of his,) who was received by the Love and Likeing, of almost all sorts of People. After him the Revrd. Mr. Alderson, visited again his second Time; and then began to conclude to come and Settle; and bought Land, and then came, and through the Grace of God, was instrumental in gathering the Church, by whom also She was constituted, and the first Pastor of the Church of Christ, at Smiths and Linvilles Creeks, in Frederick and Augusta County's, as in the Covenant afore written specified.

"Thus was the Labours of those Gentlemen aforenamed, for the Space of Eleven Years, from the First Setler, as above named, and about one Year before the Constitution of the Church. William Castle Berry and his Wife came and settled on Muddy Creek, in Augusta County, being both Members of Newbritain Church, and of these were the Church at first Built. And others there were none, till gathered by the preaching of the Word, where of was only two, which were added to the Church at the first Communion, as hath been already related. Our Revnd. Pastor Mr. John Alderson, and Mrs. Jane Alderson his Wife, being both Members of Newbritain Church in the County of Bucks; moved their Residence, and came to us the same Spring before we were Constituted &c.

"Thus have I noted, First, the First coming here of the Religion of the Baptists, in the first Settlers. Secondly, who they were. Thirdly, the Coming of the Word, by the first Baptist Ministers. Fourthly, who they were. Fifthly, when they were constituted into Church Order. Sixthly, by whom they were constituted. Seventhly, who it was God in his great Mercy and Wisdom, chose as his Instrument, to carry on his Work in the Church, for their first Minister. And, Eighthly, When She actually, as a Church of Christ, entered into her milatary State.

"And now Oh! Father of all Mercies, own us in Christ, for thine, who hath purchased us with his own Blood. Let us Oh! God of Love, rest assured of thy Love, in our dear Redeemer, the Son of thy Love, the Lord our Righteousness. Let us experiance thy Love to us, by a Sense of our Love flowing to thee; and to one another, in Christ our Head; who is Love, according to his Command given us. John 1, 4 & 21. And this Commandment have we from him, That he who loveth God, loves his Brother also. From which Text I shall conclude with the following Poem, on the Nature of Love; having briefly shown our Rise here &c. . . . ."

It may be noted that while the above account states that Samuel Newman and his wife were the first members of any Baptist church that settled in the neighborhood, this does not necessarily mean that John Harrison was not an earlier settler. It is established that Harrison was referred to as an old man at the time of the organization of the church and that at an advanced age he made the long hazardous journey from Augusta County, Virginia, to Oyster Bay, Long Island, for baptism, "some short time" after Newman's settlement in 1744, and before 1756.

Benedict, above referred to, states that "At Oyster Bay on Long Island a church arose in early times, but the exact date of its origin cannot be ascertained. As early as 1700 the gospel was preached here by one William Rhodes, an unordaind minister who fled hither to avoid persecution, from whence it does not appear. By his ministry a number were brought to an acquaintance with the truth among whom was one Robert Feeks, who was ordained pastor of the church in 1724. In 1741, Elder Feeks wrote to his brethren in Newport as follows—'There has been 17 added to our little band in about three months.' When Mr. Feeks was advanced in years this church obtained for its pastor one Thomas Davis, who laboured with them several years, and then removed to other parts. After him a young man by the name of Caleb Wright, one of their members, engaged in the ministry. (The day set for ordination he died). The church then had visiting ministers until Mr. Benjamin Coles who was one of their number began to labour among them. Mr. Coles was born in the township April 6, 1737, began to preach when young, spent six years with the church at Stratfield, Conn., seven with the church at Hopewell, and two at Scotch Plains, both in New Jersey; the rest of his ministry was spent in Oyster Bay where he died August 10, 1810." (See Vol. I, p. 543.)

The first pastor of this church, the Rev. Rhodes, was a native of Chichester, England, and had migrated to Rhode Island shortly before coming to Oyster Bay. He died in 1724, and Mr. Feek was ordained the same year by Elders from Rhode Island. The Rev. Feek was a son of a Quaker, according to Thompson's History of Long Island, which relates that "the first Baptist church was erected in 1724 and still remains (1839) a curious relict of that age. It is about 20 feet square, with quadrangular pointed roof, and no longer used for 'lodging folks disposed to sleep', having been lately converted into a stable. The present church was built in 1801."

Benedict mentions that the Rev. Davis was born in the parish of L'lanfernach, and the country of Pembroke, Wales, in 1707. He arrived in America, July 27, 1713, was ordained at Great Valley, Pennsylvania, and died at Yellow Springs, this state, February 15, 1777. (Vol. I, p. 572). Wrightman, in his history of the Oyster Bay Church, states that he was settled in Oyster Bay in 1745, as a collegue of Mr. Feek, and returned to Pennsylvania in 1748.

The Rev. Wright died October 27, 1752. As Rev. Feek was pastor of the church from 1724 until he "was advanced in years", he no doubt died shortly before Mr. Wright was to be ordained, and was thus the pastor at the time the ordinance of baptism was adminstered to John Harrison, of the Linville Creek Church.

In the journal of his third voyage, De Vries relates that on June 4, 1639, he anchored "in the eastern haven, a commodious haven on Long Island. This haven is in the Island upwards of two miles wide. We found fine oysters there, from which the Dutch call it Oyster Bay." Oyster Bay, Long Island, was first permanently settled in the year 1653. The first transfer of land was by Indian deed dated this year to Peter Wright, Samuel Mayo, and the Rev. William Leveredge. The land was purchased from the Matinecocs. Of these proprietors, Wright was the only one who actually settled or remained there, but others soon followed. The proprietors were from Sandwich, on Cape Cod Bay, an old Plymouth Colony settlement, and from the first were determined to be subjects of England. In the spring of 1640 an attempt at an English settlement had been made at Oyster Bay, but this was broken up by the Dutch, who had first settled in New

Netherlands at Fort Orange, a few miles below Albany, in 1615, and on Manhattan Island in 1622 or 1623.

The territory of Long Island was settled by towns or townships, and these were not combined into counties until after the conquest. The east end of the island was settled under English authority, while the west end was settled by English people under the permission of the Dutch government. The two extremes of the island were settled first, the western, near Brooklyn about 1625—the first deed for land in Brooklyn is said to be dated in 1639—and the eastern, on Gardiners Island, by Lyon Gardiner in 1639. The first English settlements were under authority granted by Charles I, in a patent for Long Island to William, Earl of Sterling, "Secretary of the Kingdom of Scotland," the settlement on Gardiner's Island being under a purchase confirmed by the agent of Sterling. South Old was commenced in October of the next year on a tract of land purchased from the Indians by the Governor of New Haven. All of the principal towns on the island are said to have been started within a space of forty years, and in the territory afterwards erected into Queen's County, settlement was made at North Hempstead in 1643, at Flushing in 1645, at Oyster Bay in 1653, as stated, at Jamaica in 1655, and at Newton in 1656.

Oyster Bay was from its beginning within English territory. The four New England colonies, Plymouth, Massachusetts, Hartford, and New Haven formed a union for their mutual protection on May 19, 1643, and at Hartford, September 19, 1650, a treaty was signed to settle the boundary between the Dutch and the English; "upon Long Island a line was run from the wester-most part of Oyster Bay, and a straight and direct line to the sea shall be the bounds betwixt the English and Dutch there, the easterly part to belong to the English, and the westermost to the Dutch." The line was run north and south dividing the island into two halves; Oyster Bay being within the eastern half. When the town came to be settled a dispute arose with the Dutch governor in regard to the westernmost limits of the bay. In common with other English towns on the island the settlers formed a voluntary connection with Connecticut, and in 1657 men from both Oyster Bay and Hempstead sat as jurors at New Haven. (See *Early Long Island, A Colonial Study,* by Flint, p. 190).

In May, 1660, the inhabitants of Oyster Bay made a declaration of their loyalty to Charles II, and early in 1662 they again asserted their allegiance and determination to resist any other authority. They then formed a closer alliance with New Haven, and to some extent acknowledged the latter's judisdiction. The Charter of Connecticut was received in October of this year, and the liberal provisions it contained caused the several English towns to be desirous to perpetuate their voluntary connection with this province.

In 1664 the English captured New Amsterdam, and on March 12th, of the same year, Long Island was conveyed by Charles II to his brother James, the Duke of York, who would not suffer it to be dismembered by the terms of any other charter, or by agreement of any section of the inhabitants with any other colony. Thus the connection of the several English towns on the Island with Connecticut ended. (See *A Sketch of the First Settlement of the Several Towns on Long Island,* by Silas Wood, 1824.)

That the early Harrisons of Augusta and Rockingham were familiar with some of these matters will be further developed in the next Chapter.

CHAPTER III

Isaiah Harrison of Oyster Bay, and Some Early Long Island Families

ISAIAH HARRISON first appears upon the town records of Oyster Bay under date of 1687, "January ye 2nd." In those days the new year did not begin until the month of March; hence by our present calendar the date would now be written January 2nd, 1688. Later in this year occured the short revolution in England, during which the unpopular King James II was forced from the throne. From the entry in the old town book, Harrison was evidently a newly arrived resident. Subsequent records show that at this time he had undoubtedly only shortly before reached his majority; thus he was born within the first five or six years following the Restoration in 1660, and during the reign of King Charles II. The entry occurs in Book B, page 7, and reads as follows;

"Oysterbay At a town Meeting 1687: Jan. ye 2d Given & granted to Isaiah Harrison one whole Right of Comonage in & upon ye old purchase of ye Town Wthall prilivedges thereto belonging as other such Pticular rights have; on this Condicon that if he ye said Isaiah do live & Continue an Inhabitant in This Town of Oysterbay untill full seven yeares next & Imediately after ye date hereof be fully compleat & ended then the sd right shall be & remaine to him ye said Isaiah & to his Hires forevr: But if ye said Isaiah shall at any time wthin ye sd seven yeares remove himself from this to any other Town the sd Right of Comonage shall clearly & freely returne to ye Town againe & neither he nor his Heires shal have any Title or Claime to it by verture of this Grant: but if he ye sd Isaiah shal happen to dye wthin ye sd seven years ye sd Right shall be & remaine to his wife & her Heires forever; This done by ye ffreeholdrs of ye Town & by them ordered to be entred.

By John Newman, Recordr."

(See, *Oyster Bay Town Records, Vol. II*, p. 338.)

By this grant Isaiah Harrison was made a freeholder of the town. The nature of the grant appears to be that of a sort of bonus; that he was not required to wait seven years before participating in the affairs of the town as one of the freeholders is evident from subsequent records. Mention is made of the old purchase; this was the first purchase of 1653 from the Indians. On the 29th of September, 1677, a patent of confirmation for the lands previously bought from the natives was obtained of Governor Andros in which the proprietors were named as Henry Townsend Senr, Nicholas Wright, Thomas Townsend, Gideon Wright, Richard Hacker, Joseph Carpenter and Josias Latting, "on ye behalf of themselves and their Associates ye ffreeholders & Inhabitants of ye Said Towne their Heirs Successors and Assignes." This patent was recorded by order of the Governor at the request of the inhabitants 20th November, 1685. As these men were at the time of the patent the influential townsmen of Oyster Bay, no doubt it was through the inducement of one of these, or some member of their families, that Isaiah Harrison came to locate in the town.

Prior to Isaiah's settlement at Oyster Bay no other Harrisons appear on the town records. Other Harrisons are found in the vicinity however, and across the sound there had been settled, at New Haven, for a number of years a family of this name, but the many detailed accounts given of this clan make no mention of an Isaiah. While these details appear to preclude any direct descent of the Oyster Bay settler from the Connecticut family, numerous names appear in common among the descendants of Isaiah and those of the immigrant to New Haven, and as such similarity of names frequently is found in related families, it may be that some relationship existed between the two settlers.

The Connecticut family was founded by Richard Harrison, who came to New Haven with his grown children from West Kirby, in Cheshire, England. He took the oath of allegiance at New Haven, August 5th, 1644, and removed to Branford, where he signed the divsions of land July 1st, 1646, and died October 25th, 1653. His children were; Richard, Jr., Thomas, Mary or Maria, Elizabeth, and probably Samuel and Ellen. Of these; Richard, Jr. m. Sarah Hubbard and removed with his family in 1666, with the Rev. Abraham Pierson, to Newark, New Jersey, where he was one of the founders of the town. Richard, Jr's. children were; John d. 1676, Joseph b. 1649, Samuel b. 1652, Benjamin b. 1655, George b. 1658, Daniel b. 1661, and Mary b. 1664. Richard, Jr. died at Newark prior to 1691. Thomas, the son of Richard, Sr., was born about 1630; he m. first, February 1655-6, Dorothy, the widow of John Thompson and had, Thomas, Jr. b. 1656-7, and Nathaniel b. 1658. Thomas, Sr. m. second, the widow Elizabeth Stent, whose first husband had died on the way to America, and had; Elizabeth b. 1667-8, Mary b. 1668-9, John b. 1670-1, Samuel b. 1673, and Isaac b. 1678. Samuel, who was probably the son of Richard, Sr., does not appear to have left any children; he married Sarah Johnson and died at Newark in 1705. (See, Collections of the New Jersey Historical Society, Vol. VI, *Proceedings Commemorative of the Settlement of Newark*, p. 119, and "*Five Generations of Connecticut Harrisons*," by Mrs. Francis Harrison Corbin, 1916.)

"The Harrison family on Long Island" has been referred to in a general way by some writers, similar to references frequently found to the Connecticut family. Unfortunately details are not given in regard to the members of the Long Island family, and thus it is that such a family is difficult to identify. An instance of this occurs in Lee's Genealogical and Personal Memoirs of Mercer County, New Jersey—Vol. I, page 207—as follows; "John Hinchman Jr. was the son of John Hinchman, the progenitor of that family, and Sarah Harrison, the daughter of Samuel Harrison the progenitor of the Harrison family who came from England and settled on Long Island."

John Hinchman and Samuel Harrison both settled in Newton township, Gloucester County, New Jersey. Hinchman was born at Flushing, Long Island, and located his first survey in Gloucester in 1699, and died in this county in 1721 leaving a will. His father, John Hinchman, who also had a wife Sarah, was settled at Flushing as early, at least, as the "1st day of January 1685," when he and his wife signed a deed for land there to their son Robert. (See, Liber A, Queens County Deeds, p. 58). This John appears to have been the one who previously had resided at Oyster Bay, according to a deed made by one John Hinksman for land he sold there in February, 1659. Clement, in his *Sketches of the First Emigrant Settlers in Newton Township, Old Gloucester County, West Jersey*, in speaking of the emigrant to Gloucester, says; "His wife was Sarah, a daughter of Samuel Harrison, whom he married while a resident of Long Island." The presumption is that Harrison also at one time resided at Flushing. Clement relates that the Harrisons removed to Gloucester from Long Island about 1700; however, Samuel Harrison owned land at Gloucester as early as 1688-9. His name appears on "a Plat of the River Delaware before the town of Gloucester, 1689," as the owner of a lot. "J. & W. Harrison" are also given as owners of another lot there. (See, *Reminiscences of Old Gloucester,* by Isaac Mickle, 1845, p. 36.)

Samuel Harrison was a mariner; he died in Gloucester in February, 1703-4, without leaving a will. His wife Sarah was granted letters of administration on her husband's estate March 1, 1703-4. The will of William Hunt, of Gloucester, September 3, 1688, names Hunt's daughter Sarah Harrison, and the will of Thomas Penston of the same county, August 26, 1697, mentions Samuel Harrison's sons William and Samuel, Jr. The widow, Sarah, afterwards married a Bull; she died in August, 1744, leaving a will naming children Samuel and William Harrison, and grandchildren Joseph Harrison, John Hinchman, William Hinchman, Eilzabeth Hinchman, Samuel Clement, and Priscilla Harrison. (See, *Abstracts of New Jersey Wills,* Vols. I and II.)

At the time of Isaiah Harrison's settlement at Oyster Bay there was a John Harrison located at Flushing. Queen's County, Long Island, which at this time included the towns of Flushing and Oyster Bay, was established March 1, 1683. A patent for the town of Flushing was granted March 23, 1685, and among the proprietors named in this were Thomas Willett, John Lawrence, Sr., John Harrison, John Hinchman, Joseph, John and Samuel Thorne, and John Talman. (See a copy of the patent in *Flushing, Past and Present,* by Rev. C. Henry Mandeville, 1860, p. 19.) John Harrison was made High Sheriff of Queen's County on December 1, 1692. In 1698 he is given in a census list of the inhabitants of Flushing, along with his wife Elizabeth, and children William, Edward, Henry, Elizbeth, and Ann. (See, *Documentary History of New York,* by Christopher Morgan, p. 664.) John Harrison and his wife also appear within the years 1692 to 1702 on some of the town records of Jamaica, the county seat, where, no doubt, he had a residence in connection with his office as High Sheriff. On these records the name Harrison is spelled Harresson at times. (See, Vols. I and II, *Records of the Town of Jamaica,* by Long Island Historical Society). He was the owner of many tracts of land scattered from Long Island through the Jerseys to Pennsylvania. On July 22, 1697, he applied for a patent to a tract at Oyster Bay, having previously purchased the land from the Indians. Between the years 1697 and 1708, he disposed of his Oyster Bay holdings, and the deeds made give his location as Flushing in 1697, as Perth Amboy in 1701, as Elizabeth Town in 1702, and as Rockyhill in 1708; the last three places being in East Jersey.

The "purchase" or deed for the town of Harrison in Westchester County, New York, was among his various holdings. This town is just across the sound from Long Island and was named for him. The town was first settled largely by Quakers, many of them being from Flushing and the vicinity. John Harrison sold his interest in the purchase May 23, 1702, to Major William Lawrence of Flushing, and from this time he seems to have centered his main activities in New Jersey, where he was a prominent character in the settlement of East Jersey as an agent for the proprietors in buying up large tracts of land from the Indians and disposing of them to numerous settlers. One of these Indian purchases was made September 6, 1701, for 17,000 acres, the deed for the land being recorded at Jamaica, and signed by him December 14, 1702, in which he is styled "John Harrison of East Jersey." (See, *Records of the Town of Jamaica,* Vol. II, p. 130.) His son John, Jr. was a Captain of the militia and seems to have been associated with him. He succeeded him as an agent for the proprietors and as a member of the Provincial Assembly.

John Harrison, Sr. made his will while on his death bed at Perth Amboy, February 8, 1709, and died there three days later. (See, Vol. 10, p. 55, Unrecorded Wills,

Trenton, N. J.) The will names his wife Elizabeth, and four daughters, Elizabeth, Ann, Mary and Sarah, the last three under age, and sons, John, William, Edward, and Henry, the last under age. He mentions his lands, dwelling house, houses, tenements and meadows in Perth Amboy and states that he confirms the lands already given by deeds to the first three of the above named sons. He appointed his son John, Jr. as executor.

Of the children above; John, Jr. m. Elizabeth, the widow of Thomas Higgins, about 1705, and died at Perth Amboy, 1724-5, leaving his wife, and a son Benjamin under age; Mary m. Samuel Moore, "carpenter," June 2, 1718; Anne b. 11 mo. 14, 1696, m. July 6, 1721, Richard Allison b. in England 3rd mo. 20, 1695-6; Edward died in 1716 leaving wife Ruth, and daughters, Sarah and Elizabeth; Henry b. 1691-2, d. 1730-1, leaving wife Grace and children John, Henry, Thomas, Ann and Elizabeth; William m. Gawennetta, the daughter of John Campbell; she died in 1758, and he, before this time. (See, *Abstracts of New Jersey Wills,* Vols. I-III, *History of Elizabeth Town, N. J.,* by Rev. E. F. Hatfield, 1868, p. 260, *Contributions to the Early History of Perth Amboy and Adjoining County,* by Wm. A. Whitehead, p. 86, *History of Hunterdon and Somerset Counties, N. J.,* by James P. Snell, p. 735, *Biographical and Genealogical Notes from the Volumes of the New Jersey Archives,* by Wm. Nelson, p. 13, *New England Historical and Genealogical Register,* Vol. 22, p. 344, *New York Genealogical and Biographical Record,* Vol. 42, p. 29.)

As Long Island was first settled by townships which were much later combined into counties, the oldest records generally of the island are the town records. From an examination of numerous such records available, it appears that the first Harrison settlers on Long Island were John and Isaiah. No record of Samuel on Long Island had been found beyond what has been given, and his name does not appear in the index of deeds to Queen's County, but as the town records of Flushing were destroyed during the Revolution this, and the fact that he was a mariner, may account for the lack of further details. There appear to be many common circumstances in regard to these three Harrisons; they all make their first appearance on the records at about the same time; that is, John at Flushing in 1685, Isaiah at Oyster Bay in 1687, and Samuel at Gloucester in 1688. They were evidently all young men at this time and of about the same age; John's widow was living in 1724, and Samuel's died in 1744, and their known children were mostly all under age in 1698 when the census of Flushing was taken. All three settled in Quaker communities and all were allied with Quaker families. Bolton, in his *History of Westchester County, New York,* states that John Harrison, the patentee of the town of Harrison, had a brother Samuel and that they were the sons of John Harrison, who apparently resided at Newton, Long Island, in 1655, whence he removed to Flushing. But as this author goes on to name the daughters of Samuel, as Hannah, who married Joshua Cornell, and Sarah, who married Gilbert Palmer, and then mentions their sons as living (1848), clearly a generation or two were overlooked, particularly as Joshua Cornell was not born until 1726. (See, *Genalogy of the Cornell Family,* by Rev. John Cornell, p. 288.) A Samuel Harrison married Sarah, the widow of Soloman Palmer, October 8, 1719, she was the daughter of John Ferris of Westchester County, and may have been the mother of Sarah to whom Bolton was referring. (See, *Ye Historie of Ye Town of Greenwich,* Conn., By Mead, p. 535.) A John Harrison appeared in a list of the settlers of Newton in 1655-6, as given in Thompson's *History of Long Island,* of 1839, but the last edition of this book (1918) gives this list under the date of 1686, and as Riker in his *Annals of Newtown,* 1852, mentions no Harrison family of this town, it appears that John of Flushing, of 1685, no doubt owned land in the adjoining township of Newton in 1686.

An examination of the inventories of the movable estates of John Harrison of Flushing and Perth Amboy, and of Samuel of Gloucester, shows that they were possessed of considerable personal property for their day and time, and that much of this evidently came from England. Among John's effects were such items as three dozen puter plates, thirteen puter dishes, three puter tankards, two brass kettles, one half dozen red leather chairs, a dozen cane chairs, a dozen matted chairs, six tablecloths and four dozen napkins, three counterpaines, one chest of drawers, three looking glasses, books, four large pictures and sixteen smaller ones, five large trunks and one smaller one, one "Howse" clock, two pair money scales, plate 110½ ounces valued at 44 pounds two shillings, one negro woman, on Indian boy valued at thirty pounds, a gun, sword and pistol. Samuel's effects included brass kitchen ware, a dozen leather chairs and half a dozen "Girky work" chairs, carpet, pillow cases, three dozen napkins and several table cloths, three dozen plates outside the puter ones enumerated, five night looking glasses, a great flagon, a black walnut table, one pair brass "hand" irons, three mariner's compasses, two quadrants, a pair of dividers, a watch, one safe, three trunks, a case of drawers, one clock, books, and plate (china ware) to the amount of twenty eight pounds, iron for building a vessel, one negro man, and a woman, and two boys, two small copper stills, and two guns. Both inventories mention numerous other pieces of furniture, such as beds, tables, and various kitchen utensils. As the items noted were scarce in the colonies as early as 1703-9, it would appear that they were too numerous to have been inherited here and that John and Samuel Harrison were undoubtedly immigrants. As has been observed, Lee states that Samuel was an immigrant. (See, Vol. 9, p. 15, *Unrecorded Wills of N. J. at Trenton,* and *Calendar of N. J. Wills,* Vol. I, p. 213.)

Isaiah Harrison came to Oyster Bay as a "Black Smith"—

"By hammer and hand
All arts do stand,"

So ran the motto of the ancient Blacksmith's Guild, of England, and from the trouble the townsmen of Oyster Bay had previously been put to in order to "entertain" a blacksmith among them, evidently Isaiah was, by repute, a skilled craftsman in his art. Some idea of their difficulty in this regard is related in *A Memorial of John, Henry, and Richard Townsend,* by W. A. Townsend, (1865), as follows: "Their chief trouble was the want of a competent blacksmith. They no doubt required an accomplished artist, who could keep their iron ware of all kinds as good as new for twice its natural life, and then contrive something to answer the purpose out of the remains. The first as mentioned was John Thompson, whom the town receives as blacksmith and allots to him a home lot which if he die in the Town is to belong to his heirs, but if he leaves is to return to the Town. they paying for his improvements . . . . Suddenly there was a change; at a Town Meeting, in 1677, the Constable, Thomas Townsend, was ordered to "give notice to John Thompson to resine up the land, which the Town formerly gave him, for a breach of covenant, being then entertained as the Town Smith, or to answer the Town's complaints the next session at Jamaica". . . . Soon after that Abraham Alling, or Allen, was accepted as smith. There were other negotiations with blacksmiths, showing that for many years the settlement of one in the village was a public concern" (p. 35). According to another writer, Oyster Bay in its early days was a point of shipbuilding for vessels in the coastwise trade among the colonies. This may account in some measure for the town's solicitude in regard to blacksmithing. That the craft was highly regarded is evidenced from the town records.

Hist. of Lawrence Fam

A blacksmith in those days furnished the main supply of hardware for building and farming, and was thus the forerunner of the hardware merchant of the present day. (See, *Historical Genealogy of the Lawrence Family,* by Thomas Lawrence.)

The year following Isaiah Harrison's election as a freeholder of Oyster Bay he bought one hundred acres of land on which he made his residence. The deed for this land is found recorded in Book B, page 173, of the town records, and reads as follows:—

"TO ALL CHRISTIAN people to whom this prsent writing Shall come or in any wise ApPtaine Be it known that I John Davis of Littleworth in ye Bounds of Oysterbay on Long Island in ye Pvince of Newyork for & in ye Consideration of an Exchange of Land Lying & being at Littleworth aforesd wth John Wright of Oysterbay, which Land was fformerly Jacob Brookins and ye Sd John Wright hath Confirm'd ye Same to me undr his hand & Seal by a Deed of Sale Bearing Date ye Same Day of these prsents to my full content & Satisfaction and for other good Causes & Considrations me ye Sd John Davis especially Moving HAVE GIVEN, GRANTED, Alienated, Made over, Bargained, Sold & Confirm'd And by these presnts I ye Sd John Davis do Give, Grant, Alienate, make over, Bargaine Sell & Confirme unto John Wright aforesd a Certaine Tract, or Pcel of Land Lying & being near Suckscalls Wigwam So Called it being Pt of ye Last General Purchase by ye Inhabitants of Oysterbay of ye Indeans of Matenacocke Lands as by ye Indians Deed bearing Date ye Nineth Day of January 1685 doth at Large appear wch Sd Tract of Land was Granted to ye Sd Davis on a Good and valuable Consideration by ye purchasers of ye Sd Land; And was Surveyed & Laid out to ye Sd Davis by ye Surveyors of Oysterbay aforesd as it appears in ye Records of Town Grants & Surveys in ye Book B: ffoleo ye 6: and ffoleo ye 7: And Bounded as ffolloweth it Begins at Suckscals Wigwams Hollow on ye South Side of Caleb John & Edmond Wrights Land, Ranging west two hundred Rod to a white Oake Tree Marked, and Southward by ye Sd Hollow, Eighty rod, And is ye Same Breadth at ye west end as at the East: Having ye Sd Wrights Land on ye North The Sd Hollow on ye East, And on ye South & West ye Comons, Including and Containing in ye Sd Bounds, one hundred Acres, be it More or Less and is Wthin ye Bounds of ye Pattent of Oysterbay aforesd Together wthall my Right Title & Interest Claime & Demand wtsoever wch I ye Sd John Davis now have or wch any or either of my Heirs, Executrs Administratrs or Assignes may hereaftr have of, to or in ye Sd Land wthall Issues & Pfits from thence arising or Growing or in any wise ApPtaining TO HAVE & TO HOLD unto him ye Sd John Wright his Heires & Assignes all & Singular ye Sd Hundred Acres of Land wth its Appurtences to ye only PPuse & behoofe of him ye Sd John Wright his Heires & Assignes forever And ye Sd John Davis hath put ye Sd John Wright into a Lawfull & peaceable possession of all & singular ye prmises by ye Delivery of these prsents, And ye Sd John Davis doth for himself his Heirs, Executrs & Administratrs & Assignes further Convenant & agree to & with ye Sd John Wright yt it Shall & may be Lawful for him ye Sd John Wright his Heirs Executrs or Assignes quietly & peacably to have hold occuy, possess & enjoy all & Singular ye prmises forever without the Lawful Let hindrance or Interuption of him ye Sd John Davis his Heirs Executrs or Assignes or any other Pson or Psons Lawfully Claiming for, by or undr him or any or either of them Notwithstanding any former Gifts, Grants Bargains or Sales wtsoever IN WITNESS whereof I have hereunto Set my hand & Seal the sixteenth Day of January in ye year of our Lord one Thousand Six hundred eighty eight:

Signed Sealed & dd in prsence of
John Newman; Job Wright.

John Davis O
The marke of
Mercy (X) Davis O

Be it known by these prsents that I John Wright ye wthin Mentioned in this wthin written Deed, have Assigned, Madover & Confirmed, And by these prsents does Assigne Make over & Confirme this wthin written Deed wch beareth Date ye Sixteenth Day of January 1688: unto Isayah Harrison of Oysterbay in Queens County on Long Island in ye pvince of New Yorke wthall ye Right, Title & Interest wch I ye Sd John Wright my Heires Executrs or Assignes Shall or may have to ye Land therein Mentioned in every Clause & Convenant thereof as ffully & Amply as it is made unto me from ye Within Named John Davis for him ye Sd Isaiah his Heirs Executrs or Assignes to have hold occupy posess & enjoy forever; he having Satisfied & pd me for ye Same Sixty pounds in Merchantable pay of this Pvince to my full Content & Satisfaction In Witness whereof I have hereunto Set my hand & Seal the Sixteenth Day of January one thousand Six hundred eighty & eight.

Signed, Sealed & dd in prsnce of	John Whight	O
John Newman	The (M) marke of	
Job Wright.	Mary Wright	O

This Assignmt is written on ye Backside of ye Deed above entred in this page."

(See, *Oyster Bay Town Records,* Vol. I, 1653-1690, Published by order of the town, p. 530.)

This deed shows that Isaiah's 100 acres of land was located at Suckscall's Wigwam and was a part of the general purchase from the Matenacocke Indians of January 9, 1685, which was included in the patent for Oyster Bay. The land was first laid out to John Davis who exchanged it January 16, 1688, for land of John Wright's at Littleworth which had formerly belonged to Jacob Brookins. Wright then sold it the day of the exchange to Isaiah Harrison for sixty pounds current money of New York. Suckscall was an Indian chief; his wigwam was located at what is now known as Brookville (Wolver Hollow), Long Island, on the North Hempstead Turnpike, a few miles southwest of the town spot of Oyster Bay. As the land had only been purchased from the Indians three years previous to its sale to Isaiah Harrison, and as there is no mention in the deed of a dwelling house, no doubt Isaiah was the first white man to live on it. It was characteristic of the Quakers that they always bought their lands from the natives, and while there is no record that Isaiah himself was a Quaker, yet the community was in general largely of this sentiment, and there appears to have been no molestation by the Indians during Isaiah's possession of the land.

In 1690 the freeholders of Oyster Bay made a second division of their land. This division recorded in Book B, Fol. 11, reads as follows;

"Be it known by these prsents that wheras ye ffreeholdrs of this Town of Oystebay have made an agreemt at Town Meetings & otherwise to make a New or second division of their Lands in ye Bounds of ye old Pchase of ye Town to each man a Lott of ffifty Acres or Twenty acres or wch they shall see cause; Now thereupon wee ye sd ffreeholdrs whose names are undrneath subscribed do by these prsents bind ourselves our Heires Executrs & Administratrs ffirmly by these prsents each to other to stand by one another agt all or any Pson or Psons yt shall make any Claime or Demand to ye Lotts yt shall be Laid out on ye acct aforsd or yt are already Laid out, and to bear our equall charge in all Law suits, trouble, charge Incumbrance or other expence that shall happen in ye

Defending our right in ye sd Lotts in Generall or in Pticular to wch wee subscribe our hands the third day of May in ye yeare of our Lord 1690:

Nathaneell Coles
Thomas Weekes
Edward White
Joseph Ludlam
Daniel Townsend
Peter Wright
Jno Rogers
Joseph Dickinson
William Simpkins
Robert Chain
Jno Pratt
Simon Cooper
Thomas Willitts
Wm. Frost
Isaiah Harison
Wm. ffry
Jno Newman
Aaron fforman
Isaac Daughty
Thomas Miller
Wm. Buckler
Robt Cooper
Thomas Cheshire
. . . . *(eighteen others).*"

This shows that Isaiah Harrison was a freeholder of the town. There were forty-one subscribers to this division and no doubt all the names of the freeholders at this time were recorded; their family names were as given above. (See page 355, Vol. II, *Oyster Bay Town Records.)*

That Isaiah's land was at a juncture of the early highways is revealed by the following entries in Book B of the town records—

Fol. 10a. 4. "Laid out to Isayah Harrison 5 Acres of Land wch he Bought of John Newman it being Pt of ye New purchase of Matenacock Lands Lying neer Suckscall Wigwam adjoyning to ye Highway going from Matenacock to Jerico on ye North 25 pole; On ye west adjoyning to a Haighway of ffour rod wide Leading to Westbury 34 pole; on ye south to ye Comons 25 pole, and on ye East to ye Comons 34 pole April 23d 1692:

P Thomas Weekes, John Townsend } Surveyors.

Fol. 10a. 5. "Laid out also to Isayah Harrison a piece of Land in ye Old purchase of Oysterbay Town Lying Neer Suckscalls Wigwam: The first Boundr is a Red Oake Tree Markt by ye Highway Leading to Oysterbay Town; Ranging by sd way 50 pole North-east to a red Oake tree markt, thence southeast 80 pole to a White Oake Tree markt Thence Southwest 50 pole to a Black Oake Mrk'd, Thence 80 pole to ye ffirst Boundr Including wthin sd Bounds 25 Acres; this belongs to ye 2d division
Aprill 23: 1692

P Thomas Weekes, John Townsend } Surveyors.

Fol 14a. 17. "Old purchase Novembr ye 10: 1695:
Laid out to Isaiah Harrison a peece of Land on ye Northwest side of ye Highway from sd Isaiahs House to Oysterbay, the first Boundr begins by a Hollow on ye northwest sid of sd Highway, Thence by sd Highway Northeast 100 rod, thence Northwest by ye Comons 82 rod & half, thence southwest by ye Comons 100: rod, Thence s[outh] East

by ye Commons 82 rod & half to ye first Boundr Containing 51 acres of La[nd] of ye second division Leaving sd Highway 6: rod wide

By John Townsend & John Townsend } Surveyrs"

(See pp. 354, 374, *Oyster Bay Town Records,* Vol. II.)

By these three entries eighty one more acres were added to Isaiah's home land at Suckscall's Wigwam. The first mention of his house occurs in the last entry. In addition to the lands so far noted, he purchased of Daniel Townsend two tracts; the first on April 25, 1699, for seven pounds six shillings, "One Right of Land In the New Purchase of Oysterbaye;" and the second on August 30, 1700, for four pounds ten shillings, "all that of a Certaine two thirds parts of a whole Right of Land and priviledge In the new Generall purchase of Oysterbay." Also, on February 18, 1700, he bought of Hope Williams "of Jerico In ye Bounds of Oysterbay," for six pounds six shillings, "a Certain whole Right of Land in ye New Generall purchase of Oysterbay," the deeds being on record for these tracts in Book C of the town, pp. 2, 54 and 69. (See, *Oyster Bay Town Records,* Vol. II, pp. 396, 471, 492.)

In the ancient town Book B, of Oyster Bay, fol. 19a, there occurs a quaint old record reading as follows;—

"Isaiah Harrison the Sone of Isaiah Harrison was Borne
In Oysterbay ye 27th Day of September Annoq Domini 1689

"John Harrison the Sone of abovesaid Isaiah Harrison Was
Borne in Oysterbay the 25th Day of September Annoq Domini 1691

"Gideon Harrison the Sone of the abovesaid Isaiah Harrison was
Born in Oysterbay ye 25th Day of June Annoq Domini 1694

"Mary Harrison the Daughter of ye said Isaiah Harrison was
Born in Oysterbay ye 25th Day of May Annoq Domini 1696

"Elizabeth Harrison the Daughter of ye said Isaiah Harrison
was Borne In Oysterbay ye 30th of March Annoq Domini 1698.

"These are the Sons and Daughters which the said Isaiah
Harrison begat by Elizabeth Harrison His wife the Daughter
of Gideon Wright of Oysterbay aforesaid Deceased."

Immediately before this record occurs a similar account of the birth of three of Daniel Weeks' children, and a statement of the death of Daniel Weeks, who died the 23rd of March, 1698. These records are sandwiched between the regular land entries; the one immediately preceeding the birth records being an entry of land laid out to Samuel Macoune. This last entry is undated, but the next following, which is for land laid out to Daniel Coles Junr, bears date July ye 27th Annoq Domini 1698. The above record of Isaiah's family was therefore entered in the town book between May 10th and July 27, 1698. (See, *Oyster Bay Town Records,* Vol. II, 1691-1704, p. 390.)

This account shows that Isaiah Harrison married Elizabeth, the daughter of Gideon Wright, and that they had the five children, Isaiah, John, Gideon, Mary, and Elizabeth, whose birth dates are given.

Gideon Wright died in June, 1685. Among his children was a son Gideon, Jr., who died in 1722. Gideon, Jr. married Margaret, the daughter of John Urquehart, of Oyster Bay, in 1702, and had, among others, a son Zebulon who married Clemence, the daughter of Rev. Robert and Clemence (Ludlam) Feke, of Oyster Bay, in 1734.

The Rev. Feke was the pastor of the Oyster Bay Baptist church at the time John Harrison of Augusta County, Virginia, was baptized, as before related. John Harrison, the son of Isaiah, was thus a first cousin by marriage of two of Rev. Feke's children.

John, of Augusta, had a son Zebulon Harrison, who no doubt was named for his cousin Zebulon Wright, who died at Oyster Bay in November, 1746. Of the other Harrisons whose birth dates are given above, the court records of Augusta County, Virginia, show that Isaiah (Jr.) settled in Augusta before 1748, and by 1750 had "removed to Carolina"; thus the brother of the tradition, "who went south," is identified. A Gideon Harrison, probably a son of the above, died in Augusta County in 1761; the appraisment of his estate being recorded, and an administrator appointed, this year. Mary Harrison married Robert Cravens, before noted, and they also settled in Augusta County. The Rev. John Craig, of the Old Stone Church, of Augusta, baptized Elizabeth Herison, "an adult person," July 27, 1744, and it is presumed that she died in Augusta unmarried.

Isaiah Harrison, of Oyster Bay, married Elizabeth Wright in 1688. The ancient town record says that she was "the Dughter of Gideon Wright of Oysterbay aforesaid Deceased." This was written in 1698, while Gideon Wright died in 1685. As there is nothing in the records, immediately preceeding the mention of Elizabeth, that refers to Gideon's death, and as subsequent records show that she must have died about this time—1698—, no doubt the word "Deceased," refers to her, instead of to her father, owning to the peculiar style of phraseology used.

John Harrison, of Augusta, returned to Oyster Bay between 1744 and 1756 to be baptized; there he had been born, there he had grown up in childhood, there many of his relatives were living, there ministered the venerable Feek, two of whose children had married his first cousins, and who was no doubt an old friend of the family, and there his mother had died and was buried. Thus the tender ties of sentiment and association explains his selection of the old town as the place of his baptism, and the undertaking of the long difficult journey at his age from Virginia to Oyster Bay and return. That there were other Baptist churches and ministers much nearer Augusta County is shown by Benedict, before quoted.

The above date of Isaiah's marriage to Elizabeth Wright, and the date of the death of her father, is found in *The Wright Family of Oyster Bay*, a valuable and charming work by Howland Delano Perrine, 1923. (See p. 71.) The author also gives the above years of birth of Isaiah's children, and from this volume much valuable history of the Wright family is gleaned.

Gideon Wright was born in the decade following 1630. His father, Peter Wright, migrated with his (Peter's) two brothers, Anothony and Nicholas, from Norfolk County, England, landing at Sangus—now Lynn—in the Massachusetts Colony, in August, 1635. From here they removed two years later to Sandwich in the old Plymouth Colony, where various records of them may be found on the ancient town books. From Sandwich the brothers came to Oyster Bay, Peter being the first brother to settle at the new location. Some account has been given of him previously and, as stated, he was among the original proprietors of the town and the only one of its first settlers to remain in it permanently; in fact, he was practically the founder of the town. Perrine traces the ancestry of the Wright emigrants back through sixteen generations to one Gilbert de Lyn, an old feudal lord, of the time of Henry I, (1100-1133).

Peter Wright, the eldest of the three brothers, was born within the years 1590 to 1600, in Norfolk county, England. His wife was Alice, whom he married in England prior to 1635. Peter died at Oyster Bay between 1660 and 1663. His widow married Richard Crabb by the latter date. Crabb came to Oyster Bay about 1660. He died there in 1680, and his wife died there February 24, 1685. Peter Wright and his wife Alice had eleven children, viz.; Gideon, born 163—, died June, 1685; Job, born 1636, died September 13, 1706; William, born 164—, died 1648; Mary, born 1642, died 1688; Hannah, born 1646, died March 3, 1675; Sarah, born February 11, 1648; Mordecay, born 1649, died 1650; Peter, died February 28, 1651; Adam, born March 20, 1650, died 1698; Elizbeth, born 1653-4, died before 1677; and Lydia, born 1655, died before 1707. Of these children, Job married Rachel, the daughter of John, 2nd, and Susannah (Harcourt) Townsend; Mary married Samuel Andrews, of Oyster Bay, in 1663, and Lydia married Isaac Horner, also of Oyster Bay, in 1683-4, and both of these last two couples removed to Burlington county, New Jersey, in 1685; Sarah married Edmund Wright; and Elizabeth married James, the son of John 1st, and Elizabeth (Montgomerie) Townsend. Quakers

Peter Wright and his family were Quakers; his daughters being particularly prominent members of the Society of Friends. Perrine (pp. 48-50) furnishes many interesting details as to the persecution of the Quakers by the authorities of the Massachusetts Colony. The execution of Mary Dyer, a Quakeress, June 1, 1660, aroused deep indignation, and among the Friends who flocked to Boston were Hannah and Mary Wright, the daughters of Peter. They were especially "bold in speech," according to an old account, in denouncing the magistrates, and Mary gave her "testimony" against the authorities for their cruelty in putting Mary Dyer to death. She was accused of witchcraft, tried and acquitted, but was convicted of being a Quaker and was detained in Boston, along with her sister Hannah. Both were banished in 1661, after suffering many hardships. In 1662, Hannah, then thirteen or fourteen years old, returned to Boston and appeared in open court there warning the magistrates to spill no more innocent blood. She was especially prominent in the Oyster Bay Soicety of Friends and never married. She was drowned while traveling in Virginia on a visit to the Quakers in 1675; her brother Gideon was granted letters of administration April 12, of this year.

Gideon Wright, son of Peter, married Elizabeth, the daughter of John, 1st, and Elizabeth (Montgomerie) Townsend. His sister, Elizabeth Wright, married James Townsend, his wife's brother, and his brother, Job Wright, married Rachel Townsend, his wife's niece. The children of Gideon and his wife Elizabeth were; Elizabeth; Peter, who died between 1685 and 1694, supposedly unmarried; Gideon, Jr., who died in 1722; Anthony; Silvanus, who was living in 1736; Hannah; John, who died in 1737; and Tabitha.

Elizabeth married Isaiah Harrison, 1688. Gideon, Jr. married Margaret Urquehart, as before related, and had: John, d. 1750, m. 1st, Ruth Ludlam, 2nd, Ruth Bailey, 1729 or 39; Zebulon, d 1746, m. Clemence Feke, 1734, lived at the "Mill River Hollow"; Elijah, b. April 4, 1713, d. November 1766, m. Ann Durland of Oyster Bay, 1742, lived at Norwick, L. I.; Elizabeth, d. May 15, 1782, m. Edmond Weeks of Oyster Bay, 1735; Abigail, m. John Feke, a brother of Zebulon's wife; and Margaret or Mary, m. Daniel Ludlum of Long Island. Anothony Wright, the son of Gideon, married Mary, the daughter of Rev. John and Dinah Rhodes of Oyster Bay. The Rev. Rhodes was the first Baptist minister, as before noted. Anthony's children were: Peter, b. 1703, and Dinah, b. 1705. Silvanus Wright, son of Gideon, married Mary Proctor, of Long Island, and had at least a son Charles. John Wright, son of Gideon, married Abigail, the daughter of James and Sarah (Jeffery) Barker, of Newport, Rhode Island, January 27, 1707-8, and went there "to Dwell the 14th day of April in ye year of our Lord 1707." Their children were: Abigial, b. 1712-13; Gideon, b. 1715, d. after 1770, Tabitha, and John. Tabitha Wright, daughter of Gideon, married John Brook, of Rhode Island, August 16, 1711.

Gideon Wright (Sr.) was a farmer and shoemaker. He lived on land now (1923) owned by Edward Weeks, Esq. His widow, Elizabeth, after his death in June, 1685, married Gershom Lockwood in August, 1697, and removed to Stamford, Connecticut, Lockwood being from this place.

The Townsends were also Friends, and like the Wrights, three brothers, John, Henry, and Richard, came to America from Norfolk County, England, being from the town of Norwich. John settled first at New Amsterdam—New York—some years before 1645, where he "was seized of a certain parcel of land, containing eight acres by estimation, lying and being at the Fresh Water (Collect)," according to a petition of his widow, Elizabeth, to Governor Andros, which further recites that upon this land her husband "did build and make large improvements, and peacably enjoyed the same divers years in the time of great calamity, being daily alarmed by the Indians, etc."

In 1645, Governor Keift issued a patent for the town of Flushing to John Townsend and others, and here he (John) was joined by his brother Henry. On account of his failure to contribute to the Established Church, John, with other Friends, was summoned to appear January 23, 1648, before the Director General, Governor and Council, at Ft. Amsterdam. Thompson states that the Townsends left Flushing and removed to Warwick, Rhode Island, where all three brothers were members of the Provincial Assembly, besides holding municiple offices. In 1656 they returned to Long Island and obtained a patent, along with others, for the town of Jamaica, then called Rusdrop. Their religious difficulties continued however, and in January, 1661, two of the magistrates furnished the names of twelve persons, including John and Henry Townsend and their wives, "who counternanced Quakers." This year the Townsend brothers removed to Oyster Bay, where they are first mentioned on the records September 16, 1661.

John Townsend died in 1668. His wife was Elizabeth Montgomerie whom he married in England. Elizabeth divided her estate in writing in "the 23rd year of the reign of Charles II, King of England, 10th day, 5th mo., 1671." In this paper she mentions her "two eldest sons, John and Thomas," her "six younger children, James, Rose, Anne, Sarah, George & Daniel," and her "eldest daughter Elizabeth & husband Gideon Wright."

John Towsend, Jr. lived at Jerico. In 1698 his wife's name was Phoebe. His first wife was Susannah, the daughter of Richard Harcourt, of Oyster Bay. Thomas Townsend was one of the most active men in the affairs of Oyster Bay, being Captain of Militia, Constable, Recorder, Surveyor, and Justice. He married 2nd, Mary, the daughter of Job Almy of Rhode Island, and removed to Portsmouth, this colony, in 1686, returning to Oyster Bay in 1697. A little later he went to Tiberton, in the Boston Colony, but returned to Oyster Bay in 1709. He is though to have died in Rhode

Island. James Townsend married Elizabeth, the daughter of Peter Wright, as before stated. Rose Townsend married John Weeks, of Warwick, Rhode Island, the brother of Richard Townsend's second wife. After his death she married Samuel Hayden. George Townsend was born after 1661 in Oyster Bay. He married Mary Hawxhurst in 1684, and died in "the great sickness." Daniel Townsend married Susannah, the daughter of Samuel Furman, and died July 2, 1702. He had sons, Robert and Daniel.

The above is based on "A memorial of John, Henry, and Richard Townsend," before quoted, (See pp. 81, 84, 92, 93) which also gives the names of the children of Elizabeth and her husband Gideon Wright—(see page 132)—and which states that their daughter Elizabeth Wright married Isaiah Harrison, and that "her family removed from Oyster Bay, and nothing is known of them or of Hannah (Wright.)"

On April 20, 1702, Isaiah Harrison sold his entire possessions of ſand in Oyster Bay; the deed on record in the town Book C, page 101, reads as follows;—

THIS INDENTURE made the twentyeth Day of Aprill in the ffourteenth Yeare of the Reign of our Soveraigne Lord William ye third by the Grace of god of England Scotland ffrance and Ireland King Annoq Domini 1702 by and between Isaiah Harrison of Oysterbay in Queens County on Nassaw Island in the Collony of Newyorke Black Smith on ye one part and Daniel and Abraham Underhill of Oysterbay aforesaid on ye other part Witnesseth that ye Said Isaiah Harrison ffor and in Consideration of ye Sum of ffour hundred pounds In Currant Lawfull money of New Yorke aforesaid in hand paid and by him ye Said Isaiah Harrison Received of ye Said Daniel and Abraham Underhill In ffull payment before ye Ensealing and Dilivery of these presents the Receopt whereof the Said Isaiah Harrison Doth hereby acknowledge and himselfe to be there with fully Satisfied and Doth ffully and Clearly acquit Exhonerate and Discharge ye Said Daniel and Abraham Underhill theire Heires Executors adminisstrators and assignes from him ye Said Isaiah Harrison his Heires Executors adminisstrators and assignes and ffor other good Causes and Considerations Especially Moveing Hath Given Granted alienated Infeoffed assigned released Sold and Confirmed and by these presents Doth ffully ffreelly Clearly and absolutely Give Grant alienate Infeoff assigne release Sell and Confirme unto ye Said Daniel and Abraham Underhill theire Heires and assignes ffor Ever all that of One Hundred Acrees of Land which he Bought of John Wright whereon his House now Stands and ffive Acrees of Land which he Bought of John Newman and two whole rights and two third parts of a right of Land in the New generall purchase of Oysterbay which Rights he Bought of Daniel Townsend and Hope Williams which Rights are Equall wth the purchasers Entered In ye record of Oysterbay in Libr B page 42 & 43 and also a whole right of Land in ye old purchase of Oysterbay Equall with any propriators right yt are Entred in ye Record of Oysterbay in Libr A page 240 Withall ye Land he hath taken up upon ye ffirst or Second Divitions with what Else of right is Belonging to him Within the Patten and Township of Oysterbay Together withall the Right title Interest Claime and Demand whatsoEver which ye Said Isaiah Harrison now hath or which any or Either of his Heires Executors administrators or assignes may hereafter have of to or in ye Said granted percels of Land or any part or percell thereof Withall the profits Comodities Customes Immunities privileges Housen apple trees or what Else is arising Standing or growing or becoming Due upon ye Same to HAVE & to HOLD unto them ye Said Daniel and Abraham Underhill theire Heires and assignes ffor Ever all and Singular ye Said granted premises and ye appurtenances thereof to ye only proper use and behove of them the Said Daniel and Abraham

Underhill theire Heires and assignes ffor Ever and the Said Isaiah Harrison hath put ye Said Daniel and Abraham into Lawful and peaceable posession of all and Singular ye Said granted percels of Land and premises and Every part and percell thereof by the Dilivery of Turffe and Twigg and by these presents the Said Isaiah Harrison Doth ffor him Self his Heires Executors administrators and asignes ffurther Convenant and agree to and with ye Said Daniel and Abraham Underhill that itt Shall and may be Lawfull for them ye Said Daniel and Abrah[am] theire Heires and assignes Quitely and peaceably to Have hold occupy posess and Enjoy all Singular ye Said granted percels of Land and premises ass theire ffree and Cleare Estate of Inheritance forEever without the Lawfull Lett hindrnace or Mollestation of him ye Sd Isaiah Harrison his Heires Executors administrators and assignes or any other person or persons Lawfully Claiming any part or percel thereof Notwithstanding any fformer Gift Grant Mortgage Judgment or Execution had made or Comitted by him or any other ffrom by or under him or any other Conveyance or Incumbrance whatsoEver and ye Said Isaiah Harrison Doth find himself his Heires Executors and adminsstrators ffirmly by these presents to warrent and Defend the Said Daniel and Abraham theire Hieres and assignes in Quite and peaceable possesion of all and Singular ye Said granted premises against any Just and Lawfull Claim whatsoEver In Witness whereof he the Said Isaiah Harrison hath hereunto Sett his hand and Seale the Day and Yeare first above writt[en]

Signed Sealed and Delivered — Isaiah Harrison O.
in the presence of — L
John Townsend — her
Nathaneill Coles — Abigail X Harrison O.
Anthony Wright. — mark

Memorandum yt on ye Day and Date within written the within Named Isaiah Harrison personlly appeared before me Nathaniel Coles Esqr one of his majesties Justices of the peace ffor Queens County and acknowledged the within written Deed to be his reall act and Voluntary Deed.

Nathaniel Coles.

(See, *Oyster Bay Town Records*, Volume II, 1691-1704, pp. 530-531.)

The name of Long Island was changed to the "Island of Nassau" on April 10,1693. (See—*Flushing Past and Present*, by Rev. G. Henry Mandeville, 1860, p. 29.)

CHAPTER IV

A Settlement on the Banks of the Nissequogue

THE INDENTURE signed by Isaiah Harrison "the twentyeth Day of Aprill in the ffourteenth yeare of the Reign of our Soveraigne Lord William ye third," disposing of all his lands in "the Patten and Township of Oysterbay," discloses many interesting details of his residence in the town. This deed mentions specifically the "One Hundred Acres of Land which he bought of John Wright whereon his House now Stands," showing that he resided on the land bought January 16, 1688, "Lying & being near Suckscalls Wigwam." On this land stood his "Housen apple trees" "by ye Highway leading to Oysterbay Town". This land he had originally obtained from John Wright, the son of Nicholas, and a first cousin of his wife's father. John Wright was the builder, and no doubt helped to erect Isaiah's dwelling. To this land Isaiah had added from time to time several tracts as he became more associated with the affairs of the town in which he held a "propriator's right". Here his wife, Elizabeth, had died, between 1698 and 1702, leaving him with five small motherless children. By the latter date he had married again, as his second wife Abigail joined him in signing the deed disposing of all his holdings in the town this year.

The town records of Oyster Bay are silent as to Isaiah's further whereabouts, and evidently his association in the town's affairs ceased with the disposal of his land. His family "removed from Oyster Bay, and nothing is known of them", states the Memorial to the Townsends, and here arises one of those problems so baffling to the genealogist. Isaiah's children, born at Oyster Bay, are found about thirty years after his removal from the town to be among the pioneers of Augusta County, Virginia, but where was he in the meantime? Fortunately, after considerable search, it was found that the key to the answer to this occurs in the published "*Records of the Town of Smithtown, Long Island*", 1898, in the notes in this volume by Wm. S. Pelletreau. In regard to the mention of a certain tract of land in the town records, Pelletreau states that "according to a deed recorded in Suffolk County Clerk's office, Liber A, page 113, William Lawrence sold this tract to Isaiah Harrison, April 20, 1702, for 400 pounds, and Isaiah and wife Abigail sold it to Amos Willits of Islip, June 12, 1721." (See p. 330.) Thus the day that Isaiah signed the deed of sale at Oyster Bay he was given a deed for land at Smithtown, Long Island, about fifteen miles to the east of his old home, and in in the adjoining county of Suffolk. Moreover, for his new land he paid the whole amount he had received from the sale of his old lands, but this time he bought an estate of five hundred acres. The first book of the town records of Smithtown has become lost or destroyed, but as the deed books for Suffolk County begin about 1689, the deed is found as given above, at Riverhead, Long Island, and reads as follows:

"THIS INDENTURE, Made ye twientieth day of April in ye 14th year of ye reign of our Soverign lord William ye 3d by ye grace of God of England Scotland, France & Ireland King anno doni 1702 by & between William Lawrence of Flushing in Queens County on Nassau Island in ye Province of New York on ye one parte & Isaiah Harrisson of ye county aforesd. on ye other part.

WITNESSETH that ye sd William Lawrence for & in consideration of ye sum of four hundred pounds in current lawfull money of New York aforesaid in hand paid &

by him ye said William Lawrence received of ye said Isaiah Harrison in full payment before ye ensealing & delivery of these presents ye receit whereof ye said William Lawrence doth hereby acknowledge and himself to be therewith to be fully satisfied and doth fully & clarely acquit exonerate & discharge ye sd Isaiah Harrisson his heirs executors administrators & assigns, and for other good causes and consideration especially moving hath given granted aliened enfeoffed assigned released sould & confirmed & by these presents doth fully freely clearly & absolutely give grante alienate enfeoff assign release sell & confirm unto ye sd Isaiah Harrisson his heirs & assigns forever all-of certain 500 acres of woodland which he hath lying & joyning on ye west side of Nesequogue River in ye County of Suffolk which is bounded as followeth:
It begins at ye southwardmost of ye branch next to ye river & next to ye house on ye south side of ye road & from thence to run west tw hundred roddes and from thence to run northerly keeping the same breadth adjoyning to ye river untill it comes to Jonathan Smiths frost medow and then to keep ye same breadth on ye upland untill it makes up just five hundred acres of land and also a piece of salt meadow joyning to ye sd. river it was drawn by his wife whose name was Debora Smith and also a piece of meadow lying on ye east side of ye river being by estimation four acres of meadow-land.

TOGETHER with all right title interest, claime & demand whatsoever which ye said William Lawrence now hath or which any or either of his heirs executors, administators or assignes may hereafter have of to or in ye sd. granted land or meadow or any part of parcell thereof, with all ye profits commodity, customes, immunity ,privileges, houses, barnes or what else arising standing or growing or becoming and upon ye same. TO HAVE AND TO HOLD unto him ye sd. Isaiah Harrisson his heires & assignes forever or & singular ye said granted premises and ye appurtenances thereof to ye only proper use & behoofe of him ye said Isaiah Harrison his heires & assignes forever and ye sd. Wm. Lawrence hath put ye said Isaiah Harrison into lawfull & peaceable possession of all & singular ye sd. granted land & meadow & premises & every parte and parcell thereof by ye delivery . . . . . and by these presents ye sd Wm. Lawrence doth for himselfe his heires executors, adminstrators and assignes futher convenant & agree to & with ye sd. Isaiah Harrison that it shall & may be lawful for him ye sd. Isaiah Harrison his heires & assignes quietly & peaceably to have, hold, occupy posses & enjoy all & singular of ye sd. granted land & meadow and premises as their free & clear estate of inheritance forever without ye lawfull let hindrance of molestation of him ye sd. Wm. Lawrence his heires exec. admin. & assigne or any other . . . . . lawfully claiming any part or parcell notwithstanding any former gift, grant mortgage judgment or execution have made or committed by him or any other form by or under him or any other conveyance or incumbrance wt. soever & ye said Wm. Lawrence doth bind himself his heires exec. & admin. firmily by these presents to warrant & defend ye sd. Isaiah Harrison his heires & assignes in quiet & peaceable possesion of all & singular ye sd. granted premises agt. any just & lawfull claime wt. soever.

IN WITNESSSE WHEREOF, he ye sd. Wm. Lawrence hath hereunto set my hand & seal ye day & year first above written.

Wm. LAWRENCE (Seal)

Sealed and delivered
in presence of
John Townsend
Nath Coles Anthony

Memorand if on ye day and date within written ye w'in named Wm. Lawrence personally appeared before me Nathanaell Coles Esq. one of his ——— Justices of ye Peace for Queens County and acknowledged ye within written to be his reall act & voluntary deed.

Nathanaell Coles"

(See, Liber A of deeds, p. 113, Riverhead, L. I.)

Smithtown, Long Island, is situated on the Nissequogue River. The township was largely a free gift to Lyon Gardiner, July 14, 1659, from Wyandanch, the grand sachem of Long Island, in recognition of Gardiner's services to this chief in redeeming his daughter from the savages across the sound. As the Nissequogue tribe of Indians also claimed the land Gardiner later obtained a grant from them in 1662. The next year he conveyed the premises to Richard Smith, who was an inhabitant of Southampton as early as October 26, 1643. In 1664 Smith obtained a further title to the lands in the form of a release from David Gardiner, the son of Lyon, and on March 3, 1665, he was granted a patent of confirmation by Governor Nicholl on condition that he would settle ten families in three years. This land appears to have been largely or wholly on the eastern side of the Nessequogue river, as this year he obtained from the Nessequogue sechem a title to an extensive tract on the western side of the river and a new patent was issued to him by Nicholl, March 25, 1667, in which the western boundary was ommitted. This ommission led to a controversy with Huntington, as this town claimed all the lands on the western side of the river. In 1675 the court rendered a decision in favor of Smith, establishing the western limits "as the Fresh Pond" on the west side of the river "and so to the Hollow". On March 25, 1677, Smith obtained another patent from Govenor Andros in consideration of "one good fatt lamb yearly quitrent". Between the years 1665 and 1666 the patentee removed from Southampton to Smithtown, where he spent the remainder of his life between his possessions here and those in Rhode Island; he died in 1692. (See, Thompson's *History of Long Island*, Vol III, p. 3, and *Records of Smithtown*—introduction).

Isaiah Harrison's 500 acres of land was located on the western banks of the Nissequogue, as stated in the deed. This tract was conveyed by Richard Smith, the patentee of Smithtown, on March 25, 1684, to his son-in-law William Lawrence who had married Smith's daughter Debora, thus the mention of her name in the above deed. According to the Records of Smithtown, above quoted, which gives the history of this land—p. 458,— this tract laid at the common passage over the river and was bounded on the east by the river. "It begins at ye southwardmost of ye branch next to ye river & next to ye house on ye south side of ye road", so runs the deed; thus the house evidently stood in a clearing on the banks of the Nissequogue, and overlooking it near the jucture of a branch with the river, and at the common passage of the road over it. Here Isaiah and his wife Abigail made their home, and raised their children along with his children by his first wife Elizabeth. Here he prospered as the "husbandman" and in 1708 added 200 more acres to his estate, this additional land being on the eastern side of the river, as shown by the following deed found at Riverhead:

"THIS INDENTURE, Made twenty third day of Sept. in ye 7th year of ye reigne of our Sovereign Lady Anne by ye Grace of God Queen of Great Brittain France & Ireland defender of ye faith anno dni 1708 BETWEEN RICHARD LAWRENCE of Smithtowne in ye County of Suffolke of ye Colony of New Yorke Yeoman on ye one parte, and ESAIAH HARRISON of ye same place husbandman on ye other parte

WITNESSETH that ye sd Richard Lawrence for & in consideration of eighty pounds good & lawfull money of New Yorke above sd., to him in hand paid by ye said Esayah Harrison ye receit whereof ye said Richard Lawrence doth hereby acknowledge, and himselfe to be therewith fully satisfyed contented & paid, and thereof and therefrom by these presents doth fully acquitt & discharge the sd. Esayah Harrison & his heirs executors & administrators forever, hath bargained sould given granted aliened enfeoffd released & confirmed, and by these presents doth for himself his heires executors and administrators & either of them fully freely & absolutely bargain sell give grante alien enfeoffe release & confirm unto ye sd. Esaiah Harrison his heirs & assignes

ALL that two hundred acres of land scituate lying & being within ye bounds of Smithtowne above sd. on ye east side of ye river called Nessequague River bounded on ye south side by ye Common Path or Country Roade, westward by ye said river & extending northward one hundred poles & soe to extend in length in a parallel line to make up ye complement of two hundred acres, taking in all Swamps Meadow Creek thatch with all ye benefits and priviledges thereunt obelonging, with liberty of fishing hunting & fowling on ye necke on ye west side of ye sd. Nessequague River and also the liberty to take up any hollow that is not disposed of & ye liberty of commonage for all creatures & to cut creeke thatch in ye said Nessequage River,

TO HAVE AND TO HOLD ye said two hundred acres of land and all & singular ye within granted premises, with appurtentances, to ye said Esaiah Harrison his heires & assignes forever to ye use & behoofe of him ye said Esaiah Harrison his heires & assignes forever. And ye said Richard *Richard* Lawrence for himselfe & his heires executors and administrators doth hereby convenant promise & grante to & with ye said Esayah Harrison his heires & assignes that he ye said Richard Lawrence is ye rightful owner of ye said land and premises and that ye ensealing thereof hath full power and lawfull authority to dispose & convey ye same with ye sd. Esaiah Harrison his heires & assignes and that ye said Esayah Harrison his heires or assignes shall or may at all times hereafter, & from time to time, quietly & peaceably have hold & enjoy ye within granted premises freely & clearely acquitted from all incumberances wtsoever, and ye sd. Richard Lawrence for himselfe & his heires, doth hereby warrent ye within granted premises against all persons whatsoever claiming or to claime any right title or pretence wtsoever, by from or under him ye sd. Richard Lawrence his heires or either of them, and futher to give any better confirmation hereof, as shall be reasonably advised or devised by ye said Esaiah Harrison his heires or assigns by his or their counsell learned in ye law and at their costs.

IN WITNESSE WHEREOF ye sd. Richard Lawrence hath to these presents set his hand and seal ye day & year above written.

Sealed & delivered in the presence of
Geo. Phillips
Richard Floyd

RICHARD LAWRENCE (Seal)

Sept. ye 23 1708 The within named Richard Lawrence acknowledged this deed within mentioned to be his free act & deed.

Coram Tho. Helme one of her majesties justices of ye Peace in ye County of Suffolke

Entered Oct. ye 6 1708 Tho. Helme cler."

(See, Liber A of Deeds, p. 157, Riverhead, Long Island).

As the Smithtown records that have been preserved begin with the year 1715, no mention of Isaiah Harrison's ownership of this land appears in the published volume before referred to. The deed is important however as through the disposal of this land Isaiah left record of his new location. In fact, this deed was found while making an investigation at Riverhead to establish this point. This land added two hundred acres on the eastern side of the Nissequogue to his five hundred acres on the western side, making an estate of seven hundred acres divided by the river. The first tract, Isaiah's home place, was bought from Major William Lawrence of Flushing, and in the deed Harrison's name is frequently spelled Harrisson, as was the case in connection with deeds relating to John Harrison of Flushing and Perth Amboy. It will be recalled that this John Harrison sold his interest in the town of Harrison to Major William Lawrence, May 23, 1702, or about one month after Lawrence sold his land at Smithtown to Isaiah Harrison, thus Major Lawrence knew both Harrisons, and from other common circumstances, as related, it appears likely that Isaiah and John Harrison were at least kinsmen. Several of Isaiah's children used the double "S" in spelling their name on the Augusta County records, and this perculiarity persisted in this family in Virginia as late as the first census of the United States.

Isaiah Harrison bought all of his land at Smithtown from the Lawrences; the second tract being obtained from Richard Lawrence of this town. Major William, above, and Richard Lawrence were the sons of Capt. William Lawrence, who was born in England. Capt. William settled on Long Island about 1645. He was twice married, both of his wives being named Elizabeth; his second wife, whom he married in 1664, was the daughter of Richard Smith, the patentee of Smithtown. Capt. William Lawrence died in 1680, and after his death his widow married Capt. Phillip Carteret, Governor of New Jersey. Major William Lawrence, the oldest son by his father's first wife, the year of his father's death, married Debora Smith, the sister of his father's second wife. Richard Lawrence was the son of Capt. William and his second wife Elizabeth Smith, thus the desent of Isaiah's land from Richard Smith the patentee. (See, Thompson, Vol. IV, p. 411, and *Genealogical Memoir of the Family of John Lawrence*, by John Lawrence, p. 59.)

After having resided fourteen years at Oyster Bay, and nineteen years at Smithtown, Long Island, Isaiah Harrison disposed of his homeland at Smithtown, in 1721, as disclosed in the following deed previously alluded to:

"THIS INDENTURE, made the Twelfth day of June in the seventh year of our Sovereign Lord George by the Grant of God of Great Britian, France and Ireland King Defender of the faith or Between Isaiah Harrison of the Riverhead in the limits of Smithtown in Suffolk County on Nassau Island in the Province of New York in America yoeman of the one part and Amos Willitts of Islip Grangue in the said County yoeman on the other part WHEREAS the said Isaiah Harrison was lately by virture of an Independence of Bargain and Sale remaining of record in the office of Clerk of the Peace for Suffolk County (Liber A) in page (113) from William Lawrence of Flushing in Queens County on the Island aforesd, dec'ed. Actually and lawfully seized and posessed of a certain Tract of land (and House) Situate lying and being at the Riverhead, afords. near Smithtown on the West side of Nissequogue River bounded as follows beginning at the Southwardmost part of the Branch of the said River west to the House on the south side the road and from thence to run west two hundred Rodds and from thence northerly (keepin the same breadth along the River) untill it comes to a fresh meadow formerly Jonathan Smiths Dec'd (purchased from him as aforesaid by the Sd.

Isaiah) and then to keep the same breadth on the Upland untill it makes up just five hundred acres of land also by virture of a certain grant or Bill of Sale dated the thirtieth day of April 1713 from the aboved named Jonathan Smith was lawfully and actually posessed of a piece of fresh meadow lying and being (the uppermost) on the West side of said River containing by estimation five acres be the same more or less bounded northerly by the meadow Adam Smith &c. Now this Indenture Witnesseth that the said Isaiah Harrison by and with the consent of Abigail his wife signified by her signing and sealing to these presents for and in consideration of the sum of Five hundred pounds lawful money of New York to him the said Isaiah in hand paid by the said Amos Willitts before the executing of these presents the receipt whereof does hereby acknowledge and therefrom and every part thereof doth by these presents forever acquit discharge and Release him the said Amos Willits his executrs and Admin. hath granted, bargained, sold, aliened, released and confirmed and by these presents for him and his heirs doth grant bargain, sell release and confirm unto him the said Amos Whillitts and his heirs and assigns ALL that the now dwelling house of the said Isaiah and all and every the above mentioned tract of land and piece of fresh meadow and also a share of salt meadow joined to the said River together with five parts of seven of all his right of commons right of cutting of timber and right of mowing of creek thatch in the marshes or thatch beds and all houses barns, stables, orchards, gardens now standing lying or being on the premises with all water ways water courses landing and houses. Together with all right title interest possession claim and demand whatsoever which the said Isaiah Harrison now hath or at any time hereafter he or his heirs may have in or to the premises with all profits customs, immunities, privileges hereditaments and appurtenances, with the reversion and remainder thereof the same land houses and meadows and other the granted premises being now in the actuall possesion and seizin of the said Amos Willitts by virture of one Indenture of Lease and Bargain and Sale, made the day next before the day of the date hereof for the term of one year by the said Isaiah Harrison of the one part and the said Amos Willitts of the other part and by virture of the Statute for transfering of Uses into posession. To Have and to Hold the said above recited and granted lands and Premises with their and every of their appurtenances unto him the said Amos Willittis and his heirs and assigns to his and their only use and behoof forever, clearly acquitted and discharged and otherwise kept harmless of and from all and all manner of former Gifts, Grants, bargains, sales jointures dowers Judgements executions and incumbrances whatsoever done or suffered by the said Isaiah Harrison for himself and heirs Executors and admin. doth hereby covenant grant and agree to and with the said Amos Willitts or assigns that he the said Isaiah Harrison and his heirs shall and will warrent and defend the said granted lands, and premises to the said Amos Willitts his heirs and assigns against all persons what sever lawfully claiming the same or any part thereof. And futher that he the said Isaiah Harrison and his heirs and assigns shall and will at any time after the expiration of one year (if desired) give and execute any other deeds of conveyeances of every the said lands and premises to the said Amos Willitts his heirs and assigns for the futher vesting the said lands and premises in him the said Amos Willitts and his heirs and assigns forever as shall be reasonably devised and required.

In Witness Whereof the parties to these presents have put their hands and seals interchangeably the day and year first above written Annoque Domini 1721.

Sealed and delivered in the presence of
Anna Smith
Mary Smith

ISAIAH HARRISON L. S.
her mark
ABIGAIL x HARRISON L. S.

Memorandum that the words as also a share of Salt meadow joining to the said River was inserted before the execution thereof by unanimous consent of all the parties duly concerned therein.

Memorandum That on the twelfth day of June in the year of Our Lord Seventeen Hundred and Twenty-one the above Isaiah Harrison and Abigail his wife named in this conveyance came personally before me Henry Smith Esqr. one of his Majesties Justices of the Peace for Suffolk County (being examined apart) and acknowledged this Instrument to be their volutary act and Deed.

Test

H. T. SMITH Just.

(See, Liber B of Deeds, p. 91, Riverhead, L. I.)

The creek thatch mentioned in these deeds was used for making roofs. In Norfolk County, England, today, the reeds of marsh land are still employed for this purpose. These reeds constitute a durable thatch lasting thirty years or more. Thatch is said to form an extremely good roof, warm in winter and cool in summer, and if saturated with a solution of lime is claimed to be incombustible.

"An exile from home splendour dazzels in vain,
Oh give me my lowly thatched cottage again."

—PAYNE, *was born at Easthampton, L. I.*

The above deed was acknowledged before Henry Tangier Smith and was evidently witnessed by his wife and eldest daughter, Mary. Smith probably drew up the deed as he had been clerk of the court for Suffolk County from 1710-1716. His daughter Mary married Edmund Smith (d. 1735) of the Smithtown family, a son of Adam Smith mentioned in the above deed. Adam was a brother of Jonathan Smith, also mentioned in the deed. Henry Tangier Smith was born in Tangiers, Africa, in 1679, and was the son of Col. William Smith, who arrived in New York, August 6, 1686. Col. Smith brought over with him his wife and two children, one of whom was his son Henry Tangier.

Col. William Smith was born at Newton, near Higham-ferrers in Northamptonshire, England, in 1655. At the age of twenty he was commissioned Colonel and appointed Governor of Tangiers, Africa, by Charles II, who had received this outpost as a wedding gift from the King of Portugal. There, 1675, he married Martha, the daughter of Henry Tunstall, Esq. of Putney, England. Tangiers was abandoned in 1683, upon which Col. Smith and wife returned to England with three children, three having died at Tangiers. After engaging in trade for a time in London he embarked from Youghall, Ireland, July 1686, with his wife and three children, leaving the remains of two infants in Brainford, England, where they had died. On the voyage to America he committed to the sea the body of his youngest child, Hibernia, a daughter of two months who had been born at Youghall.

Col. Smith early visited Brookhaven, Long Island, where, with the aid of Gov. Dongan, he made extensive purchases at Little Neck in 1687. A year or two later he took up his permanent residence there, settling with his family, afterwards erecting his holdings into St. George's Manor, through a patent from Col. Fletcher in 1693. He was appointed by Gov. Slaughter one of his Privy Council, March 19, 1691, four days after the Governor's arrival in New York. This office he held under several governors until his death in 1705. For a time he was one of the Commissioners of Oyer and Terminer, and Chief Justice, and after Governor Bellmont's death in 1701, as President of the Council, he became acting Governor of the Colony of New York. His will was dated August 20th, 1704, and his wife's September 7th, 1707; she died in 1709. Both he and his wife were buried at St. George's Manor. Six children were born to them after they came to America, and out of the fourteen only this number survived their father. The wills mention Henry Tangier, William Henry (1689-1743), Patty, Gloriania, Charles Jeffery (1693-1713), and Joane. Henry Tangier m. 1st, 1705, Anna (1685-1735), the daughter of Rev. Thomas Shephard, and had Mary, mentioned above, (died 1765), Anna b. 1706, William Henry b. 1708, Henry b. 1710, Gloria b. 1715, Martha b. 1717, Charles Jeffery b. 1721, and Catherine b. 1725. In 1737 he m. 2nd, Frances, the daughter of Rev. Henry Caner, and in 1743 he m. 3rd, Margaret Biggs, by whom he had Frances and Margaret. (See—*Thompson,* Vol. IV, p. 397; *Mementos of the Golden Wedding at Logwood,* by Mrs. Eleanor Jones Smith, p. 25, and *Wills of the Smith Families of New York and Long Island,* 1664-1694, by Wm. S. Pelletreau, pp. 4 and 11).

In the case of Isaiah's settlement at Oyster Bay, he bought his land from a relative of his wife, and from one of her family name. Had he used this as a precedent on his second marriage his wife would have been a Lawrence, but while it is likely that his Smithtown land was obtained from one of her relatives it does not appear from the various Lawrence genealogies published that she was of this family. (See—*Historical Genealogy of the Lawrence Family,* by Thomas Lawrence, p. 23, *Records of Smithtown,* by Pelletreau, p. 480, and Thompson, Vol. IV, p. 182, etc.) Isaiah and Abigail were married while he was living at Oyster Bay and before his removal from there in 1702. The probability is that they were married at Huntington, the township of which joined Oyster Bay on the east and Smithtown on the west. The first records of the old Independant or Congregational Church, organized at Huntington about 1660, have not been preserved. This was the first church established in the whole region and was attended by both Oyster Bay and Smithtown settlers. This church became Presbyterian in 1748. It may be noticed in passing that the oldest existing Presbyterian church in America is said to be the one at Jamaica, Long Island.

On June 5th, 1723, the Rev. Ebenezer Prime was ordained pastor of the Huntington church by Presbyters from Fairfield, Bridgehampton, Norwalk, Greenfarm, Southold and Huntington. From this date the records of the church are preserved. These show the marriage of a Nathaniel Harrison and Rebecca Smith of Huntington, January 16, 1751-2, by the Rev. Prime. September 25th, 1757, the Rev. Prime baptized Hannah and Sarah Harresson and Daniel Harrison, and Feb. 19, 1758, Rebecca Harreson, Nov. 1, 1761, Nathaniel Harrison, Feb. 12, 1764, Jesse Harrison, and April 27, 1766, Mary Harrison. (See—*Records of the First Church in Huntington, Long Island,* 1723-1779, printed for Moses L. Scudder, 1899, pp. 48, 49, 52, 53, 56, and 86). These are the only Harrisons mentioned in the church book and Nathaniel is the first Harrison mentioned in the Huntington town records. He was chosen Constable and Collector May 7, 1771, and is given in the list of inhabitants of the "Town Spot" at the close of the Revolution, "about 1783." In 1805 there was a David Harrison also a resident of the town. (See *Huntington Town Records,* published by the town, Vol. II, pp. 511,515, 521, 531, and Vol. III, pp. 105 and 217). It appears from a striking similarity of names of these Harrisons with those of Isaiah's known grandchildren that probably Nathaniel was also a grandchild of his, and it may be that the Daniel and Jesse mentioned were on a visit from Augusta County, Virginia, when baptized. Many Harnets are mentioned in the town books as well as Langdons, and it is significant that one of Isaiah's granddaughters of Augusta, married a Langdon, and later a David Harnet.

The maiden name of Isaiah's second wife does not appear to be known for certain, probably owing to the loss of the first records of the old Huntington church. An extensive search of various genealogies relating to many of the early Oyster Bay and Long Island families of this section, including Carpenters, Davises, Hallocks, Lawrences, Loyds, Smiths, Townsends, Underhills, Warrens, Weekes, Whiteheads, Willets and Wrights, has failed to yield anything definite in this connection. However, there are many circumstances indicating that she was a Smith, and of the Smithtown family.

Richard Smith, the immigrant and patentee of Smithtown, came to New England in the early part of 1600 and married Sarah ...., his first wife, by whom he had issue; Jonathan m. Sarah Brewster; Obediah, drowned in 1680, supposed to be the first white person buried in Smithtown; Richard II, m. 1670, Hannah Tooker and d. 1720; Job m. Elizabeth Thompson; Adam m. Elizabeth Brown; Samuel m. Hannah Longbothem; Daniel m. 1st Ruth Tooker, m. 2nd Mary Hilton; Elizabeth m. 1st 1664, Capt. William Lawrence, m. 2nd Capt. Phillip Carteret, Governor of New Jersey, as previously stated; Debora m. 1680, Major William Lawrence, also previously noted, and d. 1743.

Of these; Jonathan had Jonathan II, and Debora; Richard II, had Nathaniel, Richard, Ebenezer, Hannah and Sarah; Job had Job II, St. Richard, Timothy, Aaron, James, Joseph, and Elizabeth; Adam had Edmund who m. Mary Smith, as noted; Samuel had Obediah II, Richard (the Quaker), Mary, Phebe, Anna, and Hannah; Daniel by wife Ruth had Obediah, Daniel II, and Debora and by wife Mary; Soloman, Lorinda, Mary and Sarah. Elizabeth and Capt. Wm. Lawrence had Mary, Thomas, Joseph, Richard, Samuel, Sarah, and James. (Capt William and a first wife, Elizabeth ...., had William, the Major below, John who m. Elizabeth ...., and Elizabeth who m. Thomas Stevenson of Newton, 1672. (The Lawrences resided at Flushing). Debora and Major William Lawrence had William, Richard, Obedah, Daniel, Samuel, John, Adam, Stephen, (b. 1700), Joshua, Caleb, Debora, Sarah, Elizabeth who m. John Willits. (See, *Thompson's History of Long Island,* Vol. IV, p. 182.)

The genealogical accounts of Richard Smith's family are very fragmentary. It will be observed that Thompson only mentions two children of Jonathan and one son of Adam. As before stated, Jonathan and Adam owned land adjoining Isaiah Harrison, and it may be that Abigail, the wife of Isaiah, was a daughter of Adam Smith, and a sister of Edmund who married Mary Smith one of the witnesses of the deed. As Abigail was, however, evidently much older than Mary Smith the greater probability is that she was a daughter of Jonathan.

John Smith, the immigrant to Augusta County, Virginia, had sons both John and Jonathan as well as a son of Daniel. The coat of arms of the Smithtown patentee, as pictured in Pelletreau's Records of Smithtown, show on the shield six fleur-de-lis set three, two, and one. The fleur-de-lis was also a prominent figure on the arms of the

Augusta family, as shown by the seal on John's will. As will be further observed in succeeding pages, from the time of Isaiah Harrison's settlement at Smithtown until his death the deeds relating to him and his sons are usually witnessed by at least one Smith. Other old records to be mentioned later show that in the case of the children by his second wife there was a marked intimacy of these with various members of the above Smith family of Augusta. Thus from Isaiah's second marriage, and removal from Oyster Bay to Smithtown, may be traced a continuation of his family's long association with many Smiths.

As Isaiah Harrison bought both of his tracts of land from Lawrence brothers, so he sold both of these tracts to Willits brothers. The 500 acre home tract was sold to Amos Willitts, as given by the above deed, while the 200 acres east of the Nissequogue was sold to Richard Willetts. These Willits were the sons of Thomas Willits (1650-1710) and his wife Dinah, the daughter of Richard and Deliverance (Cole) Townsend. As Richard Townsend was a brother of John, the ancestor of Isaiah's first wife, the Willits were kinsmen of hers. Thomas and Dinah Willitts had nine children, viz; Isaac, Amos, Richard, Thomas, Mary, Elizabeth, Hannah, Sarah, and Dinah. Thomas was a son of Richard the immigrant who came from England and settled at Hempstead by 1657. Richard the immigrant married Mary, the daughter of William and Jane Washburn and died before 1666, when his widow removed to Oyster Bay and settled at Jerico. She joined the Quakers and became a minister of the sect. Thomas Sr. settled at Islip which was named for a town of this name in Oxfordshire, England.

Of the children of Thomas and Dinah Willits, Isaac m. 1716, Clement Hallock; Amos m. 1st, 1713, Mary Hallock, m. 2nd, 1719, Rebecca Whiston; Richard m. 1st, Sarah Hallock, m. 2nd, Margaret Hallock, widow of John Powell; Thomas m. 1st 1706, Catherine Hallock, m. 2nd, Rachel, daughter of Thomas Powell; Mary m. 1691, Thomas Powell, son of Thomas; Elizabeth m. John Underhill; Hannah m. Samuel Underhill; and Dinah m. perhaps William Hallock. The wives of Isaac, Amos, Richard and Thomas Willits were sisters, the daughters of John and Abigail (Sweezy) Hallock. John and Abigail Hallock were married in 1679, and had besides these, sons John, Jr. b. 1680; Benjamin; and Peter, who m. Abigail, the daughter of Thomas and Mary Willits Powell; and daughter Abigail, b. 1688, d. unmarried. John and Samuel Underhill were brothers, the sons of John and Mary Underhill. Thomas and Catherine Hallock Willits had among others, sons Jesse, b. 1714, and Isaiah, both of whom removed to Pennsylvania, probably Bucks County. (See, *Long Island Genealogies,* by Mary Powell Bunker, pp. 73 and 85, *The Willet Genealogy* by J. E. Bookstover, p. 103, *Ancestors and Descendants of James and Ann Willits of Little Egg Habor, N. J.,* by A. C. Willits).

The old road from Oyster Bay and Huntington joins the Jerico turnpike on the western banks of the Nissequogue just to the north of Smithtown, At this juncture the turnpike crosses the river eastward and continues on into the town. Several handsome views of this beautiful river are given by Pelletreau in his Smithtown volume. The river empties into Smithtown Bay on Long Island Sound. The mention in the deed of the common passage over the river indentifies closely the location of Isaiah Harrison's dwelling. Evidently his house stood on the western banks of the river by the south side of the road leading to Huntington, and was near the present jucture of this road and the turnpike. Here passed the old settlers on their way to and from the east of the

Island, and here, no doubt, many of them accepted Isaiah's friendship and aid in crossing the river—

"Let me live in my house by the
side of the road,
Where the race of men go by,
They are good, they are bad, they
are weak, they are strong,
Wise, foolish, so am I,
Then why should I sit in the
scorner's seat,
Or hurl the cynic's band?
Let me live in my house by the
side of the road
And be friend to man."

—SAM WALTER FOSS,

Isaiah's location was advantageous, and after his removal part of his land early became a mill site. In reference to the "Mill on the Nissequogue" Pelletreau gives the following account, which he says was probably written about 1775,

"On the 25th. Day of March 1684, Richard Smith Patentee of Smithtown, conveyed to his son in law, William Lawrence, 500 acres of land at the Common passage over the river Nissequague, Bounded East by the river.

"In some period after, William Lawrence conveys the 500 acres of land to Isaiah Harrison.

"Isaiah Harrison conveys the 500 acres to Amos Willits of Islip. Amos Willits while in posession of the above 500 acres of land, about 50 years past, in conjunction with his brother Richard Willits, Daniel Smith and Richard Smith, built a dam across the river and erected a saw mill, each building and owning a quarter of said Mill.

"Daniel Smith and Richard Smith convey each their quarter to Daniel Bates after two or three years, with their right to the pond, upon which Daniel Bates erects the first fulling mill, and Amos Willits afterward the first grist mill.

"Daniel Bates conveys his title to saw mill and fulling mill to James Chipman, and Amos Willits conveys his half of the saw mill and grist mill to Richard Smith, surnamed the Quaker.

"On the 28th. of December, 1730, James Chipman conveys to the above Richard Smith and his brother Obediah, his half of the saw mill and the fulling mill with half the privilege of stream and water, and so much land as is needful for the pond to flow.

"On the 21st. of August, 1735, the above Richard Smith conveys the whole of his title to the said mill to his brother Obediah Smith, bounding him east by the eastermost part or side of the stream and pond as they run."

(See p. 458).

Pelletreau notes from the above that "it is plain that the dam and the first mill were built as early as 1725, and probably a few years earlier". A futher reference to this tract reads as follows—see p. 282;

"May 14 day 1736, then layd out a certain tract of land on the right of Debora Lawrence, containing five hundred ackers, lying on the west side of Smithtown River a place where the mills now stand, bounded as followeth. Beginning at the Said river at a certain branch of said river lying southward of the said mills Called Peasapunk branch, from thence running north thirty one degrees west one hundred and ninety six rods, then east thirty degrees north 404 rods to a marked tree being the northwest bounds of said tract, then running south thirty degreese one hundred and ninety six rods, to the meadows, then running southward betweene the meadows and upland one hundred and eight rods, then running east to the said river, then running southwardly up the middle of said river to the first bound at the mouth of the said Peasapunk branch, excluding out of the said tract two acres of land layd out to Daniel Smith joyning to the sayd meadows, and a piece of land twentyfive rods in length and 4 rods in width layd out to Aaron Smith joyning to the Sayd meadows. The above sayd tract is said formerly to have been sold by William Lawrence deceased and his wife Debora Lawrence to Isaiah Harason, one hundred and thirty acres of the above sayd tract lying southward of the highway that leads over the said river towards the house of Obediah Smith is layd out to the sayd Obediah Smith on the right of the said Debora Lawrence, and the remaining part of the said 500 acres lying northbound of the said highway is layd out on the right of the sayd Debora Lawrence to the heirs of Richard Smith, deceased, son of Samuel Smith deceased." (Book 1715-1747).

As disclosed by the following deed, the year after Isaiah's removal from the Colony of New York he disposed of his final holding on the Island of Nassau.

"THIS INDENTURE, MADE the 28th. day of April in the eigth year of the Reign of Our Soverian Lord George by the Grace of God King of Great Brittain France and Ireland -x-x-x-x-x-x- Defender of the faith &c. Anno Domini 1722 BETWEEN ISAIAH HARRISON Senior of the County of Sussex upon Delaware Blacksmith on the one part and RICHARD WILLETTS of the Islip in the County of Suffolk and Colony of New York on the Isle of Nassau Husbandman of the other part.

WITTNESSETH, that the said Isaiah Harrison for and in consideration of the sum of two hundred pounds current money of New York to him in hand paid before the ensealy and delivery hereof by the said Richard Willetts the receipt whereof the said Isaiah Harrison doth hereby acknowledg and himself therewith fully satisfyed and contented and paid and thereof end every part and parcell thereof do exonerate acquitt and discharge the said Richard Willetts his heirs executors and administrators forever by these presents hath given granted bargained sold alienated enfeoffed released conveyed and confirmed and by these presents doth for himself his heirs executors administrators and assignes fully freely and absolutely give grant bargain sell alien enfeoff release convey and confirm unto the said Richard Willetts his heires and assignes.

ALL that two hundred acres of land situate lying and being in the bounds of Smithtown in the County of Suffolk in the Colony of New York on the Isle of Nassau aforesaid on the east side of the River called Nessoquage bounded south by the Common Path; west by the aforesaid River from thence eastward in length a mile and from the aforesaid Common Path northward in breadth one hundred poles taking in all Swamps Meadow Creek thatch with the benefitts priviledges improvements and commodities thereunto belonging or in any wise appurtaining thereunto with liberty of fishing fowling & hunting on the neck ye west side of the river aforesd. and ye liberty off commonage for creatures cutt creek thatch in the said River Nessoquage.

TO HAVE AND TO HOLD the said two hundred acres of land and all and singular the within granted premises with their appurtenances to the said Richard Willetts his heirs and assignes for is and there own proper use benefitt and behoofe forever and the said Isaiah Harrison for himself and his heirs executors and administrators doth hereby covenant promise and grant to and with the said Richard Willetts his heires and assignes that he the said Isaiah Harrison is at the ensea-ling and delivery hereof the true sole a-ad lawfull owner of the above bargained premises and hath in himself good right full power and lawfull authoryty to sell and dispose of the same in manner as above said and that the Said Richard Willittes his heires and assignes shall and may from time to time and at all times for ever hereafter have hold use and occupy posess and enjoy the said granted premises freely and clearly acquited and of and from any incumberances whatsoever and the said Isaiah Harrison for himself and his heires, and assignes doth hereby *hereby* warrent and defend the above granter premises against the just and lawfull claim of any person or persons whatsoever and further to give any better confirmation hereof as shall be reasonably advised or devised by ye sd. Richard Willetts his heires or assignes or his or their counsell learned *learned* at their cost,

IN WITNESS WHEREOF the said Isaiah Harrison hath to these presents set his hand and seal the day & year first above written.

ISIAH HARRISON (Seal)
ABIGAEL HARRISON (Seal)
her mark

Sealed & delivered in presence of us
William Moleston
Rot. Newcombe

Sussex) SS: The above deed of sale was signed sealed & acknowledged by the within Isaiah Harrison and Abigail his wife before me Philip Russell, one of his majesties Justices of the Peace for the County of Sussex afsd. according to the contents thereof.

Test Philip Russell.

Recorded the 13th. day of September 1722.
L. Congreve

Liber B of Deeds page 95.
(See—Liber B of Deeds, p. 95, at Riverhead, Long Island).

CHAPTER V

Maiden Plantation—"Sussex on the Delaware"

THIS INDENTURE made the twenty Second day of June in the Year of our Lord one thousand Seven hundred twenty one & in the Seventh year of his Majts Reign Between Henry Loyd of the mannor of Queens Village in Queens County on the Island Nassaw in the Province of New York Gent, on the one part & Isaiah Harrison of Smithtown in the County of Suffolk on the Island & in the Province aforesaid black Smith on the other part WHEREAS there is a Tract piece or parcell of Land commonly called or known by the name of Maiden Plantation Situate lying & being about Eight miles from the Town of Lewes in the County of Sussex in the Province of Pensilvania wch was here to fore Laid out to William Darvel of the County of Kent in sd. Province of Pensilvania by warrent from the Court of the County of Sussex for one thousand acres & by said Darvel sold & conveyed by Deed Poll to John Nelson of Boston in New England Merchant bearing date the 2nd day of Febuary in the Year of our Lord 1687 who by Deed of Gift made over the same to his son in Law Henry Loyd of Queens Village aforesaid dated the 16 day of November 1713 which said Tract of Land was resurveyed in purtuance of a warrent from the Comisioners of Property the first day of January 1717/8 to the said Henry Loyd by Jacob Taylor Surveyr Genrl & found to Contain nine hundred & seven acres bounded as follows beginning at a white oak Tree near the Land of James Fisher from thence Runing South Seventy four degrees fourty mints Westerly four hundred Perches to a Corner tree flan near Brights Beaver dam from thnce South twenty degrees fiveteen mints Eastenly Three hundred ninety eight Perches to a stump Thence North sixty nine degrees East one hundred seventy eight Perches to a red Oak from thence North seventy two degrees thirty mints East one one hundred & Eighty Perches to a Hickory Tree & from thnece north fourteen degrees thirty mints West Three hundred Seventy six Perches to a white oake a foursaid as by reference being had to Deeds above mentioned & Surveyors return may more fully appear.

Now THIS INDENTURE witnesseth that the said Henry Loyd for & in Consideration of the Sum of One hundred Pounds Current money of New York to him the Sd Henry Loyd in hand well & truly paid by Sd Isaiah Harrison before the Executing of these Presents the Receit where of he does hereby acknowledge & therefrom & every part There of doth by these presents of ever acquit discharge & Release to him the sd. Isaiah Harrison his Heirs Executrs adminrs Hath Granted Bargained Sold Alined Released & Confirmed & by these presents for him & his Heirs Doth grant Bargain Sell alien Release & Confirm unto him the sd Isaiah Harrison & his Heirs & assignes for ever all ye above mentioned Tract piece or parcell of Land as Laid out to William Darvel a foresaid for one thousand Acres to be the same more or Less & by him Sold and conveyed as aforesaid but more especially as the said Land was resurveyed as aforesaid for nine hundred & seven acres Together with all & Singular the trees woods underwoods buildings Pastures fences fields meadows marshes swamps Brooks Creeks Rivers Rivnlets Islands ponds proffits privileges rights Commodites hereditaments Emoluments & appurtenances whatsoever to the said Tract of Land belonging or in any wise appartaining and the reversion & Reversions Remainder & Remainders rents Isues & Proffits thereof &

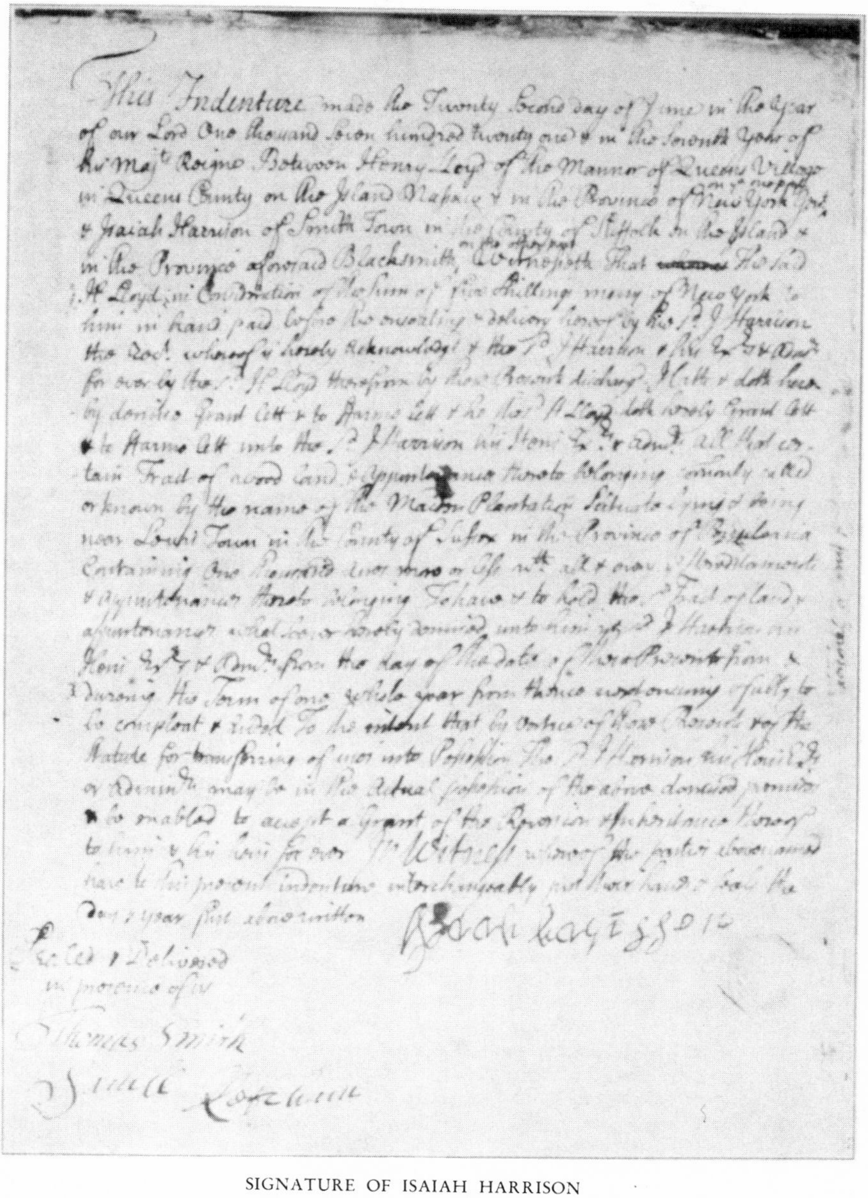

This Indenture made the Twenty Second day of June in the year of our Lord One thousand seven hundred twenty one & in the seventh year of his Maj^t Reigne Between Henry Loyd of the Mannor of Queens Village in Queens County on the Island Nassau & in the Province of New York Gent & Isaiah Harrison of Smith Town in the County of Suffolk on the Island & in the Province aforesaid Blacksmith Witnesseth That the said H Loyd in Consideration of the sum of five shillings money of New York to him in hand paid before the ensealing & delivery hereof by the s^d I Harrison the Rec^t whereof is hereby acknowledged [illegible] by these Presents [illegible] doth [illegible] Grant [illegible] unto the s^d I Harrison his Heirs [illegible] all that certain Tract of [illegible] Land & Appurtenances thereto belonging [illegible] known by the name of the Maiden Plantation Situate lying & being near Lewis Town in the County of Sussex in the Province of [illegible] Containing One Hundred acres more or less with all & every [illegible] & Appurtenances thereto belonging To have & to hold the s^d Tract of land & appurtenances [illegible] unto him the s^d I Harrison his Heirs [illegible] from the day of the date of these Presents from & during the Term of one whole year from thence next ensuing [illegible] to be compleat & ended To the intent that by Virtue of these Presents [illegible] the Statute for transferring of uses into Possession the s^d I Harrison his Heirs [illegible] may be in the Actual possession of the above [illegible] premises & be enabled to accept a Grant of the Reversion & Inheritance thereof to him & his heirs for ever In Witness whereof the parties above named have to these present Indentures interchangeably put their hands & seals the day & year first above written

Sealed & Delivered in presence of us

Thomas Smith

[illegible]

SIGNATURE OF ISAIAH HARRISON

In connection with his purchase of Maiden Plantation.

See pages 42 and 71.

(By permission of the New York Historical Society.)

also all the Estate Right Title Interest inheritance property claim & Demand whatsoever of me the said Henry Loyd & my heirs respectivly of in or to the Same or any part there- of TO HAVE & TO HOLD the said Tract or parcell of Land with the appurtenances There of unto the said Iasiah Harrison his heirs & asignes for ever to his or their only Sole & proper use benefit & behoof from henceforth & forevermore absolutely without any maner of reclaim challenge or Contradiction of me the said Henry Loyd or any other person claiming any interest herein from by or under me my heirs Executrs or ad- minrs the said tract or parcell of Land & appurtenances being now in the posession & Seisin of the said Isaiah Harrison by vesture of one Indenture of Grant & Lease & made the day before the date here of for the term of one year by the said Henry Loyd of the one part & the said Isaiah Harrison on the other part and by virture of the statute for trans- ferring of uses into posession and the said Henry Loyd for himself his heirs Executrs & adminrs Doth hereby convenant Grant & agree to & with the said Isaiah Harrison his heirs & asignes that he the said Henry Loyd & his heirs shall & will warrent & defend the said Tract of Land & premises (as resurveyed by Jacob Taylor as aforesd for nine hundred & seven acres) to the Said Isaiah Harrison & his heirs & assgnes against all Per- sons what so ever lawfully claiming the same or any part There of and futher that the said Henry Loyd his heirs shall & will at any time within Three years after the date here of at the reasonable request & at the Cost & charge of him the said Isaiah Harrison give & execute any other deeds or Conveyances for the sd Land & premises to the sd. Isaiah Harrison his heirs & asignes for the futher vesting the sd. Land & premises to the sd. Isaiah Harriason his heirs & assignes for ever as by council Learned in the Law shall be judged requisite IN WITNESS where of the said Henry Loyd hath here unto set his hand & seal the day & year here in mentioned

Signed Sealed & Delivered in presence of us the words on the other side near the land of James Fisher first interlined. Thomas Everet, Small. Pecton.

Henry Loyd. Seal.

Received of Mr Isaiah Harrison the Consideration money herein mentioned being one hundred pounds. June 22, 1721.

Henry Loyd.

Suffolk SS. June 23, 1721.
The above named Henry Loyd personally appearing before me the Subscriber one of his majts justices of ye Peace for the sd. County acknowledged the foregoing instrument to be his free act & Deed.

John Wickes.

Sussex SS. The within Deed of sale was acknowledged & made over In an open Court of Common pleas held at Lewes for the County afsd on the sixth day of August 1722 by Capt. Jonathan Baily Lawfull Atorney of the within Henry Loyd unto the within Isaiah Harrison his heirs & assignes according to Law & the within contents.

Teste Phil Russel D. Clk.

The above deed is found in Deed Book F-6, 1721-1733, page 53, of Sussex County at Georgetown, Deleware, under "Deed of Sale Henry Loyd to Isaiah Harrison". The following three deeds on pages four, seven, and ten, respectively of Deed Book G. N. No. 7, 1733 at Georgetown, are significant, as they disclose the names of three of Isaiah Harrison's sons by his second wife, Abigail.

"Deed of Sale Isiah Harrison To his Son Thoms Harrison".

THIS INDENTURE Made the tenth day of October in the year of Our Lord one thousand Seven hundred & thirty two Between Isiah Harrison of the Broadkill hundred in the County of Sussex & in the province of Pensilvania yeomn of the One part & Thoms Harrison his Son of ye county & Province aforesd Yeomn of ye other part Whereas there is a certain tract piece or Percel of Land commonly called & known by the name of Maiden plantation—Situate Lying & Being about Eight Miles from the Town of Lewis in the County afsd Which was heretofore Laid out to Willm Darval in ye county of Kent in ye Province of Pensilvania By Warrant from ye Court of County of Sussex for One thousand Acres & By ye Sd Darval Sold & Conveyed By deed Poll To Jno Nelson of Boston in New england Marcht Bearing date ye Second day of February in the year of Our Lord 1687 Who By deed of Gift Made Over ye Same To his Son in Law Henry Loyd of queens vilage of queens County in the Island of Nassaw in ye province of New York Gent dated ye 16th day of November 1713 Which Said Tract of Land was resurveyed in pursuance of a Warnt from ye Comisr of Property the first day of January 1717/8 To ye Sd Henry Loyd By Jacob Taylor Surveyor Genl. & found to Contain Nine hundred and Seven Acres Bounded as follows Begining at a white oak tree Near the Land of James Fisher from thence running South Seventy four degrees forty five Minutes Westerly four hundred perches to a corner tree fallen Near Brights Beaverdam from Thence South twenty degrees fifteen Minutes Easterly three hundred Ninety eight perches to a Stump thence North Sixty Nine degrees East One hundred Seventy Eight perch to a red Oak from thence North Seventy two degrees thirty Minutes East One hundred & eighty perches To a hickory Tree thence North fourteen degrees thirty Minutes West three hundred Seventy Six perch to ye White oak Aforesd. as By reference Being had to the deeds above Mentioned & Surveyors return may more fully appear And Whereas the Sd Henry Loyd By Certain deeds of Lease & release bearing date ye [twenty] first and second days of June in ye year of our Lord One thousand Seven hundred and Twenty one and for ye Consideration Therein Mentioned grant release & Confirm unto ye Sd Isiah Harrison his heirs Executs. & administrators all ye above described tract of Land To hold to him the Sd. Isiah Harrison his heirs & assigns for Ever As By ye Last recited deeds of Lease & release May More fully & at Large appear

Now THIS INDENTURE Witnesseth that ye Sd Isiah Harrison for & in consideration of ye Sum of five Shillings of Lawfull Money of America to him in hand paid by the Sd Thomas Harrison Before ye Executing of these presents ye receipt Whereof he doth hereby acknowledge & therefrom & every part thereof doth by these presents forever acquit & discharge & release ye Sd. Thomas Harrison his heirs Executors & adminsistrators hath granted Bargained Sold Ailiened released & Confirmed & By these presents for him & his heirs doth grant Bargain Sell Alien release & Confirm unto him the Sd Thomas Harrison his heirs & asigns forever Two Hundred & fifty acres of Land Bounded at One End By a line runing North fourteen degrees Thirty Minutes West & Thence Joyning to his Brother Daniel Harrisons Land To a Line running South Twenty degrees fourteen Minutes East thence along that Line so far As to Make up the Sd Tract Two hundred & fifty acres of Land & Being part of pt. abovesaid Nine hundred & Seven Acres Together With all & Singular ye Woods trees underwoods

Edifices Buildings pastures fences fields meadows Marshes Swamps brooks creeks rivers rivelets Island Ponds profits rights privileges Commodities Hereditaments Emoluments & appertenances Whatsoever to the Sd Two hundred & fifty Acres of Land belonging or in Any Wise Appertaining & ye reversion & reversions remainder remainders rents Isues & profits thereof & also all ye estate right title Interest inheritance property claim & Demand Whatsoever of him ye Sd Isiah Harrison & his heirs respectivly of in & to the Last described Tract of Land or Any part or parcel thereof

TO HAVE & TO HOLD ye Sd Tract or parcel of Land With ye appurtenances unto him ye Sd Thomas Harrison his heirs & Asigns forever To his & their only Sole & proper use Benefit & Behoof from henceforth & forever Aboslutely & Without Any Let reclaim chalenge & Contradiction of him ye sd. Isiah Harrison or any other person claiming or to Claim Any right Titile or Interest therein by from or under him his heirs Executors or administrs the Sd Tract or parcel of Land & appurtenances Hereby granted Being now in ye posession & Seizin of the Sd Thomas Harrison By verture of One Indenture of Lease made ye day Before ye day of ye date hereof for the Term of One year By the Sd Isiah Harrison of the One part & ye sd. Thos Harrison of ye other part & By verture of ye Statute for Transfering of uses into posession and the Sd Isiah Harrison for him Self his heirs Executs & adminrs doth hereby Covenant & agree To & with the Sd Thomas Harrison his heirs & assigns that the Sd Isiah Harrison & his heirs Shall & Will Warrent & forever Defend the Last described tract of Land & premises To ye Sd. Thomas Harrison his heirs & asigns against all persons whatsoever Lawfully claiming or to claim ye Same or Any part thereof and further that he ye Sd Isiah Harrison & his heirs shall & will at any time Within the space of three years after ye date hereof at the Reasonable request cost & Charges of him ye Sd Thomas Harrison Make give and Execute any other deeds or Conveyances for the sd. Two hundred & fifty Acres of Land & premises unto ye Sd Thoms Harrison his heirs & assigns for Ever the further & Better Securing & Vesting ye Sd Land & premises to the Sd. Thos Harrison his heirs & assigns forever As By his or their Council Learned in ye Law Shall Be reasonably Devised Advised & required IN WITNESS Whereof the Sd Isiah Harrison hath hereunto Set his hand & Seal dated ye day & year first above written

Isiah Harrison Seal.

Sealed & Delivered in the presence of us
Robt. Smith. Robt. Shankland.
Sussex County SS.

The above deed of release was acknowledged & Made Over in Open Court held at Lewis for the County of Sussex on delaware the Seventh day of Novemb Anno Dom 1733 By the above Named Isiah Harrison To his son Thomas Harrison according to Law and the above Contents.

Test. Phil Russel, Porthonotary.

Then follows "Lease of Isiah Harrison to Thomas Harrison his son, Oct. 9, 1732."

"Deed of Release Isiah Harrison to Danl Harrison."

THIS INDENTURE Made the tenth day of October in the Year of Our Lord One thousand Seven hundred & Thirty Two Between Isiah Harrison of Broadkill Hundred in ye County of Sussex in the province of Pensilvania Yeoman of ye one part & Daniel Harrison of ye sd. County & province yeoman his son of the other part. Whereas there is a certain Tract piece or percel of Land comonly Called or known

By the Name of ye Maiden Plantation Situate Lying & Being about Eight Miles from the Town of Lewis in the County afsd Which was heretofore Laid out to Willm Darval in the County of Kent in ye sd Province of Pensilvania By Warrent from ye Court of County of Sussex for One thousand Acres & By ye said darval Sold & Conveyed By deed Poll To John Nelson of Boston in New england Marcht Bearing date ye Second day of February in the year of Our Lord 1687 Who By deed of Gift Made Over ye Same To his Son in Law Henry Loyd of queens vilage of queens County in the Island of Nassaw in the province of New york Gent dated ye 16th day of November 1713 Which Said Tract of Land was resurveyed in pursuance of a Warrent from the Commissioners of property the first day of January 1717/8 To the sd. Henry Loyd By Jacob Taylor Surveyor Genr. & found to Contain Nine Hundred and Seven acres Bounded as follows Beginning at a white oak tree Near the Land of James Fisher from thence running South Seventy four degrees fourty five Minutes Westerly four hundred perches to a corner tree fallen Near Brights Beaverdam from Thence South Twenty Degrees fifteen Minutes Easterly three hundred Ninety eight perches to a Stump thence North Sixty Nine degrees east One hundred Seventy Eight perch to a red Oak from Thence North Seventy two degrees thirty Minutes East One hundred & eighty perches To a hickory Tree thence North fourteen degrees thirty Minutes West three hundred Seventy Six perch to ye White oak A foresd. as by reference Being had to ye deeds above mentioned & Surveyors return may more fully appear & whereas the Sd Henry Loyd By Certain deeds of Lease & release bearing date ye [twenty] first and second days of June in ye year of Our Lord one thousand Seven hundred & Twenty One and for ye consideration therein Mentioned grant release & Confirm unto ye Sd Isiah Harrison his heirs Executs. & adminstrators all ye above described tract of Land To hold to him ye sd. Isiah Harrison his heirs assigns for Ever As By ye Last recited deeds of Lease & release May more fully and at Large appear

Now THIS INDENTURE Witnesseth that ye Sd Isiah Harrison for & in consideration of ye Sum of five Shillings of Lawfull Money of America to him in hand paid By ye Sd Daniel Harrison before ye Executing of these presents ye receipt Whereof he doth hereby acknowledge & therefrom & every part thereof doth by these presents forever Acquit discharge & release him ye Sd Daniel Harrison his heirs Executors & administrators Hath Granted Bargained Sold Aliened released & Confirmed & By these presents for him and his heirs Doth grant Bargain Sell Alien release & Confirm unto him the Sd Daniel Harrison his heirs & assigns forever Two Hundred & fifty acres of Land Bounded at One End By a line running North fourteen degress Thirty Minutes West to the abovesaid Beginning Whiteoak thence by ye Sd Line running Seventy four degrees fourty five Minuts Westerly four hundred perches To the above Corner tree fallen near Brights Beaver dam Thence South Twenty degrees fifteen Minutes Easterly & thence to the place of Beginning So that ye Said Tract May Contain Two hundred & fifty Acres of Land & part of the abovesd. Nine Hundered & Seven Acres Together With all & Singular the woods trees underwoods Edifices Buildings pastures fences fields meadows Marshes Swamps brooks creeks rivers rivelets Islands ponds Proffits Priveleges rights Comodities Hereditaments Emoluments & appertenances Whatsoever to the Sd Two hundred & fifty Acres of Land belonging or in Any Wise Appertaining & ye reversion & reversions remainder and Remainders rents Isues & profits Thereof & also all ye Estate right Title Inheritance Property claim & Demand Whatsoever of him the sd. Isiah Harrison & his heirs respectively of in or to the Last described Tract of Land Or Any part or parcel thereof.

TO HAVE & TO HOLD ye Sd Tract or parcel of Land With ye appurtenances unto him the sd. Daniel Harrison his heirs & Assigns forever To his & their only Sole & proper use Benifit & behoof from henceforth & forever Absolutely & Without Any Let reclaim chalenge or contradiction of him ye sd. Isiah Harrison or any other persons claiming or to Claim Any right Title or Interest therein by from or under him his heirs Executors or administrs the Sd Tract or parcel of Land & appurtenances Hereby granted Being now in ye posession & Seizin of the Sd. Daniel Harrison By vertue of One Indenture of Lease made ye Day Before the day of date hereof for the Term of One year By the Sd Isiah Harrison of the One part & the sd. Daniel Harrison of the other part & by vertue of ye Statute for Transfering of uses into possesion and the Sd Isiah Harrison for him Self his heirs Executs & adminrs doth hereby Covenant & agree To & with the sd. Daniel Harrison his heirs & assigns that the Sd Isiah Harrison & his heirs Shall & Will Warrant & forever Defend ye Last described tract of Land & Premises to ye Sd. Daniel Harrison his heirs and assignes against all persons whatsoever Lawfully claiming or to claim ye Same or Any part thereof and further that he ye Sd. Isiah Harrison & his heirs shall & will at any time Within the space of three years after the date hereof at the Reasonable request cost & Charges of him the sd. Daniel Harrison Make give and Execute any other deeds or Conveyances for ye ed. Two hundred & fifty acres of Land & premises unto the sd. Daniel Harrison his heirs & essigns for ye further & Better Securing & vesting ye Sd Land & premises to ye Sd. daniel Harrison his heirs & assigns forever As By his or their Council Learned in ye Law Shall Be reasonably Devised Advised & required in WITNESS Whereof the Sd. Isiah Harrison hath hereunto Set his hand & Seal Dated the day & year first above Written

.... *(Signature not copied on deed book).*

Sealed & Delivered in the presence of us
Robt. Smith. Robt. Shankland.
Sussex County S. S.

The above deed of release was acknowledged & Made Over in Open Court held at Lewis for the county of Sussex on delaware the Seventh day of November Anno. Dom. 1733 By the above Named Isiah Harrison unto his Sd. Son Daniel Harrison according to Law and the above Contents.

Test. Phil Russel. Prothonry.

Then follows the lease for one year of the above tract, Isiah Harrison to Daniel Harrison his son, Oct. 9, 1732.

"Deed of Release Isaiah Harrison to Jeremih. Harrison".

THIS INDENTURE Made the tenth day of October in the year of Our Lord one thousand Seven hundred & thirty two Between Isaiah Harrison of Broadkill hundred in the County of Sussex & in ye Province of pensilvania yeoman of the One part and Jeremiah Harrison his Son of ye Sd County & province yeoman of ye other part Wheras there is a certain tract piece or Parcel of Land commonly called or known by ye Name of Maiden Plantation Situate Lying & Being about Eight Miles from the Town of Lewis in the County afsd Which was heretofore Laid out for William Darvall in ye county of Kent in ye province of pensilvania By Warrent from ye Court of Sussex for One Thousand Acres And By ye Sd Darval Sold & conveyed By deed Poll to John Nelson of Boston in New england Marcht Bearing date ye Second day of February in the year of Our Lord 1687 Who By deed of Gift Made Over ye Same To his Son in Law Henry Loyd of queens vilage of queens County in ye Island of Nassaw in ye province of New York Gent dated ye Sixteenth day of Novemb. 1713 Which Sd tract of Land was resurveyed in pursuance of a Warrnt from ye Commiss. of property ye first day of January 1717/8 To ye Sd Hnry Loyd By Jacob Taylor Surveyor Genl. & found to Contain Nine hundred & Seven Acres Bounded as follows Beginning at a White Oak tree Near ye Land of James Fisher from thence Running South Seventy four degrees fourty five Minutes Westerly four hundred perches to a corner tree fallen Near Brights Beaverdam from thence Running South Twenty degrees & fifteen Minutes Easterly three hundred ninety eight perches to a Stump thenec North Sixty Nine degrees East One hundred Seventy Eight perch to a red Oak from Thence North Seventy two degrees thirty Minutes East One hundred & eighty perches To a hickory Tree thence North fourteen degrees thirty Minutes West three hundred Seventy Six perch to ye White oak Aforesd. as By reference Being had to ye deeds Above Mentioned & Surveyors return more fully appear And Whereas the Sd Henry Loyd By Certain deeds of Lease & release bearing date ye [twenty] first and Second Dayes of June in ye year of Our Lord One thousand Seven hundred and Twenty One and for ye Consideration Therein Mentioned grant release & Confirm unto ye Sd Isaiah Harrison his heirs Executs. & administrators all the above Described Tract of Land to hold to him ye Sd Isaiah Harrison his heirs & asigns forever As By ye Sd Last recited Deeds of Lease & release May More fully & at Large appear

Now THIS INDENTURE Witnesseth that ye Sd Isaiah Harrison for & in consideration of ye Sum of five Shillings of Lawfull Money of America to him paid By ye Sd Jeremiah Harrison Before ye Executing of these presents the receipt Whereof he doth hereby acknowledge & therefrom and Every part thereof doth by these presents forever Acquit discharge & release ye Sd Jeremiah Harrison his heirs Executors & administrators Hath granted Bargained Sold Aliened released & Confirmed & By these presents for him & his heirs doth grant Bargain Sell Alien release & Confirm unto him the Sd Jeremiah Harrison his heirs & asigns forever Two Hundred & fifty acres of Land Bounded at One End By A Line runing South Twenty Degr. & fifteen Minutes East To a Stump Thence North Sixty nine degrees East One hundred Seventy Eight perches To a red Oak thence North Seventy Two degr. & Thirty Minutes East one hundred & Eighty perch. To a Hickory Thence North fourteen Degrees Thirty Minutes West till A line from Thence To the Beginning May Make ye Sd. Tract Two hundred & fifty acres and Being part of ye Sd. Nine hundred & Seven acres To gether With all & Singular ye Woods trees underwoods Edfices Buildings pastures fences fields meadows Marshes Swamps brooks creeks rivers rivelets Islands Profits rights priveleges Comodities Hereditaments Emoluments & appertenances Whatsoever to the Sd Two hundred & fifty Acres of Land belonging or in Any Wise Appertaining & ye reversion & reversions remainder & remaindres rents Isues and profits thereof & also all ye estate right title Interest inheritance property claim & Demand Whatsoever of him ye Sd Isaiah Harrison & his heirs respectivly of in & to ye Last described Tract of Land Or Any part or parcel thereof

TO HAVE & TO HOLD ye Sd Tract or parcel of Land With ye appurtenances unto him ye Sd Jeremiah Harrison his heirs & Asigns forever To his & their only Sole & proper use Benifit & behoof from henceforth & forever Absolutely & Without Any Let reclaim chalenge & Contradiction of him the Sd Isaiah Harrison or any other person claiming or to Claim Any right Title or Interest therein by from or under him his heirs

Executors or administrs the Sd Tract or parcel of Land & appurtenances Hereby granted Being now in ye posession & Seazin of ye Sd Jeremiah Harrison By Vertue of One Indenture of Lease made ye day Before ye day of the date hereof for the Term of One year By ye Sd Isaiah Harrison of the One part & the Sd Jeremiah Harrison of ye other part & By vertue of ye Statute for Transfering of uses into posession and the Sd Isaiah Harrison for him Self his heirs Executrs andministrs doth hereby Covenant & agree To & with ye Sd Jeremi. Harrison his heirs & assigns to claim ye Sd Two hundred & fifty acres of Land he the Sd. Isaiah his heirs Executrs & Adminis. Shall and Will Warrent & forever defend To ye Sd Jeremiah Harrison his heirs & asigns Forever and Further that he ye Sd Isaiah Harrison & his heirs Shall and Will at Any Time Within ye Space of three years after ye date hereof at ye reasonable request cost & Charges of him the Sd Jeremia. Harrison Make give and Execute any other deeds or Conveyances for the sd. Two hundred & fifty Acres of Land & premises unto ye Sd Jeremi. Harrison his heirs & assigns for ye further & Better Securing & Vesting ye Sd Land & premises to the Sd. Jeremi. Harrison his heirs & asigns forever As By his or their Council Learned in ye Law Shall Be reasonably Devised Advised & required IN WITNESS Whereof the Sd Isaiah Harrison hath hereunto Set his hand & Seal dated ye day & year first above writ- ten

Isaiah Harrison Seal

Sealed & Delivered in the presence of us
Robt. Smith. Robt. Shankland.
Sussex County SS.

The above deed of release was acknowledged & Made Over in Open Court held at Lewis for the county of Sussex on delaware the Seventh day of Novemb An Dom 1733 By the above Named Isaiah Harrison unto his Sd. Son Jeremiah Harrison according to Law and the above contents.

Test. Phil Russel, Prothonotary. Ct.

Then follows "Lease of Isaiah Harrison to Jeremiah Harrison his son, Oct. 9, 1732."

The three preceeding deeds show that Isaiah's Maiden Plantation lay within the limits of Broadkill Hundred. On October 10th, 1732, he gave to each of his three sons, Thomas, Daniel, and Jeremiah Harrison, two hundred and fifty acres of this plantation. These deeds disclose the names of three of his sons by his second marriage.

The remaining one hundred and fifty acres of Maiden Plantation was disposed of by Isaiah in the following deed—the last ever made by him. This deed besides more particularly locating the land than heretofore, is also interesting in that it gives in its closing paragraph an inkling as to some of the likely causes leading to the family's removal from Delaware.

"Deed of Sale of Isaiah Harrison to Robt. Frame".

THIS INDENTURE Made the Seventh day of May in the year of Our Lord One thousand Seven Hundred & thirty Six Between Isaiah Harrison of the County of Sussex upon the delaware Blacksmith of the One part and Robert Frame of The Same County yeomn of the other part. Whereas there is a Tract of Land in the County afsd Lying Nigh the head of the Cold Spring Branch that was formerly Surveyed for One Wm Dervall & Laid Out for One thousand Acres known By the Name of the Maiden Plantation Which was afterwards Sold unto one John Nelson of Boston in Newengland As by deed of Sale Bearing date the second day of February Annoq Dom. 1687 and the

Sd John Nelson By deed of Gift Bearing date the Sixteenth day of November 1713 Granted the Sd Land to his Son in Law Henry Loyed of queens village in the Government of New york & The Sd Henry Loyed By his attorney Mr Saml Hold of the City of Philadelphia obtained of the Honble Commissioner of ppty out of the Land office of Philadelphia a Warrent of resurvey By Jacob Taylor Surveyor General Bearing date the second day of qber (Decembr) 1717 To me directed requiring Me to run Lines of the Sd Land Which was pusuant to the Sd Warrent resurveyed & Laid outffor Nine hundred & Seven Acres as the Certificate of Survey Bearing date of the first day of January 1717 and the Sd Henry Loyed Sold the afsd Nine hundred and Seven acres unto the above named Isaiah Harrison.

Now THIS INDENTURE Witnesseth that the Sd Isaiah Harrison For & in Consideration of the Just Sum of thirtee nine pounds Current Lawfull Money of America To Me in hand paid By the Sd Robert Frame Before the ensealing and Delivery hereof the receipt Whereof he the Sd Isaiah Harrison doth hereby acknowledge and thereof and Every part & pcell doth Clearly Acquit Exhonerate & Discharge the Sd Robert Frame his heirs & assigns forever By these psents Hath given granted Bargained Sold Aliened Enfeoffed released Conveyed & Confirmed & By these presents doth give grant Bargain Sell Alien Enffeoff release convey & Confirm unto the Sd Robert Frame his Heires and asigns forever a certain part or quanity of ye Afsd Tract of Land Butted & Bounded as ffolloweth Viz.

BEGINING at a Corner White Oak of Thomas Harrisons part of the afsd Tract of Land and running with the Line of the above dividend South Twenty & a quarter degrees East Sixty foure & a quarter perchs To a Corner White Oak Standing in the Sd Line and Thence With a dividing line North Seventy four and three quarters East three Hundred thirty & Six pches to a Corner Staked red Oak in the Line of Willm Pettijons Land & thence with the line of ditto land North Twenty Six and a half degrees West Sixty four & a half pchs To a Corner tree of Thomas Harrisons Tract and Thence running With ye Line o f the Sd Harrisons Land South Seventy four & three quarters degrees West three hundred thirty and one pchs home To the first Bounder Containing and Laid Out for one Hundred thirty and four acres of Land as also his right of a small quantity of Land lying at the Bottom of the Sd Land and deemed to Be the dividing line Between the afsd Tract of Land & Wm Pettijons Land containing By Estimations Sixteen acres of Land Together with all & Singular the Improvement and appurtenances Thereunto Belonging or to any part or pcell Thereof and the reversions & remainders rents Issues and pfits thereof and all Premises or any part or pcell thereof

TO HAVE AND TO HOLD the afsd Mentioned or Intended To be hereby granted Bargained & Sold and The Sd Robert Frame his heirs & asigns To the Only ppuse & Behoof of Him the Sd Robert fframe & of his heirs & asigns fforever The rents and Services Which Are already due & Which hereafter Shall Become due and Payable To the Chief Lord or Lords of the ffee or fees thereof Excepted and the Said Isaiah Harrison doth Covenant ffor him Self his heirs Executors and administrators to and With the Sd Robert fframe his heirs & asignes Thatt Before the Ensealing hereof he is the true and Sole Owner of the above Bargained Land and premises & is Lawfull Seized ' Posessed of the Same in his own right As a good & Absolue Estate of Inheritance & hath in him Self good right full power & Lawfull Authority To grant Bargain & Sell the afsd One hundred and Thirty four Acres of Land and that the afsd Robert fframe his heirs & asigns Shall & May from time to time and at all Times for ever hereafter By vertue of these presen^{ts} Lawfully Peaceably and quitely have hold use occupy Posess & enjoy the afsd Land and premises With the appurtenances ffree and Clear and freely and Clearly acquited Exonerated & discharged of & from all and all Manner of former gifts Grants Bargains Sales Leases Mortgages Wills Entails Joyntures dowers Judgements Execution Incumbrances & Troubles Whatsoever & I the Sd Isaiah Harrison to further Bound My Self My heirs Executors & administrators firmily By these Presents To Warrant & defend the afsd Robert Frame his heirs & asigns in quite and pecably Posession of all & Singular the afsd Land & premises With their and every of their appurtenances against him the Sd Isaiah Harrison his heirs Executors and Administrastors & all and every other person and persons Whatsoever (The Sixteen Acres of Land Excepted) Lawfully Claiming or to Claim the afsd Land and premises or any Part or percell thereof (excepted as Before exceptet) Shall and Will Warrent and for ever defend By virtue of these Presnts IN WITNESS Whereof I the Sd Isaiah Harrison have hereunto Sett my hand & Seal the day and year first Within Written

Sealed and Delivered
In the Presence of us
Daniell Harrison, John Russell.

Isaiah Harrison Seal.

Sussex SS.

The above deed of Sale Isaiah Harrisson to Robert Frame for One hundred & Thirty four Acres of Land was acknowledged Made over & Delivered at May Term 1736 By the abovesaid Isaiah Harrisson unto the above named Robert Frame according to Law & ye contents of the above deed

John Welbore Depty. Clk.

From Deed Book G. N. 7, 1733, p. 155,
Georgetown, Delaware.

Shortly after his father's purchase of Maiden Plantation, Gideon Harrison also bought land in the neighborhood of the Broadkill. This is shown by the following—

"Deed of Sale for 75 Acres of Land Jno. Fisher & wife to Gideon Harrison."

THIS INDENTURE Made the fifth day of February in the ninth year of the reign of our Sovereign Lord George by the grace of God of Great Brittain Anno Domino One thousand seven hundred & twenty two Between John Fisher of the County of Sussex upon Delaware Afs. of the one part and Gideon Harrison of the same County Afs. of the other part Witnesseth that the Afs. John Fisher for & in Consideration of the sum of thirty pounds Curr: money of America to him in hand at & before the Ensealing & delivery hereof by the Afs. Gideon Harrison well & truly paid the rect. whereof he doth hereby acknowledge himselfe therewith to be fully Satisfied Contented & paid And thereof of every part & parcel thereof doth clearly acquitt Exonerate & discharge the sd. Gideon Harrison his heirs Executtrs. Adminrs & Assigns forever Hath granted bargained Sold Aliened Enfeoffed & Confirmed and by these presents doth fully & absolutely Grant Bargain sell alien enfeoff & Confirm unto the sd. Gideon Harrison his heirs executrs & assigns forever a certain Tract or parcel of Land Situate Lying & being on a branch of the broad Creek in the County of Sussex Afsd. Beginning at a stake standing on the lower side of the Kings Road at the Round pole branch and running from thence down the sd. branch binding with the run thereof on severale courses two hundred & twenty perches to a Corner marked Maple standing in the fork of the said branch and from thence up the sd. fork on the severale courses of the run thereof binding with it one hundred & fourteen perches to a corner gum Sappling standing by the side of the sd. branch at the going over at the Kings road, And from thence along the sd. Road on severale courses binding with it One hundred & seventy six perches to the first mentioned stake Containing & laid out for Seventy five Acres of Land being part of a Larger Tract Containing One thousand Acres Called Millford And purchased by the sd. John Fisher from Thomas Bedwell & Honour his wife Executer of the Last will and Testament of William Clark late of Lewes Town in the County afsd. Gent: decd. as by Deed thereof bearing date the seventh day of May one thousand seven hundred & thirteen recourse being thereunto had more at large appears The afs. Seventy five acres of Land Together with all houses Edifices buildings Barns Orchards Gardens fencing Timber Woods underwoods ways Easments hereditaments appurtenances whatsoever thereunto belonging or in anywise appertaining and all Deeds writings & Evidences touching or Concering the same or any part thereof

TO HAVE & TO HOLD the same unto him the sd. Gideon Harrison his heirs & assigns To the only proper use behoofe of him the sd. Gideon Harrison his heirs Executrs adminrs & assigns for ever clear & free & clearly & freely acquitted Exonerated discharged of & from other & former Gifts Grants Bargains sales Dowers Mortgages & Incumbrances whatsoever the rents & Services heretofore or that which shall hereafter be arising & growing due to the Lord or Lords of the Ffee or fees for or in respect of the premisses only expected & foreprized And that sd. John Fisher for himself his heirs & assigns against him the sd. John Fisher his heirs & Assigns & all & every other person & persons whatsoever Lawfully claiming Shall & will Warr. & forever defend by vertue of these presents And Lastly Elizabeth the wife of the sd. John Fisher doth hereby relinquish her right of Dower of & in the above bargained Land & premises in Witness whereof the sd. John Fisher & Elizabeth his wife hath hereunto put their hand & Seal the day & year first above written.

Sealed & Delivered In presence of
William Selthridge Phil. Russel.

his
John X Fisher Seal.
mark.
her
Elizabeth E Fisher Seal.
mark.

The within Written Deed of Sale was by the within named John Fisher & Elizabeth his wife in an open Court held at Lewes for the County of Sussex on Delaware In Feb. Anno Domino One thousand Seven hundred & twenty two Acknowledged and made over unto Gideon Harrison his heirs Executors Administrators & assignes for ever according to Law.

Witness the County Seal. Test. Preserved Coggeshall Clk. Jr.

(See Deed Book F-6 p. 49, at Georgetown, Del.)

Gideon died by 1729, according to a reference given in the "Index to Guardians Bonds in Orphans Court, 1728-1846" for Sussex County. This reads as follows— "Harrison, Gideon, Decd. Account of his Administratrix, 1729, Book No. 1, page 10". (The first records of this court have been removed to Dover). No doubt the widow was appointed administratrix. Daniel Harrison appears to have come to her aid at this time, and her brother's land passed to him in the following manner—

"Deed of Sale Ryves Hold Sheriff to Daniel Harrison. To All Christian People to whom these presents shall come Ryves Holt Esq. Shffe. of the County of Sussex

Sendeth Greeting WHEREAS William Till Esq. Trustee of General Loan office of the county of Sussex in the Court of comon Pleas held at Lewis for the county of Sussex the fourth day of November in the Year of our Lord One thousand Seven Hundred & Twenty Nine By the Consideration of the sd. Court had recovered Agst. Gideon Harrison as Well the Sum of Sixteen pounds fifteen Shillings & Sevenpence of debt as Sixty Six Shillings which the sd. Will. Till in the sd. Court were adjudged for his damages which he had Sustained by Occasion of the dentention of the sd. debt and Whereas By writt of Levare facias issuing out of the Court of Comon pleas afsd. Bearing date the Fourth day of december in the year of our Lord One Thousand Seven Hundred & Twenty Nine to Me the sd. Shffe. directed I was command that of the goods and chattells Lands & tenemts. of the Afsd. Gideon Harrison in my Bailywick Being I should cause to Be Levied as Well the afsd. Sum of Sixteen pounds fifteen Shill: & Seven pence of debt as Sixty Six Shill. damages afsd. that I should have that Money Before the Justices afsd. in the court of comon pleas afsd. the first Tuesday in May Next Ensueing to render to the afsd. Wm. Till Esq. for his debt & damages afsd. Whereof the afsd. Gideon Harrison was convided et. & that Writter. at Which day I the afsd. Shffe. returned that By Virtue of the Afsd. Writt. To Me directed I had Seized & taken in Execucon a Certain Tract or parcel of Land of the afsd. Gideon Scituate Lying & Being in the County afsd. Beginning at A stake on the Lower Side of the Kings Road at the round pole Branch thence down the sd. Branch Binding with the run thereof Two hundred & twenty perches to a corner Marked Maple Standing in the fork of the sd. Brnch thence up the sd fork on the several courses Binding with it One hundred & fourteen perches to a corner Gum Sapling Standing By the Side of the sd. Branch at the going over at the Kings road and from thence a Long the sd. road on Several Courses Binding with it one Hundred & Seventy Six perches to the first Mencond Stake Containing Seventy five Acres and that in persuance of an act of assembly of this Governor. I had Caused the Same to Be Appraised By Simon Kollock and Anderson Parker Who have Valued the Same at Eighteen pounds Ten Shill. & that I had the sd. Money to render to ye sd Will. Till at the day & Place afsd. for his debt & damages afsd. as By the afsd. Writt I was comanded having exposed the Same to Sale by publick Vendue Where the Same was purchased by Daniel Harrison he being the Highest Bidder for the Sum of Twenty pounds Currt: Money of this govermt.

Now Know Ye that I the sd. Shffe. for & in Consideration of the afsd. Sum of Twenty pounds afsd. to me in Hand paid By the Afsd. Daniel Harrison at or Before the Sealing and delivery of these presents the receipt whereof I do Hereby Acknowledge & thereof do acquitt the sd. Daniel Harrison his heirs Executs: & Admin: By these presents By Virtue of the writt of Levari Facias afsd. & of act of assembly of this Govermt. & of power to Me thereby given Have granted Bargained & sold & By these presents do grant Bargain & Sell unto the sd. Daniel Harrison his Heirs & afsd.: the afsd. Piece or parcel of Land With all & Singular the rights Members & Appurts. & all the right title and Interest of the afsd. Gideon Harrison of in or to the afsd. premisses or any part thereof

To Have & to Hold the afsd. piece or parcel of Land & premisses With the Appurtas. unto the sd. Daniel Harrison his heirs & afs: for Ever to the only proper use & Behoofe of the sd. daniel Harrison his heirs & Assns for Ever In Witness Whereof I the sd.

Ryves Holt Shffe have hereunto set My hand & Seal this Eighth day of May in the Third Year of His Majestys Reign Anno Dom. 1730.

Sealed and delivered in the presence of Henry Fisher, Joseph Pemberton.

R. Holt Seal
Vie: Com.

Com. Sussex.

The within deed of Sale was acknowledged & Made over in open Court held at Lewis for the County afsd: the Eighth day of May 1730 By the Within Ryves Holt Sher: unto the within Daniel Harrison according to Law & Within Contents.

Test. Phil. Russel Pthons. et."

(See Deed Book F-6, 1721-1733, p. 368, at Georgetown, Delaware.)

The second son of Isaiah to purchase land near his father was John Harrison, who acquired one hundred acres on Broad Creek—the Broadkill—in 1729.

"Deed of Release Abraham Wiltbank to Jno. Harrison."

To all Htion People to whom these psents Shall come Know ye that Abraham Wiltbank of the County of Sussex on Delaware yeom. for the consideration of Twelve pounds Curr. Money of America to him in hand (pald) at & Before the Ensealing & Delivery Hereof By John Harrison of the County afsd. well & truly paid the rect. whereof is hereby Acknowledged Hath Remised released & for Ever quitt Claimed and By these psents for him Self & his heirs doth fully clearly & absolutely Remise, release, & for Ever Quitt claim unto the Sd John Harrison in his full & peaceable posession & Seizin & to his Heirs & assigns for ever, all Such right Estate Title Interest & demand Whatsoever as he the Sd. Abraham Wiltbank had hath or ought to have, of in, or, to, One Certain Tract or parcell of Land Situate Lying & Being on the North Side of the Broad Creek in the County of Sussex afsd. Bounded on the North East with the Land wch was formerly John Donnovans But Lately purchased by Edward Naws & on the South west with a parcell of Land Sometime Since Sold By Cornelius Wiltbank to John Jones & on the South East with the Creek afsd. reputed to contain One hundred Acres (Be the Same More or Less) Together with the Houses Improvements Woods, under Woods ways Easments hereditaments appurtenances thereunto Belonging, or in any wise appertaining

TO HAVE & TO HOLD the afsd. purcell of Land & premises unto the Sd John Harrison his Heirs & asigns To the only proper use Behoofe of him the Sd John Harrison his Heirs Exec. Administ & Asigns for ever, So that Neither he the Sd Abraham Wiltbank nor his Heirs nor any other pson or psons for Him or them or in his or their Names Shall or will By any ways or Means hereafter Have claim Challenge or Demand any Estate right Title or Interest of in or to the premisses or any part or parcell thereof. But from all & Every Aim, right Estate Title Interest & Demand of in, or to the premises, or any part or parcell thereof they & Every of them Shall Be utterly Excluded & Barred for ever By these psents And also the sd. Abraham Wiltbank & his Heirs the afsd. Land & premises with the appurtenances to the Sd John Harrison his Heirs & assigns. To his & their Own proper use & uses in Maner & form Above Specified Against their Heires & assigns & Every of them shall Warrt. & Defend By these psents IN WITNESS Whereof the Sd. Abraham Wiltbank Hath hereunto Set his hand & Seal the Second Day of Decemb. Anno Dom. One thousand seven Hundred & twenty Nine.

Sealed & Delivered In the psence of
Alexander Draper. Phil Russel.

his
Abraham A Wiltbank Seal.
marke

County of Sussex SS.

The within Deed of Release was acknowledged & made over in an Open Court Held at Lewes for the County of Sussex afsd. the fourth day of Decembr Anno Dom. 1729 By the Within Abraham Wiltbank unto the within John Harrison According to Law & the Within Contents.

Teste Phil. Russel pthon.

(See Deed Book F-6, p.341, Georgetown, Delaware).

Settled near the Harrisons in the neighborhood of Maiden Plantation was Robert Cravens, who married, as previously noted, one of Isaiah's daughters. The following abstract is taken from a deed recorded in Deed Book F-6 page 354, of Sussex County. This deed is the first on record in Sussex relating to a Cravens.

"Deed of Sale Samuell Stewart To Robert Cravens for 244 A."

THIS INDENTURE Made the third day of February In the year of Our Lord God One Thousand Seven hundred & twenty nine Between Samuell Stewart of the County of Sussex on Delaware Yeomn. of the one part and Robert Cravens of the Same County Yeomn. of the other part . . . . for Sixty Pounds Current Money of America . . . . . a certain Tract or pcell of Land Scituat Lying & Being on the North West side of the Cypress Branch, Being one of the Branches of the Broad Kill in the County of Sussex . . . . it being the same land which was Capt. Thomas Pemberton Lately dyed posessed of . . . . Containing & Laid out for two hundred and twenty four acres of Land . . . .

Recorded February 3rd. 1729/30 Samll Stewart Seal.

Deed Book No. 1 for Sussex County begins with the year 1681. On page 245 of this book occurs the first reference to Alexander Herron, the father of another son-in-law of Isaiah Harrison.

"Edward Bran of This County weaver Appeared In This Court and by Deed of sale Duly Perfected under his Hand and seal Bearing date the fourth day of November 1719 made over Acknowledged Conveyed and Confirmed unto Alexander Herron of The same County yeoman, a certain Hundred and Eighty Nine Acres of Land Situate Lying and being on the South side of a Branch called Ivery Branch proceeding from Rehoboth Bay. In this County of Sussex, Butted and Bounded as in the Said Deed Exprest according to Law and contents of the said Deed, and to his Heirs or Asigns forever . . . . ."

CHAPTER VI

Some Preparations For An Early Western Migration

IN THE WILL of John Harrison of the Linville Creek Baptist church, previously referred to, he is styled a cordwinder. On the 12th day of April, 1737, he and his brother Daniel each executed an instrument of writing, and in the paper signed by him he is identified as in his will. These instruments are the first of a series on record disposing of all the lands of Harrisons in Sussex on the Delaware. The paper signed by John is a bond, reading—

"Know all Men By These presents that I John Harrison of ye County of Sussex on delaware Cordwind. am Held & firmly Bound unto John Sollovant of dorset County in Maryland Planter in ye Sum of One Hundred & Twenty pounds Currant Money of America to Be paid unto the Said John Sollovant or to his Certain attorney heirs Exect. Administra. or Assigns for ye Which payment well & Truly to Me Made & dune I doe hereby Bind my Self my heirs Exect. & Administr. Joyntly & Severally for ye Whole & in the Whole firmly By these presents Sealed With my Seal dated this Twelfth day of Aprill Anno dom. 1737

The Condition of this Obligation is Such that the above Bounden John Harrison his heirs Execut. or Administr. Shall well and Truly at the Next Court of Comon pleas to Be held at Lewes in ye County aforsd on ye first Tuesday in May Next in Open Court According to Law Acknowledge a firm release & Conveyance of a Certain Tract of Land & Marsh Situate Lying & Being at the Broad Kill in the County of Sussex Now in the posession of the Sd John Harrison Bounded By Edgar Naws on the East and John Jones on the West formerly Belonging to Abraham Wiltbank dcd. Containing One hundred & fourty acres More or less As by his platt May More fully appear and ye sd. John Sullovant His Heirs Exec. & Administrs in the Sd Conveyance defend Generally against all & all Manner of persons Laying Claim to the Sd. land and Marchs then this obligation TO Be Void otherwise to remain In full force & Vertue

Sealed & Delivered In presence of us John Harrison Seal."
Jacob Kollock Robt. Smith.
(See Deed Book No. 7, p. 231, Georgetown, Delaware).

This bond shows that John Harrison sold his land at this time to John Sullovan of Dorset County, Maryland, and that he was to acknowledge the deed at Court the first Tuesday in May, 1737.

The other writing mentioned above, dated the 12th day of April, 1737, is signed by Daniel Harrison and reads as follows—

"Deed of Sale Daniel Harrison To Henry Scidmore".

THIS INDENTURE Made the twelfth day of April in the Tenth year of the reign of our Soverign Lord George the second By the grace of god King of great Brittain &c Annio Dom. One thousand Seven hundred & thirty Seven Between Daniel Harrison of the County of Sussex upon delaware yeomn. of the One part and Henry Scidmore of the Same County yeomn. of the other part Witnesseth that ye Sd. Daniel Harrison for and in Consideration of the Sum of thirty pounds Curt Money of America to him in hand at & Before the insealing & delivery hereof By the Sd. Henry Scidmore well and truely paid ye rect. Whereof he doth Hereby acknowledge himself therewith To Be fully Sattisfied Contented & paid & thereof & of Every part & percell thereof doth Clearly Aquit Exonerate and Discharge the sd. Henry Scidmore his heirs Executrs. Administ and asigns forever Hath granted Bargained Sold Aliened Enefeoffed and Confirmed By these prsnts do fully & absolutely grant Bargain Sell Aline enfeoffe and Confirm unto the sd. Henry Scidmore His heirs Executs. Administs. and asigns forever a Certain tract or parcell of Land Scituate Lying & Being on a Branch of the Broad Creek in the County of Sussex afsd. Beginning at a stake Standing on the Lower Side of the Kings road at the round pole Branch and running from Thence down the Sd. Branch Binding with ye run thereof on Severall Courses Two hundred & twenty perches to a certain Marked Maple Standing in the fork of the Sd. Branch & from thence up ye sd. fork on the Severall Courses of the run thereof Binding With it One hundred & fourteen perches to a corner gum Sappling Standing By the side of The Sd. Branch at ye going Over at the Kings road & from thence along the sd. road on ye severall Courses Binding With it One hundred & Seventy Six perches To the first Mentioned Stake Containing & Laid Out for Seventy five Acres of Land Being part of a Larger tract Containing One Thousand Acres Called Millford & purchased By ye By ye Sd. John Fisher from Thomas Bedwell & Honour his Wife Executr of the Last Will and Testament of Willm Clark Late of Lewes town in the County Asd. gent. decd. As by ye Sd. deed thereof Bearing date the Seventh day of May One thousand Seven hundred and Thirteen recourse Being thereunto had more at Large appears & the sd Gideon Harrison for and in Consideration of ye Sum of Thirty pounds in Bills of Credit to him in hand paid By Willm. Till Esq. Trustee of ye general Loan office for ye County of Sussex Afd. did Mortgage the afsd. Tract of Land & premisses unto Willm. Till Esq. Trustee As Afd. his Successors & asigns and ye sd. Willm. Till trustee As afd. for his not Complying With the Annual payments Menconed in ye Sd Mortgage deed in Caus One Writt of Sevariffacious To Issue of the Court of Comon pleas held for the County of Sussex Afd. Bearing date the fourth day of december in ye year of Our Lord One thousand Seven Hundred & Twenty Nine directed unto Ryves Holt Esq. Sheriff of the County Afd. Wherein he was Commanded that of the goods & Chattels Lands & Tentmts of ye Afsd. Gideon Harrison in his Bailwick Being he Should Cause to be levied as well a Certain debt of Sixteen pounds fifteen Shillings & seven pence of debt As Sixty Six Shillings, damages, afd. & that he Should Have that Before the Justices Afd. in the Court of Comon pleas Afd. The first Tuesday in May Next Ensuing To render to Willm. Till Esq. for his debt & Damages Afd. Whereof ye Sd. Gideon Harrison was Convicted & That Writt yt which day he ye Sd Sheriff rendered that by Vertue of the Sd. Writt to him directed he had Levied & taken in Execution a Certain Tract or pcell of Land of the Afd. Gedion Situate Lying & Being in ye County afd. Butted and Bounded As Afsd. & that In pysuance of an Act of Assembly of this govermt he had Caused the Same To Be appraised By Simon Kollock & Anderson Parker who have valued ye Same at Eighteen Pounds Ten Shillings & that he had ye sd. Money to render to ye sd. Will Till at ye day & place afsd. for his debts & damages afd. As By ye Sd. Writ he was Comanded Having exposed The Same To Sale By Publick Vendue Where of Same was purchased By Daniel Harrison he Being the Highest Bider for ye Sum of Twenty pounds Curt. Money of the Government as By ye sd. deed Bearing date the Eight day of May in the year of Our Lord Christ One thousand Seven Hundred & thirty recourse Being thereunto had May at Large Appear The Within Mentioned Seventy five Acres of Land together With all Houses edefaces Buildings Orchards gardens Fencing Timber Woods under woods Ways Easments Hereditaments & appurtenances Whatsoever thereto Belonging or in any wise appurtaining & all deeds Writings & Evidences Touching or Concerning The Same or Any part thereof

TO HAVE & TO HOLD the Same unto Him the Sd. Henry Scidmore his heirs Executs Administrs & Asignes forever clear and free & clearly and Freely acquitted Exonerated and discharged of and from other & former gifts grants Bargains Sales Leases dowers Mortgages & Incumbrances Whatsoever The rents & Services Heretofore or that wich Shall Hereafter Be Arising & growing due To the Lord or Lords of the fee or fees for or in respect of the premises Only Excepted & fore said and the Sd. Daniel Harrison for himself his heirs &c the Sd Seventy five acres of Land & premises unto ye Sd. Henry Scidmore his heirs & asigns against him the Sd Daniel Harrison his heirs and asigns and all & Every other pson & psons Whatsoever Lawfully Claiming Shall & Will Warrant & forever defend By Vertue of these presents & Lastly the sd. Daniel Harrison hath Made ordained Constituted and appointed & By these presents doth make & apoint Jacob Kollock of Lewes Town in the County afsd. my True & Lawful attorney Irevokable and in My Name and for the use Aforsd. To Acknowledge the above & Within deed in open Court according to Law ratifying Confirming & allowing all and Whatsoever My Sd. attorney Shall do in these premises In Witness Whereof I the sd. Daniel Harrison have hereunto Set my hand & Seal the day and year first Within Written.

Sealed and Delivered In the presence of us Daniel Harrison Seal.
Jacob Phillips, Jacob Kollock.
Evidence Sworn Jacob Phillips.

Sussex SS.

The Within Deed of Sale for Seventy five acres of Land Was acknowledged at May Session 1737 By Jacob Kollock Attorney To the Within Named Daniel Harrison unto Henry Skidmore Within Mentioned according to Law & enterd. In Libr C

Phil Rusell Clerk.

(See Deed Book No. 7, p. 215, Georgetown, Delaware).

This deed was for the land that Daniel had bought at the Sheriff's sale when his brother Gideon's estate was sold. It will be noted that Daniel arranged to have his deed acknowledged by an attorney at the May term of Court, 1737. This was the same term at which John Harrison had bound himself to acknowledge his deed of sale. Neither John nor Daniel appear to have personally presented themselves at this court. By this term Jeremiah Harrison had also sold his land, as shown by his acknowledgement of the sale at this time. Curiously enough, the acknowledgement appears to have been made shortly before the deed was written.

"Deed of Sale Jerm. Harrison To Saml. Black".

THIS INDENTURE Made the Seventh day of June in the year of our Lord One thousand Seven hundred & thirty seven Between Jeremiah Harrison of the Co. of Sussex upon Delaware yeom. of The One pt. and Samuel Black of the Same County yeom. of the other pt. Whereas there is A Certain Tract or pcell of Land Lying & Being About Eight Miles from the Town of Lewes In the County of Sussex on Delaware afsd. Beginning at One End of the Whole tract & By a Line running South twenty degrees & fifteen Minutes East to a Stump Then North Sixty Nine degrees East One hundred & Seventy eight pchs. to a red oak Thence North Seventy two degrees & thirty Minutes East One

Hundred & Eighty pchs To a hickory Then North fourteen degrees & thirty Minutes West till a Line from thence to the Beginning May Make the Complement Two Hundred and Fifty Acres Being pt of a larger tract of Nine hundred and seven acres Called & Known By the Name of the Maiden Plantation Formerly granted By the Coms. of the Court of Sussex afsd. unto one Willm Darvell Who By his Deed Poll under his hand and Seal duly pfected Bearing date the second day of Feby. One Thousand Six hundred & Eighty Seven did Convey and Confirm the same Land & premises unto one John Nellson of Boston in New England Mercht. Who By his deed of gift Made over the Same To his Son in Law Henry Loyd dated the Sixteenth day of Novbr. One thousand Seven hundred & thirteen Who By his deed or release under His hand & Seal duly pfected Bearing date the Twenty Second day of June One thousand Seven hundred & twenty One did Sell & Confirm The Same Land & premises unto Isaiah Harrison Who By his deed of release under his hand & seal duly pfected Bearing date the Tenth day of Octbr. One thousand Seven hundred & thirty two did convey & Confirm the above Bounded Two hundred & fifty Acres of Land with all Houses Improvements Hereditaments & appurtenances Whatsoever thereunto Belonging or appertaining unto the above named Jeremiah Harrison his Heirs & assigns forever as By The Sd. Several Writings and deeds recourse Being thereunto had More at Large May appear

Now THIS INDENTURE WITNESSETH that the Sd. Jeremiah Harrison for & in Consideration of the Sum of fifty pounds Curt. Money of America To him in hand at or Before the ensealing and Delivery hereof By the Sd Samuel Black well & truly paid The rect Whereof is hereby acknowledged Hath granted Bargained Sold alined Enfeoffed & confirmed and By these presents doth fully & absolutely grant Bargain Sell Alien Enfeoffe & Confirm unto the Sd Samuel Black his heirs & Asign forever The Above recited Two hundred & fifty Acres of Land with all Singular The Houses, Improvements, Woods underwoods Ways Easiments Hereditaments & appurtenances Whatsoever to the Same Bargained Land Belonging or appurtaining & all deeds Writing and evidences Concerning the Same

TO HAVE AND TO HOLD the afsd Two hundred & fifty Acres of Land & all & singular other the premises Before hereby granted Bargained and Sold or Menconed or Intended to Be herein or hereby granted Bargained & Sold With their & Every of their rights Members & appurtenances Whatsoever unto the sd. Saml. Black his Heirs To the Only pper use & Behoofe of him the Sd. Samuel Black his heirs Execur Admin. & Assigns for free & clear of & from ye Lawfull Claim or Claims of the Sd. Jeremiah Harrison his Heirs Execur. Arministr. & asigns & of & from Lawful Claim or Claims of all & Every other pson & psons Whatsoever or Wherefoever Shall & Will Warrt & forever defend By Vertue of These presents (the rents & Services hereafter Arising and growing due To the Lord or Lords of the ffee or fees for or in respect of The premises Excepted & fore prized)

In Witness Whereof the Sd. Jeremiah Harrison hath hereunto Set his hand & Seal the day and year first Above Written

Sealed & Delivered In Psence of
John Welbore, Phil Russel

Jeremiah Harrison Seal.

Sussex SS.

The Within Deed of Sale for Two hundred & fifty acres of Land was acknowledged Made over & delivered In open Court held at Lewes Town Being May Sessions 1737

By the within Named Jeremiah Harrison To the Within Named Samuel Black according to Law & Contents of ye Within Deed Entered in Libr G.

Teste Phil Russel Prothon. ct.

(See Deed Book No. 7, p. 203, Georgetown, Delaware).

This deed was for the part of Maiden Plantation that was given to Jeremiah Harrison by his father Isaiah. The three above records show that John, Daniel, and Jeremiah had arranged to dispose of their lands by the May term of Court, 1737. In the fall of this year John formerly acknowledged his deed of sale to John Sullovan as guaranteed by his bond.

"Deed of Releas Jno Harrison To John Sullovan".

To all Christian People To Whom these psents. Shall Come Know ye that John Harrison of the County of Sussex on delaware yeom. for ye Consideration of Sixty pounds Curt. Money of America to him in hand at or Before ye Ensealing & delivery Hereof By John Sullovan of ye County afsd. Well and Truly paid the rect Whereof is hereby acknowledged Hath remised Relased and forever quit Claimed and By these present. for himself and his heirs doth fully Clearly & absolutely remise release & forever quit Claime unto the Sd John Sullovan in his full & peaceable posesion & Seizin & to his heirs & asigns forever all Such right Estate Title Interest & demand Wtsoever As the Sd John Harrison had hath or Aught to have By Virtue of a deed of release from Abraham Wiltbank unto ye Sd. John Harrison Bearing date ye Second day of december One thousand Seven hundred & Twenty nine of in or to One Certain tract or pcell of Land Situate Lying & Being on ye North Side of ye Broad Creek in ye Conty. of Sussex afsd. Bounded on the North East With ye Land Wch. was formerly John donnovans But Lately purchased By Edward Naws & on ye Southwest With a Parcell of Land Sometime Since Sold By Cornelius Wittbank to John Jones & on ye South East with ye Creek Afsd. Containing One hundred Thirty & five Acres as ye Survey under the hand of Robert Shankland Eq. deputy Surveyor for ye County of Sussex afsd. Bearing date the twenty & fourth day of aprill One thousand seven hundred & thirty one May at Large appear Together With ye Houses Improvements or in Any wise appurtaining unto the Sd. John Sullovan his heirs and asigns To the only proper use & Behoof of him ye Sd. John Harrison Nor his heirs Nor any Other pson or psons for him or them or in his or their Names or in the right Name or Stead of Any of Them Shall or Will By any ways or Means hereafter have Claim Challeng or demand Any Estate right Title or Interest or in or to The Premises or Any part or parcel thereof But from all and Every Acon right Estate Title Interest & demand of in or to The Premises or any part o r percell thereof they & Every of them Shall Be utterly Excluded and Bared for Ever By these pGents and also the Sd. John Harrison & his heirs ye afsd Land & premises With the Appurtenances To the Sd. John Sullovan his heirs & asigns To his & their Own proper use & uses in Manner & form specified against Their Heirs & Asigns & Every of them Shall Warrent defend By These pGsents In Witness Whereof ye Sd John Harrison Hath hereunto Sett his hand & Seal the fourth day of October One thousand Seven Hundred & Thirty Seven

Sealed & Delivrd In psence of us
Simon Kollock, Willm Burton
Josa. Fisher.

John Harrison Seal.

Sussex Co. S. S. delaware.

The above deed of release was acknowledged made over and delivered at a private

Cot. held at Lewes Town for the County afsd the fifth day of Octo. One Thousand Seven hundred & Thirty seven By ye abovesd. John Harrison unto the abovesd. John Syllovan According To Law & Contents of ye Above.

Phil Russel. Prothon. ct.

(See Deed Book No. 7, p. 230, Georgetown, Delaware).
Immediately following this deed is the Bond of John Harrison, as quoted at the beginning of this chapter.

That both Thomas and Daniel Harrison had disposed of their homes and removed from Delaware before the fall of 1738, is disclosed by the following deed of sale by Thomas Harrison, disposing of his part of Maiden Plantation.

"Deed of Sale Thomas Harrisson to James Hood."

THIS INDENTURE MADE the Fourteenth day of October In the year of Our Lord One Thousand Seven Hundred & Thirty Eight Between Thomas Harrison Late of Sussex County on delaware yeoman of the One part and James Hood of the County of Sussex yeoman of the other part Whereas there is a certain Tract or parcell of Land lying and Being in the County aforesd about eight Miles from Lewstown Being part of a larger Tract Containing Nine hundred & Seven Acres Commonly Called or known By the name of Maiden Plantation Butted and Bounded As follows Beginning at One end By a line Running North fourteen degrees thirty Minutes West and Thence joyning to the Land that was Daniel Harrisons land late of This County aforesd. & now Belonging To George Campbell of the County of Sussex To a line runing South Twenty degrees fifteen Min. East Then along that line So far as to Make up the Sd. tract Two hundred & fifty acres of Land Being part of the abovesaid Nine hundred and Seaven Acres of Land As By pattent Will further declare & appear Which Sd two hundred & fifty acres of Land & premises the above Named Thomas Harrisson Granted for and in Consideration of the Sum of eighty five pounds Current Money of America to him in hand paid By the aforsd. James Hood Have Granted Bargained Sold Aliened Enfeoffed and Confirmed and By these presents do fully and absolutely Grant Bargain Sell Alien Enfeoffe and Confirm unto the above Named James Hood his heirs & asigns forever the above recited Two hundred and fifty acres of Land With all and Singellar the Houses Edifices Improvements Woods under woods Ways Easments herditaments and appurtenances Whatsoever thereunto Belonging or in any wise appurtaining and all deeds of Sail or deeds of Gift Lease or release Writing and Evidences Touching or Concerning the Same Or any part Thereof

To HAVE & TO hold the Said two hundred and fifty acres of Land and all & Singular other the premises Before hereby granted Bargained & Sold or Mentioned Or Intended to Be herein or Hereby Granted Bargained and Sold With his or their & Every of His and their Right Members and appurtenances Whatsoever unto the Sd James Hood his heirs and asigns To the Only propr use and Behoofe of him the Sd. James Hood his heirs Executors Administratrs. and asigns forever Clear and free of and from the Lawfull Claim & Clames of All & Every person and persons Whatsoever or Wheresoever Shall and Will Warrent and forever Defend By Vertue of these presents and that the Same Bargained Land Shall Be well and Sufficiently discharged from all Manner of Incumbrances Whatsoever (The rents & Services hereafter or arising & Growing due To the Lord or Lords of the fee or fees for or in respect of the premises Only Excepted and fore praised)

IN WITNESS WHEREOF the Sd. Thomas Harrison hath hereunto put his hand and Seal dated the day and year first above Written

Sealed & Delivered In the presence of
Robt Smith Jean Smith
James Smith

his
Thomas T Harrison Seal.
mark

Sussex SS. The Within Deed was acknowledged at February Term 1738
Phil Russel Clck.

(See Deed Book No. 7, p. 277, at Georgetown, Delaware).

While the foregoing deeds show that Daniel had sold all of his land before the time given in the formal deed below, this deed is interesting in that it completes the series relating to the disposal of Maiden Plantation, and fixes within a close period the time of the death of Isaiah Harrison.

"Deed of Sale Daniel Harrisson to George Campbell".

THIS INDENTURE made ye third Day of March in ye Year of our Lord one thousand Seven hundred & forty between Daniel Harrisson of ye County of Sussex upon Delaware of ye one part & George Campbell of ye Same County Cooper of ye other part Witnesseth that ye L: Daniel Harrisson for & In Consideration of ye full & True Sum of one hundred & fifty Pounds Current Lawfull Money of america to him in hand at & before ye Ensealing & Delivery hereof by ye L: George Campbell well & Truly paid ye Receipt Whereof he doth hereby Acknowledge him Self Therewith to be fully Satisfied Contented and paid & thereof & every part & parcel thereof Doth fully & absolutely acquit Exonerate & Discharge ye Sd. George Campbell his heirs & assigns for ever by these presents hath given granted bargained Sold aliened endowed Conveyed & Confirmed A Certain Tract or parcel of Land Scituate Lying & being in ye County of Sussex Afs. BEGINNING at one end of ye Tract of Land Called maiden Plantation by a Line Running North fourteen Degrees Thirty minutes west to ye beginning white oak of the Tract Afs. thence by ye Afs. line Running Seventy four Degrees fourty five minutes West by four hundred perches to a Corner Tree fallen near Brights beaver Dam Thence South Twenty Dgrees fifteen Minutes Easterly & thence to ye place of Beginning So that ye Afs. Tract or parcel Contains Two hundred & fifty acres of Land being part of ye Tract Afs. Called Maiden Plantation which by Vertue of a Warrent from ye Court of Sussex was Granted unto a Certain Willim. Darval of ye County of Kent upon Delaware Dew: for one Thousand acres of Land & afterwards by ye Afs. Darval Sold & Conveyed ye Afs. Tract of Land by Deed of Sale bearing Date ye Second Day of February Annoq Domini one thousand Six hundred Eighty Seven to a Certain John Nellson of Boston in New England his heirs & asigns Who by Deed of Gift made over ye Same to his Son in Law Henry Loyd of Queens County in ye Island of Nassaw in ye Province of New York Gent: bearing Date ye Sixteenth Day of November in ye Year of our Lord one thousand seven hundred & thirteen & was Resurveyed in persuance of a Warrent from ye Commissioners of Property ye first Day of January in ye Year of our Lord one thousand Seven hundred & Eighteen to ye Afs. Henry Loyd by Jacob Taylor Surveyor General & found to be but Nine hundred & Seven acres of Land and ye Afs. Henrv Loyd by his Deed of Lease and Release bearing Date ye first & Second Days of June In ye Year of Our Lord one thousand Seven hundred & twenty one Did for ye Consideration Mentioned therein Did Grant Release & Confirm all ye Afs. Nine hundred & Seven acres of Land unto one Isaiah Harrisson Late of Sussex County Dec: his heirs & assigns forever & ye Afs. Isaiah Harrisson in his Life time by his Deeds of Lease & Release bearing Date ye Ninth & Tenth Days of October in ye Year of our Lord one thousand Seven hundred & thirty two Did grant Release & Confirm ye above Recited two hundred & fifty acres of Land part of ye Tract Afs. unto his Son Daniel Harrisson his heirs & assigns forever Recourse being had to ye Several Deeds will make it more fully & amply appear TOGETHER with all houses Edifices woods underwoods ways easements hereditaments & appurtenances whatsoever to ye Afs. two hundred & fifty acres of Land & premises in any wise appertaining or to any part or parcel thereof & all Deeds writings & Evidences touching or Concerning ye Same Land or any part thereof.

TO HAVE & TO HOLD ye Afs. Land & premises all & Singular other ye appurtenances belonging or appertaining unto ye Afs. George Campbell his heirs & assigns to ye only proper use & behoof of him ye Afsd George Campbell his heirs Executors Administrators & Assigns for ever free & Clear freely & Clearly acquited Exonerated & Discharged of & from all other former gifts grants bargains Sales Cases mortgages & Incumbrances whatsoever ye Rents & Services which are already due & which hereafter shall become Due & pay able to ye Chief Lord or Lords of ye fee or fees for in Respects of ye Premisses always Excepted & foreprized & ye Afs. Daniel Harrisson for himself his heirs Executors & Administrators Doth Convey & agree to & with ye Afs. George Campbell his heirs & assigns to warrent & Defend ye Afs. Two hundred & fifty acres of Land & premises unto ye Afs. George Campbell his heirs assigns for ever against him ye Afs Daniel Harrisson his heirs & assigns & all & every other person & persons whatsoever or wheresoever Shall & will warrent & forever Defend by Vertue of these presents in Witness whereof ye Afs. Daniel Harrisson hath hereunto Set his hand & affixed his Seal ye Day & Year first within written

Sealed & Delivered in Presence of — Daniel Harrisson Seal.
Christopher Dingee Russel.

Sussex Com. }
Sup: Delaware. } p.

The within Deed was acknowledged & made over at a Special Court held at Lewes Town for the County Afs. the 4th. Day of March 1740 before Simon Kollock Jacob Kollock Abraham Wynkoope Rives Holt Esq'es. by ye within Daniel Harrisson to ye within named George Campbell according to Law & ye Contents of ye within Deed

Teste. Shepard Kollock Dp: Prothon.

(See Deed Book No. 7, p. 336, Georgetown, Del.)

That Robert Cravens removed from Sussex on the Delaware to Augusta County, Virginia, in 1739, is shown by the following abstracts taken from Deed Book H, No. 8, pages 161, and 162, of Sussex County.

"James Hood Attorney to Robert Cravans to Robert Talbert Deed"

This Indenture made the third day of February Seventeen hundred fourty seven Eight Between Robert Cravans in Augustine County in the Collony of Virginia on the one part and Robert Talbert of Sussex County on Delaware in the Province of Pensilvania and Territories thereunto adjacent on the other part Witnesseth Whereas Robert Cravens afsd by his Power of Attorney bearing date the first day of June in the year of our Lord Seventeen hundred thirty nine did Constitute Ordain and impower a certain James Hood of Sussex County afsd Yeo. to be his true and lawfull Attorney also to make sale of any lands belonging to the said Robert Cravens and to give Deed or Deeds for the same as by the said Power of Attorney may more fully and at large appear by virtue of which said power of Attorney the afsd James Hood made sale of a certain tract lying and being in the County afsd to the afsd Robert Talbert party of these presents And before an Deed of Conveyance was duly executed the Evidences of the afsd Power of Attorney were deceased So that the afsd James could not make a good title to the Land afsd according to an Act of Assembly of this Government in Such Cases made and provided And the same being represented to the afsd Robert Cravans by James Hood his Attorney afsd the said Robert Cravens did by an other Power of Attorney renew the Sfsd Power of Attorney to the afsd James Hood bearing date the twenty fifth day of December Seventeen hundred and forty seven Now this Indenture witnesseth that the afsd Robert Cravans for and in Consideration of the Sum of ninety Pounds Current money of the Province of Pensilvania to him in hand paid........................one certain tract of land........................in the County of Sussex on the North Side of the Cypress Branch being one of the Branches of the Broad Kiln of the County afsd............containing and laid out for two hundred and twenty four acres of Land ....

James Hood Seal.

Recorded February 3rd, 1747.

Then follows a record of Robert Cravens giving power of Attorney to James Hood beginning........

"Know all men by these Presents that I Robt Cravens of the county of Sussex afsd yeomen. Have made and by these Presents............(dated) First day of June Anno Domo. 1739....................

his
(Signed) Robert R Crevans Seal
mark

(Witnessed by)
Horman Harmonson
Robert Smith

Then follows a renewal beginning........

"Know all men by these Presents that I Robt Cravens of the County of Augusta and Collony of Virginia being sensible that the Last Evidences to my Letter of Attorney are deceased.............. dated twenty fourth day of December Seventeen hundred and forty seven. (Signed as above.)

Witnessed by William Hopkins, Samuel Hopkins.
Both powers of Attorney recorded Feb, 3rd, 1747.

It only remains to complete the cycle of Sussex County deeds begun in Chapter V, by giving one more short abstract. Alexander Herring, or Herron, disposed of his land in Sussex, in May 1742.

THIS INDENTURE made the fifth day of May One thousand Seven hundred & forty two between Alexander Herring of the County of Sussex upon Delaware yeoman of the one part and Peter Dale of the Same County Yeoman on the other part............... forty Pounds Current Lawfull Money of America . . . . Tract Situate in the County of Sussex.................. Lying & being on the South Side of a Branch Called Key Branch proceeding out of Rehobeth Bay taken up by Thomas Blizard late of the County afsd deceased....................by the said Blizard sold............to a certain John Hastings as per

Deed............and laid out for one hundred and eighty nine acres of Land................which sd land by Deed of Sale bearing date fourth day of November In the year of our Lord One Thousand Seven hundred & nineteen made over and conveyed unto a certain Alexander Herring late of the County deceased father to the above named Alexander Herring by a certain Edward Bran late of the County aforesaid........................

Sealed & Delivered in the presence of us William Harding Russell. Alexander Herring Seal.

Recorded and proved first Tuesday in May, 1742, by the above Alexander Herring. (See—Deed Book H, No. 8, p. 9, Georgetown, Del.)

This Alexander Herron, or Herring, married Abigail, the only known daughter of Isaiah Harrison by his second wife—Abigail.

The foregoing are all the deeds found, prior to the Revolution, recorded in Sussex on the Delaware, under the names of Harrison, Cravens, or Herring. These deeds dispose of all the lands acquired by deeds given in the previous Chapter.

Following the explorations of Henry Hudson in 1609, and of Cornelius Hendrickson in 1615-16, the first settlement of Delaware was made by the Dutch West India Company in 1631, near the present site of Lewes. One of the leaders of this company was Capt. David P. de Vries, the early explorer of Oyster Bay. This settlement was soon destroyed by the Indians, and the next year another attempt was made which was abandoned after two years. A more successful effort was later made under the South Company of Sweden. This corporation was organized in 1624 by William Usselinx, the chief organizer of the Dutch West India Company, under a charter from Gustavus Adolphus. The Dutch members were bought out about 1640. Under this company, in 1638, Peter Minuit established a settlement at Ft. Christina, now Wilmington. Minuit's territory was bought from the Minquas Indians and was known as New Sweden. A new South Company was chartered in 1642, and a governor, Johan Printz, sent over in 1643. Printz established settlements at the mouth of Salem Creek (New Jersey), near the mouth of the Schuylkill River, and near present Chester, Pennsylvania. Friction later arose with the Dutch, and in 1651, Peter Stuyvestant, the governor of New Netherlands, built Ft. Casimer, near where New Castle now stands. In 1654 the Dutch were expelled by John Claduius Rising, Printz's successor, but in retaliation Stuyvestant with seven vessels recaptured the fort and in addition took Ft. Christina. Thus the whole of New Sweden passed to the Dutch. In 1657 the Dutch established a settlement at Ft. Casimir, and in 1658 a trading post near what is now Lewes. At this latter point a fort was erected in 1659. In 1663 the whole of the Delaware country came under the city of Amsterdam.

The "three lower counties of the Delaware", along with New Netherlands, were seized by the English from the Dutch in 1664. For a short time in 1673-4 the Dutch were again in control, but by the treaty of Westminister (1674) this territory was formally surrendered to the English, and became a part of the holdings of the Duke of York, later James II. The actual grant from Charles II to his brother was delayed until March 1683. New Castle, the northern boundary, was fixed by drawing the arc of a circle, twelve miles in radius, with New Castle as a center. The Duke was an old friend of the father of William Penn, and in August 1680, leased the country to the son for 10,000 years. Following Penn's grant from Charles II, in 1681, for the territory of Pennsylvania, the Duke of York deeded "the three lower counties" to Penn, in August, 1682. On account of various differences arising with the colonial government of Pennsylvania, Penn, in 1691, appointed a special deputy governor for Delaware. Although reunited with the Province of Pennsylvania in 1693, the "territories" obtained a separate Assembly in 1704, and a separate executive council in 1710. The Governor of Pennsylvania was the chief executive until 1776.

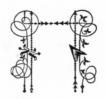

BARNARD CASTLE
Showing the River Tees, and the Hills of Yorkshire
(From an Old Print)
See Page 81

CHAPTER VII

The Long Flight of an Ancient Golden Eagle

"The harp that once through Tara's halls
The soul of music shed,"

* * * * *

"As slow our ship her foamy track
Against the wind was cleaving,
Her trembling pennant still look'd back
To that dear isle 'twas leaving."

—THOMAS MOORE

AS THE WILL OF John Harrison, earlier noticed, furnishes a clue to the origin of his family in America, so the will of his brother Daniel, and a few other "exhibits"' furnish some further clues regarding the English origin of the family. "Daniell Harrisson" signed his will in Old Augusta County, Virginia June 8, 1767. This will was proven Aug. 25, 1770. The original as preserved at Augusta court still bears the seal as affixed at the time of signing.

This seal, kown as a "seal upon a label," was applied by first placing a lump of melted wax directly on the body of the paper on which the will was written. On the top of the wax was then placed a little square of paper on which the seal in turn was impressed. The seal used was circular (or slightly elliptical) in shape, making an impression about the size of our present penny. This impression is yet distinct over approximately one half of the surface to which the seal was applied. The figure of the impression is that of a clearly defined shield on which is displayed an eagle with its wings expanded. (The tail, legs, and feet, of the eagle are for the most part indistinct, but a trace of one foot remains). Around the neck of the eagle may be discerned a collar of the outline of a coronet. The shield is surrounded with a border decoration, similar to a wreath; the same being joined together at the top by a small figure in place of the usual knot, resembling a cap. A full sized photograph of the impression submitted to Mr. Marc J. Rowe, one of the foremost heraldic artists of this country, (a former Londoner, and for many years with Baily, Banks, and Biddle, of Philadelphia), discloses that the will bears on its seal the following Coat of Arms, described in Burke's General Armory, 1851, as—

HARRISON, (London, descended from Durham; Heralds Office c 24).
"Azure an eagle displayed or, ducally gorged ar," Crest—"On a chapeau azure turned up and indented ermine a bird with wings endorsed sable."

The colors being *azure,* or blue, for the shield, *or.,* (aurum), or gold, for the figure, and *argent,* or silver, for the decoration, show that the chief motif of the arms is a golden eagle. The bird is depicted on the shield with its wings expanded as specified by the word "displayed," and is embellished by a ducal coronet encircling its neck. Thus, the golden eagle displayed was the heraldic emblem of Isaiah Harrison's family.

The flight of this eagle was noted in the reign of Charles I, as will appear anon, but how long the old bird had been in captivity before this time is unknown. From the fact that it was allowed to wear a metal "collar," thus violating a rule of heraldry now long since established of *no metal on metal,* it appears that this particular bird was already of venerable age by the time of the first Cavaliers. Orginially there may have been three eagles turned loose, this number being mentioned in the arms of "Harrison of the North," granted in 1574, as described by Burke, and as pictured elswhere for those of "Harrison of London," granted in 1613 in connection with a pedigree of a family dating from 1374. A second pedigree, however, of evident equal, or earlier, age is found represented by only the one eagle.

The arms on Daniel Harrison's seal, identified as above, were those of a London family of Harrisons descended from Durham. The significance of the seal therefore, regarding Harrison's descent, is that his father is inferentially traced as a connection of the London family, or as the descendant of a sometime resident of London.

* * * * * *

Considering the tradition regarding the origin of the Rockingham Harrisons, as given on a previous page of this work, in the light of what has so far been disclosed as to the actual records of the family, it will be noted that the tradition is borne out by a surprisingly large number of facts. The few errors found may be accounted for as those incident to the losing trace of some of the early members of the Valley family. Seven sons of Iasiah Harrison have been identified; in some way this may partially explained the mention of the fourteen brothers, although it would seem more likely that there were originally four.

The old tradition says: "Our ancestors came from England, and settled on Long Island." Isaiah Harrison is accordingly found a new settler at Oyster Bay, and has been in turn revealed as the immediate ancestor of the Valley family. That he was an immigrant is evident from the consideration of a number of circumstances.

* * * * * *

In the first place his characteristics, as shown by the records, were those of an immigrant. Beginning with his arrival at Oyster Bay in 1687 he makes his appearance as a young man unmarried. There are no indications of any home ties whatsoever. That he was unsettled, bold and adventurous, is manifest in his subsequent career. Thus he is observed first locating in the virgin forest on the site of the old Indian chief Suckscal's wigwam, soon after his marriage in 1688, and establishing himself near his wife's people. After her death, leaving him with five small motherless children, he is found remarrying and 1702 severing his connection with Oyster Bay, and removing to Smithtown, Long Island. Here he prospered and raised a second family of five more children, yet he was not permantently settled. In 1721 he is seen on the move again; this time migrating south with his family to Sussex County, Delaware, where he acquired a large tract of land known as Maiden Plantation. Here, once more he disposed of his land, following probably his second wife's death, and a little later, in 1737, ventured with his grown family into the wilds of the unsettled country "West of the Great Mountains," in Virginia. On this venture death overtook him while camping on the banks of the Shenandoah near the eastern foothills of the picturesque Massanutten Mountain. He did not quite live to see the lands on the western side of the mountain; the region in which his family finally settled. Like Moses of old—

"By Nebo's lonely mountain,
On this side Jordan's wave,
In a vale in the land of Moab,
There lies a lonely grave."
—MRS. CECIL FRANCIS ALEXANDER.

In the next place, the old account quoted fits the known details of Isaiah Harrison's history. This account indicates that the immigrant of the Valley of Virginia family was a young unmarried man when he came to America. No mention is made of the four, or fourteen, brothers having families on their arrival. This first ancestor first settled on Long Island, having come directly from England, or "Great Britain".

There is no allusion whatever to any previous settlement. The Valley pioneers in turn removed from Long Island. Thus the family was established on Long Island from the time of the immigrant until the removal of the later Virginia settlers. From this it is evident that Isaiah was either an immigrant or a native of Long Island. If he was the latter he would have been born on Long Island about 1666. The Oyster Bay Records begin with 1653, but there is no mention of a Harrison until the time of the first reference to Isaiah. Neither is there found in the numerous published records of the various other older towns of the Island any mention of a Harrison prior to John Harrison of Flushing, of 1685, or to Isaiah of Oyster Bay, 1687.

The first wills of New York down to the time of the Revolution have been published, and in addition the first wills of Long Island in particular are published elsewhere in a separate work, but there is no mention in these volumes of an Isaiah Harrison, or of any other earlier Harrisons on Long Island. An examination of the old deed books of Queens and Suffolk counties also fails to disclose any earlier Harrisons than the two above.

* * * * *

That John Harrison of Flushing was an immigrant, and probably a close kinsman of Isaiah has been noted, but certainly he was not Isaiah's father. This John is mentioned as a settler of Elizabethtown, New Jersey, in 1702. He finally located at Perth Amboy, the same state, where he died in 1709. (See page 17.) An old tradition in a Harrison family of East Orange, New Jersey, state that John Harrison, their ancestor, came from England to Perth Amboy in or about the year 1665 in a vessel "White Oak," and that his wife was Arabella Talbot, whom he married in England. The first settlements in New Jersey were made, however, at Elizabethtown in 1665, and at Newark in 1666, Perth Amboy being settled later, in 1683. This John seems to be embraced in the following curious quotation found in Nelson's genealogical notes in reference to Moses Bloomfield of Woodbridge, New Jersey. "His (Moses') first wife was a grand-daughter of Jonathan Ogden, whose mother's maiden name was Harrison, (a daughter of) one of the original proprietors of Elizabethtown, New Jersey, her father, John likewise migrated with him and his two brothers, from England, after ye restoration in 1666." (See, *Biographical and Genealogical Notes from the Volumes of the New Jersey Archives*, by Wm. Nelson, p. 33.)

The first wife of Moses Bloomfield, (b. 1729), it may be added in this connection, was Sarah, (1733-1773), the daughter of Robert and Phoebe (Baldwin) Ogden. Robert was a son of Jonathan Ogden (d. 1732) of Elizabethtown, son of John Ogden, an original settler and patentee of the town. John Ogden was at Stamford, Connecticut in 1641, within a year after its settlement. "He had previously married Jane, who as tradition reports, was a sister of Robert Bond." Early in 1644 John removed from Stamford and settled at Hempstead, Long Island, where he was made a freeman in 1650. He is mentioned in the old charter of Connecticut obtained by Winthrop. From Long Island he migrated to Elizabethtown in 1665. His sons were John, Jonathan, David, Joseph, and Benjamin. (See, Hatfield's *History of Elizabethtown*, p. 64.)

John Harrison, originally of Flushing, Long Island, and his son John, Jr., are the first Harrisons mentioned in the records of Perth Amboy, and of Elizabethtown. At the time of John's death his wife was Elizabeth. His settlement in New Jersey was much later than 1665. As elsewhere pointed out the evidence is that he, himself, was an immigrant, and that he came to America about 1685, prepared and equipped to speculate in land on a large scale.

* * * * * *

After having located John and Isaiah Harrison on Long Island the descendants of both may be traced continually through later generations. Hence it may be set down as a practical certainty that families of their known characteristics could not have been located on Long Island from 1660 to 1687 without leaving any trace of the name, especially in those days of early land owners. Then there is no tradition in the Valley of Virginia family of the birth of any ancestor of the pioneers on Long Island; only the hint that the Valley settlers themselves were born there is conveyed in the allusion to their father in the old account.

* * * * * *

One singular indentifying characteristic of Isaiah Harrison was his given name. The name Isaiah was extremely rare for a Harrison, and is not known to have ever been used except by Isaiah of Oyster Bay, and his descendants. In fact, the more one is familiar with the history of the Harrison family in general the more singular this fact appears. Extensive genealogies have been published of the Connecticut family and of the James River family of Virginia. Some of these may be seen in the various volumes of the *New England Historical and Genealogical Register,* and of the *Virginia Magazine of History and Biography*. Both families date back prior to 1645, and hundreds of names of Harrisons occur in these genealogies, but not once does the name Isaiah Harrison appear. Neither does this name appear in any of the various volumes of the *New York Biographical and Genealogical Society;* nor in those of Savage's *Genealogical Dictionary of New England.* (1927.)

A numerous family of Harrisons were early settled in Maryland, as shown by the several volumes of the *Maryland Calendar of Wills,* so far published, but the name Isaiah Harrison does not appear in these volumes. The same is true in regard to the first wills of Delaware. The early wills of New Jersey are also published, but no Isaiah Harrison occurs in these before 1737, as will be noted later. In the Pennsylvania Historical Society's extensive series of volumes there are notices of various early Harrison families, but these show the same absence of an Isaiah. The old records of the Puritan Colony, and the early records of Boston, and of other early towns in Massachusetts, Connecticut, Rhode Island, New Hampshire, Maine and Vermont, have been examined with the same result. Many sources of genealogical information could be cited, including works on the Carolinas, but a comprehensive and extended search of such sources at the Congressional Library, the New York Public Library, the Pennsylvania Historical Society, and elsewhere, has only resulted in the same reward. The name Isaiah Harrison was absolutely unique, and manifestly it was not inherited from any similar named ancestor in any of the earlier Harrison families on this side of the Atlantic.

* * * * * *

It may be recalled that Waddell's *Annals of Augusta County* states that, "The Harrisons of Rockingham . . . are said to have come from Connecticut." Just how this came to be said is unknown, but it is readily seen how the idea may have originated. Isaiah Harrison's mother-in-law, Elizabeth Wright, after her second marriage to Gershom

Lockwood, in 1697, removed from Oyster Bay, Long Island, to Stamford, Connecticut. The record of this marriage reads:

> "These are to Infform all people to whom It may Any wise Consern that Gershom Loockwood of Greenwitch In ye Collony of Connecticut & &c & ye Widow Elizabeth Wright of Oysterbay In Quuens County on Long Island were published According to order and stood up & took themselves as man and wife before Edward White Justice of ye peace ye 3 day of August 1697."

(See—*Oyster Bay Town Records,* Vol. I, p. 515.)

This Quaker wedding occurred about the time that Isaiah Harrison's first wife died, or a little before. As John Harrison, Isaiah's son, was born in 1691, he no doubt frequently visited his grandmother across the Sound, and likely passed on to his children some remembrance of his stopping with her in the interval between his mother's death and his father's second marriage.

* * * * * *

At the time of Isaiah Harrison's boyhood, relatively few of the native born white children of the American settlements were taught to write. The older deeds and wills are as frequently found signed by a witnessed mark, as by a full signature. The fact that a person who owned property made his mark merely indicated in a great number of instances that he had been born and reared in America. The early natives, as has been aptly said, were far "more handy with the rifle than the pen." On all the deeds and papers signed by Isaiah Harrison his full signature appears. That he had been taught to write in his youth is shown by the early date of the records signed by him at Oyster Bay. A specimen of his original signature (1721) as preserved among the Papers of the Lloyd Family., (New York Historical Society) bears witness that he had been carefully tutored in the use of his quill; in fact the formation of his letters hint of a knowledge of what present-day draughtsmen term lettering. (See—*Papers of the Lloyd Family,* Vol. I, p. 243. The original paper shows a seal on which the arms are indistinct, but the border engraving is apparently the same as, or similar to, the seal on Daniel Harrison's will.)

* * * * * *

Among the effects of John and Daniel Harrison, and of the latter's son Robert, as disclosed by their wills and inventories, are found articles of evident English origin, which, considering their scarcity in the Valley of Virginia in the days of these pioneers, are readily accounted for as heirlooms inherited from Isaiah Harrison, and brought over by him to this country. Thus John's inventory, (November 21, 1771) mentions a "silver hedet cane," a pair of kneebuckles, and an expensive pair of sleeve buttons. Daniel's inventory, (August 21, 1771) mentions a pair of silver shoe buckles, a pair of silver kneebuckles and clasps, a pair of money scales, and "a pair of (surveyor's, or hunter's) cumpuses." Robert in his will, (May 4, 1761), disposed of his "Best Hatt" and watch. John Harrison had also three "old chests" that may have crossed the ocean. The seal bearing the coat of arms, as used by Daniel, the rarest article of the lot, had most assuredly taken the trip and been handed down by Isaiah. All these personal effects combined were no more than what one might expect an immigrant of Isaiah's day to possess on his arrival in this country. That there were no duplicates of such articles among the brothers is shown by their inventories.

THE OLD WATER BOTTLE

It may be a curious commentary on the family, but the only known article once owned by Isaiah Harrison that has survived amongst his descendants to this day is an ancient bottle. The old heirloom is now in the possession of a member of the Ewing family of Harrisonburg. (See later mention.)

This interesting example of the ceramic art is a very flat bellied bottle with a long narrow tapering neck. It is very heavy for its size, being made of thick, evidently lead, glass. The colour is a decided dark green, almost black, showing small flakes of brown or yellow in places. The surface of the glass is covered with millions of scratches owing to the wear incident to its age, but none of these show the semblance of a date mark. In size, the bottle is about five and one-fourth inches in diameter at its belly, and about this same dimension in height from its bottom to its mouth. The mouth is about an inch in diameter outside. One pint of water fills the whole neatly; the fluid in the neck just touching the bottom of an ordinary stopper. The workmanship shows that the vessel was hand blown. There are slight markings of a twist in the texture of the glass forming the neck such as were caused by strain as the molten glass was twirled in the process of blowing. The bottom of the bottle is flat with a rough coarse concave circular patch in its center, further distinguishing its hand-made nature. The neck is finished at the top rather roughly, and a lip or rim, surrounds it just below its mouth.

A little sketch and description of the old heirloom submitted to an authority at the National Museum, Washington, D. C., in a kindly granted interview, developed that this remarkably preserved relict is none other than an Old English ale flagon, of the type of three or four hundred years ago. Bottles of this type date back to the time of Shakespeare, and are said to have been introduced into England by the Dutch. Wherever the English colonists went these old bottles went with them, and the Atlantic Ocean is supposed to be paved with them. Some of these ancient flagons are yet to be found in our older seaport towns among various other mementoes of early colonial times, as exhibited by the antiquarian. The glass used was thick and strong to prevent the gases of fermentation from bursting the vessel. The rim around the neck was used in tying down the stopper. The long neck provided an easy grip for the hand, and the wide bottom prevented accidental tipping over.

"But see you the CROWN how it waves in the air?
There a big-bellied bottle still eases my care."

—BURNS.

The story of the bottle, however, leads to no inference that such was ever its use, although at the beginning of its journey across the Atlantic it may have been stored with some such potentiality. The tradition of the bottle, as preserved by its late owner, Miss Mary E. Ewing, (1824-1916), a great-grandaughter of John Harrison, son of Isaiah, discloses that on its arrival on this side of the ocean it was leading a very temperate existence, and certainly since that time it has so continued. The tradition relates:

> The bottle is of very ancient date, and was brought over from England on a ship called the *Spotted Calf* by "one of the Harrison ancestors,"—the immigrant of the Rockingham family,—on his voyage to America. The vessel was three or more months in crossing the Atlantic, and during the time the drinking water supply ran low. In the emergency a pint of water per day was

THE OLD WATER BOTTLE

See page 72.

rationed out to each passenger, and the bottle was used by the immigrant to store his portion of the water. On his trip to Virginia, (Delaware), the tradition continues, the Harrison settler of Rockingham, (ancestor of the Ewing line), used the bottle to store an extra supply of water issued to his family for the baby.

THE PIED COW, AND SOME BOSTON HARRISONS

In Hotten's *Lists of Emigrants* to Virginia, under "persons sailing from London, 1635," 18th of July, appears the following, page 106:

"The under written names are to be transported to New England, imbarqued in the *Pide-Cowe*, p. cert. from the Minister of his conformitie, and from Sir Edward Spencer, resident near Branford, that he is no subsidy man; hath taken the oath of allegiance and supremacie.

William Harrison	55	Wm. Baldwin	9.
Jo. Baldwin	13		

In a further notation of the 23rd of July, it is learned that the Master of the vessel was Mr. .... Ashley. According to the *New England Historical and Genealogical Register*, (Vol. 6, p. 34), the original entry is in a volume in the Rolls Office, London. Some further comments on the entry appear in a later volume of the *Register*, (Vol. 20, p. 31), from which it is further gleaned that Sir Edward Spencer occupied the manor of Boston, near Brentford, Middlesex County, England. (Branford, Connecticut, was named for this town.) Of William Harrison, Savage, in his *Genealogical Dictionary of New England*, remarks: "He came in the *Pied Cow*, 1635, aged 55, from London, but we know no more." (Vol. II, p. 366.) This about sums up the situation.

A William Harrison, so called, of the province of Lygenia, later York County, Maine, witnessed a deed from Geo. Cleeve, Gent., to land at "bla: poynt," the "last day of July, 1648." (See—*York County, Maine, Deeds*, Vol. I, Part 1, Fol. 84.) He signed by making his mark, and later records indicate that he was in reality named William Harris.

William Harrison, of Boston, is named in the tax lists of Division No. 5, in 1674. (See—*Tax Lists of Boston*, 1674-1695, City Document No. 92, p. 51.) William, John, and "Ri:" Harrison, took the oath of allegiance in Boston, 11th of November, 1678. *(Records, Early History of Boston, Miscellaneous Papers*, Document 100, pp. 166, 164, and 167.) Rebecca, the daughter of William and Prudence Harrison, was born October 31, 1679, and Edward, a son of the same couple, February 9, 1684. *(Report of Records Commissioners of Boston, Births, Baptisms, Marriages, and Deaths*, 1630-1699, pp. 148 and 163.) William was one of the first members of the first Church of England organized in Boston, June 15, 1686. He died the same year. Under date of August 5, 1686, Samuel Sewall, in his Diary, notes—"William Harrison, the Bodies-maker, is buried, which is the first that I know of buried with the Common-Prayer Book in Boston. He was formerly Mr. Randolph's Landlord." (Sewall's *Diary*, p. 146.) He left a will dated July 3rd, and proven August 4, 1686. (Hoyt's *Old Families of Salisbury and Amesbury*, Vol. I, p. 195.)

In the 1681 tax lists, William is styled "body maker," and in his deed to John Button, 18th of August, the same year, "Bodys Maker." *(Suffolk Deeds*, Liber XII, p. 96.) The "Widdow Harrisone" was taxed in 1686, and in 1687; the later year being reported as "Housing 12." (Tax Lists, as above, pp. 83 and 109.) Besides the two children noted there was a son William, and all were under age at the time of the body maker's death. William Harrison, son of William and Sarah Harrison, was born March 8, 1698, in Boston. (Boston, Births, Baptisms, etc., p. 241.)

The earliest Harrison mentioned on the Boston records is apparently John Harrison, Gent., ordinarily styled "Ropemaker," who was settled in the vicinity by 1638 or 9. He is presumed by some authorities to have been the father of William, the "bodys maker." In 1647, he was one of the attorneys of John Hodges, "citizen and cooper of London." (See—*The Pioneers of Massachusetts,* by C. H. Pope, 1900, p. 215.)

"John Harrison, Gent." was granted an attachment by the Gen. Court, (of Massachusetts Bay Colony), 4, (10), 1638. (See—*Pope,* p. 215.) In 1639-40, as Jn[o] Harrison," his name appears on a list of those that "yt have lotts & propertions granted pr. the Towne of Colchester in the first division." *(Hoyt,* Vol I, p. 8.) In 1639, John Harrison was settled at Salisbury, proper. In 1641, "2nd, 4th mo," he was made a freeman of Boston. *(Massachusetts Bay Colony Records,* Printed by the Legislature, Vol. I, p. 378.) He sold his land in Salisbury to Ralph Blasdale 25, (1), 1643, and the same year removed to Boston, being received in the church there, with wife Grace, from Salisbury, 17, (12), 1643. *(Pope,* as above; also see *Boston Records, Book of Possessions,* 1634-60, Document 46, 1881, pp. 37, 38, and 77.) In 1676, he is listed as "John Harrison, Senr.," in the Boston Tax List, and as owning "Houses & wharfs 40, Horses 1, cows 1, estates 40." *(City Document* No. 92, 2nd edition, 1881, p. 62.) He was twice married, his first wife being named Grace, and his second, Persis. The latter was formerly the widow of Wm. Bridges. On 16th November, 1677, she stated that she and her husband, John, had been married "neere twenty Seven years since." *(Suffolk Deeds,* Liber XI, p. 9.) She was admitted to the church as his wife, April 9, 1654. *(Pope,* p. 215), and died March 7, 1682-3. Her tombstone stands in old Granary graveyard, Boston. John Harrison died in Boston, December 11, 1684, aged 77. *(Genealogies and Estates of Charleston, Mass.,* by Thos. B. Wyman, Vol. I, p. 475.)

His children were: by wife Grace—John, b. June 26, 1642, d. young; William, the bodys maker, probably, (aged 18 in 1666 ? See, *New England Hist. and Genealogical Register,* Vol. 6, p. 341); by wife Persis; John, b. April 2, 1652; Elizabeth, b. August 2, 1653; *Eliashib,* bapt. March 18, 1655; Anne, b. December 21, 1656, m. John Morrison, Jr., of Boston, both living there 1684; Bethiah, b. September 7, 1658, m. 1684-5, Thomas Garrett; Ebenezer, b. May 31, 1660; Abraham, b. September 3, 1661, shipwright (and clerk; see—"A List of Inhabitants in Boston 1695," Tax Lists of Boston, 1674-1695, p. 163), married Elizabeth . . . . (to whom he left all of his property by will of June 7, 1690, proved November 14, 1695); and Isaac, b. June 18, 1664, (so named on both the town record of his birth and on the baptismal record of the church a few days later). (See—*Pope,* p. 215; *Hoyt,* p. 63, and letter, J. G. B., *pens me,* 14th April, 1927.)

Of whom: John Jr. is named by his father, "John Harrison Senior of Boston in New England Ropemaker," as my "Son John Harrison of sd. Boston Ropemaker," in the elders deed of gift to him of a house and lot (with respect to a promise made unto the said son upon his marriage), 3rd, January, 1678. *(Suffolk Deeds,* Liber XI, p. 278.) And of whom, further; "John Harrison junr of sd Boston ropemaker", is again named as a "Sone," Abraham Harrison "of sd. Boston Shipwright," as my "Loveing sonne," John Morrison of sd. Boston Cordwainer, as "my Sonne in law," and "Anna his (Morrison's) wife, and Bethiah Harrison of sd Boston Spinster," as "my 2 Daughters" by John Harrison their father, of "Boston in N. E. Ropemaker," in a deed of gift to them of his personal property, signed 2nd May, 1684, "John Harrison & a Seale upon Label."

This deed was evidently a substitute for a will, and embraces an inventory of the grantor's effects listing feather beds with furniture, brass kettles, peweter dishes, plates, porringers, brass candle sticks, brass "And Irons", large long table clothes, napkins, a silver pint pot, three silver cups, seven silver spoons, one silver tankard marked I H P, money, ropes, rigging, "household stuff," etc. (*Suffolk Deeds,* Liber XIII, p. 338.)

Another early Harrison of Boston was Edward, who was admitted a townsman, 23rd, 12 mo., 1645, (*Boston Records,* Document 46, 1881, p. 86), and who appears the most likely to have been the father of William, the "Bodys maker." Savage states that Edward came from Virginia, "where, says the record, he was a member of the church." He was granted 500 acres of land in Virginia in 1640. His wife was Eleanor, by whom he had; Joseph, b. 20th May, 1646, John baptized 21st May, 1648, and Elizabeth, baptized 28th October, 1649, "aged about 7 days." At the time of John's baptism his father was, according to the baptismal record, pastor of the church in Virginia. (See, *Savage,* Vol. II, p. 366; *Pope,* p. 215, and Boston records of Births as above.)

No further trace appearing of William Harrison of the voyage of the Peid Cow, he may have accompained the Baldwin boys to America and returned shortly thereafter to London. From the fact that he was known to Sir Edward Spencer of Brentford, (a short distance west of London), he is thought likely to have been a member of the "Harrison of Braintford" family, settled in Brentford three generations by 1621. In any case, while interesting, the record of William and the Boston Harrisons only serves to accentuate a particular instance of what has already been stated in general; ie. that no reference is found in any of the early Harrison records of the colonies to Isaiah of Oyster Bay prior to his arrival in 1687-8.

THE SPOTTED CALF

The Pied Cow suggests the possibility of a Spotted Calf. Such, in fact, was the actual case. There were two boats, and as would naturally be expected, the Spotted Calf was a later boat than the Pied Cow, likely of the same line. Moreover the Spotted Calf was manifestly in existance at the time of Isaiah Harrison's arrival at Oyster Bay. An enquiry addressed to the Public Record Office, London, elicited the following—

> "The Calendar of State Papers Domestic shows that there was a ship called the Spotted Calf about the year 1690. The Port Books would probably show whether she sailed to America in 1687, but they do not give the names of passengers. The Register you mention gives them, but belongs to a series which ends before 1687." (C. F. F., Secretary, *pens me,* 25th September, 1927.)

A search of the port books of London, Ipswich, Sandwich, Yarmouth, Bristol, and Southampton, for the year 1687 (as catalogued in the manuscrip calendar at the Public Record Office), while revealing nothing further of the boat, discloses that the books of the day refer mainly to customs and subsidies, and that in various instances they are badly mutilated or faded, and in several cases in regard to the port of London no names of ships are given. In one instance a book of the series was unavailable.

The record of the Spotted Calf in the Calendar of State Papers Domestic, 1690-1691, as referred to, is found on page 233, and reads—

"Jan. 24, 1691.

Clancarty House, Dublin — "The Lords—Justices to Viscount Sydney. We have directed the ship Spotted Calf to be delivered to the Dutch Consul here, and have ordered satisfaction to be given to the captain of the frigrate and the seamen who brought her in. We send you some proposals made by Col. Venner (?) touching a marching hospital . . . . ".

This follows a notation of the same date, page 232, as follows —

"Viscount Sydney to the Lords Justices of Ireland. I have received your letter of the 16th. instant, giving an account of the late expedition against the rebels in Connaugt, which have taken a copy of, and sent the original to the King at the Hague." *(Calendar of State Papers Domestic,* as above, edited by by John Hardy, London, 1898. Copy in Congressional Library, original in *State Papers, Ireland,* 353, No. 5.)

England at this period was engaged in a war with France during the reign of William and Mary, who had succeeded James II upon the latter's forciable removal from the throne in 1688. "War against Louis XIV," observes the historian Andrews, "was William's mission in life." As steadholder of Holland he joined the League of Augsburg in 1689, and five days later, as king of England, declared war upon France. Trouble developed with the Scottish Highlanders, and with the greater part of Ireland, led by the deposed James II, and aided by Louis XIV. James arrived in Ireland in 1689, and a fight to the death with the English was on for the possession of the country. The famous seige of Londonderry ended in August, 1689, with a victory for William. July 1, 1690, James and William met at the battle of Boyne, (to the north of Dublin), and there James' hopes were decisively ended. He fled to France, but for four months longer the Irish held out. The uprising terminated with the peace of Limerick, October, 1691.

From the context of the reference to the Spotted Calf it appears that the boat had been used by the Irish in the uprising, and after being captured was loaned to the Dutch in the aid of William's struggle with France.

During the reign of James II, (1685-1688), the fortunes of London, history records, were at their lowest ebb, and nowhere was the arrival of the Prince of Orange more welcomed. The price of a passage to America at that time, (1686), for a man and wife was £11-0-0, or about $55.00.

* * * * * *

In reviewing the circumstances of the time surrounding the arrival of Isaiah Harrison at Oyster Bay, and everything known in regard to him from his first appearance on Long Island, seeking as a young man to carve out his fortune in America, until the close of his life as a pioneer in the Valley of the Shenandoah; the singularity of his name, the evident lack of home ties with any other old community prior to his first settlement, the story of the seal, the old water bottle, and the Spotted Calf, and finally, the actual verification of the name of the boat, and the indentification of the vessel with the period of Isaiah's first days on Long Island—all available data points to the same conclusion, and stamps him unmistakably the immigrant ancestor of his line in this country. That he was of good family is shown by his reception at Oyster Bay, and his subsequent life. The old seal at Augusta court bears testimony that he came of a line of worthy forbears, long settled in Old England.

"Dear old England, ever leading
Onward through the files of Fate,
Foremost where the brave are bleeding,
Foremost where the wise debate;
Mistress of the willing sea,
Mother of the nations free,

Friend of Genius, Learning, Art,
Honest friend of honest heart;
Source of social elevation,
Schemes of wide benevolence,
Pioneer to every nation,
Up the steps of Providence!"

—JOSEPH SALYARDS

Such were the sentiments of Isaiah and his people.

II.

EARLY ENGLISH HARRISONS

THE HARRISONS are said to have come into England with the Sea Kings who finally under Canute, (1016-1035) conquered and posessed the whole of the country. They were among the "free Danes" of whom Kingsley's hero, "Hereward the Wake" was one, and who were the last to withstand William the Conqueror. Thus they were in England a generation or more before the time of the battle of Hastings, (October 14, 1066), and the period of the Domesday Book, (1085-1086), from which many old English families date their origin.

Northumberland, the Danish portion of England, is said to be filled with Harrisons now, and the name there is variously spelled, sometimes without an "H", and sometimes with only one "r". The name being of Danish origin it is claimed that it is properly spelled Aryson, which is common to this day in Denmark, Sweden, and Norway. (See —*Richmond Virginia Standard,* No. 41, June 12, 1880.)

Surnames began to be hereditary in England in the eleventh century and became common after 1160, when Henry II enfranchised the land. They were legally recognized in the "*Statute of Additions*", under Henry V, (1413-1422). Given names the most popular have always been those made famous by some great king or national hero. William and Robert, and a little later John, were such names introduced at the Norman conquest, and have maintained their ground ever since.

The old chronicles of England end with the close of the fourteenth century, and the offical records begin in 1509. With the introduction into the kingdom of parish registers, 1538, by Thomas Cromwell, vicar-general, and the further growth of the system under Queen Elizabeth, accelerated by the laws of 1601, placing the affairs of the civil parish under the vestry and overseers of the poor, a more definite idea of the distribution of family names of the time, and of their specific locations in the shires is obtained.

That Daniel and Robert were early given names among the Harrisons of Northumberland is shown by a record of the baptism of "Daniell son of Robert Harrison" in the parish of Berwick-upon-Tweed, under date of December 26, 1610. (See— *The Register of Berwick-upon-Tweed, County of Northumberland,* by Durham and Northumberland Parish Register Society, Vol. I, p. 72.)

Northumberland, it may be observed, is the northernmost shire of England. To the east it borders on the North Sea, and to the north on the river Tweed, which separates it from Scotland. Its southern boundry is the river Tyne, and from Newcastle, near the mouth of this river, extends the ruins of the old Roman wall which ran across the country to Solway Firth on the west coast. This wall was the northern limit of definite Roman occupation. During the time of Canute, (and the earlier kings), Northumberland embraced the "whole tract of England from the Humber river northwards to Scotland, together with Lancashire, Westmoreland and Cumberland". (See— *The Baronage of England,* by Wm. Dugdale, London, 1675, p. 2.) Berwick, Northumberland, at the mouth of the Tweed, is furthest north of any city of England. From the old kingdom "of the North", the Harrisons drifted south among the various other shires of the country.

Directly south of Northumberland, and bordering also on the North Sea, lies the county of Durham, referred to at the beginning of this Chapter, known at the time of the above (Berwick) records as the County Palatine of Durham. Formerly, in the time of the Romans, it was a part of the general region called by them Ebor. The Romans found settled in the region the Brigantes, an ancient British tribe that inhabited most of present Yorkshire, Lancashire, Durham, Westmoreland, and Cumberland. Caer Efroc was their capital. During the Roman occupation the legionaries made the town their military headquarters, and changed the name to Eboracum; now known as the city of York. From Eboracum a Roman road, yet in use today, led south connecting the region with London.

The name Durham is taken from the peninsula which was anciently called Dunholme, or Hill Island. In Norman times this was softened to Duresme, whence Durham. The county was one of the Counties Palatine; the other two being Lancashire and Cheshire. The Palatine was abolished in 1646, but was revived after the Restoration, and with some restrictions continued to 1836. Durham, the principal city of the county, obtained its first charter in 1179-80. A bill for securing representation to the county and city of Durham and the borough of Barnard Castle, was introduced in Parliment in 1614. The city is the seat of the cathedral of St. Cuthbert, begun in 1093, the view of which from the river is said to be surpassed in beauty by no other English cathedral. The town grew up about the early church which in Canute's time was presided over by Bishop Aldune, whose daughter, says Dugdale, married Uchtred, one of Canute's earls. (See— Dugdale, as above.)

The parish registers of St. Margaret's, Durham, begin in 1559. Among the first marriages recorded were—"Wm. Herrison et Margrett Farles," November 9, 1559; "Thom Herrison et Isabel Whitfield", June 16, 1560; "Xpofor Herrison et An Walton", November 12, 1593; "Thomm Herrisson et Elizabeth Gryndye," November 7, 1598; "Rollande Haryson et Jeneta Thompson," June 29, 1600; and "Johannem Harryson et Bettram Wrangham, Jiduam," July 4, 1602. (*Publications of the Harleian Society, Registers of St. Margaret's*, Durham, pp. 1, 6, 7.)

South of Durham, and skirting the North Sea to the Humber, lies Yorkshire, and to the west borders Cumberland and Westmoreland, the three counties, with Durham, being embraced in both the old Roman region Ebor, and the later region Northumbria. In each of these counties were seated by 1575 Harrison families whose records, as collected by the College of Arms, some dating back to the days of the old chronicles, show that they had long since—

> *"Stood forth—fully mewed,*
> *From brown soar feathers of dull yeomanry,*
> *To th' glorious bloom of gentry."*
>
> —ALBUMAZAR, A. III, SC. 4,—DRYDEN

THE COLLEGE OF ARMS, AND VARIOUS OLD HARRISON PEDIGREES

The College of Arms, London, the famous official depository of English pedigrees, was incorporated in 1483. The visitations of the nobility and gentry began in 1528.

The last commission under the great seal for registering descents was issued in 1686. Some pedigrees under this commission were registered as late as 1704, but since then it has been left to the choice of individuals to continue or not their pedigrees with the College. The more noted visitations were made at intervals of about once a generation; familiar examples being those made under the Norry Kings of Arms, William Flower, Richard St. George, and William Dugdale, about the years 1575, 1615, and 1666, respectively, in which years Durham and other counties of the North were visited.

Probably the oldest Harrison pedigree of record is that styled simply HARRISON, (alluded to on page 68), tracing the descent of a London family of Tower Ward, 1633, from the year 1374. Ten generations are embraced. The arms pictured are as certified by Sir Richard St. George, Knight, Norry King of Arms, 7th July, 1613,—"Or, on a fesse sable, three eagles displayed of the field, a crescent for difference. Crest—On a chapeau Sable turned up and indented azure an eagle's head or changed with a crescent." (The colours of the crescents are not shown.)

The pedigree begins with Henry de Hede, who died 31 March, 1374, and continues through; (2) Adam, his son, "surnamed Harrison", d. May 1391; (3) Thomas Harrison, d. at Gilcalvon, 10 August, 1430; (4) William Harrison, d. 1475; (5) John Harrison, d. 9 July, 1505, wife Margaret; (6) John Harrison, d. 30 November, 1530, wife daughter of an Alonby, brothers Thomas and William Harrison; (7) Michael Harrison, of Penrith, Cumberland, brothers William and Peter Harrison; to (8) William Harrison, a merchant of London, deceased, (9) his children, and (10) a grandaughter. (See—*Publications of the Harleian Society*, Vol. XV, *Visitations of London*, 1633, 34 , 35, Vol. I, *London*, 1880, p. 355.)

Thomas Harrison who died at Gilcalvon, now Greystock, Cumberland, is said to have been buried in the church at Greystock. The arms, with the exception of the crest, are similar to those of "Harrison of the North", mentioned by Burke, as granted in 1574, in that three eagles appear in both cases.

The "Harrison of the North" arms, (granted to Thomas of Finchampstead—out of Cumberland), are described by Burke as—"Or on a chief gu. three eagles displayed of the field. Crest—Out of a ducal coronet a talbots head or, guttee de poix". Substituting the word *in* for *Out of*, in the description of the crest, and adding over it the motto "Victus in ardus," these arms are as those described for "Harrison of London, and North Riding, county York." (See—Burke's *Gen. Armory, London,* 1851, and *Grantees of Arms to the end of the 17th Century*, by Joseph Foster, ed. by W. Harry Rylands, Harleian Society, Vol. LXVI, 1915, p. 116.)

A second early Harrison pedigree of manifest equal age of the above is found among the Middlesex pedigrees of 1593 and 1634, as collected by Richard Mundy.

This pedigree, styled "HARRISON OF BRAINTFORD, (see page 75), begins with Stephen Harisonn of Kendall, Westmoreland, and continued through; (2) John Harisonn of Kendall, wife Jane, sister of Wm. Eland; (3) Thomas Harisonn, (second son), wife Mary, dau. of Henry Blackwell, brother John Harisonn; (4) William Harrifsonn, wife Jane, dau. of Henry Colombell; (5) John Harrisonn, wife Elizabeth, dau. and heir of Richard Nynesor; (6) John Harrisonn, wife Jane, dau. of Richard Kendall; (7) Willm. Harrisonn, of Braintfford, county Middlesex, (second son), wife dau. of . . . . Skeggs, brothers, John, (first son, d. without issue), Robert, (third son), and George Harrifsonn, (fourth son); (8) John Harrisonn of Braintfford, wife dau. of . . . . Edwards; to (9) Thomas Harrisonn of Braintfford, d. without issue 17 May, 1621, wife Margaret, dau. of Lawrence Lepton in York.

The descent of Richard Nynesor from his great grandfather, William Nynesor, is noted; and also various descents from Robert and George Harrifson. Robert's son is named in the pedigree as Robert, and his grandson, as John. (*Publications of the Harleian Society,* Vol. LXV, *Middlesex Pedigrees,* London, 1914, p. 148.)

No arms appear on this pedigree. However, in the pedigree of HARRISON OF GOBIONS MANOR, found in the Visitation of Northamptonshire, 1618-19, tracing the descendants of George above, the arms are stated to be: "Quartely—1 and 4, Gules, an eagle displayed and a cheif Or: 2 and 3, Sable, a chevron Ermine between three clenched dexter hands Argent erased Gules. Crest—A snake vert entwined round a broken column Or". The first and fourth quartering, and the crest, pertains to the Harrison descent.

This pedigree begins with John Harrison who married Elizabeth Nynesor. From George the descent is through; (1) Robert Harrison, of Stow, Northampton, wife Elizabeth, dau. of .... Fritz-Geffry of co. Bedford; (2) Thomas Harrison of Northampton, wife Elizabeth, dau. of Francis Bernard of Abington, Northampton, brothers John and Robert Harrison, (last s. p.), and four sisters; to (3) Thomas Harrison of Gobyons Manor in the Towne of Northampton, 1618, (second son), brothers, Francis, eldest, died without issue, Jonathan (third son), Joseph, (fourth son), William, Benjamin, and Richard Harrison, sisters Prudence and Sarah. (*Visitations of Northamptonshire,* 1564, 1618-19, ed. by Walter C. Metcalfe, 1887, p. 98.)

* * * * * *

In county Durham, (Chester Ward, Wickham Parish), just to the south of the old Roman wall, the estate of Byermoor descended in 1566 to the heirs of Richard Hodshon, whose sister Agnes married William Harrison of Wickham. The whole tenure was reunited by a purchase in the Harrison family, and in 1616 William Harrison, son of William and Agnes, died seized of Byermoor, "containing a messuage, a hundred acres of arable, as many of meadow, twice as much pasture, 40 acres of woodland, and two hundred of moor, held by the 20th. part of a knight's service", leaving William Harrison of Byermoor, Gent., his son and heir.

William Harrison, son and heir of Agnes, inherited one fourth of the estate in 1566. He was buried 9th November, 1616, and his administration granted to his son Richard, 14th December, 1616. His wife was Margery, the daughter of James Rawe, who was living, aged 66, in 1606.

The pedigree of HARRISON OF BYERMOOR and BRIANS LEAP appears in Surtee's *History of Durham,* from which the above details are gleaned. The descent is traced from Thomas Hogeson of Biermore, "son and heir of Jane Robson, who was daughter and heir of John Gilford, Ing. p.m. 4 Sinews," through two Hogeson generations, (Hugh, the heir 1505, and George, 1508), to Agnes, wife of William Harrison, of Whickham, and thence through William's son William two further generations. William and Margery's children are named as—Richard, of Brian's Leap, in the Chapelry of Tanfield, Gent. buried 25 March, 1654; Isabel, living 1623, m. 1st, John Hedworth, about 1594, m. 2nd, John Heron, of Birkley Hall, Gent., 18 February, 1599; and William, of Byermoor; Gent, died 1635.

Of whom; Richard of Brians Leap m. 1st, Isabel, who d. 1618, m. 2nd, in 1631, Anne, dau. of Thomas Smith, Gent., and widow of John Meaburne. William of Byermoor m. 1606, Isable, dau. of Nicholas Tempest. Richard's children were, by 1st wife: Jane, b. 1615; William b. 1616; Anne, d. 1624; by 2nd wife: John, of Brians Leap, Gent., (1633-1710), admr. granted to his half brother Anthony Meaborne; Ralph, of Brians Leap, Gent., b. 1634-5, will 1687, o.b. coel; Thomas, d. 1699; Anne, Jane, and Elizabeth. William and Isabel had—Ralph, of Byermoor, Gent., (1607-1637), o.b. sp., Robert, b. 1610, Charles, (1614-1632), William, b. 1616, d. same year, Matthew, b. 1619, (last four named sp.), Lionel, of Byermoor, Gent., (1608-164-), sp., m. Elizabeth Scurfield, 1641, Margery, Eleanor, Margaret, Anne, Barbara, and Elizabeth. (See—*The History and Antiquities of the County Palatine of Durham,* by Robert Surtees, London, 1816, Vol. II, pp. 256-7.)

No arms are mentioned by Surtees, but the family is listed in St. George's Visitation, 1615, and was obviously of the landed gentry. *(Ibid,* Vol. I, Appendix III, p. cliv.)

Enough herewith has been set forth to show that there were early Harrisons of genteel blood in Durham and adjacent counties, and that the oldest lines of decent are found represented by arms emblazoning the golden eagle.

THE LONDON FAMILY DESCENDED FROM BARNARD CASTLE, DURHAM

Continuing the story of the old seal. From the College of Arms, London, through the advice of the Norry King of Arms, Registrar, it is learned that—

(a) A search of the records of the College developed that no mention of an Isaiah Harrison is found on any pedigree recorded with the College.

(b) The "Crest on a chapeau Azure turned up ermine a bird with wings addorsed Sable", together with the Arms "Azure an eagle displayed gorged with a ducal coronet Or a chief ermine, was recorded in 1634 bv Robert Harrison, one of the Cursitors of His Majesty's High Court of Chancery. At the same time he recorded a Pedigree of three generations going back to his grandfather Royland Harrison of Bernard Castle, Co. Durham."

(Letters March 23, 1926, and October 14, 1927, *pens me.)*

The passion for recording pedigrees had greatly abated by the time of Dugdale's visitations, thus it was not to be expected that there was much likelihood of Isaiah Harrison's name appearing. No arms were found recorded at any time by any Harrison of "just an eagle displayed ducally gorged" (ie. without the chief), mentioned by Burke.

Coat of Arms, however, were in use long before the time of the founding of the College, and many arms used, even since the founding, were never recorded with the College. Burke's *Genral Armory* is understood to be a record of all arms used, whether recorded by the College or not; and while it is recognized as a standard authority it is not what the College terms official. The manuscripts of older or other pedigrees, and of other records showing arms, are in the British Museum.

"The attempt to regulate the use of arms by means of heralds appointed by the King, and incorporated into a college," says the *Journal of American History,* (Vol. XII, No. 2), was a late device to squeeze money out of the people by creating a heraldic monoply. The whole idea was decadent, and . . . . added greatly to the chaos and led to numerous heraldic blunders which are so many pitfalls to the unwary genealogist . . . . The doctrine taught by Fox-Davies some years back, that armorial bearings are not used lawfully unless the Heralds' College at London contains a record either of their grant or confirmation, is a bit of humbug. . . . . The most ancient and most interesting coats-of-arms are precisely those with the adoption of which the College of Arms had nothing to do."

The *chief,* or emblazoning of the upper portion of the shield in a different colour from the rest thereof, was often used by an eldest son to distinguish him. Other members of the family frequently ommitted it. Ignoring the chief, the arms described by

Burke, as quoted at the beginning of this Chapter,—with the slight exception of Burke's mention of the colour argent for the coronet,—are those described above (Page 81). Burke's description is accompanied by the notation "Heralds Office c 24," and on the same page he mentions the exact arms above without any crest, for "Harrison of London," with the same notation. Hence the arms were manifestly used both with and without the chief. On the pedigree referred to by the Registrar (page 81) the arms are pictured with the chief, and the colour of the coronet is shown "Or", the same as the eagle. The cap, or chapeau, is shown indented as described by Burke.

The arms and the pedigree are found in *The Visitation of London*, 1633, 1634, 1635, by Sir Richard St. George, Kt. (*The Publications of the Harleian Society*, London, 1880, Vol. XV, *London*, Vol. I, p. 356.) The arms were recorded "Under the hand of Sr. William Segar, Garter King of Arms", whose patent under the great seal was dated January, 1606-7, and who died December 1633, a year before the visitation. (See—*Dict. of Natl. Biog.*, Vol. XVII, p. 1135.) They were therefore recorded sometime between the years 1607 and 1633.

The pedigree is styled HARRISON, is signed by ROBERT HARRISON, and shows the following descents—

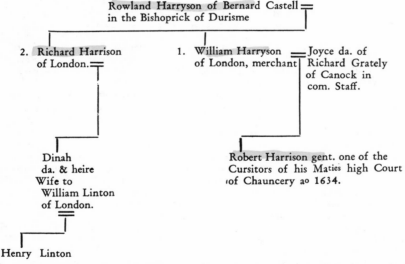

Rowland Harryson of Bernard Castell =
in the Bishoprick of Durisme

2. Richard Harrison
of London. =

Dinah
da. & heire
Wife to
William Linton
of London.
=

Henry Linton

1. William Harryson = Joyce da. of
of London, merchant | Richard Grately
of Canock in
com. Staff.

Robert Harrison gent. one of the
Cursitors of his Maties high Court
of Chauncery ao 1634.

As pedigrees are concerned with the tracing of particular lines of descent, they are more or less fragmentary in naming all of the children of an ancestor. It is possible that Robert Harrison may have had brothers and sisters, and that Richard may have had other children, although in the latter case as Dinah was his heir it seems likely there were no sons living.

The Bishopric of Durham is the old name for the region out of which the county was evolved. It dates back to the days of the early kings. The region was not included in the inquest made at the time of the *Domesday Book*, but was surveyed a century later, (1186), and its inquest recorded in *Boldon Book*. One of the old communities so listed was Newbottle, located a short distance south-east of Wickham. This village at the time consisted of sixteen cottagers who each held twelve acres of land, and three others who each held six acres. The demesne, consisting of four carucates of land, with the sheep and pasture, were in the bishop's hands. The whole arrangement was feudal, with the bishop the chief lord of the region.

The country was early divided into wards and parishes, and among the vicars or curates of Queen Elizabeth's time was one John Herrison of St. Helen, Auckland, parish of St. Andrews, 1564. The list of curates on which his name appears begins with John Drawles, vicar of Gridon 1421. (See—*History and Antiquities of the Co. Palatine of Durham,* by Wm. Hutchinson, Vol. III, p. 420.) A "Rowland, son of John Herrison," of Bishop Middleham, was baptized at Bishop Middleham, December 29, 1589. (See—*Registers of Bishop Middleham, Co. Durham,* by Durham and Northumberland Parish Register Society, 1906, p. 10.) "Isabell Herrisone," of the same place was baptized September 14, 1578. *(Ibid,* p. 7; the register begins in 1559.) Rowland Harrison of the pedigree was evidently born before 1570, and likely around 1550.

The Auckland country lies to the southwest of Durham city, the principal town being Bishop Aukland on the road from Durham to Barnard Castle, which last is located about ten miles southwest of Bishop Aukland, and is on the Tees, the boundry with Yorkshire.

Barnard Castle is a town in Darlington Ward, one of the largest of the five wards of the county. The ward comprises the ancient boroughs of Darlington, and Aukland, in addition to that of Barnard Castle. The town grew up about the castle walls, and about the middle of the twelfth century the men of the town were given a charter by the owner of the castle, making them burgess, and granting them the same privileges as the burgess of Richmond in Yorkshire.

The castle, from which the town derives its name, is the principal scene of Sir Walter Scott's *Rokeby.* The ruins extend over an area of six acres. It was built by Guy Baliol Barnard, son of Guy Baliol, to whom the land, as a part of the lordship of Gainford, is said to have been granted by William Rufus, son of William the Conqueror. The castle and the lordship continued in the posession of the Baliols until forfeited by John Baliol, King of Scotland, with his other English estates, in 1296. It was then seized by Anthony, bishop of Durham, as being within his palatinate. King Edward I, denied the bishop's rights, and granted the castle and town to Guy Beauchamp, Earl of Warwick, whose descendants held them until they passed to the Crown through the marriage of Anne Neville to Richard III, (1483-1485), then the Duke of Gloucester. In 1630 the castle was sold to Sir Henry Vane, and the same year it is said to have been dismantled for building materials.

Presumably the ducal coronet in Robert Harrison's (the cursitor's) arms is an allusion to the ducal lordship with which the town had been connected. In 1641, among those yet paying the "ancient rent" of the town and borough of Barnard Castle, was Jane Harrison, whose assessment was £0-6s-6d. *(Surtees,* Vol. IV, p. 76.)

The above arms, with a change in the color of the shield and the omission of the coronet, it may be observed in passing, are similar to those of Harrison of Gobions Manor (see page 80), Northampton. Robert Harrison of Stowe-Nine-Churches, this line, died in 1558 leaving a widow Elizabeth, sons Robert and Thomas, the latter of whom, in 1601, married a Bernard or Barnard, whose pedigree dating back to 1381-2, may be seen in the *History and Antiquities of the County of Northampton,* by George Baker. (London, 1822, p. 10: also see *The Records of the Borough of Northampton,* pub. by the City of Northampton, 1898, Vol. II, p. 168.)

MAJ. GEN. THOMAS HARRISON, THE REGICIDE

The Harrisons of Rockingham, relates the historian of Augusta County, Virginia, in his notice of the family earlier quoted, are said to have been descendants of Thomas Harrison, one of the judges who condemned King Charles I, to death. *(Annals of Augusta County,* p. 152.)The statement is more specifically presented by a later writer probably conversant with the above, who says; "Harrisonburg (Virginia) was named after Thomas Harrison a grand son of Thomas Harrison, one of the judges sentencing Charles I, to death." *(Richmond Virginia Times Dispatch,* March 2, 1924.) Of this Thomas, Inderwick, in his *Side Lights on the Stuarts,* remarks—"He was in reality, as I think has been satisfactorily established, the son of a good family of Durham, having an estate in that county, which had descended to him in a direct line from his great grandfather." (Page 289.) As a young man he is said to have been employed in the office of Thoma Houlker, an attorney in Clifford's Inn, one of the Inns of Chancery attached to the four Inns of Court, London. (See, *Murray's Handbook to London,* 1876, p. 146.)

The trial of Charles I lasted from January 21st to the 27th, 1649. On the last day the sentence was read. Among the judges who signed the death warrent was Thomas Harrison, on officer of Cromwell's army. The King was beheaded on the third day following the sentence, and on May 19th, the same year, the Republic was proclaimed. This was followed in 1654 by the Protectorate. Cromwell died September 3, 1658, and on May 25th, 1660, Charles II, landed at Dover, having been invited to return to England. Shortly thereafter thirteen of the judges who had condemned his father to death were in turn executed; one of them being Major-General Thomas Harrison, who was hung, drawn and quartered, at Charing Cross, London, October 13, 1660.

Thomas Harrison at one time, i. e. during Cromwell's absence in Ireland, was appointed to the chief military command in England. He early rose to prominence in the cause of the parliamentarians. He took part in the battle of Marston Moor, was a Major in the Earl of Manchester's army, 1644, and was present at Naseby, 1645, and the seige of Oxford, 1646. In the latter year he entered Parliament as a member from Wendover. Early in 1647 he served under Lord Lisle in Ireland, and upon his return to England was thanked by the Commons. In the quarrel with Parliament he sided with the army, and was appointed by Fairfax to treat with the parliamentary commissioners. He displayed much zeal in bringing the king to trial, and escorted him from Hurst Castle to London.

Much has been written in regard to Harrison; the most detailed account being a biography entitled *Thomas Harrison, Regicide and Major General,* by C. H. Simpkinson, (London, 1905.) This account says that he was born in the town of New-castle-under-Lyme, Staffordshire, 1606, and was baptized 2nd July, that year, (although other authorities state that the entry is not found in the baptismal register of New-castle-under-Lyme,—compare *Dict. of Natl. Biog.,* Vol. IX, 1908, p. 41.) His father (Richard, buried May 25, 1653, m. Mary, buried May 18, 1658), was four times chosen Mayor of the town, "an office which twice at least had been held by his father (Richard Sr.) before him." In the year 1647 Thomas married Katherine, (died 1700), daughter of Ralph Harrison, (died 1656), "a distinguished officer in the London train-bands, and a man of importance in the City." About 1656 Thomas Harrison and his wife joined the Baptist sect and were publicly baptized. *(Simpkinson,* pp. 2, 46, and 218; names and dates in parenthesis supplied—see later.)

The story of his descendants, as would naturally be expected in view of the cir-

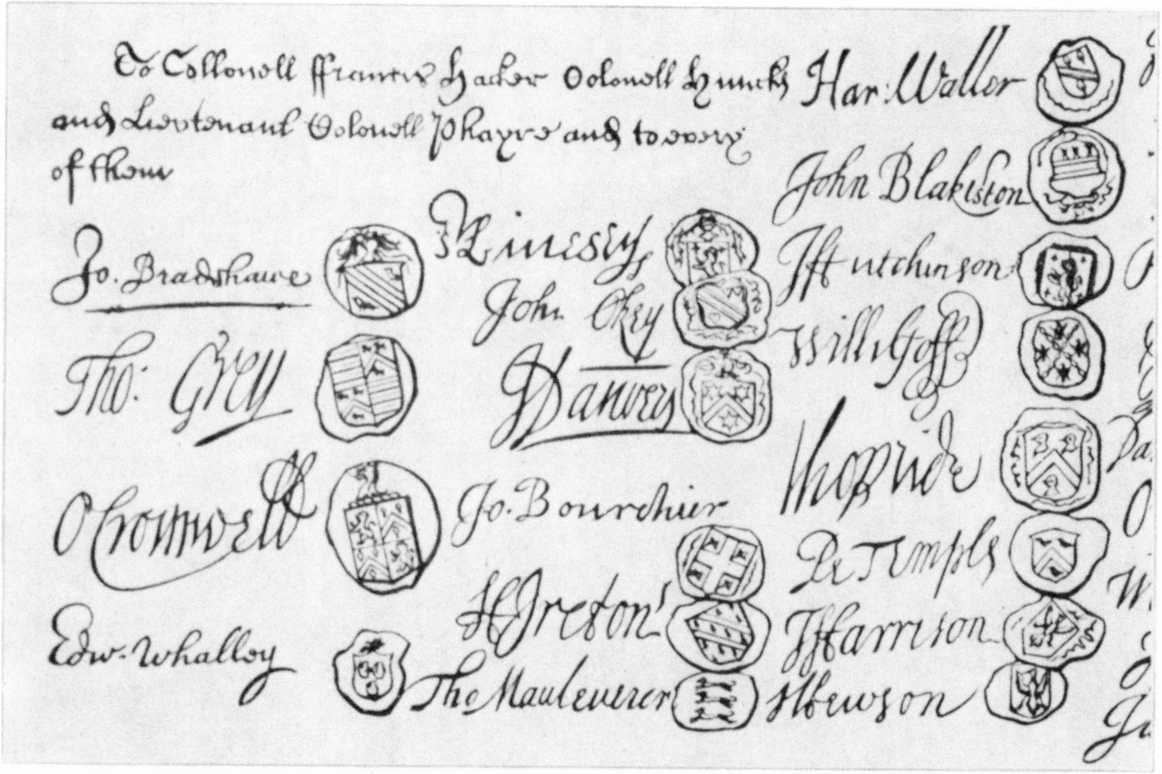

FROM—A FACSIMILE OF THE WARRANT TO EXECUTE KING CHARLES I.

(First engraved by the Society of Antiquarians, London, 1750.)

Showing the first eighteen signatures, and a copy of the seals as etched in by the engraver.

See pages 84 and 100.

cumstances, seems to be involved in much conjecture. "One of his descendants," says Inderwick, "a son, was in Vienna at the Restoration, and thus possibly escaped his father's fate. Another son emigrated to Virginia, where he became a man of note . . . . and was the ancestor of Benjamin Harrison, of Surry in Virginia . . . . one of the signers of the Declaration of Independence . . . . Harrison's daughters remained in England and made good marriages, among their descendants being found members of the aristocratic families of Stirling and Ashburton." (Page 289.) Elsewhere it is stated that Hamburg, Germany, was the point of refuge of a son (Stanley) whence his descendant came to America, (New York) after 1800. *(American Anecestry,* Vol. III, p. 172.) The Virginia ancestor of Benjamin Harrison, the signer, was however, in America by 1633. (The Grymes tradition in the James River family refers to a daughter of the Regicide—see Keith's *Ancestry of Benjamin Harrison.)* Charles H. Firth, in a *Memoir of Major-General Thomas Harrison,* 1892-3, states that Harrison had no children alive at the time of his death, and that none are mentioned in his wife's will. *(Proceedings of the American Antiquarian Society,* Vol, VIII, 1892-3, p. 390.)

His biographer sums up the matter thus—"The touching parting recorded at his death is indeed still in our hands, to exhibit his affection for his wife Catherine; and three entries in the burial registers of St. Anne's, Blackfriars, tell us of the death of three sons, (Thomas, buried February 1), 1649, (Ralph, buried April 10), 1652, (Richard, buried January 12), 1653, respectively." "But we cannot even tell whether he left any descendants behind him; if he did it must have been by a previous marriage to that of 1647 with Catherine Harrison; at all events no children appear in the story of his farewell to his relations. Then his only relation present was his wife to whom he left his Bible, the sole piece of property which his condemnation had spared him." *(Simpkinson,* pp. 273-4; dates and names in parentheses from Firth.)

* * * * * *

Isaiah Harrison, the Long Island immigrant, was born within a few years of the Restoration, but most likely following this event, or about 1666. The idea of the Major-General having descendants in America is now generally discredited, although in an indefinite way it has lingered persistently among several of the Rockingham lines, and was widely accepted long before Inderwick's day.

Thomas Harrison, as contemporary evidence shows, was identified with Staffordshire. On February 3, 1654, during his difference with Cromwell, he was ordered to return to his father's home in Staffordshire, and not to leave until further ordered. *(Calendar of State Papers, Domestic,* 1653-4, p. 387.) He was arrested at his own house in Staffordshire, May, 1660, by Col. John Bowyer, and committed to the tower. Ralph Harrison, his father-in-law, was a resident of Bread Street Ward, London, 1640, and was considered one of the principal inhabitants of the city; his name appearing on a list of such at the time, who were thought able to lend Charles I, money towards raising a sum of 200,000 pounds. (See, *Miscellanea Genealogica Et. Heraldica,* ed. by J. J. Howard, 1892, Vol. II, 2nd series, p. 37.) One of the name of St. Mary Woolnoth, London, clothworker, was licensed 7th November, 1590, to marry Judith Starkey, spinster, of St. Mary Axe, London. (See, *London Marriage Licenses,* 1521-1869, ed. by Joseph Foster, p. 635.) Katherine Harrison, Thomas' wife, following her husband's death married Col. Barrow, "one of Oliver's Colonels in Ireland," who lived in Hundsditch without Cripplegate, London, 1671. (See, *Calendar of State Papers, Domestic,* 1671, p. 476.) (One account states that she married Thomas Legh, of London.) She died in 1700.

THE SECOND SEAL AT STAUNTON AND SOME YORKSHIRE FAMILIES

Robert Harrison, son of Daniel, and grandson of Isaiah, the immigrant, also left a will on which there is a seal bearing a Coat of Arms. Robert signed his will May 4, 1761, while on his death-bed at the home of his brother-in-law, Daniel Smith. The will was proved August 18th, following, and on October 15, 1765, Capt. Daniel Smith's settlement of Robert's estate was recorded, one item of which reads: "To attendance and necessaries found for the deceased during the time he remained sick at my house, where he died, from the 10th February to 25th May, 1761, being 3 months & 15 days." (See Augusta County Will Book No. 3, pp. 60 and 429.)

The seal was applied to Robert's will in a manner similar to that of his father's, and the two are of the same size, so far as can be discerned. The seal shows a very pretty border, and a shield on which there are three identical figures set in a triangle, two at the top. A rubbing of the seal (photography being found impracticable) submitted to the College of Arms, London, was by the Register "made out to be"—

"Azure three demi lions erased Or"

"recorded in 1612 by Thomas Harrison of Eaton, (Caton), Co. York, who at the same time entered a Pedigree of four generations. This pedigree was continued by the family in 1666." (Letter, 23 March, 1926, *pens me*—Caton in parenthesis supplied.)

As Robert Harrison signed his will under unusual circumstances, it would appear off hand that he possibly used a Smith seal. Luckily, however, by chance the unrecorded and heretofore unknown will of Capt. John Smith, the immigrant, and father of Daniel, was found during a search to guard against this point. John Smith's will shows an emblem on its seal—a prominent figure being the fluer-de-lis, as elsewhere observed,—entirely different from Robert Harrison's seal. Neither was the seal a Hart seal, Silas Hart being one of the witnesses—and also "Gent." Thus there were two sets of HARRISON arms used in the Daniel Harrison branch of Isaiah' family.

In the old court records of Augusta, Daniel is often styled "Gent," and due to his seniority and station in the family he would have, it appears, been careful to use the arms most directly bearing on his ancestral line. He was the eldest son by Isaiah's second wife, and, as observed, had evidently inherited the two seals among his father's effects upon the latter's death. Robert Harrison, on the other hand, Daniel's eldest son, was a young bachelor who traded and dealt in land, and merely needing a seal in this connection, was likely handed the unused one inherited by his father. Robert's seal bears no discernable crest, which was only, but not necessarily, used by a man.

The pedigree of HARRISON OF CAYTON, appears in the *Visitation of Yorkshire* in 1612, and is signed "Per me, Mathewe Ellye, pro Thome Harryson de Caton." Over the title appears to the left the notation "Libertas De Knaresburg." This pedigree begins with Thomas Harrison, Lord Mayor of Yorke, 1575, and 1592, (wife's name not entered) to whom the above arms were granted, with the crest—"A demi lion as in the arms, holding a laurel wreath vert," "p. Edm. Knight, Norry, 1592, 2 Aug. 34 Q. Eliz." Thomas the Lord Mayor's children are give as; John Harrison, (from whom Harrison of Acaster, descends) 2nd son, Lord Mayor of York, 1612; Thomas Harrison son and heir; and Robert Harrison alderman of

York, 1612, (wives of neither of the sons given.) The descent from Thomas is shown: his children being, Thomas Harrison of Cayton, (as above), wife Elizabeth, dau. of Henry Atkinson, of Little Cattall; Mary and Joane Harrison. Thomas and Elizabeth's children are named as Beatrix, Joane, Mary, and Alice. (See—*The Visitation of Yorkshire,* 1584-5, and 1612, Publications of the Harleian Society, ed. by Joseph Foster, London, 1875, p. 527.)

From Dugdale's *Visitation of Yorkshire,* (ed. by J. W. Clay, London, 1917), which traces the descendants of Thomas, the Lord Mayor, in more detail, it is learned that the Lord Mayor's wife was Johan, who died in 1595, and that he died in January, 1604-5. His son John, Ld. Mayor of York, and Lord of the Manor of Acaster Selby, had arms granted to him 2nd. August, 1592. He died in 1625. Thomas, the eldest son, was a lawyer of York. Robert, the third son, was Ld. Mayor of York in 1607, (prior to being Alderman), and died in 1616. His wife was Frances, the daughter of William Robinson, Alderman of York and Allerthorpe, and of their children—Thomas, "late of Copgrave," was knighted 11th October, 1640, and was the High Sheriff of Yorkshire, 1656-7. Thomas of Cayton, son of Thomas the lawyer, died in 1642. He married in 1605, and had besides the children named in the above pedigree—Thomas, who died unmarried, Robert, of Cayton, aged 36, in 1665, admitted to Gray's Inn, London, 23rd October, 1646, and William, who died unmarried. Of his daughters—Beatrice and Joane died unmarried, Mary married Edward Wise, and Alice, John Warenner. (See, Vol. III, pp. 80, 269, and 500; also *Publications of the Surtees Society,* Vol. XXXVI, 1859, *The Visitation of York,* by Wm. Dugdale, pp. 172, 216, and 217.)

The descendants of Thomas, the Lord Mayor of York, (1575) were very numerous by the time of Dugdale's visitation. Of his son John's children, Robert Harrison, in Dugdale's time was settled at Bishop Auckland, in Durham. On his pedigree labeled, HARRISON OF BISHOP AUCKLAND, are pictured his arms showing three demi lions, set exactly on the shield in the position of those on the seal of Robert Harrison, son of Daniel, of Augusta County, Virginia, son of Isaiah, the immigrant. In the case of Robert of Bishop Auckland there is a small trefoil added in the center of the triangular position of the three demi-lions, for difference. (from the arms of his grandfather). This trefoil being very small would scarcely show on a seal, if at all. In any event, both Daniel and Robert's seals at Staunton point back to Harrison families of England, members of which resided in Durham within twelve miles of each other, in 1641.

Harrison of Bishop Auckland's arms are described as—"Azure, 3 demi-lions rampant maned or, a trefoil slipped arg. for difference. Crest—A demi-lion as in the arms charged with a trefoil slipped gu. holding between its paws a laurel garland ppr." The pedigree begins with John Harrison, Ld. Mayor of York, 1612, wife Isabell, daughter and heir of . . . Fryer. Their children are named as; 1. Thomas, of Acaster, York; 2. John, Dr. of Physic, died unm.; 3. Stephen, died unm.; and 4. Robert of Bishop Auckland, co. pal. Duram, aged 59, 4th September, 1666, wife Isabell, dau. of Linley Wrenn, of Binchester, co. pal. Durham, Esq. Of whom—the last couple had sons: 1. Robert Harrison, son and heir, aged 9, 4th September, 1666; 2. Frances (Francis) aged 3 yrs.; and daughters, 1. Barbara, aged 11; 2. Isabel, aged 8, and 3. Dorothy, aged 10 weeks, (4th September, 1666, date of visitation), "certified by ROBERT HARRISON." (See, *Durham Visitation Pedigrees,* 1575, 1615, and 1666, ed and pub. by Wm. Foster, London, 1887, pp. 154-155.)

Robert Harrison's brother, Thomas of Acaster, had a son Cuthbert, of Acaster, who was a "Capt. of Foote," in the service of Charles I. He (the Capt.) died in 1699, aged 81 years. Evidently this branch of the family were Royalists. Robert Harrison of Bishop Auckland, following the Restoration, was one of the signers of the petition of the inhabitants of the county Palatine of Durham for the restoration of the Church of England. Sir Thomas Harrison, the High Sheriff of Yorkshire, 1656-7, however, sided with the Parliamentarians, and in 1657 was appointed by Cromwell, along with "Thomas Lord Fairfax, baron of Cameron," Col. Charles Fairfax, and others, as one of the visitors to the college at Durham, founded by Cromwell the year before. *(Hutchinson,* Vol. I, p. 641.)

Sir Thomas Harrison, died in 1664, leaving two sons, Thomas of Allerthorpe, in Richmondshire, York, age 38, and Henry of Holtby, York, age 31, in 1665, and four daughters. The sons had families of young children in 1665. Thomas of Allerthrope, and his wife, Mary, and also his mother, Margaret, were all buried at Burneston church, Southwick, county Durham. *(Clay,* Vol. III, p. 269.) (Richmond is about fourteen miles southeast of Barnard Castle.)

REV. THOMAS HARRISON, GOVERNOR BERKLEY'S CHAPLAIN AT JAMESTOWN, VA.

THE JAMES RIVER HARRISONS

THOMAS HARRISON, D. D. (1619-1682), an intimate of the Cromwell family, and previous thereto Chaplain of the early Jamestown colony of Virginia during Governor Berkeley's first term, (1645-1652), was a native of Kingston-upon-Hull, Yorkshire. He was born in 1619, and arrived in Virginia before 1640, in which year he qualified as the minister of Elizabeth River Parish. (See, *Hening's Statutes at Large,* Vol. I, p. 242.) The same year the Sewell's Point church agreed to pay him 100 pounds sterling annually as long as he occupied the pulpit. He used his influence against the Puritans who were numerous on the south side of the James, but following the second Indian massacre (April 18, 1644) turned Puritan himself and in 1648, after refusing to read the Book of Common Prayer or administer the Sacraments, abandoned his ministerial office. (See, *Institutional History of Virginia in the Seventeenth Century,* by Philip A. Bruce, Vol. I, pp. 132, 149, and 166, and *Encyclopaedia of Virginia Biography,* by Lyon G. Tyler, Vol. I, p. 253.) He removed to New England, and visited Boston. Savage mentions him as having been perhaps a brother of Edward Harrison of this town. (See page 75.) About 1648-9, he married, in New England, Dorothy, (bapt. November 9, 1619), the daughter of Samuel Symonds of Ipswich, (1595-1678), Deputy Governor of Massachusetts, 1638, and native of Great Yeldham, Essex County, England. (See, *Old Families of Salisbury and Amesbury, Mass.,* by D. W. Hoyt, p. 598, and *The Pioneers of Mass.,* by C. H. Pope, p. 445.)

From Massachusetts, the year following his daughter Elizabeth's birth, (bapt. 28th October, 1649, age 7 days) Harrison returned to England, and about 1650 succeeded Dr. Goodwin in his "gathered church" as St. Dunstans-in-the-East, London. (See, *Savage,* Vol. II, p. 366.) Here, having the confidence of the parliamentarians, a commission granted by "Charles Stuart to William Davenet, to have command of some English plantation in America," fell into his hands, and on November 10, 1652, he was directed by the Council of State to bring the commission to the Council. (See, *The Virginia Carolorum,* by Ed. D. Neill, p. 418.) As a resident of St. Dunstans-in-the-East he and his wife sent power of attorney, 10th February, 1653, to her brothers Samuel and William Symonds, of Massachusetts. After remaining for a few years in

London he removed to Brombrough Hall, Warrall, Cheshire, and in 1655, accompained Henry Cromwell, (son of the Protector), to Ireland, when the latter went there as lord-deputy. During this time he resided with Cromwell's family.

Upon the Restoration, Rev. Harrison returned to Chester, where he preached to large congregations in the Cathedral. Following the passing of the "Act of Uniformity" he settled permanently in Dublin, and founded there a flourishing dissenting church. He died in Dublin in 1682, "amidst general mourning." "He was a complete gentleman," says Calamy, "much courted for his conversation." He was the author of several works, among them, *Old Jacob's Account Cast Up, &c., A Funeral Sermon for Lady Susannah Reynolds,* 1654, and *Threni Hibernici, or Ireland Sympathising with England and Scotland in a Sad Lamentation for the Loss of Their Josiah,* a sermon preached at Christ Church, Dublin, on the death of Oliver Cromwell, London, 1659, dedicated to Richard, Lord Protector, &c. He left a valuable library. (See, *Dictionary of National Biography,* Vol. IX, 1908, p. 41.)

Harrisons were in Dublin much earlier than Rev. Thomas. Under date of 13th August, 1584, Robert Harrison of Dublin, was granted a lease by the government of three islands in Galway called Aaron More, Irishmany and Inishery, and possession of the religious houses of Fynibour, Anaghcoine, Kilecany, and Corcomore, to hold for twenty-one years at the rent of maintaining twenty English footmen. In 1599 a patent or grant was given him to "40 messuages, a water mill, and five carucates of land in the lordship of Maybrecke alias Maybreckre, co. Westmeath . . . To hold forever, by fealty, in common soccage Rent £8-18s-2d, In consideration of £411-17s-0d, due him for vituals in the time of the late earl of Essex in Ireland." (Faints—Elizabeth; *Ireland Pub. Records,* 13th Rept. of Deputy Keeper, p. 170, and 16th. Report, p. 249.)

Rev. Thomas Harrison was at Jamestown, Virginia, at the time of Edward Harrison, later of Boston (see page 75), and of Benjamin Harrison, Clerk of the Jamestown colony, founder of the James River family, and was also a contemporary of Richard Harrison of New Haven, founder of the Connecticut family, (see page 16). Richard of New Haven, was a resident of West Kirby, Cheshire, near Liverpool, prior to his emigration to American: "1668, Juene 18, Certificate, that Hopestill Lyne, 6 to 7 years old, the daughter of Henry Lyne of New Haven, in New England, son of John Lyne of Badby, Northamptonshire, which Henry died, January 14, 1662, and had the child Hopestill by his wife Elizabeth, daughter of Richard Harrison of West Kerby, Cheshire, is still alvie as sworn to by Richard Harrison (Jr.), Thomas Johnson, William Meaker, and Ellen Johnson," of New Haven. (See, *New Jersey Archives,* Vol. XXI, p. 29.)

Richard of New Haven, came to America with his grown children. Several writers of the history of the New Haven family unhesitatingly state that he was a brother of Benjamin Harrison, the Clerk, of Virginia. The two, with Rev. Thomas and Edward of Boston, are included in an interesting account preserved by Keith.

"Very soon after 1640 appeared Thomas and Edward, the former figuring in Neil's works on Virginia history, first as Governor Berkeley's chaplain and then as a nonconformist divine. . . . They are embraced in the following tradition brought over from England by Rev. Joseph Harrison, a native of Skipton, Yorkshire, who lived in the city of New York in the early part of the present century (1800-1900), viz: four brothers of the name went to America, whom the Rev. Joseph called, Thomas, Richard, Benjamin, and Nathaniel, of whom his own father told him, two went north and two south, a fifth brother, Edward, a clergyman remaining in England, Cromwell being a member of his church. Now we have seen the name of the clergyman was Thomas, and he was one of those who came to America. Yet afterwards he preachd in London and accompanid Henry Cromwell to Ireland. Edward was one of those who came to America. I can find no Nathaniel here at that time nor any Benjamin in such registers of Yorkshire as have been examined; but the Richard of the tradition, appears to be identical with the Richard living in New Haven in 1644, and of Branford, (Conn.), in 1666, (one of whose sons was called Nathaniel), as well as of Richard, who had a son Benjamin, born in 1655 . . . among the other Harrisons that came to Virginia were Dr. Jeremy and his wife Frances . . ." etc. (See, *Ancestry of President Benjamin Harrison,* by Charles P. Keith, p. 43.)

None of the accounts of Richard Harrison of New Haven, mention any Coat-of-Arms in the family. The only reference to a semblance of arms is apparently the one made by Atwater in his statement that Richard, Jr., when signing the deed disposing of his home in Branford, in 1667, "affixed his mark with a seal bearing the design of three roses." (See, Atwater's *History of New Haven,* Vol. II.) No further record seems to be extant of Edward who settled at Boston, or Hartford. John Harrison of Wethersfield, near Hartford, died in 1664, leaving children, John (b. 1642), Joseph, Thomas, Mary, and Sarah. (See, *Puritan Settlers of Connecticut,* by R. R. Hinman, p. 31; A search of the Wethersfield town books developed no mention of an Isaiah Harrison.)

The James River, Virginia, family of Harrisons used the Yorkshire arms as in the case of Robert Harrison of Augusta County, Virginia. According to the *Richmond Standard* of February 14, 1880, the following arms appear on some of the plate of the late William Byrd Harrison, Esq., of Upper Brandon on the James; "Az. three demi-lions rampant. Crest—A demi-lion rampant with a wreath in his paw." (The colours of the demi-lions and of the wreath are evidentaly omitted in error.) The arms, "Az. three demi-lions rampant Or," with Crest—"A demi-lion rampant arg. holding a laurel branch vert." appear also on an obelisk of the tomb of Henry Harrison, (1692?-1732), son of Benjamin II, at Brandon. (See, *Virginia Magazine of History and Biography,* Vol. 32, p. 199.) A second Coat-of-Arms used by the James River family, and the arms usually cited for them, are described as—"Az. two bars ermine between six estoiles, three, two, and one, ar. Crest—An escallop shell."

Benjamin Harrison, (d. about 1648), Clerk of the Council, of Virginia, 1633, and Member of the House of Burgesses, 1642, was the immigrant ancestor of the James River family. The earliest grant to any Harrison on record in the Virginia Land Registry Office was made to him for 200 acres in "Warrosquinoake County," July 20, 1635,—Book No. I, p. 207. (See, *Richmond Standard,* No. 24.) On March 15, 1633-4, he certified to a copy of the will of Abraham Piersey, signing himself "Ben Harryson, Clec. Con." After much research by many authorities in regard to his origin, his English ancestry is unknown.

A most delightfully interesting account of the family of the two Presidents is a work by Willis Abbott, entitled, "*Carter Henry Harrison a Memoir.*" While this volume relates particularly to the World's Fair Mayor of Chicago, a detailed account is given of the origin of the family in Virginia. Benjamin Harrison, I, the Clerk, married Mary . . . . ., and had two children, both of whom survived him, viz.; Benjamin, II, (1645-1713), and Peter. The latter died before middle age without issue. Benjamin II was born upon the family estate of Southwark parish, Surry County. He was a member and Speaker of the House of Burgesses and from 1700 to 1704 sat in the Governor's Council.

He married Hannah, who by tradition is said to have been a daughter of Thomas Harrison, the Regicide, and had: Sarah, (1670-1713), Benjamin, III, (1673-1710), Nathaniel, (1677-1727), Hannah, (1678-1731), and Henry, (b. about 1693, d. without issue, 1732).

Of whom—Sarah married Rev. James Blair, first President of William and Mary College, (1693-1743); Benjamin, II, Member and Speaker of the House of Burgess, Treasurer and later Attorney General of the Colony, married Elizabeth Burwell, and settled at Berkeley; Nathaniel, Member of the Governor's Council, married Mary Young, nee Cary, (b. 1678), and settled at Brandon, on the James; Hannah, married, 1697, Philip Ludwell, (d. 1726), the son of the Governor of North Carolina. The grave of Benjamin Harrison, II, son of the immigrant, is near Cabin Point, Virginia. (The town of Brandon, England, is in Norfolk County.)

III.

CONCLUSION

ISAIAH HARRISON'S PARENTAGE AND REV. THOMAS HARRISON'S CAREER

Every man shall camp by his own standard
with the ensign of his father's house.

—Numbr. 2:2.

Coming now to a more particular reference as to Isaiah Harrison's parentage; any account of his people necessarily involves furnishing a basis of some explanation regarding the various points of his background upon his arrival in America, such as the circumstances surrounding his departure from Great Britain; the date of his emmigration; the boat on which he sailed; the old water bottle; his occupation; the similarity of his arms with those of the James River Harrisons, and traditional kinship with this family; the Regicide tradition; the occurence of the Durham and Yorkshire arms in his family; his age at settlement; the uniqueness of his name, and the spelling thereof; his point of settlement; his religious affiliations, and other known characteristics.

While no extended research among original English parish registers has been attempted; it being deemed sufficient for the purpose of an American genealogy to begin with the immigrant; yet considering the above points of his background, or lines of enquiry, it may be observed that in reconciling them as a whole the only apparent reasonable explanation lies in the conclusion that the father of the immigrant was Thomas Harrison, D. D., before referred to, the former Chaplain to Governor Berkeley at James town, Virginia, a native of Kingston-upon-Hull, Yorkshire, who died an Independent or Congregational minister of the gospel in Dublin, Ireland, 1682.

Isaiah himself is thought to have been born in or near the city of Chester, England, and as a refugee from Dublin to have sailed from this old port, or her more modern nearby sister, Liverpool, which at the time was rapidly supplanting Chester as a point of departure owing to the silting up of the river Dee.

The year 1687, during which he arrived at Oyster Bay, was a significant one in English history in the way of emigration from Ireland. Especially was this the year of a notable exodus from Dublin. On the sailing of Lord Clarendon from the city in February, 1687, "he was accompanied," says Fitzpatrick, in his history of Dublin, "by 1500 Protestant families." (See, *Dublin, a Historical and Topographical Account of the City,* by Samuel A. C. Fitzpatrick, London, 1907, p. 91.) "Something like a panic reigned among the English inhabitants," remarks another authority, "at the news of Tyrconnell's appointment as Lord Lieutenant. The quays of Dublin were thronged with families fleeing in terror from the country." (See, *The Story of Dublin,* by D. A. Chart, London, 1907, p. 89.)

Ireland in January, 1686-7, was handed over by James II, to the notorious Earl of Tyrconnell, whom the king appointed at the time his lord-deputy to succeed Clarendon, his former lord-lieutenant, and Protestant brother-in-law. Richard Talbot, Earl of Tyrconnell, was the son of a Catholic lawyer and politician, and the brother of a onetime Catholic archbishop of Dublin. He had been introduced to James II, in the days when James was in exile, as a person willing to assassinate Oliver Cromwell, and was attached to James household forthwith. On taking charge of Ireland he established himself in Dublin, and proceeded to turn the country over to the Catholics, who under him were made almost everywhere predominent. In the army whole batallions of Protestant soldiers were discharged without even their own clothes which they had paid for themselves. The disarmed Protestants were at the mercy of marauders, and were soon reduced to dispair. A letter from Dublin in 1688, within a year of Harrison's settlement at Oyster Bay, states that in eighteen months Tyrconnell had reduced Ireland "from a place of briskest trade and best paid rents in Christendom to ruin and desolation." *(Dict. of Natl. Biog.,* XIX, p. 331.)

It was to Dublin that the boat, *Spotted Calf,* on which Isaiah Harrison embarked to America, was brought in 1691, during the Irish uprising against William, Prince of Orange. The boat having figured on the side of James II, was evidently an Irish boat whose home port was in the southern section of Ireland, most likely Dublin itself. A noted sandbar and a rock guarding the entrance to the harbor were known respectively as the Bull and the Bullock, the names being suggestive of the roaring of the serf at the two points. The city has long been the chief cattle market of Ireland, and is today the largest such market in the British Isles.

Recalling the story of the old ale bottle; it may be remarked that as early as the seventeenth century Dublin was famous for its brown ale. Out of this fame has grown today's well known largest brewey in the world. The high reputation of Irish glass too, goes back to early times, and manifestly there was no derth of this material for the blowing of "big bellied bottles" in which to store the ale.

Probably nowhere in the British Isles were the guilds of Isaiah's Harrison's time more influential in city affairs than in Dublin. From the fact that Isaiah succeeded as the Town Smith of Oyster Bay, where several other smiths before him had failed, and that he appears to have arrived well recommended, the presumption is strong that he had served his apprenticeship under some master artizan. It was cutomary in his day for boys of genteel families, and the younger sons of noble families, to be trained to some trade, and in Dublin the restrictions regarding the selection of apprentices were peculiarly such that this may well count for the careful preservation of the seals later used by his son and grandson.

As the headquarters of a real and not a mythical English rule, in the midst of the native Irish, every effort was made to maintain Dublin predominently English. Under the watchful eye of the able governors appointed by Queen Elizabeth the town slowly became Protestant. The use of the *Book of Common Prayer* was enjoined on every church and printed Bibles were set forth for public reading in Christ Church and St. Patrick Cathedrals. It was during Elizabeth's reign that Trinity College, now richly endowed, was founded—"whereby knowledge and civility might be increased by the instruction of our people there, whereof many have usually heretofore used to travell into ffrance, Italy and Spaine to gett learning in such foreign universities, whereby they have become infected with poperie and other ill qualities and soe become evill subjects." Like London, Dublin in the time of the great rebellion became a stronghold of the Parliamentary party, and due to her English and Welsh ancestry rather leaned to Puritanism and Calvinism in her relegious opinions. Of an estimated population of 24,000 in 1644, approximately seventy percent are said to have been Protestant. Following the exodus due to the Earl of Tyrconnell's brief ascendency under James II, the people eagerly welcomed William of Orange.

About the close of the seventeenth century a more complete control of the city was placed in the hands of the civic authorities, and for nearly two centuries thereafter they "continued to rule it with a rod of iron." Its government closely resembled that of Florence, Italy, in the thirteenth century, by the guilds, and had nothing in common with modern municipal rule. New rules for the better government of the city were introduced in 1672, and in 1759 a further act for regulating the corporation became law, whereby the junior guilds received considerable privileges. "It must be remembered," says Fitzpatrick, in speaking of these acts, "that no person was qualified to be elected to the common council of the city 'who for some time does not, or sometime theretofore did not follow as his public and known occupation some trade, or did not serve an apprenticeship,' that is to say was not a member of one of the guilds." The members of the council were chosen by ballot from the different guilds, at the head of which stood the Guild of the Holy Trinity, or Merchants' Guild, which returned twenty one representatives out of a total ninety-six.

The regulations of the guilds in regard to apprentices were "at all times stringent." In 1417 the Taylors Guild stipulated that all apprentices to their fraternity should be of English birth. Similarly in the charter granted to the various guilds of Elizabeth's time it was enacted that "apprentices should be Free, of the English nation, and of good conversation, and should be bound for seven years." Under the ordinance of 1652-3, only Protestants were admissible to apprenticeships in the guilds of the city. In a royal charter of Charles II, 1670, it was set forth that all members must swear allegiance to the king and be of the Protestant faith. While apprentices were liable to a seven year term of apprenticeship, they had some special privileges, such as being entitled to wages after the first year of service,—not under eight pounds in the case of the Merchants Guild.

* * * * * *

A comparison of the four or fourteen brother tradition, as preserved among Isaiah Harrison's descendants, (see page 9), with the four brother tradition of the James River Harrison family, (see page 89), indicates that the two families are descended from two of these brothers. This is further evidenced or partially confirmed by the occurence of the demi-lion or Yarkshire arms in both families, and by the prevalence of such distinctive Harrison names as Benjamin, Nathaniel, Robert, and Thomas, etc., in the two lines in their early generations. A traditional relationship has been the understanding from time out of mind in the Valley of Virginia family.

One of these brothers in Keith's account, it will be recalled, was Thomas Harrison, the Chaplain of the Jamestown colony, while a second tradition in the Rockingham family, (see page 91), names as their ancestor Thomas Harrison, the regicide.

All traditions, observes an eminent historian, were originally based on fact. It is natural for blood relations to retain a reasonably accurate recollection of those in their family whose personal history is of material importance to them. These recollections being passed on to the future generations may in time become somewhat distorted as to details, but an element of truth remains. Major-General Thomas Harrison and Rev. Thomas Harrison, both of the same name, and both having been an associate of Cromwell and both having figured in Irish history under him, their indentities as preserved by tradition were easly confused. Obviously the common germ of truth of the three traditions, so far as they could refer to the ancestor of the Valley of Virginia family, involves the identification of Thomas Harrison of Cromwell's time, as the former Chaplain of the Jamestown colony, and as the ancestor of the Rockingham line.

Not only were the Major-General and the former Chaplain of the same name, but both had wives named Katherine living at the same time, and both were identified with Staffordshire. This interesting coincidence is disclosed by two references found in the *Calendar of State Papers Domestic,* (of the Public Record Office), in conjunction with a further reference appearing in Dugdale's *Visitation of Straffordshire,* 1663-1664.

The first is a copy of Edward Bradshaw's letter, dated at London, March 19, 1661, addressed to "his son Doctor Harrison" at Chester, stating that he "had a convenient place to see the City election . . . . The Lord Mayor and Recorder were proposed, but the commons had pitched upon . . . . Alderman Foulke and three other Presbyterians. A courtier . . . . said it was a warning for the Bishops. Sir George Booth is very desirous to have Mr. Recorder chosen for Chester,"etc. *(Calendar of State Papers Domestic,* 1660-1661, p. 538.)

The second reference is dated at Chester, July 3, 1665, and identifies "Doctor Harrison" beyond question:—"Sir Geoffry Shakerley to Williamson, Great strictness is observed in keeping out strangers suspected to bring in the sickness, but the pest of disobedience and nonconformity continues rife. A conventicle of 100 persons assembled at the house of Dr. Thomas Harrison, late chaplain to Harry Cromwell, broke open the house and, though many escaped, some were taken hidden under beds or in closets, &c, and 30 or 40 brought before the mayor. The chief were examined, and paid their money to escape puishment, this being their first conviction, as Harrison himself, Edw. Bradshaw, and Peter Lee, late alderman, Mayor Joseph Jolly and others. These are not Anabaptists, but of the first and worst stamp of sectaries, and therefore require the more severity. The parties are so linked together in the city that it will be difficult to suppress them, unless it be by a special commission for their punishment, directed at those of no affinity with them. Some of them threaten to complain of the writer for breaking down the door and disturbing them." *(Ibid,* 1664-1665, p. 461.)

The third reference is dated in 1663 and records a brief pedigree embracing "Thomas Harrison, Dr. in Divinity, Prebend of Lichfield," and his wife "Catherine, daughter of Edward Bradshaw, Alderman of Chester, sister to Sr. James Bradshaw Knt." *(Staffordshire Pedigrees,* based on the Visitation of Sir Wm. Dugdale, 1663-1664, from the original manuscript by Gregory King; Harleian Society, Vol. 63, London, 1912, p. 121.)

This Katherine Bradshaw was moreover a kinswoman of John Bradshaw of Chester, the celebrated president of the High Court of Justice which condemned King Charles I to death. John Bradshaw thus even more than Major-General Thomas Harrison qualified among the Royalists as a socalled regicide. In fact, he stood preeminent in this respect, his name heading the list of those signing the death warrent, Cromwell being third and Harrison seventeenth. Following the Restoration his remains, like those of Cromwell's, were disinterred and removed from Westminister Abbey.

That Major-General Thomas Harrison left any descendants is highly unlikely in view of Firth's and Simpkinson's exhaustive effort to discover some trace of them. Both authorities are agreed that there were no children by his wife Katherine living at the time of her death, and Isaiah Harrison to have been his son would have been a child of this marriage. On the other hand the pedigree above referred to, while fragmentary and not actually naming any children, shows clearly that Dr. Thomas Harrison and wife Katherine had issue. This is further confirmed by other records as will appear anon.

* * * * * *

Benjamin Harrison, founder of the James River family, appears to have been bred to the profession of a clerk at law, or cursitor. Thomas Harrison, the Chaplain, named by the Rev. Joseph Harrison as Benjamin's brother, married in Massachusetts a daughter of Samuel Symonds, who prior to his arrival in America "was one of the cursitors," according to his pedigree which may be seen in *The Visitation of Essex*, 1634. (Harleian Society, Vol. XIII, p. 495.) Symonds at the time of the visitation was a resident of Topsfield, Essex. The *estoile* arms of the James River line were similar to those of the Harrisons of Essex, which county adjoins London on the east. In the city resided in Symonds' time Robert Harrison, the cursitor of the high court of chancery, before named. Harrison and Symonds being both cursitors connected with nearby courts of chancery, one jurisdiction higher than the other, were likely known to each other. Robert Harrison may have been a kinsman of Benjamin and Thomas, as many of the Jamestown colony were associated in one way or another with London people. Upon his return to England Thomas Harrison resided in London in the region towards Essex.

Thus the arms on Daniel Harrison's seal, considered in connection with the courts of chancery and the associations of Rev. Thomas Harrison, afford the suggestion of a Harrison and Symonds family acquaintance prior to Thomas' and Samuel's migration from England, and in addition supply a reasonable hypothesis in explanation of Isaiah Harrison's implied descent from a sometime resident of London. As a native of Yorkshire where many of the Harrisons were related to those of Durham, Rev. Harrison may have quite naturally inherited the right to bear either of the Coats of Arms found at Staunton. These arms specify Durham and Yorkshire strains and allude to a residence in London, and certainly Thomas was of Yorkshire parentage and a one time inhabitant of the city.

Following his settlement in London, Rev. Harrison resided for a short time in Cheshire, whence he removed in 1655 (prior to July 23rd), to Dublin, Ireland, where with the exception of about twelve years immediately following the Restoration he remained until his death.

From four separate and distinct considerations therefore, whether the question of Isaiah Harrison's former home is approached from the point of view of the year of his emigration, the name of the boat on which he sailed, the traditions of his family, or the seals at Staunton, the indications point to his having been a former resident of Dublin.

* * * * * *

At his death in 1682, Rev. Harrison left a will which was recorded the same year. (See—Index to the *Act or Grant Books* and to *Original Wills of the Diocese of Dublin* to the year 1800. Appendix to the 26th *Report of the Deputy Keeper of Public Records and Keeper of the State Papers of Ireland*, p. 392. Manuscript Div. Library of Congress.) This will unfortunately was destroyed in the Four Courts fire of the Public Record Office of Ireland in the late rebellion of 1922. (Letter—The Deputy Keeper *pens me*, 23rd of March, 1931.)

Rev. Harrison's congregation is said to have met on Cook Street, Dublin, near St. Audoens church. The presumption is that he resided nearby. At St. Audoens Arch, a relic of one of the old city gates of the neighborhood, was still standing at the close of the eighteenth century, the Hall of the Smiths, or Guild of St. Loy (Eloi), one of the guilds before alluded to. This guild was chartered as early as 1474. Its *Entry Book of Apprentices,* 1638-1670, with the admission of Freemen, was among the records also destroyed in the Four Courts fire.

Owing to the loss of the vast treasure of Ireland's early English records in this fire, research in Dublin has disclosed little regarding Rev. Harrison's family. The earliest deed now on file at the Record Office is dated in 1708. No port books or boat lists of Isaiah Harrison's time remain. No abstract of Rev. Harrison's will is known at the Office of Arms, and no pedigree regarding him or his family is found there. The directories of the city begin about 1750. The Quaker Registers on Eustice Street remain, but as would be expected reveal no record of Isaiah.

From the Registers of St. Michaels Parish Church of Wood Street is gleaned under date of 1675, September 2; "Doctor Timothy Bifield, physisian & Mrs. (Miss) Dorothy Harrison, daur of Dr. Thom. Harrison, married by license," (Letter, V. E. T. *pens me* June 6, 1931), from which it is manifest that Dr. Harrison and his first wife had at least two daughters, Elizabeth, earlier named, and Dorothy. While Dorothy's marriage was recorded in the regular parish register the marriages of many nonconformists were entered in a volume farmiliarly known as the Couple Beggers Register. In such instances the ceremony usually was preformed by a minister of their own sect. This volume was another that was consumed in the Four Courts fire.

According to a "list of names of men who entered Trinity College between the years 1593 and 1846," appearing in *Alumni Dublinenses*—by Burtchcall and Sadler—"Thomas Harrison, D. D. (Chaplain to the governor of Virginia)" was entered under date "circa 1658." (See also *Early History of Trinity College,* Dublin, 1591-1660, by Wm. Urwick.) Dr. Calamy, in his account of the nonconformist ministers states also that Harrison obtained his Doctor's degree from Trinity. Neither of these authorities, however, reveal anything regarding Dr. Harrison's family. (See—*An Account of the Ejected Ministers* by Edward Calamy, 1702, p. 607.)

An examination of the parish registers of Dublin, the oldest dating from 1619, (twelve volumes, including one volume on Derry Cathedral, Londonderry, as published by the Dublin Parish Register Society), discloses no record of Isaiah Harrison's birth. This, as in the instance of the Quaker records, is as would be expected, Rev. Harrison having settled in Chester upon the Restoration, and Isaiah having been born shortly thereafter—he being manifestly very little, if any, past twenty-one years of age upon his arrival at Oyster Bay, 1687, and about seventy-two or three at his death, 1737-9.

Dorothy, the first wife of Dr. Harrison, died sometime between the years 1653 and 1659, and in view of the state of the times it appears unlikely that she accompanied her husband on his first trip to Dublin. She may have remained at Bromborough Hall in Cheshire, which by 1668, was in the posession of Edward Bradshaw, his second wife's father, as lord of the manor. (See—*The History of Chester,* by Thos. Helsby, Vol. 2. p. 428.)

* * * * * *

Among the Dublin Harrisons prior to and during Dr. Harrison's time, the following left wills—Hadrain Harrisonne, smith, 1584, Thomas Harrison, tailor, 1609, Peter Harrison, Gent., 1630, Mathew Harrisone, Esquire., 1667, John Harrison, merchant, 1670, and Michael Harrison, Esq., 1709. (See—*Vicar's Index to Perogatiove Wills of Ireland,* pp. 219-220.)

Mary, the daughter of Thomas Harrisson, yeoman, and wife, was christened January 3, 1668, and buried January 5, 1668. Elizabeth, the daughter of Thomas Harrisson, carpenter, and wife Ann, was baptized January 9, 1669. Elizabeth, the daughter of Thomas Harrisson, trunkmaker, and "Catherin," his wife, was baptized June 21, 1687. John, the son of Thomas Harrisson, "tayler," and Catherin, his wife, was buried 1689, October 25. Elizabeth, the daughter of Thomas Harrisson, "taylor," and Catherin, his wife, was buried December 29, 1694. Jane, and Sarah, two other daughters of Thomas, the tailor, and Catherin, were buried June 16, 1698 and May 3, 1700, respectively. "Michaell Harrisson", Soldier of Captn. Jno. Baxter's Company, was buried March 29, 1679. Samuel Harrisson, the son of Samuel and Catherine, was baptized September 12, 1681. "Beniamin," son of George Harrisson, gent., and Elizabeth, his wife, was buried July ye 9, 1676. Mary, the daughter of "Georg" Harrison, inkeeper, and Elizabeth, his wife, was buried March 3, 1678. "Georg," son of Georg Harrisson, drover, and Elizabeth, his deceased wife, was buried Nobr. ye 7, 1682. *(St. Michan's Parish,* 1636-1685, pp. 99, 101, 174, 286, 382, 411, 442, 468, 227, 29, 212, 226, and 250.)

Josias, the "sonn" of William and Margaret Harrison of St. Kevins Street, was born "December ye one and twentieth," 1673. Jasiah, the sonn of William Harrison of St. Kevins Street, was buried "Tuesday, January the fifth," 1674. Other children of William were—Joseph "ye son of William Harrison, buried Mar. 2d," 1669. "Shusannah," daugr. of Willm. and Margaret Harrison, born in St. Kevins Street, July 31, 1670, Mary Daughter of William Harrison of St. Kevins Street, buried May 14, 1673, and Deborah, daughter of William and Margaret Harrison of St. Kevins Street, born Tuesday, June 15, 1675. *(Ibid,* Vol. IX, Parish of St. Peter & St. Kevin, 1669-1761, pp. 33, 40, 6, 14, 26, and 47.) William Harrison, the son of Joseph and Jane, was born ye 13 and bapt. ye 14, Nov. 1687. Elinor Harrison, the daughter of Joseph and Jane, was born ye 15th. and bapt. ye 16th. Nov. 1689. Ann, a daughter of the same couple was baptized ye 26th. Nov. 1690; "Serah," another daughter, was baptized 15th. June, 1698, and Clements, another son, was baptized 23rd. Sept. 1700. *(Ibid* Vol. V, Parishes of S. Catherine and S. James, 1636-1715, pp. 77, 91, 100, 112, and 129.) William, the son of Joseph Harrisson, fidler, and Ann, his wife, of St. Michans Parish, was buried 24th. April, 1691. Elizabeth, the daughter of William Harrisson, gent., and Ann, his wife, of the same parish, was buried 28th April 1697. *(Ibid,* Vol. III, pp. 397 and 430.)

* * * * * *

Passing over the Irish Sea to the opposite port of Chester, which at the time was linked very closely to Dublin; it was to this point that the Protestants first fled on the departure of Clarendon from Ireland, and from here most likely, as earlier observed, Isaiah Harrison sailed to America. "Our ancestors came from England," says the old tradition, (see page 9). Chester for many centuries was one of the main seaports of England and corresponded closely in this respect to present day Liverpool, which in fact owes its rise to the decline of Chester as a port.

In Chester and the surrounding shire, Harrisons of Isaiah's day were very numerous, and had been long settled. The bare indexing of their wills occupies many pages. (See —*Index to Wills and Inventories now Preserved in the Court of Probate, Chester,* pub. by The Record Society, ed. by J. E. Earwaker, Vols. XV, 1660-1680, XVIII, 1681-1700, XX, 1701-1720, and XXII, 1721-1740.) In 1667-8 Richard Harrison was mayor of the City. (The Record Society, Vol. LI, p. 154, *Rolls of Freemen,* Part I, 1392-1700.)

Among those of rarer names who left wills were—Josiah Harrison of Minshull Vernon, yeoman, 1664, Joshua Harrison, of Warrington, Adminstration with Inventory, 1675, Jeremiah Harrison, of Manchester, 1685, Jeremiah Harrison of Sollom, 1706, Catherine Harrison of Kinderton, spinster, 1727, Catherine Harrison of Melling, Admon. 1727, Catherine Harrison of Aldford, widow, 1734, etc.

Earwaker, in his *History of the Ancient Parish of Sanbach, Cheshire,* (page 202) notes a pedigree of the Harrisons of Cranage Hall, arms "Argent, a fess between 3 pheons, Gules, a mullet for difference," embracing the brothers (Rev.) William d. 1686, Samuel, d. 1709, Edmund, d. 1676, Daniel, John, and Joseph Harrison, the last thee living in 1685, the sons of . . . . Harrison, and wife Anne, of whom, Daniel had children, John, William, Alexander, Daniel, Benjamin, Mary, Anne, Elizabeth, and Sarah, all living and under age in 1685, but Mary. Samuel's line is traced in some detail. The Rev. William was vicar of Icklesham, county Sussex, and purchased the Hall in 1679. He left his estate to his brother Samuel, whose sons were Samuel and Strathill.

It was to Chester that Rev. Thomas Harrison returned upon the Restoration, where, says the record, he preached in the Cathedral, and remained until after the passing of the Act of Uniformity, (1662.)

Bromborough Hall, his old home, (prior to his first residence in Dublin ?), is situated about eleven miles from Chester on the river Mersey, and immediately across the river from Liverpool, over which city it commands an interesting view. After passing through various hands it was purchased from . . . . Green by Edward Bradshaw, from whom at his death in 1671 it descended to his son James Bradshaw, and was later purchased from the latter by his (James') nephew, James Mainwaring, son of George Mainwaring, (Manwaring), (d. 1695.) The last named married Elizabeth Bradshaw, sister to James Bradshaw, and of Dr. Harrison's wife. James Mainwaring's wife was Mary Johnson. (See—Helsby's *History of Chester*, Vol. II, pp. 428-429.)

Dr. Harrison's return to Chester was followed in a short time by his second marriage. As disclosed by the registers of St. Peter's Church, Chester, under date of—

Febv. 28a, 1659-60: "Mr. Thomas Harrison Doctor in Divinity & Mis Katherine Bradshaw, spinster, (were) married."

At this time she was twenty-three years of age, as is also disclosed by these registers—

10 Septr. 1637: "Katherine Bradshaw ye daugr of Mr Edward Bradshaw, Mercer & Sheriff of Chester was baptized."

Two other entries record the births of two children—

"1661. Thomas the son of Mr Thomas Harrison, Doctor in Divinitye born April 23, Baptized May 22."

"1663. Katherine daugr to Mr Thomas Harrison, Doctor in Divinitie, born the 15th. day of August & Baptized the 26th August."

(Letter—F. B., *pens me* March 4, 1933.)

With the last entry the St. Peter's record as to Thomas and Katharine closes. These registers were kept by the Established Church, and down to this time, (1663) Rev. Harrison was associated with this church, as disclosed by his being named as a prebendary of Lichfield Cathedral this same year. (See page 94.) About 1665 persecution of the nonconformists arose, and as manifested from Shakerley's report to Williamson, (see page 94), Dr. Harrison was considered by the authorities one of the prime movers of nonconformity in Chester. It is apparent that by this date he had served his connection with the state church. During this year Parliament passed the "Five Mile Act," forbidding an noncomformist minister to reside within five miles of any city or corporated town. With the plague in Chester also threating, he evidently moved his residence about this time from the bounds of St. Peter's jurisdiction. In any event his views as to Independency from this time forward would seem to account sufficiently for his omission of baptism by the Episcopal authorities of any of his later children, regardless of his location.

There was a number of state churches in Chester, among them St. Peter's, St. Oswald's, The Holy Trinity, and the Cathedral, (the latter containing the episcopal throne of the Bishop), dating back to mediaeval times. The registers of the Cathedral, (Marriages and Baptisms, published by The Parish Register Society), as preserved, begin with the year 1687. Aside from these registers and those of the Parish of the Holy and Undivided Trinity, (Baptisms from 1656, marriages from 1654), the records of the various parishes of Chester appear to be available only in the original. In the instance of the records at Bromborough, an examination of the registers is not allowed by the present rector. (Letter— F. B. *pens me,* 18 of November, 1933, inclosing original from pastor, 20-ix-1933.)

It was about the time of the outbreak of the persecution of the nonconformists that Bromborough Hall came into posession of Dr. Harrison's father-in-law, and while the *Dictionary of National Biography* has been followed as to Dr. Harrison's residence there, it may well be that he resided at the Hall for a time during the persecutions. It was in or near West Kirby (on the Dee), of the Bromborough neighborhood, that Richard Harrison, founder of the New Haven, Connecticut line, said to have been a brother of Rev. Thomas Harrison, resided prior to his emigration to America. (Note— Theophilus Eaton, founder and Governor of New Haven, married the eldest daughter of George Lloyd, Bishop of Chester, 1604-1615.) From New Haven to Oyster Bay would have been an easy step in the way of Isaiah Harrison's settlement, and it appears that on his sailing from England his first aim was likely to get in touch with the family of New Haven. The remarkable similarity of the early New Haven Harrison names to those of Isaiah's family continues for several generations. Such names among his descendants as Ezekiel, Gideon, Jeremiah, Joseph, Josiah, Nehemiah, Ruben, and Zebulon, indicate an undoubted Puritan origin.

* * * * * *

The name Isaiah fittingly suggests a Puritan preacher's son; particularly considering that the time of his birth was undoubtely at that critical period in Puritan history illustrated above—when the Cromwells had past and the Restoration was an accomplished fact, driving Presbyterians and Congregationalists alike into nonconformity. Old Ironsides himself, was referred to as a Josiah by Rev. Thomas Harrison in his sermon preached at Christ Church Cathedral, Dublin, on the occasion of the Lord Proctector's death. (See page 89.) That Isaiah as a name for a Harrison was a distinct innovation is evident the deeper the matter is gone into, and too much stress cannot be laid on this fact.

Harrison as spelled by Isaiah and his sons in their signatures was spelled with the double "s" (Harrisson.) While instances of this older form of spelling may be found in English records alongside other variations and the usual way, the Harrisons of Dublin, judging from the parish registers, seem to have adhered to the double "s" more consistently than their kinsmen of England, where the usual spelling appears predominent.

Rev. Thomas Harrison continued a resident of Cheshire as late as 1672, in which year his name appears as "Thomas Harrison of Chester" in a list of nonconformists clergymen licensed to preach; his name being listed under "Place General, Denomination, Independent." (*Calendar of State Papers, Domestic,* 1672, p. 575.)

The Independents were Congregationalists, and while Isaiah Harrison's religious affiliation is not known, it is assured that he was of nonconformity stock. He is thought to have been a member of the early Congregational church of Huntington, Long Island, later Presbyterian. The town is located midway between Oyster Bay and Smithtown, two points of his settlement. The first records of the church have been destroyed, but in 1751 is recorded here the marriage of Nathaniel Harrison, and a short time later the baptism of Daniel and Jesse Harrison, names familiar among Isaiah's sons and grandsons. (See page 36.)

In fleeing from Ireland in view of these premises it would have been natural for Isaiah Harrison to have come to New England, where Congregational churches were flourishing, and his relatives of New Haven resided.

New York at the time was under an able Irish governor, Thomas Dongan, (1683-1688) and the colony was well known in Ireland. In 1686 it was placed under the jurisdiction of Sir. Edmund Andros, (1686-1689) when the latter took charge of the whole region from Delaware to the St. Croix, with Boston as the capital. King James' persecution of the Scotch Convenanters about this time led thousands of them to emigrate to New Jersey, where many were landed at Perth Amboy. John Harrison of Flushing, Long Island, who owned land at Oyster Bay during Isaiah's residence there, became the agent for the proprietors of East Jersey in the settlement of the Scotch. Two of these proprietors were natives of Ireland.

* * * * * *

Out of the distant past the two old seals at Staunton remain, pointing unmistakably to Isaiah Harrison's descent from a member of the gentry, to which class Dr. Thomas Harrison obviously belonged. It was from this class that Cromwell had sprung, and his close followers would have been careful to preserve the tokens of such standing; "I was born a gentleman," said he, in an address to Parliament, "and in the old social arrangement of a nobleman, a gentleman, and a yeoman, I see a good interest of the nation and a great one." (Bruce's *Social Life of Virginia in the 17th. Century,* p. 113.)

It is significant that of the two Thomas Harrisons, the Major-General, and the Doctor of Divinity, no pedigree or Coat of Arms regarding the former is found recorded in the various visitations of the Heralds College, while a pedigree embracing the latter and his wife is recorded. The fact of the recording of the pedigree, brief though it is without the arms stated, is evidence conclusive that Dr. Harrison was recognized as entitled to bear arms. Moreover the pedigrees and arms of the families of both of his wives were recorded, showing further that all were of genteel stock. The existance of the two seals bearing different arms may well explain, in fact, the omission of either arms in the pedigree; it not being determined at the time which to enter.

Throughout the seventeenth century, and the earlier part of the eighteenth, there resided at Chester one or more of the four Randle Holmes of four successive generations, each of whom was in turn a deputy of the Heralds College. Randle Holme, III, (b. 1627) became involved in disputes with the College, the authorities asserting that he had usurped their privileges in preparing Coats of Arms, hatchments, etc., instances of which were later nullified by Dugdale, as noted in the *Diary of his Visitations* of 1663-4. In the end Holmes seems to have come to terms with the College, and in 1688 published his great work *The Academy of Armoury.* He began his collections for the book in 1649, and his papers together with the notes of the other three Randles are now a part of the

Harleian MSS. of the British Museum. (See —*Chester, A Historical and Topograprical Account of the City,* by Bertram C. A. Windle, p. 261.)

In a general way the two seals at Staunton may be accepted as representative of different periods in the ancestral history of the immigrant. Of the two Coats of Arms the *eagle* arms refer obviously to the older strain of ancestry. The *eagle displayed* as an emblem dates back to the time of Charlemagne, and is found much less frequently in English arms, it is said, than in those of Teutonic origin. It is accounted one of the most noble bearings. The lion is a more distinctly English emblem, although found in the arms of Denmark and Norway. The demi-lion is referred to by authorities on heraldry as usually associated with the Harrison family. A touch of sable is a marked characteristic of Harrison arms, and alludes doubtless to the Danish orign of the family; the *bird sable* in the instance of the Durham line is a striking reminder of the time—

"*When Denmark's raven soared on high,*
Triumphant through Northumbrian sky."

Rokeby—SIR WALTER SCOTT.

Although both Coats of Arms were recorded, (the Durham arms with the addition of the chief) near the beginning of the seventeenth century, this gives no clew as to how long either "achievement" may have been in existance before this time. It is assured that by 1634 there were Harrisons of Durham descent in London, one of whom was a public official there, who under the laws then prevailing was using there the eagle arms, and that by this time also the demi-lion arms were widely known in Yorkshire where for three successive generations from 1592, they continued to spell THOMAS HARRISON, the name of the founder of a numerous family from which sprang Sir. Thomas Harrison, High Sheriff under Cromwell, of Yorkshire, Dr. Harrison's native county.

* * * * * *

Such are some of the explanations afforded in view of the history of the seals and of Rev. Thomas Harrison's career of the various circumstances of Isaiah Harrison's settlement. Enough, it is believed, has been set forth demonstrating that these circumstances are entirely too numerous in their indicated connection with Dr. Harrison for this connection to be ignored on the grounds of mere coincidence. Thus while absolute record proof is unavailable, considering the congruency of the circumstances ample warrent is furnished for the statement first made at the beginning of this discussion.

* * * * * *

On the occasion of his arrival in Dublin, under Henry Cromwell, Rev. Harrison, the 21st July, 1655, was assigned to preach at Christ Church Cathedral on Lord's Days in turn with Rev. Samuel Winter, Provost of Trinity College, and others. A few days later (July 23rd) he was directed to preach at St. John's, and on the 8th of September of the same year was settled as the stated minister of Christ Church Cathedral with a stipend of 300 pounds a year, the largest amount until then ever paid a clergyman in Ireland. The Cathedral was the state church for Henry Cromwell and the Commissioners, and was considered the most important place of worship in the country. In effect it became the Cathedral of the Independents.

Dr. Harrison was considered a highly effective preacher. It was a popular saying "that Mr. Charnock's invention, Dr. Harrison's expression and Mr. Samuel Mather's logic would make the 'perfectest' preacher in the world." (See—*Puritans in Ireland,* 1647-1661, by Rev. St. John D. Seymour, *Oxford Historical & Literary Studies,* Vol.

XII, pp. 33, 110, and 141.) Rev. Mather, it may be observed in passing, was the pastor of St. Nicholas Church, Dublin, and was the son of Increase Mather, Independent, the well known New England divine, who among a number of Puritan preachers from New England was also in Ireland at the time.

Little beyond what has been stated appears to be known of Rev. Thomas Harrison's life following the Restoration. Having been so closely allied with the Cromwell party his fortune doubtless suffered irreparable reverses upon the return of Charles II to the throne. In 1663, he was receiving a stipend from the Cathedral of Lichfield. This church although located in Staffordshire seems to have been at the time connected with the See, or city, of Chester. It was from Staffordshire that Major-General Thomas Harrison hailed, and thus doubtless part of the confusion as to him and Rev. Thomas in the old tradition. From Staffordshire also came "Jeremy Harrison, Dr. of Physic," mentioned in *St. George's Visitation* of 1614, in the pedigree of Thomas Whitgreave, as the latter's son-in-law; he having married Frances, the daughter of Thomas.

Dr. Jeremy and his wife emigrated to Virginia prior to 1654, in which year she is named a widow. (See later; also *Visitation of Staffordshire,* by Sir Richard St. George, 1614, and by Sir Wm. Dugdale, 1663-1664, Ed. by H. Sydney Glazebrook, London, 1885, p. 310, and *Early Va. Immingrants,* by George Cabell Greer, p. 149.)

Rev. Harrison's (second) settlement in Dublin was in 1672, or shortly thereafter, by which time he had manifestly been disassociated from the state church eight or nine years. During the interim the development of the Clarendon Code, of which the Act of Uniformity, the Five Mile Act, and the Conventicle Act were intergal parts, as an instrument in the persecution of the Puritan element, reached its climax. The Conventicle Act, passed in 1670, forbade all meetings for the purpose of worship under any other form than that prescribed by the Established Church. With the close of the Dutch war and the fall of Clarendon, the king took matters into his own hands and in 1672 released all nonconformists, Roman Catholics and dissenters alike, from the operation of the Code. With the ban lifted Rev. Harrison obtained his license as an Independent clergymen, and about the same time settled in Dublin. With the rise of the Catholic element there under James II, all hope for the advancement of any of his children was definitely cut off; Tyrconnell and his party having scant sympathy with any former follower of Cromwell, or his children—to say the least.

Kingston-upon-Hull, ordinarily known as Hull, England, where Rev. Harrison was born, was granted a charter by Edward I, in 1299. In 1381 Edward III granted the burgess power to choose a mayor, but it was not until 1576 that the present city was incorporated. In 1511, Robert Harrison, and in 1537, John Harrison were the mayors. Among the aldermen were John Harrison, 1548, John Harrison, 1576, Chistopher Harrison, 1593, and Thomas Harrison, 1687. (See—*History of Kingston-upon-Hull,* by Rev. John Tickall, 1796, pp. 106 117, 124, 127, and 183, and *Hisotry of Kingston-upon-Hull,* by J. J. Shehan, 1864, p. 389.) On July 8, 1548, "John Herryson, with Thomas Dalton, the mayor, James Johnson, William Johnson, and others, aldermen and burgess of "Kyngston upon Hull," granted to William Knolles, Knight, a tentment in a street called "High Gate," in the said town. *(Yorkshire Deeds,* Ed. by Wm. Brown, Vol. III, p. 56, The Yorkshire Archaelogical Society Record Series, Vol. LXIII.)

A curious sepulchural brass in memory of John Harrison, the mayor of 1537, who died in 1545, is yet in a good state of preservation in the church of St. Mary. His son John Harrison, the alderman of 1548, died in 1550, leaving a will naming wife Elizabeth, and establishing Harrison's Hospital of Chapel-Lane, the first charitable institution founded in Hull after the Reformation. Presumably Rev. Harrison was of a family of the same line as some of these aldermen and burgess, thus originating his right by interhitance to bear arms.

Thomas Harrison married first, as stated, Dorothy, the daughter of Samuel Symonds, and second, Katherine, the daughter of Edward Bradshaw.

Samuel Symonds' father was Richard Symonds of "great Yeldham," county Essex, son of John Symonds of Newport, county Salop, and wife Anne, (daughter of Thomas Benbow of Shropshire), and grandson of John Symonds of Newport, with whom the Symonds pedigree as recorded begins. Richard was granted, 10th July, 1625, the following arms, to him "& his posterity for ever"—"Azure, a chevron engrailed between three trefoils slipped or. Crest—Out of a murial coronet or, a boar's head argent, tusked of the first, crined gules." He married Elizabeth, the daughter of Robert Plume of Yeldham, and had issue; John Symonds of Yeldham, "one of the cursitors of the Chancery," Edward Symonds of Black-Notley, "one of the cursitors," Margaret, the wife of Edward Eyre, "one of the cursitors of the court of Chancery," Samuel Symonds, of Topsfield, (Dorothy's father), "one of the cursitors," and Richard Symonds of Yeldham, 1634, "utter barrister of Lincoln's Inn."

Samuel Symonds was thrice married. His first wife, and the only one mentioned in the pedigree, was Dorothy, the daughter of Thomas Harlakenden of Earls Colne, Essex, and by her he had sons Richard, Samuel, Harlakenden, John, and William, and daughters Dorothy, Jane, Anne, and Elizabeth, all of whom are named in the pedigree. (See—Harleian Society, Vol. XIII, *The Visitations of Eessex*, by Hawley, 1552, Hervey, 1558, Cooke, 1570, Raven, 1612, and Owen and Lilly 1634, Ed. by Walter C. Metcalf, London, 1878, Vol. I, p. 495.)

The Harlakenden arms are described as: "Argent, three chevronels within a bordure gules. Crest—Between th attires of a stag or, an eagle regardent, with wings expanded argent, belled or." *(Ibid*, p. 210.)

Symonds married second, in Massachusetts, Martha, nee Reade, the widow of Daniel Epps, and third, Rebecca, nee Swayne, the widow first of Henry Biley, second of John Hall, and third of Rev. Wm. Worchester. Samuel died in 1678, (will proven March 6, 1678.) His widow Rebecca was yet living when Isaiah Harrison came to America. She died July 21, 1695.

Katherine Bradshaw was of the "Bradshaw of Pennington" line. Her father's pedigree may be seen in Dugdale's *Visitation of Lancashire,* 1664-5. *(Remains Historical and Literary* connected with the counties of Lancester and Chester, pub. by The Chetham Society, Vol. 84, p. 54.) A more complete pedigree, however, naming "Catherine" herself occurs in the *Piccope MMS.* of the Chetham Collection, in which her family is traced from "Robert de Bradshaw, Lord of Bradshaw, 23 Edward I," (1295.) (See —*The Genealogist,* New Series, Vol. XVII, London, 1901, pp. 14-15.)

This Robert de Bradshaw was the ancestor of the numerous Bradshaws of Lancashire and Cheshire of Rev. Harrison's time. He had sons Henry de Bradshaw, "son and heir," 12 Edw. II, (1319), and William de Bradshaw. From Henry descended the Bradshaws of Bradshaw, and from William the Bradshaws of Pennington. Beginning with William the line descends through, 1st, Adam de Bradshaw, and wife Margaret, the daughter of Adam de Aspull, near Wigan; 2nd, William de Bradshaw of Aspull, (wife unnamed); 3rd, Youett de Bradshaw of Aspull, (wife unnamed); 4th, Rafe de Bradshaw of Aspull, and wife Catherine, the daughter of John Chetham of Nuthurst; 5th, Henry Bradshaw, and wife Janet, the daughter of John Risley of Risley; 6th, Henry Bradshaw, and wife Elizabeth, daughter of Wm. Gerard of Ince; 7th, William Bradshaw of Aspull, gent., d. 1558, and wife Margery, the daughter of Hugh Hindley of Hindley 8th, James Bradshaw of Aspull, land in Wigan, and lease of Pennington, wife Elizabeth, daughter of John Hassocke of Wigan; to 9th, Raphe Bradshaw of Aspull, County Lancaster, from whom descends immediately "Bradshaw of Pennington."

Rafe Bradshaw married Anne, the daughter of Rafe Orrel of Turton, and had among others Roger Bradshaw of Aspull and Pennington, d. 1625, (will proved at Chester.) Roger married as his third wife Ellen, the daughter of John Owen of Manchester, and by her had sons Henry Bradshaw of Bradshaw, Richard Bradshaw of Chester and Pennington, John Bradshaw of Farnsworth, and Edward Bradshaw, (Katherine's father) Alderman and Mercer of Chester, and Sheriff of Chester, 1636. (Will dated 3rd of September, 1670, proved 1671.)

Edward Bradshaw married Mary, the daughter of Matthew Stone of London, as his second wife. He was buried in St. Peter's Church, Chester, where his epitaph may be seen reading—

> "Near this place lieth the body of Edward Bradshaw, esquire, who by his first wife Susannah, daughter and heir of Christopher Blease of this city alderman, had 12 children, and by his second wife Mary, the relickt of Mr. Christopher Love, had 7 children; he was exemplary for his piety and charity when living, and departed this life 21st. October, 1671, in the 67th. year of his age leaving 5 children yet alive, to continue whose memory, his son and heir Sir. James Bradshaw, of Risby in the east rideing of y[e] county of York, has erected this monument." (See—*History of Chester,* by Thomas Helsby, Vol. I, p. 324.)

Five of Edward and Mary's children are named in the pedigree; viz., Elizabeth, who married George Manwaring, of Chester, 1672; Mary, who married Roger Manwaring of Kermoncham, 1672; James, Knighted 28th June, 1673) who married Dorothy, the daughter of John Ellerker of Risby (and left two daughters); Edward, and Catherine (Katherine), the last named the wife of Rev. Harrison. Le Neve's *Pedigrees of the Knights* names a third son, Christopher Bradshaw. *Harleian Society,* Vol. VIII, p. 284.)

The pedigree is in error, in naming all of the above children of Edward Bradshaw as those of his second wife. Probably only one or two were such. Rev. Christopher Love, (b. 1618), did not die until 1651. In the case of Catherine Bradshaw, she being born in 1637, was thus the daughter of Edward by his first wife, nee Blease. (See—*Dict. Natl. Biog.,* London, 1893, Vol 34, p. 155.)

In his will, proven by his son James, the sole executor, 5th December, 1671, Edward Bradshaw names the following— James Bradshaw, his son and heir; Edward Bradshaw, his second son; his daughter Elizabeth; his daughter Mary (devised legacy left by grandfather Blease); his daughter Elizabeth by his last wife; his daughter Katherine Harrison, "and her husband, Dr. Harrison, and her children," (unnamed); his daughter-in-law (stepdaughter) Mary Love; his kinswoman Elizabeth Bradshaw, "that lives in Bolton;" his brother Richard Bradshaw and wife (unnamed); his brothers and sisters, (unnamed); his cousins John Ratcliffe, and wife (unnamed), and Robert Greggs and wife (unnamed); "six silenced ministers" (unnamed); Mrs. Anne Clarke, Mrs. Furnice, Mrs. Slater, and Mrs. Elock, ministers' widows; the widow Blease; the widow Anne Hespith; his servant Richard Taylor; his maid servant (unnamed); the poor householders of Chester; the poor of Aspull, where he was born; his nephew, Wm. Lyme; Mr. Wm. Barneston, desceased; and his friend Richard Green; all but the last three receiving bequests. (Relationships as stated in the will.)

He desired to "be buried in The Parish Church of St. Peter in the City of Chester in the same grave where my first and second wifes were buried and to the end my grave may be made very deep I give 20s for the making thereof." All of his lands in Aspull and Hindley, the rent of the Rectory of Westleigh, his land in Whiston, of county Lancaster, the Manor and Manor House with the appurtenances in Bromborough, his lands in Taltonhall, and Mollington Bannister, county Chester, his lands and buildings in the city of Chester, (except a piece of property left to his second son), his gold watch and signet ring, he devised to his son James. To Edward he left his lands in Huntington, county Chester, and a "House, Shoppe & Seller in Northgate Street in Shoemakers Rowe," in the city of Chester. To the other children he left various Sums of Money, (totaling about 3,300 pounds) and in addition devised to his daughter Elizabeth, "that Diamond Ring & Necklace of pearls that was her Mothers."

His bequest to his daughter Katherine and her husband runs as follows: "I give to my daughter Katherine Harrison 40 pounds for her own disposal and to her husband Dr. Harrison I give 10 pounds & to her children 400 pounds to be equally divided amongst them." (Abstract—F. B. *pens me* Feburuary 17, 1933, from Chester.)

From the fact that Edward Bradshaw was an Alderman and Mercer of the city of Chester it is evident that he was a member of the Merchants Guild. His arms are described as: "1 and 4: Argent, between two bends Sable three mullets of the second; Bradshaw: 2 and 3; Vert, a chevron or, on an escocheon of pretence, Argent, a salter sable: between four crescents of the second; on a chief Azure a garb or between two martletts of the fourth". With the exception of azure for vert in 2 and 3, and the addition of the escocheon of pretence, these arms are the same as those of Bradshaw of Pennington, 1663, where the Crest is described as—"On a mount vert, in front of an oak tree a stag trippent, proper."

As for Isaiah Harrison, although possessed of the tokens of gentle birth, the fortunes of his family having been depleted, he made no pretense of displaying them. Rather for his posterity he desired no sign—

"Save men's opinions and their living blood,
To show the world that they were gentlemen."
—*Richard II, Act* 3, *Sec.* 1

CHAPTER VIII

The Valley of Virginia Pioneers

"Can you feel again the romance
Of this ancient long grey trail?
Can you hear the stages rattling,
And the trav'lers lusty hail?
Can you see the long procession
Of the endless marching years?
Hear the laughter that has kissed them
Or the splash of blood and tears?"

—WAYLAND.

LONG BEFORE the stage's rattle over this ancient trail was heard there passed this way, according to tradition, a simple old two-wheeled cart, which is claimed to have been the first wheeled vehicle to appear in the Valley. This was brought in by the Harrisons on their way from Delaware. As Isaiah Harrison had been a blacksmith back in his younger days at Oyster Bay, Long Island, he no doubt had fashioned this old cart with his own hands.

It was at the May term of Sussex court, 1737, that John, Daniel, and Jeremiah began disposing of their lands in Delaware. By the next year Thomas also was "late of Sussex County on delaware," as stated in the deed signed by him executing the sale of his land. While Daniel did not release his final tract in Sussex until March 3rd, 1740, the deed of his brother Thomas shows that he too, was "late of This County" by 1738.

The first patent on record granted to a member of Isaiah Harrison's family for land in the Valley of Virginia was issued to Daniel Harrison the 22nd day of September, 1739, for 400 acres. A year or two was usually required between the application for and the final issuing of a patent. In this instance the survey appears to have been made in 1738. Under date of December 8th, this year, a survey of 400 acres entered for the above patentee is found recorded at Orange. (Deed Book 3, page 208, Surveys made in Orange County since June 1738.) This was only six years after the settlement of Lewis and Hite. Daniel's grant was followed at short intervals by a long series of other patents to various members of Isaiah's descendants, showing that in the early days of Old Augusta these Harrisons patented over 17,400 acres, (including about 3,200 acres granted to Cravens and Herrings), of what is now largely the choicest land in Rockingham County. As subsequent patents were made out in a manner similar to Daniel's, only this one will be given in full. It reads as follows:

"GEORGE the Second by the Grace of God Great Britain France and Ireland, King Defender of the Faith &c. TO ALL TO WHOM these Presents shall come Greeting. Know ye that for divers good causes and consideration but more Especially for and in Consideration of the Sum of Forty Shillings of good and lawful Money for our Use paid to our Receiver General of our Revenues in this our Colony and Dominion of Virginia WE HAVE Given Granted and confirmed and by these presents for us our heirs and successors do give grant and confirm unto Daniel Harrison one certain tract or parcel of land containing four hundred acres lying and being in the

THE LONG GREY TRAIL

Looking North at the crossing of the "Fairfax Line," now the Rockingham-Shenandoah County Line. See page 151

County of Orange on the east draft of the west fork of the Naked Creek and bounded as follows to-wit; BEGINNING at a white oak on the west side of the said Creek, thence S 86 degrees 80 Poles, thence S 43 degrees E 80 poles near three blazed white oak saplings N 73 degrees E 260 poles to a spanish oak near a large rock, N 17 degrees W 74 poles to a hickory on a ridge, N 73 degrees E80 poles to two hickories N 17 degrees W 1666 poles to a stake near a blazed white oak on the North side of the said draft, thence S 55 degrees W 464 poles to the beginning. With all woods underwoods swamps marches low-grounds meadows feedings and his due share of all veins mines and quarries as well discovered as not discouvered with the bounds aforesaid and being part of the said quantity of said four hundred acres of land and the rivers waters and water courses therein contained, Together with the privileges of hunting hawking fowling fishing and all other profits and commodities and hereditaments whatsoever to the same or any part thereof belonging or in any wise appertaining; To have hold posess and enjoy the said tract or parcel of land and all other the before granted premises and ever part thereof. With their and every of their appurts unto the said Daniel Harrison and to his heirs and assigns forever. To the only use and behoof of him the said Daniel Harrison and to his heirs and assigns forever; To be held of us our heirs and sucessors of our mannor of East Greenwich, in the County of Kent in Free and Common Soccage and not in Capite or by Knights service. Yealding and paying unto us our heirs and successors for every fifty acres of land and so proportionably for a lesser or greater quantity that fifty acres the fee rent of one Shilling yearly to be paid upon the feast of St. Michel the Arch Angel, and also cultivating three acres part of every fifty of the tract above mentioned within three years after the date of these presents. Provided always that if three years of the said fee rent shall at any time be in arrears or upaid, or if the said Daniel Harrison his heirs or assigns do not within the space of three years next coming after the date of these presents cultivate and improve three acres part of every fifty of the tract above mentioned, then the estate hereby granted shall cease and be utterly determined and thereafter it shall and may be lawful to and for us our heirs and successors to grant the same land and premises with the appurts unto such other preson or persons as we our heirs and successors shall think fit.

IN WITNESS whereof we have caused these our letters patent to be made; WITNESS our trusty and well beloved William Gooch Esquire our Lieutenant Governor and Commander in Cheif of our said Colony and Dominion at Williamsburgh under seal of our said colony the 22nd day of September one thousand seven hundred and thirty nine, in the 13th. year of our reign.

William Gooch.

(See—Book No. 18, p. 381, State Land Office, Richmond, Virginia.)

This was the 222nd patent made for the land in Orange County. The Orange patents begin with book No. 15, in 1734. The first patent is dated 20th August, 1734 and was granted to Jost Hite.

The Valley of Virginia was settled under the administration of Lieut. Governor Gooch, a native of Scotland, who arrived in Virginia October 13, 1727, the year that King George II came to the throne of England. In 1697 the office of Governor-in-Chief of Virginia became a pensionary sinecure enjoyed by one residing in England. George Hamilton Douglas, the Earl of Orkney, enjoyed this privilege from 1704 until his death in 1737. He was one of the sixteen peers of Scotland, a Colonel in the English Army, and had been in the battle of Blenheim (August 13, 1704) with the Duke of

Marlborough. He was succeeded by William Anne Keppel, the Earl of Albemarle, who served until 1754. Williamsburg at this time was the capital of Virginia, the seat of government having been removed from Jamestown in 1698, by Lieut. Governor Nicholson, who had formerly been Governor of New York.

The first organized effort by the English to explore the Valley of Virginia was made under Colonel Alexander Spotswood, a descendant of an old Scottish family, who arrived in Virginia as Lieutenant-Governor in 1710. Like the Earl of Orkney, Spotswood had also been in the battle of Blenhiem. He was wounded in this fight.

Spotswood headed a party of explorers, afterwards familiarily known as the "Knights of the Golden Horseshoe," in 1716. Leaving Williamsburg August 20th, they arrived about two weeks later at the top of the Blue Ridge at what is now Swift Run Gap, near Elkton. From here they appear to have turned back on account of the difficult path, and finally the same day crossed the mountain through present Milan's Gap. They reached the Shenandoah River near where the town of Shenandoah now stands. There they camped for two days, exploring and fishing, and consuming a plentiful supply of a variety of liquors, and then turned back on September 7th, after leaving a few rangers to make further surveys. Ten days later the party returned to Williamsburg, having travelled about 440 miles out and back.

According to the historian Campbell, Col. Spotswood was born in 1676, in an English colony in Africa. From this it appears that he was born at Tangiers while this outpost was under Col. William Smith, before noticed. (See page 35.) Spotswood retired as Governor in 1722, and was succeeded by Hugh Drysdale, who died in 1726. Drysdale was in turn succeeded by Edmund Jennings, who was suspended July 8th the same year. Upon Jennings suspension Col. Robert Carter, president of the Governor's Council, and agent of Lord Fairfax, became acting Governor until Gooch's arrival. Spotswood settled at Germanna, and died in 1740. Col. Gooch served as Lieut. Governor until June 29th, 1749, when he sailed for England, amid the regrets of his people.

At the time of the Tramontane expedition the Colony of Virginia contained 72,000 whites and 23,000 negroes, and was next to Massachusetts in population. Four years after this expedition the frontier of Virginia was extended to the Blue Ridge mountains, Spottsylvania County being formed in 1720 from Essex. Orange County was formed from Spottsylvania in 1734 and at this time included all of the Colony of Virginia west of the Blue Ridge.

"What Governor Spotswood saw filled his party," says Cartmell, in his *Shenandoah Valley Pioneers,* "not only with wonder and admiration, but a desire to hastily spread the news, inviting immigration from the settlements lying along the Jersey coast and the more thickly settled parts of Pennsylvania." The first settlement south of the Cohongoroota River—Indian name of the Potomac—and west of the Blue Ridge, appears to have been a more or less natural overflow from the Colony of Maryland at or near Packhorse Ford, where Shepherdstown in West Virginia is now located. It is fairly well established that there were some settlers there as early as 1717-20. This, of course, was within the Colony of Virginia at this time.

Various individual explorations followed the Spotswood expedition, and the year 1730 saw the first recorded legal grants for land in the Valley. The first actual grant found on record in the books of the Land Office at Richmond to land in this section evidently was a family affair between Col. Robert Carter above, as the agent of Lord Fairfax, and his sons and grandsons. This grant mentions Benjamin Harrison, IV, and his son Benjamin, Jr. The former was a son of Benjamin, III, previously noted; the latter was a signer of the Declaration of Independence and the father of President William Henry Harrison. President William Henry was in turn the grandfather of President Benjamin Harrison. This old "Northern Neck grant" is dated 22, September, 1730, and in part reads as follows:

"The Right Hon. Thomas Lord Fairfax Baron of Cameron in that part of Great Britain called Scotland Proprietor of the Northern Neck of Virginia . . . etc. . . give grant and confirm unto Landon Carter and Geo. Carter sons of Robert Carter Senr. Esquire, Carter Burwell and Robert Burwell, sons of Major Nathaniel Burwell, dec. Carter Page and Robin Page sons of Mann Page Esq., Robert Carter Nicholas son of Dr. Geo. Nicholas, Robert Carter Junior, son of John Carter Esq., Benjamin Harrison Junior, son of Benjamin Harrison Esquire, and Robert Carter, Jr. son of Robert Carter, Junior, Esq. one certain tract or parcel of land containing fifty thousand two hundred and twelve acres situate lying and being in Stafford County on the North side of a branch that juts out of Potomac River on ye upper side of the Blue Ridge, commonly called Chenandoah Creek and is bounded as follows, viz. BEGINNING

At a large walnut tree marked R. C. standing near the bank of the said creek on the lower side of the mouth of a Spout Run that falls into the said creek, on the North West side thereof opposite the lower Gap or Thoroughfare of the aforesaid Blue Ridge, about twelve or fifteen miles above the mouth of the said creek and a little above an Island commonaly called Mattisons Island and extending thence . . . . . . to a hickory tree near the Drafts of Cedar Lick being a branch of the aforesaid creek . . .

TO HAVE AND TO HOLD the said fifty thousand two hundred and twelve acres of land and the six islands included within the said creek . . . . . etc.
(See—Book C, 1729-1731, p. 77, Land Office, Richmond, Virginia.)

Col. Robert Carter (b. 1663, d. Aug. 4, 1732) resided at "Corotoman" in Lancaster County, Here the old "grant book" was no doubt kept at the time. Col. Carter had served as Speaker and Member of the House of Burgesses, and in 1699 was appointed a member of the Governor's Council, a position which he held until his death. From 1699 to 1705 he was also Treasurer of the Colony. In 1726 he became acting Governor, as related above. As the agent of Lord Fairfax, the Proprietor of the Northern Neck of Virginia, he handled vast bodies of land and by his will left over 300,000 acres to his children. On account of a certain lordliness of manner he acquired the sobriquet of "King Carter," a name by which he is commonly referred to. He married 1st, 1688, Judith, the daughter of John Armistead, and 2nd, 1701, Elizabeth, the daughter of Thomas Landon and widow of Richard Willis. His children were: John, of "Corotoman" and "Shirley"; Elizabeth (d. 1721) m. 1st Nathaniel Burwell of Carter's Creek, m. 2nd, Dr. George Nicholas; Judith m. 2nd, Mann Page of "Roswell", Gloucester Co.; Anne, m. Benjamin Harrison IV, of "Berkeley"; Robert, of "Nomini", Westmoreland Co.; Sarah (d. young); Betty (d. young); Ludlow (d. young); Charles, of "Cleve," King George Co.; Landon, of "Sabine Hill", Richmond Co.; Lucy, m. Henry Fitzhugh, of "Eagles Nest," King George Co.; and George, d. unmarried. (See, *Va. Magazine of History and Biography,* Vol. 32, pp. 18 and 97.)

Benjamin Harrison, III, (1673-1710) of Berkeley, Member of the House of Burgesses, and wife, Elizabeth Burwell, had only two children who survived him, viz.; Benjamin, IV, (Esquire, above) and Elizabeth who m. a Randolph. Benjamin, IV, Member of the House of Burgesses, and Anne, the daughter of Robert "King" Carter, had—Anne, m. William Randolph; Elizabeth, m. Peyton Randolph, President of the 1st Continental

Congress; Benjamin, V., (Junior, above), 1726-1791, Member of the House of Burgesses and of the Continental Congress, Signer of the Declaration of Independence, Governor of Virginia, (1781-1784), m. Elizabeth Bassitt; Charles, Brig-Gen. of the Continental Army; Henry (d. young); Nathaniel, m. Anne Gilliam; Henry; Robert, m. a Collier; Carter Henry, m. Susannah Randolph; Lucy, and Hannah. Benjamin IV, and his last two named daughters were killed at Berkeley by a stroke of lightening July 12, 1745.

So far as traditions go regarding descent from Major-Gen. Thomas Harrison, the regicide, it is interesting to note in comparing them that they make Hannah—the mother of Benjamin, III—a sister of Isaiah Harrison, from which circumstance Bejamin, III, (the father of Benjamin Harrison Esquire, of the Carter grant, and grandfather of the signer), would have been a first cousin of Daniel Harrison of the 1739 patent. Had Hannah been instead a child of the Rev. Thomas Harrison, as well as Isaiah, an even closer relationship would have existed between the patentees, presuming the four brother tradition of Keith correct. (See page 89.) Daniel Harrison had a son Benjamin born two years after the date of the patent. It was Henry Harrison, 1692 ?—1732, a brother of Benjamin, III, on whose tombstone at Brandon the before described arms similar to those on Robert Harrison's seal appear.

Many of the pioneers at the beginning of their settlement "on the West side of the Great Mountains" were, in the eyes of the law, mere squatters on the public domain. The country being uninhabited, the usual proceedure in taking up land, after exploration and choice, was by first establishing what was known as tomahawk right. That is, the land selected was marked by blazing certain trees with the tomahawk, or similar instrument, thus locating the boundries, reserving for a future date the process of legal formalities. After the tomahawk right followed a petition for a grant of survey and settlement, which was issued providing no other restriction or previous orders were found in the way. This in turn was followed by a patent establishing legal owenership. A patent was not granted before a survey had been entered in the records. No deed of bargain and sale could be made until the patent was granted and complied with. All prior legal trasactions were directly under the supervision and consent of the Governor in Council, in whose journal they were recorded. The first "grants" were merely orders of the Virginia Council and are not therefore found in the land office books.

As stated, the year 1730 marks the beginning of *grants* to land in the Valley of the Shenandoah. This year the first two *grants for settlement* appear. The Fairfax grant of September 22, 1730, has been noted. In addition to these, three *grants for survey* were also made this year.

The two grants for settlement were issued by Governor Gooch on the same date, 17th, June, 1730, and were to the Van Meter brothers, John and Isaac. On this date also a grant for survey was made by the Governor to Jacob Stover. Later, on the 28th of October, 1730, an order granting Alexander Ross and others *a right to survey* was made by the Governor in Council. Finally, in 1730, Joist Hite, of Pennsylvania, through the influence of the Governor there, obtained a conditional grant from the Virginia Council for land "West of the Great Mountains" not heretofore granted.

These grants were all for large areas of land in order to induce settlement, and were powerful factors in getting the Valley populated. After this time only three other such grants were made, viz.; to William Russell and Larkin Chew in 1733-4, to William Beverly, (patent) September 6, 1736, and to Benjamin Borden, (patent) November 8th, 1739. With the exception of the grant to Stover all but the last two were for land in the lower Shenandoah Valley. The Stover land was approximately midway between the extremes of the early settlements, but outside the general course of these, being in the region now known as Page Valley. This section of the Shenandoah Valley lies between the Massanutten Mountain and the Blue Ridge.

While the Van Meter entries occur a few months prior to the date of the above deed, or patent, by Robert Carter, as the agent of Lord Fairfax, these grants show, however that they were made subsequent to a survey of the Carter land. John Van Meter was granted 10,000 acres for the settlement of himself and family of eleven children, and "leave for surveying" an additional 20,000 acres when he had settled on it twenty families, or the Council was satisfied so many were to move thither. Isaac Van Meter was granted 10,000 acres for the settlement of ten families, the condition of both grants being that the required number of families would be seated within two years. Their lands were located in "the fork between the river Shenando and the river Cohonguroota," (Potomac), and extended to the Opequon. The southern boundary was the Carter tract which was mentioned in the grant. Surveys were made of this land within the time limit and confirmed May 12, 1732, which was sometime after the date of the Carter grant.

The Carter land was also between the Shenandoah and Opequon, and embraced a large territory north of the present town of Front Royal, now mostly included in the southern part of Clarke County. According to John Esten Cooke, the noted native author of the Valley, in his *Virginia, a History of the People*, "on this tract, around the present village of Millwood, settled (later) numerous friends and relatives of the proprietor, (Lord Fairfax), bringing with them the traits of the lowland: the cordial sentiments, the love of social intercourse, and the attachments to the English Church, which characterized the race."

Jacob Stover was given permission to survey two tracts of 5,000 acres each. These tracts were yet further south along the South Fork of the Shenandoah in the region before described. He did not receive patents for this land until December 15, 1733, and in the meantime seems to have changed the location of one of his tracts from that first proposed. One tract known as "Massanutten" was to be surveyed on "both sides of the South Fork," and the other on the "south side of the North Fork." These forks join near present Front Royal, and the latter tract was to be located in this vicinity at, or near, today's town of Strasburg. On the date mentioned patent was granted him for the Massanutten land and another 5,000 acres south of where the village of Port Republic is now located. These patents were issued in consideration of the settlement of 100 individuals on each tract. (See—*Cartmell*, p. 267, and *Massanutten*, by H. M. Strickler, pp. 30, and 122.)

On January 6, 1728, Russell and Chew had filed application for an order to survey 50,000 acres of land and settle families "between the Great Mountain and Sherando River" near the Front Royal locality mentioned. This land was intended to embrace a territory on the south and east side of the river and was somewhat between the Carter and Stover lands. A question arose as to the boundary of the Carter grant and in settling this the Governor limited Russell and Chew to 10,000 acres, and delayed issuing their grant until the session of 1733-4. This may explain, in a measure, the apparent change in Stover's plans.

In a general way all these lands were scattered along the Shenandoah River and the South Fork thereof, in the strip of territory extending from the Potomac River on up through Page Valley. The eastern boundary was roughly the Blue Ridge while the western was the course of the Opequon at the north, and the range of the Massanutten at the south. This territory now runs southward through the counties of Jefferson, Clarke, Warren and Page. As will be noted is was to a degree parceled out in 1730.

Alexander Ross was given the right to lay out contiguous tracts not exceeding 100,000 acres "from such waste land not embraced in any order heretofore made." This grant was very liberal and general, and did not limit the time as to when the families would have to be seated, which later caused confusion and litigation. Ross's surveys were located on the west side of the Opequon, in the section now north of Winchester, and never aggregated 100,000 acres, as he ran into the Van Meter land. The first grant confirmed to him appears November 22, 1734, for 2,373 arces, part of a 40,000 acre survey of the same year. Among these associated with him were Josiah Ballenger, James Wright, Evan Thomas, and other "Friends from Pennsylvania, and Elk River in Maryland." The first deed on record in Frederick County made by Ross was to Joseph Bryan, one of the "other Friends," April 13, 1744.

Joist Hite received a conditional grant for 100,000 acres of land to be located "West of the Great Mountains," the condition being that he would settle forty families within two years, but later this number was reduced to twenty. Hite was not required to locate his surveys in one tract, but was allowed to make selections southward from the Potomac on up the Valley.

It is said that John Van Meter led Joist Hite into this land of promise. Van Meter had been granted 200 acres of land near what is now Frederick, Maryland, November 3, 1726, by Lord Baltimore, and the following year he is found at Germanna lending his aid to Spotswood's settlers. Tradition states that from there he set out to explore the Valley, blazing his way through the dense forests. He was a typical backwoodsman, an Indian trader, and familiar with the savages' ways. Previously he had accompanied the Delawares on a hunt through some of this country, and had engaged with them in a skirmish with the Catawbas near present Franklin, West Virginia. According to the petition of Isaac Van Meter, he too, "had been to view the lands in these parts." Both brothers were granted their petition at the same time, and it appears that both were together on the trip from Germanna. They explored the Valley "from the forks of the Shenandoah," in the region of today's Front Royal. The old Van Meter house, which stood near the town of Kearneysville, is said to have had the date 1727 cut in a locust slab still owned by the family. This slab was probably a timber of a mere hunter's lodge, or cabin, erected by the brothers while on their explorations, as it was not until later that these Dutchmen settled on their land.

Outside of the settlements of some squatters around what later became Shepherdstown, and a little band of German and Swiss immigrants who had settled in 1726-7, at "Massanutten," on the land later granted to Jacob Stover, no settlements had been made in the country "West of the Great Mountains" when the above grants of 1730 were executed.

The first settlers at Massanutten were Adam Miller, and others, who had previously immigrated to Lancaster County, Pennsylvania. They called themselves "Dutchmen." Tradition states that in 1716 Miller made a trip from Lancaster County to Williamsburg and there learned of the Spotswood expedition, and later, following the Governor's old trail, finally arrived at Massanutten. By 1729 Stover appears to have been the leading spirit in the little colony. It is said that he recruited some of his settlers at Germanna. The settlement was not far from where Spotswood had camped while on his exploration, and as some of his rangers had been enlisted at Germanna this may account for the selection of the location of the settlement. As revealed by the petition of Miller and his friends to the General Court, in 1733, they had bought their land—5,000 acres—from Jacob Stover, "about four years past," and had paid him "upwards of four hundred pounds" for the same. Long before his application for a survey was granted Stover had located his settlers and disposed of the land to them for cash, apparently all unknown to the Governor and Council. He was evidently the first man to sell land in the Valley of Virginia. At the time of the petition he was "Daily Expected to Run Away."

Some sort of an agreement must have later been made, as he was finally given permission for a survey in 1730, and a patent in 1733, as stated. He died prior to 1754, in which year on February, 13th, his son Jacob Stover, Jr., of Lunenburg County, conveyed to William Russell, of Culpeper, 4,000 acres, the reversion of one of the 5,000 acre tracts patened to Jacob Stover, Sr., December 15, 1733. (See Deed Book 6, page 427, *Chalkley*, Vol. III, p. 329.)

According to Waddell, "Miller and his associates, if any, locating out of the tract of the tide of immigration which afterwards poured in, remained unknown, or unoticed, by the English-Speaking people." *(Annals of Augusta County*, p. 22.)

Hite arrived in the Valley in 1731, and in his explorations found the Van Meter land in his way. The result was that on August 5, 1731, he bought out the Van Meter brothers. The conditions of these grants, with that of his own, now required him to locate about 140 families. He later obtained from the Governor an extension of time to December 25, 1734, and, as indicated by an order of the Governor in Council of October 31, 1731, in the meantime formed a partnership with Robert McKay. By March, 1736, Hite and Mc Kay had taken into their firm two others, William Duff, and Robert Green. This was, no doubt, the first firm organized in the Valley. It does not appear that the partners of Hite were ever interested in his Van Meter land. On June 12, 1734, an order of the Governor in Council was recorded stating that Hite had made due proof of his compliance with the terms of his Van Meter grant, and it was directed that patents issue to him or his assigns. He received his first patent in August, 1734. This was the first patent issued by the Governor to land in this region of the Valley.

Generally speaking, the year 1732 marks the beginning of organized pioneer life in the Valley of Virginia. Two characteristic settlements were made this year that were to become a nucleus for future development. These settlements were those of John Lewis in the upper Shenandoah Valley and Joist Hite in the lower part of this valley. Hite fixed his settlement on the Opequon, within his Van Meter grant, in the present vicinity of Kernstown. The site was on the old Indian trail and is now marked by the crossing of the Opequon by the Valley Turnpike. John Lewis was the first settler in what is now Augusta County; he located near the old trail about two miles east of the present city of Staunton. His old home, known as Fort Lewis, is yet standing.

Hite had rather extensively traded in land in Pennsylvania before his removal to the Valley. After his removal he was almost continually engaged in this occupation until his death. He recruited his settlers mostly from the colonies north of Virginia, the remainder being largely Scotch-Irish immigrants direct from Ulster, Ireland. About the year 1738 eighty such immigrants were brought over in one boat load by his son Jacob, among whom was Catherine O'Bannon, Jacob's future wife. A great number of Hite's settlers from the north had previously located in Pennsylvania, whence they came direct to Virginia. Hite himself was a typical example.

Lewis is said to have come to the Valley with Hite, but his settlement was in striking contrast to that of the latter. He settled on land then entirely unclaimed, and about eighty-five miles farther south. He had no colonization scheme under way and was entirely alone in his forest home. Later his family joined him. John Lewis (1678-1762) was a native of Ulster, Ireland, and according to Cooke, was a member of a Huguenot family that had taken refuge in Ulster. Through his mother he was descended from an ancient Scottish family. Having killed his landlord in defense of his home —"a deplorable affair, but one alike honorable to his spirit and manhood"—he escaped to America. He was later exonerated from blame. Soon after his settlement in Virginia there began to locate around him various others from his native country; the first of the Scotch-Irish, that a little later were to begin to arrive in such great numbers by 1740.

As shown by the patent to Daniel Harrison and the grant to Carter's descendants, two authorities had begun disposing of land in the Valley of the Shenandoah. Despite the well laid plans of the Governor, and the ambition of Carter and Hite to induce settlement in the lower Valley first, the upper regions of the Shenandoah were destined to be as quickly populated, if not even more so. Several causes led to this, among which was largely the conflict of authority in granting land between the Governor, representing the Crown, and Lord Fairfax.

The Valley of the Shenandoah was at this time the extreme western frontier of the Colony of Virginia. In order to greatly facilitate the protection of the country on the east, and to prevent the encroachments of the French on the west, the government encouraged rapid settlement of this region. It being detached by the Blue Ridge from immediate contact with the thinly settled bordering sections on the eastern side of the mountain, inducements were offered to invite settlers from more thickly populated centers. While the eastern territory of Virginia had always been a stronghold of the Established Church, the nearby northern colonies had from their beginning been a refuge to dissenters; thus the Governor early in the Valley's history let it be known that he would be inclined to deal leniently with various Protestant sects differing in points of doctrine from those of the state religion.

As late as 1777 the historian, Backus, wrote; "Whether Britain would have had any colonies in America at this day, if religion had not been the grand inducement is doubtful." Certainly this inducement was the great motive that rapidly accelerated the settlement of the Valley of Virginia.

The first settlers were mainly of the Calvanistic faith. The earliest of these, Hite found located on his Van Meter purchase around what became old Mecklenburg, later Shepherdstown. After his settlement more of this class also came from Pennsylvania, and located in various places on his land. In their church records they styled themselves the "Reformed Calvinist Ministry from the Palatinate". Hite, himself, had come over from this country prior to 1710, or following the war of 1688-1697, in which the country had been annexed by Louis XIV, of France. Being familiar with the stern religious persecution this territory on the left bank of the Rhine had long suffered, the political upheavals of the War of the Spanish Succession (1701-1714) which almost immediately followed, and conditions generally of the people on both banks of the river, and using their language, Hite early endeavored to draw his settlers from among various of his countrymen, and others, immigrants to the German localities in Pennsylvania. These immigrants began pouring into the Quaker province in large numbers following the war of 1701-1714, and continued thus on down to and after the War of the Austrian Succession, 1740-1748. (See, Rupp's *Thirty Thousand Names of Foreign Immigrants to Pa., 1727-1776.*) In this way a large part of Hite's settlers were of German origin, but he by no means neglected to induce the English to buy and locate on his land, and took advantage of all opportunities offered.

The first settlers of the upper Valley were Calvinists, of the Presbyterian denomination. John Lewis was of this faith. His native land had also been subjected to long and harsh religious persecutions. His escape and settlement attracted the attention of others of his countrymen of similar faith on both sides of the water, and before long many of this class began to look to the Valley of Virginia as a haven of refuge from religious persecution.

The Northern Neck of Virginia embraced all the territory from the Chesapeake Bay as enclosed between the Potomac and Rappahannock Rivers, back to the head springs thereof. The western boundary, as finally closed, was found to include the whole of the lower, or northern, section of the Shenandoah Valley. Proprietary grants for the "Northern Neck" were made by the king under charters of 1649, 1669, and 1688. At the time of the beginning of the settlements in the region of the Shenandoah, and down until his death, Thomas, Lord Fairfax (1693-1781), originially of Leeds Castle, county Kent, England, was the sole proprietor of this vast area of over five million acres of land. In 1710 he succeeded as sixth Lord Fairfax and one sixth proprietor of the Northern Neck, and in 1719 became the sole proprietor. He inherited the proprietary from his Culpeper ancestors.

The first or 1649 charter for the Northern Neck was drawn up while Charles II was in exile in Holland. The original is now in the British Museum. The grantees named were, Ralph, Lord Hopton; Henry, Lord Jermyn; John, Lord Culpeper (Baron of Thoresway); Sir John Barkeley; Sir William Morton; Sir Dudley Wyatt; and Thomas Culpeper, Esq. The fathers of the Culpeper grantees were brothers, Thomas and John, both of whom became members of the Virginia Company in 1609, or two years after the founding of Jamestown. These members of the Virginia Company, together with another brother, Sir Alexander Culpeper of Greenway Court, county Kent, England, were the sons of John Culpeper (1530-1612) of Wigsell, Sussex County, England. Thomas, the last mentioned 1649 grantee, a son of John of the Virginia Company, and a brother John, both emigrated to Virginia, where they died; John being the Clerk of Northampton County at his death in 1674. Among the children of Thomas was a son, Alexander (1629-1694), Surveyor-General of Virginia, 1671-1694, and a one sixth proprietor of the Northern Neck under the 1669 and 1688 charters, and a daughter, Frances, who m. 1st, Samuel Stephens, Governor of Albemarle, m. 2nd, 1670, Sir William Berkeley, Governor of Virginia, m. 3rd, Philip Ludwell, the Governor of Carolina before alluded to. John Lord Culpeper of the 1649 charter, (also a member of the Virginia Company, (1617-1623), was created Lord Culpeper in 1644. He died the year of the Restoration, and his son Thomas (1635-1689) succeeded to the title.

In 1669 Charles II issued a new charter for the Northern Neck, various grantees of the old charter having died or sold out their interests. Among the new grantees were Thomas, (1635-1689), Lord Culpeper above, and his cousin Alexander, the Surveyor-General. In recognition of the debts owed his father by Charles II, for material aid given the Crown, both before and while in exile, Thomas, Lord Culpeper was made a one sixth proprietor of the Northern Neck under the new charter, a member of the Council of Foreign Plantations, 1671-1674, one third proprietor of all Virginia under the Arlington charter of 1673, and Governor of Virginia, 1677-1683. In 1681 he became five sixth proprietor of the Northern Neck, and from this year to 1684, when he surrendered to the Crown, was the proprietor of all Virginia. In 1688 James II confirmed his title to the Northern Neck in granting a new charter. He married, 1660, Margaret van Hesse (1635-1710), who became a one sixth proprietor of the Northern Neck under the will of Alexander Culpeper, the Surveyor-General. Lord Culpeper's daughter, Catherine, (1670-1719), inherited her father's proprietary, and in 1690 married Thomas, the fifth Lord Fairfax of Cameron (1657-1710.) Among their children were, Thomas, the sixth Lord Fairfax above, Robert, succeeded as seventh Lord Fairfax, in 1781, and Frances, who m. Denny Martin, of Loose, county Kent, England. Thomas, the sixth Lord Fairfax, became one sixth proprietor of the Northern Neck under the will of his grandmother, Margaret van Hesse, and sole proprietor upon the death of his mother. (See—*Virginia Magazine of History and Biography*, Vol 33, p. 113, etc.)

An early difficulty in connection with the Northern Neck grant was the location of its western boundary, or closing line. For many years after the 1688 charter this line was undefined. On June 29th, 1729, Governor Gooch called the attention of the home government to the ambiguity of the charter, expressing his determination "to refuse the suspension of granting patents, until the case should be fairly stated and determined." The next year the final attack of the colonial government on the proprietary was launched. On June 30, 1730, among other matters of complaint, the House of Burgesses concurred in a petition of the Governor to the King in Council, stating "that the head springs of the Rappahannock and Potomac are not yet known to any of your Majesty's subjects, but much inconvenience had resulted to grantees therefrom, and praying the adoption of such measures as might lead to its ascertainment to the satisfaction of all interested."

Upon Carter's death, in 1732, the double necessity of meeting the attack of the colonial government, and of appointing Carter's successor, stirred Lord Fairfax to action. In 1733 he induced his kinsman, William Fairfax, the Royal Collector of Customs at the Port of Salem, Massachusetts, to remove to Virginia, as his resident agent, and petitioned the King in Council to appoint a commission to run and mark the bounds of his land. This petition was granted, and accordingly on November 29th, of the same year, an order was issued by the king directing Governor Gooch to appoint from three to five commissioners, representing the Crown, to meet with a like number appointed by Lord Fairfax, and employ surveyors to settle the "marks and boundaries" of the proprietary.

Lord Fairfax himself came over to Virginia in May, 1735, and remained until September, 1737, looking after his interests. During this time he resided with William Fairfax, first in Westmoreland, and later at Falmouth on the Rappahannock. He was instrumental in getting an Act passed by the Virginia Assembly, in 1736, recognizing him as having inherited Lord Culpeper's charter. This year he fired his broadside at Hite by entering a "caveat" against him, thus beginning the long legal battle that was to last for fifty years, or until after both principals were dead, and which resulted in such great damage to Hite's plans for bringing in settlers. This year also, commissioners were appointed, in compliance with the former instructions issued to the Governor, to ascertain the true fountains of the Rappahannock and Potomac rivers.

These commissioners met at Fredericksburg, September 25, 1736, and on October 12th began their surveys, fiinishing the 14th of December following, on which day they marked what they reported to be the first fountain of the Potomac river. Plans were drawn up which were referred to the Council of Foreign Plantations, December 21st, 1738. Here the matter rested until after the beginning of King George's War. On April 6th, 1745, the Council decided that the closing line of the grant ought to be a straight line from the first spring of the South Branch of the Rappahannock to the "place in the Alleghaney Mountains where that part of the Potomac River, which is now called Cohongoroota, first arises." This decision was confirmed by the king April 11, 1745, and at the same time another commission was ordered to be appointed to run the line. This famous dividing line "between his Majesty, King George II, and Lord Fairfax," was run in the fall of 1746.

In 1739 William Fairfax purchased of Edward Washington a plantation on the Potomac, known as Belvoir, just south of where Mt. Vernon now stands. Here, in 1741, he built a large brick house, which became his residence and the office of the proprietary. The ruins of the old house, partially demolished by British gunboats in the War of 1812, are now within the bounds of Camp Humphreys. (It is interesting to note that the first step in the long journey to Richmond of the old Northern Neck grant books, was from Corotoman to Belvoir.)

The litigation that Hite found himself entangled in, determined many of the settlers of the lower Valley to remove further south, and as others came pouring in they passed over this section to regions not involved in Fairfax's claims. It is said that at the time of the caveat some six hundred of Hite's settlers were affected.

As stated, only two grants of large areas of land were made by the Governor for land in the upper Shenandoah Valley; these were to Beverly in 1736, and to Borden in 1739. Both Beverly and Borden received their grants in time to benefit by the Fairfax-Hite litigation. Beverly's territority covered 118,491 acres centered around the present city of Staunton, and embraced a large part of what is now Augusta County. He had first petitioned, in 1732, for the Massanutten section, which resulted in the appearance of Miller and his associates.

William Beverley was a member of the House of Burgesses and of the Governor's Council. He was a son of Robert Beverly, the historian and "Knight of the Golden Horseshoe," and a grandson of Robert Beverly, the commander of the Royal forces at the time of Bacon's Rebellion, 1676. He was Clerk of Essex County 1720-1740, and died in 1756. Beverley grant 118,491 acres

Borden's land was in the extreme southern section of the Shenandoah region; in fact it bordered on the forks of the James river. His tract consisted of 92,100 acres, or about half of what is now Rockbridge County. Borden tract 92,100 acres

Benjamin Borden was a native of New Jersey, whence he came to the lower Valley. He settled in this section on his "Spout Run plantation" on the Opequon; which was granted him October, 3rd, 1734. He died in 1743. His will shows that he owned considerable land in various sections of the Shenandoah Valley, besides other holdings in New Jersey. His Valley lands were on the Bullshire, Smiths Creek, North Shenandoah, and James rivers. He was a land agent for Lord Fairfax, and appears to have been largely responsible for inducing more settlers to locate in the Valley of Virginia than any other one man. His efforts contributed greatly to the rapid settlement of the upper Valley, and both he and Beverley were indefagitable in bringing over settlers from Ulster, Ireland. In this they were aided by Col. James Patton, a native of Ulster, and commander of a passenger ship, who is said by Brock, in the *Dinwiddie Papers,* to have crossed the Atlantic twenty five times in bringing over Irish immigrants. Patton traded to Hobbes' Hole, on the Rappahannock. The settlers on Beverly and Borden's grants, in Old Augusta, were almost without exception Scotch-Irish. Patton himself finally located on Beverly's Manor.

The Van Meters and Hite were originally from the Province of New York. Various Hites were living in Queens County, Long Island, at the time of Isaiah Harrisons residence there. John and Isaac Van Meter were born at Marbleton, Ulster County New York, and later settled in Pilesgrove township, Salem County, New Jersey.

According to Shourd's *History and Genealogy of Fenwick's Colony*, which gives some particulars of their settlement in this old Quaker colony, another brother, Joseph, settled in Monmouth County, New Jersey.

Joist Hite, as stated by Stapleton, in his *Memorials of the Huguenots in America*, was a native of Strasburg, in Alsace, France. From there, says Cartmell, he came direct to the Hudson River with his wife, Anna Maria Du Bois, and a daughter, Mary. He was located at Kingston, on the Hudson, in 1710, where two daughters, Magdaline and Elizabeth, were born, their births being entered in the records of the old Dutch Reformed Church at this point. He next appears at Old Salem, New Jersey, where he was a fur trader for seven years.

From Salem, John Van Meter removed to Maryland, and Hite to the present site of Germantown, above Philadelphia, where the latter was living in 1717. Here Hite purchased a large tract of land which he later exchanged for another tract on the Schuylkill at the mouth of Percoman Creek. On Percoman Creek he built a mill, opened up farms, traded in land, and became prominent in the community. His emigrant train from the Schuylkill to the Valley of Virginia consisted of about twenty families, including his own, and those of his married daughters. It is said that this train left the Schulykill in 1730. While exploring and waiting the order for his surveys to be made he and his party spent about a year camping near the present site of Shepardstown.

John Van Meter's grant of 1730, recites that he had petitioned, "that he is desirous to take up a tract of land in this colony—on the west side of the Great Mountains for the settlement of himself and eleven children and also divers of his relations and friends living in the Government of New York." The grant to Isaac Van Meter describes him as, "of the Province of West Jersey," and states that his petition, "set forth that he and divers other German families are desirous to settle themselves on the West side of the Great Mountain in this colony . . . . . . praying that ten thousand acres of land lying between the lands surveyed for Robert Carter, Esq. and the forks of the Shenado river and the river Operkon" be granted him, "for the accommodation and settlement of ten families." (See MSS. *Journal of the Governor and Council of Virginia*, 1721-1734, pp. 363 and 364, at the State Library, Richmond, Virginia.) It is barely possible that these brothers may have had a suspicion that their lands would later be found to be in Fairfax's territory.

According to B. F. Fackenthal, in *A Collection of Papers Read Before the Bucks County, Pennsylvania, Historical Society*, "Ann Wyncoop baptized August 21, 1698, married, about 1717, Isaac Van Meter of Salem, New Jersey, and went there to live." Fackenthal further states, "that the subsequent history of this couple would fill pages of very interesting reading, for a generation later they went pioneering into the wilderness of Virginia where the family figured extensively in the annals of its western development. In 1744 Isaac offered his Salem lands for sale and with his older sons departed for the South Branch of the Potomac." (Vol. III, p. 384.)

Old Salem County, New Jersey, is just across the river from Delaware. Here Isaiah Harrison, Jr. appears to have been located at the time of his brother's residence further down the western side of the river. No reference to Isaiah, Jr. is found among the Delaware records, but an Isaiah Harrison appears as a witness to a Salem County will in 1737. This is the only instance so far discovered of the name occuring in the New Jersey wills, or in any other records found outside of those of Long Island, Delaware, or Old Augusta County, Virginia. (See p. 70.)

An abstract of the will found among the volumes of the N. J. Historical Society, is as follows: "1737, Aug. 29, Brick, John Esq. of Cohansie, Salem Co., will of; Wife Hannah, Children, William, Elizabeth Dunlop, Hannah Hancock, Joshua, Joseph, John. Grandsons, John and Ephraim Worthington. Home farm; land on or near Tindall's Island; land on Stoke Creek, bought of Anthony Woodhouse; farm bought of Leonard Gibbon; 300 acres at Carle Town, said Co. bought of Clement Plumstead and Israel Pemberton; personal estate, including 6 negro slaves. Executors—the wife and sons John and Joseph. Witnesses—Thomas Bright, Isaiah Harrison, John Podmore. Proved April 26, 1753. Lib. 6 p. 453." (See—*New Jersey Wills*, pub. by New Jersey Historical Society, Vol. III, p. 40.)

The colonial deed and will books of New Jersey are in the State Capitol at Trenton. The original will book referred to shows that John Brick, Jr. was the executor appointed, and that the will was proven by him only. Isaiah Harrison, Jr. at this time was in Augusta County, Virginia. It will be observed that the will was written a few months after the Harrisons in Delaware began disposing of their lands, and when Isaiah Sr. was past seventy years old, hence he was evidently not the witness. The index to the early deeds at Trenton makes no mention of an Isaiah Harrison, and neither is there any reference found to one of this name in the old Court Order books at Salem, but Isaiah, Jr. could readily have owned land and lived in this county without being thus mentioned. A large part of the early deeds of New Jersey were never recorded, so it is said on authority. After the first deed for a tract of land was made and recorded, subsequent transfers were frequently merely noted on the back of the original deed, which in turn was then handed over to the new owner of the land.

John Brick's name occurs regularly in the old Court Order books of Salem, as he was one of the justices of this court.

There was an Israel Harrison settled in Old Salem at an early date. According to Shourd, above—p. 465—Israel "Married at Salem in 1685 . . . . Hester White, daughter of Christopher White." He died in 1697-8 and an inventory was taken of his personal estate "4th. day, 1st. Mo. (March) 1697-8." (See—*New Jersey Wills*, Vol. I, pp. 213 and 504.) White's widow, Hester, made her will, 11th day, 3rd mo., 1698, mentioning her daughter, Hester, and her daughter's children, Joseph and Sarah Harrison. The abstracts of the records of the "Salem Monthly Meeting" of Friends, at the Historical Society of Pennsylvania, in Philadelphia, give: "Sarah Harrison the daughter of Israel Harrison by Hester his wife was Born ye 14th. day of 12th. mo. 1696." Apparently there were only two children. It will be recalled, in passing, that Samuel Harrison, the mariner, formerly of Flushing, Long Island, was settled at this time a little further up the Delaware River at Gloucester, West Jersey.

The indications are that it was through their brother, Isaiah, Jr. that the Harrisons of Sussex, Delaware, received their first information in regard to the region on the Shenandoah. Isaiah, Jr. likely obtained his account direct from Isaac Van Meter of Old Salem. As noted, Van Meter himself had explored the lower Valley prior to 1730.

Under Charles II, (1660-1685), the proprietary system of land grants flourished in America. While this system was a great aid to the Crown in the setlement of the new country, it became more or less unpopular with the increasing number of settlers. The Lords Proprietors were frequently exacting and many of the colonists resented being forced to pay taxes to them in the form of quit-rents and various fees. During the time of Lord Culpeper's partial and whole proprietary of the Colony of Virginia two rebellions blazed forth, viz: Bacon's Rebellion of 1676, and the Tobacco Rebellion of 1682. The first deeds to the Harrisons of Delaware make no mention of any "Rents and Services Due and payable to ye Chief Lord or Lords of ye fee," but by the time of their removal, as revealed by the deeds disposing of their lands, this system was in evidence. This was probably one of the chief reasons for their "western migration."

Isaiah Harrison and his sons and daughters, with the exception of Gideon, who had died, and possibly Elizabeth, were all emigrants to the Valley of Virginia. The old tradition—page 9—states that there were sixteen in the party that came to the Valley together. The little band is said to have been composed of five brothers and their father, together with the wives and children of the married brothers. All indications are that the party left Delaware in the spring of 1737. As Isaiah, Jr. appears later this year to have been living in Salem County, New Jersey, and as he is not found settled in Old Augusta, with his brothers and sisters, until shortly after the opening of the first court, the five brothers of the tradition are indentified as John, Daniel, Thomas, Jeremiah, and Samuel. They came in by the way of what is now Alexandria, Virginia, and crossed the Blue Ridge at Thornton's Gap. As their former home in Delaware was only eight miles from Lewes, they had no doubt embarked at Lewes on a sailing vessel, journeying by water to the old town of Bellhaven on the Potomac.

Lewes was an early colonial port; the Delaware Bay pilots formerly made their headquarters there. Henlopen Light, just south of Lewes, is one of the oldest lighthouses in America.

About a week was probably required to make the long trip around Cape Charles. On their arrival at Bellhaven the long tedious journey over land began. Bellhaven was later incorporated as Alexandria, in 1748.

Thornton's Gap, in the Blue Ridge, is a few miles east of the present town of Luray. This gap was on one of the earliest routes from the eastern section of Virginia to the Valley. Crossing the Ridge through this gap, and heading westward, the emigrants struck the South Fork of the Shenandoah near the present "White House." This old landmark is now at the intersection of the Lee Highway and the river. This location was well within the early Massanutten settlement previously noted. Here the party is said to have camped for some time, but finding the climate malarious, and sickness breaking out among them, they later removed to the western side of the Massanutten. As the old road through Massanutten Gap to the Rockingham section was not established until 1740, the party must have worked their way along up the river, passing "The Peak," continuing by the end of the Massanutten to the region in which they finally made their settlement.

By following the general course of the South Fork of the Shenandoah and its tributary, the North River, they would have come on the land along Naked Creek. For a short distance this creek now separates Rockingham and Augusta counties near the village of Burketown. According to the patent to Daniel Harrison, of 1739, his land is described as being "on the east draft of the west fork of the Naked Creek." While there is also another creek of this name forming a small part of the present boundary of Rockingham, seperating it from Page, which the emigrants would have first passed by the above route, the fact that Daniel again later—in 1746— patented 215 acres more on the "West Fork of Naked Creek," and at the same time patented two tracts on Muddy Creek, and one on Linville's Creek, shows that his original land was in the first mentioned region. Muddy Creek heads some five or six miles west of Harrisonburg and flows into the North river a few miles northwest of Naked Creek This latter creek moreover forks to the west of the Valley Pike, thus futher identifying the location of the 1739 patent.

The indications are that the Harrisons camped on the Shenandoah—the South Fork—for probably two years while exploring and preparing to take up land. Here sickness breaking out among them, their father, Isaiah, died. After his death they then removed to the western side of the Massanutten, settling on higher ground. The date of Daniel's patent shows that this removal occurred by 1738.

Isaiah Harrison, the old Oyster Bay settler and immigrant ancestor of his line in America, died about 1738. He was one of the first casualties of the new country. The Delaware deeds show that he was living in 1736, and deceased by 1740. He left no will. He was born about 1666, some five or six years following the Restoration, and about fifty years after the death of Shakespeare. His father, the indications are, as heretofore related, was Thomas Harrison, one time chaplain to Governor Berkeley of Virginia, and later to Henry Cromwell, son of the Lord Protector of England. His boyhood days appear to have been spent on the banks of the Mersey and the Dee, and doubtless his childish eyes had eagerly watched many a proud ship as she gently drifted down stream bound for the New World.

Isaiah lived through an interesting period of colonial development. He grew to manhood during the reign of Charles II, and emigrated to America in the closing years of that of James II. He appears continually on the old colonial records from 1687, "January ye 2d," until 7th, May 1736. On the first mentioned date he was made a freeholder of Oyster Bay, Long Island, in the province of New York, and was granted a proprietor's right in the common town land. This was only some thirty-four years after the first settlement of the town by Peter Wright, his future wife's grandfather. At this time Jamestown was yet the capital of Virginia.

He is said to have been buried by the banks of the Shenandoah, in the later White House neighborhood. There is a very old burial ground in this locality, only a short distance from the old house; but it is not known just where by the river his body was laid. The scene of his death was in a region wildly beautiful, and in striking contrast to the sea-shore country he so long had known. In the distance to the east, towered the Blue Ridge, while near his camp the silvery Shenandoah tumbled along, as it wandered on its winding course by the evergreened foothills of the lonely Massanutten. Isaiah's death was typical of his life; he was on his way to a new country—

"Nothing dies; it only passes,
Like the hills which I have trod;
Lives are but mysterious glasses,
Linking all our days to God,
And the Good Old Man is living,
In the young, the fond, the fair,
Life melodious drinking, giving
Down the chords of light and air,
Minstrel of the mountain heather,
We shall always live together."

—JOSEPH SALYARDS.

CHAPTER IX

Among the First Settlers in the Region of Harrisonburg

"Ninety miles and more it stretches
Up the Valley, towards the South;
Firm it is to wheel and hoof-beat,
Firm it holds in flood and drouth;
And it links the towns and cities,
Jewels on a silver chain,
Shining in their emerald settings,
In the broad and fertile plain."

—WAYLAND.

THESE NINETY MILES for the most of their distance stretch over the broad and fertile plain bordering on the western slope of the Massanutten. This region extends southward from Strasburg to above Harrisonburg, and westward, across the Valley, to the Alleghaney Mountains. It is drained mainly by the North Fork of the Shenandoah. This stream joins the South Fork, forming the main river, a little to the east of the northern end of the Massanutten. The mountain rises between the two forks. The broad region west of the Massanutten is immediately in the central part of the Shenandoah Valley. It lies about midway between what was Hite's land on the north, and Beverly's land on the south.

After burying their father, and breaking camp on the South Fork of the Shenandoah, the Harrisons explored their way southwesterly along up the river, and around Peaked Mountain, the southern end of the Massanutten. Here they came into the region enclosed between the North River and the South Fork. Together these streams describe a wide circle around the end of the mountain. The North River in flowing southeasterly across the Valley joins the South River, forming the South Fork, some five miles southwest of "The Peak." Keeping within this circle the party headed directly into the section lying at the southern end of the above broad central region. In this way they shortly came onto the high lands in the present vicinity of Harrisonburg. This was about the year 1738.

Today this city is the central jewel, among the three larger ones, on the long silver chain. Its emerald setting is some six miles northwest of Peaked Mountain, on about the highest elevation of any town in the Valley.

In this region the little band of five brothers divided, each choosing for himself and family a separate camp. Thus they spread about, all locating at large springs. At these they proceeded to fix their permanent homes. Here they were joined by their other brother, and by their two married sisters who came in with their husbands.

(1) ISAIAH HARRISON (1666-1738), the father of these Harrisons, was, as elsewhere set forth, twice married. (See page 29.) All ten of his known children were natives of Long Island, New York. To summarize briefly in carrying forward the genealogy of his descendants: Isaiah married first, 1688, about a year after his settlement at Oyster Bay, Elizabeth, the daughter of Gideon and Elizabeth (Townsend) Wright. He bought his home place, consisting of 100 acres, at Suckscall's Wigwam, of John Wright, his wife's cousin, January 16, 1688. Gideon was a son of Peter

Wright, the immigrant from Norfolk County, England, 1635, to Sangus, now Lynn, Massachusetts. From Sangus, Peter Wright removed to Sandwich, in the Plymouth Colony, 1637, and from there to Oyster Bay, where he was the first settler and principal founder of the town, 1653. The children of Isaiah Harrison and his wife Elizabeth were as follows—their births being recorded in the old Oyster Bay town book—see page 23:

(11) ISAIAH—b. September 27, 1689; d. ——.
(12) JOHN—b. September 25, 1691; d. May 1771; m. about 1720, Phebe ——, b. 1686, d. December 6, 1793.
(13) GIDEON—b. June 25, 1694; d. — 1729; m. ——.
(14) MARY—b. May 25, 1696; d. 1781; m. about 1721, Robert Cravens, b. 1696 c, d. May 1762.
(15) ELIZABETH—b. March 30, 1698; d. ——; m. ——.

See further record for all of the above.

Elizabeth, the first wife of Isaiah, died shortly after her daughter Elizabeth was born.

About 1700 Isaiah Harrison married, second, Abigail (Smith ?). On April 20, 1702, he sold all of his Oyster Bay lands, his wife Abigail joining him in signing the deeds. (See page 28.) The same day he bought 500 acres of land on the western bank of the Nissequogue River, at Smithtown, Long Island, to which he removed with his family. There he bought 200 acres more, September 23, 1708; this land being on the eastern side of the river opposite his home tract. His second wife is thought to have been a Smith, and of the Smithtown family. The children of Isaiah and his wife Abigail, born at Smithtown, Long Island, were;

(16) DANIEL—b. about 1701; d. July 10, 1770; m. 1st, Margaret Cravens, sister of Robert above; m. 2nd, Sarah Stephenson, widow of William.
(17) THOMAS—b. about 1704; d. 1785; m. 1st, Jane De La Haye; m. 2nd, Sarah (Cravens?).
(18) JEREMIAH—b. 1707 c; d. 1777 c; m. Catherine ——.
(19) ABIGAIL—b. 1710 c; d. 1780 c; m. Alexander Herring.
(20) SAMUEL—b. 1712 c; d. 1790 c; m. Mary ——.

See further record for all of the above.

Isaiah sold his home place at Smithtown, June 12, 1721, and very shortly thereafter removed with his family to Sussex County, Delaware, where he bought 900 acres of land known as Maiden Plantation—about eight miles west of Lewes—June 22, 1721. After his removal to Delaware he sold his remaining 200 acres at Smithtown, April 28, 1722, his wife Abigail also signing the deed. She is thought to have died about 1732. This year, on October 10th, for a nominal sum, he deeded to each of his sons, Daniel, Thomas, and Jeremiah, 250 acres of Maiden Plantation, her name being missing from these deeds. Later, on May 7th, 1736, he disposed of his remaining 150 acres of Maiden Plantation, also without her signature. (See pp. 33, 40, 42, 44, 45, 47.)

All of the above sons and daughters of Isaiah, with the exception of Gideon, and possibly Elizabeth, settled in the region now around Harrisonburg, Virginia.

The five brothers in the little band of Harrison emigrants from Delaware have been identified as John, Daniel, Thomas, Jeremiah, and Samuel. All of them appear on the early records of Orange court. Isaiah, Jr. evidently arrived somewhat later as no record of him is found until after the Court of Augusta County was established. Samuel does not appear in the Delaware deeds, probably owing to his not being of age when his father divided Maiden Plantation. Mary, the eldest daughter of Isaiah, and her husband, Robert Cravens, either came into the region west of the Massanutten with her five brothers or shortly joined them here after their settlement. As will be recalled, Robert signed his "power of attorney" to dispose of his Delaware land June 1, 1739. Elizabeth too, is thought to have come to the Valley, in the little party of sixteen. She, however, may have been the wife of John Fisher, who sold land to Gideon Harrison, February 5, 1722. Abigail and Alexander Herring were, as indicated by the Augusta records before quoted, the last to arrive. Alexander's deed releasing his land in Delaware was dated May 5, 1742. Gideon Harrison died before his brothers' removal from Delaware, but some circumstances indicate that his widow and children were also among the first settlers in the early Harrisonburg region.

In fact, it is thought that all of Isaiah's living descendents settled here; certainly with the possible exceptions just noted all were a part of that early band of adventurous spirits—

> "*Who climbed the blue embattled hills*
> *Against uncounted foes,*
> *And planted there, in valleys fair,*
> *The Lily and the Rose!*
> *Whose fragrance lives in many lands,*
> *Whose beauty stars the earth;*
> *And lights the hearths of happy homes*
> *With loveliness and worth!*"
>
> —TICKNOR.

That the Harrisons were the first to locate in the region in which they settled is shown by their land patents. They were evidently unhampered by the prior claims of others. Their first patents embraced land scattered over a wide territory in the central part of the present county of Rockingham. Besides being centrally located in a beautiful and fertile section these lands were finely watered. Several of the largest and most noted springs in the county were first owned by the Harrisons.

Land was plentiful, and the whole region lay open to their choice. There was no hurry in completing the legal formalities necessary in applying for a patent. To Williamsburg, the seat of the land office, and capital of the Colony, was a long tedious journey almost as difficult as when Governor Spotswood first covered this distance. Orange court was scarcely more accessable; as in both cases the Massanutten and Blue Ridge mountains furnished considerable obstacles in the way of travel. Thus the first settlers bided their time and waited, so long as there was no danger of others coming in to claim the lands they had chosen. In this way many were unmolested for several years; the case af Adam Miller and his associates on the South Fork has been noted, and that of John Lewis elsewhere is another example. The Harrisons also, as indicated by the old tradition and the dates of their first patents, delayed a time before applying to the Governor and Council for their lands, and no doubt camped for the first year or so while awaiting their surveys and making various improvements.

The earliest surveys found are dated as follows: for Daniel Harrison, December 8, 1738, for Thomas Harrison, December 18, 1739, for John Harrison, Sr., November 12, 1740, for Jeremiah Harrison, November 13, 1740, and for Samuel Harrison, November 14, 1740, the last four surveys being recorded in an old surveyors' book at Winchester.

The first mention of any of these Harrisons found on the Court Order books at Orange occurs in an order of the July court, 1741, in regard to a suit brought by

John Harrison. The following month, August 20th, Daniel Harrison was granted by patent his second tract of land in Old Augusta County. At this time his son Robert was also given a patent to land in the same locality. Daniel's original tract on Naked Creek was in what is now Augusta County, just south of the line that today divides this territory from Rockingham. This was some ten miles south of the present city of Harrisonburg. The indications are, therefore, that the brothers approached the immedaite vicinity of this city from the south; probably by exploring the lands along Cook's and Muddy creeks, or by following the old Indian Trail from North River.

Daniel and Robert's 1741 patents were the first of the long series granted to Harrisons embracing land in this particular vicinity. The grant to Daniel included 400 acres on the Dry Fork of Smiths Creek, while that to Robert was for 206 acres along this fork "on Daniel Harrison's land." Both of these patents embraced the tract later known as Smithland. This historic old county seat is some two miles north of Harrisonburg on the Long Grey Trail. (See— Book 19, pp. 1118, and 1131, of Patents, at Land Office, Richmond, Virginia.)

The reference to John Harrison at Orange court, reads as follows: "In the suit by petition brought by John Harrison against Robert Luney, Deft. for one long gun of the value of 5 pounds current money the defendant not appearing judgement is granted the plaintiff." A further proceeding in regard to this appears under date of August 28, 1742; "In the suit by Scare facias brought by John Harrison pet. agt. Robert Lundy Deft. the Deft not appearing the sheriff having returned there is nothing found in my bailiwick whereby I could cause the Deft. to know neither is he found in my bailiwick Yts. therefore (ordered) at pltfs. motion that an Alias Jura facias issue against sd. Deft. returnable at next court." This matter was finally disposed of apparently September 25, 1742: "John Harrison vs. Robert Luney deft. for 40 shillings Current Money . . . . Luney ordered to pay 40 shillings 133 pounds tobacco and costs of suit." (See, Court Order Book 1739-1741, p. 359, and book 1741-1743, pp. 222 and 280, at Orange, Virginia.)

Thomas and Daniel Harrison also had some business before Orange court in 1742. The first reference to Thomas is dated July 22nd of this year; "The suit by petition brought by Thomas Harrison pet. agt. James Pollard Gent. deft. being agreed is dismissed." Also on August 27th, 1742; "Thomas Hard appearing on Last Court's order to be fined for not appearing as an Evidence for Thomas Harrison agt. William Triplet and on oath declared that he was prevented from coming by sickness Yts ordered that he be discharged from paying the fine." Finally, September 24th, the same year, the court "Ordered the Lewis Stephens, James Bond, John Sheldon, Daniel Harrison, Abraham Hollingsworth & Elizabeth Cantrell severly be fined three hundred and fifty pounds of tobacco each for not appearing to give their Evidence in behalf of William Linville dt. ye suit of Nathaniel Chapman unless they appear by next court to show sufficient cause for their not appearing." (See—last mentioned book above, pp. 175, 205, and 257.) John Sheldon

The older books bear much testimony to the difficulty the people west of the Blue Ridge had in attending court at Orange. The seat of the court was at the present town of Orange, Virginia. The first session of this court was held January 21, 1734, and, according to Waddell, the first reference to Valley people occurs under the date of July 20, 1736.

That John Harrison and his sons were settled in the Dry Fork of Smiths Creek region of Old Augusta by 1742, is shown by a reference found in the *Virginia Magazine of History and Biography* under "Militia Companies in Augusta County, 1742." Among the members of "Capt. Peter Schowll's Company" are listed, And. Burd, Lieut., Math. Skeens, Ens., ... John Harrison . . . . Zebulon Harrison . . . . John Harrison . . . . Thomas Moore . . . . etc. (See—Vol. 8, p. 280.) Peter Scholl lived on Smiths Creek—as given by the Orange Court records: "Feb. 23, 1743, Petition of Peter Schole and other inhabitants on Smiths Creek on West Side of North Mountain, hardship to work on a road thirty miles distant from their plantations . . . . petition for a road, etc." Also, May 24, 1744—"Peter School (or Scholl) Gent. is hereby appointed to take the list of tithables the present year in ye lower part of Augusta county as far as John Harrison and round ye pooked Mountain through ye Gap to ye north Mountain at Peter Cravens." "John Lewis . . . . appointed to take . . . . from Linvilles Creek and Cravens upwards to Colonel Patton's Mill. John Buchanan Gent. . . . . appointed . . . . for remainder of county." (See, Order Book 1743-46, pp. 49 and 108, at Orange, Virginia.)

Among the early records of this time at Orange are the following "Military Commissions." as found in the old Court Order Books—

"At a Court held for Orange County on Thursday the 24th. day of February 1742. Present—Robert Slaughter, Robert Greene, John Finlasson, William Russell and Goodrich Lightfoot—Gentlemen Justices."

"George Hobson, Jacob Hite, John Harrison, Samuel Morris, Joseph Carter and Edward Watts having taken the oaths prescribed by act of parliament to be taken instead of the oaths of allegiance and supremacy and the abjuration oath prescribed the tests and whereof severally sworn to their military commission of Lieutenant accordingly—Present George Taylor Gent.
Absent Robert Slaughter Gent."

(See, Order Book, 1741-43.)

"March 22, 1743, William Linville and Benjamin Allen Gent. produced their Military Commissions for Captain of Horse. Thomas West, Gent. for his Lieutenant of said Linville's Troop and Thomas Linville and Thomas Harrison their commissions as Cornetts having severly taken the Oath appointed by act of Parliament instead of the Oath of Abjuration and Supremacy and the abjuration Oath Subscribed the Test and were severly sworn to their said Military Commissions accordingly." (See, Order Book, 1743-46, p. 58.)

"At a Court continued and held for Orange County on Friday the 29th. day of July 1743. Present George Taylor and James Pendelton, Gents."

"Daniel Harrison Gent. having taken the oaths prescribed by act of Parliament instead of the oaths of allegience and supremacy and abjuration oath subscribed the test and was sworn into his Military Commission of Captain of Horses."

"Robert Craven, Gent. having taken the oaths prescribed by act of parliament instead of the oaths of allegiance and supremacy and the oath of abjuration, subscribed the test and was sworn into his Military Commission as Captain of Horses." (See, Order Book, 1741-43, p. 506.)

John Harrison, as shown in Chapter I, in connection with the court order of 1745 for the Indian Road, settled at the Big Spring, now Lacey Spring. This spring is a head water of Smiths Creek.

The creek empties into the North Fork of the Shenandoah near the present town of Mt. Jackson. Dry Fork, a branch of the creek, rises about eight miles to the south of the "Big Spring," and somewhat to the southeast of Harrisonburg, and flows northward generally between the Valley Pike and the Massanutten.

Between Daniel and his son Robert, and John and his sons John, Zebulon, and Reuben, the Harrisons at one time or another fairly well covered this beautiful region. John, Sr. first patented two tracts on Smiths Creek, totaling 400 acres, June 25, 1747. (See, Augusta County Deed Book 12, p. 426.) The next year, February 10, 1748, he patented 400 acres more on the "Dry Fork of Smith's Creek," and on the same date his son John patented 200 acres "on the draft of Smith's Creek," and 400 acres "on the Dry Fork of Smith's Creek." John, Jr. handled many large tracts of land in Old Augusta. His first patent was dated February 12, 1742, embracing 366 acres "on a branch of James River called Luney's Mill Creek." He evidently did not reside on this for any length of time as he sold it February 2, 1744, to James Letherdale or Lidderdale, Blacksmith, giving a deed in August, 1749.

Thomas Harrison has been mentioned under the dates of 1739, 1742, and 1743. On March 15, 1744, he was granted his first patents. At this time he took out three patents, two of them totaling 591 acres "on the Head Spring of the East Fork of Cook's Creek," while the third patent embraced 250 acres "on the East Branch of Cook's Creek." Robert Cravens also patented 400 acres on this creek at the same time (1744). Harrison's land was located on the site of the present city of Harrisonburg.

According to the Orange court records, on August 22, 1745, "Jeremiah Harrison (was) appointed Constable in the Room of Thomas Stewart who is Discharged from this office, and he having taken the usual Oath to his Majesties Person and Government taken and subscribed the abjuration Oath and the Test was sworn into his office and then took the oath appointed by the Tobacco Law." (See, Order Book 1743-46, p. 412.) A little later the same year—September 26—"Jeremiah Harrison and . . . (others) bond for Robert Leaper to keep the peace towards James Patton Gent. in that part of the county called Augusta." (Same book, p. 427.) As given by Augusta County Land Entry Book No. 1, Jeremiah Harrison entered 100 acres on the "south side of Cook's Creek, joining Robert Cravens land," December 7, 1745. His first patent was granted 10th February, 1748; "370 acres on the drafts of Cook's and Linville's Creek." At this time John Harrison, Jr. also patented 600 acres, Robert Cravens, 336 acres, John Harrison, 400 acres, Reuben Harrison 233 acres and Zebulon Harrison 165 acres.

Samuel Harrison first appears on the Orange Court Order records, 30th June, 1744. "Robert Green Gent. vs. Samuel Harrison. In Debt. The sheriff having returned not executed by reason of sickness, at the motion of Zachary Lewis Gent. capias is ordered returnable at next court." Same date; "Robert Green Gent. vs. Daniel Harrison—On Petetion—The sheriff having returned, not executed at the motion of Mr. Lewis attorney for the Petitioner—process is ordered returnable at the next court." Also a little later, 23rd November, 1744; "Robert Green Gent vs. Samuel Harrison—The sheriff having returned on the Plures Capias not executed it is ordered that a P. L. Cap's Issue against the Deft. returnable to the next court." Same date; "Robert Green Gent. vs. Daniel Harrison—Petetion—this suit is Dismissed not executed." (See, Order Book 1743-46, pp. 167 and 235, at Orange, Virginia.) Samuel first patented land the 25th of September, 1746; "200 acres on a branch of Cook's Creek." On this date Daniel also received four patents totaling 1402 acres, and John Harrison, Jr. five patents totaling 1566 acres.

The old tradition in regard to the five brothers emigrating from Long Island to the Valley relates that one of these brothers "stopped off east of the Ridge" and was later lost track of as to his family. No doubt this refers to Gideon, who had died in Delaware. Only four brothers are mentioned as settling at the various springs; one evidently having been omitted or overlooked. Five springs are named in the two versions of the tradition, however, these being the Big Spring, Flook's Spring, the Head Spring of the East Fork of Cook's Creek, the Head Spring of Cook's Creek, and Krotzer's Spring.

John Harrison, as stated, settled at the "Big Spring," now Lacey. This spring is slightly west of the Dry Fork into which it flows, forming Smiths Creek. A few miles further south, near the foot of the Massanutten, and to the east of this fork, a small branch rises which also flows into Smiths Creek near Lacey. Flook's Spring is on the headwaters of this branch. From the fact that Daniel Harrison patented land as early as 1741 on the Dry Fork, somewhat in this vicinity, and in the neighborhood now to the east of Harrisonburg, he may have at first camped awhile at this spring. However, another account—to be given a little later—more positively identifies John Harrison, Jr. as settling here.

Daniel Harrison finally settled on the Head Spring of Cook's Creek, now Dayton. Several of his early patents embraced land on Muddy Creek, which is a little to the west of this town. Muddy Creek heads near the present village of Mt. Clinton, through which it flows. That Daniel settled at the above spring is established by two records. In the first place he willed his "Home Plantation" to his son Benjamin. Secondly, Benjamin resided on this in the large stone dwelling still standing at the eastern edge of Dayton. Among the petitions and orders of December, 1790, on record at Augusta court, as given by Chalkley, there occurs in part the following:

"Rockingham Co. 12th September, 1801. By order of Rockingham County Court, surveyed for Benjamin Harrison 1,129½ acres on both sides of Cook's Creek (including the *spring of the main branch* of said creek), including the 10 following tracts, viz. 83½ acres, part of 100 acres, part of 1264 acres patented, 26th March, 1739, to McKay, Hite, Duff, and Green, and conveyed by deeds 18th June, 1749, to Robert McKay, Jost. Hyte, Robert Green, and Robert Green, sole heir of the will of William Duff to Samuel Wilkins, and by him to Daniel Harrison, 27th February, 1749 . . . acres patented to . . . Harrison, 25th September, 1746; . . . acres patented to Daniel Harrison, 10th September, 1755. These three tracts willed by Daniel Harrison to said Benjamin Harrison by will 8th of June, 1767 . . . etc." (See, Vol. I, p. 482.)

Thomas Harrison, like his brother John, also settled on the later Great Road. His settlement was about seven miles south of the latter, and at the Head Spring of the East Fork of Cook's Creek on the land he first patented at the present site of Harrisonburg. This "Fork" flows southward joining the main creek some six miles southwest of the city. About two miles beyond this juncture the creek empties into North River. It somewhat parallels Muddy Creek, which also flows southward emptying into the same river some three miles farther west.

Jeremiah Harrison, besides his brothers, owned various tracts of land on Cook's and Linville's creeks. From his first patent for "370 acres on the drafts of Cook's and Linville's Creek" it appears that he settled in the section now traversed by the Raleigh Springs Turnpike; probably near the present juncture of this pike with the road leading to Mt. Clinton. Just to the east of this juncture the pike crosses the northernmost branch of Cook's Creek while a little to the west the Mt. Clinton road crosses the southernmost branch of Linville's Creek. In the old church book of the Rev. John Craig, the first resident Presbyterian minister in Augusta, Jeremiah is spoken of as living at the "Half Way House." His name occurs on a petition for a road filed at Augusta court in 1753-4, by the "Inhabitants of North Mountain, at the head of Muddy Creek." (*Chalkley*, Vol. I, p. 440.) The above juncture of roads is approximately midway between Harrisonburg and Mt. Clinton, and Jeremiah was probably about half way between "Thomas Harrison's" and the Muddy Creek community. In 1759 and 1760, he acquired several hundred acres on Linville's Creek, and the South Branch thereof, the 1759 patent including nineteen acres of land "at the great Spring" on the head of the South Branch. (See, Deed Book 9, p. 129, of Augusta County, at Staunton, Virginia.)

Samuel Harrison has been identified as the brother who settled at Krotzer's Spring, now Linville. The court record of 1764—see page 8—states that he "moved to Virginia and settled on Linville's Creek where he took up 400 acres." September 5, 1749, he patented this quantity of land on the South Branch of the creek and on August 16, 1756, he patented 245 acres more "on the northwest side" of this branch. Krotzer's Spring is almost directly on Linville's Creek and as both Jeremiah and Samuel located land on the South Branch, presumably the main branch of this creek, it may be that they both at first camped for a time at the spring. Jeremiah evidently did not live at the "great Spring" mentioned in his patent, as he sold this, including nineteen acres, February 17, 1761.

It may be observed, Linville's Creek rises a little to the west of Harrisonburg, while the Dry Fork rises a little to the east of the city. Both of these streams flow northward. The former empties into the North Fork of the Shenandoah near the town of Broadway; the latter, continuing as Smiths Creek, joins this river near Mt. Jackson. Dry Fork and Smith Creek run through the lands immediately bordering the western foothills of the Massanutten. This may also be said of the North Fork of the Shenandoah, north of Mt. Jackson. This river rises to the west of Broadway, beyond Brock's Gap in the Allegheny Mountains. While the waters of the above creeks head near Harrisonburg and flow northward, on the other hand, those of Cook's and Muddy creeks, which rise in this vicinity, flow southward, emptying into a branch of the South Fork of the Shenandoah. These Forks of the Shenandoah, or rivers, traverse regions on opposite sides of the Massanutten. Harrisonburg is almost directly on the brow of the watershed between these rivers. The Valley Turnpike crosses this brow about a mile north of the town and continues northward through the fertile lands lying between Smiths and Linville's creeks.

In the region watered by the four creeks named, and now traversed by "The Long Grey Trail," the Harrisons patented practically all of their lands; and here they fixed their pioneer homes.

* * * * *

Scattered among the early records at Orange there occur various references to William, Charles, Andrew, Battaile, George and Lawrence Harrison. These Harrisons were not of the Augusta County family and nothing in regard to them is found on the records of this county. They apparently came into Orange from Pennsylvania, evidently settling in that part of the county east of the Ridge. In his *Sketches of Southwest Pennsylvania*, principally Fayette County, James Veech mentions a family of Harrisons, the elder manifestly being Lawrence, Sr. Among the younger members appear Benjamin William, Charles, Battle, and Lawrence, Jr. (See p. 119, etc.) One William Harrison died in Orange County by 1738, as on the 23rd of March, this year, William Christopher brought suit against his estate. Further reference to this suit occurs under date of July 26, 1739. (Order Books 1734-39, p. 453 and 1739-41, p. 34.) Andrew, Battle,

Charles George and William all appear in 1739, and the first two with Lawrence in 1741. Andrew Harrison and his two sons—not named—are mentioned October 25, 1744; the sons among others being allowed "26 pounds of tobacco" for patroling and guarding a prisoner. (Order Book, 1743-46, p. 224.) Lawrence Harrison was a witness to a suit in 1745. Following the Revolution, one Battaile or Battle Harrison, of Virginia, settled in Ohio on land granted him for services as an officer in this war. He is prominently mentioned in William Harrison's notes, *A Partial History of the Harrison Family...* One of this name (Battle) received deeds for land in Orange County from Thomas Chew, Gent. and Martha his wife, November 26, 1741. (See Order Book 1741-43, p. 52.)

The first courts established west of the Blue Ridge were those of Frederick and Augusta Counties. Frederick court was organized November 11, 1743, and Augusta, December 9, 1745. The House of Burgesses had passed an Act establishing these counties November, 1738. The former county was named in honor of Frederick, Prince of Wales, while the latter was named for his consort, the Princess Augusta. The new counties were taken out of Orange and included all the territory of the Colony west, of the Blue Ridge "to the utmost limits of Virginia." Of the two counties, Augusta was much the larger; to the west and northwest it embraced all of the country claimed by Great Britain in this direction, including nearly all of the present state of West Virginia, all of Kentucky, Ohio, Indiana, Illinois, and "as contended by Virginians" a part of western Pennsylvania.

In the Act creating the new counties the dividing line was defined to run "from the head spring of Hedgman river to the head spring of the river Potowmack." At this time the final locations of these springs were still undetermined. At the January term of Frederick court following its organization, Col. James Wood was ordered "to run the dividing line between this and Augusta County, according to the Act of the Assembly, from the head springing of Hedeman river to Patterson's creek." However, there was some delay in carrying out the order owing to the court of Augusta not having as yet been established. By 1744 the line was run. This year an Act was passed by the Assembly in regard to Augusta's share of the costs, stating that Frederick had engaged a surveyor to do the work.

As shown by the order of Orange court of May 24, 1745, previously quoted in regard to the Indian Road, Toms Brook at this time was on the Frederick County line. Hedgman's River is not given on present maps of Virginia, but by comparison with a map dated in 1796, as bound with *Heads of Families—First Census of the United States*—it appears that this stream is now known as the Rush River, a branch of the Thornton. It heads in the Blue Ridge to the west of Flint Hill. The 1744 line ended on Patterson's Creek, and was evidently only tentative owing to the indfieniteness of the true terminals. The aim of the Assembly was apparently to use the boundry of the Northern Neck, and in 1753 this was done; the line between Frederick and Augusta being finally made identical with the "Fairfax Line." This now separates the counties of Rockingham and Shenandoah.

The Act establishing Frederick and Augusta provided that they should remain a part of the County of Orange, and parish of St. Mark, until it should be made apparent to the Governor and Council that there "were a sufficient number of inhabitants for appointing justices of the peace and other officers, and erecting courts therein." Until this time the inhabitants were exempted from "the payment of all public, county, and parish levies in the County of Orange, and parish of St. Mark." (See, Hening's *Statutes at Large of Virginia.)*

As evidenced by the organization of the courts of Augusta and Frederick, the county West of the Great Mountains was beginning to be fairly rapidly peopled by this time. Settlers had begun pouring in, the flood having started in earnest about 1740. In the words of John Esten Cooke: "the wave of population like a steady rising tide, had advanced up the lowland rivers, reached the mountains at last, and flowed over into the sweet fields of the Shenandoah." Concurrently with the rise of the tide about them, the Harrisons began bestirring themselves in regard to establishing full titles to the lands they had chosen. Thus the various dates of their patents. Prospects for investment had begun to brighten—and have continued ever since!

There are several noted natural gateways to the Valley of the Shenandoah, all of which are now on main highways, and were first used by these early settlers. From the north they began coming in by the old Indian trail to the east of Falling Waters, crossing the Potomac at Pack Horse Ford, lated Mecklenburg, now Shepherdstown. By 1740 their main route from this direction had begun to swerve to the east. This entered the Valley at the picturesque jucture of the Shenandoah and Potomac. Here for the accommodation of the immigrants in crossing the latter, Robert Harper erected his famous ferry. The ferry was made a public one in March 1761. From the east the tide of immigrantion poured in through the various gaps in the Blue Ridge. Of these, Thoroughfare Gap, Thornton's Gap, Swift Run Gap, and Rockfish Gap were the earliest used, and most noted.

Various writers have left the impression that the Shenandoah Valley was very nearly entirely settled by Pennsylvanians. An instance of this reads: "The counties of Augusta and Rockingham, in Virginia, were settled almost exclusively by Pennsylvanians from Bucks, Berkes, and the Cumberland Valley." Another authority goes so far as to say that, "Most of the early settlers of the Shenandoah Valley in Virginia were Pennsylvania Germans with a few Scotch Irish and Quakers from the same Province." (See, *The American Aarat*, by W. S. Ely, p. 2, and Stapleton's *Memorials of the Huguenots*, p. 135.)

A study of the early records of these settlers, however, warrents the assertion that such impressions are entirely erroneous. In fact, in the light of such monumental works as Chalkley, Waddell, and Cartmell, it would seem modern research has disclosed that the Pennsylvania emigration to the Valley of Virginia has been overemphasized. Pennsylvania, being in fairly close proximity to the Valley of Virginia, was naturally on the route of emigration from other northern colonies. Ports of debarkation from England were also located on the Delaware, particularly at Lewes, and at Philadelphia. While a very large number—possibly the larger number—of early settlers did come to the Shenanadoah direct from Pennsylvania, a very large proportion of them, more strictly speaking, came *through* Pennsylvania. Campbell, in his history of Virginia, says; "the Indians had been so wisely dealt with by Penn that the handful of first settlers could more securely venture into this country as coming from the Province of Pennsylvania, a colony indeared to the Indian by its founder, hence the movement to the Valley was not interrupted by them." It is well known that for about twenty years the Valley settlers were unmolested by the savages. "Some," says Foote, "who had known war in Ireland, lived and died in that peace in this wilderness for which their hearts had longed in their native land."

Of the first settlers, John Van Meter came in from Maryland, and Isaac from Salem, New Jersey. Both were natives of New York. The grant to John Van

Meter distinctly states that he proposed to locate his relatives and friends from this Province. Many Dutch names are found among the early settlers of the lower Valley. Joist Hite was a native of Alsace, France, also an emigrant from New York, first to New Jersey, and then to Pennsylvania. John Lewis was a native of Ulster, Ireland. The settlers on Stover's Massanutten tract were immigrants from Switzerland and nearby German Provinces to Pennsylvania. Benjamin Borden and Morgan Morgan, two of the first men appointed as Justices of Frederick Court, were from New Jersey. Morgan was a native of Wales, and a very early settler in the lower Valley. Col. James Wood, the founder of Winchester, the first Clerk of Frederick Court, and a former Surveyor of Orange County, was from that part of Orange east of the Ridge. In the lower Valley the Scotch-Irish were prominent and numerous. Regarding these, Cooke remarks; "they established their homesteads along the Opequon, from the Potomac to above what is now Winchester. As soon as they had built their houses they proceeded to build their churches and the Tuscarora Meeting House, near Martinsburg, and the Opequon Church, a little south of Winchester, are it is said, the oldest churches in the Valley of Virginia,—they are still standing." Lord Fairfax, himself, the Proprietor of this whole region, in the summer of 1747 made his final voyage from England to Virginia, and this year laid out his "quarters" at Greenway Court some thirteen miles southeast of the present city of Winchester. Here he came to live in 1751, and here he died 9th, December, 1781, thirty years later. *(Va. Magazine of History and Biography,* Vol. 34, pp. 37 and 40.) Around him settled a host of Virginians from East of the Ridge.

Benjamin Borden, a land agent for Lord Fairfax, was a native of New Jersey, of Rhode Island descent, and as previously stated owned land in various parts of the Valley. Perth Amboy is a reminder that the Scotch Presbyterians were immigrating to East Jersey by 1685. The principal and most active Proprietors of this region were natives of Scotland. John Harrison, of Perth Amboy, formerly mentioned as the agent of the Proprietors, was largely instrumental in locating many of these immigrants. In regard to the migration of the English and Scotch from this section Franklin Ellis, in his *History of Monmouth County, New Jersey,* remarks—

"From Monmouth County, which has afforded an asylum for these victims of religious persecution in Europe and New England, many of their descendants removed to other provinces and states, and made for themselves new homes in the valleys of the Delaware, the Susquehanna, the Potomac, the Shenandoah and Kanawah. 'Among the first settlers of the Valley of Virginia who began to locate there about 1732', says the Hon. Edwin Salter—in an address delivered at the celebration of the bi-centennial anniversary of the New Jersey Legislature in 1883—'were Formans, Taylors, Stocktons, Throckmortons, Van Meters, Pattersons, Vances, Allens, Willets, (or Willis), Larues, Lucases and others of familiar New Jersey names. Fourteen or fifteen Baptist families from this region settled near Gerrardstown, and there were also many Scotch Presbyterians from New Jersey, among whom were Crawfords, McDowells, Stuarts, Alexanders, Kerrs, Browns, and Cummingses. Many of these families eventually passed into the Carolinas, Kentucky, and elsewhere, and descendants of some became noted not only in the localities or State where they settled, but in the annals of the Nation." (p. 84.)

In this connection the case of Ezekiel Clements furnishes an interesting detail, as disclosed by the Augusta court records. "District Court Judgements, September 1794 (K-Z) Abraham Clements, demise 18th June, 1746. Mary Roberts deposes, February 28, 1788, in Frederick County, Maryland, that she was a neighbor of Ezekiel Clements, of Hopewell Township, County Hunterdon, New Jersey, and knew the family

15-20 years. Ezekiel and eldest son Abraham, went out to purchase land; said they had bought in the backwoods. Abraham married and had three children, one of whom was a son Abraham. Copy deed from Borden's executors to Ezekiel Clements, 1746." This land was on the Mary Branch of James River. *(Chalkley,* Vol. II, p. 8.)

Numerous references to emigrants from New Jersey appear in the records at Orange. Of these may be cited several cases under one date, 25th July, 1743. "Jacobus Johnson vs. Thomas Gray, otherwise called Thomas Gray of Loabanon in ye county of Hunterdon and West of New Jersey, Yeoman." "Abraham Frisbie and Daniel Roso, both of ye Township of Bethlehem, Co. of Hunterdon and certain Division of the province of New Jersey, Yeoman." "In the action of Debt between John Baldwin pet. and Daniel McKay otherwise called Daniel McKay of Capomay (Cape May) County in West Jersey, Deft." (Order Book 1741-43, pp. 479-481.) Another case taken at random; "Nov. 27, 1741, Peter Syeans Pet. and James Hogeland otherwise called James Hogeland of East Jersey and County of Middlesex, house Carpenter." (Same Book, p. 60.)

In the upper Valley the Scotch-Irish practically covered the lands of Beverly and Borden. Many of them had come in through the port of Philadelphia, as shown by the numerous lists of importations at Orange court. On one day, May 22, 1740, sixteen heads of families appeared at Orange "to prove their importations," all having come "from Ireland to Philadelphia and from thence to this colony" at their own charge. (See, Order Book 1739-41, pp. 155-157.) The first settlers on Borden's land were John McDowell and his family, his aged father Ephraim, and his sister Mary and her husband James Greenlee. They located on the land in 1737. *(Chalkley,* Vol. II, p. 268.) Ephraim lived to be over 100 years old. In his youth he was one of the defenders of Londonderry. He was a kinsman of John Lewis. On the 28th February 1739, John McDowell made oath at Orange "that he imported himself, Magdaline, his wife, and Samuel McDowell, his son, and John Rutter, his servant, at his own charge from Great Britain, in the year 1737, to dwell in this colony . . . etc." *(Waddell* p. 37.) There were other McDowells early in the lower Valley also.

Others of the Scotch-Irish were brought over by Col. James Patton and landed on the Rappahannock. Thornton's Gap being on one of the earliest routes to the Valley, through here doubtless came many of those so landed. From this gap their way in general led along that followed by the Harrisons until the region of Naked Creek was reached. Continuing southward only a few miles they came on the lands of Beverly—near what is now Ft. Defiance—and finally further on those of Borden. The Harrisons themselves no doubt used the trail blazed by some of the earliest of these immigrants, breaking camp on the South Fork of the Shenandoah and coming into the region at the end of the Massanutten, with the harbingers of the tide that was to shortly rise, flooding the country south of the present Augusta County line.

In the central part of the Shenandoah Valley, the present county of Rockingham was settled by emigrants from particularly widely scattered sections. The beginnings of this county were mainly centered about the early region of Harrisonburg, before described. Here are found settlers from all the northern Provinces, at least south of Rhode Island, some from Eastern Virginia, many from Ulster, Ireland, a few Germans, one or more from Scotland, and even the capital of the British Empire was represented—by the son of a Frenchman. Among those more or less intimately associated with the Harrisons were Cravens, Herrings, Smiths, Stephensons, Warrens, Davisons, Moores, Lincolns, Tallmans, Ewings, Dyers, McClures, Woodleys, Bryans, Shanklins, Matthews,

Stewarts or Stuarts, McWilliams, Chrismans, Howards, Birds, or Byrds, Wrights, Carpenters, Davises, Newmans, Thomases, Aldersons, Harts, Linvilles, Caldwells, Hopkins, Whites, Seviers, and others as will appear later.

Of these, Robert Cravens, and Alexander Herron or Herring, brothers-in-law of the Harrisons, like them, came in from Sussex County, Delaware. Following the settlement of these families others of their neighbors and friends also came in from here. In this county today may yet be found many family names familiar in old Rockingham, such as Layton, Conrad, Jones, Houston, etc. Here various Stewarts and Shanklins frequently appear on the early records. At the time of the Harrisons' residence in Sussex, Robert Shanklin was the County Surveyor. One of this name, and evidently the same person, signed as a witness on the deeds to Thomas, Daniel and Jeremiah Harrison when their father divided Maiden Plantation. A little later John and Robert Shanklin appear as the first clerks of the Church at "Thomas Harrison's" in Old Augusta. Robert Cravens bought his land in Sussex of Samuel Stewart. Next is found on the Orange records Samuel Stuart appointed as one of the "Overseers," along with John and Daniel Harrison, for building the old Indian Road. Also Jeremiah Harrison succeeded Thomas Stewart as Constable. David Stewart too is mentioned in the early "processioners" lists of first settlers in the Cook's Creek region. Another early settler on this creek, near Cravens, was Abraham Potter, "otherwise called 'Abraham Potter of Sussex upon Delaware,' bond by him to Robert Cravens, dated 1745." (*Chalkley*, Vol. I, p. 309.) Potter bought his land from James Fisher, who too was probably from Delaware. It will be recalled that one John Fisher sold land in Delaware to Gideon Harrison.

Potter

One of the early New Castle County, Delaware, families was that of Valentine Hollingsworth, a Friend, who came over from County Armagh, Ireland, in 1682. Abraham, his grandson, was among the prominent Friends first in Old Frederick County, Virginia. He died there in 1748. (See, *Descendants of Valentine Hollingsworth, Sr.*, by J. Adgar Stewart, 1925.) A later emigrant to the Valley was Anthony Houston, whose father, according to an old account, came over from England and settled in Delaware. From there—sometime before the Revolution—the son migrated to near Jamestown, and then to what is now Rockbridge County, Virginia. One of this name appears among the Delaware settlers on the Manor of Stenning, of around 1710, as given by a map of this Manor in Myers' *Immigration of Irish Quakers into Pennsylvania.* This Manor later became New Garden Township. Anthony's land was just within the circular boundary of New Castle County. (See p. 133.) He does not appear as a Friend. Various references to the Hollingsworths are also given in this work. Descendants of both Valley immigrants later inter-married with the Harrisons of Rockingham.

The first regular minister to settle west of the Blue Ridge was the Rev. John Craig who landed at New Castle, Delaware, August 17, 1734, having emigrated from County Antrim, Ireland, where he was born in 1709. He was educated at Edinburg, Scotland. He came to Augusta in 1740, and was the pastor of two Presbyterian congregations. The one in which he lived met at the Old Stone Church, the other at Tinkling Spring.

Among the early families associated with the Harrisons at Oyster Bay, Queen's County, Long Island, were Warrens, Carpenters, Wrights, Davises, Newmans, and Whites. One of the oldest tombstones yet standing in the New Erection cemetary, to the west of Harrisonburg, is in memory of Michael Warren. This recites that "M. Warren, Sen. was born in Queens County on Long Island, July the 5th in the year of Our Lord, 1711. . . . M. Warren, Sen. died. . . . 1795, and was buried in Rockingham County, Virginia." Joseph Carpenter is mentioned on the Augusta records under date of March 1764. "County Court Judgements, Seely vs. Carpenter—Jeremiah Seely married the daughter of Joseph Carpenter, lately of the Province of New York, Joseph, in 1746, and after the above marriage, moved to Jacksons River, where he and most of his children then unmarried settled." (*Chalkley*, Vol. I, p. 339.) John Wright and his wife Lydia were also among the pioneers associated with the Harrisons of Old Augusta. The Tallmans were another early Queens County, Long Island, family. Many of the first inhabitants of this county were from Rhode Island, and there was much going to and fro from the one to the other locality. According to the Tallman family Bible, as quoted by Lea and Hutchison in their *Ancestry of Abraham Lincoln*, William Tallman was born in Rhode Island, 25th March, 1720, and died in Rockingham County, Virginia, 13th February, 1791. (See p. 176.)

Daniel Davison was probably a native of Long Island also; at least his father, Josiah, was a resident of Southold in 1715. Josiah removed with his family from there to near New Brunswick, New Jersey, where he bought land of John Harrison, Jr. of Perth Amboy, before noticed. From New Jersey, Daniel came to the Valley. He married Phoebe, a daughter of John Harrison of the "Big Spring," and had among others a son Josiah, the first Sheriff—barring Silas Hart—of Rockingham. In 1750, Daniel died and his widow later married Thomas Moore, the ancester of another early Rockingham family, of whom more later.

The parents of John, William and Archibald Hopkins migrated from Ulster, Ireland, to Albany, New York. From there the father, with a second wife and his family, removed to Baltimore, Maryland, whence the three brothers came early to Augusta and settled on Muddy Creek. (See, *A Chapter of Hopkins Genealogy*, by Ella W. Harrison, p. 17.)

Another of the Scotch-Irish settlers in this section was John McClure. The first of this family in Augusta was James McClure, who was born in the north of Ireland about 1690. In 1738, he immigrated to Augusta with his family, one of whom was his eldest son John. This year John settled on the South River about six miles south of present Waynesboro. (See, *The McClure Family*, by James A. McClure, p. 23.) On November 27, 1751, the Muddy Creek settler of this name bought 387 acres of Daniel Harrison and his wife Margaret. He also appears in March, 1756, among others, as a signer of a petition "of sundry inhabitants of the County by this North Mountain, in Captain Harrison's and Captain Love's Companies." (See,*Chalkley*, Vol. III, p. 299, and Vol. I, pp. 313, 440.)

One of the earliest communities in Rockingham was that on Linville's Creek. Hite is said to have had a mill on this creek before 1742, which he rented this year to Thomas Linville. Among those early settled here was William Ewing. He too came over from Ireland, but according to Johnson's *Memorials of Old Virginia Clerks*, he was a native of Scotland. Being a strong Calvinist he fled to Londonderry, whence he came to America, first stopping in Bucks County, Pennsylvania. From there he came to the Shenandoah Valley. He is said to have made his first purchase in 1742, locating "some three miles northwest of where Harrisonburg now stands." Another account relates that he came over with three cousins. They had a stormy voyage and landed at Philadelphia. He went to school in Pennsylvania for three years to Ann Shannon whom he married at the age of twenty-two, she being three years his senior. His first deed in Augusta was recorded November 17, 1761. On this date he purchased from Hite et als. 708 acres "on easternmost branch of Linville's Creek." (See, *Clan Ewing of Scotland*, by E. W. R. Ewing, pp. 256-9.)

The first pastor of the old Linville Creek Baptist Church was the Rev. John Alderson. This noted pastor was a native of Yorkshire, England, who as a young man immigrated to New Jersey. On landing he was hired by the Captain of the ship for his passage over to a respectable farmer of the name of Custis. He later married Custis' daughter. Subsequent to his marriage he was baptized. From New Jersey he removed to Germantown, Pennsylvania, and from Germantown, in 1755, to the Linville Creek Church. He served this church about sixteen years and then went to another in Botetourt County, where he died in 1781. His son John Alderson, Jr., born in New Jersey in 1738, succeeded him at the Linville Creek Church, October, 1775. (See, Taylor's *Lives of Virginia Baptist Ministers*, 1837, pp. 21 and 147.)

Associated with the families of John and Jeremiah Harrison in this early church were various Lincolns. John Lincoln, the emigrant, and native of New Jersey, settled on Linville's Creek. His son Abraham married a daughter of Alexander Herring, and his daughter Hannah married a grandson of John Harrison of the Big Spring. In reference to the early emigrants from New Jersey, Ellis, before quoted, continues—

"Another man still more noted in the history of the nation, who descended from an early settler of New Jersey, and whose ancestors went from Monmouth County to Eastern Pennsylvania and thence to the Valley of Virginia, was President Abraham Lincoln, one of whose ancestors was John Bowne, of Monmouth, Speaker of the House of Assembly more than two hundred years ago. The founder of this family was Samuel Lincoln, who came from Norwich (Norfolk County), England, to Massachusetts (d. 1690); he had a son Mordecai; (1st) of Hingham, (1657-1727); he in turn had sons, Mordecai (2d) b. April 24, 1686, (d. 1736); Abraham, b. January 13, 1689; Isaac, b. October 21, 1691, and a daughter, Sarah, b. July 29, 1694, as stated in Savage's *Genealogical Dictionary*. Mordecai (2d) and Abraham moved to Monmouth County, New Jersey, where the first named married a granddaughter (Hannah Salter) of Capt. John Bowne, and his eldest son born in Monmouth, was named John. About 1730 the Lincolns moved to Eastern Pennsylvania, where Mordecai's first wife died, and he married again. He died at Amity, Pennsylvania, and his will dated February 23, 1735, and proven June 7, 1736, mentions his wife Mary, and children, John, Thomas, Hannah, Mary, Ann, Sarah, Mordecai (b. 1730) and a 'prospective child.' The latter (Abraham) proved a boy and subsequently married Ann Boone, a cousin of Daniel Boone. John Lincoln, the eldest son, with some of his neighbors, moved to Rockingham County, Virginia; he had sons, Abraham, Isaac, Jacob, Thomas, and John. John (1st) died at Harrisonburg, Virginia. . . ." (Dates in parenthesis supplied.)

Many instances could be given of typical settlers in the Valley of the Shenandoah descending from families having a previous history in the early provinces; but enough has been set forth showing whence these first immigrants came. Further notice of others of the old Rockingham families named will appear in succeeding pages. Various members of at least the first twenty-one families mentioned intermarried with the Harrisons; some of the whole number were their kinfolks; many were affiliated with them through their church connections; and all were their neighbors and friends. Aside from the Scotch-Irish who had crossed the Atlantic, most of the Old Augusta pioneers were clearly of English stock. Of such were a great number of the early "Virginians of the Valley".

"The Knightliest of the Knightly race,
That since the days of old,
Have kept the lamp of chivalry
Alight in hearts of gold.
The kindliest of the kindly band
That rarely hated ease!
That rode with Raleigh round the land,
With Smith around the seas."

—TICKNOR.

Of such, also, were largely those among the *first* settlers in the region of Harrisonburg.

CHAPTER X

First Days Just South of the "Fairfax Line"

"Leading out from fair Winchester,
'Cross Opequon's silver stream,
Through the fields of hard-fought battles,
And where Shendo's waters gleam,
Far along the Massanutten,
Where the shadows blend and play,
On it leads to the hills of Staunton—
Besty Bell and Mary Gray!"

—WAYLAND

THE FIRST COURTS organized West of the Great Mountains were held on the sites of the present cities of Winchester and Staunton. Frederick court being erected at the former point, while that of Augusta was at the latter. Here they have remained ever since: their early records a silent memorial of the courage, struggles and hardships, hopes and disappointments, marriages and deaths, and lasting achievements, of the sturdy pioneers on the frontier of America. While there was some delay in deciding just where the jurisdiction of these courts met this was finally determined at the "Fairfax Line." This crossed the Valley—bisecting the country "far along the Massanutten"—some sixteen miles north of "Thomas Harrison's," today's city of Harrisonburg.

Winchester, Harrisonburg, and Staunton, these are the three cities of the Valley of the Shenandoah. All are on "The Long Grey Trail." At the time of the establishment of the above courts these cities were not even villages, and their names were entirely unknown. Their founders were all living however—Col. James Wood, Thomas Harrison, and Col. William Beverly.

As indicated, the Harrisons had settled in the open region immediately separating Fairfax and Beverly. Of the brothers, Thomas, in particular, came just about midway of this region when finally the Fairfax Line was run. John was the nearest to this line, being only about seven miles south of it. All of the brothers were evidently careful to keep entirely outside of the territory claimed by Lord Fairfax. This is further confirmed by the absence of their names in the old Northern Neck "Grant Books" at Richmond, and in the various early deeds dealing with Northern Neck land, at Orange and Winchester. Neither, as shown by the Orange and Winchester records, did they come in under Beverly, Borden, or Hite. Their first lands were all obtained by patent direct from the Crown, as represented by the Governor of the Colony.

While Hite and Borden were interested in some lands in the country "just south of the Fairfax Line" these were of comparatively small quantities, their large holdings being elsewhere in the Valley. According to the reference before quoted the early firm of Hite, McKay, Duff, and Green, had patented 1264 acres on Linville's Creek in March, 1739. This same amount of land is later mentioned in a deed of John Wilkins to Alexander Herron—30th October, 1766—for 400 acres on Naked Creek, adjoining Daniel Harrison's land, hence, apparently some of this, at least, was located here. (Augusta County Deed Book, No. 13, p. 129.) Cartmell states that the Linville Creek survey was a part of a grant of 7,000 acres made to the above firm in March, 1739, most of which was located in the present neighborhood of Front Royal. Borden's tract was on Smiths Creek. His will also mentions land on the North Fork of the Shenandoah.

* * * * * *

The first sessions of Frederick court were held "at the house of Mr. Wood," and the records were kept there for about two years, when they were ordered transferred "to the Clerk's Office at the Court House." Kercheval relates that in 1755 the court house at Winchester consisted of a small log cabin.

Prior to this time the Colonel had built his fine old colonial brick mansion, known as "Glen Burnie"—still standing within the limits of Winchester. Before this house was built he was living in an earlier one at some point on the great lawn as early at least as 1743, when he qualified as the first Clerk of the Court.

According to Campbell, both Winchester and Staunton were started with a cabin or two in 1736. On the 9th of March, 1744, Col. Wood petitioned the Court to allow him to dedicate a number of lots—taken from his home plantation of 1241 acres—for the use of the county. This petition was granted on condition that Lord Fairfax would later affirm his title to the land, and accordingly the same year he sold to the county for five shillings, twenty-six lots of one half acre each, "together with two streets running through said lots of the breadth of thirty-four feet, etc." Thus was started the town of Winchester. It was begun on the site of old Shawnee Springs. Lord Fairfax afterwards made an addition to the town. On this the court house, Episcopal Church, and jail were built. The town was established by law in February, 1752. It is thus only ten years younger than Richmond, Virginia.

* * * * * *

In the year following the founding of Winchester, and in the spring preceeding the establishment of Augusta court, the route of the old "Indian Road" was "Blazed and laid off with Two notches and a Cross." This was the first road authorized up the Valley and the forerunner of the Valley Turnpike, "The Long Grey Trail." As stated, John and Capt. Daniel Harrison, Robert Cravens, Samuel Stuart, William Thompson, and John Stenson, were appointed "Surveyors and Overseers," from "Benjamin Allen's Ford and Robert Colnell's Path, Cross Beard's Ford on North River," to "Alexander Thompson's Ford on the Middle River". This section crossed the region later "just south of the Fairfax line" and completely spanned the territory now known as Rockingham. In fact, it began about eight or ten miles north of the above line and extended somewhat south of the present Rockingham—Augusta line. Middle River—flowing northward—joins the North River on this latter line a little to the east of Naked Creek.

South of "Thomas Harrison's" the road was to the east of the present pike. Various circumstances indicate that the route from Harrison's was by way of what is now Cross Keys, Mt. Meridan, and New Hope. Alexander Thompson's Ford was at or near the second named point, which is just west of Cave Hill. Thompson, at this time lived on the South River near the early known today's Grand Caverns. On February 19, 1746, he sold to William Beard 100 acres "on the south branch of Shenando, known by Cave Bottom; Alexander Thompson's ford; next to the Great Mountain; Cave Hill; (etc.) part of tract patented to Alexander, 13th July, 1742." In 1754 one of this name, a tailor, bought land in Beverly's manor of Samuel Lusk. This he sold "by William Thompson attorney" to William Dean, February 17, 1762. At this time he was living in "Mill Creek Hundred, County of New Castle on Delaware." (See, Augusta County Deed Book, No. 1, p. 180, *Chalkley,* Vol. III, pp. 252, 258, 330, 381.)

At or near Thompson's Ford the road evidently joined the first one ordered opened across the Blue Ridge through Swift Run Gap. "26th Feb. 1741. On the petition of Alexander Thompson and others for a road or bridleway the convenientest Way from Jackson's Mill over the ridge by the way of Swift run gap Yts ordered that Jacob Dyer, James Barton, Jacob Cassell and James Dyer or any two or more of them mark view and lay off a road and make return of their proceedings to ye next court." (See, Orange Court Order Book, 1741-43, p. 109.)

Leaving Thompson's Ford the next section of the Indian Road ended at Tinkling Spring, another early community. This spring is about a mile south of Fishersville, and five or six miles southeast of Staunton. Thus the seat of Augusta court, when founded, was not quite on the new highway. It was not until a little later that the "Great Road to the Court House" became a part of "The Long Grey Trail."

It is grey with the dust of limestone,
Ground by myraid pounding feet,
And by wheels that turn unceasing
Through the hours and minutes fleet;
For the whole long trail is bordered
With the native rocks of gray,
Strewn in scattered heaps about it,
As from giant hands at play."

—Wayland.

The region of the Shenanadoah is a natural limestone and blue grass country—similar to Kentucky. The pioneer "Overseers" found plenty of road material near at hand, but they never dreamed that about one hundred years later they would be followed by one of the great Napoleon's distinguished engineers—Col. Claude Crozet—who would build on their foundations a magnificent highway—the route of which would be even then famous in the annals of a new nation. Nor could they vision the time when the hosts of the Blue and the Grey would contend for every inch of their route.

* * * * * *

From the beginning Augusta court met in a building erected especially for its own use. Anticipating the establishment of the court Col. Beverley, who was then living in Williamsburg, had built a court house on his manor at his "mill place." This he promised to deed to the county, along with two acres of land, by the spring of 1746. The court house at Staunton today stands on this land. The first building was of logs "hewn on both sides not laid close," and had openings for windows, but there was no glass in them. According to the early records it was thirty-eight feet, three inches long, and eighteen feet, three inches wide. Later, by 1748, the jail was built; this was of "square logs near one foot thick" and was about twenty-two feet long by seventeen feet wide.

On July 15, 1747, Thomas Lewis laid off for Col. Beverly several streets and thirteen town lots of the present city of Staunton. By a further survey of Lewis the next year thirty-one more lots and other streets were added, and a plot of twenty-five acres was reserved for the use of the county. A plan of the town was then drawn up; this was produced in court by Beverly and recorded February 27, 1749. (See, Deed Book No. 2, p. 410.) The twenty five acre reserve was conveyed by Beverly to the county on April 21st of the same year. Campbell relates that the town was named for Lady Staunton, the wife of Governor Gooch. In 1748 an Act of Assembly was passed establishing the town. This however, was "disallowed" by George II. Staunton was finally established by law November 1761, five years after its founder's death.

Gov. Gooch

Col Beverly, like Col. Wood, was a native of Eastern Virginia, but unlike the latter, he did not make his permanent home in the Valley. In 1736, along with William Fairfax, of Belvoir, and Charles Carter, he was one of the commissioners appointed by Lord Fairfax to ascertain the true fountains of the Rappahannock and Potomac rivers. (See p. 116.) Governor Gooch appointed Col. William Byrd, of Westover, John Robinson, of Piscataway, and John Grymes, of Brandon, as the King's representatives on this commission.

In the fall of 1742 Col. Beverly was the County Lieutenant, or commander-in-chief, of the military forces of Augusta. James Patton was the Colonel, and John Smith, Andrew Lewis, John Buchanan, James Cathrey, John Christian, Samuel Gay, Peter Scholl, James Gill, John Willson, Hugh Thompson, George Robinson, and John McDowell were the Captains.

From the number of companies the population of the county has been estimated at about 2,500.

Of the above officers Capt. John Smith has been given some account of as the ancestor of the family early associated with the Harrisons. He was born in England in 1698, according to Boogher, and settled with his parents in the Province of Ulster, Ireland. From Ulster he removed with his family to Chester County, Pennsylvania, about 1730. He is said to have been a former officer of the British army. He proved his importation at Orange court in 1740. (See, p. 8, also *Waddell,* p. 39.) On June 24, 1742, he was commissioned Captain, along with Buchanan, Gay, Cathrey, and Christian. (Orange Court Order Book, 1741-43, p. 160.) March 30, 1745, John Smith, Gentlemen, patented 400 acres of land in the great survey of Mossy Creek and 400 acres on Spring Creek. During the French and Indian War Capt. Smith and his son Joseph were captured at Ft. Vause, June 25, 1756. His son John, a Lieutenant, was killed in this fight. (See *Draper MSS,* Wisconsin Historical Society.) Joseph died on the way to New Orleans. The Captain was taken to France, where he remained two years. Peyton relates that a street in London is said to have been named for him. At least two of his sons, Colonels Abraham and Daniel, served with the Virginia militia during the Revolution. The latter's son married a daughter of Capt. Daniel Harrison, and was one of the wealthiest men of the county. Capt. John Smith, the immigrant, died at Smithland, the home of his son Daniel, shortly after the beginning of the Revolution. (See later.)

SMiths

Andrew Lewis was a son of John Lewis, the pioneer. He was later the noted General Andrew Lewis, the hero of Point Pleasant, whom Washington considered the foremost military man of America at the outbreak of the Revolution. It is related that Washington recommended him to the Continental Congress for the post of Commander-in-Chief. *(Campbell,* p. 588, *Waddell,* p. 243.) Lewis was one of Washington's Brigadier Generals, of whom the Valley furnished two—he and John Peter Gabriel Muhlenberg, the preacher patriot. It was Gen. Lewis who early in the Revolution drove out of the Colony, July 9, 1776, the last of a long line of Virginia's colonial Governors; John Murray, Earl of Dunmore. The General died in 1781, and was buried at his old home near Salem, Virginia. His statue is one of those adorning the base of the monument to Washington, in Capitol Square, Richmond, Virginia.

Capt. John Willson, later Colonel, was one of the two first representatives of Augusta County, in the House of Burgesses. According to the inscription on his tomb, in the old glebe burial ground, near present Swoope's Depot, as preserved by Waddell, he died in 1773, aged 72, "having served his county twenty-seven years . . . . . in the Honorable Hous of Burjesis, in Virginia, &c." Foote mentions that the first tombstone reared in the Valley of Virginia to mark the resting place of an immigrant stands in the old burial ground of the Opequon church, south of Winchester. The stone was erected by the husband who inscribed the letters himself; "John Willson Intered here The Bodys of His 2 Childer & Wife Ye Mother Mary Marcus, Who Dyed Ag'st The 4—1742 Aged—22 Years." On the opposite side "FROM IRL,AND July Vi, th 1737 Co y Arg ma GH." (*Cartmell* p. 169.) Tradition says that John Willson was the early School Master. It is thought that he was the later Burgess.

John McDowell was the first settler on Borden's grant. He was killed on the North River in one of the earliest fights with the Indians, December 14, 1742. A party of thirty-three Indians in passing down the Valley had professed friendship for the whites, but in tarrying about a week camping on the south branch of the river they alarmed the settlers. Capt. McDowell called out a company of about thirty men to conduct them beyond the settlements. A lame Indian fell behind and was shot by one of McDowell's men. This started a fight in which two Indians were killed and five wounded. Ten whites were killed. The Indians took to the Blue Ridge and only two of them reached their home in Pennsylvania. Gov. Gooch afterwards ordered that 100 Pounds damages be paid the settlers. For more than a year a state of war existed, but peace was restored in 1744, by the treaty of Lancaster, Pennsylvania. McDowell's widow married Benjamin Borden, Jr., who, upon the death of his father in 1742, succeeded to the management of the elder Borden's lands.

* * * * * *

The first court of Augusta was organized December 9, 1745, and consisted of the following "Gentleman Justices," as appointed by a "Commission of the Peace" issued under the hand of Governor Gooch, October 30th previously,—James Patton, John Lewis, John Buchanan, George Robinson, Peter Scholl, James Bell, Robert Campbell, John Brown, Robert Pogue, John Pickens, Thomas Lewis, Hugh Thompson, Robert Cunningham, John Tinla (Finley?), Richard Woods, John Christian, Robert Cravens, James Kerr, Adam Dickenson, Andrew Pickens, and John Anderson. On the same date the Governor also commissioned James Patton, High Sheriff, John Madison was commissioned Clerk of the Court under the hand and seal of Thomas Nelson, Esq., Secretary of Virginia, and Thomas Lewis was commissioned County Surveyor, by "William Dawson president and masters of the college of William and Mary."

Twenty-one first magistrates of the county would seem to have been an ample number. As all were not required to meet at the same time, and as they served without pay—with the exception of the rotation of the office of High Sheriff among them—no doubt the difficulty of holding court at stated intervals was lessened in this manner. It required at least four of the Justices to constitute a court. The sessions began on the second Monday of the month until 1748, when quarterly courts were established by Act of Assembly an account of the burden of attendence.

Several of this historic group, viz. Patton, Buchanan, Christian, Robinson, Scholl, and Thompson, have been named as officers of the militia under Beverly in 1742. Col.

Patton was the former ship owner. John Lewis was the pioneer. John Buchanan was a son-in-law of Col. Patton's. Thomas Lewis was a son of John, and the brother of Andrew above. "24th. Jan 1744—Thomas Lewis Gent. having taken the oath appointed by act of Parliament instead of the Oath of Allegiance and Supremacy and having subscribed the Test afterwards took the oath of Surveyor for the county of Augusta." (Orange Court Order Book, 1743-46, p. 245.) He was thus the county surveyor before the court of Augusta was organized. James Bell came to Augusta from Ulster about 1740; he was a school teacher and surveyor. Robert Campbell was a son of John Campbell who had migrated from Ulster in 1726 to Pennsylvania and thence to Augusta about 1743. Robert Pogue and John Anderson were among those who proved their importation from Ireland at Orange in 1740. Four of Anderson's sons were officers in the Revolution; one was for many years a member of the Virginia Assembly; Anderson, South Carolina, is named for another. Robert Cunningham was a native of Ireland also. He settled in Augusta about 1735, and with Col. Willson was one of the first two representatives of the county in the House of Burgesses. John and Andrew Pickens were probably brothers. One of them was the father of the distinguished South Carolinian, Gen. Andrew Pickens, and had immigrated to Pennsylvania from Ulster prior to 1739, the year of the General's birth.

Captain Robert Cravens and Peter Scholl represented the lower part of the county, their homes being in the region of "Thomas Harrison's"—or of Craven's brother-in-law. Peter Scholl was the early resident on Smiths Creek. He appears to have been a nephew-in-law of Daniel Boone and to have later removed to Kentucky, where one of this name was living in 1776. (See, Collins' *History of Kentucky.)* Boone is known to have spent a year or two camping on Linville's Creek while migrating to North Carolina from Berkes County, Pennsylvania. Scholl probably came in also from this county. In 1742, as mentioned above, he was one of the Captains under Col. Beverly. Some of the members of his company have been named, the full roster being:

And. Burd, Lieutenant; Math. Skeens, Ensign; Abraham Harden, John Hill, Jonathan Burley, John Harrison, Georg. Clemens, Wm. Halimes, Zebulon Harrison, Jno. Davis, Jno. Taylor, Joseph Burley, William White, Isaac Lotos, Wm. Sherral, Valentine Sevier, John Cumberland, Jacob Jacobs, Thos. Moore, Stephanes Haweworth, (Haworth.) Jas. Haweworth, John Beeson, Steph. Howard, Absolom Howard, Joseph Howard, John Benson, Benj. Hames (Haines), John Harrison, Thos. Lowker, Griffiths Thomas, John White, Adam Sherral, Robt. Caldwell, John Miller, Will Brizes, (Briges), Wm. Carrel, John Hodg, Absolom Haweworth, and John Haweworth. (See, *The Preston Papers, Copies of Musters of Augusta County*, 1742, Capt. Peter Shoull's list, *Chalkey* Vol. II, p. 509.)

This early militia company was known as "No. 5." (See, *Virginia County Records, Colonial Militia*, by Wm. A. Crozier, Vol. I, p. 93.) These were the men of military age at the time in the Smiths Creek vicinity. For the most part their names are no longer represented among the inhabitants of this region, but still today may be found here Byrds, Harrisons, Howards, Moores, and Whites.

The Harrisons of this company were John, Sr., and his sons John, Jr. and Zebulon. Reuben, another son of John, Sr., was at this time too young for military service. Altogether, John, Sr., and his sons later patented about 3,000 acres of land in this region, (Smiths Creek and the Dry Fork thereof.) In addition Daniel Harrison and his son Robert patented 660 acres on the Dry Fork. Thus the two families were the first holders of about 3,600 acres of land here. Later other lands were bought in this same region by John, Jr. and his brothers. It is difficult to even estimate the amount of the Harrisons' total holdings in the vicinity, but 3,600 acres were only a beginning.

The first patents by any of John Harrison Sr's. family were two dated 25th September, 1746, to John Harrison, Jr.; one for 175 acres, the other for 400 acres; both tracts being on Smiths Creek. (See, Book No. 24, pp. 415, 417, of *Patents of Land Office*, Richmond, Virginia.) The original of these patents, written on parchment and now yellow with age, (as well as one to Zebulon Harrison dated 16th, February, 1771), are yet in existance, being now in possesion of Miss Anna K. Harrison, of Harrisonburg. These patents to John, Jr. were the beginning of the Harrisons' formal titles to lands in and around what is now Lacy Spring.

Lieut. Andrew Bird, or Byrd, and Thomas Moore, were in the region between John Harrison Sr. and the Fairfax line. In fact, their lands were about midway of this region—or some three or four miles north of the "Big Spring." Here were also located Valentine Sevier and Daniel Davison. In 1753 Sevier and his wife Joanna sold to Bird 184 acres of land "Between Limestone Ridge and Smiths Creek; corner Andrew Bird's survey, Robert Milsap's survey," etc. (*Chalkley*, Vol. III, p. 315.) Lieutenant Bird was commissioned Captain, 28th February, 1744. (Orange Court Order Book, 1743-46, p. 269.) He evidently enjoyed the diversions of his day: "Aug. 1772. Joseph Pearse deposition 8th April, 1771. Edward Sampson kept school in the neighborhood of Capt. Andrew Bird's and boarded with Bird, and Thomas Moore's children went to him. He (Sampson) and Bird frequently got drunk together, and had frequent frolics, when Bird became violent and threatened to kill everybody." (*Chalkley*, Vol. I, p. 366.) Tradition has it that two Byrd brothers from the James River started on a trip north and in passing through the Valley decided to make their home here. One of them was probably the Captain.

Captain Byrd was not the only one, however, who enjoyed the spirits of those days. "May 1768. Alexander Herron vs. Patrick Quinn.—Enjectment. Daniel Harrison, aged about sixty-six or seven, deposes; That he was present when Col. James Wood, the surveyor of the County of Orange (now Augusta), ran off the lands in dispute, and that the first line run by Thomas Lewis this day extends as far, etc., the corner of Samuel Wilkins, and that of Green & Co., under whom said Wilkins claims he has ever since been well acquainted with the lands, etc. that the lines were not marked until the patent issued, and the reason Wood gave for it was that when he was about to survey the same, he himself was d. . . . d drunk and the rest concerned were in the same condition, etc. (Signed) Daniel Harrison, 16th Dec. 1767. John Cravens deposes same time and place (age forty-five or thereabouts,); He was present when Col. James Wood surveyed the lands in dispute, now upwards of 22 years" . . . etc. (Augusta County Court Judgements, May, 1768 (A); *Chalkley*, Vol. I, p. 467.) The lands referred to were those of the Hite firm on Linville's Creek. Wood had run the first lines, but had no further interest in the survey. While Suveyor of Orange County though, he became interested in the region "just south of the Fairfax line," and patented various tracts here. His son-in-law, Matthew Harrison, through his wife Mary, the Colonel's daughter, was later posessed of large holdings in the "Great Plains" on the North Fork of the Shenandoah. Another tract was on Muddy Creek. Some of the Colonel's lands were also on Smiths Creek and passed into the possesion of Thomas Moore.

Thomas Moore as early as 1741 appears on the records at Orange. "26th November, 1741,—Certificate for obtaining Letters of Admon. of the Estate of Reuben Allen decd.

is granted to Reuben Allen the Eldest son of the decd. who having taken his Affirmation in Lieu of the oath of an Admr. and entered into bond with Thomas Moore and Benjamin Allen his securities." Another reference occurs later,—"27th. June 1745, Indenture of Lease and Release between James Gill and Elenor his wife of that part called Augusta joining to Orange in the Colony of Virginia on the one prt. and Thomas Moore of the aforesaid County and colony of the other part were acknowledged by said James and ordered to be Recorded." (Orange Court Order Books, 1741-43, p. 52, and 1743-46, p. 356.)

The Moores and Allens were Quakers. Benjamin Allen was the owner of the ford before referred to, on the old Indian Road. The Allens settled in this region now between Mt. Jackson and Edinburg,—or south of Woodstock. Benjamin is said to have migrated from the Monocacy Valley, Maryland, 1734. In regard to the early settlers in this section Cartmell remarks; "Near the site of Woodstock, long before the Muellerstadt village was started, the English, Scotch and Irish had founded their homes, and have maintained a foothold through the passing generations. We can barely mention a few: Benjamin Allen, Reily Moore, Wm. White, Jno. Branson, Levi Fawcett, Briscoe, Calvert, Crawford, Newman, Walker, and Sibert were on the ground about 1734-36 . . . . Some evidence can be produced that the pioneers on the North Fork disputed all claims which the German pioneers presented for settlement, and they were thus hindered for some time. Many passed further South, and peopled the rich sections of what became Rockingham County." (See p. 446.)

On the 26 July, 1753, Thomas Moore and Mary his wife deeded 200 acres of land on Smiths Creek to Samuel Newman. This land had originally been obtained from Fairfax by Newman, who in turn sold it to Moore. "Teste: Wm. Carrel and John Hughes." (See, Augusta County Deed Book No. 5, p. 349, *Chalkley,* Vol. III, p. 315.) This was the year that the county line between Augusta and Frederick was finally adjusted, but at that the land was evidently outside of Fairfax's territory. Hence the title was not clear. This doubtless explains why Moore returned it to Newman. Newman was one of the original members of the Linville Creek Baptist Church, and had come in from Pennsylvania. (See, p. 11.) A deed of gift, May 22, 1769, of Mary Wood of Frederick, to Alexander White and wife Elizabeth,—daughter of Mary,— of 165 acres, "on North River of Shenandoah, part of a tract called the Great Plains patented to James Wood, deceased, 12th January 1746," describes the land as having a "corner on the line between Matthew Harrison and said Alexander White according to the division of said plain made by Robert Rutherford, Daniel Holeman and Thomas Moore, line between His Majesty and Lord Fairfax." (Deed Book 16, p. 111; *Chalkley,* Vol. III, p. 492.) On May 22, 1762, the court of Augusta appointed Thomas Moore, Quaker, an arbiter in a matter involving the value of Pennsylvania money in terms of that of Virginia, £42, 3, 9, of the former equals £33, 15, of the latter. (Augusta County Court Order Book, VII, p. 233; *Chalkley,* Vol. I, p. 98.) This Thomas was obviously acquainted with the value of Pennsylvania currency, and thus probably came to the Valley immediately from one of the Provinces on the Delaware. On August 20, 1768, Thomas Moore's will was produced in Augusta court and witnesses summonsed. *(Chalkley,* Vol. I, p. 151.)

Thomas Moore who married the widow Phoebe Davison, a daughter of John Harrison, Sr., owned 1,700 acres of land on Smiths Creek. His location was on the old Indian Road about five miles south of present New Market. Part of this land is yet in the possession of his descendants, being the home place of the late Newton G. Moore, in whose family there are still several originial records. One of these is the old parchment patent to Col. James Wood for 370 acres, dated 12th January, 1746. On the back of this is Wood's acknowledgement of the sale of this land to Daniel Davison, 4th June, 1748. The deed on record describes the land as being on Smiths Creek, "on south side of wagon road." (Deed Book 2, p. 21.) The land was delivered to John Harrison, Jr., November 1756. Harrison was the guardian of Josiah Davison. Another paper is the original deed of Josiah Davison, "son and heir at law of Daniel Davison of the County of Augusta, deceased," to Thomas Moore, Blacksmith, for the above 370 acres, "on both sides of Smiths Creek," dated 7th November, 1767. This Thomas Moore Sr., according to his tombstone, died in 1797, "aged about 70 years." He is said to have been a Quaker. Evidently he was not the Thomas Moore of the Orange records of 1741-45, or of the militia company of 1742, etc.; neither, according to his estate settlement, does he appear to have been the owner of the lands in the "Great Plains." He is buried in the old family burial ground at the home place above, and just outside the family plot, as fenced in, are other graves that tradition says are those of several old slaves brought to Virginia by the first ancestor of the family. As Thomas of the militia company was the first in the vicinity, the indications are that he was a near relative of Thomas who died in 1797. Both were likely from New Jersey or Maryland.

Patrick McDonald

Valentine Sevier originally owned 200 acres of the 1,700 acre plantation of Thomas Moore, Sr., above, This land was on "Smiths Creek crossing Daniel James' Branch" and was patented by Sevier 27th June, 1767. The consideration was the importation of four persons, viz: James Porteus, John Roe, Patrick McDonald, and Daniel Warner. (*Chalkley*, Vol. II, p. 26.) That Sevier lived on Smiths Creek very near this land is shown by a deed of Alexander Buchanan and Isabella, of North Carolina, to Michael Bowyer, 10th April, 1769, in which the land is described as being "the tract commonly known by the place whereon Valentine Sevier formerly lived, containing 400 acres, side of Daniel James' Branch. Absolom Hayworth's (Haworth's) line." Deed Book 15, p. 492, *Chalkley*, Vol. III, p. 487.) This tract was patented by Sevier, 12th January, 1746, and was conveyed by Bower to Sebestian Martz, 19th March, 1777. (Deed Book 21, p. 264.) It is now owned by Mr. J. C. Bradford.

Sevier proved his importation at Orange court, 28th May, 1742: "Valentine Sevier & Margaret Gibson came into Court and made oath that they were immediately imported from Great Brittain & Ireland and that this is the first time of proving their importation in order to obtain right to land ye woman in open Court assigned over her right to sd. Valentine Siveier which is ordered to be certified." (Orange Court Order Book, 1741-1743, p. 159.)

Sevier was the son of Valentine Xavier (French for Sevier), a Huguenot, who upon the revocation of the Edict of Nantes, (1685), fled to London, where he became a prosperous merchant. He married an English girl, named Mary Smith. Valentine, the immigrant, was born in London, in 1702. He married Joanna Goade (or Good), of Virginia, about 1744, by whom he had seven children; John, Robert, Joseph, Valentine, Abraham, Polly, and Catherine. He moved to the Watauga settlement in Tenn. December 25th, 1773, and died in 1803. (See, *Notable Southern Families*, Vol. IV, *The Sevier Family*, by Zella Armstrong, 1926.) He owned various tracts of land on Smiths Creek and the North Fork of the Shenandoah.

Some of this appears to have been that on which the town of New Market was started. His son John Sevier, born September 23, 1745, probably on Smiths Creek, is said to have laid out the town soon after the French and Indian War. The town site was later owned by Peter Palsel, who laid off thirty-two lots in 1785. The town was incorporated December 14, 1796.

John Sevier moved to Holston 1773

John Sevier, in 1773, moved to the North Holston. He fought in the battle of Point Pleasant, and later became the noted Gen. John Sevier; the hero of King's Mountain, the first Governor of Tennessee, (for six terms from 1796), and member of Congress from 1811, until his death, September 24, 1815. His wife was Sarah Hawkins, whom he married in 1761.

* * * * * *

James Porteus above was probably a kinsman of the one of this name who was the first "Kings Attorney" of Frederick and the first to practice law west of the Blue Ridge. The attorney, like Sevier, was from London. He appears on the Orange records as early, at least, as June 28, 1739, when he moved the court to admit to record a deed from Beverly to William Smith. (Order Book 1739-1741, p. 4.) He and Gabriel Jones, William Russell, John Quinn, and Thomas Chew were the first to qualify for the practice of law in Augusta County. The first records of the county were largely penned by the hand of James Porteus. He died in 1751; on August 27th, his administrator was appointed. His last record was penned 26th, February, 1750, noting Charles Gallagher's appraisement by Jeremiah Harrison, Daniel Harrison and Robert Cravens. (*Chalkley*, Vol. III, pp. 22, 19.)

Among the early settlers in the region of the North Fork were the brothers John and Silas Hart. Thomas, another brother, settled in the lower Valley. All three are mentioned on the Orange records: "25th Sept. 1741, John Hart sworn under sheriff for the part of the county called Irish Tract." "25th March, 1742, Thomas Hart appointed Constable." "25th. Aug. 1743, Silas Hart appointed Adminstrator of his Brother and Next of Kin John Hart." "24th. Nov. 1743, Silas Hart appointed Under Sheriff." "24th. Feb. 1743, Deposition of Silas Hart aged about 24 years ....That he weigh some money for Robert Breckenridge, etc." (Orange Court Order Books 1741-43, pp. 24, 113; 1743-46, pp. 6, 29, and 55.) The Irish Tract was an alternate name for Beverly's Manor.

The Harts were from Bucks County, Pennsylvania. John and Eleanor (Crispin) Hart of this county had ten children, among whom were Joseph and Oliver and the three brothers above. Joseph (1715-1788), the eldest, was a prominent patriot of Bucks County during the Revolution. Thomas, the second son, m. Mary Combs at Philadelphia Monthly Meeting, in 1722. With other Bucks County Friends he settled on the Elk Branch of the Opequon, where he purchased 1,500 acres of land of Joist Hite in 1735. Oliver Hart, A. M., (1723-1795), entered the Baptist ministry in 1748, and from 1749 for over thirty years was pastor of the church at Charleston, South Carolina. He was a noted divine and the author of a number of religious works. During the Revolution he took an active part in the patriot cause. When Charleston was captured by the British in 1780 he returned to his birthplace, and later bcame pastor of the church at Hopewell, New Jersey, where he died, (*Bucks County Pioneers in the Valley of Virginia*, by S. Gordon Smyth; paper read at Friends Meeting House, Wrightstown, Pa., November 8, 1923.)

Silas Hart (b. May 5, 1718, d. October 29, 1795), in 1749 owned over 900 acres of land on the "South Fork of North River of Shenandore, James Wood's line." Some 800 acres of this was patented to John Smith, Gent. 25th June, 1747, 400 acres of which were sold by him and his wife Margaret to Silas Hart, mason, 5th June 1749. (Deed Book 2, p. 250; *Chalkley*, Vol. III, p. 274.) Hart was intimately acquainted with both the Smith and Harrison families and was early associated with them in many ways. He and Daniel Harrison were appointed by Capt. John Smith as the executor of his will, dated May 7, 1753. He was a witness to Robert Harrison's will, before noticed. His wife was Jane Robertson, (probably a widow before her marriage to him) whom he married in present Rockingham County, September 28, 1749. (See, *Waddell,* p. 292.) His widow married John Smith, a son of Col. Abraham Smith, and grandson of the Captain. Waddell states that she was Mary Jane Smith of a Culpeper family. (The early deeds show that his wife's name was Jane.) Hart was among the first settlers to locate within the later bounds of the Smiths and Linville's Creek Baptist Church and became an active member shortly after its organization. On April 21, 1749, he was one of the justices of Augusta court to whom Beverly deeded the twenty-five acres for the use of the county. (Deed Book 2, p. 246.) At the November term of court, 1764, he qualified as High Sheriff. On the 21st of this month, Daniel Harrison, John and Archibald Hopkins, and three others, furnished bond with him to collect the county taxes (Will Book III, p. 370.) When the first court of Rockingham County was organized he was the senior justice commissioned, and was accordingly appointed High Sheriff. He left no issue and by his will devised sufficient property to yield an annuity of fifty pounds to the Philadelphia Baptist Association. His executors refused to pay the Association on the ground that it was unincorporated. The case finally went to the United States Supreme Court, which decided that the Association could not receive under the will.

Of the little band of first members of the Linville Creek Baptist Church, it may be observed that at least John Alderson, Silas Hart, the Harrisons and the Lincolns, all trace back in ancestry to the eastern counties of England. Rev. Alderson was from Yorkshire. The Harts were of a family originating near Islip, in Oxfordshire. The Lincolns were of a Norfolk county family, and the Harrisons, through the Wrights and Townsends, also trace back to this county, and otherwise to Yorkshire. The Lincoln and Townsend emigrants were from the same town—Norwich.

John Hart, the immigrant, was of Whitney, Oxfordshire. He was a member of the Society of Friends, and reached Pennsylvania in 1682. After his settlement in Bucks County he became a Baptist. He married Susannah Rush, and died in 1714, aged 63, leaving, besides his widow, children John, Thomas, Josiah, and Mary. John (1684-1763), the eldest son, married Eleanor Crispin, (b. 1687), the daughter of Silas and Esther (Holme) Crispin, and had Silas, and the others above. John Rush the father of Susannah, was the ancestor of a noted Pennsylvania family, and was the great-grandfather of the celebrated Dr. Benjamin Rush, signer of the Declaration of Independence. John Rush is said to have been a Captain of Horse in the Cromwellian army. He married at Horton, Oxfordshire, Susannah Lucas, 1648. They emigrated to Pennsylvania in 1683. He joined the Quakers in 1660, but in 1691 forsook the faith and later became a Baptist. He died in 1698. His children were: William, John, Jane, and Susannah Rush. (See, *Bucks County Pioneers,* as above.)

The first "King's Attorney" of Augusta to become a resident of the county was Gabriel Jones. He succeeded John Nicholas in this office, May 1746, at the age of twenty-two. At this time he was living in Frederick, where he had succeeded Porteus in March, 1744. He was born near Williamsburg, the son of John and Elizabeth Jones, of North Wales. After his father's death his mother returned to England and resided in London where Gabriel was educated. On the completion of his schooling he returned to Virginia and settled in Frederick County. In 1751, he purchased a part of the original Jacob Stover tract on the South Fork, in present Rockingham, some eight or ten miles southeast of "Thomas Harrison's." To this point he removed by 1753. He was highly regarded by Lord Fairfax, who in his will, dated November 8, 1777, named him as one of his three executors. He proved this will May 5, 1782. Gabriel Jones, Thomas Lewis, and John Madison married Strother sisters. Each were members of the House of Burgesses at different times. All lived in the same neighborhood, and when Rockingham was formed became citizens of the new county. Jones was immediately appointed its first prosecuting attorney. He and Lewis were members of the State Convention for the adoption of the Federal Constitution. His son served as a Captain in the Revolution. Attorney Jones died in 1806. The old road from his home to "Thomas Harrison's" is still known as the "Lawyers' Road."

* * * * * *

The first term of Augusta court was principally concerned with the swearing in of officers, and in general with the routine of organization. At this term attorneys named all qualified and doubtless, judging from the bulk of early court orders and land records, soon found plenty of business on hand. From the day of organization until the county of Rockingham was formed the Harrisons are found continually transacting their legal affairs at this court. Here are recorded their voluminous deeds concerning land, here are their wills, and here are the records of their services to others—to their neighbors and their country. On the second day of the court, Thomas Harrison, Wm. Williams, Jeremiah Harrison, and Hugh Douglass, were appointed appraisers of John Levenson's estate. (Order Book No. I, p. 4.)

The year following the organization of the court, the first Vestrymen of Augusta Parish were elected, and representatives chosen for the House of Burgesses. It is thought that these events took place on the same day. The vestrymen elected were: Col. James Patton, (Col.) John Buchanan, John Madison, John Christian, Patrick Hays, (Mr.) John Buchanan, Robert Alexander, Thomas Gordon, James Lockart, John Archer, John Mathews, and John Smith. Their first meeting was held at the court house April 6, 1747, and John Madison was elected Clerk.

The first four named were members of the court. John Smith was the Captain of 1742. John Madison, the Clerk of the Court, and brother-in-law of Thomas Lewis and Gabriel Jones, was a cousin of Col. James Madison, of Orange—father of the later President. His son became the distinguished Rev. James Madison, D. D., the first Bishop of the Episcopal Church of Virginia. Patrick Hays proved his importation at Orange, May 22, 1740. (See p. 133.) Robert Alexander was the founder of the first classical school west of the Blue Ridge. This was opened in 1749 near where Old Providence Church now stands, a few miles southwest of Greenville. According to Campbell, Alexander is believed to have been educated in Edinburgh, Scotland. He emigrated to Pennsylvania in 1736, and to the Valley in 1745. Archibald, his brother, was an agent for Borden. John Mathews settled on Borden's grant about 1737. Withers, in his *Border Warfare,* states that five of his seven sons were at Braddock's defeat. His son George served under Washington at Brandywine, and Germantown, was Governor of Georgia, 1786 and 1797, and the first representative of the state in Congress. During the War of 1812, Gen. Mathews erected the first United States Flag in Florida.

Vacancies on the vestry were filled by the board. The minister of the Established Church was "ex-officio" president of the board. Two members were annually appointed to act as church wardens and to look after matters pertaining to religion and public morals. The vestrymen laid the levy for the general expenses of the church; they had care of the poor and attended to the "processioning" of lands. The minister was paid a fixed salary and given a farm—or glebe—and a parsonage for his use. Prior to 1784 only ministers authorized by the Established Church were permitted to perform the marriage ceremony. The register of marriages was kept by the vestry. The Rev. John Hindman appeared at the first vestry meeting with a recommendation from Governor Gooch and after some parley was engaged as "rector of the parish." The glebe was purchased later, and a plot laid off for a public burial ground. Rev. Hindman died in 1749, and was succeeded in 1752 by the Rev. John Jones, who served the parish for more than twenty years.

The first churches of Augusta were Presbyterian, and the vestrymen were largely of this faith. They appear to have been in no hurry to build a church for the Rev. Hindman. However, at a meeting of the vestry, 20th July, 1747, John Smith, Gent. and others were granted "leave to build a Chappel of Ease on Daniel Harrison's Plantation, provided it doth not affect the Parish now or hereafter." At this meeting arrangements were made "to purchase land for the Glebe convenient to the lands of Col. Patton near Leeper's Old Plantation, which is adjudged the most convenient place to build a church." Col. Patton agreed to give timber, stone and five acres convenient to a spring for the building of a parsonage to be finished by October, 1748. The dwelling was to be 32x18 feet, "with a partition staircase, a brick or stone chimney at each end, floored above and below." A stable 14x18 feet and a dairy ten feet square were also arranged for. Mr. Hindman was allowed twenty Pounds yearly for his board until the parsonage was completed. (Augusta Parish Vestry Book, p. 3; *Chalkley*, Vol. II, p. 432.)

This year the number of "tithables" of the county was 1,670, and the tax as levied by the vestry six shillings per head. In 1744 the number of tithables in Frederick was 1,283. The head of the Established Church in Virginia was the Rev. William Dawson, Commissary to the Bishop of London, and President of William and Mary College. He had succeeded the Rev. John Blair, the first to hold these offices, on the latter's death in 1743. Rev. Blair was President of William and Mary for fifty years. He was appointed Commissary in 1698. William Fairfax succeeded Dr. Blair as a member of the Governor's Council, November, 1743.

* * * * * *

The first churches organized in Augusta were those of Tinkling Spring and Old Stone Church. These were originally one congregation and in 1739 presented a call to Rev. John Thompson of the Presbytery of Donegal. He remained only a short time, and they next presented a call to Rev. John Craig who arrived in 1740. "February 22, 1740—John Craigg a presbyterian Minister in open court took the Oaths appointed by act of Parliament to be taken instead of the Oaths of Allegiance and Supremacy and the oaths of Abjuration and subscribed the test which is ordered to be certified." (Orange Court Order Book 1739-41, p. 311.) According to the register kept by Rev. Craig the first meeting at Tinkling Spring was held April 14, 1745, when the meeting house was "about half built." The corner stone of Old Stone Church was laid by Rev. Craig in August, 1747, and he preached in the present building for the first time January 22, 1749. Previous to this, there had been a log church on the site. On May 16, 1746, an entry was made in the county land records of "200 acres for ye Meeting house of ye Lower congregation, where it is now Built, including a spring adjoining Thomas Stephenson's land." (Entry Book p. 2.) With the exception of Tuscarora Meeting House, before mentioned, Old Stone Church is about the oldest building now standing in the Valley of Virginia. It is at Ft. Defiance, on "The Long Grey Trail," some fifteen miles south of Harrisonburg.

The pioneer minister kept an interesting list of baptisms during his pastorate. "A record of the names of the children baptized by the Rev. John Craig, both in his

Maxwell History & Genealogy by Florence Wilson Houston

own and neighboring congregations, where God in his Providence ordered his labours." This begins October 5, 1740 and ends September 28, 1749, during which time he baptized 463 males and 420 females. Outside the record of baptisms, other items are entered and altogether the book is said to contain 1,474 names. Some extracts from this book are given by Waddell, and a full list of the baptisms, may be found in Florence Wilson Houston's *Maxwell History and Genealogy*. Among those baptized within the time above were Jeremiah Harrison and two children, Lida Donnell and Nehemiah. Elizabeth Herison "an adult person," was baptized July 27, 1744, and Abigail Herrison, another "adult person,"January 21, 1747. *(Houston,* p. 584; *Waddell,* pp. 49-50.) See Maxwell History

In regard to the first churches in what is now Rockingham, Mr. Charles E. Kemper, in the *Virginia Historical Magazine* remarks: "The old Peaked Mountain Presbyterian Church, now Massanutten, is the oldest of all the various congregations in Rockingham County, Virginia. Rev. John Hindman preached there in 1742 and the congregation was organized in 1745. In 1747, he changed his church affiliations and became a Church of England minister, and in that year two chapels of the Established Church were built in present Rockingham County, one on the plantation of Daniel Harrison near the present town of Dayton and the other at Cross Keys about 200 yards east of the old Peaked Mountain Church. The records are clear in showing that the Presbyterian and Established (present Episcopal) Church were the first religious denominations definitely founded in the present County of Rockingham, Virginia." (Vol. 33, p. 76.) The old *Session Book of Cook's Creek and P'yked Mountain Congregation* containing the records of the church from 1759 to 1835 is yet in existence. This was the parent church of the later Harrisonburg and New Erection congregations. Many items in the old church book, including the dates of various baptisms, are given in the *Hopkins Genealogy* before referred to. (See p. 135.)

The above "chapels" appear to have been the first buildings of public worship erected in Augusta County for the use of the Established Church. In 1755 the vestry ordered that the "Rev. Mr. John Jones preach at James Neeley's on Roan Oke, at John Mathew's, Sr., in Forks of James, at Augusta Court House, at Captain Daniel Harrison's, and at any place contiguous to Mr. Madison's, at such times as he shall think proper." (Vesty Book, p. 165; *Chalkley,* Vol. II, p. 443.) Down until 1760 the vestry evidently made no effort to erect a church building. At a vestry meeting of November, 1758, James Lockhart moved to "lay a levy for building a church in the parish" but this was defeated. At a meeting in May, 1760, the vestry unanimously agreed to erect a church at Staunton on ground given by Beverly, April 3, 1750. A committee was appointed to contract for a brick building to be finished by December 1, 1762. This building was finished in 1763. Prior to the completion of this church, however, according to the Vestry book, 20th November, 1761, Thomas Harrison's (was) designated as a place of worship. (See p. 348; *Chalkley,* Vol. II, p. 448.)

* * * * * *

The long deferred line "between His Majesty, George II, and Lord Fairfax," was finally run in the fall of 1746, the year of the election of the first vestrymen of Augusta. The commissioners and surveyors of 1736 had located the head springs of the Rappahannock and Potomac rivers; their finding being finally approved by the Crown in 1745. The task of those of 1746 was to find the old terminals, and to place marks defining a straight line—some seventy-six miles in length and over the various mountains encountered—from one terminal to the other. Actually two lines near each other were run; one, a base or preliminary line, on the outgoing trip, the other, a straight or the true line, as a verification, on the return. From the data, plans were later drawn up establishing further detail points on the true line.

After about a week of preliminary surveying to locate the branch of the Conway previously marked, the line was started at the head of this river,—a branch of the Rapidan now dividing Madison and Greene counties—at a "Red oak & 5 Cotton trees," 110 poles east of the top of the Blue Ridge, on Thursday the 25th of September. On October 22nd following, according to Thomas Lewis, one of the surveyors, they "Dined on a Loyn Roasted Venison" and then "Drank his Majestys health" at the "Spring head" of the Potomac. The next day they planted there the "Fairfax Stone," thus marking the western terminal of the line. Today a large concrete monument erected by the United States Government stands on the spot. (See, *Bulletin* 689, *Department of Interior,* p. 125.) It was planted at the head of the North Fork of the Potomac, about 4,000 feet south of the present southwestern corner of Maryland. After elaborately marking the terminal the surveyors set out eastward the same day, and finally arrived back at the head of the Conway, November 13th. Here they came out below their starting point only about 100 yards. This, in the days before the telescopic transit, and under such conditions as were encountered in 1746!

The commissioners appointed by Governor Gooch to run the line were: Cols. Joshua Fry and Lunsford Lomax, and Major Peter Hedgman. Those representing Lord Fairfax were the same as in 1736. (See p. 141.) The entire outfit consisted of about forty men, and probably as many horses. The commissioners went by the easier routes, arranged for the supplies, the camps, the moving of the baggage, etc., leaving the surveyors to contend with the greater difficulties of the mountains. The surveyors employed were Robert Brooke, one of the "Knights of the Golden Horseshoe," and Col. Peter Jefferson, the father of the later President, for the Governor, and Thomas Lewis and Capt. Benjamin Winslow, for Lord Fairfax. Lewis was the Surveyor of Augusta County, then twenty-eight years old, (d. 1790). He kept an interesting journal of the survey.

Lewis's Journal starts with Wednesday, September 10, 1746; that being the dey he set out from home to join the Company at Capt. Downs' near Orange court. On their way westward the surveyors started their course N. 41-2/3 degrees W. They arrived at the South Fork of the Shenandoah on the 27th, and camped that night with the commissioners at "Loungs" (Long's.) The next day, Sunday, all continued in camp. There they took "ye varation of the Needle" and decided to correct their course to N. 43.5 degrees W. On Monday the commissioners with the horses and baggage crossed "Peaked Mountain," through "masenuten Gap," while the surveyors began at the "West Side of the Shenandoah River." That day they crossed the three ranges of the mountain encounterd—and between the second and third, a branch called "the fountain of life"—and finally, about dark, found their company camped at "Peter Shouls". Here the next morning Lewis bought a pair of shoes—"price 7 Sh." Continuing Tuesday from where they left off the evening before, 216 poles from this point they crossed Smiths Creek, and 213 poles further on, "ye Indian Road," and then 381 poles more, "ye North Br. of Shenando." Their total distance for the day was 1,600 poles, ending at a pine marked "21 miles". This day's work was done by Col. Jefferson and Capt. Winslow; Lewis and Booke having run the line over the mountain were in the meantime helping to move the camp. The company being misdirected they camped that night on the North Fork without finding their surveyors. The next morning they caught up with them at John Dobins, and Lewis resumed his survey. In the evening it rained, and after progressing 1,000 poles from the 21 mile mark the surveyors returned to the camp at Dobins'. The following day, Thursday, 620 poles from the 1,000 pole mark, they crossed the "head of Benj. Allens mill Creek." It had continued to rain, and Col. Fairfax returned home, being unable "to undergo the fautauge of Journey."

On the return trip their compass bearing was continually S. 46 degrees E. November 8th, they crossed the Indian Road, 487 poles from the North Fork, and after going 354 poles further ended their day's work on the eastern bank of Smiths Creek. "Went Down to Lockharts & Encampd here we had left Some Rum & Wine which Contributed to our Spending the Evining very Pleasantly Rejoycing we had Surmounted Somany Difficultys." The next day, Sunday, they continued at Lockhart's and on Monday Lewis and Jefferson began where they had left off at the creek the Saturday before. The same day they crossed the two ranges of the Massanutten here, and ended their day's work on the South Fork—about three miles below their first line. The others of the company went by way of Massanutten Gap, and all camped that and the succeeding night at Long's, where they had stopped on the way out. On arriving at their eastern terminal on Thursday the surveyors met there the Commissioners, who in the meantime had come from Long's the day before, and all assembled at their "old Camp." "Dined Drank his majesties & L. Fairfax heaths which was accompanyd with a Discharge of nine Guns to Each health."

The above distances show that the Indian Road was about where the Valley Pike is today. On their way out the surveyors crossed the country between Smiths Creek and the river at, or slightly north, of the present New Market. Benjamin Allen's Mill Creek is now Mill Creek; this flows into the North Fork at Mt. Jackson. On their return trip the distance given from the North Fork to Smiths Creek corresponds with that measured today on the Rockingham County line.

Lockhart appears to have lived on Smiths Creek south of Scholl. He was probably the vestryman.

Upon completing their survey the company gradually disbanded, and on the 17th, of November, Lewis left Capt. Downs', arriving home two days later. The surveyors agreed to meet at Col. Jefferson's on January 1st, following, to draw up their final plans or maps. Lewis arrived there on the 3rd, and after considerable delay awaiting the others all began work on the 24th, sending to Williamsburg for paper. By February 21st Lewis and Winslow completed seven plans of the Northern Neck on "Ld. Fairfax Account," according to their "Instructions from Col. Beverly by Capt. Winslow." (See, *The Fairfax Line, Thomas Lewis's Journal of* 1746, ed. by John W. Wayland.) Following the drawing up of the "plans," later in the year 1747, Lord Fairfax came over to Virginia to live, finally (1751) establishing his home at Greenway Court in Frederick County—now Clarke. To here about 1760, or after the death of William Fairfax, 1757, the office of the Proprietary was removed from Belvior.

On March 11, 1748, young George Washington, then only sixteen years of age, with George William Fairfax as his only companion, crossed the Blue Ridge to report himself to "His Lordship's Quarters over the Mountains." His engagement was, to use his own words, "to measure out plantations for Thomas Lord Fairfax, the reputed owner of the Northern Neck." His companion was his friend and former instructor in surveying, a son of William Fairfax above, who is said to have given him this his first remunerative employment. Young Washington kept a diary of his trip, *A Journal of my Journey over the Mountains*, long since published, in which he mentions many of the early settlers of Old Frederick, in the region in which his surveys were made

—along the Shenandoah and the South Branch of the Potomac. In a sense his career dates from his indentification with the county. In 1749 he was commissioned public surveyor by the President and Masters of William and Mary, and continued at this profession until 1751-2. His old offices, both at Greenway Court, and at Winchester, are yet standing. In his early military campaigns Winchester was largely used as a base, and there, in 1756, he built Ft. Loudoun. He was the county's representative in the House of Burgesses from 1758 to 1761.

* * * * * *

It was in the early days following the running of the Fairfax Line, and while young Washington was beginning his surveys in the lower county on the Shenandoah, that the final Harrison brother makes his first appearance on the records of Old Augusta. This was Isaiah Harrison, Jr., who has been mentioned as the last brother to arrive in the Valley. He was the eldest of the family.

Continuing the genealogy noted at the beginnig of the last chapter (see pages 122); of the children of Isaiah Harrison, and his wife Elizabeth:

(11) ISAIAH HARRISON, Jr., born at Oyster Bay, Long Island, September 27, 1689, appears to have been living in the southern part of West Jersey, across the river from Delaware, in 1737. (See page 129.) That he removed from Long Island to Delaware with his father in 1721 is indicated by the elder being styled "Senior" in the deed releasing his final tract on Long Island, April 28, 1722. (See page 40.) Isaiah, Jr., has been identified as the brother who removed south, as embraced in the accounts given on pages ten, and twenty-six.

According to the first will book of Augusta County, page 78, on the 18th May, 1748, Isaiah Harrison qualified as administrator of Joseph Harrison, with Jeremiah Harrison and William White as his sureties. An appraisment of Joseph's estate was made on the 27th of July, the same year, by Samuel Wilkins, William McGill, and David Logan. On September 1st, following, a "vendue" of the goods of Joseph was held at the house of Samuel Stewart by Jeremiah Harrison. Among those who bought part of his effects were Samuel Harrison, Arthur Johnson, Abraham Smith, and Ephraim Love. (Will Book I, pp. 84 and 208.) Finally under date of 23rd May, 1750—Order Book No. II, .p 365—is recorded; "Isaiah Harrison admr. of Joseph Harrison (has) removed to Carolina." (*Chalkley*, Vol. I, p. 40.)

Only a fleeting glimpse is thus given of Isaiah, Jr. Later his brother Samuel also "removed to Carolina," settling in Craven County, where he remained for a short time before he returned to Augusta; hence, it is presumed that Isaiah, Jr., had located there, (Old Craven County, South Carolina.) Nothing is known of his family, or of the date of his death. Joseph Harrison above was probably his son.

Isaiah, Jr. was one of the vanguard in the great stream of migration that had started to flow from the northern and eastern colonies to the southern and western parts of the new world. The annals of Old Augusta bear mute witness that this stream early flowed through the Valley of the Shenandoah. The migration of Isaiah, Jr., was a little later to be followed by the numerous descendants of his brothers and sisters to pioneer homes in the South and West. Many whose fathers had passed by "The Long Grey Trail" died on other frontiers far removed from the secenes of their childhood —the spirit of Isaiah Harrison, Sr., the Oyster Bay immigrant, was marching on:

> "*O to die advancing on!*
> *Are there some of us to droop and die? has the hour come?*
> *Then upon the march we fittest die, soon and sure the gap is fill'd,*
> *Pioneers! O pioneers!*"
>
> —Walt Whitman.

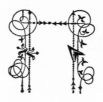

CHAPTER XI

John Harrison of the Old Linville Creek Baptist Church and His Family

THE PIONEER PERIOD

JOHN HARRISSON, (1691-1771), for so he spelled his name, the son of Isaiah Harrison and wife Elizabeth (Wright), was born at "Suckscall's Wigwam," Oyster Bay, Long Island, in the Province of New York, according to the ancient Town Book "B," fol. 19a, "the 25th Day of September Annoq Domini 1691," and died testate, May (?), 1771, in what is now Rockingham County, Virginia. (See pages 21, 23, and 123.) His will, dated July 30, 1769, and proven May 21, 1771, recorded in Augusta County Will Book No. 4, page 398, at Staunton, Virginia, reads as follows:

IN THE NAME OF GOD AMEN—written the 30th day of July 1769 in the year of our Lord God one thousand seven hundred and Sixty Nine

I John Harrison of Augusta County and Colony of Virginia—Cordwinder being of Perfect Mind and Memory & no disorder but that of old age thanks be given unto God for his Mercy and therefore Calling unto mind the Mortality of my body and knowing that it is Appointed unto all men once to dye do make Ordain this my last Will & testament in writing that is to say

Principally and first of all I recommend my soul into the hands of God that who gave it and as for my Body I recommend to the earth to be buried in a Christian like and desant Manner at the discretion of my executors nothing doubting but at the General resurrection I shall receive the same again by the Mighty power of God and as touching such Worldly estate wherewith it hath Pleased God to bless me in this life I give devise and dispose of the same in the following manner and form

imprimiss it is my Will & I ordain in the first Place that my well beloved Wife Phebe Harrison enjoy my Plantation on which I now dwell without Disturbance during her natural life together with my Movable estate and with my slaves and increase of them to worke for her Maintainence during her Natural life

and it is further my Will and I do order my land whereon I now dwell being a part of two surveys which has been divided I do Leave my well beloved son Zebulon Harrison his heirs and Assigns forever

and further my survey which is also Pattained known by the name of the long Meadow which is Part thereof and is described in the Pattain I give my son Reuben Harrison and his heirs and assigns forever

which land above named shall be freely Posessed and enjoyed by my above named sons and their heirs after their above named Mother decease and not before

I furthermore I will that after her decease all my Movable estate be apraised and sold According to law except my negro wench Jenny if my daughter Phebe Moore shall see cause to take her at the Praisment for so much of her shire of my estate as she shall be Appraised to if it shall amount to More than her shire she shall pay the overplus to the other heirs and if she does not see Cause to take her she shall be sold with the rest of my Slaves in being

in the first Part the half of my Movable estate is to be equally divided between

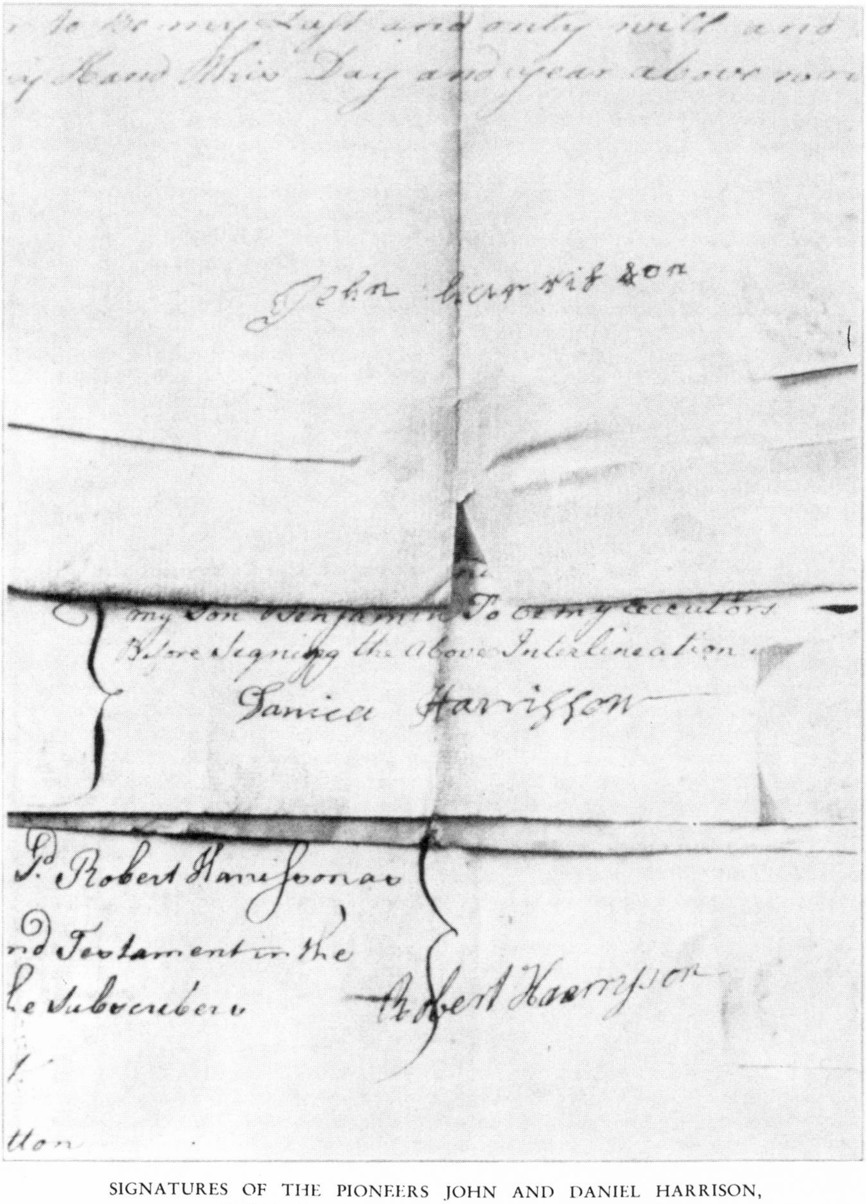

SIGNATURES OF THE PIONEERS JOHN AND DANIEL HARRISON,
and of the latter's son Robert, to their respective wills.
See pages 157, 192, and 193.

Zebulon Harrison and Phebe Moore and the other half of my Movable Estate to Reuben Harrison and for my Daughter Ann Langdon I leave her one shilling Starling

and I do make Constitute and ordain my well Beloved sons Zebulon Harrison and Reuben Harrison that is above mentioned my sole Executors of this my last will and testament

and I furthermore ordain my said Executors that they provide a Baptist Minister if they can so do with Conveniency to Preach my Funeral Sarment if noon of them is to be had that then they Provide some other Christian Minister for it as Proposed for that Service to pay him twenty Shillings

I furthermore order that they Pay all my Just debts and funeral Charges out of my movables and such Charges shall be levied before such estate suffers division as aforesaid

and I do hereby disalow revoke & disanul all and every other and former wills Legaisse & Executors by me before this time named willed Bequeathed Ratifing & Confirming this & no other to be my last and only will and testament

In Witness whereof I have set my hand this day & year above written.

John harrisson. (Seal.)

Felix Sheltman
John Ray
John Harrisson, Junior.

"At a Court held for Augusta County May 21, 1771 the last Will and Testament of John Harrison was Proved by the oaths of John Ray and John Harrison, Junior two of the witnesses thereto and ordered to be recorded" . . . . etc. Reuben and Zebulon Harrison qualified as executors.

As copied in the will book the Harrison signatures are given with only one "S" However, the original will is also on record at Staunton, and in this both John and his witness John, Jr., signed as above, using the double"S", one letter being the old style long "S". Daniel Harrison, John's brother, in his signature, also spelled his name thus, as so did his sons Robert and Benjamin. In the first census of the United States the double "S" is used in giving the names of various Rockingham Harrisons, among them being Zebulon, the son of John above, and the father of John Jr. the witness.

The body of the original will is in a different handwriting than that of the signer. The seal was applied in the same manner as that of Daniel's before described. (See page 67.) It bears no discernible figure, and is slightly larger than that of Daniel's, the circular disk being about the size of our modern "Buffalo nickle." John's signature is very similar in handwriting to that of his brother's, showing a much feebler hand, however.

John Harrison, Jr., the son of John, is not mentioned in his father's will, as prior to this time he had been killed. He also left a will. This was signed August 23, 1758, and proven November 16, 1763, as given below:

Will of John Harrison, Jr.

IN THE NAME OF GOD AMEN—the twenty third day of August in the year of our Lord one Thousand Seven hundred & fifty Eight I John Harrison Junior of Augusta County and Colony of Virginia, Yeoman—Being in Good Health and of perfect mind and Memory thanks be given unto God for his mercy Therefore Calling unto Mind the Mortality of my Body & Knowing it is appointed for all men once to Die do therefore make and ordain this my last will & Testament in writing That is to say

Principally and first of all I reccommend my Soul into the hands of God that gave it and my body to the Earth to be buried in a Christian and Decent manner at the Discretion of my Executors hoping at the General Resurrection when all that sleeps in Jesus Shall arise I shall Receive the Same again by the Mighty power of God and as touching such worldly Estate wherewith it Hath pleased God to Bless me with in this Life I give Devise & Dispose of the same in the following manner & form

Item I Give & bequeath unto my well beloved brother Zebulon Harrison Eldest Son John Harrison one certain tract of Land Lying and being in Augusta County on Smiths Creek Containing four hundred acres

and to Phel Harrison Eldest Dafter of Zebulon Harrison I give & bequeath Two tracts of Land lying and being in Augusta County on Smiths Creek one containing an hundred & Seventy five acres and the other Containing Seventy acres

Item I give unto my well beloved Sister Phebe moore the Sum of thirty pounds Current and Lawful money of Virginia to be paid out of my movable Estate within two years after my Decease

and to her Daughter Ann Davison I give an certain tract of Land Containing four hundred acres Lying and being on the dry fork a branch of Smiths Creek

and to her Daughter Phebe Davison I give and bequeath one certain tract of Land Lying and being between dry fork and Smiths Creek containing two hundred acres.

Item I give and Bequeath unto my Brothers Zebulon Harrison & Reuben Harrison all my other Estate Lands and movable Estate

I do hereby make Constitute and ordain my Brothers Zebulon Harrison and Reuben Harrison my only and sole Exters of this my last will and Testament

I order that my Brothers Zebulon Harrison and Reuben Harrison do make Equal Division of the Same Between themselves Quantity & Quality alike

and I do hereby utterly Dissalow Revoke & Dissanul all and every other former Testament & Legacies

In witness whereof I hereunto set my hand and Seal the Day and year above written

Signed Sealed in the presence of us the Subscribers

Jonathan Douglass John (SEAL) Harrison.
John Hopkins
James Breane

"Proved in a court for Augusta County November 15, 1763, by John Hopkins, November 16, 1763, by Jonathan Douglass. Reuben & Zebulon Harrison with Daniel Love and Robert Cravens their sureties entered into and acknowledged their Bond according to Law." (See, Augusta County Will Book No. 3, p. 296, at Staunton, Virginia—original will also on record.)

John Harrison, Sr. in his will styled himself a "cordwinder." This, it will be recalled, is the term by which he identified himself in his bond to John Sullovant, April 12, 1737, when disposing of his land in Sussex, Delaware. (See page 56.) In his younger days he had evidently been taught the trade of a *cordwainer,* or maker of high grade footwear—boots and shoes, such as were worn by military officers and others among the gentry. Cordwain was the term applied to Spanish shoe leather; this was considered the best to be had. In the Coat of Arms used by the old Cordwainers' Guild of London, which came to be a very influential organization, three goat heads "erased" were emblazoned on the shield, thus probably cordwain was tanned from goat hides. John Harrison's grandfather, Gideon Wright, was by occupation a shoemaker, as well as a farmer, and doubtless John had been taught the trade by one of his mother's family.

Those who had been brought up in mechanical trades were proud of their special pursuits, and were generally careful to refer to them in their legal documents. Such reference indicated that the individual had been well reared. It was customary in the best of families, where funds were not sufficient to establish the sons in a profession, to apprentice them in trade. Frequently in the early deeds the same man is found referred to at one place as a "carpenter," or "mason," etc., and in another as a "gentleman." An instance of this occurs in the Augusta records in deeds relating to Silas Hart. Bruce, in his *Social Life of Virginia in the 17th Century*, relates that Major William Barber,who had charge of building the capitol at Williamsburg, in some deeds described himself as a "cooper," and in others as a "carpenter," yet he was a member of the House of Burgesses, and the son-in-law of Henry Cary, who was always designated as a "gentleman." In his first deeds John Harrison's father, the Oyster Bay immigrant, is mentioned as a "blacksmith," and in later records as variously, "freeholder," "proprietor", "husbandman," "yeoman," "blacksmith," and "Mr."—the last two terms being used in the same deed. (See page 43.) According to Bruce, the word "Mister" when used in the older legal documents denoted one whose claim to be a gentleman in the broad social sense was admitted by all. (p. 115.)

John Harrison, Jr. in his will described himself as a "yeoman." This designation frequently occurs in the colonial records, and in early times it too was employed with discrimination. Originally a yeoman meant a freeman owning sufficient land to qualify him to serve on juries, to vote for the knight of the shire, etc. As the required amount of land was not large the term was applied in general to small land owners, but in the Colonies it came to designate an agriculturest, or farmer, without special significance as to the size of his lands. In a deed of about 1649, Robert Beverly—a kinsman of Col. William, before mentioned— one of the largest landowners of Virginia, described himself as a yeoman. Of all the Augusta Harrisons, John, Jr. was the largest, or next to the largest landowner. His patents alone totaled nearly 3,500 acres. In the early deeds of Augusta, Thomas Harrison, John Sr's. brother, is first mentioned as a "yeoman" and later as "farmer," thus by this time the terms were synonymous here. Daniel, another brother, in his first deeds was also styled "yeoman," later in Augusta, he frequently appears on the records as "Gent," or gentleman. Such too is the case in regard to Robert Cravens.

The boyhood of John Harrison Sr. was passed at Oyster Bay until he was eleven years old, when his father removed to Smithtown, Long Island. When he was about seven years of age his mother died, and a few years later, while still living at Oyster Bay, his father married a second time. Their new home was on the western bank of the beautiful Nissequogue river, where the boy grew to manhood. In 1721 the elder Harrison removed to Delaware; thus John and his full brothers and sisters came of age while the family was on Long Island.

As Smithtown was only a short distance from Oyster Bay, no doubt John frequently returned to his birthplace during his youth to visit his mother's people, and there are many indications that he was attached to them by tender ties. On December 2nd, 1729, or some eight years after his father's removal to Delaware, he bought land near Maiden Plantation, his father's home, and settled on Broad Creek in the same county. Close by his brother Gideon had also previously located, in 1722.

Phoebe Harrison, the wife of John, was about five years his senior. Three, at least, of their children were born before he purchased his land in Delaware. Phoebe was a popular name among the Townsend and other Oyster Bay families of the time, but it is not known what her maiden name was.

The Harrisons located in Delaware about eight miles west of Lewes, which at the time was one of the ports of entry for immigrants to Pennsylvania. When a little later the Valley of Virginia migration set in from the Quaker Province, doubtless the news quickly spread to the "three lower counties on the Delaware," inducing various of those who had passed through the old port to later find their way to the western frontier of Virginia. On April 12, 1737, John Harrison entered into bond to dispose of his Delaware home, and on October 4th, of the same year, completed the sale by signing the deed to his land. With his father and brothers in a party of sixteen, as elsewhere related, he removed with his family, a pioneer to the Valley of the Shenandoah.

Many events of John's life and various circumstances regarding this move have already been touched on. It is a curious fact, but all of the traditions relating to the origin of the Harrisons of Rockingham seem to have been preserved through this branch of the family, particularly through John's daughter Phoebe, and his son Reuben. Among the latter's grandchildren, John Harrison, who died in 1880, in his eightieth year, is said to have been especially well versed in the history of the family. The late Mr. John Harrison, a son of this John, and a brother of Elizabeth, earlier quoted, (page 9), recalled his father stating that the Harrisons came immediately to the Valley from one of the smaller provinces on the Deleware, and thought that Delaware was the province named. Out of the distant past this appears to be the only recollection late in the family of the old days in Sussex County. While all of the pioneer Harrisons, but Isaiah, Jr., came in from Delaware, likely New Jersey may have been also included in John Harrison's account, owing to the eldest brother's removal from this colony.

John Harrison, the pioneer, made his final settlement at the Great Spring, on the old Indian trail. Today this point is known as Lacy Spring, in Rockingham County, Virginia. His house is said to have stood on the little knoll overlooking the spiring, which rises immediately to the north or west of it, and over which the Valley Pike now runs (the house being just to the east of the pike and about in front of the present building, lately known as Rinehart's store.) A short distance to the east of the spring is an old mill site on Smiths Creek, and in the meadow opposite the mill race, and between the race and creek, was located on the western bank of the latter, the family burial ground, traces of which remain to this day.

In the neighborhood to the south and west of John Harrison were settled his half brothers, Thomas, at present Harrisonburg, Capt. Daniel, at present Dayton, Jeremiah, in the region between Thomas and Daniel, and Samuel at what is now Linville. Near Thomas was also settled Robert Cravens, who had married Mary Harrison, John's full sister, and near Daniel was Alexander Herron, who married John's half sister Abigail. In this section too, there settled for a short time before his removal to Carolina, Isaiah Harrison, Jr., the eldest of the family, and the only full brother of John then living.

Owing to the practically uninhabited condition of the country at the time of their settlement, as shown by the early and numerous dates of their land patents, it was several years after their arrival in the neighborhood before they made effort to establish formal titles to their lands. John's first survey is dated November 12, 1740. The first reference found on the Court Order books at Orange to John, or any of his family, is that pertaining to his suit vs. Robert Luney (Looney), at July court in 1741, in regard to "one long Gun." By 1742 John, Sr., and his sons John, Jr. and Zebulon, were members of Peter Scholl's militia company on Smiths Creek.

With Orange court having jurisdiction at this time over the region West of the Great Mountains, the seat of the court was very much detached from the settlers on the

Shenandoah. The organization of the militia was one of the first events to take place in establishing the local government. On February 24, 1742, John Harrison was commissioned "Lieutenant."

In the John Harrison branch of the family John Harrison, Junior, appears the first to patent land. Oddly enough this first patent was for a tract on a "branch of the James River." The date was February 12, 1742, and the land embraced 366 acres on "Luney's Mill Creek." This patent was granted only a few days before the elder John was commissioned Lieutenant.

Several references concerning this land appear under the County Court Judgements of Augusta. Harrison sold the land to one James Louderdale or Lidderdale, who gave bond, 2nd February, 1744-5. In the subsequent litigation, September 1747, Harrison brought suit for debt, the writ being dated 23rd June, previously. At this time the defendant was living on the James River. In August 1749, Harrison again brought suit in which a writ of 20th February, 1747, is mentioned. Later, in November, 1756, in the suit of Lidderdale vs. John Harrison, Jr., it is stated that the former bought land of John on the "South Branch of James River" in March 1744-5. John, Jr. finally gave "Letherdale" a deed for land in 1749, and another on August 28, 1750. (See, *Chalkley,* Vol. I, pp. 297, 301, 315, and Augusta County Deed Book No. 2, pp. 287, 868, and 871.)

Manifestly the James River patent was merely a speculative venture on the part of John Harrison, Jr. Looney's Mill Creek was probably named for Robert Looney, the defendant in the suit regarding the gun. The creek is in the region now between Buchanan and Roanoke, and is bordered for a part of its distance by the Lee Highway. It was somewhat south of Borden's territory, and was thus not within his grant.

Borden had land on Smiths Creek at the time of his death in 1743, and John Harrison, Jr. was the first of the Harrisons to patent land on the creek, but his uncle Daniel had preceeded him on the Dry Fork in 1741. The first Smith Creek patents were two granted to John Harrison, Jr., still in existance, and written on parchment, under date of 25th September, 1746.

On the whole John Harrison, Sr. and his sons were granted twenty-three, or more, patents covering about 5,000 acres of Valley lands distributed as follows—

To JOHN HARRISON, JR.

Date		Acres		Book No.	Pages
12th. Feb. ,	1742,	366	"on a branch of James River called Luney's Mill Creek"	20	164
25th. Sept. ,	1746,	175	"on Smith's Creek"	24	415
" "	"	350	"on South Side of Woods River and north Side of North Fork of Naked Creek"	24	416
" "	"	400	"on Smith's Creek"	24	417
" "	"	400	"on a Branch of Woods River called Meadow Creek"	24	418
" "	"	241	"on a branch of James River at the east end of Short Hill"	24	419
10th. Feb. ,	1748,	200	on a draft of Smith's Creek"	27	110
" "	"	400	"on the Dry Fork of Smith's Creek"	XIII	495
10th. July ,	1755,	175	"on Smith's Creek"	XVIII	417
" "	"	70	"on Smith's Creek"	XVIII	417
10th. Sept. ,	1755,	272	"on both sides of Cook's Creek"	32	642

10th Sept.,	1755,	400	"on a branch of the South Branch of Potomac called West Fork of Mill Creek"	32	643
TOTAL		3,449	acres		

To JOHN HARRISON, SR.

25th. June ,	1747,	234	"on Smith's Creek"	XII	426
" "	"	166	"on Smith's Creek"	XII	426
10th. Feb. ,	1748,	400	"on the Dry Fork a branch of Smith's Creek"	27	125
20th. Sept. ,	1751,	19	"on the Head Spring of the Long Meadow"	31	25
26th. July	,1765,	18	(sold by executors)	XVII	187
TOTAL		837	acres		

To ZEBULON HARRISON

10th. Feb. ,	1748,	165	"on Smith's Creek"	27	123
12th. May ,	1770,	169	"on both sides of Smith's Creek"	39	50
16th. Feb. ,	1771,	84	"on Smith's Creek"	39	303
TOTAL		418	acres		

To REUBEN HARRISON

10th. Feb. ,	1748,	233	"on the Dry Fork of Smith's Creek adjoining John Harrison survey"	27	126
14th. July ,	1769,	48	"on the branches of Smith's Creek"	38	750
12th. May ,	1770,	20	"on the Dry Fork a branch of Smith's Creek"	38	901
TOTAL		301	acres		

(See, Patent Books, numbered as above, except Roman numerals, Land Office, at Richmond, Virginia. Roman numerals refer to Augusta County Deed Books.)

At the time of the settlement of the family, the country was a lonely wilderness. The hardships endured, and the difficulties encountered, have been graphically described by Campbell, but half will never be told. Only the rudest of log cabins were at first constructed. While wild game was plentiful the problem of obtaining other food by tilling the soil must have been solved by slow laborious effort. According to Mrs. Dandridge, in her *Historic Shepherdstown*, the Valley at this time was not one unbroken primeval forest. In their great annual hunts the Indians had burned over large areas of land, thus there were large prairies interspersed between the woodlands, where the grass is said to have been so tall that a man passing through it on horseback could tie it across his saddle-bow. These were fat pasture lands on which the early settlers raised quantities of horses and hogs, without the trouble of planting timothy or clover for their use.

Roads at this time were of course unknown. The location and laying out of the Indian Road, the first highway up the Valley, has been described. This occurred in 1745, and before the erection of Augusta court. As the name indicated, this first road followed the old Indian trail. Today its route closely approximates the Valley Turnpike. For the section traversing present Rockingham, John, and Capt. Daniel Harrison, and Robert Cravens, were among the overseers appointed to begin this historic thoroughfare. At the time John had not yet patented his land, but had located on the old trail. A few miles further south Daniel had patented land along its route at what is now Smithland, and Thomas, at present Harrisonburg. Robert Cravens too was on or near the old trail somewhat south of the last named point. Daniel's land on Naked Creek, yet further to the south, was also near The Long Grey Trail, as it runs today.

Following the organization of Augusta court, in 1745, the next year the Fairfax Line was run. The running of this line permanently established that the later Rockingham territory was outside the Northern Neck, and therefore entirely subject to the jurisdiction of Governor Gooch in the matter of issuing patents to land. On the very day that the survey of the Fairfax Line was started the first Smiths Creek patents were granted to the Harrisons for land a few miles south of the line. These were the two to John Harrison, Jr. Down to this time the Harrisons had taken out only seven patents, but from now on their acquisition of lands went rapidly ahead. As John Harrison Sr., and his sons, were in the region nearest to the line, they particularly had evidently been considerably in doubt as to the final outcome.

Some idea of the names of the various early landowners, and of the numerous Harrison tracts in the neighborhood, just south of the line in 1747, is given by the old Augusta Parish Vestry Book, in the processioners list therein contained. This year the first Vestry met, and as before stated, one of its duties was to attend to the processioning of lands. The boundary lines of the early tracts owned by the settlers were more or less temporarily marked, or ill defined, and the processioners were appointed by the Vestry to preserve the lines, and to settle disputes in connection therewith. The law required that every four years the boundaries of each person be marked. Among the processioners appointed 3rd September, 1747, were Robert Cravens and Thomas Harrison, "from Samuel Wilkins' to the lower end of the Great Plain to Fairfax line, thence with said line to the South Mountain; Daniel Harrison and Morgan Bryan, from Samuel Wilkins to the great Plain to Lord Fairfax's line, thence with the said line to Henry Smith's.

On the 8th of March, following, Daniel Harrison and Morgan Bryan, in brief, reported; "Processioned for Samuel Harrison, present Daniel Love, John Wright. Processioned for Robert Cravens, present Daniel Love, John Wright; processioned for Daniel Harrison, present John Rutlege, Richard Wainscot; Daniel Harrison not processioned, there being a dispute; processioned for James Anderson, lines unknown; processioned for Col. James Wood; processioned for Daniel Harrison, present Archibald Hopkins; processioned for Daniel Harrison, present Jacob Dye, Richard Wincot; . . . . processioned for Thomas Moore, present Francis Hughs; processioned for John Miller, present Thomas Hughes, Thomas Moore; processioned for Thomas Moore, present Francis Hughes; . . . processioned for Jacob Chrisman, present David Stuart, Sam'l Harrison; processioned for Robert McKay, present Thomas Bryan," etc.

Thomas Harrison and Robert Cravens made their returns, also at the same time. "Processioned for Daniel Harrison, present Daniel Harrison; processioned for Robert Harrison, present Daniel Harrison; Pocessioned for Robert Cravens, present Daniel Harrison; processioned for John Harrison, present Zebulon Harrison; . . . processioned for John Harrison, Jr., present John Harrison; processioned for John Harrison, Jr., present John Harrison; processioned for Thomas Harrison, Samuel Minefee; processioned for Thomas Harrison, present Samuel Minefee; processioned for Thomas Harrison, present Samuel Minefee; . . . . Henry Downs not processioned; Valetine Sevier not processioned. (See, Augusta Parish Vestry Book, pp. 4, 19, and 23; *Chalkley*, Vol. II, p. 435.)

John Harrison, Jr. never married. He is said to have settled at Flook's Spring, in the neighborhood to the south of his father. Some of his land on Smiths Creek adjoined the latter, some adjoined Valentine Sevier, and some joined Benjamin Borden, Jr. In the Land Entry Book No. I, of Augusta County entries were made May 20, 1748, to Valentine Sevier, for 400 acres on Smiths Creek, and to John Harrison, Jr., for 400 acres adjoining this, and for 400 acres joining Borden. On May 20, 1749, two entries were made to John (Jr.); "400 (acres) on Smith's Creek, between his land and John Davis, and 200 acres, between his own and his father's land, on Smith Creek." (*Chalkley*, Vol. II, pp. 379, 383.)

The will of John Harrison, Jr., mentions his brothers Zebulon and Reuben, Zebulon being named as the eldest son of John, Sr., his father. In the old tradition, before quoted, it is stated that Reuben Harrison was engaged to marry a lady on Long Island at the time of his removal to the Valley of Virginia, but that finding frontier life in such striking contrast to her more luxurious surroundings, he concluded he would be asking too much of her to give up her style of living, and instead, later married his first cousin Lydia Harrison, from the Potomac River. This account is obviously mixed in several details. Reuben was born in 1731, while his father was living in Delaware, and thus was only about six years old when the family removed to Virginia. There is no evidence found whatever that any of his father's brothers ever lived on the Potomac River. Jeremiah Harrison, as recorded by the Rev. John Craig of the Old Stone Church, had a daughter "Lida Donnell," whom the Rev. Craig baptized, about 1744. She was Reuben's half first cousin, and doubtless his future wife.

Zebulon Harrison, Reuben's brother, however, did return north for a wife, and as he married his first cousin, the tradition is explained as a distorted account of this, and the above. Zebulon was old enough to belong to Capt. Peter Scholl's military company in 1742. According to the list of marriages as given in the *History of the First Presbyterian Church of Morristown, New Jersey*—published by the church— "Zebulon Harrison of Augusta County, Virginia, married (there) 23rd July, 1747, Margaret Primrose." (See pp. 7, 100, and 196.) The pastor was Rev. Timothy Jones, the first minister of the church, who began his services August 13, 1742. Boogher, in his *Gleanings of Virginia History*, states that Margaret Cravens, the daughter of Robert, married "her Cousin Zebulon Harrison." (see p. 379) and this is confirmed by Robert's will, dated October 2, 1761, in which he mentions his daughter Margaret Harrison, and grand-children, Zebulon and Robert Harrison. Margaret had evidently married a Primrose as her first husband. The year following Zebulon's marriage he was granted his first land patent, and settled on Smiths Creek a little north of his father.

Besides being infested by roving bands of Indians at this time, the country was occasionally subjected to the excursions of white outlaws bent on robbery. In 1749 the Harrisons on Smiths Creek were attacked by a party of outlaws, under one Ute Perkins. In the tradition regarding this, it is stated that the robbers came in from Alexandria, Virginia and that they attacked first John Harrison, Jr. He was seized on what is now the Keezeltown road, robbed, and carried back to his house at Flook's Spring. There he was bound while the robbers ransacked the place. As they were doing this, he overheard one of them remark that they next intended to proceed to the home of his father, a few miles further down the creek. Upon their leaving, he quickly mounted a fleet horse, and rode to the Big Spring, giving the alarm to his father, and to his brother Reuben. When the outlaws arrived they were met by a spirited defence of the elder John's home, in which one of them was killed, another mortally wounded, and the rest dispersed. The old account continues that John, Jr., rode to Winchester for a doctor, for the wounded robber. The man dying, the bodies of both he and his companion were buried, by the two brothers, in a large sink-hole just over the brow of the hill, to the north of present Lacy Spring. This natural decavity is within sight of and slightly to the east of the Valley Pike. A further detail related is that on examining the body of the robber killed outright, a bottle of whiskey was discovered, whereupon John is said to have exclaimed to his brother, "By faith, Reuben, let us have a drahm!"

Among the original petitions and papers filed in the County Court of Augusta in 1749, is the following—"To ye worshipful his majesties' justices in Court sitting. The petition of John Harrison humbly prayeth that your worships will please to take into consideration the following account for as much as the goodness of God (delivered?) unto my hands those that sought my life and my . . . goods and whereas I thought it my duty to act toward my fellow creatures as such and not as if ye were altogether brutes and I have been at this charge following which I humbly pray that your worships shall please to allow and your petitioner as in duty bound shall pray, etc. The chargs of burying ye robbers £2, 0, 0. Three shillings for ye man I sent for ye surgeon £0, 3, 0. To ye surgeon £0, 15, 0. By me, John Harrison, Jr."

According to Augusta Court Order Book No. II, (p. 522), February 27, 1750, "John Harrison's petition to be reimbursed out of the estate of William Young, who was killed in attempting to rob John Harrison, granted." Also, Order Book No. III, (p. 241), February 19, 1751-2, "Petition of John and Reubin Harrison for reward for killing 2 persons under Ute Perkins; certified to Genl. Assy." The real name of Ute Perkins was James Anderson, as appears in an action brought in August, 1749, by Col. James Patton against Rev. John Hindman, the first minister of the Established Church. "In 1747 defendant married James Anderson (Alias Ute Perkins) and Elizabeth Skeleron, widow and relict of William Skeleron, late of Augusta, without license." *(Chalkley,* Vol. I. pp. 435, 43, 50, and 302.)

Phoebe Davison Moore, the daughter of John Harrison, Sr., is named in the wills of both her father, and of her brother John, Jr. Her daughters, Ann and Phoebe Davison, are also mentioned in her brother's will. Her first husband, Daniel Davison, died about 1750. On the 26th of February, 1750-51, "Phoebe Davison relict of Daniel Davison," petitioned to administer on her husband's estate. (See, Originial Petitions filed in County Court.) This petition was granted as the next day, according to Will Book No. I (p. 288), she gave bond as administratrix "of Daniel Davison, with sureties John Harrison, (and) Samuel Newman." Besides the two daughters, she also had a son, Josiah, by her first marriage; Order Book, VII, (p. 6), 19th May, 1761, "Josiah Davidson, orphan of Daniel Davidson, aged 16 years, chose John Harrison his guardian;" Will Book III, (p. 235), same date, "John Harrison, Jr's bond (with Thomas Moore) as guardian (chosen) to Josiah Davison, orphan of Daniel Davison." Phoebe Harrison Davison and Thomas Moore were married between 1751 and 1755; "Judgements at Rules (C) May, 1755, Thomas Moore and Phebe his wife, vs. Abraham Smith and Gabriel Pickens,—Phebe, late Phebe Davison, (and) 'Phebe Davison spinster., Bond dated 1751." Also, Order Book X, (p. 328), August 26, 1766, "Phebe Moore, wife of Thomas Moore, late wife of Daniel Davidson, assigned dower." (See, *Chalkley,* Vol. I, pp. 435, 90, 312, 130; Vol. III, pp. 19, 77.)

At the time of her father's removal to Augusta, Phoebe was about nine years old. She has been identified as the baby, on the voyage of the family to Delaware, associated with the tradition of the so carefully preserved old heirloom—"the big bellied bottle," which descended to her daughter, Phoebe Ewing. Her marriage to Daniel Davison occured about 1745, and after his removal to the Valley from New Jersey. It will be recalled that Davison settled on Smiths Creek, near the old Indian Road, and a few miles north of his father-in-law, where he bought 370 acres of land of Col. James Wood, June 4, 1748. (See pp. 135 and 146.) Another tract which he owned there had originally belonged to John Harrison—Deed Book II, p. 253, 22nd August, 1749, "Daniel Davison, yeoman, and Phoebe, to Zebulon Harrison, yeoman, Daniel James's branch. Delivered, John Harrison, Nov. 1746, Witness; John Denton and John Phillips. Teste: John Denton, Jr., Robert Breckenridge, John Phillips." *(Chalkley,* Vol. III, p. 274.)

On August 23, 1766, Daniel Davison's estate settlement by his administratrix was recorded, and account rendered—

> To estate of Daniel Davidson deceased—
> To paid Thomas Harrison the balance of his account........
> To paid John Miller ....
> To paid Daniel Harrison, Depy Sheriff a Levyr's Acct.........
> To paid Samuel Lusk for Smith work........
> To paid John Riddle for linen........
> To paid David Jones for assisting to take care of and providing (or foddering) the creatures three months after Deceased death........
> To one cow belonging to the estate bought of Thomas Harrison which died soon after appraisement............
> To paid Randolph Loker the Quit rents of the land........
> To paid ....etc.
> To trouble and expense going to ye Jersies at three Different times but desire but allowance for one.
> This service was done by the widow and Administratrix........£9.
> Total estate £140, 2, 01."

(See, Augusta Co. Will Book III, p. 464, at Staunton, Va.)

Thus, not once, but three different times, Phoebe had journeyed northward, from old Augusta, on—

A VISIT TO NEW JERSEY

Phoebe's three trips to New Jersey were made between 1750, and 1766. In Colonial days this province was frequently referred to as "the Jersies," owing to it originally having been divided, in 1676, into East and West Jersey, under separate groups of proprietors. Some of the old monuments on the dividing line, which ran from near the Delaware Water Gap to Little Egg Harbour, are said to be yet standing. Phoebe's journeys to "ye Jersies" were due to several circumstances.

Josiah Davisson, the father of Daniel, settled in Middlesex County on the east bank of the Millstone river, about two miles from the center of present Princeton, where he reared his family. His mill was located at the juncture of Rocky Creek and the Millstone. Near him there also settled his brother, Daniel Brinton Davison, a physican. Daniel Brinton, in will dated at Prince Town, Somerset County, January, 1741, proved, March 18, 1746-7, named no children, but left land and a house in "Prince Town," to Frances Horner, and at her death, to "Daniel, son of my brother Josiah Davison," and to two daughters of Joshua Anderson. (*Abstracts N. J. Wills*, Vol. II, p. 136.) This last Daniel was the husband of Phoebe, and her trips to New Jersey were mainly to settle his estate there. Josiah Davison outlived his son Daniel nine years. His will, dated 13th August, 1757, proven 24th November, 1759, names his wife Mary, and children, John, Obediah, Andrew, James, Amaziah, Nathaniel, Ananias, and Mary, the wife of Joseph Skelton. In his will he mentions 202 acres of land conveyed to him by deed from James Alexander, of New York, and directs his executors "to sell all my lands and buildings in Princeton and to pay to my grandson Josiah Davison 150 pounds at the age of 21 years, but if he dies in non age said 150 pounds be divided between his two eldest sisters." (See, 3217-3222, L. of Wills, Office Sec. of State, Trenton, N. J.; also *Abstracts of Wills,* Vol. II, p. 68.) This grandson was the son of Daniel and Phoebe; he became of age in 1766, the year of Pheobe's account above; thus besides settling her husbands estate, she was evidently also looking after her son's interest in the legacy left by his grandfather.

The Davisons, like the Lincolns, were descended from an old New England family. Daniel Brinton, and Josiah, were both born at Ipswich, Mass., the former in 1690, the latter in 1692. Their father, Daniel Davison, married Sarah Dodge in 1685, and lived in the eastern part of Ipswich until he removed with his family to New London, Connecticut. From New London the brothers migrated to Long Island, Josiah being at Southold in 1715, and from Long Island both removed to New Jersey, settling at the above point. At least three sons of Josiah; viz. Daniel, Amaziah, and Ananias, came to the Valley of Virginia. Amaziah later located in what is now Harrison County, West Virginia. Ananias probably went to Tennessee. One of this name, mentioned in the Augusta records, *(Chalkley,* Vol. II, p. 263), apparently his son, and a sister Mary, the wife of Abraham Sevier, removed from the Shenandoah Valley, to near Knoxville, by 1820.

While Phoebe, in her final account of Daniel Davison's estate settlement, mentioned the trouble and expense of going to "ye Jersies" at three different times, she desired to be reimbursed but for only one time. Manifestly, she had used the opportunity for visiting. Besides seeing her late husband's people, the indications are, that she also saw some of her own relations.

* * * * * *

In Book D, of the Town of Oyster Bay, Long Island (page 466), under date of April 8th, 1708, there is a deed beginning; "I John Harrison of Rockyhill in the County of Middlesex in the province of New Jersey . . . . etc." by which Harrison disposed of a tract of land at Oyster Bay to Thomas Jones. The granter was John Harrison, previously mentioned, formerly of Flushing, and later of Perth Amboy. "1698, March 1, Deed, Josiah Pricket of Burlington to John Harrison of Flushing, Long Island, for all his improvements at Cranbury Brook, now occupied by Anthony Ashmore." "1698, April 1, License to purchase Indian land at Cranbury Brook granted to John Harrison to improve road from Burlington to New York." "1699, May 8, Indian Deed, Hughon and Lumoseecon, Sachems, to John Harrison, for a tract between Cranbury brook and Millstone River, York-road, and Thomas Budd." *(N. J. Archives,* Vol. 21, pp. 142-3.) Cranbury brook empties into the Millstone about three miles south of Rocky Creek.

"Between 1685, and 1700, large quantities of land in Somerset were either patented to Campbell, Gordon, Hamilton, Willocks, Johnston, or John Harrison," say a writer in the *Somerset Quartely,* (Vol. 6, p. 13), in an article regarding the early Scotch element of Somerset, Middlesex and Monmouth. He continues, "but neither they nor their families except those of Campbell and Harrison (but Harrison was not a Scotchman) ever settled on these lands." John Harrison, in his will of 1709, states that he ratifies and confirms the lands he had already given by deeds or otherwise to his sons John, William, and Edward. John, Jr. (Capt. John), was an early settler at Rocky Hill, and in 1717 built the first mill on the Millstone. "His land was afterwards known as the Berrian place and it is supposed that he resided where the old Berrian house stands in which Washington wrote his Farewell Address—to the Army, Nov. 2, 1783. (*History of Hunterdon and Somerset Counties, N. J.*, by Snell, p. 804.) William the brother of Capt. John, also owned land at Rocky Hill, and Henry, another brother, was a resident of Somerset County at his death, in 1730. After Capt. John's death, in 1724, at Perth Amboy, his widow, Elizabeth, was residing at Rocky Hill when she signed her will, April 22, 1730, the year of her death. (See, *Centennial History of Sommerset Co., N. J.*, by Messler, p. 11; *Abstracts N. J. Wills*, Vol. I, pp. 212-3.)

The Harrisons of Rocky Hill, now Somerset County, resided not more than four miles from the Davisons. Daniel Brinton Davison bought his land from the executors of Capt. John Harrison. Book E-2, N. J. Deeds, (at Trenton) p. 97, "To Daniel Brinton Davison of New Brunswick, 23rd May, 1726, by John Parker of Perth Amboy, Middlesex, County, Extr. of John Harrison of said city, of the one part and Daniel Brinton Davison, of New Brunswick Twp. Physician, of the second part; Where as John Harrison by will of 2nd March, 1723, made George Willocks and John Parker his Exrs, and George Willocks being about to leave America, 3rd Oct., 1724, renounced, and now Parker grants lands in New Brunswrick Twp.—etc.." At this time Benjamin, the only son of Capt. John, was under age. By the will he was to become sole executor on reaching his majority. Curiously enough, six silver spoons, marked S. R., and two marked I. H., were bequeathed by his will. (*Abstracts N. J. Wills*, Vol. I, pp. 212-13.)

At the time of Phoebe Harrison Davison's visits to New Jersey the Somerset Harrisons were mostly of the third generation from John, Sr., of Perth Amboy. Of John, Sr's. sons—Edward, in will, November 27, 1715, proven October 22, 1716, names wife Elizabeth; daughters Sarah and Elizabeth; nephews Benjamin, son of brother John, and William, son of brother William; and brother Henry. Ganatta, wife of William, last named, in will, November 24, 1756, at Perth Amboy, proven September 6, 1758, mentions children, Mary Lyell, Ganennetta, and William Harrison, and Mary Moore, sister of deceased husband; "land and share of mines at Rocky Hill, house and lot at Amboy." Henry, "of Somerset County, in will January 28, 1728-9, (about 37 years old), proven February 25, 1730- 1, refers to lot in Amboy received from brother (Capt.) John, and names wife Grace, and children John, Henry, Thomas, Ann, and Elizabeth. (*Abstracts N. J. Wills*, Vol. I, pp. 212-13; Vol. III, 147.)

Snell states that "the old Indian Path (from New York to Pennsylvania?) ran through the whole of the upper and a part of the lower section of the Harrison tract" at Rocky Hill. This old trail was first used by the Dutch.

In the Colonial deed Books of New Jersey—at Trenton— there appear about one hundred deeds devoted to the lands of Capt. John, and to his father. The earliest of these is dated October 18, 1697, by which Thomas Kendall conveyed a tract of land at Burlington to John Harrison (Sr.) Also; "1698, Sept. 30, Deed, John Harrison of Queens County, Long Island, Gent. to Anthony Woodward of Monmouth County, East Jersey, for a house and water lot on the Island of Burlington, 34½ feet front on Delaware River." (*N. J. Archives*, Vol. 21, p. 517.) Benjamin Harrison's deeds run from 1727 to 1731. His wife's name was Rachel, as given by his mother's will. "Rachell Harrison of Middlesex County," in will, August 10, 1760, divided her property between her son John, then absent, and others. (*Abstracts N. J. Wills*, Vol.

III, p. 147.) According to an inscription on a tombstone in the old churchyard of St. Peter's Church, Perth Amboy; "Here Lyes ye body of Mr. Benjamin Harrison who Departed this Life Febry 26th. 1731, in ye 26 year of his age." (See photograph, p. 300, *History of St. Peter's Church,* by W. N. Jones.)

Gideon Wright, the grandfather of John Harrison, of Augusta County, Virginia, had sisters Mary Andrews, and Lydia Horner, who removed with their husbands to Burlington, New Jersey, in 1685. (See p. 25.) In 1680 Burlington was the only town in West Jersey except New Salem, in Fenwick's colony. The town was first settled about 1676, which was five years before the first colonists to Pennsylvania arrived in three ships at the present site of Philadelphia.

The first Harrison to own land in West Jersey was James Harrison, who came over from Yorkshire, England, and settled in Maryland. "1677, July 5, Deed; Thomas Hutchinson of Beverley, Thomas Peirson, of Bonwick, Joseph Helmeley of Kelk, yeoman, George Hutchenson of Sheffield, distiller, and Mahon Stacey of Dorehouse, tanner, all of the County of York, to James Harrison of Stainton Dale, Yorkshire, Yeoman, for ¼ of a share of West Jersey." "1697, Oct. 18, Deed, William Harrison of Choptank, Maryland, yeoman, son and heir of James Harrison of the same place, deceased, to George Hutcheson, for 1/4 and 1/2 of a share of the Province (N. J.)" Part of this land was at Burlington. "1697-8, Feb. 5, Deed, Christopher Wetherill of Burlington, tailor, to Thomas Brain of Northampton. Burlington County, husbandman, for 1-32 of a share, excepting the town, water and townbounds lots, as bought of George Hutcheson Nov. 2, 1697, who purchased it from William Harrison, October 16, 1697." *(N. J. Archives,* Vol. 21, pp. 500, 502.)

In the fall of 1677 the flie-boat "Martha", from Burlington, to Yorkshire, arrived at Burlington, New Jersey, with 114 passengers. One of these was Richard Harrison, a Quaker, who was the first Harrison apparently to settle in West Jersey. He later removed to Chesterfield Township, Burlington County. His marriage to Ruth Buckman, "late of Nottingham," New Jersey, 3rd mo. 4th, 1687, appears on the records of Crosswick's Monthly Meeting. On March 6th and 20th, 1690, he purchased of Thomas Wright, Yeoman, who had also come over in the "Martha," a large tract of land near Jacobstown. His will, December 20, 1739, proven October 5, 1742, names (2nd) wife Alse, and children, William, Peter, George, Richard, Ruth Starkey, and Sarah Rodgers. Of these: Peter m. Sarah Starkey—will, July 27, 1749, names children Isaac, Joseph, Thomas, Sarah Fox, Mary, Ruth, and Debora, Richard m. 1720, Alice Stewart, widow of Joseph; Ruth m. 1714, James Starkey; Sarah m. 1721, Joseph Rodgers. *(History of Burlington & Mercer Counties, N. J.* pp. 10, 267, Woodward & Hageman; *Abstracts N. J. Wills,* Vol. II, p. 223.)

A rare old tract printed in London, England, by Thomas Milburn, in 1681, entitled, *An Abstract or Abbreviation of some Few of the Many (Later and Former) Testimonys from the Inhabitants of New Jersey, and other Eminent Persons, who have Wrote particularly concerning That Place* includes "An Abstarct of a letter from Thomas Harrison to his brother: wherein he writes of many private things: But of the country in short thus."

"Dear Brother:
This is a pleasant country, the woods are like a Garden; for all sorts of Flowers and Herbs grow in them, and Strawberries and other Fruits in abundance, and our Land far exceeds England for one thing; for three Pecks of Wheat will sow an acre of this land, which in England two Bushels will hardly do it. I can not express all Things that we have in this Country.

"Dear Brother, Pray send me a brass compass, with a Dyal for this Latitude; whereby the more easie to find the markd Trees of my own Land, from other Men's. Few in this Country have done more than I have. I shall have fenc'd and Clear'd a Quarter of a Mile this Summer. I have set four Acres of Indian-Corn; and in the fall I shall plow Twelve Acres of Wheat, and six of Pease. I and my family are very well; and for my own part, never better in my life; for I never *coughed since I came into this Country.

*Who was greatly troubled with a cough heretofore.

Burlington, 27th of March, 1681.
Who has not been There above a Year and a half; and being a poor man had not any servants.

Subscribed
Thomas Harrison.

One, Thomas Harrison, yeoman, carpenter, of Amwell, Hunterdon County, who may have been the above, in will, December 22, 1721, proven January 20, 1721-2, names wife "Rebeckah," as sole heiress, and Richard Kirby and John Wright as executors. "Witness Richard Harrison, George Fox, Sam'll Green." *(Abstracts N. J. Wills,* Vol. I, p. 213.) The township of Amwell was slightly northwest of Rocky Hill.

Samuel Harrison of Gloucester, 1688, mariner, (Captain of the ship Pennsylvania Merchant, 80 tons, London to Philadelphia?—*Maryland Historical Magazine,* Vol. I, p. 17) and Israell Harrison, further down on the Delaware, in Old Salem, 1685, have been mentioned. (pp. 16, 119.) An Xpopher (Christopher) Harrison was also living in Salem about this time; "1691, Nov. 17, Clarke, John, Inventory of—notes and bills due by . . . . . Xpopher Harrison," (Salem Wills A 65-68; *Abstracts N. J. Wills,* Vol. I, p. 94.) Samuel of Glouchester, formerly of Long Island, may also have had a brother William of Gloucester, 1689, (see p. 16). He had at least sons Samuel and William. Samuel, the younger, had wife Sarah, (which also was the name of his mother), and may have been early at Philadelphia; "Flushing Friends Monthly Meeting, 1719, 5, 9mo., Samuel Harrison of Philadelphia, Pennsylvania, (married) to Sarah Feris, dau. of John & Mary Feris." (See,*Flushing Friends Monthly Meeting—Marriage Intentions,* by Wm. A. Eardly, p. 3.) As before noted, this Sarah was a widow of Soloman Palmer. (p. 18.) Among the early Quaker records of New York, as published by the *New York Genealogical and Biographical Register,* (Vol. IV, p. 94) there is a particularly detailed account, giving besides the dates, the time of day, attendants, etc., for the births of the children of Samuel Harrison of New York, and Sarah his wife; "Mary b. 25 day, 7th mo., 1720; John b. 26d. 12 mo. 1721-2; Margery b. 1st d. 2nd mo. 1724; Sarah b. 18d. 9 mo. 1725; Samuel b. 9d. 1st mo. 1727; Hannah b. 2nd d. 8th mo; Elizabeth b. 30 d. 8 mo. 1729." (Prior to the introduction of the present Gregorian Calendar into England, and her Colonies, in 1752, the year began on March 25th.)

Old Nova Caesara, or New Jersey, was the early home of probably more different Harrison families than any other Colony. The first of the name to settle in the province was Richard Harrison, who came to Newark in 1666, with the founders of the town from New Haven, Connecticut. (see p. 16.) The descendants of Richard spread through the Oranges (see *Founders and Builders of the Oranges,* by Whittemore) and some evidently drifted westward of the Passaic, towards the mountains of Schooley, into Old Hunterdon, now Morris. Among the numerous descendants of Richard, mentioned in the *Records of the Town of Newark,* (Collections of N. J. Historical Society Vol. VI; Supplementary Proceedings commemorative of the Settlement of Newark, on its

200th Anniversary), there occurs a reference to "Rheuben Harrison," 12th March, 1765 and to a Reuben Harrison, Freeholder, 14th March, 1769. (pp. 48, and 151.) Here are also found, in the first days of the town, Abraham, Benjamin, Daniel, David, George, John, Joseph, Samuel, and Thomas Harrison, etc., and if Phoebe Harrison Davison Moore stopped at this point, on any of her trips to New Jersey, she was certainly among familiar names. Her brother, Zebulon, had been married at Morristown, in 1747, at the first Presbyterian Church. Among later Harrisons married there, were John, to Betsy Day, September 29, 1804, and Reuben, to Phoebe Merry, October 10, 1824. This last named was the daughter of Samuel Merry, Jr.; she was born 12th June, 1804, and died at Palestine, Illinois,—bapt. August 1884. *(History of 1st Pres. Church.) Morristown;* Part II, The Combined Registers, pp. 55, 100, 156.)

II

John Harrison, Senior, one of the nine founders of the pioneer Smiths and Linville's Creek Baptist Church, as revealed by the extant records of the church—and as noted by both Benedict and Semple—sometime between 1744 and 1756, made the long journey from Augusta County, Virginia, to Oyster Bay, Long Island, (his birthplace), to be baptized. (See Chapter II.) His daughter Phoebe on her trips to New Jersey, (1750-1766) most certainly did not travel alone. Her escort, on at least one of these trips, was assuredly her father, and being his favorite daughter, as very pointly shown by his will, she doubtless continued on to Oyster Bay with him, and there witnessed his baptism. This evidently occurred between 1750 and 1754, most probably shortly after Daniel Davison's death. At this time John was about sixty years old.

According to Chalkley's *Extracts from the Records of Augusta County*—"Original Petitions Filed in County Court House 1751-1752"; "John Harrison, aged 64 (1751)," petitioned "to be delivered from County levy." (Vol. I, p. 439.) To have been in his 64th year at this time he would have been born in 1687-8. This however, owing either to a misscopy, or forgetfulness of John, as to the exact date of his birth, is about three years too early. Most of the old pioneers of Augusta, the records show, only stated their ages approximately, John's daughter Phoebe, and his brother Daniel among them. (See p. 144.) Phoebe, his wife, was about the age mentioned, and he may have had her in mind. As further recorded—Order Book III, p. 202—his petition to be levy free was rejected, 27th November, 1751. *(Ibid* p. 48.)

That by this date he was feeling the weight of his years is evidenced by Samuel Newman's mention of him as "old Mr. Harrison" when writing of the days just before the organization of the church, August 6, 1756.

The old session or record book of the Smiths and Linville's Creek Church is the oldest such volume found among the Baptists west of the Blue Ridge. It bears lasting witness to the deep piety, sincere zeal, loving charity, and abiding faith of the "covenanters."

"Howe'er it be, it seems to me,
'Tis only noble to be good.
Kind hearts are more than coronets,
And simple faith than Norman blood."
—TENNYSON

It was a solemn occasion on which that little band met, that 6th day of August,

1756, to sign their covenant, and establish a new church, to the Glory of God, in "this lonesome wilderness Part of the World."

"THE PROVIDENCE of God, in all Ages of the World"—so begins the old record; "in carrying on his glorious Church-Building, hath been from Time to Time, by God himself, and the People of God, exactly chronicled and observed, for the Honor of God, the Soverign Disposer of his People, who will have his Works admired and notified by those that he makes the Monuments of his free Grace, and Love: As we may see, by the Declaration he makes, of his carrying on the rising Church from his Servant Abraham, (the Beginer of the Nation of the Jews) unto whom the Promises were made untill the Coming of Christ in the Flesh. In all which Time, the national Church of the Jews, did worship God in the Forms, and Prescriptions, by him appointed. By the legal Purification, and Sacrifices, under the Dispensation; which held forth, and typified, a Saviour, or Mesiah to come; who was when he came, to be the End of the law for Righteousness, to all that believe in him. And consiquently the End, of the national Dispensation of the Church Government.

And secondly we are to observe, how Gloriously God hath displayed his soverign Grace, in the Rise, and Progress, of his Gospel—Church, since the glorious promised Saviour did come, and act in the ministerial Office, in order to display his divine Love, to perishing Sinners, and to gather himself a Church, no more national, but congregational, promising, that in all Places, they that, fear God, and work Righteousness, shall be *ex*cepted of him.

And oh! hear his gracious Promise to that purpose. Where two or three are gathered in my Name, I will be with them, and grant their Request. Oh! dear Lord, may two or three weary and heavy laden Sinners, meet together and expect thy special Presence; hearing their burdend Complaints, and be assured, of being heard, and answered. Assist then Oh! precious Saviour thy Churches, every where, to lift up their waiting Eyes to thee, and shower down thy Bleesings of Love, into their Souls and cause them to experience the Sweetness of thy Grace, flowing to each one of them, as a Stream from the Fountain of Life, into their Souls; that they, as they have gifted themselves to thee, and bound themselves in Covenant with thee, may by thee, be owned as Covenant-Children, and obtain thy promised Presence with them, through the Stage of Action; And at Length receive, the promised Inheritance: And be welcomed Home, with, Come ye blessed of my Father, inherit the Kingdom prepared for you. Come! Come! and enter ye into the Joy of your Lord.

And now, Shall not we, be engaged to admire his condesending Love and to record his wonderous Dealings with us, who are now entering into Covenant with thee. Dearest Lord shall not we adore thy free Grace who are gathering us into thy Fold, who were scattered therefrom, and gone astray into this lonesome wilderness Part of the World, where but a few Days ago, the glorious gospel Scheme had not reached, nor the glad Tidings of Salvation by . . . . glorious Jesus sounded. Dear Saviour, hath any two or three of us, met together in thy Name, and ask'd this Request of thee, that thou are granting us a Privilege of? Hath any of us pleaded thy Promise with thee, That the dark Corners of thine Earth should be enlightened, and thou hast graciously heard? Precious Saviour take the Glory to thy self, for thou art worthy; and help us to praise thy great Name. That ever thou put it into our Hearts, to perform the least Duty faithfully for thee.

And now oh! Come! Come dear Lord into thy Garden; let the Spices thereof flow out. Let the Gifts, and Graces of thy Spirit flow into every soul, entering into Convenant with thee. And bring in oh! Father of Mercies, bring into thy Garden, hereafter such Plants of thy free Grace, that may bring forth much Fruit, to thy great and glorious Name, to the advancement of their glorious Head, King Jesus, & his Interest. And now eternal King of Zion, Let thy Church according to thy Promise, Be a garden enclosed, a Spring shut up, a Fountain Sealed, Let her be built upon the great Foundation of thy Word.

The appostles, & Prophets: Jesus Christ himself being the chief Corner Stone. Eternal Jehova! Upon this Rock build thy Church, that thy Promise may take Place; and that the Gates of Hell may not prevail against it; is the earnest Prayer of, Lord, thy poor worthless Creatures, who have, in the following Covenant, with our Names annexed, at our first Constitution, of this Gospel Order, given ourselves to thee, dear Saviour, and to oneanother by the Will of God; Set us then as a Seal upon thine Arm; and let thy Banner over us be love."

THE COVENANT:

"For as much, as God hath been graciously pleased, to make known unto us, by his revealed Will, his Word of Truth, the great Privileges of the blessed Gospel, of our dear Lord Jesus Christ; and hath made us experience his Love, and Favor; in that he called us, from our State of Nature, in which state we were Enimies to God, by wicked Works, and hath revealed Christ, in us, the hope of Glory.

Therefore for the better carrying on, to our mutal Comfort, and the Adavancement of the great Privilege of the true Religion; to the Glory of God, and to the praise of his glorious Grace.

We whose Names are hereunto Subscribed, Inhabitants of Frederick County, & Augusta County, in the Colony of Virginia; being all of us baptized, upon Profession of our Faith, and belief of one only, ever living, and true God; and of a Trinity of Persons, in unity of Essence; The Father, the Son, and the Holy Ghost; Subsisting in the Unity of the God-head. And secondly that the enternally begotten Son of God, one with the Father in Essence, and equal Power, and Glory; did, in the Fullness of Time, Take human Nature, in to that inseparable Union, with his divine Person.

And thirdly; that he, in the same did fulfill the Law; died on the Cross; thereby making Attonement for Sin; and satisfied divine Justice; and procured Peace for Sinners.

And fourthly; That all Mankind fell from the Estate of created Innocency, in, by, and with Adam's first Sin, and became liable to the Wrath of God, by the Breach of his holy Law, and in this State and Condition, consiquently have no Hope of Eternal Life, till by the same Law, convinced of this fallen Estate; and of the damning Nature of all Sin in us from this Root: And so made to seek for eternal Life by Faith in the Lord, Jesus Christ, who alone is the Mediator, of the New Covenant and alone Redeemer of God's Elect; who, (without any Merit in us, or moving Cause of Good, in us, forseen to Merit his Mercy,) was delivered to death for our Offences. And, that we might be freely justified, by his free, and Soverign Grace, was raised again for our Justification and in whom only, we have Redemption, through his precious Blood, even the Forgiveness of our Sins.

And fifthly we believe, that he ascended into Heaven, and sitteth at the Right Hand of God, from whence he will come, to judge the Quick, and the Dead, at the last great Day.

And Sixthly, we believe the Scriptures, of the old and new Testaments, to be the Word of God; and the Doctrines therein contained, to be the Commands of God, and our Duties to comply with, as such without Variableness, or Shadow of Turning.

And Seventhly, we believe the Doctrine of Baptism, and the Lords Supper; the Doctrine of Laying on of Hands; of final Perserverance in Grace; of the Resurrection, of the dead Bodies of Men, and eternal Judgement; together with all those Principals of Doctrine and, religious Practice, contained in the Confession of Faith, adopted by the Baptist Association at Philadelphia, Anno Domini 1742, and Reprinted in 1743, and having unanimously appointed this sixth Day of August in the Year of our Lord one Thousand, seven Hundred, and Fifty-six, To join together in a Gospel Church Relation, and Fellowship. And having spent Part of the Day in Fasting and Prayer; We give ourselves to the Lord, and to one another by the Will of God, according to 2nd Cor. 8 & 5th. And as a Church of Christ Do, solemnly, voluntarily & mutually covenant, with one another, to be found in, and continue to practice, the following Duties, and Disciplines, as far as God shall enable us, agreeable with the Rule of his Word.

AND first, That we will meet together on every Lords Day as many as conveniently can, to celebrate the Worship of God, and to edify one another in Love, and to keep the Day holy, And to watch over our Children, and each of our Families, that they do the same; as becometh the Gospel of our dear Redeemer, whom we now take for our Head, and King; our Prophet, and Priest; according to our Ability, to promote the Glory of God, our own Benefit, and the Good of others.

Secondly; That we will walk according to Gospel-Rule, by not taking to ourselves any Office, or Dignity, in the Church, of the Ministry, or other, till thereunto called, by the Voice of the Church, according to God's Ordinance; Knowing, that he that exalteth himself, shall be abased: And he that humbleth himself, shall be exalted. And that no Man taketh this Honor, unto himself, but he that is called thereunto &c.

And Thirdly, The minister shall not impose Members on the Church; nor Lord over the Church; nor act any Matter belonging to the Church, without their Consent; Neither shall the Church weaken his Hands; but obey him, or them in the Lord, as they that watch for their Souls. See 1 Pet. 5 & 3. Heb. 13-17.

Fourthly, that we take due Care, to receive only into the Church Fellowship, as our found in the Faith, Baptized on personal Professional and Evidence their Conversion, by a Holy Life. Acts 2:41.

Fifthly, That particular Care be taken, not to refuse any weaker Believer, whom we have Reason in the Judgement of Charity to believe, the Lord hath received; for he hath Children in his House, as well as Fathers. Rom. 14:1.

Sixthly, That every one, for the promoting of Peace and Purity, endeavor to avoid defaming Speeches; revealing Church Secrets, or any Thing, that may grieve and trouble one another. Titus 3:2. James 4:11 Rom. 14:13.

Seventhly, That if any Member, be absent from divine Service, on Church Days, or celebration of the Lords Supper, he, or She, shall give their Reason, or be set aside as disorderly Persons. 2 Thesl. 3. 6.

Eightly, That no member shall uncharitably, receive, or raise an evil Report, against a Fellow Member upon Suspicion, and groundless Jealously, as Tale-bearers use to do. Levit. 19, 16 James 4. 11.

Ninthly, That if any Member be overtaken in a Fault, that is openly scandalous, to deal with him, according to the Nature of the Fault, in Gospel-Rule; and Labour to restore him, or them in the Spirit of Meekness. Galat. 6, 1.

Tenthly, That if any evil Report, be brought against a Member, by any of the World, (whose Business it generally is, to revile the Professors of Godliness,) and the Charge doth not appear certain, nor their Accuser able to make it so appear, the Brother or Sister, shall be believed, before the Non-Member, until clear Proof had &c. Psalms 15. 3. 4. first of Cor. 13. 6.

Eleventhly, That if any Difference arise, between Members to their Damage, and the Disturbance of the Church, let them consult the Minister, or some able Person, to advise in the Cause. 1 Cor. 6. 5.

Twelvthly, That all the Church diligently avoid evil Surmising, one of another; and rash proceedings one against another, Tim. 6. 4. Prov. 25. 8.

Thirteenthly, That if any Member privately hear or know, any Thing of evil Behavior, of a Fellow-Member, a Brother, or Sister, he shall not publish it, but go, according to the Command of Christ, to him, and use those Means, and the Method by him appointed, before he bring it to the Church, and faithfully reprove them as directed, Math. 18. 15.

Fourteenthly, That all Labour to compose Differences, so much as can be, without bringing it to the Chruch; and manage it with Wisdom, and Tenderness, if it must come there. Math. 18. 15. Eph. 4. 3. 32.

Fifteenth, That no Matter of Debate, be handled in the Church on the Lords Day, least a Contention should arise, to the polution of the Day, the Dishonor of God, and the Disturbance of the Churches Peace &c.

Sixteenthly, That if Controversies should arise, which cannot mutally, with one Consent, be decided, let it then go by Majority of Voices, or Votes, and a final End be made, in this Form, to save further Grief or Trouble &c.

Seventeenthly, That no Member remove him, or herself from the Church disorderly; but seek regular Dismission, if God in the Course of his Providence, call them to remove to any other Church, of the same Faith, and Gospel-Order, that they may seek regular Admission with them, and be by them watched over, taught and if Need be, reproved in Gospel-Rule.

Eighteenthly, That in all Things, Care be taken, to deal chartiably, truly and impartially, as we serve the Lord Christ; as we are to Judge for him, and be judged by him, 1 Cor. 6. 14. Rom. 14. 10.

WE therefore, hoping and relying upon Almighty God, for Grace, Wisdom and Spiritual Understanding, Guidance, and Ability, to adorn this our Profession, and covenant Promises; and to perform our Duties, each to the other; and to bless us with Grace, sutable to our Privileges, that he in his Goodness & Mercy hath bestoneed upon us in his House; through Jesus Christ our Lord. To whom be Glory in the Church, throughout all Ages, World without End. Amen. ....

Subscribed on the Day aforesaid.

John Alderson.
Samuel Newman.
John Harrison.
William Castle Berry.

Jane Alderson.
Martha Newman.
Margaret Castle Berry.

The historical account immediately following is quoted in Chapter II. (See page 11.) The whole concludes with a poem, or hymn (of eight verses) which was probably sung at their first gathering:

(7)

"Oh precious Love, sweet Jesus come
Breathe on thy Spouse, with Love divine,
To this small Branch, in Love come Home
Till Love, meets Love, in Christ the Vine.

(8)

Oh! make our Love, thy Love obey
That when we leave our dark Abode;
Let Wings of Love bear us away,
In Christ to meet our loving God."

This early church was the second Baptist church organized "West of the Great Mountains" and the first of this denomination to be gathered in the Valley of Virginia, within the present limits of the State.

The first Baptist church west of the Blue Ridge was the Opequon, or Mill Creek Church, at present Gerrardstown, (now West Virginia) which was organized about 1746, by a company of settlers that had removed hither in 1743 from Chestnut Ridge, Maryland. The Chestnut Ridge church, at Baltimore, Maryland, was the 24th oldest church of the Baptists in America. See, *Henry Sator* 1690-1754. The recital of the life and character of an early adventurer to Virginia, etc. by Isaac W. Maclay, p. LXV.) Of the first members of the Mill Creek church, Edward Hays and Thomas Yates were the most noted. Norris, in his *History of the Lower Shenaandoah Valley,* states (p. 58) that fifteen Baptist families from New Jersey settled in this region in 1742. This is confirmed by Ellis, the historian of Monmouth County, N. J. (See p. 132.) The first pastor of the church was Rev. Henry Loveall, a native of Cambridge, England, and former resident of Newport, Rhode Island, 1729, and Piscataway, New Jersey, 1730. From New Jersey he removed to Chestnut Ridge, Maryland, in 1742, and to Virginia, in 1746. The Rev. Loveall was forced to resign, and in 1751-2 was succeeded by Rev. Samuel Heaton, mentioned in the Linville Creek Church Book as an early preacher "at old Mr. Harrison's the only Disciple he knew to be in the Place."

Rev. Heaton (or Eaton) was a native of Wrentham, Massachusetts, whence he emigrated with his three brothers to Morris County, New Jersey, about 1734. He settled near the Black River, and set up an iron works. At this time he appears to have been of the Presbyterian faith, but later "went to Kingwood and was baptized by Mr. Bonham." He began to preach in the mountains of Schooley, and from his efforts there dates the beginning of the church at Schooley. In 1751 he was ordained, and the next year he came to the Mill Creek church above. He served this church until 1754, when he removed to Knolowa, Pennsylvania, being succeeded by Rev. John Gerrard. (See, Benedict's *Gen. History of the Baptist Denomination,* 1813, Vol. I, p. 578, Vol. II, pp. 12, 27.)

According to Semple, in 1754 another company of Baptists also settled on the Opequon, "where there was a church under the care of S. Eaton." These emigrants came in from New England. Among them was their pastor, the noted Rev. Shubal Stearns, a native of Boston, who was baptized at Towland, Connecticut, in 1751. (Semples' *History of the Rise and Progrees of the Baptists in Virginia,* 1810, p. 366.)

Owing to the disruption of the Mill Creek church by the Indians, during the French and Indian War, Rev. Gerrard and many of his flock removed east of the Ridge and resided for a time in Fairfax, now Loudoun County. While there he founded a church on Catocton (Ketocton) Creek, about 1756. After the war he returned to the Mill Creek church where he died a very old man, in 1784. He is thought to have been a native of Pennsylvania. The present Mill Creek church was (re)organized, May 25th, 1761, by Rev. Gerrard, on which date their oldest church book yet in existance begins. At this time there were 159 members.

Beyond that held on the date of organization, only one other meeting in the year 1756 is recorded in the old session or minute book of the Smiths and Linville's Creek Church. The minute regarding this is the first entry made following the "poem," and states that "At a general Meeting held in October 1756 by the three congregational Churches of Christ, baptized on personal Profession of Faith in Fairfax & Frederick Counties, in Virginia; it was agreed that the sd. Churches, do Annually Meet at some one of their several Meeting-Houses, to hold Communion and Fellowship together, on the second Sabbath of June in each year hereafter, to begin with the Church of Christ at Smith's Creek in June, the Second Sabbath 1757." (Page 10.)

Aside from those already mentioned "The next (first) member that was added, was Mary Banot, the wife of Arthur Banot, she being brought up in Quakerism . . . was convinced by a sermon preached in the Beginning of the year 1757 . . . Submitted to Gospel Ordinances; was received in April 1757 . . . etc." (p. 10.)

"The next was Catherine Harrison the wife of Jeremiah Harrison, who submitted to the Order of the Gospel, and was baptized and received a Member of the Church, on the Second Sabbath of May 1757, at which time our Third Commemoration of the dying Love of our dear Redeemer was held, by apointment of the Church in its Order since our constitution; and was in Communion with us our Rev. Brother Mr. Malechi Bonam of East Jersey," (p. 10.)

"The next Communion was held the 2nd Sabbath in June 1757, by Appointment of the three Churches above sd. in Annual Meeting, where was present with our Rev. Brother Alderson, the Rev. Mr. John Ganot, (Minister of the Church of Christ of the same Faith and Gospel Order, with us, in Fairfax County; and likewise of Mill Creek in Frederick County), which two carried on the solemn Public Worship of God three Days sucessively, in which Time the following Persons gave Obediance to the Commands of God, in his Gospel Ordinances of Baptism, and Laving on of Hands, and was received Members of ye Church of Christ, at the North River of Shenandoah, and Linville's Creek. The first was the Wife of George Nicholas; she was a Presbyterian, and zealous in their Cause, and well reported of . . . &c. The other was a Gentleman of no mean Character, a Man in Authority both civil and military; Cornelius Ruddell, by Name, who often opposed the Truths we profess publickly; yet he, was convinced of the Truth of the Cause he had opposed . . . and was accordingly received a Member of the sd. Church with the other. He was formerly by Profession, a Church of England Man &c. This was our Fourth Communion since Constitution, at which Time *they* sd. three Churches mutually agreed, That the next Yearly Meeting should be held with the Church of Christ at Catockton in Fairfax County, at the Time before appointed viz. the Second Sabbath in June 1758." (p. 10.)

In regard to this historic gathering, the first yearly Baptist "Association" held in the Valley of Virginia, Semple remarks—"on the second Sunday in June 1757 the Mill Creek, Ketocton, and Smiths and Linvilles Creek churches had their first yearly meeting at the meeting house of the last named church. These churches became members of the Philadelphia Association soon after their constitution. They were dismissed from this in 1765 and the next year formed the Ketocton Association." *(Semple* pp. 288, 290, 299.)

The Philadelphia Association was the first Association formed in America, and was organized in 1707 of the following five churches; viz.—Pennepeck, founded 1688, now the oldest Baptist church in Pennsylvania; Middletown, Monmouth County, New Jersey, founded 1688, oldest Baptist church of New Jersey; Piscataway, at Elizabeth, New Jersey, founded 1689; Cohansey, Hopewell township, Cumberland County, New Jersey, founded by 1690, (some Baptists from Tipperary, Ireland, had settled here about 1683—Benedict, Vol. I, p. 567); and "The Welsh Tract" church, at Pencader, New Castle County, Delaware, founded 1703.

As indicated in the above minute, "ye Church of Christ at the North River of Shenandoah, and Linville's Creek" was the beginning of two congregations. Meeting at first were doubtless held at various homes of the members, but at an early date three church buildings were erected. The old Linville Creek building stood near the western bank of the creek in the neighborhood now between Daphna and Linville. A later building erected by this congregation, a little west of the original location, was until recently, standing. For many years it has been in the possession of the Tunkers, the Baptists having moved their point of meeting to Brock's Gap. The Smiths Creek, or North River of Shenandoah, congregation met at present New Market. For a long time, down until about 1900, the Baptists worshiped here in a quaint old brick meeting house that stood a little off the main street, and near the center of the town. It is said that John Sevier gave the land for this old church. The new Smiths Creek church building is a few blocks north of the old site.

The Smiths and Linville's Creek Church was gathered early in the second year of the French and Indian War, and about thirteen months following Braddock's defeat, of July 9, 1755. The year of its organization, Washington built Ft. Loudoun at Winchester; this year also, the Seven Years War (1756-1763) in Europe began, from which time on the war in America became a phase of the general European conflagration. From Virginia to the Great Lakes the whole western frontier of the English Colonies, and various parts beyond, were the scenes of bloody conflict, one of the principal events being the capture of Quebec, in 1759. During this period, especially following the defeat of Braddock, and prior to the capture of Ft. Duquesne (1758), by young Washington, the Valley of Virginia was in an alarmingly exposed condition. The country was subjected to numerous inroads of roving bands of Indians, and frequent horrible massacres of families occured. The settlers flocked to rudely constructed forts; a number removed to the Carolinas; all protected themselves as best they could, and the whole region continued in a state of armed defence.

From August, 1757, to September, 1759, was particularly trying, and only one opportunity for the church to hold communion was available. The last gathering in 1757 was "At a Monthly Meeting the Day before the Second Sabbath in August" at which "Mary Denham, the Wife of Joseph Denham offered herself to the Church and proposed for Baptism." . . . (She had been brought up a Quaker.) The intention was to hold a meeting the next day, the minute stating that she was found "satisfactory to the Church, and was baptized, and received by them accordingly . . . on the 2nd Sabbath of August, which was our sixth Communion since Constitution," but continues immediately—"N. B. This last Church Act took no Place, being let, by Satans Emesaries, who with him, are always endeavoring to break the Churches Peace" (p. 11). Then follows—

"ABOUT this time arose certain of the Favorers of that Scriptureless Practice Infant sprinkling, and, in a Disorderly manner, called one Alexander Miller (a Presbyterian Minister) to their Assistance, to go Ridicule & slander our Minister, and our Church Officer, who at that Time did officiate the Office of Deacon by the Churches Appointment, (which sd. Miller had before, rediculously aspersed our Rev. (Mr. Alderson) Brother of being a Papist). Accordingly, on Wednesday the 21st of Septem. 1757, the sd. Miller and a rude Assembly with him in a disorderly Manner, without Leave, or previous Notice given to the Church, or Persons by him accused, opened our *Meeting*

House, and assumed our Pulpit, and there slanderously, falsely, and contrary to Christian Rule and Order, dispitefully use our Minister, and Brother, the Deacon, with approbrious Speeches, of Spite and Malice, entirely untruth, and unknown to sd. Parties; and of which we are fully convinced, neither of them were guilty of the Errors by him charged, neither in Thought, Word, or Deed, which sd. Irregular and disorderly Practice of his, has since occasioned Animosities in the Neighborhood, and he the sd. Miller, hath been thereby instrumental, in the hands of Satan, to disturb the Churches Peace, and the Peace of the Neighborhood, this being a Time of noted Peace with us, in the Midst of Difficulties elsewhere. The Wednesday following this riotous Action, it pleased God to permit the Heathen to fall on our Settlement, and disordered the whole worse than they had done themselves, the Week before. A just retaliation for such unheard of Proceedings, and Measures they had taken &c. The aforesaid Proceedings, together with the Indian troubles hindered our Church Meetings, from that Time, till the first Saturday in January 1758; at which time the kind Providence of God, enabled us to regulate so many of the Disorders that attended us, as that with Comfort and Peace, we could proceed in the Ordinance the day following, our meeting of Business, and Regulation of our Church Affairs. The first part of the sd. Day of Business, was spent in solemn Humiliation, with Prayer and fasting, (under a Consideration of our Unworthyness of the great Favor we enjoyed in such perillous Times), by Way of Preperation for the Work of the Day following, being the second Sabbath in January, when we held our Seventh Communion since Constitution." (p. 12.)

"After this time Spring coming on, the Indian Troubles continued, and all oppertunities of Meetings were taken from us, and not only so, but the whole Neighborhood forced either to go into Forts or over the Mountains, to escape the Rage, in the month of June following. During which Time of Troubles, divine Providence seemed entirely against us, and the whole Neighborhood; and some Disorders happened in these Troubles amongst our own Members. . . . These Disconveniences continued and got no better, till the Summer of the Year 1759, when it pleased God to make our Armies victorious, in the North Part of our Continent, (which drew the Enemy form us,) so that the Forts that had harboured them to our Hurt, fell in our Hands without Bloodshead."

"And when the Summer of 1759 was ended, and the Enemy not permitted to break in upon us, in the Month of September, the church assembled together, on Saturday the 22nd and by the good Hand of God with us settled the Disorders of her Body, so that on Sunday the 23rd the Lords Supper was celebrated in its usual Solemnity and was our Eighth Communion since Constitution. At this Time there were two Members added viz. Jeremiah Ozban & Mary Ozban his Wife, and all our Members were together save two, one by Reason of Distance and Cumber; the other disobediant and disorderly, refused to come, who having walked disorderly and riotous, was by the Church set aside, and not allowed Communion, nor any Act as a Member thereof, till Satisfaction given, viz. Cornelious Ruddle."

"From the time last noted (above) by Reason of the Length of the Way, the Difficulty of Winter, the Troubles of removing back from our Flights, caused by the Enemy, and great Affliction of the Small-Pox raging in the Land, we had not an Oppertunity to meet in Church Order, nor hold Communion till the 10th of August 1760, when it pleased God in his great Mercy to permit some few of us to meet, to commemorate his dying Love, and preserved us from all Enemies, even those present behaved with uncommon Silence, and seemed to listen and hear the Word with awful Reverance, (the Lord grant it might be with a God like fear). This was our Ninth Communion, since Constitution." . . . (p. 12.)

But the old church went on—a beacon light in the wilderness, and at two meetings in 1761, new communicants are mentioned. On the "Fourth Sabbath of May," this year, "Phillip Fegans was added a member." Their next meeting was "The last Sabbath of August, at which was admitted and baptized, Thomas Porter, Jeremiah Harrison, John Ozban, and his Wife, Elizabeth Ozban, and Esther North, the Wife of John North, and the sd. North having been baptized elsewhere, was admitted to transient Communion, and Sarah Thomas, the Wife of James Thomas, who was before his sd. Wife a Member with us. (Six persons offered for baptism, and were examined as to their Faith, and gave clear and satisfactory Answers, and were admitted and baptized, These are their names, (as above)." (p. 13.)

Jeremiah Harrison was the half-brother of John, Sr.; his wife, Catherine, had very early united with the church. As will be recalled, he had previously been baptized by the Rev. John Craig, (Presbyterian), prior to 1749. (See pp. 151, and 164.) Of the five Harrison emigrant brothers, two were now members of the Linville Creek Church. As the former faith of neither is mentioned in the old church book, the inference is that they had originally been Church of England men. Daniel and Thomas were evidently such. At the time of John, Sr.'s birth there were only eleven Baptist churches in America. (See list of early churches in Maclay's Account of the Chestnut Ridge, Maryland, Congregation, "*Henry Sator,*" etc.)

The first Baptist church in this country was that founded at Providence, Rhode Island, in 1639, by Roger Williams, the founder of the Colony. (Robert Williams, a brother of Roger, was one of the original propiretors—along with Peter Wright, and others—of Oyster Bay, Long Island, 1653.) In 1644 and 1656 the First and Second Baptist churches, respectively, of Newport, Rhode Island, were founded. Then followed the First Church of Swansea, Mass., 1663, First Church of Boston, 1665, North Kingston, Rhode Island, 1665, Charleston, South Carolina, 1683, Cold Spring, Bucks County, Penn., 1684, and the three New Jersey churches, 1688-1690, previously noticed.

Following the above gathering no more meetings of the Smiths and Linville's Creek Church were held in 1761; their next gathering being on the Second Sabbath of May, 1762, "when we had another Member added, viz. Sarah Porter, the Wife of Thomas Porter." (p. 13.) The next meeting was, "Saturday the Day before Second Sabbath in August," at which, "Thomas George and his Wife [were] baptized and admitted." "The Day following, being the Day appointed for the ordinance of the Lords Supper, there was a great Congregation of People gathered . . . Mr. John Alderson was appointed Messenger to go to the Association." The next meeting was scheduled to be held the second Sabbath in November, 1762. "This last Appointment was frustrated and no Meeting till 25th of December and was then celebrated the 14th Communion since Constitution." (p. 14.)

On the 2nd Sabbath of March, 1763, "the Church was dissapointed for lack of Wine for its Use but the Association Letter was read and the Church of *Smiths Creek, a Branch of North Shenandoah, in Frederick County,* was received into Fellowship with the Association of the associate Churches, of the same Faith and Gospel Order at Philadelphia, October 12th, 1762." . . . Following this their next gathering was the 5th Sabbath in May, (1763) at which the sacrament was administered by "the Rev. Mr. David Thomas Minister of the Gospel of the same Faith & Order, in Fauquier County, in Virginia." (15th communion.) They next appointed to meet—"Saturady before fourth Lords Day in August." (p. 14.) Here again—

"N. B. These Church Appointments, was by the barbarous Enemy the Indians, dissapointed; the church being scattered . . . But at a public Meeting on Linvilles

Creek, the Church was called to meet as a Church for business, on the last Saturday of September, next, being the 24th Day, which they did at the Dwelling house of Samuel Newman, where they recalled that Brother to the Office of an Elder." (p. 15.) At this meeting appointment was made for the last Saturday in October and preaching the Sunday following with communion, "But it (the Church) was dissapointed by the Deacons not providing Wine, so that no communion was held; nor no Appointment further made for any &c." (p. 15.)

The above is the last mention of the Indians in the old church book; this year the war closed, and the old pioneers then living, had come to see the day when the war cry of the savage was all but ended, in the Valley of the Shenandoah, forever. Prior to the French and Indian War, the Indians had given the settlers, as a whole, comparatively little trouble. While some, who had known the privations and hardships incident to their removal to this lonesome wilderness, had been permitted to spend their closing years in peace, in their new found home, many others there were, who too, having known these prviations, had yet to pass through the perilous times of ten long years of the most treacherous and savage warfare of the Colonial period. Such were some of the circumstances, and trials encountered, by the members of this pioneer church, in their first days by "The Long Grey Trail"—

"*It is grey with age and hoary*
From the passing of the years,
Long unknown in white man's story,
Though beset with hopes and fears;
For the red men in their journeys
Passed this way in the long ago,
Now to visit friendly neighbors,
Now to attack some distant foe."

—WAYLAND.

III

It was in the fall of 1763, following the last Indian irruption above, that John Harrison, Jr. was murdered. His will was proven on November 15th and 16th of this year. (See p. 158.) He was killed by one of his negro slaves, who shot him in the back. The crime is said to have been committed in a cornfield, and as the body was not discovered for some time, when found, immediate burial was necessary. His grave was prepared by the spot where he fell. On November 9, 1763, as noted in Augusta Court Order Book No. VIII, (p. 324), at a "Court of Oyer and Terminer for trial of Tom, slave, for murder of John Harrison by shooting in back," the slave confessed, was judged guilty and was sentenced—"that he be hanged by the neck on Saturday, 19th inst., and his head be severed and affixed on a pole on the top of the hill that leads from the Court House to Edward Tarr's. Memo—Tom valued at £50." Same Order Book (p. 385) January 2, 1764, at a Court of "Oyer and Terminer for trial of Fanner, a negro slave of John Harrison, for aiding and abetting Tom in the murder of John"—this slave was acquitted. (*Chalkley*, Vol. I, pp. 109, 111.)

The Harrisons were among the very first settlers of Augusta to own slaves. Later, as witnessed by will after will, they were also among the first inhabitants of their county to voluntarily begin freeing them.

An entirely different class of help occasionally referred to in the early records was indentured servants. Such servants were simply white men of small means, who for a stated sum of money had bound themselves to their debtor for a definite length of time to work out their indebtedness. They were not necessarily of humble origin and many were educated and highly respected. Poor boys were frequently befriended and given a start in this way. As early as May 23, 1750—Order Book II, p. 365—one William O'Briant, is mentioned as a servant of John Harrison.

From his youth John Harrison, Jr. had helped to defend his country. In 1742, he is found a member of Peter Scholl's militia company on Smiths Creek. The year of Braddock's defeat he appears as a member of Capt. Daniel Harrison's company. On 27th November, 1755, the Vestry of Augusta Parish met, and designated processioners (to report before March 1st next) as follows: viz., "John Harrison, Jr., and Daniel Smith, in Capt. Daniel Harrison's Company. Thomas Moore and David Robinson, in Capt. Ephraim Love's Company, and to head of Brock's Gap. Mathew Patton and Wm. Dyer, on South Fork of the Branch of Potowmack, Jacob Peters and Henry Landcisco, on Mill Creek and Shelton's tract," etc., thus naming the companies in which he, and the others, were serving at the time.

In their returns of 1756, John, Jr., and his cousin Daniel Smith, just about turned in a list of their neighbors and kin among the land owners of the region along the old Indian Road, from the county line to a little south of "Thomas Harrison's." As compared to similar returns of 1748 (see p. 163) the population had considerably increased; "Processioned from Fairfax's line to North River, by John Harrison and Danl. Smith, viz.: For John McClure, for Richd. Dear, for Pat Quen (Quinn), for Danl. Love, for Mathew Black, for Arter (Arthur) Johnson, for Thomas Harrison, for John Wight, for David Walston (Ralston), for William Logan, for John Davis, for Thomas Lokey, for Jacob Wooly (Woodley), for Valentine Sevier, for John Phillips, for Andw. Bird, for Thos. Millsaps, for John Obryan (O'Bryan), for Michael Wearen (Warren), for John Fawler, for David Logan, for Randolph McDonald, for John Cravens, for Joseph Cravens, for Robert Cravens, for John Shelpman, (Sheltman), for Alex. Herring, for Jeremiah Harrison, for Reuben Harrison, fo John Harrison, Sr., for John Harrison, Jr., for Zebulon Harrison, for Thomas Moore, for Moses Bird, for Wm. McGee, for Col. Wood's Plains, for Robert Harrison. Naid Creek Patten part not processioned because Capt. Daniel Harrison and John Edwards objected because there was no patent nor course to know the lines. Niles Run tract not processioned by reason none to show the lines. Capn. Harrison's not processioned, none to show lines." (Augusta Parish Vestry Book, pp. 157, 164, 174; *Chalkley*, Vol. II, pp. 442-4.)

About this time during the war the House of Burgesses passed an Act for the further protection of the Colony from invasion by the French and Indians, in which the sum of £25,000 was appropriated—thus beginning:

"ANNO REGNI
GEORGII II.
REGIS MAGNAE, BRITANNIAE, FRANCIAE,
ET HIBERNIAE, TRICESIMO SECUNDO.

At a Generaly Assembly, begun and held at the Capitol, in Williamsburg on Thursday the fourteenth day of September, in the thirty-second year of the reign of our sovereign lord GEORGE II, by the grace of God, of Great Britain, France, and Ireland, King, Defender of the faith, &c. and in the year of our Lord 1758; being the first session of this assembly.

Francis Fauquier esq. Governor.

An act for the defence of the Frontiers of this Colony, and for other purposes therein mentioned.

The SCHEDULE to which this Act refers.

To the Militia of the County of Augusta, and Provisions furnished by sundry inhabitants of the said county viz. . . . *(including the following)*—

"To Arthur Trader, Robert Patterson, Robert M'Geary, Mathew Black, Jonas Friend, Nathaniel Harrison, etc. . .. seven shillings each	£8	1	0
To Nathaniel Harrison, Robert Black, etc. seventeen shillings each	1	14	0
To John Fulse		19	
To Lieut. Daniel Smith		15	
To William Cravens, Willry Cunrod, George Moffett, James Stephenson, Thomas & John Stephenson, Adam Miller, etc. . . . five shillings each			
To William Cravens seargeant	2	12	
To James Fowler		12	
To John Harrison	1	9	
To Leonard Herren		18	
To Cornelius Sulivan	1	16	
To Nathaniel Harrison		12	
To Robert M'Corney	1	0	
To Gideon Harrison		18	
To Leonard Herring		13	
To John Harrison, Nathaniel Harrison, Thomas Paterson eighteen shillings each			
To Reuben Harrison, for provisions for Indians	1	1	8
To George Matthews, Richard Matthews, etc. eighteen shillings each			
To William Matthews		8	
To Sampson Matthews, as ensign		10	
To Capt. John Smith and his son as lieutenant in the said company	20	15	
etc., etc."			

See, Hening's *Statutes at Large of Virginia,* Vol. VII, pp. 179-194.)

Notwithstanding the war, and the consternation generally immediately following Braddock's defeat, the Harrisons went right ahead patenting lands. The two patents to John, Jr. for 245 acres, dated July 10, 1755, (the day after the defeat), were followed, on September 10th, by two more to John, Jr., for 672 acres, and two to Thomas for 379 acres. (See p. 161.) This year also, on December 15, Daniel patented 120 acres. The next year, on the 10th of March, Thomas was granted by patent 120 acres, and on August 16th, Daniel, Thomas, and Samuel, each obtained similarily 200, 379, and 245 acres respectively.

Prior to the date of his will John Harrison, Jr. disposed of 1,357, acres of his land, embraced in four patents, as follows—

(1st). May 23, 1750, by deed to Richard Hall, 400 acres on "Meadow Creek of Woods River," patented to John, Jr., September [2]5, 1746; Delivered William Hall,

July, 1763." (Further record: "Richard Hall of Halifax, to Abraham Chrisman of Frederick County," £175, "400 acres on a branch of Wood's River, alias New River, called Meadow Creek, conveyed by John Harrison, Jr., to Richard, 23d May, 1750. . . . Delivered Abraham Christman, 4th September, 1773.") (Deed Books 2, p. 760; 11, p. 369—*Chalkley*, Vol. III, pp. 286, 402.)

(2nd). The Luney's Mill Creek tract, patented to John, Jr., February 12, 1742, was deeded by him to James Letherdale, blacksmith, 28th August, 1750, as before noted.

(3rd). November 28, 1750, deed by John, [Jr.] to Cornelius Brown, 350 acres on Woods River—"Neck Creek." (Further record: 4th November, 1766, "Cornelius Brown of Congras in South Carolina, taylor, power of attorney to Abraham Brown, his brother, planter, of Augusta County, to make deed to William Davis, of County Philadelphia, Pennsylvania, to 175 acres on Woods River, otherwise called, New River, part of 350 acres conveyed by John Harrison to Cornelius. Teste: John Paxton, James Trimble, John Hickman," etc. Also, 17th November, 1767, deed, "Cornelius Brown of Congrees in South Carolina, taylor, by Abraham Brown of Augusta County, brother of Cornelius," to "William Davis of Philadelphia, Penn., skinner," £43, 175 acres, one-half of 350 acres on south side of Wood's river, commonly called New River . . . patented to John Harrison, 25th September, 1746, on side of Neck Creek." (Deed Books, 3, p. 81; 13, p. 223; and 14, p. 34; *Chalkley*, Vol. III, pp. 291, 450, 460.)

(4th.) 27th November, 1757, deed, John Harrison, farmer," to "Robert Renick, farmer," 241 acres—this appears to have been the tract patented to John, Jr., 25th September, 1746, "on a branch of James River at east end of Short Hill." Earlier, on November 8, 1752, a "valuation of Robert Renix improvements on plantation formerly called John Harrison's place" was recorded. (Deed Book 4, p. 25, Will Book I, p. 422; *Chalkley*, Vol. III, pp. 25, 299; Vol. I, p. 436.) (The old deed books not always being clear as to whether John, Sr., or John, Jr., is referred to, identification in such cases is as given by the patent books at Richmond.)

On March 10, 1764, the appraisment of John Harrison, Jr.'s estate by Daniel Smith, Michael Warren, and Michael Shirley was recorded. Among the items mentioned was money(£10 ?) due by Jonathan Langdon. (Will Book 3, p. 317.) This year on 21st November, Zebulon and Reuben, the executors, for £90, deeded 400 acres "on a branch of South Branch of Potomac called West Fork of Mill Creek" to Jacob Peters—"Delivered, Moses Hinkle, 31st July, 1793." (Deed Book 11, p. 738.) The sale of this tract, granted by patent to John, Jr., 10th September, 1755, disposed of the last of his patented lands elsewhere than in the immediate region of his home. (Further mention of the home lands devised will appear later.) On November 18, 1767, his final estate settlement was made. Of those who bought part of his "movables" were John and "Alickander Mecdonnold," Robert Dickey, Joseph English, John Needham, Josiah Davison—"one Steel Trap," Joseph Langdon—"one Mare & Coult," Robert Cravens "one horse," etc. "To Cash paid Thomas Moore, Legase, £30. Joseph Langdon one Debt £10." Total £318, 1, 9. (Will Book 4, p. 59.)

* * * * * *

Ann Langdon, the daughter of John Harrison, Sr., while not exactly her father's favorite daughter was nevertheless remembered by him in his will. Doubtless her history, if more fully known, would at least prove interesting. According to a genealogical table in the Ewing family, her first husband was John Davison. Whether or not he was a kinsman of her sister's first husband, Daniel Davison, appears unknown. Besides the

New Jersey Davisons there were others of the name early in Old Augusta. "July 24, 1741—Importation—John Davison came into court and made oath that he imported himself, Jane, George, Thomas, William, and Samuel Davison at his own charge from Ireland to Philadelphia and from there into this colony and that this is the first time of proving his and their rights in order to obtain land, which is ordered to be certified." (Orange County Court Order Book 1739-41, p. 209.)

Ann's second husband was doubtless one of the Langdons mentioned in her brother John's estate settlement above, probably Joseph, and was likely of the Queens County, Long Island, family. Many Langdons, among them, John, Thomas, and Joseph, appear on the early records of Hempstead, Long Island, the adjoining township of Oyster Bay. (See, *Records of North and South Hempstead, L. I., New York,* pub. by the town, 1896, Vols. I-VIII.)

In an Act of Assembly, of March, 1761, establishing the town of Woodstock, Virginia, Clause II begins—"And be it further enacted, by the authority aforesaid, that Cornelius Riddel, John Skeen, Burr Harrison, Mathew Harrison, Joseph Langdon, Moses Striker, Adam Yeaker, Jacob Miller, and Peter Hainger, gentlemen shall be, and they are hereby, nominated, constituted and appointed, directors and trustees for the said town:" etc. (Hening's *Statutes at Large of Virginia,* Vol. VII, p. 406.)

David Harnet, one of Rockingham's patriots of Revolutionary days, was the third, and final, husband of Ann. He too, is thought to have been a descendant of an old Long Island family. On April 6, 1666, "Edward harnet" was chosen to chose fremen," of Huntington. "Jonathan harnett" was one of the owners of the ten farms there April 16, 1672. (See, *Huntington Town Records,* pub. by the town, Vol. I, 1653-88, pp. 45, 88.) Huntington township joined Oyster Bay on the east.

According to an old deed recently found among some Moore papers stored in the attic of the late residence of Mr. George Harrison, who for many years was the owner of the following land—23rd July, 1792, James Brewster, and Eleanor his wife, of Rockingham County, Virginia, conveyed to David Harned of the same County and State, for £800, "360 acres of an inclusive survey bearing date February 7, 1783, 100 acres part thereof granted David Brewster by patent bearing date August 6, 1756, also 71 acres by patent date July 20, 1768, also 100 acres granted to Brewster by deed of Lease and release date March 20, 1759, from John Scott and wife .... together with 89 acres of unpatented land to make the above quantity, which said land is lying in Rockingham County on Cub run and Branches thereof which said land was granted to the said James Brewster inclusively by patent dated 1785, bounded as follows, Beginning on East side of a run on a point of a stony ridge running thense south 72 degrees, west 350 poles to a Black oak, etc." Teste—"George Huston, John Waest, Reuben Harrison, John Huston, Thos. Herron."

This land was just north of that of Thomas and Phoebe Harrison Moore, on the old Indian Road, and became a part of the Moore estate when later sold by David Harnet to Reuben Moore, son of Thomas and Phoebe. At present it is included in one of the finest estates in the Valley, "Court-Manor," the Virginia stock farm of Mr. Willis Sharpe Kilmer. Part of the consideration in Harnet's sale was that "Reuben should support David's wife, Ann Harnet" (Reuben's aunt). Ann, however, could not see it this way, evidently, and spent her closing years with her nephew John Harrison, son of Reuben Harrison, who as next friend brought suit in a "bill for maintainence" in 1802. Ann died at John's house, 9th August, 1805. On October 25th, following, Harnet brought suit against Moore, in "Bill of Revivor," and by this time "David had determined to live in New Jersey." He died prior to 30th September, 1815. (See—Judgements Circuit Court Causes Ended, Harnet vs. Moore, OS. 267, NS. 94, Bill of Revivor; *Chalkley*, Vol. II, p. 201.)

* * * * * *

Zebulon Harrison only, among the children of John Sr., and his wife Phoebe, is mentioned in the Smiths and Linville's Creek Church book. Notations of new members, however, were not always made; thus others of John's family may have also been connected with the church. Zebulon first appears on the record under date of 15th December, 1787. The church had met in a business session "at the house of Brother Jno. Lincoln's," and near the close of the meeting, " a Motion was made by Brother Thomas, When and where our next Church Meeting should be held, and it was agreed, that we will hold it on the Saturday before the 3rd Sabbath in February next, at Mr. Zebulon Harrisons House on Smiths Creek." (p. 24.) From this time on Zebulon is mentioned.

Zebulon's father had probably leaned towards the Baptists when in Delaware. The "Welsh Tract" Church had as its first pastor the noted Thomas Griffith. He with fifteen others embarked from Wales, England, on board the *William & Mary*, in June, 1701 and landed at Philadelphia 8th of September, following. Rev. Griffith was born in Lauvernach parish, county of Pembroke, 1645, and after serving the above church twenty-four years, died at Pennepeck, Penn, July 25, 1725. (Benedict, Vol. II, p. 4.) From New Castle County the Baptists spread to other points in the Colony. Various names among the early members of the Welsh Tract Church, such as Griffith, Thomas, Davis, Philips, Evans, etc. are later found in Rockingham. (See, *Records of the Welsh Tract Baptist Meetings*, 1701-1828, Part II, p. 6, Vol. IV, publications of Historical Society of Delaware.)

It may be observed in passing, that in his account of the early history of the Linville Creek Church, Samuel Newman appears to have been at some pains to note that he was the first Baptist to settle in the community. While not actually stating that he was settled before John Harrison, he leaves the impression that he and John had been somewhat rival claiments to being the first Baptist of the neighborhood. Newman probably had known of John before either removed to Virginia. It is a curious coincidence, if such, that the first record of John's father, Isaiah, at Oyster Bay, appears over the signature of a John Newman, and the first record of John Harrison in the old church book was written by a Samuel Newman.

* * * * * *

Following the pause in the meetings of the church in 1763, their next meeting aparently was held on the 26th day of May, 1764, at which time a letter was "approved of," to be sent to the "Church at Cumis (Cunmis ?), in Berks County, Pennsylvania," regarding "our Sister Jane Rodgers," a member of the Pennsylvania church. Her son-in-law Thomas Evans is also mentioned. At the "next meeting Saturday 20th April, 1765, Samuel Newman and Martha his wife," who were moving away to "some parts of North, or South Carolina, sued for Letter of Dismission," which was granted. And likewise Phillip Fegans, "to some place or places as Providence may direct which was likewise granted by the Church." And as Mary Banot, is by her husband moved away she desired a letter of dismissal be sent by Samuel Newman (as messenger) which was granted." (p. 15.) At a meeting on the 2nd Sabbath in June, 1765, "then was added two Members viz. Joseph Thomas, and a Negro Man called Joe"—17th Communion. "Met according to appointment the Second Sabbath of August, then was added two more Members, viz. John Ray, and Thomas Evans. And then was admitted into transient communion a Person of Quality viz. Silas Hart by name. Then the Church appointed . . . and every Male Member to pay seven Shillings for Mr. Aldersons journey to the Association in Philadelphia." (p. 16.)

Silas Hart was the early Justice of the court. John Ray was a little later one of the witnesses to John Harrison, Sr.'s will.

* * * * * *

John, Sr., was getting up in years, and about this time, following in his father's footsteps, sold off a part of his home plantation to his son Reuben; 20th September, 1765, deed, John Harrison, Sr., to Reuben Harrison, his son; £10, "part of two tracts: 1st containing 117 acres, part of 234 acres patented to John, 25th June, 1747, on Smith's Creek; the other tract containing 83 acres, part of 166 acres patented to John 25th June, 1747, on Smith's Creek. Teste: Daniel Smith, Jos. Rutherford, Wm. Kavanaugh, Jane Smith." (Deed Book 12, p. 426; *Chalkley*, Vol. III, p. 438.)

John Harrison, Sr., the Old Augusta County pioneer, and founder of the Smiths and Linville's Creek Church, died in the spring of 1771. He had kept the faith, and his "Covenant."

(1)

"*Happy the Soul where Graces reign*
Where heavenly Love inspires the Breast,
Love is the brightest of the Train.
Love flows and strengthens all the rest.

(4)

'Tis precious Love, shall live & sing,
When Sisters Faith & Hope, shall cease:
'Tis Love shall tune our joyful String,
In the sweet chanting Realms of Bliss."
—*The Old Church Book.*

On the day of the proving of his will, 21st May, 1771, his sons, Zebulon and Reuben, after qualifying as executors—with sureties Archibald Huston, and James Beard—conveyed to Robert Dickey for £30, 18 acres "patented to John Harrison, deceased, 26th July, 1765, and by him devised to grantors." "Delivered Robert Dickey, April, 1773." Later, on 10th August, 1772, "Reuben Harrison and Lydia" deeded to Christopher Waggoner the "tract patented to John Harrison, deceased, 20th September, 1751, and devised to Reuben by John his father." "Teste, Abraham Lincoln." (Deed Books 17, p. 187; and 18, p. 487; *Chalkley*, Vol. III, pp. 509, 524.)

The final settlement of John's estate was delayed until after his wife's death, but on 3rd October, 1771, the first "vendue" of a part of his estate was held. The "sale bill of widow Harrison," includes as an item, "the apparel of Zebulon Harrison" (formerly John's.) A second vendue is recorded under date of 17th October, 1775, and a third, 16th September, 1779. Among those who bought property at the second sale was John Conner, and Joseph Scothron, and at the third, John Reeves and Thomas

Alderson, etc. (Will Books, 5, p. 533, and 6, p. 440.) On November 21st, following the first sale, the "Appraisment of the estate of John Harrison lately deceased," by Michael Warren, John Hinton and Wm. Henton, was recorded. Of the "movables" listed, the items below show that for an old pioneer he was among those of good circumstances—

"3 Beasons & large Puter dish.
5 Beasons & 2 large Puter dishes.
6 old plates and 12 old spoons.
3 tin cups & streaming (steaming ?) Boal.
a Bed furnature & Bead stead.
a nother Bed & furnature & Bead Stead.
2 Collars.
To old Lumbox
Spoon moulds.
2 old Chests
1 old Chest & 2 sacks
a Ruggat
7 chairs
a walnut Table & pine table
a warming pan

a silver headet cane, a pair of neebuckles	£0	11	0
a pair of sleeve buttons	1	03	0
The apparel	6	00	0

A Horn Sow and old gun
3 old wheels—52 lbs woolen yarn.
A smothering iron, 19 yards linen.
Leather
Old plow irons and some Shue tools and old trunk
A side saddle
A young Bea house
4 augers, 3 axes
4 iron pots & Beak Cittle (Kettle) & a frying pan.
½ share cross cut saw.
16 Harrow teeth
Negro Sip.
Negro Giney.
Negro Cate"
....etc. etc.
(Will Book 4, pp. 398, 466, original also on file.)

By his will John had provided that his wife Phoebe would have the use of his home plantation, "without Disturbance during her natural life." However, he doubtless had no idea of thus deferring his final estate settlement as long as he did. As recorded in the old church book (p. 52)—

"Met according to appointment on Saturday Dec. 7, 1793, and after Praise and Prayer Proceeded to Business, &

1st. Brother Johnson & Lincoln reported that they had wrote, signed and delivered Brother (Absalom) Graves & Wifes Letter of Dismission.

2nd. Agreed that Brother Johnson disappoint his preaching here To-morrow, on account of his being requested to attend and preach the Funeral of Mrs. Phebe Harrison on Smiths Creek who departed this Life in the 108 Year of her Age.

Adjourned till meeting in course."

John Harrison, Sr., died during the reign of King George III, but Phoebe, his wife, lived on to see the dawn of a new era; the rise of another George; and their sons' and grandsons' former commander-in-chief, the first President of the United States. She died during Washington's first administration. Her funeral was preached by the Rev. James Johnson, formerly of the Buckmarth Church in Frederick, who was ordained "to the Pastorship" of the Smiths and Linville's Creek Church, "Saturday 8th. of October, 1791." (The old church book, pp. 38, 40.)

On the 11th March, 1794, the final appraisment of John Harrison's estate, by Benj. Fawsett, Benj. Tallman, Jno. Bright, and Geo. Henton was recorded, and in June, of the same year, the final settlement in account with Reuben Harrison, the surviving executor, was likewise disposed of. £312-13-3¾." "Dec. 5, 1793, To paid Alexander W. Farling for making a Coffin for the Widow Harrison $1-10S;" "June 17, 1794, to paid for a Copy of the former settlement of the estate, 4S, etc." (Will Book VIII, pp. 105, 119.)

The bodies of John and Phoebe were laid away in the old family burial ground, before mentioned—to the westward of the foothills of the sheltering Massanutten, in thier peaceful meadow, by the drowsy waters of Smiths Creek.

Their children were, as named—

(121) Zebulon—b. 1718 (circa); d. 1792; m. July 23, 1747, at Morristown, New Jersey, Margaret Primrose (widow), daughter of Robert Cravens. See further record.

(122) John, Jr.—b. 1721 (circa); murdered by negro slave, Oct. 1763; died unmarried.

(123) Phoebe—b. 1728; d. 1807; m. 1st, 1744-5 (circa), Daniel Davison, son of Josiah, of New Jersey, b. ——, d. Jan. 1751; m. 2nd, 1753 (circa), Thomas Moore, b. 1727, d. 1797. See further record.

(124) Ann—b. ——; d. Aug. 9, 1805; m. 1st., John Davison; m. 2nd, Joseph Langdon; m. 3rd, David Harnet, living 1805, d. by Sept. 1815. Harnet removed to New Jersey between these last dates. No. issue.

(125) Reuben—b. 1731, in Del.; d. April 1807; m. 1st, Lydia Harrison, baptized by Rev. John Craig about 1745, living in 1777, daughter of Jeremiah Harrison (18); m. 2nd, Mary McDonald, b. ——, d. ——. See further record.

---

(13) GIDEON HARRISON, son of Isaiah Harrison and wife Elizabeth, born at Oyster Bay, Long Island, New York, June 25, 1694, (see p. 23), died in Sussex County, Delaware, 1729. Following his father's removal to Sussex in 1721, Gideon bought 75 acres of land on the "broad Creek" (the Broadkill) "on the lower side of the Kings Road," of John Fisher and wife Elizabeth. February 5, 1722. This land was near his brother John's, and was sold to their half-brother, Daniel, May 8th, 1730. The

latter in turn sold it, April 12, 1737, to Henry Scidmore. (See pp. 51-52, 56.) Gideon was married, and his widow served as administratrix.

A Gideon Harrison, probably his son, died in Old Augusta County, Virginia, in 1761 On May 20th, of this year, Benjamin Harrison (son of Daniel) qualified as his administrator. (Order Book III, p. 15.) The appraisment of his estate by Daniel Love, Saml. Hemphill, and William Gragg was recorded, November 17, 1761. (Will Book III, p. 93.) His sale bill of November 10th indicates that he was a young unmarried man, and includes only the following—

"Mary Harrison to 16 yards stripes & Stuffa
Daniel Love to velvet and Calamanco
Benjamin Harrison to 5 yds. Camblet
" " to 1 Green Jaccoat
" " " 1 Coat and Jaccoat
" " " 1 Jaccoat & Cravat
" " " 1 pair Britches
" " " 1 Colt Bridle
" " " 3 shirts
" " " 1 Gray Horse
Patrick Guin (Quinn) to 2 deer skins
William Cravens to 2 deer skins.
Daniel Smith " 2 " "
John Faris " Cash for sale
Total £16-19-00."

According to a suit at law brought by Mathias Lair and Catherine, 28th May, 1765, a John Harrison and Mary (his wife) had "left the Colony" just prior to this time. (County Court Judgements August 1756; *Chalkley*, Vol. I, p. 334.) This John may have been also a son of Gideon, Sr. (13.) He does not appear to have been a land owner.

CHAPTER XII

Capt. Daniel Harrison, of the French and Indian War, and His Family

THE INDIAN WAR PERIOD

DANIELL HARRISSON, (1701-1770), the eldest child of Isaiah Harrison, and his second wife Abigail, according to a deposition made by him the 16th December, 1767 (see page 144), gave his age at this time as "about 66 or 7" years. Thus he was born in 1701-2; the latter date placing him in his 66th year in 1767. His birthplace was either Oyster Bay, or Smithtown, Long Island, New York, most probably the former; his father having remarried about two years prior to the spring of 1702, the time of his removal from the first to the second named point. Daniel died testate in present Rockingham County, Virginia, July 10th, 1770. His will signed June 8, 1767, and proven, August 25, 1770, follows:

IN THE NAME OF GOD AMEN—the eighth day of June in the Year of our lord one thousand seven hundred and Sixty Seven I Daniel Harrison in the County of Augusta and Colony of Virginia being in Reasonable health & of Perfect mind and Memory thanks be Given to God therefore Calling to Mind the Mortality of the Body & knowing that it is appointed for all men once to die do make and ordain this my last will and testament

that is to say Principally and first of all I give and recommend my soul unto the hands of God that gave it and for my Body I recommend it to the earth to be Buried in a Christian and decent manner at the discretion of my Executors nothing doubting that at the General Resurrection I shall receive the same again by the Mighty Power of God and Touching such worldly estate wherewith it hath pleased God to Bless me with in this life I give devise and dispose of the same in the following manner and form viz.

Imprimis I give and bequeath first to my beloved Wife two Negroes one called Hannah and the other Called Simon during her Widow hood next again I leave her my Dwelling house and the store house kitchen and all the rest of the Buildings with a third part of the Plantation during her life with a third part of the stock and household furniture

Secondly I give and bequeath unto Sarah Stevenson my Wife's daughter one good bed and furniture and a young Breeding Mare

Thirdly I leave and bequeath unto my son Benjamin Harrison my youngest son all my home Plantation with Mill and still at my wifes decease or Marriage he paying unto the rest of my Children Thirty Pounds to be equally divided Amongst the rest of my Children

and all the out lands that I now Posess to be sold and when all my Just debts is Paid the Residue or Remainder of said Money to be equally divided and the remaining two thirds of my stock to be sold at Publick Vendue & equally divided

and my Negroes Cesar Kate and Moses to be sold at Publick Vendue to be equally diveded amongst my Children and the two Negroes Hannah and Simon that I left unto my Wife till her decease or Marriage to be sold at Publick Vendue & equally divided amongst my Children and I do hereby utterly disannul disallow and revoke all and every other former Wills legacies request or anything whatsoever Relating to a Will any ways named or Bequeathed

Ratifying and Confirming this and no other then to be my last will and Testament In Witness hereof I have hereunto sett my hand and seal the day and year above Written

before signing I appoint my wife and my son Benjamin to be my Executors (before signing, the above interlination was made)

Signed and Sealed & Delivered in presence of

Andrew Johnson Daniell Harrisson. SEAL.
John Johnson
Robert Brown.

Proved by John Johnson, August 25, 1770.

Proved by Andrew Johnson, May 13, 1771; deposition taken in Culpeper County, this date. (See, Augusta County Will Book No. 4, p. 408, Staunton, Virginia; original will also on record.)

Prior to the making of his will, Daniel Harrison, like his half-brother John, had lost a son. This son was Robert, whose death occurred at the home of his brother-in-law, Daniel Smith, May 25, 1761. (See page 86.) Robert's will signed while on his deathbed, reads as given below—

Will of Robert Harrison.

IN THE NAME OF GOD AMEN—the fourth day of May in the year of our Lord One Thousand seven hundred and sixty one I Robert Harison of Augusta County and Colony of Virginia being very sick & weak in body but of perfect Mind and Memory Thanks be given unto god therefore Calling unto mind the Mortality of my Body and knowing that it is appointed of all men to Die do make and Ordain this my last will and Testament that is to say—

Principally and first of all I give and Recommend my soul into the hands of God that gave it and for my Body I Recommend it to the Earth to be buried in a christian Like and Decent Manner at the Descretion of my Executors nothing Doubting but at the General Resurrection I shall receive the same again by the Almighty Power of God and as touching such Wordly Estate wherewith it hath pleased God to bless me in this Life I give and Devise— I dispose of the same in the following manner and form

Imprimis I give and bequeath to my Father Daniel Harrison my best Hatt and Eight Pounds Current Money of Virginia to be delivered and paid by my executors on Demand

Item I give and bequeath to my brother Jesse Harrison Eight Pounds Current Money aforesaid which he is Now Indebted to me and Ten pounds like Money I allow to be at his Disposal to be put to interest or Lay out as he shall think most Beneficial for the Youse of his Daughter Ann when she arrives at the age Eighteen Years

Item I give and bequeath to my brother Daniel Harrison all my wearing Apearil Except my Hatt before Mentioned

Item I give and bequeath to my Brother in Law Daniel Smith my watch and twenty pounds Current Money I alow to Remain in his hands for the schooling and Educating of his son Robert Smith which he is to pay for that Youse

Item I give my lands and stock and all Remaining part of my Personalty Estate to be sold by my Executors and the Money Acruing by such sale with what I now have or will Remain after paying my Just Debts and Funeral expense and Legacies before Mentioned to be Equally divided between my Brothers Jesse Harrison Daniel Harrison and Benjamin Harrison and my sisters Mary and Abigail Harrison and my Brother in Law Daniel Smith

I do hereby constitute make and ordain the Above mentioned Daniel Smith & Jesse Harrison my Executors of this my last will and Testament

in Witness Whereof I hereunto set my hand & seal the day and year first Above Written.

Signed Sealed published pronounced
& Declaired by the sd. Rob. Harrison
as his last will and Testament in
presents of the subscribers

Robert Harrisson. SEAL.

Silas Hart
Hugh Hamilton
Wm. Minter
Wm. Gragg.

Proved August 18, 1761, by Hamilton and Minter;
executors qualified with Wm. Preston and Michael Warren.
(See, Augusta County Will Book No. 3, p. 60, Staunton, Virginia, original will also on record.)

Together, these wills mention all of the children of Daniel Harrison, with the exception of his daughter Jane, the wife of Daniel Smith. The seals on the wills, with the Coats of Arms impressed, have been described (See Chapter VII.) The spelling above in the signatures is as given on the originals; "Harrison" being spelled with the "double S", the same as in the case of John, Sr.

Daniel Harrison's childhood was passed at Smithtown, Long Island. The year of his birth (1701), Capt. William Kidd, of pirate fame, came to the close of his meteoric career, and no doubt the young children of Daniel's day were highly entertained with many a story of the bold Captain, and of buried treasure on Long Island.

Kid originally was commissioned by the British Government. His sailing orders, dated in London, 25th February, 1695-6, and signed by Earl of Bellomont (who in in 1695 had been appointed Governor of New York) instructed him to sail directly to Boston in New England, to bring all prizes captured to London, and to direct his letters to Sir Edmund Harrison, etc. He was commissioned Commander of the ship Adventure Galley, which had been fitted out by the Governor, and Sir Edmund Harrison, a merchant, and others, all of London. The plan was to capture Spanish pirate prizes for the King; the backers being allowed to divide their treasure. The authorities later withdrew their support, and Kidd was finally convicted of piracy. He seems to have died a victim of unfortunate cirmstances. (See, *The Real Captain Kidd, A Vindication,* by Sir Cornelius Neal Dalton, 1911.)

It may be remarked in this connection, that the Rev. Jacob Henderson, a missionary of the Church of England, stationed at Dover Hundred, in Pennsylvania, in his short account of the Church in the Province of New York and New Jersey, dated June, 1712, to which was appended a "Scheme of the Charge in New Jersey," made reference to a John Harrison; "who, I am audibly informed, was brought up with one Kidd, a pirate, to take the place of Daniel Cox, a worthy gentleman and a zealous Churchman, who had given 200 acres of land to the church at Hopewell." (*New Jersey Archives,* Vol. IV,

p. 155, New York Colonial Documents.) This John Harrison was Capt. John, the son of John Harrison, formerly of Flushing, Long Island. The later was one of the first members of the church at Perth Amboy, New Jersey, in whose memory a tablet today bears testimony of his early generosity. The whole charge was political, but Kidd (who seems to have been a native of Scotland) before his wild-goose chase after pirates, had up to this time been settled in New York, where he was a reputable sea-faring man of easy circumstances, and married to a lady of considerable fortune.

In 1721, Daniel Harrison migrated with his father, Isaiah, to Sussex County, Delaware. There May 8th, 1730, after his first mariage, he purchased 75 acres of land, which had belonged to his half-brother Gideon Harrison, who had died the year before. On October 10, 1732, he was one of the sons to whom his father deeded a 250 acres share of Maiden Plantation, when the latter divided this, his tract of 907 acres of land. (See Chapter V.)

Daniel's first wife, and the mother of his children, was Margaret Cravens, whom he married about 1724, or shortly before this time. She was a sister of Robert Cravens, who had previously married Daniel's half-sister, Mary, very soon after the Harrisons' removal to Delaware.

As earlier identified, Daniel was among the party of five Harrison brothers, who, with their father, migrated from Delaware to what was then Orange County, Virginia, in the spring of 1737. The brothers began disposing of their Delaware lands in April of this year, and on the 12th of this month, Daniel sold his Gideon Harrison tract to Henry Scidmore. They arrived in the region of the Shenandoah, in what had been set apart for Augusta County, before the tide of emigration had begun rapidly to set in. Several years were spent in camping and exploring, during which time their surveys and preperations to take up land were developing. Daniel's earliest surveys are dated, December 8th, 1738, and November 15th, 18th, 19th, 1740. (Last three dates from records at Winchester, Va.; kindly supplied by Dr J. W. Wayland.) He was the first of the three brothers to begin the long list of numerous Harrison land patents; his first patent bearing date 22nd September, 1739, has been quoted in full in Chapter VIII. The following year, on March 3rd, he released his final tract in Delaware to George Campbell. (See Chapter VI.)

Altogether, Daniel Harrison and his sons were granted some 4,294 acres of Augusta County lands in seventeen patents—all but three of these being issued to Daniel himself, as follows—

To DANIEL HARRISON, SR.

Date	Acres	Location	Book No.	Page
22nd. Sept., 1739,	400	"on east draft of West fork of Naked Creek"	18	381
20th. Aug., 1741,	400	"on Dry Fork of Smith's Creek"	19	1131
25th. Sept., 1746,	100	"on Cook's Creek" (willed to Benjamin.)		
" " "	387	"on South east side of Muddy Creek."	24	422
" " "	400	"on a branch of Muddy Creek"	24	423
" " "	215	"on the West Fork of Naked Creek"	24	424
" " "	400	"on the head of Linville's Mill Creek"	24	425
5th. Sept., 1749,	200	"on a branch of Muddy Creek"	27	356
10th. Sept., 1755,	65	"on Cook's Creek" (willed to Benjamin.)		
15th. Dec., 1755,	100	"on the North Fork of Linville's Creek, for importing Joseph Roberts and Richard Simpson	32	660
" " "	120	"on the North River of Shenandoah above the		

		Gap in the mountain including the 3rd. fork of said river.."	32	661
15th. Dec., 1755	250	"On a draft of Linville's Creek on the west side of the land Bryan and Linvel lives on"	32	661
16th. Aug., 1756,	200	"on Muddy Creek and Dry River"	33	124
30th. July, 1763,	365	"on a branch of Linville's Creek called Johns Run."	35	321
TOTAL	3,602	acres		
		To ROBERT HARRISON		
20th. Aug., 1741,	260	"on Dry Fork of Smith's Creek on Daniel Harrison's land and on Robert Craven's line"	19	1118
		To DANIEL HARRISON, JR.		
5th. Sept., 1749,	262	"on a branch of Muddy Creek adjoining Daniel Harrison Sr."	27	325
		To JESSE HARRISON.		
10th. July, 1766,	170	"near one of the main branches of Linville's Creek, etc."		

(See, Patent Books numbers as above, at Land Office, Richmond, Virginia; also page 128 of *this* volume.)

September 25, 1746, appears to have been a notable day for the Harrisons in general in the way of Land Patents. This day the survey of the Fairfax Line was started. Besides the grants to Daniel on this date, his nephew, John Harrison, Jr., patented 1,566 acres, and his brother Samuel, 200 acres. On the next date September 5, 1749, besides the patents to Daniel and Daniel, Jr., Samuel was granted 400 acres. Also, 16th August, 1756, Samuel and Thomas (another brother) patented 245 and 212 acres respectively.

Following his second patent, Daniel is found first mentioned on the Orange court records in 1742. This, and various other references have been quoted. (Chapters I, and IX.) A further record shows that some time prior to 1743 he had loaned out a sum of Pennsylvania money, the currency used in Delaware. Here again the name of Robert Smith, probably the same who had witnessed so many Harrison deeds in Delaware, makes its appearance.

"July 3, 1743—Daniel Harrison having obtained an attachment against ye estate of Thomas Renix under the hand of James Wood Gent, £7.10, Sheriff having returned he had attached ye estate of Thomas Renix in ye hand of Robert Smith . . . ordered that an attachment issue against ye Deft. Garnashee returnable next court if suit is till then continued." The suit was continued July 29, 1743; "In a list by attachment brought by Daniel Harrison pet. against ye estate of Thomas Renix Deft. the Pet. in open court made Oath to his acct. against the Deft. for £7.10, Pa. Money the value of £7.10 current money of Virginia which is ordered to be certified on the account and Its further Ordered that the Pet. be lodged in ye suit." Again, 25th August, 1743; "In the suit by attachment brought (by) Daniel Harrison vs. one Renox, Robert Smith Garnashee being summonsed & sworn declared that he was indebted to the S[aid] Renox in the sum of £7 . . . current money of Pennsylvania." Also, 23rd March, 1743-4: "Daniel

Harrison vs. Thomas Rennox, Deft.—Robert Smith Garnashee . . . etc." (Orange Court Order Books, 1741-43, pp. 506, 529; 1743-46, pp. 3, 75.)

On the date of the second continuance of this suit, July 29, 1743, Daniel was in court in person. It was at this time that he and Robert Cravens were each sworn into their "Military Commission of Captain of Horses." (See p. 126.) From this time on he is frequently found referred to (except on the land records) as Capt. Daniel Harrison.

Capt. Daniel was one of the overseers appointed, along with his brother John Harrison and Robert Cravens, by the Court of Orange, May 24, 1745, to lay out and clear the old Indian Road, "The Long Grey Trail," through what is now Rockingham County. (See pp. 2, 139, 162.) This was destined to be the most traveled highway in the Valley, and was the first to traverse it lengthwise; affording access from the northern to the southern settlements of the region on the Shenandoah.

Prior to the organization of the county courts of Augusta and Frederick, very few public roads had been authorized west of the Blue Ridge. These were generally connecting links with the territory of Orange east of the mountain. An instance of this was the Swift Run Gap road ordered opened in February, 1741. (See p. 140.)

At June Court, 1739, David Davis presented a "petition for a road from John Young's at N. Mountain to top of Blue Ridge to bounds of Goochland." At this time also it was "Ordered Road be cleared from Hite's mill to the ford of Shenandoah River at Sihley's bent and that Charles McDowell clear the same from the Mill to John Nation . . . etc." (Orange Court Order Book, 1739-41, p. 3.) McDowell was a settler of Frederick, and Hite's mill is said to have been at present Bartonville in this county.

Among the first roads ordered opened by Frederick court after its organization (1743), according to a list given by Cartmell (p. 51) was one from Hite's Mill to Nation's run, one from Cedar Creek to (John) Funk's Mill, one from Funk's Mill to the Augusta line, etc. This last joined here the northernmost link of the Indian Road as ordered opened by the Orange court order. Funk's Mill was at the present town of Strasburg.

On 23rd May, 1745, the day before the final order regarding the Indian Road was issued "Upon the petition of Philip Long and several of the inhabitants of Massanutten" it was set forth that it was a hardship for them to help "clear a road near the foot of Blue Mountain." (Orange Court Order Book, 1743-46, p. 324.) The Massanutten settlers, being on the eastern side of this mountain, were later exempted (Sept. 28, 1745) from working on the Indian Road. (See Chapter I.)

While Captain Daniel Harrison's first patents embraced land on Naked Creek, and the Dry Fork—a headwater of Smiths Creek—his permanent settlement was made on his Cook's Creek land. He located some five or six miles to the southwest of his brother Thomas, on what is now the Warm Springs Turnpike, at the present town of Dayton. This point is at the head spring of the western branch of Cook's Creek. A little further west is Muddy Creek, and a little to the south begin the head streams of Linville's Creek, in which region ran one of the earliest roads of present Rockingham—known by 1743 as "Daniel Harrison's path," the "Irish Road," and by 1764 as "Daniel Harrison's road": "Patent by Gooch, 30th August, 1743, to William Skillern, 343 acres on Linville's Creek on both sides the Irish Road, Daniel Harrison's path" (*Chalkley*, Vol. II, pp. 46-47); June 21, 1764, deed, George and William Skilleren to Walter Crow, 243 acres "on the head of a draft of Linville's Creek on Daniel Harrison's road"; land patented to William Skillern, (Sr.), deceased, 30th August, 1743, and devised to his sons to be disposed of. (Deed Book 11, p. 706.)

Patent by Gooch

To the 165 acres patented by Daniel on Cook's Creek, he added $83\frac{1}{2}$ acres by purchase from Samuel Wilkins, 27th February, 1749; this land having been a part of 1264 acres originally patented to Robert McKay, Joist Hite, William Duff and Robert Green, 26th March, 1739. By 1801 Daniel's son Benjamin had enlarged the "home plantation," thus started, to $1129\frac{1}{2}$ acres. (See p. 128.)

The region "West of the Great Mountains" being sufficiently filled up by settlers, the organization of Augusta County was completed in 1745, by the establishment of the first court. From this time on many of the activities of Daniel Harrison's life are gleaned from the old records at Staunton; his name appearing here almost continually (with the possible exception of 1746 and 1762) each year until his death.

At one of the first meetings of the vestry, July 20, 1747, leave was granted John Smith, Gent. (Capt. John) and others to build a "Chapel of Ease on Daniel Harrison's Plantation." This was no doubt the first building erected for public worship by a congregation of the Established Church in Old Augusta County. As will be recalled this was one of the points at which Rev. John Jones was ordered to preach in 1755. (See pp. 150, 151.)

The first reference to Daniel on the court records appears a month following the vestry meeting; August 20, 1747, Order Book No. I, (p. 225) "John O'Neal ordered to be recognized to the peace, especially towards Daniel Harrison." This year also, September 3rd, Daniel was appointed a processioner, as elsewhere noted. (See p. 163.)

One of the first mills of present Rockingham was owned by Capt. Harrison; July 26, 1748—Land Entry Book No. 1, "Charles Driver 400 acres between Daniel Harrison's mill and Ro. Patterson." This mill, according to his will, was on his home plantation. The will also mentions his still, the date of the origin of which appears to be unknown; doubtless it too, was one of the first of Rockingham. Driver and Patterson were obviously near neighbors of Daniel. Among other nearby land owners of the time were Jacob Dye (Dyer), farmer, and wife Mary, who on 29th July, 1748, sold a tract of land on Muddy Creek, "corner Daniel Harrison, Wm. White, Wm. Carroll," to Ephraim Love, "late of Lancaster County, Pennsylvania"—Delivered Wm. Hopkins, 5th March, 1753. (Deed Book 2, p. 16.) Ephraim was later Capt. Ephraim Love, mentioned along with Capt. Daniel in the lists of 1755. (See p. 182.)

Capt. Harrison was also one of the first to use the plentiful supply of limestone near at hand for building. The old mansion house built of this material, probably by him, and certainly resided in by his son Benjamin, until the latter's death, is still standing. (See illustration.) It is said to have been used as a fort at one time. His first "stone house" is referred to under date, 28th February, 1749, at which time his first deeds appear. Deed Book No. 2, (p. 582), "Samuel Wilkins to Daniel Harrison, 190 acres near the head of Cook's Creek; Delivered, Alexander Herron, March, 1762"; Same date (p. 586), "Daniel Harrison, Gent. to Arthur Johnson, 190 acres; 10 acres; Cook's Creek—Harrison's stonehouse." (*Chalkley*, Vol. III, p. 282.) Daniel appears to have been quite a builder. In May, 1750, he petitioned the court stating that his was the lowest bid for building the (new) court house, and enquiring the reason why the commissioners refused to give him their contract. (County Court Judgements A.) Earlier this year he had joined his brother, Jeremiah Harrison and Robert Cravens, as an appraiser of Charles Gallagher's estate. (See p. 147.)

Conditions in the county at this period were generally quiet, but regardless of the dangers from without, incident to the times, there were some unscrupulous characters within always ready on opportunity to furnish a disturbance. One such character was John O'Neal, whose early differences with Daniel came to a head in 1747. In 1751, O'Neal flared up again—"June 1, 1751—Daniel Harrison appointed next friend to his son Robert Harrison in order to bring suit vs. John O'Neal" (Order Book II, p. 609); also, Fee book of Augusta Court; August-November, 1751, (p. 135)—"Robert Harrison, Capt. Harrison's son, vs. O,Neal." This suit appears in August of the next year; "Harrison vs. O'Neal—Robert Harrison infant, by Daniel Harrison his father and next friend." (Judgements at Rules, *Chalkley,* Vol. I, pp. 45, 305; Vol. II, p. 397.) In the meantime, on November 29, 1751, Daniel qualified "Under Sheriff" of Augusta County (Order Book III, p. 216) and for several years O'Neal appears to have been effectively curbed as a general nuisance in the neighborhood. (Robert, the Captain's son, at this time, according to Boogher's date of his birth, was twenty-six years old; he had patented land in 1741. Evidently the term "infant" was used very leniently; or probably this Robert was actually a grandson.)

Two days prior to his induction into office Daniel's first sale of patented lands was recorded. Here too, occurs the first and only mention of his first wife, Margaret—"27th November, 1751, deed, Daniel Harrison and Margaret to John McCluer, 387 acres on Muddy Creek, on North side of North River; patented to Daniel, 5th September, 1746; Teste, James Kilburn, Ro. Renick." (Deed Book 4, p. 29.)

The year 1751, saw the dawn of a new era in the Colony's history. On November 20th, Robert Dinwiddie (b. 1693—d. 1770), Lieutenant-Governor of Virginia, arrived from England. Governor Gooch had left the Colony with his family June 29, 1749. He had resigned, but remained a steady friend of Virginia. On his leaving, John Robinson, Sr., president of the Council, succeeded as acting Governor, but he dying on September 5th, following, was in turn succeeded by Thomas Lee, as president and acting Governor. The Earl of Albemarle, William Anne Keppel, was still titular Governor-in-Chief in England. Lee died February 12, 1751, and was succeeded by Lewis Burwell, of Gloucester—also president of the Council—who served until Dinwiddie's arrival. Dinwiddie had been born in Scotland, and educated in the Church of the same. He was appointed Lieut-Governor, July 20, 1751. This year also, George Washington was appointed one of the adjutants-general of Virginia, with the rank of Major. The same year his brother Lawrence died at Mt. Vernon, aged 34 years.

One of the new Governor's first acts was the division of the Colony, in 1752, into four military districts, the northern one being allotted to Major Washington. France was now undertaking to stretch a chain of forts from Canada to Louisiana, to secure control west of the Alleghanies, which she claimed on account of La Salle's discovery. Posts were established on the Ohio in territory claimed by Virginia.

In Augusta—following Daniel's appointment as Under Sheriff, on August 19, 1752, (Order Book III, p. 312), "Charles Campbell, Ebenezer Westcourt, Daniel Harrison, and Peter Scholl, each qualified Captain of a Company of Foot," and William Jameson, Coroner. This was the second time Harrison and Scholl had qualified as Captains, their former appointment being under the jurisdiction of Orange County. (Other Captains of the day had also formerly served under this jurisdiction.)

Winchester was incorporated this year, but settlers to the upper Valley were pouring in also, and the Clerk of the Court of Augusta was rapidly nearing the end of his forth book of deeds. And these were large books too. By November 15, 1752, he had arrived at page 527. On this date Daniel and Thomas Harrison, along with Edward Shanklin, were witnesses to a deed of James Downing and Mary, to James White—120 acres patented to Hugh Douglass, 25th June, 1747, John Stevenson's line. The same day Deed Book No. 5 was started; here too, Daniel was again on hand and witnessed another deed (p. 11) with his neighbors John Smith and John Anderson; "John Poage and Mary to William Cleghorn, blacksmith, 214 acres on Cedar Creek of James."

Margaret Cravens Harrison, the first wife of Daniel, died in 1753. She was born probably about 1702. From her death until 1760, Daniel remained a widower. She too had "climbed the blue embattled hills," and while there is ample testimony of her husband's resourcefulness and fortitude, certainly hers was no less. Coming into a wild and unsettled country with six little children, one a baby in arms, she had ministered to their, and her husbands, needs, and brought fourth another—this last, one of Rockingham's most distinguished soldiers of the Revolution.

THE SMITHS

It has been well said that the Harrisons of Rockingham were intimately connected with the Smiths. Reference here is to the family of the immigrant Capt. John Smith, some account of whom has been given, and the accidental finding of whose will among the unindexed records at Staunton has been noted. (See pp. 8, 37, 86 and 141.) This will, in the original, written on a single sheet of paper on the back of which occurs the notation, "John Smith Senr Will," is dated May 7, 1753, and reads as follows—

"IN THE NAME OF GOD AMEN—

I John Smith of Augusta County and Colony of Virginia being very Sick in Body but in my Perfect Sences do make this my Last will and testament first of all I Leave to Margaret my well beloved wife all my Stock of Horses and Cattle Household Goods and all my Movables Whatsoever She shall also make Choice of any one Tract of Land that I have which She is to hold During her Life and at her Death the sd. Land to fall to my daughter Louisa I also Constitute and appoint Daniel Harrison Silas Hart and my son Abraham Smith to be my Executors and it is my will that they Shall Sell all or so much of my Land Excepting the above Tracts as will Pay all of my Debts and funeral Charges and what Ever of my Land Remains un sold to pay my Debts to be Divided Equally between my sons William Joseph David Jonathan and James Jordon my Executors to Pay five Shillings Each to my Sons Abraham Henry Daniel and John & I Do hereby Revoke make null and void all other wills made by me before this Date and hereby Pronounce and Publickly Declare this to be my Last Will and Testament in Witness whereof I have Hereunto Set my hand and Seal this Seventh Day of May one Thousand Seven Hundred & Fifty three—

In Presents of
James Patton — Jno Smith." (SEAL).
Robt. Renick
Humphrey Madison.

(See original wills, Box 3, Staunton, Virginia.)

The signature of Capt. Smith is in a very bold hand. The seal is of red wax bearing embossed on it the figure of a "horn of plenty," out of which pours a "fleur-de-lis," and water (?), onto a sprig, or branch of a vine, placed underneath, and curved as an inverted rainbow. The fleur-de-lis was the Royal emblem of France, and is also the name for a species of iris. Probably the vine of the seal alludes to the latter, particularly as the iris of mythology was associated with the rainbow. In one way or another the fleur-de-lis occurs frequently in the arms of Smith families. Its significance in pouring from a horn of plenty would seem to be evident. On the arms of Richard Smith, the Smithtown, Long Isiland, immigrant, the fluer-de-lis, was a prominent figure. (See p. 37.) Among Richard's sons were Jonathan and Daniel, names which appear above.

Robert Renick was doubtless a kinsman of Thomas to whom Daniel Harrison had made the loan mentioned in the Orange records. James Patton was the colonel, and Silas Hart was the justice.

The will is interesting, in that it mentions more children than appear to have heretofore credited to Capt. Smith. At the proving of his importation at Orange (See page 8) he included his wife Margaret, and sons Abraham, Henry, Daniel, John, and Joseph. Of these Abraham, b. in Ulster, Ireland, 1722, m. Sarah Caldwell, of Augusta County; Daniel, b. in Ulster, 1724, m. about 1751, Jane, the daughter of Capt. Daniel Harrison; Henry, b. 1727, m. Camey ———; John, Jr., b. 1730, was killed at Ft. Vause, June 25, 1756; and Joseph, b. 1734, in Chester County Pennsylvania (?), was captured with his father at Ft. Vause, June 25, 1756, and died a prisoner on the way to New Orleans. A daughter Margaret, according to Boogher (p. 330) b. 1741, m. Hugh Reece Bowen, who d. October 7, 1870. The will names a daughter Louisa, probably Margaret Louisa, and adds sons William, David, Jonathan, and James Jordan. The last may have been named for his mother's family. Evidently these five were the youngest children.

* * * * *

Early in 1754 the French and Indian War opened; April this year found Washington with two companies proceeding to Great Meadows. The year before he had been sent by Dinwiddie to the French Commander, Pierre, at Ft. Le Boeuf, on French Creek, a short distance south of Lake Erie, to remonstrate against the French encroachments. On this trip, leaving Williamsburg, October 31st, and travelling by way of Alexandria and Winchester, (Ft.) Cumberland, the farthest frontier settlement was reached, November 14th. Continuing over the tractless mountains and ascending the Allegheny, he and five attendants selected the confluence of the Monogahela and Allegheny Rivers—at present Pittsburgh—as a site for a fort. Here Ft. Duquesne was afterwards erected by the French. Washington arrived back at Williamsburg with Pierre's sealed reply, January 16, 1754. April 17th, following, marked the first open act of hostilities between France and England in America. On this date an Ensign left in command of the unfinished fort at the fork of the Ohio was forced to surrender. Hearing of this April 25th, Washington marched slowly to the mouth of Red Stone Creek and camped. Here he had a skirmish, May 28th, but his provisions becoming exhausted, he then fell back to the post at Great Meadows, styled Ft. Necessity, July 1st. Two days later, with overwhelming numbers, the French captured this fort, and on the 4th, under terms of an agreement with the enemy allowing him to return with his troops to Virginia unmolested, Washington surrendered. Accordingly he retired by way of Wills Creek to Williamsburg. The Assembly voted him and his officers thanks.

In the fall two independent companies, ordered by Dinwiddie from New York, arrived in Hampton Roads and were sent to Wills Creek, where they built Ft. Cumberland—about 50 miles northwest of Winchester. In October the Assembly granted 20,000 Pounds for public exigencies, and the Governor enlarged the Virginia forces to ten companies. These he made independent to terminate disputes between the regular and provincial officers, under which plan Washington, as he would have been reduced to the grade of Captain, and inferior in rank to those of his command who held a king's commission, resigned and passed the winter at Mt. Vernon. He had lately come into this estate through the death of his brother Lawrence.

At the outbreak of the war the population of the Colonies was 1,485,000, including 292,000 blacks. Virginians were described by Dinwiddie as indolent, and without military ardour.

In Augusta, at the time, Col. James Patton was the County-Lieutenant, or commander-in-chief of the local military forces. In January the Governor wrote to him ordering him to "draw out" the militia, and from them obtain by volunteering, or drafting, fifty men who were to be at Alexandria by February 20th, to join the command of Major Washington. It is thought that this company was led by Andrew Lewis, who was with Washington at the capitulation of Ft. Necessity. Writing on the 6th of September, the Governor stated that he had heard "complaints from our frontier in Augusta County of many parties of Indians, etc., robbing and ill-treating our people." On the 11th he ordered Washington to give a detachment of forty or fifty men to Capt. Lewis, who was to march immediately to Augusta, and apply to Col. Patton to "direct him where to proceed that he may be the most useful." On the same day Dinwiddie addressed a letter to Lewis and on the 6th of October, the Captain was on his march. Somewhere south, or west, of Staunton he built a stockade fort. Here he appears to have remained until after February 12th, following, on which date he was ordered to march immediately to Winchester to remain for further orders. The fort was left in command of Ensign William Wright.

On October 10, 1754, (Order Book No. 11, p. 319), John Brown and Daniel Harrison were each allowed pay for patrolling. Daniel was now about fifty-three years old, and was probably assigned to local duty. His Lieutenant, at least for a part of the time, was Benjamin Kendley, as disclosed by a suit brought by the latter vs. Capt. Daniel Harrison—1754: "To 20 days service as Lieutenant of Militia under your command at 25 pounds tobacco per day." (County Court Judgements—August, 1759.)

Among the settlers in the region to the west of present Harrisonburg at this time, were the following before alluded to, (p. 129) who as "Inhabitants of North Mountain, at head of Muddy Creek," in 1753 or 1754, petitioned for a road from Ephraim Love's to the road from "South Branch to Swift Run Gap"; viz. Ephraim Love, John Hardman, Jeremiah Harrison, Aaron Oliver, Thomas Campbell, Robert Pattison, John Slaven, Patrick Black, Robert Rollston, John Negarry, Thomas Shanklin, John Taler, Daniel Harrison, John Foolston, Jesse Harrison, and Patrick Cain. (Original Petitions filed in County Court 1753-4, Part I.) In this region also probably resided John Bowyers, Francis Bealey and James Thompson, the last two of whom, with Daniel Harrison, are mentioned 22nd August, 1754, as witnesses to Bowyer's idemnifying bond to Archibald Alexander, with sureties James Lockhart, Andrew Hays and Wm. Woods. Alexander was an agent of Borden and had given Bowyer power to sign deeds to Borden's lands. (Will Book 2, p. 67.)

Other settlers of old West Rockingham in 1754, appear as signers of a petition regarding John O'Neal, who, regardless of the war, continued with his outbursts, adding to the general alarm. This curious document may be of interest here—

"To the Worshipful Court of Augusta County. The petition of sundry inhabitants of this County by this North Mountain, in Capt. Harrison's and Capt. Love's Companies, humbly sheweth: That your petitioners are daily troubled by John O'Neal, a person of evil fame, who being ill natured, evil, designing, citigious, wicked man, he often takes occasion to come to the houses of some of your petitioners and then designedly raises and foments disputes with them in which he makes use of the most opprobrious and abused words he can invent, and as he is bound to the peace, dares any one to strike him, therefore, should any of us strike or beat him we know not what might be the consequences as we are unacquainted with the law and his usual manner threatens to shoot us if he sees any of us out of our own plantations, that he will do us all the damage he can by killing our horses, cattle, &c., and when reproved of his misbehavior he tells us that if he does any action, be it ever so bad, that he will be cleared by this Court for two pieces of eight. His behavior is such that your petitioners are afraid to leave their families to go about their lawful affairs, not knowing but he may fulfill his thcreats before our return by killing our wives or children, burning our houses, or doing some other irreparable damage, and as doubtless your Worships is well acquainted with the behavior of this malicious man, we hope you will take our case into consideration and fall upon some method to hinder him from being guilty of such outrages and irregularities for the future. That we, being subjects to his Majesty and the laws of the Domain, may be no longer abused by such a person in the above manner, and your petitioners, as in duty bound, shall ever pray.—Daniel Harrison, James Magill, Daniel Smith, John McGarry, Robert Harrison, Gawin Black, John Lonkill, Patrick Cain, Aaron Oliver, Robert Gray, Henry Smith, Benjamin Kinley, John Smith, John McClewer, Gabriel Pickens, John Hinton, and Robert Patterson."

November 8, 1754, Cain and Patterson denied signatures, and Black stated that he was overpersuaded by some of the petitioners, but during the dark days of 1756, O'Neal was found guilty through a writ of "Scire facias on recognizance," issued in connection with a suit brought against him by the King. (Judgements at Rules, March, 1756 (A), King vs. O'Neal; *Chalkley,* Vol. I, p. 313.) (*Waddell,* p. 131.)

The year 1755 was marked indelibly in the memory of the Valley settlers by Braddock's defeat. Gen. Edward Braddock arrived in Virginia, in February, this year, as the newly appointed commander-in-chief of all the military forces of America. After proceeding immediately to Williamsburg to confer with the Governor, on March 2nd, he invited Washington to join his army as a volunteer, retaining his former rank. This was accepted. The General established his headquarters at Alexandria. Here, on April 13th, at the now famous old home of John Carlyle, he met the Governors of Massachusetts, New York, Pennsylvania, Maryland, and Virginia, to outline a plan of campaign. At this meeting by invitation were also Washington and Benjamin Franklin, the latter being deputy postmaster-general of Pennsylvania. On April 20th, Braddock began his march to the country beyond the Blue Ridge. On the way he was joined by Washington, who accompanied him to Winchester, and thence to Ft. Cumberland. In May, young Washington was made his aide-de-camp. Braddock's army consisted of 1,000 British, and 1,400 Virginia and Maryland troops, besides a troop of Virginia light horse and a few Indians. From Ft. Cumberland, in June, was launched the second expedition against Ft. Duquesne, the army cutting its way and building a road through the dense forest, as it moved forward. When within about ten miles of the fort, as the troops had just completed fording the river, and as those in advance were reaching the heights above it, they were met by a detachment of the French at about one o'clock in the afternoon, and thus began the terrible battle of the Monongahela, July 9, 1755.

The enemy detachment numbered 230 French and Candians, and 630 Indians, and at the first skirmish their commander was killed. They however, had the advantage of position, and concealed their forces so skilfully that their hot fire created consternation in Braddock's advance guard. This fell back on the main army in great confusion, communicating their panic to the rest of his forces. Braddock was unused to the Indian mode of warfare, and in vain threatened and entreatied, endeavoring to form his men in platoons and columns, as if maneuvering on the plains of Flanders, but in the confusion they remained in a road twelve feet wide, enclosed by woods, for three hours huddled together, exposed to the enemy, shooting into the air, often hitting each other, and doing little hurt to their unseen foe. Washington and Sir Peter Halket, urged the General to allow his men to shelter themselves, but he called them cowards and struck at them with his sword. In spite of his orders the Virginia troops concealed themselves, and preserving their presence of mind fought with the utmost bravery. The French and Indians aimed particularly at the officers, and Washington was the only mounted aide not wounded. More than half of Braddock's men were killed or wounded, about two-thirds of their casualties being by their own bullets. Braddock himself, after having had three horses killed under him and two disabled, was mortally wounded, falling from his horse about five o'clock in the evening. Their ammunition used up, his army fled in disorder back to the Monongahela; the regulars throwing away their arms and accountrements as they ran. Many were tomahawked at the fording place, but those that crossed the river were not pursued, as the Indians stopped to collect the plunder. The French lost only 28 killed, and 29 badly wounded.

Not one of Braddock's British soldiers could be persuaded to stay and aid in bearing off their wounded General. Orme and Capt. Stewart of the Virginia light-horse, and his servant, together with another American officer, carried Braddock from the field. He continued to give orders for two days. On dying, he bequeathed his charger and body servant to Washington. His death occurred at Great Meadows, Sunday, 8 p. m., July 13, and the next day he was buried in the road near Ft. Necessity. In the absence of a Chaplain, Washington read the burial service. On returning to Mt. Vernon his reputation was greatly elevated by his signal gallantry on this occasion. Braddock was succeeded by Col. Dunbar, a Britisher, who retreated with the reminent of the army to Winchester. Fearing for his safety even here, Dunbar further retired with his regulars to Philadelphia, where he went into winter quarters, in the midst of summer; much to the disgust of Governor Dinwiddie.

While Braddock's defeat occurred in the region to the north of the Potomac, its consequences were immediately felt by the Valley settlers to the south, they being the nearest of Virginia's Colonists to the territory claimed by the French. News of the disaster spread like wildfire, and widespread consternation, anxiety, and alarm, was universal. The Rev. John Craig at this time did valiant service in rallying the spirits of the Augusta inhabitants. He states that they were in dreaful confusion, and discouraged to the highest degree. Some of the richer sort were for flying to safer parts of the country, but he advised eloquently against this, and urged the building of forts, one of which was to be his church. The people readily followed, and within less than two months his congregation was well fortified.

About a week following Braddock's defeat, Col. James Patton was killed by the Indians. He had gone on business to the upper country, and was resting from his journey at the house of William Ingles and the Drapers. While the men of the house were in the fields a party of savages surprised the Colonel sitting at a table writing. His broadsword being before him, he cut down two of them, before he was shot by another out of his reach. The Indians also killed Mrs. George Draper, and one Casper Barrier, and after plundering the premises set fire to the house, and carried away as prisoners Henry Leonard, Mrs, John Draper, and Mrs. Ingles and her two children. Mrs. Draper was released six or seven years afterwards. Mrs. Ingles was taken to Ohio, and separated from her children, one of whom died in captivity. She later escaped and after about five months absence made her way to New River, where she found her husband, who then took her to Ft. Vause, near the head of the Roanoke—about one half mile west of present Shawsville. Persuading her husband to take her to the east of the Ridge they left here, and the day they did so the fort was captured by the Indians, and all were killed or taken prisoners.

On the 11th of August, Gov. Dinwiddie wrote Capt. Andrew Lewis, recognizing him as next in command to Col. Patton. This month the Assembly voted 40,000 Pounds for public service, and augmented the Virginia regiment to sixteen companies—1,500 men. Washington was commissioned commander-in-chief of the Colony's forces, and allowed to appoint his own officers. He appointed next in rank to him Col. Adam Stephens, and Major Andrew Lewis, of Augusta. By October 11th, Washington was in command at Winchester. The militia still refused to stir, as confusion and alarm yet prevailed. No orders were obeyed which were not inforced by a party of soldiers or at the commander's drawn sword. The Governor wrote Lord Fairfax, the County-Lieutenant of Frederick, condoling him for having to live amongst such people.

On October 25, 1755, the court of Augusta allowed Samuel and James McDowell pay for patrolling. Andrew Scott pay for a horse impressed, and Daniel Harrison pay for patrolling. (Order Book IV, p. 492.) Andrew Scott was probably a near relative of Samuel, whose orphan John Scott had chosen Daniel Harrison as his guardian. Daniel's bond, as guardian, was recorded March 20, 1755, with sureties, David Stewart and Robert McClenachan. (Will Book 2, p. 97.)

With the county patrolled, the court continued to hold sessions, and while some were leaving for quieter parts evidently their debts were not being overlooked. November 20th, Daniel Harrison is again mentioned, this time in a suit vs. Joseph Bryan regarding an attachment levied on the latter "before his removal from the county." (Order Book IV, p. 504.)

In February, 1756, Washington visited Gen. Shirley, the new Commander-in-Chief of the British armies in America, at Boston, to obtain a king's commission for himself and officers. This month, from Ft. Frederick, on New River in Augusta County, was begun the Sandy Creek expedition. This was against the Shawness in Ohio, and with the exception of a few Cherokees it consisted exclusively of Virginia troops under Major Andrew Lewis. Among the Captains were John Smith, William Preston, and David Stewart, the last named being the commissary. The whole force numbered 340 men. They marched on the 18th, and passing by the Holston, and Clinch, the head of Sandy Creek was reached on the 25th. In March their provisions ran out, and when they arrived near the Ohio the expedition was abandoned. All made the best of their way home, it requiring two weeks to reach the nearest settlement. Some perished on the way back, and all endured great hardships from cold and hunger, being forced to eat, it is said, the strings of their moccasins and the belts of their hunting shirts.

In April another Indian irruption, led by the French, spread consternation throughout the country on the Shenandoah. The woods appeared to be alive with savages, and each day brought fresh alarms, and disasters. Winchester was now the principal fortified settlement west of the Blue Ridge. Here Washington established his headquarters, and erected Ft. Loudoun. Other forts, or places of refuge, were hastily constructed amongst the settlements. To these the inhabitants fled for shelter, their plantations being almost entirely deserted. In Augusta at the time, the number of tithables was 2,273 whites and 40 blacks, from which the population was estimated at 9,000 whites and 80 blacks. About the close of the month, the Indians returned to Ft. Duquesne laden with prisoners, scalps, and plunder. Washington plead with Dinwiddie for reinforcements. The Governor called out the militia of ten counties, the total for the Colony being estimated at 35,000 fit to bear arms, but found great difficulty in completing a single regiment. Major Lewis was ordered to the country of the Cherokees—East Tennessee—to build there a fort for these friendly allies. Col. Jefferson of Albemarle (the father of the later President) was ordered in the meantime to take half of his militia to Augusta. From June to September, Lewis was absent from the county. His fort (like Washington's called Ft. Loudoun) was built on the Tennessee river, about 30 miles south of present Knoxville.

Throughout the summer and fall Dinwiddie was busy issuing instructions to the militia, dispatching numerous letters to the variuos officers, and to his Commander-in-Chief at Winchester. Washington was ever on the alert attending local "Councils of War" and making frequent tours of inspection to different parts of the Valley; all the while rendering all the succor in his power to the settlers in their defense.

Among the Captains of militia of Augusta this year, as given by the Courts Martial record book of the county were—Captains of Horse: Israel Christian, Patrick Martin, and John Dickenson. Captains of Foot: Samuel Norwood, James Allen, George Willson, John Mathews, Joseph Lapsley, James Mitchell, Ludovick Francisco, Robert Bratton, Joseph Culton, Robert Scott, William Christian, Robert Breckenridge, William Preston, Samuel Stalnicker, Thomas Armstrong, Robert McClenachan, Peter Hogg, James Lockhart, Ephraim Love, John Smith, Abraham Smith, and Daniel Harrison. David Stewart and John Buchanan are mentioned as Colonels, and John Brown as a Major.

Captains John and Abraham Smith were father and son. Two other sons of John—Daniel and John, Jr.—were Lieutenants. Daniel was also later a Captain. It was during the year 1756 (June 25th), that Capt. John Smith was captured, along with yet another son, Joseph, in the attack on Ft. Vause. In this fight Lieut. John Smith was killed. (See, *The Preston Register*, Collections, of Dr. Lyman C. Draper—State Historical Society of Wisconsin.) Earlier in the year Capt. John Smith had been in the Sandy Creek expedition. While preparing for this, it seems that he had wanted biscuit for his men; but the Governor, ever a Scotchman with a watchful eye for economy, took pains to write him that he must provide flour or corn-meal instead. Along with this advice he was forwarded £100 in money—for which "you must account for on your return." The old Captain evidently had not taken to heart Dinwiddie's first lesson in economics sent him only the year before—informing him that forty shillings was too much to give for a coat for some friendly Indian brave. *(Waddell,* pp. 116, 130.) The pay of Capt. John Smith's company to June 25, 1756, was £575-13. (Hening's *Statutes at Large of Virginia*, Vol. 7, p. 200.) Following his capture he was taken (along with his son Joseph, who died on the way) to New Orleans, and, as elsewhere related, thence to France, whence he finally returned after two years, by way of London, to Augusta.

John Smith, Jr., made his will January 22, 1756. (Will Book 2, p. 155.) In this he mentions his brothers Daniel, Abraham, and Henry, and Daniel's son John, to whom he devised his plantation on "North River Shenedoe" which he bought of Silas Hart. Daniel qualified as executor with sureties Hart and Robert Harrison.

The danger of invasion being thought much lessened during the cold season; about the middle of November, Major Lewis was ordered to recall his men from the frontiers and to reduce the Augusta companies in service to three. Among the claims filed with the court, December 3, 1756, (Order Book V, p. 302), was one from Daniel Harrison for ranging, and provisions expended in his company. Likewise one from Thomas Armstrong for his company. The local taxes were being collected about this time; 24th November, 1756, James Lockhart's bond, with John Trumble, William Long, and Daniel Harrison, for the collection of the county levy having been recorded. (Will Book II, p. 180.)

The spring and summer of 1757, in Augusta, was passed in comparative quiet—"this being a time of noted peace with us, in the midst of difficulties elsewhere," to quote the words of the old Smiths and Linville's Creek church book. On June 20th there was a new alarm at Winchester, and weekly alarms in July. In August a detachment was sent by Washington to Augusta, and the House of Burgesses voted to raise 300 rangers, 200 of whom were intended for this county's frontier. Washington remained stationed at Winchester. Towards the close of September, according to the old record above, "the Heathen" again were permitted "to fall on our Settlement" the "Indian troubles" continuing to the first Saturday in January. In October, the Augusta rangers went into service. On the 19th of this month, the Governor refused Washington permission to visit Williamsburg, reminding him at the time, of previous frequent similar indulgences—"you know the fort is to be finished, and I fear in your absence little will be done," etc.

The ocassion of one of the above alarms in July, appears to have been a penetration this month of the settlement on the headwaters of the James, near present Buchanan, by a party of Shawnees. According to the *Preston Register,* July 25, 1757, Robert Renick and Thomas Moon at "Fork of James River" were killed, and Mrs. Renick and seven children, and a Mrs. Denis were taken prisoners. Wither's in his *Border Warfare,* mentions the children as William, Robert, Thomas, Joshua and Betsy; and states that the elder Renick was killed at the home of Thomas Smith, who was also slain at the time, and Mrs. Smith captured; but places the date in 1761. Robert Renick was probably a kinsman of Thomas to whom Daniel Harrison had loaned the Pennsylvania money of early Orange court days. One of the name by 1752 had made improvements "on plantation formerly called John Harrison's place," and was deeded by John, Jr., 241 acres "on a branch of James River at east end of Short Hill," 27th November, 1757. A Robert Renick was also among the witness to Capt. John Smith's will, in 1753.

Coming first to the house of Renick, whom they found away from home, after capturing Mrs. Renick and the children, the Indians next proceeded to the home of Smith. Here they found both Smith and Renick, whom they scalped, and captured Mrs. Smith and her servant girl. The captives were taken to the Indian towns on the Sciota and there divided. On the way little Robert Renick, (about eighteen months old) whose crying irritated the Indians, was grasped from the arms of his mother and his brains dashed out against a tree. Joshua, about eleven years old, was carried to Piqua and there reared in the family of Tecumseh's parents, and after that celebrated Indian's birth was a companion of him and his brother, the Prophet. Shortly after arriving at the Indian towns, Mrs. Renick gave birth to a son, whom she named Robert, after his murdered father and brother. William Renick, of Greenbrier, b. 1792, was his son. Mrs. Renick remained in captivity until 1767. *(Waddell,* p. 165.)

During the year 1757, Lord Loudoun, the newly appointed Commander-in-Chief of the Colonies, arrived in America, and called a conference of Governors and military officers at Philadelphia. Washington attended the conference, and Dinwiddie urged his promotion to the British establishment. Loudoun determined to direct his main efforts against Canada, leaving only 1,000 men in the middle and southern provinces. Instead of receiving the aid Washington had asked, Virginia was required to send 400 troops to South Carolina, and her own regiment was reduced in number to one thousand. Towards the close of the year Washington relinquished his post temporarily, and retired for several months to Mt. Vernon.

The war was still far from being over—in fact, the worst was yet to come. In England, William Pitt had only recently arisen to the head of affairs, and it was quickly felt in every part of the empire that there was a *man* at the helm. In January, 1758,

John Campbell

Dinwiddie sailed from Virginia. His place was filled by John Blair, president of the Council, until the arrival of Francis Fauquier, as Lieut. Governor, June 7, 1758. (John Campbell, the Earl of Loudoun, had been commissioned Governor General of all the American Colonies, February 16, 1756, but it is thought that his military avocations prevented him from ever visiting Virginia.) Prior to the arrival of Fauquier, Gen. Forbes, the commander of the Middle and Southern Colonies, was ordered to undertake an expedition (the thrid) against Ft. Duquesne. Washington rejoined the army. The campaign was deferred in getting under way, and the Indians resumed their merciless warfare—"Spring coming on, the Indian Troubles continued, and . . . the whole neighborhood forced either to go into Forts or over the Mountains, to escape the Rage, in the month of June following," says the old Linville Creek church book. In Augusta, relates the historian Campbell, sixty persons were murdered. This probably alludes to the massacre at Seybert's Fort (now Pendelton County,) which was attacked by the Shawnees, April 28, 1758, forty-one persons being taken prisoners. *(The Preston Register.)* Nearly all of those captured were lined up in rows and tomahawked—young James Dyer was the only one to ever return.

The Virginia troops were increased to about 2,000 men, in two regiments; one under Washington, who was still Commander-in-Chief of the Colony's forces, the other under Col. William Byrd, of Westover. Washington gathered his troops at Winchester, several companies being recalled from Augusta, and late in June marched for Ft. Cumberland, which was reached July 2nd. Forbes' command consisted of 1,600 British regulars, Highlanders, and Royal Americans, 2,700 Provincials from Pennsylvania, the two Virginia regiments, and some Indian allies, making in all between six and seven thousand. This army was five months in reaching the Ohio. Instead of marching immediately upon the river by Braddock's road, as Washington advised, Forbes undertook to build another road from Raystown, Pennsylvania; the delay detaining the Virginia troops at Ft. Cumberland until the middle of September. Forbes arrived at Raystown this month, and dispatched Col. Bouquet, who had been stationed there awaiting him, to make a further advance. Disregarding again Washington's advice, Major Grant was detached from the camp at Loyal Hannah, about fifty miles from Ft. Duquesne, and sent forward to reconnoitre. Grant's detachment, consisting of 800 picked men, including 162 Virginians under Major Andrew Lewis, was surprised and involved in a defeat similar to Braddock's. Grant and Lewis were both captured. Lewis was taken to Quebec, later returning home about the close of the war. The total loss was 273 killed and 42 wounded, Washington's regiment losing six officers and 62 privates. Capt. Thomas Bullitt, and 50 Virginians, defended the baggage, and helped to save the remnant of the detachment.

When the main army was put in motion Washington requested to be put in advance, and Forbes complied with his wish. October 8th, Raystown was left, and the camp at Loyal Hannah reached early in November. Winter had set in, and the troops being worn out with fatigue and exposure, it was deemed unadvisable to proceed further. In a short time, however, three prisoners were taken, who gave a report of the feeble state of the garrison. It was then determined to push forward at once—Washington and his provincials opening the way. Arriving at the site of the fort, it was found to have been abandoned. The French, deserted by the Indians, and reduced to 500 men, had set fire to the premises and retired down the Ohio. On November 25, 1758, Washington marched in and took possession. The Fort was repaired and renamed Ft. Pitt in honor of the Prime Minister. After leaving a detachment of his regiment as a garrison, Washington returned with his men to Winchester. From there he went to

Williamsburg to take his seat in the House of Burgesses, as the representative of Frederick County. In December, he resigned his military commission, the last he was to hold under the Colonial Government, and retired for the winter to Mt. Vernon. January 6, 1759, he married Martha, the daughter of John Dandridge, and widow of Daniel Parke Custis.

Notwithstanding the interruption due to the Indian alarms, and the state of defense under which the settlers lived, the Augusta court managed to hold regular sessions throughout the year. Among the deeds recorded was one from Daniel Harrison to his son Robert, 16th March, 1758, for £40, "400 acres on the head of Dry Fork of Smiths Creek." (Deed Book 7, p. 539.) This land was patented to Daniel, August 20, 1741, and was later conveyed to Daniel Smith, his son-in-law, in 1764. It was the third Augusta tract sold by Daniel Harrison, and the first Harrison patent in the Smiths Creek region. Together with the land patented by Robert at the same time it was the beginning of the later Smithland estate.

On the date of the sale of this land, Daniel signed Martha Claypole's bond, as administratrix of William Claypole. August 17th, following, with Matthew Patton, he also signed Margaret Dyer's bond as administratrix of William Dyer. (Will Book 2, pp. 233, 264.) Claypole at least was an old Sussex County, Delaware name, and Daniel was probably an old friend of William's family—19th August, 1761, Daniel Harrison was appointed and qualified guardian to Jane Claypole, infant orphan of William. (Order Book VII, p. 61; also, Will Book 3, p. 241.) Among those named in the "Commission of Peace" issued for Sussex County, Delaware, September 23, 1726, was Jeremiah Claypoole, Robert Shanklin, Philip Russel, Samuel Davis, George Walton, etc. (*Some Records of Sussex County, Del.*, by Turner, p. 46.)

The Indian troubles "continued and got no better, till the Summer of the Year 1759, when it pleased God to make our Armies victorious, in the North Part of our Continent, (which drew the Enemv from us)", so runs the old church record. The main theatre of war had now shifted to the conflict leading to the seige of Quebec. This great stronghold of the French, defended by Montcalm, was captured by the English under Wolfe, September 13, 1759. This was the great event of the war, and rapidly led to its final conclusion—"the forts that had harboured them to our Hurt," now "fell in our Hands without Bloodshed." "And when the Summer of 1759 was ended, and the Enemy not permitted to break in upon us, in the Month of September, the church assembled together," etc. From this time on until the close of the war the Indians were unorganized, and from 1759 to 1761, appear to have been particularly quiet in the region of the Augusta settlements.

* * * * * *

January 20, 1759, Daniel Harrison with Samuel Hemphill, and Edward Mc. Garry, witnessed Arthur Johnson's will. The will was proven August 15th, of the same year, by Harrison, and Hemphill; the widow Margaret qualified as executrix, with sureties Daniel Love and Robert Cravens. The children named were sons, John, Andrew, and Arthur, and daughters Jane, Sarah, and Mary, the first two being bequeathed the home place with an "adjoining survey called Hunter's Gulley," and Arthur, Jr. a "tract adjoining Ellick (Alexander) Herrin's line." The estate was appraised 19th March, 1760, and again 13th August, 1762, by Harrison, Hemphill, and John Cravens. (Will Books, 2, pp. 325, 354; and 3, p. 180.) The Johnsons were near neighbors of Daniel Harrison. It was to Arthur Johnson that Daniel sold his first land. (p. 197.) In 1770 (August 25), John Johnson and Mary deeded to William Bowyer, for 50 Pounds, 124 acres "part of 200 acres left by Arthur Johnson, deceased to his two sons John and Andrew . . . .

corner Daniel Harrison," also 18 1/2 acres adjoining, part of 37, "left by said Johnson to his said sons." (Deed Book 17, p. 5.) December 19th, 1772, this land, "on the head springs of Hunter's Gully (Cook's Creek)," was the subject of litigation between Daniel Smith and Bowyer. (County Court Judgements Aug. 1773 A; *Chalkley,* Vol. I, p. 368.)

Mary, the daughter of Daniel Harrison, married Henry Bowyer, or Bowyers. "He was lost at sea in 1760. Their son Henry married Agatha Madison, their daughter Emiline married Judge Eliu Johnson, and were the grandparents of Mary Johnson the novelist." Following Henry Bowyer's death, Mary his widow, married 2nd, William Kavanaugh.

In 1760, George III came to the throne of England. This year the Processioners again made their rounds in Augusta. In the Cook's Creek neighborhood the officers appointed were John Hopkins, and David Ralston, of Capt. Ephraim Love's company, and the lines viewed were those of—Francis Green, Jeremiah Harrison, Daniel Love, Daniel Callkin, Robert Cravens, Thomas Harrison, Ephraim Love, Widow Johnson, Alex. Herring, Edward Shanklin, Widow Logan, William Logan, John Cravens, Widow McDonel (McDonald), Joseph Cravens, William Hopkins, John Hopkins, Thomas Shanklin, Alex. Miller, Matthew Black, Thomas Campbell, Daniel Harrison, Daniel Harrison, Jr., Samuel Harrison, Robert Harrison, Pat Quin (Quinn), Wm. Snoding, John Fowler, David Nelson, Samuel Bridges, John McGill, Christopher Thompson, Archibald Hopkins, John Wright, and Thomas Gordon. (Augusta Parish Vestry Book, p. 295.)

John Wright was doubtless a kinsman of Daniel Harrison's half-sister Mary Cravens, the wife of Robert. November 9, 1760, John Wright, and "Lydda," and John Cravens (son of Robert) and Margaret, deeded to David Pounder 510 acres, "Daniel Harrison's land," on the "head of the east fork of Cook's Creek and a draft of Smith's Creek." The land seems to have been a part of Daniel's original survey or "tomakawk right" on the head of the Dry Fork of Smiths Creek, and was patented to Jacob Gardiner, 16th August, 1756; "Teste Daniel Harrison, Jonathan Douglass." On 1st February, 1757, Gardiner deeded 310 acres of his patent to John Cravens and John Wright—witness Robert Cravens, Samuel Hemphill, Matthew and Robert Black, "delivered to John Wright, Aug. 1758." This last tract was later conveyed by Daniel and Jeremiah Pounder, 10th September, 1763, to Joseph Rutherford, and in May, 1768, delivered to Reuben Rutherford. (Deed Books 7, p. 381; 9, p. 19; 11, p. 282.)

Captain Daniel Harrison's second marriage occured in July, 1761. (Marriage Licenses in Augusta County—*Chalkley,* Vol. II, p. 276.) His second wife was Sarah Stephenson, widow of William. *(Boogher's Gleanings.)* William's will was proven May 16, 1759.

The Stephensons were early in Old Augusta—"22nd. May, 1740, John Stephenson came into court and made oath that he imported himself Sarah and Mary Stephenson from Ireland to Philadelphia, and thence to this colony." On the same date Thomas Stephenson and Rachel also proved their importation by the same route. (Orange Court Order Book, 1739-41; pp. 159, and 157.)

It was during the year 1761 that Robert Harrison, the first child of Daniel, died. He was born in Sussex County, Delaware, in 1725. As noted, his will was signed while on his death-bed at the home of his sister Jane, and brother-in-law Capt. Daniel Smith, May 4, 1761. His death occurred on the 25th, of this month. On August 18th, following, his will was proven, and November 17th, 1761, his estate was appraised by Hugh Hamilton, John Hopkins, and Robert Cravens. (Will book, 3, pp. 60 and 92.)

The ten long years of war were now rapidly drawing to a close. The treaty of peace, marking the high tide of British dominion in America, was finally signed at Paris, February 10, 1763. Following the capture of Canada, in 1760, little was done by England to conciliate the Indians, and they were treated with contempt by her soldiers. They again became restless, and in 1761 renewed their ravages, and in 1763 open warfare. The war, originating in the so called "conspiracy of Pontiac," was begun by the Ottowa chief's attack on the fort at Detroit, May 1763. On August 6th, the same year, Col. Bouquet decisively defeated the Indians at Bushy Run, in western Pennsylvania, and in October headed an expedition from Ft. Pitt to the Ohio country. In the expedition were two companies raised by Col. Andrew Lewis; one under his brother Charles, the other under Alexander McClenachan. A treaty of peace was concluded by Bouquet with the Delawares and Shawnees, November 9th, 1763.

During these hostilities the murderous activities of the savages again spread to the region of the Valley of the Shenandoah. In Augusta their depredations were now restricted almost wholly to the outlying border settlements, or to the more or less unprotected mountainous districts. In July, 1763, the Greenbrier settlements were entirely extinguished. Cornstalk, the famous Shawnee warrior, headed his first expedition against the whites there this year. As late as September there was universal alarm —and as disclosed by the Baptist Church book, even an appearance of "the barbarous enemy" on Linville's Creek.

With the prospects of peace in the spring of 1763, the Augusta settlers seem to have renewed afresh their real estate activities. As shown by the deed books, one of Daniel Harrison's numerous tracts at this time was near what is now known as "Tide Spring," on Linville's Creek, evidently then called "Sinking Spring"—3rd May 1763, deed; Benjamin Kinley to Martin Humble, 215 acres "adjoining Rees Thomas and Daniel Harrison, and a survey of said Kinley commonly called Sinking Spring." (Deed Book 11, p. 546.) Rees and Evan Thomas both owned land on Linville's Creek near Daniel; 16th May, 1768, Evan bought of Francis Green and Margaret, for five shillings, 240 acres "on Middle Branch of Linville's Creek, joining one Hite and near a survey of Daniel Harrison," also 20 acres "joining his own land" and Daniel Harrison's line. (Deed Book 15, p. 21.) Rees Thomas was an early member of the Linville Creek Church. One of the name is also found among the first members of the old Welsh Tract Church (Baptist), of New Castle County, Delaware. (See page 186.)

Beginning with 1763, Daniel Harrison manifestly contributed his share to the increasing burden on the court scribe, and to the lengthening of the old deed book of the time—No. 11. On June 21, 1763, he disposed of a third tract granted him by patent, and on the next day followed with another. The first embraced 120 acres, patented 15th December, 1755, "on North River of Shanando above the Gap in the mountain—including the 3rd fork of said river, and an island below the fork." This was deeded to Charles Mann. The second tract, "100 acres on North fork of Linville's Creek," (also patented 15th December, 1755) was deeded by Daniel and Sarah to James Green. On the date of the second conveyance Daniel, with Daniel Smith and Felix Gilbert, witnessed a deed of James McCowan, and Margaret, to Gabriel Jones: "300 acres on Catawba of James River." The next day (June 23rd) Jonathan Douglass mortgaged to Daniel, for 40 Pounds, 306 acres, "part of two tracts of 400 acres each . . . . one tract granted to Jonathan by Thomas Beal of Frederick County, Maryland, 1755, the other patented to Jonathan, 11th July, 1761, on the head of Broad Run, a branch of North river of Shendoe, whereon Douglass now lives." (Deed Book 11, pp. 303, 238, 305, and 336.)

As his father before him, and as his brother John, when getting along in years,

Daniel now began disposing of his lands amongst his sons; he even went farther, and included his grandsons—14th November, 1763, deed; Daniel Harrison and Sarah to Daniel and Jesse Harrison, his grandchildren, sons of Jesse Harrison, 400 acres (patented September 25, 1746) on the head of Linville's Creek, Joseph Hite's line (delivered to Benjamin Bowman by order of Jesse Harrison, 18th February, 1793.) Also—22nd March, 1764, deed; Daniel Harrison and Sarah to Jesse Harrison, his son, two tracts, 1st, 200 acres on a branch of Muddy Creek, patented by Daniel, 5th September, 1749, 2nd, 200 acres adjoining the former, part of 400 acres patented by Daniel 25th September 1746, Love's line corner Daniel Harrison (Jr.'s) part of said tract, (delivered Jesse Harrison, March 1783.) Finally—21st August, 1764, deed; Daniel Harrison and Sarah, to Daniel his son, 200 acres, part of 400 (above), corner Jesse Harrison's part of same. The consideration in these conveyances was 20 Pounds for the first and last tracts, and 40 Pounds for the second. (Deed Book 11, pp. 553, 556, and 699.)

SMITHLAND

In his will, Robert Harrison appointed as his executors his brother Jesse, and brother-in-law Daniel Smith. These executors on the 16th November, 1764, sold to Abraham Smith, for 243 Pounds, Robert's land—two tracts adjoining each other "on the head of the dry fork of Smiths Creek;" A, 400 acres patented to Daniel Harrison 20th August, 1741, and conveyed by him to his son Robert, 16th March, 1758, "end of Timber Bottom:" B. 260 acres patented to Robert, 20th August, 1741, end of Timber Bottom, corner Daniel Harrison, Robert Craven's line." On November 22nd following, Abraham Smith and Sarah deeded this land to Daniel Smith at cost. (Deed Book 11, pp. 759, 761.) Thus was begun the historic Smithland estate, a few miles north of Harrisonburg on the Valley Pike. Here Daniel Smith and his wife Jane Harrison made their home. The old house erected by him, one of the first brick residences of the Valley, is said to have been built of brick brought from England to Alexandria, as ballast in a sailing vessel. It stood until about 1895, a short distance south-west of the present fine old colonial home built by his descendant. Smithland from its beginning has always been one of the noted estates of the Valley of Virginia. In the old house was held the first court of Rockingham County. Here Daniel's father, Capt. John Smith, the immigrant, died. (See page 141.)

The final settlement of Robert Harrison's estate, by "Capt Daniel Smith," was allowed and recorded, 6th October, 1765—"To cash paid Edmon Pendleton . . ., to John Harrison . . ., to Joseph Langdon to approved account, to James McDowell . . ., to John Cravens . . ., to Thomas Moore . . ., to Legase left Anne Harrison . . ., to Legase left Robert Smith . . ., to one thousand nails 7 s.-6d., Mary Harrison one mear (mare) . . . Daniel Harrison one young mear, Jesse Harrison one branding iron . . ., William Cravens one fork . . ., William Cravens one chest . . ., benuman (Benjamin) Harrison one horse . . ., Samuel Harrison 9 Pounds-10s," etc. Among the names mentioned on the sale bill, with their purchases, are the following, "Capt. Harrison one ax; Jesse Harrison one blanket; beneman Harrison to a pair of Sadel baggs; Mary Harrison one cow; Abraham Smith one Steer; Thomas Harrison one Steare; beneman Harrison one mear; Daniel Harrison one Colt;" etc. (Will Book 3, p. 427.)

October 14th, a few days following the settlement, Daniel Harrison conveyed to Daniel Smith for 50 pounds, 200 acres on Muddy Creek and Dry River, including a "high bank opposite an island." This land had been patented to Daniel, 16th August, 1756. (Deed Book 12, p. 298.)

About this time Daniel was Deputy Sheriff of the county, as disclosed by a suit appearing against him, October 1765, brought by one John Hapes. As the "Spa" was issued September, 1763, he had evidently been serving several years. Hapes had been employed as Deputy Sheriff for two years under Robert McClenanchan, with sureties Daniel Harrison and John Cravens. As the end of his term drew near, fearing that he would be behind in his accounts, he "withdrew himself to Carolina," leaving his Sheriff's books for the satisfaction of his bondsmen. Daniel was appointed Deputy Sheriff in his place, and immediately attached his effects. Hapes later returned to Augusta and now petitioned for an account. This was granted—Daniel showing by the same that "orator is still in his debt." (District Court Executions D; *Chalkley* Vol. I, p. 491.) Silas Hart at the time was the High Sheriff—the year before, November 21, Daniel with Andrew Erwin, Jno. Hopkins, Arch. Hopkins, and Geo. Anderson, had gone on Hart's (sheriff's) bond to collect the taxes. (Will Book 3, p. 370.)

Capt. Harrison's last years were spent in quiet—from 1764 to 1774 the country was at peace. The times were stirring however; this being the prelude to the great conflict for American Independence. In 1767 he signed his will, when "in Reasonable health," although getting along in years. Ten days following the date of his will; according to a deposition of Abraham Smith, 18th June, 1767; (in connection with the Herron vs. Quinn ejectment before referred to—page 144), "This day Patrick Quinn came . . . and says that *Capt.* Daniel Harrison is very ailing; he is afraid that he will soon change his natural life, as he doth believe that he will die very soon." But the old Captain recovered, and made his deposition 16th December, 1767—at which time he stated his age—and an additional deposition the next day, regarding land, that he and Alexander Herring had bought of Samuel Wilkins.

Many Colonial governors had come and gone during Daniel's day. Virginia's long line was now rapidly drawing to a close. Fauquier died March 3, 1768, and was succeeded by John Blair, president of the Council, as acting governor. Blair at times had served before. (He was President of William and Mary, and Commissary, or head of the Established Church.) In October, arrived Norborne Berkeley, Baron de Botetourt, as Governor-General, the first of the title since Lord Culpeper, who had condescended to come over to Virginia. Botetourt succeeded Sir Jeffry Amherst, the successor of Loudoun, in 1763.

In his famous essay on old age, Cicero argues that regardless of a man's age he never gets too old to remember the debts owing him. On 21st March, 1770, only a few months before his death, Daniel Harrison and Sarah deeded to Felix Gilbert the land mortgaged to him by Jonathan Douglass, in 1763. Jonathan had failed to pay his debt, now 55 Pounds, and Daniel had brought suit, the decree having been rendered 25th March, 1769—Witness James McDowell, William Patton. (Deed Book 16, p. 244.)

(16) Captain Daniel Harrison, the old French and Indian War soldier, and pioneer to Old Augusta County, Virginia, died July 10, 1770. *(Boogher.)* He is thought to have been buried in the early Episcopal Churchyard near his home, at present Dayton, in the north section of today's cemetery. In recent years the site of "Old Erection," the church of the early Presbyterians, in the same locality, has become submerged, being now under Silver Lake. In making way for improvements all bodies that could be found were moved to the newer part of the cemetery, but all traces of the present location of Daniel's grave, whether in either location, as well as those of many others of his day, have become lost.

"These noble Knights Tramontane rode
On many a wild foray
Did battle with the Indian tribes
In fierce and bloody fray,
And year by year they slowly pressed
The savage hordes toward the West."
—ALDINE S. KIEFFER.

On 25th August, 1770, Benjamin Harrison's bond, with sureties Andrew Bird and David Bell as Administrator of Daniel's estate, and Sarah Harrison's bond, with surety Abraham Smith, as executrix of the same, were recorded. A year later, 21st August 1771, "Daniel Harrison's appraisement" by Solomon Turpin, Robert Cravens (Jr.) and John Gratton, was also recorded. (Will Book 4, pp. 399-340.) Among the numerous items mentioned in the appraisement were the following taken at random; he was one of the wealthy men of his day—

One pair of silver Shoe Buckles, Nee (knee) do. (ditto) & Clasps 0-15-00
One pair of cumpuses, ... One pair of money Scales ....
One branding iron ....
3 table cloths & napkin, ... 1 doz. & 10 spoons ...., 1 doz. knives & forks
One dutch oven,
1 Bed & furniture with short steads .... 1 bed & furniture & Do. ....
1 Bed and furniture plank stead
1 bed & furniture steads .... 1 Bed & Furniture do.
1 Negro fellow, Seaser .... 1 Negro boy Moses .... 1 Negro child Cate.
1 Negro woman .... 1 Negro boy Simon .... etc."

Sarah, the executrix of Daniel Harrison, made her "O" mark in signing. Daniel's second wife, now twice a widow, seems to have outlived her husband by only a few years; but the date of her death is unknown. There were no children by this marriage.

The children of Capt. Daniel Harrison (Sr.), and his first wife, Margaret Cravens, were briefly—

(161) ROBERT—b. 1725, d. May 25, 1761, unmarried.
(162) DANIEL—b. 1727; d. ——; m. Sarah ——.
See further record.
(163) JESSE—b. 1729; d. 1817 c; m. between 1750-55; Sarah ——. P/317
See further record.
(164) MARY—b. 1733; d. ——; m. 1st, Henry Bowyers, d. 1760, at sea; m. 2nd, William Kavanaugh.
(165) JANE—b. 1735; d. 1796; m. 1751, Capt. Daniel Smith, son of Capt. John Smith.
See further record.
(166) ABIGAIL—b. 1738; d. ——; m. October, 1764, Jeremiah Ragen.
See further record.
(167) BENJAMIN—b. 1741; d. 1819; m. Aug. 8, 1763, Mary McClure, d. 1815, daughter of John McClure.
See further record.

(Birth dates from Boogher.)

All, but the last named, were born in "Sussex on the Delaware," on Maiden Plantation.

CHAPTER XIII

Thomas Harrison, the Founder of Harrisonburg, Virginia, and His Family

THE REVOLUTIONARY WAR PERIOD

"From distant lands, to this wild waste he came,
This seat he chose, and here he fixed his name.
Long may his sons, this peaceful spot enjoy,
And no ill fate, his offspring here annoy."
—ANONYMOUS.

AND WHEREAS it hath been represented to the present general assembly that Thomas Harrison of the county of Rockingham hath laid off fifty acres of land where the courthouse for the said county now stands into lots and streets which would be of great advantage to the inhabitants of that county if established a town for the reception of traders. Be it therefore enacted, That from and after the passing of this act, the said fifty acres of land so laid off as aforesaid shall be and the same is hereby established a town by the name of Harrisonburg; that the freeholders and inhabitants of the said town so soon as they shall have built upon and saved their lots according to the conditions of their deeds of conveyance shall then be entitled to and have and enjoy all the rights, privileges, and immunities granted to, or enjoyed by, the freeholders and inhabitants of other towns not incorporated."

So runs the old act establishing the town of Harrisonburg, passed May, 1780, "AT A GENERAL ASSEMBLY, begun and held, At the Capitol in the city of Williamsburg, on Monday the fourth day of October, in the year of our Lord one thousand seven hundred and seventy-nine, and in the fourth year of the commonwealth. Thomas Jefferson Gov." (See, Hening's *Statutes at Large of Virginia*, Vol. 10, p. 295.)

At the same time the town of Louisville, (now in Kentucky), was also established by law—the whole act being entitled: "An act for establishing the town of Louisville at the falls of the Ohio, and one other town in the county of Rockingham."

Later at Richmond, Virginia, December 1797, the Assembly further passed "An Act concerning the town of Harrisonburg, in the county of Rockingham;" the first clause of which reads—

"1. Be it enacted by the general assembly, That twenty-three and one-half acres of land as the same are already laid off into lots and streets in the town of Harrisonburg in the county of Rockingham, by Robert and Reuben Harrison, the proprietors thereof, shall be and they are hereby added to and made part of the said town to all intents and purposes." *(Ibid.,* Vol. 15, p. 132.)

(17) THOMAS HARRISON, the founder of Harrisonburg, Virginia, was born, about 1704, on the western bank of the Nissequogue River, at Smithtown, Suffolk County, Long Island, in the Province of New York. He was the second, or third, son of Isaiah Harrison, (1), the immigrant, and his second, wife Abigail. Thomas died at Harrisonburg, in 1785. His founding of the town, and having it established as

THE COURT HOUSE AT HARRISONBURG, VIRGINIA
By The Long Grey Trail
Showing the old "Head Spring" before the present pavement was laid.
See page 220.

the county seat of Rockingham, was the successful culmination of the last years of his life.

He died testate, his will being dated, 21st, February, 1776, as shown by a deed—24th, February, 1794, George Sights (Sites) and Elizabeth, his wife, and Robert Harrison, Reuben Harrison, and Mary, his wife, James Mitchell, and Mary, his wife, of Rockingham, to Thos Sulivan (Sullivan), one half acre, one half of lot No. 2, in N. W. Square of Harrisonburg, formerly conveyed to James Mitchell by the said Harrisons, and by him to Geo. Sights 27th, September, 1790, part of an inclusive survey of 1,290 acres granted to Thomas Harrison by "Patent Rains," 1st March, 1773, under signature of Governor Dunmore, " & by the last will and Testament of the (said) Thomas Harrison Deceased Bearing date the twenty first Day of February, 1776, Left to his two sons the said Robert & Reuben Harrison" . . . (Deed Book 00, of Rockingham, burnt records, page 20.)

Owing to the all but complete burning of the original first records of Rockingham, in the War-between-the-States, his will has been lost. However, the following deed from Reuben Harrison, in Burnt Record Deed Book, No. 00, page 278, at Harrisonburg, is of more than equal value in naming all of the founder's heirs—

"THIS INDENTURE made the twenty seventh day of February in the year of our Lord one thousand seven Hundred and ninety eight Between Reuben Harrison and Mary his wife of the one part and Alexander Wason of the other part witnesseth

that for and in consideration of the sum of Two hundred pounds current Money of Virginia, to the said Reuben Harrison and Mary his wife in hand paid by the said Alexander Wason at or before the sealing and delivery of these presents, the receipt whereof he doth hereby acknowledge, and thereof doth release, acquit and discharge the said Alexander Wason, Executors and Administrators, by these Presents, the said Reuben Harrison and Mary his wife hath granted, bargained, sold, alienated released and confirmed, and by these presents doth grant, bargain, sell, alien, release and confirm unto the said Alexander Wason and his heirs one certain lot or parcel of land in the Town of Harrisonburg containing and known and distinguished on the plat of the said town by No. 13, in the South East Square fronting on Irish Street, and bounded as follows to wit . . . .

which said lot of land is a part of a greater tract of one thousand two hundred and ninety acres, first granted by and including Patent unto Thomas Harrison due and dated the first day of March, 1773, and by him 620 (acres) of which including said lot was devised unto his two sons as joint Tenants Robert and Reuben Harrison and the said Robert Harrison dying intestate and thereby the fee simple Estate of and in one half of the aforesaid six hundred and twenty acres descend unto Jeremiah Harrison, John Harrison, Thomas Harrison, Ezekiel Harrison, Davis Harrison, Reuben Harrison, Leonard Haring and Abigail his wife, and Sara (h) Waren (Warren), as Heirs and legal representatives of the aforesaid Intestate Robert Harrison deceased and by them the said Estate of Inheritance in the Joint tenancy aforesaid of the said Intestate conveyed unto the aforesaid Reuben Harrison by and of Bargain & Sale dated the . . . day of . . . 1797, as fully and at large appear by the Record of the County Court of Rockingham, reference thereunto being had—TO HAVE AND TO HOLD the lot hereby conveyed, and all singular other the Premises granted, with its appurtenances, unto the said Alexander Wason" . . . etc.

Robert Harrison, similar to his first-cousin of the same name, the son of Capt.

Daniel Harrison, died unmarried; thus the descent of the land to his brothers and sisters. No mention is made of Thomas, Sr's. wife; she too, had died by this time .

The Act of the Assembly of 1780, establishing the town, refers to the courthouse then standing on the land. The courthouse of Rockingham County today still stands on the the old location, the Public Square of Harrisonburg. Just within the main entrance of the imposing structure may be seen a stone tablet affixed to its walls, on which is engraved:

Formation of Rockingham County
1778
Public Square donated by
Thomas Harrison
Aug. 5, 1779.
Court Houses
First 1784 Stone
Second 1833 Brick
Third 1874 Brick
Fourth 1897 Stone.

The "Square" was conveyed by "Deed to Silas Hart, Gent, first Justice in the Commission of the Peace, for the said County, from Thomas Harrison, Senr. and Sarah Harrison," for, "consideration, five shillings for and in behalf and for the sole use and behoof of the said County of Rockingham and their successors—a certain tract or piece of land contaning Two Acres and Half to build the Court House and other public buildings necessary for the said County of Rockingham." (Deed Book "O", p. 291, Burnt Records.)

Sarah Harrison was Thomas' second wife. Together the above deeds name her and all of his children.

Thomas Harrison's father before him had been a town builder; "At a town Meeting 1687, Jan. ye 2d," or very soon after his arrival in America, he had been "Given and granted one whole Right of Comonage," or a proprietorship in the old purchase of the town of Oyster Bay, Long Island. He also was among the eight proprietors, who on the 3rd May, 1690, agreed to make a "New or second division of their Lands in ye Bounds of ye old Purchase," of Oyster Bay, at which time each proprietor was granted a "Lott of fifty or Twenty Acres." (See pp. 15 and 21.) The development of Oyster Bay was largely a family affair of the Wrights, and Isaiah Harrison had as his first wife the granddaughter of Peter Wright, the founder of the town,

Smithtown too, Thomas' birthplace, was a comparatively new development in his father's day. While the son was born on an estate of 500 acres, which his father bought here in 1702, on his removal from Oyster Bay, the land was within the township limits. Also Isaiah's additional tract of 200 acres, purchased in 1708, included "ye liberty of commonage" in the lands of the town. All the early setlements of Long Island, in fact, as well as most of those of New England, were organized by townships, in contrast to the plantations and hundreds of the more southern Colonies. Thomas was thus familar, long before his arrival in Virginia, with the development of towns. His own father had been among those interested in two such projects.

In his youth, Thomas was taken by his father to Sussex County, Delaware, where the elder Harrison removed with his family upon his purchase of 900 acres, known as Maiden Plantation, in 1721, as elsewhere related. On the 10th of October, 1732,

Thomas was among the three sons to whom his father deeded to each 250 acres of his plantation. It is about this time, probably, that he was first married.

His first wife, according to tradition, was Jane Delahaye, (De La Haye, sometimes erroneously spelled Delahague), a Huguenot. The Delahayes were in old Talbot County, Maryland, family. This county is on the eastern shore of Maryland, and just west of Sussex County, Delaware. There were also Maryland Harrisons in the vicinity, and some of them in a way had long been allied with the Delahayes.

EARLY MARYLAND HARRISONS

Francis Harrison, who died in Talbot in 1711, married a daughter of William Riche, and wife Alice (d. 1692), of the same county. Among Riche's daughters was one Eve, who married Thomas Delahaye (d. 1699), of Calvert County, the owner of "Taylor's Ridge." Thomas and Eve had children, Thomas, James, Sarah, and Mary (all "to be brought up Protestants.") Thomas and James are mentioned in the will of Richard Holmes of Talbot (d. 1721), as his sons-in-law. Holmes' widow Eve (d. 1724), likewise names daughters Jane, and Cornelia Delahaye. Taylors Ridge passed into the hands of Francis Harrison, who willed it to his three sons; Francis Jr., William, and John. Francis appears to have been the son of Joseph Harrison, of Charles County (d. 1673), who married Elizabeth, the daughter of Capt. Robert Troope (d. 1666), of the same place. Joseph, of Charles County, had children, Francis, Joseph Jr., Benjamin, Elizabeth, Katherine, and Richard. Richard Harrison, of Charles County, who died in 1710, had brothers Francis, and Joseph. He married Jane,, evidently the sister of George and Thomas Delahaye above, and left children—Joseph, who inherited part of "Delahaye's Chance," in Charles County, Thomas under 21 years, Benjamin under 18 years, Eliza, who married a Hambleton, Tibithia, and Richard. To the last was bequeathed "Lane's Land" near Maryland Point. (See, *Maryland Calendar of Wills*, by Jane Baldwin, Vols., I; pp. 35, 78; II, pp. 57, 170, 190; III, pp. 87, 117, 179, and 200.)

Richard Harrison, of Calvert County, died in 1716-17, possessed of considerable land, some of which was located on Herring Creek. His will names wife Elizabeth, and sons, Samuel, and Richard, and daughters, Mary, the wife of Samuel Chew, Jr., and Eliza, the wife of John Chew. To Richard, Jr., and heirs, was bequeathed "Abington Manor," and "Dowlsdall," near Patuxent River in Calvert. (*Baldwin*, Vol. IV, p. 50.) As related in a paper read before the Historical Society of Montogomery County, Pennsylvania—"Sometime in the year 1717, Richard Harrison, Jr. came into the Province of Pennsylvania, from the western shore of Maryland, where his people had settled two generations before, in what was then Calvert County. The elder Harrison was said to have been the friend of the great Quaker, Geo. Fox. The son was of the same religious belief, and strong in his convictions. During Harrison's stay in Pennsylvania he married Mary Norris, whose father, Isaac Norris, was one of Penn's Counselors. This lady became Richard Harrison's second wife. It had been previously arranged that Mrs. Harrison was to go into Maryland where her husband, a large tobacco grower and slave holder, had an extensive plantation." Richard, however, died in Pennsylvania, in 1747. A small stone meeting house erected by him, on his plantation "Harrington", in 1730, stood until 1819. (See *Pa. Magazine, Historical Society of Pa.*, Vol. 13, p. 477, also *Historical Society of Montgomery Co., Pa.* Vol. I, p. 395.)

A later Richard Harrison, of Maryland, married Dorothy Hanson, by whom he had Robert Hanson Harrison (b. 1745, d. April 1790), the later Private Secretary to Gen. Washington, 1755-81, with the rank of Lieut. Col., and who was appointed Chief

Judge of the General Court, 10th March, 1781. (See *Md. Historical Society Magazine*, Vol. 6, p. 162; compare *Hayden*, p. 341.)

Following Boogher, some have surmised that the founder of Harrisonburg was descended from the Charles County, Maryland family. While Thomas was not so descended, there were in his time some Maryland Harrisons settled in the Valley of Virginia. These though, were located beyond the region of the Shenandoah.

According to one account, a Thomas Harrison, born in England, 1695, married there, Hannah Morrison by whom he had six sons—John, Benjamin, Thomas, Jr., Samuel, Daniel, and James, all of whom came to America after the death of their parents, and settled in Maryland. All are said to have enlisted in the American Army at the outbreak of the Revolution; John, and Thomas, being soon promoted, the former to the rank of Captain, the latter to that of Colonel. Capt. John Harrison married a Miss Malone, of Maryland, and settled in Botetourt County, Virginia. He had sons, Thomas, Samuel, John, Benjamin, Daniel, and James. Col. Thomas never married. While in the army he made a large amount of money, which he invested in Valley of Virginia lands; these at his death, he left to Thomas, son of Capt. John. This Thomas married Margaret Billops, of Virginia, and removed with his parents to South Carolina. After their deaths he returned to Virginia, and settled in Montgomery County. By wife Margaret, he had ten children, of whom he raised eight—Edward, John, Thomas, Samuel, James, Elizabeth, Sarah, and Polly. He married, 2nd, Nancy Crawley, of Virginia, and had, Nancy, Margaret, and William D. He marreid, 3rd, Jane Childress, of Virginia, and had Cynthia, Andrew L., Eliza J., and Benjamin R. In the fall of 1819 he removed with his family to Missouri, and settled on the Boonslick Road, in Callaway County, where he died in his 75th year, July 3, 1840. His eldest son Edward, died in Virginia. John, the second son, was born in Botetourt County, Virginia, October 7, 1791. (See, *A History of the Pioneer Families of Missouri*, by Bryan and Rose, p. 341.)

Various Harrisons were in Maryland at a very early date; on 28th July, 1652, Thomas Harrison petitioned the Council of State "in behalf of some well affected inhabitants in Virginia and Marieland." Joseph Harrison, Gent., appeared as a burgess for Charles County, 15th September, 1663, and is again mentioned as a member from this county in 1670. Robert Harrison, in 1689, was among the petitioners of, "We your Majestie's most loyal and dutiful Subjects, the ancient Protestant Inhabitants of Talbot County." (*Archives of Maryland*, Vol. I, p. 460; II, p. 279; VIII, p. 132.) One of the name died in Talbot, in 1718, leaving will, naming wife Alice, and children, Robert, Joseph, John, William, Benjamin, Alice, Sarah, and Abigail, and grandsons James and John, sons of son James, deceased. A James Harrison, of Talbot County, died in 1680. He was a Quaker, and has been mentioned as the first Harrison to own land in West Jersey. (See p. 169.) His will names wife Isabella, as executrix—to whom was bequeathed his plantation, "Dover," during the minority of son James—son James to receive the said plantation at 21 years of age, also rights to land in New Jersey, and sons William and Marke, 1,000 acres on Tuckahoe Creek, etc. (*Maryand Calendar of Wills*, Vols. IV, p. 151; I, p. 96.)

Among the most prominent immigrants to Pennsylvania, in 1682, were James Harrison, shoemaker, and Phineas Pemberton, grocer, of Lancashire, England, who sailed in the ship *Submission*, from Liverpool, 6th, 7th mo., landing in Maryland, 2nd, 9th mo., being fifty eight days from port to port. Mrs. Harrison accompanied her husband wtih several servants, and Pemberton brought with him his wife Phoebe, the daughter of Harrison, and children, Abigail and Joseph, and his aged father and mother. They stopped at the home of William Dickinson, of Choptank, Maryland.

Leaving their families there, Harrison and Pemberton set out by land for their destination, near the falls of the Delaware. Harrison was much esteemed by William Penn; "his certificate from the Hartshaw Monthly Meeting gives him an exalted character, and his wife is called 'a mother in Israel'." On their arrival in Pennsylvania the immigrants stopped at William Yardley's, in Bucks County, and Pemberton bought near there 300 acres of land, which he named "Grove Place." Harrison also located 1,000 acres in the same county, by virtue of a patent from Penn, dated 11th mo., 1682. They returned to Maryland for the winter, and the next spring brought their famiiles to Pennsylvania.

Prior to his emigration from England, Harrison had been granted by Penn, 5,000 acres of land, the whole of which he finally located in Bucks County. He however, never became a settler. He was one of the Proprietary's Commissioners of Property, and the agent to manage Penn's personal affairs. In 1685, he was appointed one of the Provincial judges. At his death his land (with the exception of 200 acres which he had sold) descended to his daughter, Phoebe Pemberton, and by 1718 her son Israel was the sole possessor. Phineas and Phoebe had in all nine children, three of whom left issue; Israel, m. Rachel Kirkbride and Mary Jordan; James, m. Hannah Lloyd, Mary Smith, and a Miss Morton; and Abigail, m. Stephen Jenkins. (*History of Bucks County, Pa.*, by Davis, Vol. I, p. 52.)

II

It was in the spring of 1737 (see Chapter VIII), that several of the Harrisons of later Rockingham County, Virginia, began disposing of their lands in Delaware, and in a little party of sixteen, including five brothers and their aged father, set out for the Virginia country "West of the Great Mountains." Thomas Harrison, the founder of Harrisonburg, was one of this little band, the other brothers being John, Daniel, Jeremiah and Samuel. On the 14th day of October, 1738, Thomas Harrison, "late of Sussex County," Delaware, conveyed to James Hood, for eighty-five pounds "Current Money of America," his 250 acre share of Maiden Plantation. (See p. 61.)

On their arrival in the Valley of the Shenandoah, in that part of Orange set off for Augusta County, the brothers finally chose for their place of settlement the beautiful and fertile country lying to the west of the southern end of the Massanutten. Here they all located near each other, each at a large spring, and in the general region watered by Cook's, Smiths, and Linville's creeks—Thomas himself, settled at the "Head Spring of the East Fork of Cook's Creek."

This old spring until late years was one of the noted landmarks of Harrisonburg. Although yet in existence it is now arched over and out of sight beneath the paved street surrounding the "Public Square" of the city. Today only a prosaic manhole cover identifies the spot. It is located near the curbing at the southwest corner of the Square, and the little branch into which the spring flows emerges from under the paving at the opposite side of the street.

The country roundabout being practically uninhabited, the newly arrived settlers took their time in selecting their lands, and making application for their patents. Orange court was all but inaccessible, owing to the distance to be traversed, and the mountains encountered. The first reference to Thomas found on the Orange Court Order Books appears under date of 22nd July, 1742. By this time he had brought suit by petition against James Pollard, Gent., which being agreed was dismissed on this date. (See p. 125.)

On the 22nd of March, 1743, Thomas Harrison and Thomas Linville each produced at Orange court their military commissions as "Cornetts," in Capt. William Linville's company. (See p. 126.) Linville was a Captain of Horse. A Cornet was a commissioned officer of the cavalry troop who carried the colors. Thomas Linville is elsewhere referred to on the court records as, "otherwise called I, Thomas Linville above the Ridge." (Orange Court Order Book 1743-46, p. 313.)

While Orange County yet included "that part designed to be Called Augusta," Thomas Harrison was granted his first land patents. In all, his grants totaled 2,742 acres, but as one of these was an inclusive patent the land embraced was 641 acres less. His patents were eight as follows—

To THOMAS HARRISON

Date		Acres	Location	Book No.	Page
15th March,	1744,	258	"on the Head Spring of the East Fork of Cook's Creek"	22	217.
15th March,	1744,	250	"on the East Branch of Cook's Creek	23	854.
15th March,	1744,	233	"on the East Fork of Cook's Creek."	22	213.
10th Sept.,	1755,	150	"On a Sinking Spring branch of Linville's Creek"	32	640
10th Sept.	1755,	229	"On Muddy Creek."	32	641.
10th March,	1756,	120	"On a branch of Linville's Creek at a place called Harrison's Cotton Patch"	32	685
16th Aug.,	1756,	212	"on the North West side of the South Branch of Linville's Creek.	34	131.
1st March,	1773,	1290	Inclusive patent; embracing the 233 and 250 acre patents of 1744, and 158 acres of the 258 acre patent of 1744, together with 120 acres formerly granted to Jeremiah Harrison and 529 acres never before granted.	41	179.
TOTAL		2742	less 641 or 2101 acres.		

(See Patent Books, numbers as above, at Land Office, Richmond, Virginia.)

The first 1744 patent above included the old Head Spring, now arched over, and the present land in the center of Harrisonburg.

Thomas settled within a stone's throw to the southeast of the spring and directly on the west side of what became a little later "the Great Road to the Court House—today the Main Street of Harrisonburg, a part of "The Long Grey Trail." His old house is yet standing. It stands directly across the street opposite the northside entrance to the new Methodist Church, and until recent years was long used as a law office. It is now incorporated in a more modern building, being the stone or rear section of the late Gen. John E. Roller's residence, on the corner of Main and Bruce streets.

In regard to this historic structure, the *Virginia Magazine of History and Biography* says—"The first house built in Harrisonburg, Rockingham County, Virginia, is constructed of limestone and was built by Thomas Harrison, founder of the place. It was the mansion house of 1290 acres of land, and was (later) occupied by Reuben Harrison. It changed hands several times. It was the headquarters of militia officers at interesting times, and was the scene of several bloody rows." (Vol. 10. pp. 42-43.)

The building is one of the oldest still standing in the Valley of Virginia, vieing with

THE OLD THOMAS HARRISON HOUSE
In Harrisonburg
By THE LONG GREY TRAIL. See page 220.

Old Stone Church in this respect. According to tradition, it too, was often used as a fortification against the Indians. It is said to have been built over a small spring, access to which was obtained by a stairway leading down from the first floor, in order to afford protection from the savages when obtaining water.

The founder of Harrisonburg was the first of the Harrisons to patent land on Cook's Creek. Shortly prior to Thomas' first patents his brother Daniel had been granted land on the headwaters of the Dry Fork of Smiths Creek. (See Chapter XII.) The founder's first land was a little to the southwest of this. In 1746, Daniel also patented land on Cook's Creek—but on the western branch, and in an opposite direction from his brother—and on this made his home. Of Thomas' brothers of the neighborhood, Jeremiah located the nearest to him. John settled the farthest away, and at the Big Spring, now Lacy. Both John and Thomas, as elsewhere observed, fixed their homes directly on "The Long Grey Trail" as it runs today. Near Thomas there also settled his brother-in-law, Robert Cravens. Both patented their first lands on the same day—the 1744 date above.

On the second day following the opening of the first court of Augusta County, December 9, 1745, the justices appointed Thomas and Jeremiah Harrison, Wm. Williams, and Hugh Douglas, as appraisers of the estate of John Levenson, deceased. (See p. 149.) Following the opening of the court, Thomas is found frequently referred to on the old records, and from these some of the activities of his life, preceeding the establishment of Rockingham County, are gleaned.

Prior to, and from the organization of Augusta County, he, and his brothers, were manifestly much interested in the opening of public roads. His brothers, John and Daniel were among the overseers appointed by Orange court in the spring of 1745 to open the Indian Road, the first highway up the Valley. Two early orders of the court of Augusta mentioning a connecting link to this old road, in which the founder, and his brother Jeremiah, together with Robert Cravens, and another brother-in-law, Alexander Herring, are named, have been quoted. (Chapter I.) The first of these orders is dated June 20, 1746, the other August 20, 1747, both being in regard to the appointment of Thomas and his brothers as overseers.

About the time of the first order, Thomas appeared as a planitiff in his first action at law before the court. The defendant was Edward McGill, and the subject of controversy was an oft heard old and familiar one—debt. , This particular writ was dated 14th February, 1746. (County Court Judgements, April and June, 1746.) Two other suits of this nature, in both of which Thomas was also plaintiff, were as follows—"Thomas Harrison vs. Andrew Mitchell," writ dated 18th August, 1748, and "Thomas Harrison vs. John Craig," November, 1750, note dated 12 September, 1749. (Supra—February and March, 1748, and November, 1750.)

On the 3rd of September, 1747, Thomas Harrison, and Robert Cravens, were appointed processioners, "from Samuel Wilkins' to the lower end of the Great Plain to Fairfax's line, thence with the said line to the South Mountain." Their returns made to the vestry on the 8th of March following, disclose that they had practically made a tour of the lands of their relatives. At this early date the region was evidently thinly inhabited. Wilkins appears to have lived near and somewhat to the south of Thomas. The Fairfax line was later made the northern boundary of the county. It had been run in the fall of 1746.

Thomas and Robert were next appointed, along with Jeremiah Harrison, to appraise the estate of Peter Dyer, deceased. Their appraisment was recorded 15th May, 1749.

(See, Will Book No. 1, p. 174.) Jacob and James Dyer are mentioned on the Orange records as early as 1741. (See page 140.) Peter was probably a brother.

In the autumn of 1753 a party of Moravians, from Pennsylvania, passed through the Shenandoah Valley on their way to establish their new colony in North Carolina, at present Winston-Salem. These travellers kept a journal of their trip. They found the roads well nigh impassable for their wagons, and at times had to unload part of their effects at the foot of the various hills encountered, and make two trips up the grade before continuing on. One stop overnight was made at "Thomas Harrison's," regarding which they left the following testimonial of the founder's hospitality—

"WE inquired about the way, but could not get good information. After travelling 3 1/2 miles we found two passable roads. Two of the Bretheren preceeded us on the left hand road. They met a woman who informed them about the way, then they came back to us again and we took the road to the right. We travelled ten miles without finding water. It was late already and we were compelled to travel five miles during the dark night. We had to climb two mountains which forced us to push the wagon along or we could not have proceeded, for our horses were completely fagged out. We thus arrived late at Thomas Harrison's plantation.

Here we bought food for our horses and pitched our tents a short distance from his house. These people are very friendly. They lodged strangers very willingly. (*Va. Magazine of History & Biography*, Vol. 12, p. 145.)

With the beginning of the French and Indian War, on May 15th, 1754, or within a month following the first hostilities, "Thomas Harrison qualified Lieutenant." (Order Book IV, p. 193; *Chalkley*, Vol. I. p. 63.) Two years before, his brother Daniel had qualified as a Captain. As the case of many of Augusta's Colonial soldiers, further details of Thomas' enlistment have been buried in the sands of time. Doubtless, as in the instance of others, he served on ferquent tours throughout the war.

November 20th, 1761, the vestry designated "Thomas Harrison's" as a place of worship. "A Register Book, with Alphabet, a Bible and 2 Prayer Books were ordered to be purchased for the Church." "To John Shanklin, Clerk, at Thomas Harrison's . . . .," etc. At this meeting the parish levy was laid. The number of tithable was now 2,283, and the tax assessed was five shillings each. (See pages 348 and 351.)

As before observed, the Established Church had early erected a place of worship on Capt. Daniel Harrison's plantation, and at present Cross Keys. At the last named point the Presbyterians, too, had built their first church within the present limits of Rockingham. In fact, they had preceeded the Episcopalians. Out of these two congregations grew the first churches at Harrisonburg. The fixing on Thomas Harrison's as a place of worship was thus the first step by the Established Church in the removal of its meeting place to a more central location. While it is not known what influence the founder may have had concerning this move, the step was manifiestly of considerable importance, tending towards the early growth of the village of Harrisonburg.

John and Robert Shanklin at different times served as Clerks of the Church. A further reference to John occurs under date, 20, November, 1767, at which time the vestry allowed his salary "for being Clerke at Harrison's." At this meeting the parish levy was again laid, and the next day three pounds were levied for "Robert Shanklin, Clerk at Capt. Harrison's in the yeare 1763, to be paid to John Shanklin." Among the 1764 vestry accounts is an item mentioning the pay of "Robert Shanklin to acting as Clerk at Capt. Harrison's." (Augusta Parish Vestry Book, pp. 425, 437, and 376.) Capt. Harrison was Thomas' brother. (See page 197.)

One, Robert Shanklin, was a witness to the deeds to Thomas, Daniel and Jeremiah Harrison, when their father divided his lands amongst these sons in Delaware. (See Chapter V.) For a time this Robert was the County Surveyor of Sussex. Robert, the Clerk of Augusta Parish, settled near Daniel Harrison. He came directly to the Valley from Lancaster County, Pennsylvania, which borders Delaware on the east; Deed—29th Sept., 1749, James Wood of Frederick, to Robert Shankland of Lancaster, Pennsylvania, 300 acres of land on Muddy Creek, corner Jacob Dye(r), patented to Wood 12th January, 1746. Witness—Wm. Dobbin, James Caroll, Thomas Wood, Valentine Sevier, Edward Shanklin. (Deed Book 2, p. 342.)

Among the settlers, of the time of the first meeting of the church at Thomas Harrison's, scattered in and about the neighborhood to the northwest of Thomas, were the following, who on the second of January, 1761, petitioned for a road "from Adam Reader's Mines to Isaac Robertson's, from thence to Widow Wright's Mill; thence to Thomas Harrison's in the Great Road to the Court House;" viz—Thomas Pickens, Isaac Robertson, James Wright, Tunes Van Pelt, John Chrisman, Lydia Wright, William Munsey, Robert Bellshe, Jacob Gum, Jacob Gum, Jr., John White, Leonard Herring, Thomas Harrison, William Dunlop, Robert Kearr, Alexander Painter, Jacob Miller, Scidmore Munsey, William Pickens, John Jackson, David Robertson, Henry Mase, James Thomas. (See, Various old papers filed by the Court, 1760-1770; *Chalkley,* Vol. I, p. 429.)

This year a marriage was celebrated in Thomas Harrison's family, whereby his daughter was destined to become the great-aunt of a future President of the United States. Abigail, a daughter of the founder, married Leonard Herring, (see the 1798 deed at the beginning of this Chapter), reputed by some authorities to have been a great-grandfather of Abraham Lincoln. (See, *Ancestry of Abraham Lincoln,* by Lea Hutchinson, pp. 76, and 109.) The license was dated in August 1761. (Marriage Licenses of Augusta, 1761.) Leonard was the eldest son of Alexander Herring, who married Abigail Harrison, a sister of Thomas, while they were yet living in Delaware. (See Chapter VI.)

A deed of 1800, on record in the "ruined files" (burnt records), at Harrisonburg, from "Leonard Herring and wife Abigail," recites that the said Leonard was a son of Alexander Herring who died intestate, leaving said Leonard his heir at law. (See Chapter XV, later.)

Leonard and Abigail established their home on Linville's Creek, on land deeded to him by his father. It was the latter and his wife, the elder Abigail Harrison, who were the parents of Capt. Abraham Lincoln's wife.

On the 2nd of January, 1763, the year of the closing of the French and Indian War, the appraisement of John Wright's estate, by Thomas Harrison, John Cravens, and John Sheltman, was recorded. (Will Book 2, p. 208.)

Wright and John Cravens in 1757 together owned land on the head of the Dry Fork, which they later sold. This tract was only a little to the east of Thomas. (See page 209.) Wright also owned land on Linville's Creek on which he seems to have made his home. His wife's name was Lydia. The widow Wright, and James Wright, appear as two signers of the 1761 road petition above. Among the assets listed of John's estate were numerous notes for money which he had loaned to various inhabitants of the neighborhood, one of which was from David Smith, son of Capt. John. While Wright's connection with the Oyster Bay family of the same name is not disclosed, from the circumstances of his settlement in the community, and association with the Harrisons and Cravens, it appears likely that he was a kinsman of theirs.

Prior to the close of the Indian war, Thomas Harrison had patented 1452 acres of land, all of which was on Cook's, Linville's, and Muddy Creeks. In 1764, concurrently with the rise of the tide of general activity in land trading, is found the first record of his deeding land in Augusta. On the 19th November, this year, he, and wife Sarah, conveyed to Jeremiah Harrison, 212 acres of land, "on the Dry Fork of Smiths Creek." Three days later, (November 22nd), he and Sarah also deeded to David Berry 229 acres. This land was in two tracts on Muddy Creek which he had patented in 1755. (Deed Book 11; pp. 752, 756.)

The following year, or on the 23rd May, 1765, Thomas Harrison, "farmer," for 50 Pounds, deeded to John Sheltman, 61 acres of land, "on the head spring of Cook's Creek, part of 250 acres patented to the said Thomas 15th March, 1744." (Deed Book 12, p. 11.) On the same date his wife released dower—Order Book IX (page 355) "Private examination of Sarah, wife of Thomas Harrison," etc.

This conveyance embraced a tract included in one of Thomas' first patents to land at Harrisonburg. Back in the days of Maiden Plantation, in Sussex on the Delaware, when Thomas disposed of his part of the plantation to James Hood, preparatory to his settlement in the Valley, he signed his deed of release by making his mark. (See Chapter VI). Such also is the way he identifies himself in the deeds above, including the last. Later, just before the formation of Rockingham, in probably his final signature on the Augusta records, he again so signed; this time as a witness to a deed—along with Joseph Smith, Henry Ewing, and John Warren, his son-in-law—to land patented to Thomas Gragg (wife Elizabeth), 1st March, 1773. (Deed Book 19, p. 349.)

As noted by Mrs. Danske Dandridge, in her interesting work, *Historic Sheperdstown;* "The first settlers of the Valley of Virginia were more handy with the rifle than the pen." Certainly, as evidenced by the records, a great number of such settlers, both influential and substantial, were largely unacquainted with the latter. Particularly amongst those of Colonial origin was such often necessarly the case.

Sarah, the second wife of Thomas, and the only one found named on the Augusta records, is aparently first mentioned in the 1764 deeds above. Her name however, would not likely appear before Thomas' first conveyances. As given by these, she too signed by making her mark. No record of Thomas' marriage appearing at Staunton, the indications are that they were married prior to the establishment of Augusta Parish. The marriage records of the Parish of St. Mark (out of which Augusta was taken), have become lost or destroyed. Sarah's maiden name is unknown; she was probably a Davis, one of Thomas' sons being thus named. Some have thought that she was a Cravens, a sister of Daniel Harrison's first wife; others have confused her with Thomas' first wife, mentioning her as Delahaye. She was evidently early married to Thomas and was the mother of most, if not all, of his children. She died in 1782.

Davis Harrison on the 22nd August, 1766, was appointed road surveyor. At this time he was also constable. The following year, on August 24th, Thomas Fulton was appointed to this office, "vice Davis Harrison." (Order Books X, p. 233, and XI, p. 333.)

The road to early Harrisonburg petitioned for in 1761 seems to have been slow in materializing, doubtless owing to the French and Indian War. In 1767 another petition was presented—"To the Worshipful Court of Augusta County. We, your humble petitioners, pray that your worships would be pleased to grant a road to be cleared from Adam Reader's to Isaac Robertson's, from thence to Widow Wright's Mill, from thence to Thomas Harrison's, on the great road to the Court House, which will be the covenants' road to travel either north or south, to mill or to market. May ye second day, year 1767. Your favor will oblige your humble Petitioners." The signers were the same as those to the first petition except that Tunes Van Pelt had dropped out, and with the addition of James Van Pelt, William Blear (Bear ?), Francis Munsey, Mathias Kinder, and Timothy Warren. (Petitions to May Court, 1767; *Chalkley,* Vol. I, p. 489.)

This year (1767), Jeremiah Harrison, son of Thomas, and Robert Cravens, son of Robert, were appointed processioners. Their returns of 1768 name various other settlers of the day in the neighborhood of present Harrisonburg; the lands viewed by them being those of—Daniel Smith, Leonard Herron, (Herring), Samuel Sample, Thomas Harrison, John Harrison, Wm. Shaddone, John McClure, Saml. Briggs, John McGill, John Fowler, Saml. Hemphill, Jeremiah Harrison, William Gregg, Pat. Guin (Quin), Jno. Cravens, Robt. Cravens, (Jr.), Daniel Love, Daniel Harrison, John Brown, David Rolston, John Hinton, Valentine Sevier, Francis Hughs, Alex. Harrison, James Fowler, Edward Shanklin, Jenett McDonald, Alex. Miller, Jno. Hardman, Henry Ewen, (Ewing), William Erwin, Andw. Erwin, Walter Crow, Michael Waren, (Warren), and John Curry. (Augusta Parish Vestry Book, p. 444.)

* * * * *

Events throughout the country were now rapidly leading towards the beginning of the Revolution. In 1765 the Stamp Act had been passed, in February, by the English Parliament—to take effect November 1st—and replied to in the Virginia House of Burgesses, May 30th. On this latter occasion, Patrick Henry had delivered his famous warning —"Tarquin and Caesar had each his Brutus, Charles I, his Cromwell, . . . and George III may profit by their example." Further replies had been prepared in October, by various delegates from nine of the Colonies at their meeting in New York, (called at the instance of Massachusetts), in the form of a "Declaration of Rights," and addresses of protest to the king and Parliament. Opposition to the act had blazed forth everywhere, and the resultant storm of indignation had caused it to be repealed, March, 17, 1766; but new taxes had been substituted on tea, glass, and painters materials, July 2, 1767, and authority had been granted to send British soldiers to America, two regiments of which had arrived in Boston, to be housed and fed by the colonists.

Early in 1769 Parliament advised the king to take vigorous measures against Massachusetts, and if sufficient grounds appeared for accusition of treason to transport the accused to England for trial. To this the king concurred. In February the House of Burgesses of Virginia passed resolutions affirming the rights of the Colonies to act in concert against the encroachments of Parliament, claiming for the different assemblies the sole right to tax their constituents, and warning the king of the dangers that would ensue should an American be transported to England for trial. Governor Botetourt, in alarm, dissolved the House. The members repaired immediately to the Raleigh Tavern, and adopted a non-importation agreement (particularly as to slaves), introduced by Washington, and drawn up by George Mason.

With the resignation of Grafton, January 28, 1770, the long years of Whig rule in England ended. Lord North was made the new Prime Minister, and although nominally the head of the government (1770-1781), George III, the personal leader of the Tory party, became the actual prime minister and cabinet in one. Impressed by the firmness of America, in March, 1770, all import taxes except those on tea were repealed, but North avowed the government's determination not to yield in its right of taxing the Colonies.

Later in 1770,—October 15th—Governor Botetourt, of Virginia, died. He had tried to bring about a better understanding in England of Virginia's problems, and his death was deeply lamented. He was succeeded by William Nelson, president of the

Council, as acting Governor. In February, 1772, John Murray, Earl of Dunmore, the new Governor-in-chief arrived. His wife, the Countess of Dunmore, joined him in April 1774, and the same year their three sons became students at William and Mary. Dunmore had been transferred from New York. He was the last of his line; the last Colonial Governor of Virginia.

Dunmore's short term was a crowded one—thoroughly ineffectual, he was as chaff before the wind fanning the embers of wrath now smouldering; nor were his troubles long in beginning. On March 12, 1773, another series of resolutions were moved in the House of Burgesses. Smuggling, by 1772, had become prevalent off the coast of Rhode Island, and a British armed schooner had been sent over to lie at the mouth of Naragansett Bay to examine all craft passing in or out. Recently, by accident, she had been grounded, whereupon citizens from Providence, after forcibly removing her crew had siezed and burned her. Parliament then made such offences punishable by death, and authorized that the accused be taken to England for trial. Virginia having already remonstrated against such removal, a "Committee of Correspondence" was now recommended to inquire into the newly established court in Rhode Island.

III.

For Augusta, her days were those of happy peace—seed time and harvest were following each other quietly. As the sun arose out of old Massanutten's wonderfully even and unbroken skyline, it looked down on a picture serene, such as no artist could hope to portray. Scattered clear across the wide Valley, on Nature's green canvas, were now to be seen outlined numerous sturdy log cabins, each hard by some ever-widening stream, as it flowed to join the gentle Shenandoah. Where only a few short years before could be found but an occasional thin grey line of smoke, ascending lazily from some lonely Indian's camp, there now floated briskly from the tops of broad-bottomed stone chimneys, glistening in the morning's light, silent evidence of the many bright hearth-fires in the cabins below. Surrounding these, innumerable patterns of clearings and grain fields appeared, and interwoven could be noted the delicate markings of many roads; all traced by the same hands that had outlined the cabins, the hands of the bold pioneers and their hardy sons. On the hills where shortly before had grazed the buffalo, and the deer, could be observed now feeding numerous herds of cattle and sheep. Far in the background could be discerned faintly the tops of the jagged Allegheny, standing as a kind of barrier, guarding this peaceful scene; but ever beckoning to the wide country beyond.

The woods abounded in game, and the streams in fish, and the country was a young hunter's paradise. One of the main articles of commerce being exported was deer skins. In 1770 a single merchant of Staunton alone, shipped to Richmond 795 of these, including four elk hides; likewise four years later the rate was 332, all elk hides. Other exports of the day were hemp, beeswax, ginseng, butter and cheese, and an occasional barrel of flour. Wagoners on their trips with merchandise sometimes went as far north as Boston.

Always a deeply religious people, the churches too, were flourishing, and were at the same time the main centers of social life. Meetings on Sunday frequently lasted all day, and in the summer, when the weather permitted, were often held in some shady well watered grove. Here, the larger crowds could be accommodated, especially at the annual meetings, when various congregations of the same denomination assembled

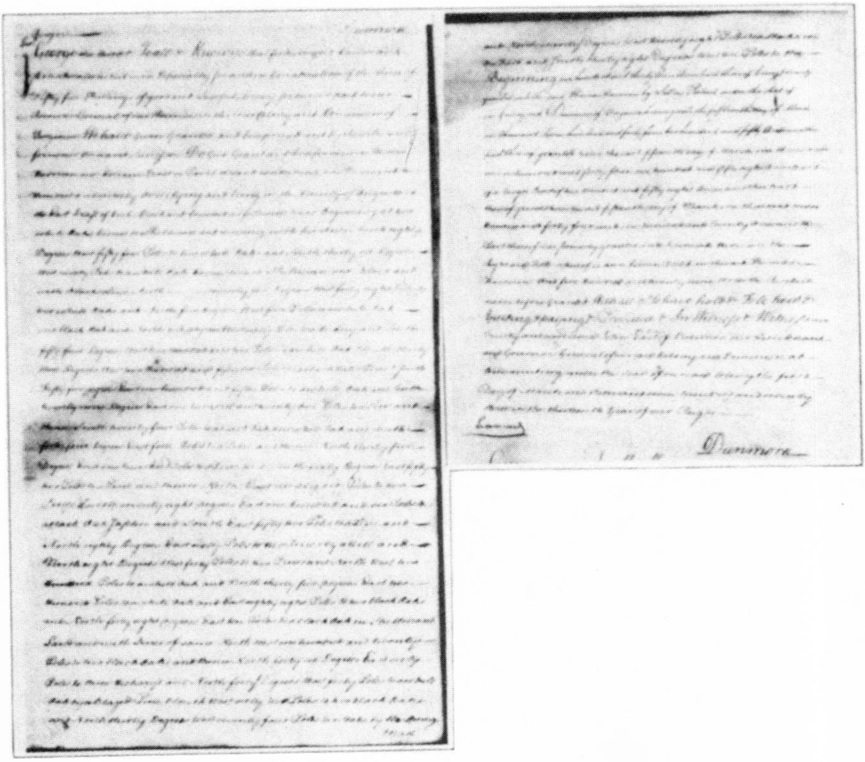

THOMAS HARRISON'S INCLUSIVE PATENT OF 1773
For his land at Harrisonburg, as Recorded in the Patent Book at Richmond, Virginia. See pages 220 and 227.

together. These meetings generally continued several days, and were usually held in the latter part of the summer, or shortly after hay-making and harvest—

"We plow the fields and scatter
The good seed on the land,
But it is fed and watered
By God's almighty hand;
He sends the snow in winter,
The warmth to swell the grain,
The breezes and the sunshine,
And soft refreshing rain,"

In the autumn of 1773—November, 18th—the Vestry of Augusta "determined to build a chapel in the neighborhood of Cook's Creek, now Rockingham." *(Waddell,* p. 218.) Down until this time preaching at "Thomas Harrison's," when not held out of doors, had probably taken place in a building erected by him. Earlier this year (March 1st), Thomas had obtained his inclusive patent for 1,290 acres of land at Harrisonburg.

But the happy years of peace were soon to end. One month to the day following the vestry meeting there occured in Boston the famous "Tea Party." This act aroused great wrath in England, and strong measures were at once determined on. Parliament early in 1774, (March-May), annulled the charter of Massachusetts, and ordered that the port of Boston be closed on June 1st. Such proceedings were the equivalent of a declaration of war.

In May 1774, the House of Burgesses met in Williamsburg, and the town was a scene of gaiety. The Governor's lady had just arrived, and it was agreed to give a ball in her honor on the 27th. In the meantime, word came from Boston telling of the closing of the port. To this the Assembly made an indignant protest, and set apart June 1st, as a day of fasting and prayer. Dunmore in wrath dissolved the House. The members, as in the days of Botetourt, again immediately repaired to the Raleigh Tavern, and then, and there, adopted resolutions discontinuing the use of tea, and other East India articles, and recommending that a "Congress of all the Colonies" be annually convened.

July 1st, as set apart, was observed; the use of tea was discontinued, and the good housewives sealed up their stock. Messages of sympathy and encouragement were sent to Boston, and contributions of money and provisions for the relief of the inhabitants followed. Neither was Augusta lacking in forwarding her share—"When the sheaves had been harvested," says Bancroft, the historian, "and the corn thrashed and ground in a country as yet poorly provided with barns or mills, the backwoodsmen of Augusta County, without any pass through the mountains that could be called a road, noiselessly and modestly delivered at Frederick one hundred and thirty-seven barrels of flour as their remittance to the poor of Boston." (Vol. VIII, p. 74.)

On August 1st, a Convention met at Williamsburg to appoint delegates to Congress. September 5th, 1774, the First Continental Congress convened at Philadelphia. All the colonies except Georgia were represented. The delegates numbered fifty-five. Peyton Randolph, of Virginia, was elected President. The proceedings were held in secret session, and lasted fifty-one days. A declaration of rights was made, the king was petitioned, the inhabitants of Great Britain were addressed, and a memorial to the colonies was written. Of Virginia's statesmen, Henry stood foremost from the beginning for Independence; on this point he had been years in advance of his compatriots. On the second day he declared, "that all government was dissolved and they were reduced to a state of nature; and that the Congress which he was addressing was the first of a perpetual series of Congresses." *(Campbell.)*

Already for Augusta her short years of peace had ended—her soldiers were even now on their way to Point Pleasant. Her warlike activities, however, were against her old savage foe, the Indian. In the spring of 1774 a party of whites, in the region of Ft. Pitt, had murdered the family of Logan, a celebrated Cayuga chief. Logan accused Col. Cresap of instigating the massacre, and began raising an army. Lately, he had formed an alliance with Cornstalk, chief of the Shawnees; a general war thus threatened. Apprehending the danger, Dunmore appointed Gen. Andrew Lewis (at the time a member of the Assembly), to command the forces raised in Augusta, Botetourt, and adjoining counties east of the Ridge, and himself arranged to head troops from Frederick, Dunmore, (now Shenandoah), and adjacent counties. The Governor planned to march by way of Ft. Pitt, and thence down the Ohio, while Lewis was to proceed down the valley of the Kanawha to Point Pleasant, the juncture of the rivers. Here the two forces were to meet to penetrate the Ohio country. Early in September, Lewis' troops rendezvoused at Camp Union, now Lewisburg, Greenbrier County, and on the 11th, began their march through the wilderness, 1,100 strong.

The Augusta forces consisted of 400 men, in eight companies, under Col. Charles Lewis, a brother of the General. The Captains were George Mathews, Alexander McClenachan, John Dickinson, John Lewis (son of Thomas, brother of the General), William Paul, Joseph Harris, Samuel Wilson, and Benjamin Harrison, son of Capt. Daniel. The Botetourt troops were of about the same number, in seven companies under Col. William Fleming, one company of which was commanded by Capt. John Lewis, son of the General. The remaining forces consisted of six independent companies, one under Col. John Field from Culpeper, and others, including a company of rangers, under Col. William Christian. Several of the latter's companies were from the Holston and New River settlements, and joined Lewis on the way.

Point Pleasant was reached September 30th; but no word had come from Dunmore. After a short wait, runners were sent out in quest of him. Before these returned an express arrived at the Point, Sunday, October 9th, with orders from the Governor for Lewis to march to the Chillicothe towns, and there to join him. Preparations at once were started to cross the Ohio. In the meantime, unknown to the Virginians, the Indians, under Cornstalk, the night of the 9th crossed the river further up, and were on their way through the darkness to surprise the camp. Cornstalk headed Delawares, Mingoes, Cayugas, Iowas, Wyandots, and Shawnees; his warriors composing the flower of the Northern Confederated Tribes. Very early in the morning the savages were met by two of Lewis' men out hunting; one hunter was killed, but the other escaped unhurt, and gave the alarm before sunrise. The General sent forward two divisions; the first under his brother, Col. Charles Lewis, and the second under Col. Fleming, while he himself remained with the reserve to defend the camp. Both divisions were attacked; Col. Lewis was mortally wounded, and Col. Fleming so severly that he had to retire to camp. Reenforcements under Col. Field arrived, and the Indians were driven back, but he too was killed. Capt. Shelby took his place. The engagement now became general and all day the battle raged—the Virginians being hemmed in between the rivers, with the enemy in front. Finally, by evening, Lewis was able to get some of his men secretly in behind the savages; this turned their attack, and soon they were thouroughly routed; with great loss they broke and fled, recrossing the Ohio in the night.

The Indians had made their last great stand for the Virginia country east of the Alleghanies; their power in fact was broken east of the Ohio—from now on their faces were to be turned westward to the country beyond the Mississippi. The battle was one of the most noted conflicts in the annals of the Indian warfare. Cornstalk, the Indian commander, displayed great skill and bravery. Some say Logan was not in the fight. The Indian losses were never ascertained, as many of their dead were thrown into the river during their flight. The Virginians lost seventy killed and the same number wounded. Many of the officers afterwards became distinguished men. The whites actually engaged were not over 550 in number; 100 were absent hunting, and knew nothing of the battle.

After erecting a small fort at the Point, and leaving a garrison to provide for the wounded, Lewis proceeded to join Dunmore, who had halted at a place called Camp Charlotte, near the Indian town Chillicothe, on the Sciota. Here eight chiefs, with Cornstalk as their leader, came to the Governor and sued for peace. Dunmore then sent orders to Lewis, to return to the mouth of the Kanawha, but suspecting the Governor's good faith, and believing that he was seeking to win the Indians over to the side of Great Britain against the Colonies, the regiment disregarded the order, and continued on. When within about three miles of the camp they were met by the Governor, and it was with difficulty that Lewis restrained his men from killing their commander-in-chief, and his Indian companions. Following a brief conference, Lewis at the Governor's further orders, reluctantly turned towards home with his troops. A short time following his departure, the Governor concluded his treaty with the Indians. On this occasion Cornstalk made a long speech, charging the whites with having provoked the war. Logan, while still indignant at the murder of his family, consented to the treaty, but refused to attend, saying, that "he was a warrior, not a councillor." His speech—afterwards immortalized by Jefferson, in his *Notes on Virginia*—was sent in a wampum belt, and delivered by an interpreter.

At home, for many days, the fate of the expedition was unknown, and anxiety was universal. The October term of Augusta court met on the 18th, only to adjourn the next day; scarcely any business was transacted. By November term the surviving heroes had returned. At the January court, 1775, numerous accounts in regard to the expenses of the expedition were presented. Among these on January 18th, were admitted to record the accounts "of Thomas Harrison, for diets of Malitia," and of Elizabeth Harrison for the same. (Order Book XVI, p. 36.) Diets included cattle, of which a large number had been driven along to supply food for the army.

Ezekiel Harrison, one of Thomas's sons, is known to have gone out with the expedition. He marched as a volunteer under Capt. Joseph Harris, and many years later in testifying in open court, mentioned that in the battle at the mouth of the Kanawha, 10th October, 1774, "I was wounded in the right breast." (State of Illinois, S. S.; Sangamon County, Oct. 9, 1832.)

* * * * * *

The year 1775 was an eventful one throughout the colonies. Early in 1775 preparations were under way to hold a Second Continental Congress. In this Virginia was in the forefront, and her western frontier stood as one with the mother state in her noble advance to face the coming storm. On February 22nd, "after due notice given the freeholders of Augusta to meet in Staunton," the first recorded patriotic meeting of the inhabitants of the said county was held, "for the purpose of electing delegates to represent them in Colony Convention at the town of Richmond, on the 20th March, 1775." Thomas Lewis, the former surveyor, and Capt. Samuel McDowell, were unanimously chosen as delegates.

Instructions to the honored pair were drawn up, and delivered them—"you may consider the people of Augusta county as impressed with just sentiments of loyalty and allegiance to his Majesty King George . . . We have also respect for the parent State, which respect is founded on religion, on law, and on the genuine principals of the constitution. On these principals do we earnestly desire to see harmony and good understanding restored between Great Britain and America. Many of us and our forefathers left our native land and explored this once-savage wilderness to enjoy the free exercise of the rights of consience and of human nature. These rights we are fully resolved with our lives and fortunes, inviolably to preserve; nor will we surrender such inestimable blessings, the purchase of toil and danger, to any Ministry, to any Parliament, or any body of men upon the earth, by whom we are not represented, and in whose decisions therefore we have no voice, ... Fully convinced that the safety and happiness of America depend, next to the blessings of Almighty God, on the unanimity and wisdom of her people, we doubt not you will, on your parts, comply with the recommendations of the late Continental Congress, by appointing delegates from this colony to meet in Philadelphia on the 10th of May, next, unless American greviences be redressed before that . . . . . Placing our ultimate trust in the Supreme Disposer of every event . . . we desire you to move the Convention that some day, . . . convenient, be set apart for imploring the blessing of Almighty God on such plans as human wisdom and integrity may think necessary to adopt for preserving America happy, virtuous, and free." (*Waddell*, p. 235.)

The second Virginia Convention met on the date proposed, at St. John's Church, Richmond , Virginia. The town had a few straggling houses. At this meeting Patrick Henry made his impassioned speech for liberty—"Are fleets and armies necessary to a work of love and reconciliation? We have petitioned—we have remonstrated—we have supplicated, and we have been spurned from the foot of the throne. I repeat it sir we must fight! A just God presides over the destines of nations, and will raise up friends for us. The battle is not to the strong alone; it is also to the viligant, the active, the brave. There is no retreat but in submission and slavery. Is life so dear, or peace so sweet, as to be purchased at the price of chains and slavery? Forbid it Almighty God! I know not what course others may take, but as for me, give me liberty, or give me death!"

Henry's speech carried the resolutions he had introduced for putting the Colony in a state of defence, and a committee was appointed to prepare a plan. Each county was to raise one, or more, volunteer companies, and troops of horse; these were to be in constant training to act at a moment's warning—thus called "minute men". All the former delegates to Congress were reelected, except that Jefferson was substituted in lieu of Randolph, the Speaker of the Houses of Burgesses, in case the latter could not attend. Dunmore at Williamsburg, on March 28th, issued a proclamation to prevent the appointment of deputies from Virginia to the Congress.

April 19, 1775—

". . . the first oath of Freedom's gun
Came on the blast from Lexington;
And Concord, roused, no longer tame,
Forgot her old baptismal name,
Made bare her patriot arm of power,
And swell'd the discord of the hour."

Following the battle of Lexington, Colonial days in Virginia fast came to an end, and among the first to see that his own were briefly numbered, was Lord Dunmore. In alarm on the night of April 20th, he secretly removed Virginia's powder stored at Williamsburg, to the Magdalen, a British war vessel lying at Burwell's Ferry. Upon being remonstrated with by the indignant citizens of the town, who had rushed to arms, he pretended that he had removed it on account of its being in an insecure place, and threatened, in case of trouble, to free the slaves, and burn the town. His act brought down the wrath of all Virginia; many companies of volunteers immediately assembled for action. The Governor promised to return the powder, but would set no date. Finally on May 2nd, Patrick Henry, at the head of an independent company from Hanover, marched on Williamsburg, resolved to either recover the powder, or make a reprisal for it. On his way other companies joined him on all sides. Lady Dunmore fled to the Fowey, lying at Yorktown, for safety. Sixteen miles from Williamsburg, Henry halted, and was met by a friend, sent at the Governor's request, who, after some parley, delivered a bill of exchange for the amount demanded as value of the powder. Henry thereupon returned with his troops to Hanover. On May 6th the Governor issued a proclamation denouncing him, but on the 11th he set out for Congress, and was escorted in triumph by his countrymen to Harper's Ferry.

The Second Continental Congress met May 10th, at the State House in Philadelphia. Randolph was again elected President, but soon had to return to Virginia to perform his duties as Speaker of the House of Burgesses. He was succeeded by John Hancock, of Massachusetts. A second petition to the king was adopted, as many yet hoped for the restoration of harmony with Britain. At the same time measures were taken towards the formation of a federal union, and for organizing a continental army to serve seven months. Washington was early appointed chairman of the military committees.

Dunmore's troubles with Virginia continued, and powder was a touchy subject. About this time Lord North, of England, offered the Colony a conciliatory proposition, commonly known as the "Olive Branch." The Governor convened the House of Burgesses, and his lady returned with her family from the Fowey. On June 1st the Assembly met. The Council gave a satisfactory answer to Lord North's proposal, but on the night of June 5th, and before the Burgesses could reply, the powder magazine exploded. A number of persons had assembled at the magazine to supply themselves with arms, and several were wounded by spring guns placed therein by the Governor. A mine was also found planted in the magazine. June 6th, Lord Dunmore, and his family, fled from Williamsburg to the Fowey—to return no more. The Assembly, however, assured him of protection, and requested his return, but instead he communicated terms on which a recònciliation might take place; these he conditioned on acceptance of the Olive Branch. To this the Assembly, in a reply, composed by Jefferson, refused to consent, leaving the subject of dispute to the determination of Congress. It was then moved that the Governor had voluntarily abdicated, and Thomas Nelson was chosen to discharge his duties.

On June 15th, Congress appointed Gen. Washington Commander-in-Chief of the Continental Army. He received his commission on the 20th, and on the next day set out for Boston. While on his way he was met by an express bringing news of the battle of Bunker Hill—fought on the 17th. On July 3, 1775, at Cambridge, he took command of the army. The war was now on in earnest.

"That seat of science, Athens,
And Earth's great mistress, Rome,
Where now are all their glories?
We scarce can find their tombs:
Then guard your rights, Americans,
Nor stoop the pliant knee,
Oppose, oppose, oppose, oppose,
The landing of the tea."

—*War Song,* 10th June, 1775.

IV

The Third Virginia Convention assembled at Richmond, July 17, 1775. At this sessions measures were taken to raise two regiments of regular troops, for one year, and two companies for the protection of the western frontier. The executive authority was lodged in a Committee of Safety consisting of eleven members. The Colony was divided into sixteen districts of militia, as minute men. Buckingham, Amherst, Albemarle, and Augusta counties constituted one district. An ordinance was passed to provide local government, particularly for putting into effect the measures of Congress, and of the Convention, through the election of county committees by the qualified voters of each county. The County Committee of Augusta, when formed, was headed by Silas Hart, the elderly justice, and old friend of Thomas Harrison, and prominent member of the Smiths and Linville's Creek Baptist Church.

* * * * * *

Hart, as elsewhere noted, had been admitted to transient communion in the church the second Sabbath in August, 1765. (See p. 187.) The next year he became a full member. The second Sabbath in April, 1766, "Nicholas Fain was received into transient communion, and Joseph Thomas excommunicated," etc., and at the following meeting, the third Sabbath in May, "then was Silas Hart received into full Communion with us by a letter from Penypack Church in Pennsylvania"—21st Communion. At three later meetings the same year members were also added—"Third Sabbath in June; Then did Benjamin Alderson and Ann his Wife submit to the Ordinances of Baptism and the Lords Supper." "Last Sabbath in July—Grace Lockhart, the Wife of Daniel Lockhart submitted to Baptism &c. and then it was appointed by the Church to meet the last Sabbath in August for Communion at *Linville's Creek.* "Met according to appointment the last Sabbath in August . . . And then was baptized Ann Mace." (Page 17.)

By this time meetings were evidently being held both on Linville's Creek, near "Thomas Harrison's," and on Smiths Creek, at present New Market. A further entry on the same page mentions, "An Yearly Meeting held in our Meeting House on *Smiths Creek,* the Second Sabbath in June 1767." Also (next page); "Met . . . last Saturday in June 1768, . . . and John Ray was censured in the highest Degree next to excommunication . . ., and then appointed to meet at Linvilles Creek the first Saturday in August next." Again—"The Association (was) held at Smiths Creek the second Saturday in August in the year of our Lord 1768." (Pages 17-18.)

Business meetings of the church were held on Saturday, prior to the preaching on Sunday. New applicants for membership were examined at the Saturday meetings, and sometimes baptized the same day. "At a Meeting . . . on the first Saturday in March Anno Domini 1769. Then was baptized John Alderson junior, who gave clear and satisfactory answers to such questions as were asked concerning his Faith . . . &c." Alderson a little later succeeded his father as the second pastor of the church, and was the pastor at the beginning of the Revolution.

From the date of Hart's joining the church to the outbreak of the war, the congregation on the whole went forward in gaining new membership. No new members appear to have been added in 1770, but "In the Year of our Lord 1771 . . . was baptized on Profession of Faith four Persons viz. Isaac Morris, & Ruth his Wife, Samuel Nicholas & Curtis Alderson." (Then follows) "In the Year of our Lord 1772, was baptized . . . the following persons, Mary Henton the Wife of Evan Henton, Ann Needham, the Wife of Jno. Needham, Hester Wright, Susannah Ray, the Wife of Jno. Ray, and Mary Alderson, the Wife of John Alderson junior." (Page 18.) The same year there were also "received into this Church by Letter, the following Persons viz. Joshua Lewis, being dismissed from new Valley Church, (Pa.), David Perguin & Mary his Wife, being dismissed from the Great Valley Church, in Pennsylvania, and Thomas Woolsey being dismissed from a church in New York Government, and now ordained for the Ministry by Order of this Church, by Rev. Mr. Jno. Alderson." "On Saturday the Eighth Day of August, 1772, the Church met . . . and then was baptized the following persons, viz. Andrew Davison, Hannah Alderson, the wife of Thomas Alderson, Hannah Harrison the Wife of Jno. Harrison, Ann Dedrage, and Catherine Waren the Wife of Timothy Waren." (Page 19.)

John Harrison was the son of Zebulon, and the grandson of John Harrison, Sr., brother of Thomas, the founder of Harrisonburg. Hannah Harrison was the daughter of John Lincoln, the emigrant, and a sister of Abraham Lincoln, the later husband of Bathsheba Herring. Andrew Davison was probably a nephew of Daniel Davison, son-in-law of John Harrison, Sr.

In the years 1773 and 1774, several members were lost. "At a Meeting held on Saturday before the 2nd Sabbath in August 1773, the church entered upon Business and ordered a Letter for the Association &c. And that Thomas Woolsey is to be dismissed, and Ruth Morris is to be dismissed. Ordered that Brother Jon. Alderson Jr. preach at the Association, on the Trial of his Gifts to exercise among us," etc. (Page 20.) At a meeting 11th June, 1774, it was ordered "That Brother Isaac Morris, be dismissed by a letter to the Church at great Bethel. (Page 21.) "August 13, 1774. Then was held a Meeting by the Church for the Business of her own Body, and it was agreed, 1st, That John Conner be suspended of having any Church Privilege . . . 2ndly That Sister Sarah Porter be suspended . . . 3rdly That Esther North (the Wife of John North) be suspended for Inconsistency. 4thly That Mr. Jno. Alderson jr. be suspended," etc. (Page 22.)

By the next year Alderson had been reinstated; "August 12, 1775, At a Monthly Meeting held at Linville's Creek, it was agreed, . . . 2ndly That Brother John Alderson Jr. be sent to the Association, and be presented to the Trial of his Qualifications for Ordination. About the last of October 1775, our Brother John Alderson jun. was according to regular Order, ordained the Minister of our Church, by the Rev. Jno. Marks." This year two members were added. "The second Saturday in November 1775, our monthly Meeting, and Communion was held at Brother Jno. Needhams House, & two persons were baptized, namely Jno. Needham and Ann Bland." (Page 22.)

Of Thomas, the founder of Harrisonburg's family, Ezekiel his son, later became a member of the Smiths and Linville's Creek Church. Ezekiel was married during the stirring days of 1775. (See, *History of the Early Settlers of Sangamon County, Illinois,* by John Caroll Power, p. 358.) His wife was Sarah Bryan. The Bryans are said to have come into Augusta from Culpeper County, and, according to tradition, were near kinfolks of Thomas Bryan Martin, the nephew of Lord Fairfax. Sarah's brothers were John, Morgan, and William Bryan. The last named became one of the first Methodist ministers of Rockingham. (See, Judgments, Circuit Causes Ended. Bryan vs. Bible. OS. 33, NS. 11; *Chalkley,* Vol. II, p. 73.)

* * * * * *

During the summer and fall of 1775 military preparations throughout the Colony rapidly went forward. For the two regiments authorized by the Third Virginia Convention, Patrick Henry, in August, was commissioned Colonel, of the first, and William Woodford, of the second. Henry was also made commander of all the Colony's forces, raised, and to be raised. George Wythe was elected a member of Congress in place of Washington. In September, Colonel Henry selected Williamsburg as the place of his encampment, and recruits rapidly poured in.

For six long years more, the struggle for Independence raged. The beginning of the war found most of Augusta's soldiers already drilled, and a large number of her officers and men had had their baptism of fire in previous conflicts when fighting the Indians. Many an old settler's home was now to dedicate a strong son to freedom's cause, and in this Thomas Harrison, the founder of Harrisonburg, was no exception. Several of his sons (as will appear in a later Chapter) are known to have participated on America's side in the glorious struggle, and manifestly the old gentleman saw them go forth with a hearty good will.

"And there was tumult in the air,
The fife's shrill note, the drum's loud beat,
And through the wild land everywhere
The answering tread of hurrying feet."
—Thomas Buchanan Read.

After Dunmore's sudden departure from Williamsburg he issued a proclamation calling on all Virginians to repair to his standard, and early in July stationed himself at Portsmouth. His wife and children late in June had sailed from New York on the *Magdalen*. On November 7, 1775, he proclaimed martial law, again summonsing all persons able to bear arms to his standard, this time on the penalty of being proclaimed traitors. To servants and slaves he offered their freedom, should they join him. At Portsmouth he rallied a band of Tories, run-away negroes, British soldiers, and collected a naval force. Here he carried on a petty warfare while engaged in fortifying Norfolk, and erecting a small fort on an island near the Dismal Swamp.

Late in 1775 occurred the battle of Great Bridge, the first bloodshed of the Revolution in Virginia. While Henry was at Williamsburg the Committee of Safety sent Woodford to engage Dunmore. Woodford entrenched his force within cannon shot of the Governor's fort. On December 9th the Governor attacked, and was repulsed with heavy slaughter, every grenadier in the action being killed. In striking contrast Woodford suffered no loss. In the night Dunmore evacuated the fort, and once again took refuge on board the fleet. Woodford was now joined by Col. Howe with troops from North Carolina, and as the latter held a senior commission he was voluntarily allowed to assume command. Soon thereafter Howe took possession of Norfolk.

On January 1, 1776, the town was burned. Dunmore having been reinforced by the Liverpool, a British Man-of-War, and the inhabitants having refused to furnish him supplies, a detachment of marines were landed, who set fire to the nearest houses of the town. No attempt was made by the provincials to arrest the flames, and after most of the town was burned, Col. Howe, with the permission of the Convention, completed its destruction. Dunmore continued his petty warfare, burning and plundering along the coasts, and was the object of general execration. Under the protection of his fleet he finally entrenched himself on Gwynn's Island.

In instructing Woodford to proceed against Dunmore, the Convention had ignored Henry, and Woodford had thereupon refused to report to him. This led to dissatisfaction on Henry's part. While Woodford was at Norfolk the Convention passed an ordinance providing that six additional regiments be raised for two years service. Shortly thereafter Congress took over into the Continental establishment four of these, together with the two originally raised. Henry being Colonel of the First, a commission dated February 13, 1776, for the command of this regiment was sent to him, but at the same time commissions of Brigadier-General were sent to Colonels Howe and Andrew Lewis. At this, Henry refused to accept his commission from Congress, and resigned that which he held from Virginia, whereupon his troops went into mourning and applauded his just resentment at "the glaring indignity." Washington, however, thought his countrymen erred "when they took Henry out of the Senate to place him into the field." Henry returned to Hanover, and was immediately elected a delegate to the Convention about to meet.

The last Court of Augusta County under the authority of the King was held May 1, 1776. Five days later the Fourth Virginia Convention met at Williamsburg. Thomas Ludwell Lee was elected President, Randolph having died September 22nd, the year previously. On the 15th of May, resolutions instructing the Virginia delegates in Congress to declare for independence were reported. The next day these resolutions were read to the troops at Williamsburg, now under command of Gen. Andrew Lewis, and a Union Flag of the American States was first waved from the Capitol, amid the celebration. On June 15th the "Declaration of Rights" was adopted, and on the 29th, the first Constitution of Virginia likewise came into being. Both were from the pen of George Mason. On this latter date, also, the Assembly elected Patrick Henry the first commonwealth Governor of Virginia.

Congress at the time was busily engaged in drafting the Declaration of Independence. On June 7th a resolution in favor of total immediate separation from Great Britain had been moved by Richard Henry Lee, of Virginia, and seconded by John Adams, of Massachussetts. On June 28th a committee was appointed to prepare the declaration. The members of the committee were Thomas Jefferson, John Adams, Benjamin Franklin, Robert R. Livingston, and Richard Henry Lee. On account of the illness of Mrs. Lee the last named had to leave Congress on the day of his appointment, and his place was filled by Rodger Sherman. The Declaration was composed by Jefferson, but was some modified by Congress. July 4th, the immortal charter of liberty was adopted and signed. Virginia's signer's were seven—George Wythe, Richard Henry Lee, Thomas Jefferson, Benjamin Harrison of Berkeley (see p. 110.), Thomas Nelson, Jr., Francis Lightfoot Lee, and Carter Braxton. As Chairman of the Committee of the Whole House, Harrison had introduced the resolution declaring the independence of the Colonies, and on the 4th reported to Congress the completed document.

Colonial days at last were over—concurrently the departure of Lord Dunmore from Virginia was immediately speeded. Gen. Andrew Lewis, on the evening of July 8th, arrived before Gwynn's Island. During the night batteries were placed, and the next morning, Dunmore's fleet being within range, fire was opened upon his flagship. The vessel was damaged, and her cabin shattered; some men on the boat were killed, and Dunmore, himself, was wounded in the leg by a splinter. After returning the fire with a few guns the ship retreated, being towed off by smaller boats. Other vessels of the fleet then received Lewis' fire, and all retired in confusion out of range. The batteries were next trained on the island camp from two directions, and soon the men there were scattered. The next morning, with the aid of canoes, Lewis captured two small armed vessels and landed a force on the island. Dunmore's men were immediately seized with panic, and precipitately took to the boats of the fleet—eighty sail. Valuable stores were left behind; besides these a few Tories from Maryland, and some cattle fell into Lewis' hands. Early following his departure, Dunmore dispatched the remnant of his followers to Florida, and the West Indies, while he himself retired to the North, and thence returned to England. In 1786, he was appointed Governor of Bermuda. He died in 1809.

July 16, 1776, the first Court of Augusta County under the Commonwealth of Virginia was organized. The justices were Samuel McDowell, Sampson Mathews, and Archibald Alexander. The first two administered the oath to Alexander, who in turn administered it to them. Richard Madison qualified as deputy Clerk, and John Christian as Sheriff. In August, Alexander was recommended to Governor Henry for High Sheriff and on November 19th, qualified as such. Alexander's appointment probably awaited the convening of the first General Assembly under the State Constitution. This met on October 7, 1776.

* * * * * *

Throughout the war the Valley was remote from the scenes of actual conflict. Only once was there an alarm of imminent invasion of the enemy. The country, however, was yet on the frontier, and exposed to the threat of British alliance with the Indians. On at least three occasions; viz. in 1776, 1777, and 1779, the militia was called on to furnish troops for Indian campaigns. Local companies, too, were frequently being raised for various tours of duty with the regular army. As regiments of the Line were depleted, recruits and supplies were constantly being furnished. Recruits were obtained by calling for volunteers, by the offering of bounties, and by drafts from the militia—this last was composed of all able bodied men of the county, up to a designated number, in ages from 16 to 50.

While the business of the court, and in general most of the domestic activities of the people, were continued fairly uninterrupted, life in Augusta was lived under conditions far from normal. During the year 1776 mention of only four meetings of the Smiths and Linville's Creek Church is made in the old church book.

"May 10, 1776, The Church met according to appointment, and agreed that Church Meeting be held at Linville's Creek, the Saturday before the 2nd Sabbath in June next, and Sarah Porter to be excommunicated." "At a Church Meeting, held at Linville's Creek the 2nd Saturday in August 1776, . . . it was agreed 4thly That the Church do meet, by Order, the last Saturday in this month, at Brother Thomas Evans, to know whether the Acusation, said against him by Sister Ann Dedrage, be Matter of Fact, or not." "Church met at the *Big Spring* November 9, 1776, and John Ray was sentenced to be excommunicated & likewise Jno. Conner; agreed to be executed the Day following. . . . Agreed that Abraham Elger be received." "December 7, 1776, The sd. Elger gave in his Letter and was received into full Communion of the Church & Bro. Lincoln was delegated to go & acquaint Brother Hart of the Times of our Stated Meetings." (Page 23.)

Brother Hart, being Chairman of the County Committee, had doubtless been too occupied with Revolutionary matters to attend regular services. Bro. Lincoln was John Lincoln, the Clerk of the church. The above is the first mention of a meeting being held at the Big Spring—now Lacey Spring.

In 1777 three further meetings were held; January 11th, "the Church met and agreed to set for experiences, and offered but none was received," February 9th, "the Church met, and agreed . . . 3rdly That Brother Alderson be delegated to the Separate Church, for a Correspondence with them." Wednesday the 13th of March, "Called a Meeting, upon the Account of the Rev. Jno. Alderson jr. who gave us Grounds to hope that the Lord has restored him by sound Repentance, and we received him into his Place, in the Church." (Page 23.)

This was the last meeting recorded of the old church during the Revolution. For ten long years there was a pause. Alderson later in 1777 removed to what is now

Greenbrier County, where he became the pastor of another Baptist congregation. He died March 5, 1821, eighty-three years old to the day. He lies buried in the burial ground of the Greenbrier church. His wife was Mary Carroll, whom he married in his twenty-first year. She died in 1805. (See,Taylor's *Lives of Virginia Baptist Ministers,* 1837, p. 147.)

* * * * * *

The year 1777 marked the turning point of the war. October 17th, saw the surrender of Gen. Burgoyne, and his army (6,000 troops), to Gen. Gates, at Saratoga, New York. Earlier this year—in April—Lafayette had arrived in America, and tendered his services to Congress. Encouraged by the surrender of Burgoyne, and still smarting under her defeats of the Seven Years War, France now showed her readiness to formally join the American cause. Benjamin Franklin and Arthur Lee were dispatched to Paris as Commissioners. The battle of Saratoga is ranked as one of "The Fifteen Decisive Battles of the World." *(Creasy,* Chapter 13.) Most of the Hessians captured at this great event were later sent as prisoners to Virginia. Many of these were quartered at Charlottesville, and in the Valley, at Staunton and Winchester.

The terrible winter of 1777-8 was passed by Washington and his troops in camp at Valley Forge. On February 6, 1778, in a treaty of friendship, France became the first country to recognize the "United States of America" a nation among the powers of the world. The same month a fleet under D'Estang was sent over to the West Indies, and soon money, powder and arms were reaching America from this friendly ally. Late in February also, Baron von Steuben, a Prussian officer in the army of Frederick the Great, arrived at Valley Forge, and undertook the task of whipping the wretched troops into shape for further victories. So menacing did the danger to England appear that Lord North declared he was ready to grant the Colonies almost everything they wanted except independence. The Massachusetts charter was restored, and the tax repealed on tea. Commissioners were appointed to treat for peace, with the promise of amnesty to all, and the suspension of all acts relating to America passed since 1763. The Commissioners even went further, and promised that no more troops would be sent to America and that the Colonies should have representation in Parliament. (Andrew's *History of England,* 1903, p. 465.) The offer came too late; the war had now become a part of the great struggle between England and France, and America stood by her ally. Congress determined to hold no conference with the envoys, unless the British forces be completely withdrawn, or the independence of the United States be distinctly acknowledged.

V.

Rockingham County was established by an Act passed at the second session of the General Assembly of Virginia, as held under the first State Constitution. This session began Monday, October 20, 1777. The act was entitled "An act for forming several new counties and reforming the boundaries of two others."

The formation of Rockingham, and the erection of Harrisonburg as the county-seat, were to a degree wartime considerations. Owing to the exigency of the day, the large areas of Augusta and Botetourt were proving to be too unwieldly for the best administration by the local authorities. As given in the preamble to the above act—"WHEREAS it is represented to this present session of assembly, by the inhabitants of Augusta and Botetourt counties, that they labour under many inconveniences by reason of the great extent of the said counties and parishes: Be it therefore enacted by the

General Assembly, That from and after the first day of March next the said county and parish of Augusta shall be divided," etc. (*Hening*, Vol. 9, Chapter XVIII, p. 420.)

The new counties formed were Rockingham, Rockbridge, and Greenbrier. Rockingham was taken wholly from Augusta, and Rockbridge from both Augusta and Botetourt. Botetourt had been created in 1769, and was the first county carved from Augusta.

In the act referred to, the territory of Rockingham and its line with Augusta are described as follows—"And that the residue of the county and parish of Augusta be divided by a line to begin at the South Mountain, and running thence to Benjamin Yardley's plantation so as to strike the north river below Benjamin Byrd's house, thence up the said river to the mouth of Naked Creek, thence leaving the river a direct course so as to cross the said river at the mouth of Cunningham's branch, in the upper end of Silas Hart's land, to the foot of North Mountain, thence fifty-five degrees west to the Allegheney mountain, and with the same to the line of Hampshire; and all that part which lies north eastward of the said line shall be one distinct (county and) parish called and known by the name of Rockingham."

The county is said to have been named in honor of Charles Watson Wentworth, (1730-1782), the Marquis of Rockingham, and Prime Minister of England, 1765-6. It was during Rockingham's ministry that the Stamp Act was repealed, and he would have probably gone further had not the king and his friends succeeded in driving him from office. He resigned in February, 1766, and was succeeded by Pitt, the earl of Chatham.

The County of Rockingham was organized in 1778—April 27th this year, the first court met. As ordered in the establishing Act the "first court" was "held at the house of Daniel Smith." Col. Smith resided at Smithland, on "The Long Grey Trail," about two miles north of Thomas Harrison's. His wife, it will be recalled, was a daughter of Daniel Harrison, Thomas' brother. (Chapter XIII.)

The justices commissioned were: Silas Hart, Daniel Smith, Abraham Smith, brother of Daniel, John Grattan, Josiah Davison, grandson of John Harrison, Sr. (Chapter XI), John Skidmore, George Boswell, Thomas Hewitt, John Thomas, William Nalle, Robert Davis, James Dyer, (see pages 140 and 222), Henry Ewing, son of William, (page 135), William McDowell, Anthony Ryder (Rader), John Fitzwater, and Isaac Hinkle (Hinckle, Henkel).

Of these, all but Skidmore, Nalle, and Davis, qualified, or took the oath, at the time of organization. Silas Hart, for the purpose of organization, having been commissioned Sheriff, qualified as such with Gabriel Jones and Robert Cravens, as his sureties. Thomas Lewis qualified as County Surveyor. Organization being completed, on the second day Hart and Daniel Smith, the senior justices, "in consideration of their having enjoyed the office lately in Augusta," relinquished their claim to the "Office of Sheriff," and requested the Court to recommend another, whereupon Josiah Davison, John Skidmore and George Boswell were named to the Governor as suitable persons. (See Rockingham Court Order Book No. 1, Part 1, pp. 1, 2, and 3.) Davison was chosen; his commission signed by Patrick Henry, May 7, 1778, was sixty days in arriving. (The original commission, yet in existence, is now treasured among Josiah's descendants of Bloomington, Indiana.)—(See MSS sketch, *The Life of Josiah Davison II*, by Schuyler C. Davison, Indiana University.)

Having no suitable public building in which the court could meet, the selection of a county seat and the erection of a court house were among the first considerations of the new county. As revealed by the old first Order, or Minute Book, of the court (which happened to be saved from complete destruction at the hands of the "Yankees" in the War-between-the-States), now on file among the archives at the State Library, at Richmond:

> 28th April 1778,—"The court having taken into Consideration the properest place for holding Courts untill the public Buildings are erected have unanimously resolved to hold Court at the house of Daniel Smith Gent in the meantime until the public buildings are completed & the Sheriff ordered to give Notice thereof to the Inhabitants of the County.
>
> Ordered that Daniel Smith & Josiah Davison Gents be empowered to contract with some person for building a secure Log Jayl or prison 12 feet square, laid with logs above and below . . . one window and a door made of iron bars . . . to be fixed on the most convenient spot of the Sd. Daniel Smith's plantation" . . . etc. (Page 4.)
>
> 25th May, 1779,—"On a majority of the Justices being present & conformable to a resolution of the Court in March last for fixing a place for the Court house the several members having proposed three different places a Majority were for fixing it on the plantation of Thomas Harrison near the head of the Spring." (Page 38.)

By this time several of Thomas' nephews were members of the court, the justices present being—Daniel Smith, William McDowell, Reuben Harrison (son of John, Sr.), Isaac Hankle (Henkel), George Boswell, John Davis, William Herring, (son of Alexander), Abraham Smith, Anthony Reader (Rader), John Fitzwater, Michael Coyer (Coger?), James Dyer, John Thomas, and Benjamin Harrison, (son of Daniel.)

Under the same date the old Order Book continues—

> "John Davis, William McDowell, John Fitzwater & Benjamin Harrison Gents are appointed Commissioners to let out the building of a Court house of Stone 36 feet Long by 26 in Breadth one Story of 12 feet in height with a partition at one End twelve feet wide to be divided into two Jury rooms with two angle fire places in each of the Jury rooms as also a prison built with Square Logs 12 inches thick in inside, 18 feet Square in the Clear & walled with stone 2 feet thick in the lower Story & the wall 18 inches thick in the upper Story." (Page 39.)
>
> 28th June, 1779,—"The Commissioners appointed to let the building of the Court house and Jayl are empowered to choose a spot not less than two acres for the public Buildings & to take Deeds for the same in the Name of the Justices & their successors for the use of the County from Thomas Harrison the proprietor together with the Liberty of Stone and Timber from the Sd. Harrisons plantation for the said buildings." Signed, Daniel Smith. (Page 40.)
>
> 23rd August, 1779: "Thomas Harrison acknowledged his Deed of Barg. & Sale to Silas Hart &c. Gent Justice on behalf of the County (ordered) to be recorded." (Page 44.)
>
> 20th November, 1779: "The Court taking into Consideration the dangerously malignant Fever that for some Months past has raged in the Family of Daniel Smith Gent. and the Apprehensions of the people that there is Danger of the Disorder being contagious to remove any Obstruction to the Administration of Justice & to quiet the Minds of the Suitors & others

who may have Business at Court are of the Opinion that the Court should be adjourned to the plantation of Thomas Harrison & it is hereby adjourned accordingly." Signed, Daniel Smith. (Page 49.)

23rd November, 1779: "Ordered that Benjamin Harrison, William Harren (Herring) & John Davis Gents or any two (of them) let out the Building of a Court ho (house) of square Logs Wh hewed (?) Corners Thirty feet Long by 20 feet wide from out to out with a partition twelve feet in the Clear across the house divided into two rooms one twelve feet wide & the other 8 feet wide the room 12 feet wide to have a neat stone Chimney inside at the Gable End of it the whole to be floored with Earth as far as the Lawyers ward (?) & then to be raised, with plank floor to the Justices Bench which is to be raised three feet above the floor & the Breast of the Bench to be studed with a rail at the Top, the pitch of the house to be 10 feet clear Cieling & Lofted with Inch plank with two windows on each side of the ho (house) facing the Clks. Table & one on Each of the Jury rooms . . . windows 18 L . . . (lights ?) each Glass 8x10 Inches with a Door on . . . just Clear of the Jury rooms." (Page 51.)

According to the tablet in today's Court House, the land for the public buildings was donated by Thomas Harrison to the county, August 5, 1779. By the following May the first court house was erected (as above, with some minor modifications), both events occurring prior to the establishment of Harrisonburg, in the latter month. While the building had been erected, it appears unlikely that it was ready for occupancy before November, 1780. As late as the 28th of this month, the sheriff was ordered to pay Thomas Harrison, £100 "for holding 3 courts in his house." (See, Wayland's *History of Rockingham*, p. 83.)

The old Order Book shows that three different locations had been proposed for the home of the court. Daniel Smith's plantation was probably one, and, as given by tradition, present Keezeltown was another. It is said that there was much rivalry between Thomas Harrison and Mr. Keezell regarding the selection of their respective lands for the county seat, and that the two raced each other to Williamsburg by different routes to obtain the support of Rockingham's members of the Assembly concerning their desires. Harrison is credited with having arrived first. Silas Hart and John Smith (son of Abraham), were at the time the county's first delegates.

A long ride across Virginia during the days of the Revolution would seem to have been attended not without difficulty and danger, and Thomas, at least, was getting along in years. By 1779 the main action of the conflict had, however, shifted to Georgia and South Carolina—in December, 1778, Savannah fell to the British, and from February to May, following, Charleston was seriously threatened.

Whatever the conflict of opinions, the selection made was a logical one. Besides being centrally located with regard to Rockingham's territory, the place chosen was in other respects a splendid site for town or camp. Already one building, a chapel, had been erected here by former county authorities. The site was well watered, high, and naturally drained, and by this time several roads from the country roundabout led to the point. One of these was the main highway of the Valley, an important link in any plan of the region's defence, and a weighty consideration, especially at this time. Moreover, it was the custom to assemble the militia at the county seat on its being called out. "Thomas Harrison's" was ideally situated for this. Even before the new county was formed it appears likely that the local troops had been furnished a plot of ground by

Thomas for their musters, and for rendezvous preparatory to joining their comrades at Staunton, or elsewhere. Harrison's residence, as noted in the Virginia Historical Society's article, was "at interesting times" the headquarters of militia officers. Many of the founder's close kinsmen were such officers during the war now in porgress, and manifestly the times referred to were mainly of this period.

With the site for the new court house fixed upon, no time was lost by Thomas in donating fifty surrounding acres of his land, and laying it off into lots, and streets, for the use of a town. May, 1780, the Assembly at Williamsburg gave its approval to his patriotic labours, by establishing the site so laid off as the town of Harrisonburg. The act of establishment named no trustees—a significant omission. At the time the founder's early residence, and probably one or two others, and whatever other buildings he may have theretofore erected, together with the chapel, and the new court house, were evidently the only structures within the bounds of the town, and Thomas and his family (with possibly one exception) the entire population. The Assembly was certainly optimistic, but no more so than in the case of Lexington, the new county-seat of Rockingham's twin-sister. Lexington was legalized and named even before it had a single habitation.

The only possible exception as to there being any other resident of Harrisonburg at the time, outside of Thomas, and his family, may have been Godfrey Haga. On the 28 of June, 1779, Thomas and Sarah, his wife, acknowledged a "Deed of Bar. & Sale" to Haga, which was ordered to be recorded. On the same date Thomas and Sarah also acknowledged another conveyance to John Warren, his son-in-law, but in neither case is mention made in the Order Book as to the location or extent of either tract. (See, Order Book, as above, pp. 40 and 43.) On May 1, 1748, as the assignee of Martin Grider and Andrew Greer, Haga(or Hagey) patented 400 acres of land on Smiths Creek. (*Chalkley*, Vol. II, p. 245.)

The first building of record erected in Harrisonburg, after its establishment, appears to have been the county jail—"28th November, 1780; Silas Hart, John Davis, Henry Ewing & William Herring Gent. Commissioners appointed to let the building of the County Jayl reported that they had let out the building of the same to Cornilius Cain for Eleven Thousand nine hundred Seventy three pounds." (Rockingham Court Order Book I, at Richmond, p. 81.)

Henry Ewing

* * * * * *

The spring of 1780 followed the coldest winter of the century. This winter was passed by Washington and his army in camp at Morristown, New Jersey, and the suffering of the troops, if possible, was even worse than at Valley Forge two years before. The country was, by now, fast becoming more, and more, bare of supplies. Bands of British and Tories continued to ravage the coasts; in Virginia entering the James and Potomac. On the 12th of May, Charleston, South Carolina, fell to the enemy, and soon the entire state was overrun by plunderers. For repelling invasion there, and in the North Carolina, the whole of Virginia's militia, if necessary, as early provided for by the Assembly, was subject to duty. Following the fall of Charleston, Gen. Gates was placed in command of the south. Gates took charge with much boasting about "Burgoyning Cornwallis," the British commander. He however, in August, was badly defeated at Camden. Hopes were revived at King's Mountain by the victory of October 7th, but by this time his army had dwindled to about 2,000 men, and he was soon replaced by Gen. Greene. During the year the Capital of Virginia was removed from Williamsburg to Richmond. Thomas Jefferson at this interval was the Governor of the Commonwealth, having succeeded Patrick Henry, in 1779.

Heretofore, soldiers from the Shenandoah Valley had been in various engagements, all the way from the storming of Stony Point, in New York, to the battle of King's Mountain, in North Carolina. But with the arrival of 1781, they were to find plenty of action on the soil of their own State. From this time until the surrender of Cornwallis, the militia of the Valley, as well as of the remainder of Virginia, had no rest.

With January came Arnold, the former hero of Saratoga, but now a traitor to his country, to the mouth of the James. Arnold aimed straight for Governor Jefferson, and the General Assembly, and on January 4th, with 900 men, landed at Westover. The next day he took possession of Richmond. Here he found his victory an empty one, as the Governor and inhabitants had fled. After spending two days in pillaging, he leisurely returned to his boats, and embarked down the James. From the river, with his fleet as a base, he continued for a time, with little opposition, his plundering expedition in lower Virginia. March 26th, Gen Phillips, his superior in command, arrived at Portmouth, and on April 24th, after some resistance, entered Petersburg. Great exertions in the meantime were being made by the Governor, and by Baron Steuben, then in command of Virginia's militia, to prepare the State for a posture of defence. Nor were preparations begun any too soon; all the while portentious events had been happening further south, rapidly shifting the main theatre of war towards the Old Dominion.

In the first scene, of the final great act of the war's drama, a Valley soldier played a leading part. Although Arnold had early aspired to the role, the same was reserved for a Saratoga hero of a different stamp. Among the cast supporting him was a militia company, or more, also from the region of the Shenandoah.

Gen. Daniel Morgan, in "the most extraordinary victory of the war," the battle of Cowpens, South Carolina, January 17, 1781, signally defeated a British force, under Gen. Banastre Tarleton. Following the battle, Morgan, with his more than 500 prisoners, moved to join Gen. Greene and the main army. Cornwallis, as soon as he heard of the fight, set out in hot pursuit, but the juncture was made. Greene, being hard pressed for men and supplies, routed his prisoners to Virginia, and retired in the same direction. A race was now started northward with Cornwallis, who was close in his rear. The British commander, however, was badly delayed by rain at both the Catawba and Yadkin. At the fords of the Dan a similar fate awaited him; and by this he was brought to a halt. The prisoners were conducted immediately in charge of Virginia troops—many of whom were from the Valley—and from the Dan were finally removed to the Shenandoah County. After being reenforced by Virginia and North Carolina militia, Gen. Greene turned on his pursuer, and gave battle at Guilford Court House, near present Greensboro, March 15th. Here, although defeated, he so weakened and baffled Cornwallis that the latter abandoned the Carolinas to join Gen. Phillips in Virginia.

Valley soldiers by this time were more than in demand—they were being used on all sides. On Arnold's invasion, considerable reenforcements of the militia from this region, including many companies from Augusta, and Rockingham, were hastily dispatched to Fredericksburg, and lower Virginia, to Gen. Peter Muhlenberg, the former pastor of the Woodstock church—now one of Washington's Brigadiers. A little later a company or more were sent to meet Morgan's prisoners coming from the south, and near the end of February, there went forward seven or more companies to join Gen. Greene. These last saw service at Guilford Court House—in one little Augusta community alone, it is said, eight or ten brave women were made widows as a result of this fight. With these calls supplied, exposure to Indian depredations on the frontier increased to a point of serious need for further protection at home. By the end of March the supply of Valley recruits for the Continental Army was well nigh exhausted, and authority was being sought of Governor Jefferson to accept men under Steuben's standard of five feet, four inches, in height. Gen. Lafayette about this time was placed in charge of Virginia's defence, and doubtless viewed the question of height more leniently—certainly even more troops were furnished.

Two armies, although, as yet, Gen. Phillips was unaware of either, were now converging on the vicinity of Richmond. April 29th, Gen. Lafayette entered the Capital at the head of a small body of regulars, and soon his army numbered 3,000 men, Continentals and militia. Two days following Lafayette's arrival, Phillips with Arnold, appeared at Manchester, but finding Richmond defended they returned to their boats at Bermuda Hundred, and sailed for the Bay. On their way a dispatch arrived from Cornwallis, ordering Phillips to join him at Petersburg. Phillips then turned back, reentering the town May 9th. The next day the Assembly, at Richmond, adjourned to meet in Charlottesville on May 24th. While awaiting Cornwallis' arrival Phillips died, and Arnold again assumed command, Having sent Tarleton ahead of him to prepare the way, on May 20th, Gen. Cornwallis effected the juncture of his armies at Petersburg, as proposed. With a price on his head in Virginia, Arnold hastily obtained a transfer to New York.

Virginia all the while was girding herself for a supreme effort. From the Valley country another "draft of the militia" went forward in May. Flushed with the superiority of his numbers, and being informed that Richmond was held by Lafayette, Cornwallis proceeded to move to the Capital, confident "the boy cannot escape me." Forewarned, Lafayette wisely evacuated the town, retiring towards Fredericksburg, and from there to Culpeper County, where he awaited reenforcements.

Finding that stores of supplies had been collected at the juncture of the Rivanna and James, and that the Assembly was meeting at Charlottesville, Cornwallis sent two of his cavalry officers, Col. Simcoe, and the dashing Tarleton, afterwards, a baronet, and a member of Parliament, to destroy the stores and to capture the Governor and the Assembly. To Tarleton was intrusted the latter task, after which he was to join Simcoe.

Tarleton reached Charlottesville on June 4th, only to find his quarry dispersed. On his way he stopped in Louisa to pick up a few scattered members of the Assembly found there, and the inhabitants suspecting the main object of his raid had hastily sent warning ahead. On receiving the warning, only a few short hours before Tarleton's arrival, the Assembly had hastily adjourned to meet in Staunton, on June 7th. Mr. Jefferson being at home at the time, his term as Governor having expired on June 1st, was warned at Monticello. One of Tarleton's officers is said to have ridden his charger up the stone steps onto the north portico of this noted residence, and to this day his horses hoof-prints in the stone flagging are pointed out to visitors. On finding the house deserted he, however, allowed nothing to be disturbed.

Simcoe, on his part, was more successful, but warning of his approach had also preceded him. Prior to his arrival the stores had been removed to the farther side of the river, where they were being guarded by Baron Steuben. Through a ruse of building camp fires over a wide territory at night, Semcoe led the Baron to believe that he was greatly outnumbered. Having with him only a few companies of raw militia, Steuben retired with the lighter baggage, leaving the remainder behind. This Simcoe destroyed and then moved to join Cornwallis the next day.

As proposed, the Assembly convened in the old parish church at Staunton, on June 7th, but three days later it was stampeded again by a new report of Tarleton. This time adjournment was moved to meet in Warm Springs, yet further west, and such seemed to be the need for hurry that Patrick Henry, according to tradition, left town in only one boot. Tarleton on this occasion was represented as pursuing across the Blue Ridge. From Lexington to Harrisonburg an alarm was quickly spread, and men were rushed to Rockfish Gap, fast lining it with soldiers. Col. Samuel McDowell at this time is said to have had some 800 or 1,000 men with him at present Waynesboro. The day preceding the alarm report was current in Staunton that the enemy was within twelve miles of Charlottesville. A detatchment of British troops had attempted a raid on Scottsville, to the east of Monticello, where further military stores had been accumulated. The attempt failed; on the approach of the raiders they were sharply turned back by the quick arm of Lafayette.

Virginia as last was able to parry the thrusts of Cornwallis, and to hold him at bay. Help was also coming from the North. The day of the Assembly's hasty adjournment at Staunton, Gen. Lafayette was joined in Culpeper County by Gen Anthony Wayne, with 800 men of the Pennsylvania Line. On June 16th, having received orders from New York, Cornwallis turned towards the coast, and was closely followed by Lafayette. The Legislature in the meantime reassembled at Staunton, and on June 12th elected Gen. Thomas Nelson, Governor of the State. In the short interval following Jefferson's term, Col. William Fleming had been acting Governor. Gen. Nelson was sworn into his office on June 19th, at Staunton, and five days later the Assembly adjourned, at their leisure, to meet in Richmond, in October.

Gen. Cornwallis was fated to find his stay in Virginia prolonged to the point of serious embarrassment to his lordship. He was being drawn to the coast by Washington's threat of attacking Sir Henry Clinton, the Commander-in-Chief of all the British forces in America, at New York. Sir Henry, becoming apprehensive as to his ability to defend himself, had directed his commander in the South to proceed at once to the coast, and to send him all the troops he could spare. Cornwallis, on his part, perceived that he would be forced to move cautiously. On crossing the James, at Jamestown Island, July 6th, he found Lafayette awaiting his passing, and watching every step he made. On his way eastward he received further dispatches from Sir Henry, advising that the situation in New York appeared to be somewhat relieved, and ordering that he now retain all his forces in Virgina, but to occupy Yorktown as a base, from which to conduct his campaign, while awaiting further developments in the North.

Further developments though, much to the surprise of Sir Henry, were not all scheduled for New York. As Cornwallis neared the Bay the tighter, and tighter, Lafayette's semi-circle of steel closed in about him. Still, more American soldiers were needed. Virginia, herself, was fast rushing forward every available man. Near the end of July another call went forth in the Valley country for militia. On August 22nd, after much sharp skirmishing while on his way, Cornwallis occupied Yorktown. No time was lost by Lafayette in informing his chief of the situation. Washington, in the meantime, had been maturing plans with Count De Grasse, the commander of the French fleet, then in West Indian waters, regarding a combined campaign, and on August 14th received word from the latter, advising of his leaving for the Chesapeake Bay. (With the fleet were some 3,000 troops.) In view of these advices Washington, with his French and American army, promptly turned towards Virginia.

In vain Cornwallis called on Sir Henry Clinton for help, but until the last moment before leaving Washington kept Sir Henry under the impression that he was about to attack New York. A short time before the close of September, the allied army arrived in the James, off Williamsburg, and immediately debarked for Yorktown. For about a month, with all help cut off by the French fleet, Cornwallis held out, striving all the while to escape. At length he was forced to yield, and after two days of preliminaries, on October 19th, 1781, at 12 o'clock, he agreed to surrender. Two hours later his 8,000 British troops marched out to lay down their arms. Independence at last was won, although peace was not formally declared until 1783.

Then up rose Joe, all at the word;
And took his master's arm,
And to his bed he softly led
The lord of Green-way farm.

There oft he call'd on Britain's name,
"And oft he wept full sore."—
And sigh'd—thy will, O Lord, be done—
"And word spake never more."

Such, according to Parson Weems, in his famous *Life of Washington,* was the way the great commander's early patron, Lord Fairfax, received the news at Greenway Court, in Old Frederick—he died December 9th, following.

* * * * * *

Word of Cornwallis' surrender was fast borne throughout the country, seemingly on the wings of the wind, and a universal welcome awaited the homecoming of America's heroes. Spontaneous celebrations were everywhere organized, and in these Rockingham County had just cause to join. Says Waddell—"on the return of the troops from Yorktown the victory was celebrated by the militia of Rockingham at a grand review in 1781." The occasion was a gala day for the new county seat, and its aged founder was doubtless particularly proud to extend his well known hospitality. Many of Rockingham's soldiers had served in the Yorktown campaign, and Harrisonburg, and its environs, had been well represented. Most unfortunately the celebration was marred by the untimely death of one of these, Col. Daniel Smith, of Smithland. Continues Waddell—"Col. Smith's horse taking fright at the firing sprang aside, and spraining his rider's back caused his death in a few days." (Page 150.) His will was proven November 28, 1781.

Numerous accounts for services rendered, supplies furnished, etc., for the Yorktown campaign, by various inhabitants of Rockingham, were allowed by the court in 1782.

Among the accounts so allowed were three under the name of "Thomas Harrison," recorded April 24th, May 29th, and May 30th, respectively. One of these was obviously the founder's. (See, *Wayland,* pp. 100, and 101.)

As amply attested by many records, the site now Harrisonburg prior to the Act of 1780 officially naming the town, was down to this time called "Thomas Harrison's." Later, in the early days of the village, Harrisonburg was commonly referred to as "Rocktown" by the local residents. Limestone rock was abundantly in evidence, in and near the place. The renowned Bishop Asbury, the first Methodist Bishop in orders in America, and the great organizer of the Church here, in the diary of his travels, mentions his visits to "Rocktown," on two occasions, and to "Harrisonburg" on the third:

"Saturday June 1, 1793. We came to Staunton, a very unpleasant place to me . . . . took lodging at the tavern. Thence we proceeded on to *Rocktown,* a beautiful place; . . . . sweet sleep was quite welcome. My congregation was small the people not having notice of my coming. Satan has been sowing discord here, and has hindered the work of God . . . . Rose and took the rain the next morning as usual."

Four years later—"Thursday 6th April 1797. My fever never left me, as I thought from Monday until Friday night—I am kept cheerful, but very weak, ... from 9th. April to 27th. May I have kept no journal. I have traveled about 600 miles with an inflammatory fever, and fixed pain in my breast. I cannot help expressing the distinguished kindness of some families where I have been forced by weakness to stop. Capt. Shannon, on Walker's Creek—Col Moffet and brother Young in Augusta; neither can I forget Mr. Lee and Moore—The Harrisons, at *Rocktown,* and brother and sister M'Williams."

Finally—"Sabbath 5th Nov. 1815. I declined preaching, being exceedingly weak. Tuesday we stopped with Wesley Harrison, son of Thomas Harrison, in *Harrisonburg.* The father was the first man under whose roof I lodged on my first visit to that town; his pious wife, and simple-hearted pious Robert Harrison, are I trust both in glory. Monday 6th we came to Captain Hills, ... very kind and attentive. Tuesday came to Thomas Harrison's son of Thomas." *(Journal of Rev. Francis Asbury,* Bishop of the M. E. Church from Aug. 7th, 1771 to Dec. 7th, 1815, pub. by N. Bangs and T. Mason, 1821; Vols, II, pp. 166, and 288; III, p. 294.)

Thomas Harrison, the first above, was the son of Thomas the founder, and a brother of Robert. By the time of the Bishop's first visit the founder had died, but Robert was yet living.

With the war over, the village of Harrisonburg began rapidly to assume the shape of a town. The month following Cornwallis' surrender, Thomas, the founder and proprietor, and Sarah, sold lots Nos. 2, and 3, in the "North Square," to Tobias Rheams of Rockingham—"Deed, 28th November, 1781; Thomas and Sarah Harrison of Rockingham to Tobias Rheams of same place, 2 lots in Harrisonburg numbered 2 and 3 of the North Square, part of 1290 acres patented to Thomas by inclusive patent, 1st March, 1773; on each lot to be built one good dwelling house 20 feet long and 17 feet wide, with a stone or brick chimney. Recorded in Rockingham, 26th November, 1781." Lot 2, then called "lot 2 of Northwest Square," was later—16th September, 1786, deeded by David Harrow and Mary of Rockingham, to Peter Conrad—Recorded in Rockingham, September, 1794. (See Judgements, Circuit Court Causes Ended: OS. 241, NS. 85, at Staunton, "Henry Sprinkle vs. Conrad's heirs;" *Chalkley* Vol. II, p. 187.)

Lot No. 1, of Harrisonburg, as related in the *Virginia Magazine of History and Biography,* (Vol. 10, page 43) was conveyed by deed to Thomas Lounsdon, on November 2, 1783, in consideration that Lounsdon would before March 1st, 1784, erect a dwelling house on it 20 x 16 feet with stone or brick chimney.

Harrison was evidently determined that all of his lots would be improved by the erection of dwellings with good chimneys.

On November 25th, 1783, lot No. 2, (square not given, part of 1290 acres, etc.) was deeded by Thomas Harrison to Elizabeth Mc. Neal, widow, of Rockingham. Elizabeth a little later married James Martin, who soon thereafter became deranged and disappeared. She remained in Harrisonburg until 1798, when she made her will (dated 7th of March, and recorded in July following) devising the land unto one James Brown, whom as a boy she had taken to raise. In her will the lot is described as on a "corner opposite Mr. Thom. Scott's lot, fronting on Irish Street and Elizabeth Street." On May 13th, 1817, James Brown and Nancy, of Licking County, Ohio, deeded this lot to Wm. Mahon, of Harrisonburg—"Gordon McWilliams desposes, he came to Harrisonburg in May 1797, when he met James Martin, husband of Elizabeth

Mc Neal," etc. (See, Mc. Mahon vs. Brown—O.S. 307, N. S., 109, Bill, 28th January., 1829, at Staunton; *Chalkley* Vol. II,p. 227.)

"In 1785," continues the *Virginia Magazine of History and Biography,* as above, "we find twenty persons owning lots in Harrisonburg, namely, John Apler, Henry Burges, Conrad Bradley, James Curry, Peter Conrad, William Cravens, trustee for Frederick Spangler, John Ewing, Sr., Thomas Henry, Dennis Leanchan (Lanachan, Lanahan), James Mitchell, Charles McClain, Brewer Reeves, Richard Rankin, Thomas Scott, J. Shipman (Jonathan Shipman), Anthony Sourbeer, Andrew Shanklin, Thomas Soolvain (Sullivan), Hugh Tiffney, and John Turner."

Of these—William Cravens was a nephew of Thomas Harrison, the founder. John Ewing was a brother of Henry, the Justice before mentioned. His wife was a grand-niece of Harrison. Dennis Lanahan was the 3rd husband of Margaret, nee Hiatt, who married first, William Dyer, and second, John Cravens, son of Robert, Sr. Of the remainder, Conrad, Shanklin, and Sullivan, were doubtless old acquaintences of Thomas—these names, like those of Cravens and Harrison, being found in Sussex on the Delaware prior to Valley of Virginia times.

Dennis Lanahan was an Irishman. He was a brickmaker, stonemason, and, what would be called today, a general contractor. He built many of the first houses of the town, and in his later life kept one of the first taverns therein.

No trustees of Harrisonburg appear to have been named until the additional twenty-three and one-half acres of 1797 were donated to the town, some years after the founder's death, by his sons Robert and Reuben Harrison. Clause 2, of the Act, authorizing this (see page 214) reads—

"2. And be it further enacted, That Thomas Scott, Joseph Koontz, Asher Waterman, Frederick Spangler, and Samuel M'Williams, gentlemen, shall be and they are hereby constituted trustees of the said town; and that they, or a majority of them shall have power to remove nuisances out of the streets, alleys and public grounds of the said town, at the expense of those who occasion them, when they shall refuse to remove them; to open the streets and alleys and keep the same in repair, and to determine all disputes concerning the bounds of the lots, which determination shall be final unless controverted at law within two years; they shall also have power to levy a tax, not exceeding one hundred dollars on the tithables and property within said town, annually, for the purpose of this act, and the surplus in such manner as the said trustees, or majority of them, shall judge most benefical for the inhabitants of the said town; to appoint a collector from time to time, who shall be subject to the same rules and regulations, and accountable for the said taxes in like manner as the collectors of the county levies are by law."

That the above were the first trustees appointed is further indicated by the remainder of the Act—

"4. In the case of death, removal, or other legal disability, of any one or more of the said trustees, such vacancy from time to time shall be supplied in the manner prescribed by the act passed the eleventh day of December seventeen hundred and seventy eight entitled, An act to empower the freeholders of the several towns not incorporated to supply the vacancies of the trustees and directors thereof.

5. This act shall commence and be in force from and after the passing thereof."

Samuel McWilliams, one of the trustees, was the Clerk of Rockingham County Court, from 1792 to 1817. His wife was the daughter of the founder's nephew, Col. Benjamin Harrison.

By this addition to the town, Thomas Harrison's sons, Robert and Reuben, became co-founders of Harrisonburg. In fact, owing to their father's death in the first year's of the town's existence, they were the virtual developers of the site into a town. Robert dying in 1797, Reuben succeeded as the sole proprietor. Page after page of the old (restored) deed books, at Harrisonburg, record the transactions of the brothers, and amply attest to their many activities in carrying on the work of their father had begun. (See later Chapters wherein many of the first settlers of the town are mentioned.)

Among the founder's sons, John, Thomas, Robert, and Reuben, lived and died in Harrisonburg. Following their father's death, Thomas and Reuben married, Thomas in 1790, and Reuben in 1791. Thomas' wife was Sally, nee Oliver. Reuben married Mary, the daughter of Solomon and Agnes Matthews. Solomon was a wealthy landowner of Rockingham, and probably a kinsman of Sampson Mathews, Rockingham's first member of the State Senate, 1780, and 1791.

Of the remainder of Thomas' sons, Jeremiah and Davis Harrison, about 1792, emigrated to Woodford County, Kentucky. Ezekial from 1796 to 1799, and from 1814 to 1815-16, was the Sheriff of Rockingham County. On August 5, 1815, he applied to the Smiths Creek Baptist Church, at New Market, for a letter of dismissal, for himself and his wife, "to which the church agreed," and soon thereafter removed to near Hopkinsville, Kentucky, and from there, about 1822, to Sangamon County, Illinois. (See, Original Minutes of the Smiths Creek Church, Book I, p. 11, and *History of the Early Settlers of Sangamon Co., Ill.*, by J. C. Power, p. 358.)

(17) Thomas Harrison, the Augusta County pioneer, Revolutionary patriot, and founder of Harrisonburg, Virginia, died, as related, in 1785.

> "At a Court held for Rockingham County on Monday, the 24th day of January, 1785: The last will and testament of Thomas Harrison, deceased, was produced in court and proven by the oath of Benjamin Smith, who also made oath that he saw Robert Smith, deceased, one of the other witnesses, affix his name as a witness to the said will, and the same is or(dered) to l(a)y for further proof"
>
> "At a Court held for Rockingham County on Monday, the 25th of April, 1785: The last will and testament of Thomas Harrison, deceased, was further proven by the oath of Mathew Reeves, late mar. . ed Smith, and O. to be recorded." (Minute Book, Rockingham County Court, 1778-1792, at State Library, Richmond, Va., p. 398.)

Sarah, the wife of Thomas, died in 1782. Both Thomas and his wife are thought to have been buried in the early churchyard on the brow of the hill overlooking the scene of his pioneer home, and of the town that he had founded. This old burial ground is located only a small distance west of the Public Square, and about a block beyond the present Southern Railway, and Baltimore and Ohio Passenger station. Many of the graves in this first cemetery are marked only by crude limestone markers on which there are no inscriptions. The land was set apart for a burial ground by Thomas, or his sons Robert and Reuben. The latter, and his wife, and his wife's mother, were buried here. In the early years of the town the first Methodist Church was erected in the churchyard of which the cemetery is a part. The site was probably that of the pioneer Episcopal chapel (see page 222). It was given to the Methodists by Robert and Reuben Harrison, in 1789.

> Deed: 26th October, 1789; Robert and Reuben Harrison to the Methodist Episcopal Church. Trustees, David Horner, Jeremiah Ragan, Richard Ragan, John Hicks, James Mitchell, John Harrison, Joseph Denny; One Acre of Land,

> Five Shillings, Lot No. 12, on South West Square of Harrisonburg . . . . "and shall permit Francis Asbury Bishop of the Methodist Episcopal Church and such other persons as he shall from time to time and at all times . . . . . . appoint and no other persons to have or enjoy the free use and benefit of the said premises . . . . . provided always that the said persons Preach no other Doctrine than is contained in Mr. John Wesley's Notes upon the New Testament and four volumes of sermons," etc. (Rockingham Co. Deed Book "O", burnt records, p. 391.)

The church building today on the site is used by another denomination, the Methodists having removed their place of worship to South Main Street, near Thomas' old home. Owing to the growth of the town the old burial ground has all but been abandoned, and many of the bodies have been removed to the new and much larger cemetery, Woodbine.

In recent years a tablet has been erected to Thomas, by the Daughters of the American Revolution. This is affixed to one of the stone pillars adorning the main entrance to the Public Square, and bears, besides the insignia, the following inscription—

Erected by
Massanutten Chapter
D. A. R.

To the Memory of
THOMAS HARRISON.
Patriot who on August 5, 1779,
Gave the Land for the
County Court House
And other Public Buildings,
in Harrisonburg,
Which was named after him.
1927

Thomas' children were briefly as follows—

(171) ABIGAIL—b. ———; d.———; m. August, 1761, Leonard Herring.

(172) JEREMIAH—b. 1740, c; d. ———; m. Mary ———, d. about 1779. Emigrated to Kentucky about 1792.

(173) DAVIS—b. 1743, c; d. ———; m. ———. Emigrated to Kentucky, about 1792, with brother Jeremiah.

(174) ROBERT—b. ———; d. unmarried, December, 1797.

(175) JOHN—b. ———; d. 1806; m. Elizabeth (Betsy) ———.

(176) THOMAS—b. ———; d. 1800; m. Dec. 22, 1790, Sarah (Sally) Oliver. She m. 2nd, Sept. 20, 1802, Richard Kyle.

(177) EZEKIEL—b. Oct. 3rd., 1751; d. 1834; m. 1775, Sarah Bryan. Emigrated to Kentucky 1815, and to Illinois, 1822.

(178) REUBEN—b.1754; d. Aug. 15, 1840; m. April 28, 1791, Mary Matthews, b. July 3, 1772, d. April 5, 1854, daughter of Solomon Matthews.

(179) SARAH—b. 1760, c; d. ———; m. John Warren, about 1779, son of Michael Warren (?).

See further record (Chapter XVII) for all but Robert above.

CHAPTER XIV

Capt. Robert Cravens, "Gentleman Justice," and His Family

ROBERT CRAVENS, (1696c-1762), on the first of November, 1729, witnessed a deed of conveyance, of this date, from "Zachariah Grifforth of Kent County, Delaware, yeoman, & Elizabeth his wife," to Samuel Stewart of Sussex County, Delaware, for 224 acres of land, value 59 Pounds. (Deed Book F-7, p. 253, at Georgetown.) On the 3rd of the following February (1729, old style), Samuel Stewart conveyed to Robert Cravens, "for Sixty Pounds Current Money of America," 224 acres of land in Sussex, on the northwest side of Cypress Branch, a tributary of the Broadkill—Broad Creek. (See page 55.) On this Robert and his wife Mary made their home.

(14) MARY HARRISON, (1696-1781), the wife of Robert Cravens, was born at Oyster Bay, Long Island, in the Province of New York, "ye 25th Day of May Annoq Domini 1696." (See pages 23 and 123.) She was the fourth child of Isaiah Harrison (1), the immigrant, and his first wife, Elizabeth Wright. Her childhood was spent at Oyster Bay and at Smithtown, Long Island. She and Robert were married about 1721, or a short time after her removal, with her father, to Maiden Plantation, Sussex on the Delaware.

Robert Cravens died testate in what is now Rockingham County, then Augusta, Virginia, in 1762. His will, as recorded at Staunton, in Will Book No. 3, page 122, reads as follows—

IN THE NAME OF GOD AMEN, October Ye Second in the year of our Lord one thousand Seven hundred and Sixty one viz 1761 and I Robert Cravens of the County of Augusta and Colony of Virginia being sick and weak in body but of perfect mind and memory blessed be God for it and calling to mind the mortality of my body and knowing that it is appointed for all men once to die, do make and ordain and appoint this as my last Will and Testament that is to Say

first and principally of all I give and Humbly Recommend my soul to God who gave it and my body to the earth to be buried in a Christain like and decent manner at the direction of my loving wife and son John Cravens whom I do make and appoint my whole and sole Executors in this my last will and Testament and as touching such worldly estate as it has pleased God to bless me in this life with I give, devise and dispose of the same in the following manner:

First, I desire all my lawful Debts to be paid which I have legally contracted.

Imprimis, I give and bequeath to Mary, my Dearly beloved Wife one young four year old dapple gray horse and side saddle her own bed and bed cloths and her great and little Wheel five cows and calves ten head of sheep five head of hogs Sixty pounds in cash and all the house hold goods three beds and furniture thereunto (The great iron pot only excepted) and and the negro wench called Knelly during her natural life and at my wifes decease I will the wench shall be sold and if Knelly has any children during my wife's lifetime I will my wife shall give and bequeath them to any of my children that their Mother please and half of my dwelling house and half of my plantation dureing her natural life and five acres of the Great Meadow.

Item. I give unto my son John Cravens one negro Boy named Tom and the smooth bore gun that he has now in posession to him and his heirs forever.

Item. I gave unto my son William Cravens the tract or parcel of land commonly known by the name of the Great Meadow containing 141 acres (five acres only excepted for his mother) to him and his heirs forever but in case he has no issue it shall become his Brethrens and their heirs forever and sixty pounds in money and forty pounds to be paid by his Brother John for the negro boy named Sip which I will to John but if John refuses to pay the forty pounds the negro Sip shall become Williams, and I allow a receipt for Thirty Seven pounds to be given on a bond that I have of Williams.

Item. I give unto My Daughter Mary the tract or percel of land she now lives on containing 124 acres to her and the heirs begotten of her body forever and one great Iron pot.

Item. I give unto my two Grand Children Zebulon and Robert Harrison that tract or percel of land containing 200 acres lying and being on the East side of Linvills Creek to them and their heirs forever and one negro child called Dina and her increase for them and their heirs forever but I will that my Daughter Margaret Harrison shall have the service of the girl Dina if she desires it during her natural life.

Item. I give unto my Daughter Agnes the tract or percel of land she now lives on to her and her heirs begotten of her own body forever.

Item. I give unto Magie my Daughter sixty pounds in money.

Item. I give unto my son Robert Cravens the half of my dwelling house and half of my plantation I now live on during his Mothers Natural life and at her decease the whole to him and his heirs forever but in case he should die without legitimate male issue the land to become his Brethrens and their heirs forever.

Item. I give unto my daughter Elizabeth Cravens one bay horse with a white foot four year old three cows and calves sixty pounds in money and one negro girl named Venus about six years old and in case she should decease without issue her part to become her sisters to be equally divided among them.

Item. I give unto my grandson Robert Cravens that tract or percel of land containing 160 acres of land commonly known by the name of Wait's Cabbin lying on the Creek below Joseph Cravens to him and his heirs forever but in case he should die without heirs legally begotten of his own body the sd. land shall become his fathers and his heirs forever.

And to his Brother John Cravens my grandson I give ten pounds in cash to help to school him and ten pounds to Mary Black my Grand daughter and the tract of land containing 470 acres of land I will to be sold where Samuel Mowry now lives on.

Item. and all my debts, lega*cis* and funeral charges being first paid I will and desire the remr. of my estate to be divided among my loving wife and nine children John, Agnes and Magee to have two shares for each others one share.

This I trust will be done and all truly fulfilled by my loving wife and son John Cravens whom I do appoint whole and sole Exors. of this my last will and Testament and I do hereby utterly disallow revoke and disannul all and every other former Testaments wills, legacies and Bequests and Executors by me in any ways before this time willed and bequeathed.

Ratifying and confirming this and no other to be my last will and testament in witness whereof I have hereunto set my hand and seal this day and year above written.

his
Robert R Cravens (Seal.)
mark

Signed sealed published pronounced
and declared by the said Robert Cravens
as his last will and testament in the
presence of us the subrs.
viz. Archd. Huston
Matthew Thompson
Daniel Love.

At a Court held for Augusta County May 18th, 1762.
This last will & testament of Robert Craven decd. was proved by the oaths of Archd Huston and Danl Love two of the witnesses and ordered to be recorded and on the motion of Mary and John Craven the Executors therein named who made oath according to law certificate is granted then for obtaining a probat thereof in due form they having with security entered into bond."

Test.

(Original will also on record.)

In his will Robert mentions "nine children," but names only eight. Joseph Cravens is referred to, as owning land near by. Joseph was the unnamed child—Deed, 22nd August, 1768; John Madison to son John, 141 acres called Great Meadow, upon a branch of Cook's Creek . . . . . "lying between the lands of John Cravens and his brother Joseph Cravens," land purchased by John Madison, Sr., 19th March, 1764, "of William Cravens brother of said John and Robert Cravens." (Deed Book XV, p. 148, at Staunton.)

A "Joseph Crauan" (Cravan, Craven), signed as witness, 30th June, 1709, at "Lews Town," to a deed of Edmund Rutter and wife Mary, to Richard Paynter, all of Sussex County, Delaware, for 322 acres of land "partly on Rehobeth Bay Called Marions Neck"— (See, Original deed, Sussex County Delaware Papers, Vol. I, p. 8, Historical Society of Pennsylvania, at Philadelphia; also Deed Book A, No. 1, p. 234 —acknowledgement, wherein the names of the witness do not appear—at Georgetown, Delaware.)

This, aside from the references to Robert, is apparently the only other mention of a Cravens on the Sussex records; neither is anything further gleaned from the index to the Colonial wills of the State, at Dover. That the witness was a sea-faring man is probable, and that in some way he was identified with Rutter or Paynter seems assured.

From the fact that not only Robert, but his sister Margaret also, married into the Harrison family of Sussex, indications point strongly to their parents as having been residents of the county, or vicinity, by 1721, and to the brother and sister as having come of age there.

Another early Cravens to locate in Augusta County, Virginia, was one Peter Cravens, who resided in the region of the "North Mountain," and is mentioned along with John Harrison, (Sr.), under date of May 24, 1744. (See page 126.) A reference to Peter also occurs under date of 24th November, 1753, on the Augusta records: ". . . . ordered that a Road be Cleared the nearest and best way from the End of William Curravans Road on his Plantation to William Bryans on Roan Oak and that the said Bryan be Overseer of the same with Peter Craven (and other) Tithables . . . . clear and keep the Sd. Road in repair." (Order Book No. 4, p. 76.)

Peter Craven from England genealogy

In an account manifestly somewhat uncertain as to the time of the migrations, it is stated that Peter Craven, with two brothers, came from England to Pennsylvania, and that "a short time before the Revolutionary War, the Peter Cravens family, together with five other families, removed to North Carolina and settled near Deep River." Peter had "six sons, the eldest of whom was Thomas." Thomas, the account continues, was born August 25, 1742, and died in 1817; but the place of his birth is given as "now Randolph County, North Carolina." (See, booklet, *Genalogy of the Craven and Barker Families,* by John W. and Oscar H. Cravens, 1913, printed by The World-Courier of Bloomington, Indiana.)

SOME EARLY CRAVEN FAMILIES

CRAVEN was a name of prominence and antiquity in England, and particularly well known in London, where one of the name had twice been the Lord Mayor of the City. An interesting epitaph of Sir William Craven, Kt., of Winwick, Northamptonshire, who died in 1707, aged 73 years, is preserved in Bridge's *History and Antiquities of Northamptonshire,* 1791, (page 602). This recites that the deceased was the "youngest son of Thomas Craven of Appletreewick near Skipton in Craven in County York and *Margaret* his wife. He was the grandson by his father's side of Anthony Craven. He was grandson by his mother's side of *Robert Craven.* He was great-grandson by his father's side of William Craven, and great-grandson by the mother's side of Henry Craven, which Henry Craven was a brother to Sir William Craven, Kt., twice Lord Mayor of the City of London . . . . ." etc.

The Lord Mayor of London died in 1618, possessed of a vast fortune. He had sons William (1608-1697), and John (d. 1648), both of whom were created barons, the title being conferred on William in 1624. John was the founder of Oxford and Cambridge Scholarships. In 1664, William was created an earl, and dying unmarried, the barony passed to his cousin William, from whose brother, John, the present title is descended. William, the first Earl of Craven, like Lord Culpeper, contributed large sums to the aid of Charles II while in exile,. and following the Restoration was in turn the recipient of many favors from the Crown, one of them being his appointment as one of the Lords Proprietors of the Carolinas, from which circumstance Old Craven County, South Carolina, (erected 1674 as one of the original four counties), and present Craven County, North Carolina, derived their names.

Among the early immigrants to America,, Hotten lists Richard Craven under "Patents granted Settlers in Virginia," 1626, and Thomas Craven, aged 17 years, as licensed to go beyond the seas to Virginia, 24th July, 1635, "imbargoed in the Assurance of London." *(Hotten,* pp. 272, 112.) James Craven of 1639, and Thomas of 1642, appear in Greer's lists as immigrants to Virginia, also, but the earliest of the name in the Colonies to leave known descendants seems to have been the widow Ann Craven, who settled under Fenwick, in Old Salem, New Jersey, about 1677.

On "the Tenth day of the Seventh Moth Commonly called September In the yeare by the English Act. One thousand Sixe hundred seventie and nyne." John Fenwick, the Proprietor of Salem Tenth, executed a deed, "for and in consideration of the sume on Nyne pounds good and Lawfull money of England, to . . . Ann Craven late of lyme house in the parish of Stepency in the Countie of Middl. (sex) Wthin the said Kingdome of England and now of the Towne of New Salem in the said colony (New Jersey) widow," for 300 acres of land, "to be called Cravens Choyce," on "Munmouth River heretofore called Allowayes Creek." (See, Salem Deeds, Liber B, p. 67, at Secretary of State's Office, in Capitol at Trenton, N. J.)

According to a paper entitled *Cravens Choyce,* by Richard Sharpe, (Salem Co. Historical Society) the widow Craven, while a resident of Shadwell, London, had bought of John Eldridge, also of Shadwell, 500 acres of Salem land, March 20, 1676-7, stipulating that her purchase should adjoin the widow Elizabeth Smith's, "as it runneth up Monmouth River." (Salem Deeds No. 2; Charles Bagaley to Henry Jennings, and wife Margaret, June 22, 1683.) The widow Smith though deferred her coming to America until long after her friend, the widow Craven, had died at Salem.

On the "5th 11th mo. (Jan.) 1679," a marriage contract was drawn up "between Charles Bagley now or late of Mary Land . . . . and Ann Craven of New Salem in west Jersey Widdow," in which Bagley promised to pay 15 Pounds, in English money, or 18 Pounds, 15 shillings, in goods, to Thomas Craven, eldest son of the said Ann, when 21 years old; 15 Pounds in English money, or 18 Pounds, 15 shillings, in goods, to Peter Craven the youngest son of the said Ann, when 21 years old; and 20 Pounds in English money, or 25 Pounds in goods, unto Ann Craven, daughter of the said Ann, when 16 years old. (See, Collections of the Genealogical Society of Pa., Vol. IV, Monthly Meetings, Mens Minutes—Quaker Records of Salem, N. J., 1676-1740, p. 222, at Pa. Historical Society.)

In view of her approaching marriage, the widow, on the day of the above contract, deeded the 300 acres purchased of Fenwick to "Charles Bagaley late of Choptank in the Countie of Talbot wthin the Province of Mary-Land, tanner." (Salem Deeds as above Liber B., p. 68.) The marriage was solemnized, and by 1681 the former widow Craven had died, possessed of considerable estate for her day. Bagley married again, and deceased in 1700, leaving will dated April 15, 1699, naming wife Elizabeth, and Thomas Craven (who refused to act) as executors. (See, *Calendar of N. J. Wills,* Vol. I. p. 22.)

An instrument of writing between Charles Bagley and Martha Smith on the one hand, and George Deacon on the other, was drawn 4th 2nd mo., 1681, for the last named to take Peter Craven, "orphan to tutor and bring up for eleven years to come." Ann Craven, the 27th of 7th mo., 1686, "being upwards of the age of 16 years, chose edward Cradway and William Killey to be her guardians." (Quaker Records, as above, pp. 30 and 90.)

In "A Memoriall of ye Evidence" given before Thomas Olive, Robert Stacey, Mahon Stacey, Thomas Budd, and Thomas Lambert, Commissioners for the Province of West Jersey, in "a Case of Charles Bagaley of Salem in ye Sd Pvince," under date of 31st 6th mo., 1681, "George Deacon affirms after a Solemn manr. in our Prsents That whereas Charles Bagley Stands Obligated by an Instrunt. Bearing date ye 5th of ye 11th Month, 1679, to pay to three children (Viz) Thomas, Peeter, & Ann Craven being the issue of his late Deceased Wife to her first husband *Robt. Craven* by Severall Spells the sum of fifty pounds or more. . . . That he was to have an Estate of 800 Acres of Land made Over to him Wth. so much psonal Estate together Wth ye Sum before Marryage as amounted to ye Sum of four score & fifteen pounds Sterl. . . . And for as much as ye Land was near made over but neglected. Therefore this Evidence is given before uss" . . . etc. (Salem Wills, 1676, p. 32, at Trenton.)

Six years later, on the 12th of April, 1687, "Charles Bagley of Caesariee River in the Province of West Jersey aforesd. Plantr. on the accompt of the Estate of *Richard Craven* of Lime house in the Countie of Middlex," purchased 500 acres of land "neare the head of Mun Muth River alias Allawayes Creek and next adjoining the Widdow Smiths 500 acres," from William Penn, Proprietor, and Governor of Pennsylvania, Sam Hodge, of Hodgefield, John Smith, of Smithfield, and Richard Tindall, of Tindall's Bowery, in the Tenth and Province of West Jersey, executors of John Fenwick, of Fenwick's Colony, Esq., late Proprietor of Salem Tenth, etc. (Salem Deeds, at Trenton.)

This conveyance apparently refers to the Robert Craven of the "evidence" above. Salem land, however, had been long known in London, and Richard may have been an executor, or a brother, of Robert. As related by Thomas Shourds, "in 1676 the wife of John Smith of Amesbury wrote to her sister Rachel, and her husband Richard Craven . . . . . advising them to come to America, which they accordingly did and landed at New Castle (Delaware) in 1690 and came to Salem the same year." (See, Our Early Settlers—Salem Historical Society, also *Cravens Choyce* above.)

For more than a century, says Sharp, the Cravens "were prominent citizens in the public affairs of Salem." Neither did they long remain Quakers.

Thomas Craven was deeded 200 acres of land, near the head of Alloway's Creek, by Bagley, April 15th, 1687, and in 1696, and 1698, bought other tracts. (Salem Deeds, Books 3, p. 259; 6, p. 104, and 7, p. 213.) His will dated 13th September, 1721, and proven 23rd December, 1730, names a son Nehemiah under age, and daughters Elizabeth, Rachel, and Ann. Nehemiah, of Cumberland County, in will of April 22, 1749, proven May 10, 1749, names minor children Thomas and Mary. (*Calendar of N. J. Wills*, Vol. I, p. 32; Vol. II, p. 123.)

Peter Craven, "husbandman," on October 18th, 1697, was assigned land by Bagley and wife Elizabeth. (Salem Deeds, Book 6, p. 192.) He left no will in New Jersey, and apparently died at Salem without issue. He was born in 1671, and is mentioned as late as 1734 in the settlement of Thomas Crabb's estate, of Salem, May 27, this year. "Wm Allen and Joseph Turner merchants of Philadelphia have paid debts due . . . . Daniel Smith, . . . Peter Cravin . . . " etc. (*Calendar N. J. Wills*, Vol. I; p. 115.) Other incidental references to him appear in the 1727-1742 minute book of Salem court.

Richard Craven, son of the 1690 immigrant to Salem, in will of 27th October, 1748, proven 15th November, 1748, names wife Patience, and sons, John and Wheat, under 15 years, and daughters, Grace and Rachel, under 16. (*Calendar N. J. Wills*, Vol. II, p. 123) John Craven, of Salem, m. April 18, 1764, Phoebe Smith, and Richard Wheat Craven, of Cumberland, m. October 10th, 1766, Rhoda Shepherd. (*Archives of N. J.*, 1st Series, Vol. 22, p. 79.) The daughter Rachel is said to have married Joseph, the son of Richard and Mary Pledger Woodnut.

One of the sons of Richard, the immigrant, according to Shourds, settled in Delaware. John and Ann Craven are mentioned in the will of David Stewart, of New Castle, Delaware, 13th November, 1776, proven 24th December, the same year. Ann was the daughter of Stewart. (See, *Calendar Delaware Wills*, 1682-1800, *New Castle Co.*, by Colonial Dames of Del., p. 83.)

A somewhat later Craven immigrant to New Jersey was Thomas Craven, who arrived in 1728, and settled in Monmouth County. He was by occupation a classical and mathematical teacher. He married Elizabeth Walling, of Monmouth, and became the father of a large number of children, including four sons, Thomas, John, Gershom, and Joseph, all of whom left descendants. Thomas early in life setled in Ohio. John sometime before the Revolution entered the employ of Robert Morris, the great financier, and following the war was in the civil service of the Continental Congress, at Philadelphia, and later of the Government at Washington, where he died in 1831. Gershom graduated at Princeton, in 1765, and located at Ringoes as a physician. Two of his descendants were Commander (later Admiral) Thomas T. Craven, and his brother, Commander Augustus M. Craven, of the U. S. Navy, both of whom served under Farragut in the War between the States. Alfred W. Craven, another brother, was for many years chief engineer of the Croton Aqueduct Department of New York city. (See, *History of Essex and Hudson Counties, N. J.*, by Shaw, Vol. I, p. 471.)

Commander Thomas T. Craven married a daughter of Dr. Thomas Henderson, U. S. Army, and wife Anna Maria Truxton, and in 1858 was living in Staunton, Virginia, where on October 19th, this year, at the residence of her son-in-law, the widow Henderson died. (*New England Historical and Genealogical Register*, Vol. XII, p. 91.)

To Pennsylvania, some time between the years 1700 and 1723, immigrated one Jacobus (James) Craven, said to have been of Holland descent. He settled in Bucks County, where he became a large landowner in Warminster township. In 1743 he was one of the trustees of Neshaminy Presbyterian Church, of Warwick. He died about 1760. His children were, Thomas, Giles, James, Alice, wife of Herman Vansent, Elenor, wife of Clement Dungan, Hannah, wife of William McDowell, (married 11th, 11th mo., 1738, at 1st Presbyterian Church, Philadelphia), Esther, wife of William Gilbert, and Mary, wife, of Anthony Stout. Thomas married Lena, daughter of William and Janet Bennett. (One of this name also married Catherine, daughter of Peter Van Horn, and is mentioned in the will of Peter, 1749.) Giles died without issue, James migrated to Loudoun County, Virginia, married, and had a son John, who in 1800 settled at Charlottesville, where he became a prominent citizen, and raised a large family. (See, *History of Bucks County Pa.*, by Davis, Vol. III, p. 247; Abstracts of Bucks Co. Pa. Wills, 1685-1795, pp. 136 and 201, at Historical Society of Pa.; *Pa. Archives*, Vol. IX, p. 16, Record of Pa. Marriages prior to 1810—Vol. II; *History of Albemarle Co., Va.*, by Woods, p. 173.)

* * * * * *

Among the earlier of these Cravens of the Augusta settler's day, only the name Joseph—whatever its significance—is found common to any of Robert's sons. Joseph of "Lews Town," 1709, was probably his father, and may have been the immigrant, or a son of Richard, the 1690 immigrant to Salem, but nothing for a certainty, is known as to this, or of the location of Robert's birthplace. Richard, the 1690 immigrant, was married by 1676, according to the date given of the receipt of his sister-in-law's letter in London, and had a son who settled in Delaware, but Richard of Salem, son of the immigrant, and brother of the Delaware settler, would seem to have been somewhat young for Joseph's generation. No Richard appears on the Augusta records, neither is any relationship known to have existed between Robert and Peter of Augusta, whoever the latter may have been.

An old tradition said to have been handed down in John Craven's family naming him as a Scotch-Irishman, would seem to intimate that Robert, his father, was a native of Ulster, as certainly the son was not. Englishmen, as well as Scotchmen, had settled in this Province, and there was much emigration from there to Delaware in the period of Robert's childhood.

Cravens were settled in the neighborhood of Londonderry prior to 1663; Baptism, August 24th, 1663; "James ye son of William Baxter; James Ruddy, James Cravens & Agnes Donnell goss." (gossips.) (*Dublin Parish Register Society*, Vol. 8, Derry Cathedral. Parish of Templemore, Londonderry, p. 155.) James resided at Coleraine.

Robert and his sister, if not born in the lower region of the Delaware, were likely brought to Sussex as immigrant children by their parents. It is barely possible, of course, that Robert as an adult may have immigrated to Delaware, and following his marriage imported his sister, but this appears doubtful.

Robert bought his land in Delaware of Samuel Stewart, and later in Augusta was associated with one of this name, along with John and Daniel Harrison, in laying out the Indian Road (1745). Following Joseph Harrison's death in Augusta, in 1748, a sale of Joseph's property was held at the house of Samuel Stewart, by Jeremiah Harrison. (See pages 2, and 154.) In September, 1747, David Stewart, of Augusta, brought suit at law against William Harrison. (*Chalkley* Vol. I, p. 296.) Also, March 20, 1755, Daniel Harrison furnished bond as guardian of John Scott, an orphan, with sureties David Stewart and Robert McClenachan. (Page 204.) On August 22, 1745, the court of Orange appointed Jeremiah Harrison, constable, in place of Thomas Stewart, (Page 127.) John Stewart, on February 17, 1761, purchased of Jeremiah Harrison, and Catherine, 275 acres of land on Cook's Creek. (Deed Book 9, p. 217.)

David Stewart of New Castle County, Delaware, who died in 1776, leaving will naming sons, Samuel and David, and a daughter Ann Craven (wife of John, one of the witnesses of the will ?) and "her children" may have been a kinsman of the Sussex and Augusta Stewarts. Stewarts appear to have been in Sussex at an early date—"The Court grant unto John Struate four Hundred Acres of Land warrent given out the—12 mo. 1682." *(Rodney's Diary and Other Delaware Records; Georgetown Records, Deal Court* 1681, p. 115.)

On May 16, 1732, "Robert (R) Cravins" witnessed a deed of Mary Kollock, widow of "Jacob Kollock of Sussex upon Delaware, Esqr," Jean Hirons, Capt. Jacob Phillips, and Hester his wife, children and heirs of the said Jacob Kollock, deceased, all of Sussex, to George Campble (Campbell) of the same county, "Cooper," for land on the north side of "Love Long Branch that runs into Rehobeth Bay." (Sussex Deed Book GN-7, p. 40, at Georgetown, Del.)

Whatever Robert's birthplace, whether in Great Britain, or on the Delaware, he was associated in Sussex with people of influence and means, and came to the Valley of the Shenandoah well supplied with funds for the adventure. He is found first mentioned on the Orange records as Robert Cravens, Gent., at which time, 29th July, 1743, he appeared along with Daniel Harrison, Gent., before the court, and was sworn into "his Military Commission of Captain of Horses." (See page 126.) That he was of good report and well recommended is further attested by his being commissioned one of the "Gentlemen Justices" for the first court of Augusta, by Governor Gooch, 30th October, 1745. (See page 142.)

Robert's removal from Delaware to Orange, later Augusta County, Virginia, occurred about the year 1739. On the 1st of June, this year, he placed his Sussex land in the hands of his attorney, James Hood, for sale. (See page 64.) Like his brothers-in-law, who had preceeded him, he found on his arrival west of the Massanutten that there was no need for undue haste in choosing a site for his new home. His first land patent is dated in 1744. In all, he and his sons were granted some 2, 513 acres of land, in ten patents, as follows—

To ROBERT CRAVENS

Date	Acres	Location	Book No.	Page
15th. March, 1744,	400	"on the Head of the dry Fork of Smith Creek and bounded as followeth to Wit . . . to a black Oak on the north West Side of the Irish Road . . . ."	22	207.

15th March, 1744	400	"on a North Branch of the North River of Shenando called Cooks Creek in the East Fork of the said Creek"	22	209.
10th. Feb., 1748,	200	"on both sides of Cooks Creek including Dyes (Dyers) meadow."	27	115.
" " "	136	"on the Drafts of the South Branch of Linvilles Mill Creek, corner Samuel Harrison."	27	116.
" " "	123	"on the Head of Cooks Creek"	27	118.
" " "	169	"on both sides of Cooks Creek corner survey of James Fisher."	27	120.
10th. Sept., 1755,	300	"on a Branch of Cooks Creek, corner Samuel Harrison"	31	610
16th. Aug., 1756,	320	"on the Head of Custiss Creek a branch of the North River Shenando."	33-1	79.
TOTAL 2,048				

To JOHN CRAVENS

10th. Sept., 1755,	400	"on both sides of Cooks Creek above a Tract of Land belonging to Robert Cravens"	31	700.

To WILLIAM CRAVENS

15th. June, 1773,	65	"on some Drafts of Cooks Creek . . . bounded as followeth . . . to a pine on John Cravens line . . . corner to John Maddison's land."	41-1	322.

(See, Patent Books, numbers as above, at Land Office, Richmond, Virginia.)

In addition to the above tracts, Capt. Cravens purchased for £40-4, 670 acres of land on the "north side of Linville's Creek", 19th June, 1746, of "McKay, Hite, Green, and the said Green sole heir exr. of Wm. Duff," part of "7009 acres granted Robert McKay, Just Hite, Wm. Duff, Robert Green, Gent.,by patent 26th March, 1739"—Delivered to John Cravens (executor) 1762. Also some time prior to 1760, Robert purchased of "Epipha Fowler", 165 acres on the "South Side of the North Branch of Shenando River, against the mouth of Fort run," which land he and wife Mary deeded to John Halpe, 18th August, 1760. (Deed Book 8, p. 426.)

Robert and his brother-in-law, Thomas Harrison, the founder of Harrisonburg, settled as near neighbors; their first patents were granted on the same day, and their lands were practically adjacent. Thomas' first surveys are dated December 18th, and 19th, 1739, and evidently Robert's were also made about this time. Robert's Dry Fork tract was located as early, at least, as August, 1741, and joined Robert Harrison's line of the later Smithland estate, to the northeast of Harrisonburg. (See pages 195 and 211.)

The head spring of the Dry Fork is commonly called Flook's Spring, but a small tributary of the fork rises further to the south, and directly to the east of Harrisonburg, and it was on this somewhere, manifestly, that Robert's land lay. The old tradition of the Harrisons mentions one of the brothers as having early located at the spring, and probably Robert had camped at it for a time also. The Irish Road mentioned in Robert's first patent was first known as Daniel Harrison's path, in the Linville Creek neighborhood, and apparently led across the country via the Dry Fork region to the early Swift Run Gap Road. (See pages 147 and 196.)

By far the greater part of Capt. Cravens land was located on the waters of Cook's Creek, to the south of Thomas, and it was in this direction that he settled. Some of his Cook's Creek land joined Samuel Harrison, but his first tract was nearer Jeremiah —"Land Entry Book No. 1, Augusta County, 7th December, 1745, Jeremiah Harrison, 100 acres, south side Cook's Creek, joining Robert Craven's land." (*Chalkley*, Vol. II, p. 379.) In 1761, February 18th, Jeremiah Harrison and Catherine deeded to Thomas Harrison, for 20 pounds, 120 acres by patent . . . 1760, "on the east draft of Cook's Creek, ... joining Robert Craven." (Deed Book 9, p. 151.) This last was embraced in Thomas' 1290 acre patent, of 1773, for his land at Harrisonburg. (See page 220.)

Robert's home was on the "Great Road" of 1755, today's Long Grey Trail, and was probably within a mile or two of the present southern limits of Harrisonburg.

The Captain was evidently one of the first inhabitants to accomodate "Valley tourists"—14th April, 1746, "License is Granted to Robert Craven Gent. to keep Ordinary at his House he having Paid the Governors fee & with John Lewis and Robert Pickens Gentlemen his securities Acknowledge their Bond for the same which is Admd. to record." (Order Book No. 1, p. 22.) On the 20th of August, 1747, the court appointed Robert Cravens and Samuel Wilkins road overseers, vice Alexander Herron, Thomas and Jeremiah Harrison, "from the Court House (Staunton) *to the Indian Road near said Cravens*." (See page 7.)

The day license was granted him to keep an ordinary, Capt. Cravens declined the honor of reappointment as a justice under the Governor's forthcoming commission of June 13, 1746. (Order Book 1, p. 68.) Shortly thereafter he bought his 670 acres of land on Linville's Creek, and from this time on his activities were mainly those of a large land owner, but his interest in public affairs continued. His appointment as a road overseer in 1747 was followed on September 3rd, the same year, by his appointment as processioner, along with Thomas Harrison, from Samuel Wilkins to the Fairfax line, etc. (See page 221.)

In all this while his land in Delaware had remained unsold, although provision for the sale had been made in 1739. His witnesses thereto, in the meantime, having died, on the 24th of December, 1747, as a resident of the "County of Augusta and Collony of Virginia" he renewed Hood's power of attorney with new witnesses; doubtless journeying himself back to Delaware for this purpose. On the 3rd of the following Feburary, through Hood, he deeded his Sussex land to Robert Talbert, of the same county, for "ninety Pounds Current money of the Province of Pennsylvania." (See page 63.)

In many of his services to Augusta, Robert was associated with his brothers-in-law, the Harrisons and Alexander Herring. His appraisement of Peter Dyer's estate with Thomas and Jeremiah Harrison, in 1749, and of Charles Gallagher's estate, with Jeremiah and Daniel Harrison, in 1750, have been mentioned in previous Chapters. (See pages 147 and 221.) On the 29th of August, 1751, he and Daniel were named again,—"Daniel Harrison & Henry Smith having according to an Order of this Court laid a way from the South branch (of Shenandoah or Linville's Creek?) to Swift run Pass, It is Ordered that Robert Craven and James Bally be surveyors of the same, and that the said Harrison lay off their Precints & appoint the Tithable persons that shall clear the same." (Order Book 3, p. 187.)

Henry Smith was a brother of Capts. Abraham and Daniel Smith, the later first justices of Rockingham court, and a son of Capt. John Smith, the pioneer. Henry, a son of Capt. Abraham, and Benjamin, a son of Capt. Daniel, married sisters, respectively,

Margaret and Elizabeth Cravens, Capt. Robert Cravens' granddaughters, sometimes confused with his own daughters, Maggie and Elizabeth, but evidently the daughters of his son Robert, Jr. (See, *Boogher*, pp. 336, 347, and 379.) Henry Smith, son of Capt. Abraham, was not born until 1758, nor Benjamin, his cousin, until 1761. Henry and his wife Margaret were married April 2, 1792. Elizabeth, the wife of Benjamin Smith, was born in 1762, and died in 1837. She and her husband married about 1782-3. He died in 1812. Both lie buried in the old Methodist churchyard at Lancaster, Ohio. (*Ibid*, pp. 338, 347, and Marriage Records of Rockingham County, Va.)

As an appraiser of land values Capt. Cravens was manifestly highly regarded, the court naming him twice at the same term, 27th November, 1751. First—along with his son John, and Daniel Stringer, to value the improvements made by James Wood, Gent. on 400 acres of his Muddy Creek land. Second—"On the motion of John Harrison for a View and Valuation of the Improvements by him made on four hundred acres of Land on the Dry Fork of Smith's Creek, It is Ordered that Robert Craven, Michael Warren & Alexander Herron (Herring) or any two of them being first Sworn before a Justice of the Peace of this County do meet to Value the Same having regard to expenses and make report of their proceedings to the next Court." (Order Book 3, pp. 203, and 207.)

These valuations were to establish record that the conditions of the patents to the land had been complied with; no controversy being involved, the relationship of the viewers to the owners was manifestly no bar to appointment. Both Cravens and Herring were brothers-in-law of Harrison, and Warren was his close friend.

Wolves at the time were yet infesting the country, and a bounty had long been offered for their heads. For the head of an old one Robert Cravens and Hugh Campbell were paid 160 pounds of tobacco, at this sitting of the court. (*Ibid*, p. 204.) Although now past military age the Captain doubtless was still familiar with his gun—that he treasured it highly is assured by his passing it on to his son John, when he came to make his will.

John Cravens—styled "John Cravens eldest son & heir & executor of Robert Cravens, farmer, deceased," in a joint deed to Archibald Huston, 8th August 1767, from himself, "& Mary Cravens, widow and executrix of Robert," conveying 470 acres of land of the testator's Linville Creek purchase, "corner to tract devised to Zebulon and Robert Harrison," etc.—was the first born of Robert and Mary. (Deed Book 13, p. 373.) He was born about 1722, in Sussex on the Delaware, being aged "45 or thereabouts" in 1767, according to a deposition made by him 16th December, this year. (See page 144.)

John and William Cravens at different times served as tax collectors of the county; John in 1748, and William in 1755. Both were also constables. John's first land was obtained by purchase 21st February, 1751; Deed, John Wright and Lydia his wife, to John Cravens, 40 Pounds, 200 acres on a branch of Cook's Creek, land formerly conveyed to Wright by Samuel Harrison and wife, Mary. Teste, Peter Scholl and Samuel Newman. (Deed Book 3, p. 97.)

On the same day Robert and Mary Cravens, with Scholl and Newman as their witnesses, also deeded the first 400 acre tract patented in 1744, to Wright, this being Robert's first conveyance in Augusta. He signed as in Delaware, with his characteristic "R" mark, and Mary with a simple plus mark.

Wright, as elsewhere observed, was undoubtedly a near kinsman of Mary Cravens. Samuel Harrison was her half-brother. James Wright on the 16th August, 1756, patented 175 acres "on the head of the Dry Fork of Smith's Creek, on the east side of a Tract of Land belonging to Robert Cravens." (Patent Book 33-1,p. 109, Land Office, Richmond, Virginia.) This land later descended to John Wright, the surviving heir, and was devised by him to James Wright, Jr. (*Chalkley*, Vol. III, p. 547.) John Wright and John Cravens in 1757 were associated together in owning land near James.

Cravens appears to have settled on his Cook's Creek land, a few miles southwest of his father, near a place called Fisher's Spring. As several of his children when small attended school at the spring, along with one or two of Benjamin Harrison's children, his plantation manifestly was not far from present Dayton.

James Fisher was probably the first owner of the spring. One of this name was an early acquaintance of the Harrisons in Delaware (see page 51.), and assuredly James of Augusta, in the early days of the county, was no new acquaintance of the elder Cravens. In 1744, while preparing to remove from Augusta, Fisher sold 350 acres of land, on Cook's Creek, to Abraham Potter, arranging with Robert Cravens to give Potter a good title. Potter agreed to make payment, at the request of Fisher and Cravens, by the last of August 1745.

Potter was from an old Sussex, Delaware, family early known to the Fishers of this county, his grandfather, Abraham Potter (Sr.), having bought land on the north side of Broad Creek, in Sussex, of Thomas Fisher and Charles Bright, in 1696. Abraham, Sr.'s widow, Jane, in will 1703, proved 1704, names son Abraham about 14 years old, and friends Frances Gum, Richard Dobson, and "John Davises son John." Abraham, 2nd, died in Sussex in 1742, leaving will dated March 27th, this year, naming wife Mary, and sons John, Joshua and Abraham (above), and a daughter Jane Russell—Witnesses, John Stuart and Enoch Cummings. (Sussex Deeds, Book A-1, p. 147; Wills, Book A-1 pp. 48, and 331.)

Following the sale of his Augusta land, James Fisher "went to Carolina." Potter failed to pay, and instead signed a new bond to Robert Cravens in 1745. In May, 1753, the matter was brought to court for adjustment. (See page 134.)

John Cravens married, sometime between 1758 and 1762, Margaret, the widow of William Dyer. On 15th September, 1758, Henry Smith signed Thomas Fulton's bond as security for Margaret Dyer. Following her marriage to John Cravens the latter assigned the bond to his father Robert. (Augusta Court Judgements, October, 1765, D; Henry Smith vs. Samuel Cowden.) In 1762 "John Cravens and Margaret his wife, late Margaret Dyer administratrix of William Dyer, deceased," brought a bill of complaint vs. Charles Wilson, regarding payment of a bond of Wilson to Dyer, dated 24th December, 1752. (Augusta Court Judgements A, 1762.) On the 20th March, 1765, Cravens was appointed guardian of Roger and John Dyer, "infant orphans of William Dyer, deceased." (Order Book 9, p. 248.)

Margaret was the daughter of John and Margaret Hiatt. The Hiatts were Quakers, and are said to have come in from the British Isles. John Hiatt, Sr. and his son John were both granted land by Lord Fairfax between the years 1759 and 1762. (See, Fairfax Grants; Book K, pp. 260, 261, 299, and 302, Land Office, Richmond, Va.,)

The name Margaret was a popular one in Robert Cravens' family. Besides his sister, the wife of Capt. Daniel Harrison, one of Robert's own daughters was of this name.

Margaret Cravens, the daughter of Robert, was likely the first of his children to be married, and was evidently near her brother John in age. Her first husband was a Primrose, and her second Zebulon Harrison, the son of John Harrison, Sr. (Chapter XI), whom she married at the First Presbyterian Church, Morristown, New Jersey, 23rd

July, 1747. (See page 164.) Various Primroses are mentioned on the old records of the church at Morristown—Mary, in 1745, m. James Watkins; Henry, in 1748, m. Rebbeca Stites; John, d. 1756, aged 89; Henry, d. 1780, aged 70, etc.—and doubtless Margaret's first husband had been a resident of the neighborhood. The town was settled about 1700, and the county formed from Hunterdon in 1739.

"Mage," Madge or Maggie Cravens, sister of Margaret, was also early married, her daughter being Mary Black, one of the grandchildren named in her father's will. She herself, by the will, was devised sixty pounds in money. In her brother John's settlement of their father's estate, "approved and recorded," 21st September, 1763, mention in his account is made of, "Legacy to Robert Black in part of his wife's legacy." (Will Book 3, p. 288; *Chalkley*, Vol. III, p. 81.) None of Maggie's sisters having a husband of this name, Black is identified as that of her own. He was doubtless the witness, along with Robert Cravens and Samuel Hemphill, of Gardiner's conveyance of Dry Fork land to John Cravens and John Wright. (See page 209.) On 11th August, 1766, "William Cravens, Robert Black, and Magey ( ) Black," witnessed a deed of "Samuel Stewart & Lydia, of North Carolina, yeoman," to Jacob Calpin of Augusta, conveying 153 acres on the South Fork of Linville's Creek, patented to Samuel, 5th September, 1749. On the 3rd September, 1766, "Robert Black & Magey ( ) of Mecklenburg County, North Carolina," deeded to Martin Archenbright 232 acres on Cook's Creek, patented to Thomas Stevenson, 25th June, 1747, and conveyed to Robert 22nd June, 1763. (Deed Book 13, pp. 56, and 143.)

Several Blacks were early in Augusta. Rev. William Black, a Presbyterian minister, on 22nd May, 1747, appeared before the court and took the prescribed oaths. He lived in Pennsylvania, and in 1758 was a member of Donegal Persbytery. (*Waddell*, p. 62.) Maggie's husband likely came in from this direction also. His father was probably Robert Black, Sr. On the 18th February, 1746, Elizabeth Skilleren was appointed administratrix of her husband William, deceased, with sureties Robert Black and John Miller. Robert Black, Sr., and Robert Black, Jr., furnished bond for affiance of Elizabeth Anderson, "formerly the widow Skilran," 27th January, 1748. On 19th May, the same year, Robert Black (Sr. ?) deeded to John Miller 200 acres, on the Beverly Manor line, corner to William Skilleren, part of Beverly Manor, formerly conveyed by Beverly to Black, 25th September, 1741. (*Chalkley*, Vol. I, p. 432; Vol. III, pp. 6, and 268.)

Whether or not Robert and his wife Maggie, nee Cravens, settled permanently in North Carolina is unknown. In Thomas Harrison's inclusive patent of 1773, to his land at Harrisonburg, "Black's line" is mentioned. Black joined Harrison on the north. His land was on Black's Run, a headwater of the East Fork of Cook's Creek. Through Harrisonburg the run and the fork together form a continous stream, locally known by the name of the run, but strictly speaking the juncture of the waters is alongside the old Head Spring in the center of the town. (See page 219.)

Joseph Cravens, although not specifically named in his father's will, nevertheless received a bequest under it, due to its residuary clause; Robert including his "loving wife and *nine* children" in this. Several years before signing his will Robert had given Joseph what he doubtless considered his share of his land: Deed, April 20, 1759, "Robert Cravens to his son Joseph Cravens," 300 acres "on a branch of Cook's Creek," corner Samuel Harrison; the consideration being a nominal amount, five shillings. The next day, for 50 Pounds, Robert deeded to Joseph another 300 acres "on a branch of Cook's Creek," corner Samuel Harrison, Teste, Samuel Hemphill, John () Jones. (Deed Book 8, pp. 126, 127.) Under date of February 21, 1763, in the cause of

Malcom Campbell vs. Joseph Cravens, the notation occurs that the suit "Abates by death of Defendant." *(Chalkley,* Vol. I, p. 104.) The first tract of land in August, 1772, was delivered to Robert Cravens, probably a son of William, and of the second, on the 11th and 18th, October, 1773, Joseph Cravens, probably a son of William also, conveyed to John Cravens, two tracts; each for 60 Pounds, each embracing 150 acres on "one of the branches of Cook's Creek, and each a part of the tract patented to Robert Cravens, 10th September, 1755. Some of Joseph's land also included a part of the 200 acres patented by his father (Robert) 10th February, 1748. (Deed Book 20, pp. 2, and 182.)

In his will Robert Cravens names two of his grandchildren, Robert and John Cravens, identifying them as brothers. One of these grandsons was bequeathed land lying below Joseph Cravens, but no mention is made of Joseph being their father. In the deeds disposing of the above 300 acres of land, in 1773, no wife signed with Joseph, the younger. These grandsons appear to have been the sons of William Cravens, who is said to have had sons Robert, James, John, and Joseph. Among the children of 1788, attending the school at Fisher's Spring before referred to, were Joseph and James Cravens, sons of John. Jeremiah and William Cravens, sons of Robert, Jr., about the same time, attended a school at Harrisonburg. Nehemiah Cravens, another son of Robert, Jr., was also among the grandchildren of Robert, Sr. living at the time. On December 20th, 1802, in the presence of A. Waterman and Peachy Harrison of Rockingham County, "Nehemiah Cravens of Ohio County in the State of Virginia," appointed Reuben Harrison, and Joseph Cravens (son of John), of Rockingham, his lawful attorneys, to sell four tracts of land, three of which contained inclusively 1,618 acres "surveyed for me in the month of August last in the County of Ohio . . . . . on Wheelin Creek about twelve miles from the mouth thereof," the fourth, "lying in the County of Rockingham, ... and in the waters of the east branch of Cook's Creek," embracing 113 1/2 acres, etc.—Presented March Court, 1805. (Rockingham Deed Book "OO", p. 248.)

William Cravens, son of Robert, was undoubtedly married at the time of his father's will. His wife, according to Boogher, was Jane ———. William, his nephew (b. 1766), the son of John Cravens, had a wife of this name, having married (1794) Jane Harrison, daughter of Benjamin, son of Capt. Daniel. William, the elder, served as a sergeant in the French and Indian War, his name appearing among the lists of Augusta's soldiers, first under Lieut. Abraham Smith, next under Lieut Daniel Smith, and later under Capt. Ephraim Love, in the Act of Assembly passed March, 1756, granting pay for the various services rendered. *(Hening,* Vol. 7, pp. 179-200.) Among others granted pay by the same act were Capt. Abraham Smith, Lieut. Sampson Archer, John Cravens, Joseph Dictum, Robert Black, Samuel Hemphill, Mathew Black, Leonard Herring, John Harrison, Gideon Harrison, Nathaniel Harrison, etc., most of whom, including Sergeant Cravens, were also later named in an act of 1758. (See page 182.) In 1759, William was promoted to an Ensign,—23rd November, this year, "William Cravens took the Usual Oaths to his Majesty's person and Government Subscribed the Abjuration and Test which is Ordered to be Certified on his commission of Ensign of the Militia." (Order Book 6, p. 335.) Following the close of the war William evidently went on a journey of some distance, probably with George Anderson as his companion, the two being mentioned together under date of 29th September, 1764, as "going out of the Colony." (County Court Judgements, March 1767 (A); "John Pharis vs. Daniel Harrison"), *(Chalkley,* Vol . I, p. 350.) In 1773 he patented land on Cook's Creek, adjoining his brother John, and in this region doubtless made his home. He had sold his Great Meadow tract in 1764. He was very much among the living of 1778, and one of his name, most likely the same, signed as a juror of Rockingham, along with John Lincoln, Benjamin Smith, William Herring, Samuel McWilliams, Reuben and Benjamin Harrison, and others, 26th July, 1796.

The year of William's promotion to Ensign, and of his father's deeds to Joseph, Robert Cravens with Daniel Love signed Margaret Johnson's bond as administratrix of her husband Arthur Johnson deceased. (See page 208) A short time before this, or on the 15th November, 1758, Robert Cravens with Ephraim Love had furnished bond to Abraham Smith as the administrator of Ludwick Fulk, deceased, (Will Book II, p. 280.) Ephraim Love, in 1748, was "late of Lancaster County, Pennsylvania." (See page 197.) Daniel Love was probably his son. He was one of the witnesses of Robert Cravens' will. On 15th November, 1763, Daniel Love, and Robert Cravens (Jr.), acknowledged their bond as sureties for Reuben and Zebulon Harrison, administrators of John Harrison, Jr., deceased, (See page 158.) By this last date Robert Cravens, senior, was also deceased, thus the identification.

Robert Cravens, Jr., had doubtless only recently passed his majority at the time of his father's will. That he was of age in 1763 is certain. No notation of senior or junior appearing in the above references, it is presumed that Robert, senior, was the bondsman in the first two cases. That Robert, Jr., owned no land prior to his father's death is evidenced by the processioners' returns for the Cook's Creek neighborhood, in 1760. This year the processioners made their rounds and among the various landowners listed in their returns were Robert Cravens, John Cavens, and Joseph Cravens, but no Robert Cravens, Jr. (See page 209.) Here Robert senior was manifestly the landowner. In 1767 Robert, Jr., was himself a processioner, and by this time owned land, as shown in his returns. (See page 225.) Either the senior or the junior, most likely the latter, was one of the appraisers, along with John Hopkins, and Hugh Hamilton, of Robert Harrison's estate in November, 1761, the month following the signing of the elder Cravens' will. Ten years later Robert, Jr., was one of the appraisers of Capt. Daniel Harrison's estate. (See pages 209 and 213.) Robert Cravens, Jr., inherited his father's home plantation, and on this lived and died. His wife's name, as revealed by the records of Rockingham, was Hester. His history belongs to a later Chapter, but more of him anon.

Mary Cravens, daughter of Robert (Sr.), by her father's will was bequeathed 124 acres of land, on which she then resided. Mary married, sometime before her father's death, Samuel Hemphill, frequently mentioned in the foregoing pages. She died in 1801. Samuel signed his will 19th March, 1802, and died in 1809, his will being proved at Rockingham Court in April, the latter year. (See, Judgements Circuit Court Causes Ended, Miller Vs. Hemphill, OS. 284, NS. 100; and Kyle vs. Smith, OS. 283, NS. 100, 5th May, 1816; *Chalkley*, Vol. II, p. 215.) The Hemphills are said to have emigrated to Pennsylvania from Ireland, and previous thereto were from England.

Of the remaining daughters of Capt. Cravens, Agnes was married at the time of her father's will, and Elizabeth was yet single in 1763, although doubtless married later, but the name of the husband of neither is directly disclosed. One of the sisters, it appears, married John Magill, and the other a Miller. John McGill, or Magill, is listed as a landowner in the Cook's Creek neighborhood by 1760. (See pages 209 and 225.) Agnes being the first of the sisters married, he is presumed to have been her husband. The Millers were also residents of the Cook's Creek neighborhood, or in any case were no further away than Muddy Creek. Elizabeth, the wife of Jacob Miller, signed with her husband in 1776, and Elizabeth, the widow of Abraham Miller, was living in 1787. One account states that one of Capt. Cravens' daughters, either Elizabeth, Maggie, or Agnes, married William Horton. (See, *D. A. R. Magazine,* Vol. 61, No. 2, p. 151.) Horton may have been Elizabeth's second husband.

Capt. Robert Cravens, the pioneer, and Justice of the first Court of Augusta County, died, as revealed by the proving of his will, in the spring of 1762, during the French and Indian War. In the previous autumn when he signed his will he was in failing health, from which apparently he never rallied. By his passing Old Augusta lost one of her noble company of first settlers, whose descendants were to add further luster to her name, and whose children's children, like those of so many others, were to go forth from Virginia to help "make other states great."

By his will Capt. Cravens appointed his wife Mary, and his son John, his executrix and executor, who on the 18th May, 1762, the day of the proving of his will, gave bond, with Edward Shankland and Andrew Erwin, for 2,000 Pounds. On the 5th July, 1762, his estate was appraised by Matthew Thompson, Archibald Huston, and John Stewart, the appraisement being recorded 17th August, the same year. (Will Book 3, p. 162.) Among the various movables listed were the following—

71 head of live stock, consisting of 3 horses, 2 mares, 2 colts, 2 oxen, 8 steers, 10 yearlings, 10 cows, 6 calves, 4 heifers, 11 sheep, and 13 hogs.
To 1 smoothe case gun . . . . one ax . . . . . . 1 pair stilyards
1 dressed buck skin
1 waggon
1 bed stead and furniture
1 bed-stead
1 bedstead and furniture
Ditto
Ditto
1 old couch . . . . . 1 chest . . . . . 1 box and chest
a table and cloth . . . . a looking glass, brush and strap
1 table . . . 6 chairs . . . . 1 Bible . . . . 10 books.
8 spoons & 1 doz. plates . . . . . a parcel of knives and forks.
4 small basons, ... 4 Pewter Basons . . . . . 5 porringers
31 pewter plates . . . . . 4 pewter dishes . . . . . 6 wooden plates .
1 brass kettle . . . . .. 6 tins . . . . a pint & $\frac{1}{2}$ pint pot.
various articles of apparel (of the deceased) including one "white collourd coat"
1 Negro boy Tom
1 negro wench
1 Negro girl Venie
1 Negro girl Dine
1 Negro boy Sippio
a bond due by Robt. McGerry and Jeremiah Harrison 25-00-00
Cash 47-9-3$\frac{1}{2}$
Total £573-15-10

Mary Cravens, the widow of Robert, being bequeathed her share of his estate for her use "during her natural life," a final settlement of the whole under his will could not be made until after her decease. A partial settlement, by John Cravens, was approved and admitted to record, 21st September, 1763. (See page 262.) In this, mention is made of payments to Samuel Hemphill, Robert Cravens (Jr.), William Cravens, John Stewart, Matthew Black, Patrick and John Frazier, Margaret Perkey,

Patrick Given, William Minter, and John Brown. Also. "to Cash paid the widow Mary," to "Cash paid John Cravens," to "Legacy of negro delivered to Zebulon Harrison for his two sons," to "Legacy to Elizabeth Cravens," and to the legacy paid Robert Black, etc.

In 1767 the Linville Creek land devised by Capt. Cravens to be sold was so disposed of. John Cravens and Margaret ( ) his wife, on the 15th March, this year, conveyed to Robert Bellshie, Jr., 230 acres "on the North East side of Linville's Creek," corner to George Speec, and to the tract bequeathed Zebulon and Robert Harrison, part of 670 acres devised by Robert Cravens, who by his will "appointed said John his Executor" to sell "this lot". (Deed Book 14, p. 127.) A part of this 230 acre tract was doubtless owned by John Cravens in his own right, thus the signature of Margaret. On the 8th August, following, John Cravens and his mother, Mary, conveyed to Archibald Huston 470 acres, part of the 670, this being the tract on which Samuel Mowry lived at the time of the testator's will. (See page 260.)

This last conveyance seems to have been in view of an arrangement made by John Cravens to acquire the same land, or a tract adjoining, for himself. Ten days later, "Archibald Huston, farmer" and wife Mary, deeded to "John Cravens, farmer," for 171 Pounds, 470 acres of land on Linville's Creek, corner to tract devised to Zebulon and Robert Harrison, etc., tract conveyed by (to) Archibald, "by deed dated 8th this instant." (Deed Book 13, p. 383.) Of this, 240 acres, "on North West side of Linville's Creek, sold to John Cravens 8th (18th) August, 1767," part of 7009 acres patented by McKay, Hite, etc., was conveyed by John Cravens and Margaret, to John Bear, 15th March, 1770. (Deed Book 16, p. 285.)

John Cravens died 24th July, 1778. (Cravens vs. Lanachan, OS. 291, NS. 103, Augusta Court.) His widow Margaret and brother Robert Cravens, Jr., with Daniel Smith and Benjamin Harrison, as their sureties, furnished bond to the justices of Rockingham court, as "Administrators of all the goods and chattels . . . of John Cravens, deceased," 24th August, 1778. (Administrators Bonds 1778-1815, at Harrisonburg, Va.) On Monday, 22nd March, 1779, the appraisement of John's estate was recorded. (Rockingham Court Order Book No. 1, Part 1, p. 25, at State Library, Richmond, Va.) At the time of his death, according to the records, he was possessed of "three tracts of land," one of which was manifestly on Linville's Creek, (230 acres), another the land bought from his nephew, Joseph, in 1773, (300 acres), and the third his home plantation on Cook's Creek.

Margaret Cravens, in 1782, is listed as owning 750 acres of land in Rockingham. (Land Book, Rockingham Co.—Personal Property List—at State Library.) On the 20th of March, 1782, she married, as her third husband, Dennis Lanahan, and with him a little later became one of the early residents of Harrisonburg. (See page 247.)

Following John Cravens' death, his mother, Mary Cravens, the widow, being the sole executor of Robert living, was also granted administration on John's estate, in so far, manifestly, as her husband's estate was concerned, "At a Court held for Rockingham County Monday, 24th August 1778, Administran of the Estate of John Cravens deceased is granted to Mary Cravens, widow of Robert Cravens . . . . who having entered into Bond . . . made Oath according to law," (Rockingham Court Order Book, No. 1, Part. 1, p. 13, at State Library.)

(14) Mary Harrison Cravens, the widow of Capt. Robert Cravens, the pioneer, died testate in Rockingham County, Virginia, in April or May, 1781, the spring preceeding the surrender of Cornwallis at Yorktown.

"At a Court held for Rockingham County Monday the 28th day of May 1781— The last Will & Testament of Mary Cravens decd. was proved by Alexr Miller & John Gwine two of theWits & admitted to record, also a Codicil was proven by the Oath of Alexr Miller & Jno Miller two of the Wits & admitted to Record whereupon Saml Hemphill & Jno Magill the Executors therein named . . . . certifications . . granted." . . etc. Also 28th May, 1781, Bond of Samuel Hemphill, John Magill, Francis Erwine, and James Shannon to Daniel Smith, William Nalle, Henry Ewing and Reuben Harrison, Gentlemen Justices of the Court of Rockingham County, for 100,000 Pounds current money of Virginia, as executors of the last Will and Tetament of Mary Cravens, deceased. (Rockingham Co. Executors Bonds, 1778-1815, No. 24, at Harrisonburg, Va.) On the 24th September, 1781, the "Appraismt of Mary Cravens Estate retd & O to be recorded, also the Vendue Bill retd & O to be recorded." (Rockingham Court Order Book No. 1, Part 1, pp. 92 and 101, at State Library.)

Owing to the destruction of the Rockingham records in the War of 1861-65, Mary's will has been reduced to ashes—such being the respect of the "preservers of the Republic" for the records of the founders of the same . She and Robert contributed at least two sons as soldiers in the Cause of Independence, and she herself furnished supplies, her executors filing claim with the court June 9th, 1781, for payment on "7 Bushels of Corn @ 2/ Each .14s" furnished by her for the "Continental" Army, the same being recorded and forwarded to Richmond by the Clerk of Rockingham Court amongst the "Filed MS Claims against the Revolutionary Army"—Folio 22. "The different Accts Sent you In this Book is A true Acct of the different Claims as they were Produced in Court, Certified by me, Henery Ewin (Ewing) C. R. C. " (State Library, Richmond, Va.)

Mary's executors gave bond in Revolutionary wartime currency. One of these executors, Hemphill, was certainly her son-in-law, and most likely Magill was also. Alexander and John Miller were probably her grand-sons, or brothers-in-law of her daughter, Elizabeth.

On the 27th August, 1781, the "Administran of the Estate of Robt. Cravens, the elder not administer'd by his executor, deced." was "granted to Robt Cravens his Son he having entd into Bond & Made Oath according to Law"which was "O to be certified." (Rockingham Court Order Book, No. 1, Part 1, p. 100, at State Library.) The same day Robert, Jr., with George Chrisman, furnished bond to "Daniel Smith, Henry Ewing, William Nalle & Reuben Harrison . . . . Gentlemen Justices of the Court of Rockingham County, now fitting, in the Sum of one hundred Thousand pounds" as "Administrator of all the Goods, Chattles, and Credits of Robert Cravens the Elder not administered by his Exrs now deceased." (Rockingham Adminisration Bonds, 1781, at Harrisonburg, Va.

Robert, Sr., and Mary Harrison Craven's children were, as named, briefly as follows—

(141) JOHN—b. 1722; d. July, 24, 1778; m. 1759 c., Margaret, nee Hiatt, the widow of William Dyer. After John's death she married, 3rd, Dennis Lanahan.

(142) MARGARET—b. 1724 c; d. 1800 c; m. 1st a Primrose; m. 2nd, July 23rd, 1747, Zebulon Harrison, (121), son of John Harrison, Sr.

(143) MAGGIE—b. ———; d. ———; m. before 1761, Robert Black, and removed with him to Mecklenburg County, North Carolina, about 1764.

(144) JOSEPH—b. ———; d. 1763; m. ———, no further record.

(145) WILLIAM—b. 1730 c; d. ———; m. ——— "and is said to have had four sons,

Maj. Bob, James, John, and Joe, and that Maj. Bob and his uncle Robert Cravens married sisters," etc.

(146) MARY—b. ———; d. 1801; m. before 1761, Samuel Hemphill, d. 1809.

(147) AGNES—b. ———; d. ———; m. before 1761, John Magill (?).

(148) ROBERT—b. 1733 c; d. March, 1784; m. Hester Harrison, dau. of Jeremiah Harrison, (18).

(149) ELIZABETH—b. ———; d. ———; m. Jacob Miller (?).

(See further record for all but Joseph, Agnes, and Elizabeth.)

---

(15) ELIZABETH HARRISON, (1698-), the second daughter of Isaiah Harrison, (1), the immigrant, and his 1st wife, Elizabeth Wright—and the full sister of John Harrison, Sr., (Chapter XI), and Mary Cravens, the wife of Capt. Robert Cravens—was born at Oyster Bay, Long Island, New York, 30th March, 1698. (See pages 23 and 123.)

Elizabeth is presumed to have been the "Elizabeth Herison, an adult person," baptized by the Rev. John Craig, of the Old Stone Church, July 27, 1744, and the individual whose account for "diets of the Militia," or supplies furnished the troops for the Point Pleasant expedition, was admitted to record, along with those of Thomas Harrison, January 18th, 1775. (See pages 151 and 229.)

She is thought to have lived and died unmarried, likely making her home with one of her brothers, probably Jeremiah. In any case no record, or tradition, has been found identifying her husband. (See however, page 124.)

Should this conjecture be correct, she was obviously "up and doing" in 1775, and likely died after the formation of Rockingham.

CHAPTER XV

Jeremiah and Samuel Harrison, and Alexander Herring

AN ANCESTOR OF ABRAHAM LINCOLN

JEREMIAH and SAMUEL HARRISON, with ALEXANDER HERRING, their brother-in-law, were among the first landowners in the Linville Creek neighborhood, one of the oldest settlements in present Rockingham County, Virginia. It was to this community that John Lincoln removed on his migration from Berks County, Pennsylvania, and it was here that fate thus began to weave the threads of that half-forgotten romance—so beautifully described by Herring Chrisman in his *Memoirs of Lincoln*—which was destined to infuse two new strains of high spirited ancestry into the veins of a future native of Old Rockingham—Thomas Lincoln, the father of the President.

Of the three families, the Harrisons, Herrings, and Lincolns, the Harrisons were the first in the Linville Creek community. Manifestly, several of the brothers of this name were familiar with the lay of the land here as early, at least, as 1740, the date of the disposal of their last lands in Delaware. Following Samuel Harrison's settlement on the creek, Alexander Herring came into the Valley, from Delaware also, and finding that Samuel had already reserved more land than he was in any immediate need of, accepted Harrison's offer allowing him to take up a part of the said Samuel's survey. After becoming more acquainted with the country roundabout, Herring a little later acquired other broad acres on Cook's Creek, at Herring Ford—a few miles further south, and nearer Jeremiah and Daniel Harrison—and here erected his permanent home. He, however, retained possession of his Linville Creek land, and it was on this that he established his son, Leonard, upon the young man's marriage to Abigial, the daughter of the founder of Harrisonburg. Leonard was a brother of the fair Bathsheba Herring, who a little later became the young wife of Capt. Abraham Lincoln.

Out of the Harrison-Herring Linville Creek land agreement grew the litigation of 1764, "Samuel Harrison vs. Alexander Herron"—referred to at the beginning of this work—identifying Samuel, and further furnishing the interesting testimony that both contestants had removed from the same Province, thus completing the identification of both the Harrison and Herring families as having come in from Delaware. The leaving of the name of the Province blank in the testimony was probably due to the fact that the government of Delaware was under the jurisdiction of the Governor of Pennsylvania, thus the court was likely placed in a quandry as to whether or not Delaware could be legally termed a Province. Aside from the records, family tradition, according to Chrisman, states that Herring removed to the Valley from Delaware. The tradition though errs in naming the county as New Castle. Neither the Harrisons nor Herrings were landowners in this county, while on the other hand they were such in Sussex.

* * * * * *

(18) JEREMIAH HARRISON, (1707 c-1777 c), born at Smithtown, Long Island, New York, the son of Isaiah Harrison, (1), the immigrant, and his second wife Abigail, on October 10th, 1732, was deeded by his father 250 acres of land in Sussex, Delaware, as his share of Maiden Plantation. On the 7th of June, 1737, Jeremiah con-

veyed this land, by deed of bargain and sale, to Samuel Black, and at about the same time, in the little party of sixteen—including his brothers John, Daniel Thomas, and Samuel —set out for the country on the Shenandoah. (See, pages 47, 58, 120, 123.)

Various references to him having been made in previous Chapters, in connection with the family in general, and with the first three of these brothers in particular, these may be briefly summarized as follows: His appointment August 22, 1745, by Orange court as constable, vice Thomas Stewart, discharged, was followed by the recording of his bond, at the same court, September 26th, 1745, insuring that Robert Leaper would keep the peace towards James Patton, Gent. On December 10th, 1745, he was appointed by the first court of Augusta as an appraiser, along with Thomas Harrison, Wm. Williams, and Hugh Douglass, of the estate of John Levenson, deceased, and on June 20th, 1746, along with Thomas Harrison, and Alexander Herron, was next appointed a road overseer, in which capacity he served until August 20th, 1747. On May 18th, 1748, his bond as surety for Isaiah Harrison (Jr.), as administrator of Joseph Harrison, deceased, was recorded, following which his sale of the goods of Joseph at the house of Samuel Stewart occurred, September 1st, 1750. (See pages 127, 221, 7, 154, and 147.)

That his home, mentioned as the "Half-Way House," by the Rev. John Craig, in his journal, was in the region to the west of his brother Thomas, is shown by his signature appearing on the road petition of the "Inhabitants of North Mountain, at head of Muddy Creek," 1753 or 4, and by the inclusion of his name as a landowner in the processioners' list of John Harrison and Daniel Smith, 1756, and of John Hopkins and David Ralston, 1760. His house is thought to have stood at or near the present juncture of the Raleigh Springs Turnpike with the road to New Erection and Mt. Clinton, or about half way between the Muddy Creek community and Harrisonburg. (See, pages 201, 182, 209, and 128.)

In comparison with his brothers, Jeremiah appears to have been somewhat slow in making his permanent settlement. It seems he may have investigated the possibilities for locating in the lower Valley before making his final decision. He evidently camped for a time, probably with his brother Samuel at the spring at present Linville and thereafter lived at the home of one of his brothers until his land entries were in the course of completion. His first survey is dated November 13, 1740, and his first land entry on the Augusta court records, December 7th, 1745; "100 acres on the south side of Cooks Creek, joining Robert Cravens." His first patent was granted 10th February, 1748. (See page 127.) In all he patented some 1,023 acres, in five tracts, as given below—

To JEREMIAH HARRISON

Date	Acres	Location	Book No.	Page
10th. Feb., 1748,	370	"on the drafts of Cooks and Linvilles Creek."	27	108.
16th. Aug., 1756,	245	"on the south side of Linvilles Creek, adjoining land of Abraham Hill's."	34-1	131.
10th. Aug., 1759,	18	"at the Great Spring on the Head of the South Branch of Linvilles Creek"	34-1	385.
2nd. June, 1760,	120	"on the East draft of Cooks creek"	34-1	476.
2nd. June, 1760,	270	"on the Head of the South Branch of Linvilles Creek."	34-1	477.
TOTAL	1,023	acres.		

(See, Land Patent Books, as above, at Richmond, Va.)

Besides the lands embraced in these patents, Jeremiah acquired by purchase other tracts, as disclosed in the following deeds to him: 21st November, 1755, from John Harrison (Jr.), yeoman, for 38 Pounds, 272 acres on Crabb's (Cooks ?) Creek, corner John Hopes, one line presumed to interfere with Robert Cravens; 31st December 1760, from the same, for 150 Pounds, 400 acres in Linville's Creek, part of 1200, etc., adjoining John Wright and David Ralston; 31st December, 1760, from Rebecca, wife of Abraham Hite, "Ditto"; 19th November 1764, from Thomas and Sarah Harrison, for ——— Pounds, 212 acres on the Dry Fork of Smiths Creek—this last may refer to Jeremiah Harrison, son of Thomas. (See, Deed Books, 7, p. 265; 9, p. 115; 11, pp. 102 and 752.)

Of these tracts, the 18 acres patented in 1759, (corner Samuel Stewart), were conveyed by Jeremiah Harrison, and Catherine (), to Samuel Semple, for 22 Pounds, by deed 17th, February,1761. Also the same day, for 95 Pounds, Jeremiah and Catherine deeded to John Stewart the 272 acres on Crabb's Creek purchased in 1755. Likewise, on the next day, the 120 acres patented in 1760, (corner Robert Cravens), was deeded to Thomas Harrison, for 20 Pounds—this being a tract later included in Thomas' 1773 patent to his land at Harrisonburg. Also, on the 15th, October, 1765, for 276 Pounds, 10 shillings, Jeremiah and Catherine deeded the 400 acres on Linville's Creek purchased of John Harrison, Jr., in 1760, to "John Hinton of County of Berks, Province Pennsylvania." (See, Deed Books; 9, pp. 129, 151, and 217; and 12 p. 304.)

With these transactions over, Jeremiah was the owner of about 1,300 acres on Linville's Creek and the head-waters thereof. His home plantation—the tract first patented—lay on the watershed between Linville's and Cook's Creeks, in the locality already noticed.

Catherine Harrison, as named in the deeds above, was the wife of Jeremiah—Court Order Book X, page 8; 16th, October, 1765, "Catherine, wife of Jeremiah Harrison, commission for private examination," this being in regard to her releasing dower to the land sold Hinton. On the second Sabbath of May, 1757, the day of the third communion held by the Smiths and Linville's Creek Baptist Church, "Catherine Harrison the wife of Jeremiah Harrison . . . . . submitted to the Order of the Gospel, and was baptized and received a member of the church." (See page 177.) Sometime during the Rev. Craig's pastorate of the Old Stone Church, (1740-1749), Jeremiah, and two of his children, Lydia Donnell, and Nehemiah, had been baptized by the Rev. Craig, in the Presbyterian faith. (See page 151.) Later, on the last Sabbath of August, 1761, Jeremiah again submitted himself to baptism, this time in his wife's church, thus becoming a member with her in the congregation in which his half-brother John had been a laborer from the day of its organization. (See page 180.)

In 1772 Jeremiah and Catherine were yet among the living, but little else beyond this is gleaned from further records. He is mentioned as a surety for Grabiel Powell in an attachment filed by Esther Cobb, 13, November, 1768, as Powell was preparing to remove from the county, and on the 18th August, 1772, he and "Katherine" () signed a deed to Nehemiah and Josias (Josiah) Harrison, both evidently their sons. (County Court Judgements, and Deed Book 18, p. 327.) In addition to these sons, Jeremiah and Catherine appear to have had also a son Jeremiah, Jr., and probably a Benjamin. In the proceedings of the Harrison-Herring suit of 1762, on November 18th, a commission was appointed to take the depositions of "Jeremiah Harrison, Senior and Junior." (Order Book 7, p. 364.) A Jeremiah Harrison is mentioned as having been a settler for a short time around 1770, on land of the Loyal Company, known as Peach Bottom, in what was Grayson County, 1805. (Beavins vs. Newell, 27th

September, 1805; Circuit Court Causes Ended; *Chalkley*, Vol. II, p. 143.) Summers, in his *History of Southwest Virginia*, lists also a Jeremiah Harrison, under date of May 23rd, 1774, among the landowners named in the first surveys on the waters of the Holston and Clinch rivers. (*Sommers* p. 812.) According to the Preston Register, a Benjamin Harrison was killed by the Indians on the Holston River, in October, 1754. (*Supra*, p. 58.)

With the formation of Rockingham County, the Augusta pioneer's land passed under the jurisdiction of Rockingham, and owing to the destruction of so large a part of this county's early records, the details of the final disposition of the lands, whether by will, or otherwise, or the date of his, or of his wife's death is unknown. Both likely spent their last days on the old home plantation.

Briefly, as given above, Jeremiah Harrison (18), and wife Catherine, had issue—

(181) LYDIA DONNELL—b. 1732 c; d. 1780 c ;m. Reuben Harrison (125), son of John Harrison, Sr.
See further record.

(182) NEHEMIAH—
See further reference.

(183) JOSIAH—
See further reference.

(184) JEREMIAH—May have removed to the Holston River, about 1770.

And probably others, including, Benjamin, killed by the Indians, October, 1754, during the French and Indian War, and Hester, who m. Robert Cravens, Jr., (148.)

* * * * * *

(20) SAMUEL HARRISON, (1713 c.-1790 c.), the son of Isaiah Harrison, (1), and wife Abigail, like his brothers Thomas and Jeremiah, was born while his parents were yet residents of Smithtown, Long Island. Of the seven sons of the immigrant, Samuel was manifestly the youngest, and likely the youngest of his ten children. That he was under age when his father divided Maiden Plantation among his (other) sons in Delaware by his second wife, is indicated by a fourth share being reserved at the time, and later sold, in 1736, to Robert Frame.

Upon Samuel's removal with his brothers to the country west of the Massanutten, he stopped on Linville Creek, spending his camping days, as inferred from the old tradition, at the "Great Spring," now Krotzer's, near present Linville, probably in company with his brother Jeremiah. In this vicinity he located the greater part of his land, and finally made his settlement.

One of the first surveys on the creek was made by the early Hite firm, and possibly the Harrisons were attracted thither by some of the glowing accounts sent out by this enterprising organization. According to a deed to Robert Cravens, in 1746, for land on the north side of Linville's Creek, the said land was a part of 7,009 acres patented to this firm, 26th March, 1739. (See page 258.) On the same date a patent was granted the same firm for 1,264 acres, on the waters of Cook's, Linville's, and Naked Creeks. (See page 197.) (This last may have been included in the 7,000 however.) The surveys having been made previous to the granting of the patent, the land was doubtless explored several years earlier.

Associated with Hite, in this historic company, were Robert McKay, William Duff, and Robert Green. Green was a member of an old Culpeper family, and in 1742 was one of the justices of Orange court, and like Col. James Wood, the County Surveyor, became early interested in Valley lands. In some manner he became acquainted with Samuel Harrison, and evidently made some sort of a deal with him, probably in regard to land, the outcome of which was the suit entered 30th June, 1744, "Robert Green, Gent vs. Samuel Harrison," calling for Samuel's first appearance at Orange court. The sheriff, however, owing to sickness, could not execute the summons, and the case was continued until the next court, apparently coming up again 23rd November, 1744, at which time the sheriff again reported the summons "not executed." whereupon another continuation was granted .(See page 127.) Winter passed, and on March 30th, 1745, the case came up once more, with the same result. Finally, on the 28th June, 1745, the defendant at last having been summonsed, "was Solemnly Called but came not, therefore on the motion of the said Lewis (Green's attorney) it is ordered that unless he appears at next court and answers the plantiffs action Judgement shall then be entered for the Plantiff against him the said Defendant and Daniel Harrison his security for the Debt in the Declaration mentioned and costs.—Present Robert Green, Gent." (Orange Court Order Book, 1743-1746, pp. 306, and 377.)

The above is an interesting illustration of the inconvenient location of Orange court with respect to the settlers beyond the Blue Ridge. Apparently the case came up no more, and probably a settlement was made out of court.

On the 25th September, 1746, within a year following the establishment of the court of Augusta, Samuel was granted his first patent. His first survey is dated November 14, 1740. In all he was granted three patents, totaling 845 acres, as follows—

To SAMUEL HARRISON

Date	Acres	Location	Book No.	Page
25th. Sept., 1746	200	"on a branch of Cooks Creek"	24	421.
5th. Sept., 1749	400	"on the South Branch of Linvilles Creek."	31	25.
16th. Aug., 1756	245	"on the N. W. side of the South Branch of Linvilles Creek."	34	131.
TOTAL	845			

(See, Patent Books, as above, at Richmond, Va.)

Among Harrison's first neighbors were Daniel Love, John Wright, David Stewart, and Jacob Chrisman. In March 1747, the processioners, Daniel Harrison and Morgan Bryan, in making their returns, noted Daniel Love and John Wright present as they viewed Samuel Harrison's lines, and David Stewart and Samuel Harrison present as they viewed Chrisman's lines. (See page 163.)

An old sandstone marker in memory of George Chrisman, still standing in the churchyard burial ground of New Erection Church, Presbyterian, a few miles south of Linville, bears the interesting inscription—"George Chrisman, son of Jacob Chrisman, a native of Swabia in Germany who emigrated to Virginia about 1740. He died August 29, 1816, Aged 71 years." Hard by, stands a similar marker to "Hannah Chrisman, wife of George Chrisman, died January 24, 1817, aged 70 years."

Samuel did not long retain possession of his Cook's Creek land, and it appears doubtful that he ever made other than a temporary settlement on it. On the 20th, August, 1748, "Samuel Harrison and Mary his wife," deeded this land to John Wright, "witness—Daniel Harrison and Samuel Newman." (Deed Book 2, p. 144.) In 1751 Wright conveyed the same to John Cravens, as stated elsewhere. (See, page 260.)

Rockingham Co. Va.
Samuel Hill 1748 Augusta Co, Va

Samuel's next conveyance is found under date, 17th May, 1751—"Samuel Harrison and Mary to Alexander Herron, 265 acres on Linvilles Creek, part of 400 acres patented to Samuel, 5th Sept., 1749." (Deed Book 3, p. 318.)

Just before, and between, the time of these deeds occurred some minor litigation, "Samuel Hill and Ann his wife vs. Samuel Harrison," the writ being dated 20th March, 1748, and judgement rendered at the May term of court, 1749. (County Court Judgements; *Chalkley,* Vol. I, p. 301.) As the subject of dispute was probably a bond this may in a way explain Samuel's first conveyance.

Samuel was among those whom the Rev. Craig called "of the richer sort," who removed to the South with their families during the dark days of the French and Indian War. (See page 203.) At the time his second tract of land on Linville's Creek was evidently in the course of being patented. The patent was granted the following year, notwithstanding his absence, with probably one of his kinsman acting as his agent in completing the formalities. According to the testimony in the proceedings, "George Parks vs. Samuel Harrison," 14th March, 1755, Samuel was then "removing himself from the County." (Judgements at Rules, May, 1755, C; *Chalkley,* Vol. I, p. 312.) His removal thus occured several months prior to Braddock's defeat, and the general exodus thereafter.

That the indignation of the court, however, was directed to include those who fled before, as well as after, is indicated pointedly by his being returned "runaway," in the delinquent tax lists of 1755. (See, *Chalkley,* Vol. II, p. 416.)

On the 18th October, 1762, Samuel Harrison and Mary (), of Craven County, South Carolina, deeded to William Minter, millright, for 125 Pounds, the 245 acres "on the South Branch of Linvilles Creek," patented 16th August, 1756. (Deed Book 11, p. 79; also North Carolina Historical and Genealogical Register.) Minter in 1767 conveyed this land to John Currey "by deed recorded in Amherst" (Walter Crow's land), and by 1784 it was in the possession of Col. Benjamin Harrison, son of Daniel. (McWilliams vs. Hollingshead, 1803; *Chalkley,* Vol. II, pp. 46-7.)

Shortly following their sale of this land, Samuel and Mary returned to Augusta to resume their residence, and by November 18th, 1762, Samuel had instituted his interesting suit vs. Alexander Herron. (See page 8.) This case dragged along in the court for two years or more, being recorded partly in March 1764, and further in November of the same year.

"Only the answer," says Judge Chalkley, [appears] "in the papers, but that shows that complainent, Samuel Harrison, came to Augusta from the Colony of ————, Defendant, Alexander Herron, came from the same place. Harrison came first and settled on Linville's Creek. About the time of Braddock's defeat Harrison went to Carolina. Robert Harrison was nephew of Samuel." (Vol. I. p. 340, County Court Judgements.)

In passing, it may be observed that not only Daniel Harrison, but his brother, Thomas, too, had a son Robert, thus, regardless of which Robert was referred to, Samuel was his uncle.

Upon Samuel's return to Augusta, he having sold previously the lands patented in 1746, and 1756, and 265 acres of the 1749 patent, apparently owned only the 135 acres remaining of this last. On the 9th April, 1764, for 100 Pounds, he deeded "100 acres on the South Branch of Linvilles Creek patented 5th Sept., 1749." to Daniel Smith; witness—Walter Crow, Peter Kinder, Felix Sheltman, and Joseph Rutherford. (Deed Book 11, p. 647.)

Mary Harrison, the wife of Samuel, had probably died by this time, her name being missing from the deed. Following this date further trace of Samuel, owing to the loss of the records, is involved in conjecture. Whether or not he and Mary left any children is unknown.

A curious reference to a Samuel Harrison occurs on the records of Frederick County (at Winchester),—"5th March, 1767; Samuel Harrison (Harison) vs. John King—This day came as well the plaintiff by his attorney as the said defendant in his own Proper Person who sayeth that he cannot gainsay but that he doth owe 2814 pounds tobacco to the plaintiff. It is therefore considered by the court that the said plaintiff recover against the said defendant his damages as aforesaid, in form aforesaid, confessed, and his costs by him about the suit, in the behalf expended and the said defendant in money &c and the Plaintiff Residing out of the colony (meaning county?) Francis Dale undertakes to pay the cost and charges of the suit." (Order Book 13, p. 309.)

On March 1st, 1773, a patent was granted by Lord Dunmore,
To MARY ANN HARRISON, ELIZABETH HARRISON, and MARY HARRISON, for—965 acres of land in Augusta County, "on North River of Shenandoah." (See, Patent Book 40-1, p. 185, at Richmond, Va.)

These women evidently belonged to the Rockingham Harrisons, and may have been the daughters of either Jeremiah or Samuel, the pioneers.

One, Samuel Harrison, according to the Minute Book of Rockingham County, —Court Order Book I,—on April 29th, 1783, was granted a "certificate of good character and Wiggish principles" on leaving the county, and on the same date Ezekiel, Reuben, and Isaiah Harrison, were granted an order regarding their "going to Georgia. (*Chalkley*, Vol. II, p. 369, —Order Book now at Richmond, Va.)

II.

ALEXANDER HERRON, (HERRING), (1708 c-1778), the Augusta County pioneer, and the progenitor of the Rockingham line of Alexander Herrings, was the only son of Alexander Herron, Sr. (died about 1735), and wife Margaret, of Sussex County Delaware. Will, 19th September, 1735, (abstract)—

"Alexander Herring of Sussex County, sick: To loving son Alexander Herring, house and 189 acres. To loving wife Margaret Herring one feather bed and furniture. To loving daughter Eady Herring beds and furniture when 16 years of age. To my daughter Esther Wood one shilling. To my daughter Sarah Prettyman one shilling.
Witness: John ( ) Mariner, John Russell, his
Elizabeth ( ) Mariner. (Signed) Alexand X Herring (SEAL).
mark

(See, Sussex Co., Del. Wills, A No. 1, pp. 288-9.)

(19) ABIGAIL HARRISON, (1710 c-1780 c), the daughter of Isaiah Harrison (1), and 2nd wife Abigial, and the wife of Alexander Herron, the pioneer, was one of the younger children born to her parents at Smithtown, Long Island. Following her removal with the family to Sussex, Delaware, in 1721, she and Alexander were married during their residence in this county, and several years prior to their migration to Virginia.

Abigail's identity as a Harrison has been preserved by her descendants, through the generations from her day to the present. Says the late Daniel S. Harrison, in a brief sketch of the early Herrings of Rockingham, in speaking of the pioneer ancestor; "I want to say in the first place that Alexander Herron, and Alexander Herring, are undoubtedly the same, and Capt. John A. Herring very positively claims that his (Alexander's) wife was a Harrison, of the same line as the Dayton Harrisons . . . . .This history that I am going to give, I procured from Major Chrisman, partially verified from the records here (Harrisonburg), and at Staunton, and by old deeds and grants, in the possession of Capt. John A. Herring. All the Herrings of Rockingham County are descendents of this Alexander Herron." (Letter, April 29, 1913, *pens me.)*

* * * * * *

The immigrant Herring, according to the tradition given in the *Memoirs of Lincoln,* (by the Major's brother), was an English gentleman's son (one version has it, the son of Lord Benjamin Herron), "born in Norfolk County England, not far from the beginning of the eighteenth century. His family had been settled for many centuries in that county and still clings to its coat of arms in its old home on that side . This coat of arms, of which a copy has been imported as a memento to this side, purports on the face of it to have been granted to a certain Lord Vi. Compte of the family name, a title of no great dignity and long since lapsed, and recites that he was of that 'ancient family' and bearing date of 1374. One of the emblems that appear on this coat of arms is the picture of a boar's head in allusion to a well-remembered contest between two brothers of this house and a famous wild boar in which the savage beast killed one brother and the other brother killed the boar." (The name, Benjamin Herron, given by D. S. H., as per Major Chrisman.)

The arms alluded to are undoubtedly the following: "Az. semeé of crosslets, three herrings ar. Crest—A boar's head couped in fesse, pierced through the snout with four arrows ppr.", these being the only arms listed by Burke, for Herring, mentioning a boar. The time and other circumstances of the story, however, refer evidently to a Heron family descent.

The name Alexander Herron, (Heron, Herron, Herrin, Herring, as variously spelled on the court records), was of early origin in eastern England, and Scotland. The oldest spelling of the name appears to be "Heron", as used by Burns, in his poem on "Mr. Heron's Election, 1795." In the land patents granted to Alexander, of Virginia, this spelling is also used, but on the early records of Augusta the usual spelling is Herron. Sir William Dugdale, in his *The Baronage of England,* printed in London, in 1675, (Tome I, page 730), states that William Heron, a baron, held the lordship of the Castle of Pickering, in "com. Ebor.", and was Sheriff of Northumberland, in "40 Henry III," (1256). His son, William, died at Newcastle-upon-Tyne in 25 Edward I, (1297.) A younger son, "out of doubt," was Roger Hairon, Governor of the Castle of Barnsbury, 10 Edward II, to whom succeeded William, who in 12 Edward III, obtained a license to make a castle of his house in Northumberland. In 14 Edward III, he obtained a charter for Free Warren in all his lordships of Ford (Ford Castle) . . . etc., and Heron in Northumberland. William was succeeded by his son William, who in 44 Edward III, (1371), was summonsed to Parliament among the barons of Scotland. He was succeeded by another William Heron, who was summonsed to Parliament in 17 Richard II, (1393), and until 5 Henry IV, (1404), inclusive.

Burke describes the arms for the first and last two Williams, as; "Gu. a chev. between three herons or", *(General Armory,* 1883), and for the first William, a Crest, "A heron as in the arms." James Yorke, "Blacksmith," in his *The Union of Honor,* London, 1640, sketches the "Herron" arms as, "Sable a cheveron Ermine, between 3 Herrons Or." (Page 36.)

An order of the second year of Queen Elizabeth, (1561), in regard to fortifying the borders of England, includes a schedule of the names of all "Lords, Freeholders, Tenaunts, and Inhabitants" within the county of Northumberland, "who have consented and agreed to the execution of the Articles contayned in this Book" . . . . . among whom appear as subscribers, William Herrings, (his mark), Alex. Heron, of Corbrick, (his mark), Henry Heron, John Heron, Wm. Heron, (his mark), Alex. Heron, (his mark), Jarrett Heron, (his mark), etc. (See, *History and Antiquities of North Durham,* 1832, by J. Raine, p. xxxi.)

From England the name was carried to the Province of Ulster, in Ireland. Myers, in his work elsewhere referred to, notes an "Alexander heron," as a witness to the will of John Marsh, of County Armagh, 1688. (p. 409.)

About eighteen or twenty years following young Alexander Herron's settlement in Augusta, one, Thomas Herron, immigrated from Ulster and settled in the Linville Creek region of later Rockingham. His half-brother, William, followed him, and was the Linville Creek schoolmaster of 1784-1792. William was drowned about 1803, while attempting to cross the North River, and until his death made his home with Thomas, who administered. Some small time after William's demise his full-sister, Jane, and her husband, Alexander Campbell, arrived from Ireland, and proceed to bring suit against Thomas, the bill being dated 20th, May, 1804—"Alexander Campbell and Jane his wife, of Rockingham, vs. Herring"—and the testimony disclosing that these parties were all from Ireland, and that all were the children of a William Herring, a "Minister of the Gospel," who had twice married, and who had died there, and that Thomas had "left Ireland about forty years ago." Aside from these Herrings, a Samuel Herring is mentioned as an appraiser on the Augusta records, May 22nd, 1755, but whether or not he was direct from Ireland is not known. (See, Judgements Circuit Causes Ended, and Order Book 14, p. 429; *Chalkley,* Vol. II, p. 144, Vol. I, p. 67.)

Campbell from Ireland

* * * * * *

On the 4th November, 1719, Edward Bran, of Sussex County, Delaware, weaver, "made over Acknowledged Conveyed and Confirmed unto Alexander Herron of The same County, yeoman," 189 acres of land on the south side of "Ivory Branch proceeding from Rehobeth Bay." (See page 55.) This was the land later willed to Alexander, the Augusta pioneer, by the will above.

That the immigrant was of the Episcopal faith is indicated by his name—"Alexr Herring"—appearing opposite his subscription of £1-0-0, on 25th March, 1732, among the subscribers at Lewes, of Indian River Hundred, "to Buy the Rev. Wm. Becket a farm," or glebe. Others subscribing were, Thomas Davis, Sr., Thomas Davis, Jr., and Nehemiah Davis, of Cedar Creek Hundred. The Rev. Becket died in 1743. (See, *Some Records of Sussex County, Delaware,* by C. H. B. Turner, p. 217.)

Continuing the tradition in regard to the first Alexander, (erroneously confused with his son), this goes on to say that his parents having died when he was a boy his aunt became his guardian, and sent him to a boarding school, where "he became disgusted with his idle and precarious kind of life, for the discipline was harsh enough, and incontinently ran away and hired himself to a shipmaster who was about to sail for the colonies, to work his passage over, ... When he came of age it is presumed he realized his means in England, for he married a wife about this time and bought a farm near New Castle (Lewes), Delaware, and lived on it while his four children, three boys and one girl, were being born." *(Memiors,* p. 8.)

Alexander, of Augusta, it will be observed, was of age in 1735, when his father made his will, thus the elder was manifestly married some time before buying his land of Bran. The number of children is as in the will, only there were three girls and one boy, instead of the other way around. The Augusta settler had more than three sons, as will appear anon. There is evidence from the will that the signer was of limited schooling, but his signature was made while he was sick, and is thus not wholly conclusive of his training with the quill.

Game is said to have been the great inducement that determined young Alexander to cast his lot with the settlers on the Shenandoah. Being a lover of the chase, and finding his opportunities for hunting growing limited in the coast country, owing to the spread of the settlements, "and hearing that game was plentiful in the Valley of Virginia he sold his possessions" in Delaware, and started with his family "up the Shenanadoah." So, in substance, runs the legend. His migration occurred about the spring of 1742.

On the 5th May, 1742, for "forty Pounds Current Lawful Money of America," he conveyed to Peter Dale, of Sussex, the 189 acres inherited through the will above —"which sd land by Deed of Sale bearing date fourth day of November In the year of our Lord One thousand Seven hundred & nineteen made over and conveyed unto a certain Alexander Herring late of the County deceased father to the above named Alexander Herring by a certain Edward Bran late of the County aforesaid." (See page 65.)

"And when he got to where the forest was dense enough to suit his taste and log cabins far enough apart not to crowd and jostle much, he came to a halt and began to look about for some land to buy." *(Memoirs,* p. 8.)

About this time, judging from the account later given in his testimony of 1764, he ran across his brother-in-law, Samuel Harrison, and Samuel thereupon undertook to provide him with the land. It took time, however, to institute and complete patent formalities; he discovered that the court was on the wrong side of the mountain, and further, that the land office at Williamsburg was most as far away as Delaware. But in the meantime plenty of unclaimed land was in sight, so evidently depending on Samuel, he decided to wait until the new court was established, and some roads were laid out. Court finally being organized in the winter of 1745, in the spring following, he is found being appointed, along with Thomas and Jeremiah Harrison, one of the county's first road overseers—"from the Court House to the Indian Road," a part of today's "Long Grey Trail." (See page 7.)

Finally, probably becoming impatient with the delays incident to the surveys, and the granting of his chosen land on Linville's Creek, he determined to buy some land already patented. Among the road overseers, who had succeeded him and his brothers-in-law in 1747, was Samuel Wilkins, who was somewhat experienced in land values, and who, moreover, had a tract to sell near his (Alexander's) brother-in-law, Daniel Harrison.—"Deed, 1st March, 1749, Samuel Wilkins and Sarah to Alexander Herrin, 365 acres on Cooks Creek, corner Daniel Harris(on), dower released by Sarah, wife of Samuel, 23rd May, 1750." This land was later 'delivered,' January, 1754, to Benjamin Kinley. (Deed Book 2, p. 589.)

Next followed his deed from Samuel Harrison, 17 May, 1751, for 265 acres on Linville's Creek, part of Samuel's 400 acres patented in 1749. This tract upon Alexander's death descended to his son Leonard—see presently.

In the fall of 1751, Alexander was appointed, with Robert Cravens, another of his brothers-in-law, and Michael Warren, to view the improvements made by John Harrison, brother of Samuel, on his Dry Fork of Smiths Creek land. (See page 260.)

In all this while he appears to have been living on the land first promised him by Samuel, holding it by a mere "tomahawk right," or first claim, from the fact of first and continued residence thereon. In 1755 he was finally granted the land promised him. Thereafter, so far as has been found, he only patented three small tracts, and these mostly to round out larger ones. In all, he and his son, Leonard, prior to the formation of Rockingham, were granted 674 acres, as follows—

To ALEXANDER HERRING

Date	Acres	Location	Book No.	Page
10th. Sept, 1755. (To Alexander Herrings)	200	"on the South Branch of Linvilles Creek adjoining land of Samuel Harrison."	31	680.
10th. Sept., 1755	200	"on the South Branch (Fork) of Linvilles Creek adjoining land of Samuel Harrison."	XI	853.
10th. Oct., 1757	60	"on the west branch of Cooks Creek."	See below.	
30th. Aug., 1763 (To Alex Heron.)	38	"On the East Fork of Linvilles Creek between David Ralston and Samuel Harrison's and running on one line of Hite's land."	35-1	423.
30th. Aug., 1763 (To Alexr. Heron)	88	"on the west side of Cooks Creek adjoining Edward's line and Daniel Harrison's line."	35-1	424.
		(Survey entered in Secretary's office 9th., April, 1763.)	See below.	
TOTAL	586			

TO LEONARD HERRING

Date	Acres	Location	Book No.	Page
Feb., 1781	88	"on drafts of So. Br. Linvilles creek."	Note	

(See, Patent Books, Nos. as above, except Roman numeral, etc., at Land Office, Richmond,Va.; Roman numeral refers to Augusta County Deed Book; Note, to certificate in McWilliams vs. Hollingshead, 1803, as page 274.)

The first two patents above embraced the 400 acres of Harrison land mentioned in Herring's testimony of 1764. (See page 8.) One of these tracts apparently descended to Leonard Herring, at the death of his father, and the other Alexander sold, in 1765, to Walter Crow, who seems to have combined it with another tract originally Samuel Harrison's; Deed 22nd, March, 1765, "Alexander Heron and Abigail, to Walter Crow, for 25 Pounds, 200 acres on South Fork Linville's Creek, corner Samuel Harrison's land." (Deed Book 11, p. 853; and account of Samuel above.)

The remaining "38 acres on East Fork of Linvilles Creek"—"between David Ralstone's and Samuel Harrison's land."—was deeded the same day by Alexander and Abigail to Samuel Semple, for 5 Pounds. (*Ibid*, p. 851.)

Herring's land on the creek was processioned in 1756, by John Harrison, Jr., and Daniel Smith. In 1760, John Hopkins and David Ralston, in their returns included Alexander's name among others of the Cook's Creek region, as did also Robert Cravens, Jr., and Jeremiah Harrison (son of Thomas), in 1768. (See pages 182, 209, and 225.)

On the 15th of July, the year of the first procession, "Alexander Herron qualified Lieutenant." (Order Book 5, p. 188; *Chalkley*, Vol. I, p. 73.) His services were with the militia—Washington at the time was stationed at Winchester. (See page 205.)

By far the greater part of Alexander's domain was gradually acquired by him on the West Fork of Cooks Creek, (somewhat below Daniel Harrison), "these lands won his heart," and on the plantation thus acquired he finally "made it home." A large part of this land was obtained from his early friend Samuel Wilkins, from whom he had bought his first tract. According to the first Surveyor's Book of Rockingham County—23rd January, 1769,—

"Surveyed for Alexander Herron, seven hundred and fifty acres of land, lying on the west branch of Cook's Creek. Four hundred and ninety eight acres part thereof being part of a larger tract of land containing twelve hundred acres granted by patent to Robert McKay and others the twenty sixth of March Seventeen hundred and thirty nine and by them transferred to Samuel Wilkins, who at sundry times conveyed the said four hundred and ninety eight acres to the aforesaid Herron. Also sixty acres granted to the aforesaid Herron by patent dated the tenth day of October Seventeen hundred and fifty seven; and eighty eight acres surveyed and entered in the Secretary's office the ninth of April Seventeen hundred and sixty three. The remaining one hundred and four acres unpatented land." (Book O, Part I, p. 129.)

Alexander is said to have owned 1,100 acres extending down both sides of the West Branch of Cook's Creek for a mile or two. (*Memoirs*, p. 9.) In 1762 he acquired 190 acres, "near the head of Cooks Creek," which had formerly been sold by Wilkins to Daniel Harrison. (See page 197.) Part of the original 1200 acres (1264 acres), patented to McKay et al.,was located on Naked Creek, and Alexander also acquired a part of this—Deed, 30th October, 1766, "John Wilkins of Mecklenburg county, North Carolina, to Alexander Herron, for 80 Pounds, 400 acres on Naked Creek, part of 1264 patented McKay, Hite, & Co., and surveyed to Samuel Wilkins, deceased, father to the said John, Daniel Harrison's line." (Deed Book 13, p. 129; also page 138, *this volume.*)

Jas Wood founder of Winchester

Most, or all, of Herring's Wilkins land was originally surveyed by Col. James Wood, the founder of Winchester, he having made the 1264 acre survey for McKay, Hite, & Co., as well as a further survey, about 1745, of land later Herring's. This last survey included a tract which came to form the basis of the litigation, "Alexander Herron vs. Patrick Quinn, Ejectment," furnishing the testimony of 1767, regarding Daniel Harrison's age and illness, and John Craven's age, etc. (See page 144.) By the time of these depositions Daniel Wilkins was dead. An elaborate survey, and description, of the land in dispute, as made by Thomas Lewis, the first surveyor of Rockingham, is preserved among the papers yet extant. Some of the original Herring land on Cooks Creek is still in possesion of the family.

Alexander Herring, the pioneer, died about June, 1778. On the 22nd of this month—

> "The last will & Testament of Alex. Herring deceased was proved by the witnesses thereto & Ordered to be recorded whereupon Abigail Herring Alex. & Jesse Herring the Exrs. therein named having made Oath entered into Bond according to Law. Certificate is granted for obtaining a probate. Josiah Harrison, Jno. Smith son of Danl. John Hardman & Nehemiah Harrison or any three of them (are appointed to) appraise this estate." (Rockingham Court Order Book I, p. 22, at Richmond, Va.)

Owing to the destruction of the will books for the period, the details of his last wishes are unknown. Immediately preceeding this notation on the old Court Order Book, under the same date, and on the same page, appears the following—

> "Deed of Bargain & Sale from Leonard Herring to his brothers Alex Herring Wm. Herring Bethuel Herring & Jesse Herring was acknowledged by Sd Leonard & O (ordered) to be recorded."

The next year, 25th May, 1779, (page 39) is found—

"Ordered that Benj. Harrison & Henry Ewing Gents examine the Estate deed of Alexr. Herring decd."

Six months later, under date of 22nd November, 1779, (page 49), is noted—

"Admr. of the estate of Alex. Herren decd is granted to Leond Herren his eldest Bro he having ent. into Bond & made Oath according to Law. Nehemiah Harrison Josiah Harrison Benj. Harrison & James Magil or any three being sworn appraise this estate.

This last named Alexander, the brother of Leonard, was obviously not the signer of the will, as at the exact time of the proving of the will, he, Leonard's brother, was being deeded land. Moreover, an Alexander Herring was named as one of the executors of the will, and this executor entered into bond the day of the acknowledgement of the deed.

Leonard, while the eldest of the brothers, was not named as an executor in the will. According to the *Memoirs*, the pioneer died without a will, and his property descended to the eldest son, who sold his rights to his brothers, etc. (Page 10.) Leonard doubtless sold some of his rights by the 1778 "Estate deed," but his father left a will. This however, was apparently broken, explaining a further deed made by Leonard in 1800, as follows—

"This INDENTURE made the sixteenth day of October in the year of our Lord one thousand eight hundred between Leonard Herring & Abigail his wife of the County of Rockingham and State of Virginia of the one part and Jacob Peary of the county & State aforesaid of the other part

WITNESSETH that the said Leonard Herring and Abigail his wife for and in consideration of the sum of four hundred pounds current money of Virginia in hand paid by the said Jacob Peary hath granted bargained and sold unto the said Jacob Peary one certain tract or parcel of land containing one hundred and twelve acres and 3/4 of an acres be the same more — less lying and being in the County of Rockingham on a branch of Linville Creek joining the lands of Walter Crow, Abraham Peary &c.

The same being part of two tracts the first containing 400 acres granted unto Samuel Harrison by Pattent dated the 5th day of December 1749 and afterward 265 acres of said tract was conveyed by said Samuel Harrison and Mary his wife to Alexander —ring by a Deed of bargain & sale dated the 17 day of May 1751 which will appear by the record of the County Court of Augusta reference thereto being had the said Alexander Herring d. . .ing intestate his son Leonard being his heir at law the said Tract was transfer. . .ed to him which will appear by the records of the county court of Augusta aforesaid, the other tract containing 88 acres was granted unto Leonard Herring by survey bearing date the 15 day of April 1780 and Bounded as follows to wit

Beginning at a large Hickory in a line . . . . .etc.

In witness whereof the said Leonard Herring & Abigail his wife have here unto set their hands & Seal the day and year first above written.

Signed Sealed & Delivered
In the presence of
Gordan McWilliams
John Sefferens.

Leonard Herring (SEAL).
her
Abigail X Herring (SEAL).
mark

At a court held for the County of Rockingham the 21st day of October, 1800.

This Deed of Bargain & Sale from Leonard Herring and Abigail his wife to Jacob Peary was acknowledged by the said Leonard and Abigail (she being first privately examined) and ordered to be recorded

A Copy Teste: S. Mc Williams, Clk.

Rerecorded from Original Deed under Act of Assembly approved Nov. 18, 1884.

Teste, C. H. Brunk, D. C.

(See, Burnt Deed Book No. 00—Page 429, Harrisonburg, Va.)

No record of a settlement of any Alexander Herring's estate, nor any record of any transfer of his land, at his death, to Leonard, appearing at Augusta court (Staunton), and the pioneer certainly dying after the establishment of Rockingham, as shown by the Surveyor's book, before quoted (see page 280), the writer of the deed obviously made a slip of the pen in his second reference to the records of Augusta, and may have done so also in using the word "intestate."

The breaking of the will may account for this last. Regardless of whether or not he died legally testate or intestate, the names of five of his sons, and of the eldest son's wife, the year of one of his son's death, and of his own death, are disclosed.

Besides these sons, Alexander, Sr. (the pioneer), seems to have had a son John, who died sometime prior to his father. A "John Heren" is named in the Augusta records as a witness 21st September, 1763. Also the case of John Heren vs. Wm. McGee is of record under date March 1764. (See, *Chalkley*, Vol. I, pp. 109 and 329.)

With the death of Alexander, Jr., four sons of the Augusta settler remained. Jesse Herring's will was proven 26th March, 1781, (Rockingham Court Order Book I; *Chalkley*, Vol. II, p. 367), thus leaving three. "Three boys and one girl" are the number mentioned in the *Memoirs*.

The girl, as named in these interesting reminiscenses, was an only daughter, Bathsheba. Her father, and the three brothers remaining after Jesse's death, are also named. Major Chrisman, a brother of the author, names in his account of the family the brothers, Leonard, John, William, and Bethuel, as the sons of the pioneer Herring, whom he erroneously calls John. (See also *Lea and Hutchinson*, p. 109.) Owing to the loss of Leonard's deed to his brothers, in addition to the will of his father, it appears doubtful that any court record will ever be found giving the name of Alexander Herring's daughter. (It is interesting to observe in this connection, that it was a detachment of Yankee soldiers who, in setting fire to Rockingham's records, destroyed the records of Mr. Lincoln's own ancestry.)

Much effort has been spent by various authors of repute in trying to identify Capt. Abraham Lincoln's wife. Lea and Hutchinson, in *The Ancestry of Abraham Lincoln*, Marion Dexter Learned, in his *Abraham Lincoln, An American Migration*, Waldo Lincoln, in his *History of the Lincoln Family*, and William E. Barton, in *The Lineage of Lincoln*, all the late works, agree, with little or no qualification, that she was Bathsheba Herring, of the Rockingham (Bridgewater—Dayton) family, but none have been able to go beyond Major Chrisman's assertion that she was the daughter of Leonard Herring, although Mr. Waldo Lincoln has pointed out some difficulties in this connection. No attempt, except in a causal way, incident to Capt. Lincoln's marriage, has been made, apparently, to identify Leonard Herring.

Leonard Herring was married in 1761, while Capt. Lincoln was married in 1770. No record at Staunton of any earlier marriage of either party appears. Leonard was born about 1735, and was a resident of Rockingham as late as 1805. The records of the marriage of a number of his children are at Harrisonburg, from which it is evident that they were of a later generation than Bathsheba, as in a number of instances he gave his own consent to these marriages.

Fortunately, through the generosity of Mr. William Herring Chrisman, in publishing his father's *Memoirs of Lincoln,* 1930, Bathsheba Herring's identity as a sister, not a daughter, of Leonard Herring, has been preserved. Mr. Chrisman not only identifies her as a sister of Leonard, but also as the daughter of Alexander Herring, the pioneer settler of Augusta, and further mentions her as an only daughter, thus barring her as a daughter of Leonard, or of any later Alexander.

Of the five sons left by the pioneer at his death, Alexander, who died in 1779, was evidently a widower. His daughter Abigail, in 1782, married Andrew Shanklin. His brother administered. In the "Clerk's Fee Book of Rockingham," under date of November, 1779, he is named as Alexander Herring, Jr.:

> "Nov. 1779: Leonard Herring Admr of Alexr Herring junr. Administration of Herrings Estate."

William and Bethuel Herring both married, and left families, including daughters, but no Bathsheba. Bethuel (Barthnell) Herring was appointed constable vice Robert Shanklin, August 17, 1773. (Order Book 4, p. 144, *Chalkley,* Vol. I, p. 173.) Jesse Herring died two years following his brother Alexander, and seems to have been unmarried. His brothers William and Bethuel administered. From the position of his name in the order regarding the estate deed, he appears to have been among the younger of the brothers.

Leonard Herring, the eldest son of Alexander, the pioneer, was old enough to furnish supplies to the militia in 1758. His wife, as noticed in an earlier Chapter, was his cousin, the daughter of the founder of Harrisonburg. Among their children were several daughters, as recorded in the marriage bonds referred to above. Leonard settled on one of the Samuel Harrison tracts purchased by his father, on Linville Creek. That he was residing in this neighborhood in 1781, is indicated by his patent of this year. (See pages 183 and 223.)

* * * * * *

John Lincoln, the Pennsylvania emigrant, frequently styled, "Virginia John," was born in Monmouth County, New Jersey, 3rd May, 1716, the son of Mordecai and Hannah (Salter) Lincoln, and, some time following Leonard Herring's marriage, migrated with his family from Berks County, Pennsylvania, to the Linville Creek community, where he settled. (See page 136.) His sister Ann, and her husband, William Tallman, (Taulman), also came in and settled in the same region at the same, or about the same, time. Among William Tallman's sons was one Benjamin, born in Pennsylvania, in 1745, who married there in 1764, Dinah Boone, a cousin of Daniel Boone. Daniel was a native of Berks County, Pennsylvania, and had come into the Linville Creek community in 1750. After tarrying a while on the creek he passed on to Yadkin in 1751, and later, following his explorations in what is now Kentucky, removed with his family from North Carolina to "the dark and bloody ground," in 1773. (See *Lea and Hutchinson,* pp. 76, and 176, and *Learned,* p. 122.)

Dinah Boone Daniel Boone Berks Co. Pa

Linville Creek is said to have taken its name from a member of an old "Linville" family of Lancaster County, Pennsylvania. One, "Lenivelle" took up land on the creek in 1746. *(Learned, p.* 122.) Thomas Linville, according to the Orange court order of 1743, was settled "above the Ridge" by this time. (See pages 126 and 220.)

The original Lincoln land was purchased by John Lincoln, 22nd June, 1768; "600 acres part of 1200 granted to McKay, Duff, Green, and Hite, by patent 26th March, 1739." This land, as disclosed in the proceedings, "Rymel and Ux vs. Lincoln," 1813, was conveyed by the above firm 20th June, 1746, to Robert McKay, and by him devised to his sons, Zacharia, Moses, Robert, and James, by will 7th October, 1746. The McKays in turn conveyed it to Lincoln. 210 Acres of this land were later conveyed by John Lincoln to his son Abraham (the Captain), by deed of gift, August 12th, 1773, and 200 acres more, part of his home plantation, were further devised by John to his son Thomas, by will, 8th February, 1786, recorded in Rockingham, 22nd June, 1789. (*Chalkley*, Vol. II, p. 232; and *Lincoln*, p. 193.)

The home plantation included a tract also devised by John to his widow Rebecca for her lifetime, and at her death to his daughter Rebecca Rymel. The bill for the above proceedings is dated 26th March, (1813), and recites, among other details, that John Lincoln died in November 1788, and that two year's later Thomas sold his share of the plantation to his brother Jacob. The latter's deed from Thomas and wife Elizabeth, is dated 20th September, 1791. Thomas removed to Kentucky about this time, or the following year.

The "widow Rebecca" (b. March 30th, 1720, dau. of Enoch and Rebecca Flowers), following her husband's death, "lived with her daughter Hannah Harrison." "At the time Jacob took possession she was 70 years old, and shortly before Hannah's death John (Rymel), and his wife, took her, 3rd August, 1803. She died 21st July, 1806. (Rymel vs. Lincoln, as above.)

John Lincoln's will, a copy of which was filed in the proceedings, names his wife Rebecca, and sons Thomas, Abraham, Isaac, Jacob, and John, and daughters, Hannah, Lydia, Sarah and Rebecca, and a granddaughter Hannah Bryan.

Lincoln Hist. mary ward

Of the sons—

Abraham, b. 13 May, 1744, in Berks Co., Pa., d. May, 1786-8, (Summer of 1785, says Lea), administration granted October 14, 1788, in Kentucky. (See later.)

Issac, b. March 5, 1750, Berks Co., Pa., d. June 10, 1816, at Watauga, Tenn. m. Mary Ward, b. 1758 c, d. August 27, 1834, at Watauga, Tenn.

Jacob, b. 18th November, 1751 (according to his tombstone), in Pa., d. 20th February, 1822, m. August 29, 1780, Dorcas Robinson, dau. of David and Dorcas Robinson, b. March 15th, 1763, d. January 25, 1840. Jacob and wife died near Linville. Their tombstones are yet standing in the old family burial ground.

John b. July 15th,, 1855, in Pa., d. July 13, 1835, at Lebanon, Ohio. Removed about 1819, with "most of his children" to Ohio. (on 27 June, 1810, he was residin Shelby County, Kentucky, near Hinton (Rymel vs. Lincoln) m., June 27, 1782 Mary his cousin, dau. of Francis and Mary Yarnell of Berks Co., Pa., b. 1760, d. May 27, 1832, at Lebanon, Ohio. (John and Mary were interred in the Baptist cemetery at Lebanon—tombstones yet standing.)

Thomas, b. October 23, 1761, d. 1819 c, near Lexington, Ky., m. September 23, 1782, Elizabeth Casner.

Of the daughters—

Hannah, b. March 9, 1748, married John Harrison, son of Zebulon, son of John, Sr., (12), half-brother of Alexander Herring's (the pioneer's) wife. She died near Linville, in Rockingham, and her will was proven in this county, December court, 1803. (See copy in later chapter.)

Lydia, twin sister of Hannah, was unmarried at the time of her father's will. Either she or her sister, Sarah, married a Byran, a kinsman of Ezekiel Harrison's wife. **(See page 233.)**

Greeneville Tn

Sarah, b. September 18, 1757, is said to have married a Deane.

Rebecca, b. April 18, 1767, d. September, 1840, near Greenville, Tenn., m. April 26, 1786, in Rockingham, John Rymel.

Among the subscribers to William Herron's school in 1790 were, Hannah Harrison, two scholars, James Henton, four scholars, Reuben Harrison, four scholars, and Josiah Harrison, one scholar, and in 1792, Jacob Lincoln, Soloman Mathews, Cornelius Bryan, Thomas Bryan, Thomas Bryan, Sr., David Caufman, George Chrisman, Dives (Davis ?) Bryan, John Bryan, and Michael Warren (See, Alexander Campbell vs. Herring; as above.)

John Lincoln, Jr., and his wife, and sister Hannah Harrison, were faithful members of the early Smiths and Linville's Creek Baptist Church. John was for many years the clerk of the church. (See pages 11, 233, and 236.) At a meeting the Saturday before the 3rd Sabbath in February, 1788, "at the House of Mr. Zebulon Harrison's," "Bro. John Lincoln was chosen Clerk," and delegated, along with "Brother Thomas," to transcribe the old church book into "one new covered Book."

"At a Church Meeting held at the House of Brother John Lincoln's on the Saturday before the 3rd. Sabbath in April 1788 . . . . then did our Brother Jno. Thomas and Jno. Lincoln in a Particular Manner inform the Church, then present, That they had performed the Business committed to their Charge at our last Church Meeting, viz. That of Transcribing our old Church Book &c. and declared that they had done it according to their Directions. Then a Door was opened to hear Experiances, and Mary Lincoln (the Wife of Jno. Lincoln) offered, and gave a short but very satisfactory Experiance to the Church, & was received unamimously without a dissenting Voice into the Fellowship of the Church." (The Old Church Book, pp. 24, and 25.)

Abraham Lincoln, the later Captain, son of "Virginia" John, and brother of John, of the above church, married, as stated, Bathsheba Herring. His marriage license was granted June 9, 1770. (*Chalkley,* Vol. II, p. 277.) Unfortunately the women's names were not entered in the records of the period. Early biographers of the President, beginning with Nicolay and Hay, have named Capt. Lincoln's wife as Mary Shipley, (the daughter of Robert and Sarah Shipley, of Lunenburg County, Virginia), from which the conclusion was reached by the authors of *The Ancestry of Abraham Lincoln,* that he was twice married; the second time to Bathsheba. Later investigators, however, are agreed that there was only the one wife, Bathsheba.

The Shipleys, or Chipleys, were formerly probably of the Linville Creek region. Among the few surviving wills at Harrisonburg of before the War of 1861, is that of Elizabeth Herring, the widow of William, son of Alexander, the pioneer. William died in July 1806, without leaving a will. (See Alexander Herring vs. Chipley et als., Bill 23rd February, 1810; *Chalkley,* Vol. II, p. 212.) His wife's will was proven in February, 1821, (copy in later Chapter), and in the same she names her "Grandson William Benj. Chipley son of my late daughter Abigail" . . . and her granddaughter Elizabeth H. Chipley. In the testimony of Herring vs. Chipley, it is stated that Abigail married William Chipley, who died in Carolina, in William Herring's lifetime.

Captain Lincoln remained on his Linville Creek land until about 1780; and after the birth of his son Thomas, father of the President. In his short autobiography, written out of regard for his old friend, Hon. Jesse W. Fell, and not for publication, the President says—

"My parents were both born in Virginia . . . . My paternal grandfather, Abraham Lincoln, emigrated from Rockingham County, Va., to Kentucky, about 1781 or 2, when a year or two later, he was killed by the Indians, not in battle but by stealth when he

Abraham Lincoln

was laboring to open a farm in the forest . . . . . . My father, at the death of his father, was but six years of age, and he literally grew up without education." (See, full autobiography in Power's *History of the Early Settlers of Sangamon, Co., Ill.,* p. 457)

Authorities are not in exact agreement as to the date of Thomas Lincoln's birth. Messrs. Lea and Hutchinson record it January 20, 1780, while the more recent authors record it January 5, 1778. (See *Lincoln* p. 199, and *Barton,* p. 76.)

On the 12th February, 1780, "Abraham Lincoln of the County of Rockingham & State of Virginia and Bersheaba his wife," for 5,000 Pounds current money of Virginia, deeded to "Michael Shanks & John Reuf of the County and State aforesaid," 250 acres, part of 1200 granted to McKay, Duff, Green and Hite, by patent 26th March, 1739, and by them conveyed, etc. . . . . and the aforesaid McKays, conveyed to John Lincoln 600 acres of the aforesaid Land by Deed 22nd June 1768, and John Lincoln Conveyed a part of this within mentioned 250 acres to Abraham Lincoln & Tunis Van Pelt Thos Bryan & Holton Muncey conveyed the rest of the said Land to Abraham Lincoln . . . . . Lying & being on the North side of Linvilles Creek . . . etc.

(Witnesses) (Signed) Abrm Lincoln.
Charles Mair Batsab Lincon.
Soloman Mathews
George Chrisman.

This deed "from Abraham Lincoln & Bersheba his wife" was proven 26th June, 1780, by the oaths of Charles Mair and George Chrisman, and by the "Solemn affermation" of Soloman Mathews.

Abraham's next record is found in Kentucky, in fact, on March 4, 1780, he had already secured three warrents for land there totaling 1,200 acres.

* * * * * *

Abigail Harrison Herring, (19), the wife of Alexander Herring, the pioneer, was probably yet living at this time. She apparently outlived her husband, her name being among those who proved Alexander's will, in 1788, but the exact year of her death is not known. Here the record is somewhat at variance with the *Memiors*... These mention the pioneer's wife as having died prior to his own death. Abigail Herring, the wife of Leonard, may have died before her husband.

Briefly, as given in the above, Alexander and Abigail Herring had—

(191) Leonard—b. 1735 c; d. after 1805; m. August, 1761, Abigail Harrison, (171), daughter of Thomas, founder of Harrisonburg.

(192) John (?)—b. before 1741; d. before 1778.

(193) Alexander—b. 1739 c; d. April—May, 1779; m. ———.

(194) Bathsheba—b. 1742 c; d. 1836. (Three sons and a daughter of the pioneer are said in the *Memiors* (page 8), to have been born in Delaware. She died aged above 90, and according to family tradition, nearly 100; *Barton* p. 74.) m. Abraham Lincoln, b. 13 May, 1744, d. May, 1786, son of "Virginia" John Lincoln.

(195) William—b. 1744 c; d. July, 1806; m. Elizabeth Stephenson, b. ———, d. February, 1821, sister to Major David Stephenson, of the Continental Line.

(196) Jesse—b. ———; d. March, 1781; unmarried.

(197) Bethuel—b. 1751; d. ———; m. 2nd, in October, 1800, Margaret Ervine, daughter of John.

(Sequence of births approximate.)

See further record, Chapter XVII, for all of the above but John and Jesse.

CONTEMPORARIES

About 1754 there appears on the records of Augusta the first mention of a Harrison obviously other than a member of the Rockingham family. November 22, 1754, Burr Harrison furnished bond as Assistant Surveyor, with sureties Gabriel Jones, Francis Taylor and W. Russell. (Will Book 2, p. 81.) He and Matthew Harrison were in 1761 appointed trustees at the incorporation of Woodstock. (See page 185.) Matthew was a son-in-law of Col. James Wood. (See page 144.) Both of these Harrisons came to Augusta from Frederick, and as for a short their names occur alongside those of the Rockingham family, a brief sketch of their connections may be permissible at this juncture.

Apparently, with one exception, the only reference to Burr on the Augusta records is in relation to his occupation. This exception indicates that he was settled in what is now Shenandoah; May 1779, "Burr Harrison of the County of Dunmore vs. Josiah Davidson," bond dated 11th March, 1773. (County Court Judgements.) In 1768, Matthew brought suit vs. John Alderson, Wm. McGee, and John Phillips, regarding accounts of 1766-7; likewise, August, 1768, vs. Reuben Rutherford—"contract dated 1763." Also, August, 1768, Matthew in turn was sued by one Footman relative to a debt of 1765, in which he is described as "Mathew Harrison of Frederick County." *(Chalkley,* Vol. I, pp. 348, 373, and 457.) As early as May 11, 1744, Cuthbert Harrison is named on the records of Frederick. *(Cartmell,* p. 23.) On 31, August 1747, Joist Hite deeded to George Harrison, for five shillings, 150 acres of land in the "Parish and County of Frederick," beginning at Joseph Vance's corner, etc. . . . Also 1st September 1747, for £3-10, Hite deeded to George, 150 acres in Frederick, "whereon Samuel Fulton now dwelleth . . . beginning at Joseph Vance's corner," etc. . . . March 28, 1748, George deeded the first tract to Vance, for five shillings, and the next day, for £45, George and wife Esther, disposed of the second tract to Vance, likewise. (See, Frederick County Deeds, at Winchester.)

Cuthbert, Burr, Matthew, and probably George also, were descendants of an old Stafford County family, some of whom later moved into Dettingen parish, Prince William. Bishop Meade, in his famous *Old Churches, Ministers, and Families of Virginia,* (Vol. II, p. 214,—index by Wise, separate), quotes the following, taken from the parish records of St. Margaret's Westminister, (London), and certified to by Richard Gibson of London, as entered on a leaf of the old Overwharton (Stafford County) vestry book, which in turn had been torn out and fastened to the first page of the vestry book of Dettingen Parish, likely by Rev. Thomas Harrison, the minister in charge—"Burr Harrison of Chipawamsic, born in England, son of Cuthbert Harrison, baptized in the parish of St. Margaret's Westminister, 28 Dec. 1637. His son Thomas born in 1665; grandson Burr born May 21, 1699, great grandson Thomas born 3rd of March, 1723; his sister Jane the 9th Dec. 1726; his sister Seth the 30th Nov. 1729."

The first Burr is identified by Haden *(Virginia Genealogies,* p. 512) as the immigrant. Stannard's *Some Emigrants to Virginia,* (p. 31) places him in Stafford, 1665. Both Cuthbert, described as "Cuthbert Harrison Esq. of Ancaster, Caxton and Flaxby, Yorkshire, England," and his son Burr, spoken of as "Burr Harrison of Chippawamsic," settled in Stafford County, "near Dumfries," according to Henry Tazwell Harrison, in his genealogy of the family, *A Brief History of the first Harrisons of Virginia.* (See also, HARRISON OF CAYTON, page 86, of previous Chapter.)

Burr Harrison (I), m. Mary Smith, widow of Edwin, and had William, and Thomas (I). Thomas (I), b. September 7, 1665, d. August 13, 1746, was an officer of Stafford

County, 1700, had—Burr (II), above; Cuthbert, m. Frances Barns; Thomas (II), m. Ann Grayson; William; Sarah Elizabeth; Frances, m. Valentine Peyton; and Ann Frances, m. J. McMillan. Burr (II), m. July 31, 1722, Anne Barns, and had—Thomas (III); Jane, and Seth, as above; Matthew, b. February 18, 1731, d. February 18, 1798; Burr (III), b. June 16, 1734, d. August 21, 1790; George, b. 1737; Cuthbert, b. 1739; Elizabeth, b. 1741; Anne, b. 1743; and Sarah, b. 1746. Thomas (II), known as Capt. Thomas, High Sheriff of Prince William, 1732, had—Thomas, b. 1726, d. 1827, m. Mary Butler, and moved to Kentucky; William; Burr; Mary; Benjamin, b. 1744; and Anne, b. 1749. Thomas (III), m. July 2, 1747, Ann Wye Peyton, dau. of John and Ann Wye Peyton, of Stony Hall, Strafford County, and had—Burr, Valentine, John Peyton, and Rev. Thomas. Burr (III), m. September, 1760, Mary Anne Barns, b. 1734, d. 1790, and had—Ann Catherine, b. 1761; Matthew, b. 1763, m. Catherine Elzay, and became the head of the Leesburg line; Jane, b. 1767; Cuthbert, b. 1768, d. 1795, at Staunton, Virginia; Anne Barns, b. 1771; Thomas, b. 1774; Mary Anne, b. 1776. George and Cuthbert Harrison, sons of Burr (II), removed to Kentucky after the Revolution.

Matthew Harrison, of Augusta, probably a son of Burr (II), in 1771, resided on the North Fork of the Shenandoah, a short distance south of the Fairfax line, in the territory now called "The Plains"; May 6, 1771, mortgage, Mathew Harrison, to Thomas Carson, of Fairfax County, and Henry Mitchell, of Spotsylvania, merchants, £1748, "tract whereon Matthew now lives known as the Great Plain"; 210 acres deeded to him by Mrs. Mary Wood, also 568 acres, 3 tracts surveyed 2nd December, 1768, unpatented land "on North River of Shenandoe," etc. (Deed Book 17, p. 330.) He appears to have settled here in 1769. In the cause of Scothron vs. Harrison Rutherford, August, 1773, it is stated that "Capt. Matthew Herrison was at Winchester in 1769, and requested Joseph Scathron (Scothron) to go with him to the Plains, where he would give Joseph land. (*Chalkley*, Vol. I, p. 368.) September 9th, of this year, "Matthew Harrison of Augusta," and Alexander White and Elizabeth of Frederick, conveyed to Mathias Kersh, 290 acres of land, near "Peaked Mountain," part of 2000 acres patented to Robert Green, 20th August, 1740. (Deed Book 16, p. 149.) Matthew and White married sisters, and like White (see page 145), Matthew acquired his land through his mother-in-law; 22nd May, 1769, deed, Mary Wood of Frederick to Matthew Harrison—"marriage heretofore celebrated between Matthew and Mary's daughter Mary, deceased," 210 acres on North River of Shenandoah, part of tract called the Great Plains, patented to James Wood, deceased, 12th January, 1746, also 270 acres "adjoining Fairfax's line" and the lands of Michael Ness, patented to Mary Wood, 27th June, 1764, etc." (Deed Book 16, p. 152.)

Matthew was among those recommended for appointment as justices of Augusta court, June 22nd, and August, 1769. (Order Book VIII, pp. 222, and 324.) Likewise March, 1770, and March 16, 1773, and qualified, May 24, 1773. On March 15, 1774, he was again among those mentioned for the "New Commission of Justices," and also January 17, 1775, for the "New Commission from Dunmore," but did not qualify. (Order Books, 14, p. 66; 15, pp. 1, 123, 302; 16, p. 30.)

Most of Matthew's lands were disposed of by him through a series of mortgages, beginning with 1770, and including the one above. March 8, 1770, for £287, he disposed of 210 acres, "corner tract called the Plains," to John Ashburner, of Baltimore. Also, 9th August, 1770, to Benjamin Marshall, of Philadelphia, for £233, negro slaves, and one half of the undivided 840 acres between Shenandoah River and Peaked Mountain, (Massanutten), part of 1100 acres conveyed to him and White, 6th September, 1769, by Mary Woods, et als. (Deed Books 16, p. 530; 17, p. 101.) By 1772 he had returned to Prince William—8th, May, 1772, deed, "Matthew Harrison late of Augusta County, now of Dumfries, in County of Prince William," and Alexander White of Frederick County, and Elizabeth, to Frederick Haines, tract "on Branches of Lick Run," part of patent to Robert Green, deceased, 20th, August, 1740, and divided between Green's extrs. and Mary Wood, widow and devisee of Col. James Wood; delivered Christopher Armentrout, 25th Oct. 1774." (Deed Book 19, p. 37.)

Col. James Wood, the founder of Winchester, died November 6, 1759, aged 52 years. His wife was Mary, the daughter of Capt. Thomas Rutherford, a former resident of Orange, and the first Sheriff of Frederick. Their children were—Elizabeth b. September 20, 1739, m. Hon. Alexander White; James, b. January 28, 1741, d. at Onley, near Richmond, July 16, 1813, Col. and Brig. Gen. in Revolution, Governor of Virginia 1796-1799, m. circa. 1775, Jean Moncure, 1753-1823, dau. of John, no children; Mary b. September 23, 1742, m. Col. Matthew Harrison, as above, officer in Revolutionary Army; John b. January 1, 1743-4, physician, m. Susannah Baker; and Robert, b. July 27, 1747, m. Comfort Welch. Mary Dorcas a daughter of Robert, m. 1798, Lawrence Augustine Washington, b. 1773; Stafford County, d. 1824, Wheeling, (West) Virginia, son of Col. Samuel, and grandson of Augustine Washington. The wife of Col. Wood died about 1800. (See, *Cartmell*, p. 290; *Hayden*, pp. 436, and 512.)

Aside from Burr, Matthew, and Cuthbert, of the Prince William line, there was a William Harrison an early resident of Augusta, not of the Rockingham family. With the exceptions in regard to these four Harrisons, all other references to the residents of the county, of the name, on the *early* records, are believed to apply to the descendants of Iasiah.

Among the wills of Cumberland County, is that of "William Harrison, late of the County of Chesterfield, but now of Augusta County, Virginia," dated 28th August, 1753, and probated 24th September, the same year. (Will Book I, p. 81.) In this the testator names his wife, Elizabeth, his daughter Molly Harrison, and his son, "to be baptized by the name of William Harrison," his mother, Sarah Harrison, his half-brother, Ezekiel Slaughter, and his uncle Samuel Butler, (no bequests being made to these last two,) and desires that his "land in Augusta County, containing 150 acres purchased by me of Col. John Buchanan," be sold by his executors, Ezekiel Slaughter, and Israel Winfree. His home plantation in Chesterfield (or Cumberland), known as "Long Acre," he devised to his mother for her lifetime, and to his sister, for her widowhood, and then to the children. He also mentions land in King William that he had sold. (See Tyler's *Quarterly Historical and Genealogical Magazine*, Vol. IX, October, 1927, p. 128.)

A William Harrison was removing out of the county of Augusta in 1747, according to the proceedings, "David Stewart vs. William Harrison," of September 2nd, this year. (See, County Court Judgements; *Chalkley*, Vol. I, p. 296.)

In addition to the James River and Prince William lines there was a "Skimino" Harrison family that had long been settled in Virginia when the Valley of Virginia was opened for settlement. This line was founded by Richard Harrison, (1600-1664), born in St. Nicholas Parish, in the town of Colchester, county Essex, England, who emigranted to Virginia by 1634, when he is found paying tithes in respect to a patent of land on Queens Creek, in Skimino Hundred, Middletown, later Bruton Parish, York County. His close kinsman, Dr. Jeremy Harrison settled near him.

Richard married Elizabeth Besouth, and had issue—John, William (1648-1713), James, Anne, and Ellena. William m. Mary Hubbard, the daughter of Matthew

mt. Pleasant
OHio - Quaker
Settlement

margaret maupin
Jordan
Quaker

Hubbard, a renowned planter, and had, among others, William, II, (1675-1727), who m. Ann Ratcliffe. William II, in turn, had a son William III, (1705-1771.) This last m. Margaret Maupin, and had a son William, IV,(1740-1819), whose wife was Margaret Jordan, a Quaker. William, IV, embraced his wife's faith, and in 1817, sold his Queens Creek property and removed (via Winchester, the Cumberland Road, Wheeling, etc.) to near Mt. Pleasant, Ohio, a Virginia settlement of Quakers. His eldest son, Samuel Jordan Harrison, (1771-1846), settled in Lynchburg, Virginia, 1789, and m. 1801, Sarah Hudson Burton, dau. of Capt. Jesse Burton. William, another son of William, IV, followed his brother to Lynchburg in 1811. See, *Aris Sonis Focisque, The Harrisons of Skimino,* Ed. by Fairfax Harrison, pp. 4-84.)

Dr. Jeremiah (Jeremy) Harrison, and his brother John, were the sons of Sydney Harrison, of St. Runwalds Parish, Colchester, England. John according to the parish records, was baptized December 31, 1610, and Jeremy, December 31, 1612. Jeremy's wife was Frances (Whitgreave,—see page 102), who as a widow, in 1654, received a patent for 1000 acres of land in Westmoreland County. On September 4, 1654, 1000 acres were granted to her brother-in-law, John Harrison, entail, remainder to her, remainder to Giles Brent, in said county. (Keith's *Ancestry of Benjamin Harrison.)* John seems to have settled first in Maryland, and both he and his brother appear to have left no children. On March 29, 1666, the above land, "formerly granted to John Harrison . . . . . and for want of heirs to his body, descended to his sister Mrs. Frances Harrison, and for want of heirs to her body, came to Capt. Giles Brent." *(Va. Mag. of History & Biography,* Vol. 17, p. 83.) John Harrison, in will 5th Desember, 1690, proved 3rd May, 1705, Charles County, Maryland, devised to Nathaniel Bolton and Mary his wife, personality, and 50 acres "Haphazard;" to Martha, dau. of Giles Wilson; to Thos. Spinkle and Jane his wife, personality; to Giles Dent (Brent) of St. Mary's County, and residuary legatee of his estate, real and personal, including "Harrison's Adventure," 215 acres, and "Providence," also "all land in Corretoman, Virginia." Capt. Dent (or Brent), in his administration of the estate, showed that Harrison had removed to Virginia, and left no personal estate in Maryland. (Baldwin's *Calendar of Md. Wills,* Vol. III, p. 56.) Capt. Giles Brent, of "Peace," Stafford County, Virginia, was the second husband of the widow Frances. It was he, no doubt, who administered. (See *Encyclopaedia of Virginia Biography,* by Lyon G. Tyler, Vol. I, p. 253.)

Among the descendants of Matthew Harrison, the founder of the Leesburg line, is the Hon. Thomas W. Harrison, of Winchester, long a representative from Virginia, in Congress.

Of the line from Samuel Jordan Harrison was Burton Norvell Harrison, private secretary to Jefferson Davis, during the War-between-the-States. His son, Hon. Francis Burton Harrison, of New York, representative in Congress from this State, 1903-5, and 1907-13, was Governor General of the Philippines under President Wilson. Mr. Fairfax Harrison, president of the Southern Railway System, author and historian, is also of this line, being a brother of the ex-Governor General. Through their mother Constance, nee Cary, the authoress, both are descended from William Fairfax, founder of the Belvoir line, cousin of Lord Fairfax, of Greenway Court. (See Chapter VIII, also, *Abridged Compendum of American Genealogy,* ed. by Fred A. Virkus, Vol. I, p. 646, and *Who's Who in America,* Vol. 13, pp. 1475, 1477.)

A Word of Explanation

AS TO THE PLAN OF THE GENEALOGY

Probably a brief word of explanation should be inserted here, regarding the plan of the genealogical outline continued through the following Chapters, as it pertains to the tracing of the descendants of the Harrison immigrant.

The classification begins with what are denoted as "Clans." Each Clan bears the name of one of the immigrant's sons, or sons-in-law, and consists of the descendants of this son, or son-in-law. The Clans are, in turn, subdivided by way of various "Lines"; each Line being denoted by the name of the individual through whom the ancestry is traced back to the founder of the Clan, with the exception that in the case of maternal descent the Line is denoted by the husband's name. All families listed after a particular designation of lineage are of this lineage until the designation is changed; thus obviating needless repetitions of lineages.

Individual descendants are further identified by numbers, which also trace back to the immigrant. Thus the children of the immigrant are denoted by numbers of two digits; such as 11, 12, 13, etc.; and their children in turn by numbers of three digits, the first two of which are those of the parent's number repeated; and so on, down the line. For example, number 1234 is a child of number 123, who in turn is a child of number 12, son of the immigrant, and founder of his Clan. While in the instance of families of over nine children it is not possible under this plan to repeat the last figure of the parent's number, these instances are comparatively rare, and the adjustment obvious, in the light of the lineage as outlined above. The scheme is thus little disturbed.

CHAPTER XVI

Some Soldiers of the Revolution

THIRD GENERATION

"For gold the merchant plows the main,
The farmer plows the manor;
But glory is the sodger's prize,
The sodger's wealth is honor:
The brave poor sodger ne'er despise,
Nor count him as a stranger;
Remember he's his country's stay
In day and hour of danger."
—BURNS.

* * *

"State of Virginia } ss.
County of Rockingham }

ON THE 22ND DAY OF MAY 1833 personally appeared in open court, before the Justices of the County Court of Rockingham County now sitting Reuben Harrison a resident of Rockingham County and State of Virginia aged 75 or 76 years, who being first duly sworn according to law, doth on his oath make the following declaration in order to obtain the benefit of the act of Congress passed June 7th 1832.

That he entered the service of the United States under the following named officers, and served as herein stated. The first tour he served was in what is called Tygarts Valley under Capt. Robert Cravens of the Rockingham Militia, for the protection of the inhabitants against the Indians. He entered as a volunteer, and served three months as a private, and got no written discharge, but owing to a great failure of memory he is unable say in what year this service was rendered. They had a general engagement with the Indians.

His next term of service was under Col. Hamilton then a Captain of the Rockingham militia. He volunteered to serve a tour as a soldier, but his team was taken into the service about the same time, and he was permitted to drive it. He served three months this time, principally in the lower part of Virginia, round about Norfolk, the British troops had possession of that place, and had erected a fort near it, and he understood the object of the detachment to which he belonged to be to cut off supplies of provisions from that Fort. Captains Coger, Baxter, and Riddle of the Rockingham militia, with their companies, belonged to the same detachment. They were under the command of Genl. Muhlenberg whom he frequently saw—They had no general engagement, but had some skirmishing with the enemy. He was discharged near the fort in the vicinity of Norfolk, but he is unable, from loss of memory, to state the time. He got no written discharge.

His next service was a tour of twenty days as a volunteer, although the Company with which he served were drafted, as militia man generally. They marched from Rockingham to the neighborhood of James Town, and he was in hearing of the engagement with the enemy near that place; the company to which he belonged were

THE OLD HARRISON STONE HOUSE AT DAYTON, VIRGINIA
Residence of Col. Benjamin Harrison (1741-1819.)
See pages 197 and 319.

mounted, and hastened to the battle-ground, but it had ended when they arrived. Genl. Wayne had command of the forces to which he belonged, and Col. Harrison, a near relation of his, of the Rockingham militia commanded the militia companies from this County. But he is unable to recollect the Captain under whom this term was served.

This applicant was born in this County which was then a part of Augusta, and has resided in this County to the present time. He has no record of his age, the family Bible in which his age was recorded having fallen into the hands of some other member of the family, but he believes his age to be about 75 or 76 he is positive it is not less than 75. He has no documentary evidence of his services, having never received a written discharge. He never received a commission, and all his services were rendered as a waggoner or private. For his character for veracity, and the belief of his services he refers to Dr. Cravens, and the Revd. Wm. Bryan & Capt. David Ralstone. He hereby relinguishes every claim whatever to a pension or annuity except the present, and declares that his name is not on the pension roll of the agency of any state.

Sworn to and subscribed the day & year aforesaid.

Reuben Harrison

We William Bryan a clergyman residing in the County of Rockingham and the State of Virginia, and Joseph Cravens residing in Rockingham County & State of Va. hereby certify that we are well acquainted with Reuben Harrison, who has subscribed and sworn to the above declaration, that we believe him to be 75 or 76 years of age: that he is reputed and believed in the neighborhood where he resides, to have been a soldier of the Revolution, and that we concur in that opinion.

Sworn to and subscribed the day & year aforesaid.

William Bryan.
J. Cravens.

(From—U. S. Dept. of Interior, Bureau of Pensions, Revolution, and 1812 War Section.)

In the neglected and abandoned old burial ground in the heart of the town of which he was co-founder, sleeps all that was mortal of this old soldier, with a falling old headstone, and a broken foot marker, to denote his last resting place. On the drooping stone may be discerned the inscription—

In Memory of Reuben Harrison who departed this life August 15, 1840, aged 86 years.

Alongside is a similarily neglected plot, with the headstone broken in five pieces, four of which have long since fallen to the ground, but the whole when matched together is found to be—

In Memory of Mary Harrison, Consort of Reuben Harrison, who was born July 3, 1772, and died April 5, 1854.

And the busy traffic on the street, skirting the sacred ground, rolls on, all oblivious to the debt of gratitude owing the memory of this old "unknown" soldier, who had labored so faithfully to continue for the town's benefit the work which he and his father had begun.

In Illinois, sleeps his brother—

"State of Illinois }
Sangamon County } Ss.

On the ninth day day of October in the year 1832 personally appeared in open Court before Reuben Harrison, Thomas Moffit and J. B. Smith County Commissioners of the Commissioners Court of the County aforesaid; now sitting Ezekiel Harrison a resident of the said County and State, aged eighty one years, who being first sworn according to law doth on his oath make the following declaration in order to obtain the benefit of the act of Congress passed 7th, of June 1832.

That he entered the service of the United States under the following named officers, and served as herein stated to wit I served two tours of three months each in the Virginia volunteer Militia in the year 1780, under Capt. George Ruddel in the Regt commanded by Col. All, Genl. Lafayette was the head field officer. I entered the service about the last of June or the first of July, and continued in for three months, & there was very little time, from the expiration of the first tour until I volunteered for the second tour and continued for three months more in the service in the same year 1780. I resided in Rockingham County State of Va. during these tours. We marched through Richmond & James Town to near a place called hot water.

I also served one tour of three months as a Mounted Militiaman in the year 1781, in a Company commanded by Capt. Reuben Moore, in the Reght of Col. Benjamin Harrison, also one tour in the same year, of three months, under Capt Robert Cravens as a mounted Militiaman, the Same Col. Commanding. In the tour under Capt. More, I entered the service I think, some time in September or October of 1781, and we marched, from Rockingham Co. through Capon over to the waters of the South branch of the Potomac, and thence to the north fork of the same River. This tour was against the tories who had been embodied in Capon

In addition to the above services, in 1774, I volunteered in the Company of Capt. Joseph Harris, and marched in an expedition against the Indians to Hinkles Fort, and from thence to the mouth of Kanawa River, where on the 10th October 1774, a battle was fought between the Indians and our troop under the Command of Cols Andrew and Charles Lewis, in which the latter fell. In this battle I was wounded in the right breast.

I hereby relinquish every claim whatever to a pension or annuity except the present and declare that my name is not on the pension Roll of any agency of any State. I never had a certificate of discharge.

Ez[l]. Harrison—

Sworn to and subscribed the day and year aforesaid

C. R. Matheny Clerk.

We Charles R. Matheny Clergyman, residing in the County of Sangamon, and Cornelius Bryan residing in the County of Morgan, hereby certify that we are well acquainted with Ezekiel Harrison who has subscribed & sworn to the above declaration, that, we believe him to be eighty one years of age, that he is reputed and believed in the neighborhood where he resides to have been a soldier of the Revolution, and that we concur in that opinion. Sworn to and Subscribed the day and year aforesaid.

Interrogatories put by the Court to the applicant.

1. Where and in what year was you born.
   Ans. I was born the 3[d] October 1751, in Rockingham Co. Va.

2. Have you any Record of your age, and if so where is it.
   Answer. Yes, and it is at my Son Reubens in this County.
3. Where were you living when called into service and where have you lived since the Revolutionary war, and where do you now live.
   Ans. In Rockingham Co. Va. Since the Revolutionary war I lived in Va. till 1815, and then came to Christian Co Ky. until 1822, and have since resided in this County.
4. How were you called into service, were you drafted, did you volunteer or were you a substitute.
   Ans. I was always a volunteer.
5. Genls Layfayette and Wayne, were the only regular officers whose names I can now recollect that were ingaged in the same service with us.

And the Court do hereby declare there opinion after the investigation of the Matter, and after putting the interrogatories prescribed by the War department that the above applicant was a revolutionary soldier and served as he states: And the Court further Certifies that it appears to them that Charles R Matheny who has signed the precedng certificate is a clergyman resident in the County of Sangamon and that Cornelius Bryan who has also signed the same is a resident in the County of Morgan is a credible person and that their statements are entitled to credit.

Josiah B. Smith
Reuben Harrison } County Commissioners.
Thomas Moffett

I Cornelius Bryan, do hereby make oath and say that I saw Ezekiel Harrison the above applicant during the Revolution war in the Virginia Militia at the time of the battle at hot water, and I understood that he was frequently in the service afterwards.

Sworn to in open Court C. R. Matheny Clrk.

I Charles R. Matheny Clerk of the County Commissioners Court of the County of Sanganmon, do hereby certify that the foregoing contains the original proceedings of the said court in the Matter of the application of Ezekiel Harrison for a pension.

In testimony whereof I have hereof set my hand seal of Office this ninth day of October AD 1832.

C. R. Matheny Clc."

(From, U. S. Dept. of Interior, as above—entitled, "Declaration in order to obtain the benefit of an act of Congress of the 7th June 1832.")

From Wisconsin comes another testimonial—

"BENJAMIN HARRISON was born in the year 1741 at the head of Cooks Creek in what was then Augusta County but now Rockingham: where he continued to reside till his death which occurred in the year 1819. He was at the battle at Point Pleasant and held a Captains Commission, and commanded a company, gathered out of the county of Rockingham; all of whom were engaged in the battle and were as brave men as any who fought on that bloody field. . . . . . The subject of this notice was always heard to speak with the highest commendation, when dwelling on the scenes of this bloody day, of the cool intrepidity and military skill of Col C. Lewis; and that his death was profoundly regretted by the whole army and he always spoke too with the high praise of the bravery and fine military talents of Captain Arbuckle; and to whom much of the success of the battle was attributed. If his testimony is to be relied on Justice has not been done to the fame of Capt. Arbuckle in the narrative of the battle of the point, as given by Howe in his recent history of Virginia.

The subject of this notice held a colonels Commission and commanded a regiment of Virginia Militia in what has usually been called McIntosh's Campaign. This expedition was made against some hostile tribes of Indians inhabiting a portion of the country now included in the State of Ohio. The army penetrated into the country as far as the Hockhocking River, effected the object of the expedition and we hear without any fighting; and returned home in the midst of a Severe Winter; and suffered incredible hardships from cold and hunger . . . . had to live on the hides of beeves they had slaughtered on their outward march and hung on trees of which they made broath without salt. . . . . This . . . . gave many of the men a wasting downhold which well nigh carried them off. Among these was Col. Harrison, fortunately however had a hardy little animal to Carry him which he called Bonny, which the writer of this sketch recollects well to have seen.

During the Revolutionary War the subject of this notice had entrusted to his conduct a little expedition against some tories in Hardy Co. who had assembled under the influence of a man called General Claypole. It turned out however to be a frolic rather than a battle. . . . . . The chief aim of the expedition was to capture the general, but he eluded their pursuit.

When Lord Cornwallis was in the state Col. Harrison commanded a regiment in what was called the twenty days service, and was placed under the command of General LaFayette. He had in his Regiment both officers and privates some as brave men as ever carried a rifle. This was amply tested in several alarms and skirmishes which occurred during their term of Service among these were Lieutenant, afterwards Major Regan and his brother Jeremiah Regan a private man of extraodinary cool intrepidity. Lieutenant, afterwards Capt. William Herring and his brother Bethuel, a private, no less cool and brave.

Their term of service ended before the capture of Lord Cornwallis at York Town.

After peace was established he was, for many years, Col. Commandant of the county of Rockingham . . . . gave all the energy and influence he had to promote the adoption of the federal constitution, he was elected as delegate to the legislature of the State. Was a man of unimpeached integrity, ... of ardent patriotism—a staunch republican, a devout christian—and lived and died respected of all.

Addressed: To Gen. Samuel Lewis, South River."

(See, *Draper MSS.* 8Zz 68, State Historical Society of Wisconsin, Copy kindly supplied by the late Mrs. W. W. (Mary Lynn) Williamson.)

From Tennessee comes yet another "certificate of honor"—

"Gideon Harrison was born in 1762, in Rockingham County, Virginia; the name of his parents not stated.

While residing in Washington County in the territory south of Ohio (which was later East Tennessee), he volunteered early in September, 1780, served eight months as a private in Captain James Wilson's company, Col. John Sevier's North Carlonia regiment, and was in the battle of King's Mountain. He also served as a private of cavalry on several tours against the Creek and Cherokee Indians in Captain Weir's company, Colonel Sevier's North Carolina regiment as follows: from June, 1781, six months; from the winter of 1781-1782, four months; from the spring of 1782, three months, shortly after the end of this tour he served another two months to the Greasy Cove or Cave; during his service in the Indian country, while ranging through the mountains, he was in several skirmishes in which more than twenty Indians were killed and several taken prisoner.

"The soldier lived for some years in Alabama, then moved to Murfreesborough, Rutherford County, Tennessee. He was allowed a pension on his application executed August 23, 1832, at which time he was a resident of Murfreesborough, Tennessee, where he lived nearly six years." (Extract from the papers on file in pension claim S. 2602, U. S. Veterans Administration, Washington, D. C., Revolution and 1812 War Section.)

* * * * * *

Of the above:

Col. Benjamin Harrison was the "near relation" mentioned by Reuben, of the first affidavit. Col. Benjamin was Reuben's own first cousin, being a son of Capt. Daniel Harrison, the brother of Thomas, founder of Harrisonburg, who was in turn the father of Reuben and Ezekiel of the affidavits. Captains Robert Cravens, Reuben Moore, and William Herring and the latter's brother Bethuel, were also near relations of the Harrison soldiers. Capt. Cravens was the son of Capt. Robert Cravens, the elder; Capt. Moore the grandson of John Harrison, Sr.; and the Herring brothers the sons of Alexander, the pioneer. No record has been found further identifying Gideon.

At least three sons of Thomas Harrison, founder of Harrisonburg, were in the service. In November 1779, Robert Harrison was recommended Ensign in Capt. Josiah Harrison's company, and on the 24th October, 1780, qualified as Ensign. (Rockingham Court Order Book I.) Among Rockingham's soldiers in the Continental line were privates James, Robert, and John Harrison, each of whom were certified to the Court as entitled to 100 acres of bounty land, in Document No. 34,—"A LIST OF SOLDIERS Who have been allowed bounty land by the Executive of Virginia, and who have not received warrants. The order for the same remain on file in the land office." (Page 12,—Document at Harrisonburg.)

Two of Robert Cravens' sons were Revolutionary soldiers. John Young, in his declaration of military services, states that he was born in Pennsylvania, 1760, moved to Augusta when aged four, and that he enlisted under Capt All, who raised a Company of Volunteers to repel the Indians, and on May 1, 1778, volunteered under Capt. William Cravens to succor Tygart's Valley; volunteered again September 1st, the same year, under Capt. Robert Cravens, Col. Benjamin Harrison, and Genl. McIntosh, against the Indians, etc. (*Chalkley*, Vol. II, p. 486.)

Four sons of Alexander Herring, the pioneer, are said to have been in the war; "two under Light Horse Harry Lee, and two as Morgan's riflemen." On 24th October, 1780, "William Herring took the Oath as Captain of Militia." (Rockingham Court Order Book I, p. 56, at Richmond, Va.)

Under the authority of the Third Virginia Convention, held early in the war, (see page 232), commissioners from the various counties comprising the district of which Augusta County was a part, met on 8th September, 1775, at the house of James Wood, in what is now Nelson County, and resolved that Augusta would furnish four companies of fifty men each, and that each of the other counties would furnish two companies of the same relative strength. The officers appointed for Company No. I, of Augusta, were, Benjamin Harrison, Captain, Henry Evans, Lieut., and Curord (Conrad) Custard, Ensign. (*Waddell*, p. 245.)

Benjamin Harrison had been a Captain under the old establishment some years prior to this time—18th November, 1762, Benjamin Harrison, Andrew Bird, and Abraham Bird, qualified Captains of the Militia. (Order Book VII, p. 363.)

In addition to Benjamin, another son of Capt. Daniel Harrison, Sr., was early in the service. John Sizer, in his declaration of military services, September 6, 1832, states, that in 1777 he moved to Rockingham County, and volunteered in the company of Capt. Daniel Harrison, etc. (*Chalkley*, Vol. II, p. 501.)

On the 20th August, 1777, a list of the tithables was ordered taken in the various military companies, or districts, of Augusta County, forty-five such being enumerated, including—Capt. Robert Cravens', Capt John Hopkins', Capt John Stephenson's, Capt. George Pence's, Capt. Wm. Nall's, Capt. Thomas Hewit's, Capt. Anthony Rider's, Capt. Ralph Stewart's, Capt William Robertson's, Capt. Abraham Lincoln's, Capt. Daniel Smith's, and Capt. Reuben Harrison's. (Order Book XVI, p. 222; *Chalkely*, Vol. I, p. 193.)

Capt. Reuben Harrison was the son of John Harrison, Sr., (Chapter XI.) In his affidavit above, Reuben the son of Thomas (Chapter XIII), states that "he never received a commission." Following John, Sr's., death in 1771, the final settlement of his estate was delayed until after his widow Phoebe's death, but in the meantime an accounting of the finances was rendered by his executors at various times to the court. One such account was admitted to record in 1784,—Will Book VI, page 441—

"John Harrison's estate settlement.
2. To tax Paid in the Year 1778,
3. " " " " " " 1779,
4. " " " " " " 1780,
5. " " " " " " 1781,
etc., etc.,
Sept. 1779, for whiskey to Vendue—

"Augusta Sct. Ss. This day Capt. Reuben Harrison came Before me and on his Solemn oath Declares that he paid the accounts above and the other part he furnished for use of the Estate of John Harrison Deceased to the amount of £44-18-6, as is certified under my hand this 18th May, 1784.

S. John Poage."

Reuben Harrison, it will be recalled, was one of the executors named in his father's will. (See pages 156 and 189.)

On the second day following the establishment of Rockingham County Court, the following "Recomendations to the Council" (of the Governor) were made: "Abraham Smith for County Lieutenant, Daniel Smith as Colonel, Benjamin Harrison as Lieut. Col., & John Skidmore as Major." At the same time William Herring was appointed Lieutenant in Capt. Robert Cravens' company and Richard Ragan, 2nd. Lieutenant, and Joseph Smith, Ensign, in Capt. Daniel Smith's company. (Rockingham Court Order Book I, pp. 3 and 4.)

About a month later, on 25th May, 1778, "Abraham Smith, Gent., Qualified Co. Lieut.; Daniel Smith, Gent., Col.; Benja. Harrison, Gent., as Lieut. Col., & Wm. Nalle, Gent, as Major." Also "Anthony Ryder (Rader), Gawen Hamilton, Thos. Hewitt, Thos. Baggs (?), Reuben Harrison & Daniel Smith, jun., being appointed Captains of the Militia took the Oaths according to Law which is ordered to be certified." Joseph

Smith, John Rice and Nicholas Curn, Lieuts., Wm. Smith and . . . (others) Ensigns of the Militia. *(Ibid,* p. 6.) On the same date, Josiah Harrison took the oath as Lieut. of the Militia. *(Ibid,* p. 7.) On the following day William Herring took the same. *(Ibid,* p. 10.)

Daniel Smith, as elsewhere noted, was Benjamin Harrison's brother-in-law, his wife being Benjamin's sister Jane. Capt. Daniel Smith, Jr., was a son of Daniel, the Colonel. Daniel, Jr., commanded a company at the battle of Point Pleasant. According to Waddell, three of the Colonel's sons, viz.: John, Daniel, and Benjamin, participated in the seige of Yorktown. *(Waddell,* p. 152.) Joseph, the Ensign above, was also one of Col. Daniel's sons. On the 27th April, 1779 he qualified 2nd Lieut. in Capt. Daniel Smith's company. (Rockingham Court Order Book I.)

Josiah Harrison is tentatively identified as a son of Jeremiah. (Chapter XV.) Josiah was recommended Capt., 23rd November, 1779, and on the 27th March, 1780, "took the Oath of a Capt. of Militia, Jacob Havener, Ensign." (Rockingham Court Order Book I, pp. 52 and 56.) A younger Josiah Harrison was recommended Ensign in Capt. Reuben Moore's company 26th March, 1781 and on the 29th May, following, "took the Oath of Ensign of Militia. *(Ibid* p. 92.) This Josiah is placed as the son of Zebulon Harrison. The latter lived near Moore. Josiah, the son of Zebulon is named as a Captain in 1788, and by 1810 was Col. Josiah Harrison. (See, *Virginia Valley Records,* by J. W. Wayland, p. 105; and later this present volume.) A Josiah Harrison, probably son of Capt. Reuben, was allowed pay, March 25, 1782, on his claim of March 1, 1781, "for 6 days with his team in conducting British prisoners from the South to Shando Courthouse." At the same time Josiah was allowed pay for bullock driving 1 day, January 16, 1781, and likewise Gideon Harrison, one day, January 18, 1781. *(Wayland,* pp. 88-89.)

Josiah Davison, the half-brother of Moore, and another grandson of John Harrison, Sr., was also a Captain, and is mentioned as such in 1780. (See, *Virginia Militia in the Revolutionary War,* by J. T. McAllister p. 229.)

"Robert Harrison, *son of* Zebulon, (was) appointed Constable in the room of Jacob Woodley," 24th May, 1779. (Rockingham Court Order Book I, p. 34.) This Robert was likely the Continental soldier, no such identification being applied to the Ensign in the militia. John Harrison, the Continental soldier, may have been also a son of Zebulon. An Isaiah Harrison, thought to have been Zebulon's son, is named in 1783, as having been a Revolutionary soldier. (See later reference—Ezekiel Harrison.)

Col. Abraham Smith, on the 28th November, 1780, resigned as the County Lieutenant of Rockingham, and his brother Col. Daniel Smith, was recommended to succeeed him. (Rockingham Court Order Book I, p. 81.) Upon Daniel's promotion Benjamin Harrison was in turn recommended to succeed him, 26th March, 1781. Benjamin qualified, and a few months later, on 27 November, 1781,—following Daniel's Smith's death—was "recommended County Lieutenant vice Daniel Smith, deceased." This office he held for a number of years. *(Ibid,* dates as above, and *Draper.)*

On the 26th February, 1782, Col. Benjamin Harrison ordered into service Capt. George Baxter's company to guard a party of British prisoners to Winchester, after which the company was discharged March 4th (1782.) Among the privates named on Baxter's pay roll was Daniel Harrison, a nephew of the Colonel, evidently. (See, *Virginia Soldiers of 1776,* by Louis A. Burgess, Vol. I, p. 123.)

Besides their military services, several of the foregoing were also Justices of the Court, and they and others held various offices, as will be found detailed below.

CLAN OF JOHN HARRISON

(121) ZEBULON HARRISON, (1718 c-1792), the son of John Harrison, Sr., (12), and wife Phoebe, was born on Long Island, New York, and removed with his parents, in 1729, to Sussex County, Delaware, and from there with them to Augusta, later Rockingham County, Virginia, about 1737. In 1742 he was a member of Peter Scholl's Militia company on Smiths Creek. He married at Morristown, New Jersey, 23rd July, 1747—while on a trip from Augusta County,—his cousin, Margaret Primrose, nee Cravens, (142), a young widow, the daughter of Capt. Robert Cravens, Sr., (Chapter XIV), the Rev. Timothy Jones, the first pastor of the First Presbyterian Church, of Morristown, officiating. (Chapter XI.)

Upon his marriage Zebulon settled on Smiths Creek, a mile or so north of his father. Between 1748, and 1771, he patented three tracts of land in this locality, totaling 814 acres (the original 1771 patent being yet in existence.) Near his house was an early road and a ford. Among the petitions filed with the court in 1751-2, was one from John Phillips, as overseer of the "road from Massanutten to dry fork of Smiths Creek leading to Augusta Court House," praying to be released and nominating Zebulon Harrison, Wm. McGee, and Wm. Draper, in his stead. On 19th November, 1767, Zebulon was appointed surveyor of highway vice John Phillips. (Order Book II, p. 361; *Chalkley*, Vol. II, pp. 142, and 437.) On the 26th May, 1778, "David Harnett" was appointed "overseer of the road from John Kellingers, formerly Samples, to Zeb. Harrison's ford," and John Phillips from the ford to the line of Shenandoah. At the same time Jacob Woodley was appointed overseer of the road, "from the fork on this side of Sebastian Martz's" "to Reuben Harrison's, and Jeremiah Harrison (son of Thomas) from Reuben Harrison's to Daniel Smith's Gent." (Rockingham Court Order Book I, p. 7.)

In the First Census of the United States, *Heads of Families, Virginia,* 1784, "Harrisson Zeb," of Rockingham County, is listed with "13 white souls, 1 Dwelling, 1 Other building." (Page 76.) In 1789 he is mentioned as owning 575 acres of land in Rockingham. (Wayland's *History of Rockingham County,* p. 449.) By his father's will he was bequeathed the elder's home plantation, at present Lacey Spring. Following his father's death in 1771, his mother evidently made her home with him, her funeral being preached, Sunday, December 8th, 1793, "on Smith's Creek." (See page 189.) She was doubtless included in the above thirteen.

By the will of his brother, John Harrison, Jr., proved 1763, Zebulon was devised 400 acres of land on Smiths Creek, and his eldest daughter, "Phel" (Phoebe), 245 acres in the same locality. His sons Zebulon and Robert, about the same time, inherited 200 acres on Linville's Creek from their grandfather, Robert Cravens.

In addition to the tracts patented and inherited, he purchased on the 22nd August, 1749, a tract on "Daniel James branch," a tributary of Smiths Creek, from his brother-in-law, Daniel Davison, (See page 166), and on the 20th March, 1762, from Richard Faields and Alice, for £20, 220 acres on Daniel James Branch, corner William Carroll's survey, corner Zebulon Harrison's land. On 19th August, 1767, he conveyed both tracts, the first containing 46 acres, patented to Davison, 25th September, 1746, to Thomas Looker, who in turn conveyed the while to James Looker, his son, 17th November, 1768. (Deed Books 10, p. 286; 15, p. 216.)

Among his neighbors, in the region of Daniel James Branch, was his pastor, the Rev. John Alderson, Jr., who on 20th November, 1771, purchased from Joseph Carroll, the only surviving son and heir of William Carroll, deceased, late of Frederick County, and Mary, his wife, two tracts on "Stroud's branch between Smith's Creek and

Peaked Mountain," the first embracing 158 acres, adjoining another survey of Carroll's, and the second 265 acres, called Carroll's Meadow, crossing Daniel James Branch, adjoining a "survey belonging to Zebulon Harrison." (Deed Book 17, p. 491.)

During the Revolutionary War, Zebulon was allowed, March 25, 1782, claims for furnishing supplies to the American Army, his claims being dated, February 24, March 1, August 20, and December 4, 1781, for horses, cattle, corn, hay, rations, etc. (*Wayland,* p. 88.)

* * * * * *

Zebulon Harrison, as his father before him, was one of the pillars of the early Smiths and Linville's Creek Baptist Church. Upon the Rev. Alderson's removal to Greenbrier, during the Revolution, the church for the remainder of the war period held no regular meetings (there being a pause in the records.) Following the close of the war, Zebulon Harrison, John Lincoln, and some others, got together to effect, if possible, a reorganization, and if not, to unite with "Brother Moffett's Church," the Smiths Creek wing at present New Market, which, in the meantime, had come to be allied with the Mill Creek, or Whitehouse Church, in what is now Page County. John Koontz

The Whitehouse Church was gathered in 1772, by Elders John Picket and John Koontz, largely drawing its first members from the Dutch Mennonists. Elder Koontz was the leading and resident pastor, and the first Baptist to preach within the bounds of the church. "He was by extraction, and birth, a German." At the time of his baptism in Fauquier, December, 1768, his home was near present Front Royal, where a little later he began to preach. In 1770 he resolved to visit his brother George, in the old Massanutten neighborhood, and in doing so found opportunity to preach in this locality. He settled there in 1776, when he was ordained. At the time of its organization the church consisted of seventy members, and among them were two preachers, Anderson Moffett, and Martin Kaufman.

The Smiths Creek Church, proper, was constituted in 1774, by Revs. Koontz and Moffett, assisted by Rev. James Ireland, of Culpeper, a Scotchman. It was gathered on a part of the old ground of the Smiths and Linville's Creek church. Rev. Moffett became its pastor about 1778. (See, *Semple,* pp. 174-189, and Taylor's *Lives of Va. Baptist Ministers,* 1837, p. 103.)

The meeting to decide the future policy of the remnant—or Linville's Creek wing—of the Smiths and Linville's Creek Church was the first called following the Revolutionary War.

It was "held at the House of Brother John Lincoln's (according to a certain previous Appointment) on Saturday the 15th Dec., 1787, and Bro. Anderson Moffett being present, was called as a help, and chosen Moderator, and Bro. Jno. Thomas Clerk . . . . then a Motion was made by Bro. Lincoln, viz. Whether this Church should continue to keep their Constitution, or join Bro. Moffett's Church Bodily, and dissolve its own Constitution? And after deliberating & duly considering the Matter, the Question was put by the Moderator, Whether this Church thought it would be most for the Glory of God & the Good of this Church, to keep its Constitution, or dissolve it, & join his Church on Smiths Creek? It was answered that we think it best to keep our Constitution yet for a while. Then a Motion was made by Brother Thomas, When and where our next Church Meeting should be held, and it was agreed, that we will hold it on the Saturday before the 3rd Sabbath in February next, at Mr. Zebulon Harrisons House on Smiths Creek." (Old Church Book, p. 24.)

A call was then presented the Rev. Moffett to be their pastor, which he accepted, and after agreeing to join in a "Contribution to hire a Hand to Work . . . . for him, the better to enable him to attend upon the Business of Preaching the Gospel &c.," the meeting adjourned.

"THE CHURCH met accordingly to Appointment at the House of Mr. Zebulun Harrison's on the Saturday before the third Sabbath in Feb., 1788, and Bro. John Lincoln was chosen Clerk, and it was agreed by the Church . . . . 2ndly It was agreed and Anacted by the Church That our old Church Book, should be transcribed into one new covered Book, that is to say our Constitution & Introduction preceeding sd. Constitution, and the Register of all our Church proceedings from Time to Time, both what is contained in sd. old Book, and other Papers, and it is appointed and agreed, That Brother Thomas & Lincoln do the same by the Original & make it exactly agreeable to and with the Sense of sd. Original. (p. 24.)

The succeeding meeting was the April one referred to in the last Chapter, regarding John and Mary Lincoln. (See page 285.) On this occasion, "The Church . . . . earnestly requested Brother Moffett to promise, or engage, to preach at the Baptist Meeting House on Linvilles Creek, one Sabbath Day in every Month, statedly, (or that often in the Summer Season at least.)" Rev. Moffett, could not consent, however, to "this Call" for so much regularity.

The next session was held, "at the Baptist Meeting House on Linvilles Creek" (Saturday before the) 3rd Sabbath, May, 1788, and Bro Moffett was again urged to engage himself as above, "but he . . . now answers the Church absolutely, That he cannot . . . notwithstanding he says, he will preach at the Meeting House on Sabbath, or other Days, as often as Oppertunity may offer, and . . . . will make the Appointments . . . . from one Meeting to another." At this session "Brother James Thomas & Sister Sarah Thomas his wife, made orderly Application to the Church for a letter of Dismission, to join another Church of the same Faith & Order, which was agreed to." "N. B. The Sabbath succeeding this last Church Meeting there was a large Concourse of People assembled at the Meeting House & a very excellent Sermon preached according to appointment by the Rev. Moffett, from the 2nd Verse of the last Chapter of Isaiah & latter Clause of sd. Verse . . .. . After sermon, Mary Lincoln (the Wife of Jno. Lincoln) Cheerfully submitted herself, and came under the solemn Ordinance of Baptism, by the Hands of our Rev. Brother Moffett, & under the Ordinance of laying on of Hands by him & the Elders. Then was celebrated the Ordinance of the Lords Supper, with solemnity and good order." (p. 26.)

On the Saturday before the 5th Sabbath in June, 1788, Bro. Lincoln was appointed Messenger, "to the Association that is to meet at Buckmarsh in August next."

At the 2nd Sabbath in September session at the "old Meeting House . . . . The minutes of our Association & Circular Letter and the Minutes & Circular Letter of the Philadelphia Association, were all read to the Church, which gave her great Satisfaction and Comfort." At this time "John Lockard offered & was received into fellowship." "N. B. The last Sabbath in October following this last Church Meeting, the sd. John Lockard submitted himself to the Ordinance of Baptism and laying on of Hands." (p. 29.)

"Met according to appointment, at the old Meeting House on Linvilles Creek, the Saturday before the 2nd. Sabbath in April 1789. Agreed that we seek (by the most reasonable Means we can devise) a greater intercourse, and reciprocal Union & Communion with our Sister Church on Smiths Creek. (p. 29.)

On "Saturday before the 2nd Lords Day in August 1789," Brother Lockard was appointed "Messenger to the Association to be held next Saturday at Broad Run

Faquire County, ... also Brother Aaron Soloman." At this meeting Br. Lincoln was instructed "to draw a Subscription Paper" for "The Business of Building a new Meeting house." But at the next meeting "12th Day of Sept. 1789.", Brother Lincoln reported "That upon conversing with the People at large . . . he found it expedient to drop the drawing a Subscription Paper for building a new Meeting House, but instead thereof repair the old one upon the same Plan, viz. by Subscription." (p. 31.)

"At a called Meeting of the Church, at the House of Bro. Jno. Lincoln, on Thursday the 1st of October 1789," a letter presented by Bro. Lincoln to be sent to the "District Association (to be held at Water Lick, beginning on Saturday the 3rd of this instant)" was agreed to. "The old Catocton Association was divided last August into two District Associations; containing about twelve Churches each, the Upper District, (being that which we fell into) still retaining the old Name, of the Catocton Association; and the lower, the Chapawamsic Association." (p. 32.)

On the 2nd Sabbath in December, 1789, Brothers Moffett and James Ireland were present, and held communion service.

Meetings on occasion were held all day. At a meeting Saturday before the 2nd Sabbath in April, 1790, it was "Agreed to set apart the Saturday before the 2nd Sabbath in May, next, for the Solemn Worship of God, and fasting and praying, that is to meet precisely at 9 O'clock in the Morning & hold till 1, in the Afternoon in this Duty, and then proceed upon the Business of the Church." (p. 34.)

"After Public Worship was over," the 3rd Sabbath in February, 1791, the Church "Met together to hear Experiances; when Patience Brumfield offered, and was recieved for Baptism, and the 2nd Sabbath in March was appointed for her Baptism, if the Weather was favourable, & her health would permit." (p. 37.)

On "Saturday before ye 2nd Lords Day in March . . . . . two offered and one was received for Baptism, viz. Amelia Smith, & Tomorrow fixed upon for Baptism. March 13th being the 2nd Lords Day was Baptized, Patience Brumfield, the Wife of David Brumfield, and Amelia Smith, the Wife or Widow of John Smith 7 came under the Imposition of Hands."

On the 2nd Sabbath in May, (1791), the Sacrament of the Lords Supper was administered, and "there were present, besides Brother Moffett, Administrator, and the usual Members, Bro. James Johnston and Josiah Ozburn, both Ministering Brethren." (p. 38.)

On the Saturday before the 3rd Lords Day in June, Bro. Johnston being present opened the meeting with prayer. Also, 1st. Said Brother Johnston applied for Transient Membership (not having obtained his dismission from Buckmarsh Church) and as he was sufficiently well known by our church was by her accordingly, received into Transient Membership and Communion. 3rdly. Esther Henton (now Widow of John Henton deceased) presented to the Church, a letter of Dismission, dated Nov. 23, 1766, from a Church of Christ, at Cumry Township, in the County of Berks & Province of Pennsylvania, baptized on Profession of their faith in Christ &c. And Amelia Bowen, Wife of Francis Bowen, presented a Letter of Dismission, from the United Baptist Church of Christ at Mill Creek Shenandoah County, Virginia. Each of the aforesaid Sisters, were received upon their Letters, the last Letter Dated May 28, 1791." (p. 38.)

* * * * * *

At a meeting the Saturday before the 2nd Lords Day in July, 1791, "1st. A Door was opened to hear Experiances. Eleanor Gum, Widow of Norton Gum, related hers & was received by the Church for Baptism. 2ndly. Brethern Johnston, Lockard, & Harrison, or any two of them were appointed our Messengers to the Ketocton Association."

"On the second Sabbath in July, viz. the Day after the above Meeting, was baptized the aforesaid Dinah Talman, and Eleanor Gum, (by our beloved Brother Anderson Moffett), and came under the Imposition of Hands. (p. 39.)

Brother Moffett a few months later was succeeded by Rev. Johnston, as the pastor of the church. On Saturday 10th September, 1791,—"5thly. Appointed the Saturday before the said Sabbath for Meeting of Business to begin at 10 O'clock, appointing and setting forward Brother Johnston then to be Ordained the Pastor of this Church, and should the Help for that Purpose attend according to their own, & the last Association Appointment. The following meeting was Sat. 8th of October, at which "one of the Helps viz. Brother John Monroe having come up according to appointment, Met with us. Meeting was opened in the usual Form, Brother Moffett being present was called to assist Brother Monroe, when they proceeded in a very solemn Manner to the Ordination of Brother Johnston, by Imposition of Hands, Prayers, &c. to the Pastorship of this Church & giving him Credentials of sd. Ordination." (p. 40.)

Zebulon's appointment above, as a Messenger to the Ketocton Association, is the last mention of him in the old record. Between this time and the final settlement of his father's estate in June 1794, he died, his brother Reuben being the surviving executor of his father. (See page 189.) His death occurred in 1792. Doubtless, as in the case of his mother, the Rev. Johnston preached his funeral sermon.

His wife, Margaret, outlived him. She, too, was a member of the church—Met . . . Saturday 8th of December (1792) . . . "2ndly. Nominated Brother Talman to deal with Sister Margaret Harrison, for her nonattendance so frequently of late . . Sister Margaret Thomas to deal &c. with Brother Bowen & Wife for the same." (p. 47.)

"Sister Margaret Harrison" is mentioned as late as April 11, 1795, in the old record. At this time she subscribed to help pay the salary of Bro. Moffett. She probably died soon after this. Both she and her husband were buried in the present old unmarked burial ground, east of Lacy Spring.

Zebulon (121) and Margaret (142) Harrison's children were—

(1211) John—b. 1749 c; d. ———; m. Hannah Lincoln, daughter of "Va. John Lincoln," b. Mar. 9, 1748. She d. a widow 1803.
See further record.

(1212) Zebulon—b. before 1761; d. after 1811; m. ———.

(1213) Robert—b. before 1761; d. ——; m. a daughter of Wm. Young, (?).
See further record.

(1214) Phoebe—b. before 1758; d. ——; m. James Dyer.
See further reference.

(1215) Josiah—b. ——; d. 1824 (?); m. 1786, Margaret Miller, dau. of Mrs. Janet Miller, mentioned as a widow in the marriage bond.
See further record.

(1216) Polly—b. ——; d.——; m. 1784, Robert Harrison (1621), son of Col. Benjamin.
See further reference.

And several others, including likely; Gideon, m. Mary Brian, April 26, 1784, (daughter of John), and Isaiah, living 1784. (First five above named in D. S. H. MSS.)

Gideon Harrison, who m. Mary Brian, (surety Josiah, or Isaiah Harrison), migrated to North Carolina, prior to 1788, and from there, prior to 1790, to Georgia, where he settled in Green County, and died. Letters of administration were granted

Mary and Davis Harrison, on his estate, June 2, 1797. Mary, the widow, married, in Green County, January, 1801, John Luckey, whose will is dated in 1808. Gideon's children were, Robert, William, b. September 22, 1788, d. June 1870, Margaret and Elizabeth, of whom, William, m. February, 1815, Susan Kendrick. Mr. John M. Harrison, and his brother, Mr. De Sales Harrison, of Atlanta, Ga., are descendants of William.

DAVISON—MOORE

(123) PHOEBE HARRISON, (1728-1807), the daughter of John Harrison, Sr., (12), and wife Phoebe,—and the preserver of the old water bottle of her grandfather's voyage to America—was born on Long Island, New York, about a year before her father's removal to Delaware, and died in Rockingham County, Virginia, in 1807. She was buried in the old Moore family burial ground near her home; the inscription on her tombstone reading—"In Memory of Phoebe Moore consort of Thomas Moore, who departed this life in the year 1807, aged about 79 years."

Phoebe married first, about 1743, Daniel Davison, the son of Josiah Davison, of Middlesex County, New Jersey. Josiah was a grandson of Daniel Davison, the immigrant, who was born in 1630, died 1693, buried at Weenham, Mass., and who married April 1657, Mary Low, the daughter of Thomas Low, the son of Admiral John Low. Daniel, the son of Josiah, came into Augusta County from New Jersey, a year or so prior to his marriage. He was probably a native of the same county as his wife, his father having been a resident of Southold, Long Island, before his removal to New Jersey. Daniel died about 1751, leaving wife Phoebe, and three children, the eldest of whom was Josiah, the latter justice of Augusta and Rockingham Counties, and the first commissioned sheriff of Rockingham. Subsequent to Daniel's death Phoebe made three trips to New Jersey from Virginia between the years 1750 and 1766, partly, at least, in connection with a legacy left her son, Josiah, by his grandfather Davison. On one of these trips she manifestly accompained her father on his visit back to Oyster Bay, and there witnessed his baptism. (See pages 166 and 238.)

About 1753, Phoebe married second, Thomas Moore, Sr., who a little later, 1767, upon Josiah's coming of age, bought from the latter the land he had inherited from his father, Daniel. (See page 146.) Thomas appears to have come into Augusta from Frederick County. (See Chapter X.) He died in 1797, and was the first Moore, apparently, to be buried in the old cemetery. His inscription reads—"In Memory of Thomas Moore, Senior, died 1797 aged about 70 years."

The home of Thomas and Phoebe was near the early Indian Road, on which the Davison land bordered, and was between the road and Smiths Creek. A part of his land, including the site of his house, is yet in the possession of some of his descendants. The house is said to have stood on the knoll overlooking the creek, near the site of the residence of the late Otis Moore.

As given in the first United States Census, Virginia, 1784, "Thomas Moor Senr," of Rockingham, was listed with "2 white souls," 1 dwelling, and 1 other building; "Thomas Moor Junr" with "4 white souls," 1 dwelling, and 1 other building; "John Moor", with "8 white souls," no dwellings and buildings enumerated; and "Capt Reuben Moor," with "3 white souls," no dwellings and buildings enumerated. (First Census—*Heads of Families*, p. 76.)

Among the large land owners of 1789, Thomas Moore, Sr. was entered as owning 1,070 acres, and John Quaker Moore as owning 1,088 acres. (*Wayland*, p. 449.)

At the time of his death, Thomas owned six plantations embracing 1,700 acres. He died without a will. According to the litigation instituted by his daughter, Lucretia Dunkenson, and her husband, Thomas, vs. her brothers, the greater part of his land was acquired as follows—

200 acres on Smiths Creek, between Davision's, Phillip's and Rambo's lands, corner Buchanan, patented, 26th July, 1765.

190 acres, same location, patented (to Thomas L. Moore), 12th May 1770, lines of Michael Bowyer and Thomas Loker.

190 acres on Smiths Creek adjoining J. Woodley's land, corner John Phillips, patented 12th May, 1770.

200 acres on Smiths Creek, crossing Daniel James Branch, patented 27th June, 1764, to Valentine Sevier, in consideration of importing four persons, viz. James Porteus, John Roe, Patrick McDonald, and Daniel Warner.

370 acres on Smiths Creek patented 12th January, 1746, to James Wood. (This land was the land Wood sold Davison.)

68 acres on Long Meadow, or North River Shenandoah, patented 31st October, 1765, to Thomas Looker, and conveyed by Looker to Thomas Moore, Sr., 17th February, 1791. Witness Reuben Moore, Thomas Loker, Jr., Philip Counce (Koontz), recorded in Rockingham, 27th June, 1791.

(See, Dunkenson et ux. vs. Moore, Judgements, Sept. 1802, A to R; *Chalkley*, Vol. II, p. 26.)

The first of these tracts now include several of the finest estates on the Valley Pike, one of which is the well known late N. G. Moore property, and another, a part of Court Manor, adjoining. Court Manor, is all 'Moore land,' the remainder having been acquired by Reuben Moore, the Capt., from his uncle, David Harnet, the husband of Phoebe Moore's sister Ann. (See page 185.)

In a further judgement regarding the settlement of Thomas' estate—Dunkenson vs. Moore, Bill, 31st, August, 1804—"Thomas Dunkenson and Lucretia, his wife, daughter of Thomas Moore, of Rockingham, vs. Thomas, John and Phoebe Moore, Moses Walton and Elizabeth, his wife, one of the children and heirs of Reuben Moore, deceased," it was found that Thomas Moore died intestate, leaving widow Phoebe, and children, viz. Thomas, John, Reuben, and oratrix, and that Reuben was dead. Reuben's heirs, besides Elizabeth, are named as Thomas, Reuben, Sarah, and Ann Moore, "infants and orphans of Reuben and Phoebe Moore, widow and relict of Reuben's." David Harnet is mentioned as an uncle of Reuben—"had married Reuben's aunt." Thomas Looker's wife was a half-sister of Dunkenson. (See, Circuit Court Causes Ended, Judgements, April, 1799; *Chalkley*, Vol. II, p. 131.)

Phoebe's three children by her first marriage have been named in a previous chapter. (See Chapter XI.) Her brother John Harrison, Jr., in his will, proved 1763, bequeathed land to both of her Davison daughters.

Her children by the two marriages were, as given below—

DANIEL DAVISON and PHOEBE (123), his wife, had issue:

(1231) Josiah—b. Dec. 1, 1743; d. Sept. 9, 1825, in Monroe Township, Preble County, Ohio; m. Ist, Edith Herring, said to have been a daughter of Alexander Herring(Jr. ?); m. 2nd, prior to 1797, Ann (or Nancy)

Williams. Removed about 1795, to Harrison County, now West Virginia, and from there, about 1813, to Ohio.
See further record.

(1232) ANN—b. 1746; d. 1822; m. prior to 1767, Reuben Moore, of Frederick County, Virginia.
See further reference.

(1233) PHOEBE—b. 1748; d. 1838; m. John Ewing, of Harrisonburg, son of William.
See further record.

THOMAS MOORE, SR., and PHOEBE (123), his wife, had issue:

(1234) REUBEN—b. 1755; d. Aug. 6, 1803; m. Phoebe ———, b. 1764, d. Aug. 27th, 1821.
See further record.

(1235) JOHN—b. 1760, d. Sept. 2, 1841, aged 81; m. Sarah ———, b. 1759, d. Mar. 3, 1833, aged 74; No issue. Lived at the late N. G. Moore's home site.

(1236) THOMAS—b. 1763; d. Aug. 31, 1829, aged 66; m. 1st, Sarah ———, d. Mar. 21, 1808, aged 48; m. 2nd, Mary Hughes, d. June 24, 1853; she, a widow m. 2nd, Samuel Coffman, of New Market. No issue. (Thomas resided at the present Vernon Biedler home site.)

(1237) LUCRETIA—b. ———; d. ———; m. 1785, Thomas Dunkenson.
See further record.
(The tombstones of Reuben, John, and Thomas, and their wives, except Mary Hughes, are in the Moore family burial ground, Mary Coffman's marker is in the 'Lower' Lutheran Churchyard, at New Market.)

---

(125) REUBEN HARRISON, (1731-1807), the youngest son of John Harrison, Sr., (12), and wife Phoebe, was born near Lewes, Deleware, and accompanied his father and mother, in the little band of sixteen, on their removal to Orange, later Augusta, now Rockingham County, Virginia. Frequent mention of him having been made on former pages, particularly in Chapters II, and XI, reference is here made to these as to the tradition regarding his first marriage, his encounter with the robbers, his land patents, and other details of his earlier days in Old Augusta.

He married, as his first wife, Lydia Harrison, his cousin, identified as the daughter of Jeremiah Harrison, (18). She is mentioned as late as 1772, when she joined her husband in deeding land to Christopher Waggoner. (See page 187.)

Upon establishing his home, Reuben settled directly on the early Indian Road, about a mile south of his father, at what is now known as the old Allebaugh place, on the Valley Pike, a short distance south of Lacey Spring. The site of his lawn is marked today by a fine old coffe tree which stood by his house, and which may be readily observed from the Pike—"The Long Grey Trail." The early road on which he located is said to have run immediately in the rear of the present residence, and traces of it may be found here, as well as a few miles further north, at the old Daniel Matthews place, now Locust Grove.

The greater part of Reuben's land was acquired by him through inheritance from his father, John Harrison, Sr., and his brother, John Harrison, Jr. (See their wills in Chapter XI.) The story is told that he had so much land that he gave a part of it away, explaining, in doing so, that he wanted some neighbors. He is listed as owning 1,204 acres in Rockingham, in 1789 (*Wayland*, p. 449), but this being late in his life by no means represented all the land he had handled, or possessed, in his day. By this date, too, several of his children had evidently received their share..

There is a famous old cave mentioned by the historian, Kercheval, as Harrison's Cave, on the tract Reuben gave to his son David. This natural wonder is now opened to the public under the name of "Virginia Caverns," having recently been leased to the owner of the New Market Endless Caverns by one of David's descendants, Thomas Harrison, a great grandson. The entrance to the caverns is within full view of the Pike, and almost immediately on it.

To the lands he had inherited from his brother, John, Jr., in his father's lifetime, Reuben added a tract which his brother had willed his niece, Ann Davison—Deed; 21st August, 1767, "Reuben Moore ( ) & Ann, of Frederick County," to Reuben Harrison, for 100 Pounds, "400 acres on Dry Fork of Smiths Creek, patented to John Harrison, deceased, 10th Feb. 1748, and devised to said Ann." This land was delivered to Thomas Patterson by Reuben's order, January, 1773. (Deed Book 13, p. 495.)

Besides his large Rockingham County estate, he also owned at his death 500 acres of land in Greenbrier.

As early as 1756, Reuben Harrison was appointed "Constable in ye Lower end of Augusta County." (Delinquent reports; *Chalkley*, Vol. II, p. 418.)

One, "Rubin harrison" was among the "Near 10,000 subscribers" to "The Dissenters Petition," which was presented to the Virginia House of Delegates by Thomas Jefferson, and referred to the "Committee of Religion," October 16, 1776. The Valley country having been settled predominently by dissenters, this section of the Old Dominion enthusiastically furnished an abundance of signatures. This famous appeal for religious freedom in Virginia is now preserved among the Archives at the State Library, at Richmond—

"To the Honorable the President and House of Delegates the petition of the Dissenters from the ecclesiastical Establishment in the Commonwealth Humbly Sheweth.

"That your petitioners being (in Common with the other inhabitants of this Commonwealth) delivered from British Oppression, rejoice in the Prospect of having Freedom secured and maintained to them and their posterity inviolate. The hopes of your petitioners have been raised and confirmed by the Declaration of your Honorable House with regard to Liberty. EQUAL LIBERTY! that invaluable Blessing; which though it be the Birthright of every good Member of the State, is what your Petitioners have been deprived of; in that by taxation their property hath been wrested from and given to those from whom they have received no equivalent.

"Your Petitioners therefore having long groaned under the Burden of an Ecclesiastical Establishment beg leave to move your Honorable House that this as well as every other Yoke may be Broken, and that the Oppressed may go free that so every Religious Denomination being on a Level, Animosities may cease and that Christain Forbearance, Love and Charity, may be practiced towards each other, while the Legislature interferes only to support them in their just Rights and equal Privileges

"And your petitioners shall ever pray:

Among the signers besides the above, a few others were—

Zebulun Harrisson	John Ray
Nathaniel Harrisson	John Moore
Josiah Harrisson	Reuben Moore
Burr Harrison	Jacob Lincoln

etc.

In 1777, Reuben Harrison was one of the Captains of Augusta County named, in whose companies the tithables were ordered to be taken. (See page 298.)

On the 28th April, 1778, "William Mc Dowell Gent., Thomas Moore, Aaron Hughes, and Reuben Harrison, or any three of them." were ordered to appraise the estate of Andrew Huling, deceased. (Rockingham Court Order Book I, p. 3.)

Upon the organization of the Rockingham militia, 25th May 1778, Reuben Harrison qualified as a Captain in the new county. (See page 298.) A list of the "Tithables" was ordered 22nd June, the same year, to be taken in the companies of Capt. Robert Cravens, Capt. Abraham Lincoln, Capt. Reuben Harrison, etc. *(Ibid,* p. 12.)

A few months later he was appointed one of the Justices of the Court—

> 22nd Sept. 1778—"New Justices appointed by Patrick Henry, 12th Day of August, last (were) sworn in (and) Daniel Smith Gent, Thomas Hewitt Gent, Silas Hart Gent, George Boswell Gent, John Thomas Gent, William Nalle Gent, James Dyer Gent, Henry Ewing Gent, Wm. Mc Dowell Gent, Anthony Rider Gent, John Fitzwater Gent, John Davis Gent, Reuben Harrison Gent, & Gawen Hamilton Gent, took their seats accordingly." *(Ibid,* p. 18.)
>
> 27th April, 1779—"Ordered that Reuben Harrison Gent. divide the Tithables working on the road from the Line of Shenandoah to Geo. Hustons under John Phillips and John Harrison the overseers thereof." *(Ibid,* p. 32.)

John Harrison was Zebulon's son. John Phillips was a settler probably from New Jersey. He lived in the region of Thomas Moore. A Stephen Phillips, Jr., is mentioned in the Augusta records, August, 1751, as having come in from "New Brunswick, County Middlesex. Province East Jersey." (See, *Chalkley,* Vol. I, p. 306.)

At one sitting of the Rockingham Court early in 1780, half of the justices present were allied with the Harrison family—

> 28th Feb., 1780,—Justices "Present, Daniel Smith, Benjamin Harrison, Wm. Herring, John Davis, Wm. Nalle, Thomas Hewit, Henry Ewing, Reuben Harrison." (Rockingham Court Order Book I, p. 53.)

Lydia Harrison (181), the first wife of Reuben, died about 1780. A short time later he married, as his second wife, Mary McDonald, who following his death removed with her married daughter, Hannah, to Christian County, Kentucky, in 1816.

Mary McDonald * had dau Hannah

Mary was doubtless a near kinswoman of Alexander McDonald, who bought some of John Harrison, Jr's., movables at the sale during the settlement of his estate, in 1767. (See page 184.) One, Patrick McDowell was imported to Augusta by Valentine Sevier, about 1764. (See page 306.) Colonel Angus McDonald headed a small force from Wheeling to the Indian country, a few months before the battle of Point Pleasant. *(Waddell,* p. 219.)

X Col. Angus McDonald

Capt. Reuben Harrison, the justice, died in 1807. His, and his first wife's, ashes rest in the old family cemetery on Smiths Creek—to the east of present Lacey Spring. Until the War of 1861-65, his tombstone was standing, but following the desecration of the site, at the hands of the Northern soldiers as they camped in the meadow, his marker was carried away and lost. Prior to the war the surrounding land had passed into the possession of one of the Lincoln family, who taking advantage of the scattering of the stones during the war removed as far as possible all traces of the old burial ground. Many of the tombstones are said to have been used in building the foundation of the mill nearby. The soldiers had used the old markers to build camp fires on, and had scattered them around the meadow in doing so. Reuben's is said to have been found, and removed by a relative to another burial ground. (The Moore Cemetery near the Virginia Caverns.)

A few years ago, a certified copy of Reuben's will, by rare good luck, was unexpectedly turned up among some old files in the Court House at Harrisonburg. This interesting document reads as follows—

Will of Reuben Harrison

In the Name of God Amen I Reuben Harrison of the County of Rockingham and State of Virginia being Seventy one years of age and Sensibly feeling the decline of nature although of perfect mind and memory Cauling to mind that all men are mortal & born once to Die do make and ordain this my Last Will and Testament in manner & form as followeth to wit first of all & In primis I give and bequeath my Soule into the hands of almighty god who gave it and my Body to the Earth to be decently Intered at the discretion of my executioners in a christian like manner not doubting but I shall receive the same again at the resurrection of the Just & as touching my worldly estate wherewith it hath pleased god to bless me with in this life I give and bequeath in the following manner to wit

Firstly all Just & Lawful Debts & funeral charges to be paid

Secondly I give and bequeath unto my well beloved wife Mary Harrison the full & entire privileges and sole benefits and prophets of all my old plantation with all the buildings and Improvements thereon during her natural life or as long as she continues my widow and at her decease or marriage the above old plantation to be the property of my son Abner Harrison forever also one Late Survey contan . . g thirty acres that I purcesed from Josiah Harrison also a Small survey of four acres adjoining to the above thirty acres I give and bequeath in the same manner as the above old plantation also fifty acres of another survey adjoining to said old plantation on the west side thereof as above I likewise give and bequeath unto my above named wife Mary Harrison one femel Mulato Slave named Jude also all my household and kitchen furniture with two Beds Bedsteads and Beddings that she may choose with her several suits of apparel and one horse or Mare that she may choose out of my Stock her Saddle & Bridle and three Milch cows & Six Sheep at her choise

Thirdly I give and bequeath unto my eldest Daughter Lucrese Harrison one Survey of Land contain . . g Twenty acres more or less it being the survey where the Negroes now hath a field

Fourthly I give and bequeath unto my eldest son Nathanel Harrison one Negro Slave named Jacob

Fifthly I order and it is my will that a certain obligation that I have again . . my second son John Harrison for the sum of Eighty two pounds priceseable bearing date the twelfth day of March in the year of one thousand Seven Hundred Ninety and four that at my Decease my Executors Deliver said obligation to my said Son John his heirs & so forth without money or reward in full for his part of my Estate

Sixthly I Give and bequeath unto my son Joseph Harrison one Negro Slave named Lonee—

Seventhly I Give and bequeath unto my two sons Joseph & Reuben Harrison a Tract of Land that I have in green Brier containing five Hundred acres to be Equally divided by my under named Executioners being the Land whereon the said Joseph & Reuben Harrison now lives and also I give and bequeath unto my above named Son

Joseph my large Still and also I give and bequeath unto my above named Son Reuben one Negro Slave named Peter

Eightly I give and bequeath unto my Son David Harrison three Hundred and Twenty three acres of Land in too surve . s it being the land he now lives on

Ninethly I give and bequeath unto my Son Samuel Harrison five Hundred acres of Land in two surveys to wit two Hundred and fifty acres where William Jerryholmes formerly lived and two Hundred and fifty acres lying on the west of my other lands known by Executioners

Tenthly I give and bequeath unto my too daughters Rachel the wife of Jesse Harrison and Hannah Harrison the meadow Survey Including the round Bottom with another survey containing one Hundred & fifty acres to be Equally Divided by my Executors Between the above named woemen and also my above named Daughter Rachel to have one Negro femel slave named Jin and Hannah is to have one Negro Slave named Rome and what ever lands I have not already Specified I do order my Executioners to sell for the highest price that may be Either at public O . ction or other ways & to convey the same by Deeds in fee simple to the purchasers thereof & the money arising therefrom to be Equally divided amongst and between my Eight Sons to wit Nathaniel John Josiah Joseph Reuben David Samuel & Abner Harrison and as touching my personal Estate not already Specified I order my Executioners to sell at Public O . ction and the money arising therefrom to be among and Between my four Daughters Equally Divided to wit Lucresy Harrison Lidey the wife of John Neely Elizabeth the wife of Thos Warren Ann the wife of John Chrisman

Eleventhly and Lastly I constitute & ordain my two well af . ected and Trusty sons Nathanel Harrison and David Harrison the whole and Sole Executioners of this my Last will and Testament and I do hereby revoke disannul & Disallow all former wills and Testaments by me made constituted or *or* ordained and I do constitute ordain this and no other to be my last will and Testament

In Testimony whereof I have hereunto affixed my Seal and Subscribed my name this Second day of May in the year of our Blessed Lord god one thousand Eight Hundred and too 1802.

Reuben Harrison (SEAL).

Signed Sealed pronounced published and Declared in presents of us and we in his presents and in presents of each other have hereunto subscribed our names

Wm. Dunlap
Josiah Harrison
Andrew Bowman
Samuel Lacey

N. B. It is further my will before Signing that my too old Slaves Con & Frank be free at my Deceas.

Rockingham April Court 1807
The Last Will and Testament of Reuben Harrison Deceased was presented in Court and proven by oaths of William Dunlap, Josiah Harrison and Andrew Bowman and ordered to be Recorded.

Teste: S. M. Williams C.R.C.

A COPY Teste: S. M. Williams, C.R.C.
A COPY Teste: J. F. Blackburn Clerk.
(The last named, Mr. Blackburn, was the one who found the McWilliams copy recently, and kindly supplied the above.)

Among the witnesses, Josiah Harrison was doubtless Reuben's nephew, Zebulon's son. Samuel Lacy appears to have been the one from whom Lacy Spring took its name.

"Tuesday to wit:

At a Court held for the County of Rockingham the 21st day of April 1807.

Benjamin Harrison, Josiah Harrison, Thomas Moore & Arch Rutherford—
Justices.

The Last will and Testament of Reuben Harrison dec. was presented in Court and was proven by the oaths of William Dunlap, Josiah Harrison & Andrew Bowman, and ordered to be recorded and on the Motion of David Harrison, one of the Executors named in the said Will, who with security entered into and acknowledged bond, and made oath thereto, as the Law dire . ts, a Certificate is Granted him for obtaining a probate indue form, Nathl Harrison the other Exer. named in said Will, appeared in Court and refused to Join in the said Probate and It is ordered that Benjamin Tallman Andrew Bowman, Michael Summers & Solomon Mathews or any three of them being sworn be appointed to appraise the said estate and make report to the Court." (See, Rockingham Court Order Book VI.)

As named in the foregoing will, the children of Capt, Reuben Harrison, (125), were:

By 1st wife, Lydia Harrison

(1251) LUCRETIA—b. ———; d. ———; unmarried.

(1252) NATHANIEL—b. ———; d. 1807; m. 1784, Mary Woodley, b. Feb. 18, 1764. See further record.

(1253) JOHN—b. 1761; d. 1819; m. Grace Woodley, b. Jan. 27, 1762. See further record.

(1254) JOSIAH—b. ———; d. 1827, c; m. ———; removed to Kyser, now West Va. See further record.

(1255) LYDIA—b. ———; d. ———; m. 1st., John Neely, m. 2nd., John Woodley; he b. Nov. 26, 1767, removed to Warren Co., Tenn. See further record.

(1256) JOSEPH—b. ———; d. ———; m. Polly Boyd, (?) Dec. 18, 1806, removed to Greenbrier County, now West Virginia.

(1257) REUBEN—b. ———; d. ———; removed to Greenbrier with twin brother Joseph. (Settled in present Monroe Co?).

(1258) ELIZABETH—b. ———; d. ———; m. May 2, 1793, Thomas Warren, descendant of John Warren, lived in Harrisonburg. See further reference.

(1259) DAVID—b. Apr. 20, 1775; d. Mar. 1, 1851; m. 1799, Elizabeth Pickering —dau. of William—b. Apr. 7, 1781, d. Mar. 23, 1851. See further record.

(1260) ANN—b. Jan. 28, 1777; d. Mar. 25. 1839; m. 1795, John Chrisman, b. Aug. 17, 1773, d. May 1, 1815. See further record.

(1261) SAMUEL—b. twin bro. of Ann; m. Esther Hooke, removed to Rockbridge County. See further record.

By 2nd wife, Mary McDonald

(1262) HANNAH—b. ———; d. ———; m. Oct. 17, 1805, William Brisbain, removed to Christian County, Kentucky, 1815, and later to Missouri.

(1263) RACHEL—b. ———; d. ———; m. May 26, 1801, Jesse Harrison (1771), son of Ezekiel (177), removed to Christian County, Ky., 1815, and later to Ill., and thence to Mo.
See further reference. .

(1264) ABNER—b. ———; d. Dec., 1807, unmarried, and intestate..

See further reference, under Josiah, above.

CLAN OF CAPT. DANIEL HARRISON

(162), DANIEL HARRISON, JR., (1727-), the second son of Capt. Daniel Harrison, Sr., (16), and 1st wife Margaret, was born on Maiden Plantation, Sussex County, Delaware, and settled in the Muddy Creek community a few miles north of his father, where on the 5th September, 1749, he patented 262 acres of land. On the 21st August, 1764, his father conveyed to him 200 acres in this same neighborhood, adjoining his brother Jesse, part of 400 acres patented to the elder Daniel, 25th September, 1746. (See pages 194 and 210.)

In his father's lifetime Daniel, Jr. is referred to on the Augusta records as "Daniel Harrison, Jr.", an instance of which occurs in the mention of his bond of 17th January, 1764, to James Ma Gill. (County Court Judgements March, 1765, Ma Gill vs. Daniel Harrison; *Chalkley*, Vol. I, pp. 334 and 340.)

He married prior to 1767, when he had a wife named Sarah. On the 20th June, this year, "Daniel Harrison Jr. and wife Sarah," for 53 Pounds, deeded to George Baxter 106 acres of land, "on a branch of Muddy Creek," part of the 400 acres above, "200 acres of which Daniel Harrison, Sr. conveyed to his son Daniel, Jr., of which this 106 acres is a part," corner Jesse Harrison's part of said 400 acres. This land was delivered to Jesse Harrison, 29, March, 1783. (See, Deed Book 15, p. 498.)

Daniel, (Jr.), as well as his brother Benjamin, is mentioned as a Captain early in the Revolution. (See page 298.)

About 1805, or 6, he emigrated to Kentucky, likely in company with a nephew; several of Col. Benjamin Harrison's sons, among them Fielding, having removed to Christian County about this time. (See Power's *Early Settlers of Sangamon Co., Ill.*, p. 359, and later mention.)

On the 24th February, [1806], "Daniel Har[rison] of the estate of Kentucky, and Michael Harrison of the S[tate] of tenasse," conveyed to Daniel Smith "of the state [of] Virginia and of Rockingham County," all the said Daniel Harrison's interest in his father's estate, as inherited under the latter's will; the transaction being explained as follows—"Whereas Daniel Harrison late of the County of Rock[ingham] dec'd and in and by his last will and Testament [. . . . .recorded in the County Court of Augusta] among [other] things devised that all his out lands be sold [and] after the payment of his just debts the money be [equally divided] as mentioned in said will, and wheras the sai[d] [Daniel] Harrison is one of the sons of the said Daniel Harri[son] [Sr.] as such entitled to a share of all monies arising fr[om] [the] outlands aforesaid which share he hath heretofore sol[d] [to] the said Michael Harrison and whereas the said Mi[chael] Harrison has sold all his right and interest and cl[aim] in and unto the said outlands and all monies . . . . . therefrom to the said Daniel Smith. Now this In[denture], Witnesseth," etc. [signed] Daniel Harrison, Michael Harrison, witness

George Loftus. Proved, "State of Kentucky, Christianit [y] County . . ." etc. "Rockingham July Court 1806. This Deed from Daniel & Michael Harrison to Dan[iel] Smith was presented in Court and being duly certifie[d] . . . . the County of Christianity and State of Kentucky and . . . . . to be recorded. Teste S. McWilliams." (Rockingham B. R. Deed Book 1, pp. 107-8, mutilated.)

Apparently, Daniel, Jr., left no children. In 1763, when his father deeded the land to his (Daniel, Sr's.,) grandchildren, only Jesse's sons were named. At the time of his migration to Kentucky he was nearing 80 years of age, yet at this late period of his life, instead of remaining in Rockingham with one of his children, and disposing of his inheritance through him or her, he sold out to one with whom, manifestly, he was not living, and proceeded to remove to an unsettled community. In the first census of the United States, *Heads of Families*, Virginia, 1784, "Harrison, Daniel," of Rockingham County, the only 'Head' so named, was listed by Josiah Davison, with "2 White souls, 1 Dwelling"; his name appearing among others of the Muddy Creek neighborhood, such as Joseph Hinton, Archibald Hopkins, Sr., Daniel Love, etc. (First Census, p. 76.) He, himself, being one of the white souls and his wife presumably the other, his whole family would seem to be accounted for, so far as his immediate household at the time was concerned.

In Kentucky, he is thought to have resided with some one of his nephews. His wife had no doubt died in Virginia prior to his removal thence.

---

(163) JESSE HARRISON, (1729-1817 c), the third son of Capt. Daniel Harrison, Sr., (16), and 1st wife, Margaret, as his brother above, was born on Maiden Plantation in Delaware, and was enumerated among the *Heads of Families, Virginia*, 1784, as "Harrison, Jesse, Senr," by Josiah Davison, and listed with "8 White souls, I Dwelling, 1 Other building." *(First Census*, p. 76.)

Jesse located in the Muddy Creek neighborhood, "near the head of one of the main branches of Linvilles creek." In 1753-4 he was among the "Inhabitants of North Mountain, at the head of Muddy Creek," who petitioned for a road from Ephraim Love's to the South Branch of the Shenandoah. (See page 201.) Curiously enough, his father deeded two of his (Jesse's) sons land before sharing in this respect with his own sons. On the 14th November, 1763, Daniel Harrion, Sr., (about two years following his second marriage), conveyed to his grandsons Daniel and Jesse, the sons of his son Jesse, 400 acres of land on the head of Linville's Creek. The next year, 22nd March, 1764, Daniel, Sr., conveyed to Jesse, his son, two tracts in the same neighborhood, totaling 400 acres. On the 10th July, 1766, Jesse patented 170 acres in this region—thus, all told, he was the virtual owner of about 1,000 acres here. (See pages 211 and 195.) In 1789, "Jesse Harrison Sr." is listed as owning 544 acres of land in Rockingham. *(Wayland*, p. 449.)

Jesse's wife appears to have been called Sarah—a popular name evidently in his family. His father, Daniel, Sr., his brother, Daniel, Jr., his son Jesse, Jr. his uncle Thomas, and the latter's son Thomas, were all partial to Sarahs. Sarah the wife of Jesse, Jr., was a Curry, but her mother-in-law's maiden name is unknown. She was likely a Moore. The elder Sarah probably died about 1815, and the younger about 1820.

Daniel and Jesse, Jr., the sons of Jesse, were married in 1784, and 1785, respectively. In 1787, Jesse made two conveyances on the same day, one to Daniel, and one to Jesse, Jr.,—"Jesse Harrison Sr. and wife to Jesse Harrison Jr." etc. (Rockingham

Burnt Deeds 000, p. 362.) These deeds being entirely burned, the reference here is taken from the Court Order Book.

That Sarah was the wife of Jesse, Sr., is indicated later—"This indenture made this 15th day of August in the year of our Lord one thousand eight hundred and fifteen, between Jesse Harrison and Sarah, his wife, of the County of Rockingham, State of Virginia, of the one part" . . . . and John Deter, of etc. the other part,—conveyance of a small tract, "near one of the main branches of Linvills Creek and on the Brocks Gap road containing twelve acres and one-half of land on which is a small spring, it being part of a tract of land which was granted to Jessee Harrison by patent bearing date the 10th day of July, 1766, containing one hundred and seventy acres, the residue whereof, being yet in possession of the said Harrison . . . . In witness whereof, the said Jesse Harrison and Sarah his wife, have hereunto set their hands and seals the day and year first above written. (signed) Jesse Harrison. (Rockingham B. R. Deed Book 2, p. 538.)

Several years after the above, appears a conveyance clearly from Jesse, Jr., viz. January 19, 1819, "Jesse Harrison, and Sarah, his wife, to Benjamin Bowman," tract lying "on Linvils Creek being the South end of a tract of four hundred acres conveyed to the Said Jesse Harrison and Daniel Harrison by their Grand Father Daniel Harrison and Sarah his wife divided by a line run across Said Tract as a line of partition between the Said Jesse Harrison and Daniel Harrison the Younger as will more fully appear reference being had to a Deed made by Said Daniel Harrison the Younger to Jacob Spitler," etc. (Rockingham B. R. Deed Book 4, p. 387.)

A part of the 170 acres patented to Jesse, Sr., had been conveyed to Jesse, Jr., by the 1787 deed;—Deed, April 20, 1819, "Jesse Harrison and Sarah, his wife" (signed by Jesse only), to John Bowman, a little over 21 acres, "on the North West side of the Main Branch of Linvils Creek," one of the lines running "to a leaning white oak corner of Jesse Harrison's Pattent," the land "being a part of a Tract of one hundred and seventy . . . . to Jesse Harrison by Pattent bearing date the tenth day of July one thousand seven hundred . . . . conveyed to Jesse Harrison Junr by Deed bearing date . . . . . 1787." (Rockingham B. R. Deed Book 4, p. 156, mutilated.)

On the same date, April 20, 1819, "Jesse Harrison and Sarah, his wife," conveyed to John Detrick, a "part of one hundred and seventy acres granted to Jesse Harrison by Patent bearing date the 10th day of July 1766." (*Ibid*, pp. 156-7, signed by Jesse only.)

Sometime between 1815, and 1819, Jesse Harrison, Senior, the indications are, died, and the son was now disposing of the remainder of his father's patented land, a tract obviously some distance from his home—being on the Brock's Gap road, etc. About this time Jesse, Jr's., brother, Daniel, removed to Kentucky, and in 1818, as a resident of Clark County, sold out to his brother (Jesse) of Rockingham. His land, as will appear later, was a part of the original Daniel Harrison, Sr., land, "on the head of Linville's Creek." (See page 211.) Thus Jesse, Jr., while disposing of his out lands, was establishing himself more firmly on the home plantation.

In his will of 1761, Robert Harrison, the uncle of Daniel and Jesse, Jr., left a bequest to their sister Ann. (See page 192.) The latter died unmarried at her brother's home in Kentucky, having most likely accompanied him thither on his migration, after her parents' death.

Daniel, the brother of Jesse, Jr., has frequently been confused with his cousin of the same name, the son of Col. Benjamin Harrison. Each Daniel had a wife Ann, and

Ann Patton

both removed to Kentucky. Daniel, Jesse, Sr's., son, married Ann Patton, and settled, as above noted, in Clark County, while Daniel, Col. Benjamin's son, married Ann Ervin, and settled at, or near, Hopkinsville, in Christian County. According to their tombstone inscriptions the Clark County Daniel was born in 1760, or several years before Col. Benjamin Harrison's marriage. He it was who married Ann Patton, she being the daughter of Matthew Patton, and they, Daniel and Ann, were the parents of Patton Harrison, born in 1795. (See later reference.)

Similar to the two Daniels, there were also two Benjamins, evidently, one a son of Col. Benjamin Harrison, and the other, inferentialy at least, a son of Jesse Harrison, Sr. In fact, according to the descendants of Daniel of Clark County, he had a brother Benjamin.

Elizabeth Koontz
John Koontz

A Benjamin Harrison and Polly Hall, the daughter of John Hall (of Middle River), were married by the Rev. Wm. Wilson, March 22nd, 1791. (Marriage Bonds, and Marriages of Augusta County; *Chalkley*, Vol. II, pp. 296, 352.) A Benjamin Harrison and Elizabeth Koontz, both of Rockingham, were married April 4, 1809, by the Rev. Christopher Frye. (First Marriage Book of Rockingham.) Elizabeth was the daughter of John Koontz, who signed the marriage bond. *(Strickler*, p. 62.) On May 24th, 1814, Benjamin Harrison, Jr. and Nancy, his wife, deeded to David Coffman land on Cooks Creek. (Rockingham B. R. Deed Book 0000, p. 306.)

The first and last named Benjamin was the Colonel's son. According to *The McClure Family*, and others, he married Polly Hall, but she died in 1793, as further disclosed in two letters from her father of June 5th and August 7th, this year—filed later in connection with his suit, "John Hall vs. Benjamin Harrison Jr."— in the first of which it is stated that "Polly died without children." (Judgements, April 1795; *Chalkley*, Vol. II, p. 23.)

Nancy was Benjamin, Jr's., second wife. His deed to Coffman was for a fraction over one acre of land—part of a tract he had sold to Henry Harshbarger, at whose request the conveyance was made—the whole transaction being explained in another deed of the same date, viz. 24th May, 1814, "Benjamin Harrison Jr. and Nancy his wife of the county of Rockingham and state of Virginia," to "Henry Harshbarger of the same county and state," consideration 3000 pounds lawful money of Virginia, "two certain tracts or parcels of land . . . . on Cooks Creek containing 318 three quarters [acres] and 21 poles be the same more or less and was conveyed unto the said Benjamin Harrison Jr. by Benjamin Harrison Sr. by deed of Bargain and Sale bearing date the 15th. day of September 1807" . . . the first tract 100 acres, the second 218¾ acres, 21 poles "(being the ballance of the 220 acre tract after deducting the one are 19 poles conveyed to David Coffman," by direction of said Harshbarger, etc.) (signed) Benjamin Harrison, Jr., Nancy Harrison. (Rockingham B. R. Deed Book 2, p. 331.)

Col. Benjamin Harrison in his conveyances was styled Benjamin Harrison, Sr.,—Deed, 1806, "Benjamin Harrison, Senior, and Mary, his wife, of the county of Rockingham and state of Virginia," to William Harrison and Ezekiel Logan also of Rockingham, seven and a fraction acres of land on the north branch of Cooks Creek, part of two tracts received by said Benjamin under the will of Daniel Harrison, etc. (Rocking-B. R. Deed Book 1, p. 89.)

In his own will, Col. Harrison mentions land that his son Benjamin had sold to "Harshbarger," thus confirming the above transaction, and completing the identification of Benjamin, Jr.

Among the subscribers from Virginia, to *A General History of the Baptist Denomination in America*, by David Benedict, published at Boston, 1813, was

Benjamin Harrison, Jr., whose name was sent in, along with those of Ezekiel Harrison, John Lincoln, Anderson Moffett, Samuel Harshbarger, etc., by Thomas Buck, Esq., of Belle Air, Frederick County. (See—Subscribers, end Vol. II.)

Benjamin Harrison who married Elizabeth Koontz migrated with her to Rowan County, Tennessee, and after his death she removed to Valporaiso, Indiana, where she died at the home of her son William. As this Benjamin was obviously not the above, nor the son of the above by his first wife, but was instead his contemporary, it appears fairly certain that he was the Colonel's nephew—the said brother of Daniel of Clark County.

Among the six children of Jesse Harrison, Sr's., family at the time of the 1784 census, was Michael Harrison, of the 1806 deed, who removed to Tennessee. (See page 313.) Michael married Margaret Ragan, February 9th, 1784. His marriage bond was signed by Jesse Harrison as surety. (*Wayland*, p. 444, *Strickler*, p. 61.) He settled in, or near, present Jonesboro, Tennesee, where, about 1790, he was Sheriff of Washington District, N. C.

Sarah, the wife of Jesse Harrison, Jr., following her husband's deed of 1819, dissappears from the record. On January 1st, 1825, "Jesse Harrison and Mary J. Harrison, his wife," conveyed to David Hinton two tracts of land on the "head waters of Linvilles Creek," etc. (Rockingham B. R. Deed Book 6, p. 558-9.)

On February 9th, 1826, "The last will and Testament of Jesse Harrison des. was presented in Court and proved by the oaths of Reuben Moore Jr. and Archibald Rutherford and ordered to be Recorded, and the Codicle annexed to the said Will was proved by the oaths of the witnesses thereto and also ordered to be Recorded . . . . Mary Harrison wife of Jesse Harrison, deceased, personally appeared in court, and relinguished and renounced the provisions may—for her by the will of her said Husband, which is ordered to be certified." (Rockingham Court Order Book.)

The suit of Elizabeth Moore vs. Jesse Harrison, for "breach of Promise of marriage," was recorded in Sept. 1803. (Circuit Court Judgements; *Chalkley*, Vol. II, p. 27.)

At the time of his death the decaesed was in possession of 284 acres of land, according to an assignment of dower from his estate to his widow Mary J. Harrison, in pursuance of a decree of the October term of court, 1826. The commissioners went upon the land January 25th, 1827. Jesse Ralston and John H. Ralston, as Jesse's executors, a little later conveyed 70 acres of land on Linville's Creek to John Teter or Detrick. (Rockingham B. R. Deed Book 7, p. 144.)

As named above, the children of Jesse Harrison, Sr., (163), and wife Sarah, were—

(1631) Ann— b. 1758; "departed this Life April 18, 1820, in the 62nd. year of her age." Buried in the old family cemetery on the Thomas Lewis Van Meter farm, near Winchester, Ky.

(1632) Daniel—b. Sept. 2, 1760; d. March 16, 1823; m. Jan. 29, 1784, Ann Patton, daughter of Matthew. She d. Feb. 7, 1819, "in the 50th. year of her age." Both Daniel and wife buried as above.
See further record.

(1633) Jesse—b. 1763 c; d. Jan., 1826; m. 1st, 1785, Sarah Curry, daughter of John. She d. about 1820, m., 2nd. Mary J. ——; probably Ralston, who outlived her husband.

(1634) Benjamin—b. 1772 c (?); d. 1824; m. April 4, 1809, Elizabeth Koontz, daughter of John. Removed to Tenn.
See further record.

And two or three others, including probably a daughter Mary, and likely a son Michael, who married in 1784, Margaret Ragan, and migrated to Jonesboro, Tenn.

A single old Harrison marker in the cemetery at Dayton, Virginia, recites—"Here lies the body of Mary Harrison who departed this life the 30th Day of April 1793, Aged 26."

BOWYER-KAVANAUGH

(164) MARY HARRISON, (1733-), the daughter of Capt. Daniel Harrison, Sr., (16), and first wife Margaret, married, 1st, Henry Bowyer, who was lost at sea in 1760. She married, 2nd, William Kavanaugh. One son by her first husband, viz:

(1641) HENRY—m. Agatha Madison.
See page 209 for further record.

SMITH.

(165) JANE HARRISON, (1735-1796), the eldest daughter of Capt. Daniel Harrison, Sr., (16), and 1st wife Margaret, was born in Delaware, and in childhood brought by her parents to Augusta, later Rockingham County, Virginia, where, about 1751, she married Daniel Smith, the son of Capt. John Smith, the immigrant frequently referred to on former pages. (See particularly pages 8, 37, 141, 149, 199, and 205.)

Daniel Smith and his wife, Jane, settled at historic Smithland, on the early "Great Road," a short distance north of present Harrisonburg. (See page 238.) The land, 660 acres, had been patented by Capt. Daniel Harrison, and his son Robert, and was purchased by Daniel Smith, 22nd November, 1764, from his brother Abraham, who had purchased it (a few days earlier) from Robert Harrison's executors. (See pages 194 and 211.)

At various times Daniel Smith served as one of the justices of Augusta court, his last term ending with the formation of Rockingham County. For many years, until October, 1777, he was a member of the Courtmartial for West Augusta district. In the battle of Point Pleasant he was a Captain under Gen. Andrew Lewis, and is mentioned by Waddell as of this rank in 1776. In 1775 he was a member of the Third Virginia Convention. (See page 232.) On September 20th, 1781, he was commissioned Deputy Purveyor, Southern Department, in the Revolutionary Army. Upon the formation of Rockingham County he was one of the first justices, and was commissioned Colonel of the militia (See pages 238 and 298.) On the 25th May, 1778, he took the "Oath of fidelity to the State as Vestryman." On March 26, 1781, he took the oath as oath as County Lieutenant of Rockingham.

Being one of the wealthiest men of his day in the county, his house was probably the most commodious, and in it, at the order of the Virginia Assembly, was held the first Court of Rockingham County.

It was here that his father died, in 1779, of "the dangerously malignant Fever," mentioned in the old Court Order Book. (See page 239)—

> 20th Nov. 1779, Last will of John Smith deceased proven and on motion of Margaret Smith, Robert Smith, and James Davis ordered to be recorded. Ordered that Benjamin Harrison, Leonard Herren Nehemiah Harrison & Josiah Harrison or any three of them appraise this estate." (Rockingham Court Order Book I, p. 49.)

At the outbreak of the Revolution, so it is related, the patriotic old Captain applied for a commission in the army, and was greatly offended that he was refused on account of his age. (*Waddell,* p. 151.)

Rockingham's first jail, a crude log structure, was erected on the Smithland estate. It is said to have stood on the prominence on the opposite side of the Valley Pike from the present residence, near the ruins of an old well, which still remain.

Following the resignation of Col. Abraham Smith, as the County Lieutenant, in 1780, Col. Daniel Smith (his brother) was commissioned to this office. On September 24th 1781, as the presiding justice of the court, he signed the old order or minute book for the last time, and left immediately for Yorktown, where it is stated, he joined four of his sons, viz. John, Daniel, Joseph, and Robert, in the seige. (D. S. H. MSS.) On the return of Rockingham's troops following the surrender, he summonsed them for a grand review to celebrate the victory, the last act of which was the "running salute." As the soldiers opened fire his horse became frightened, causing the accident which resulted in his death. (See page 245.) His widow outlived him fifteen years.

Col. Daniel Smith, and wife, Jane Harrison, (165), had issue—

(1651) John—b. Nov. 30, 1752; d. ——; m. 1776, Margaret Davis
See further record.

(1652) Daniel—b. June 25, 1754; d. ——; Commanded a company at the battle of Point Pleasant, after his captain was killed.

(1653) Joseph—b. Feb. 9, 1756.

(1654) Robert—b. Nov. 28, 1757; d. unmarried.

(1655) Margaret—b. Oct. 27, 1759.

(1656) Benjamin—b. May 25, 1761; d. Aug. 18, 1812; m. 1782-3, Elizabeth Cravens, (1484), dau. of Robert, Jr. She b. 1762, and d. Feb. 22, 1837. Removed, 1810, to near present Lancaster, Ohio.
See further record.

(1657) Ann—b. Sept. 6, 1763.

(1658) Jane—b. July 19, 1765; m. Smith Lofland.

(1659) Sarah—b. Oct. 13, 1767.

(1660) Abraham—b. July 23, 1770, d. unmarried.

(1661) William—b. Aug. 20, 1775; d. Oct. 6, 1806, m. Dinah Mc Donough, b. Sept. 19, 1776, d. Jan. 22, 1842. Lived at Smithland.
See further record.

(1662) James—b. Mar. 6, 1779; d. 1827 c; m. 1804, Rebecca Emmett, of Augusta County. Removed, 1807, to Mt. Vernon, Ohio.
See further record.

(D. S. H. MSS., also see *Boogher,* p. 347.)

---

(167) BENJAMIN HARRISON, (1741-1819), the youngest son of Capt. Daniel Harrison, Sr., (16), and first wife, Margaret, was born on his father's plantation at present Dayton, Rockingham County, Virginia. (See page 295.) His fine old stone mansion is yet standing near Silver Lake, at the eastern gateway to the town.

Among the Heads of Families of Virginia, Rockingham County, 1784, "Harrison, Benja." was listed (by himself) with "14 White souls, I Dwelling, 4 Other buildings." (*First U. S. Census,* p. 77.)

Under his father's will of 1767, proven 1770, Benjamin inherited his father's home plantation, to which he added from time to time. As disclosed by an inclusive survey, recorded September 12, 1801, made "Pursuant to an Order of the County Court of Rockingham," it then totaled 1129¼ acres of land, including the following tracts—

$83\frac{1}{2}$ acres willed him by his father. (See page 128.)

215 acres willed him by his father.

65 acres willed him by his father.

185 acres patented to John Edwards, 20th. Sept. 1768, and willed by the same to Benjamin 31st Oct. 1775.

30 acres, patented by Thomas Gordon, 9th Aug., 1758 and deeded by the same to Benjamin 20th. Jan. 1793.

$32\frac{1}{2}$ acres, new survey, 21st. Feb., 1801, by virtue of a warrant for which he is assignee of Alexander Herring, of George Lang, Jr., of George Picket, part of said Picket's warrant of 3000 acres No. 18619, 13th. Aug., 1783.

$38\frac{3}{4}$ acres, new survey, 21st. Feb., 1801, pursuant to the following warrants—viz. for 16 acres assignee of Alexander Herring, of William Oliver, and William Russell, part of said Russell's warrant for 1000 acres, No. 10960, 13th February., 1782, and for $23\frac{3}{4}$acres he is assignee of Jacob Bear, part of said Bear's warrant for 1000 acres No. 17531, 27th. June, 1783.

$16\frac{1}{2}$ acres, new survey, by the following warrants—for 5 acres he is assignee of Alexander Herring, of Wm. Oliver, of Wm. Russell, part of said Russell's warrant for 1000 acres, No. 10960, 13th. Feb., 1782; for $11\frac{1}{2}$ acres he is assignee of John Harrison, part of said Harrison's exchange warrant for 750 acres, No. 976, 29th. May, 1800.

1 acre, new survey, 21st. Feb., 1801, by warrant for 3000 acres No. 18619, 13th. Aug., 1783, for which he is assignee of Alexander Herring, of Geo. Lang Jr., and of George Picket.

421 acres, new survey, 20th. March, 1801, by the following warrants—50 acres he is assignee of Alexander Herring, of Wm. Oliver and of Wm. Russell, part of said Russell's warrant for 1000 acres, No. 10960, 13th. Aug., 1782; for 371 acres he is assignee of John Harrison's exchange warrant for 752 acres, No. 976, 8 th. May, 1800.

41 acres of surplus land by the following warrants—for 29 acres he is assignee of John Harrison, part of said Harrison's warrant's for 752 acres, No. 976, 8th May, 1801; for 12 acres he is assignee of Alexander Herring, of George Lang Jr., and Geo. Picket, pursuant to said Picket's warrant for 3000 acres, No. 18619, 13th. Aug. 1783.

$1{,}129\frac{1}{4}$ Total acres

(See, Rockingham County, Surveyor's Book.)

About the time of the above survey, a caveat was filed against it by Alexander Herring, probably the son of William. (See, Judgements, September, 1799, A-L; Alexr. Herring vs. Benj. Harrison; *Chalkley*, Vol. II, p. 47.)

Benjamin Harrison married, in 1763, Mary McClure, the daughter of John, and Mary McClure, who came to Augusta in 1740. (See page 135, also *The McClure Family*, p. 130.) She was baptized 28th November, 1742, and died in 1815. The marriage license was dated 8th August, 1763. (*Chalkley*, Vol. II, p. 276.)

John McClure, in 1751, purchased 387 acres of land on Muddy Creek of Daniel Harrison, Sr., 200 acres of which he and wife Mary conveyed to Barney Murry and John Huston, 21st March, 1769. (Deed Book 15, p. 296.)

In 1768, Benjamin Harrison is mentioned as a highway surveyor, "from Linville's Creek to Mole Hill," being succeeded on May 12th, the same year, by Henry Erwin.

On the 29th June, 1769, William Herring was appointed road overseer, vice Benjamin Harrison. (Order Books 12, p. 490, 13 p. 234.)

Benjamin's appointment as Captain in 1762, his services as such at the battle of Point Pleasant, and at the beginning of the Revolution, and his appointment successively, as Lieut. Colonel, in 1778 (May 25th), Colonel, in 1780, and County Lieutenant of Rockingham, in 1781, have been noted at the beginning of this Chapter.

On the 25th May, 1778, he took the oath of fidelity to the State of Virginia, as a vestryman. His appointment as a justice of the County Court of Rockingham followed soon thereafter—

> 22nd. March, 1779, "Benjamin Harrison & Wm. Herren Gents took the Oath of Justice of Peace & Justice of the County Court . . . also a Justice of Oyer & Terminer—Present Reuben Harrison, Benjamin Harrison, & Wm. Herren." (Rockingham Court Order Book I, p. 26.)
>
> 23rd. March, 1779, "Present, Daniel Smith, Benja. Harrison, Wm. Herren, Gawen Hamilton." *(Ibid*, p. 27.)
>
> 24th. May, 1779, Justices present. Daniel Smith, Abraham Smith, Henry Ewing, Reuben Harrison, Gawen Hamilton, Benj. Harrison, James Dyer." *(Ibid*, p. 33.)

Gawen Hamilton was a surveyor. On the 28th April, 1778, Hamilton was sworn in to run the "Devision Line with Augusta," under Thomas Lewis, and was at the same time recommended as deputy surveyor. *(Ibid*, p. 3.) James Dyer was the son-in-law of Zebulon Harrison. (See page 304.)

In 1787, and again in 1801-2, Benjamin Harrison was the High Sheriff of Rockingham County.

He represented his county as a member of the House of Delegates, from 1781 to 1783, and from 1799 to 1803. (Wayland's *History of Rockingham*, pp. 441 and 442.)

On June 22nd, 1789, James Curry, Brewer Reeves, Benjamin Harrison, and Thomas Scott, as trustees of the Presbyterian Church of Harrisonburg, were granted liberty by the Circuit Court of Rockingham to build a house for public worship. The deed for the lot, on East Market Street, was made out to the above trustees, September 25, 1792 by Charles McClain.

"The Presbyterian Church of Harrisonburg" was organized as a distinct church under the permission of the Presbytery of Lexington, granted April 15, 1789, in answer to a petition, October 23, 1788, of the Harrisonburg congregation, to which Rev. Benjamin Erwin had been preaching one third of his time. The Presbytery confirmed this arrangement for a pastor, and on October 20, 1789, the Mossy Creek, and Cook's Creek Church, and the Harrisonburg Church, reported that Rev. Erwin had been so "employed." As stated elsewhere the parent church of the Presbyterians of Harrisonburg was the old "Cook's Creek and Peaked Mountain Church" of near Cross Keys (See page 151.) On March 22, 1779, the deed from Robert Hill to the Presbyterian congregation, appropriating a lot for its use on the Public Square of Harrisonburg, was ordered to be recorded, "Thomas Brewster to pay fees." (Rockingham Court Order Book I; *Year Book, Presbyterian Church, Harrisonburg*, Va., 1928, p. 45.)

Col. Benjamin Harrison died in 1819. An incomplete copy if his will, found among his effects, reads as follows—

Will of Benjamin Harrison

I Benjamin Harrison, of the county of Rockingham, State of Virginia, finding my bodily strength much inpaired, through the natural effects of advance age, and deeming it my duty, while of sound and disposing mind & memory to make further distribution to that portion of my estate, whereof I have not hitherto disposed, after humbly committing my Soul to the divine Author of my being, do hereby make my last will & testament in manner and form following—to wit:

1st. It is my desire that my remains be interred in such manner as my Executors may direct.

2ndly. I wish my Executors herein after named to provide for the prompt payment of my just debts and funeral Expenses as they think most advisable.

3rdly. To my dearly beloved wife Mary Harrison I give and bequeath a plentiful incumberance and such portion of household & kitchen furniture as my Executors may deem necessary or convenient to her Situation.

4th. I give & bequeath to my son James Harrison the plantation whereon he now resides with the mill & other appurtenances thereto belonging on condition, however, that he deposit in the hands of my other Executor within five years next after this date the sum of two thousand six hundred sixty six dollars and sixty six cents and on my sd. son James complying with such Conditions the said plantation & mills with their appurtenances to belonging to him & his heirs and assigns forever.

5thly. It is my will that my son Peachy Harrison have my home plantation with its appurtenances (Execpt that part which was laid off to Ezekiel Logans) to him & his heirs & assigns forever, on condition & with the reservation following to wit: The quantity wherein appurtenances is to be estimated at £800 whatever may be the amount of land so rated my son Peachy is to pay into the hands of my Executors Subject to such disposal as hereinafter made for the payment whereof my said son Peachy is to be allowed the time of five years from the date hereof

6thly. To my sons Daniel, Benjamin, James, Peachy & William I devise all the estate interest right title claim & demand of which I am seized of posessed, or am or hereafter may be entitled to a certain tract or parcel of land be the quantity what it may, which is now in dispute between Alexander Herring & myself & for which a Suit is now pending in the Court of Appeals between the sd. Herring & my self—to them and their heirs forever.

7thly. I give and bequeath to my grandson Castle Harrison, son of Reuben Harrison . . . . . . with interest thereon from November 1813 till paid, which according to a contract between my said son Benjamin & myself is to be paid by the said Benjamin to the said Reuben for Castle's benefit in the manner and time specified in an obligation Executed by the said Benjamin for the payment thereof.

8thly. It is my will that the contract entered into between Benjamin Harrison & myself in relation to the land I conveyed to him be Strictly Executed, the said land (being the same he has since sold to Harshbarger) was rated to Benjamin at £4 .. . . . .

All that was preserved.

In addition to the above sons, according to a family tree of George Harrison, the son of James, above, Col. Benjamin Harrison had sons—Robert, John, Fielding, Jesse, and Thomas, the last two twins. (See old file, *Times Dispatch,* New Albany, Indiana.)

The marriage bonds of Rockingham record the marriages of—Samuel McWilliams, and Edith Harrison, daughter of Benjamin, 1792, surety Joseph Cravens; William Cravens and Jean Harrison, daughter of Benjamin, 1794, surety S. McWilliams; Ezekiel Logan and Margaret Harrison, daughter of Benjamin, 1797, surety S. McWilliams; Reuben Harrison and Parthenia Harrison, daughter of Benjamin (B. Harrison), 1804, surety Jesse Harrison. (See, Strickler's *Rockingham Co. Marriages.)*

Besides these daughters, the family tree of the Colonel's grandson includes a daughter Marillah. Other descendants assert there was also a daughter Eudocia.

In brief, as named, Col. Benjamin Harrison, (167), and wife Mary, had issue—

(1671) ROBERT—m. Sept. 11, 1784, Polly Harrison, (1216), "his cousin," daughter of Zebulon. Removed to Christian County Kentucky.

(1672) DANIEL—b. Feb.1, 1765; d. Feb. 8, 1837; m. Jan. 24, 1787, Ann Erwin, dau. of Francis. She b. Oct. 11, 1768, d. Jan. 29, 1838. Both Daniel and Ann buried in Hopkinsville, Kentucky.
See further record.

(1673) JOHN—m. Ann (Nancy) Tallman. Settled in Mo.—(D. S. H.).

(1674) BENJAMIN—m., 1st., March 22, 1791, Polly Hall, dau. of John. She d. 1793. m. 2nd., Nancy ——. (See page 316.)

(1675) JAMES—b. 1770 c; d. ——; m. Jan. 27, 1794, Ann Millan, dau. of John. Settled in Lebanon Co., Ohio.
See further record.

(1676) EDITH—m., Jan. 16, 1792, Samuel McWilliams. Removed to Kentucky.
See further record.

(1677) MARGARET—b. 1773; d. ——; m., May 22, 1797, Ezekiel Logan. Removed to near Madison, Ind.
See further record.

(1678) JEAN—d. 1835; m., Jan. 29, 1794, Rev. Wm. Cravens, (1414), son of John. Settled in Ind.
See further record.

(1679) PEACHY—b. April 6, 1777; d. Apr. 25, 1848; m., Feb. 29, 1804, Mary Stuart, dau. of John. She b. Sept. 12, 1783, d. Sept 19, 1857.
See further record.

(1680) FIELDING—b. 1788 c; d. June 11, 1829, m; Oct. 1 1800, Ann Quinn, dau. of James. Removed to Kentucky 1805-6, thence, in 1822 to Illinois.
See further record.

(1681) WILLIAM—m., 1st., Aug 25, 1801, Jane Young, who d. about 1807. m., 2nd., Apr. 17, 1810, Mary McClure. Settled in Illinois.
See further record.

(1682) JESSE—m., Mar., 1784, Elizabeth Wilson.

(1683) THOMAS—Twin of Jesse.

(1684) PARTHENIA—m., April 2, 1804, Reuben Harrison, (1773), son of Ezekiel. She d. in Va. He removed to Ky., thence to Illinois.
See further record.

(1685) MARILLAH—

(1686) EUDOCIA—

(See also, *The McClure Family*, by A. J. McClure, p. 130; The D. S. H. MSS. omits Robert, Benjamin, Jesse, Thomas, and Eudocia, but says "two others names unknown died in infancy." Marriage dates, all but Daniel, and Peachy, from the First Marriage Book of Rockingham, Daniel's from marriage bond, Peachy's from *Boogher*.)

CHAPTER XVII

"Heads of Families"

FURTHER MEMBERS OF THE THIRD GENERATION

CLAN OF THOMAS HARRISON

ABIGAIL HARRISON, (171), the daughter of Thomas Harrison, (17), founder of Harrisonburg, and wife, married August, 1761, Leonard Herring, (191), son of Alexander Herring, the pioneer. See Clan of Alexander Herring.

---

(172) JEREMIAH HARRISON, (1740 c.-), the son of Thomas Harrison, (17), founder of Harrisonburg, and wife, was for many years a processioner in Old Augusta. He also served for a time as road overseer of the Great Road—The Long Grey Trail—"from Reuben Harrison's to Daniel Smith's Gent." (See page 300.)

Among the processioners appointed by the Augusta vestry, 21st November, 1767, was "Jeremiah Harrison (son of Thomas)," Robert Cravens, Archibald Hopkins, Isaac McDonald, David Robinson, and Cornelius Riddle, "from Fowler's along the road to the County Line on the side of the North Mountain," and Benjamin Logan, John Frazier, David Laird, Reuben Harrison, Jacob Woodley, and Evan Phillips, "from County line to Fowler's, down North River to Mr. Jones's, thence along the Picket Mountain to County Line." (See, Augusta Parish Vestry Book, p. 429; *Chalkley*, Vol. II, pp. 454-5.)

Jeremiah married Mary ——; who died about 1779. "All deeds made by Jeremiah Harrison, and recorded in Staunton," says the late Daniel S. Harrison, in his MMS., "bear her name, and those recorded in Harrisonburg do not have her name affixed. There is nothing to show there were any children. He emigrated to Woodford County Kentucky, about 1792, leaving all his affairs in the hands of his brother John. "

He was a resident of Woodford County in 1801. On the 14th July, 1801, "Jeremiah Harrison of Woodford Courthouse," in a deposition taken before John O' Bannon, Hugh Watkins and E. Wooldidge, in connection with the suit of McWilliams vs. Hollingshead (see pages 274 and 279) testified that he had been a processioner 27 or 28 years in Augusta.

---

(173) DAVIS HARRISON, (1743 c-), the son of Thomas Harrison, (17), founder of Harrisonburg, and wife, was old enough by 1766 to be appointed highway surveyor and constable. (See page 224.) He married, but the name of his wife is not known. Sometime before 1800, (about 1792, or before that time, says the late Daniel S. Harrison), he removed to Woodford County, Kentucky, probably in company with his brother Jeremiah. According to the marriage bonds of Rockingham County, his daughter—

(1731) ELIZABETH—b. ——; d. ——; m. Sept. 10, 1799, John Dyer.
(See, also *Rockingham Co., Va., Marriages*, by H. M. Strickler, p. 49.)

---

(175) JOHN HARRISON, (-1806), the son of Thomas Harrison (17), "Proprietor of Harrisonburg," and wife, Sarah (?), lived and died in Harrisonburg.

His wife's name was Betsy, or Elizabeth, (probably Herring.) His will dated April 17th, 1806, and proven in September, the same year, is found recorded in the single surviving old burnt will book of Rockingham County (prior to 1861-5), and reads as below—

Will of John Harrison

IN THE NAME OF GOD AMEN. I John Harrison of the County of Rockingham and State of Virginia being in low state of health but of perfect mind and memory, calling to mind that it is Appointed for all men to die do make and ordain this my last will and Testament in manner and form Following, to witness

first of all I recommend my soul to God that gave it, second my body to be decently buried at the discretion of my executors, & as to my wordly goods

I first give and bequeath to Betsy my beloved wife my negro Girl named Nell during her life and at her death to be disposed of as she my said wife may think best Also my household furniture during her life Except that may be otherwise [disposed] of by this my last Will & Testament further I give to my beloved wife my sorrel Horse with a bald face and two milch Cows, all which property to be at her disposal.

Secondly I give and bequeath to Sisselah my beloved daughter one good Bed stead and furniture and my dark bay horse I got of (N ?) Dormon Loflend, and one milch cow which she has always claimed from a calf.

I further give and bequeath to my beloved wife Betsy the profits arising from my land on which Bolton as she may think . . . . .

My Executors hereafter named sell my negro Boy Joe or Joseph of the age eleven years November last past, until he . . . . . to the age of thirty years then to be free from slavery, at least from any claims from by or under me my heirs Executors and administrators .

Also my waggon and Geers and one white horse to be sold and such debts as are owing . . . . . . me be collected and my just Debts and funeral charges to be paid then the residue or remainder to be equally divided among all my children, except Thomas who has already received his full share, the three children of my daughter Phebe to take share as if the mother was alive to claim,

and after the two years lease which bolton has of my la. . the said land to be sold by my Executors either by publick or private sale as they shall think most advantageous for my heirs

the house and Lott I now live on in Harrisonburg to Continue in the posession of my beloved wife Betsy until the expiration of the lease of the land afore mentioned is Expired then to be sold as the Land at the Judgement and discretion of my executors, and the money arising from the Land . . . . Lott to be divided as follows . . . .

during her life and if any remaining at her death to be equally divided amongst my children in the same manner as before mentioned and the Remaining two thirds to be Equally divided amongst my children, my son Thomas excepted as before and my daughter Phebe Regan's children to take full share, with the rest of my children, as if their mother was living yet.

I further order and direct My Executors to take and reserve from Isaac Kiser and his wifes share one hundred and twenty five dollars which he has recieved by contract in Advance.

Also from Michael Dashner, and his wifes share ninety eight dollars which they by contract have received in advance.

Also from James Campbell and his wifes share one hundred and eight dollars which they by contract have received in advance.

Also from Henry Mc Ettee and his wifes share $46 which they by contract have received in advance

which said sums are to be deducted so as all the shares to share alike in the whole estate hereby divided and heretofore advanced except Thomas as before

and I constitute and appoint my beloved son Thomas and my Beloved Brother Reuben Harrison the Executors of this my last will and testament,

renouncing and revoking all . . . . Pronouncing this my last will and testament. In Witness whereof I have hereunto set my hand and affixed my seal the seventeenth day of April eighteen hundred and six.

John Harrison. (SEAL.)

Teste
Andrew Shankling
Bob Rutherford
Benj. Tinder
Nancy Tinder

Proved September Rockingham Court 1806.

(From Rockingham County Court, Burnt Will, or record, Book, page 450. Only two old books were saved of this nature, but one, while it has some wills in it, is not wholly a will book.)

Wash. Co., Tn

As named in the above, and the early marriage records of Rockingham, John Harrison, (175), and wife Betsy, had issue—

* (1751) Thomas—(known as Thos. Jr.) m., April 10, 1792, Mary Curry, dau. of Adam and Ann, Removed to Washington Co., Tenn. about 1820. See further reference

(1752) Jane—m., Nov. 3, 1802, Patrick Henry Mc Atee.

(1753) Phoebe—d. 1800 c.; m., Mar. 1, 1792, Daniel Ragan, He m. 2nd Melinda Harrison, Nov. 18, 1802, (1774), daughter of Ezekiel. See further record.

(1754) Cecelia—m., Sept. 8, 1807, Joseph Hicks

(1755) Mary—m., Oct. 23, 1783, Isaac Kiser. See further reference.

(1756) a daughter—m. Michael Dashner.

(1757) Amelia—m., 1795, James Campbell.

(All named in D. S. H. MSS. also.)

---

(176) THOMAS HARRISON, (-1800), the son of Thomas Harrison, founder of Harrisonburg, (17), and wife, married 29th December, 1790, Sarah Oliver, His marriage bond reads as follows—

"Know all men by these presents, that we Thomas Harrison & Andrew Shanklin of the county of Rockingham and State of Virginia are held and firmly bound unto Beverly Randolph Esquire, Governor of Virginia in the sum of fifty pounds current money, to be paid to the said Governor, or his successors in office, we bind ourselves and each of us, our, and each our heirs, executors, and administrators, jointly and severly, firmly by these presents, 1790 in the 15th year of the commonwealth.

The Condition of the above obligation is such, that whereas there is a marriage shortly intended to be solemnized between Thomas Harrison and Sally Oliver of this county: Now if there should be no just cause or impediment to hinder or obstruct the said marriage, then the above obligation to be viod; or else to remain in force.

Thomas Harrison (SEAL.)
Andrew Shanklin (SEAL.)

Rockingham, Sct.

Whereas there is a marriage shortly intended to be solemnized between Thomas Harrison and Sally Oliver of this county: I do hereby certify that all due caution has been taken in my office, for a license to issue for that purpose. Given under my hand, this 29th day of Dec., 1790.

W. T. Gwin C. R. C.

To Anthony Rader, Gent. first Justice in the
Commission of the Peace for said county, or
in his absence, the next sworn in said commission."

Elsewhere in the records, Thomas's wife is named Sarah, and this being also the name of Thomas, the founder's wife, the father and son have been confused. And further, owing to a Thomas Harrison having been mentioned as a Captain in the Revolution, on the Augusta records, it has been presumed that the founder was the Captain.

In John T. McKee's declaration of military services, January 5, 1835, in behalf of his widowed mother Nancy, the wife of James, who deceased August 14, 1832, aged 80 years, he states that his father served as an Ensign "under Col. John Bowyer, Capt. Thomas Harrison, Lieut. Alex. Wiley," etc. (*Chalkley*, Vol. II, p. 483.)

Col. Bowyer, afterwards known as Gen. Bowyer, in 1781 was a Colonel of the Rockbridge militia, and with his command served in lower Virginia at the time of Arnold's invasion. He married, as his second wife, Mary Baker, of Maryland. (See, *Waddell*, p. 180.)

Capt Thomas Harrison was also of the Rockbridge militia, and was evidently of the Maryland family earlier noticed, some of whom settled in Botetourt, out of which the portion of Rockbridge, of which Col. Bowyer was a resident, was taken. These Harrisons came to Botetourt after the county was formed, and were thus not of Augusta's jurisdiction. (See page 218.) Needless to state, the founder of Harrisonburg was much too old to have served in the Revolution as a soldier.

Thomas, the founder's son, lived and died in Harrisonburg. His death occurred in 1800. Although a merchant in the town, he, like his brothers, was a large landowner in the county roundabout; his land being in the Keezletown direction from Harrisonburg. In the *Heads of Families*, Virginia, 1784, "Harrisson, Thomas, Junr, of Rockingham County," was enumerated by Benjamin Harrison, as having only "1 White soul," himself, in his household. In 1789 he was listed as owning 860 acres of land. (See, *Wayland*, p. 449.) After his father's death he became Thomas, Sr., and his nephew, the son of his brother John, Thomas, Jr.

On his first visit to "Rocktown," Bishop Asbury, the famous Methodist circuit rider, stopped at Thomas' house, (1793). On a third visit he stopped with Thomas' son Wesley, (1815), recalling, as he did so, his earlier visit, as mentioned in his Journal. Thomas' "pious wife" was also remembered, she having died, evidently, between his second and third visit. On this last trip after leaving town his second stop was made at "Thomas Harrison's son of Thomas"—likely a grandson of John, the brother of Thomas above. (See page 246.)

Thomas Harrison's will, dated 4th June, 1799, and admitted to probate April, 15,

1800, a copy of which has been preserved at Harrisonburg (in connection with subsequent litigation in regard to the settlement of his estate), reads as follows:

Will of Thomas Harrison

In the name of God, Amen. I Thomas Harrison of the county of Rockingham & State of Virginia, do make and ordain this my last will and testament in manner and form following That is to say.

1st I desire that all my personal Estate be sold at public sale except such parts of my household furniture as may be thought necessary for the use of my family and out of that amount together with my bonds notes and book accounts, all my just debts to be paid, also to sell at private sale one hundred acres off of the upper end of the place I bought of Dickerson, which is the end next to Reuben Harrison's for the difrent purposes mentioned.

2ndly I bequeath to my beloved wife Sarah Harrison one horse four cattle, twelve sheep, and six hogs such as she may choose out of all I have, Independant of the above mentioned sale to her own use and Disposal.

3rdly I desire that one Hundred acres be cut off the north east end of my lands, next to Sprinkle's place for the purpose hereinafter mentioned, and then all my other land, except the Balance of the tracts bought of Dickeson, to be equally divided quanity and quality betwixt my two sons Wesley and Robert Harrison, Wesley to have the part occupied by James Rogers, and Robert to have the part occupied by William Wretchford.

4thly It is my desire that a dwelling house and other necessary buildings be erected on the Acre lots I last bought of Reuben Harrison, opposite his stone house for the use of my wife and such of her children as may remain with her during her natural life or widowhood.

5thly I desire that all my unsold land be rented accordingly to the judgement of my Executor until my oldest daughter Rebecca Harrison shall arrive at the age of Eighteen years. And then as soon as may be convenient the above mentioned balance bought of Dickeson together with the above excepted Hundred acres to be sold And then the one third part of the money arising from the same to be paid to my oldest Daughter and each of my other two Daughters to wit Sarah and Edith as they come to the age last mentioned to receive one equal share of the remaining two thirds and the Boys land to remain rented until as each one shall arrive at the age of twenty one years and then to receive their respective Divisions.

6thly I desire that all the moneys arising from the said rents together with the overplus of the above mentioned sales, to be applied to the support and necessary expense of my family and building the above mentioned Houses and the Balance if any to remain in the hands of my Executors on use for the comfortable maintenance of my said Belived wife as they may think necessary during her natural life or widowhood.

7th It is my will and desire that if either of my children shall die before they come to the posession of their respective Dividends not having any lawful issue then and in that case his or her share shall be equally divided amongst the rest of my children by the sale of land by my executors if found necessary.

8th I desire that all my children may be learned to labour agreeable to their sexes, also to be educated in Literature and put to such places for said purpose as they my said Executors shall think best for the correction and preservation of their morals.

9thly I do hereby authorize and desire my Executors to supply either or both of my sons as they come of age with such necessarys as they may think proper out of any money that may remain in their hands.

10thly I desire that one ton of hay and thirty bushels of grain be annually reserved out of the rents for the use of the Horses belonging to the Travelling preachers in the Methodist connection or so much thereof as my executors shall think necessary, so long as my lands remain in the posession of my children.

11thly It is also my will that the house and lot above mentioned be sold and the price thereof be equally divided amongst my children, at the death or marriage of my said beloved wife.

12th I bequeath to my yellow woman, Patty, her freedom together with the use of her own daughter, Barbara, until she shall arrive at the age of Eighteen years at which time the said Barbara also be free, and Patty also to have reasonable wages from the date of this testament so long as she is necessarily employed in the family.

13th I bequeath the services of yellow George and his sister Liddy to my said wife and children until the said George shall arrive at the age of twenty-one and Liddy to the age of Eighteen years at which time I will them both their freedom.

14th I bequeath to Black George his freedom after he has served on the place one year from this date.

15thly I do hereby authorize and empower my said Executor to sell and convey in fee simple to the purchaser or purchasers any such lands as are here mentioned for sale.

16thly It is my will and desire that Reuben Harrison and Joseph Cravens shall take charge of any such goods as may be found remaining in my store at the rates they are invoiced to me at, and carry on the business of said store, still standing accountable to my estate for the same or the amount thereof with legal interest.

Lastly I do hereby nominate and appoint Joseph Cravens, Reuben Harrison, Samuel W. Williams and Benjamin Smith Executors of this my last will and testament, hereby revoking all former wills or testaments heretofore by me made.

In testimony of which I do hereby publish and declare this my last will and testament sealed with my seal and dated this fourth day of June in the year of our Lord one thousand seven hundred and ninety nine.

Thomas Harrison (Seal)

Signed, sealed and acknowledged in presence of us.

his
James X Rogers
mark
Thomas Rumburgh

Reatea Burgess
her
Elizabeth X Rumburgh
mark

Rockingham April Court, 1800.

This last will and testament of Thomas Harrison, deceased, was presented in Court by Reuben Harrison, Joseph Cravens, Benjamin Smith and Samuel W. Williams the Executors therein named and proved by the witnesses thereto and ordered to be recorded and on motion of the said Executors who made oath thereto and with security entered into and acknowledged bond in the Penality of 5,000 Dollars conditioned as the law directs. A certificate is granted them for obtaining a probate thereof in due form.

Teste: S. W. Williams, C. R. C.
A COPY. Teste: S. W. Williams, Clk.

(Copy kindly supplied by the late
J. F. Blackburn, Clerk of the Circuit Court of Rockingham.)

Sarah, Thomas's widow, married 2nd, Richard Kyle, September 20, 1802. (Rockingham Marriage Bonds.) A short time thereafter, "Richard Kyle and Sarah, his wife, late Sarah Harrison, widow of Thomas Harrison, deceased," brought suit, recorded 18th February, 1803, vs. Joseph Cravens, Reuben Harrison, Samuel McWilliams, and Benjamin Smith, executors of Thomas Harrison and guardian of his orphans. In this a copy of his will was filed, as above. (See also, Augusta Circuit Court Judgements, Causes Ended, New Series, File 20.)

Briefly, as named in his will, Thomas Harrison, (176), and wife Sarah, had issue.

(1761) Wesley—m., Dec. 15, 1814, Peggy Custer, dau. of Jacob.
(1762) Robert—
(1763) Rebecca—m. Oct. 25, 1810, William Evans.
(1764) Sarah—
(1765) Edith—m., Samuel Hamilton. (See Strickler's *Rockingham County Marriages*, p. 62.)
See further record.

(All named in D. S. H. MSS. except Hamilton.)

---

(177) EZEKIEL HARRISON, (1751-1834), the son of Thomas Harrison, (17), "Proprietor of Harrisonburg," and wife Sarah, was born at what is now Harrisonburg, 3rd October, 1751. (See page 294), and died in Sangamon County, Illinois, "about 1835." In the *Heads of Families*, Virginia, "Harrison, Ezekiel," of Rockingham County, was listed by Benjamin Harrison with "6 White souls, I Dwelling, 2 Other buildings." *(First Census, U. S.*, p. 77.) He was a large landowner in the county.

Ezekiel married, in 1775, Sarah Bryan (Brian), born in Augusta, later Rockingham County, Virginia, 31st July, 1753. She died in Illinois, (Sangamon County), June 6, 1845. (See, Power's *History of the Early Settlers of Sangamon Co., Ill.*, p. 358.)

Sarah was evidently a descendant of Morgan Bryan, an associate of Alexander Ross, who was interested, very early in the Valley's history, in obtaining a large tract of land near what is now Winchester, for the settlement of a colony of Quakers from Maryland, and adjacent provinces. (See page 112.)

Among the first patents issued to settlers on this land, was one granted to "John Hiet junr.", 12th November, 1735, by William Gooch, Esq., Lieutenant Governor of Virginia; stating—

"KNOW YE that xxxx an order of our Lieutenant Governor and Council of our Colony and Dominion of Virginia bearing date the three and twentieth day of April 1735, Granting Leave to Alexander Ross and Morgan Bryan to survey . . . 1000 acres of land for each Family of Seventy Families by them brought into our said Colony and settled upon the Lands in the said Order mentioned and to issue out Patents for the same. We HAVE GIVEN, Granted, confirmed . . . etc. unto John Hiet junr. of the County of Lancaster in the Province of Pennsylvania one certain Tract or parcel of Land containing three hundred acres . . . . on the North side of the Opeckon . . . above the lower end of Paul Williams land." (Land Patent Book, 17, p. 332, Richmond, Va.)

A Morgan Bryan, in 1747, was a processioner of lands with Daniel Harrison . (See page 163.) He seems to have lived in the region of present Broadway. In the litigation of William Bryan vs. Lewis Bible, regarding a tract of land that the defendant had sold to Morgan in 1797, it is recorded that William, a brother of Morgan, was a Methodist preacher, and that "Ezekiel Harrison and Jmes Begs were brothers-in-law of Bryan."

John Bryan is mentioned as another brother of Morgan. Begs removed to Kentucky in 1803. Jacob Lincoln deposed 16th October, 1802, that he had known Morgan for thirty years. (See page 233.)

Ezekiel Harrison was married in the midst of exciting times. Only the year before his marriage he had returned wounded from the battle of Point Pleasant, and the year of his marriage saw the beginning of the Revolution. Soon he was on the march again —this time under a new flag.

His services to his country, as described in his testimony before the Court of Sangamon County, have been noted in Chapter XVI.

The year peace was declared, Ezekiel, and his brother Reuben, and Isaiah Harrison, evidently his cousin, appear to have made a trip to Georgia, seemingly with the intention of settling. The curious minute in the old first Court Order Book, regarding this, shows that they had been true patriots—

> "At a Court Continued and held for the County of Rockingham on Tuesday, the 29th of April, 1783.
>
> On the motion of Ezekiel Harrison, Reuben Harrison, and Isaiah Harrison, having advertised the Court of their intention of removing from this state to the state of Georgia and as they are informed it is necessary for strangers to carry with them a certificate of their character and conduct from the place where they remove from prayed the court would certifie their knowledge of them. The court therefore taking the same under consideration and willing to do justice as well to the said Isaiah Harrison, Ezekiel Harrison and Reuben Harrison as to their fellow citizens where they are about to remove to Ordered that the clerk of this court do certifie that the said Ezekiel Harrison, Reuben Harrison and Isaiah Harrison were born and brought up in the County and during the long contest with Great Britian as behaved themselves as good and faithfull citizens and soldiers and always posessed true Wiggish Principles and upon all occasions exerted them for the service of the United States."

(See also page 275.)

Their stay in the South was obviously of short duration, but Ezekiel continued to his later years to feel the urge of the pioneer spirit to find for himself a new home in a less populated region of the country.

He settled in Rockingham, in the community between the two early Baptist Meeting Houses— the Linville Creek Church, and the Smiths Creek Church. Both he and his wife were members of the latter, at present New Market, but he frequently attended the former, and on occasions his home served for a union meeting.

"Met Saturday the 11th of May, 1793 . . . 3rd A DOOR was opened to hear Experiances, Mr. Hopkins Doll offered but was not received. 4th. Brother Moffet informed the Church, that at the last Church Meeting it was agreed that they would hold a general communion with this Church at some future Period if agreeable to us, to which he moved for our Concurrence, which was agreed to, and Brother Ezekiel Harrison's house was pitched upon for the Place, and the 2nd. Lords Day in Augusta next the Time for sd. Communion." (Old Church Book, p. 49.)

As before observed, Rev. Johnston was at this time the pastor of the Linville Creek wing of the original church, Bro. Moffett being the pastor of the Smiths Creek wing, now an independent congregation.

Brother Johnston, it seems, needed a house, and it was proposed about this time to build one for him on Ezekiel Harrison's land.

"Met Oct. 12, 1793, . . . 1st a Member of the Name of Mary Woods, formerly Mary Cox, being present, was conversed with by Brother Johnston in the Churches name, concerning joining the Church, to which she appeared to have no great Objection, as soon as she could obtain a new Letter of Dismission, from ragged Mountain Church in Culpeper County, where her Membership was , and from whom she had formerly received a Letter of Dismission, but had lost it. 2ndly. the Memebers present named the Sums of Money, or Property they would be willing to Subscribe towards building a House for Brother Johnston, on Brother Ezekiel Harrisons Land which is set on a separate Piece of Paper, & to be inserted in these Minutes hereafter." (p. 51.)

* * * * * *

The first meeting under Rev. Johnston's pastorate, appears to have been that held on Saturday the 12th November," (1791), "1st a Matter of greviance was made Known by Brother Lincoln" (regarding a disorderly member, Elenor Gum, who was accordingly excommunicated.) "2ndly. Brother James Riggs presented his Letter of Dismission, from a Church on the Waters of Peters Creek, Dated Nov. 11, 1788 and was received upon the same. 3rdly. The case of Black Members or Slaves was considered, that is, whether they should be admitted to a Seat among us on Days of Business, when meeting with us on those Days. Resolved that they should. 4thly. Resolved that Mr. John Stevenson, be considerad a Member of this Church in full Fellowship. 6thly. a Door was opened to hear Experiances, Francis Bowen offered and was received."

"November 13, 1791, being Sabbath Day was baptized Francis Bowen, & came under the Imposition of Hands by our lately ordained Brother James Johnston. (p. 42.) Saturday the 10th. March (1792) . . . 3rd. Mary Webb offered, and was received, and at her particular Request was baptized the Day following."

Saturday 12th May . . . 1st. "Invited a certain Brother Woods (a Member of Brother Countz' Church) to a Seat with us who accordingly excepted. 2ndly. a Door was opened to hear Experiances, Benjamin Talman offered and was unanimously received for Baptism Tomorrow. 3rdly. Resolved unanimously, that the public Worship of God, at this Place, when Brother Johnston is to preach begin at eleven O'Clock as nearly as can be ascertained, for the future, both in Summer and Winter. The 13th. of May, being the 2nd. Sabbath was Baptized Benjamin Talman & then was celebrated the Sacred Ordinance of the Lord's Supper . . . . " (p. 44.)

Met 9th June (Sat.) . . . "3rdly. Appointed Brother Lincoln to write the letter to our next Association, which is to be held at Long Branch, Fauquier County . . . N. B. The Lords Day, August 12th was baptized the abovesaid Ruth Brigs, and came under the Imposition of Hands of Brethren Moffett and Johnston." (p. 45.)

"Met . . Sat. 12th of January, 1793, . . . 1st. Brother Absalom Graves came forward with his letter of Dismission from the Church of Christ on Rapidan River, in Culpeper County and was received into the Fellowship of this Church. 2nd. The Brethern and Sisters appointed last Meeting to deal with Certain Brethren and Sisters for their non attendance of late at Church Meetings made their Report which was prity satisfactory." (See page 304.)

"At a Meeting held the Saturday before the 2nd. Sabbath of March . . . 1st. Sister Lucinda Rice, wife of Jno. Rice, came forward with her Letter of Dismission, from crooked Run Church in Culpeper County, and was received into the Fellowship of this Church, upon said Letter, and the Answers of a few Questions respecting her Faith." (p. 47.)

Met . . on Saturday June 8, 1793, . . "1st. To the reception of Brother Lathem and

Kisandren his Wife, who came forward with their Letters of Dismission from a Church of Christ of the same Faith and Order at Chapawamsic in Stafford County, and was received into the fellowship of this Church . . . 4th. Grace Fine dismissed by letter account having removed out of the bounds of our Church some Years past." Aug. 10, 1793 . . . "Letters of dismission written for Sister Webb and Sister Smith, upon application, but held for until another application is made. (p. 50.)

Saturday Sept. 7th, 1793, . . . "1st. The Letters for our two Sisters as mentioned last Meeting was applied for and delivered for them, as also a particular Recommendation for Sister Amelia Smith was applied for wrote signed and delivered for her." (p. 51.)

Met . . . Saturday Nov. 9, 1793, . . . "2nd. As Brother Absalom Graves & Wife are about shortly to remove their Residence out of the Bounds of this Church, they through the Means of Brother Johnston applied for a Letter of Dismission, which the Church agreed they should have." (p. 52.)

Met . . . Saturday January 11, 1794. . . "agreed to draw a Subscription Paper for the purpose of raising Money, or Property, to build a Dwelling-house, for Br. Johnston on the Land of Br. Ezekiel Harrison, said Paper to be presented to Members, & Non-members, for signing." (p. 53.)

The last named minute follows the one regarding Bro. Johnston preaching the funeral sermon of Mrs. Phoebe Harrison, on Smiths Creek. (See page 189.)

Eleven years later—Sat., April 13th, 1805, . . "2nd. Brother Ezekl. Harrison and wife being Present, took their seats amongst us. 3rdly. On the motion of Brother Ezekl. Harrison the Church considers it highly necessary of offering a Subscription generally for the purpose of Building a Meeting House upon the Ground near Linvilles Creek intended for that purpose." (Brother Giles Turley mentioned as a member.) "Brother Elijah Elliot Requesting a letter of dismission it is agreed that the Clerk write one." (p. 69.)

"The Church of Christ met according to appointment at Mr. Jacob Lincolns Saturday the 8th. October 1808 . . . Brother Benjm. Davison being Present invited to a seat. Brother Ezekiel Harrison also. 5th. John Runyon came forward and Related his Experiance which was acknowledged. 6th. Nancy Hank (Hawk ?) also informed the Church of a work of Grace wrought in her Soul which was acknowledged. 7th. Anne Runion also related her Experiance and was Recd. for Baptism. (p. 76.) "On Sunday the 9th. Elizabeth Dundore gave her Experiance and submitted to the Ordinance of Baptism also the above named candidates." (p. 77.)

The succeeding meeting, dated, "Sunday preceeding the first Sabbath in Nov.", was held "at the house of Mr. Crotzers," at which time it was agreed to hold the next meeting also at Mr. Crotzer's, "Saturday preceeding the 2nd Sunday in Dec."

"The Church of Christ at Linvilles Creek met according to appointment Saturday the 3rd of December 1808 and after Praise and Prayer proceeded to Business. Brother (Samuel O.) Hendrin Moderator. Brother Ezekiel Harrison and Wife Invited to a seat." (p. 77.)

* * * * * *

Such were some of the items of interest in the life of the church, in Ezekiel Harrison's day. With the above minute his name disappears from the record.

"Mr Jacob Lincoln" was the son of "Virginia John," and the brother of Capt. Abraham Lincoln, and of John Lincoln, the clerk of the church. On March 26th, 1781, Jacob Lincoln qualified as a Lieutenant of the Rockingham militia. (See,

McAllister, p. 230.) Although mentioned as "Mr." in the church book above, he was likely a "Bro". member also. (See page 285.)

Nancy Hank lived in the region of Brock's Gap. Meetings were later occasionally held at her house—August 26, 1815 . . nominated Bro. Lincoln, Runion, Yates, & Phillip Tusinger messengers to the association. "Next Church meeting to be held at Sister Hanks in Brocks Gap," preaching there also on the Sabbath. (p. 93.)

In his own church, Ezekiel Harrison was a very active member. He frequently served on various committees, as clerk of the church, and sometimes as both Moderator and clerk of the same meeting, He was often appointed a delegate to attend the Association, and at times assisted in the preparation of the letter to the same. A few abstracts gleaned from the early records of the Smiths Creek Church (the earliest book), furnish a brief partial calendar of his services—

Sept. 5, 1789—Ezekiel Harrison appointed a delegate to attend the Association.

Oct. 24, 1789—Ezekiel Harrison contributed towards the support of the pastor, Anderson Moffett.

Apr. 5, 1790—Ezekiel Harrison one of the committee appointed to see Edward Young about the Meeting House.

Apr. 2, 1791—Church meeting held at Ezekiel Harrison's house. Sister Margaret Harrison present and invited to a seat. (See page 304.)

Oct. 1, 1791—Ezekiel Harrison one of the committee to see about puchasing land for a Meeting House. (This was in regard to a contemplated change of location, not to the lack of a church building.)

Mar. 3, 1792—Church meeting held at Ezekiel Harrison's house.

May 4, 1793—John Lockard present and served as Clerk. Bro. Ezekiel Harrison's house selected as a place to hold a union meeting with the Linville Creek Church.

Aug. 3, 1793—Ezekiel Harrison appointed a delegate to the Association.

Nov. 2, 1793—At the suggestion of Ezekiel Harrison a day was appointed for fasting and prayer, and his house selected as the place of meeting

Jan. 4, 1794—Ezekiel Harrison appointed on a committee to visit a delinquent member.

Aug. 2, 1794—Ezekiel Harrison appointed to the Association.

Sept. 6, 1794—Ezekiel Harrison, Clerk.

(From, Notes kindly supplied by Mr. Charles H. Urner.)

The oldest church book of the Smiths Creek Church under the local jurisdiction of this church, is apparently that beginning May 6th, 1810, with the Rev. Anderson Moffett, as pastor, and ending August 6th, 1858. This record also bears faithful witness to Ezekiel's zeal; as continued through his last days in Virginia.

"New Market, Jan. 2nd, 1810 . . . 2nd. Bro John Miller & Elizabeth his wife, made application to the church for a letter of Dismisison which was granted & Bro. Anderson Moffett was appointed to Right the Cert. of Dismission . . . 3rd. The church, have appointed as Delegates to the Association Bros. Anderson Moffett, Abraham Hays, Ezekiel Harrison, & Aaron Solomon to Right a letter to the Sosiation then adjourned till before the first lordes in August next. " (p. 1.)

"New Market, Feb. 29, 1812 . . . 2nd. The Minutes of the Culpeper Association was received and Distributed." (p. 3.) Sat. April 4, 1812, John Vance, Clerk. (p. 4.)

The Culpeper Association, according to Benedict, (Vol. II, p. 521), was formed in 1791, and in 1813 consisted of eighteen churches totaling 1353 members, of which the Smiths Creek Church had forty eight. To this Association also belonged the Mill Creek church of what is now Page County. John Asplund, a Swede, in his *The Annual Register of the Baptist Denomination in America,* 1790, lists the memebership of the Smiths Creek church as 50, and the Mill Creek church as 150, at the time of the first census of the United States (1790). (See, *Asplund,* p. 31; copy in Library of Congress.)

At a meeting of the Smiths Creek Church, dated "New Market—Sept. 1, 1814. . . then met according to adjournment & after praise and prear passeaced to business, with former moderator & Bro Ezekiel Harrison Clerk. a door was opened to hear greviance but none was made known." (p. 10.)

During a part of the time, viz, from 1794 to 1799, and from 1814, until his removal from Virginia, Ezekiel was the Sheriff of Rockingham County. (See page 248.) Also, for a number of years he was a justice of the peace. (D. S. H. MSS.)

In 1815, as disclosed in his testimony of 1832, (see page 294), he emigrated to Christian County, Kentucky. Says the old church book above—

"New Market, August, 5, 1815—Then met in a Church Capacity and after praise and prear pursceded to business with Bro. Jacob Harnsbarger Moderator & Bro. Ezl. Harrison, Clarkee—1st, a door was opened . . . . . 4th. Bro Ezl. Harrison aplayed for a letter of Dismisso. for him Self & wife to which the Church agreed and it is ordered that Bro. Anderson Moffett Be (appointed to write) the same & Sign it in Behaf of the church." (p. 11.)

Ezekiel settled with his family near Hopkinsville, from where, in 1822, with his wife, three sons, and one daughter, he removed to Sangamon County, Illinois, arriving November 4, 1822, north of Richland Creek, in what is now Cartwright Township. (See, Power's *History of Sangamon Co., Ill.,* p. 358.)

Briefly, Ezekiel Harrison, (177), and wife Sarah, had issue—

(1771) JESSE— b. May 25, 1777; d. Dec. 31, 1872; m. 1st., Rachel Harrison, (1263), dau. of Capt. Reuben Harrison, May 25, 1801; m. 2nd., in Missouri, Removed to Kentucky, thence to Illinois, and finally to Missouri.
See further record.

(1772) REUBEN—b. June 12, 1779; d. 1852; m., April 2, 1804, Parthenia Harrison, (1683), dau. of Col. Benjamin Harrison. Removed to Kentucky, thence with his father to Illinois.
See further record.

(1773) GEORGE W.—b. 1781; d. 1821,testate, in Harrisonburg.
See further reference.

(1774) MELINDA—b. 1783; d. ——; m., Nov. 18, 1802, Daniel Ragan, as his second wife. He was b. 1772.
See further record.

(1775) EZEKIEL B.—b. July 19, 1786; d. June 1851; m. 1st., Ann Bell, Dec. 5, 1809, m. 2nd., in Ill., Elizabeth Stuart. Removed to Kentucky, thence to Illinois.
See further record.

(1776) THOMAS—

(1777) LUCINDA—b. Mar. 13, 1792; d. Aug. 20, 1873; m., in Ill., Rev. Theophilus Sweet. Removed with her parents to Kentucky, thence to Illinois.
See further reference.

(1778) SALLY—

(178) REUBEN HARRISON, (1754-1840), the son of Thomas Harrison, "Proprietor of Harrisonburg," (17), and 2nd. wife Sarah, and himself a later Proprietor, was born at "Thomas Harrison's," now Harrisonburg, and lived and died in the town. His death occurred August 15, 1840. (See page 293.)

By his father's will, proven in 1785, he and his brother Robert were devised, "as joint Tennants," 620 acres of land, part of the 1290 acres embraced in his father's inclusive patent of 1773. This land included the town site. The founder dying a short time after securing the town as the county seat, the proprietorship thus devolved upon the two sons. In 1797 they made an addition to the town, of 23 1/2 acres, becoming in a sense co-founders with their fathers. (See page 214.) They, in fact, were substantially the town builders. Some time in December 1797, Robert died unmarried, and upon his death Reuben bought out the other heirs, establishing himself as the sole proprietor.

Reuben married, April 27, 1791, "Mary Mathes" (Matthews), the daughter of Solomon, and Agnes Van Reed Matthews. She was born July 3, 1772, and died April 5, 1854. (See page 293—marriage date from papers in Rev. War pension claim W. 7689, allowed Mary on her application of June 14, 1843.)

MATTHEWS

Solomon Matthews was a native of Pennsylvania, a wealthy Quaker, a large landowner, and the head of one of the first business firms in Rockingham. In the *Heads of Families*, Virginia, 1784, "Matthews, Solomon & Brumfield in Co.," of Rockingham County, were enumerated with "59 White souls, 6 Dwellings, 7 Other buildings;" by far the largest number of individuals and buildings listed under one head in the county.

Solomon at one time owned an iron furnace in the region of Linville's Creek, called the Mount Ery Furnace, where he appears to have been located in 1780, when he witnessed the deed of Abraham Lincoln and Bathsheba, to Shanks and Reuf. (See page 286.) In proving this deed, he affirmed. According to a deed from Daniel Matthews, of Rockingham, to Henry Shaver, of Botetourt, (recorded) 6th September, 1824, conveying 50 acres, "part of tract purchased by Daniel (Matthews) from his father Solomon, which was first granted to Jacob Lincoln," this land was on "Round Hill between Linville's and Smith Creek." Presumably the furnace was near by.

Aside from this land on Linville's Creek, Solomon was the owner of a tract on Smiths Creek, to the north of present Lacey Spring, also of a forge on the creek, known as Spring Forge. In the litigation, "Matthews vs. Fawcett," Rockingham, Feb. 1800, it is recited, that "Solomon Mathews and wife Agnes" conveyed in trust 148 acres to Wm. Herbert and John Potts, Jr., (of Alexandria), "part of tract on the north east side of the Big Spring" conveyed to Solomon by Alexander McFarland. Matthews' deed to Herbert and Potts is dated 27th January, 1790. (recorded July 1793) and conveyed "148 acres on Smiths Creek." The grantees assigned to Benjamin Fawcett, 13th February, 1793. On the 24th July, 1791, Fawcett conditionaly deeded to Matthews "all right in the the old furnace called Mount Ery Furnace on Linville's Creek and all land puchased by Fawcett from Mathews in 1786." Matthews on his part was to deliver to Fawcett the forge above. (*Chalkley*, Vol. II, p. 260.) In 1821 Benjamin Savage brought suit vs. Fawcett, stating that in 1796 he and Fawcett had formed a partnership to manufacture iron. Fawcett at that time owned a furnace called Haho Furnace, which later failed for lack of ore. In 1796 Fawcett patented 89 acres, "corner Solomon Mathews, near on iron mine." (*Ibid*, p. 257.)

Solomon was born in 1745, according to the inscription on his tombstone, which may be seen in the oldest part of the burial ground included in the churchyard of the Linville Creek Church of the Brethren, near Broadway. The Baptists, it is said, formerly held meetings here. The present building was erected in 1828. His inscription reads—

In Memory of Solomon Matthews, born Feb. 2, 1745, died April 2, 1834, aged 89 . . . . .

Alongside his grave it that of another, with a weatherbeaten old locust marker, on which the inscription is illegible. In the old cemetery at Harrisonburg, before mentioned, near the graves of Reuben Harrison and wife Mary, stands another marker reading—

In Memory of Agnes, Consort of Solomon Matthews, born Feb. 23, 1746, died May 7, 1828, aged 82 years, 2mo. & 14 days.

As disclosed in the proceedings; "Mathews vs. Warren," Bill 2nd August, 1803, Solomon was the son of Robert Mathews, weaver, who died testate in Exter Township, Berks County, Pennsylvania, leaving wife Mary, (who by 1754 married, 2nd. a Cherrington), and children, Solomon, Townsend, John and Robert Mathews, Amelia, the wife of Robert Dickey, Rebecca, the wife of Benjamin Webb, and Mary, the wife of James Webb. Michael Warren qualified as executor. John Mathews died prior to the date of the bill above, leaving daughters, Hannah, the wife of William Ratchford, and Martha Dunavan, by 1802 a widow. On the 26th July, 1754, Benjamin Webb of Exter Township, Yeoman, gave power of attorney to his "loving brother-in-law, Robert Mathews of Augusta County, cordwainer."

The Warrens, like the Mathews, were Quakers. Michael came to later Rockingham, and settled in the region of the New Erection Church, to the west of Harrisonburg. By the time of the above litigation he had died, and John Ewing and Nathaniel Harrison were summonsed as his executors. (*Chalkley*, Vol. II, p. 81.) WARRENS were Quakers

Agnes Matthews, the wife of Solomon, was the daughter of Henry Van Reed, (Reid), a Huguenot, who died testate in Pennsylvania.

Solomon and Agnes had issue: Amelia, m. Joseph Linville; Katy, m. Henry Martz; Milly (Amelia ?), m. John Green, 1794 (*Wayland* p. 448.); Elizabeth, m. a Foster, (the two last removed to Kentucky); Agnes, m. David Snyder, removed to Ohio; Mary, m. Reuben Harrison, above; Daniel, b. March 7, 1779, d. January 28, 1842, m., February 1801, Esther Blair Shaw, b. December 9, 1776, d. April 10, 1866, the daughter of John Shaw, who m. Esther Blair in Ireland, and had one child born there before coming to America; Hannah d. unmarried; Rebecca, m. George Sites, and had William, Rebecca, David, and others; Rehoboam, m. Elizabeth Robinson; and Solomon, m. a Miss Culter, and removed South.

Daniel Matthews was a Captain in the 116 Regt. of Virginia Volunteers, in the War of 1812. His company entered service July 7, 1813. From 1820, to 1821, he was a Member of the Virginia House of Delegates, and from 1833, to 1834, was the Sheriff of Rockingham County. (See *Wayland*, pp. 450, 442, and 441.) He settled on the old Great Road—The Long Grey Trail—a mile or so north of the Great Spring, now Lacey Spring. His residence, known as Locust Grove, a fine old commodious house, the home of the late Michael Martz, is still standing. Daniel, and Esther, his wife had children—

Agnes V., b. Feb. 25, 1802, m. Sept. 22, 1831, Dr. Michael Hines; and Hannah Ashbury, b. Nov. 12, 1803, d. May 22, 1861, m., April 28, 1829, Hiram Martz, b. Oct 11. 1800, d. Oct. 19, 1861, a Memeber of the Virginia House of Delegates, 1849-

1855, and 1858. (Dates from the Matthews family Bible, at Locust Grove, and from Hiram and Hannah's tombstones in the old Martz cemetery, on the present Jack Bradford farm, near Tenth Legion.)

* * * * * *

Reuben Harrison, Proprietor of Harrisonburg, and his half first-cousin, Capt. Reuben Harrison, the son of John Harrison, Sr., the pioneer, have been frequently confused by various writers. Each had a wife Mary at the same time, both were large landowners, both were constables, both were in the Revolution, and both, evidently, were justices of the court, and it is said that both, at different times, owned the land whereon the Captain lived, the Captain first, and his cousin second. One of the latter's sons certainly resided on it, which probably came about through a deed, after Capt. Reuben Harrison's death, to his son-in-law, Jesse Harrison, the son of Ezekiel, who may have, in turn, sold it before leaving for Kentucky to his uncle Reuben, the last being, as observed, a landowner in the county, as well as in the town.

Robert and Reuben Harrison, (the sons of Thomas), are listed as owning together 1620 acres of land in Rockingham, in 1789. (*Wayland*, p. 449.)

On the 27th November, 1781, "Reuben Harrison, son of Thomas," was appointed Constable. (Rockingham Court Order Book I.) His cousin of the same name by this time had been for some years a justice, and had been appointed a constable before 1756. (See pages 308-309.)

Reuben's appointment as constable followed closely upon the termination of his services as a Revolutionary soldier. During the war he volunteered on three different occasions, serving first against the Indians in Tygarts Valley, near the head of the Greenbrier, about 1778, and the other two tours in Eastern Virginia, against the British under Arnold, and Cornwallis, as stated in his testimony of 1833, before quoted in full. (See page 292.)

In the Spring of 1783, a few months after the departure of the last of the British from Charlestown, Reuben joined his brother Ezekiel, and his cousin Isaiah Harrison, in their announcement to the court of their intention of "removing" to Georgia. Whereupon, as before observed, the court certified that "they had behaved themselves as good and faithful citizens and soldiers," etc. during the long contest of the war. (See Ezekiel above.)

At the time the Continental Army had not yet been disbanded, (although preparations were about complete to this end), and in order for an ex-soldier to travel any great distance it seems it was advisable that he be prepared to present his written discharge, or certificate of good character, showing that he was no deserter.

A natural desire to see something of his country, while a young man, before permanently settling, likely prompted the trip. At any rate Rockingham continued to be his home. His father's death occuring within two years thereafter, under the terms of the old gentleman's will, he found his future work cut out for him. Nor was his father's confidence misplaced; twelve years later, and the town was needing a fifty percent addition in area. It was during this period that Reuben married. About this time too, he appears to have been appointed a justice of the court.

According to an execution of judgement in the appeal of Athony Mustoe vs. Ezekiel Harrison, recorded September, 1794, (at Staunton), an attachment was awarded against "Andrew Shanklin, Benjamin Smith, John Ewing, Samuel and Reuben Harrison, and other Justices of the County Court of Rockingham," for not granting Mustoe's appeal, as ordered 13th September, 1792. Ezekiel had originally brought suit vs. Mustoe, and judgement had been rendered by the Rockingham Court 25th August, 1790, and a mandimus awarded Mustoe 7th April 1791. (*Chalkley*, Vol. II, p. 7.) By 1794 Reuben Harrison, the Captain, was 63 years old, and, judging from the ages of the others, had most likely retired as a justice. Smith and Ewing, and obviously Samuel Harrison, also, at least, were much younger men. Samuel was a descendant of one of the younger brothers of Capt. Reuben's father, or of the Captain's brother, Zebulon.

About this time Bishop Asbury, the organizer of the Methodist Church, visited Harrisonburg, and preached in the town, stopping, with Reuben's brother, Thomas, who evidently joined the denomination, probably during the visit. Robert, too, is tenderly mentioned in the Bishop's Journal, and inferentialy also became a member.

A Church was organized, and in 1798 Robert and Reuben conveyed to the trustees a tract of land, now at the corner of High and Water Streets, on which was located the first Methodist Meeting House . (See Burnt Record Deed Book 00, p. 20.) The tract included the old cemetery in which the bodies of Reuben and Mary were later interred at their deaths. From these circumstances, it appears manifest that they were numbered among the early members of the Bishop's "Methodist Class."

Of the children of Reuben and Mary, three sons never married. Two of these were, Philip Bruce, and Jason. Jason lived at the present Allebaugh place, the early home of his cousin, Capt. Reuben Harrison, and died about 1855 or 60. Philip removed to Texas after 1856, and died some years later than his brother.

On an old undated paper handed down in the Houston family, bearing the letter head, "William A. Wilson, Attorney-at-law, 425 and 426 Dooly Block, Salt Lake City, Utah," is drawn, evidently by the attorney, a very concise chart, naming the heirs of Philip Bruce Harrison, the Houston heirs in turn, and their respective proportions of his estate. As given by this, his immediate heirs were four—William C., and Thomas Harrison, Nancy H. Houston, and Julia H. Smith.

In brief, Reuben Harrison, (178), and Mary, his wife, had issue—

(1781) THOMAS— d. unmarried. Lived in Harrisonburg.

(1782) PHILIP BRUCE—d. unmarried. Removed to Texas after 1858.

(1783) CATHERINE—"Consort of John Herron who died in this place Oct. 5, 1825, aged 28 years, 11 months, & 5 days."

(1784) NANCY—b. Dec. 6, 1798; d. May 3, 1862; m., Dec. 16, 1814, Rev. William Houston, b. Aug. 5, 1781, d. Apr. 27, 1852.
See further record.

(1785) WILLIAM CRAVENS—b. Nov. 9, 1803; d. Jan 16, 1888; m. Mildred Linza Williams, b. Mar. 27, 1838, d. Dec. 8. 1909, dau. of Geo. H. Williams. Removed to Eastern Virginia. (Both buried in Woodbine Cemetery, at Harrisonburg.)
See further record.

(1786) JULIA—b. Jan. 3, 1806; d. Feb. 23, 1883; m., Edward H. Smith, b. July 1, 1799, d. Apr. 24, 1852, son of William Smith (1661). Lived at Smithland. (Both buried in Woodbine Cemetery.)
See further reference.

(1787) MELVINA—b. Feb. 3, 1808; d. Nov. 12, 1829, unmarried.

(1788) JASON—d. unmarried.

(1789) JANETTA— b. Nov. 21, 1813; d. Mar. 31, 1832, unmarried.

(Birth and death dates from tombstones; Catherine, Melvina, and Janetta's, in the old

Methodist Cemetery at Harrisonburg. William and wife, and Julia and husband's in Woodbine Cemetery at Harrisonburg. Nancy and husband's in the old Houston cemetery on Smiths Creek, near Lacey Spring.)

WARREN

(179) SARAH HARRISON, (1760 c-), the youngest daughter of Thomas Harrison, (17), founder of Harrisonburg, and wife Sarah, married, about 1779, John Warren, whose ancestor Michael Warren, Sr., (1711-1795), frequently found mentioned with the Harrisons, was born in Queens County, on Long Island, New York, and removed thence to Pennsylvania, and later to what is now Rockingham County, Virginia. Michael's ashes rest in the old cemetery of the New Erection Church, to the west of Harrisonburg. Alongside his tombstone there stands another, in memory of Catherine Warren, who died in 1804, aged 78 years. . . . etc. (See pages 134 and 337.)

The Warrens, like the Harrisons, and most likely the Wrights, were of an Oyster Bay family connection. Several of the town's first settlers were from the old Plymouth Colony, in Massachusetts. One Richard Warren was a passenger on the Mayflower. Among the old deeds preserved in the town vault of Oyster Bay is that of "John Waring of awatie in the County of Philadelphia But lat . . of Oysterbay yeoman to Joseph Frost of Oyster bay," 10th November, 1732, proved as follows—

> "Memorandum that on ye 3d Day of april 1733 Micael Waren one of ye evidences to within Written Deed Came before me David Jones, one of ye Judges of ye Court of Common pleas for Queens County & Declared upon his oath That he was present and Saw ye within mentioned Named John Waren Execut ye within Written Deed firmly to ye Use therein mentioned which Having also Examined I allow to be entered on Record.—(signed) D. Jones. (Book F, typewritten copy of original, p. 52.)
> A little earlier appears—"To all Christian People To whome these presents Shall Come Greeting Know ye that I Jacob Wright of ye Town Shipe of Whit Land in Chester County In Pensilvaney Yeoman," etc. deed to "Jacob Townsent" of Oyster Bay, 8th October, 1730. (*Ibid*, p. 43.)

From this, it is presumed that the migrations of the Warrens and Wrights to Pennsylvania were about 1730. Michael Warren, the Rockingham settler, was residing in, or near, Berks County, above Philadelphia, at the time of Robert Mathews' will. (See page 337.)

John and Sarah Warren comprised one of the very first families to locate in Harrisonburg after its establishment as a town. On the 28th June, 1779, Thomas Harrison, the founder, and wife Sarah, acknowledged their deed to John Warren.

Thomas Warren, a later descendant of the Rockingham settler, married Elizabeth, the daughter of Capt. Reuben Harrison. This couple too, were among the early residents of the town. Thomas was obviously a son of John and Sarah. (See later.)

The old Warren House, yet standing, long a noted landmark on Court Square, was one of the town's first taverns. It doubtless took its name from John Warren, above, or else from Thomas.

CLAN OF JEREMIAH HARRISON

(181) LYDIA DONNELL HARRISON, (-1780 c), the daughter of Jeremiah

Harrison, (18), and wife Catherine, was baptized by Rev. John Craig, during his pastorate of Old Stone Church, Presbyterian, 1740-1749. Her name appears in the Rev. Craig's Baptismal Record as Lidia Donnell, child of Jeremiah Harrison. (See page 151.) She has been identified as the 1st wife of Capt. Reuben Harrison, (125.) (See Clan of John Harrison.

---

(182) NEHEMIAH HARRISON, ( ), the son of Jeremiah Harrison, (18), and wife Catherine, like his sister above, was baptized by the Rev. John Craig, as Jeremiah Harrison's child. On the 18th August, 1772, his father deeded to him and his brother, Josiah, a tract of land in the region of "Thomas Harrison's." (See page 271.) On the 15th November, 1774, Samuel Hemphill was appointed road overseer, vice John Hardman, "from Martin Argenbright's to Nehemiah Harrison's." (Order Book 16, p. 21.) Josiah and Nehemiah Harrison, and John Hardman, were among those appointed 22nd June, 1778, to appraise the estate of Alexander Herring, and on the 22nd March, 1781, Josiah and Nehemiah were appointed, along with Benjamin Harrison and Robert Cravens (Jr.), to appraise the estate of Jesse Herring. (See page 280, etc.)

Nehemiah was married, and had a number of children, but the names of his wife and children are unknown. In the *Heads of Families* census, Virginia 1784, "Harrison, Nehemiah," of Rockingham County, was listed by Benjamin Harrison, as having "9 White souls" in his family. *(First U. S. Census,* Va., p. 77.) He probably removed from the county to the south-west about 1790.

---

(183) JOSIAH HARRISON, ( ), the son of Jeremiah Harrison, (18), and wife Catherine, has been mentioned on a former page as a Captain of the militia of Rockingham, during the Revolution. In the *Heads of Families* census, Virginia, 1784, "Harrison Josiah," was listed immediately above "Harrison, Nehemiah," by Benjamin Harrison, as having in his family "5 White souls," and owning "1 Dwelling, 2 Other buildings." *(First U. S. Census,* Va., p. 77.) He was obviously a near neighbor of his brother Nehemiah. Both were deeded land together by their father, in 1772.

It is evident that Josiah and his brothers early removed from Rockingham. Mention has been made of his brother Jeremiah's apparent settlement on the Holston. In a deposition of 3rd February, 1807, Josiah Harrison deposed in Kanawha County (now West Virginia) that he came to Kanawha in 1790. (Mathews vs. Upton, Augusta-Rockingham Circuit Court Causes ended; *Chalkley,* Vol. II, p. 117.)

Besides Josiah, Nehemiah and Jeremiah, Jr., there were probably other sons of Jeremiah, Sr., but their identity is not disclosed. Both Josiah and Nehemiah, as observed. were appointed appraisers of the estates of Alexander and Jesse Herring. An Alexander Harrison, probably a son of Jeremiah, Sr., was a landowner in the Cook's Creek neighborhood in 1768. (See page 225.) A Nathaniel Harrison, evidently of the same community, furnished supplies to the militia (1758) in the course of the French and Indian War. (See page 183.) One of Capt. Reuben Harrison's sons, by his wife Lydia, was so named. (See also page 36.)

---

(185) HESTER HARRISON, ( ), the daughter of Jeremiah Harrison, (18), and wife Catherine, married her cousin, Robert Cravens, Jr. (148). See Clan of Capt. Robert Cravens. In the Heads of Families census, Virginia, 1784, "Cravens, Esther," of Rockingham County, probably Robert, Jr's., widow, was listed by Benjamin

Harrison as having "9 White souls," in her family, and owning "1 Dwelling 3 other buildings." *(First U. S. Census,* Va., p. 77.)

CLAN OF CAPT. ROBERT CRAVENS

(141) JOHN CRAVENS, (1722-1778), the eldest son of Capt. Robert Cravens, and wife Mary, (14), was born in Sussex County, Delaware, and brought, in childhood, by his parents to Augusta, later Rockingham County, Virginia, about 1739. About 1759 he married Margaret Dyer, the widow of William, and daughter of John and Margaret Hiatt. (See pages 261, and 330.)

John and Margaret Cravens made their home on Cook's Creek, some four miles southwest of "Thomas Harrison's," near a place called Fishers Spring. In addition to his home plantation and another, here, he also acquired land in the old Linville Creek community, through the death of his father. At the time of his own death in 1778, he was a large landowner of the county. (See page 266.)

Frequent mention of him, and various references to his lands have been made on preceeding pages, particularly in the Chapter regarding his father. It remains to herein supply more especially the names of his children, several of whom became prominent men in the history of the county.

He died intestate, and as observed in the forgoing, his widow in 1782, married as her third husband, Dennis Lanahan, an early resident of Harrisonburg. Lanahan was an immigrant from Ulster, Ireland. By occupation he was a stone-mason and builder. His marriage to Margaret was apparently his first and only one; at any rate he had no children at this time or thereafter . Upon his marriage, he established himself in his wife's home; she continuing to reside on the farm for some time, until their removal to town, about 1787.

In the *Heads of Families,* Virginia, 1784, "Leanaham, Dennis," of Rockingham County, was listed by Benjamin Harrison, with "6 White souls, 1 Dwelling, 2 Other buildings." *(First U. S. Census,* Va., p. 77.) By this time two of the Cravens children were married, and one other was about of age, and perhaps not residing with the family.

Margaret's marriage to Lanahan, instead of proving fortunate for her children, as she no doubt anticipated, resulted in some dissapointment in this respect. Closely following her former husband's death, she and his brother, Robert Cravens, (Jr.), were granted administration upon his estate. (See page 266.) Robert was the principal executor, and legal guardian of the children, and after Lanahan's marriage came into conflict with him. The year of the above census, Robert died, and ere long several the children were openly accusing their step-father of having diminished their estate. About this time, also, Dennis changed his will, leaving his property to his nephew, Thomas Lanahan. From the papers in the resultant litigation many interesting facts are gleaned.

The proceedings first appear at the March term of court, 1785, "Cravens' Adms vs. Denis Lenchan." (Rockingham Court Order Book I.) About 1809 the controversy was renewed, later appearing in the Circuit Court of the Augusta-Rockingham District, under whose jurisdiction the papers below were filed, (at Staunton—Box 100, "Cravens vs. Lanahan," N. S. 103.) A Commissioner was appointed by the Superior Court of Chancery, 18th July, 1816, to take depositions, some of which were dated, "at the house of Denis Lanahan in the Town of Harrisonburg, Thursday morning Sept. 13th, 1816," and sealed 12th November, 1819.

In brief, the records may be broadly classified, for the present purpose, under six heads, viz: the Bill of complaint; Lanahan's answer, 29th February 1816; Margaret's answer, 7th March, 1817; a certificate of records (regarding the several appointments of guardian), 18th September, 1818; John Hemphill's deposition, September 13, 1816; and other depositions of a few days later.

"John Cravens her former husband," says Margaret, "departed this life on or about the 25th day of July 1778, (on the 24th July, 1778, says Hemphill) seized of an estate both real and personal—three separate plantations." The home place consisted of "upwards of 100 acres of good plow land, 70 acres excellent meadow, and 45 or 50 acres of pasture, exclusive of meadow, together with a grist mill"—200 or 300 bushels of toll grain annually. (Bill of complaint.) Robert Cravens, the brother of John, was the active administrator until his death, according to Lanahan, but, says Margaret, further, "It is also true that Robert Cravens, brother of the deceased and this respondent took upon themselves the adminstration of the said personal estate, which has devolved almost exclusively upon herself. It being in the time of the Revolutionary War the said Robert Cravens was seldom at home."

As recited in the Bill of complaint—"To the Honorable John Brown judge of the Chancery District Court holden at Staunton—Humbly complaining sheweth to your Honor your Orator & Oratrix William Cravens, Joseph Cravens, James Cravens, and Joseph Snap & Peggy his wife formerly Peggy Cravens that their father John Cravens on or about the . . . day of July, 1778 being seized and posessed of a very valuable real estate, departed this life intestate, leaving his widow Margaret Cravens and seven children, to wit, Mary, Hannah, Robert, William, Joseph, James & Peggy. Shortly after the death of the said John Cravens administration of his estate was by the County Court of Rockingham granted to the said Margaret Cravens the widow and a certain Robert Cravens, brother of the intestate . . . . . widow remained in posession . . . . until her intermarriage with Dennis Lanahan, who immediately posessed himself thereof and continued to receive the rents and profits until Robert Cravens, the younger, became of age, to wit about the fall of 1785 when he, being sole heir at law, had the widow's dower laid off (which Lanahan afterwards sold) and made what was then considered an equal division of the lands between his brothers. Some time after that, to wit, about the year 1792 or 1793 the said Robert Cravens the younger, died intestate without issue . . . . . further, ... on or about . . . . the said Robert Cravens, the elder, departed this life, whereby the change of the administration devolved entirely on the said Lehanan & wife . . . that no accounts have been rendered of any portion of the estate . . . . except a kind of . . settlement a copy of which is hereunto attached," etc.

Of the above named; "Peggy was between 3 and 4 years old at the time of her father's death . . . . Hannah was married in June 1779 . . . . Mary was married in the same year and after her sister's marriage and before cold weather . . . They were both living at their mother's at the time of their marriage." (Hemphill's deposition.) Dennis Lanahan and Margaret's marriage "happened on the 20th March 1782." (Lanahan's answer.) Robert Cravens, (Jr.), the elder, died in March, 1784. (Hemphill's deposition.) Robert (III), the younger, "the heir at law was fourteen years old at the death of his father." (Lanahan's answer.) He died on the 10th December, 1793. (Hemphill's deposition.) At July Court, 1787, he was chosen guardian by James Cravens, and at the same term was appointed guardian of Margaret (Peggy) Cravens. At October Court, 1778, Joseph Cravens " made choice of the said Robert as his Guardian." (Certificate of appointment.)

Continues the mother—"It is true that the children to wit, Robert, William, Joseph,

James, and Peggy all lived with her. . (Leanahan bought a lot in Harrisonburg.) She well recollects Also that William Cravens entered with Wm. Lenahan as his apprentice to the Masons had within a few months after her marriage; that Joseph Cravens was kept by him at such employment as would better have suited a boy of more advanced age until he was sent to school by his Brother Robert as soon as he became his guardian, and James was kept by him at making brick in Staunton one season until he became sick there and was taken so down to Harrisonburg and the same fall after he had recovered he was taken by a relative to Kentucky where he remained until he was of sufficient age to choose his Guardian and never returned to us any more, and Peggy was also taken away by her Brother Robert who became her guardian. But she believes that the other three to wit, Mary, Hannah, and William have received each 1/7 part of what was considered a settlement [of] the personal estate . . . . that in the consideration betwixt Wm. Leanhan and her self he observed to her he wished to rent out or sell her Dower right which was laid off on the Home tract during her life time. Sworn to before me the 7th day of March, 1817"—(signed) Peachy Harrison.

The final outcome of the case is unknown. Considering the circumstances, the controversy manifestly largely hinged on the fluctuating value of the currency of the day. Lanahan states that paper money depreciated 45 to 1. The defendant died between March 1817, and November 1819. He acknowledged changing his will, which he believed accounted "for all this bustle," explaining, "His nephew having come in from Ireland he thought he was well entitled to enjoy the fruits of his labor as those who had so long lived on him before . . . After his arrival the friendship of his pretended friends who before were all love soon subsided and the Deft. then became a stepfather."

On May 21st, 1810, "Dennis Lanahan, and Margaret, his wife, late Margaret Cravens, Josiah Harrison, Jonathan Evans and Hannah, his wife, late [Cr]avens, Wm. Cravens [and Jane, his wife, James Cravens and Nancy, his wife, Joseph Snapp and Margaret] his wife, late Margaret Cravens, heirs, . . . Rob[ert]. [dec]eased who was eldest son and heir at law of John Crav[ens]" conveyed to "Joseph Cravens (who is also one of the sons of [the] said John Cravens decd)," for $1.00 "all their undivided . . . . and in 470 acres of land on Linvil Creek and is a part of . . . . a larger tract originally granted unto J . . . . . and others and was conveyed unto the said John Cravens (by) Archibald Huston, 17th & 18th Aug., 1767." "Recorded May Court 1811. This deed from Denis Lanahan and Margaret, his wife, Josiah Harrison, Jonathan Evans, and Hannah, his wife, Wm. Cravens and Jane his wife, James Cravens and Nancy, his wife, Joseph Snapp and Margaret, his wife, to Joseph Cravens," etc. (Rockingham B. R. Deed Book I, p. 510, mutilated.)

By this time Joseph, too, was married—"To the Clerk of Augusta County"—25th November, 1790, Certificate of willingness, "License shoulld issue to Join together in the Stat of Matrimony my Daughter Polly & Joseph Cravens"— (signed) John Nickel. (Augusta Marriage Bonds.)

Joseph seems to have been Lanahan's favorite, it being to him that Lanahan had originally willed the remainder of his estate, after bequeathing one third to his wife Margaret.

Margaret outlived her husband for some years. During the Revolution she furnished supplies to the army, two instances of which appear—

Nov. 7, 1781, Margaret Cravens 400 lb. of Beef a 2 d pounds, £3-6-8.

June 10, 1781, Margaret Cravens 1 sheep 15 s.

(Claims agst. Rev. Army—Rockingham.)

Briefly as named in the above, John Cravens, (141), and Margaret his wife had issue—

(1411) MARY—b. 1760 c; d. before 1810; m. Josiah Harrison, son of Capt. Reuben, (125)?
See further reference.

(1412) HANNAH—b. 1762 c; d. ——; m., June 1779, Jonathan Evans.

(1413) ROBERT—b. 1764; d. Dec. 10th, 1793, unmarried.

(1414) WILLIAM (Rev.)—b. Apr. 2, 1766; d. 1826; m., 1794, Jean Harrison, (1678) daughter of Col. Benjamin. Removed to Indiana.
See further record.

(1415) JOSEPH (M. D.)—b. May 20, 1769; d. 1842; m., Nov. 30, 1790, Mary (Polly) Nickel, dau. of John; b. April 10, 1774; d. Nov. 28, 1847.
See further record.

(1416) JAMES—b. Apr. 12, 1773; d. 1821; m., Ann (Nancy) Love, 1797, dau. of Thomas. Removed before marriage to Green Co., Tenn., thence after marriage to Selma, Ala., where he died.
See further record.

(1417) MARGARET (Peggy)—b. Aug. 26, 1775; d. ——; m., Joseph Snapp.
See further reference.

(Birth dates of last four Cravens given by Lanahan in his answer above—Birth of Polly Nickel (Nickle) from *James Nourse and his Descendants,* by Maria C. N. Lyle.)

---

(142) MARGARET CRAVENS, (1724 c-1800 c), the eldest daughter of Capt. Robert Cravens, and wife Mary, (14), was born near Lewes, Delaware, and married, probably there, ——— Primrose. In 1747 she was residing at or near Morristown, New Jersey, when the same year she married, 2nd., Zebulon Harrison, (121). See Clan of John Harrison.

---

(145) WILLIAM CRAVENS, (1730 c-), son of Capt. Robert Cravens, and wife Mary, (14), served as an Ensign in the French and Indian War, and as a Captain in the Revolutionary War. (See pages 263 and 297.) His wife is said to have been named Jane, but if so, his nephew William, the son of John Cravens, also had a wife of the same name. He settled near his father on Cook's Creek, where he owned a tract of land called "Great Meadow." About the time of Robert Black's removal to North Carolina, William sold his Great Meadow land, and a few months later is mentioned as "going out of the colony." In 1766 he was in Mecklenburg County, North Carolina, when he joined Black in witnessing Samuel Stewart's deed to Jacob Calpin. (See pages 252, 262 and 263.)

William's stay in North Carolina apparently was of comparatively short duration. In 1773 he patented land on Cook's Creek near his old home, and in 1778 was repelling the Indians in Tygarts Valley. (See pages 258 and 297.) The next year he was again out on another tour, "Claims against Revolutionary Army," Rockingham—"At a Court held for ye Cty of Rockingham was certified ye 20th Aug. 1782—

29th April, 1779, to William Cravens for 1 horse 18 dys. at 1/6 per day."
(Va. State Library, Richmond, Va.)

On the 27th October, 1788, Robert Cravens and William Cravens gave bond, that "Robert shall truly pay and deliver to Joseph Cravens Orphan of John Cravens deceased all effects due said Orphan." (Guardian's Bonds, 1788, Rockingham.)

William seems to have been living in the country as late as 1792. He may have removed to West Virginia, or Kentucky, after this date. (See pages 263 and 267.)

CONTEMPORARIES—NORTH CAROLINA

There were some fairly early Cravens and Harrisons in North Carolina around Edenton, Chowan County. These Cravens were from Yorkshire, England. Will, September, 1755—James Craven, Late of Donghton near Skipton in Craven in the County of York in Great Britain now of Edenton, North Carolina . . . . "I give to my wife Penople Craven (formerly Hodgson)" . . . etc. One witness was John Walton of Suffolk, Virginia. A James Craven was appointed Clerk of the Court in 1740. One of the name petitioned for a mill at Rockyhock, which was granted, in 1747.

Also will, March, 1766—Dr John Craven of Edenton, North Carolina. Son John, daughter Margaret . . . . "If my wife should wish to return to her friends and native country with our children," etc. Wife, and brother Samuel Sands, of Lancaster, Great Britain, guardians.

Deed, February, 1729—Joseph Harrison to Daniel Harrison, 200 acres on Rockyhock Creek, bequeathed to said Joseph by his father. Will, 1726—Daniel Harrison of Chowan County, wife Elizabeth, son Joseph, as above.

Among those of Edenton, in 1777, were—Benjamin Harrison, son of Thomas, Thomas Harrison, son of John, and James Harrison, son of James. One, John Harrison of 1693, had sons William and John, and a daughter Elizabeth. Another John, or the same, in 1710 had a brother Thomas, and sister Hannah. *(North Carolina Historical & Genealogical Register.)*

HEMPHILL

(146) MARY CRAVENS, (-1801), the daughter of Capt. Robert Cravens, and wife Mary, (14), some time prior to the date of her father's will, married Samuel Hemphill, who died testate in Rockingham County, Virginia, in 1809. She died in 1801. (See page 264.) The Hemphills were from Pennsylvania.

Samuel's will, dated 19th March, 1802, and proven in April, 1809, a copy of which appears in "Kyle vs. Smith, 5th May, 1816," names besides John Pottorff, and three grandchildren, the following children—

(1461) JOHN—b. 1759, "eldest son" (aged about 57 at time of deposition in Cravens vs. Lanahan.)

(1462) AGNES—m., ——— Miller.
See further record.

(1463) ROBERT—"second son".

(1464) SAMUEL—"youngest son"; m., 1799, Clarinda Solfora (Solford.)
See further record.

(Marriage of Samuel, from Strickler's *Rockingham Co. Marriages*, p. 64.)

---

(148) ROBERT CRAVENS, JR. (1735 c-1784), son of Capt. Robert Crevans, and wife Mary, (14), was among the younger children brought by his parents from Sussex County, Delaware, on their removal to Virginia. Under his father's will, proven 1762, he inherited his father's home plantation on Cook's Creek, a mile or so southwest of "Thomas Harrison's". He married, a few years before his father's death, Hester, said to have been the daughter of Jeremiah Harrison, (18). (See page 341.)

Robert, Jr., as his father before him, was a Captain of the militia. His services were in the Revolution. He was early in the conflict, and during the war, according to the record, "the said Robert Cravens was seldom at home." (See page 343.) He added luster to the family name, and before the armies were disbanded was promoted to a Major.

He was among the officers named by the Court of Augusta County, in whose companies the tithables were ordered taken, August 20, 1777. (See page 298.) Upon the formation of Rockingham, he was one of the Captains taken over into the new military organization of this county—28th April, 1778, "Wm. Herring appointed Lieut. in Capt. Robert Cravens Company," etc. (See page 298.) In the fall of the same year he served under Col. Benjamin Harrison, in Gen. McIntosh's campaign against the Indians in Ohio. (See page 296.)

As stated by John Hemphill, in his testimony, Cravens vs. Lanahan,—"Robert Cravens (the administrator of his brother John) started a few days after the sale say the 14th day of September, 1778, on what was called McIntosh's campaign. He does not know of his having anything to do with the Estate afterwards . . . he died in March 1784 . . . .but supposes the widow must have done the business . . . Question—At what time did Robert Cravens the admr. return from the campaign called McIntoshs. Ans. He returned a few days previous to the first of January 1779.

His commission expiring a short time after his return, he again offered his services —"At a Court contd & held for Rockingham County, Tuesday 23d March 1779 Robt Davis, Robt Cravens, Andrew Johnson & John Rush produced commissions as Captains of the Militia in this County & were Sworn into their office which is ordered to be certified." (Rockingham Court Order Book I, p. 30.)

Capt. Cravens and his company, as a part of the Virginia militia, participated in the brilliant campaign of Gens. Greene and Morgan, which resulted in Lord Cornwallis' retirement from North Carolina. Among Robert's men at the time was one John Young, who had served under him in the McIntosh campaign, and whose declaration of service has been noticed. (See page 297.) In his testimony, Young further relates that he volunteered in September 1780, under Capt. Robert Cravens of the Virginia Militia as a volunteer rifleman, and served under Gen. Greene and Gen. Morgan. According to McAllister's *Virginia Militia in the Revolutionary War*, Capt Robert Cravens' Company was at the battle of Cowpens, 1781. *(McAllister,* p. 43, Rockingham.)

On the 26th August, 1782, Robert Cravens qualified Major. (Rockingham Court Order Book I.) Col. Benjamin Harrison at the time was County Lieutenant. While hostilities had ceased, not all of the British were yet out of the country—only the month before they had departed from Savannah, and it was not until the 30th of November, the same year, that the Independence of the United States was acknowledged by England.

Major Cravens died in March 1784. On the 27th April, 1784, the administration of his estate was granted to Hester Cravens, his widow, and Benjamin Smith, (his son-in-law.) (Rockingham Court Order Book I, and Cravens vs. Lanahan.)

Robert Cravens, Jr. (148), and wife Hester, had issue—

(1481) JEREMIAH—b. 1762; d.——; m. Margaret (Peggy) Harrison, in Rockingham, dau. of Zebulon, (121)? Removed to S. C., thence to Ky., and finally to Missouri.
See further record.

(1482) ELIZABETH (Nancy)—b. 1762 or 3; d. 1837; m. 1782-3, Benjamin Smith, (1656), son of Col. Daniel Smith. Removed to Ohio. See further record.

(1483) WILLIAM—b. 1764; d. 1832; m. Mary Lamma, of Va., d. 1832, in Madison Co., Mo. Removed as bro. Jeremiah. See further record.

(1484) NEHEMIAH (Mi.)—m. Sallie McCullough, of Wheeling, now West Va., (See page 263.) "Went to Kentucky," from there to Washington Co., Mo. See further record

(1485) MARGARET (Peggy)—m., Apr. 2, 1792, Henry Smith, son of Capt. Abraham Smith. (See page 259, and Strickler's *Rockingham Co. Marriages.)* See further record.

(1486) ROBERT—b. (youngest son) d. ——; m. -——; Lived for a time in Ky., and then moved to Ga. (Said to have had a son Robert who lived on Lookout Mt., Tenn., d. 1885.)

(1487) ELEANOR—m., —— Hawkins. Removed to Miss.

(1488) ABIGAIL—m., —— Hays. Removed to Miss.

(All eight born in Rockingham.)

CLAN OF ALEXANDER HERRING

(191) LEONARD HERRING, (1735 c-), the eldest son of Alexander Herron (Herring), the pioneer, and wife Abigail (19), was born near Lewes, Delaware, and about 1744 brought by his parents, as a child, to later Rockingham County, Virginia. He married in August, 1761, Abigail Harrison (171), the daughter of Thomas Harrison, founder of Harrisonburg. (See pages 215, 223, 249, 283, and 286.)

Leonard settled in the old Linville Creek community, on land purchased by his father from Samuel Harrison in 1751. To this tract he added 88 acres, by patent, in 1781. His father had first settled on the land, or a tract nearby, but sometime during the French and Indian War, or before, had established himself a short distance further south on Cook's Creek. After the elder Herring's death, 1778, the son appears to have removed to Cook's Creek also.

Upon the organization of Rockingham, Leonard was appointed one of the first Vestrymen, taking the oath 26th May, 1778. (Rockingham Court Order Book, I, p. 10.)

Unfortunately, owing to the destruction of so large a part of the early records of the county, little regarding him, or his family, appears. Further, in the 1784 census, *Heads of Families,* his name is omitted, this being also a complilation of fragmentary records. According to Lea and Hutchinson, he is said to have had thirteen children, "of whom the memory of only one has been preserved."

As given by the marriage bonds of Augusta County; William Herring the "son of Leonard Herring," was licensed 28th December, 1786, to marry Hannah Robertson, the daughter of Peter; witness Sarah Herring. *(Chalkley,* Vol. II, p. 281.) Other children of Leonard are named on the marriage bonds of Rockingham County—September 26, 1780, Joseph Hall and Edith Herring, daughter of Leonard, who consents, surety Robert Harrison, witness Benj. Crow and Wm. Herring. March 9, 1783, William Lowery and Sarah Herring, daughter of Leonard, witness Richard Dictum and Michael Warren. 1800, John Ervin and Ester Herring, daughter of Leonard, who

John Erwin

consents, witness Wm. Lowery and Joseph Hall. 1801, Daniel Curry and Abigail Herring, daughter of Leonard, surety Adam Curry. 1801, Robert Irvine and Nancy Herring, daughter of L. Herring, surety John Erwin (Irvin.) 1805, Leonard Herring and Ann Ervin, daughter of Benjamin, who consents. Leonard son of Leonard Herring (Herron), who also consents, witness Robert Erwin and Daniel Curry. (See, Strickler's *Rockingham County Marriages*, 1778-1816; dates of Edith and Sarah from D. S. H. MSS..)

Their father consenting, four of the above were no doubt under age at the time of their marriage, including the two sons. All were married between the years 1780 and 1805.

HERRING—LINCOLN—CHRISMAN

As to the remaining children, if any, of Leonard Herring, the fair Bathsheba, Capt. Abraham Lincoln's wife, was much too old, it will be observed, to have been one of them, unless a child of a previous marriage to that of him and Abigail Harrison; but as before pointed out, there is no evidence whatever that he was twice married. Moreover, his daughters were too many, and his wife lived too long after Capt. Lincoln's marriage, for any Bathsheba of his to have given rise to the Herring tradition, wherein the Captain's bride is represented as the chief joy, and only daughter, of a doting widowered father.

"Her father," so the story goes, "looked with scorn on the alliance, and gave his daughter the choice of giving up her lover or being disinherited. The high spirited young woman did not hesitate. She married the man she loved and went with him to the savage wilds of Kentucky in 1782." (Charles Griffin Herring's letter, in *Lea and Hutchinson*, p. 202.)

The recent Chrisman data, written entirely from memory, without any reference to "worm-eaten old books," as the author expresses it, are remarkably consistent with the records, (so far as the latter go), and are worthy of the most careful consideration in any outline of Lincoln genealogy. Both Herring Chrisman, and his brother, Major George, (who also relied relied entirely on his memory), were gentlemen of the highest type, splendidly connected and educated, and well deserving of the honors bestowed upon them by their fellow citizens. Herring Chrisman was for several years before his migration to Illinois, in 1858, the Commonwealth Attorney of Rockingham County. George was a prominent landowner and agriculturist in the county, and during the War-between-the-States was a Major in the Confederate army. (See later Chapter.)

While Major George was under the impression that Bathsheba Herring Lincoln was Leonard Herring's daughter, he was in complete agreement with his brother as to their own kinship with Bathsheba. In the course of a nephew's visit to him, in 1912, he stated that Abraham Lincoln's grandmother and his own "Great Grand Father were brother and Sister." (From—Notes kindly supplied by Wm. H. Chrisman, of Mapleton, Iowa.) This kinship is subtatianted in the *Memoirs* by the elder brother, in his identification of Bathsheba as Leonard's SISTER; the only identification possible on which this kinship can be explained. Both brothers were great grandsons of William Herring, a brother of Leonard.

Although inferentially represented as an only daughter, it is possible that Bathsheba may have had a sister Edith, who married prior to her own marriage.

Among the inhabitants of the Linville Creek neighborhood, in Capt Lincoln and Leonard Herring's day, was Capt. Josiah Davison, the first active sheriff of Rockingham, son of Daniel Davison, and wife, Phoebe, nee Harrison. Deed; 17th August, 1771, Francis McBride and Mary, to Thos. Hood, of Frederick County, 200 acres on

Linville Creek between Josiah Boone and Josiah Davison, part of 1200 acres patented to McKay Hite & Co., and by them conveyed to William Linvil, by him to Jos. Briant, by him to Jacob Chrisman, Sr., by him to Francis McBride, by him to John Bear, and by him to Francis again, 17th Aug. 1768, corner Josiah Boone's part of same, Witness Abraham Miller, Michael Warren, Daniel Smith, John Thomas, etc. (Deed Book 17, p. 401.)

Josiah, along with "Corneliays Briant," and Ann Briant, was a witness to the deed of John Lincoln and Rebecca to Abraham Lincoln, 12th August, 1773,—part of 1200 acres patented to Duff, Green and Hite, 26th March, 1739, and by them conveyed to Robert McKay, etc., corner Isaac Lincoln. (Deed Book 19, p. 361, see also page 286 above.)

In 1782, Josiah Davison, as surety, signed the marriage bond of Andrew Shanklin to marry Abigail Herring, the daughter of Alexander Herring, (Jr.) (Strickler's *Rockingham Co. Marriages*, p. 104.) This Alexander was a brother of Leonard.

Davison was about a year older than Capt. Lincoln. His first wife was Edith Herring, and among his descendants by her, living in 1919, was one Alexander Herron Davison, aged 102, of Earlville, Illinois, near Chicago. Edith, so the Davisons have it, was a sister of President Lincoln's grandmother, Capt. Abraham Lincoln's wife.

Like Abigail, Edith was a frequent Herring name. Leonard's father had a sister so named, and each of his brother's William, and Bethuel, had also an Edith. Josiah Davison's wife, Edith, was not a daughter of either of these brothers, but was apparently of the right age to have been their sister. Capt. Lincoln, it may be observed, had a son Josiah, who may have been named for his uncle Davison.

In the *Memoirs* the author mentions having visited the house in which Bathsheba was married. The old residence, it is understood, is yet standing on Linville's Creek. From this, it seems likely that she was married at the home of her brother Leonard, and perhaps it was here that she met Capt. Lincoln.

Following the sale of her husband's land, in 1780, the deed was recorded June 17th, the same year, without her examination, and renunciation of dower. On September 8th, 1781, the court ordered a commission for her examination, she "being unable to travel to our Sd. County Court of Rockingham." The commission reported back to the court September 24, 1781. (Rockingham Court Order Book I.) Her husband having already acquired his land in Kentucky, returned for her and the children about this time, or a little later. (1782, says one authority.), and removed with them to their new home.

The administration of Abraham Lincoln's estate was granted in Nelson County, Kentucky, October 14, 1788. His land was in Jefferson. Following his death, his widow removed to Washington County with her family, where she was residing in 1792. She died in 1836. Their children were—

Mordecia—b. about 1771; d. Dec. 1830; m. 1729, Mary Mudd, b. ——, d. about 1859. Removed to Howard Co., Ind., and thence to Hancock Co., Ill., about 1828.

Josiah—b. about 1773; d. Sept., 1835; m. Feb. 28, 1801, Catherine Barlow, dau. of Christopher. Removed to Harrison Co., Ind.

Mary—b. ——; d——; m., August 5, 1801, Ralph Crume, of Nelson Co., Ky., son of Philip and Anne Crume.

Thomas—b. Jan. 5, 1778; d. Jan. 17, 1851, near Janesville, Ill.; m., 1st, June 12, 1806, at Beechland, Ky., Nancy Hanks, b. 1783-4, d. Oct. 5, 1818, near Gentryville, Ind., granddaughter of Joseph and Nancy (Ann) Hanks. Thomas m. 2nd., Dec. 2, 1819, at Elizabethton, Ky., Sarah, nee Bush, the widow of Daniel Johnston. She b. Dec. 13, 1788, d. Dec. 10, 1869, near Janesville, Ill. No children.

Children of Thomas and 1st. wife, Nancy Hanks—

Sarah—b. Feb. 10, 1807; d. 1828; m. 1826, Aaron Grigsby, of Spencer Co., Ind.

Abraham, the President—b. Feb. 12, 1809, at Buffalo, Hardin, (now La Rue), Co., Ky.; d. Apr. 15, 1865; m., Nov. 4, 1842, at Springfield, Ill., Mary Todd, dau. of Robert, of Lexington, Ky. Mary Todd dau. of Robert

Thomas—b. 1811, died in infancy.

Nancy—b. Mar. 25, 1780; d. Oct. 9, 1845, Hardin Co., Ky.; m. Jan. 12, 1801, William Brumfield.

* * * * * *

Leonard Herring is said to have "gone west" with his family in 1782, but as shown by the marriage bonds of his children, he was yet a resident of Rockingham in 1805. By this time he was nearing, or past, 70 years of age, and if his removal occurred, it appears likely that he accompanied one of his sons to the West after his wife Abigail's death.

As named above, Leonard Herring, (191), and wife Abigail, (171), had issue—

(1911) WILLIAM—b. ——; d. ——; m. 28th Dec., 1786, Hannah Robertson, dau. of Peter.

(1912) EDITH—b. ——; d. ——; m. 26th Sept., 1780, Joseph Hall.

(1913) SARAH—b. ——; d. ——; m. 9th Mar., 1783, William Lowery.

(1914) ESTHER—b. ——; d. ——; m. 1800, John Ervin, son of Benjamin.

(1915) ABIGAIL—b. ——; d.——; m. 1801, Daniel Curry.

(1916) NANCY—b. ——; d. ——; m. 1801, Robert Irvine.

(1917) LEONARD—b. ——; d. ——; m. 1805, Anne Ervin, dau. of Benjamin.

And possibly six others.

---

(193) ALEXANDER HERRING (-1779), the son of Alexander Herring, and wife Abigail (19), was married prior to 1761, as inferred from the *Memoirs of Lincoln,* but the name of his wife is unknown. She probably died before he did. His brother Leonard was appointed the administrator of his estate in Rockingham court, 22nd November, 1779.) His daughter—

(1931) ABIGAIL—m., 1782, Andrew Shanklin. (See page 281,)

---

(194) BATHSHEBA HERRING, (1742 c.-1836), the daughter of Alexander Herring, and wife Abigail, (19), as the daughter of Alexander Herring, (the pioneer), is named in Herring Chrisman's *Memoirs of Lincoln,* as the wife of Abraham Lincoln, the son of John, the emigrant to Rockingham County, Virginia. *(Memoirs,* pp. 6-11.) For further record, and the evidence regarding her identity, see Chapter XV, and Leonard Herring, (191), above.

---

(195) WILLIAM HERRING, (-1806), the son of Alexander Herring, and wife Abigail, (19), settled on Cook's Creek, in the region of his father, near present Dayton, Virginia. In the *Heads of Families* census, Virginia, 1784, "Herring, William," of Rockingham County, is named in the "List of Capt. William Herring" (himself), as having in his family, "4 White souls," and owning "2 Dwellings, 2 Other Buildings." (First Census U. S.—Virginia, p. 77.)

One of the earliest references to him on the Augusta records is that of 29th June, 1769, when he was apointed road overseer, vice Benjamin Harrison. (See page 321.)

During the Revolutionary War, William for a time served under Capt. Robert Cravens. Later he was a captain himself. On the 28th April, 1778, he was apointed Lieutenant in Capt. Cravens' company, and on the following 28th May, took the oath. He is mentioned in the Draper MSS. as serving in the regiment of Col. Benjamin Harrison when Cornwallis was in the State. (See pages 298, 299, 297, 296.) On the 29th April, 1783, Cornelius Cain was appointed Captain, vice Wm. Herring. Ulrich Gorton appointed Lieut., and Michael Mullen, Ensign, in Capt. Wm. Herring's company. (Rockingham Court Order Book No. I.)

As a civil officer of the county, William Herring was appointed first a vestryman, and later a justice of the court. On 25th May, 1778, Daniel Smith, John Thomas, George Boswell, Gawen Hamilton, Benjamin Harrison, and William Herring took the "oath of fidelity to the State as Vestrymen." (Rockingham Court Order Book, I, p. 7.) The last two took the oath as a justice 22nd March, 1779. (See page 321.)

From 1789 to 1790, William Herring was the High Sheriff of Rockingham County. (*Wayland*, p. 441.) At the court held on Monday August 23, 1790, "at the Court house of said County . . . Wm. Cravens was Sworn in deputy Sheriff under William Herring." (Rockingham Court Order Book, I, part II,, p. 481.)

In December, 1790, James Curry, William Herring, Benjamin Harrison, John Rice, Reuben Harrison, John Hardman, George Baxter, Richard Ragen, Samuel McWilliams, Jonathan Shipman, Benjamin Smith, James Burgess, George Sites, Thomas Shanklin, John Lincoln and William Cravens as jurors of Rockingham, signed a paper declaring a tract of land on the waters of Linville and Middy creeks formerly belonging to the Rev. Thomas Jackson, lately deceased, escheatable. An act entitled, "An Act concerning Escheators at the Court House of Rockingham County," was later passed, 26th July, 1796, by the State legislature, as a result, to terminate the proceedings. (*Chalkley*, Vol. I, p. 481.)

Captain Herring married Elizabeth Stephenson, a daughter of William, whose widow, Sarah, married as her second husband Capt. Daniel Harrison, (16). (See page 209.) William Stephenson, in will proved 16th, May, 1759, names his wife Sarah, and children, Adam, John, James, William, David, Elizabeth, Mathew, and Sarah. (Will Book II, p. 299; *Chalkley*, Vol. III. p. 52.) David Stephenson was a Major in the Virginia Continental Line, 1778-1783. (See Heitman's *Historical Register of Officers of Continental Army*, p. 381.)

Mary Stephenson, the widow of Major David Stephenson, in will dated 5th March, 1816, and proven in February 1818, divided her estate into two equal parts—one to her husband's relations, and the other to her own. David's relations named were, his deceased brother Adam's children, his deceased brother James' family, his deceased brother William's family, his sister Elizabeth Herring, and his nephew Robert Shanklin, the son of another sister. (*Chalkley*, Vol. III, p. 247.)

William Herring died in July, 1806, intestate, leaving besides wife Elizabeth, children, Alexander, Sarah, the wife of R. Huston, Elizabeth, Rebecca, Edith, Margaret, William S. and grandchildren William and Edith Chipley, the children of his deceased daughter Abigail, who married William Chipley; as disclosed in the son Alexander's bill of 23 February, 1810, vs. Chipley et als., petitioning for title to a part of his father's estate. In this Alexander was joined by his brother-in-law R. Huston. He recites that he married in 1793, and that his father had given him a part of his estate, but had never made title. It is further disclosed that Huston and Sarah were married in 1797. (See page 285.)

Elizabeth, the widow of William Herring, outlived her husband many years. She died in 1821, testate. Her will proven at February court, this year, was recorded in the single old will book now remaining of the early days of Rockingham. The edges of the book being badly charred in the bonfire through which it had passed, during the War of 1861-65, part of the writing is gone, but, so far as it remains, the will reads as follows—

"..

....in..

....g Dollars to him this ....

....ter Elizabeth Herring One bed and furni..........................

..........................& one hundred Dollars to her & her heirs forever ....

..................ter Rebecah Davis a Chest of drawers that was her father—

..........................purchase a set of Silver table Spoons to her other heirs forever . . . . my daughter Edith Shanklin Fifty Dollars to her other heirs . . . bequeath to my daughter Margaret Porter Fifty Dollars to her . . . . I give and bequeath to my son William S. Herring my best bed and furniture Viz. a red Green & white Coverlid and white Counterpine two pair of fine cotton sheets and pillow Cases also half dozen silve . . . presented to me by the late Gabriel Jones Esq and all marked with . . . also Scott's family bible in four volumes & one hundred dollars to . . . . heirs forever I give and bequeath to my Grandsons William H. Porter . . . . . Wilson Porter the sum of Fifty Dollars each (they being Children of m . . . Margret Porter) to them & their heirs forever I Give and bequeth to my . . . . Elizabeth S. Shanklin a Child of my daughter Sarah Huston dec'd twenty fi. . . . her and her heirs forever I Give and bequeath to my Grand daughter Ca . . . . the second daughter of my last daughter Sarah Huston dec'd Twenty . . . . to her and her heirs forever. I give and bequeath to my Grand sons . . . . H. Huston & William H. Huston and my Grand daughter Sarah Husto . . . . of my late daughter Sarah Huston dec'd the sum of one Hundred doll . . . Equally divided between them to them and their heirs forever. I Give a . . . . to my Grandson William Benja Chipley son of my late daughter Abegail . . . . Twenty dollars to him & his heirs forever. I give and bequeath to my G . . . . ter Elizabeth H. Chipley my second best bed & furniture also half a dozen . . all blue edged which formerly belonged to her mother to her and her . . I Give and bequeath to My Grand daughter Elizabeth S. Herring daughter . . . . . . Alexander Herring one white counterpine to her and her heirs forever I give . . . . bequeath to my daughters Elizabeth Herring and Rebecca Davis al. . . . . wearing apparel to be used and disposed of as they may think proper I . . . and desire that all the remainder of my Estate real and personal be so . . . . my Executors herein after named and the money arising therefrom and all the money due me I allow to be equally divided between my Children Alexand . . . Elizabeth Herring Edith Shanklin Rebecca Davis Margaret Porter & Willi . . . Herring and the Children of my daughter Sarah Huston dec'd and the . . . . of my daughter Abegail Chipley dec'd the Children of my said daughter . . . . Huston dec'd to draw one share to be equally divided between them and . . . children of my sd daughter Abigal Chipley dec'd to draw one share . . . . equally devided between them to them and their heirs forever.

I do hereby Constitute and appoint my son William . . . . . and my son in law Walter Davis Executors of this . . . . and testament hereby ratifying and confirming . . . .

. . . .

Gabriel Jones

. . . . request and in
. . . .
. . . . Lockridge
. . . . Lockridge
. . . . . . S. Smith
. . . . .Smith

Rockingham County February Court 1821
The last will and testament of Elizabeth Herring dec'd was presented in court and proved by the oaths of William Lockridge and Daniel Smith and ordered to be recorded and on the motion of Walter Davis and William S. Herring the executors named in the said will who entered into bond with security and made oath thereto as the law directs a certificate is granted them for obtaining a probate in due form.

R. J. Gambill, C. R. C.

(Burnt Will Book, Page 69.)

As named in the above, William Herring (195), and wife Elizabeth, had issue—

(1951) ALEXANDER—b. 1766; d. ——; m., 1793, Margaret Reed Smith, dau. of John Smith, (1651). She b. Apr. 23, 1777, d. ——. See further record.
(1952) SARAH—d. before 1821; m., 1797, Robert Huston.
(1953) ELIZABETH—d. unmarried.
(1954) REBECCA—m., 1809, Walter Davis.
(1955) ABIGAIL—d. before 1806; m. 1800, William Chipley, of N. C.
(1956) EDITH—m., Dec, 16, 1808, Jesse Shanklin.
(1957) MARGARET—m., 1806, Thomas Porter.
(1958) WILLIAM S.—m., ———;

(All of the above but William S. named in *Lea and Hutchinson.* See also, Strickler's *Rockingham County, Va., Marriages.)*

---

(196) JESSE HERRING, (-1781), the son of Alexander Herring, and wife Abigail, (19), seems to have died unmarried. His death occurred in 1781. The minute entered in the old first Court Order Book, of Rockingham, (1778-1792), regarding the settlement of his estate reads as follows—

"At a Court held for Rockingham County on Monday, the 26th day of March, 1781. Present: Daniel Smith, James Davis, William Herrin, Reuben Harrison, William McDowell, Anto. Reader, Gent. Justices.

The last will and testament of Jessse Herring, deceased, was produced and proven by the witnesses thereto, and William Herring and Bethuel Herring the Exors. therein named, having entered into bond with security, and made oath according to law, certificate is granted them etc.

Ordered that Nehemiah Harrison, Josiah Harrison, Benjamin Harrison and Robert Cravens, or any three first being sworn, do appraise said estate."

---

(197) BETHUEL HERRING, (1751-), the son of Alexander Herring, and wife Abigail, (19), like his brother William, settled near his father at Herring-ford on Cook's Creek, a short distance south of the present Dayton. In the *Heads of Families* census, Virginia, 1784, "Herring, Bethewel," of Rockingham County, was listed by Capt. Wm. Herring, with "4 White souls, 2 Dwellings, 2 Other buildings." (First U. S. Census, Va., p. 77.)

Bethuel was old enough to be appointed Constable in 1773, vice Robert Shanklin. (See page 283.) Among the witnesses examined in the cause of Cravens vs. Lanahan, at Lanahan's house in Harrisonburg, Friday, September 20, 1816, was "Bethuel Herring about the age of 62 or 63 years,—witness for the defendant. (See page 343.)

Of all the sons of Alexander Herron, the pioneer; Bethuel appears to have been the only one who could possibly have been referred to by the author of the *Memoirs of Lincoln*, as the "gentle and kindly old man", the writer had remembered seeing in his youth. (See the *Memoirs*, p. 13.)

In the Draper MSS., Bethuel Herring is mentioned as a private in Col. Benjamin Harrison's regiment during the Revolution. (See page 296.)

According to the Lincoln *Ancestry*, Bethuel married an Irven, or Erwin, and had seven children, four of whom are named as, Philander, Edith, Betsy, and Jane. A Bethuel Herring and Mary Miller of Rockingham were married August 16, 1782. (First Marriage Book of Rockingham.) On October 11, 1800, Bethuel Herring, a widower, with Thomas Erwin as security, gave bond in Augusta court to marry Thomas' sister Margaret, who gave her own consent. *(Chalkley,* Vol. II, p. 340.)

The marriage bonds of Rockingham list, James Davis and Nancy Herring, daughter of Bethuel, married 1808; Samuel Davis and Mary Herring, daughter of Bethuel, who consents,—Jacob C. Erwin, guardian of Samuel, also consents,— 1815; and Jesse Harrison and Mitilda Herring, daughter of Bethuel, 1815. (See, Strickler's *Rockingham Co. Marriages.)*

In lieu of these daughters, three sons, among them a Bethuel living in 1797, are named in the *Ancestry*, but at least two of these, viz. John, killed in the Revolution, and William who married a Stephenson, were obviously not Bethuel's sons. The Bethuel of 1797 may have been a son. In any case no son of the Bethuel, who was born 1752, would have been old enough to have been married in 1782, and no child of this marriage could have had the married daughters above.

In brief, therefore, based on the foregoing, Bethuel Herring's (197), children were—

(1971) PHILANDER—
(1972) NANCY—m., 1808, James Davis.
(1973) EDITH—
(1974) BETSY—
(1975) MARY—m., 1815, Samuel Davis.
(1976) MATILDA—m., 1815, Jesse Harrison, son of ———.
(1977) JANE—
And probably a Bethuel, Jr.

CHAPTER XVIII

Lines and Allied Lines

FOURTH GENERATION

"Two children in two neighbor villages
Playing mad pranks along the healthy leas:
Two strangers meeting at a festival;
Two lovers whispering by an orchard wall;
Two lives bound fast in one with golden ease;
Two graves grass-grown beside a gray church-tower,
Wash'd with still rains and daisy-blossomed;
Two children in one hamlet born and bred:
So runs the round of life from hour to hour."

—Tennyson.

IN ROCKINGHAM, there dwelt at the close of the Revolution, about 1132 white families, as shown by the data of the first census. Of these, about 714 families embraced all of the family names. By this time the population had increased, from a mere handfull of settlers in 1740, to 7,449 inhabitants, including 772 negro slaves.

Social life, as from the beginning, naturally centered largely around various congenial groups and gatherings, and of all the opportunities afforded for this last, the church undoubtedly furnished the greater part. There were other congregatings, however, of more or less regularity, in which the men folk of the community had opportunity to form contacts, and make congenial acquaintances, such as at political meetings, elections, sales, musters, and court-day assemblages. In the more intimate groups the occasion of a house-raising, corn-husking, applebutter-boiling, quilting-bee , spelling match, tournament, fox hunt, or wedding, furnished the young folk particularly an opportunity of intermingling, and acquiring new friendships. The great social event of all was the wedding; and this was usually celebrated long and with much merriment.

The social distinctions prevailing were the outgrowth of those which the early settlers had brought in, modified by the conditions under which the country had grown.

In the first days, when the inhabitants were few, congenial families had oft times settled in groups for their own protection. Frequently all in the group had come in together, or else some had first settled, and others, their relatives or friends, had followed, all having known each other in the place of their former abode. But each head of a family being desirous of acquiring as large a home plantation as his circumstances would justify, an appreciable distance was necessarily placed between even the closest neighbors, and in the case of a stranger, later arriving, the average distance to him was all the greater. This comparative isolation, especially in the event of Indian alarms, or disaster, only served to emphasize the dependence of what few nearer neighbors there were on each other. Thus were begun, and fostered, those frequent close associations of families, continued through several generations.

As the roads were built, and the surrounding country became settled, the social interests of the neighborhood widened. The Indian War coming on, and then the Revolution, brought inumerable further contacts, and afforded the young men generally

HOME SITE OF DAVID HARRISON (1775-1851)
By The Long Grey Trail
Present residence built by Madison Moore
See pages 378, 499, 589, 607

with a far greater circle of acquaintances. The same, to a lesser degree, also applied to the young women, particularly in the Indian War, when the whole countryside was forced to flee to various forts for protection. Schools, too, in the meantime, were being opened, and these also lent their influence to the social life of the day. The establishment of the county court added its prestige to the whole, and in a very real sense the court immediately became the great arbiter socially, as well as legally. No appointment to office, civil or military, was considered too insignificant to be sought for, and each confirmed social recognition.

Among the 700 early families alluded to, over fifty, in one generation or another, by the time of the fourth generation of the Harrisons, were allied to the latter, through one or more marriages. Including the older alliances, the Cravens, Herring, Smith, Davison, and Moore families, the descendants of the pioneer Harrisons had by this time intermarried with over one tenth of the 700 original lines. The significance of these alliances is all the more marked, when it is understood that to the lines involved belonged a great proportion of the long roll of Rockingham's foremost citizens, from the beginning of her history.

Long before the first census, the Harrison family had begun to branch out into what may be termed its own lines. Some of these have already been treated of as Clans, in connection with which a number of the earlier allied lines too have been noticed. These Clans each, in turn, gave rise to a series of new lines, which through their common kinship, three generations back, as well as by some later intermarriages, may broadly be termed allied lines also. These lines, or divisions of the Clans, and something of the others of the seventy odd lines above, more particularly follow in tracing the generation herein considered.

CLAN OF JOHN HARRISON

LINE OF ZEBULON HARRISON

(1211) JOHN HARRISON, (1749 c-),the son of Zebulon Harrison, (121), and wife Margaret, married Hannah Lincoln, the daughter of "Va. John Lincoln," the Pennsylvania emigrant. He died some years before his wife. (See page 304.) His will was dated, 1st, May, 1788. He resided near present Lacy Spring, some of his land being a part of that originally patented to John Harrison, Sr., the pioneer. (See, D. B. 000, of Rockingham, p. 167.)

Hannah Harrison, as before observed, was a sister of John Lincoln, the clerk of the Linville Creek Baptist Church, and of Capt. Abraham Lincoln, the late President's grandfather, also of Jacob Lincoln, who lived and died at the old Lincoln homestead on Linville Creek. (See pages 284 and 333.)

Among Jacob's children was a daughter, Elizabeth, and a son, John, d. 17th July, 1818, aged 35 years, 5 mo., 4 days; Abraham, b. Mar. 15th 1799, d. June 13, 1851, m. Mary (Horman), b. Oct. 24th, 1802, d. Mar. 8th, 1874, all of whose tombstones, but that of Elizabeth, are standing in the old family burial ground, near the site of the old home, a small distance from the present Pennybacker residence. Another of Jacob's sons was David Lincoln, b. June 28th, 1781, d. April 26th, 1840, whose tombstone along with that of his wife, Catherine, b. Feb. 6th, 1784, d. May 15th, 1873, may be seen in Lacey Spring Cemetery, he having settled at the "Big Spring," where he acquired a tract of the original Harrison land from Col. John Koontz. (See later, this Chapter.)

"Of the children of David Lincoln," says an article in the *Baltimore Sun*, of February 13, 1909, "three spent their entire lives in Rockingham County—Mrs. Peter

Lincoln Koontz, of Athlone; Jacob Lincoln, and Abraham L. Lincoln, all deceased." The present Rockingham family is headed by Mr. Samuel Lincoln, a son of the latter, of the Tenth Legion neighborhood.

Hannah Lincoln, the wife of John Harrison, like her brother John, was an active member of the early Smith and Linville's Creek Baptist Church.

* * * * * *

"Met—Sat. July 26, 1794. . . 3rd. Appointed Brother Lathem and Talman, & Sister Hannah Harrison, (if she can go) to wait upon Sister Margaret Harrison, in Order, if possible, that her Greviance against Brother Joe may be done away, & that Matters of Dispute, or Difference may be amicably settled between them." (Old Church Book, p. 55.)

Sister Margaret was Sister Hannah's mother-in-law, and evidently the latter was too tactful to accept this particular commission. "Met Sat. Aug. 9, 1794—1st. Brother Lathem being the only Member that awaited on Sister Margaret Harrison according to appointment reported accordingly, but said Sister being present herself, was enquired of concerning the Nonfellowship between her and Moore's Joe," etc.

Margaret's grievance had first appeared under date of May 10, 1794, at which time she had accused Joe, (a negro slave), of propagating "a slanderous Report as a Truth, against a Member of Sister Harrison's Family." At this meeting "Joe was laid under the Senser of the Church", after which—

"3rd. A Door was opened to hear Experiances, Absalom Lynn & Jenny his wife came forward and related theirs, and were Joyfully & unanimously received by the Church. N. B. On Sunday, or Lords Day, May 11, was baptized the aforesaid Absalom Lyn & Jenny his Wife, & then was celebrated the . . . . Lords Supper." (p. 53.)

Various mention of negro slaves appear in the church book. At a later meeting—"N. B. On the Lords Day, June 8, 1794, was baptized the aforesaid Mollato Lucky." (Brother Lathem's Mollato Woman . . . . called Lucky.) (p.54.)

Following his suspension, Joe was summonsed before the church—"Met . . . . Sat. July 26, 1794, . . . 2nd. Brother Joe being now present, had a hearing concerning the Charges brought against him by Sister Margaret Harrison, and which was the Cause of his Supposition," etc. At this meeting Joe's suspension was continued, but in addition it was decided to also suspend his accuser, upon which Bros. Lathem and Talman, and Sister Hannah Harrison, as above, were appointed to await upon her. At an Aug. 9th meeting, (1794), Margaret "came so far as to forgive sd. Brother Joe his Fault against her, or that which she viewed as a Fault in him, and agreed that he might keep his Place in the Church, as well as herself and that she would not neglect her Duty in the Church on this Account," but on condition that Joe should not have the privilege of her negro Dine as his wife, whereupon, 2nd. . . . . "the said two contending Members were both restored from under Suspension to full Previlege in the Church." (p. 55.)

Sat. Sept. 13, 1794, . . . "3rdly. Received Sister Margaret Briten into transient Communion of the Church, she being a Member of Buchmarsh Church." (p. 56.) Met Sat. Nov. 8, 1794. . . . "Proceeded to appoint Brother Lincoln Moderator for the Present, our Minister Br. Johnston, being removed from us." etc. (p. 57.)

Brother Johnston had removed from the church about a month previously. On October 11, 1794, Brother Lincoln was directed to prepare Rev. Johnston's letter of dismission.

Met. Dec. 13, 1794. . . "2nd. it is . . . . . agreed by the Church to give Brother Moffett a Call to preach . . . among us one Lords Day in each month till we can be more conveniently supplied . . . . . 6th. Agreed to pay Tom, or Jem, (who are black members of the church) six shillings if either of them will sweep the Meeting house & make Fires when necessary for one year." (p. 57.)

On Satudray, April 11, 1795 . . . 1st. "Br. Talman & Lincoln made their report concerning a contribution to be made by the Members of this Church to Br. Moffett" . . . the following contributing—Br. Talman and Wife, Lincoln and Wife, Lathem and Wife, Bowen and Wife, Lyn and Wife, McFarland and Wife, Sister Hannah Harrison (10 s), Margaret Harrison (10s), M. Thomas, E. Henton, Br. Lockard, sister Brumfield, and . . . Britton . . . total £6-00-00. (p. 58.)

Bro Lathem at a meeting, Sat. Nov. 7, 1795, requested a letter of dismission for his "Molato Woman Lucky" whom he "expects will shortly remove out of the bounds of the church." March 12, 1796, "Bro. Lincoln reported that he prepared a Letter for Molato Lucky according to appointed which was signed by himself & several other Memebers next Day & delivered, also upon Application, he had prepared similar Letters for Brothers Lathem & Wife & Lynn & Wife, signed by himself and Brother Talman & delivered." (p. 59.)

June 11, 1796, ... "NB. our Return to the Association was 20 Members." Oct. 8, 1796, ... "Met . . after divine Service by Brother James Ireland who had come to visit us and preach, proceeded to Business sd. Brother being chosen Moderator, & Letter of Recommendation & Dismission, was presented to (by) Rhoda Jeffres, Wife of . . . . Jeffres, Member of Baptist Church of Christ on lost River, upon which she was received into the fellowship & under the care of this church." (p. 60.)

"The Church Met Sat. Dec. 8, 1798, according to appointment, and after praise and prayer proceeded to Business & 1st. Brother Thomas Yates gave in his Letter of dismission from F. T. Church and was received into full fellowship. 2ndly. Agreed to keep up dicipline strictly, if possible for the future. Adjourned." (p. 63.)

(This last minute brings the notes down to 1800. Page 58 is the last page numbered, and from there on the pages are whiter than the preceeding, being evidently a separate insert over to the Brock's Gap Confession of Faith, at the end of the book. Page 60 is apparently the last of a similar handwriting. Only two other meetings of 1798 are mentioned—April 7th, and August 11th—and none in 1799, and 1800. One meeting August 8th, is noted in 1801.)

In 1802 the church joined the Culpeper Association. Met . . Sat. Sept. 11, 1802, . . "1st. Brother Lockhard brought forward a Letter of dismission from the Ketocton Association, to join the Culpeper Association." At this meeting Nancy Green was suspended and given notice to appear at the next meeting. (p. 63.) Sat. Nov. 13, 1802 . . . "2ndly. Appointed Brothers Talman, Lincoln and Lockard to meet with any members of the Methodist Class on Linvilles Creek that may be properly authorized to meet with them, to consult on a plan for building a new meeting house." (p. 64.) Lockhart

Met . . . Oct. 8, 1803, . . "1st. Nansy (wife of John Harrison) came forward & related her experiance, and was received for Baptism 2nd. Rachel Britten from Hill-Town-Church, in Bucks County, Pennsylvania, came forward with her letter of Dismission from said Church, and was received into the fellowship of this Church. Hannah Lincoln, daughter of John Lincoln, came forward & related her experiance and was received for Baptism. Sunday Oct. 9, 1803, before Sermon, the Church being collected, Set for Experiance, Rachel Lincoln came forward & related what the Lord had done for her Soul, & was received for Baptism, ... After Sermon the aforesaid three

Candidates were baptized, according to our Lords command, by Br. Moffett, after which the Lords Supper was commemorated." (p. 65.)

Nancy Harrison was the daughter of Benjamin Tallman, a near relation of Hannah Harrison. As given by the marriage bonds of Rockingham, John Harrison and Ann Tallman, the daughter of Benjamin, were married in 1797. Two brothers of John also married sisters of Ann. A part of Tallman's land was obtained from Zebulon Harrison—Deed. 25th Aug. 1783, Zebulon Harrison and wife Margaret, of Rockingham, to Benjamin Tallman, 165 acres on Smith's Creek. (Mathews vs. Johnston, N. S. 132; *Chalkley*, Vol. II, p. 250.)

Hannah Harrison, the widow of John, died about August 1803. Prior to her last illness her mother Rebecca Lincoln had made her home with her. (See page 284.) Hannah's will, as recorded at Harrisonburg, in one of the two old burned books before referred to, reads as follows—

Will of Hannah Harrison

IN THE NAME OF GOD AMEN. I Hannah Harrison widow and relict of John Harrison Decd. being sick and weak in body but of sound mind and memory thanks be to God for his mercies and knowing it is appointed for all Once to die do make and ordain this my last will and Testament and in the following manner and form

first I Recommend my soul to God who gave it and my body to the earth from whence it came to be buried in a decent and Chistian manner at the discretion of . . . executors and at the charge of son Zebulon Harrison.

Item I give and bequest to my eidest son William Harrison half stock of sheep . . .

Item I give and bequeath to my second son Zebulon Harrison the two Hors creatures and the Hogs that I now own, also what is indebted to me and what Corn and Rye that is . . . . made besides that will discharge my Debts with my whole stock of Ca. . .

Item it is my will and desire that the third of the land left me . . . Husbands last will and Testament be sold by my executors . . . . six sons and Daughter Phebe to wit—William, Zebulon, Henry, John, Isaac, and Abraham Harrison with the above named Phebe Harrison.

Item I do will and bequeath to my daughter Phebe two cows which she has sometimes Claimed and her own property with all the kitchen and Household furniture that I have not above willed away, with the other half of the stock of sheep that I have not willed to my son William Harrison, with a small room upstairs which she claims her own till her brother Abraham is of age,

and I do hereby constitute and ordain my well beloved brothers Jacob Lincoln and [John] Lincoln my soul Executors of this my last Will and Testament—in witness my hand and seal . . . . this twelvth day of September 1803.

her
Hannah Harrison (SEAL.)
mark.

Test.
Nathaniel Harrison.
Josiah Harrison.
William Tallman.

Proved December Court 1803 at Harrisonburg
(See, Rockingham Court Old Burnt Book, p. 47.)

Briefly, as named in the foregoing, John Harrison, (1211), and wife Hannah, had issue—

(12111) WILLIAM—m., 1797, Mary Fawcett, dau. of Benjamin.
See further record.

(12112) ZEBULON A.—b. Mar. 1775; d. June 6, 1825, m. 1803, Mary Tallman, dau. of Benjamin.
See further record.
(12113) HENRY—m., Susan Tallman, dau. of Benjamin.
(12114) JOHN—m., 1797, Ann Tallman, dau. of Benjamin.
See further reference.
(12115) ISAAC—
(12116) ABRAHAM—m., Grace Harrison, dau. of Nathaniel, (1252.)
(12117) PHOEBE—m. Mar. 12, 1807, William Cooper; Removed to Franklin Co., Ohio, before 1811.

(All in D. H. S. MSS.; see also Rockingham Co. D. B. 000, p. 167, wherein John's heirs are also named. Dates from Strickler's *Rockingham Co. Marriages.)*

(1213) ROBERT HARRISON ( ), the son of Zebulon Harrison (121), and wife Margaret, was devised land by his grandfather Capt. Robert Cravens, in 1761, and in 1779 was appointed a constable. (See pages 251 and 299.) He married, but his wife's name is not directly disclosed. William Young in his will 22nd October 1810, proved 27th May, 1811, in Augusta, names among others, "Him who was my son-in-law Robert Harrison," and Robert's children, Robert, William and James. (Will Book 11, p. 25.) This Robert may have been Zebulon's son.

In an agreement, 10th March, 1813, between William C. Davis and Robert Harrison, Sr., of Christian County, Kentucky, witnessed by R. Harrison, Jr., and Davis Harrison, William sold to Robert 667 acres of land, three surveys, including 495 acres of Military land devised to William and his brother Abraham by their father James, all three tracts lying on "the Montgomeries fork of Red River Christain County . . . . 200 acres being the place where the said Harrison now lives, . . . also a part of a survey now owned by Reuben Harrison, and the whole being divided from said Reubens farm where he now lives by the Big Road leading from Hopkinsville to Russelsville." (Original record.)

Among the papers handed down in the family of the above Robert are two parchment patents granted to Zebulon Harrison; the first dated 12th May, 1770, before noticed, the second, a Commonwealth grant, dated 6th Dec., 1790, for 137 acres "in the county of Rockingham on the South side of Smith's Creek;" also a deed, 26th August, 1812, from "Reuben Harrison and Sally () his wife & Robert Harrison and Sally his wife all of the County of Christian and State of Kentucky" to John Brock of Rockingham County, Virginia, for 240 Pounds, 137 acres, the same survey as the 1790 patent.

This Robert was born in Rockingham, in August 1783, and died in Christian County, Kentucky, June 17, 1853, aged 69 yrs. 10 mo. He married there, April 11, 1811, Sally Davis, the daughter of James Davis, son of Walter and Martha (Cunningham) Davis, and granddaughter of Robert Cuningham, of Augusta, who with Col. John Willson, served as a first Burgess of the county. She died Dec. 29, 1861. Their children were—Naomi (m. Wm. H. Forston), Sarah, Martha, Debora (m. Geo. Fortson, bro. of Wm.), Davis, William, and Fayette, (b. Mar. 15, 1815, d. Paduach, Ky.,1897.) The last named married October, 1838, Harriette, the daughter of James Bradshaw, of Christian County, Ky, and had—James H., Mary Elizabeth, Robert B., William D., Gustavus, Edward, Elbridge B., Lafayette, and Sally; of whom Mary Elizabeth, b. July 1841, m. Aug. 4, 1864, William Boase Trewolla. (From data kindly supplied by Rev. James A. Trewolla, of Braddock, Pa., a grandson of the last named, through his son Charles. B.)

(1214) PHOEBE HARRISON, ( ), the eldest daughter of Zebulon Harrison, (121), and wife Margaret, by the will of her uncle, John Harrison, Jr., proved 1763, was bequeathed 254 acres of land on Smiths Creek. (See page 157.) According to Augusta County Deed Book XVIII, (page 417), the said land was patented to John, 10th July, 1755, and devised to "Feby Harrison, wife of said James Dyer." Dyer in 1779 was one of the justices of Rockingham court. (See page 321.) He is thought to have removed to Pendleton County, now West Virginia, which was carved out of Rockingham, in December, 1787.

(1215) JOSIAH HARRISON, (-1824), the son of Zebulon Harrison, (121), and wife Margaret, married, 1786, Margaret Miller, daughter of the widow Janet Miller, who, with William Bryan, gave her consent. (See page 304.) Janet was the wife of Alexander Miller, who patented 169 1/2 acres of land on Muddy Creek, 14th May, 1787, and died intestate—Deed; 21st Dec., 1793; John Millier and Jane, his mother; Margaret, his wife; Samuel Miller, and Anna, his wife; Josiah Harrison, and Margaret, his wife; Isaac Miller, and Polly, his wife, all of Rockingham, to Thomas and Gad Gilmore, land as above, etc. Recorded, Dec. 1793. (Gilmore vs. Gilmore, N. S. 82; *Chalkley*, Vol. II, p. 182.)

Josiah Harrison joined the "Great Western Migration" about 1810. He appears to have settled first in Barren County, Kentucky, whence he removed about 1811 to Christian County. Among the papers of the Robert Harrison family, above referred to, is a deed, dated 14th March, 1823, from Benjamin Harrison and Ann H. Harrison, his wife, to Josiah Harrison, Reuben Harrison and Robert Harrison, "all of the County of Christian and State of Kentucky" for 172 1/2 acres of land, part of "the Military Claim of Craig and Johnson," on the East Branch of Little River; witness William C. Gray, Benjamin Harrison. On the back of this deed, under date March 15, 1823, occurs a notation—"We Josiah Harrison Reuben Harrison & Robert Harrison Sen. do request James Bradley Sheriff of Christian County to Levy an execution now in his hands in the name of Finis Ewing against Robert Harrison Jr. John Harrison and us upon the tract named in the within deed. . . Signed, Josiah Harrison, Reuben Harrison, Robert Harrison. Recorded, March 15, 1823, in Christian County.

Josiah, in will of November 19, 1820 recorded in Christian County, November Court, 1824, names his wife Margaret, his nephew Josiah, son of his brother Reuben, to whom he devised land on Little River, his brothers Reuben and Robert, his sisters Neomia and Rutha and Margaret Cravens, his nieces Betty Wright and Peggy Harrison, "daughters of my brother Gideon Harrison," Cyrina Laney, Matilda and Caroline McCoy, "and my wife's nieces Betsy and Jenny Miller." A bequest was also made to Margaret Matilda Burgess (when she came of age), and freedom was granted to his slave Pompey, to whom he willed a field during the latter's lifetime. His friend Thomas Moore of Rockingham County, Virginia, is also named. A codicil mentions Sirene Laney, to whom he devised "that part that was intended for my sister Polly Laney."

No children are mentioned. His brothers Reuben and Robert were appointed executors. The sister Ruth ( ) Harrison, in a separate paper, April 15, 1834, witnessed by Zebulon Harrison, and Elvirea Harrison, acknowledged receipt of her share of the estate, also a sum for Samuel and Polly Laney. Ruth was residing in Howard County, Missouri, at this time. The sister Naomi married Zebulon Dyer, of Pendleton County, Virginia, who was residing in this county in 1845, and she in Christian County, Kentucky. She died in 1856. (Will dated May, 1852). The Gideon named appears identical with the one who settled in Georgia prior to 1790. (See page 304.) His daughter Margaret (b. about 1792) m., 1817, Isaac Vinson, and Elizabeth (b. 1790) m., about 1817, Isham Wright. (Received too late for mention in Chapter XVI.)

LACEY SPRING

It was Col. Josiah Harrison, the son of Zebulon, and grandson of John Harrison, the pioneer, who sold out of the Harrison family the Big Spring tract of land, the original home plantation patented by John Harrison, 25th June, 1747. The land was devised by the pioneer to his son Zebulon, in will dated, 30th July, 1769. (See pages 156 and 162.)

In all of the county records down to August 15, 1849, mention is made of the spring as the Big Spring, and not Lacey Spring. Just how the name came to be adopted for the present town is not indicated by the records, there being no reference to any Lacey found among the various deeds in connection with the ownership of the land. One, Samuel Lacey was a witness to Capt. Reuben Harrison's will, 2nd. May, 1802. (See page 311.) He seems to have lived in the old log house near the spring originally built by John Harrison, and he, or one of his decendants, may have for a time kept the tavern owned by Col. John Koontz, in 1818, in which year on the 4th of August, Col. Koontz signed an article of agreement with Samuel Butler, wherein he "this day rented to Said Butler the big Spring Tavern House, Kitchen Stable & garden thereto attached together with one acre of land, to 1st Oct., 1819." The post office was established March, 14, 1850, with William H. Barley as postmaster. (U. S. Govt. Post Office Records, Washington, D. C.)

Josiah Harrison conveyed his land, 421 acres, to Col. Koontz, 7th May, 1810, by deed, reading so far as preserved, as follows:

THIS INDENTURE made this 7th day of May one thousand eixx . . . . . and ten Between Josiah Harrison and Margaret his wife of the Coxxxxxx . . . Rockingham and State of Virginia of the one part and John . . . . the County and State aforesaid of the other part, WITNESSETH . . . said Josiah Harrison and Margaret his wife for and in . . . . .ration of the sum of two Thousand pounds Virginia cuxxxx . . . him in hand paid by the said John Koontz the receipt whexxx . . . hereby acknowledged have bargained & sold and do hereby . . . . and sell unto the said John Koontz and his heirs and assxxx . . . ever, Several adjoining tracts or parcels of land containixx . . . hundred & twenty one acres more or less lying and being ix . . County of Rockingham on the waters of Smith Creek in . . . the following tracts, grants, or part of grants of lanx . . . part of a tract of land granted by patent to Alexander . . and by him conveyed to said Josiah Harrison, a tract of lxxx . . four acres granted by patent to Zebulon Harrison, and by . . . .and bequeathed to his son the said Josiah Harrison—part . . . of two hundred and thirty four acres granted by patent . . (John) Harrison and *and* by him devised and bequeathed to his soxxx . .(Zebulon) Harrison and by him to his said son Josiah Harrison, . . . of another tract of one hundred & fifty six acres granted to said John Harrison, by him Devised to the said . . . . (Zebulon) by him to his son the said Josiah Harrison . . . . . tract containing twenty eight acx . . . . . . by hxx . . . . .ng . . . . parcels of lanx . . un . . . . to the said Koontz by the following lines tx . . . . Beginning at two pines corner of the above traxx . . . . running thence N 26 W 13 poles to a double pxxx . . . . . eight four acre tract with the lines of . . . poles to a stake instead of a white oak and . . . corner Henry Isles land thence S. 10½ W 135 poles . . . sapling corner to Michael Summers land Thence . . . to a stake also Summers corner thence S. 38 E 4 poles to a coxxxx . . . and black oak corner of said 234

acre pattent thence with the line of the same S 34 W 23 poles to a white oak and black oak Grubs on the said line and Thos Bears corner thence with this line crossing the tract S 51¼ E 100 poles to a Stake on another line of this pattent also Bears corner thence with this pattent N 61 E 78 poles to a white oak and cedar instead of a pine now down Thence N. 50 E 38 poles to three cedar rushes near the big Spring rn thence S. 34 E. 30 poles to a white oak and cedar near John Brocks corner Instead of two hickories now down a corner of the eighty four acre pattent thence S 78 E 36 poles to a walnut also a corner of the 84 acre pattent pattent near John Brocks line thence to Brocks line and then with the same N 44 E. 42 poles crossing Smiths creek twice to two white oak Saplings now stumps also Brocks corner thence S. 53 E. 90 poles crossing the said creek to 3 pines in John Dippos line and corner to Brock and to the tract conveyed by the said Wm. & Jno. Armstrong thence with the lines of the same and Dippos land N 45½ E 130 poles to a white oak and hickory also corner to Dippos & John Armstrong land thence N 3 W 66 poles to a white oak corner to Armentrout and the said 166 Acre pattent thence with the lines of the said last mentioned pattent N 52½ W 72 poles crossing Mathews forge down down to a stake instead of the new pattent corner now down Thence S. 33 W 98 poles to a scrub white oak and hickory a corner to the land conveyed by Mc Farlin and near said pattent line thence N 26½ W 90 poles to three pines another of Mc Farlins corner containing on the lines of the same N 75 W 73 poles to a black oak and white oak instead of two pines now down thence, S 87¾ W 63 poles to the beginning. The above corners, courses and distances. Including a dam and Griss and saw mill &c. Together with all appurtenances thereunto belonging to the said tract of land unto him the said John Koontz and his heirs and assigns forever, to the sole use and behoofe of him the said John . . . . .ontz and his heirs and assigns forever and the said Josiah Harxxxxxx . . . Margaret his wife do bind themselves their heirs, executors. . . . . said tract of four . . . . .Koontz and his heirs or assigns forever . . . . . claim of any person or persons whatsoever claixx . . . . . from or under them, or any or either of them . . . . whatsoever will warrant and forever defend . . . . . said Josiah Harrison & Margaret his wife hath . . . . .ed their names and affixed their seals the day anx . . . . . . ove written
. . . . sealed and delivered
in presence of

	Josiah Harrison	(Seal.)
David Ragan	her	
S. McWilliams	Margaret X Harrison	(Seal.)
John Laffaner	mark	
J. Knootz		
Peachy Harrison.		

(Copy kindly supplied by the late J. F. Blackburn, Clerk of the Rockingham Circuit Court. From Burnt Record Deeds.)

Koontz

KOONTZ

In 1821, Col. Koontz was residing on this land: Deed of Trust; 19th Nov, 1821; John Koontz of Rockingham, to William McClung of Bath, to secure payments to David Given of Bath . . . . "all that Tract or parcel of Land lying and being in the County of Rockingham on which he the Said John Koontz now lives . . . Containing Four hundred and Twenty One Acres and purchased by the Said John Koontz from Josiah Harrison and Margaret his Wife as appears by Deed bearing date the 7th of May in the Year One Thousand Eight Hundred and Ten . . . with the following reservations to Wit

Thirty Five Acres Conveyed to Reuben Harrison and three fourth Acre Conveyed to Jacob Cole." Recorded in Bath, Nov. 21, 1821, in Rockingham, Mar. 6, 1822. Signed—John Koontz, David Given, Wm. McClung.

Col. Koontz, in will dated 25th January, 1826, directed—

"3rd. I give to my Son Horatio all this part of my home plantation including my Mills house and barn that is to say beginning at the mouth of the Bigg Spring branch . . . . and running up the said branch . . . between said line and the Mill dam . . . to within Twenty poles of My dwelling House thence to within twenty poles opisit my Barn towards the bigg Spring . . . so as to strike my out line at the mouth of Danl. Matthews line at the Stage Road thence with my line running with Houstons and others Crossing the Creek . . . Stevens line . . . to include about Seventy acres of pine land . . . between the lands of Brock and Stevins . . to leave out the bottom known by the name of Gaund bottom and so to the mill dam . . . . also the privilege of water anywhere out of Sd spring Branch to the Head for Cooking or other hous use. . . ."

4thly I Give to my Son Shroder all and Singular the Ballance of my land I Hold on Sd Smiths Creek including the aforesaid Spring branch the Spring the Tanyard the Tavern House the place called Iles place and the aforesaid Gaund Bottom and the Ballance of the Harrison tract of land with all its appurtenances."

His will names, aside from the above sons, his wife, Jane; his daughter Elizabeth, "now widow of Benjamin Harrison," ($800 to be paid in 10 years after my death with interest for 5 years before due), his daughter Polly Hite; his daughter Jane Allen; his son George, (1/2 of my tract of land on Bigg Sandy containing 1154 acres in the state of Virginia); his son Coskey, (the other moiety of the Big Sandy land); and his " grand Daughter Mariah Graham Koontz, the only Daughter of my Son Jacob Koontz—I have advanced considerable sums of Money to her Father my son Jacob during his life." In the first section of the will he directs that his slaves and two tracts of land near the "Town of Harrisonburge" be sold. He appoints as his executors, Dan Matthews, Reuben Allen, and Jacob Cole. Signed—John Koontz. Witnesses —William Pickering, Robert ( ) Jones, Brewer Reeves, George ( ) Hollensworth, Henry M. Durvall, Henry Stahl. Codicil, undated, appoints "my friend Archibald Brock" an executor. (From original, kindly loaned by Mr. Jacob Cole, of Lacey Spring.)

Mrs. Maria G. Carr, the granddaughter named, (nee Koontz), in her *My Recollections of Rockingham, Now Known as Harrisonburg, From 1817-1820,* states—

> "My Grandfather Koontz had a store (in Harrisonburg) before I remember—he bought a farm ten miles N. of H. . . . . called Big Spring—and built his house there which is now occupied by the Lincoln Family. He built his house when I was three years old and it is in a good state of preservation. He had a fine tanyard which was carried on by Isaac Hite, son of Mrs. Hite (before mentioned), he married Polly Koontz, daughter of Col. John Koontz, sister of my Father. My Grandfather had a large merchant and saw mill near his dwelling,—there was also a large log house just above the spring which was used as a house of entertainment. Mrs. Patton lived there when I first remember, afterward some of the Lincoln family got it. . . . . My Grandfathers Graham and Koontz were among the first trustees of H(arrisonburg.)" (Page 22.)

Col. Koontz's will was probated in Rockingham County Court, in August 1830, but prior to this time he sold by deed to David Lincoln (see page 357), September 15, 1829, two tracts of land; the first containing "15 acres, 1 rood, and 15 poles," including the Big Spring, the second containing 111 acres, both of which tracts also appear in the report of the commissioners assigning dower to the widow Lincoln. (Deed Book No. 9, p. 426.) Owning to the destruction of the records, the only record of Col. Koontz's will at Harrisonburg is a memorandum stating that it was proved, and that Jacob Cole qualified as executor, on the date mentioned.

(1216) POLLY HARRISON, ( ), the daughter of Zebulon Harrison, (121), and wife Margaret, married, 1784, Robert Harrison, (1671), son of Col. Benjamin Harrison. Robert removed with his family to Christian County, Kentucky. No further record. See Josiah above.

LINE OF DANIEL DAVISON

(1231) JOSIAH DAVISON, (1743-1825), the son of Daniel Davison, and wife, Phoebe, (123), nee Harrison, during his youth received a legacy from his grandfather, Josiah Davison, a resident of New Jersey, and at his father's death inherited land on Smiths Creek. On coming of age, he sold his Smiths Creek land to Thomas Moore, who married his mother, as her second husband. (See pages 166, 146, and 305.) A memorandum of July 17, 1767, regarding the settling of his grandfather's legacy is yet in existence among his descendants. His original deed to Moore, dated 7th November, 1767, is also extant. (See page 146.)

Josiah settled in the old Linville Creek community, near Leonard Herring, Josiah Boone, and the Lincolns. (See page 349.) His land was a part of the original Hite land, and adjoined an early tract of one of the Harrisons. On the 18th August, 1766, Daniel Smith (later Col.), and Lydia Wright, as the executors of John Wright, deceased, conveyed to John Johnston, 300 acres on Linville Creek, part of 550 acres conveyed to Wright by Abraham Hite, 31st December, 1760, adjoining Green and Harrison's land. This tract was delivered to Josiah Davison, November, 1767. (Deed Book 13, p. 81.) An inclusive survey of 510 acres was made for Josiah in 1774, according to a receipted bill of April 19th, the same year.

In the *Heads of Families* census, Virginia, 1784, "Davisson Josiah," of Rockingham County, was enumerated in his own list as having in his family "8 White souls," and owning "1 Dwelling." *(First U. S. Census, Va.,* p. 76.)

Josiah Davison has been frequently mentioned as Rockingham's first Sheriff. (See page 238, etc.) Prior to the establishment of Rockingham, he had been a justice of the County Court of Augusta for at least two terms, having qualified 17th August, 1773, and 21st May, 1777. (Court Order Books 15, p. 148, and 16, p. 191.) On the 28th June, 1779, as disclosed by the first Court Order Book of Rockingham, "Josiah Davison refuses to perform the duties of Sheriff," whereupon Abraham Smith, John Grattan, and George Boswell, were each recommended for the office, of whom, Smith qualified, 26th July, following.

Josiah's resignation was likely due to his desire to enter the military establishment as an officer. In 1780 he is named as a Captain of the militia. (See page 299.) On November 4, 1784, he was commissioned Coroner of Rockingham, by Gov. Benjamin Harrison.

The same year, October 29, 1784, he purchased from Benjamin Smith a warrant for 1,000 acres of land, which he probably located a short time later in what is now West Virginia. Sometime between January 13, 1794, and April 9, 1795, he moved to Harrison County, that state. In a bill of sale, of the 1794 date, of a negro woman, and her three children, sold to him, he is named as "Josiah Davisson of the County of

Rockingham," while in a bond of the 1795 date, to John Ashren, he is named as "Josiah Davisson, of Harrison County and State of Virginia." On January 19, 1795, the County Court of Harrison ordered its Surveyor to survey for him three tracts of land on the waters of Pleasant Creek.

About 1813, Josiah Davison migrated to Ohio, (from present West Virginia) settling first near Wilmington, in Clinton County, and finally, on April 24, 1816, in Monroe township, Preble County, where he patented 640 acres of land. His removal to Ohio, says a descendant, was largely due to his detestation of slavery, and his desire to reside in a free state. (Richard L. Davison, in an address, *The Life of Josiah Davison II*, made on the occasion of the Centennial Anniversary of Josiah's settlement on the above land.) At the time of his settlement in Preble, the country was practically a wilderness, and the Indians still roamed the woods. His land was entirely covered by forest, and it is related that he was the first white man to settle in Monroe township. Part of his land has been continually occupied by his descendants from his day to the present.

His death occurred in 1825. He was buried in the old Baptist churchyard at the southeast corner of his farm; his inscription reading—"In Memory of Josiah Davisson who died Sept. 9th, A. D., 1825, aged 81 years, 9 months, and 8 days."

Josiah Davison, (1231), was twice married; first to Edith Herring, elsewhere noticed, (see page 350), who is thought to have died in Harrison County (West Virginia), and second, to Ann, or Nancy, Williams. His children were fifteen, as follows—

By first wife Edith—all, or most all, of whom remained in West Virginia on their father's removal to Ohio—

Col. Benj. Watson

(12311) Daniel—b. 1772; d. ——.
(12312) Abigail—b. 1774; d. 1794.
(12313) Phoebe—b. 1776; d. 1864; m. Col. Benjamin Watson, as his 2nd wife.
(12314) William—b. 1779; d. 1846; m. ——.
(12315) Ann—b. 1781; d.——;
(12316) Reuben—b. 1783; d. ——; m.———.
(12317) Jesse—b. 1786; d. 1821; m. ——.
See futher reference.
(12318) Edith—b. 1789; d.——.

By second wife Nancy—

(12319) George—b. Aug. 1800; d. ——; m. ——.
(12320) Absalom—b. Sept. 18, 1802; d. ——; m.——.
(12321) Hannah—b. Sept. 7, 1804; d. ——; m. —— Woolard.
(12322) Jonathan William—b. Nov. 16, 1806; d. ——; m.——.
See further record.
(12323) Josiah—b. Nov. 6, 1808; d. 1863; m. ——.
See further record.
(12324) Mary—b. June 2, 1811; d. ——; m. —— Paddock.
(12325) Amaziah—b. Aug. 19, 1813; d. ——; m.——.

(All but George named in a list prepared by Prof. Schuyler C. Davison, a descendant of Jonathan above. Birth dates of the last seven found written on the margin of the printed pages of an old book entitled, *Meditations and Contemplations*, printed in London,

1784, and handed down in the family of Josiah (12323), as noticed by Richard L. Davison, in his address.)

MOORE

(1232) ANN DAVISON, (1746-1822), the daughter of Daniel Davison, and wife Phoebe (123), nee Harrison, by will of her uncle, John Harrison, Jr., proved, 1763, was devised 400 acres of land on the Dry Fork of Smiths Creek. (See page 157.) Sometime prior to 1767 she married Reuben Moore, of Frederick County, later Shenandoah. On the 21st of August, this year, she joined her husband in conveying the above land to her uncle, Reuben Harrison, the Captain. (See page 308.)

Reuben Moore's residence, a fine old country seat, was known as Mt. Pleasant. It was here that Ann died on April 8, 1822. According to a brief death notice appearing in the *Shenandoah Herald* of the same month—"On Monday the 8th at the residence of the venerable Reuben Moore, in Mt. Pleasant, in this County, his pious and Aimable consort, Mrs. Ann Moore, in the 75th year of her age, after an indisposition of only 8 days."

Reuben Moore was apparently the son of Thomas Moore, who at an early date settled in the present Forrestville -Moore's store community, to the west of Mt. Jackson. In 1753, Thomas, and wife Mary, conveyed to Samuel Newman, a tract of land on Smiths Creek, in what was evidently now Rockingham. (See page 145.) Thomas's will, recorded at Woodstock, 1790, (Will Book C, page 244), names, his wife, Mary, and children; John, Reuben, Joseph, Lydia, Ann, Elizabeth, and Hannah, and a nephew Thomas George. (See, Wayland's *History of Shenandoah County*, p. 715; also Strickler's *Forerunners*, p. 55.)

EWING

Ewing

(1233) PHOEBE DAVISON, (1748-1838), the daughter of Daniel Davison, and wife Phoebe (123), nee Harrison, like her sister Ann above, was devised Dry Fork land by her uncle, John Harrison, Jr., in his will of 1758, her share being 200 acres. This land, says Augusta County Deed Book XX, (page 248) was "patented to John Harrison, Jr., 10th Feb., 1748, and bequeathed to Phoebe Davis[son], now wife of John Ewin, by said John's will."

Phoebe and John Ewing were married in 1768. He was born in 1741, and died May 15, 1822, in his 82nd year. She died in 1838. It was to her that her mother handed the interesting old water bottle, the trophy of her great-grandfather's voyage to America. (See Chapter VII.)

John and Phoebe Ewing, and their daughter Mary, were among the witnesses examined at Dennis Lanahan's house in Harrisonburg, September 13, 1816, in the Cravens vs. Lanahan case. (See page 342.) All three were questioned by Joseph Cravens (son of John, deceased), concerning the time he spent at Ewing's home in his childhood—a school season or more. As given by the record—

"John Ewing of Lawfull age, says about the age of seventy six or seventy seven being first sworn . . . a witness for the plaintiff deposeth & saith . . . Question by Joseph Cravens, 1st. At what time was I sent to and boarded at your house to go to school when William Herron was the Teacher & who paid the expenses for me. Ans. I do not perfectly remember the time you came there but I believe it was about the year 1784-1785 and remained part of two years . . . deponent does not recollect who paid the schooling . . . . the boarding he did not charge as he thought his work sufficient.

As you were at that time a strong active boy about fourteen or fifteen years of age." . . etc.

"Phoebe Ewing, about the age of sixty-eight years, being first sworn . . . Question by Joseph Cravens, 1. Where did I get my clothing whilst I stayed at your house? Ans. I do not know; you brought some with you but they were but few, we washed and mended for you" . . .etc.

"Mary Pence, daughter of John & Phoebe Ewing, about forty two years of age, being first sworn," also "deposeth . . . Question by Joseph Cravens. 1st. At what time did I come to your fathers to go to school and how long did I continue there and at your uncle Davisons. Answer—I do not recollect the year—you came early in the summer and stayed the next winter at my fathers & the following summer and winter at my uncle Davisons—after you left the school at Mr. Davisons you staid sometime at my fathers how long I do not recollect . . . Question by defendants counsel. What was your age at the time Joseph Cravens came to live at your fathers? Answer. I do not remember but was at that time going to school and might have been about nine or ten years of age things happening at that age I can recollect better than things at a later date"—(signed) Mary Pence.

John Ewing was the son of William Ewing, the immigrant, who settled in the early Linville Creek communtiy, in the region of the New Erection Church. (See page 135.) The ashes of both William, and wife, Ann, rest in the churchyard of this church. She died in 1801, at 90 years of age, says one authority.

William Ewing is asserted to have been a descendant of the Ewing family of Scotland, whose ancestral home was Tullichewan Castle, on or near Loch Lomond, a short distance northwest of Glasgow. The name Ewing, in the Augusta and Rockingham records is variously spelled, Ewen, Ewin, and Ewing, but on the old tombs of the family in the Bonhill churchyard, Scotland, Ewing is the spelling invariably used. The arms are described as: "A shield argent; a chevron azure between three star gules, the star at the base afterwards changed to a sun in splendor, gules." (Stoddard's *Scottish Arms*, Vol. II.) An old document handed down in the family of John Ewing, above, bears the original signature of William Ewing, and the arms depicting the "sun in splendor," on the immigrant's seal.

William's children were—Henry (1736-1796), Andrew (1740-1813), John, as above, Elizabeth, and Nancy. Of these, Andrew appears to have inherited the home plantation, his father's land, purchased in 1761; this being delivered him, October, 1769. Henry, and John, were each at different times, justices of the Rockingham County Court. (See pages 238, 309, 321, and 338.) Henry was among the first justices appointed, and in 1782, succeded Peter Hogg as Clerk of the Court. Hogg was the first clerk. Henry served until 1792, when he was succeeded by Samuel McWilliams. During his term, February 7, 1786. "John Ewing took oath of Deputy Clerk." (Rockingham Court Order Book, I.) Soon afterwards, John qualified as a "Gentleman Justice," which office he continually held until his death.

John Ewing, and wife Phoebe, (1233), had issue—

(12331) Ann—b. July 9, 1770; d. 1845; m. 1790, Thomas Shanklin, Jr. Removed to Kentucky.

(12332) James—b. April 4, 1773; d. ——; m., April 15, 1795, Grace Shanklin, dau. of Thomas. Removed to Kentucky, and afterward to Missouri. Issue—Joseph, Elizabeth, Cyrus, Jesse, Ruth, Sophronia, and William G.

(12333) Mary—b. Oct. 8, 1775; d. ——; m. 1st, April 19th, 1791, Benjamin Smith; m. 2nd, Oct. 6, 1794, John Pence.

(12334) WILLIAM—b. Aug. 15, 1780; d. Jan. 14, 1857; m. 1807, Elizabeth Bryan, dau. of William. She b. 1791, d. May 5, 1830. See further record.

(12335) HANNAH—b. Dec. 8, 1782; d. ——; m. April 13, 1809, James Mallory. Removed to Missouri.

(12336) ELIZABETH—b. Nov. 7, 1786; d. ——; m. Col. Harrison Conner. Removed to Kentucky.

(12337) JOHN DAVISON, (Rev.)—b. Apr. 2, 1788; d. ——; m. Drusilla Del Tate. See further record.

(12338) JESSE—b. July 2, 1791; d. June 16, 1809. (marker in New Erection Cemetery.)

(First five given in a list kindly supplied by Miss Lucy Barbour Ewing, of Washington, D. C., a descendant of William. Also see W. R. Ewing's *Clan Ewing of Scotland*, p. 276; *The Ewing Genealogy*, by Presley Kitteredge Ewing, p. 38; and Strickler's *Rockingham Co. Marriages.)*

LINE OF THOMAS MOORE

(1234) REUBEN MOORE, (1755-1803), the son of Thomas Moore, Sr., and wife Phoebe, (123), nee Harrison, settled on the "Great Road," today's Long Grey Trail, on a tract of land originally owned by his father, and just to the north of the latter, his plantation embracing the land now known as "Court Manor," a fine old estate recently acquired by Mr. Willis Sharpe Kilmer from Mr. George Harrison. (See pages 185, and 306.) The site of his home was about that of the present residence, later built by his son.

To his original tract, Reuben added land purchased from David Harnet, who married the widow Ann Langdon, the sister of Phoebe Moore, as her third husband. David acquired his land by purchase in 1792, and in selling to Reuben, oddly enough, part of the consideration was that Reuben should support David's wife—Reuben's aunt. This arrangement rapidly led to complications—Ann, instead, went to live with another of her nephews, John Harrison, who as next friend filed a bill for maintainence in 1802, which was followed by Harnet's suit of 1805, after Reuben and Ann's deaths, and revived by Harrison about 1815, following Harnet's death. In his deposition of 1815, John Harrison states, among other things, that Ann was a sister of Reuben Harrison, his father. (See page 185.)

Thomas Mooore, another deponent in the case, (son of Reuben above?), deposed that he was a brother of Reuben Moore, and that they had an uncle Reuben Moore. Other deponents were John Walton, of New Market, 1810, and Richard and Susannah Weeks, of New Lancaster, Fairfield County, Ohio, the same year.

Reuben Moore, the son of Thomas, Sr., married about 1779, Phoebe, whose maiden name is unknown. Theirs was manifestly a war time romance—the struggle for Independence being then in progress.

During the Revolutionary War, Reuben served as an officer in the Rockingham militia, under Col. Benjamin Harrison. (See page 294.) On the 26th March, 1781, Reuben Moore and George Chrisman qualified Captains. (Rockingham Court Order Book, I.) In 1781, Capt. Moore participated in an expedition to the North Fork of the Potomac against a band of tories "embodied" at Capon Springs, some of whom had likely been former residents of Rockingham.

On the 13th August, 1777, according to a deposition of David Harnet, above, before Daniel Smith, August 16th, one Hinton with an armed force came to David's house "and declared himself in favor of the Crown of Great Britain . . . and enquired for Capt. Hite and Joseph Smith," whom he declared he would impress into his service, if found. Hinton and two Gryders were promptly convicted of trying to raise an armed force, and each were sentenced to a fine and imprisonment. Among the witnesses summonsed for the defence were Robert Harrison, son of Thomas, Catherine Keezell, Daniel Smith, Sr., Isaiah Harrison, and Thomas Moore, all patriots. (District Court Judgements, Commonwealth vs. Hinton, etc.; *Chalkley*, Vol. I, p. 509.)

In the 1784 census, *Heads of Families*, of Virginia, "Capt. Reuben Moore," of Rockingham, was enumerated as having three in his family, including himself. At the time, besides his wife, there was only one child, a daughter, his four later children being named as late as 1804 as infants. (See page 306.)

In 1789, Reuben Moore was one of the Commissioners of Rockingham, as appears from his list of the landowners of the county returned this year. In this, incidently, Harnet, of whom he later bought his land, was listed as the owner of 795 acres. (See, *Wayland*, p. 449.)

Capt. Moore died in 1803. Phoebe, his wife, outlived him for a number of years. The remains of both were buried in the old Moore family cemetery on Smiths Creek. His inscription reads—"In Memory of Reuben Moore who died Aug. 6, 1803, aged 48 years, 1 mo., 26 days." "Phoebe Moore, Consort of Reuben Moore," according to her marker, "died Aug. 27, 1821, aged 57 years. . . ."

Reuben Moore died testate. A copy of his will, as found recorded in the historical old burned record book at Harrisonburg (see page 326), is as follows—

Will of Reuben Moore

IN THE NAME OF GOD AMEN. I Reuben Moore of Rockingham County and State of Virginia being of perfect mind & memory thanks be to God for his mercies. Calling to mind the mortality of my body and knowing it is appointed Once for all men to dye do make this my last Will and Testament in writing, that is to say principally and first of all I Recommend my Soul to God who gave it & my Body to the earth to be buried in a decent Christian like manner at the discretion of my well beloved wife and Executors here mentioned; and as touching Such worldly Goods as it hath pleased God to bless me with in this life I give devise and dispose in Manner as follows—

Item—It is my will and I Order That all my Just debts be Paid.

2ndly. I give to my dear and loving wife the use of two Rooms in the house where I now live with one third of my other buildings and 1/3 the land on this place, Or Otherwise if she chooses to live on the land my father owned, to have all that house with one third of my Other buildings on the place where she makes her choice with one third of the land of Said Place so as not to have more than one third of One

and the son that posesses the other Plantation not to be disturbed by any claim of his mothers but it is my will that he pay to the brother that Suffers by his mother the One half of said . . . . . berage yearly and likewise my negro man . . . work for her on the Plantation and . . . . To be set free & if incapable to work . . . maintained by my two sons Likewise it . . . . . will that my negro wench naney Should . . . to her mistress and Wait on her Induri . . . . Life and at her death said wench and . . . . . crease if any to be disposed of by my wife amongst her three daughters Elizabeth . . . . ann and Sarah I further will and desire that She should have One horse best two cows six sheep, the choise of my stock with t . . feather beds and furniture the one third of my house and kitchen furniture.

Item I give to my son Thomas Moore all my lands that I hold of my father's Estate the following slaves Joe, Harry & Frede . . . & Cate millys Child. Said lands and slaves . . . . . him the said Thomas Moore his heirs Assigns forever with one horse which he now has, one bedstead and furniture.

Item I give unto my son Reuben all the Plantation which I Purchased of David Harnet with the following slaves M . . . . . her two sons Cers and George and if . . . . should have any increase after the date of this will to be his likewise which land and Slaves to belong to the said Reuben Moore his heirs and assigns forever, all which land and slaves to be fully Posessed by my two sons Thomas and Reuben as . . . . mentioned after the Plantation . . . . . . of David Harnet is fully Paid . . . . until discharged their to Injoy each his own.

Item I further will and desire that my daughter Elizabeth Walton late Elizabeth Moore Should have the negro wench named Nance and her child Pleas with their increase to her and [her] heirs and assigns forever with the stock and furniture she has received . . . . but of the negros now given to my daughter Elizabeth should be taken from her by any means through the settlement of my father's estate she shall Receive redres One hundred Pounds from my two sons Thomas and Reuben Moore out of the Estate I left them.

Item I give to my daughter ann The negro wench named Grace with her increase to her heirs and assigns forever & One Good mare four cows 6 sheep Out of my stock at the Old Place with two feather beds and furniture.

Item I give my daughter Sarah the negro girl named Frank with her increase to her heirs and assigns forever & One Good Mare, five cows, 6 sheep, out of my stock at the Other place, with two feather beds and furniture.

Item, it is farder my will and I do order that all stock farmer utensils and house furniture my Waggons and team with debts Remaining and not here to fore disposed of to be kept together on my land . . . . . Plantation by my two Sons to assist . . . make the annual Payments to . . . . said Payments . . . . To be equally divided between my two sons Thomas . . . . .

Item I further will and Postively Order that if my well Beloved wife Phebe Moore shall not be Satisfied with the contents of the within will so far as concerns her but goes forward and brakes the same or any Part thereof that will injure my two sons contrary to my Said Will, that in so doing . . . . negro wench named nancy with her incerease . . . . . of being disposed of at the discretion of my . . . . I will to my two Sons Thomas and Reuben at the . . . . of my wife to make then in such Injurie . . . . I . . . . . them suffer

further it is my will & I do constitute and appoint my well Beloved Wife Phebe Moor Executrix with John Moore and Thomas Moore Sen. Executors to this my last will and Testament,

disannulling Revoking & Recalling Other wills and Testaments, in Witness whereof I have hereunto Set my hand and Seal this . . . . . of August 1803.

Signed Sealed & Delivered in Presence of Reuben Moore. (SEAL.)
Jacob Pirkey
Solomon Kingree
Josiah Harrison.

Proved Rockingham November Court 1803.
(Rockingham Burnt Record Book, p. 24.)

In brief, as named in the above, Reuben Moore, (1234), and wife Phoebe, had issue—

(12341) ELIZABETH—b. 1781; d. 1864; m. 1798, Moses Walton.
See further record.

(12342) THOMAS, JR.—b. 1786; d. Sept. 15, 1818; m., Feb. 5, 1805, Elizabeth Hite.
She m. 2nd. Benjamin Long, April 10, 1823.

(12343) REUBEN—b. 1791; d. 1859; m., 1st., Martha Jane McWilliams, dau. of Gordon, b. 1797, d. 1833, "aged about 33 years." m. 2nd. Mildred Hughs, from Eastern Virginia, d. June 23, 1865, aged 70 years.
See further record.

(12344) SARAH—

(12345) ANN—m., 1808, Henry Devier, removed to St. Louis, Mo.
See further reference.

(See p. 306.) Tombstones of Thomas and Reuben, and of Reuben's wife Martha, in the Moore family burial ground. Mildred's marker in "Lower Lutheran" Cemetery, New Market.

DUNKENSON

(1237) LUCRETIA MOORE, ( ), the daughter of Thomas Moore, Sr., and wife Phoebe, (123), nee Harrison, in 1785, married Thomas Dunkenson—Witness, Reuben and Thomas Moore. (See page 306; alos *Strickler*, p. 49.)

Sometime between 1799 and 1823, Thomas Dunkenson removed to Kentucky, as disclosed in Sarah Looker's bill of 6th, January, 1823, vs. Dunkenson. (Judgements, Circuit Court Causes Ended, N. S. 137; *Chalkley*, Vol. II, p. 256.) Sarah was the daughter of John Reeves of Rockingham, whose will, 5th May, 1799, proved the same year, appointed Elijah Moore, his son-in-law, and Thomas Dunkenson, administrators. John Reeves left a widow, Margaret, who died in 1814, and children, Sarah, William, John and Mary Reeves, and Lydia, the wife of Elijah Moore. Of these, Sarah married a Looker, and Mary married Charles Moore. Among the deponents in the above litigation was Robert Dunkenson, who deposed that he was the nephew of John Reeves, Jr., and the son of Thomas Dunkenson, and that his father settled in Christian County, Kentucky, and sent him to school in Hopkins County, to the said John Reeves, etc.

As gleaned from this, Thomas Dunkenson, and wife Lucretia, (1237), had at least the one child—

(12371) THOMAS—
(No further record).

LINE OF CAPT. REUBEN HARRISON

(1252) NATHANIEL HARRISON, (-1807), the son of Capt. Reuben Harrison, (125), and wife Lydia, by his father's will, proven 1807, was devised one "Negro Slave named Jacob." Prior to this his father had conveyed to him 446 acres of land on the Dry Fork of Smiths Creek—Deed, 19th August, 1817, Michael Howard and Lydia, his wife, of Rockingham, to Christian Burkholder, "their undivided 1/11th. of 446 acres patented to John Harrison (Jr.) 10th. Feb., 1748, and by him devised to Ann Moore, and by her conveyed to Reuben Harrison, and by him to his son, Nathaniel Harrison." (See page 368, and presently.)

Nathaniel Harrison married, in 1784, Mary Woodley, the daughter of "Capt. Jacob Woodley"—witness Richard Ragen. (*Strickler*, p. 61.) The same year in the *Heads of Families* census, Virginia, "Woodley, Jacob," of Rockingham County, was enumerated as having in his family, "8 White souls," and owning "1 Dwelling 1 Other building."

WOODLEY

Jacob Woodley was among the early settlers on Smiths Creek. He had probably come in from Eastern Virginia. One James Woodley's estate is mentioned on the Orange County Records, under date of 26th February, 1741. (William Glover vs. James Woodley; Orange Court Order Book, 1739-1741, p. 108.) In 1756, Jacob Woodley's Smiths Creek land was processioned by John Harrison, Jr., and Daniel Smith. On the 17th March, 1756, Jacob furnished bond as administrator of George Handy, with surety John Harrison. (Will Book 2, p. 139.) In 1767, he was a processioner, along with Reuben Harrison. He was appointed road overseer from the fork on "this side Sebastain Martz's to Reuben Harrison's," in 1778. The following year he is mentioned as a constable. (See pages 182, 324, 300, and 299.) His land lay to the east of the "Great Road," in the region of present Tenth Legion, and is today identified by the old cemetery (now Strickler's) at the curve of the road leading from the village, towards the Massanutten, as it approaches the mill site. (See will below.) The land, purchased 4th February, 1749, by Jacob, from John Hodge, included Valentine Sevier's Mill tract. (D. B. 2, p. 149.)

Besides Nathaniel Harrison, John Harrison, his brother, and Lydia Neely (nee Harrison), his sister, also married a daughter and son, respectively, of Jacob Woodley.

Jacob died in 1804. His will, as recorded in one of the two old burnt Rockingham Court Record books (see page 326), reads as follows—

Will of Jacob Woodley

"IN THE NAME OF GOD AMEN—I Jacob Woodley of the County of Rockingham and State of Virginia being weak in Body but of sound Memory (blessed . . . . do this sixth day of March in the year of our Lord Eighteen hundred and two do make and publish this my last will and testament in ma . . . . following (that is to say) first of all I give and recommend my soul unto the hands of Almighty God that gave it and my body to the earth, to be decently Interred at the discretion of my executors hereafter mentioned, as concerning my worldly estate where with it . leased God to bless me with in this life I give & bequeath in the following manner to witness

First of all my lawful debts and funeral charges to be paid—

Secondly I give and Bequeath my son John Woodley's two sons Jacob and John Woodley all my old plantation that I now live on the survey that adjoins the same to them & their heirs Assigns forever. One quarter of an acre excepted for burying ground forever.

Thirdly as touching my . . . . . hannah, she being well . . .during my life, will . . . . . her fee by deed of Gift before my death.

As to my other lands not above bequeathed I give and Bequeath in manner following unto my son . . . . Law John Harrison's wife Grace Harrison during her life time all my lands that lie on the . . . . meadows, that the said John Harrison now lives on, and their children heirs . . . . executors and assigns forever after,

as touching my tract of . . . . . to William Pickering during her life time and at her decease to be divided . . . . legimate children their heirs and assigns equally forever, Abraham Pickering excepted in the above division if not a certain Bond is not paid up of one hundred dollars by barbara Pickering or her heirs then said Pickering is entitled to part of the lands as far as that bond extends to his Heirs & Assigns forever.

And I do hereby Otherwise and Impower my trusty friends and executors Nathaniel Harrison & John Phillips to make over my movable estate unto Ulrich Philips, Barbara Pickering, grace Harrison & Polly Harrison their heirs and assigns forever, one bed and furniture excepted to grace Harison and her assigns,

and further I do will and bequeath my son John Woodley one Guinea.

In witness whereof I the said Jacob Woodley have to this my last will & Testament set my hand & seal this sixth day of March in the Grace of Our Lord eighteen hundred and two.

(Witnesses) Jacob Woodley." (SEAL.)
his mark

Samuel Marks
Jacob Spehr
John phillips
Daniel Cummings. Proved Rockingham September Court, 1804.

(Rockingham Burnt Record Book, p. 141.)

Jacob Woodley's wife was Grace Looker, the daughter of Thomas. Their children were; Uriah, b. February 13, 1749; Jacob b. August 25, 1753; Barbara b. November 21, 1758; Grace, b. January 27, 1762; Mary (Polly), b. February 18, 1764; and John, b. November 26, 1767. Of these; Barbara, married William Pickering; Grace, married John Harrison; Mary, married Nathaniel Harrison, above; and John, married Lydia Harrison, as her second husband. Subsequent to his father's death, John Woodley, and wife Lydia, removed to near McMinnville, Tennessee, where they died. (See page 312.)

McMinnvil Tenn

* * * * * *

Nathaniel Harrison died in 1807, the year of his father's death: Bill 18th December, 1825, by Christian Burkholder vs. Harrison's heirs, reciting that Nathaniel Harrison died testate in 1807 leaving no widow, but the following children, viz. "Lydia, Phebe, Gracy, Anna, Elizabeth, Mary, Jerusha, Edith, Lucretia, and Samuel and Nathaniel, infants." Regarding these Burkeholder's bill further states, that "Lydia married Michael Howard, Phebe married Noah Bowers, Gracy married Abraham Harrison, Anna married Jacob Dehart, Elizabeth married John Tallman, Mary married Solomon Bowers, Jerusha married Christopher Shultz."

Among other papers in the case was the Howard deed herein before noticed, also Deed, 10th March, 1817, Abraham Harrison, and wife Grace, and John Tallman, and wife Elizabeth, of Fairfield County, Ohio, to Burkeholder, for 2/11th. of the same land; also Deed, 18th March, 1817, Noah Bowers, and wife Phoebe, and Solomon Bowers, and wife Polly, of Augusta, and Jerusha Harrison of Rockingham, to Burkholder, for 121½ acres, their share in the same.

(Circuit Court Causes Ended, N. S. 116; *Chalkley*, Vol. II, p. 238.)

As named, Nathaniel Harrison (1252), and wife Mary's Children were—

(12521) LYDIA—b. 1784; d. 1869; m., 1807, Michael Howard. See further record.

(12522) PHOEBE—m. Nov. 2, 1809, Noah Bowers.

(12523) GRACE—m., Abraham Harrison, (12116), son of John.

(12524) ANNA—m., 1810, Jacob De Hart (or Dehart.)

(12525) ELIZABETH—m., 1808, John Tallman, removed to Ohio.

(12526) MARY—m., Oct. 6, 1812, Solomon Bowers.

(12527) JERUSHA—m. Christopher Shultz.

(12528) EDITH—m., Milford (Mifford) Hannah.
See further record.
(12529) LUCRETIA—m., Abraham Leonard.
(12530) SAMUEL—m. Mrs. Summers. "went west, 1840."
(12531) NATHANIEL—m., Anne Fught, removed to Indiana, arriving there Oct. 15, 1835.
(Dates from D. S. H. MSS., and Strickler's *Rockingham Co. Marriages.)*

(1253) JOHN HARRISON, (1761-1819), the son of Capt. Reuben Harrison, (125), and wife Lydia, at the time of his deposition, 30th September, 1815, in "Harnet vs. Moore" (see pages 186 and 370), gave his age as 54 years. John settled on the "Long Meadows," a short distance west of present Mauzy, on the road now leading from Mauzy to Broadway. The land whereon he lived originally belonged to Jacob Woodley. (See Woodley's will above.) His house is said to have stood about where the late Ambrose Spitzer's house now stands. In the same neighborhood was settled Ezekiel Harrison, the son of Thomas, founder of Harrisonburg, and Thomas Dunkenson, who married Lucretia Moore.

An original patent, of 27 April, 1801, now in the possession of Mr. Joseph Mauzy, of Mauzy, to Ezekiel Harrison, for 710 acres of land, "by survey bearing date 19th Oct., 1799, lying and being in the County of Rockingham on the West side of the long meadows and between said meadows and Linville Creek," mentions as various points on the boundry, "corner to his own & Michael Holsinger's land near a road, ... corner Thomas Dunkason, . . . his own, John Harrison's and John Kring's corner, ... line of Jacob Rife's land . . . . Yount's & Bowman's corners" etc. Patent granted, "By virtue of two land warrants To wit, 400 acres by No. 21,149, issued 1st Dec., 1783, 310 acres by No. 2,559, issued 26th Oct., 1798."

John Harrison married, as stated, Grace Woodley, the daughter of Jacob. He died about January 1819, and she sometime thereafter. His will dated 6th May, 1815, recorded Rockingham February court, 1819, a copy of which appears in "Harrison vs. Ragen et als.," (Circuit Court Causes Ended, N. S., 135; *Chalkley,* Vol. II, p. 253), names wife Grace, daughter Phebe Bowman and her children, Margaret and Jacob, daughter Lidda Taulman, wife of Benjamin Taulman, daughter Ann Suter, late Ann Kring, and brother David. Under his will freedom was granted to a slave, when the latter reached the age of twenty one years, this finally leading to the litigation mentioned; "Bill by a free man of color to declare free his son who was a slave of John Harrison, of Rockingham," etc.

Briefly, John Harrison, (1253), and wife Grace had—

(12531) PHOEBE—b. 1791; d. 1859; m., Dec. 24, 1812, Miller Bowman.
See further record.
(12532) LYDIA—m., 1805, Benjamin Tallman, Jr., who at the time was under age. (Consent, Benjamin Tallman, Sr.) Removed to Tennessee.
(12533) ANN—m., 1st., 1802, Henry Kring. m., 2nd., 1811, James Suter.
(First and last named in D. S. H. MSS.; See also Strickler's *Rockingham Co. Marriages.)*

(1254) JOSIAH HARRISON, ( ), the son of Capt. Reuben Harrison, (125), and wife Lydia, is said to have lived for a time in Kiser, now West Virginia, "but the records show," says the late Daniel S. Harrison, "that he eventually moved to

Franklin County, Missouri." He is thought to have been the individual named in the Cravens data as the husband of Mary Cravens, the daughter of John. (See pages 344 and 345.)

Josiah died in Franklin County, Missouri, prior to 1827: Deed, 23rd July, 1827; "Josiah Harrison, Samuel Harrison, Lethe Harrison, John B. Harrison, and Thomas Groff and Elizabeth his wife, formerly Elizabeth Harrison, the Children and Legal heirs of Josiah Harrison deceased of the county of Franklin and State of Missouri, to Jacob Cole of the County of Rockingham and State of Virginia, ... all the right title interest and claim in and to the lands of Abner Harrison deceased which he heired by will of his Father Reuben Harrison deceased, of them the said Josiah Harrison, Samuel Harrison, Lethe Harrison, John B. Harrison, and Thomas Groff and Elizabeth his wife formerly Elizabeth Harrison, said children and legal heirs of Josiah Harrison deceased who died intestate, in and to a Certain tract or parcel of land lying and being in the County of Rockingham . . . . and on the Stage road leading from Harrisonburg to New Market which tract . . . . formerly belonged to Abner Harrison who died intestate said Abner having derived his title to said land from the last Will and Testament of his Father Reuben Harrison, deceased." Proven, Franklin Co., Mo., 23, July, 1827. Elizabeth Groff released dower. (From Cole papers previously referred to.)

Another conveyance of the same year from (or to) Jacob Cole, and Sarah, "his wife, legal heir of Josiah Harrison, deceased, of Franklin County, Missouri," conveys all interest in the land of Abner Harrison, deceased, and names Sarah as "formerly Sarah Harrison, legal heir of Josiah Harrison." (Rockingham Deed Book 8, p. 47.) It appears that Jacob Cole was the son of John and Catherine Cole, who migrated to Pulaski County, Kentucky, before 1821. (See, Rockingham Burnt Record Deed Book 5, p. 415.) Among the descendants of Jacob is the present Mr. Jacob Cole, of Lacy Spring.

As named in the above, Josiah Harrison, (1254), and wife, had issue—

(12541) Josiah—
(12542 Samuel—
(12543) Lethe—
(12544) John B.—
(12545) Elizabeth—m. Thomas Groff.
(12546) Sarah—m. Jacob Cole.

(First five named in D. S. H. MSS.)

WOODLEY

(1255) LYDIA HARRISON, (   ), the daughter of Capt. Reuben Harrison, (125), and wife Lydia, married, first, John Neely, and second, John Woodley, the son of Jacob. (See page 374.)

John Woodley, and wife Lydia, migrated to near McMinnville, Tennesee. Their children were—

(12551) Jacob—b. Nov. 1789.
(12552) Mary—b. Mar. 24, 1792.
(12553) John—b. Aug. 29, 179—.
(12554) ————b. Nov. 25, 1796.
(12555) Betsy—b. July 27, 1797.
(12556) Daniel—b. Oct. 30, 1800.

(12557) HARRISON—b. Aug. 11, 1802.
(12558) GREER—b. Feb. 17, 1805.
(12559) JEFFERSON—b. Dec. 18, 1806.
(12560) ABNER—b. Oct. 30, 1808.
(12561) JAMES—b. Oct. 12, 1812.
(D. S. H. MSS.)

WARREN

(1258) ELIZABETH HARRISON, ( ), the daughter of Capt. Reuben Harrison, (125), and wife Lydia, married, May 2nd, 1793, Thomas Warren, "a descendant of John Warren," evidently his son. (See pages 312, 340, and later.) Thomas and Elizabeth made their home in Harrisonburg, Virginia. Their children were—

(12581) NANCY—m., John Gordon.
See further record.
(12582) LYDIA—m., 1814, Andrew Bear.
See further record.
(12583) an infant—d. in infancy.
(12584) CATHERINE—m. 1814, Jack Chrisman.
See further record.
(12585) JEHU—b. 1801; d. Apr. 18, 1851, m. Harriet Rice, b. Nov. 4, 1807, d. June 3, 1886.
See further record.
(12586) LUCRETIA—d. unmarried.
(12587) SOPHIA—b. 1804; d. Dec. 3, 1867; m. Joseph Burkholder, b. Nov. 24, 1801 d. July 4, 1879.
See further record.

(All named in D. S. H. MSS. Dates of marriages from Strickler's *Rockingham Co. Marriages*. John Krotzer was guardian of Lydia and Catherine at the time of their marriages. Jehu Warren, and wife, and Joseph Burkeholder, and wife, buried in New Erection Churchyard.)

(1259) DAVID HARRISON, (1775-1851), the son of Capt Reuben Harrison, (125), and wife Lydia, settled near his parents, on "The Long Gray Trail," on land willed him by his father. The site of his home was that of the present residence of Mr. Thomas Harrison, at Virginia Caverns, a few miles south of Lacey Spring. (See page 307.)

The stately old trees on the hospitable lawn whisper of long forgotten ante-bellum days when their owner was truly the master of a great part, if not all, that his eyes could survey. In front of and below him, to the east, spread his broad meadows, drained by the Dry Fork of Smiths Creek; beyond lay his more rolling land, stretching towards the foothills of the distant Massanutten, while to the west rose the ragged and rocky old ridge, his woodland, under which today's historic caverns are located.

The Great Stage Road on which his land bordered, came in his day to be the Valley Turnpike. It ran through his land a mile or so, and out of his estate is now carved a half dozen fine farms, including several given to his sons in his lifetime.

David Harrison married, in 1799, Elizabeth Pickering, the daughter of William Pickering, and wife Barbara. The Pickering land was at present Mauzy, some distance further north on The Long Grey Trail.

PICKERING

William Pickering's wife, Barbara, was the daughter of Jacob Woodley, of the 1802, will. (See page 374.) William and Barbara had issue— Abraham, b. July 8, 1775, m. Ann Looker, moved to Pickerington, Licking County, Ohio, of which he was the founder; Mary, b. August 27, 1779, m. John Cowan, of Rockingham; Elizabeth, b. April 7, 1781, m. David Harrison, above; Jacob, b. January 26, 1783, m. Hannah Miller, moved to Ohio; John, b. August 21, 1784, m. Nancy Browne, moved to Ohio; Daniel, b. June 29, 1786, d. August 24, 1843, m. Hannah Dunlap, d. December 23, 1830, aged 46 yrs., 1 mo., 27 days, resided in Rockingham, drowned in Brock's Gap; Grace, b. August 13, 1789, m. Michael Heistand, of Ohio; William, Jr., b. December 27, 1791, m. Mathia Martz (?), resided in Rockingham; Richard, b. November 16, 1793, m. Lucy Nicholas, resided in Rockingham, buried at McGhaeysville; Uriah, b. March 15, 1795, died in Rockingham, unmarried; Susannah, b. March 3, 1796, m. Jacob Cowan, moved to Ohio; James, b. June 5, 1798, m. Mary Loker, resided in Rockingham; Catherine, b. November 9, 1801, m. William Cowan, moved to Ohio—he m. 2nd., and removed to Bonango County, Pennsylvania.

Among Daniel Pickering's children, was a son, William, b. October 6, 1811, d. November 20, 1855, m., November 23, 1836, Mathia Cowan, b. October 5, 1814, d. April 11, 1885, one of whose sons, the late Abraham Pickering, of near Tenth Legion, b. 1838, was one of the oldest residents of Rockingham at the time of his death. Among James' children, was the late James Pickering, of near New Market, whose widow, Mrs. Anne Pickering (nee Shirley) continues her residence there.

Samuel Pickering was an early settler in the old Quaker community, near Winchester. (See pages 112 and 330.) He was a native of Bucks County, Pennsylvania, where he married, before his removal to Virginia, Grace Stackhouse. The certificate of their removal is perserved among the records in the Friends Library at Baltimore, Maryland. Samuel was a son of Samuel Pickering, Sr., who, about 1700, emigrated from Bristol, England, to Pennsylvania, and settled in Bucks County. His wife was Mary Scarborough, some of whose people also came to the Valley from Pennsylvania. Among the sons of Samuel, the younger, was one Levi, who migrated to Belmont County, Ohio. This last is thought to have been a near relative, probably a brother, of the Rockingham settler.

* * * * * *

David Harrison died in 1851, and his wife, Elizabeth, within the same month thereafter. Both were buried in the old family burial ground, now on the Lilburn Long place, a short distance east of the Pike, and near an old log house, marking the site of his son Nathaniel's home. The Inscription on his tombstone reads—

"In Memory of David Harrison, Born April 20, 1775, Died March 1, 1851, Aged 75 years, 10 mo., 11 days . Reader Remember thou too art Mortal." Alongside stands Elizabeth's marker—"In Memory of Elizabeth, Consort of David Harrison, Born April 7, 1781, Died March 23, 1851, Aged 69 years, 11 mo., 16 days."

Among his effects, as listed in his inventory, was a copy of Ballou's Sermons. Hosea Ballou (1771-1852), was a famous Universalist, who at an early age joined the Baptist Church, and later embraced the Universalist faith. At the time of his death he was the pastor of the Second Universalist Society at Boston. He was an industrious writer, and in 1819, commenced the Universalist Magazine, and in 1831, the Universalist Expositor. Several volumes of his sermons were published, besides numerous other of his controversial works. Between 1780 and 1789, says Benedict, the historian of the Baptists, "a considerable number of brethern fell in with Elhanan Winchester's notion of Universal

Restoration. The rage for this doctrine prevailed for a time to a considerable extent ..... Mr. Winchester, the author or rather reviver of it in modern times, was for a while a very popular preacher among the Baptists." *(Benedict,* Vol. I, p. 275, and Whittemore's *Life of Ballou.)*

David Harrison died testate. A copy of his will, as preserved in the battered and charred old record book, at Harrisonburg (see page 326), in which also his inventory may been seen, reads as follows:

Will of David Harrison

"I David Harrison of the County of Rockingham and State of Virginia, being of sound mind and disposing memory, do make and constitute this my last Will and Testament; in the following manner and form:

..... first after paying the funeral expenses and all just debts I give . . . bequeath unto my wife Elizabeth Harrison all the estate both personal and real of which I may be posessed at my decease to have and to hold all of sd personal and real property during her life time unto the said Elizabeth Harrison for her own proper use and behoof, to use and apply as she may need and see fit, during her lifetime or as long as she may remain my widow. At her death or marriage, I desire that my son William Shall have one hundred acres of my land to include the buildings of which I am at present in posession, it being his share and the share of my son Reuben, which my son William purchased of my son Reuben and which is bounded as follows,

Beginning at Dan Harrison's corner in the middle of the Valley Turnpike road and thence with said Dan . . . Harrison's line crossing the dry fork. N. 38 1/4 degrees W. 150-4/10 poles to a stake in a line, said Daniel Harrison's corner, thence with his line N. 77 ½ degrees W. 32-4/10 poles to two pines Wenger's corner, S. 8½ degrees W. 99-2/10 poles to a white oak sapling, said Wenger corner thence . . . . 35½ degrees E. through the outer tract of my land 154 poles to the middle of the Valley Turnpike road and thence with sd. road N. 26¾ E. 110 poles to the place of beginning.

And at my wifes death or marriage I desire that the balance of my land be equally divided between my four daughters to do with as they may think proper;

My sons John, Nathaniel, Daniel and Reuben having received their shares

My stock in the Valley Turnpike, I give and bequeath to my two youngest daughters to dispose of as they may think proper.

At the death of my wife I desire that my executors shall sell any and all my personal property that . . . . may leave and the proceeds of sd. personal estate to be equally divided between my four daughters.

It is my will and desire that each of my children may be charged in the settlement of my estate with the accounts I may have against them in my book or books with interest thereon from their dates . I have now in my hands a small sum of money for the heirs of my brother Josiah Harrison not exceeding thirty six dollars, which if not paid before my death I wish my Executors to pay without interest.

I hereby appoint my son Reuben N. Harrison Executor of this my last will and testament. In testimony whereof I have hereunto subscribed my name and affixed my seal on the 27th day of February, 1846.

his
David Harrison. (Seal.)
mark

Sealed and published by ......
at and for his . . . . Testament
in our . . . . . the same in . . . .
request . . . . . .

This . . . last Will and Testament of David Harrison dec'd was . . . by the oaths of Michael Sellers and George W. Gaither, two of . . . . . and ordered to be recorded. An . . . .on the motion of Reuben N. Harrison . . . . named who made oath thereto and entered into bond in the penalty of . . . . as the law directs. A certificate is granted him for obtaining a probate in due form. Atteste,

E. Coffman. C . . . .

(Will follows an entry March 14, 1851.)

That the testator was probably in failing health at the time of signing, is indicated by his using a mark for his signature. Earlier papers are found signed by him in full, among them a deed, December 17, 1811—"David Harrison, Surviving Extr. of the last will and Testament of Reuben Harrison Decd, of the County of Rockingham and State of Virgina, to Jacob Cole of same county, 463 Pounds, two Shillings, 103 acres, part of a larger tract of 198 acres granted to Reuben Harrison Deceased, by patent dated the first day of March 1781. Also the Said Tract . . . . hereby conveyed was by the Last will and Testament of the Said Reuben Harrison, Deceased, bearing date the 2d day of May 1802, was therein directed to be sold by his Said Exrs . . . . corner John Koontz's Land . . . . . to 3 Cedar Bushes near the Big Spring run on line of the patent . . . . to the west Side of the road . . . . Crossing a Spring Run . . . . John Brock's corner on John Koontz line," etc. Signed, David Harrison. Proved by David in Rockingham Sept. Court, 1811. Teste; S. McWilliams, C. R. C. (Original deed in possession of Mr. Jacob Cole, of Lacey Spring—the patent mentioned may have been a partial duplication of the one of the earlier colonial grants, and is not included in the list given on page 162.)

"Four daughters," are mentioned in David's will, but are not named. This deficiency, however, is supplied by another paper of David's, yet preserved, viz. a *Family Register*, published by Ambrose Henkle & Co., of New Market, 1811, wherein blank spaces for names and dates, etc., were left by the printer to be filled in by pen, which in David's case was done, as to the names of his children and their dates of birth, and the paper passed on to his son Reuben—it being now in the possession of the family of the latter's son—the late Mr. Charles D. Harrison, of Harrisonburg.

As named in the foregoing, David Harrison, (1259), and wife Elizabeth, had issue—

(12591) JOHN—b. 15th. July, 1800; d. Jan. 19, 1880; m., Jan. 25, 1838, Barbara Hollingsworth, dau. of George. She b. Dec. 16, 1817, d. Jan. 14, 1890. See further record.

(12592) NATHANIEL—b. 22nd Jan. 1803; d. Feb. 26, 1839; m., Mary High, b. Feb. 9, 1810, d. Dec. 31, 1898.
See further record.

(12593) MARY—b. 24th July, 1805; d. Dec. 18, 1872; m. Reuben Walton, b. July 7, 1799, d. May 16, 1874, son of Moses Walton, and wife Elizabeth Moore, (12341).
See further record.

(12594) DANIEL—b. 22nd Oct., 1807; d. July 17, 1871; m. 1st., Rhoda Brown, b. May 30, 1808, d. Feb. 8, 1844. m. 2nd, Hulda Hayne, b. Aug. 10, 1824, d. May 13, 1882. Removed to Tennessee, and thence to Carroll County Missouri.
See further record.

(12595) LYDIA—b. 4th Aug., 1809; d. Aug. 16, 1893; m., Nov. 14, 1839, Madison

Moore, b. Dec. 19, 1812, d. Jan. 9, 1878, son of Reuben Moore, (12343.)
See further record.

(12596) REUBEN N.—b. 18th July, 1812; d. July 17, 1885; m., 20th Feb. 1840, Catherine Allebaugh, b. 1811, d. Nov. 12, 1875, dau. of John.
See further record.

(12597) WILLIAM—b. Sept 6, 1814; d. May 9, 1853, unmarried.
"Behold for peace I had great bitterness but Thou hast in love to my soul delivered it"; inscription on tombstone in family cemetery, as above. He was an invalid.

(12598) ELIZABETH ANN—b. 19th January, 1816; d. Apr. 9, 1895; m. John Moore, b. July 27, 1818, d. Jan. 29, 1864, son of Reuben above.
See further record.

(12599) BARBARA CATHERINE—b. 13th. Aug., 1823; d. Jan. 28, 1877; m. Andrew S. Henton, son of Peter and Elizabeth (?) Henton.
See further record.

(Birth dates from *Family Register,* and verified as to John, Nathaniel, William, and Elizabeth by tombstone records, from which their dates of death are also gleaned. See later individual mention.)

CHRISMAN

(1260) ANN HARRISON (1777-1839), the daughter of Capt. Reuben Harrison, (125), and wife Lydia, married in 1796, John Chrisman, "Gentleman Jack Chrisman," as he was frequently styled. (See page 349.) Ann's father, Reuben, Sr., gave his consent, and the groom's surety was John Lincoln. The witness signing was David Harrison. (Strickler's *Rockingham Co. Marriages.)*

Jack Chrisman (1773-1815), was the son of George, and Hannah Chrisman, whose tombstones have been mentioned as standing in the old churchyard at New Erection Church. (See page 273.) George was born in 1745, the son of Jacob Chrisman, who emigrated from Barvaria, about 1730. In 1747 a tract of land in the Linville Creek community was "processioned for Jacob Chrisman," by Daniel Harrison and Morgan Bryan. (See pages 163 and 273.) Jacob was settled in Frederick County—Deed, 14th Nov., 1746, "Thomas Linvell and Hannah, his wife, to Jacob Chrisman of Frederick County," 500 acres, part of 1,200 on Linville Creek, purchased from "Jost Hite." (Deed Book 1, p. 165.)

One of the daughters of Joist Hite, the famous pioneer, whose early firm patented land on the creek in 1739, was Magdaline, baptized at Kingston, on the Hudson, 13th September, 1713, who married "Jacob Chrisman, a German" (Jacob above.) "And it is highly probable," says Cartmell, "that their bridal trip was part of the emigrant train that the elder Hite headed for the Colony of Virginia in 1730." (See page 118; and *Cartmell,* p. 261.)

Hite, it will be recalled, came directly to the Valley from York, Pennsylvania. It was to this county that Jacob Chrisman, with his brothers Abraham and Isaac, immigrated from Germany. Jacob and Magdaline, his wife, were married prior to his removal to Virginia.

Jacob settled in Frederick, near Winchester, at a great spring, known as early as 1735, as Chrisman's Spring. He and Madgaline had children—Abraham, b. Oct. 15, 1733; Sarah, b. Sept. 23, 1734; Anna Maria, b. Nov. 9, 1735; Isaac, b. Nov. 9, 1736;

Johannes, b. March 9, 1739, d. 1772-3, m. Mary Hinton; Jacob; George, b. 1745, as above, m. Hannah McDowell, dau. of Gen. Joseph McDowell; Henry, m. a Scott; Rebecca, m. a Stephens; Sindy; and Elizabeth. Jacob's will was probated at Winchester, October, 1778. (See also *Cartmell,* p. 262.)

On the 5th May, 1761, "Jacob Chrisman and Magdalina," his wife, "of Frederick County," conveyed to George Chrisman, of Frederick, 376 acres of land on Linville's Creek, part of a larger tract, corner to John Chrisman. (Deed Book 9, p. 369.) A month earlier, Jacob had deeded to Francis McBride, 300 acres, near by, which he had originally purchased from Joseph Bryan. In McBride's deed of 1771, he is styled "Jacob Chrisman, Sr." (See page 236, and Deed Book 13, p. 188.) Besides George Chrisman, his brother Abraham, of Frederick, also owned land in Augusta in 1763. (See page 184.) John Chrisman, on whose land George cornered, in will, 27 May, 1772, proved 17th August, 1773, names wife Mary, and minor children, Jacob, Joseph, Abraham, and Isaac; witness George Chrisman. (Will Book 5, p. 114.)

George Chrisman, and wife Hannah, are said to have had "four sons, and three daughters," viz: Hugh, Joseph, Charles, John, Margaret, Hannah, and one other daughter; of whom, Joseph and Charles migrated to Kentucky, Margaret married John Spears, and removed to Kentucky with him, along with her brothers, Hannah married Joshua Kring, and resided in Rockingham. There was probably a Jacob, also. The third daughter's name was Elizabeth.

The next earliest Chrisman to George of the Rockingham family, so far as the old tombstones at New Erection disclose, was Jacob Chrisman, who died August 27, 1818, aged 49 years, 8 mo., 12 days; then follows, John Chrisman, of whom more hereafter, and Charles Chrisman, died July 28, 1812, aged 37 years, etc. (b. 1775), and Elizabeth, "daughter of George and Hannah Chrisman," born April 25, 1779, died, December 16, 1835, after which, apparently, there is a pause of seventeen years in birth dates.

The marker, "Erected to the Memory of John Chrisman, son of George Chrisman," recites that he was born August 27th, 1773, and died, May 1st, 1815.

George Chrisman, the father of John, (and of Charles above,), settled in the region to the west of Linville Creek. In 1780 he was one of the witnesses to Abraham and Bathsheba Lincoln's deed to Shanks and Reuf. (See page 286.) During the Revolution he served as a Captain of the militia of Rockingham, qualifying as such, 26th March, 1781, (see page 286.) In *Heads of Families* census, Virginia, 1784, "Christman, Capt. George," of Rockingham County, was enumerated as having in his household "9 White souls," and owning "1 Building, 3 other buildings." *(First U. S. Census, Va.,* p. 77.) In 1801 he was one of the jurors in the Dunkenson et. ux vs. Moore litigation. (See page 306.)

John Chrisman, son of George, located in the Linville-Muddy Creek neighborhood, on the land of his father, at what came to be known as Chrisman Post Office, a few miles northwest of present Mt. Clinton; where he was a large landowner. Some of his land was purchased 19th, November, 1805, and had formerly belonged to Joshua Wright, who sold to Handle Vance, Sr., 8th June, 1772. Vance died, and his son Handle, Jr., conveyed his interest in the estate to Chrisman, and removed to Ohio. (Vance vs. Vance admrs.—*Chalkley,* Vol. II, p. 244.)

Ann Chrisman outlived her husband many years. Her tombstone, standing alongside that of his, in New Erection Churchyard, bears the interesting inscription:

"Erected to the Memory of Ann Chrisman wife of John Chrisman and

Daughter of Reuben and Lydia Harrison and the Mother of Joseph, George H, and Margaret M. Chrisman . Born Jan. 28, 1777, Died March 25, 1839, Aged 62 years, 1 mo., & 28 days."

As named thus, John Chrisman, and wife Ann, (1260), had issue—

(12601) JOSEPH—b. Nov. 11, 1797; d. 1874; m. 1st., Elizabeth Lincoln, d. Jan. 4, 1824, "aged 20 years, 4 months," dau. of Jacob Lincoln— son of "Va." John. m. 2nd., Jane Chrisman, dau. of Isaac, of Stephens City, son of John, son of the immigrant. Removed to Missouri, 1837.
See further record.

(12602) GEORGE H.—b. Sept. 23, 1799; d. Sept. 15, 1870; m., Mar. 14, 1822, Martha Davis Herring, dau. of Alexander, (1931), b. April 2, 1799, d. Jan. 19, 1866.
See further record.

(12603) MARGARET M.—b. Jan. 16, 1801; d. 1854; m., about 1825, Charles C. Spears, of Kentucky.
See further record.

(Tombstones of Elizabeth, George and Martha D., in New Erection Churchyard, from which their dates are gleaned; other dates from D. S. H. MSS.)

Hook fam. info in Virginia Valley Records – Wayland

(1261) SAMUEL HARRISON (1777-), the son of Capt. Reuben Harrison (125), and wife Lydia, married, February 5, 1810, Esther Hooke, born April 6, 1785, the daughter of George Hooke, of Rockingham, (founder of the Highland County family), and wife Mary Ann. (See Hooke Family Data, in *Va. Valley Records*, by J. W. Wayland, p. 217.) Following his marriage he and his wife removed to Rockbridge County, Virginia.

Samuel and wife Esther had issue—

(12611) ABNER—d. unmarried.
(12612) JAMES—m. Susan Schultz.
See further record.
(12613) HARVEY—m. Isabel Campbell (?).
(12614) MARY—m. John Campbell.
See further record.
(12615) ELIZABETH—
(12616) DELILAH—

(D. S. H. MSS.)

(1263) RACHEL HARRISON, ( ), the daughter of Capt. Reuben Harrison, (125), and 2nd wife Mary, married, May 26, 1801, Jesse Harrison, (1771), son of Ezekiel. See Clan of Thomas Harrison, Line of Ezekiel Harrison.

SMITHLAND
By The Long Grey Trail
See pages 211, 318, 391, 410, and 485

CHAPTER XIX

The Great Western Migration

FOURTH GENERATION, CONTINUED

"We led fair freedom hither,
And lo, the deserts smiled,
A paradise of pleasure
Just opened in the wild;
Your harvest, bold Americans,
No power shall snatch away,
Then let's huzza, huzza, huzza,
For brave America."

—REVOLUTIONARY WAR SONG.

ABOUT THE YEAR 1805, there began what may be termed the great western migration of many of Rockingham's sons from their native heath. Of the Harrisons, the fourth generation in particular, heeded the beckoning of the towering Alleghanies to the wide country beyond. While there was not such a complete removal of this generation as that of the second from Delaware, yet this 'later western migration' was in many respects much more marked than the first.

Several causes, some more evident than others, contributed to this detail of the trend of the times. The Revolution, now happily an event of the past, had given birth to the new Federal government, which was lending its might to the protection and fostering of new homes in the West. The war, too, had supplied a further incentive in that Virginia, through her bounty warrants, had granted much land in Kentucky, and Ohio, to her soldiers, as a result of their services. These warrants enjoyed a brisk circulation. (See, Wilson's *Catalogue of Revolutionary Soldiers and Sailors of the Commonwealth of Virginia, from Official Records in Ky. State Land Office—Year Book of Society Sons of the Revolution in Ky.* 1894-1913, p. 190, etc.)

This country being new, and largely uninhabited, appealed strongly to the pioneer blood coursing so abundantly in the veins of the sons and grandsons of the Valley settlers. The region now West Virginia lay just over the great mountains, and Ohio and Kentucky were neighboring commonwealths. With Virginia's contribution to the nation of her broad western territories, 1784-89, had gone these old "counties," together with that of Illinois—including Indiana,—formed 1776-78. Ere long the first two had joined the great sisterhood of States, Kentucky in 1792, and Ohio in 1803. To the south bordered Tennessee, which had also felt the quickened pulse of the times, and had joined her sisters of the Union in 1796. Much of this whole region was early and favorably known to the Valley pioneers, through their various campaigns against the Indians, and many had already drifted thither in search of adventure and fortune.

Of the two routes available to Kentucky and the West, in 1780, one led from Philadelphia to Pittsburgh, and thence by way of the Ohio; the other from Pennsylvania southwesterly through the Valley of Virginia, by way of the "Great Road," and the Wilderness Road, to Cumberland Gap, and thence northwesterly, by the Wilderness

Road, to the Falls of the Ohio, at Louisville. The southern route, on account of the hostility of the Indians, was considered the more practical, and less dangerous, and by it the greater number of the early emigrants journeyed. Rockingham County, lying directly athwart this route, came immediately under the influence of a great "moving procession of restless seekers after new lands and unknown goods." (See, *Tarbell*, p. 3.) By 1790 over 100,000 had gone West. Kentucky at this time boasted 73, 677 inhabitants. By 1820 her population had grown to 564,317. Her emigrants were almost exclusively from Virginia and North Carolina. (See, Beveridge's *Abraham Lincoln*, p. 9.)

Down until the time of the French Revolution (1792), Rockingham was a tobacco growing country. The first settlers were, is is said, under the impression that cereals, particularly corn, exhausted the soil, and rarely cultivated more than enough for their own needs. Following the beginning of the settlements in Kentucky word was soon passed back to Rockingham that this region afforded a soil better adapted to the raising of tobacco than the Valley country. Glowing reports, too, were received as to the fertility of the land for growing corn and wheat, claiming that no crop rotation was necessary. With the upheaval in France, famine stalked in Europe, causing the price of wheat in America to soar to the then fabulous price of $14.00 a barrel at the ports. The character of Rockingham's staple crop was accordingly changed; tobacco was forgotten, and the demand for wheat and other grain land correspondingly increased.

In 1804, the vast empire of the Mississippi, purchased of Napoleon was delivered to the young nation. The same year saw the beginning of the expedition of Lewis and Clarke to the Pacific. Quickly followed the opening of new routes to the West, and a period of expansion of the country's industries. From the beginning of the second decade of the new century may roughly be dated the great era of the development of transportation. The first steamboat on the Ohio and Mississippi appeared in 1812.

The home country, due to the natural increase in population, was fast becoming too crowded to supply the rising generation with adequate plantations. By now too, the owning of slaves was in many instances becoming highly distasteful. Thus there were both factors urging, and factors appealing, all culminating in that far hunt for new lands —the great move to the West.

* * * * * *

That the slavery question was even as early as 1797, agitating the minds of some of Rockingham's citizens, is shown by a rare old pamphlet printed this year, and now preserved in the Library of Congress—the "Minutes of the Ketockton Baptist Association, held at Frying Pan, Loudoun County, Virginia, August 1797, beginning Tuesday the 17th."

At this meeting, "The Committee appointed to prepare a Plan of Gradual Emancipation" brought in the following—

1st. All slaves 14 years old, and under, to be free at 22 years of age.
2nd. All slaves above 14 years, and under 20, to be free at 25.
3rd. All slaves above 20, and under 25, to be free at 28.
4th. All slaves above 25, to serve 5 years.
5th. All slaves born after this date shall be entitled to the same rights and privileges as children born of Negroes heretofore emancipated.
6th. All who have been purchased with money, shall serve 10 years, from time of such purchase.

(15th minute.)

The churches forming this historic Association at the time, their respective

Messengers, and the number of members reported, were —Linville Creek, Benjamin Talman, 21; Mill Creek (Gerrardstown), David Thomas, 16; Ketocton, Thomas Humphrey and Timothy Hickson, 21; Difficult, Jeremiah Moore and Chris. Neille, 29; "Opiquan," John and David Van Meter, and Wm. Burns, 18.

Plans for the next meeting, as adopted, read—"The Yearly Meeting to be held at Linvilles Creek, in Rockingham County the second Lordes Day in June 1798. And Saturday preceeding Elders Jeremiah Moore, Wm. Mason, John Hickerson, and John Hutcheson are to attend the same." (10th minute.)

CLAN OF CAPT. DANIEL HARRISON

LINE OF JESSE HARRISON, SR.

(1632) DANIEL HARRISON, (1760-1823), the son of Jesse Harrison, Sr., (163), and wife, on the 14th November, 1763, along with his brother Jesse, was deeded by his grandfather, Capt. Daniel Harrison, 400 acres of land on the head of Linville's Creek. (pages 211, and 315.) Both the grantees being infants, their father acted as trustee.

On the 26th February, 1782, among the members of Capt. George Baxter's company ordered to guard a party of British prisoners to Winchester, was Daniel Harrison, evidently the above, (Daniel, the Colonel's son, at this time was too young; see pages 299 and 323.)

In 1784, Daniel, the son of Jesse, Sr., married Ann Patton, the daughter of Matthew Patton, who is said to have emigrated from the region on the Bull Pasture about 1785, to Clark County, Kentucky, and died there in 1802. "Patton, Matthew," of Rockingham County, Virginia, was enumerated in the *Heads of Families* census, 1784, as having in his household, "8 White souls," and owning "1 Dwelling, 6 Other buildings." *(First U. S. Census, Va.*, p. 77.) Matthew was a descendant of Col. James Patton, the immigrant. (See pages 117 and 203.) ann Patton

Daniel Harrison's marriage bond was dated, January 29, 1784, with Benjamin Harrison as surety. Ann Patton is mentioned as of Rockingham County, but the name of her father is not given. The signature of Daniel is of a distinctly different handwrite than that of the groom of the same name on the 1787 bond to marry Ann Erwin, while the same Benjamin, it appears, may have signed both bonds; the latter as a witness. (See page 316.)

About 1815, Daniel, and wife, removed to Clark County, Kentucky, and as a resident there, in 1818, conveyed the above land to his brother Jesse Harrison of Rockingham. Their deed, so far as it has been preserved, reads—

"This Indenture made this 14th day of May in the Year of our Lord one Thousand Eight-hundred and Eighteen Between Daniel Harrison and Ann his wife of the County of Clarke and State of Kentucky of the one part and Jesse Harrison of the County of Rockingham and State of Virginia of the other part; Witnesseth that they the said Daniel Harrison and Ann his wife for and in consideration of the sum of one Dollar to them in hand paid by him the said Jesse Harrison the receipt whereof is hereby acknowledged hath granted, Bargained and Sold unto the said Jesse Harrison all that tract or parcel of land on which he the said Jesse . . .ison being the North end of the tract of four hundred acres conveyed . . . . .id Daniel Harrison and Jesse Harrison by their Grand . . . . . . l Harrison and Sarah his wife Deceased by a line running . . . . as a line of partition between the said Daniel Harrison . . . . . . the said Jesse Harrison as reference will more fu . . . . .de by sd Harrison to Jacob Spitler w . . . was the division line between sd Harrison & Jesse H . . . . appurtenances to him the said Jesse Harrison his heirs . . . . ever to have and to hold the said tract or parcel of land with . . . . .ances and they the said Daniel Harrison and Ann his wife for the xxxx . . . . their heirs exors & Admr . . . . do covenant with him the said Jesse Harrison . . . . they *they* the said Daniel Harrison and Ann his wife the said tract or par . . . land with all its appurtenances to him the said Jesse Harrison and . . . . &c. will forever warrant and defend against the claim of them their h. . . . Exors & Admr. or any person or persons claiming through by or under . . . . against the claim of *me* other person whatever in Witness whereof the x. . . . . . Daniel Harrison and wife have set their hands and seals the dxx. . . . . above written.

Daniel Harrison (Seal.)
Ann Harrison (Seal).

State of Kentucky Clarke County *Set*. Clerks office May 14th. 1814. I James Bullick Clark of the Court in and for the aforesaid County of Clarke do hereby certify that this Deed of Bargain and Sale from Daniel Harrison and Ann his wife to Jesse Harrison was produced before me and acknowledged by the said Daniel Harrison and Ann his wife to be their Act and deed for the purpose therein mentioned she the said Ann being first privily examined according to Law freely and voluntarily relinquished her right of Dower therein and the same is certified accordingly to the state of Virginia Rockingham County.
In testimony whereof I the Clerk aforesaid have hereunto set my hand and affixed the seal of the said County of Clark the above

(SEAL.) James P. Bullock.

Recorded in the Clerks Office of the County Court of Rockingham December 21st. 1819.
Re-recorded from Burnt Records under act of Assembly Approved November 18th, 1884.

Teste: D. H. Lee Martz, D. C.

(See, Burnt Deed Book 4, p. 384.
The deed to Jacob Spitler referred to was recorded, September, 1787.)

The home of Daniel Harrison in Kentucky was near present Winchester, on the Van Meter Pike, his estate today being known as "The Pines," or the Thomas Lewis Van Meter farm, on which the old family burial ground is located. (See page 317.) The land since his day has been associated with his descendants.

Daniel Harrison died in 1823. His inscription runs—"In Memory of Daniel Harrison, born Sept. 2, 1760, and departed this life March 16, 1823." "By his son P. D. Harrison." His wife died in 1819. Her inscription runs—"In Memory of Ann Harrison Consort of Daniel Harrison who departed this life Feb. 7, 1819, in the 50th. yr. of her age." (The last figure of the year of her death being indistinct, the same is based on the deed above.) Near by stands the marker, "In Memory of Ann Harrison," Daniel's sister—erected "By her nephew P. D. Harrison."

Daniel Harrison, (1632), and wife Ann, had issue—

(16321) "Margery Maxwell, late Margery Harrison, born May 16, 1785, and departed this life Aug. 1838." (Buried as above, marker erected "By her brother P. D. Harrison.")

(16322) Benjamin—b. ——; d. ——; lived in Kentucky, no further record.

(16323) Patton D.— b. 2nd Nov. 1795; d. March 26, 1841; m. Sept. 28, 1820, Polly Elgin, b. Aug. 9, 1804, d. Aug. 9, 1870.
See further record.

(List of children kindly furnished by a descendant of the last named.)

(1634) BENJAMIN HARRISON, (1772 c-1824), identified tentatively as the son of Jesse Harrison, Sr., (163), and wife, by the meagre reference to him available, but more particularly by the elimination of these references from any connection with various other records pertaining to the individuals of his name, married in 1809, Elizabeth Koontz, of Rockingham County, the daughter of Col. John Koontz, a resident of Lacey Spring, probably son of Rev. John Koontz. (See pages 301, 316, and 365.)

Benjamin's marriage bond was filed in Rockingham court, and the marriage recorded in the first record book of marriages, as kept by the clerk. As entered therein, the date was April 4, 1809, and the officiating minister the Rev. Christopher Frye. Seemingly the date was that of the actual ceremony, and the place Rockingham County. However, according to the record in the family Bible handed down among his descendants, "Benjamin Harrison and Elizabeth Koontz were married April 2, 1809, at McNunelville, Tennessee." April 4th was likely the date of the dispatch of the return of the license, which in this instance was apparently erroneously entered in the record book as the date of the wedding.

Benjamin's full name was Benjamin Peachy Harrison, and that he was of the Dayton line of the Rockingham family is assured. His migration to Tennessee obviously occurred about the time of his marriage. Michael Harrison, likely his brother, had removed to the same State about 1806. (See page 313.) An old tradition of 1835 relates that Benjamin's plantation and Sam. Houston's (the later General) adjoined in Tennessee. (Several of Benjamin's sons served under Houston in Texas in the 1836 Rebellion.) In 1823, at the time of his son William's birth, he was living in Roane County.

Benjamin Harrison died September, 5, 1824. (Bible record.) Following his death his widow removed to Valporaiso, Indiana, where she died. Says the inscription on her tombstone—"Elizabeth Koontz Harrison, Born in Rockingham Co., Va., Feb. 15, 1792, Died (at) Valporaiso, Indiana, Jan. 21, 1870." (Same date of death recorded in the family Bible, also.)

Briefly, Benjamin Harrison, (1634), and wife Elizabeth had—

(16341) Achiles L.—b. Feb. 13, 1810, d. 1836. Second Lieutenant in the Texas Army during the 1836 Rebellion. Died at San Antonio, of yellow fever. Buried there.

(16342) Erasmus Darwin—b. Apr. 24, 1811, "departed this life March 1836, at the taking of the Alimo." (Shot at Farming's Massacre, Goliad, Texas.)

(16343) Jane— F.—b. Dec. 30, 1813; d. Oct. 8, 1814.

(16344) Eliza Jane—b. Apr. 9, 1817; d. Jan. 20, 1841; m. Oct. 19, 1836, Rev. Michael Decker, son of Levi Decker, of Staunton, Va.
See further record.

(16345) John S. K.—b. Aug. 20, 1818; d. Dec. 31, 1864; m. ——. Served with Sam Houston in the Texas Rebellion. Lieut. Gen. in Confederate Army—Texas troops. Captured with Pemberton at Vicksburg. Died in Texas.
See further reference.

(16346) JOSEPH L.—b. Aug. 15, 1820; d. Dec. 20. 1822.
(16347) WILLIAM M.—b. Nov. 18, 1823; d. July 11, 1852, at Valparaiso, Indiana; m. June 15, 1847 Eliza Gwinn.
See further record.

(Dates from copy of Bible record as sworn to June 14, 1928, in Porter Co., Ind., by Grace L. Axe Wiltfong (Mrs. Charles O.), the owner of the Bible. A copy kindly supplied by Wm. H. Decker, of Page, Nebraska.)

LINE OF COL. DANIEL SMITH

(1651) JOHN SMITH, (1752——), the son of Col. Daniel Smith, and wife Jane, (165), nee Harrison, on March 14, 1776, was commissioned Ensign in the Fourth Regiment, following which he was promoted to Second Lieutenant, August, 1776, and First Lieutenant, February 21, 1777. On May 26, 1778 he resigned. He was again commissioned First Lieutenant, September 12, 1778, and was present at Cornwallis' surrender at Yorktown, 1781.

He married in 1776, Margaret Davis, who as his widow in 1793 gave her consent to her daughter's marriage, as below. Their children were two, viz.:

(16511) MARGARET REED—b. April 23, 1777; d. ——; m. 1793, Alexander Herring, (1951), son of William.
See further record.
(16512) DANIEL, (the Judge)—b. Mar. 12, 1779; d. Nov. 8, 1850; m. June 10, 1809, Frances Strother Duff, dau. of James, b. Feb. 11, 1792, d. Oct. 4, 1849. (Both buried in Woodbine Cemetery, at Harrisonburg.)
See further record.

(Also named in D. S. H. MSS; Margaret's birth date from this; Daniel and wife's from monument.)

(1656) BENJAMIN SMITH, (1761-1812), the son of Col. Daniel Smith, and wife Jane, (165), nee Harrison, as his brother John, above, was among Rockingham's Lieutenants in the Revolutionary War, and present at the surrender at Yorktown.

Benjamin Smith was the owner of a fine old estate near Harrisonburg,—within about two miles of Smithland, his father's home. His house, familiarily known as the "Old Stone House," has long been a landmark of the county. "Being opposed to slavery he removed in September, 1810, with his family, to near present Lancaster, Ohio." (House there destroyed by fire in 1859.)

About 1782, Benjamin married Elizabeth Cravens, (1484), the daughter of Robert Cravens, Jr. (See page 260.) He died in 1812, and she, February 22, 1837, "aged 75 years." Their children were:

(16561) JOHN—b. 1783; d. 1827, (from accident); m. 1809, Adamena Carthae, dau. of John, b. July 28, 1783, d. June 16, 1848.
See further record.
(16562) NANCY—b. 1784; d. ——; m. 1802, Major Joseph Brown, of Rockingham, Co., Va.
See further record.
(16563) ROBERT—b. 1785; d. Feb. 21, 1870; m. 1834, Phoebe Searle, of Providence, R. I., b. 1810, d. Feb. 22, 1884.
See further record.

(16564) Daniel—b. 1787 c.; d. 1854, at Charleston, now West Virginia; m. Mrs. Nancy Harriman.
See further reference.

(16565) Margaret—b. 1792; d. Sept. 11, 1823; m. 1811, John Creed.
See further record.

(16566) Elizabeth—b. 1795; d. Sept. 4, 1827; m. 1826, Hugh McElroy; only child died in infancy.

(16567) Benjamin Harrison—b. Oct. 31, 1797; d. Dec. 10, 1887, at Charleston, now W. Va.; m. Dec. 19, 1826, Roxalana Noyes, d. Feb. 10, 1859.
See further record.

(16568) James Harrison—b. 1798; d. Aug. 9, 1830; m. Nov. 1828, Elizabeth Standeland White, dau. of Rev. William White, of Philadelphia.
See further record.

(16569) Jane Harrison—b. ——; d. ——, young.

(D. S. H. MSS.)

(1661) WILLIAM SMITH, (1775-1806), the son of Col. Daniel Smith, and wife Jane, (165), nee Harrison, lived at his father's home, Smithland. He married in 1797, Diana McDonough, the daughter of "Jan." deceased. She was born in 1776, and died in 1842. (See page 319.) Their children were:

(16611) Edward Harrison—b. July 1, 1799; d. April 24, 1852; m. Julia Harrison, (1786), dau. of Reuben. She b. 1806, d. 1883. Lived at Smithland.
See further reference.

(16612) Jane H.—b. Dec. 18, 1800; d. ——; m. Dr. Michael Harris.
See further record.

(16613) James—b. July 7, 1802; d. Oct. 18, 1827; unmarried.

(16614) Mary—b. 1804; d. ——; m. Col. William B. Yancey.
See further record.

Col. Wm B. Yancey

(16615) William—b. 1806; d. ——.

(D. S. H. MSS.)

(1662) JAMES SMITH, (1779-1827 c.), the son of Col. Daniel Smith, and wife Jane, (165), nee Harrison, "in 1807, having conscientious scruples on the question of slavery . . . moved to Ohio." He settled at Mt. Vernon, (now Knox County). A short time after his settlement he was appointed Clerk of the County Court, in which capacity he served for twenty years. Besides attending to his secular duties he filled the pulpit of the Christian Church, wherein he was an ardent worker. He was the author of several books on The Trinity. Whilst returning from court at Marion, Ohio, he was thrown from his horse and fatally injured.

Rev. Smith married, in 1804, Rebecca Emmett, of Augusta County, Virginia, by whom he had:

(16621) Jane Harrison—b. Nov. 18, 1805; d. ——; m. Sept. 25, 1823, Col. Charles Sagar, at Mt. Vernon, O.
See further record.

(16622) Diana—b. 1808; d.——.

(16623) Benjamin F.—b. 1811; d. ——; m. 1830, Julia Stilly.
See further record.

(16624) James—b. 1815; d. 1882; m. 1848, Elizabeth L. Morton.
See further record.

(16625) Vespasian—b. Oct. 21, 1818; d. Oct. 9, 1897; m. 1846, Charlotte Neely, of Pa., b. 1824, d. 1899.
See further record.

(16626) Adeline T.—b. July 31, 1821; d. ——; m. June 25, 1850, Rev. A. A. Davis.
See further record.

(16627) Henrietta Clay—b. 1824; d. 1847; m. 1846, Charles Lybrand.
See further record.

(D. S. H. MSS.)

LINE OF COL. BENJAMIN HARRISON

(1672) DANIEL HARRISON, (1765-1837), the son of Col. Benjamin Harrison, (167), and wife Mary, married in 1787, Ann Erwin, the daughter of Francis, who gave his consent; surety John Erwin, Jr.; witness Samuel and Mary Erwin, and Benjamin Harrison. (See page 316.)

In the marriage bond, dated January 24, 1787, her name is given as Ann, while in the Clerk's certificate it is Anna, and on her tombstone Nancy, from which it is gleaned that her name was Ann or Nancy Erwin. Francis, her father, is referred to in the bond as of Rockingham County. "Erwin, Francis," of this county, was enumerated in the *Heads of Families* census, Virginia, 1784, as having in his family "9 White souls," and owning "1 Dwelling, 6 Other buildings." *(First U. S. Census, Va.*, p. 77.)

ERWIN

Francis Erwin was the son of Francis and Jean Curry Erwin, of Augusta County. He was probably born on the Cowpasture, where he is said to have resided for a time. His wife was Elizabeth Clements, the daughter of Jacob, of this region. (See page 132.) He and Elizabeth had issue—Ann, b. October 11, 1768, m. Daniel Harrison, as above; Mary, b. June 25, 1771, m. Robert Scott, 1790; Jacob Clements, b. June 29, 1772, m. 1797, Jean (Stuart) (?); Sarah, b. July 25, 1775, m, Thomas Hopkins, 1795; Andrew, b. June 5, 1778, m. Polly Huston; Rebecca, b. March 22, 1781, m. David Usher, 1803; Ruth, b. April 22, 1784, m. Michael Fridley, Jr.; and Francis Eugene, b. November 27, 1787. (Names and birth dates in letter, Mrs. Lafayette Marks, *pens me,* September 11, 1923; marriage dates from *Strickler;* see also *Margaret Logan Morrison Records,* by E. M. Houston.)

Of these—those whose marriage dates are given, married in Rockingham, and the first, second, fourth, and sixth couples, "sometime between 1793 and 1818, probably 1805, removed to, or near, Hopkinsville, Kentucky."

* * * * * *

In Kentucky, Daniel Harrison is said to have been known as Capt. Harrison. He had no doubt served in the militia of Rockingham as a Captain prior to his removal; his father having been the county lieutenant. On the return of a summons of witnesses from Rockingham, in "Matthews vs. Burns, executrix," dated 15th October, 1794, the notation was made, "Thomas Harrison not at home, Daniel Harrison and Ralph Given in the army." *(Chalkley,* Vol. I, p. 403.)

Daniel's home in Kentucky was in Christian County. His removal from Virginia was likely in company with several of his brothers, two of whom, Robert and Fielding, stopped in this county also. The latter is mentioned as having removed from Rockingham about 1805 or 6. Their uncle Daniel, too—who seems to have made his home with one of the brothers,—was obviously a newly arrived resident of Christian, in 1806. (See page 313.)

Daniel Harrison died in 1837, and his wife Ann, or Nancy, as she was called, the year thereafter. Both were buried in Hopkinsville. Their inscriptions recite that Daniel Harrison was born in Rockingham County, Virginia, February 1, 1765, and died February 8, 1837, and that Nancy Harrison, his wife, was born in Augusta County, Virginia, October 11, 1768, and died January 29, 1838. (Pioneer Cemetary.)

An old sampler handed down in the family, as worked by their daughter, Betsy Clementina, in 1803, bears the initials, "D. H.," in one corner, and "N. I.," in the diagonally opposite one.

Daniel Harrison, (1672), and wife Nancy, had issue:

(16721) Betsy Clementina—b. April 24, 1792; d. unmarried.
(16722) Theodocia—m. Thomas Hawks.
See further record.
(16723) Maria—d. ——; unmarried.
(16724) Edith McWilliams—b. Jan. 25, 1797; d. 1865; m. Aug. 27, 1818, William Hopper, b. 1791, d. 1876.
See further record.
(16725) Daniel Harvey—b. Dec 2, 1805; d. ——; m. 1st, Elvira Byron; m. 2nd, Norah ——.
See further record.
(16726) Sallie Taliaferro—m. —— Craig, "believed to have been from S. C."

(First five named in a list kindly supplied by Eunice O. Marks, (Mrs. Lafayette Marks), of Springdale, Arkansas. Last buried in the cemetery at Hopkinsville, as advised by her granddaughter, Mrs. A. M. Bradley, of Abington, Virginia, who kindly furnished the tombstone dates regarding Daniel and Nancy.)

(1675) JAMES HARRISON, (1770 c.), the son of Col. Benjamin Harrison, (167), and wife Mary, married, January 27, 1794, Ann Millan, (Milton?), daughter of John Millan, of Rockingham County; surety Andrew Shanklin.

Among those taxed for the year 1788, in Company No. 3, of Rockingham, was "Harrison, Benjamin, and sons over 16, John, Benjamin, and James." (See—Rockingham tax lists, original.)

James Harrison is said to have been among those of Col. Benjamin Harrison's sons who migrated to Christian County, Kentucky. He eventually, however, settled in Lebanon County, Ohio. His removal from Rockingham was evidently after his father's death. (See page 322.)

James Harrison, (1675), and wife Ann, had issue:

(16751) Elizabeth—m. John Clarkson.
(16752) Isabella—
(16753) Junebella—
(16754) Parthenia—
(16755) Maria M.—
(16756) Cynthia—

(16757) George—m. Aug. 9, 1832, Sarah Paul Grover, dau. of Josiah. See further record.

(16758) Julia Ann—

(16759) Jane Madison—

(Named in the New Albany, Ind. *Times Dispatch* article before referred to—see page 322—and verified by letter in D. S. H. papers.)

McWILLIAMS

(1676) EDITH HARRISON, ( ), the daughter of Col. Benjamin Harrison, (167), and wife Mary, married in 1792, Samuel McWilliams; surety Joseph Cravens. (See—Strickler's *Rockingham Co. Marriages*, p. 83; and below.)

Samuel McWilliams, (1766-1817), was a short time later Clerk of Rockingham County Court. He was the third to so qualify, and served twenty-five years. In a brief notice regarding him, Johnston, in his *Memorials of Old Virginia Clerks*, states—"Samuel McWilliams was appointed to succeed Mr. Ewing in July, 1792 and continued to hold the office until his death, in February, 1817. Mr. McWilliams married Edith Harrison, a daughter of Col. Benjamin Harrison, January 16, 1792, and resided on what is now known as Watemamo farm, northeast of Harrisonburg. His death was caused by a fall from a wagon. Mr. McWilliam's family has disappeared from the county, and nothing can now be gathered of his history" (page 346).

In the Act of Assembly, December, 1797, authorizing the adidtion of 23½ acres of land to the town of Harrisonburg, the first trustees of the town were appointed, among whom were Samuel M' Williams, and Asher Waterman, gentlemen. (See page 247.)

Samuel McWilliams is presumed to have been a brother of Gordon McWilliams, who as a witness in the litigation, "McMahon vs. Brown," 1829, (see page 246.), deposed that "he came to Harrisonburg in May, 1797."

Gordon McWilliams was conveyed land (Water Crow's land) on Linville's Creek in May, 1799, by Abraham Peary and Joseph Hall, as shown by the papers in "McWilliams vs. Hollingshead, 1803." (See pages 196, 274, 279, and 324.) The land was near Leonard Herring, and in 1800 he witnessed Herring's deed to Jacob Peary. (See page 281.)

Gordon McWilliams' eldest daughter, Martha Jane McWilliams, 1797-1833, married, Reuben Moore, the son of Capt. Reuben, and among the Moore records it is stated that Gordon was the son of James McWilliams, 1716-1783, and wife Ann McWilliams, 1727-1780. Gordon married November 25, 1795, Martha Botherton, the daughter of William Botherton, 1729-1812, and wife Martha, 1738-1794. (See page 373.) He is thought to have come to the Valley from east of the Ridge, first stopping probably in Staunton.

In the *Heads of Families* census,, Virginia, only three Mc Williams are named—Hugh and John, of Albemarle, and Hugh, of Greenbrier.

Samuel McWilliams came to Harrisonburg likely as a schoolmaster. He was born about 1766. As a witness for the defendant, Samuel McWilliams, "about 50 years of age," testified September 19, 1816, in the "Cravens vs. Lanahan" litigation (see page 343.)

"Question. Was not James and Peggy Cravens sent to your school sometime between the years 1784 to 1788? Ans. I taught school in Harrisonburg in the year 1787, at the time Denis Lanahan subscribed for two scholars. . . . I recollect that James

Cravens was at my school, but what part of the time he attended I do not remember. Peggy Cravens I do not recollect, but suppose she might have been there. . . . Lanahan at the time lived in Town. Question by Joseph Cravens. Did not yourself & Robert Cravens ride sheriffs about the year 1791 or 1792? Ans. I think we did about the year 1792 under Andw. Shanklin," etc.

In December, 1790, Samuel signed as a juror of Rockingham, along with William Cravens, and others, in declaring a tract of land on Linville Creek escheatable. (See page 352.)

Following his death, his family removed to Christian County, Kentucky, likely in company with some of his wife's brothers and their families. (See—*The McClure Family,* p. 130.)

Samuel McWilliams and wife Edith, (1676), had issue:

(16761) PEACHY—
(16762) ASHBURY—
(16763) AGATHA—m. Alexander Logan.
(16764) NANCY—m. Resin Hammond.
(16765) MARY—

(First four named in the *Times Dispatch* account—see page 322. Mary, a "pretty widow," named in Mrs. Carr's *My Recollection of Rocktown,* p. 11.)

LOGAN

(1677) MARGARET HARRISON, (1773-), the daughter of Col. Benjamin Harrison, (167), and wife Mary, married, "Tuesday, May 23, 1797," Ezekiel Logan; surety S. McWilliams.

Ezekiel Logan was born the 31st of August, 1770, and "departed this life June 15, 1825, aged 54 years, 10 months and 2 days." Margaret Harrison, his wife, was born "on Sunday, October 4, 1773."

These dates are taken from the "Old Bible Records," entered in their family Bible, extant among their descendants. At the time of their marriage both were residents of Rockingham County.

Ezekiel and Margaret Logan settled in the neighborhood of her father; the Colonel setting off a part of his home plantation for them, as indicated in his will. (See also page 316.) Sometime after 1806, and probably before the Colonel's death, they joined the great western migration, and removed by way of Kentucky, to southern Indiana, near Madison, or New Albany, where their children are next found residing.

Named all, in the Bible record above, Ezekiel Logan and wife Margaret, (1677), had:

(16771) BENJAMIN HARRISON—b. Thursday morning, Apr. 5, 1798; d. ——; m. 1821, Catherine Keplinger.
See further record.

(16772) POLLY MARIA—b. Monday morning, Sept. 9, 1799; d. 1900; m. Samuel Culbertson.
See further record.

(16773) BETSY EVELINE—b. Sunday Morning, Dec. 1, 1800; d. 1886; m. John (Charles) Goodnow.
See further record.

(16774) WILLIAM LONG MCWILLIAMS—b. Sunday morning, Apr. 4, 1802; d. Mar. 26, 1809.

(16775) JANE LYLE—b. July 16, 1804; d. ——; m. Isaac Delay.

(16776) PEACHY—b. Friday, July 18, 1806; d. Sept. 6, 1812.
(16777) ANGELINA—b. Feb. 11, 1809; d. 1904; m. 1831, John Williams.
See further record.
(16778) FRANCIS ASBURY—b. Mar. 8, 1811; d. Mar. 18, 1902; m. Aug. 15, 1843, Elizabeth Ireland.
See further record.
(16779) EDITH PARTHENIA—b. June 5, 1813; d. Dec. 16, 1889.

(1678) JEAN HARRISON, (-1835), the daughter of Col. Benjamin Harrison, (167), and wife Mary, married in 1794, Rev. William Cravens, (1414), the son of John Cravens. See Clan of Capt. Robert Cravens, Line of John Cravens.

(1679) PEACHY HARRISON, (1777-1848), the son of Col. Benjamin Harrison, (167), and wife Mary, by his father's will was devised the old home plantation, at present Dayton, Virginia. Of all the Colonel's children, Peachy appears to have been the only one to remain in Rockingham. He lived and died in Harrisonburg.

Something of his childhood school days is learned from his testimony in Cravens vs. Lanahan, he being one of the numerous witnesses in this long contested controversy. (See page 343.)

"Saturday morning, September 21, 1816, Peachy Harrison about 38 years, witness summonsed by the Deft. being sworn" deposed, etc. "Went to school at a place called Fisher's Spring with Joseph and James Cravens (sons of John, deceased) and am inclined to think that Peggy also went there. I remember to have (gone) home with the children from school . . . first time had ever seen Denis Lanahan. (went to school to best of his recollection to Matthew Bowyers; commenced about age of four and went to . . . Bowyers three years.) Question by Joseph Cravens. Can you recollect that when myself & Brother James Cravens went to school that we went week about—so as to make one scholler between us? Answer. It is not my recollection. Signed, Peachy Harrison."

Peachy's school days were finished at the famous early medical school conducted by Dr. Benjamin Rush, in Philadelphia, from which he graduated. He became a distinguished practicing physician, and, as remarked by *Boogher*, "was an active Christian, and characterized through life by public spirit, integrity and benevolence."

From 1824 to 1826, Dr. Harrison was Sheriff of Rockingham County, and later represented the county at Richmond, in the House of Delegates.

Dr. Harrison married, February 29, 1804, Mary Stuart, the daughter of John and Frances (Burnsides) Stuart. (See—*Boogher.)* "Frances and John had a daughter Polly, who married Peachy Harrison," says a line of testimony, in the *Extracts from the Augusta Records*—Bill of Complaint, 18th June, 1805, John Baxter and Margaret, his wife, "daughter of John Stuart, whose will was recorded in Augusta." Herein it is further revealed that the widow Frances married Joseph Moore, and that she was the daughter of John and Martha Burnsides. Her answer, sworn to in Shenandoah County, 14th November, 1805, mentions her son Samuel,—Margaret's brother,—born after his father's death. (Baxter vs. Stuart's executors; *Chalkley*, Vol. II, p. 90.)

John Stuart was probably a descendant of Samuel, the early associate of the Harrisons, although Samuel's name appears to have been spelled "Stewart," to follow the questionable orthography of the old court scribes. (Stewart was the original Scotch mode of spelling.) John Stuart resided in the Old Stone Church neighborhood. (See—*Waddell*, p. 367.)

Dr. Harrison's death occurred in 1848. Says the *Baltimore Sun* of May 3rd, this year—"The last Rockingham (Va.) Register announces the death of Dr. Peachy Harrison, a venerable and distinguished citizen in the 72d year of his age. He represented Rockingham in the Leigslature, and was a member of the Convention that met at Richmond in 1829, to revise the State Constitution." (His will was dated February 26, 1848 (?), and proven May, 1848; see—*Virginia Valley Records,* by J. W. Wayland, p. 410.)

His wife, Mary, died in 1857. Both lie buried in Woodbine Cemetery, in Harrisonburg, where their markers may be seen. His inscription runs—"Sacred to the Memory of Dr. Peachy Harrison, Born April 6, 1777, Died April 25, 1848." Mary Harrison, his wife, says her inscription, was born September 12, 1783, and died September 19, 1857.

Of their sons, two died in early manhood; one before his father's death, the other, after becoming a practicing physician in the office of his father, was called in the midst of a promising career, a few years following his father's death. A third son became the distinguished educator; but of him more in a later Chapter.

Briefly, Dr. Peachy Harrison, (1679), and wife Mary, had issue:

(16791) Edward Tiffin—b. Aug. 21, 1805; d. June 21, 1828; unmarried.

(16792) Gessner—b. June 26, 1807; d. Apr. 7, 1862; m. Dec. 15, 1830, Eliza Lewis Carter, dau. of Prof. Geo. Tucker.
See further record.

(16793) Frances Moore—b. Feb. 23, 1809; d. July 10, 1810.

(16794) An infant—b. Feb. 28, 1815; d. young.

(16795) Mary Jane—b. Nov. 5, 1816; d. Dec. 7, 1889; unmarried.
See further reference.

(16796) Margaret Frances—b. Apr. 24, 1818; d. June 13, 1858; m. Wm. F. Stephens. A daughter, Williett, m. —— Baughman, and they had a son, Greer Baughman (of Richmond, Va. ?).

(16797) Caroline Elizabeth—b. May 22, 1822; d. unmarried.

(16798) Peachy Rush (Dr.)—b. Jan. 4, 1825; d. May 22, 1852; m. June 6, 1848, Mary Frances Rhodes, dau. of William. She b. Jan. 14, 1828; d. July 14, 1899.
See further record.

(Tombstones of Edward Tiffin, Mary Jane, Caroline, and Dr. Peachy Rush, in Woodbine Cemetery, Harrisonburg, and of Mary Francis Rhodes in "Lower Lutheran" Churchyard, at New Market—dates of births and deaths from these . See also Boogher's *Gleanings of Virginia History*.)

(1680) FIELDING HARRISON, (1778-1829), the son of Col. Benjamin Harrison, (167), and wife Mary, married October 1, 1800, Ann Quinn, the daughter of James, who signed the marriage bond as surety. The officiating minister was the Rev. John Walsh, who also married Samuel McWilliams and Edith Harrison, and Ezekiel Logan and Margaret Harrison; both brides Fielding's sisters. (See—Old Marriage Book of Rockingham.)

Quinn

Fielding Harrison was born about 1777, and his wife Ann Quinn about 1779, says John Carroll Power, in his *History of the Early Settlers of Sangamon County, Illinois,* who adds, that he was born in Rockingham County, Virginia, and she in Culpeper

County, Virginia. At the time of their marriage she, as well as her father, was a resident of Rockingham; the bond being filed in this county.

Upon his marriage, Fielding settled near his father, to the west of Harrisonburg, but about 1805, he migrated with his wife, and one child, to Christian County, Kentucky, where five more of his children were born. From there he removed with his family to Sangamon County, Illinois, arriving at the north side of Richland Creek, in what is now Salisbury township, in November, 1822, likely in company with his brother, William, and his cousin Ezekiel, both of whom settled in the same county. (See page 335.)

Says a writer, in speaking of Fielding and his brother; "I have heard the daughters of both tell of the elegance in which Anna Quinn Harrison travelled from Virginia to Kentucky in a carriage, with a retinue of slaves, which her father had given her, on horseback; one slave went with them to Illinois and lived to be very old, and is buried in the front door yard of the old Fielding Harrison, afterwards the Peyton Harrison homestead." (Miss J. B. to D. S. H., Mar. 30, 1914.)

THE WILDERNESS ROAD

From Rockingham, their way led, likely, over the route of the famous "Great Road through Virginia," and the Wilderness Road; passing by way of Staunton, "North Branch of James River," Botetourt Court House (Fincastle), and "Alleghaney Mountain," to a point somewhere about today's Salem, Virginia, probably "New River," and thence westward, on leaving this point, by way of "Ft. Chiswell," "Head of the Holston," Washington Court House, (Abingdon), "Black Horse," Powell's Mountain, and Cumberland Mountain (Cumberland Gap), to Crab Orchard, Lincoln County, Kentucky, an early frontier post, "from which emigrants branched off to their respective destinations." From here the Wilderness Road continued on to the "Falls of the Ohio," by way of Logan's Station, (Stanford), Herod's Station, (Harrodsburg), and Bardstown.

Such were the names of some of the early points along the way, noted in reverse order, as early as 1786, by John Filson, in his journal, on passing from Louisville to Delaware, his native home. Filson was one of Kentucky's earliest settlers. He records the distance from Louisville to Staunton as 509 miles. (See—Durritt's *Life of Filson; Waddell*, pp. 315 and 318.)

The old route led through several county seats; two of which, Staunton, and Botetourt Court House, were the oldest.

In an Act of October, 1776, abolishing the county of Fincastle, and out of its territory creating instead the counties of Kentucky, Washington, and Montgomery, the justices of the new counties formed were ordered "to meet and hold Court," for Montogomery County, at Fort Chiswell, for Washington County, at Black's Fort, and for Kentucky County, at Harrodsburg. (See—*Middle River Settlements,* by D. E. Johnston, p. 57.)

From Crab Orchard to Christian County, Kentucky, the way probably led for its greater part by way of the Green River.

* * * * * *

Fielding's settlement in Christian County was likely in that part now Trigg, in which he was residing in 1816. From here to Sangamon County, Illinois, was a comparatively short journey by way of the Tennessee, Ohio, Mississippi, Illinois, and Sangamon rivers. The intervening country was obviously too sparsely settled for an overland route. A Methodist circuit rider in passing from Terre Haute to the Sangamon River two years later (1824), went six days without seeing a human habitation. (See—Beveridge's *Abraham Lincoln*, p. 103.)

In Sangamon County, the scene of Lincoln's later rise to prominence, and the home of the State Capitol since 1837, Fielding Harrison settled on an adjoining farm to the noted pioneer evangelist, Peter Cartwright, Lincoln's opponent for Congress in 1846. Thus was begun the acquaintance of the two families leading later to several alliances.

Springfield, at the time, was scarcely a village, and in 1824 it is described by the circuit rider, as "a little cluster of cabins . . . all squatters on government land." Fielding's home was a short distance northwest of the town. "I Have seen," continues the writer before quoted, "the Harrison homes in Sangamon . . . and they are elegant examples of Virginia plantation architecture."

Fielding Harrison, (1680), died, June 11, 1829, in Sangamon. His ashes rest in the old family burial ground near the site of his home. His widow, Ann, died in Alton, Illinois, in August, 1835.

In brief, their children were:

(16801) PEYTON L.—b. Sept. 7, 1804; d. ——; m. Nov. 13, 1827, Elizabeth B. Cartwright, dau. of Rev. Peter Cartwright.
See further record.

(16802) JOHN F.—b. Feb. 5, 1807; d. ——; m. Parthenia Harrison, dau. of Ezekiel B. (1775).
See further reference.

(16803) PEACHY A.—b. Nov. 19, 1809, d. 1866, m. Robert Harrison, "her cousin," son of William, (1681).
See further record.

(16804) MARY E.—b. June 5, 1811, d. ——; m. Irwin Randall, of Sangamon. Resided in Edwardsville, Ill. One account says no issue.

(16805) SIMEON QUINN—b. Sept. 27, 1816; d. June 1, 1883; m. Mary A. Renshaw.
See further record.

(16806) MARTHA JANE—b. Jan. 31, 1820; d. ——; m. James Harrison, d. July 8, 1873, son of William, (1681).
See below.

(See Power's *History of Sangamon Co., Ill.*, p. 359; all but Martha J. named in the letter to D. S. H., 1914, from which the date of Simeon Q. is gleaned.)

(1681) WILLIAM HARRISON, ( ), the son of Col. Benjamin Harrison, (167), and wife Mary, married, August 25, 1801, Jane Young. She was living in 1806, and died before 1810. On April 17, 1810, he married, 2nd, Mary McClure.

Both of William's marriage bonds were recorded in Rockingham; his surety in the second instance being Peachy Harrison, (his brother). From these circumstances it is apparent that both wives were residents of the county at the time of their marriages.

One, Samuel Young, Jr., is named in the *Heads of Families* census, 1784, as a resident of Rockingham, having in his family, "9 White souls." William Young of Augusta, whose will was proven in 1811, had a Harrison son-in-law, but his name is given as Robert, although three of this Young's Harrison grandchildren had names similar to three of William Harrison's children. (See page 361.) The testator left a wife Elizabeth, sons James and William, and a daughter Margaret, who married Robert Anderson.

A William Young, of Kingsoss, Philadelphia County, cordwainer, February 15, 1763, gave power of attorney to John Madison of Augusta County, Virginia, to convey to William Davis, of Philadelphia, 400 acres of land on New or Woods River. The paper was acknowledged by Isaac Vato and John Kirke, of Philadelphia, before Henry Harrison, the mayor thereof. Daniel Young of Augusta on the 10th December, 1764, conveyed to Samuel Beard 260 acres "at Snoden's Spring." His deed was witnessed by Thomas and Jeremiah Harrison, and one other. (Deed Book 11, pp. 400 and 842.)

John Young, the Revolutionary soldier who served in the Rockingham militia under Capt. Robert Cravens, Jr., in 1780, mentions in his declaration that he was born in Lancaster County, Pennsylvania. In March, 1783, he moved to Kanawha, but later appears to have returned to Augusta, his declaration being filed there. (See page 297.)

Mary McClure, the second wife of William Harrison, was likely a kinswoman of his mother.

Sometime following his second marriage (and the date of his father's will), William Harrison emigrated to Christian County, Kentucky, where his brother Fielding had earlier located. From there he removed, about the same time as the latter, to Sangamon County, Illinois. (See Fielding Harrison above.)

William Harrison's (1681), children by his two marirages were:

(16811) William Henry—

(16812) Robert—d. 1855 or 56; m. Peachy A. Harrison, (16803), dau. of Fielding. See further reference.

(16813) James—d. July 8, 1873; m. Martha Jane Harrison, (16806), dau. of Fielding. Removed to Shullsburg, Wis. See further record.

(16814) Martha—

(16815) Maria—

(16816) Benjamin—

(16817) Elizabeth—

(Same references as Fielding, above. All but William Henry named also in D. S. H. MSS.)

(1684), PARTHENIA HARRISON, ( ), the daughter of Col. Benjamin Harrison, (167), and wife Mary, married, April 2, 1804, Reuben Harrison, (1772), the son of Ezekiel Harrison. See Clan of Thomas Harrison, Line of Ezekiel Harrison.

CLAN OF THOMAS HARRISON

LINE OF JOHN HARRISON

(1751) THOMAS HARRISON, ( ), the son of John Harrison, (175), and wife Betty, about 1820 removed with his family to Washington County, Tennessee; thus passed from Rockingham the only "Harrison" heirs of John Harrison's line.

Three of the founder of Harrisonburg's sons had early heard the call of the great West, and of the three with families remaining, all the sons and daughters of two, with an exception or so in the case of a daughter, or of a death, are believed to have answered. Only the family of Reuben is known to have remained in Rockingham; and even among his children there was a later migration.

Thomas Harrison's wife was Mary Curry, the daughter of Adam and Ann Curry.

He and Mary were married April 10, 1792. They are thought to have settled in the region of Rogersville, Tennessee.

The Currys were another instance of Rockingham's settlers being early interested in western lands. Their name, like those of several other prominent lines at the time allied with the Harrisons, has long since largely disappeared from the county. The family appears to have come in about the close of the French and Indian War. Nicholas Curry, of Fayette County, Kentucky, in a deposition, 19th, November, 1800, in McWilliams vs. Hollingshead, states that his father settled in Augusta in the fall of 1767.

RAGAN

(1753) PHOEBE HARRISON, (-1800 c), the daughter of John Harrison, (175), and wife Betty, married March 1, 1792, Daniel Ragan (or Reagan). In her father's will, proven 1806, a bequest was made to her children, "as if their mother was yet living." (See page 325.) She was deceased by 1802, in which year, November 18th Daniel Ragan married, 2nd, Malinda Harrison, (1774), the daughter of his first wife's uncle, Ezekiel Harrison.

Daniel Ragan was undoubtedly a near kinsman of Jeremiah Ragan, who married Capt. Daniel Harrison's daughter Abigail, (166.) (See page 213.) The Ragans, similar to the Currys, began early to remove from Rockingham, and as completely passed from her history. Jeremiah, by 1802, was living in Washington County, Virginia. In a letter from James Crow, of this county, dated 3rd August., 1802, as filed among the papers in McWilliam vs. Hollingshead, the writer acknowledges a request to obtain a deposition of Jeremiah Ragan, whom he knew "35 years ago." At the time Jeremiah and James' father were residing as near neighbors.

Daniel Ragan, and wife Phoebe, (1753), had issue—

(17531) Nancy—
(17532) Sally—
(17533) Polly—

Daniel Ragan, and wife Malinda, (1774), had issue—

(17741) Jeanetta—
(17742) Preston—
(17743) George Washington—
(17744) Lucinda—
(17745) Betty—
(17746) Malinda—
(17747) Peggy H.—
(17748) Robert—
(All named in D. S. H. MSS.; no further record.)

KISER

(1755), MARY HARRISON, (   ), the daughter of John Harrison, (175), and wife Betty, married October 23, 1783, Isaac Kiser.

The Kisers were an early family in the region of what is now Page County, Virginia, and came into the Valley from Pennsylvania. One Charles Keyser, the son of Johannes

Kiser Farm

and Barbara (Funk) Keyser, (c. 1744), a descendant of Direk Keyser, of Amsterdam, Holland, the immigrant, married a daughter of Dr. Shelly, of Philadelphia, "and moved from Germantown, Pennsylvania, to Page County, prior to the Revolution." (See, * *The Keyser Family*, by Charles S. Keyser, 1889, p. 153.)

Isaac, Kiser or Keiser, is presumed to have settled in Ohio, where various of his descendants now reside, some in Greenville, and Mansfield.

LINE OF THOMAS HARRISON, JR.

HAMILTON

(1765) EDITH HARRISON, (   ), the daughter of Thomas Harrison, Jr., (176), and wife Sarah, married Rev. Samuel Hamilton, of Hagerstown, Maryland. The Rev. Hamilton migrated with his family to the West, and "preached in Ohio, Indiana, and Charleston, Virginia." He was a member of the Ohio Conference (Methodist ?), and appears to have finally located in Lancaster, Ohio, where his wife died, and was buried. About 1855 he employed an eniment lawyer, Thomas Ewing, of Lancaster, to "go to Harrisonburg to collect money due from the estate of Edith's father, $2,000 more or less, which he got as Mrs. Hamilton's share."

Rev. Hamilton and wife Edith, (1765), had issue—

(17651) MARY—
(17652) JANE—
(17653) SUSAN—
(17654) EDITH—

One of these married John Milton Balthis, b. 1827, Zanesville, Ohio, who in 1915 was residing at "Orchard Farm," Clifton, Illinois. (Letter from same February 5, 1915, to D. S. H., wherein all four, and his own daughter, Edith, are named—see also *History of Iroquois Co., Ill.*, for further account of Mr. Balthis.)

LINE OF EZEKIEL HARRISON

(1771) JESSE HARRISON, (1777-1872), the son of Ezekiel Harrison, (177), and wife Sarah, born in Rockingham County, Virginia, married there, May 26, 1801, "his cousin," Rachel Harrison, (1263), the daughter of Reuben Harrison, Sr. (Capt. Reuben), who gave his consent. The Rev. Anderson Moffett performed the marriage ceremony. (See pages 311 and 312, and Old Marriage Record Book of Rockingham.)

Jesse's *maison natle*, the home of his father, was in the neighborhood known as Long Meadows, to the west of the recent Mauzy P. O., now Mauzy. Near by lived John Harrison, a brother of his future wife. (See page 376.) Following his marriage and Capt. Reuben Harrison's death, Jesse probably resided on some of the Captain's land; his wife having inherited a tract under the will of her father.

From Rockingham, Jesse and his family emigrated, about 1816, to Christian County, Kentucky, and from there, in 1822, to Sangamon County, Illinois. After a stay of but two years in Sangamon he passed on to Missouri. He is presumed to have accompained his father on his migration to Kentucky, and was with him on his removal to Illinois.

Rachel, his wife, died after reaching Missouri. Says Power, "he married again, had five children, and died on the evening of Dec. 31, 1872, at Mexico, Audrain County, Missouri." *(History of Sangamon Co., Ill.*, p. 358.)

His death occurred at the home of Abner Harrison, his adopted son and nephew, who cared for him in his declining years.

Abner Harrison was born in Rockingham County, Virginia, October 14, 1808, and died at Mexico, Missouri, in 1877. His father and mother, one of whom—presumably the latter—is thought to have been a Pitts, died when he was very young, and his uncle Jesse raised him as one of his own children, not informing him that he (Jesse) was his uncle until grown. Owing to some disagreement between the families of his parents as to who should adopt him, it seems that Jesse, when he took him, changed his name, and in doing so eliminated the name Pitt therefrom. Rachel Harrison, Jesse's wife, had a brother Abner, who died in December 1807, from which circumstances it would appear that young Abner may have been named for him, although the late D. S. Harrison, in his correspondence says—"I have a faint recollection of having seen the record of a Harrison marrying a Pitts, and if my recollection is correct, that Harrison's name was Abner. I also think that he was a brother of Jesse Harrison."

An Abner Harrison, likely of the Rockingham line, was settled sometime before the War of 1812 in Tennessee. He served in the war from this state, being commissioned therefrom 2nd Lieutenant of the 3rd rifle regt., 13th March, 1814, and honorably discharged 15th June, 1815. (See, Heitman's *Historical Register of U. S. Army,* Vol. I, p. 504.) One of the name, a "second cousin" of Daniel Harrison, son of David, Rachel's brother, lived in Washington County, Tennessee, by the time of, and directly after, the War-between-the-States, and was known personally to Jacob Harrison, son of Daniel, as stated in Jacob's writings.

Jesse Harrison, (1771), and wife Rachel, (1263), had issue—

(17711) EMILY—m. Andrew Monroe.
See further record.
Likely others.

(The names of Jesse's 2nd wife, and children are unknown.)

(17801) ABNER—b. 1808; d. 1877; Jesse's adopted son, married and raised a family. Youngest daughter, Mrs. Loutie Harrison Brannock, living at Mexico, Mo., 1921.

(1772) REUBEN HARRISON, (1779-1852), the son of Ezekiel Harrison, (177), and wife Sarah, born in Rockingham County, Virginia, June 12, 1779, married in Rockingham, April 2, 1804. Parthenia Frances Harrison, (1684), the daughter of Col. Benjamin Harrison. The Rev. William Hughs was the officiating minister.

To this union was born one child, named in Col. Harrison's will as Castle Harrison. Some years prior to the Colonel's death, Parthenia died, after which her husband married again.

Reuben's second wife was Barbara A. Harnsberger, (Anna Barbara), whom he married in Rockingham, November 29, 1810. The minister on this occasion was Rev. Gerard Morgan. (See Old Marriage Record Book of Rockingham.)

Barbara Harnsberger, (1788-1842), was the daughter of Conard Harnsberger, (1758-1814), of Rockingham, who served, in 1777, in Capt. Thomas Buck's Company, 8th Virginia Regt., and who married, in 1778, Anna Barbara Miller, (b. 1751), the daughter of Henry Miller, son of Adam Miller, the Massanutten settler. (See page 112; also *Lineage Book*, 65, p. 18, National Society Daughters of the American Revolution; and letter Mrs. A. H. L. to D. S. H. February 20, 1922.)

Three children were born to Reuben and Barbara in Virginia. In 1815, or 1818, he emigrated to Christian County, Kentucky, where one more child was born. Thence, with his wife and children, he removed in company with his father, several brothers and their families, to Sangamon County, Illinois, in 1822, arriving on Richland Creek November 4th, that year.

Reuben settled as a near neighbor of his father. In 1832, as revealed by the latter's declaration of military services, he (Reuben) was one of the County Commissioners of his county. (See page 295.) His office was in Springfield.

Sangamon, owing to its great extent and natural wealth, was called, "The Empire County," of Illinois. By 1835, the population was 17,573. Springfield in 1837, (when Lincoln went there to live), boasted about 1,500 inhabitants. Her broad streets were unpaved, and sidewalks and street lights were unknown. The court house, a brick structure, "surrounded by a green pleasant lawn enclosed by a railing," stood in the center of the public square. There were six churches in the town, two Presbyterian, two Baptists, and one each Methodist and Episcopalian.

Reuben Harrison's wife, Barbara, died in Sangamon, August 23, 1842. After her death he appears to have made his home with his eldest son, Leonard Castle (or Cassel) Harrison, who resided by this time at Summerfield, near Selma, Alabama. He died at Summerfield, May 3, 1852.

Reuben Harrison's (1772), children were—

By 1st wife, Parthenia, (1684),

(17721) Leonard Castle, (Rev.)—b. Feb. 4, 1805; d. 1867; m. Sarah J. Wynne. Resided in Alabama.
See further record.

By 2nd wife, Barbara,

(17722) George M. (M. D.)—b. Mar. 20, 1813; d. Sept. 1, 1873; m. 1st., May 28, 1840, Maria B. C. J. Houston, dau. of Rev. Wm. and wife Nancy, (1784.) She d. Jan. 11, 1845. He m., 2nd, Mary A. Megredy, living 1873.
See further record.

(17723) John H.—b. Apr. 6, 1815; d. ——; m. May 17, 1843, Sarah A. Conover, b. Mar. 15, 1825.
See further record.

(17724) Sarah U.—b. Dec. 20, 1817; d. July 4, 1849; m. Feb. 14, 1849, Daniel Megredy, of Sangamon.

(17725) Malinda A—b. Mar. 20, 1820; d. ——; m. in Sangamon, Henry M. Harnsberger.

(See, Power's *History of Sangamon Co., Ill.*, p. 358.)

(1773) GEORGE W. HARRISON, (1781-1821), the son of Ezekiel Harrison, (177), wife Sarah, was born in Rockingham County, Virginia, August 1, 1781. On April 22, 1807, he was admitted to the bar at Harrisonburg. (See, *Wayland*, p. 351.) In 1810, he signed, as surety, his brother Reuben's marriage bond to marry Barbara Harnsberger. (See, Strickler's *Rockingham Co., Va. Marriages.*). He removed with his father and brothers in 1815, to Christian County, Kentucky, and after a short stay there returned to Harrisonburg. The house which he built was known as the Old Castle, and contained, besides the rooms for his residence, his library and law office. Says Mrs. Carr, in her *My Recollection of Rocktown*, "I remember him well . . . He was a perfect gentleman, was sick for a long time with white swelling—when I was a little child, I went to see him every day—he was generally reclining on a lounge. He would call me to him and kiss me, telling me about my mother, whom he was very fond of. I remember when he died and went to see him . . ." etc. (Pages 4, and 29.) By his will, proven in Christian County, Kentucky, 1821, he devised the residue of his estate to "Catherine Harrison, daughter of my Uncle Reuben Harrison of Harrisonburg, Va." (See page 336.)

(1774) MALINDA HARRISON, (1783-), the daughter of Ezekiel Harrison, (177), and wife Sarah, born in Rockingham County, November 19, 1783, married there November 18, 1802, Daniel Ragan. The minister was the Rev. Anderson Moffett, pastor of the Smiths Creek Baptist Church. (See, Old Marriage Record Book of Rockingham.) She was Daniel's second wife, his first having been Phoebe Harrison, (1753), the daughter of John. See line of John Harrison above.

(1775) EZEKIEL B. HARRISON, (1786-1851), the son of Ezekiel Harrison, (177), and wife Sarah, born in Rockingham County, July 19, 1786, married in Rockingham December 5, 1809, Ann Bell. The minister was "Bro. Reynolds." (Old Marriage Book, as above.) Bell

Four Bell families were very early in Augusta. Three of these were each headed by James Bell, the other by Joseph Bell. All four families were distinguished. It is presumed that Ann belonged to "The South River Bells", of whom one of the above James Bells was the head. (See, *Waddell*, p. 288.)

Ezekiel B., and wife, passed by the same route to Sangamon County, Illinois, as his father and brothers; settling first in Christian County, Kentucky, and later removing in company with them to Sangamon. Six children were born to the couple in Kentucky, one of whom, a twin, died on the way to Illinois. Four more children were born to them in Sangamon, after which the mother died in that county. Ezekiel later married, as his second wife, Elizabeth Stewart. He died at Petersburg, Illinois, June, 1851.

Of the children of Ezekiel B. Harrison, (1775), and wife Ann—

(17751) Milton B.—m. Mrs. Martha Sutton, nee Hunter. Residing in Petersburg, Ill., 1873.
See further record.

(17752) Lucinda P.—m. Enoch Megredy, of Sangamon.

(17753) Parthenia—m. John F. Harrison, (16802), son of Fielding.

(1777) LUCINDA B. HARRISON, (1792-1873), the daughter of Ezekiel Harrison, (177), and wife Sarah, born in Rockingham, March 13, 1792, emigrated with her parents, first to Kentucky, and from there to Illinois. She married in Sangamon, Rev. Theophilus Sweet, and died at the home of her nephew, John H. Harrison, August 20, 1873.

LINE OF REUBEN HARRISON

p139

HOUSTON

(1784) NANCY HARRISON (1798-1862), the daughter of Reuben Harrison, (178), Proprietor of Harrisonburg, and wife Mary, was born in Harrisonburg, and died in Rockingham County. She married December 15, 1814, Rev. William Houston, (1781-1852), a minister of the Methodist Episcopal Church.

"William Houston, had travelled twelve years in the Kentucky Conference," says Armstrong, the historian of the Old Baltimore Conference, "entering in 1798 at the age of nineteen, was sent as a Missionary to the Southwestern Territories, enduring great hardships, was transferred in 1813 to the Baltimore Conference, and travelled a few years, when his health failing, he was made supernumerary and died April 27, 1852. He had a vigorous mind, an extensive knowledge of history and geography, and was proficient in biblical and theological lore. He died in full hope of immortal life." (See, *History of the Old Baltimore Conference,* by J. E. Armstrong, p. 400.)

Rev. Houston was the son of Athony Houston, and wife Mary, and the grandson of Anthony Houston, Sr., who emigrated from England, and settled about 1710 in New Castle County, Delaware. (See page 134.) The Delaware connection, and something of the history of Anthony, II, is disclosed in an old letter penned by William's daughter (Amantha) to an enquiring neice—

> "My great grandfather Houston came from England and settled in the state of Delaware, U. S.. I think his son Anthony who was my grandfather moved to Jamestown, Virginia, from thence to Rockbridge County, Virginia, and when my father William Houston was five years of age the family removed to Scott County, Kentucky, 12 miles from Lexington the county seat.
>
> My father William and his brother Anthony were Methodist ministers. John Houston my father's brother went to Darke County, Ohio. Anthony Houston (my grandfather's) children were, Anthony, Wm., (my father), John, Stevens, Charles, and one other son James, I think; daughters Ruth, Hannah, Elizabeth, Jacyntha, Phoebe and Judith.
>
> My father (Wm.) died in Rockingham County, April 27, 1852, aged 71 years, 8 mo. 22 days, sustaining a supernumerary relation to the Methodist E. Church. He told us often of the name of the shire from which they emigrated to U. S."

Anthony "Huston," on May 21, 1778, was among those allowed a bounty for wolf scalps by the Court of Augusta County. (See, List of wolf scalps, *Chalkley,* Vol I, p. 483)

The name Houston on the court records is variously spelled Houston and Huston. Rev. William pronounced it as it was spelled, Houston, not Huston. This is also the pronunciation commonly used in Delaware today, where the family has long been a distinguished one.

Anthony Houston, the father of William, died in Scott County, Kentucky, in 1831. A copy of his will, as recorded at Georgetown, the county seat—in an old volume whose edges have been badly charred on passing through a fire—follows—

Will of Anthony Houston

"In the name of God Amen, I Anthony Houston of the County of Scott in the State of Kentucky, being weak in body but of sound and disposing mind and memory taking into consideration the certainty of death and the uncertainty of the term thereof and that I may be the better prepared in my worldly concern to leave this world when it shall please Almighty God to call me hence do make and ordain this my last will and testament consisting of one sheet of paper.

Imprimes—I commit my soul into the hand of God who gave it and my body to the earth to be decently burried in Christian burrial at the discretion of my Exor hereinafter named.

Item. I will that all my just debts be paid . . . .

. . . .

and fire wood together with all the black people during . . . . their boys Amos, Samuel and George to be hers during . . . . and bedding on Plugh two horses and gear for the same . . . . . Chest of drawers and one spinning wheel which is in lien of her right of . . . .

Item. I give and devise all my land except what I have already devised to my sons . . . . bequeath to my wife as aforesaid during her natural life or widowhood. . . . . to William Houston Anthony G. Houston and Ina M. Houston . . . . . . heirs and assigns forever to be divided so as to make them three equal . . . . estate in a fair and equatable settlement and they the said William . . . . shall pay to the female heirs of my estate Eight Hundred dollars in the following . . . . . . to my daughter Hanna Shuff One hundred dollars to the children of my . . . . Hill decd one hundred dollars to my daughter Mary McMillan one hundred dollars to the children of my daughter Phebe Coleman decd one hundred dollars to my daughter Sallie one hundred dollars and no more of my estate to my daughter Cynthia Tilford one hundred dollars to my daughter Ina M. Houston one hundred dollars which said bequest of one hundred dollars to my said daughters are not to be paid by my sons William, Anthony . . . . until after they shall have come into posession of my real estate after the deceased or widowhodd of my said wife Mary Houston.

Item.—I give and bequeath to the heirs of my son Jas Houston decd fifty one dollars worth of household furniture and live property to-wit; Madaline twenty dollars Mary Jane one dollar, Lura Ann five dollars Jas. W. H. Houston five dollars and no more of my estate.

Item—I give and bequeath unto my daughter Judith Houston her choice of all my horses and a good saddle and bridle and first rate bed and bedding with a high post bed stead one beaureau two cows four . . . . . five dollars worth of cupboard ware.

Iem—After the payment of the aforesaid legacys of anything remain of my personal estate I will it to be equally divided among my daughters Hanna Shuff the children of Elizabeth Hill, decd . . . McMillan the children of Phebe Coleman decd Sallie Rotell, Cynthia Tilford and Jacob Houston.

Item—It is my will and desire in case it shoud become necessary for my said sons . . . . Anthony and John to sell the premises devised to them on which I now reside that they . . . . . half acre of groud to include the burrying ground in the Orchard and the . . . . . . and regress to the same for all family connections who may at any time freely visit there to burry their dead there if they chose.

Lastly I do appoint my thwo sons Anthony G. Houston and Charles C. Houston to be Exors of this my last will and testament and do hereby invest them with full authority to carry it into effect acording to the true intent and meaning thereof, hereby revoking and annulling all other and former will or wills or codicils by me made, declaring and publishing . . . and only last will and testament . . . . and acknowledged by Anthony Houston the testator . . . . . . presence of us who at his request do witness the same

Anthony Houston, (Seal.)

. . . . Hume
Thos Sherritt
Auston Bradford. Jun

Scott County Sct. October Court 1831.
The foregoing last will and testament of Anthony Houston decd was this day returned to Court and proven by the oath of George Hume . . . . and Austin Bradford Jr and ordered . . . .

Att Ben B. Ford, Clk.

(Will Book E, 1829-32, p. 274.)

The Houston land was at Newton, and in Harrison County. Scott County was formed from Fayette in 1792. Numerous records of other Houstons, members of another Rockbridge family, are found at Lexington, the county seat of Fayette. Anthony is said to have been a kinsman of this family.

John Houston, the immigrant of this family, came to America about 1735, from the north of Ireland, in company with his mother, his wife, nee Cunningham, and six children. He located first in Pennsylvaia, whence he removed to Old Augusta (now Rockbridge) County, Virginia, and settled on the "Borden Tract," near where Old Providence Church was a little later built. He was born in 1690, and died testate in Augusta, in 1754, and was buried at Old Providence Church. (Will at Staunton; Will Book 2, p. 40.) Two of his sons were Robert (b. 1720), who married Margaret Davidson, (dau. of Samuel and Ann Dunlop Davidson), and John, who married Sarah Todd. Robert had a son Samuel who married Elizabeth Paxton. (The Paxtons immigrated to America with the Houstons). Samuel died in 1806, and his widow removed with her family to Blount County, Tennessee. Among their children was a son Samuel, (born in Rockbridge, March 2, 1793, died in Texas, July 26, 1863), the later Gen. Sam Houston of Texas fame. Of the sons of John Houston and Sarah Todd, John (b. 1750), and Robert, removed to Kentucky. Samuel, another son, became a Presbyterian minister, and lived in Rockbridge County, Virginia. (See, *The Houston Family,* by Rev. Samuel Rutherford Houston, D. D., pub. at Cincinnati, O. 1882.)

This family of Houstons was predominently Presbyterian from its beginning in Augusta. The immigrant was one of the founders of Old Providence Church. The Anthony Houston line is said to have been Presbyterian also, down to the time of Revs. William and Anthony. The story is told of the disappointment of some of John Houston's descendants at their "cousins" becoming Methodist ministers.

Following his retirement from the ministry as an active pastor, Rev. William Houston resided in Rockingham on Smiths Creek, a short distance north of Lacey Spring. He had lost the sight of one eye, and on retirement engaged in farming and operating a mill.

The great wheel of his day has long ceased to turn, and the property has changed hands many times since Sheridan passed that way, but the fires of the great boaster's wrath could not blot the old minister's name from the site, nor cease for a season so much as one wild goose from being guided on his homeward flight by the familiar old landmark—the Old Houston Mill.

Near by, on the slope of the hill, as it arose to the westward from the mill site, stood the old home. High up on the crest of the slope grew a spreading tree, overlooking the whole landscape for miles around. Today under its deep shade, and guarded by the ruins of a once fine old stone wall, marking the bounds of the residue of the Houston land, there stands a dark grey headstone—

"In Memory of Rev. William Houston, Born on August 5th 1781, Died April 27th 1852, aged 70 years 8 months and 22 days."

Nancy Houston, his wife, died May 3, 1862, aged 63 years, 4 mo., 27 days.

William Houston, and wife Nancy, (1784), had issue—

(17841) William Parker Harrison—b. Feb. 11, 1816; d. Nov. 4, 1816.

(17842) Maria B. C. J.—b. ——; d. Jan. 11, 1845; m. May 28, 1840, Dr. Geo. M. Harrison, (17722), son of Reuben. Removed to Ill. See further record.

(17843) AMANTHA L.—b. Aug. 22, 1821; d.1897; m. Theodore N. Jordan, 1844 c, See further record.

(17844) ALSCINDA B.—b. Jan. 25, 1823; d. Nov. 28, 1887; m. Mar. 20, 1848; Samuel Bowman, b. May 16, 1825, d. July 1, 1858. See further record.

(17845) JOHN WESLEY CLARKE—b. Jan. 20, 1828; d. Nov. 22, 1869; m. Jan. 20, 1853, Rachel Huffman, dau. of John, b. Oct. 6, 1826, d. April 15, 1900. She m. 2nd. Louis Berry, of Ohio. See further record.

(17846) PHILIP GEORGE ASBURY—b. Mar. 23, 1830; d. Mar. 24, 1830.

(17847) FRANCES—b. ——; d.——; m. Shelton Carrier, of Keezeltown, Va.; no issue.

(17848) W. LEE O.—b. Mar. 15, 1834; d. Sept. 19, 1869; m., Jan. 17, 1861, Grizzell Ann Earnest, b. 1838, d. Apr. 12, 1871. See further record.

(17849) ZERUIAH A. B.—b. ——; d. Sept. 12, 1907, m. James Hall, removed to Iowa. See further record.

(17850) CATHERINE—b. Mar. 10, 1838; d. same day.

(17851) JULIA—b. Sept. 23, 1839; d. June 15, 1868; m. William I. Paul, son of Isaac. See further record.

(All but the first, 6th, and 10th named in the Wilson chart, as children of Nancy H. Houston. Wm. Parker, John W. C., Philip Geo. Asbury, and Catherine, buried in the old Houston cemetery. Alscinda, and her husband, buried in Lacey Spring Cemetery, and Julia Paul, in Woodbine Cemetery, Harrisonburg.)

(1785) WILLIAM CRAVENS HARRISON, (1803-1888), the son of Reuben Harrison, (178), "Proprietor of Harrisonburg," and wife Mary, born in Harrisonburg, November 9, 1803, married, at the old Daniel Matthews home, Locust Grove, (see page (337) Mildred Linza Williams, the daughter of George Henson Williams, (b. November 25, 1809, d. August 30, 1887), and wife Elmira. She (Mildred) was born March 27, 1838.

William Harrison resided in Harrisonburg. He married somewhat late in life, and following his death his family removed to Eastern Virginia, in or near Emporia. His death occurred January 16, 1888. His wife died December 8, 1909. (See page 339.) Their children were three, viz.:

(17851) MYRA—Resides at Warrenton, N. C.; owner of two of the original land patents to Thomas Harrison, founder of Harrisonburg; the first for 258 acres, the second for 1290 acres.

(17852) GEORGE—Residing at Warrenton, N. C., (1930).

(17853) BRUCE—Residing at Warrenton, N. C., (1930.)

SMITH

(1786), JULIA HARRISON, (1806-1883), the daughter of Reuben Harrison, (178), Proprietor of Harrisonburg, and wife Mary, born at Harrisonburg, January 3, 1806, married Edward H. Smith, (16611), born July 1, 1799, the son of William Smith, and wife Diana, nee McDonough. (See page 391.)

Edward and Julia Smith resided at Smithland, near Harrisonburg, on the old plantation of his grandfather, Col. Daniel Smith. They lived in the present residence, which stands somewhat nearer the pike—The Long Grey Trail— than the original, and was built sometime before the War-between-the-States, either by Edward, himself, or his father. When the new house was built the old one was allowed to remain standing, and it was since the property has passed out of the possession of the family that the original house has been dismantled. (See page 211 and 318.)

Smithland, the home of Ed. Smith, was built of generous proportions, and built to last. Possessed of ample means, and a great number of slaves, no expense or labor was spared by its builder to build it one of the finest residences in Rockingham; and so it stands today. Its tall columned portico and massive brick walls, its wide center hall and ascending stairway, its great high-ceilinged rooms, and deep-throated fireplaces, have welcomed, sheltered, and cheered a host of its master's and mistress's relatives and friends.

But its floors have not always felt the tread of friendly feet; nor its windows looked out on peaceful scenes. Murder has been plotted in its old slave quarters, to be further done in its kitchen. Haughty Yankee officers have pounded at its door, and demanded admitttance; rude foreign tongued subalterns have ransacked its interior from rock-ribbed celler to slate-roofed attic; and hostile soldiers have lolled under the trees on its lawns, trampled its boxwoods, denuded its gardens, and camped within the penciled shadows of its chimneys. The forbidden lover, too, has trespassed on its premises, as Romeo like, under the curtain of night, he awaited at the base of its high second-storied rear porch for his fair Juliet to drop from her balcony into his welcoming arms, and with him to swiftly fly over the hills, to the nearest friendly parson.

It was left for its proud mistress in the loneliness of her widowhood to experience these trying days. On April 24, 1852, Ed Smith signed his will, and died. He left no children. By his will he devised that at his wife's death his slaves were to be set free and transported out of Virginia, and that the remainder of his estate was to go to thirteen nephews and neices. (See, Old Burnt Will Book of Rockingham, before referred to.)

Julia, the widow, a short time after her husband's decease, engaged as her manager and overseer her nephew, John Houston. (See page 409.) He, having in the meantime married, established his home in the original Smithland residence. A few years before the war, and subsequent to his settlement, some of the slaves got word of their coming freedom under the provisions of the Smith will, and decided to hasten the event. They plotted to murder both their mistress and overseer by poisoning the breakfast coffee at the two residences. Houston owned a negro house boy who was taken into the plot. He was instructed to apply the poison at his master's home, while one of the others on the same morning was to apply it at the Smithland residence, proper. The boy carried out his part, and Mr. Houston and his family were made violently ill, but fortunately, due to an overdose, their stomachs refused to retain the stuff. The quick aid of a physician was also employed. The other plotters failed, for some cause, to fulfil their intentions, on the morning arranged. About eight, or ten, of the slaves involved were convicted, and sent to the penitentiary, or sold, among whom was a portly old negro mammy, who loudly proclaimed her innocence.

The old mammy after a short term was released by the war, and of her own free will returned immediately to Smithland, On her arrival, in the pride of her newly won freedom, she knocked at the front door, and Mrs. Smith, all unsuspecting, happened to answer by opening the door in person. At the sight of her former mistress the old negro in her joy completely forgot her new "dignity"; threw her arms around her much astonished mistress, kissed her and wept, before the aristocratic old lady had time to realize it.

Mrs. Smith was very fond of children, and always had some of her small grand-nephews or nieces around. Several of these remembered the incident. Mammy was allowed to remain. The war, of course freed all the slaves but a few of the older ones —the old mammy among them—were given a home in their old quarters until death.

The war not only freed the slaves, long before Edward Smith's intention, but very much impoverished his widow otherwise. During its course she invested heavily in Confederate bonds. Peace found her fields in desolation, fences torn down, barn in ruins, farm implements stolen, stock driven off, slaves gone, and bonds worthless.

Such, however, was the lot of a Southerner, and with true southern fortitude she faced the future. Following the death of John Houston, her nephew, in 1869, another nephew, the late T. A. Jordan, managed the property for her.

"Julia Harrison, wife of Edward H. Smith," died February 23, 1883. Her body was laid beside that of her husband, in Woodbine Cemetery, Harrisonburg,—the spot is marked by a chaste monument (enclosed by an ornate iron fence)—on which the names and dates of both appear.

CLAN OF CAPT. ROBERT CRAVENS

LINE OF JOHN CRAVENS

(1414) WILLIAM CRAVENS, (1766-1826), the son of John Cravens, (141), and wife Margaret, married, 1749, Jean Harrison, (1678), the daughter of Col. Benjamin Harrison; surety S. McWilliams. (See pages 323, 345, and *Wayland*, p. 444.)

William Cravens, upon his marriage, settled in or near Harrisonburg. He is said to have been somewhat inclined to intemperance as a young man, before joining the church and entering its ministry. He was a man of powerful physique, and was doubtless the individual of the same name who had served as Deputy Sheriff in 1790. (See page 352.) The story is told, that on one occasion during his church services, finding himself interrupted in the midst of his sermon by some rowdies in the congregation, he stopped short in his discourse, calmly descended from the pulpit, walked quietly down the isle to where his disturbers sat, and ejected them bodily, after which he resumed his sermon as unperturbed as if nothing had happened.

He was one of the first Methodist ministers of Rockingham; and a beloved and prominent one. The fragrance of his memory long lingered in the county after his removal therefrom.

Today there are no Cravens in Rockingham, all having passed from her hills; either by death, or by way of "the great western migration." Both John Cravens, and his brother Robert, the Major, left sons, later founders of distinguished lines in the South and West. Their descendants have numbered many eminent men in their chosen professions, and several—among them a grandson, and a nephew of Rev. William—have graced the legislative halls of the nation.

As one of the heirs of John Cravens, deceased, William, (and wife) in 1810, signed the deed conveying his interest in his late father's 470 acres of land on Linville Creek, to his brother Joseph. (See page 344.) In November, 1810, he joined his brothers Joseph and James, and his brother-in-law, Joseph Snapp, in executing a deed to Robert Belshe, "in completion of a sale made in 1768 by John Cravens deceased,"

—200 acres on the banks of Linville Creek—"the bed thereof . . . .of the water does not appear to have been conveyed," etc. (Rockingham D. B. 1, p. 533.)

The exact date of Rev. Cravens ordination as a pastor is not known. His name appears on the first marriage book of Rockingham, as that of the officiating clergyman, at a marriage February 4, 1811, and continues as such to as late as March 15, 1814. (See Strickler's *Rockingham Co. Marriages*, p. 110 and 49.)

About 1815, he removed, with his family, to Indiana. His removal occurred, says the Nourse genealogy, while Indiana was a territory, The state was admitted to the Union in 1816. He became a noted circuit rider and travelled in both Indiana and Illinois. He settled at Madison, in Indiana, but in his old age bought land four miles south of Salem, in the same State, on the Martinsburg and Salem Road, in Washington County, where he was buried. (One account states that he died, October 10, 1826.) His wife died in 1835.

Rev. William Cravens, (1414), and wife Jean, had issue—

(14141) Hannah—m. Rev. William Shanks.
(14142) John—m., 1818 c, Ann Christopher Newman, of Va.
See further record.
(14143) Benjamin—m. Margaret Blackburn.
(All named in the *Times Dispatch* article, wherein the wife of John is named as Ann C. Newman. (See page 322.)

(1415) JOSEPH CRAVENS, (1769-1842), the son of John Cravens, (141), and wife Margaret, married November 30, 1790, Mary Nickle, the daughter of John Nickle, of Augusta County. (See page 345.) The officiating clergyman was Rev. Benjamin Irvin, the pastor of the Cooks Creek Presbyterian Church. (See page 321—Rev. Erwin's name appears spelled various ways.)

John Nickel, Sr., (Nickle, Nichol), the grand-father of Mary Nickle, (Polly as she was called), in will, 24th March, 1755, names wife Barbara, eldest son John, sons Joseph and Thomas, and daughter Elizabeth. Executors, wife and her brother, and . . . McComb. Witness, Alexander Blair, and James Reaburn. Will proved August 17, 1774. Barbara Nickel and Andw McComb, qualified executors. (Original Wills, Augusta Co., 1774.)

Edwin Nichol, of the " County of Madison," of Virginia, on November 6, 1822, was deeded by Joseph Cravens, and Mary his wife, "of the Town of Harrisonburg," 17 acres of land adjoining the said town, and "lying on the northwest square of said town and known by the name of said Cravens lot, beginning on Main or German St. . . . part of inclusive survey, 1773, to Thomas Harrison," Land conveyed by Reuben Harrison to Geo. Sites, and by Sites to Joseph Cravens. (Rockingham D. B. 6, p. 126.)

Joseph Cravens and Mary, following their marriage, made their home in Harrisonburg, Virginia, where he was a prominent physician "for about fifty years." He was one of Rockingham's distinguished citizens, and among the first of his profession to practice in the town. He is thought to have attended Rush Medical College, in Philadelphia, as did his cousin, Dr. Peachy Harrison, his contemporary.

From 1831 to 1833, Dr. Cravens represented the Valley country in the Virginia State Senate. He was a man of fine intellect and an influential public speaker. During the Cravens vs. Lanahan cause, although he had engaged counsel, he frequently conducted the cross-examination himself.

Joseph Cravens is named as a member of Rockingham Militia Company No. 5, in 1792. In the personal property tax list of 1797, he appears as the owner of one slave and three horses; in 1811, as the owner of two slaves and two horses; and 1812, as the owner of one slave and six horses. From 1811 to 1813 he was assessed for two "White tithables," and prior thereto for only one—himself. (Original Tax Lists of Rockingham.)

Dr. Cravens became early interested in Harrisonburg's development, and between September 1791, and July 1826, was the granter and grantee of some twenty-six deeds, about thirteen of each class. A few of these of more particular interest mentioning some of the old landmarks of the town follow—

> Sept. 6, 1791; Joseph Cravens and Mary, his wife, to William Carroll, Lot 36 feet front, 100 back, part of lot sold by Robert and Reuben Harrison to said Cravens, part of an Acre Lott known by the name of No. 12, in the South East Square, adjoining John Smith's. (Rockingham Original Deeds.)
>
> Dec. 20, 1794; Joseph Cravens and Mary, his wife, to James Cravens, Part of that Acre Lot No. 12, in the South East Square, etc. part of a Tract of 1290 acres, Granted to Thomas Harrison, Deceased, by Patent bearing date 1st. March, 1773, "and Left by Said Thomas Harrison Decd, to His two sons Robt & Reuben as will appear from his last will and testament now on record in this county office. Beginning at a Stake on the edge of the Street Near the Public Lott." (Rockingham Original Deeds.)
>
> Feb. 15, 1803; Joseph Cravens and Mary, his wife, of Rockingham, to Jeremiah Kyle of the same county, "a small lott of land in Harrisonburg" that Joseph sold to James Cravens, and he to Alexander Humphres, and Humphres to Kyle; correction of former conveyance. (Rockingham D. B. 000, p. 217.)
>
> May 1814; Joseph Cravens and Polly, his wife, to George Sites, 40 Acres adjoining the town of Harrisonburg, part of same conveyed to Thomas Harrison (Jr.) by Daniel Dickenson, and by Exors. of said Harrison conveyed to J. Gambill, 1810, and to Joseph Cravens in Sept. 1810. "Except that the tan yard is entitled to the privilege of linking a pipe . . . to receive the water from the spring 18 inches below the surface . . . then to be elevated by a pump for family purposes only but not to be employed in the supply of Water Poll or vats." (Rockingham D. B. 2, p. 310.)
>
> July 12, 1821; Joseph Cravens and Mary, his wife, Reuben Harrison and Mary, his wife, to Francis A. Hite. Land adjacent to town of Harrisonburg, 1¾ acres 10 poles, adjoining Samuel McWilliams, north side of Great Road leading from town to Geo. Sites . . . spring near a willow—run mentioned—Reuben Harrison, P. Harrison's corner, near the tan yard. Part of two tracts; 1st. part of 41-5/8 acres conveyed to said Cravens by Henry J. Gambill, the other part of a well known tract of 1291 acres first granted to Thomas Harrison in 1773. (Rockingham D. B. 2, p. 552.)
>
> June 22, 1809; John Rogers to Joseph Cravens, "sell to the Said Joseph Cravens. . . for an during the lifetime of Sarah Kyle, late Sarah Harrison, one certain tract adjoining the Town of Harrisonburg, 100 acres that was laid off to her late husband Thomas Harrison (Jr) deceased, Reference to deed of March 12, 1803. Except 23 acres being a part of the above described land conveyed by Richard Kyle and Sarah his wife to Samuel McWilliams.

Witness Henry Burgess, John Sheltman, Reuben Harrison. (Recorded Feb. 1810. (Rockingham D. B. 0000, p. 504; also No. 1, p. 314, mutilated.)

May 2, 1814; George Sites and Elizabeth, his wife, to Joseph Cravens of the Town of Harrisonburg. One Lott in said town in the north west Square . . . of Lott No. 3. It is on German or Main St., adjoining John Jenkins' Lott. Lott No. 4, Jacob Googler's Lott, Rutherford's lott . . . . Elizabeth St. . . . conveyed to said Sites, the 1st. by Robert and Reuben Harrison, the 2nd. by Thomas Sulivan, and one lott on German St. part of lands of Thomas Harrison contained in inclusive survey, 1773, of 1291 acres. (Rockingham D. B. 2, p. 309, mutilated.)

For a time during his residence in Harrisonburg, Dr. Cravens was associated with Reuben Harrison, his cousin, in conducting a store. By his will of 1799, proved in April 1800, Thomas Harrison, Jr., appointed as his executors, Joseph Cravens, Reuben Harrison, (the testator's brother), Samuel McWilliams, and Benjamin Smith. (See page 329.) In the will Thomas directed his executors to carry on the business of his store for a time.

Further proof that Dr. Cravens was highly regarded by Thomas, is shown by other clauses of the will, one of which provided that a dwelling house be built for his (the testator's) wife and children, "on the Acre lots I last Bought of Reuben Harrison, opposite his stone house," and another, desiring that all of his children "be learned to labor agreeable to their sexes, also to be educated in Literature and put to such places for said purpose as they my said Executors shall think best."

In 1823, Joseph Cravens was one of the executors of the will of Samuel Hemphill, deceased, another relative. (See page 346.) Incidently, in this connection, it is revealed that he (Joseph) was the owner of a "medical shop," or one of the first drug stores of Harrisonburg.

As Hemphill's executor, Joseph Cravens (and John Cravens, his son ?), entered into bond to William Jenkins of Baltimore, Maryland. Joseph's security was Reuben Harrison, above named, and to secure the latter he pledged a part of his personal property, 17th July, 1823, (recorded 12th March, 1824). Among the items listed was one negro boy William, about five years old, 1 desk, 1 book case with 200 books . . . part worn, 1 case of Dramns, etc., . . . and "All the medicines with the medical shop furniture consisting of bottles, mortars, Slabs, surgical & other instruments of the said Joseph Cravens."

Dr. Cravens, and his wife, following his service in the State Senate, removed late in life to Madison, Indiana. Several of his children had settled in Indiana, among them his sons Dr. Robert Cravens, and James Harrison Cravens, the later congressman. He died at Madison in 1842, at the home of his daughter-in-law, Mrs. Stevenson, who had married, as her first husband, his son Robert. Three of her granddaughters live in the same house today (1930), one being the widow (2nd. wife) of Dr. Edward Eggleston, the author.

Dr. Joseph Cravens, (1415), and wife Mary, were the parents of nine children—three of whom followed in his profession, one becoming an eminent physican of Missouri, a fourth—the last named above—inherited his father's predilection for the law.

Briefly, their children were—

(14151) MARGARET, (Peggy)—b. 1792; d. 1833; m. 1811, Francis Asbury Hite, of Harrisonburg. Removed to Madison, Ind. prior to 1830.

(14152) Robert (M. D.)—b. 1794; d. 1821; m. 1818, Sarah Grover Paul, dau. of Col. John Paul, founder of Madison, Indiana. Settled at Madison.
See further record.

(14153) John (M. D.)—b. Oct. 28, 1797; d. Mar. 15, 1882; m. Feb. 15, 1821, Ruhama Chapline, of Maryland, b. Mar. 26, 1805, d. Nov. 26, 1882. Removed to Daviess Co., Mo., 1837.
See further record.

(14154) Sallie—b. 1800; d. 1833; m. 1818, Abraham Hite.

(14155) James Harrison (Congressman)—b. Aug. 2, 1802; d. Dec. 4, 1876; m. 1824, Sophia Capito, b. 1803, d. 1895, dau. of Daniel Capito, of Franklin, now W. Va. Removed to Franklin, 1823, and thence to Madison, Ind., 1829.
See further record.

(14156) Amanda Fitzallen—b. 1804; d. 1884; m. 1820, Jacob R. Kennerly, of Indiana.
See further record.

(14157) Oscar Fitzallen (M. D.),—b. 1808; d. 1841; m. Mary E. McMahon, dau. of Col. William McMahon. Settled in Courtland, Ala., 1836.

(14158) William—b. 1810; d. ——; Removed to Cravensville, Davis Co., Mo., 1840.

(14159) Joseph— . . . . "In Memory of JOSEPH son of Joseph and Mary Cravens who died in this place Feb. 6, 1817, Aged 1 Yr. 3 mo. and 18 days. Suffer little children to come unto me and forbid them not for of such is the Kingdom of God." (Epitaph in old Methodist Churchyard at Harrisonburg.)

(Robert, John, and James, named in *James Nourse and his Descendants*, by Maria Catherine Nourse Lyle, Lexington, Ky., 1897, p. 38.)

(1416) JAMES CRAVENS, (1773-1821), the son of John Cravens, (141), and wife Margaret, born in Rockingham County, Virginia, April 12, 1773, was conveyed "Part of that Acre Lott No. 12, in the South East Square," of Harrisonburg, by his brother Joseph Cravens, in 1794. (See above.) In 1810 along with his brothers, William and Joseph, he joined in confirming his deceased father's sale of Linville Creek land, originally sold in 1768.

A part of the days of his youth—between the years 1782 and 1787— were spent in the home of a relative in Tennessee, (not Kentucky—see page 344.) He married in Greene County, this State, in 1797, Ann Love, the daughter of Thomas and Dorothy Love, of the said county. Although back in Rockingham again for a period following his marriage, he returned after his third child was born to Green County, and settled.

Thomas Love and wife were from Fauquier County, Virginia. His first deed in Tennessee is dated in 1787. His will, proved in Green County, May 1810, names besides his wife, children, Mary, Lucy, Martha, Ann, Dorothy, John, Philip, William, and Charles.

After residing for a time in Tennessee, James Cravens removed with his family to Selma, Alabama. Both he and his wife died in Alabama, in 1821.

Their children were eight in number, viz;

(14161) MARY—m. in Ala., Jacob Shelly; Col. in the Mexican War. See further record.
(14162) MARGARET—m. Samuel Swan.
(14163) ROBERT—b. 1805, in Rockingham County, Va.; d. Dec. 1886; m. 1st., in Rockingham, Catherine Roddy, dau. of Jesse Roddy, of Tenn. m. 2nd., Caroline Cunningham; no issue by last marriage. See further record.
(14164) ANN—m. ——; Roberts.
(14165) DOROTHY—m. Thomas Ball.
(14166) ELIZABETH—m. Jacob Haley.
(14167) MARTHA—m. Pleasant Lea.
(14168) SARAH—d. unmarried.
(From list kindly supplied by Mrs. (Dr.) Geo. R. West, of Chattanooga, Tenn., a descendant of Robert.)

SNAPP

(1417) MARGARET CRAVENS, (1775-), the daughter of John Cravens, (141), and wife Margaret, married in Rockingham, October 1, 1793, Joseph Snapp; surety Robert Cravens. (See, *Strickler*, p. 107; *Wayland*, p. 444.)

Joseph Snapp appears to have been the son of John Snapp, Sr., who, in 1813, owned land on Mill Creek, in Rockingham. On January 20, 1821, Joseph Cravens and Mary, his wife, conveyed to Philip Rymell, 81 acres, "Land on Mill Creek first conveyed by Jno. Snapp Sen. to Joseph Snapp, Mar. 16, 1813." (Rockingham D. B. 5, p. 176.)

One branch of the Snapp family, probably descendants of Joseph, or of his brother, have long been residents on Smiths Creek in southern Shenandoah County, in the region of New Market.

LINE OF SAMUEL HEMPHILL

MILLER

(1462) AGNES HEMPHILL, ( ), the daughter of Samuel Hemphill, and wife Mary, (146), nee Cravens, married in 1795, Jacob Miller. (See, *Strickler*, p. 84.) In her father's will, recorded in Rockingham, April 1809, a bequest was made to his three Miller grandchildren, viz;

(14621) MARY—
(14622) JOHN—
(14623) BENJAMIN—
(See page 346; no further record.)

(1464) SAMUEL HEMPHILL, JR., ( ), the youngest son of Samuel Hemphill (Sr.) and wife Mary, (164), nee Cravens, married, in 1799, Clarinda Solford; surety James Smith. By his father's will Samuel, Jr., was devised land, which he later sold, by 1815, to Jeremiah Kyle, of Rockingahm. In "Miller vs. Hemphill," bill 1815, (See page 264), it is stated that Samuel Senr's son Samuel is now dead, leaving besides his widow, Clarinda, children, all infants, viz;

(14641) RUTH—
(14642) ROBERT—
(14643) MARY—
(14644) JOHN—
(14645) SAMUEL—
(No further record.)

LINE OF MAJOR ROBERT CRAVENS

(1481) JEREMIAH CRAVENS, (1762-), the son of Major Robert Cravens (148), and wife Hester, married Margaret Harrison, of Rockingahm, thought to have been a daughter of Zebulon Harrison, (121). (See page 362.)

From Rockingham, Jeremiah Cravens "emigrated to South Carlonia, and afterwards moved to Kentucky (settled in Christian County), and from there to Scott County, Missouri, where he died,". Issue, two children—

(14811) HESTER—m. Jesse Cravens, son of Nehemiah, (1484) of Kentucky. See further record.

(14812) ELIZABETH—m. Robert Harrison, "a second cousin," in Christian Co., Ky. "Emigrated South."

(1482), ELIZABETH CRAVENS, (1763-1837), the daughter of Major Robert Cravens, (148), and wife Hester, married in 1782-3, Benjamin Smith, (1656), son of Col. Daniel Smith. See Clan of Capt. Daniel Harrison, Line of Col. Daniel Smith. (Page 390.)

(1483), WILLIAM CRAVENS, (1764-1832), the son of Major Robert Cravens, (148), and wife Hester, born in Augusta, later Rockingham County, Virginia, died in Madison County, Missouri. His route from Rockingham to Missouri was by way of the Indian Lands in South Carolina, where he remained two years, thence to Frankfort, Kentucky, where he stopped one year, thence to Christian County, Kentucky, and finally, in 1810, to Cape Giradeau, later Madison County, Missouri.

William Cravens married, in "1789 odd", Mary Lamma (pronounced Lamb), "born in Rockingham Co., about 1768," probably daughter of William Lam of Rockingham, who in the *Heads of Families* census, 1784, was enumerated as having in his family, "7 White souls," and owning "2 Dwellings, 2 Other buildings." (Jacob, Henry, and Michael Lame, are also listed in this census.) One Natham "Lammy", of Rockingham, married in 1782, Nancy Ralston, of near Harrisonburg. (See, Strickler's *Rockingham Co. Marriages*, p. 75.)

William Cravens and wife both died in 1832, within two or three days of each other—she first. Their children were—

(14831) ROBERT—b. ——; d. ——, in S. C. in infancy.

(14832) MARGARET—b. ——, in S. C.; d. ——; m. Jeremiah Cravens, in Ky., son of Robert Cravens, "being second cousins." Removed to Missouri, about 1808, and thence to Arkansas.

(14833) ELEANOR—b. Nov. 1791, near Frankfort, Ky.; d.——; m. 1st, Henry Straim, in Ky., m. 2nd., in Mo., James McFadden. See further record.

(14834) NANCY—b. ——; d. 1827 c; m. 1816 c, in Mo., Samuel H. Thompson, removed to Ill.

(14835) JEREMIAH—b. Nov. 20, 1796; d. Mar. 16, 1849; m. Mar. 28, 1818, in Madison Co., Mo., Kiturah (Kitty) Murphy, dau. of William and Rachel (Henderson) Murphy. See further record.

(14836) JESSE J.—b. 1799 c; d. ——; m. in Mo., Martha Logan.

(14837) ELIZABETH—b. 1801 c; d. ——; m. 1826, in Mo., Moses Vandivirs.

(14838) NEHEMIAH—b. Dec. 15, 1803; m. 1825, in Mo., Sophia Thompson, d. 1862.

Removed to present Logan Co., Arkansas, 1831, where was living 1889. See further record.

(14839) FINIS—b. 1806; d. ——; m. 1830 c, in Mo., Susan McFadden.

(14840) ABIGAIL—b. 1808; d. ——; m. 1826 c., Squire Stiles.

(All but first two born in Kentucky.)

(1484) NEHEMIAH CRAVENS, ( ),—sometimes called "Mi.", or Michael Cravens,—son of Major Robert Cravens, (148), and wife Hester, born in Augusta, later Rockingham County, Virginia, migrated prior to 1802, to "Ohio County in the State of Virginia," where in 1806 he sold a tract of land on "Wheeling Creek" (see page 263.) He married Sallie McCullough (or McCullock), of Wheeling, present West Virginia. He resided for a time in Christian County, Kentucky, and from there moved to Washington County, Missouri, in which county he died. Following his death his wife returned to Wheeling. A son—

(14841) JESSE—m. Hester Cravens, (14811), the daughter of Jeremiah. See further record.

SMITH

(1485) MARGARET CRAVENS, ( ), the daughter of Major Robert Cravens, (148), and wife Hester, married April 2, 1792, Henry Smith, (b. 1758) the son of Capt. Abraham Smith, and wife Sarah Caldwell; surety Wm. Cravens. (See pages 199, 238, and 259.)

Abraham Smith was a brother of Col. Daniel Smith. He was a Captain in the French and Indian War from September 11, 1756 to April 19, 1760. Upon the organization of Rockingham County he became one of the first justices, and was the county's first County Lieutenant. He resided near North Mountain on a large estate called "Egypt". His children were two sons, of whom John (b. Dec. 16, 1775), the eldest, participated in the battle of Point Pleasant, as an Ensign in his uncle Daniel Smith's company, and was later a Revolutionary soldier. John married, in 1755, Mary Jane Smith, of Culpeper County, whose first husband was Silas Hart. Henry, the youngest son, inherited the home plantation. (See *Waddell*, p. 51.) One account relates that he later migrated to Ohio.

Henry Smith and wife Margaret, (1485), had issue—

(14851) BENJAMIN—removed to Kentucky.

(14852) WILLIAM—removed to Georgia.

(14853) ABRAHAM—

(See *Boogher*, p. 336.)

CLAN OF ALEXANDER HERRING

LINE OF WILLIAM HERRING

(1951) ALEXANDER HERRING, (1766-), the son of William Herring, (195), and wife Elizabeth, married in Rockingham, in 1793, (1797 ?), Margaret Reed Smith, (16511), the daughter of John Smith. (See page 390.) She was born in 1777, and at the time of her marriage her father was deceased, thus her mother's consent—surety Samuel McWilliams. It is related that four of her uncles served in Gen. Morgan's riflemen during the Revolution.

Alexander and Margaret Herring resided in Rockingham on a part of the original Herring land, near Dayton. In speaking of the grandsons of the pioneer Herring, the author of the *Memoirs of Lincoln* remarks—"They held and their descendants continue to hold every acre of the original rich fertile land . . . One of these farmers left to his heirs 6,800 acres originally granted to his mother's brother for revolutionary services, having been one of Washington's generals. Two others of these grandsons left over a thousand acres each of fine farm land in a high state of cultivation, still held by their heirs." (Pages 44-45.)

The 6,800 acres of bounty land were located mostly, if not all, beyond the Alleghanies. Reference here is evidently made to Major David Stephenson. (Major, 5th, 11th, and 6th Va. Regiments, Continental Line, 4th May 1778, to 1st Jan. 1783; Heitman's *Historical Register of Officers of the Continental Army,* p. 381.) Aside from this land, whether inherited by Alexander, or his brother William S., or both, the former was the owner of a large tract of land in Rockingham.

From 1789 to 1825, Alexander Herring was the county surveyor. *(Wayland,* p. 442.). He was a man of considerable wealth for his day, and a public spirited and influential citizen. It is said that he offered his services in the War of 1812, when over 60 years of age, (over 46) along with one of his sons only sixteen.

As a witness for the defendant, September 20, 1816, in Cravens vs. Lanahan, "Alexander Herring about the age of 50" deposed—"he went to school to Michael Mullin who taught at a place called Fisher's Spring. . . and that Joseph Cravens & James Cravens went at the same time, and he thinks Peggy Cravens also. Question. Was there a man by the name of Mathew Boyers who kept school in that neighborhood? Ans. There was a man who lived in that neighborhood . . . who taught school . . . but none of my father's family went to him," etc.

Alexander Herring, (1951), and wife Margaret, had issue—

(19511) John Smith—b. 1798; d. 1830, unmarried, at Lexington, Ky. Grad. of law at Washington University, now Washington & Lee. Member of Va. State Senate. At time of death was commissioned to survey "Virginia's large military reservation in western Kentucky."

(19512) Martha Davis—b. Apr. 2, 1799; d. Jan. 19, 1866; m. Mar. 14, 1822, George Harrison Chrisman, (12602), son of John Chrisman, b. Sept. 23, 1799, d. Sept. 15, 1870.
See further record.

(19513) Eliza—b. 1800; d. ——; unmarried.

(19514) William—b. 1804; d. ——.

(19515) Alexander—b. 1806; d. ——. Is said to have died young on Illinois River, at Pekin. Student at Washington University, and West Point. Settled in Ohio.

(19516) Daniel Smith—b. 1808; d. —— young, unmarried, "among the everglades in Florida while fighting Osceola under Gen. Taylor." Grad. from West Point.

(19517) Margaret Davis—b. Aug. 11, 1810; d. Oct. 7, 1902, unmarried.

(19518) Stephenson—b. 1812; d. —— unmarried, "on Mississippi River."

(19519) Rebecca—b. 1814; d. in childhood.

(19520) Ann Harrison—b. 1816; d. Nov. 27, 1887; m. 1st. Judge Madison McAfee, of Miss., m. 2nd., Dr. William C. Richardson, of Rockingham.

(All named in D. S. H. MSS. Tombstones of second in New Erection Churchyard, and of seventh, and tenth, in Woodbine Cemetery, at Harrisonburg, from which their dates are taken. See also *Lea and Hutchinson,* p. 108, and Chrisman's *Memoirs of Lincoln,* p. 45.)

CHAPTER XX

"Missouri Bound"–1822

JOHN HARRISON'S JOURNAL

AMONG THE TRAVELLERS to the West, in 1822, from Virginia, was JOHN HARRISON, of Rockingham County—the eldest son of David Harrison, (1259) —who set out from Harrisonburg on horse back, "Monday the 7th October." His companion was his cousin, Jehu Warren, (12585), of Harrisonburg, the son of Thomas Warren. (See pages 378 and 381.) The object of his trip was to see the country, possibly with some thought of settling. His way led through a number of localities in which various of his relatives, whose migrations have been followed, had settled, and doubtless many of these were visited.

On his journey John Harrison wrote a description of the country over which he passed, appending thereto a detailed account of his expenses, his mileage made from day to day, his lodging points, etc. Much attention was paid to the kinds of soil, and varieties of timber found. Numerous rivers were encountered over which it was necessary to ferry, or to pay toll. Many of the towns noticed, then mere struggling villages, are today large and important cities.

He travelled as far west as "Journeys," Montgomery County, Missouri, some distance beyond St. Louis, where on the 26th November, he turned his course "towards Virginia." Taking a different route east than that over which he had passed on his way west, he arrived the last day of the year (1822) at "Woodley's," the home of a relative at Town Creek, near McMinnville, Tennessee, at which point his journal ends. After stopping there for several months, during which interval he taught a school, he continued home, arriving back in Rockingham after an absence of about six months.

His original Journal, of which the following is a copy in full, (except that the title has been adopted), is in booklet form, penned in an excellent hand, and is now in the possession of his daughter, Miss Fannie Harrison, of Harrisonburg. She also owns the pistol which he carried on the trip.

JOHN HARRISON'S DESCRIPTION OF HIS TRIP TO THE COUNTY WEST OF ST. LOUIS IN 1822

THE following is a full account of my expenditures preparatory to my departure from Rockingham Oct. the 7th 1822.

Sept. the 9th 1822
Then Bought in the Town of New Market

	Dol. cts.
1 Pair of Saddle Bags	5.00
1 H(at?)	2.22-¾
1 Whip	.75
1 Shirt	1.45-¾
1 Waist Coat	1.50
1 Pocket Knife	.37-½
1 Pocket Comb	.25
Had my Saddle Pad stuffed	.25
1 Pocket Book	.37-½

September the 14th 1822.

Then Bought in the Town of Harrisonburgh

		Dol. cts.
	Trimmings for one Coat	2.00
1	Blanket	.25
	MAKING one Coat	3.50
1	Pair of Boots	6.50
1	Pair of Leggins	1.25
1	Saddle cover	2.00
1	Umbrella	3.75
1	Pair of Martaingill Hooks and putting them on	.50
1	Saddle Bag Lock	.25
2	Gerths	.75
	Preparatory Expense	$ 33.96

SEPTEMBER the 9th. 1822	D. cts.
Then Received	5.31
Sept. the 26th. Received	10.00
Same day Received	13.00
Sept. the 18th. Received	3.50
October the 5th. Received	6.50
Oct. the 6th Received	50.00
Total	$88.31

MONDAY the 7th Oct. 1822.

Left Harrisonburg and directed our course towards Ohio, through Gennings Gap: On leaving Harrisonburg, about 6 miles; we began to leave behind us the blue Limestone Rock, so peculiar to that place and with it that richness of soil peculiar to Limestone: We now began to approach a Sandy, Gravely, and Mountainous; in some places the soil is mixed with Sand, in others with Gravel, and in others with a kind of Slate Gravel, both of white, and red, colors; the latter however is peculiar to the Mountains;

This country is covered principally, with Black Oak, White Oak, and Pine, both Pitch and Spruce, interspersed; which continues to be the case untill you leave the head waters of James River: Also it is full of stupendous Mountains, and watered by a Great number of delightful Springs, especially in Bath county, which particularly is abundant in Springs and well adapted to Grass: The soil in the whole scope of country, from a distance of 6 or 8 miles, beyond Harrisonburg, is of on inferior quality, except along the Rivers, which afford now and then a good plantation. The Rivers, are first the N. Fork of Shenandoah, which affords but little good Bottoms; second the Calf Pasture; which affords but little more, the Bull Pasture, which none; the Cow Pasture, which affords but little; Jacksons River which affords some excellent bottoms, and nice plantations; this River is the largest yet mentioned, and is the principal branch of James River.

In passing from Rockingham, to Green Brier; we passed through Augusta, Bath, by the Warm Spring, and then took the Antonys Creek road, and crossed the Aleghany Mountain, to Green Brier County: Here the soil appears to be of a better quality as soon as you get on the Western waters: But to the full as broken, with hills, and Mountains, and, (if possible) better adapted to Grass.

The soil is not of so fertile a quality except along the Rivers, and Creeks; Which are 1st. Anthonys Creek, & Howards Creek, both of which have some excelent bottoms; But of inferior wedth, Green Brier River, has no good bottoms as I saw; but is a considerable River, and is the principal branch of New River, crossed this River near Lewisburg, after passing the White Sulphur Spring.

These Springs, are the resort of numerous Gentry, during the months of July, August, and September, Who visit them for their health, numbers of whom receive unquestionable benefit from the waters; as is also the case with the warm, and hot Springs, in Bath County. The warm, and hot Springs, is undoubtedly a great natural curiosity; the water issues from the former, in a sufficient quantity to turn a Mill, and is above the temperature of Blood, the hot Springs, I am told, does not afford such a quantity of water, but is about the temperature or near, that of scalding: near each there is a beautiful Spring of cold water.

Passing LEWISBURG, which is an inconsiderable town, and the first (that deserves the Name) after leaving Harrisonburg; The country for a small distance on this side of the Town resembles Rockingham, except the hills, which are more in number and higher, more natural to Grass &c. Crossing Meadow Mountain, from here; wee came on Meadow River, which is on inconsiderable stream, But remarkable for the immense quantity of Alder, that grows on its banks; stops the brush, and forms frifts, which keeps the bottoms a Swamp; which are in places of considerable wedth; and ware it not for this impediment, would make excellent meadows; the adjacent country is poor, and hilly.

Leaving Meadow River, we passed Suel Mountain, New River, and the New River clifts. This River is the main branch of Kanhawa, and would be navigable were it not for it falls near Kanhawa, above which it affords a navigation at Spring freshets. Passing from here, wee passed through a narrow strip of Giles County, thence crossing Cotton hill to Kanhawa County. The country from Green Brier county, to the Kanhawa is scarcely any thing but an uninterrupted range of Mountains, in many places of stupendious hight, forming with their abrupt ends, and turns, many astonishing scenes; Precipices! rising almost perpendicular, to the height of a hundred feet, with trees, standing up their sides in places, and in others bear; with the sun scorching their naked Rock, giving it a portion of Grandure, and Awe. enraptures the eye of the beholder. Mounting one of these precipices and casting a look around you would imagine (for a moment,) the whole United States, ware Mountains.

Desending Cotton hill, to the Kanhawa river; I was much transported with the beauty of the scene, that then presented itself to my view: On either side, the mountains rose magestically, almost to the height of the clouds,—At their base rolled the river, delightfully, wafting away the surplus produce to distant markets—the land exhibiting the most abundant fertility along its banks.—Soon as wee passed down it a few miles, the Salt furnaces, began to make their appearance, they are on both sides of the River, for about 7 miles down it;—they are an immens avenue of wealth the owners thereof,—close on the bank of the River, there is a natural curiosity called the Burning spring (a small puddle of water) which takes fire on presenting a torch, and burns untill extinguished with so much heat as to boil water; Stone coal, is also abundant here; Passed down the River through CHARLESTON which is the county seat of Kanhawa and a handsome little town: crossed Elk river at the mouth, and took a right hand road, which penetrated again into the mountains, and hills; which continue without any striking variation, until we came on Mill Creek, which has excellent bottoms which are peculiarly adapted to grass, but not exceeding 4 hundred yards wide in many places; these continue to be our road to the Ohio river. The country from Kanhawa to Mill creek is one continual range of hills, and mountains producing excellent range and not very stony, but too steep by far for cultivation.

In passing from Kanhawa to the Ohio river wee passed over 3 mile creek, and Pokatalico each of which have now and then a good spot of Land along their banks. The hills from Kanhawa, to the Ohio, are generally covered with Oak, and the bottoms (where there are any) with sugar, ash and Buckeye. Mason county lies between Kanhawa and Ohio rver. The Ohio is undoubtedly the handsomest of any of the western rivers that I have seen; being about 5 or 6 hundred yards wide at low water, and of a sufficient depth to float the largest of boats, even Ships at Spring freshets. The bottoms along this River are abundantly fertile, and about from 1 to 2 miles wide, exhibiting some delightful, and well watered farms for a new country, crossed this river, at Seelart Falls. Timber on these bottoms is generally Walnut, Elm, Hackberry, Hickory, Grape Vine, and Pawpaw.

Leaving the Ohio river, wee began to take a Hilly, and on some places a Mountainous country; generally poor, (except along the Hockhocking, covered with White Oak, Black Oak, Poplar occasionally, and Hickory: which continued until wee reached New Landcaster; except along the Hockhocking, the bottoms of which ware generally covered with Beach, Poplar and Walnut &c. In passing from the Ohio river, to New Landcaster; wee passed first, through Meigs county, cross Shade river, in this county; which is an inconsiderable stream; but which affords some good land along its banks; though in but small quantities; second through Athen county; crossed the Hockhocking at ATHENS; This is but a small river, in many places, not more than 30 or 40 feet wide; yet so deep as to be navigable for boats to Athens, 40 or 50 miles from its mouth: Its current runs but slow, and its bottoms extremely low and wet, the banks in many places being higher than the adjacent bottoms: it is however the better adapted to grass, for which Ohio is famous.

Athens, on this river is a delightful little place, well built, and is the seat of the OHIO UNIVERSITY. The bottoms along the Hockhocking, are much inferior to those of the Ohio, or Kanhawa, in producing corn. Passed from Athens through Hocking county to NEW LANDCASTER on the Hockhocking, Fairfield County: This is a delightful Town; and well built; generally of Brick: It contains several handsome Public buildings: particularily Churches, on the Methodist, and Catholic order; a Brewery and, Millinery. Leaving New Landcaster, wee began to take a delightful fertile and level country, covered with Beach, Black Walnut, Honey Locus, Elm, Sugar Maple, White Oak, (Occasionally) Black and White Ash &c., peculiarly adapted to the culture of grass or grain. Leaving New Landcaster we passed Over Walnut creek, to JACKSONVILLE, which is an inconsiderable town, same county: Where I tarried some time, which time I employed in viewing the country round about, which I found the most fertile of any that ever I had seen; also bying level, and of an elegant soil to cultivate; this kind of soil continues untill you leave the opposite side of the Scioto river. In passing from New Landcaster to the Scioto, we passed over Black lick, and Big Belly, which are inconsiderable streams; the bottoms along them are little superior to the adjacent land, it all resembling bottom more than uplan; then to COLUMBUS, and elegant and promising town about 3 quarters of a mile in length along the Scioto, it is the present metropolis of the State; and contains the United States court house, and a Penetentiary: The town is generally built of brick; and I am informed was a wilderness in 1812.

FRANKLETON on the opposite side of the river, is an elegant little town, and contains a jail court house &c and (if I mistake not) is the county seat of Union Co.; Columbus, is situated in Franklin County. The Scioto on which these two Towns are situated is a neat little river, about 100 yards wide at Columbus, at low water; Clear, of a rapid current, and Gravelly bottom; it is only navigable this high at high water: This river affords some elegant and fertile bottoms from 1 to 2 miles wide.

Leaving Columbus, we began to take country apparently poorer; with more Oake, Less Beach less Ash &c: which continued about 12 miles. when we came to an opening containing perhaps 1000 Acres; Called the big Prairie; the land in and about which was almost like unto a dung-hill; being covered in the Prairie, with grass as high as a mans head; and round the edge with Swamp Oak, White Elm, and Grape Vine &c.

Leaving the big Prairie we began to take a country somewhat more hilly and poor; with no beach, but covered principally with Oak, and Hazel brush, of which there is an abundance, especially, about Big Darby creek; Crossed big Darby, (which is an inconsiderable stream, and has no bottoms) and began to take the Prairies of Ohio; which are covered with grass, similar to the big Prairie, with now and then a small Grove of Burr Oaks, interspersed, but not of as fertile soil, as the big Prairie, but of much greater extent being perhaps 10, or 12 miles in breadth:—water is uncommonly scarce all over this Prairie.

Leaving the Prairie, all around there appears to be springs, of water as usual in this country, they are small. Crossed little Darby, about the head of which there are some good land, and nice Springs. Leaving little Darby wee began to take a country, somewhat poorer; covered with White Oak, Hickory and Burr Oak, where there is any Prairies: which are to be seen occasionally untill you reach SPRINGFIELD though not so large as those between big and little Darby. Springfield is a snug little town, the county seat of Clark County situated on . . . . *(two lines blank)*

Passed through Springfield and began to take the hill, which lie between Springfield, and DAYTON; these hills are tolerable land, covered with Oak, Hickory, Ash, and Beach, occasionally mix ed: In passing from Springfield, to Dayton, we passed along the banks of Mad river, which are very fertile, and well watered; the bottoms along the River, in some places are Prairies; in others covered with Sugar, Beach, and Hackberry: They are generally from ½ to a mile wide.

Leaving Mad river, we went on over a country somewhat leveler than that about Mad river, to Dayton, (Green County,) This is a beautiful town, and the Largest from Rockingham to it, by the rout that wee travelled; situated on the bank of the Great Miama; which is a swift runing river, with gravelly bottom, about 100 yards wide; and navigable at high water: The bottoms along it are excelent, about from 1 to 2 miles wide, affording many an elegant farm; and is said by some to be the best part of the State: Dayton is the seat of justice for Green County, crossing the Great Miama, we imediately took a Beach county, similar to that about Jacksonville; which continued to Paint Creek: covered intirely with Beach, Ash, and Sugar; but not of sich a soil as that about Jacksonville altogether. In passing from Deyton, to Paint creek, we passed through Montgomery County and EATON, town, Preble county. Leaving Paint creek, which has some excellent bottoms; (though narrow;) The upland along it is very hilly, and poor; covered principally, with Oak.

Leaving Paint creek, we traveled through an elegant, and well cultivated country to CINCINATTA; especially along the rivers and Creeks: which are first 7 Mile Creek, which bottoms are narrow; but very fertile; the Great Miami, which bottoms are similar to whare last (?) crossed, crossed this River, at FT. HAMILTON, an elegant little town, and the county seat of Butler county. Thence to SPRINGFIELD, another snug villiage: Hamilton county. Thence crossed Mill creek, which is but a tolerable stream; but affords excellent bottoms, from ½ to 1 mile wide; thence to Cincinatta. The country from Paint creek to Cincinatta, is covered along the bottoms with Sugar Maple, Beach, Walnut and Hackberry: The uplands with Beach, Sugar, and Oak. We arrived in Cincinatta on the 10th. of November and tarried there two days; during which time I took a complete view of the place. It is a most delightful, and flourishing town; situated on the N. side of the Ohio river, just above the mouth of the Great . . . . . and is by far the largest town and most comercial one in the State: Steam boats and others are daily arriving and departing from this place, it keeps up an extensive commerce with PHILADELPHIA, and ORLEANS; with the former, by way of WHEELING; thence by the U. S. road; with the latter by the river Ohio, to its junction with the Missisippi; thence by that River. The inhabitants are very enterprising and much given to Mechanical, as well as Commercial persuits: There is here a Mill, 7 stories high; whose operations are performed by steam: Spinning, Carding, and Fulling Machines; are carried on within its walls: all by the same power. Also an Iron and Brass Foundry in this town whare the largest of Bells are cast: and Steam engines, for boats are made of enormous size. The casting of Iron utentials is also carried on at this place. There is also a Musuem here which contains many Natural and Artificial, curiosities: such as the different Savage implements; Grecian, and Roman coins; Monsters of nature, and almost all kinds of wild animals of the West, (skins stuffed) together with bones of the Mammoth. The streets of this Town, are spacious, cross at right angles, and are well paved in many places; There is here also an elegant Church; belonging to the Presbyterians, which (I am told) cost 41,000 dollars: Just below the town there is also a Paper, and Saw Mill; the operations of which are performed by steam. There is also just in the edge of town, a Glass factory.

Leaving Cincinatta we went down the Ohio river; which is about, ¼ of a mile wide here, and much beautifuler than where we crossed it: Crossed Mill creek, and the Great Miami, again, which took us into the State of Indiana. Leaving the Gt. Miami, we passed along the Ohio; over a very hilly, and extremely fertile country: covered with Elm, Ash, Sugar, and Hackberry, which continued, untill we crossed Hogans creek the second time. In passing from the Great Miami to the head water of Hogan Creek: we passed through LAWRENCEBURG, Dearbourn County, which is an inconsiderable place. Over Tanners creek; which is an inconsiderable stream: but affords some excellent bottoms, covered with Hackberry, and Walnut; but not more than 1 quarter of a mile in wedth: Through ARORA; which is a small town: and Over Hogan creek; which is at times sufficiently deep to navigate. It affords some narrow; but fertile bottoms: covered with Walnut, and Hackberry.

Leaving the head waters of Hogan Creek, we began to take Country, recembling that about Jacksonville; but of somewhat poorer soil, and covered with Beach, and Poplar generally; which kind of land continues until you come on the waters of White River. In passing from Hogan, to the waters of White river; we passed 1st. through VERSAILS, crossed Lochra Creek just in the edge of town which is a considerable Creek and navigable for boats at high water: Versails is an inconsiderable town, yet the seat of justice for Ripley county. Thence crossing Graham Creek, and Muskakitak, which is another considerable creek, and navigable for boats at high water; but like Lochra, has no good bottoms: crosses the Muskakitak at VERNON, another inconsiderable town, yet the county seat of Gennings county: Leaving Vernon about 15 miles we came to the water of White River: As soon as we came on the waters of the driftwood fork of White river, the soil became Sandy, somewhat richer, and covered with Beach, Poplar, and Walnut, on the upland; and Beach, Ash, and Hackberry, on the bottoms; which are from ¾ of a mile, to 1½ mile wide and amazeingly fertily, but subject to annual indutations. This, and the other fork of White river, is navigable for the most part of the year, but much filled with drift wood, sand bars &c. Their width is about 60, or 70 yards at low water, the sandy soil continued untill we left the driftwood fork of this river. In passing this river, which we three times crossed we passed first through BROWNSTOWN, which is a little decaying and Sickley town yet, the county seat of Jackson county; then across Driftwood near this place; then crossed Drift *(here ends book one)*

Leaving the River, the country began to be hilly and poor, covered with White Oak, Hickory, and Black Oak; which continued to be the case untill we crossed Driftwood the last time; when we began to take the barrens which lie between this and the other fork of White river, which are covered with Scruby Oaks, Grass, and small Brush, &c. and of an inferior quality; which continued untill wee reached the a little town on the mane fork of White river, called WASHINGTON. In passing from near BONO, to the main fork of White river, we passed first through ORLEANS, which is an inconsiderable town . . . . . county, then through HINDOSTAN, which is another small town, situated on the Driftwood fork of White river; Then crossed White river (Hindostan is in Martian county). Then through Washington, which is a neat, but small town, situated on the mane branch of White river, Davis County. Leaving Washington, we began to take the bottoms along the W. fork of White river, which are remarkable fertile, covered with Beach, Sugar, Walnut, Hackberry, and Pawpa: Crossed the river which is a considerable river, about 100 yds. wide, and navigable at all seasons of the year.

Leaving the river we began to take a country of tolerable fertility, covered with Oaks, White and Black, Popler, Hickery, and Hasel, in places where there are small taverns, which country to VINCENNS; in passing from Washington, to Vincenns, we passed through Honer county. Vincenns, is a tolerable vilage situated on the Wabash river, which is navigable for Stream boats at high water, and for others at all times; it is about 150 yards wide, of a gentle current and gravelly bottom. Vincenns was at first built on the French plan, of low frame houses, plastered without, it however is improving after the American Style. The bottoms along the Wabash, are excellent and generally from 1 to 2 miles wide. Crossing the Wabash to the Illinoi side, we began to take the Prairies of this State; they are of various size, from 5, to 20 miles across, with groves of timber from ½ to 4 or 5 miles wide, seperating them: they are covered with Grass from 8 to 2 feet high without any thing, except a few scattered Oaks, to interrupt the sight. The groves are generally of Scrub Oak, entirely without any thing else, in places, and in places with White, and Red Oak; generally in separate groves. This country is without a hill, that deserves the name; and astonishingly fertile; mostly of a clay soil, although after going 6 or 8 feet they generally come on sand. The country continued thus, without any variation scarcely to St. Louis. I was much delighted with the beauty of the senes that were presented to my view; at one time we would be in the midst of the Prairie in sight of nothing but Grass, and sky, together with the appearance of the distant grove; and at others hemmed in on every side with timber, and at all times surrounded to an unknown distance with the most fertile of Land.

In passing from the Wabash, to the Mississippi; we passed first, through Ellison Prairie, (which is a sand Prairie,) then through LAWRENCEVILLE, which is a small town, built of cabins, Lawrence County: Then through Clubs Prairie; Then through 6 mile Prairie: Then across Tex. river, and the E. and W. forks of the little Wabash; Then through Wayne county; Then through the 12 mile Prairie; Then through Jefferson county, and the Grand Prairie, and Washington country; Then across Kakaskia river and Shoal creek. Then, through LABANON, a small town St. Clair county; Then, through the American (bottoms, which are about 8 miles wide and of a most astonishing fertility) to the Mississippi, which is here about 1 mile and 1 chain in wedth, of rapid current, and of depth sufficient to float the largest of ships: crossed this river to ST. LOUIS; which is an elegant town situated on the W. bank of this river; it was built at first after the French order, but is now improving after the American: it contains a Catholic Church, and U. S. Store. The people of this place are of a very motly complexion, some black, a few White, and numbers of indian colour, Molattos, and Samboos. St. Louis, is situated in St. Louis county, Missouri:

Leaving St. Louis, we began to take a barren, and Prairie like country, covered thinly, with Grass, and Timber ocasionally, generally of Scrub Oak and Hazel, with some Hickory, on the hills; the bottoms, which are those of the Missouri are covered with Elm, Hackberry, Pawpa, Grape vine, and Cotton wood, which country continued to ST. CHARLES, on the Missouri river, this is a small village, built like St. Louis, at first by the French; but is fast improving, it is the present seat of government for the State of Missouri. The river here is about 3/4 of a mile wide, and navigable, of a rapid current, and always of a muddy cast, full of logs which are a great impediment to navigation: The bottoms along it are from 1 to 2 miles wide,, and of the most fertile soil that ever I have seen. The land between St. Louis and St. Charles, rises gradually in to hills, though no hills of magnitude occur. St. Charles is situated in St. Charles county.

Leaving St. Charles, we began to take the country thinly timbered with B. Jack, and Hazel, (though not so poor as Black Jack, land usually is) some what Grevelly, and the intervals between the thickest of the timber, filled with Sedge grass, the country rising gradually into hills; this country continues about 10 miles, when the country began to be of some better quality, and to open into Prairies, the groves between which are mixed with Black and Scrub Oaks; the Prairies here are more hilly than those of Illinois, and the Grass on them is not altogether so high; this kind of country continued until we reached JOURNEYS, Montgomery county.

Leaving Journeys we *turned our course towards Virginia,* and turned to the right for the nearest Ferry in the Missouri river; travelled through a very hilly country, covered with Black and White Oaks, Hickory and Scrub Oak, (Popler occasionally) and of but tolerable soil, to the river which has elegant bottoms here, covered as aforesaid; crossed to NEWPORT, which is a small and indifferent town, Franklin county. Leaving New-Port we traveled down the river about 14 miles, through a country of but tolerable fertility, and much broken with hills, covered principally, with Black Oak, Poplar, and Hickory, Dogwood &c. Leaving the river we began to take a poor hilly, and gravelly country; covered principally with Black Oak, and Black Jack, which continued about 20 miles, when the country began to be barren like in many places, more level, and of a richer soil, covered as aforesaid, which country continues to St. Louis.

Leaving St. Louis, we again took the Prairies of Illinois, which are similar to those of this state, before mentioned, with this exception these groves are more of Red Oak, especially near Big Muddy. Prairies continue without any interruption scarcely, until you reach Big Muddy, after you leave St. Louis. In passing from St. Louis to Big Muddy, we first passed over the Mississippi river; then through St. Clair County; then over

O-Kaw, through Washington County, Over Buckoo and Little Muddy, and through Franklin county, to Big Muddy. It is useless to say anything about the bottoms along the rivers in this State, the upland, and bottoms, being so very much alike, (as it respects fertility) that the difference is not worth nameing: we can only say, the bottoms are more swampy, of a looser soil, and covered with timbers denoting the richest kind of earth: as to the navigation of the rivers of this State, it will be the most easy of any State in the Union: Where ever they are wide enough to admit boats, they are, (in my opinion) deep enough to float them: they are of a muddy cast, and dull current, so that it will be almost as easy navigating them up stream, as down it.

Crossing Big Muddy, we began to take a country somewhat poorer, tolerably level, and covered with Red Oak, White Oak and Hickory, interspersed in some places, which continued to Saline Creek, when the country, began to rise into hills, and be covered with White Oak, Black Oak, Scrub Oak, and Hickory, interspersed and of not altogether so rich a soil, as where the country lay more level. (Viz. North of the Saline Creek.) this country continues to the Ohio river. In passing from Big Muddy, to the Ohio river, we passed, first throngh White county; then over Saline creek, which is an inconsiderable stream, but famous for the Salt works, carried on, on its banks, which are however at this time in a low state of cultivation; it may be noted again, I think, for the number of Gum swamps, along its banks. Then crossing Eagle creek, which is another inconsiderable creek, but like unto Saline, it has a number of Gum Swamps, along its banks. Then through Gallatin County, to the Ohio. There are no rivers, of note from the Mississippi, at St. Louis, to Ohio, on our way from St. Louis, to HOPKINSVILLE, except the Okaw, yet I think that the Big and little Muddy, Saline, and Eagle, may be navigated with success, at any rise of water.

The Illinois, is certainly the most sightly country, I have yet seen, the most fertile in Corn, and has the largest quantity of fertile and tilable Land: yet, in my opinion the Ohio will always exceed it in the production of tame Grass: For although this country is of a clay soil, (generally,) and of soil abundantly rich; yet, it is not possessed of that moistness of soil, requisite to its production.

Crossed the Ohio river, which is here about 1 mile wide, at high water, and began to take the lands of Kentucky, which are tolerable compared with the Illinois, and somewhat broken, and rocky, covered with Black Oak, White Oak Hickory, and Popler, Scrub Oak &c. interspersed; which continued to the Barrens of Kentucky, which are of some richer, though similar soil except the hill and rock, which are some scarcer. These Barrens, are covered with Black Oak, Black Jack, and Hickory, Saplings, interspersed with Hazel, and Sedge grass, which continued untill we reached Red river. In passing from the Ohio river to Red river we first passed through Livingston County; then, through Cauldwell county, and PRINCETON, which is an inconsiderable town though the County seat of Cauldwell county; then across the North Fork of little River to HOPKINSVILLE, Christian Co. This is a neat little village, and in a thriving condition, situated between the N. and S. Fork of Little river, it is the seat of justice for Christian County: Little river, between the Forks of which it is situated, is an inconsiderable stream: Then across the South Fork of Little river; to the West Fork of Red river, which we passed to Red river.

Crossing Red river, which is a small river; (not more than 100 yards wide,) but navigable, and rapid current &c. This river affords but little good bottoms, as I saw. Leaving Red river, we began to take a country, somewhat Generally, and very poor and hilly, covered with Black Oak, White Oak, Hickory, and Dogberry, with a popler, interspersed occasionally; which, continued about 30 miles, when we began to come on the waters of White creek, when the land began to be of a better soil and covered with Beach, Ash, Walnut and Hackberry Buckeye &c. but as much broken with hills, and more with rock, than before; which continued to Cumberland river, about 4 miles, from Whites creek, when we immediately took a poor hilly country, covered with White Oak, Black Oak, and Chestnut, near their sumet; which continued about 4 miles, when we came into a barren like country, very poor and Gravelly, covered with Black Oak, and Black Jack, Saplings, with now and then a Hickory interspersed; which continued untill we reached the spurs of Cumberland Mountain. In passing from Stones river, to Cumberland Mountain, we passed through Marion Co. Over the barren fork of Collins river and over Hickory creek; Passed the first spur of Cumberland Mountain, to town creek along which the land is excellent as it runs through, and heads in, what may be called a Cone; This creek, makes a part of the head waters of the mane branch of Collins river.

Tarried in TOWN CREEK, and *taught a School,* for the term of three Months, in which time I visited the settlements on Collins river about McMINVILLE, and BATTLE CREEK, the Widows creek &c.

But to return to the country we have passed over: it would be well enough to say something about the water, and timber, of the country we have passed over. Leaving the Kanhawa, to which place the country is both watered, and timbered, with the best of Springs, and most beautiful of Oak, the country began to be scarcer of Springs; but still remains well Timbered, with Oak, untill you leave New Landcaster, when the country begans to be covered with Beach, (principally,) and Springs, are somewhat more plenty. Ohio is timbered in parts, almost entirely, with Beach but where it is not timbered with Beach, it may be said to be a heavy timbered country; as is the case with Indiana: The Springs, continue to be tolerably plenty to the barrens of Ohio, when they begin to dissappear, and you see few good Springs, again untill you come on the waters of Mad river, where there are some springs, after which you see few more, untill you reach EATON; Leaving this place we saw few Springs untill we took the Beach, of Indiana, that and beyond that, somed distance there are a tolerable share of springs, after which, a Spring would be about a Phenomina untill you reach St. Louis. Leaving this place we scarcely saw a Spring untill we reached Franklin County. Leaving this place we saw no Springs (save one) untill we came near the Ohio river, where there are a few, on both sides of the river, after which we saw but few untill we reached the barren fork of Collins river; after which we saw them plenty to this place. Leaving the State of Indiana the timber, (whare there is any) is of a low groth and mostly Scrub Oak, Hickory, and Black Jack, untill we reached this place. Water is obtained in the State of Ohio, generally by digging from 6 to 20 feet, and in the Illinois, in from 20, to 60 feet. In both places the digging is uninterrupted by rock.

Next follows tables of expenses. Spelling, punctuation, and capitalization, as in original (The names of the principle towns have been capitalized to better show the route).

EXPENSES other than Lodging, and Ferriage, Toll, &c.	cts.
2 shoes put on my Mare at K,ks.	67
1 shoe nailed on in Vernon,	12-½
Admittance in the Museum,	25
Stuffing my Saddle pad	25
Fixing my Saddle Bags.	12-½

Camphor	19
For Papper	25
Wafers	12-½
Mare shod all around in Hop.	1.12-½
Saddle pad Stuffed	50
unnoticable Expenses	$3.61

		Miles.
MONDAY the 7 October, 1822.		
	Went from Harrisonburg to Nichols	18
8th	From Nichols, to Pauleys,	14
	Same day From Pauleys to O Kanis	24
9th	From O Kans. to the Warm Spring	10
	Same day, From the W,am. Springs to K-g-kads	25
10th	From Kingkads, to the White Sul. Springs	16
	Same day to Lewisburgh	29
11th	From Lewisburgh to Youngs	14
	Same day to Tyrees	26
12th	From Tyrees, to Vandells,	12
	Same day to Morrises	18
13th	From Morrises, to Starks	10
	Same day to Hills	3
14th	From Hills, to Castors	13
	Same day to Fishers	11
15th	From Fishers, to Harrisons	8
17th	From Harrisons to Carneys	15
	Same day to Smiths	20
18th	From Smiths to Steadmans	15
	Same day to Athens	25
19th	From Athens to Nelsonville	12
	Same day to Smiths	14
20th	From Smiths, to N. Landcaster	16
	Same day to Brumfielas	3
21st	From Brumfields to Talmans	16
	Then to Jacksonville	3
Sud. the 3rd November, went,		
	From Jacksonville to Columbus	20
4th	From Columbus to Hoppers	8
	Same day to Sagars	14
6th	From Sagars to Springfield	36
7th	From Springfield to Fairfield	13
	Same day to Millers	22
8th	From Millers to Eaton	14
	Same day to Longinekers	5
9th	From Longinekers, Hamilton	20
	Same day to Springfield	10
10th	From S,p. to Cincinatta	13
12th	From Cincinatta, to Arora	24
13th	From Arora, to Versailles	25

14th	From Versailles to Browens	8
	Same day to Vernon	20
15th	From Vernon to Brownstown	30
16th	From Brownstown to Woods,s	8
	Same day to Trimbles	16
17th	From Trimbles to Orleans	8
	Same day to Johnsons	21
18th	From Johnsons to Hindostan	4
	Same day to Washington	19
19th	From Washington to an Irshmans	12
	Same day to Lawrenceburg	14
20th	From Law. to Clubs	6
	Same day to Mc Cauleys	29
21st	From Mc. C,s. to Illiots	14
	Same day to Roberts	20
22nd	From Roberts to Houstons	15
	Same day to Molicars	28
23rd	From Mar,'s. to Labanon	10
	Same day to St. Louis	10
24th	From St. Louis to St Charles	20
25th	From St. C. to W. Koontz's	10
	Same day to Journeys,	25
26th	From Journeys to N. Port	15
27th	From N. Port to Morrises	14
8th	Dec. From Morris' to Balls	20
9th	From Balls to St. Louis	25
10th	From St. Louis to OGles	9
11th	From O Gles to W. Wleelises	30
12th	From W. Whee's to Vinsons	8
	Same dat to Kirk Patricks	36
13th	From K. P. to Causuawys	35
14th	From Cau's. Waldons	30
15th	From Wal,s. to Williams,s	24
16th	From Wim,s. to Rochesters	25
17th	From Roch,s. to Hopkinville	25
26th	From Hopk'e. to Gardners	33
27th	From Gardeners to Summers	29
29th	From Summers to Marribles	25
30th	From Mar,s. to Capt. Carsons	29
31st	From Carsons to Youngs	10
	Same day to Woodlees	20
		1448

Ferriages.	cts.	Toll over	cts.
Over Newriver	12-1/2	the Hocking at N. L.	6-1/2
the Kanhawa	12-1/2	G. Miami at H.	6-1/4
Elk	12-1/2	Kaskaskia	12-1/2
Great Miami	12-1/2	Shoul Creek	12-1/2
Fanners creek	6-1/4	Ferriage over	
Driftwood 3 times	37-1/2	the Okaw	12-1/2
W. F. of W. river	12-1/2	B. Muddy	12-1/2
Wabash	12-1/2	Saline Creek	12-1/2
E. F. of L Wabash	12-1/2	Ohio	75
Mississippi	50	Red river	12-1/2
Misouri	50	Cumberland	6-1/4
Mississippi	1.00		
Toll over		Tem	$ 5.37-3/4

(Next page torn across about at middle, leaving top missing. Evidently expenses of lodging listed—)

at the W. Spring	30		
Kinkades	87-1/2		
at the W. S. Spring	12-1/2	. . . arks	37-1/2
in Louisburg	87-1/2	Carneys	25
Youngs	37-1/2	Smiths	70
Tyrees	87-1/2	Steadmans	31
Vandells	50	in Athens	67-1/2
Morriss	75	Thomsoons	12-1/2
		Smiths	50
		in N. Landcaster	37-1/2

(. . . . bottom of page . . . .)

(after torn part)—

in Columbus			
Hoppers	31	in Brownstown	75
in Springfield	75	Woods	25
in Fairfield	37-1/2	Trimbles	37-1/2
Millers	31	in Orleans	37-1/2
in Eaton	37-1/2	Johnsons	75
in Hamilton	12-1/2	in Hindostan	37-1/2
in Springfield	67-1/2	in Washington	75

(. . . . last page . . . .)

Tushmans	37-1/2
in Lawrenceburg	75
Cluks	37-1/2
McCauleys	75
Illiots	37-1/2
Roberts	50
Huestons	37-1/2
Mollicers	75
in St. Louis	1.50
in St Charles	1.00
in Labanon	67-1/2
W. Koontzes	37-1/2
Journeys	1.00
in Newport	1.00
Balls	37-1/2
in St. Louis	1.62-1/2
O Glees	75

(then begins second column on page.)

W. Weeliss	torn off.
Winsons	25
Kirkpatricks	1.00
Gasways	75
Waldons	87-1/2
Williams,s.	1.25
Rochesters	1.00
in Hopkinsville	62-1/2
Gardners	1.00
Sumners	1.62-1/2
Marables	87-1/2
Capt. Carsons	50
Youngs	37-1/2
Exps	$ 43.49-3/4

Handwriting very clear, but second book is coming apart badly, and is badly shelf worn.
All copied that was not torn out.

NATHANIEL HARRISON'S JOURNAL.

1823

The year following John Harrison's trip to Missouri, his brother, Nathaniel, made a trip to Champaign County, Ohio, regarding which he wrote a brief account. The original of this was found among the papers of his brother Reuben N. Harrison, and is now in the possession of the family of the latter's son, (the late Charles D. Harrison), of Harrisonburg.

Nathaniel's route to Ohio was by way of a different course than that followed by his brother, John, thus different early towns are named. His Journal reads as below.

* * * * * *

A JOURNAL

From David Harrison's,
On Dry fork Rockingham County
Virginia
To the Western States—
October 1823.

Leaving Dry Fork on the 21st we travelled a N. W. direction to Turlytown about ten miles. Thence a N. E. course to the little Shenandoah river; thence we turned a little N. of W. to Custards among the mountains where we got entertainment that night. The country we seen to day is poor and hilly except on Linvilles Creek where is some good farming lands, but broken with hills: the land is generally broken to the river where it becomes mountain.

Leaving Custards on the 22nd we travelled a north eastern course into Hardy County to Mrs. Wourden's. In the morning we travelled through a very barren part of country among the mountains until we got some distance on Lost river. The people back appear to be lost as well as the river, for we called at several places before we could see any body that would get us breakfast. The bottoms along the river are very narrow but apparently good. These bottoms being situated between the mountains which afford good range, and being well adapted to grass. I think it a good country along the river for raising stock.

Leaving Wardens on the 23 rd we after going a small distance the same course we went the day before left loss river on the right and travelled a west course for several miles in Hampshire County and crossed North river. Thence north course to the Buck Tavern. Thence a north west direction to Romney. Romney is a thriving little village pleasantly situated in a poor part of the country. The land is generally poor; covered principally by pine, whiteoak and blackwalnut—some round oak and a good many whertlebury-bushes. The land is however well adapted to potatoes and the fine ones I saw people digging, being the largest I have ever yet seen.

Leaving Romney on the 24th we travelled a north west direction along the South Branch river till we left it on the right and came to Springfield. From Springfield we travelled a W. course through a little village called Frankfort on Patison Creek. We continued the same course through a little shady vilage called Cressip—across the N. Branch mountain and crossed at a place called Washington's Bottoms into the state of Maryland, Allegghany County and struck the Pavement at Carter's tavern. We travelled the same course on the pavement to Frostborough about five miles; thence a north west course across the Savage mountains to Shavers four miles. The Savage mountain is next to the highest ridge of the alleghany we had to cross. The country we have seen today is gererally mountainously situated and poor with the exception of the S. and N. Branch river bottoms which are very fertile. The part of the bottoms that is timbered is covered principally with sicamore, walnut, and hackberry; the balance of the land from romney to the N. Branch river is covered chiefly with pine, some blackoak, and a good many whurtleberry and scrubby bushes. On entering Maryland the soil became slaty covered mostly with whiteoak to Frostborough. The savage mountain is covered with chestnut Shemistoak & scrubby bushes except on the north west side is some nice white pine timber: in fact the whole of the west side along the pavement to little crossing is covered principally with white pine. The bridge at little crossing over the little Yohoghany river is a very elegant with one arch. It cost 19000 dollars.

Leaving Shavers on the 25th we continued on the pavement across the river above mentioned over Negro Mountain, Kisers Ridge and thence into Pennsylvania Somerset County—across the Winding Ridge to Smithfield 25 miles: thence over the Yohoghany River at Big Crossing. This is a superb bridge with three arches, one 90 one 60 and the other 30 feet high. This bridge cost 45000 dollars. From this bridge we crossed the barren ridge to Wiggins 15 miles, in Fayette County. The land that we have seen today is poor whiteoak except from Little Crossing to Pennsylvania: this part of the mountains are covered principally with Chestnut, Whiteoak, Maple, Beach and Hackberry. There are some places among the mountains that produce good oats and rye.

Leaving Wiggins on the 26th we crossed the Lorrel Hill the highest and most ruggid ridge of the alleghany range of mountains we had to cross to Monrow 7 miles & from Monroe to Union 2 miles. Union is a tolerable little place and would be handsome if it was not so black with stone coal smoke. From Union to Brownville 12 miles. Brownville has an ugly situation on the banks of the Monongahal River but some elegant building. Thence across the river to a little village called Bellville 8 miles, thence to another village called Hillsberry 3 miles—thence to Dunlap's in Washington County. When we came to Union we left the alleghanies behind, and glad I am of it, (into a roaling country of a tolerable fertile soil covered principally with whiteoak, some beach and some blackoak bushes) for the alleghanies are cold and tough, and God knows we have had alleghany mountains enough. This is a fruit country, it affords the finest apples I have ever seen.

Leaving Dunlaps on the 27th we continued our course N. W. on the pavement to Washington (which is the county town of Washington Cty.) 2-½ miles. Washington is a handsome town situated on a rising ground and affords some very nice buildings. Thence a west course to a little village called Claysville 9½ miles. From Claysville to W. Alexander 6 miles. Leaving Washington County at W. Alexander we got into Virgina again Ohio City—thence to Wheling 3 miles. Wheling lies in a string along the east side of the Ohio River. It is not large but appears to be a place of considerable trade, being on a river that affords the safest navigation of any in the United states. From Wheling across the river to Nicle's in Belmont County. The Ohio River is about ¾ of a mile wide at Wheling. The stream is gentle and the water very clare. We have travelled today through a country hilly much as yesterday—the soil much the same and covered with the same kind of timber untill we entered Ohio County Va. On entering Ohio County Va. the country becomes more hilly—more fertile, less whiteoak timber, more shugar maple and some beach. The pavement in Ohio County crossing a little stream called Wheling Creek in a great many places over which a number of elegant bridges at one of which is a Statute of marble in the shape of a woman with some handsome inscriptions on it. The Ohio River affords but little good bottom where we crossed. The land on the west side is more hilly; the soil is of a different coulour and more fertile producing from 50 to 60 bushels of corn to the acre. This land is covered with a different kind of timber to that on the eastern side; some elm, some hackberry, some honeylocas, some sugarmaple and some beach.

Leaving Nichol's on the 28th we travelled so many courses that I cannot tell what course we went, however we passed through a very hilly country and three towns, the first was St. Claresville which is the largest and handsomest being the county town of Belmont, the 2nd. Mouristown the third a little town called Fairfield. Thence into Gwrnsey County to Hayse's. The land we have seen today is of tolerable fertility being well addapted to grass and producing good wheat and corn. It is covered with many kinds of timber, such as whiteoak, beachchestnut, sugarmaple, poplar, walnut, dogwood, blackoak, and some hackberry in the hollows, but the principle timber on the hills is whiteoak.

Leaving Hayse's on the 29th we travelled many courses through a very hilly country to Silver's Muskingum County. We passed through two town the first was a little town called Washington and the next the county town of Gurnsey County called Cambridge. The part of Ohio we have seen today is poor with the exception of the narrow bottoms along the creeks and hollows covered principally with large whiteoak timber. Although the land is poor and very hilly it produces fine grass.

Leaving Silvers on the 30th we travelled a west course to Zanesville—crossed the Muskingum River to a little town called Washington, from that to Somerset. Thence a nort west course to a town called Thornville in Perry County. The land we have seen today is not quite so hilly as that we seen yesterday, but of about the same fertility. It continues hilly to somerset and then becomes tolerable level; covered principally with whiteoak timber. The Muskingum is a beautiful river one quarter of a mile wide at Zanesville, but has not much good bottom where we crossed. There is a small creek some miles on the west side called Jonathans creek that has some good bottoms.

These bottoms are covered with many kinds of timber, such as Sicamore, ash, elm, hackberry, swapeak &c. Zanesville is a thriving town, well situated for travel and manufactories, being on a river that affords an easy and uninterrupted navigation to the place. Somerset is the county town of Perry County.

Leaving Thornville on the 31st we travelled a west course to Jacksonville in Fairfield County. From thornville to jacksonville is level fertile country of a black soil covered on the highest places principally with beach and some whiteoak: and the marshy places with elm, walnut, sugar maple, ash, beach, buckeye &c. Dogwood is plenty through the whole of the state that I have seen.

Leaving Jacksonville on the 9th of November we travelled a north west course through a level country across Blacklic, Bigbelly and Alum Creek on to Columbus in Frankleton County—crossed the Scioto River—passed through Frankleton through a paririe to Big Darby, thence to Jonathan Alders in Madison County. The land from Jacksonville to the Scioto is of a very fertile soil where it is not too wet, covered chiefly with beach and ash except on the creeks where it is mostly sicamore, elm, &c. The land from the Scioto to Alders on darby is ot tolerable fertility covered with white and swamp oak, elm, sugar, dogwood, &c., except the bottoms and pariries and near about them. The on the Scioto are wide and abundantly fertile. The soil is from three to four feet deep. The pariries appear also to be very rich, being covered with grass from three to 5 feet high. The Scioto is a handsome river and is navigable when high 40 miles above columbus. Columbus is the seat of the government. Frankleton is a little town one mile from columbus on the west side of the river.

Leaving Alders on the 11th we went a north course for several miles through the darby plains, thence a N. W. direction up darby on the edge of the plains—through the edges of Delaware and Union Counties—through Milfort a little town in Union County—through the edge of Champaign County into Logan County—across Mad river to a little town called Zanesfield. The land except on the plains and on the darby is tolerable poor and a little rolling, covered principally with white & black oak, hickory, dogwood &c. The plains and bottoms on darby and on mad river are very fertile where they are not too wet. The bottoms on mad river are dryer than those on darby. What timber is on the plains is bur or swamp oak, some sugar maple, Lynn, Hackberry, walnut, honeylocus, Buckeye, and dogwood.

Leaving Zanesfield on the 12th we travelled a N. W. course through a rolling fertile country up the head waters of mad river to Standfields and Smiths. The principle timber in this part of the country is lynn, hackberry, walnut, elm, and sycamore on the bottoms, and lynn, ash, beach, &c on the hills.

Leaving Smiths on the 13th we travelled a west direction through a paririe country to Lewistown. The paririe soil appears good, but is very wet and mire covered in its natural state with grass from 3 to 5 feet high. The little rises (which are covered with groves of timber) between the pariries are poor.

Leaving Colo. Lewises (a Shawnee Chief) on the 14th. we went in a W. course through Bellfountain which is the county town of Logan—crossed mad river into Champaign County; thence the same course through a fine level stretch of country, the finest I have seen in the state,—crossed Mickacheck and King Creek to Urbana which is the county town of Champaign.

The land until we crossed Md. river is poor and tolerable hilly, covered with whiteoak. After crossing Md. river it is mostly paririe and barren country. The pariries are lower than the barrens and more fertile, covered chiefly where they are not cultivated with grass from 3 to 5 and 6 feet high which is cut in large quantities by the farmers for hay. I seen on the paririe bottoms along Md. river I think not less than 1000 stacks of paririe grass hay. The barrens are of a thinner soil, but produce fine corn, wheat &c. They are in places covered with grass and shrubs. Md. River is a small stream affording a number of excellent mill seats. Urbana is a thriving little town, pleasantly situated in a level fertile part of the country with a handsome little stream running through it called town run.

Leaving Urbana on the 15th we travelled along Md. river to Mrs. Hisers. The bottoms on mad river are abundantly fertile, covered principally with walnut, buckeye, sicamore and hackberry.

. . . . *All* . . . .

From a little home-made pamphlet of twenty pages, not including backs, sewed together. The writing in fine penmanship covers 17 pages, and about two lines on the 18th page. Remainder of pages blank.

On back of pamphlet is written by Reuben N. Harrison, "Journal of Nath. Harrison decd."

Spelling, punctuation, and capitalization copied from original.

CHAPTER XXI

Sons and Grandsons of Old Rockingham

FIFTH GENERATION

"Children's children are the crown of old men;
and the glory of children are their fathers."
—PROV. 17-6

BY THE TIME OF THE fifth generation of the descendants of Isaiah, the numerous lines from which they had sprung had become widely scattered. Many a native of Old Rockingham had by this time been borne forth from the scenes of his childhood, on the stream of migration, which, starting with the county's first settlement, had continued to pour through the Valley of the Shenandoah, and which had at length, reached its flood tide in "the great move to the West." Many more now, the sons of these natives, were to rear their children as part and parcel of the life of the young sisterhood of States, formed and being formed, out of the vast region of the Mississippi, and her tributaries.

While many had thus departed from the county—anticipating Mr. Greely's general admonition to young men by a considerable season—by no means all of the representatives of the older families had left. In fact, a large proportion of the old family names may yet be found in Rockingham today. Opportunity awaited at home; as witness the general prosperity of those who continued in the neighborhoods of their ancestral acres.

Of the various Harrison "Clans" of the fifth generation, that of John, in particular, remained largely in Rockingham. Daniel's Clan saw further departures from the old county, while Thomas' persisted therein only in several female lines. The same may be remarked as to Robert Cravens'.

The fifth generation quite naturally gave rise to the largest number of descendants of any generation so far considered. Something of over 400 of these are hereinafter named, but it is recognized that even this list is incomplete. Owing to the wide scattering of the various lines involved, the records are in many instances necessarily fragmentary; but regardless of the line to which any particular family belonged, there is evident a pride, and a thread of a tender memory, in its having been stemmed in Old Rockingham.

CLAN OF JOHN HARRISON

1. LINE OF ZEBULON HARRISON
2. LINE OF JOHN HARRISON

(12111) WILLIAM HARRISON, ( ), the son of John Harrison, (1211), and wife Hannah, married, in 1797, Mary Fawcett, the daughter of Benjamin Fawcett, who signed the marriage bond. (See page 360.) Benjamin Fawcett is thought to have resided on Smiths Creek, near present Lacey Spring, and to have been the individual interested, along with Benjamin Savage and Solomon Matthews, in the early manufacture of iron. (See page 336; *Chalkley* Vol. II, p. 257.)

William Harrison, (12111), and wife Mary, had issue—

OLD HARRISON LOG CABIN

By The Long Grey Trail

Near Lacey Spring, on land formerly belonging to Capt. Reuben Harrison

See pages 311, 378, and 459

(121111) DELILAH—b. May 21, 1798; d. April 25, 1883; m., Jan. 22, 1824, Henry Carrier, as his second wife.
See further record.

Probably others.
(D. S. H. MSS.).

(12112) ZEBULON A. HARRISON, (1775-1825), the son of John Harrison, (1211), and wife Hannah, married, June 21, 1803, Mary Tallman, the daughter of Benjamin Tallman, who gave his consent.

Benjamin Tallman, (born 9th January, 1745, in Pennsylvania), was the son of William Tallman, (son of Benjamin, and Patience Tallman, of Warwick, Rhode Island), who was born in Rhode Island 25th March, 1720, and died in Rockingham County, Virginia, 13th February, 1791. William Tallman married, 20th October, 174-, Ann Lincoln, born 8th March, 1725, died December 22, 1812 c, a sister of "Virginia John" Lincoln. (See pages 135, and 283.)

William Tallman, and wife, had issue; Patience, d. 1761; Benjamin, as above; Mary, b. 22nd May 1747, d. 1751; Sarah, b. 19th Dec., 1749, d. 6 Aug. 1770; Thomas, d. 15 May, 1753; Mary d. in infancy; Thomas b. 12 May, 1757, d. in infancy; William, d. in infancy; Ann, d. in infancy; Hannah, d. in infancy, and Anna, d. in infancy.

Benjamin Tallman married, in Pennsylvania, 9th Nov., 1764, Dinah Boone, the daughter of Benjamin and Susannah Boone. He and wife Dinah had fourteen children, viz: William, b. 27 Jan. 1766, d. 1850; Patience, b. 20 Oct., 1767, d. 21 July, 1816; Sarah, b. 11 April, 1769, d. June 3, 1844; James, b. 8 April, 1771, d. 1846; Samuel, b. 18 Nov. 1772; Thomas, b. 8 July 1774, d. 1794; Benjamin, b. 20 May, 1776, d. same month; Annah, b. 9 May 1777, d. 5 Sept., 1778; Annah, b. 15 Dec., 1778, d. 1866; Nancy, b. 20 May, 1781, d. 1826; Susannah b. 6 Feb., 1783, d. 1825; Mary, b. 20 Nov. (or 2 Dec.) 1784, d. 20 May, 1849; Benjamin, Jr., b. 10 Nov. 1786, d. 1833 c; John, b. 10 Aug. 1788, d. 1857. (See, *Lea and Hutchinson*, pp. 176-177; also D. S. H. MSS.)

In 1783, Benjamin Tallman acquired by purchase a tract of land on Smiths Creek from Zebulon Harrison, Sr., grandfather of Zebulon above. (See page 360.) Tallman about 1810 removed to Ohio, where he died (near Gilbert ?), June 4, 1820. Two of his sons, and four of his daughters, married Harrisons: viz; Benjamin, Jr., who married Lydia Harrison, dau. of John (1253); John, who married Elizabeth Harrison, dau. of Nathaniel, (1252); Nancy, who married John Harrison, son of Col. Benjamin, (167); Ann, who married John Harrison, bro. of Zebulon A., above; Susan, who married Henry Harrison, bro. of Zebulon A., above; and Mary who married Zebulon A., above, (See pages 376, 375, 323, and 361.)

Zebulon and Mary resided on Smiths Creek, about a mile east of Mauzy. Their land (or a part of the same) is now in the possession of Mr. Walter Sellers.

Zebulon A. Harrison, (12112), and wife Mary, had children—

(121121) PATSY—b. April 1, 1807; d. ——; m. —— Hostetter.
See further reference.

(121122) LYDIA—b. Oct. 15, 1809; d. ——, unmarried.

(121123) SUSANNA—b. Feb. 1812; d. ——; m. COLEMAN BRIGHT, b. 1808, d. ——.
Issue—
1. Minerva—m. WM. LIVENGOOD, of Ind. Two daughters: Grace; and Daisy, m. —— Tate.

2. Jane Ann—b. Jan. 3, 1840; d. Jan. 2, 1916. m. GEO. CRESSWELL GILL, b. Aug. 5, 1842, Olympian Springs, Ky.; d. Sept. 20, 1927. Five children: Albin Bright; Blanche (of Quincy, Ill.); Harrison; Grace, m. —— Kingsbury; and Bruce Lausdowne.

(Six others died in infancy.)

(121124) ABRAHAM—b. Mar. 7, 1814; d. Mar. 17, 1888; m. Delilah Rhodes, b. 1817, d. 1899. Resided on Smiths Creek, above Lacey.
See further record.

(121125) ABNER—b. July 9, 1816; d. ——; m. Elizah Sellers.

(121126) NANCY—b. Mar. 14, 1823; d. ——; m. Oct. 1839, William Sellers. No issue.

(D. S. H. MSS. and other papers.)

(12114) JOHN HARRISON, ( ), the son of John Harrison, (1211), and wife Hannah, married, 1797, Ann Tallman, the daughter of Benjamin Tallman. She was a sister of the wife of her husband's brother Zebulon A., and of Nancy Harrison, wife of John Harrison, Col. Benjamin's son.

"Nansy Harrison (wife of Jno. Harrison)," was received for baptism in the Linville Creek Baptist Church, October 8, 1803, and was baptized the following day. (See page 359.) Her father, Benjamin Tallman, had been a member of the church since 13th May, 1792. (See page 332.) She and her sister Ann, were both members of the church. Apparently the latter did not long remain a member.

At a meeting of the church Saturday, April 9, 1804, . . . 1st. "On the Application of our beloved Sister Ann Harrison, a Letter of Dismission and recommendation was granted her, that she (in case of removal, as she expects) out of the bounds of this Church, may have it in her power to join the same. Appointed Sat. before the 2nd Sunday in May next for meeting of Business. Brn. Talman & Lockard to press Br. Moffett to preach at Br. Brumfields said Sunday." (Old Church Book, p. 66.)

With this minute further trace of John and Ann Harrison is lost. They are thought to have removed from the county, probably to Ohio, the same as her father. (See, however, page 323.)

* * * * * *

With the exception of an occasional minute mentioning Ezekiel Harrison (as elsewhere quoted), the foregoing entry is the last in the old record regarding a Harrison. The minutes close with the year 1818. During the short intervening period, the church struggled against the loss of members, due in a great measure to the removal of various of the older families from her environs. The Methodists, too, in their zeal, were appealing to the same community for new members. Devotedly, Bros. John Lincoln, and Benjamin Tallman, two stalwart pillars of the church, labored to offset the loss. New converts were recruited, largely from the Brock's Gap region. A new minister was engaged, and a new church building erected. Gradually the Brock's Gap element came more and more in the ascendant, and meetings were frequently held in this region, sometimes at the home of Sister Nancy Hanks. Finally, about 1818, the parent church was abandoned, Brs. Tallman and Lincoln, themselves, having about this time succumbed, at last, "to the western fever." Following their removal the Brock's Gap Church was organized.

In this connection, and having, in the course of these pages, followed somewhat in detail the minutes of the old church, down to the time of the last above, it may be of interest to continue here brifly with a few notes, gleaned from the record through its closing period.

LAST YEARS OF THE LINVILLE CREEK BAPTIST CHURCH

NANCY HANKS AND OTHERS

"Met Sat. June 9, 1804. 2ndly. Brother Giles Turley came forward with his letter of Dism. from Little River Church, Loudoun County & was received." (p. 66.) Saturday, October 13, 1804—2nd. "Sister Clara Yates, wife of Abner Yates, came forward with her Letter of dismission & recommendation from F. T. Church in . . . County, Virginia, and was received in to . . . this Church." 3rdly. the said Abner Yates came forward and related an Experience of a work of Grace in his Soul & was received a candidate for Baptism. (p. 67.) Sat. Oct. 27, 1804, ". . . 2nd. Mrs. Terry came forward . . . (but) . . . was not received. Delphe, a black woman of Mrs. Kinseys came forward and offered . . . and was received a candidate for baptism. 4thly. Brothers Talman and Lincoln Ordained Deacons. N. B. On Sunday Oct. 28, 1804, Mr. Hay (Floy ?)Mr. Abner Yates, & Delphe, a black Woman were baptized by Br. Moffett." (p. 68.)

Sat. Dec. 8, 1804, "Collection for Bro. Moffett of $4.50 were made," (and promise of $4.00 more—this is the first mention of dollars and cents).

Mar. 9, 1805, "1st. Brother Lincolns request to discontinue acting as writing Clerk for the Church . . . it is agreed to give him up as soon as another Brother shall take his place. 3rdly. We as a Church agree that it is necessary to try to have a meeting house built, at or near this Place, (viz. Linville Creek old meeting house) for the worship of God." (p. 69.)

(From here the handwriting is different and smaller, and much more difficult to read—the previous penmanship has been beautifully done.)

Sat. Aug. 10, 1805 . . . Brother (John) Lockard and Brother Yates appointed Messengers to the Culpeper Association to begin Friday before the first Sunday in October. Sat. Sept. 1805, . . . "2nd. Lucy Rice Wife of John Rice discontinued as a Member for Transgressing the order of this Church by joining the Methodist Society." (p. 71.)

Sat. Oct. 12, 1805 . . . 2nd. "Brother Lockard according to his statement to this Church is about to travel to the western cty. he applies for a Recommendation for a letter setting forth the standing he is in both as a Private and Public Member of this Church." 7th June 1806 . . . 2nd. John Miller came forward and Related what the Lord had done for his Soul was Received by the Church unanimously. 3rd Brother Stevenson making application for a letter of Dismission was granted. (p. 71—The last joined the New Market Church.) "The Second Sunday in June Brother John Miller was Baptized by Brother Moffett. Brother Lockart being about to remove his Place of Residence Requesting a Letter of Dismission which is granted. Received by Letter sister Phobe Burnsides." (p. 72.)

11 April, 1807 . . . "2nd at the Request of the Dover and Goshen association for Material to publish the writing a History of the Baptist we agree to furnish such things as come to our knowledge and appoint Brother Lincoln to collect such as he may think most suitable for that purpose." (p. 72.)

Aug. 8, 1807 . . . 3rd "The Church taking the business of Respecting Sister Talman under their consideration . . . think it best to discontinue her Membership" . . . etc. (She was disciplined for non-attendance.)

** "Saturday 9th April 1808 . . . 1st Brother Samuel Hendrin being present Preached a short Discourse from Malacia 3rd Chapter, first clause of 16th verse." 7th May 1808, . . . "3rd Rebecca Dunlap offered her Experience to the Church who in judgement of Charity Acknowledged." (p. 74.) "On Sunday the 12th of June the following Brethren and Sisters Submitted to the Ordinance of Baptism. Brother Hendrin being the administrator. Rebeckah Dunlap, Eliza. Dunlap and (John) Horman's Aaron. Also was received into this Church Brother Peter Branner formerly a Member of Coffman Church." (p. 75.)

"Friday 17th June 1808 . . . 5th Brother Samuel Hendrin accepts the Churches Call to attend this once a month on the first Saturday and Sunday, in August, (?) The Church agree to support the preaching of the Gospel to the best of their abilities." At this meeting also, "Mr. Dunlap's Woman Ede" was received for baptism. (p. 75.) "Sat. Aug. 6, 1808 . . . 1st Esther Runyan Wife of John Runyan . . . was Received for Baptism." (p. 76.)

"Lewis, a man of Color" was baptized 5th Feb. 1809. (p. 77.) 4th March, 1809, "Lewis received into full fellowship agreeable to the rules of the Church." John Peck, another "man of Color" was baptized the next day. Saturday 15th April 1809 . . . 1st John Peck . . . "was received by giving the Right Hand in full fellowship." (p. 78.)

"Saturday 17th June 1809 . . . 2. M. T. Trumbo came forward and Related his Experience and was unanimously received. The next Church Meeting to be held at the new Meeting House the Saturday preceeding the third Sunday in August next."

"Sat. before 3rd Sun. in August . . . 3rd Brother Lincoln appointed to write the letter to the Association Brothers Lincoln and Turley appointed Messengers to the sd. Association To be held at F. T. Meeting House in Culpeper County Friday before the third Lords day in September." (p. 79.)

"The Church of Christ at Linvilles Creek, being Convened (met) at the new Meeting House agreeable to appointment Saturday the 19th May 1810." (p. 80.)

"The Church being convened Aug. 17, 1811 proceeded to business. Brother John Lincoln prepared a letter to the Culpeper Association to be held at Smiths Creek Church Shenandoah County to begin friday before the first Sunday in Sept. which was read . . . John Lincoln Giles Turley and Abner Yates appointed Messengers to said association." (p. 82.)

"Met . . . Saturday the . . . of November 1812 . . . Brother John Runion jun. chosen moderator, and br. Abner Yates Clerk. Sister Hester Trumboe and sisters Betsy & Rebeckah Dunlap applied for a letter of dismission." (p. 83.) Met . . . at Sister Caldwells house, sometime Brother Turley's Decem. 19, 1812." (p. 84.)

Sat. Apr. 17, 1813 . . . First, sister Betsy and Rebecca Dunlap related that they had given up the idea of requesting a letter of dismission, etc. 3rdly. The church requested Br. Lincoln to write to Elders Mason and Sims, requesting them . . . to attend our meeting-house the first Lords Day in June next & Sat. before . . ." (p. 84.)

"Elders Mason and Sims attended our meeting house last thursday in May & first Lords Day in June & preached the latter time,—to a very large congregation, but no communion held for want of a table." (p. 85.)

Aug. 20, 1814 . . . "Anderson Runyan . . . received a candidate for baptism, without a dissenting voice." 3rd. At this meeting Mrs. Dunlaps Edith was cited to appear before the church at the next meeting "to answer for her gross misconduct." Sept. 17, 1814 . . . Elder Hashberger being present . . . chosen moderator." Mrs. Dunlap's Edith excommunicated. "Anderson Runyan being baptized in Brocks Gap the last Lords Day in August last . . . by Elder Hershbarger was received into . . . the church. Also John Runyon junior of junior & Ester his sister & Jacob Runyan, having been baptized by the same Administrator, at the same place . . . Mary Beaver, wife of Mathias Beaver related her Experience . . . . & was received for baptism" . . . Next meeting to be held at said Mathias Beavers house on Linville Creek, Sat. before 2nd Sabbath in October next." (p. 87.)

Sat. Oct. 8, 1814 . . . 1st. "Received Samuel Price, and his ancient mother Hannah Price into . . . the church, he having related his experience . . . Aug. last . . . at old Br. Runyans on Saturday & was with some others baptized on Sunday, and she in the same manner . . . sometime afterwards. Also received Hannah Bare, daughter of John Bare on her experience . . . as a candidate for Baptism, when she and Mary Beaver were immediately baptized," by Elder Hashbarger. 2ndly. Excommunicated the aforesaid Delph" etc. N. B. At a Union meeting Sunday the 30th Oct. and Saturday before, present, Elders Jones Harshberger & Booten, all preached . . . both days & on Sabbath, was administered the Lords Supper, by said El. Jones, immediately previous to which, the said church received into fellowship John Tusinger & his brother Philip Tusinger Hannah Price & Mary Price, daughters of Samuel Price, all of whom being baptized by Elder Harshberger the 2nd Sabbath of October . . . This was a happy season for our little church." (p. 88.)

Nov. 12, 1814 . . . the church unanimously gave her call to Br. Harshbarger to supply her a part of his time, which he agreed to do monthly . . . (p. 89.) Saturday Dec. 24, 1814 . . . 1st. Daniel Runion and Wife Margaret, Jacob Price & Katherine Williams, wife of Peter Williams being previously baptized . . . by Elder H. our pastor . . . received the right hand of fellowship of the church.

"N. B. On the evening of the above day after preaching at Br. Hanks . . . Susannah Tusinger wife of John Tusinger . . . was received a candidate for baptism & having . . . acquiced in the rules of the church . . . is to be considered a member . . ., in full fellowship, immediately after Baptism & on Sabbath day the church gave the righ hand of fellowship to Eve Price, wife of Andrew Price & received her into . . . full fellowship . . . she being by our pastor previously baptized . . . (p. 90.)

Sat. Jan. 21, 1815 . . . "And that of absent members being taken up, Br. Lincoln agreed to write to Br. Trumbo again, also Sisters, Betsy Bowman, Burnsides, & Briton . . . Br. Hashbarger to see . . . Br. & Sister Turley." (p. 90.) May 27th 1815 . . . Old brother Trumbo (who lives on the South Fork of the Potomack,) being present related, in a very humble & affecting manner, his reasons for his long absence . . . at the same time expressing his great attachment to the church & sincer desire to attend . . . more frequently for the future; his reasons &c . . . considered . . . satisfactory. Received Rebecca Bealer in full, as a candidate for baptism. N. B. . . . present . . . 23 members. On the Sabbath following Elder P. Sperry . . . preached immediately after Elder Hershberger . . . then was baptized, Sissy Runyan, and Rebecca Bealer." (These . . . received into full fellowship on Saturday, June 24, 1815, according to next entry—p. 92.)

Oct. 21, 1815 . . . "Br. Hershberger reported that . . . Sister Trumbo, who, considering the great distance that she lives from this church . . . wishes to obtain a letter of dismission, that she may join the South Branch Church . . . Sister Betsy Bowman, who lives near (er) Salem Church than this . . . applied for a similar letter to join that Church . . . both ordered . . . written." (p. 93.)

"Nov. 25, 1815, Hannah Price daughter of Samuel Price, having been visited by sister Hank and Ann Runyen . . . etc. . . . the church was . . . of opinion she ought to be excluded . . . fellowship, which accordingly she was." (p. 94.)

June 22nd 1816, "at Br. Lincolns. Br. and Sister Turley being present applied for a letter of dismission to join the Salem Church which was agreed to . . . On the Lords day the Supper was celebrated in a very solemn manner." 24 Communicants. July 27, 1816 . . . appointed Br. Harshberger & Br. Beaver to visit our delinquint sisters Beaver and Bear & excite them to their duty. Br. Lincoln to visit or write to Sister Hannah Carrier, for the same purpose. (p. 95.) Aug. 24, 1816 . . . 3rd. Sister Rebecca Gilkins being about to remove to the State of Ohio requested a letter of dismission, which was agreed to" . . . etc. Members returned to the Association 38, there being 4 dismissed by letter, 1 excluded, & 1 dead (viz. Sisters Trumbo, Bowman, Br. Turley and wife, excluded H. Price jun. dead Sister Brumfield.

"Met Sept. 21, 1816 at the meeting house and after worship appointed next church meeting at Br. John Tusingers high up in Brocks Gap." (p. 96.)

"The Church met, Saturday December 21, 1816 at sister Hanks, and after worship, Anne Runyan, Daughter of John Runyan, came forward and related her Experiance of faith in Jesus Christ & was received for baptism. Likewise . . . Madeline Runyan, wife of Daniel Runyan . . . and the next day they were both baptized and received into the church." (p. 97.)

"Saturday May 24, 1817 . . . Brother Yates having previously undertaken brought forward a new walnut table for the use of the church, for which he was allowed $3.25, to be paid him . . . in a reasonable time." (p. 97.)

"The Church met at Sister Hanks Saturday Sept. 27, 1817, and after praise and prayer proceeded to Business and first . . . Resolved to change their times of church meetings from the 4th to the Saturday before ye 2nd Sabbath in each month wherein any meeting is held." Contributions at different times "to pay for a communion table furnished by Br. Yates" . . . Those contributing—Anderson Runyan, Danl. Runyan, Jno. Lincoln & Family, Sist. Price, Jn. Tusing & Samuel Price, Br. Runyan 2nd and sist. Hank, Jacob Price, Jacob Runyan, and Phillip Tusing. "Br. Lincoln to pay Br. Yates 1/9. N. B. this . . . pays for a phamphlet the property of the church . . . ye 3rd annual report of the Baptist Board of Missions &c." (p. 97.)

Feb. 7, 1818. "Church met a old Br. Runyans . . . Br. Runyan younger, or 3rd against Br. John Tusinger . . . brought in a . . . grieviance," debt of $6.00. An inquiry and report was ordered. (p. 98.) Mar. 7, 1818, . . . all the witnesses being heard on both sides . . . it was agreed . . . that Br. Tusing should pay but $2.75 to Br. Runyan, upon which each partie . . . appeared to be satisfied." Saturday May 9, 1818, at our meeting house . . . Sister Rebecca Bealer . . . excluded from fellowship & communion . . . till repentance & reformation shall appear." (p. 99.)

"Met Aug. 8, 1818, at Nancy Hanks, . . . widow Dunlap having been baptized some weeks ago & having expressed her desire to join this Church, it was . . . agreed that she should be considered a member . . . Appointed Anderson Runyan, Samuel Price, Jno. Runyan & Jno. Lincoln our messenger to next Association, & contributed ab. 6 s. to send by them. Appointed next meeting in course at Linvilles Creek." (p. 100.)

* * * * * *

"Sister Nancy Hanks" lived in the region of Brock's Gap. (See page 334.) One "Nancy Hank," evidently the same, was acknowledged a candidate for baptism at a meeting Oct. 8, 1808, at "Mr. Jacob Lincolns," at which Ezekiel Harrison was present. (See page 333—in the entry regarding this particular meeting the letter "n" in Hank is not clearly formed, and judging from this instance alone, might be assumed a "w".) A meeting was held at "Br. Hanks," Dec. 24, 1814, (see above), but from the more frequent mention of those held at "Sister Hanks," it appears likely that she was a widow, and the head of her own household.

Joseph Hanks (1725-1793), native of Richmond County, Virginia, and the ancestor of Nancy Hanks, the mother of Lincoln, according to Barton's *The Lineage of Lincoln*, removed from Hampshire, now Mineral County, West Virginia, to Nelson County, Kentucky, 1784, where in 1793 he died, leaving will, dated and proven this year, naming wife "Nannie," sons Thomas, Joshua, William, Charles, Joseph, and daughters Elizabeth, (m. Thomas Sparrow of Ky. 1795), Polly, and Nancy, (m. Levi Hall.) He also had a daughter Lucy, (the eldest), who married Henry Sparrow, (bro. of Thomas), in Kentucky, 1790. On Jan. 10, 1794, the widow Nancy, (dau. of Wm. Lee of Richmond Co., Va.), and her son Joseph, joined in selling the contract under which the Hanks land was held, to William, her son, following which she and Joseph "returned to Virginia," where she died.

The county in which the widow Hanks died, and the time of her death is unknown. Thomas Hanks, when the family went to Kentucky, remained in Hampshire, and it is presumed that she returned to this county. In 1800 he removed from Hampshire to Rose County, Ohio. Joseph Hanks, on March 8, 1817, testified in Nelson County, Kentucky, to having "migrated to Virginia and back again." *(Barton*, p. 189.)

Nancy Hanks, the mother of Lincoln, was born about 1783. The account of her childhood is involved in much conjecture. She is said to have been reared in the home of her grandmother Hanks until the latter returned to Virginia, when, so it is assumed, Lucy took her. Sometime following Elizabeth's marriage she went to live with her, and continued as one of Thomas Sparrow's family until her own marriage, in 1806, to Thomas Lincoln.

Chrisman states that Thomas first met his future wife Nancy at the home of a relative of his, in Rockingham, while he (Thomas) was on a visit back from Kentucky. Nancy at the time, relates the *Memoirs*, "lived just over the hill," and later emigrated from this neighborhood to Kentucky with her people. The Kentucky Hanks were Baptists (also Thomas Lincoln), as was "Sister Nancy Hanks" of the Brock's Gap region. Considering the circumstances, it appears highly probable that "Br. Hanks" was Joseph, who resided with his mother Nancy, and that Nancy, the future wife of Thomas Lincoln, was stopping with her grandmother and Joseph, when some occasion of the neighborhood, perchance one of the identical church meetings of these old minutes, happened to lead to their introduction.

* * * * * *

One more minute, and the record is closed. "At a Church meeting at Linvilles Creek, Sat. Sept. 12, 1818. After worship Br. Runyan was chosen moderator, sister Dunlaps coloured woman Edith came forward and related . . . that she had seen, and was now, and for some time past made fully sensible of the impriety & sin of her conduct, . . . that she heartily repented thereof, and hoped God had, for Christ's sake, pardoned her sins, and that she wished to join the Church again; but her reception was deferred till another opportunity. Next Church meeting in course at Bro. Prices. (p. 100.)

This last, is the final entry in the book before "The Confession of Faith of the Regular Baptist Church Called Brocks Gap," but in the space intervening there appears to have been eight pages cut out—these many stubs showing.

The Brock's Gap records cover ten pages, including the "Confession of Faith." This church was organized 18th February, 1843, and the records run to February 17, 1844, in the book. Nine leaves following the last entry appear to have been eliminated. (The church is still in existence.) Below the "Confession of Faith" is listed the names of the members at the time of organization, viz.:—(Brothers) Jacob Trumbo, Adam

Tusing, Samuel Price, Daniel Price, John Hess, Christian Biller, Jacob Fowley, Anderson Runyon, Levi Hess, John Hulve, James Hay, Philip Tusing, John Bosey, John Minnich, and Samuel, "a Collerd man." (Sisters) Elisabeth Trumbo, Lydia Tusing, Susan Price, Mary Price, Catherine Hess, Hannah Biller, Sarah Fawley, Sarah Runyen, Dorothy Hess, Margaret Hulve, Hannah Henester, Elisabeth Thomas, Melvina Peterson, Mary Bull, Margaret Painter, Sarah Riggleman, Catherine Tusing, Lena Runion, Katherine S. Henkle, Nancy Biller, Barbary Turner, and Margaret Dwyer. The names of the Sisters being arranged in a parallel column to that of the Brothers, it is assumed that the first ten persons of the two columns were husbands and wives.

---

1. LINE OF DANIEL DAVISON
2. LINE OF JOSIAH DAVISON

(12317) JESSE DAVISON, (1786-1821), the son of Josiah Davison, (1231), and wife Edith, removed with his parents to Harrison County, now West Virginia. Two old copy books, as used by Jesse and his brother William, are extant. Regarding these, Richard L. Davisson, in his address before referred to, states; "The one in my father's posession is inscribed: 'William Davisson, Harrison County, Booth's Creek,' dated 'July 5, 1800-November 1, 1800.' The one in my Uncle Frank's posession is inscribed, 'Jessie Davisson's Copy Book,' which has dates from February 9, 1804, to April 17, 1806, and contained the following; 'Monongalia Co., State of Va., September 5, 1804'."

Jesse Davison married, and left two sons, one—

(123171) Alexander Heron—living at Earlville, Illinois, in 1919, was then 102 years of age.

(12322) JONATHAN WILLIAM DAVISON, (1806-), the son of Josiah Davison, (1231), and second wife Nancy, was born in Harrison County, now West Virginia, and settled in Preble County, Ohio, where he was a County Commissioner, and the Assessor of Monroe township. He married, and had issue—

(123221) Lewis—
(123222) Amaziah—
(123223) David—m. ——;
See further record.
(123224) Susan—
(123225) Elizabeth—
(123226) Isabel—m. —— Samsel. Living at Galveston, Cass Co., Ind. 1916.
(First five, from a list by Prof. S. C. Davisson; last mentioned by Richard L. Davisson.)

(12323) JOSIAH DAVISSON, (1808-1863), the son of Josiah Davison, (Davisson), (1231), and second wife Nancy, born in Harrison County, now West Virginia, Oct. 6, 1808, removed with his father at the age of eight years to Preble County, Ohio. He married in Ohio, Hannah Foos, born in Warren County, this State, February 13, 1819, the daughter of Jacob and Elizabeth (Roberts) Foos, from Pennsylvania to Ohio. She died July 15, 1896.

Josiah and Hannah Davison resided on the home plantation of his father in Preble. He served as a Justice of the Peace and as township treasurer. Both he and his wife were members of the Baptist Church, which denomination had in Josiah Sr's. day erected a meeting house on land adjacent to his farm.

Josiah Davisson, (12323), and wife Hannah, had issue—

(123231) FRANK M.—Residing at the old homestead, 1900. (Residence at the time built, said to have been one of the finest in the county.) Student at Christian Univ., Indianapolis, and 3 yrs. at Ann Harbor, Mich. Civil Engr. Followed profession 10 yrs.
(123232) AMELIA ELIZABETH—Residing, 1900, with bro. above.
(123233) OSCAR FULTON—Attorney, Dayton, Ohio. (1900.)
(123234) EDWARD CLINTON—Physican, Dayton, Ohio. (1900.)
(123235) SARAH ALICE—No further record.

(See, Genealogical and Biographical Record, Preble Co., O. *Compendum of National Biography,* Lewis Pub. Co., 1900, p. 377.)

---

2. LINE OF JOHN EWING

(12334) WILLIAM EWING, (1780-1857), the son of John Ewing, and wife Phoebe, (1233), nee Davison, lived and died in Rockingham County, Virginia, near Harrisonburg. He married, in 1807, Elizabeth Bryan, the daughter of William Bryan, who signed the marriage bond as surety. (See, *Strickler,* p. 51.)

William Byran was of the family to whom Ezekiel Harrison's wife belonged. (See page 330.) He served as a Major in the War of 1812. His son Daniel, for many years postmaster at Alexandria, Virginia, was a gifted poet and author. *(Wayland,* p. 316.)

On August 19, 1812, William Ewing was commissioned a Captain of Cavalry, serving in the 116 Regt. Rockingham militia.

William Ewing, (12334), and wife Elizabeth, had issue—

(123341) JESSE HARRISON—b. 1808; d. 1867; m. Lavina Bryan, settled in Mo.
(123342) NANCY BRYAN—b. 1810; d. 1889, unmarried.
(123343) GEORGE WASHINGTON—b. 1812; d. 1846, unmarried.
(123344) HENRIETTA DAVISON—b. 1815; d. 1884; m. Dec. 30, 1840, Robert Stithington.
(123345) BENJAMIN BRYAN—b. 1817; d. 1862, unmarried, at Richmond, Va. Served in Gen. J. E. B. Stuart's Cavalry, Confederate Army.
(123346) PHOEBE ANN—b. 1819; d. 1893, unmarried
(123347) DANIEL BAKER, (Rev.—D. D.)—b. July 7, 1821; d. Feb. 13, 1886; m. Oct. 18, 1852, Francis Todd Barbour, of Orange Co., Va. See further record.
(123348) ROBERT D.—b. 1823; d. 1889, unmarried.
(123349) MARY ELIZABETH—b. 1824; d. July 8, 1916, unmarried. See further reference.
(123350) ELIZABETH ALLEN—b. 1827; d. 1902; m. Sept. 15, 1875, John T. Brown. Lived near Harrisonburg.
(123351) WILLIAM DAVIS, (Dr.)—b. 1828; d. 1902; m. Oct. 29, 1859, Margaret Sellers. Served as a surgeon in the Confederate Army. Resided at Cave Station, Augusta Co. See further record.

(12337) JOHN DAVISON EWING, (1788-), the son of John Ewing, and wife Phoebe, (1233), nee Davison, was for many years a minister of the Gospel at Falling Springs, (Rockbridge Co.), Virginia. He married Drusilla Del Tate. Issue—

(123371) Philander—d. unmarried.
(123372) Phoebe Jane—m. Daniel Morgan.
(123373) William P.—m. Anne Sturgess.
(123374) Anne Eliza—m. Samuel Jetter.

---

1. LINE OF THOMAS MOORE
2. LINE OF CAPT. REUBEN MOORE

WALTON

(12341) ELIZABETH MOORE, (1781-1864), the daughter of Capt. Reuben Moore, (1234), and wife Phoebe, born Oct. 24, 1781, died March 4, 1864, married in 1798, Moses Walton, born April 20, 1775, died March 13, 1847, son of Moses Walton, Sr., b. 1740, and wife Eunice, nee Rogers. Moses, Sr., was the son of Moses Walton, the pioneer,whose will was proven in Frederick County, about 1763.

Moses Walton was a Virginia State Senator from 1826 to 1830. His father, Moses Walton, Sr., is thought to have been descended from the early Walton family of Eastern Virginia, (from Lancaster, in England), and a near relative of George Walton, a signer of the Declaration of Independence from Georgia. George was born in Frederick County, Virginia, (or Cumberland), in 1740. He died February 2, 1804. (Meadow Garden, his old home in Augusta, Georgia, is owned by the Augusta Chapter, D. A. R. Most of his early biographers name him as a native of Frederick Co., Va.)

Among the children of Robert Walton, of Prince Edward County, Virginia, were sons, Robert and George, who married respectively, sisters Martha and Mary Hughs, daughters of Robert Hughs, who left will dated, July 13, 1750, proved in Cumberland County, Oct. 25, 1752. Robert and Martha Walton had sons, Robert, John, Jesse, Thomas, and George "double first cousins of George the signer," son of George and Mary Walton. (See, *Baltimore Sun,* Nov. 20, 1904; Hearst's *Sunday American,* Atlanta, Ga., May 18, 1930.)

Moses Walton, Sr., resided in that part of Frederick, now Shenandoah, in or near Woodstock, where many of his descendants have long been seated. His children, in addition to Moses, Jr., above, were, Samuel, d. July 27, 1843, Eunice (Walton) Chandlee, d. March 1822, Anna (Walton) Hawkins, d. September 20, 1842.

The children of Moses Walton, Jr., and wife Elizabeth, (12341), were—

(123411) Reuben—b. July 7, 1799; d. May 16, 1874; m. Mary Harrison, (12593), daughter of David. Resided at Woodstock, Va. See further record.
(123412) John—b. Oct. 9, 1801; d. ——; m. Lydia Allen. See further record.
(123413) Mary Ann—b. Feb. 25, 1807; d. unmarried.

(Dates from Walton family Bible, now in possession of Mr. M. Lauck Walton, of Woodstock, Va.)

(12343) REUBEN MOORE, (1791-1859), the son of Capt. Reuben Moore, (1234), and wife Phoebe, born August 24, 1791, married, first, about 1812, Martha Jane McWilliams, the daughter of Gordon McWilliams, elsewhere noticed. (See page 394.)

A sister of Martha, Betsy McWilliams, married George Wright.

Reuben Moore resided at the old home of his father, on the property now widely known as Court Manor, one of the finest estates in the Valley of Virginia. (See pages 185 and 370.) It was he who built Moreland Hall, the present residence. While an extension to the northern wing, and a new Colonial portico, at the front of the house, has recently been added, the latter is a restoration of the original, which since Reuben's day had come to be replaced by a more morden porch. The old log house of Reuben's father stood about on the location of Moreland Hall today. After the new residence was built, the logs of the old one were sold to an inhabitant of "Burketown," who used them to build himself a new house.

The present Court Manor estate, embraces only a part of Reuben Moore's land. His territory included several other fine farms, among them those of the late N. G. Moore, adjacent to Court Manor, the present Biedler land, adjacent to Moore, the Zirkle land, east of Smiths Creek, and other properties; an estate of over 1,200 acres, extending from the foothills of the Massanutten westward across "The Long Grey Trail," to the top of the distant ridge beyond the highway.

Moreland Hall, the mansion house of these broad acres, was erected in proportions amply in keeping with the surrounding plantation. Set on a wide lawn, shaded by magnificent old trees, and facing the "Big Road," a few hundred yards to the west, it presented a perfect picture of Rockingham's best in the great days "befo de wah."

The bricks of which it was built were made on the place, largely by slave labor. Its architecture, barring the recent modifications, is very similar to that of Smithland, before noticed, but owing to the later additions the Hall today is much the larger.

Beyond the meadow to the east, and nestling by the side of Smiths Creek, as it ran through the estate,, was the mill. (On the site of Mr. Stultz's today.) The ground flour and other products of the mill and plantation, were transported by wagons to Fredericksburg. Moore is said to have had several fine teams on the road almost continuously. Many were the stories of adventure brought back by his young sons, when occasionally they were allowed to make the long trip down the Valley and over the mountains, in company with some trusty teamster.

Martha Jane, the first wife of Reuben Moore, died January 6, 1833. Sometime thereafter he married Mildred Hughs, from Eastern Virginia, likely of the family related to the Waltons. (See page 448.) She was born May 19, 1797, and died without issue.

Reuben Moore died January 30, 1859, and Mildred, his wife, June 23, 1865. His will dated November (?) 30, 1858, and proven in 1859, reads as follows—

Will of Reuben Moore

I, Reuben Moore, of the County of Rockingham and State of Virginia do make and ordain this my last will and testament as follows:

First: I direct that all my just debts and funeral expenses shall be paid out of the first monies that may come into the hands of my executors.

As to my worldly estate, I dispose of the same as follows: First, I give to my wife Mildred Moore four thousand dollars, to be paid her out of my estate as dower money, with all the furniture in her bed room and all the furniture in the adjoining room. It is my wish that my wife remain in my family as long as they wish to remain a family. I wish all my household and kitchen furniture to be kept together for the benefit and use of all the single members of my family, including my wife, who I wish to remain as the head of the family as long as she may see proper to do so, and share alike in the enjoyments and benefits of my home residence under the management of my son

Thomas, for the family's mutial benefit as long as they may see proper to remain together. If they see proper to separate then each can take their property as set forth in this will.

I also leave my negro girl named Charlotte to wait on my wife during her life if she sees proper to take her for that purpose, but she is not to be hired out, and at the death of my wife, or at any time she may see proper to give her up, I give her to my son Thomas. The balance of my negroes I give to my son Thomas, except those that may be hereafter be named and otherwise disposed of, which he is to take good care of and provide for agreeable to their age and condition.

I give to my daughter Phoebe Ann Price and her heirs and assigns the tract of land she is now living upon, containing by recent survey two hundred acres and is known in said survey as Lot No. 4, which was made by P. P. Koontz in the fall of 1858. The money which she has already received and the bonds I hold against Price are to be given up to her and that is to be in full of her share of my estate.

I give to my two sons, John and Thomas Moore, all my lands on the west side of Smith's Creek to be divided in the following manner. It is to be divided as it was between my father and John Moore, except it is to be a straight line commencing at the walnut tree on the side of the mill dam, formerly a corner of my father and John Moore and running a straight line to the top of the hill to a cedar and from that cedar a straight line to a black oak, formerly a corner of my father and John Moore; thence from said black oak a straight line to the corner of the woods; thence a straight line to the division fence; thence with the division fence up to Beam's corner on the back line, but the lines are to remain as they are at present as long as the widow of my son holds the lands which I gave her, each to be entitled to the full use and benefit of said land as divided, except that part included in the land laid off for my son Reuben Moore's widow, which I suppose to be about one hundred acres, which she is to have as long as she may live or remain Reuben Moore's widow, for the purpose of raising her children on; but if she should marry then she is to have no further use of said land and it is to fall to my two sons John and Thomas, agreeable to the division line, reserving for John a water way from the black oak corner to a point before the spring house on said widow's part.

I give to my son Thomas that tract I purchased of William Zirkle and I give to John that tract I purchased of Byrd.

I give to my daughter Catherine Gaines, and her heirs or assigns, all that tract of land included in the survey referred to and is Lot No. 5, containing two hundred thirty-eight acres, thirty-eight acres of which William F. Gaines has paid me for. The other two hundred acres and eighteen hundred dollars, which is to be paid by executors to him, is in full of her share of my estate.

I give to my sons John and Thomas Moore, the mill and saw mill and water right to said mill, also the balance of my land on the east side of the creek in Lots No. 6 and No. 1, containing No. 6 thirty-four acres and twelve perches, No. 1, seven and one-half acres. I also give to my two son, John and Thomas Moore, all my personal estate, bonds and monies and stock of every description, except the negro houses and farming utensils on my place. I give them to my son Thomas and out of the estate given to my two sons I bind them to pay to the balance of my children not yet named the following sums of money.

To my daughter Virginia Moore, seven thousand dollars and a negro girl which she has got and which I purchased of Martz, which is in full of her share of my estate.

I give to my daughter, Elizabeth, seven thousand dollars and a negro girl named Amanda, which is to be in full of her share of my estate.

I give to my son Madison Moore, seven thousand eight hundred dollars, which is to be in full of his share of my estate. All claims held by me against any of the above named heirs, either by note or account is to be offset against their legacies.

I also give to my three grand children [children] of my son Reuben, Frances, Mary, and Oscar two thousand dollars each, to be paid to them at the age of eighteen, but it is to remain in the hands of my executors until they arrive at the age of eighteen without inter est unless some circumstances should throw the land I leave to the widow to raise them out of her hands or control, then in that event they must pay the interest on the amount after the children arrive at the age of fifteen years.

I further bind my two sons, John and Thomas' real estate to pay the above named legacies in the following manner. The four thousand dollars to be paid to my wife in six months after my death or the interest on the amount. The balance of my legatees are to be paid three thousand dollars a piece in twelve months after my death and the balance in two equal yearly payments.

Also I give to my three grandchildren, Frances, Mary and Oscar, Maria and her three children and their increase. Frances to have Susan and Mary her choice of the others after giving George to Oscar, and her and her increase to be equally divided among them. If either of them should die before they arrive at the age of eighteen then their portion is to go to the other two surviving children.

It is my wish that Edmond remain and work for the widow to aid in raising the children and then to go to Thomas, and if my wife should be dissatisfied with the proportion of the will and take her dower in land, then in that event John's part of the land must lose its equal part of the dower. Elizabeth is to have full privilege of her room and furniture, also my wife to enjoy the use of her two rooms, especially as long as she may see proper.

Lastly, I appoint my two sons, John and Thomas Moore, my executors of this my last will and testament, hereby revoking all former wills by me at any time made and request the County Court of Rockingham to require no security of them in their bonds, as I have bound all their real estate for their performance.

In witness whereof I have hereunto affixed my hand and seal this 30th day of March . . . .

Reuben Moore. (Seal.)

(From the Records at Harrisonburg. Copy kindly furnished by Miss Josephine Moore.)

* * * * * *

As named in his will, the children of Reuben Moore, (12343), were—

(123431) MADISON—b. Dec. 19, 1812; d. Jan. 9, 1878; m. Lydia Harrison, (12595), dau. of David Harrison.
See further record.

(123432) PHOEBE ANN—b. Apr. 15, 1817; d. 1864; m., 1838 c., Joshua Price.
See further record.

(123433) JOHN—b. July 27, 1818; d. Jan. 29, 1864; m. Elizabeth Ann Harrison, (12598), dau. of David Harrison.
See further record.

(123434) THOMAS—b. Dec. 18, 1819; d. 1878, unmarried.

(123435) MARTHA JANE—b. Dec. 26, 1821; d. 1849, unmarried.

(123436) SARAH ELIZABETH—b. Nov. 3,1823; d. 1870, unmarried.

(123437) VIRGINIA—b. Dec. 4, 1825; d. 1902; m. Joseph Moore, of Shenandoah County.
See further record.

(123438) REUBEN—b. Feb. 16, 1828; d. 1859; m. Annis Beaver, b. 1824, d. 1890, dau. of John Beaver.
See further record.

(123439) MARGARET FRANCES—b. 1830; d. 1848,unmarried.

(123440) MARY CATHERINE—b. Oct. 31, 1832; d. 1874; m. William Gaines.
See further record.

(John and wife, Thomas, Martha, Elizabeth, Reuben and wife, Mary and husband, and Frances interred in the old Moore family burial ground on the late N. G. Moore's place. Madison and wife, interred in the Moore cemetery at Virginia Caverns; dates from tombstones and family Bible.)

---

1. LINE OF CAPT. REUBEN HARRISON
2. LINE OF NATHANIEL HARRISON

HOWARD

Howards Stephen Joseph Absalom

(12521) LYDIA HARRISON, (1784-1869), the daughter of Nathaniel Harrison, (1252), and wife Mary, born November 15, 1784, married in 1807, Michael Howard. Her father signed the marriage bond as surety. She died in March 1869.

The Howards have long since been seated in the region traversed by The Long Grey Trail, to the north of Harrisonburg. (Somewhat below Smithland.) Stephen, Absalom and Joseph Howard were members of Capt. Peter Scholl's militia company as early as 1742.

Michael Howard, and wife Lydia, (12521), had children—

(125211) MARY—b. Feb. 27, 1808; d. ——; m. John Stover.
See further record.

(125212) ELIZABETH—b. July 9, 1809; d. June 4, 1889, unmarried.

(125213) LYDIA—b. Jan. 21, 1811; d. 1887, unmarried.

(125214) ANN—b. Dec. 22, 1813; d. Oct. 3, 1896, unmarried.

(125215) JOHN—b. Sept. 15, 1815; d. Dec. 28, 1896; m. Nov. 11, 1847. Lena Andes, b.Mar. 17, 1819. Resided at the homestead above.
See further record.

(125216) MICHAEL—b. Mar. 25, 1817; d. Mar. 28, 1892; m. 1st ———, m., 2nd., ———;

(125217) EDITH—b. Jan. 15, 1819; d. Apr. 10, 1892; m. ——.

(125218) MARGARET—b. Sept. 17, 1822; d. Jun. 10, 1907, unmarried.

(125219) NATHANIEL—b. Sept. 30, 1823; d. Nov. 6, 1893, unmarried.

(D. S. H. MSS.)

HANNAH

(12528) EDITH HARRISON, (   ), the daughter of Nathaniel Harrison, (1252), and wife Mary, married Mifford Hannah, (Hanna), of Rockingham. Issue—

(125281) MARY—m. —— Wagner.

(125282) ANN— m. —— Sweeker.

(125283) EDA—m. W. V. Queen.

(125284) NATHANIEL—b. Mar. 5, 1824; d. July 6, 1863, at "Camp Chase," Columbus, Ohio; m., 1849, Belle C. Rhodes, b. Nov. 22, 1828, d. Jan. 19, 1867.
See further record.

(125285) John—
(D. S. H. MSS.)

---

2. LINE OF JOHN HARRISON

BOWMAN

(12531) PHOEBE HARRISON, (1791-1859), the daughter of John Harrison, (1253), and wife Grace, married Dec. 24, 1812, Miller (Wm.) Bowman; surety Benjaman Tallman. Her age "21 last May," was affirmed by Barbara Pickering before Thomas Moore. (Strickler's *Rockingham Co. Marriages,* p. 33.)

Miller Bowman is said to have been a son of John Bowman, born July 1st, or August 26, 1750. Miller was drowned about 1832, and some time thereafter his widow went to live with her youngest son, at whose home she died, in Centerville, Tennessee.

Miller Bowman, and wife Phoebe (12531), had issue—

(125311) Margaret—m. —— Tallman?
(125312) Jacob Smith—
(125313) Andrew Jackson—b. Aug. 4, 1816; d. ——; m., 1st, Ann Welsh, m., 2nd. Sarah Miller See. Removed to Hopkinsville, Ky., and later to Centerville, Tenn.
See further record.

(Date of birth of last, from family Bible reference, kindly supplied by Callie Bowman Kane (Mrs. Charles de Lisle Kane) of St. Louis, Mo.)

---

2. LINE OF THOMAS WARREN

GORDON

(12581) NANCY WARREN, ( ), the daughter of Thomas Warren, and wife Elizabeth, (1258), nee Harrison, married May 29, 1821, John Gordon of Rockingham, a descendant of James Gordon, an early vestryman of Augusta, who settled on Muddy Creek, about 1754.

Issue—

(125811) David—d. unmarried.
(125812) Thomas—m. Catherine Bear.
See further record.
(125813) John Newton, (M. D.)—b. Mar. 8, 1825; d. July 27, 1882; m. Elizabeth Warren, dau. of Jehu Warren, (12585).
See further record.
(125814) Jehu—
(125815) Caroline—
(125816) Cassie (M. Catherine)—
(125817) Lydia—m. Erasmus Byrd, son of Abraham. Removed to Texas.
(125818) Addison—

(D. S. H. MSS. Date of John Newton, from tombstone in New Erection churchyard.)

BEAR

(12582) LYDIA WARREN, (1794-1851), the daughter of Thomas Warren, and wife Elizabeth, (1258), nee Harrison, married, October 20, 1814, Andrew Bear, of Rockingham; surety John Crotzer. Andrew Bear was born in 1788, and died January 4, 1868. Issue—

(125821) Betsy Ellehorn—m. John Strother Effinger, of Harrisonburg. No Issue.
(125822) Frances—m. Harvey Bear.
(125823) Harriett—b. 1828; d. 1899; m. T. D. Bell of Rockingham.
See further record.
(125824) Catherine—m. Thomas Gordon, above.
(125825) Nancy—d. young.
(125826) John K.—d. Dec. 1857; m. Nancy Campbell.
(125827) Jehu—m. Margaret Conrad.
(125828) Hester—m. Milton Ervine.
(125829) Peter (David)—b. Sallie Rice.
(D.S.H. MSS.)

CHRISMAN

(12584) CATHERINE WARREN, ( ), the daughter of Thomas Warren, and wife Elizabeth, (1258), nee Harrison, married, April 28, 1814, John Chrisman, of Rockingham, b. January 10, 1794, d. October 25, 1846, son of Jacob (b. Dec. 15, 1763), and wife Barbara, son of John and Mary Chrisman. (See page 383.) She died January 10, 1815. Following her death John Chrisman married, 2nd, Eleanor Ralston, January 23, 1816, who died September 14, 1860. John and Catherine Chrisman had issue—

(125841) Elizabeth Ann—b. Jan. 9, 1815; d. Jan. 11, 1815.

(Among the children of John and Eleanor Chrisman was a son Henry Alexander, b. December 13, 1817, d. October 8, 1871, and a daughter Fannie Eleanor, b. November 22, 1838, d. April 17, 1900, m. Reuben W. Moore, son of Madison Moore (123431). Last four interred in the Moore family cemetery at Virginia Caverns.)

(12585) JEHU WARREN, (1801-1851), the son of Thomas Warren, and wife Elizabeth, (1258), nee Harrison, married Harriett Rice. She was born in 1807, and died in 1886. Jehu and wife resided in Harrisonburg, in what has long been known as the Warren House, on Court Square. It was he who accompained John Harrison, (12591), on his trip to Missouri in 1822. (See last Chapter.)

Jehu Warren, and wife Harriett's, children were—

(125851) William Rice—b. 1826; d. 1884; m. Rebecca Spears, dau. of Charles C. and wife Margaret, (12603), nee Chrisman.
See further record.
(125852) E. Tiffin (Col.)—b. 1829; d. 1864; m. Virginia Magruder.
See further record.
(125853) Elizabeth—b. Apr. 7, 1832; d. Oct. 29, 1867; m. Dr. John Newton Gordon, (125813), of Harrisonburg, son of John Gordon.
See further record.
(125854) Sallie—
(125855) Amelia—
(125856) Ella—d. unmarried. Resided at Florence, S. C. ?
(D. S. H. MSS.)

BURKHOLDER

(12587) SOPHIA WARREN, (1804-1867), the daughter of Thomas Warren, and wife Elizabeth, (1258), nee Harrison, married Joseph Burkholder, (1801-1879), of Rockingham. Their children were—

(125871) Elizabeth W.—b. 1825; d. Sept. 18, 1863, unmarried.
(125872) Catherine C.—b. 1827; d. 1903; m. William P. Byrd, b. June 6, 1817, d. Aug. 2, 1887, son of Abraham.
See further record.
(125873) Preston T.—b. ——; d. Feb. 8, 1911; m. 1st., Rettie Hanger, m. 2nd., Molly Armentrout.
See further record.
(125874) Lydia A.—b. Mar. 25,1838; d. ——; m. Oct. 31, 1866, William Arey, b. Aug. 8, 1808, d. July 5, 1884.
See further record.

(D. S. H. MSS.)

---

2. LINE OF DAVID HARRISON

(12591) JOHN HARRISON, (1800-1880), the son of David Harrison, (1259), and wife Elizabeth, is mentioned in his father's will, as having received his share of the testator's estate. In 1832, David had conveyed by deed of gift a part of his homestead land to his sons, John, Nathaniel, and Daniel. A few days thereafter John sold his share to the other two brothers. (See Nathaniel below.)

In 1822, a year after reaching his majority, John Harrison visited the West, journeying as far as Missouri, and returning by way of Tennessee, where he stopped the first several months of 1823, among some of his Woodley kin, to teach a term of school. The Journal of his trip appears in the preceeding Chapter.

John Harrison married, January 25, 1838, Barbara Katherine Hollingsworth, (1817-1890), the daughter of George Hollingsworth, and wife Nancy.

George Hollingsworth resided in the Lacey Spring neighborhood. The old cemetery in which he was interred, and which probably marks the site of his land, is on a farm to the north of Locust Grove. He came to Rockingham from present Page County (formed from Shenandoah, 1831), and was a descendant of the early Hollingsworth family of Frederick. (See page 134.)

HOLLINGSWORTH

Valentine Hollingsworth, Sr., the immigrant, it is related, came to America with William Penn. He was born about 1635, and was living in 1710. By tradition, he married, as his first wife, Catherine, the daughter of Henry Cornish, High Sheriff of London. His wife Ann Calvert died in 1697. In 1682, he patented 986 acres of land in Brandywine Hundred, New Castle County, Delaware, and on this settled. He was a member of the Society of Friends, and filled many important positions in the Colony, among them serving in the Assembly, 1683, 1687, and 1695.

One of his sons, who came to America with him, was Thomas, of Rockland Manor, New Castle County, Delaware, who died near what is now Winchester, Virginia, 1732. Thomas married, first, Margaret ——. She died in 1686-7. He married second, 1692, Grace Cook. By his first wife he had one son Abraham, and by the second four sons, three of whom lived to be married, viz., Thomas b. 1698, Jacob, b. 1704, and Joseph, b. 1709. Abraham and Joseph settled in Virginia.

Abraham Hollingsworth, the son of Thomas, was born 1st Mo. 19, 1686. He married in 1710, Ann Robinson, who died in 1747. In 1732, he purchased, of Alexander Ross, 582 acres of land near later Winchester, Virginia, on which he resided until his death in 1748. (See page 112.) He had two sons George, b. 1712, and Isaac, b. 1722, d. 1759. George married, 1st, Hannah McKay, 1734, the daughter of Robert McKay, Sr., associate of Joist Hite, and 2nd, Jane ——, and in 1762 removed to South Carolina. Among his sons was Robert, b. 1744, d. 1799, who married Hannah Rice about 1769, and resided near Winchester. She died in 1833. Their sons were George, b. 1770, Joseph, b. 1773, Lewis, b. 1775, Robert, Abraham, Isaac, John, James, and Edmund, several of whom removed to Shelby County, Kentucky. George married in Frederick, 1799, Mary Gaunt. Lewis married in Frederick, 1814, Abigail Parkins.

Isaac Hollingsworth, son of Abraham, inherited his father's original 582 acres, a part of which, "The Homestead," is still in the possession of his descendants. He married in 1748, Rachel Parkins, b. 1724, d. 1806. In 1757, as a minister of the Quaker sect, he removed to Loudoun County, Virginia. He and wife Rachel had two sons, Abraham, b. 1749, and Jonah, b. 1754, d. 1801, of whom the latter inherited the Winchester homestead. Jonah married, 1778, Hannah Miller of Maryland, b. 1755, d. 1836. A son Samuel, b. 1784, was residing in Shenandoah County in 1821. (See, *Hollingsworth Genealogical Memoranda*, by W. B. Hollingsworth, Baltimore, Md., 1884.)

George Hollingsworth, of Rockingham, (probably grandson of Abraham, brother of Jonah) had children, Barbara Katherine, Mary, Jane, Susan, George, John, b. June 20, 1829, James, and Amanda, b. November 19, 1827. Of these; Barbara married John Harrison above; Mary married William Bowyers, and had Joseph, Daniel, George, David, John Newton, Houston, William, Luther, Edward, Dorcas, and Maggie; Jane married Isaac Graves, of Frederick County; Susan (d. about 1856, aged 33 ?) married Philip Webster, (d. 1904 c. aged 67), of Page County, and removed with him to Vigo County, Indiana, and had: James Ira, John William, Amanda Jane, b. July 26, 1849, Barbara Ann, b. 1851, and Mary Elizabeth; George moved to Vigo County, Indiana, married Eliza Evans, moved to Kansas, and then to Arkansas; John died in Rockingham, Dec. 20, 1902; James married Catherine Dovel, and moved to Vigo County, Indiana; Amanda died in Rockingham, Dec. 16, 1898, unmarried. Of Susan and Philip Webster's children, James Ira, married Emma Ripetoe, in Illinois, and died in Indiana; John William died young; Amanda Jane married, 3rd Sept., 1868, in Indiana, Daniel B. Shank, (b. in Ohio, Oct. 8, 1838, d. Aug 20, 1924), son of Daniel Shank of Augusta County, Virginia, and wife Elizabeth Conway, removed to Coffeyville, Kansas, and had: Anna Myrtle, b. Dec. 22, 1871, m. Rev. Frank F. Walters, and Hattie Estella, b. Dec. 18, 1877, drowned June 15, 1890; Barbara Ann married Frank Warren Warner, (d. 1927), Mary Elizabeth died in infancy.

* * * * * *

John and Barbara Harrison resided on Smiths Creek, to the east of Mauzy, where he owned a fine farm; since his day, and until recently, the home of his daughter, Frances, and now (1931) the property of his Byrd grandchildren. His land was obtained by purchase from James Pickering, a relative. His home stood on the eastern, or opposite side of the creek from the present residence. The old stone spring-house by the creek, the upper story of which housed the spinning wheel and loom, is yet standing.

John Harrison served for a time as a "Justice of the Peace" of Rockingham. He was a man of strong convictions and high integrity. He refused to own slaves, and bitterly opposed Secession, holding that it was a great mistake for the South to give up her representation in Congress. Believing as he did, he voted against Virginia's withdrawal from the Union, and was illegally arrested at the polls for his act.

During the war, his barn was the only one of two or three in the county not burned. On the occasion of Sheridan's raid, the latter's troops camped on the place and it was threatened, a fire was started in its stables, but the officer in charge of the incendiary squad, upon being paid a sum of money, was induced to withdraw his men in time for the blaze to be readily extinguished after his departure.

In religion, Mr. Harrison was of the Universalist faith, although not known to have belonged to any church. On one occasion he was instrumental in having a minister of this denomination preach at Bethlehem Stone Church. He was of a studious mind, well versed in the Scriptures, and always ready to maintain his point of view; particularly enjoying a friendly debate with a pastor of some other faith. Being of a hospitable nature and widely acquainted, and the father of a large family of children, his home was the center of much social activity of the neighborhood.

His death occurred Jan. 19, 1880. His wife survived him ten years, lacking five days. Both were interred in the old family cemetery on their place, where their markers may be seen. His will, dated March 23, 1858, and proved at the February term of court, 1880, reads—

Will of John Harrison

I, John Harrison, of the County of Rockingham, State of Virginia, being of sound mind and disposing memory, do make and publish this my last will and testament.

First: I will that my Executor herein named, shall, so soon after my death as he my said Executor shall deem best for the interests of my Estate, make sale of all my property both real and personal on such terms as he shall think best, and so far as my Real Estate is concerned my said Executor has full power and authority to sell either publicly or privately according as he in his good discretion may consider the most advantageous to the interests of my Estate.

Second: Out of the proceeds of such sales and collections of moneys due me I will that all my just debts & charges of administration shall first be paid, and all of my Estate of whatever kind that may remain after such payments, I devise, give and bequeath to my wife Barbara Catherine, while she remains my widow, and if she remains my widow until her death then to dispose of the same in such manner as she thinks proper.

Third: I nominate and appoint as my Executor my friend Wm. W. Carpenter.

In Testimony whereof I have hereunto set my hand & seal this 23rd day of March 1858.

John Harrison (SEAL.)

Signed, sealed, published and declared by the testator, John Harrison, as and for his last will and testament, in presence of us, who in his presence at his request and in the presence of each other, have hereunto subscribed our names as witnesses.

E. T. H. Warren.
Wm. W. Carpenter.
Joseph Roades.

I have determined to alter the above will so as to constitute my beloved wife, Barbara Catherine, my Executor, and without her giving security. In witness whereof, I have hereunto set my hand and seal this 9th. August, 1863.

John Harrison (SEAL.)

Signed, sealed, published and declared by the testator, John Harrison, as and for a codicil to his last will and testament, in presence of us, who in his presence and at his request, and in the presence of each other, has hereunto subscribed our names as witnesses.

John B. Smith.
Curtis Yates.
John Moore.

Virginia: In the County Court of Rockingham County, February Term 1880.

The writing purporting to be the last will and testament of John Harrison, dec'd, together with a codicil thereto attached, was this day presented in Court, and the will being proved by the oaths of Wm. W. Carpenter & Joseph Roades, two of the subscribing witnesses thereto, and the codicil thereto attached by the oaths of John B. Smith and Curtis Yates, two of the subscribing witnesses thereto, were admitted to probate, and said will and codicil ordered to be recorded. And thereupon, on the motion of Barbara Catherine Harrison, the Executrix therein named, who made oath according to law, appeared in Court and entered into and acknowledged bond in the penalty of $18,000.00 conditioned according to law, waving the benefit of the Homestead Exemption as to this obligation; a certificate is granted her for obtaining a probat of said will of John Harrison, dec'd. in due form (said will providing that no security be required of her.)

Atteste J. T. Logan, Clerk.

* * * * * *

John Harrison, (12591), and wife Barbara Katherine's children were—

(125911) Mary—b. Dec. 24, 1838; d Jan. 3, 1839.

(125912) Barbara Katherine (Kate)—b. Jan. 5, 1840; d. Sept. 21, 1918; m. Nov. 12, 1868, Michael Jackson Martz, son of Hiram, b. May 30, 1843, d. Aug. 25, 1922.
See further record.

(125913) Elizabeth Ann, (Betty)—b. July 14, 1841; d. Aug. 1, 1902, unmarried.

(125914) Julia Smith—b. April 13, 1843; d. Feb. 2, 1917, unmarried.

(125915) David Warren—b. April 15, 1845; d. Jan 21, 1933; m., Nov. 22, 1880, Anna Amantha Houston, dau. of John Houston, (17845), b. Sept. 24, 1856, d. Feb. 19, 1921.
See further record.

(125916) William Carpenter—b. April 15, 1845; d. Aug. 9, 1925; m. June 12, 1884, Emma Jane Brubaker, dau. of Peter, b. Sept. 4, 1845, d. Oct. 6, 1899.
See further record.

(125917) George Hollingsworth—b. May 23, 1847; d. Mar. 6, 1932; m. 1st., May 24, 1878, Mary C. Moore, dau. of Reuben, (123438), b. 1853, d. 1883. m. 2nd., Oct. 28, 1896, Josephine (Jo) Moore, dau. of Joseph Moore, of Shenandoah.
See further record.

(125918) John Walton—b. July 1, 1849; d. Aug. 22, 1929; m. Jennie C. Rosenberger, dau. of Gideon, b. Oct. 1, 1854.
See further record.

(125919) Amanda Virginia (Jennie)—b. June 16, 1851; d. Feb. 26, 1917, unmarried.

(125920) Phocion—b. June 28, 1853; d. July 7, 1898, unmarried.

(125921) Lydia Frances (Fannie)—b. Sept. 13, 1855.
See further reference.

(125922) Emma Strickler—b. Dec. 18, 1857; m. Nov. 16, 1897, Joseph Mauzy, b. April 12, 1851.
See further record.

(125923) Nancy Gordon—b. May 9, 1860; m. Oct. 14, 1891, Joseph Byrd, b. May 14, 1860, son of Wm. P., and wife Catherine (125872).
See further record.

(125924) Lucy Pickering—b. Sept. 27, 1862; d. May 3, 1915, unmarried.

(Barbara K. and husband interred in Lacey Spring Cemetery; Mary, Elizabeth, Julia, William, and wife, John, Virginia, Phocion, and Lucy, in Harrison cemetery above, and Mary C. in the old Moore cemetery on Smiths Creek.)

(12592) NATHANIEL HARRISON, (1803-1839), the son of David Harrison, (1259), and wife Elizabeth, married, July 29, 1829, Mary High, (1810-1898), of Rockingham. On the eve of reaching his majority he journeyed to Ohio, probably with the intention of settling. The journal of his trip shows a familarity with different kinds of soil, and species of timber, very similar to that displayed by his brother John on his trip to Missouri. (See Chapter XX.)

Nathaniel Harrison settled on a tract of land given him by his father—Deed: April 2, 1834, Daniel Harrison of Rockingham to Nathaniel Harrison of the same county, "part of the Land conveyed by David Harrison to John Harrison, Nathaniel Harrison & Daniel Harrison by Deed of Gift bearing date the 1 day of September in the year 1832, as also the interest of the Said John Harrison in Said tract of land as conveyed by him to the said Nathaniel Harrison & Danl Harrison by Deed (of) bargain & Sale bearing date the fifth day of September 1832," etc. (Burnt Record D. B. 11, pp. 381-382.)

Nathaniel's land lay to the east of the Valley Pike, and is now marked by the site of the old family cemetery, and the long since abandoned old log house in which he resided. (See page 380.) His home was within a short distance of his father, and to the north of the latter.

His death occurred early in life. As recited by the inscription on his tombstone (in the cemetery above), "Nathaniel Harrison (son of david & Elizabeth) . . . was born Jan. 22, 1803, and died Feb. 26, 1839, aged 36 yrs. 1 mo. 4 days." (The stone having become broken, is now replaced by a more modern one, with the same dates). The inscription on his wife's marker, nearby, reads, "Our Mother Mary, wife of Nathaniel Harrison, born Feb. 9, 1810, died Dec. 31, 1898. Died in the Lord."

Nathaniel Harrison, (12592), and wife Mary, had issue—

(125921) Reuben W.—b. May 27, 1830; d. Aug. 19, 1913; m., Nov. 26, 1850, Hannah Sellers, b. Feb. 29, 1832, d. July 3, 1900.
See further record.

(125922) Nathaniel P.—b. Dec. 7, 1831; d. April 8, 1894, unmarried, in California, where he went as a young man.

(125923) Jacob Cowan—b. Nov. 22, 1832; d. Mar. 14, 1912; m., Nov. 14, 1854, Elizabeth Helen Hayne, b. June 12, 1832, d. Sept. 18, 1898.
See further record.

(125924) Frances—b. Apr. 29, 1834; d. May 25, 1889, unmarried.

(125925) David—b. Sept. 22, 1835; d. Sept. 10, 1853, unmarried.

(125926) Elizabeth—b. Feb. 2, 1837 d. Nov. 18, 1916, unmarried.

(125927) Susan—b. Nov. 15, 1838; d. Feb. 26, 1914, unmarried. Lived with sister Elizabeth (Betty), at Lacey Spring.

(All but Nathaniel P., and Jacob Cowan, interred in the cemetery above, from which their dates are taken. Jacob buried in Trinity Churchyard, on Keezletown Road.)

(12593) MARY HARRISON, (1805-1872), the daughter of David Harrison, (1259), and wife Elizabeth, married Reuben Walton, (123411), the son of Moses Walton, and wife Elizabeth, nee Moore. See Clan of John Harrison, 1. Line of Thomas Moore, 2. Line of Capt Reuben Moore, 3. Line of Moses Walton.

(12594) DANIEL HARRISON, (1807-1871), the son of David Harrison, (1259), and wife Elizabeth, married, first, April 23, 1834, Rhoda M. Brown, of Rockingham. "Rhoda M. Harrison once Rhoda M. Brown", says the inscription on her tombstone, in the old Harrison cemetery above, was born May 30, 1808, and died February. 8, 1844.

Daniel, like his brother Nathaniel, settled on the land given him by his father. His line is mentioned in the will of the latter. The land, as conveyed by deed of gift, noted in connection with Nathaniel, was deeded to Daniel, and his brothers John, and Nathaniel, jointly. John sold his interest to his brothers, who, on April 2, 1834, divided it amongst themselves. Following Daniel's conveyance to his brother Nathaniel, under the same date was recorded the deed from Nathaniel Harrison, and Mary, his wife, to Daniel Harrison, etc. Daniel's home was on the opposite side of the Valley Pike— The Long Grey Trail— from his brother, at the present Lilburn Long residence.

Following his first wife's death, Daniel Harrison married, second, March 22, 1849, Huldah B. Hayne, of Rockingham—born Aug. 10, 1824, died March 13, 1882—and in 1857 removed to Green County, Tennessee, settling on the French Broad River. From there, in 1869, he removed to Carroll County, Missouri, where he died.

Daniel Harrison, (12594), and wife Rhoda, had issue—

(125941) JOHN—b. Feb. 20, 1835; d. Feb. 17, 1921, Jefferson Co., Tenn.; m. Mary Rankin.
See further record.

(125942) ELIZABETH—b. Feb. 3, 1837; d. Nov. 20, 1846.

(125943) MARY—b. Jan. 25, 1839; d. Jan. 24, 1907; m. May 19, 1859, George Hinkle, moved to Ft. Collins, Colorado.
See further record.

(125944) JOSEPH—b. Aug. 13, 1840; d. Oct. 19, 1911; m., Oct. 24, 1872, Susan Slaton, b. Stokes Co., N. C.
See further record.

(125945) WILLIAM—b. Mar. 15, 1842; d. May 12, 1887, Zephyr, Brown Co., Texas, unmarried.

(125946) NANCY MARIA BROWN—b. Dec. 30, 1843; d. Dec. 3, 1892; m. Feb. 1869, John Tarwater, of Tenn. Removed to Indian Territory.
See further record.

Daniel Harrison, and wife Huldah, had issue—

(125947) MARGARET BURNLEY—b. Feb. 15, 1850; d. 1875 ?; m. Thomas West, Removed to La Flora Co., Miss.

(125948) JACOB HAYNE—b. Apr. 26, 1851; d. Jan. 25, 1922; m. 1st., Theodocia C. Powell, m. 2nd, Lillian Kendrick Byrn; he died at San Antonio, Texas.
See further record.

(125949) ALICE RHODA—b. Aug. 21, 1852; d. Sept. 10, 1852.

(125950) LYDIA VIRGINIA—b. Aug. 9, 1853; d. Dec. 11, 1879; m. Dr. Septimus Cropp. Resided in Carroll Co., Mo.
See further record.

(125951) HARRIETT GRAHAM—b. Jan. 25, 1855; m. Dec. 31, 1880, Albert W. Beck. Resided near Hale, Carroll Co., Mo.
See further record.

(125952) CASPER MOORE—b. Sept. 26, 1856; d. July 6, 1860.

(125953) CATHERINE HELENA—b. Nov. 26, 1858; d. Sept. 4, 1878, in Chariton Co. (?), Mo., unmarried.

(125954) REUBEN DAVID—b. Mar. 2, 1860; d. July 27, 1871, Carroll Co., Missouri.

(125955) ANDREW JOHNSON—b. May 4, 1862; m. 1st., Oct. 1889, Mary Elizabeth Crose, m. 2nd; May 18, 1898, Myra Gardner. Resides in Goldthwaite, Mills Co., Texas.
See further record.

(125956) NATHANIEL DOUGLAS—b. Feb. 26, 1864; d. Nov. 3, 1877, Carroll Co., Missouri.

(125957) GILBERT NEWTON—b. May 7, 1866; d. Nov. 26, 1927; m. Feb. 15, 1905, Belle Grinnan, dau. of William Grinnan of Tyler, Texas. Removed to Brownwood, Texas.
See further record.

(125958) EMMA JULIET—b. July 27, 1869, resides with bro. Andrew J., as above. (single.)

(Dates from list kindly furnished by Mrs. Gilbert Newton Harrison, through the courtesy of Mrs. A. W. Beck. Tombstones of Elizabeth and Alice R. in the Harrison cemetery on the present Lilburn Long place, near Lacey Spring.)

(12595) LYDIA HARRISON, (1809-1893), the daughter of David Harrison, (1259), and wife Elizabeth, married Madison Moore, (123431), the son of Reuben Moore. See Clan of John Harrison, 1. Line of Thomas Moore, 2. Line of Capt. Reuben Moore, 3. Line of Reuben Moore.

(12596) REUBEN N. HARRISON, (1812-1885), the son of David Harrison, (1259), and wife Elizabeth, married February 20, 1840, Catharine, the daughter of John Allebaugh, of Rockingham.

Reuben Harrison resided for a time at Melrose, on "The Long Grey Trail," and later removed to Cross Keys, to the east of Harrisonburg, where he owned a valuable farm.

He represented his county, Rockingham, in the Virginia House of Delegates, 1860-1861, at the outbreak of the War-between-the-States, and from 1877 to 1880.

Reuben Harrison, (12596), and wife Catharine had issue—

(125961) JOHN THOMAS—b. Jan. 1, 1843; d. June 2, 1915; m., Jan. 16, 1873, Emma White, b. Oct. 28, 1853, d. Dec. 21, 1925. Removed to Missouri.
See further record.

(125962) David—d. young.
(125963) Daniel Smith—b. Nov. 15, 1845; d. April 26, 1919, unmarried.
See further reference.
(125964) James—d. young.
(125965) Elizabeth Margaret—b. June 27, 1849; d. April 4, 1917, unmarried.
Resided with brother Charles.
(125966) Charles DeWitt—b. Jan. 26, 1851; d. April 21, 1933; m. June 3, 1891, Anna M. H. Hank, b. July 17, 1864, d. May 21, 1901. Resided in Harrisonburg.
See further record.

(Daniel, Elizabeth, Charles, and Anna M., interred in Woodbine Cemetery, Harrisonburg.)

(12598) ELIZABETH ANN HARRISON, (1816-1895), the daughter of David Harrison, (1259), and wife Elizabeth, married John Moore, (123433), son of Reuben Moore. See Clan of John Harrison, 1. Line of Thomas Moore, 2. Line of Capt. Reuben Moore, 3. Line of Reuben Moore.

HENTON

(12599), BARBARA CATHERINE HARRISON, (1823-1877), the daughter of David Harrison, (1259), and wife Elizabeth, married Andrew S. Henton, of Rockingham. Andrew and wife resided on the Keezletown Road, to the south of Cross Keys, near Harrisonburg. He was born June 14, 1821, and died June 8, 1895.

William Henton from England was a settler in Berks County, Pennsylvinia, prior to the Revolution. He removed to Rockingham County, Virginia, where he died in 1786. He had three sons and five daughters. (See, Vol. 61, No. 2, Feb. 1927, Dau. ingham. Andrew and wife resided on the Keezeltown Road, to the north of Cross of Amer. Rev. Mag., p. 156.) "John Hinton of County of Berks, Province of Pennsylvania," was deeded 400 acres of land on Linville Creek by Jeremiah Harrison, in 1765. Esther Henton, the widow of John Henton, deceased, "On Saturday before the 3rd Lords Day in June," 1791, presented to the Linville Creek Baptist Church her letter of dismission, dated Nov. 23, 1766, from a church in Cumry Township, Berks County, Pennsylvania, and was received a member of the Linville Creek Church. (See pages 271 and 303.)

Andrew Henton, and wife Barbara Catherine, (12599), had children—

(125991) John—b. Dec. 7, 1846; d. April 9, 1908; m. May 9, 1882, Florence Alberta West, b. Dec. 26, 1863.
See further record.
(125992) Harrison Pickering—b. July 21, 1848; d. Sept. 6, 1851.
(125993) Mary Elizabeth—b. July 2, 1850; d. 1914; m. May 30, 1871, William H. Neff, b. July 2, 1850.
See further record.
(125994) Francis Marion—b. Feb. 12, 1853; d. Dec. 30, 1907, unmarried.
(125995) Josephine A. C.—b. May 14, 1856; d. Oct. 7, 1923, unmarried.
(125996) George W.—b. March 4, 1859; d. Jan. 26, 1861.
(125997) Nancy V. J.—b. April 25, 1863; d. May 3, 1915; m. Samuel A. Myers, b. Nov. 21, 1866, d. June 3, 1897.

(125998) Ella Gordon—b. May 22, 1867, residing in Washington, D. C. (1930.) unmarried.

(D. S. H. MSS.; Josephine and Nancy interred at Bridgewater, Rockingham Co., John, Harrison, Francis Marion, and George, in Sellars cemetery on Keezletown Road.)

---

2. LINE OF JOHN (JACK) CHRISMAN

(12601) JOSEPH CHRISMAN, (1797-1874), the son of John Chrisman, and wife Ann, (1260), nee Harrison, married, as his first wife, Elizabeth Lincoln. Her tombstone, standing in the old New Erection Churchyard, to the west of Harrisonburg, recites that "Elizabeth Chrisman, wife of Joseph Chrisman and daughter of Jacob and Dorcas Lincoln . . . . departed this life Jan. 4, 1824, aged 20 years, 4 months."

In referring to her, the author of the *Memoir* states that "her father left her a fair legacy and two slaves"—Scipio Africanus and Anne. She lived only a short time following her marriage, "and left little Jack (her only child), to the tender care of her doting slave woman. (*Memoirs*, p. 52.)

Joseph Chrisman married, as his second wife, Jane Chrisman, the daughter of Isaac Chrisman, of Stephens City, whose father, John, was in turn a brother of George, the founder of the Rockingham line. These last two, John and George, married, respectively, the sisters Elizabeth and Hannah McDowell. Isaac Chrisman, the father of Jane, lived at the old Jacob Chrisman homestead in Frederick.

Joseph Chrisman migrated with his familly from Rockingham County, Virginia, in 1837, to Lafayette County, Missouri, where he died Aug. 28, 1874.

His children were—

By first wife, Elizabeth—

(126011) John—d. (recently, 1900), at Bozeman, Montana. m. ———. See further record.

By second wife, Jane—

(126012) Isaac—

(126013) Albert—

(126014) Joseph Marcus—b. Apr. 20, 1831; d. Sept. 3, 1911, at Broken Bow, Neb.; m. 1st, Oct. 31, 1854, Isabell Richardson, of Front Royal, Va., d. May 14, 1889, dau. of Marcus Richardson, and wife Harriett Chrisman, sister of Jane, above; m. 2nd., Mrs. Mary Deerisling, of Front Royal, b. 1844.
See further record.

(126015) Ann Elizabeth—

(126016) Charles—d. 1924 c.; m. Bettie Brooks, d. 1927. Settled in Nebraska(?). See further record.

(126017) Henry—m. ——, had issue, Virginia, La Rue, and Claude.

(126018) Virginia (Jennie)—m. ——— Cooper, two children, Elizabeth and William. (probably others.)

(126019) Harrison Taylor—.

(126020) William—(d. prior to 1904). Banker of Kansas City, Missouri; m. ——; A daughter,
1. Mrs. Logan O. Swope—resides in Kansas City.

Said to have been four more.

(D. S. H. MSS., and W. H. C. papers.)

(12602) GEORGE HARRISON CHRISMAN, (1799-1870), the son of John Chrisman, and wife Ann, (1260), nee Harrison, married, March 14, 1822, Martha Davis Herring, (19512), the daughter of Alexander Herring. (See page 419.)

George Chrisman, as stated in the *Memoirs*, "was a large planter and slave owner" of Rockingham. He was a prominent resident of the county and a splendid type of the gentleman of the old school. He resided on the homestead land of his father at Chrisman Post Office, near Harrisonburg.

He and wife Martha had issue—

(126021) Herring—b. Sept. 16, 1823; d. Aug. 14, 1911; m. Sept. 25, 1854, Emma Hunt Berry, of Connecticut. Removed to Illinois, 1854, thence to Iowa.
See further record.

(126022) Burke (M. D.)—b. Sept. 5, 1827; d. July 5, 1895; m. Henrietta Warder, of Philadelphia, dau. of John H. Warder. She d. Dec. 8, 1890.
See further record.

(126023) Margaret Ann—b. Oct. 24, 1829; d. Apr. 26, 1915; m. 1st., Benjamin Buckley, of Miss.; m. 2nd., Dr. William Williams, of Harrisonburg.
See further record.

(126024) George (Major)—b. June 21, 1832; d. Nov. 23, 1915; m. Nov. 13, 1867, Lucy Gilmore Grattan, b. Aug. 19, 1835.
See further record.

(126025) William Joseph—b. June 11, 1834; d. May 24, 1912; m. 1st., May 28, 1865, Jane Giles, of Nelson Co., Va., b. Sept. 15, 1842, d. Dec. 15, 1873. m. 2nd., Jan. 13, 1875, Virginia Gay.
See further record.

(126026) Martha Grattan—b. Dec. 31, 1840; d. 1873, unmarried.

(D. S. H. MSS.; Tombstones of Burke, and wife Margaret, and Joseph and 1st wife, in New Erection Cemetery, from which their birth and death dates are taken.)

SPEARS

(12603) MARGARET M. CHRISMAN (1801-1854), the daughter of John Chrisman, and wife Ann, (1260), nee Harrison, born January 16, 1801, died November 4, 1854, married, October 26, 1825, Charles C. Spears, of Kentucky, born March 7, 1802, died November 10, 1855. (Dates of births and deaths from tombstones in cemetery at Wagner's Mill, in Rockingham.)

Charles and Margaret Spears resided at the old Capt. George Chrisman homestead, near Edom. (See page 383.) His father was John Spears, who early emigrated from the Valley to Kentucky, and whose wife was Margaret Chrisman, sister of John Chrisman, the father of Margaret M.

Charles C. Spears, and wife Margaret, (12603), had children—

(126031) Elizabeth—m. William Glasgow, of Botetourt Co., Va.
See further record.

(126032) Lina—

(126033) John—m. Sue McDowell.

(126034) Rebecca—m. Rice Warren, (12851), son of Jehu.
See further record.

(126035) Charles C.—m. Sallie Gray; issue one daughter.

(D. S. H. MSS.; a daughter "Maggie," deceased, is named in letter Mrs. C. S. T. to W. H. C., January 11, 1930, among the W. H. C. papers.)

---

2. LINE OF SAMUEL HARRISON.

(12612) JAMES HARRISON ( ), the son of Samuel Harrison, (1261), and wife Esther, married Susan Schultz. Issue—

(126121) an infant died young.
(126122) Howard H.—m. Peachy Ann Wash.
(126123) William Henry—m. Fannie ———.
(126124) Esther C.—m. Thomas Wash.
(126125) Elizabeth Jane—m. 1st, James Dixon; m. 2nd, ———;
(126126) Amanda V.—m. Jack Turner.
(126127) John P.—m. 1st., B. Bowling; m. 2nd., ———; m. 3rd ———. No further record.

(D. S. H. MSS.)

CAMPBELL

(12614) MARY HARRISON, ( ), the daughter of Samuel Harrison, (1261) and wife Esther, married John Campbell. Issue—

(126141) Isaac Newton (Rev.)—m. Eliza. C. Lockridge. See further record.
(126142) Frances Ann Gilliam—
(126143) Howard S.—m. 1st, Jennie Whitmore; m. 2nd, Margaret Taylor. See further record.

(D. S. H. MSS.)

CHAPTER XXII

Including an Early University of Virginia Family and Several Congressional Lines

FIFTH GENERATION CONTINUED

TO THE LONG ROLL of Rockingham's distinguished native sons belongs Dr. Gessner Harrison, for many years the occupant of the Chair of Ancient Languages at the University of Virginia. Harrison Hall, one of the main buildings of the Virginia State Teachers College, at Harrisonburg, is dedicated to his memory. A tablet affixed to its walls, in the lobby of the Hall, bears silent tribute to his usefulness—

HARRISON HALL

Named in Honor of Gessner Harrison: M. D.
1807-1862
Son of Harrisonburg,
Citizen of Virginia.
For thirty years professor of Latin
In the University of Virginia.
Master of Scholars
He served his people through the schools.

To this roll also belongs his contemporary, James Harrison Cravens (1802-1876), a representative from Indiana, in the Twenty-seventh Congress of the United States, and one time candidate for Governor of his State.

Both were born and reared in Harrisonburg, and as children played together on its streets, and attended the same church and school. Each was the son of an esteemed physician of the town, and their families had long been intimate.

A sister of the father of one, married a brother of the father of the other, and from this union descended a grandson, another contemporary, whose place belongs on the roll—James Addison Cravens (1818-1893), member of the Thirty-seventh and Thirty-eighth Congresses of the United States, from Indiana.

Within sight of the spot of the above State Teachers College, was born a cousin of the three, whose grandson, and great-grandson, each served in Congress, viz; Jordan Edgar Cravens (1830-1914), of the Forty-fifth, Forty-sixth, and Forty-seventh Congresses, and William Ben Cravens (b. 1872), of the Sixtieth, Sixty-first, and Sixty-second Congresses, both from Arkansas.

CLAN OF CAPT. DANIEL HARRISON

1. LINE OF JESSE HARRISON, SR.
2. LINE OF DANIEL HARRISON

(16323) PATTON DOUGLAS HARRISON, (1795- 1841), the son of Daniel Harrison, (1632), and wife Ann, married, September 28, 1820, Polly Elgin, (1804-1870) (See page 389.)

Patton Harrison and wife resided at "The Pines," the old homestead of his father, on the Van Meter Pike, near Lexington, Kentucky. He and wife Polly had issue, a daughter—

(163231) ANN PATTON—b. April 14, 1823; d. Feb. 2, 1844; m. May 19, 1842, John S. Williams.
See further record.

---

2. LINE OF BENJAMIN HARRISON

DECKER

(16344) ELIZA JANE HARRISON (1817-1841), the daughter of Benjamin Harrison, (1634), and wife Elizabeth, married, October 19, 1836, Rev. Michael Decker, thought to have been born in Virginia. Rev. Decker and wife resided at La Porte, Indiana, where she died, January 20, 1841. Issue—

(163441) ELIZABETH JANE—b. July 29, 1837; d. 1854.
(163442) WILLIAM PORTER BASCOM—b. Aug. 5, 1838; d. July 8, 1899, at Colfax, Washington; m. ———.
See further record.
(163443) SARAH ELIZA—b. July 23, 1840; d. young.

(Wm. P. interred at Colfax, Washington; Elizabeth J., in Decker lots, East Side Cemetery, Rockford, Ill; birth dates from Bible record before mentioned—see page 390.)

(16345) JOHN S. K. HARRISON (1818-1864), the son of Benjamin Harrison (1634), and wife Elizabeth, settled in Texas. He served as Chief of Scouts in 1836, and commanded Texas troops in 1848. During the War-between-the-States, he served in the Confederate Army, as Lieut. Gen. of Texas troops. He was captured with Pemberton at Vicksburg, Miss., July 4, 1863, after which he retired to his Texas ranch on the Mederia River, where he died in 1864. He married, and had two daughters—

(163451) a daughter—m. J. P. Jolly, of San Pasas, Texas.
(163452) a daughter—m. John Moore, of Texas.
(probably a son William, also.)

(16347) WILLIAM M. HARRISON, (1823-1852), the son of Benjamin Harrison, (1634), and wife Elizabeth, following his father's death in Tennessee, removed with his mother to Valparaiso, Indiana, in which city he resided until his death. He married June 15, 1847, Eliza Gwinn, (b. Feb. 17, 1826, d. July 14, 1900.) Issue—

(163471) ELLA W.—b. 16th Aug., 1851; d. May 10, 1881; m. 1875, Frank M. Axe.
See further record.

(Likely also, Fremont C., b. 28 June, 1848, and Walter C., b. 28 June, 1849, both of whom died young. Dates from Bible record above.)

1. LINE OF COL. DANIEL SMITH

2. LINE OF JOHN SMITH

(16512) DANIEL SMITH (1779-1850), the son of John Smith, and wife Margaret, married, June 10, 1809, Frances Strother Duff, the daughter of James Duff, of Rockingham, and wife Elizabeth, nee Strother.

On reaching his majority Daniel Smith came into possession of his interest in his grand-father's estate. He studied law under Judge Bushrod Washington, and began the practice of his profession at his old home in Harrisonburg. He later settled at Waverly, near the former home of his uncle, Benjamin Smith, where he generously dispensed his hospitality.

From 1803 to 1806, he served in the Virginia House of Delegates, and from 1804 to 1811, was commonwealth attorney of Rockingham. In 1811, he was appointed Judge of the Circuit Superior Court of the county, serving in this capacity to 1850, or about forty years. His portrait, which adorns the court room in the Court House at Harrisonburg, was long the only picture the officials would permit in the room. (Copy in Wayland's *History of Rockingham Co.,* p. 252.)

Judge Daniel Smith (16512), and wife Frances had issue—

(165121) MARGARET DAVIS—b. April 4, 1810, d. Aug. 25, ——; m. 1st., 1834, John Craig; m. 2nd, in 1845, M. H. Effinger.
See further record.

(165122) ELIZABETH STROTHER—b. Mar. 16, 1814; d. ——; m. Aug. 2, 1832, Judge Christopher Columbus Scott, of Arkansas, b. Apr. 22, 1807, Halifax Co., Va., d. Jan. 13, 1859.
See further record.

(165123) LUCIUS QUINTUS— b. 1816; d. 1847, in Dayton, Ohio, unmarried.

(165124) FRANCES EVELYN—b. 1819; d. ——; m., July 2, 1839, Andrew Plunkett Beirne.
See further record.

(165125) MARIE ANTOINETTE—b. Sept. 18, 1827; d. Feb. 1, 1902; m., Apr. 29, 1847, William Henry Tams, b. Dec. 8, 1824, d. Aug. 2, 1873.
See further record.

(165126) JOHN WILLIAMS GREEN—b. Sept. 17, 1829; d. ——; m. 1st, Nov. 30, 1853, Catherine M. Taylor; m. 2nd., Mar. 13, 1875, Sarah McKeldon.
See further record.

(165127) DANIEL—b. April 10, 1835; d. 1860, unmarried.

(D. S. H. MSS.)

---

2. LINE OF BENJAMIN SMITH

(16561) JOHN SMITH (1783-1827), the son of Benjamin Smith, (1656), and wife Elizabeth, married, in 1809, Adamena Carthae, the daughter of John Carthae, of Rockingham, who gave his consent.

John Carthae was a descendant of one of the early families of the Valley of Virginia. One of the name (Carthrea) was listed in the *Heads of Families* Census, of Virginia,—Rockingham—1784, as having in his family "10 White souls," and owning one dwelling, and seven other buildings. Adamena is described as having been of remarkable beauty, a devoted Christian, and universally loved.

John Smith, following his marriage, moved with his family to Charleston, now West

Virginia, where his fourth child was born, and where his wife died. He later removed to Lancaster, Ohio. In the War of 1812, he served in the comissary department.
He and wife Adamena had children—

(165611) CHARLES—b. 1810; d. 1834, c. Was elected to Virginia State Senate in 1834, but died in Vicksburg; Miss., before taking his seat.
(165612) MARY—b. 1811; d. 1837; m. 1834, George Hudson.
(165613) ELIZABETH FRANCES—b. 1819; d. ——; m. Willam Noyes, of West Va.
See further record.
(165614) JOHN BENJAMIN—b. June 22, 1822; d. Apr. 20, 1887; m. July 18, 1844, Caroline Amelia Welsh, b. Feb. 16, 1827.
See further record.
(D. S. H. MSS.)

BROWN

(16562) NANCY SMITH (1784-), the daughter of Benjamin Smith (1656), and wife Elizabeth, married, in 1802, Major Joseph Brown, of Rockingham; surety William Cravens. Issue—
(165621) BENJAMIN SMITH—m. Catherine Thomas.
See further record.
(165622) THOMAS—m. Lucy Hollister. No issue.
(165623) MARY—m. ——Pyle; no issue.
(165624) ELIZA—m. ——Knowlton.
See further record.
(165625) OPHELIA—b. Oct. 17, 1816; d. July 8, 1883; m. Worthy Paul Meacham, b. Apr. 24, 1802; d. May 17, 1853.
See further record.
(165626) ELLEN—d. 1879; m. Dr. John Russell, of Mt. Vernon, Ohio, where she died. Many descendants in California. X
(165627) ADELAIDE—m. —— Orr. Children all died young.
(D. S. H. MSS.)

(16563) ROBERT SMITH (1785-1870), the son of Benjamin Smith, (1656), and wife Elizabeth, married, in 1834, Phoebe Searle, of Providence, Rhode Island. Robert and wife settled at Lancaster, Ohio. Issue—

(165631) ELIZABETH CRAVENS—b. Apr. 5, 1835; d. 1858, unmarried.
(165632) DANIEL—b. 1837; m. Dilly Hunter.
(165633) GEORGE CREED—b. 1839; d. young.
(165634) JAMES—b. 1841; m. Rebecca McLeary.
See further record.
(165635) FRANCES (Fannie)—b. Dec. 8, 1844; m. June 2, 1870, Samuel Rutter.
See further record.
(D. S. H. MSS.)

(16564) DANIEL SMITH (1787 c.-1854), the son of Benjamin Smith (1656), and wife Elizabeth, married Mrs. Nancy Harriman, of present West Virginia. He practiced medicine in Lancaster, Ohio, and Charleston (now) West Virginia, during early life, and in the War of 1812 was a Surgeon General. He served under Gen. William Henry Harrison, and also under Commodore Perry at the battle of Lake Erie. From 1817 to 1818 he was a member of the Ohio legislature, and during the sessions of 1828, '29, '37, '38, '41, and '44, was a delegate from Kanawha County to the Virginia legislature. He was a man of fine mind, remarkably bright and witty, and weiged over 300 pounds. No issue.

CREED

(16565) MARGARET SMITH (1792-1823), the daughter of Benjamin Smith (1656), and wife Elizabeth, married, in 1811, John Creed, of Lancaster, Ohio. Issue—

(165651) Mary—b. 1812; d. 1813.
(165652) George—b. 1814; d. Aug. 29, 1845; m. Elizabeth A. Clement, d. May 7, 1889.
See further record.
(165653) Mary—b. 1816; d. ——; m. William A. Ritchie.
See further record.
(165654) Elizabeth—b. Oct. 1, 1818; m. Derius Tallmadge, d. ——. No issue.
She was residing in Trenton, New Jersey, 1903.
(165655) Margaret Davis—b. 1820; d. 1866; m. Major Andrew Parks, of Charleston, West Virginia.
See further record.
(165656) Jane Harrison—b. 1822; d. 1859; m. John C. Fall.
See further record.
(D.S.H. MSS.)

(16567) BENJAMIN HARRISON SMITH (1797-1887), the son of Benjamin Smith (1656), and wife Elizabeth, married, December 19, 1826, Roxalana Noyes, daughter of Isaac Noyes, of Charleston, West Virginia. He and wife settled at Charleston.

He was a large land owner of western Virginia, and for over sixty years a noted lawyer. In 1833, he was elected to the Virginia State Senate, and was later twice reelected. In 1849, he was appointed United States Attorney for the western district of Virginia, by President Taylor, and continued in office during the terms of Taylor and Fillmore. In 1852, he was elected a member of the Virginia Constitutional Convention, and in 1862, was a member of the convention which formed the State of West Virginia. He was again appointed District Attorney, this time by President Lincoln, and held the office five years under him, at the end of which time he resigned.

Benjamin Harrison Smith (16567), and wife Roxalana, had children—

(165671) Cynthia Elizabeth—b. Oct. 22, 1827; m. Fred C. Brooks.
See further record.
(165672) Isaac Noys—b. Apr. 6, 1831; m. Nov. 29, 1860; Caroline Shewsbury Quarrier, b. Oct. 23, 1839.
See further record.
(165673) Roxalana Emeline—b. May 13, 1841; m. Col. Amos Balfour Jones.
See further record.
(D. S. H. MSS.)

(16568) JAMES HARRISON SMITH (1798-9 - 1830), the son of Benjamin Smith, (1656), and wife Elizabeth, married Nov. 1828, Elizabeth Standeland White, daughter of Rev. William White, of Philadelphia. He settled at Lancaster, Ohio, where he was a succesful merchant. Issue—

(165681) Elizabeth Tracy—b. Aug. 3, 1829; m. Dec. 10, 1850, William Latta.
He d. Nov. 13, 1874.
See further record.

(D. S. H. MSS.)

---

2. LINE OF WILLIAM SMITH

HARRIS

(16612) JANE H. SMITH (1800-), the daughter of William Smith, (1661), of Smithland, and wife Diana, married Dr. Michael Harris, of Rockingham. Issue—

(166121) McDonough—
(166122) James—
(166123) Crampton—
(D. S. H. MSS.)

Yancey of Rockingham

YANCEY

(16614) MARY SMITH, (1804-), the daughter of William Smith (1661), of Smithland, and wife Diana, married, as his first wife, William B. Yancey, of Rockingham.

William Burbridge Yancey was the son of Layton Yancey, and wife Fannie, nee Lewis, the daughter of Thomas Lewis, son of John Lewis, the early Augusta County pioneer. He was the second child in a family of ten children, viz: Layton, Charles, John, Albert, Thomas, Fannie, Clarissa, Maria, Louisa, and himself. His father, Layton Yancey, was a Lieut in the First Continental Dragoons in the Revolutionary War. Lieut. Yancey was the son of John Yancey, from Culpeper County to Augusta. John, through his father Lewis Davis Yancey, who married Mildred Kavanaugh, was descended from one of the original four Yancey brothers (Charles, William, Joel, or Robert), who came to Virginia, with Sir William Berkeley, in 1642. The family is of Welsh origin. (See, *Genealogical and Historical Notes on Culpeper Co., Va.*, by Raleigh Travers Green, p. 81.)

Col. William B. Yancey, and wife Mary, had issue—

(166141) Diana Smith—b. 1831; d. 1895; m. George O. Conrad.
See further record.
(166142) Thomas Layton (Capt.)—b. 1833; d. 1862; m. Margaret Newman.
See further record.
(166143) William B, (Capt.)—b. 1836; d. ——; m. Julia Winsboro.
See further record.
(166144) Edward S.—b. 1838; d. 1885; m. Frances Mauzy.
See further record.
(166145) Charles Albert—b. ——; d. ——; m. Julia Morrison.
See further record.
(166146) Mary Frances—b. ——; d. ——, unmarried.

(166147) MARGARET JANE—b. 1844; d. 1895; m. Joseph Mauzy.
See further record.

(D. S. H. MSS.)

---

2. LINE OF REV. JAMES SMITH

SAGAR

(16621) JANE HARRISON SMITH (1805-), the daughter of Rev. James Smith (1662), and wife Rebecca, married, September 25, 1823, at Mt Vernon, Ohio, Col. Charles Sagar. Issue—

(166211) ELIZABETH REBECCA JACKSON—b. Oct. 18, 1824; d. Nov. 21, 1854, unmarried.
(166212) JANE CAROLINE—b. Jan 19, 1827; d. March 19, 1866, unmarried.
(166213) DIANA ELIZA—b. Oct. 16, 1829; d. June 22, 1898, unmarried.
(166214) MARCUS SMITH—b. Dec. 26, 1831; d. March 30, 1897; m., Dec. 31, 1858, Eleanor McMaster.
See further record.
(166215) CHARLES HENRY—b. Nov. 5, 1838, Lancaster, O.; m., Mar. 3, 1859, Amelia W. Starkel.
See further record.
(166216) FRANCES HENRIETTA—b. Aug. 22, 1844; m. Nov. 19, 1861, John H. Eckert.
See further record.
(166217) IRENE (twin of Frances)—d. Feb. 6, 1856, Oakland, Ohio.

(D.S.H. MSS.)

(16623) BENJAMIN F. SMITH (1811-), the son of Rev. James Smith (1662), and wife Rebecca, married, 1830, Julia Stilly. He was Auditor of Knox County, Ohio, and for four years a member of the State legislature. In 1857, he removed to Minnesota, in which state he was the mayor of Mankata, and served as a State Senator from that district. He was Grand Commander of the Knight Templars of Minnesota, Colonel of the 8th Minnesota Regiment, and commanded Ft. Snelling during the Indian war. Issue—

(166231) REBECCA—b. Feb.2, 1831; d. Aug. 26, 1849.
(166232) JAMES MONROE—b. Dec. 31, 1832; d. Mar. 17, 1836.
(166233) JOHN STILLY—b. Apr. 7, 1834; d. ——; m. Mary Dayton.
See further record.
(166234) DIANA JANE—b. Jan. 23, 1836; d. ——; m. Andrew C. Dunn.
See further record.
Bixby
(166235) SARAH— b. July 31, 1837; d. ——; m. Nahum Bixby.
See further record.
(166236) MARY HENRIETTA—b. Mar. 4, 1839; d. ——; m. George Parrot.
See further record.
(166237) ELIZA ANN—b. Aug. 13, 1840; d. ——; m. C. Brown.
See further record.
(166238) EMMETT THOMPSON—b. Apr. 17, 1842; d. June 22, 1843.
(166239) DORCAS VIRGINIA—b. June 19, 1844; d. Apr. 17, 1848.
(166240) BENJAMIN FINNEY—b. Oct.30, 1845; d. Apr. 18, 1847.
(166241) ADRIENNE ANTIONETTE—b. Mar. 6, 1847; d. ——.

(166242) JULIA ADALINE—b. Oct. 21, 1848; d. May 10, 1887.
(166243) HENRY WARDEN BURR—b. Aug. 15, 1850; m. (Miss) Ralph.
See further record.
(D. S. H. MSS.)

(16624) JAMES SMITH (1815-1882), the son of Rev. James Smith (1662), and wife Rebecca, married, 1848, Elizabeth L. Morton. He practiced law for some years in his home town, Mt. Vernon, Ohio, and was identified with municipal affairs there. In 1857 he moved to St. Paul, Minnesota, with his family. He became one of the leading lawyers of the State, and was one of the founders of Duluth. He was instrumental in building the St. Paul and Duluth railroad, of which he was president, counsel, and a director for many years. He served seven terms in the legislature, including terms in both houses. His death occurred November 22, 1882. Issue—

(166241) ELIZABETH—d. in infancy.
(166242) HENRIETTA C.—b. 1851.
(166243) ELLA AUGUSTA—b. 1852.
(166244) JAMES MORTON—b. 1854; m. Elizabeth L. Morton, Mt. Vernon, Ohio.
(166245) ALICE MORTON—b. 1858.
(D. S. H. MSS. etc.)

(16625) VESPASIAN SMITH (1818-1897), the son of Rev. James Smith (1662), and wife Rebecca, was born at Mt Vernon, Ohio, and graduated in medicine at Cleveland, Ohio. He practiced in Mt. Vernon for a time, and in 1857 moved to Superior City, Wisconsin. In 1870, he settled in Duluth, Minnesota, of which city he became one of the first mayors. He was the second Collector of Customs for the Port of Duluth, and served in this capacity for nine years. Dr. Smith married in 1846, Charlotte Neely, (1824-1899), a native of Pennsylvania. Issue—

(166251) CHARLES EMMETT—b. 1847; d. 1869.
(166252) LOUISE ELEANOR—b. 1848; m. 1871, Dr. —— McCormick.
See further record.
(166253) FRANK BRANDEN—b. 1852; m. 1878, Isabel F. Eysten. She d. 1894.
See further record.
(166254) WILLIAM NEELY—b. 1863; d. 1896.
(D. S. H. MSS. etc.)

DAVIS

(16626) ADELINE T. SMITH (1821-), the daughter of Rev. James Smith (1662), and wife Rebecca, married, at Oakland, Ohio, June 25, 1850, Rev. A. A. Davis. Issue—

(166261) ADELINE AUGUSTA—b. July 29, 1851, Fredericktown, Ohio; d. Oct. 29, 1851.
(166262) FREDERICK SCHILLER—b. Aug. 19, 1852; d. 1852, Mt. Vernon, Ohio.
(166263) ELIZABETH REBECCA—b. Oct. 13, 1853, Sunbury, Ohio; m. Dec. 8, 1881, Theodore Moore.
See further record.

(166264) James William Smith—b. Oct. 9, 1855; m. Oct. 15, 1882, Addie L. Payne, of Cardington, Ohio, at which point he settled.
(166265) Edward Douglas—b. June 9, 1858, d. Sept, 22, 1862.
(166266) Fairman Hewlett—b. May 24, 1860, Sunbury, Ohio; d. Nov. 29, 1860.
(D. S. H. MSS.)

LYBRAND

(16627) HENRIETTA CLAY SMITH (1824-1847), the daughter of Rev. James Smith (1662), and wife Rebecca, married, 1846, Charles Lybrand. Issue—

(166271) Charlesetta—b. 1847; m. Nov. 27, 1867, William Swartz.
See further record.
(D. S. H. MSS.)

---

1. LINE OF COL. BENJAMIN HARRISON
2. LINE OF DANIEL HARRISON

HAWKS

(16722) THEODOCIA HARRISON ( ), the daughter of Daniel Harrison (1672), and wife Nancy, married Thomas Hawks. Issue—

(167221) Mary—
(167222) Louis—
(167223) William—
(167224) Joseph—
(167225) Daniel—
(F. O. M. papers.)

HOPPER

(16724) EDITH McWILLIAMS HARRISON (1797-1865), the daughter of Daniel Harrison (1672), and wife Nancy, was born in Rockingham County, Virginia, and died in Warren County, Illinois. Her death occurred Dec. 1865. She married in 1818, in Todd County, Kentucky, William Hopper, who was born in Bourbon County, Kentucky, March 31, 1791, and died in Warren County, Illinois, May 12, 1876.

William Hopper was the son of John Hopper, who removed from Culpeper County, Virginia, to Bourbon County, Kentucky, in 1790. John Hopper served in the Revolutionary Army at Valley Forge. William and wife moved to near Monmouth, Warren County, Illinois, in 1835. They resided at Thorndale, their homestead, which continued in their family about seventy years. The property was sold in 1903 by Mr. Lafayette Marks and wife.

William Hopper, and wife Edith, (16724), had children—

(167241) Barbara Ann—b. 1819; m., 1835, at Hopkinsville, Ky., Hardin Coleman.
See further record.
(167242) Elijah Harrison—b. 1821; d. 1888 c.; m., 1847, Harriett Bryan.
See further record.
(167243) Frances Maria—b. 1824; d. Dec. 28, 1891; m., 1842, in Ill., John M. Owens, b. 1820, Cincinnati, Ohio.
See further record.

(167244) Daniel Harrison—b. 1827; d. 1853, unmarried.

(167245) William Logan—b. 1830; d. Feb. 26, 1894; m. 1852, Lettia Jane Clendenning, of Pennsylvania.
See further record.

(167246) Mary Thompson—b. July 20, 1834; d. 1907; m. James F. Owens, b. May 8, 1829, Cincinnati, O., (bro. of John above), d. 1901, at Thorndale.
See further record.

(E. O. M. papers.)

(16725) DANIEL HARVEY HARRISON (1805-), the son of Daniel Harrison (1672), and wife Nancy, married, first, Elvira Pennington Byron. Following her death he married, second, Nora ———. Issue by first marriage—

(167251) Thodocia—

(167252) William—

Two children by second wife. No further record.

(E. O. M. Papers.)

---

2. LINE OF JAMES HARRISON

(16757) GEORGE H. HARRISON ( ), the son of James Harrison (1675), and wife Ann, married August 9, 1832, Sarah Paul Grover, the daughter of Josiah Grover, "and neice of Sarah Grover Paul, wife of John Paul, first owner of the ground upon which New Albany, Indiana, was laid out, also first proprietor of Madison, Indiana, and Zenia, Ohio." (See *Times Dispatch* article before referred to—page 322, etc.)

An interesting letter, dated, New Albany, Indiana, October 12, 1838, addressed by George Harrison to Mr. Asbury Logan, Madison, Indiana, reads as follows—

> "Dear Cousin. I have been promising myself for some time to write you, but have not been able to attend to it, owing to a want of time: my health having been not very good since our arrival here I find myself in the rear of my business, (so to express it) & when I am pretty well I am constantly employed in some domestic arrangement if not engaged in the Seminary.
>
> Well we arrived here the day after we left Madison, found that the house which had been rented for us was not finished & if it had been I should not have been able to go to housekeeping, as I went to bed in a few minutes after stopping at tavern, having a severe attact of Sciatic pain . . . . . .
>
> After boarding for a little over two weeks we got to keeping house & are moderately well situated, though have to put up with many inconveniences until more permanently situated.
>
> Mother's health has been quite good since we have been in this place; much better than at Lebanon. She has a good appetite, sleeps, generally very well, smokes tobacco and takes her . . . . , both, as regularily as ever—and occasionally gets the blues and thinks herself misused, and without friends—as formerly—The rest of us are getting along as well as usual,

tho as above remarked, I have been taken through the flint mill rather roughly, since here, with that rascally Rheumatism.

This New Albany I find is a fine place—The citizens are industrious and moral and all things taken into account, this may be set down as a very interesting and agreeable place—The situation I have in the Seminary is quite laborious, as the classes are numerous—

The students in all the departments, amount at present to about 70 or 75. I have one Class in Greek, one in Latin, 2 in Algebra 2 or 3 in Arithmetic & Several others in the other English branches. I have an excellent assistant teacher (Marcellus Rutter) the youngest son of my old Preceptor Dr. Rutter, who died this year in Texas. The school is not so far advanced as we would like to see it but we hope to have an increasing interest in the general cause of education manifest itself here—. A young Bro. Ross formerly a teacher in this institution & a Brother of Rector Ross of Madison, stated to me, some days since, that he had been requested by a lady at Madison to make certain enquiries of me respecting the School, the boarding &c. He stated that the lady's name was Williams (of Louisana) and that she was boarding at Mrs. Logan's. You will please say to her therefore, for me, that I should have replyed promptly to the enquirie but could not—and say to her, that we concluded to take her two children to board with us, if she should finally conclude to lend them to this Seminary & should wish us to have them with me. That boarding in this place is from $3 to $5 per week for grown persons (exc. of lodging and washg. it is $3) and for smaller persons, children, it is $2.50 or $3. I cannot state precicely which but not less than 2.50 for board and lodging.

The courses of instruction in the Seminary included, has been intimated, Greek & Latin, Languages, Geography with use of globes, mathematics and the usual English branches. The terms are for Reading & Orthography per Session $6.—for Same including Arth Grammar & Geog.—$10 per Session—and for Bookkeeping History Math & Languages $16. This I believe includes all the matters of inquiry made by Bro. Ross and you will please report to the lady accordingly—presenting her my respects and the assurance of attention to her children so far as in my power, if she wishes them placed under my immediate supervision—My Mother wishes me to say to Aunt that she thot she was a great writer & that she was giving us evidence of it finely.

I am writing in haste & you will excuse my careless diction, giving our best love to all your own family, as also to Aunt Paul & to Cousin Sarah Benj. Grover's family &c &c. and believe me your friend Sincerely

(Signed) G. H. Harrison.

Write and let us hear from you—

If the lady referred to concludes to send please have her inform us must try & get a girl for housework."

(Copied from original loaned by D. L. C.)

George Harrison, (16757), and wife Sarah, had issue—

(167571) James Grover—m. Hester Hart, lived and died in New Albany, Ind.
(167572) Martha Ann—
(167573) John Harnsberger—

(167574) SARAH MARIA—m. John Beggs, a descendant of a prominent pioneer of Clark Co., Ind.
(167575) MARY ELIZABETH—
(167576) JULIA—
(167577) GEORGIANNA LOCKE—
(All listed in *Times Dispatch* account. Copy kindly furnished by Mrs. M. W. Williamson, of New Market, Va.)

---

2. LINE OF EZEKIEL LOGAN

(16771) BENJAMIN HARRISON LOGAN (1798-), the son of Ezekiel Logan, and wife Margaret (1677), nee Harrison, married, in 1821, Catherine Keplinger. Issue—

(167711) HARRISON—
(167712) GESSNER—
(167713) JACKSON—
(167714) TIFFIN PEACHY—m. ————.
See further record.

CULBERTSON

(16772) POLLY MARIA LOGAN (1799-1900), the daughter of Ezekiel Logan, and wife Margaret (1677), nee Harrison, married Samuel Culbertson. Issue—

(167721) MARGARET—m. ——— Draper.
(167722) SAMUEL—
(167723) MARIA—
(167724) JANE—
(167725) EMILY—
(167726) JULIUS—

GOODNOW

(16773) BETSY EVELINE LOGAN (1800-1886), the daughter of Ezekiel Logan, and wife Margaret (1677), nee Harrison, married John Goodnow. Issue—

(167731) JAMES HARRISON—m. 1861, Margaret Virginia Williams.
(167732) CHARLES—
(167733) JOHN—
(167734) MARGARET SUSAN—

WILLIAMS

(16777) ANGELINA LOGAN (1809-1904), the daughter of Ezekiel Logan, and wife Margaret (1677), nee Harrison, married, 1831, John Williams. Issue—

(167771) MARGARET VIRGINIA—m. James Goodnow, above named.
(167772) SARAH—m. Charles Hammant.
(167773) ELIZA MARIA—m. Joseph Christian.
See further record.

new Albany, Ind.

(16778) FRANCIS ASBURY LOGAN, (1811-1902), the son of Ezekiel Logan, and wife Margaret, (1677), nee Harrison, married, August 15, 1843, Elizabeth Ireland, who was born June 6, 1826, and died December 26, 1882. Francis and wife settled in New Albany, Indiana, where they were residing October 12, 1838, the date of George H. Harrison's letter to him. (See above.) Their children were—

(167781) MELVIN CASE—b. Oct. 1, 1844; m. Dec. 4, 1873, Ellen J. Anderson. See further record.
(167782) MARGARET VIRGINIA—b. Jan. 7, 1847; m. Nov. 16, 1865, Wm. Henry Wilson. See further record.
(167783) MARY ELIZA—b. May 3, 1849; m. Oct. 8, 1868, Levi Griffey. See further record.
(167784) SARAH PAUL—b. Sept. 6, 1851; m. —— Logan. See further record.
(167785) FRANCIS ASBURY—b. July 2, 1855; d. Oct. 22, 1874.
(167786) LAURA—b. Aug. 31, 1860: m. Sept. 19, 1888, John C. Renfro. See further record.
(167787) ANNIE ELIZABETH—b. Oct. 31, 1865; m. Mar. 6, 1889, Luther Deputy. See further record.

---

2. LINE OF DR. PEACHY HARRISON

(16792) GESSNER HARRISON (1807-1862), the son of Dr. Peachy Harrison (1679), and wife Mary, born in Harrisonburg, Virginia, was one of the nine first graduates of the University of Virginia, (founded April 13, 1819; 1st session began March 1, 1825.) As observed at the beginning of this Chapter, he became one of Virginia's distinguished educators. Of him it has been said, "he was perhaps the most important figure in the educational history of the Southern States in the period before the Civil War." His memory is cherished by the University as one of her noblest sons. He entered her halls in 1825, and graduated in the degrees of medicine and ancient languages, in July 1828.

On August 10, 1828, he was appointed Professor of the School of Ancient Languages, at the University, a position he held until near the time of his death, or for over thirty years. He was the author of an original work on the Greek preposition, a geography of Ancient Italy and Southern Greece, and a Latin grammer, which for many years was a standard text-book. An interesting sketch of his life, by Rev. John A. Broadus, his son-in-law, may be seen in *The Library of Southern Literature.* (1909, Vol. II, p. 507.)

Dr. Harrison married, December 15, 1830, Eliza Lewis Carter Tucker, born December 9, 1808, died March 11, 1893, a native of Pittsylvania County, the daughter of George Tucker, (b. in Bermuda, August 1, 1775, d. April 10, 1861), professor of moral philosophy at the University of Virginia, and the author of a life of Jefferson, and several works on political economy. Mrs. Harrison was the grand-niece of George Washington, through his sister Betty Lewis.

During his professorship at the University, Dr. Harrison and wife resided on the great lawn. His portrait now adorns the University Library in the Rotunda at the head of the lawn. At the age of fifty-three he purchased a plantation in Nelson County, on which he founded a classical school known as Belmont Academy. While nursing a soldier son, invalided home from the war through illness, he contracted a fever from which he died.

Dr. Harrison and wife had issue—

(167921) MARIA CARTER—b. Nov. 11, 1831; d. Oct. 21, 1857; m. Nov. 14, 1849, Rev. John A. Broadus.
See further record.

(167922) MARY STUART—b. Feb. 10, 1834; d. 1917; m. July 31, 1853, Prof. Francis H. Smith, of the University of Va.
See further record.

(167923) GEORGE TUCKER (M. D.)—b. July 23, 1835; living 1920; m. Lelia Bell, dau. of William Bell, of Richmond, Va.
See further record.

(167924) EDWARD TIFFIN—b. Sept. 9, 1837; d. Dec. 2, 1873.

(167925) PEACHY GESSNER—b. Dec. 24, 1839; living 1920; m. Julia Riddick.
See further record.

(167926) CHARLES CARTER—b. May 10, 1842; d. Feb. 1882.

(167927) HENRY WILLIAM (M. D.)—b. Sept. 15, 1844; practicing physican, Roanoke, Va. (1920.)

(167928) ELEANOR ROSALIE—b. July 16, 1847; d. Apr. 7, 1920; m. Dr. William M. Thornton, Dean of Engineering, Univ. of Va.
See further record.

(167929) ROBERT LEWIS—b. March 2, 1850, residence New York City, eminent attorney at law. (1920).

(167930) FRANCIS WASHINGTON—b. Feb. 15,1852; d. June 10, 1852.

(See *Boogher,* also *National Cyclopaedia American Biography,* Vol. 12, p. 136; 1914. Tombstones of Dr. Harrison and wife, and daughters, Maria C., and Eleanor, and sons, Edward T., and Francis W., in the University of Va. Cemetery, Charlottesville, Va.)

(16795) MARY JANE HARRISON (1816-1889), and her sister, Caroline Elizabeth (1822-1890), the daughters of Dr. Peachy Harrison, (1679), and wife Mary, resided in Harrisonburg, Virginia. As two estimable and kindly Christian ladies, their memory is cherished by many of the town's older citizens today. They are known to have been frequent visitors at Smithland, and to have been on the friendliest terms with its mistress, Mrs. Julia Smith, as their cousin.

(16798) PEACHY RUSH HARRISON (1825-1852), the son of Dr. Peachy Harrison (1679), and wife Mary, married June 6, 1848, Mary Frances Rhodes. He entered the University of Virginia, October 1, 1841, and graduated in medicine July 4, 1846. After attending clinical lectures in Philadelphia, he began the practice of medicine in Harrisonburg, Virginia, his home town, in which he resided until his death.

Mary Frances, the wife of Dr. Harrison, was the daughter of William Rhodes, of "Midway," Albemarle County, Va. In 1867, she and her famliy, consisting of two daughters, established their home in New Market, Virginia, where for a time she conducted a private seminary, and where she died, in 1899.

Dr. Peachy Rush Harrison (16798), and wife Mary's children were—

(167981) MINNIE LYNN—b. May 5, 1850; d. Feb. 6, 1923; m. 1874, M. White Williamson, b. Apr. 24, 1845, eldest son of Maj. J. D. Williamson.
See further record.

(167982) LUCY RUSH—b. Apr. 2, 1852; d. 1917, unmarried.

(Tombstones of both Mrs. Williamson and sister, and of their mother, in "Lower" Lutheran Cemetery, New Market, Virginia.)

---

2. LINE OF FIELDING HARRISON

(16801) PEYTON L. HARRISON (1804-), the son of Fielding Harrison (1680), and wife Ann, born in Rockingham County, Virginia, married in St. Louis, Missouri, November 13, 1827, Elizabeth B. Cartwright, of Sangamon County, Illinois, the daughter of the famous pioneer preacher, Rev. Peter Cartwright.

Peyton Harrison and wife resided at the old Fielding Harrison homestead, near Pleasant Plains, in Sangamon County, Illinois. He was yet living in 1873. Issue—

(168011) FRANCES A.—b. Nov. 27, 1828; m. William H. Purvines.
(168012) WEALTHY M. J.—m. Nathan S. Purvines.
(168013) SARAH M.—m. Amos Ely, a native of Philadelphia, Pennsylvania, Feb. 22, 1854.
See further record.
(168014) P. QUINN—b. May 20, 1837; d. ——; m. June 4; 1867, Emeline L. Lamothe, b. Dec. 12, 1843, Alton, Ill.
See further record.
(168015) CATHERINE—m. William P. Crafton.
(168016) PETER L.—m. Elizabeth F. Cartwright.
See further record.
(168017) EMILY W.—m. Benjamin Berry, of Morgan Co., Ill.
See further record.
(168018) CAROLINE A.—m. Josiah W. Owen, resided near Pleasant Plains, Sangamon Co., Ill.
(168019) VICTORIA M.—m. Dr. James T. Logan. Issue—
1. Eva May—

(See Power's *History of Sangamon Co., Ill.*, p. 359.)

(16802), JOHN F. HARRISON (1807-), the son of Fielding Harrison (1680), and wife Ann, was born in Christian County, Kentucky, on "cold Friday," Feb. 5, 1807. He married Parthenia Harrison, the daughter of Ezekiel B. Harrison, (1775), of Petersburg, Illinois. John Harrison and wife resided in Petersburg. Their family consisted of six children in 1873. No further record.

(16803) PEACHY A. HARRISON (1809-1866), the daughter of Fielding Harrison (1680), and wife Ann, married, Robert Harrison, (16812), the son of William, Fielding's brother. See below.

(16805) SIMEON Q. HARRISON (1816-1883), the son of Fielding Harrison (1680), and wife Ann, was born in what is now Trigg County, Kentucky, and married in Sangamon County, Illinois, Mary A. Renshaw. They resided in Sangamon, near Richland Station. Issue—

(168051) ROBERT P.—m. Almeda J. Bone.
(168052) ANNIE Q.—b. May 26, 1848; m. 1st, Jan. 19, 1870, Dr. Joseph B. Cloud,

son of Rev. Nathan Cloud, of Jacksonville, Ill. He d. Dec. 31, 1872, at Pleasant Plains, following which she m., 2nd, James Gardner, of Clarksville, Texas.

(168053) JENNIE E.—b. Dec. 19, 1850; m. Dec. 24, 1868, Frank Cassell. See further record.
(168054) MOLLIE E.—m. William Gardner.
(168055) IDA V.—m. Andrew Hopper, d. ——. See further record.
(168056) SUE A.—m. ———. Last three married after 1873.

(16806) MARTHA JANE HARRISON (1820-), the daughter of Fielding Harrison (1680), and wife Ann, married James Harrison, (16813), the son of William Harrison. See below.

---

2. LINE OF WILLIAM HARRISON

(16812) ROBERT HARRISON (-1855 c), the son of William Harrison (1681), and wife Jane, married Peachy A. Harrison, (16803), the daughter of Fielding Harrison, and wife Ann. Robert and wife resided in Alton, Illinois, where both died. Issue—nine children, of whom—

(168121) FIELDING T.—residing 1873, Alton, Ill.
(166122) CASTLE R.—residing 1873, Jacksonville, Ill.
(166123) JOHN H.—residing 1873, Taylorsville, Ill.
(166124) SIMEON Q.—residing 1873, Morrisville, Ill..
(168125) JAMES—residing 1873, in Kansas, m. ———.

(16813) JAMES HARRISON (-1873), the son of William Harrison (1681), and wife Jane, married, Martha Jane Harrison, (16806), the daughter of Fielding Harrison, and wife Ann. James Harrison and wife resided in or near Shullsburg, Wisconsin. Issue—

(168131) VIRGINIA—b. Jan. 1, 1838; m. Edward Ludlow Van Vorhees, a native of New York. See further record.
(168132) WILLIAM HENRY (M. D.)—b. Oct. 6, 1840, residing 1873, at Warren, Ill.
(168133) ANNA—(living 1914), m. Nicholas A. Brown. No issue.
(168134) ISABELLA—m. Amos Patton, D. D., of Northwestern University, Evanton, Ill.

(Named in letter J. B. to D. S. H., Feb. 30, 1914.)

CLAN OF THOMAS HARRISON

1. LINE OF EZEKIEL HARRISON
2. LINE OF JESSE HARRISON

MONROE

(17711) EMILY HARRISON ( ), the daughter of Jesse Harrison (1771), and wife Rachel, married Rev. Andrew Monroe. The marriage ceremony was performed by Rev. Peter Cartwright, of Sangamon County, Illinois, from which circumstance it is presumed she was married while her father was yet a resident of Sangamon.

Rev. Monroe was a member of a Hampshire County, Virginia, (now West Virginia), family, consisting of eleven children, four of whom became ministers of the Gospel. He served "50 of the 200 years the four brothers preached." At the time of his marriage he was probably residing in Sangamon County, Illinois, from which he appears to have removed to Audrain County, Missouri. Of his children—

(177111) MARGARET—m. Edward H. Dennis.
See further record.

(*D. A. R. Lineage Book*, 29, p. 22; also *Rockingham News-Record*, Sept. 28, 1929, wherein Rev. Monroe's grand-daughter, Margaret Emily Vail, of Columbus, Ohio, is named.)

---

2. LINE OF REUBEN HARRISON

(17721) LEONARD CASTLE HARRISON (1805-1867), the son of Reuben Harrison (1772), and wife Parthenia Frances, (1684), was born in Rockingham County, Virginia, and in childhood accompained his father to Kentucky, thence to Illinois. In his grand-father Col. Benjamin Harrison's will he is named as Castle Harrison, (see page 322); elsewhere he is found referred to as "Cassell" Harrison, by some of his descendants.

(A castle, name Castle Harrison, at Charleville, County Cork, Ireland, has long been the seat of a Harrison family of Ireland. It was occupied by Henry Harrison, collector of Wexford, (wife Elizabeth, son William), in 1767. See Burke's *Landed Gentry of Ireland*, 1903, p. 249.)

Leonard Castle (or Cassell) Harrison entered the ministery of the Methodist Episcopal Church, at the age of eighteen. He married, in South Carolina, Sarah J. Wynne. He and his wife resided for a time in Georgia, and later removed to Summerfield, Alabama, where he died in 1867, leaving his widow, and eight children. A daughter—

(177211) SALLIE—b. —— in Georgia; m. R. H. Pearson.

(See *Power;* also *D. A. R. Lineage Book,* Vol. IX, p. 242.)

(17722) GEORGE M. HARRISON (1813-1873), the son of Reuben Harrison (1772), and second wife Barbara, was born in Rockingham County, Virginia, and removed with his parents to Sangamon County, Illinois. After studying medicine in Springfield, under Dr. Jacob M. Early, he rode on horseback to Virginia. From here, after selling his horse, he rode by stage to Philadelphia, where he entered the Rush Medical College, from which he graduated in April 1840, being the second graduate of any medical college from Sangamon.

Dr. Harrison married, near Harirsonburg, May 28, 1840, Maria B. C. J. Houston, (17842), the daughter of Rev. William Houston. On his honeymoon he returned to Sangamon County. He entered at once upon his practice on Richland Creek, in which region, near Sailsbury, he continued to reside until his death.

Maria Houston, his wife, died in 1845, and on November 25, 1847, he married, second, Mary A. Megredy. (She d. after 1875.)

Dr. Harrison's death occurred Sept. 1, 1873. He had been to a neighbor's residence on business, and had started to return home late in the evening, but his horse arrived home without its rider. Search was immediately instituted, and his body was found at a crossing of a sharp ravine, where it is thought his horse had tripped and thrown him.

Dr. George M. Harrison (17722), had issue—

By first wife Maria (17842)—

(177221) ANNA AMANTHA—b. Aug. 13, 1841; m. in Va., June 7, 1866, Frank W. Elliot, of Sangamon.
See further record.

(177222) REUBEN H.—b. Nov. 9, 1842; m. in Nebraska, 1875, Mary J. Hendrickson. He enlisted, 1862, for 3 yrs. in Ill. Inf., 114th Regt., and served full term. Residing 1873, near York Center, York Co., Neb., on land received for his services. Two children.

(177223) SARAH B. C. (Catherine)—b. May 8, 1844; m. Thomas Cummings.

(Above three named on the Wilson chart.)

By second wife, Mary—

(177224) EMMA E.—b. April 27, 1849; m. March 28, 1872, Philip Oscar Hodgen, of Ill., b. Nov. 19, 1845, near Burlington, Iowa.
See further record.

(177225) M. JENNIE—b. May 22, 1850; m. Dec. 26, 1872, George S. Beekman, of Ill.
See further record.

(177226) JULIA S.—d. June 18, 1875; m. Jan. 1, 1874, William E. Beekman.
See further record.

(177227) ABBIE—

(177228) MELINDA—

(177229) JOHN E.—

(177230) WILLIAM H.—

(177231) MARY B.—

(177232) HENRIETTA—

All but Julia living 1875,—last six with mother at this time.

(17723) JOHN H. HARRISON (1815-), the son of Reuben Harrison (1772), and second wife, Barbara, married in Menard County, Illinois, May 17, 1843, Sarah A. Conover, who was born near Princeton, New Jersey, in 1825. John Harrison and wife resided in Sangamon County, Illinois, at the old homestead of his grand-father, Ezekiel Harrison. Their children were—

(177231) PARTHENIA E. F.—b. 1846; d. Feb. 2, 1862.

(177232) CHARLES H.—residing, 1873, in Kansas.

(177233) SUE—

(177234) SAMUEL B.—

(177235) GEORGE R.—

(177236) HOAT—

(177237) VANNIE—

Last five residing with parents, 1873.

2. LINE OF EZEKIEL B. HARRISON

(17751) MILTON B. HARRISON ( ), the son of Ezekiel B. Harrison (1775), and wife Ann, married Mrs. Martha Sutton, nee Hunter. They resided in Petersburg, Illinois. Issue—

(177511) Martha E. Anabel—residing with parents, 1873.

---

1. LINE OF REUBEN HARRISON
2. LINE OF REV. WILLIAM HOUSTON

JORDAN

(17843) AMANTHA L. HOUSTON (1821-1897), the daughter of Rev. William Houston, and wife Nancy (1784), nee Harrison, married, about 1844, Theodore Norvell Jordan, born January 29, 1814, died August 20, 1853, the son of Theodosius Jordan, (d. 1850), of Salem, Virginia. Theodore Jordan, and wife, resided for some years following their marriage, in or near Harrisonburg, and then removed to Salem, Virginia, where he died. Mrs. Jordan died in San Jose, California, in September, 1897. Issue—

(178431) Belle J.—b. 1846, c.; d. July 27, 1931, Escondido, Cal.; m. 1st, (before 1873) John (Jack) C. McCreary, of Harrisonburg; m. 2nd, James B. Wyatt, Sept. 1907, of California.
See further record.

(178432) Thodore A. H.—b. Oct. 12, 1852; d. Oct. 15, 1919; m. Claddie Wilson, b. Mar. 29, 1857, d. Nov. 26, 1932, dau. of Wm. Miller Wilson.
See further record.

BOWMAN

(17844) ALSCINDA B. HOUSTON (1823-1887), the daughter of Rev. William Houston, and wife Nancy (1784), nee Harrison, married, March 20, 1848, Samuel Bowman, (born May 16, 1825, died July 1, 1858), of Rockingham County, Virginia. Samuel and wife resided in the Lacey Spring neighborhood. Their children were—

(178441) John Robert Kyle—b. June 16, 1849; m. Nancy E. S. Harrison, b. Oct. 30, 1851, d. Mar. 4, 1900, dau. of Abraham Harrison, (121124).
See further record.

(178442) Ann N. Bruce—b. June 21, 1851; d. Feb. 15, 1927, unmarried. For many years a U. S. Govt. teacher of the Indians, at Oklahoma City.

(178443) Willoughby (William) N. T.—b. Nov. 1, 1854; m. Jennie Woodward, removed to Colorado. He d. July 6, 1930.
See further record.

(178444) Samuel O.—b. Oct. 1, 1858; d. July 24, 1910; m. Martha Allebaugh, dau. of Samuel R. and Betty (Andes) b. 1857, d. Jan. 1929. Resided a few miles north of Harrisonburg. No issue.

(All named on Wilson chart—Markers of Bruce, Samuel O., and wife, in Lacey Spring Cemetery.)

---

p/409 (17845) JOHN WESLEY CLARK HOUSTON (1828-1869), the son of Rev.

Catherine Huffman

William Houston, and wife Nancy (1784), nee Harrison, married January 20, 1853, Rachel Catherine Huffman, the daughter of John Huffman, of Page County, Virginia, and wife Catherine.

HUFFMAN

John Huffman was the son of Frederick Huffman, a descendant of an early Page County family of German extraction. He was born July 30, 1796, and died June 14, 1864. He and Catherine, his wife, nee Biedler, of Page County, were married January 28, 1821. She died October 3, 1840, leaving children:

mauzey

Rebecca A., b. Dec. 27, 1822, d. Jan. 21, 1903, m. Dec. 2, 1847, Jacob Kisling Mauzy; Rachel Catherine, as above, b. Oct. 6, 1826; Mary Jane, b. Sept. 18, 1830, d. 1904, married, 1st, Ambrose Varner, of Page; Phoebe Elizabeth, b. Mar. 3, 1838, d. June 8, 1932, married Thomas Brubaker, of Rockingham, and removed with him Mar. 4, 1893, to Dalton, Georgia, where he died, Mar. 4, 1901. Mrs. Brubaker later returned to Rockingham. Their only child, Annie Laura, (b. 1864) died in childhood (1866.)

* * * * * *

Following his marriage, John Houston resided for a brief interval at Lacey Spring, but Edward Smith having died a few years earlier, Mrs. Smith, Houston's aunt, prevailed on him to assume the management of the Smithland estate for her, and from this time until his death his home was at Smithland. (See page 410.) He resided in the original house in which the first court of Rockingham was held, and which Gen. Washington named as, "the Widow Smith's," in the diary of his travels of 1784, as he passed that way.

Throughout the War-between-the-States, John Houston served in the Confederate Army as a private. Three letters, the first, dated June 17, 1861, at Romney, Hampshire County, now West Virginia, the second, and third, at Fairfax Station, Virginia, July 11, and August 15, 1861, as penned by him to his wife, while he was stationed at these points, are yet in existence. In the last he mentions Col. Gibbons, and states that they had just elected D. L. Martz, 1st Lieut., D. Smith, 3rd Lieut, and Morris Geheen, 1st Sargt., and that Paul Briant their 2nd Lieut. was resigning account Lee Martz having been promoted over him. "So long as I can keep my health and be (of) any service to my country I will be satisfied."

At the time of the first letter, his company had assembled at Romney, after a quick march from Harpers Ferry via Winchester. "There are about three thousand of us here and Col. Johnson has gone up the Potomac River with ten thousand, and Wise is on his way to Staunton west, besides some eight or ten companies of cavalry which are cutting through the mountains in every direction; there are several regiments in Winchester and what became of the rest of the troops I don't know, but I know this much about it, they are all wide awake and on the lookout."

All of the letters breath a tender solicitude for his family; the second, in particular, expresses the soldiers anxiety at not being able to hear regularily from home. He had written several letters since receiving word that his daughter (Mary) had been ill, but so far, owing to the irregularity of the mail, had received no reply.

His wife too, as bravely bore her burdens. An instance of some of her trials occured during Sigel's encampment about Smithland, at which time the soldiers ransacked her home and carried off her kitchen utensils, among a number of other things, and even appropriated to themselves a supply of soft soap which they happened upon while plundering the attic. The soap having the consistency and color of applebutter the plunders, some German speaking troops, greedily spread it on their bread, and calmly proceeded to eat it. When warned that it was unfit to eat, they protested, saying, "gut, gut, lotverich, lotverich!" Appeal was made to the officers quartered in the Smithland residence rgarding the kitchen utensils, and to their credit be it said they ordered these returned, and granted Mrs. Houston an escort to their camp to allow her to identify her property.

John Houston died in 1869. His death occurred while he was on a tour of inspection of his place, and was due to an attack of heart failure. At the time no one was with him, and in the evening when he failed to return home for his supper, at the usual hour, it was presumed that he had gone to Harrisonburg, and had been detained on business. His dog, of which he was very fond, came home about sundown and acting queerly ran first up to one child, and then to another, as he happened to find them on the lawn, and after pawing at them in turns would whirl and lead off, only to come back and repeat this performance again, before finally desisting and going away for good. As evening wore on, the family became alarmed and a search was instituted. At daybreak, his body was found lying near a corn shock, guarded by his faithful dog. A very vicious hog had broken into the cornfield, and it was presumed that he had gone hither to run her out.

His body was buried with Masonic honors. A letter addressed to Mrs. Houston, his widow, by Henry Shaklett, Master of Rockingham Lodge, November 23, 1869, tendering the services of the lodge at his funeral, bears testimony of the esteem of his brethren.

Rachel, his widow, married, second, in "the Fall of 1875," Louis A. Berry, a widower, and a native of Rockingham, who resided near Lancaster, Ohio. He is said to have been her former suitor in his youth. She died at their home in Ohio, April 15th 1900, and was interred in Lancaster.

John Houston (17845), and wife Rachel, had issue—

(178451) MARY MATTHEWS H.—b. Jan 15, 1854; d. Jan. 11, 1913; m. William Huffman, of Page Co., Va.
See further record.

(178452) ANNA AMANTHA—b. Sept. 24, 1856; d. Feb. 19, 1921; m. Nov. 22, 1880, David W. Harrison, (125915), b. Apr. 15, 1845.
See further record.

(178453) EMMA E.—b. Sept. 7,, 1859; d. Feb. 28, 1902; m. 1st, Rev. John Lollard Murphy, (Protestant Methodist Church), of Fostoria, Ohio; m., 2nd, Rev. John T. Kitchen, (Christian Church) Windsor, Virginia. No issue.

(178454) JULIA JANETTA—b. Feb. 4, 1861; d. 1924; m. Isaac E. Rowles, of Fairfield Co., O.
See further record.

(178455) JOHN WILLIAM—b. June 30, 1865; d. July 15, 1865.

(178456) NANCY CLARK A. C.—b. Sept. 17, 1868; d. Oct. 11, 1905; m. Sept. 16, 1891, Frank G. Grove, of Page Co., Va.
See further record.

(All but John W. named on the Wilson chart—Tombstones of John W. in old Houston cemetery on Smiths Creek; of Anna, in "Upper" Lutheran Cemetery, at New Market Va.; of Clark in cemetery at Luray, Va., and of Julia and husband, and Emma and 1st husband, in cemetery at Lancaster, Ohio.)

(17848) WILLIAM LEE OLIN HOUSTON (1834-1869), the son of Rev. William Houston, and wife Nancy (1784), nee Harrison, married January 17, 1861, Grizzell Ann Earnest, b. 1838, d. April 12, 1871. On January 3, 1869, he was residing at Pleasant Valley, Iowa, on which date a letter penned by him to his brother John mentions that "Mrs. Houston and little Mary Frances have gone to church and Amantha Belle is at Aunt Rue's tonight." At the time, his health was indifferent and he was contemplating moving, probably to Kentucky. He had recently received a letter from Reuben Harrison, stating that the "friends" in Illinois were all well. He had removed to Iowa following the War of 1861-5. In his Romney, West Virginia, letter of 1861, John Houston, his brother, expressed the hope "that Lee and his wife will get home so you may all be together."

Lee Houston died in Iowa, September 19, 1869. He and wife Anna had issue—

(178481) JOHN WILLIAM—b. Mar. 5, 1862; d. Aug. 11, 1865.

(178482) AMANTHA BELLE—b. July 13, 1865; m., July 16, 1885, JOHN WILLIAM EDMOND WATSON, of Illinois. Resides at Oxford, Nebraska. Issue—

1. EARL R.—m. ——. Resides near Oxford, Neb.
   Issue—
   1. Edwin—b. 1910.
   2. Helene—b. 1914.
   3. Eldon Earl—b. 1928.

(178483) MARY FRANCES—b. ——; m. Feb. 26, 1895, C. GLENN JONES, b. Galesburg, Ill., Aug. 21, 1870. Resides in Denver, Col. Issue—

1. Genevive—(Engaged in teaching in private school, in Denver.)

(178484) ALSCINDA OLIN—b. July 8, 1869; d. Feb. 9, 1870.

(Second and third named on the Wilson chart.)

HALL

(17849) ZERUIAH A. B. HOUSTON (-1907), the daughter of Rev. William Houston, and wife Nancy (1784), nee Harrison, married prior to 1861, James Hall of Rockingham. Regarding this couple, John Houston, in his Romney letter, remarked to his wife; "you stated in your letter that Brother James and sister Zeruiah had come home; I was very glad to hear that."

James Hall and wife settled in Iowa, apparently following the War of 1861-5. They were residing near Pleasant Plains in 1869, as disclosed by her brother Lee's letter of this year (see above.) Mrs. Hall outlived her husband for some time. She died in Oklahoma City, Oklahoma, probably at the home of her daughter, September 12, 1907. Issue, an only child—

(178491) ORA LEOTA—b. Apr. 2, 1870, in Iowa; m. Fred A Dodds, residing in Oklahoma City, Oklahoma, 1933.

PAUL

(17851) JULIA HOUSTON (1839-1868), the daughter of Rev. William Houston, and wife Nancy, (1785), nee Harrison, married William I. Paul, of Harrisonburg, Virginia. They resided in Harrisonburg.

William Paul was the son of Isaac Paul. Judge John Paul, the recent representative in Congress from the Seventh Virginia District, of which Rockingham is a part, is a native of Rockingham, and senior member of the present family in the county.

In Woodbine Cemetery, at Harrisonburg, are found a number of Paul markers, among them that of Isaac, reciting that he was born in Anne Arundel County, Maryland, March 10, 1804, and died (at Harrisonburg) October 28, 1879. Mary Jane Castleman, wife of Isaac Paul, died September 5, 1901, aged 82 years . . . . Dr. Isaac Paul, (son of Isaac) born August 19, 1849, died August 15, 1872. Lieut. Samuel B. Paul, 17th Regt. Va. Inft., killed in battle near Dinwiddie Court House, Va., March 31, 1865, aged 24 years, 6 mo., 10 days. (All data from the tombstones.)

"Julia, the beloved wife of Wm. I. Paul," was born September 23, 1839, and died June 15, 1868, says her marker. Their children were—

(178511) SAMUEL—d. Oct. 12, 1925; married ———. Mrs. Paul died Oct. 18, 1926, leaving three children.

(178512) WILLIAM HOUSTON—Resides at Sedalia, Missouri. m. ———. Issue—Ora—b. ———.

(Both named on the Wilson chart.)

CLAN OF CAPT. ROBERT CRAVENS

1. LINE OF JOHN CRAVENS

2. LINE OF REV. WILLIAM CRAVENS

(14142) JOHN CRAVENS ( ), the son of Rev. William Cravens (1414), and wife Jean (1678), nee Harrison, born in Rockingham County, Virginia, married in Rockingham, about 1818, Ann C. Newman, of Virginia. As early as 1820 he migrated with his family to Washington County, Indiana, and settled a short distance south of Salem—where his father died, (see page 411.) In old age he moved into Martinsburg, and resided there until his wife's death, after which he made his home with his son—

(141421) JAMES ADDISON (Congressman)—b. Nov. 4, 1818; d. June 20, 1893; m. Susan Hardin, dau. of Aaron. Resided near Hardinsburg, Ind. See further record.

---

2. LINE OF DR. JOSEPH CRAVENS

(14152) ROBERT CRAVENS (1794-1821), the son of Dr. Joseph Cravens (1415), and wife Mary, born at Harrisonburg, Virginia, settled as a young man at Madison, Indiana. He was early educated for the medical profession, and was entering upon a promising career as a physician, at Madison, when untimely overtaken by death.

Dr. Cravens married, in 1818, Sarah Grover Paul, the daughter of Col. John Paul —first Proprietor of Madison—and Sarah Thornsberry Grover, his wife, sister of Josiah Grover, before named. (See page 475.)

Col. Paul was born in Chester County, Pennsylvania, 1758, and died at Madison, Indiana, 1830. He was the son of Michael Paul, of Chester, whose wife was Ann Parker. Michael and wife were married at Germantown, Pennsylvania, 1750, and had, among other children; John, Peter, Martha, Ruth, Elizabeth, and Jonathan,—the last born at Redstone, Old Fort, Pennsylvania. The family left Chester County, about 1766, and after stopping for a time at Redstone, and probably other points, arrived in

Hardin County, Kentucky, 1781. Col. Paul served with Gen. Geo. Rogers Clark, in his campaign against the French and Indians, in Illinois and Indiana, and was granted land in Clark County, Indiana, by the Goveror of Virginia, for his service.

Sarah Paul, the wife of Dr. Cravens, outlived her husband many years. Following his death she married, second, Dr. Goode, of Madison, whom she also outlived. She married, third, Dr. Stevenson, of Madison. (See page 414.)

Dr. Robert Cravens, (14152), and wife Sarah, had issue, an only child—

(141521) John Robert—b. 1819; d. 1899; m. Drusilla Lanier, dau. of James F. D. Lanier, of Madison, and New York City, a distinguished patriot of Indiana whose old home at Madison is now a State Memorial to him. See further record.

(14153) JOHN CRAVENS (1797-1882), the son of Dr. Joseph Cravens (1415), and wife Mary, born at Harrisonburg, Virginia, married at Harrisonburg, February 15, 1821, Ruhama (Reehannah) Chapline (Chaplain), born in Washington County, Maryland March 26, 1805. She was the daughter of Jeremiah Chapline and wife, Elizabeth Nourse, (b. in England, d. 1846, in Mo.,), the daughter of James Nourse, from England.

John Cravens was the second of Dr. Joseph Cravens' sons educated in medicine. He became a distinguished physician and surgeon, and during the War-between-the-States served in this capacity as an officer in the Confederate Army. He died one of the outstanding men of his profession in Missouri.

After practicing for a short time in Harrisonburg, where two, or three, of his children were born, he removed with his family, about 1828, to Franklin, Pendleton County, present West Virginia. In 1830, during his residence in Franklin, he was the Master of the Masonic Lodge there. (See Morton's *History of Pendleton.*) In 1837, he migrated with his family to Saline County, Missouri. He settled at Gallatin, in present Daviess County. Both he and his wife died in Gallatin, in 1882.

While on a business trip to Bloomington, Illinois, with his brother William, in 1849, he nursed the latter in his last illness, which terminated in his death on August 26th.

Dr. John Cravens (14153), and wife Ruhama's children were—

(141531) Mary Elizabeth—b. Sept. 23, 1822; d. Mar. 1, 1868; m. Apr. 23, 1842, Philip Richard Wirt, b. Apr. 8, 1815, d. Feb. 22, 1866. See further record.

(141532) Susan Caroline—b. Nov. 15, 1824; d. ——; living 1891; m. Sept. 19, 1854, John A. Leopard, b. Dec. 24, 1828. See further record.

(141533) Robert Oscar (Judge)—b. Jan. 13, 1827, living 1904; m. Mar. 4, 1855, Mary Jane Robinson, b. 1841, dau. of Marion M. Robinson. Removed to California. See further record.

(141534) Joseph Chapline—b. Sept. 17, 1829; killed by lightning, May 28, 1848, in Daviess Co., Mo.

(141535) Sarah Amanda—b. Aug. 29, 1831; living 1891; m. 1st, Feb. 3, 1848, James Henry Darnell, b. Feb. 13, 1823; m. 2nd, Oct. 12, 1858, Wm. Douglass Mc. Donald, b. Aug. 6, 1826. See further record.

Geo. R. Clark campaign

Lanier of Madison

Douglas McDonald

(141536) William James—b. Nov. 19, 1833; d. Aug. 10, 1883; m. 1855, Mary Rebecca Bryan. Settled at Springfield, Mo.
See further record.

(141537) John Marshall—b. Dec. 14, 1835; d. Apr. 23, 1876 at Gallatin, Mo., m. Aug. 23, 1870, Georgia Lowe, dau. of Dr. Alexander and Susan Boyd Lowe. She m. 2nd, 1879, James Leeper, of Chillicothe, Ohio.

(141538) Jeremiah Chapline (Lieut. Col.)—b. Feb. 18, 1838; living 1891; m. Aug. 11, 1864, Annie Desloge Smith, dau. of Robert. Settled at Springfield, Mo.
See further record.

(141539) Edgar Holmes—b. Sept. 13, 1840; living 1891; m. 1873, Love Keene, of Kentucky.
See further record.

(141540) Oscar Fitzallen—b. Mar. 19, 1843; d. Jan. 26, 1855, at Gallatin, Mo.

(First three born in Rockingham County, Va., next four in Pendleton Co., now W. Va., last three in Mo. See Lyle's, *James Nourse and his Descendants,* p. 88. etc.)

(14155) JAMES HARRISON CRAVENS (1802-1876), the son of Dr. Joseph Cravens (1415), and wife Mary, born in Harrisonburg, Virginia, served as a representative from Indiana in the Twenty-seventh Congress of the United States. (March 4, 1841—March 3, 1843.) See introduction to this Chapter.

James Cravens studied law in Harrisonburg, with John Kenney, and was admitted to the bar in 1823, in which year, after beginning his practice of law in Harrisonburg, he moved to Franklin, Pendleton County, now West Virginia, where he resumed his practice. From Franklin he removed in 1829, to Madison, Indiana, and engaged in agricultural pursuits.

CAPITO

While at Franklin, he married, in 1824, Sophia Capito, the daughter of Daniel Capito (Capiteau-French), and wife Nancy. Daniel Capito was a successful merchant and a large landowner at Franklin. He appears as the owner of land opposite the town as early as 1782; and was drowned in the Dry Fork on his way to Beverly about 1826. His children were—Isabella, m. Andrew H. Byrd; Catherine, m. —— Hamilton; Daniel, m. Jerusha ——; Sophia, m. as above; George, removed to Jefferson Co., Ind.; Peter, merchant at Beverly, removed to Ind.; Julia A., m. Henry Steenbeck; John, no further record. (See, Morton's *History of Pendleton, Co.,* W. Va., p. 319.) Daniel Captio is said to have been of an Alsatian family that went from Alsace to (near Berlin) Germany,more that 200 years ago, whence about fifty or more years later one of his sons, and his German wife, came to this country, and settled in Rockingham County, Virginia. (Pendleton County was formed from Rockingham, Augusta and Hardy Counties in 1787; Franklin being in the part formed from Rockingham.)

* * * * * *

From Franklin to Madison, James Cravens, and wife, and one child, travelled with his household goods in a wagon—with a couple of darkies along, one, an old auntie, around whose waist Mr. Cravens had sewed several hundred dollars in money.

At Madison, he rapidly arose to prominence, and represented his county, Jefferson, in the State legislature, from 1831, to 1832. In 1832, he removed with his family to Ripley County, Indiana, where he continued to reside until his death. In Ripley he practiced law, and managed a farm. In 1839 he was sent to the State Senate, and the next year was a presidential elector on the ticket of Harrison and Tyler. In 1852—following his term in Congress—he was a candidate of the Free-Soil Party for Governor of Indiana. He returned as a member of the State Legislature in 1856, and the same year ran for the office of attorney general of his State.

During the War-between-the-States, he served as a Lieut. Col. of the 83rd Regiment, Indiana Volunteer Infantry. Being a man of strong convictions, and pronounced opinions, he used his influence to get a considerable number of slaves over the line, for which he was at the time, by many, quite severely criticized. On the occasion of Morgan's raid in Indiana, he and his soldiers were taken captive.

He died at Osgood, Indiana, Dec. 4, 1876, and was interred in Versailles Cemetery, at Versailles. (See, *Biographical Directory of the American Congresses*, 1774-1927, p. 858.) His wife Sophia, died in February, 1895, aged 92 years.

James H. Cravens (14155), and wife Sophia, had issue—

(141551) JAMES WILLIAM (M. D.)—b. 1827; d. 1876; m. Mary F. Short, in Ind. See further reference.

(141552) JOSEPH ROBERT (M. D.)—b. 1830; d. ——; m. 1850, Adelia S. Edwards, of New Marion, Ind.; resided at Anderson, Ind,

(141553) JOHN OSCAR—b. 1834; d. 1914, Versailles, Ind; m. Margaret Hite, granddaughter of Abraham Hite and wife Sallie (14154), nee Cravens. See further record.

Abraham Hite

(141554) JOHN KENNEY—b. Aug. 1838; d. 1892; m. Apr. 1861, Frances Catlett Frame. Removed to Kansas City Mo., 1865. See further record.

(141555) AMANDA MEDORA—b. 1841; d. 1870; m. 1860, John Henry Ewing, of Indiana. See further record.

(141556) JUNIUS EDWARD (M. D.)—b. 1844; d. 1920; m. 1871, Emilie S. Stewart, in Ind., Resided in Paris, France, and New York City. See further record.

(Two children died in infancy.)

KENNERLY

(14156) AMANDA FITZALLEN CRAVENS (1804-1884), the daughter of Dr. Joseph Cravens (1415), and wife Mary, of Harrisonburg, married, in 1820, Major Jacob R. Kennerly (1796-1867), of Augusta County, Virginia, the son of James Kennerly, Jr. Jacob Kennerly served in the War of 1812. Following his marriage, he migrated with his family to southern Indiana. He settled at Shelbyville, in Shelby County. Issue three children—

(141561) JOSEPH ROBERT—b. 1822; d. 1899, unmarried.

(141562) VIRGINIA ANN—b. 1824; d. 1874; m. John Woodard, moved to Ill., Sept. 1868. See further record.

(141563) JAMES THOMAS—b. 1833; d. 1906; m. 1864, Susan Virginia Syrcle, b. 1842, d. 1923, native of Augusta County Va. See further record.

2. LINE OF JAMES CRAVENS

SHELLY

(14161) MARY CRAVENS ( ), the daughter of James Cravens (1416) and wife Ann, removed in childhood with her parents from Tennessee to Alabama, where she married Jacob Shelly, of Selma, or Talladega, later a Colonel in the Mexican War. At the outbreak of the war, he was clerk of his county court, and during his absence, his wife, Mary, held the office. Of their children—

(141611) JAMES—b. ——; at the age of 16, was with his father in Mexico, and during the War of 1861-65, was a Col. in the Union Army.

A second son served as a Capt. in the Confederate Army.

(14163) ROBERT CRAVENS (1805-1886), the son of James Cravens (1416), and wife Ann, born in Rockingham County, Virginia, moved with his parents to Tennessee, and later to Selma, Alabama. Following their deaths, in 1821, he and his sisters returned to Tennessee, and resided with his mother's sister, Mary Love Gordon, and her husband, who had no children. Mr. Gordon was a prospeerous business man, interested, among other things, in an iron furnace, and at the age of 21 years young Cravens became his partner. He was the first to manufacture coke in the South.

Robert Cravens married, in Greene County, Tennessee, 1830, Catherine Roddy, the daughter of Jesse and Jane Mahaffe Roddy, and grand-daughter of Col. James Roddy, who served as a Capt. in the battle of Kings Mountain. (Oct. 7, 1780.)

Continuing his interest in the manufacture of iron, Robert Cravens, about the time of his marriage, built a furnace of his own on Whites Creek, in Rhea County, Tennessee, in which neighborhood he and his wife made their home. It was here that all of his children were born. His wife died in 1845, and sometime thereafter he married, second, Caroline Cunningham, by whom there was no issue. In 1848, he moved to Chattanooga, where he built another furnace. This last was destroyed in the War-between-the-States. His home at Chattanooga was on Lookout Mountain. During the famous battle there, nine cannon balls passed through his house.

Robert Cravens (14163), and wife Catherine, had children—

(141631) NANCY—b. 1832; m. J. P. McMillin. See further record.

(141632) ELIZABETH—b. 1834; d. 1885; m., 1854, George W. Lyle. See further record.

(141633) JAMES R.—b. 1836; m., 1st, Harriet Rogers; m. 2nd, Drucilla Lyle. Residing at Ringgold, Georgia, 1889. See further record.

(141634) LYDIA—d. 1866 c; m. William W. Anderson. See further record.

(141635) JESSE RODDY—b. 1842 c; m. 1st, Mary Ellen Brown; m. 2nd, Ida Miller. See further record.

---

1. LINE OF MAJOR ROBERT CRAVENS

2. LINE OF JEREMIAH CRAVENS

(14811) HESTER CRAVENS ( ), the daughter of Jeremiah Cravens (1481), and wife Margaret, nee Harrison, married Jesse Cravens, (14841), the son of Nehemiah (Mi) Cravens, of Christian County, Kentucky. See Jesse Cravens below.

2. LINE OF WILLIAM CRAVENS

STRAIM

(14833) ELEANOR CRAVENS (1791-), the daughter of William Cravens (1483) and wife Mary, married, first, in Kentucky, Henry Straim, whom she outlived. She married, second, in Missouri, 1818, James McFadden. Issue by the first marriage, two children—

(148331) David—b. ——; no further record.
(148332) Mary—b. ——; no further record.

(14835) JEREMIAH CRAVENS (1796-1849), the son of William Cravens (1483), and wife Mary, born in Christian County, Kentucky, removed with his parents, in 1810, to Cape Giradeau, later Madison County, Missouri. He married, in Madison County, March 28, 1818, Kiturah Murphy, the daughter of William Murphy, a Revolutionary soldier, and wife Rachel, nee Henderson.

About 1821, Jeremiah Cravens moved with his family to Arkansas Territory; remaining there for about five years, then returning to Missouri, and later removing to the southwestern part of the state where he died.

Jeremiah Cravens (14835), and wife Kiturah, (Kitty), had issue seven children, five of whom lived to reach maturity, viz—

(148351) James—b. ——; d. ——; served as an officer in the Confederate Army.
(148352) Margaret—b. Nov. 3, 1820; d. Jan. 8, 1885; m. Gen. James Spencer Rains, officer of the Confederate Army.
(148353) Samuel T.—b. Apr. 8, 1824; d. Aug. 4, 1851, "in California during the Gold Rush."
(148354) Jesse Lamb (Col.)—b. ——; d. ——; served as an officer in the Confederate Army.
(148355) William Murphy (Capt.)—b. June 26, 1833, Fredericktown, Mo.; d. Jan. 2, 1919; m. Apr. 8, 1862, Mary Eloise, dau. of Col. Samuel Rutherford. Served as an officer in the Confederate Army. Removed to Ft. Smith, Arkansas.
See further record.

(14838) NEHEMIAH CRAVENS (1803-), the son of William Cravens (1483), and wife Mary, born in Christian County, Kentucky, married in 1825, in Missouri, Sophia Thompson (d. 1862.)

From Fredericktown, Missouri, Nehemiah Cravens, and family, moved to Crawford, now Logan County, Arkansas (Territory), in 1831. He settled on Shoal Creek, near Morrison's Bluff, where he was living in 1889, (June 16th), in the 86th year of his age.

Issue, four children, viz:

(148381) William L.—
(148382) James—
(148383) Jesse—
(148384) Jordan Edgar (Congressman)—b. Nov. 7, 1830, Fredericktown, Mo.; d. April 8, 1914, at Ft. Smith, Ark. Served as a Col. in Confederate Army.
See further reference.

(All born in Mo.)

2. LINE OF NEHEMIAH CRAVENS

(14841) JESSE CRAVENS (   ), the son of Nehemiah Cravens, (1484), and wife Sallie, married Hester Cravens, (14811), daughter of Jeremiah Cravens, and wife Margaret. (See page 492.) A son—

(148411) GEORGE L.—settled in Texas.

CLAN OF ALEXANDER HERRING

1. LINE OF WILLIAM HERRING

2. LINE OF ALEXANDER HERRING

(19512) MARTHA DAVIS HERRING (1799-1866), the daughter of Alexender Herring (1951), and wife Margaret (16511), nee Smith, married George Harrison Chrisman, (12602), the son of John Chrisman. See Clan of John Harrison, 1. Line of Capt. Reuben Harrison, 2. Line of John Chrisman. (Page 464.)

COURT MANOR, FORMERLY MORELAND HALL
By The Long Grey Trail
Built by Reuben Moore (1791-1859), the late home of George H. Harrison, (1847-1932)
See Pages 370, 448, 503 and 514

CHAPTER XXIII

Around and About the Old County, and Elsewhere

SIXTH GENERATION,

ALSO VARIOUS LINES OF THE SEVENTH AND EIGHTH

"Just a seam upon the surface,
Just a scar across the plain,
Just a rift that shows erosion,
Or a slight eruptive pain;
When the world was young and plastic,
And its face was tender, quite;
Possibly the smile of rapture.
At the words: "Let there be light!"

"And the minnows in your waters,
Frolic through the livelong day,
Stirring water-cress and grasses,
In their never ending play.
Break the silence of your musing,
Tell me when you first began,
Tell me, do! whence came the waters,
Which at first adown you ran."

JACOB HAYNE HARRISON, (1851-1922), a widely known poet of Texas, newspaper writer, and author, was born on the Dry Fork of Smiths Creek, in old Rockingham; and although these verses, selections from his poem, *Yellow-House Canyon*—the whole of which may be found in *The Library of Southern Literature,* (Vol. 14, page 6162)—are descriptive of a stream far removed from the scenes of his boyhood, they are fittingly reminiscent of that first stream on the banks of which, as a barefoot lad, he had stood, and which flowed immediately by the site of his birthplace, crossing there the historic Long Grey Trail.

The Dry Fork and Smiths Creek country, to the north of Harrisonburg, Virginia, has long been particularly the land of the descendants of John Harrison, the pioneer. It was in this region that he and his sons and daughters settled, and here many of his descendants have continued to reside.

In traversing this region from Harrisonburg, by way of the Valley Pike, it is interesting to note the locations of many of the old places associated with this branch of the family, and their connections. Leaving Harrisonburg, the traveller shortly passes Smithland (patented by Capt. Daniel Harrison, John's brother), on the upper waters of the Dry Fork, which stream in general parallels the route to Lacey Spring. A few miles below Smithland, the Howard lands are passed, and further on, the village of

Melrose, below which appears, in turn, the old home place of David Harrison, grandson of John, at Virginia Caverns, and then adjoining, the old lands of Daniel, and Nathaniel Harrison, sons of David, Daniel being the father of Jacob Hayne above. Next appears the old home place of Capt. Reuben Harrison, son of John, and father of David—at the present Allebaugh place—and then John's homesite, at Lacey Spring. From Lacey, the way parallels Smiths Creek, passing, just below the spring, the old lands of Zebulon Harrison, son of John, and the old Daniel Matthews home, Locust Grove, and a little further on, the early Pickering and Woodley lands, at Mauzy, then immediately beyond Tenth Legion, the old Martz Place, and next adjoining the Moore lands, including Court Manor. Further down the creek, but somewhat off the Pike in the region of Endless Caverns, is passed the old Byrd land, at Crany Island. In all, a region of approximately fifteen miles is thus traversed, extending to near the Rockingham County line, a short distance south of New Market.

Of the sixth generation; by far the greater number resident in Rockingham are found among the descendants of John Harrison, the pioneer. In fact, the Harrison name today, is believed to be represented here only in this branch of the family. As many of this generation of John Harrison's Clan have been settled in the region above, their locations may be the better understood, when named in reference to some of these older places on the trail.

CLAN OF JOHN HARRISON

1. LINE OF ZEBULON HARRISON

2. LINE OF JOHN HARRISON

3. LINE OF WILLIAM HARRISON

(121111) DELILAH HARRISON (1798-1883), the daughter of William Harrison (12111), and wife Mary, married, January 22, 1824, as his second wife, Henry Carrier, of Rockingham. Issue—

(1211111) Shelton H.— b. Apr. 29, 1825; d. Nov. 1907; m. Frances Houston, (17847), dau. of Rev. William Houston. Resided at Keezletown. No issue.
(1211112) Annie—b. May 12, 1827; d. Dec. 3, 1900.
(1211113) William—b. July 15, 1828; d. Oct. 16, 1886.
(1211114) Wilson—b. Dec. 11, 1829; d. ——.
(1211115) Henry F.—b. Feb. 2, 1833; d. Apr. 7, 1870.
(1211116) John—b. June 11, 1834; d. Sept., 1863.
(1211117) Moses E.—b. Feb. 10, 1836; d. ——.
(1211118) Elizabeth—b. May 16, 1838; d. Jan. 27, 1897.
(1211119) Hannah J.—b. July 21, 1840; d. Apr. 23, 1877.
(1211120) Amanda M. M.—b. Mar. 12, 1844; d. ——.
(1211121) Richard M.—b. June 22, 1846; d. Jan. 12, 1908.
(D. S. H. MSS.)

3. LINE OF ZEBULON A. HARRISON

HOSTETTER

(121121) PATSY HARRISON (1807-), the daughter of Zebulon A. Harrison (12112), and wife Mary, married ——— Hostetter. Her sister Nancy, married William Sellers, who, during his wife's lifetime, bought his "in-law's" shares of their father Zebulon's estate, but following his wife's death, it was found that , as he had no children, it was also necessary for him to purchase his own wife's share of the estate, thus the proceedings; "Abraham Harrison as heirs and distributors of Nancy Sellers decd. in the Cause of William Sellers, executor; vs. Zebulon A. Harrison and Children," wherein the following are named as Patsy Hostetter's heirs: Frank Hostetter, Josie L. Percey, Lillian Hostetter, Albert O. Boggs, Sadie H. Boggs, and Mrs. Martha Leiton—the first and last receiving 1/38th, and the others 1/12th of the purchase money. All at the time were residing in the West. (Account Book of Chas. D. Harrison, of Harrisonburg, attorney for the above.)

(121124) ABRAHAM HARRISON (1814-1888), the son of Zebulon A. Harrison, (12112), and wife Mary, married Delilah Rhodes, of Rockingham, born February 25, 1817, died November 19, 1899. Abraham and wife resided on Smiths Creek, a short distance south of Lacey Spring. Their children were—

(1211241) George Milton—b. May 8, 1837; d. Oct. 19, 1838.

(1211242) Robert Allen—b. May 1, 1839; d. May 9, 1912; m. Sept. 12, 1867, Mary Frances Long, b. April 19, 1845, the daughter of Adam Long. See further record.

(1211243) Erasmus Rice—b. Nov. 29, 1840; d. ——.

(1211244) James K. Polk—b. Nov. 15, 1843; d. ——; m. Mary Armentrout. Resided near Lacey Spring.

(1211245) Mary C. C. M.,—b. Aug. 28, 1846; d. Jan. 2, 1867, unmarried. (Death resulted from being thrown from a horse.)

(1211246) Minerva Jane—b. July 30, 1848; m. about 1871, William Christian (Christopher) Flook, b. May 9, 1839. See further record.

(1211247) Nancy E. S.—b. Oct. 30, 1851; d. Mar. 4, 1900; m. John Robert Kyle Bowman. (178441), son of Samuel. See further record.

(1211248) Jacob W.—b. May 3, 1853; d. Aug. 15, 1930; m. Frances Carpenter, dau. of William C. Carpenter. Resided at Ula City, Sutton County, California.

(1211249) Charles S. F. S.—b. April 8, 1855; m. ——— Sites.

(D. S. H. MSS.)

---

1. LINE OF DANIEL DAVISON

2. LINE OF JOSIAH DAVISON

3. LINE OF JONATHAN WILLIAM DAVISON

(123223) DAVID DAVISSON (   ), the son of Jonathan William Davison (Davisson) (12322), and wife, born in Preble County Ohio, married ————. Issue—

(1232231) Charles—

(1232232) John—

(1232233) Schuyler C.—Professor, Dept. of Mathematics, Indiana University, Ind. (1919).

(1232234) Lura—

(1232235) Amaziah—

2. LINE OF JOHN EWING

3. LINE OF CAPT. WILLIAM EWING

(123347) DANIEL BAKER EWING, D. D. (1821-1886), the son of Capt. William Ewing (12334), and wife Elizabeth, married, Oct. 18, 1852, Frances Todd Barbour, of Orange County, Virginia, descendant of a distinguished Virginia family, whose early history is connected with the Colonial times at Williamsburg. (See, *Some Prominent Virginia Families*, by Louise Pecquet du Bellett, chapters on the Barbours and Pendletons.) Rev. Ewing and wife, Frances, had issue—

(1233471) Bryan—d. in infancy.
(1233472) William Nicholas—m. Mitt Hall, of Texas. Resides in Houston, Texas.
(1233473) Lucy Barbour—(unmarried) Resides in Washington, D. C.
(1233474) Cornelia Bryan Summerville—m. Rev. David F. Ward, (decd). Resides with sister Lucy, as above.
(1233475) Elizabeth Bryan—m. Rev. George A. Sparrow, of North Carolina, She d. 1934.
(1233476) Maybelle—m. Edmund Harvey Simonds, of Washington, D. C.
(1233477) Jennie Pendleton—m. George Gros Hall, of Texas.

(See, *The Ewing Genealogy*, by P. K. and M. E. Ewing, p. 38.)

Miss Lucy Ewing, and her sister, Mrs. Ward, have visited the site of the ancestral home of the Ewings in Scotland, and have travelled extensively in England, and on the Continent.

(123349) MARY ELIZABETH EWING (1824-1916), the daughter of Capt. William Ewing, and wife Elizabeth, resided at the old Ewing homestead, on the Mt. Clinton Pike, a few miles west of Harrisonburg. It was she who inherited from her father the highly treasured old water bottle, of the voyage of Isaiah Harrison, the immigrant, to America. (See Chapter VII). To her, a debt of gratitude is owing, for her thoughtful care in its preservation, and the transmission of its history.

(123351) WILLIAM DAVIS EWING (1828-1902), the son of Capt. William Ewing (12334), and wife Elizabeth, married Oct. 29, 1859, Margaret Sellers, of Rockingham. He was a graduate of medicine of the University of Virginia, and during the War-between-the-States, served as a physican and surgeon in the Confederate Army. He and wife resided at Cave Station, Augusta County, where he practiced his profession. Issue—

(1233511) William T.—b. 1860; m. Blanche Ferguson.
(1233512) Elizabeth S.—b. ——; m. Luther Crickenberger.
(1233513) Isaac S. —b. 1868; m. 1897, Lelia E. Hite, of Page Co., Va. Issue—

1. Elizabeth M.—m. Edgar Chambers. He died about 1928.
2. Davis H.—d. in infancy.
3. Clarence W.—b.——.

(1233514) Lillie M.—b. ——; m. William G. Grove, of Harrisonburg, Va.

Mr. I. S. Ewing is the present owner of the old water bottle. (See, Mary Elizabeth Ewing, above.) He is a prominent business man of Harrisonburg, Virginia.

1. LINE OF THOMAS MOORE

2. LINE OF CAPT. REUBEN MOORE

3. LINE OF MOSES WALTON, JR.

(123411) REUBEN WALTON (1799-1874), the son of Moses Walton, Jr., and wife Elizabeth, (12341), nee Moore, married Mary Harrison (12593), the daughter and David Harrison, and wife Elizabeth. (See page 381.) Reuben Walton was a prominent resident of Woodstock, Shenandoah County, Virginia. He was by profession a surveyor, and served his county as the county surveyor. Issue—

(1234111) MOSES—b. Jan. 14, 1826; d. June 15, 1883; m. Feb. 5, 1851, Emily Maria Lauck, b. Mar. 27, 1826, dau. of Morgan A. Lauck.
See further record.

(1234112) ELIZABETH HARRISON—b. Mar. 7, 1829; d. 1893; m. Dec. 17, 1850, John William Ott, b. May 3, 1826.
See further record.

(1234113) DAVID HARRISON (Col.)—b. Oct. 21, 1830; d. July 7, 1876; m. Ellen L. Danner.

(1234114) ANNIE M.—b. Oct. 11, 1833; d. Apr. 24, 1878; m. Dr. JOHN L. CAMPBELL, of near Winchester, Va. Issue—
1. Harvey, d. ——; m. —— Rice.
2. William—d. ——, unmarried.

(Dates from Walton Family Bible.)

(123412) JOHN WALTON (1801-), the son of Moses Walton, Jr., and wife Elizabeth, (12341), nee Moore, married Lydia Allen. Issue—

(1234121) ELIZABETH CATHERINE—b. Feb. 24, 1832; m. Rev. JOHN McMILLAN. Issue—
1. Lydia Jeannette—b. 1853; m. George W. Allen, of St. Louis, Mo., son of Hon. Thomas Allen.

(1234122) ALLEN MOORE—b. June 11, 1834.

(1234123) VIRGINIA—b. June 30, 1840.

(See, Wayland's *History of Shenandoah Co., Va.*, p. 658.)

---

3. LINE OF REUBEN MOORE

(123431) MADISON MOORE (1812-1878), the son of Reuben Moore, (12343), married, Mar. 14, 1839, Lydia Harrison, (12595), the daughter of David Harrison, and wife Elizabeth. Madison and Lydia Moore resided at the old homestead of her father, at Virginia Caverns, on the Valley Pike. (See page 378.) Their children were—

(1234311) DAVID HARRISON—b. Feb. 13, 1840; d. Nov. 21, 1926; m. Jan. 15, 1861, Rebecca C. Sellers, b. June 19, 1842, d. May 10, 1868, dau. of Reuben and Catherine Sellers.
See further record.

(1234312) REUBEN WALTON—b. Aug. 16, 1841; d. May 21, 1911; m. May 1, 1866, Fannie E. Chrisman, dau. of Jack Chrisman. (See page 454.)
See further record.

(1234313) MARTHA VIRGINIA—b. Sept. 22, 1843; d. Feb. 1, 1916; m. Nov. 21, 1871, Dr. William Thomas Jennings, b. May 7, 1837, d. Feb. 15, 1896. See further record.

(1234314) JOHN GORDON—b. Sept. 6, 1846; d. Oct. 11, 1909; m. Nov. 1872, Alice M. Lewin, b. July 7, 1853; d. Dec. 29, 1905. See further record.

(All interred in Moore family cemetery at Virginia Caverns. Dates of births and deaths from tombstones.)

PRICE

(123432) PHOEBE (FEBE) ANN MOORE, (1817-1864), the daughter of Reuben Moore, (12343), and wife Martha Jane, married, in 1838, Joshua Comly Price, born Aug. 26, 1811, died 1864, the son of Mordecai Price (b. July 31, 1762, d. May 29, 1850), and wife Charity Ann, nee Comly, of Gunpowder, Maryland. Joshua Price came to Rockingham as an attendant at a wedding, and there met his future wife. His people were members of the Society of Friends, and had been settled in Maryland since the founding of the Colony. His grandfather, Mordecai Price, (III), married Rachel Moore, of a Maryland line of Moores, dating back to Colonial times.

* * * * * *

Thomas Price, the great-grandfather of Mordecai (III), emigrated from England to Maryland with the first settlers, who embarked from Gravesend, England, November 1633, in two vessels, the "Ark" and the "Dove". They weighed anchor from Cowes, Isle of Wight, the 22nd of November, and arrived in Maryland, (at St. Marys), late in March of the following year. Price became a member of the Common Council of St. Marys. He is said to have been a brother of Sir Edward Price, Knt. He married Elizabeth Phillips, the daughter of Robert Phillips, of Calvert County, and had a son Mordecai (I), of "North River," Anne Arundle County, who died in 1715, or 17. (will proven 1718.)

Mordecai Price (I), married Mary Parsons (will proved November 2, 1726), and had sons; John, m. 1729, Rebecca Merogard; Thomas, m. 1st, 1734, Mary Irvine, m. 2nd, Keturah Maryman; Benjamin, m. 1st, Elizabeth ——, m. 2nd, Milicent Vaughn; Stephen, m., 1716, Canstant Horne; Mordecai (II), of whom more presently; and daughters —Rachel, m. 1729, Levin Scott; Hannah, m. 1st, William Tipton, m. 2nd, John Bosley; Leah, m. ——— Ford; Elizabeth, m. Thomas Carr; Mary, m. Jonathan Hanson; and Sarah, m. 1729, (Patuxent Meeting), Thomas Taylor.

Mordecai Price (II), of Gunpowder Forest, Baltimore County, son of Mordecai Price, (I), married, 4/8, 1724, at Friends Patuxent Meeting House, Elizabeth White (1708-1769), of Cool Springs Manor, Prince George County, the daughter of Guy White, Jr., and wife Elizabeth Griffith (d. 1752), and granddaughter of Samuel Griffith, immigrant to Calvert County, Maryland, from Wales.

Mordecai (II),died about 1764, (inventory, Aug. 8, 1764.) He and wife Elizabeth had issue—Sarah, b. Sept. 1, 1730, m., 1747, Thomas Cole, Jr.; Mordecai (III), above named, b. Jan. 28, 1734, d. May 5, 1796, m. 1759, Rachel Moore; a daughter, m., 1756, Thomas Mathews, Jr.; Sophia, m. 1756, Nathan Hains; Stephen, (d. 1809), m., 1st, 1749, Rebecca Hicks, m. 2nd, 1783, Susan Rolls; Samuel, b. Dec. 28, 1739, m. Ann Moore; Elizabeth, b. June 22, 1741, m. Warwick Miller; and Mary, b. Dec. 9. 1744, m. Daniel Hains.

Mordecai Price (III), and wife Rachel, had children; Anne, m., 4/22, 1774, William Mathews; Mordecia (IV), who married, as stated, Charity Ann Comly; Rachel, b. Feb. 22, 1767, m. ——— Scott; Sarah, b. Feb. 17, 1769, m. ——— Morgan; Elizabeth, b. Dec. 2, 1771, d. Oct. 16, 1831, m. ——— Benson; Joseph, b. Oct. 28, 1774, d. May 6, 1861, m. ———; and Elijah, b. Apr. 26, 1780; of whom; Mordecai (IV), and wife, Charity Ann, had Amos; Joshua Comly; and Levi. The latter b. July 22, 1797, d. Apr. 12, 1891, m., May 15, 1831, Elizabeth Matthews, b. July 9, 1802, d. May 15, 1872.

* * * * * *

Following his marriage, Joshua C. Price and wife resided for a short time in Smithburg, Maryland, where he was engaged in business with his brother, Amos. Upon the dissolution of the firm of Price Brothers, he removed with his family to Virginia, and resided on the land later bequeathed his wife by the terms of her father's will. The site of their home was on the eastern bank of Smiths Creek, in Rockingham, where Mr. Vernon Biedler now lives. About the time of the War-between-the-States, Mr. Price returned to Maryland, and settled with his family at Ellendale, in Baltimore County, where he died. He and his wife both died the same year, she April 30, 1864.

Joshua Price was imbuded with a strong distaste for slavery, and prior to his residence in Virginia was a member of the Anti-Slavery Society. He "was a man whose very presence commanded respect and reverence," says a biographical sketch of his son, Isaiah B. Price; "plain and simple in manner, direct in speech and action, he inspired and held the confidence of even those who were opposed to his peculiar views. He had early instilled into his mind the principles of the 'Society of Friends,' and bore throughout life a strong testimony against bigotry, slavery, intemperance, and inequality of caste."

Joshua C. Price, and wife Phoebe, were the parents of nine children, several of whom became brilliant men in their chosen walks of life. Their children were—

(1234321) REUBEN MOORE—b. July 23, 1839; d. Oct.4, 1918; m. Caroline Cooper Paxion, b. Dec. 6, 1842, d. Nov. 22, 1922.
See further record.

(1234322) CHARITY ANN—b. Aug. 13, 1841; d. Dec. 15, 1873; m. John Thomas Hughs, b. July 15, 1827, d. Sept. 2, 1890.
See further record.

(1234323) MORDECAI (M. D.)—b. Feb. 4, 1844; d. Oct. 28, 1904; m. (1st), Frances Fell Remington, b. ——, d. Feb. 27, 1884.
See further record.

(1234324) ISAIAH BENJAMIN—b. Aug. 28, 1846; d. Dec. 10, 1884; m. Ellen Margaret Morton, b. Oct. 14, 1856.
See further record.

(1234325) ELIZABETH—b. Nov. 22, 1848; d. Aug. 8, 1874, unmarried.

(1234326) JOSEPH (M. D.)—b. Jan. 1, 1853; d. June 8, 1911; m. 1887, Louisa Troth (M. D.), b. June 10, 1858, d. Aug. 1, 1933.
See further record.

(1234327) THOMAS—b. Mar. 24, 1854; d. Nov. 24, 1868.

(1234328) EMILY WALTON—b. Mar.12, 1855; d. Dec. 29, 1887, unmarried.

(1234329) CORNELIA W.—b. June 11, 1857; d. Dec. 1, 1911; m. Bayard Bachus.
See further record.

(The last seven, at least, were born in Rockingham County.)

(123433) JOHN MOORE (1818-1864), the son of Reuben Moore, (12343), and wife Martha Jane, married Elizabeth Ann Harrison (12598), the daughter of David Harrison, and wife Elizabeth. John and Elizabeth Ann Moore resided on the land inherited from his father, at the site of the late Newton G. Moore's home. He died January 29, 1864. His widow outlived him thirty-one years. Their children were—

(1234331) OTTIS F.—b. Dec, 20, 1847; d. Nov. 2, 1903; m. Sallie A. Zirkle, b. 1849, d. 1883, dau. of Reuben. (a child died in infancy.)
(1234332) HARRISON—b. Nov. 25, 1849; d. Mar. 26, 1852.
(1234333) NEWTON GORDON—b. Aug. 4, 1851; d. Jan. 3, 1914; m. Sept. 27, 1876 Josephine Augusta Henkel, b. July 25, 1857, dau. of Dr. Solon P. S. Henkel.
See further record.

(First two interred in Moore family cemetery on Smiths Creek, the last in "Upper" Lutheran Churchyard, at New Market, Va.)

MOORE

(123437) VIRGINIA MOORE (1825-1902), the daughter of Reuben Moore, (12343), and wife Martha Jane, married, Aug 4, 1846, Joseph Moore, of Shenandoah County, born Jan. 19, 1819, died Aug. 30, 1881.

Joseph Moore, of Shenandoah, was a son of Reuben Moore of Moore's Store, near Forrestville, whose father, Joseph Moore, the first, is said to have been thrice married, one of his wives being Frances Stuart, the widow of John Stuart, whose will was proven in Augusta County, January 15, 1790, and whose daughter, Mary, married Dr. Peachy Harrison, (1679.) (See page 396.) Frances was yet a widow in 1794, as revealed by her mother Martha Burnsides' will. She was married to Joseph Moore prior to 1805. The latter was probably the son of Thomas Moore, who died in 1790. Among Thomas' children were sons, Joseph, and Reuben, and a daughter, Ann; Reuben being presumably the same who married Ann Davison, (1232). Ann Moore, daughter of Thomas, married Joseph Miller. (See page 368.)

Joseph Moore, the first, (three times married) had children—Mary, (1786-1848); Joseph, m. Virginia ———; John; Strother, m. Maria ———; Solomon; and Reuben. Of these; Mary m. John Newman, (1781-1839), and had, Joseph, George, Walter, Catherine, Frances, Sarah Ann, (1822-1885), Phoebe Ann, and John Strother. Sarah Ann m., 1846, Richard S. Rice, (1824-1858), and had three daughters, among them, Fanny, who married Johns Hopkins. Reuben Moore married Sally Kingree, and had—Kate, who married Benjamin Weirman, Frances, married John Allen, Belle, married Charles Wunder, Joseph, married Virginia Moore, as above, John married Minerva Crim, Solomon, married 1st, Wilelma Pennybacker, married 2nd, Sydney Granstaff, and George, married Mrs. Mary Ann Hooper.

Joseph and Virginia Moore resided at Mt. Jackson, Virginia. Their children were—

(1234371) REUBEN—b. 1847; d. in infancy.
(1234372) MARGARET FRANCES—b. Feb. 19, 1849; d. Feb. 18, 1873; m. Nov. 21, 1870, Linden Allen, b. Mar. 24, 1850, d. Apr. 17, 1912.
See further record.
(1234373) SARAH—b. Mar. 22, 1851; d. Oct. 26, 1916; m. Dec. 12, 1871, John William Miller, b. Feb. 10, 1846, d. Dec. 2, 1911.
See further record.

(1234374) Martha Virginia—b. Aug. 14, 1853; d. May 2, 1921; m. Sept. 26, 1880, Milton Neff, b. Oct. 22, 1855, d. Nov. 5, 1921.
See further record.

(1234375) Elizabeth Katherine—b. Sept. 23, 1856; d. Oct. 28, 1915; m. Apr. 15, 1887, Dr. J. William Koontz, b. Feb. 4, 1857, d. Feb., 1919. Koontz

(1234376) Thomas Earl—b. Apr. 20, 1859; d. May 5, 1929, unmarried.

(1234377) Josephine (Jo)—b. Sept. 17, 1862; m. Oct. 28, 1896, George H. Harrison, (125917), son of John. He d. Mar. 6, 1932.
See further record.

(1234378) Georgianna (George)—b. twin of Josephine. Resided at the old homestead in Mt. Jackson. She d. May. 20, 1931, unmarried.

(1234379) Louise—b. Nov. 22, 1864; m., Apr. 15, 1895, E. BAYLOR COOTES, of Norfolk, Va. Issue—
1. George Moore b. Mar. 18, 1904; m. Ethel ——, of Illinois.

(1234380) Robert Beverly—b. Dec. 10, 1866; d. Apr. 15, 1915; m. Apr. 17, 1896, Mary Cook. Resided at Gaithersburg, Md. Issue—
1. Virginia—b. July 15, 1900.

(Margaret, Sarah, Martha, Elizabeth, Thomas, and Georgianna, interred in Mt. Jackson Cemetery, also the husbands of the four respective sisters.) (See, *History of Virginia,* pub. by American Historical Society, Vol. IV, p. 249.)

(123438) REUBEN MOORE (1828-1859), the son of Reuben Moore, (12343), and wife Martha Jane, married November 5, 1851, Annis Beaver, the daughter of John Beaver, of Page County, Virginia. Reuben and wife resided on the Moreland Hall estate, as a near neighbor of his father. His home was in what was recently known as the Yates residence. Following his death, his widow and their children resided for a time at Moreland Hall. (See page 449.) Their children were—

(1234381) Margaret Frances—b. Aug. 31, 1852; d. in Fla., Mar. 7, 1886; m. Dr. Miller A. Henkel, son of Dr. Solon P. C. Henkel.
See further record.

(1234382) Mary C.—b. Nov. 26, 1853; d. Oct. 12, 1883; m. May 24, 1878, George H. Harrison, (125917), the son of John.
See further record.

(1234383) Oscar Fitz Allen—b. Jan. 11, 1855; d. 1879; m. Mary Alice Henkel, dau. of Solomon.
See further record.

(Mary C. interred in Moore cemetery on Smiths Creek.)

GAINES

(123440) MARY CATHERINE MOORE(1832-1874), the daughter of Reuben Moore, (12343), and wife Martha Jane, married William F. Gaines. They resided on the land devised to her in her father's will, their home being to the east of Smiths Creek, recently occupied by Mr. Brad Zirkle and wife, and until her death, by a sister of the latter, who made her home with Mr. and Mrs. Zirkle. These sisters were the only children, viz—

(1234401) MARTHA E.—b. Mar. 13, 1858; d. Mar. 12, 1934; m. William Hahn, d. ——; (prior to 1890.) No issue.

(1234402) LUCY—b. 1863; m. 1884, Bradford B. Zirkle, b. Oct. 28, 1854, d. Feb. 5, 1935.
See further record.

---

1. LINE OF CAPT REUBEN HARRRISON

2. LINE OF NATHANIEL HARRISON

3. LINE OF MICHAEL HOWARD

STOVER

(125211) MARY HOWARD, (1808-), the daughter of Michael Howard, and wife Lydia, (12521), nee Harrison, married John Stover, descendant of the early Page County, Virginia, family. Issue—

(1252111) JOHN W.—
(1252112) JACOB—
(1252113) DANIEL—
(1252114) SIS—
(1252115) JAMES—
(1252116) MARY—
(1252117) EDITH—
(1252118) FANNIE—
(1252119) LIVICK—
(D. S. H. MSS.)

(125215) JOHN HOWARD (1815-1896), the son of Michael Howard, and wife Lydia, (12521), nee Harrison, married, Nov. 11, 1847, Lena Andes, of Rockingham. John Howard and wife resided at the old homestead of his father, just off "The Long Grey Trail," to the north of Harrisonburg. The land lies to the east of the Valley Pike. (See introduction to this Chapter.) John and Lena Howard had issue—

(1252151) ADAM ANDES—b. Sept. 22, 1848, (unmarried.) Resides at the homestead above.
(1252152) WILLIAM S. H.—b. Nov. 12, 1851; d. ——, unmarried.
(1252153) MARY C.—b. Mar. 20, 1854; d. 1863.
(1252154) GEORGE WASHINGTON—b. Oct. 1, 1856; d. Oct. 1864.
(1252155) MICHAEL H.—b. Dec. 23, 1859; d. Oct. 1864.
(1252156) EMMA L. B.—b. Mar. 20, 1865, (unmarried.) Resides with brother Adam.
(D. S. H. MSS.)

---

3. LINE OF MIFFORD HANNAH

(125284) NATHANIEL HANNAH, (1824-1863), the son of Mifford Hannah, and wife Edith, (12528), nee Harrison, married, 1849, Bell C. Rhodes, of Rockingham. Nathaniel Hannah served as a soldier in the Confederate Army, and died a prisoner at Camp Chase, West Columbus, Ohio, July 6, 1863. Issue—

(1252841) BELLE C.—b. Aug. 21, 1850; m. George B. Keezell, (Virginia State Senator), as his 2nd wife.

(1252842) Asbury M.—b. Jan. 11, 1852; m., about 1885, ———.
Issue—
1. Katie Belle—m. ——— Stovall.
(1252843) Nathaniel B. B.—b. Sept. 10, 1856; m. 1891, ——— Burke (?).
(1252844) Mary Catherine—b. Mar. 30, 1858; d. Oct. 11, 1902; m. George B. Keezell, as his first wife.
See further record.
(1252845) John Harrison—b. July 10, 1860; m., 1888, Lenore Burtner.
(D. S. H. MSS.)

---

2. LINE OF JOHN HARRISON

3. LINE OF MILLER BOWMAN

(125313) ANDREW J. BOWMAN, (1816-), the son of Miller Bowman, and wife Phoebe, (12531), nee Harrison, married, first, Ann Welsh, and second, 1850, Sarah Miller See. He removed as a youth (aged about 16) to Hopkinsville, Kentucky, following the death of his father, and later to Centerville, Tennessee. Issue by first marriage six children, among them—

(1253131) Rebecca—
(1253132) John—
(1253133) Jacob—
(1253134) Virginia—
By second marriage—
(1253135) Callie—m. Charles de Lisle Kane, of St. Louis, Mo.
(Letter Mrs. J. L. B. *pens me*, 11-19-27.)

---

2. LINE OF THOMAS WARREN

3. LINE OF JOHN GORDON

(125812) THOMAS GORDON, ( ), the son of John Gordon, and wife Nancy, (12581), nee Warren, married Catherine Bear, (125824), daughter of Andrew Bear (d. January 4, 1868, aged 80), and wife Lydia (d. Feburary 16, 1851, aged 57), nee Warren. Thomas Gordon and wife are thought to have settled in Texas. Issue—
(1258121) Harriett—
(D. S. H. MSS.)

(125813) JOHN NEWTON GORDON, (1825-1882), the son of John Gordon, and wife Nancy, (12581), nee Warren, married Elizabeth Warren (125853), born Apr. 7, 1832, died Oct. 29, 1867, the daughter of Jehu Warren, and wife Harriett. John Newton Gordon was a prominent practicing physician of Harrisonburg. He was born March 8, 1825, and died July 27, 1882. Issue—

(1258131) Mary E.—b. May 5, 1855; d. Jan. 12, 1863.
(1258132) Harriett R.—b. Dec. 26, 1856; d. Mar. 31, 1860.
(1258133) Virginia M.—b. June 20, 1859; d. Dec. 13, 1862.
(1258134) Nancy—b.——.
(1258135) Edward Tiffin—b. ——.
(1258136) Amelia—b. Sept. 18, 1864; d. in infancy.
(1258137) Newton—b. Sept. 6, 1867; d. in infancy.
(Dates from tombstones in New Erection Churchyard; the exact sequence of Nancy and Edward Tiffin's births not known.)

Bell

3. LINE OF ANDREW BEAR

BELL

(125823) HARRIETT BEAR (1828-1899), the daughter of Andrew Bear, and wife Lydia, (12582), nee Warren, married Rev. Thomas D. Bell (D. D.), of Rockingham, born August 29, 1813, died November 22, 1889. She was born May 22, 1828, and died February 21, 1899. Rev. Bell was for many years pastor of New Erection Church, (Presbyterian). Issue—

(1258231) BESSIE ELEN—b. 1863; d. Oct. 21, 1865, in 3rd year.
(1258232) MARY J.—b.——; Resides in Richmond, Va.
(1258233) ANDREW GILBERT—b.——.
(1258234) THOMAS STILES—b. Oct. 18, 1869; d. May 8, 1924.

(Rev. Bell and wife, and first named daughter, interred in New Erection Churchyard. Dates from tombstones. Thomas S. interred in Woodbine Cemetery, at Harrisonburg.) (D. S. H. MSS.)

---

3. LINE OF JEHU WARREN

(125851) WILLIAM RICE WARREN, (1826-1884), the son of Jehu Warren, (12585), and wife Harriett, married Rebecca Spears, (126034), the daughter of Charles C., and wife Margaret, nee Chrisman. (See page 464.) Rice Warren and wife resided in Harrisonburg. He was for many years Cashier of the Rockingham National Bank. He was born Dec. 11, 1826, and died May 1, 1884. Interred in New Erection Churchyard. Issue—

(1258511) MARGARET—m. C. N. Coleman.
(1258512) SALLIE—m. Rev. ROBERT WHITE,
Issue—
1. Margaret, (see below.)
(1258513) THOMAS—resides in Harrisonburg; m. Mrs. Hill, nee Effinger.
Issue—
1. William Rice—m. Margaret White, above.
2. George—m. Sarah Maury.

(D. S. H. MSS. etc.)

(125852) EDWARD TIFFIN HARRISON WARREN (1829-1864), the son of Jehu Warren (12585), and wife Harriett, born June 19, 1829, married, December 5, 1855, at Frescita, Orange County, Virginia, Virginia Magruder, b. February 22, 1837, died April 21, 1891. He served as a Colonel in the Confederate Army and was killed in the battle of the Wilderness, May 5, 1864. At the outbreak of the war he was a practicing lawyer of Harrisonburg. (See, *Wayland*, p. 139.)

Writing under the date, January 30, 1913, from Escondido, California, Mrs. Belle J. Waytt (178431), the daughter of Mrs. Amantha Houston Jordan, remarks; "that Col. Tiffin Warren was our cousin, his father being the son of the Harrison sister who married a Warren. Col. Warren's mother, cousin Harriett, and Aunt (Julia) Smith were great friends, and cousin Harriett's daughter, Ella, and Aunt Julia Houston Paul were school mates and friends. I think Sallie Warren of whom I wrote, was Col. Warren's father's sister."

While the identity of the "Harrison sister" is here confused with Elizabeth Harrison, who married Col. Warren's grandfather, the statement is valuable testimony in confirming the latter's descent from John Warren, who married Sarah Harrison, the daughter of Thomas, founder of Harrisonburg. (See page 340.) The relationship of the writer to the Colonel is readily explained on this basis, Sarah being a sister of the writer's great grandfather. Sallie Warren was not a sister of the Colonel's father, but was likely a sister of his grandfather, Thomas Warren.

Col. Warren, (125853), and wife Virginia, had issue—

(1258531) JAMES MAGRUDER (M. D.)—b. ——; d. ——; m. Williett Sprinkle. He was a prominent physician at New Hope, and Bridgewater, in the 80's and 90's. Issue—

1. Carter—m. Wade Cochrane, (decd). Resides at Greenville, S. C.
2. Tiffin—d. in childhood.
3. James M.—m. Frances Sublett, of Harisonburg, where they reside. (2 children; twins.)

(1258532) ELIZABETH—b. Mar. 5, 1857; d. Aug. 17, 1909; m. CHARLES C. SWITZER, of Harrisonburg, d. Aug. 22, 1930. Issue—

1. Cornelia—m. Dr. Edwin Shewmake, Prof. of English, Davidson College.
2. Edward—m. Ellen Brant.
3. Virginia—m. Arthur Kent.

(1258533) VIRGINIA WATSON—b. ——; d. ——; m. Edward Lipscomb, of Staunton, Va.

---

3. LINE OF JOSEPH BURKHOLDER:

BYRD

(125872) CATHERINE C. BURKHOLDER, (1827-1903), the daughter of Joseph Burkholder, and wife Elizabeth, (12587), nee Warren, born December 3, 1827, died April 12, 1903, married June 12, 1856, William Perry Byrd, born June 6, 1817, died August 2, 1887, the son of Abraham Byrd, and wife Rebecca Samuels, whose father married Elizabeth Pennybacker.

William P. Byrd served throughout the War-between-the-States, in the Confederate Army. A short time after his enlistment, he was appointed secretary to Gen. Robert E. Lee, and served most of his time in this capacity. From the close of the war, to about 1868, he and wife resided in Harrisonburg, and then removed to Greenmount, where he was engaged in farming.

* * * * * *

Abraham Byrd, and wife, resided at Red Bank, in Shenandoah County, and at Stoneleigh Inn, in Harrisonburg. They had children—Abraham S., b. June 7, 1824, d. July 31, 1903, Capt. Quartermaster C. S. A.; Isaac d. aged about 28 yrs. unmarried;

Green, d. young; Sylvenus A., b. July 4, 1822, d. February 14, 1854, Lewisburg, now West Virginia, graduate of law University of Va.; Erasmus, m. 1st, Lydia Gordon (125817), m. 2nd, Molly Blinco, removed to Texas, m. 3rd, Julia King; William Perry (as above); Mary, m. 1st, Robert Kyle, m. 2nd, Rev. L. S. Reed, as his 2nd wife; Annie, m. Henry Wartman, as his 2nd wife; and Maggie E., b. February 7, 1829, d. June 14, 1862, single. (Dates of Abraham S., Sylvenus, and Maggie E. from tombstones in Wodbine Cemetery, Harrisonburg.)

Rev. Reed had issue, by his first wife: James, a Methodist minister, Thomas, Christopher, and Walter, the last being the distinguished Dr. Walter Reed, of the U. S. Army. By his second wife, Rev. Reed had issue, a daughter, Annie, who married Douglass T. Elam. Henry Wartman, by his first wife, had issue, a son, Edward Wartman, LLD., now resident of Florida, and for many years a member of the legislature there.

Abraham Byrd, the first named, was a descendant of Andrew Byrd, the pioneer, who (or his son Andrew) appears as a Lieut. in Peter Scholl's militia company on Smiths Creek, in 1742, and was commissioned Capt., 28th February, 1744. (See pages 143-4). Andrew Byrd, Sr., is said to have been a brother of Ordway Byrd, and by tradition, of the James River family of eastern Virginia. He died early in 1751. On the 27th February, 1750-1, Magdalena and Andrew Bird's bond, as administrators of Andrew Bird, with sureties, John Dobkin and Samuel Newman, was recorded. (Will Book I, p. 283.) In the petition to administer, Andrew states that he is the eldest son; Magdalina was the widow.

Andrew Byrd, II, and wife Mary, resided at Crany Island, on Smiths Creek, in later Rockingham. (See introduction to this Chapter.) He was commissioned Capt. of militia, 18th November 1762, was also Capt. of militia, 1752, (see page 298), and was a miller—Deed, 18th April, 1763, Valentine Sevire of Frederick, farmer, to Andrew Byrd, miller, household goods. (D. B. 11, p. 218.) Among the papers extant, handed down in his family to William P. Byrd, above, are three original land patents, two old family Bibles, the first published in London, 1763, and a volume entitled, *The New Practice of Piety*, published in London, 1749, "By his Majesty's Special Authority." On the last is noted: "Andrew Bird his property, anno domini 1 . . . given to him by a british officer," also, "Andrew Bird.—I finish reading Book Thru on Sunday 12th Day Feb., 1792. Andrew Bird his Book."

The second earliest patent, of the above series, dated at Williamsburg, 16th August, 1756, signed by Lieut. Gov. Dinwiddie, recites—

> "George the Second by the Grace of God of Great Britain France and Ireland King Defender of the Faith &c. To all to whom these Presents shall come Greeting Know ye that for the consideration mentioned in an order of our trusty welbeloved William Gooch Esquire our Lieutenant Governor and Commander in chief of our Colony and Dominion of Virginia in our Council of the said Colony the twenty first Day of October one thousand seven hundred and thirty one We have Given Granted and Confirmed and by these Presents for us our Heirs and Successors Do give Grant and Confirm unto Andrew Burd one certain Tract or Parcel of land containing two hundred and ten Acres lying and being in the County of Augusta on Smith's Creek and bounded as followeth to Wit Beginning at a white Oak Corner to John Hodge's Land on the north side of the Creek" . . . etc.

The order in Council referred to reads—

"On the petition of Robt McKay & Joost Heyd of the Province of Pensilvania setting forth that they & divers other Families to the number of one hundred are desirous to remove from thence & Seat themselves on the back of the great Mountains within this Colony & praying that one hundred thousand Acres of Land lying between the Line of Land granted to John Vanmeter Jacob Stover John Fishback & others may be assigned them and that the Residue of the sd one hundred thousand Acres may be Assigned upon & including the Several Branches of Sherundo River above the Lands of the said Stover & Fishback and his Partners The Governour with the advice of the Council is pleased to order as it is hereby Ordered that the petrs in behalf of themselves' their Partners have leave to take up the sd Qauntity of 100,000 Acres of Land within the Limits above described & that upon the above Number of Families coming to dwell there within two Years Patents shall be granted them in such manner as they Shall agree to divide the same." (See, Journal of the Council of Colonial Virginia, for 21st Oct., 1731, State Library, Richmond, Va.)

The Council order being dated in 1731, and the patent in 1756, the settlement of Byrd was obviously not within the two year limit. Hite, in the meantime, finding difficulty in obtaining 100 families, secured an extension of time and probably in the interval became acquainted with Byrd, after his actual settlement. Of the other two patents; the first dated 5th day of September, 1749, was granted to Andrew Burd, "for divers good Causes and Considerations but more especially for and in Consideration of the Sum of Twenty Shillings of good and lawful Money." This shows that Bryd was in the neighborhood long before the Hite patent was issued. The indications are that Byrd had met Borden earlier than Hite, the patent being a grant to 190 acres of land "in the County of Augusta on Smith's Creek . . . . . in a Line of the land of Benjamin Bordon, corner to the Land of Thomas and Robert Millsaps." The third patent is dated, 20th June, 1772, and was granted to "Andrew Byrd" . . . for divers good causes, etc. . . . "in Consideration of the Sum of Fifteen shillings," 150 acres of land "lying and being in the County of Augusta on the East Side of Smiths Creek joining his other Land . . . . . corner to said Byrd and Hodges Lands" etc.

On 17th November, 1752, Benjamin Bordon deeded to Andrew Bird 174 acres in "Brocks Gap on North Shenado", including "the Chimney Rock." Delivered to Abraham Bird, 27 January, 1754. (Deed Book 5, page 30.)

As recorded in the oldest family Bible, the children of (Capt.) "Andrew Bird & Mary his Wife" were—Andrew, b. November 30, 1754, Catherine, b. June 1, 1756, William, b. May 22, 1758, Abraham, b. March 1, 1761, and Isaac, b. February 4, 1763. The notations entered in *The New Practice of Piety,* state—"Mary Byrd Departed this Life 23rd Oct. 1784; Phoebe (Kranor ?) daughter of Andrew Byrd—16th Sept. 1846 (?); Andrew Byrd departed this life June the 22, 1823; Ruth Thomas departed this life Mar. 5, 1830, daughter of Andrew Bird and Ann his wife. Elizabeth Moore Daughter of Andrew bird and Ann Bird departed this life 15 Mar. 1834. Ann Bird Wife of Andrew Bird died 28 April 1834. Andrew Byrd departed this life 30th Nov. 1838."

Andrew Byrd, (III), (1754-1838), Revolutionary soldier, (qualified Capt. May 24, 1779) and wife Ann, had, as recorded in the second oldest Bible—Mary, b. Jan. 8, 1778, Elizabeth, b. June 12, 1779, John, b. May 4, 1781, Catherine, b. Jan. 20, 1783, Phoebe, b. Feb. 4, 1785, Ann, b. Apr. 4, 1787, Abraham, b. Sept. 10, 1789, Sarah. b.

Dec. 9, 1791, Andrew b. Apr. 2, 1795, Ruth, b. Apr. 10, 1797, and Thomas, b. Mar. 11, 1800.

Among these, Abraham, born Sept. 10, 1789, married Rebecca Samuels, and was the father of Abraham S., William Perry, etc.—a further notation in *The New Practice of Piety,* stating; "I finished reading this Book Sunday Feb. 21, 1892, signed, A. S. Byrd Grand Son Andrew Byrd." Abraham Byrd died, May 14, 1862. His wife, Rebecca M., was born November 23, 1794, and died July 16, 1870. (Both interred in Woodbine Cemetery, Harrisonburg.) (See also pages 182 and 298; Wayland's *History of Shenandoah Co.,* pp. 692, and 584; *Chalkley,* Vol. II, p. 365.)

* * * * * *

William P. Byrd and wife Catherine (125872), had issue—

(1258721) ELIZABETH—b.——; m. Feb. 11, 1886, Albert Henton. He d. Aug. 18, 1921.
(1258722) MARGARET—b. ——; (unmarried.)
(1258723) JOSEPH C.—b. May 14, 1860; m. Oct. 14, 1891, Nancy Gordon Harrison, (125923), the daughter of John. See further record.
(1258724) SOPHIA—b. ——; (unmarried.)
All residents of Harrisonburg.

(125873) PRESTON T. BURKHOLDER (-1911), the son of Joseph Burkholder, and wife Sophia (12587), nee Warren, married first, Henrietta Hanger, and second, Mollie Armentrout, of Rockingham. He resided near Fishersville, in Augusta County. His death occurred February 8, 1911. Issue—

By wife Henrietta, nee Hanger,

(1258731) MINNIE W.—(unmarried.)
(1258732) ALEXANDER J.—Prof. of Medicine, Univ. of Ind., m. Kate Flauver. Resides at Laland, West Virginia.
(1258733) HETTIE E.—m. ——— Shepherd, of Waynesboro, Va.
(1258734) HARRIETT—d. ——;m. Lacey Coiner, of the Waynesboro family. Resided at Fishersville.

By wife Mollie, nee Armentrout,

(1258735) THOMAS P.—b. 1880; m. Ellen ———, resides at Hartford, Conn.
(1258736) MOLLIE—d. young.
(D. S. H. MSS.)

AREY

(125874) LYDIA A. BURKHOLDER (1838-1923), the daughter of Joseph Burkholder, and wife Sophia (12587), nee Warren, married, October 31, 1866, William Arey, (1808-1884), of near Bridgewater, in Rockingham. She died February 3, 1923. Issue—

(1258741) WILLIAM L.—b. Dec. 24, 1867; m. Ella Koogler.
(1258742) J. LUTHER—b. July 8, 1869; d. Apr. 11, 1870.
(1258743) GEORGE PRESTON—b. Apr. 8, 1872; m. Lucy Early.
(1258744) MARY WARREN—b. June 17, 1878; m. 1929, B. Frank Dove.
(D. S. H. MSS., etc.)

LOCUST GROVE

By The Long Grey Trail

The Former home of Daniel Matthews (1779-1842), Late home of Michael J. Martz.

See pages 337, and 511.

2. LINE OF DAVID HARRISON

3. LINE OF JOHN HARRISON

MARTZ

(125912) BARBARA KATHERINE HARRISON (1840-1918), the daughter of John Harrison (12591), and wife Barbara, married November 12, 1868, Michael Jackson Martz (1843-1922). They resided on "The Long Grey Trail" at Locust Grove, his birthplace, the old Daniel Matthews later the Hiram Martz homestead, to the north of Lacey Spring.

Michael Jackson Martz was the son of Hiram Martz, and wife Hannah Asbury, the daughter of Daniel Matthews. (See page 337.) Hiram Martz was long a member of the General Assembly of Virginia.

* * * * * *

Among the immigrants to Pennsylvania, were Hans Michael Mertz, who arrived in 1733, Dan Martz, who arrived in 1734, and John Henrich Martz, who arrived in 1737. (See Rupp's *Thirty Thousand Names of Foreign Immigrants to Pa.*, pp. 91, 159, and 109.)

Sebastain Martz, appears as a settler in the "Big Spring" neighborhood of Rockingham, near Zebulon Harrison, in 1778. He resided on the land now owned by Mr. J. C. Bradford. (See pages 146 and 300.) His wife's name was Mary. Their son Michael Martz, born October 1, 1775, died November 30, 1841, married September 4, 1798, Sarah Hawkins, born January 17, 1780, died October 11, 1865, daughter of Benjamin and Magdalene (Byrd) Hawkins. (See page 508.)

Michael Martz, (son of Sebestian), and wife Sarah had children—John b. July 6, 1799, m. ——— Robinson; Hiram, as above; Dorilas, b. February 23, 1802, d. March 23, 1872, unmarried; Mary b. March 5, 1804, d. May 1879, unmarried; Martha, b. July 7, 1805, m. Martin Martz; Michael, b. January 13, 1807, m. ——— Huff (?); Benjamin Hawkins, b. July 22, 1808, d. July 30, 1888, m. Temperance Martz; Napoleon B., b. November 23, 1809, m. ——— Woodruff; Clareann, b. February 10, 1811, m. Benjamin Conner; Rebecca, b. July 9, 1813, m. ——— Miller; Erastus (Erasmus), b. April 26, 1815, m. Grace Cowan; Jackson, b. 1816, d. December 29, 1900, m. Catherine West. Of whom—

Hiram Martz (1800-1861), and wife Hannah (1803-1861), had—Benjamin Franklin, b. March 24, 1830, d. August 27, 1860 m., September 12, 1854, Elvira G. Fletcher; Adaline E. S. (Addie), b. October 20, 1832, d. June 2, 1909, unmarried, (resided with bro. Michael); Addison Blair, b. October 28, 1834, Confederate soldier, killed at the battle of Chancellorsville, Mary 5, 1863; Dorilas Henry Lee, b. March 23, 1837, d. October 20, 1914, Colonel in Confederate Army, m. November 14, 1860, Mary Carter, of Nelson County, b. July 16, 1838; Daniel Green, b. December 3, 1839, d. September 27, 1891, m. April 3, 1860, Lydia Ann Sellers; Michael Jackson, as above, b. May 30, 1843; Julias Jefferson, b. August 16, 1849, d. December 19, 1892, m. September 26, 1869, Hettie V. Whissen, dau. of Abraham W. (From old Martz family Bible at Locust Grove—date of death of Benjamin F. from his tombstone in Woodbine Cemetery, Harrisonburg.)

* * * * * *

During the War-between-the-States, Michael Martz, (son of Hiram), served as a Confederate soldier. Says the *Shenandoah Valley* (of New Market, Va.), of August 31, 1922, on the occasion of his death—"He was a member of the Valley Rangers, but in 1862 was detached from this organization and was enrolled in Company G., 10th Virginia Regiment, in order that he might be with his brothers, and was with Lee at the surrender at Appomattox. It will be recalled that his brother, the late Col. D. H. Lee Martz, was the distinguished commander of the regiment, and later served so many years as the clerk of the courts of Rockingham County."

"For a number of terms, Mr. Martz was land assessor in Plains district, and for thirty years . . . . crop reporter of the U. S. Agricultural Department. He was widely known and esteamed. "

Locust Grove has long been known for it famous hospitaliay, and in Michael and Kate Martz's day its reputation in this respect passed into the proverbial. As devoted parents of a cultured family of children, the host and hostess, by their genial welcome, early established it a favored rendezvous of the young, as well as of the old, and about it centered much of the social life of the community.

Barbara Katherine Martz died, September 21, 1918. She was a woman of much charm, gentle and kindly, and beloved by all who knew her. Both she and her husband were members of the Methodist Episcopal Church, South, of Lacey Spring. He died August 25, 1922.

Michael J. Martz, and wife Katherine, (125912), had issue—

(1259121) Sallie Blair—b. Sept. 9, 1869, (unmarried). Resides at Locust Grove.

(1259122) Hiram Harrison—b. Dec. 6, 1870; m. Aug. 1, 1906, Lena May Peters, of Tennessee, dau. of George Peters.
See further record.

(1259123) Lucy Lee—b. Sept. 10, 1872, (unmarried.) Resides at Locust Grove.

(1259124) Nannie Hollingsworth—b. Apr. 23, 1874; m. Aug. 14, 1902, THOMAS M. RICE, of New Market, Va., son of Dr. Eugene Rice.
Issue—
1. Michael Eugene—b. Feb. 22, 1906, m., Nov. 19, 1927, Maude Moreland, of near Edinburg, Va. Issue—
 1. Nancy Josephine—b. Oct. 26, 1930.

(1259125) Hannah Matthews—b. Feb. 6, 1876, (unmarried) Resides at Locust Grove.

(1259126) Margaret Shaw—b. Feb. 17, 1879; d. Feb. 5, 1919, unmarried. She was a talented musican, and a pupil of the New England Conservatory of Music.

(1259127) Maude Templeton—b. June 7, 1881; d. Feb. 17, 1934, unmarried. Resided at Locust Grove.

(Last two interred in Lacey Spring Cemetery.)

(125915) DAVID WARREN HARRISON (1845-1933), the son of John Harrison (12591), and wife Barbara Katherine, married in Fairfield County, Ohio, November 22, 1880, Anna Amantha Houston (178452), the daughter of John W. C. Houston, and wife Rachel. (See page 486.)

Following his marriage, David Harirson purchased the old Dorilas Martz place, a valuable tract fronting about half a mile on the Valley Pike, some three fourths of a mile north of Tenth Legion, where he was successfully engaged in farming and stock raising until 1912, when he retired from farming, and bought a residence and a plot of land a short distance west of New Market, on the depot road. During his residence on the farm, he was for a number of years a member of the Rockingham School Board. He took a keen interest in public affairs, and was widely acquainted throughout the Valley. His genial disposition, and business integrity, endeared him to a host of his kindred and friends. Following his wife's death, he made his home with his son-in-law, Thomas Moore who resides on the farm adjoining his old home in Rockingham, which last is now owned by Mr. Moore and his mother, as a part of the Moore estate managed by the son in connection with his own farm.

The war coming on during his youth, David Harrison, and his brother William, for some time were engaged in collecting saltpeter for the manufacture of powder for the Confederate Army. The year before the surrender, they enlisted in Page County, and served that year in the 7th Virginia Cavalry, Company I, Gen. Rosser's Brigade, under Capt. John Hughs. The company was disbanded late in the year, owing to the arrival of winter and lack of supplies.

Anna A. Harrison, the wife of David Harrison, was born at Lacey Spring, and reared at Smithland. Upon her mother's second marriage, she removed, with the latter, to the vicinity of Lancaster, Ohio. She died at her home near New Market, in 1921. In a more extended account regarding her passing, the *Shenandoah Valley,* (Feb. 24, 1921) remarks—"She had been a member of the Methodist Church since childhood, and was a faithful wife, devoted mother, and much esteemed lady." (See, *Daily News Record,* Harrisonburg, February 21, 1921, and January 23, 1933.)

David W. Harrison (125915), and wife Anna, had issue—

(1259151) Lester Lee—b. Mar. 30, 1882, d. at birth.

(1259152) John Houston—b. July 8, 1887; m. June 4, 1912, Berta Steptoe Watson, dau. of A. Sidney Watson, of Albemarle Co., Va., and wife Louise, nee Wheeler.
See further record.

(1259153) Rita Catherine—b. Nov. 19, 1889; m. Feb. 12, 1916, Thomas Moore, son of Newton G. Moore, (1234333), and wife Josephine, nee Henkel,
See further record.

(David W. Harrison, and wife, interred in "Upper" Lutheran Cemetery, New Market, Virginia, Lester Lee in the old Houston cemetery, near Lacey Spring.)

(125916) WILLIAM CARPENTER HARRISON (1845-1925), the son of John Harrison (12591), and wife Barbara Katherine, married, June 12, 1884, Emma Jane Brubaker, born September 4, 1845, died October 6, 1899, the daughter of Peter Brubaker (1821-1878), and wife Martha Jane, nee Ailshire (b. 1822), of Page County, Virginia.

William Harrison and wife resided, for a time following their marriage, at Moreland Hall, now Court Manor, he being then a part owner of the property, with his brother George, to whom, about 1895, he sold his interest therein, and at about the same time purchased a valuable farm at Daphna, near Broadway, in Rockingham, on which he resided as a widely known stockman and (grazing) farmer, "for about thirty years." Late in life he removed to the environs of Harrisonburg, where he died at the home of his daughter, August 9, 1925. (See, *Shenandoah Valley,* August 13, 1925; also David Harrison above.)

William C. Harrison (125916), and wife Emma, had issue—

(1259161) David Brubaker—b. May 24, 1886; d. May 15, 1921; m. Sept. 2, 1914, Nellie Beard, dau. of John and Sallie (Vaughn) Beard, b. Jan. 31, 1890. She resides in Broadway, Va. where he formerly lived Issue—

1. Eleanor—b. Oct. 10, 1916.
2. Nancy Jean—b. —— 1921.

(1259162) George Brubaker—b. Dec. 24, 1887, (unmarried.) Resides at Harrisonburg, Va.

(1259163) Martha Hollingsworth—b. Sept. 25, 1892; m. Nov. 25, 1922, Edward B. Spitzer, of Rockingham. Resides at Harrisonburg. (No issue.)

(David B. interred in Linville Creek Church Cemetery, at Broadway.)

(125917) GEORGE HOLLINGSWORTH HARRISON (1847-1932), the son of John Harrison (12591), and wife Barbara Katherine, married, first, May 24, 1878, Mary C. Moore, (1234382), the daughter of Reuben Moore, of Moreland Hall. (See page 503.) She died in 1883. He married, second, October 28, 1896, Josephine (Jo) Moore (1234377), the daughter of Joseph Moore, of Shenandoah County. (See page 503.)

George Harrison, until recent years resided at and owned Moreland Hall, the valuable Rockingham estate now known as Court Manor, the history of which has been briefly traced in the course of these pages. (See pages 185, 306, 370, and 448.) He became interested in the property through his marriage to Mary Moore, one of the heirs, at whose early death he was left a widower, with two infant children. Some years ago, upon his retirement from active business life, he sold the property, greatly improved and much enhanced in value, to Mr. Willlis Sharpe Kilmer, of Binghampton, New York, the well known turfman. He then removed to Mt. Jackson, Shenandoah County, where he resided until his death, in the old Moore homestead; the former home of Mrs. Harrison's parents, in which she continues to reside.

As one of Rockingham's most prominent stockmen, and farmers, George Harrison, during his residence at Moreland Hall, led a very active life, and in his day, grazed, fattened and marketed many thousand head of cattle. For many years, and until the Valley Pike—then a toll road—was taken over by the State of Virginia he was a member of the board of directors of the Valley Turnpike Company, representing the State's shares. At the time of the company's dissolution Harry F. Byrd, the present U. S. Senator from Virginia, was its president. (See, *Shenandoah Valley*, March 10, 1932.)

George H. Harrison (125917), had issue—

By wife Mary, nee Moore,

(1259171) William M.—b. Oct. 3, 1879; d. Aug. 22, 1932; m. Hattie P. Vest, of Rockbridge Co., b. Oct. 8, 1888, d. Apr. 30, 1924. Resided at Lacey Spring. No issue.

(1259172) Reuben N.—b. June 19, 1883; d. Jan. 2, 1933, unmarried. (Rockingham Memorial Hospital.)
See further reference.

By wife Josephine (Jo), nee Moore,

(1259173) Thomas Moore—b. Jan. 19, 1899; m. June 8, 1922, Frances Moore, b. Nov. 21, 1898, dau. of Thomas Moore, son of Reuben W. (1234312.)
See further record.

(Geo. Harrison interred in Mt. Jackson, Va. Cemetery; William, and Reuben, in Lacey Spring Cemetery.)

(125918) JOHN WALTON HARRISON (1849-1929), the son of John Harrison (12591), and wife Barbara Katherine, married, August 16, 1888, Virginia (Jennie) Carolyn Rosenberger, the daughter of Gideon Rosenberger, of Rockingham, and wife Delilah, daughter of David Sipe.

John Harrison settled near the former home of his father. His estate adjoins the old homestead, and is located about two miles east of Tenth Legion. As his brothers above, he was a prominent stockman and farmer. He was a graduate of New Market Polytechnic Institue, and a former pupil of the distinguished professor, and author, Joseph Salyards. For many years he served as land assessor of the county, and for about fifty years as a judge of elections.

Issue—

(1259181) JOHN WALTON, JR.—b. Aug. 16, 1889; (unmarried) Prof. of Music —violin—Shenandoah Collegiate Institute and School of Music, Dayton, Va. Resides at home, as above. Served in the 180th Regt. (Rainbow Div.) A. E. F. during the World War.

(1259182) HUGH ROSENBERGER—b. July 3, 1891; m. Mar. 29, 1931, (Mrs.) Ruby Sizemore. Resides at Princeton, W. Va.

(1259183) FRANK HARRIS—b. Oct. 20, 1892; m. Oct. 23, 1913, Lennie Jane Zirkle, dau. of Reuben, and Virginia (Allen) Zirkle. See further record.

(1259184) JESSE HOLLINGSWORTH—b. Sept. 1, 1894; d. Nov. 21, 1903.

(1259185) CLARENCE MOORE—b. Mar. 19, 1896; (unmarried). Resides at home, as above.

(Jesse interred in Harrison cemetery on Smiths Creek, at the old homestead of his grandfather.)

(125921) LYDIA FRANCES HARRISON (1855), the daughter of John Harrison (12591), and wife Barbara Katherine, resided, until recently, at the old homeplace of her father, on Smiths Creek, about a mile east of Mauzy. She is the surviving sister of a group of four sisters and a brother, viz: Betty, Jennie, Phocion, Lucy, and herself, who resided there during the lifetime of the other four, (their sister Julia having made her home with her brother George, during the interval he was a widower, and later, with her brother William). Upon the death of her brother Phocion, she (Frances) became the manager of the estate, and at the death of her sister Jennie, the sole heiress to the same. She was an able manager, and a worthy compeer of her brothers, and similar to them, operated her place largely as a stock farm. She conserved the property, and much improved it, and upon her retirement to Harrisonburg, where she now makes her home, with her sister, Mrs. Byrd, and her husband, disposed of the farm to her Byrd nephews and neices.

Fannie Harrison, as she is more familarily known amongst a wide circle of relatives and friends, has travelled extensively in the West and is, and has been, personally acquainted with probably more of John Harrison the pioneer's descendants, and their connections of her time, than any other person now living. She is a vertiable mental encyclopaedia regarding the genealogy of the numerous connections of the family.

As a young woman, she taught school at various points in the county, and many there are who owe her a debt of gratitude, for her gentle kindly patience, and the inspiration of her presence in the schoolroom. She early became a member of the Presbyterian Church, of Broadway, Virginia, and is a highly regarded gentlewoman.

MAUZY

(125922) EMMA STRICKLER HARRISON (1857), the daughter of John Harrison (12591), and wife Barbara Katherine, married, November 16, 1897, Joseph Huffman Mauzy, son of Jacob Kisling Mauzy, and wife Rebecca, daughter of John Huffman. (See page 485.)

Joseph Mauzy, and wife, reside at Mauzy, the former home of his father, where he was born. He is a widely known and well to do stock farmer, and the owner of a large tract of land, which, as the sole heir of his father, he inherited from the latter.

Mauzy is situated on the Valley Pike—The Long Grey Trail—a few miles north of Lacey Spring, and in the days of the stage coach, was a stopping point for a change of horses and rest. The present residence, now remodeled, stands on the opposite side of the Pike from the site of the old tavern, and for many years a post office—Sparta—and a store, were conducted in a building which stood near the site of the tavern, and later, in another building yet standing. The land was formerly owned by William Pickering. (See page 379.)

* * * * * *

Jacob Kisling Mauzy was a descendant of Henry Mauzy, a Huguenot minister of the Gospel, who fled from France to England, upon the revocation of the Edict of Nantes, 1685. Henry Mauzy is thought to have embarked from France on the same vessel that conveyed James Fontaine to England. (See Foote's *History of the Huguenots,* p. 577.) After stopping in England for a time, he came to America, and is supposed to have first landed at Charleston, South Carolina. He settled in Stafford Co., Va., where he was a planter. He married, while in England, a daughter of a Dr. Conyers. His second son, John, married Hester Foote, about 1720, and had issue—Henry, b. 1721, John b. 1723, William, b. 1725, Priscilla, b. 1727, Peter, b. 1730, Elizabeth, b. 1734, and Jemima, b. 1740. Of whom: Henry m. 1st, Ann Withers, of Stafford Co., and had—John, Peter, William, Henry, Elizabeth, Nancy, Priscilla, Hester, and another, name unknown; m. 2nd, July 23, 1765, Elizabeth Taylor, widow of James Morgan, and had—Susanna, Thomas, Richard, Margaret, Jemima, George, Michael, and Joseph, later a Colonel.

Col. Joseph Mauzy, youngest son of Henry, was born in Fauquier County, Virginia, August 14, 1779, and died near McGaheysville, Rockingham County, where he resided, December 20, 1863. From 1835 to 1849, he was the County Surveyor of Rockingham. He married, 1805, Christiana Kisling, eldest daughter of Jacob, of near McGaheysville, and had—Henry, Julia, Elizabeth, Joseph, Layton, Albert Gallatin, b. May 9, 1815, d. January 5, 1851, Lucy Gilmer, Jacob Kisling, as above, b. June 3, 1820, d. March 5, 1906, Frances, Richard, of Staunton, and George Whit--field. (See, *Genealogical Record of the Descendants of Henry Mauzy, A Huguenot Refugee,* by Richard Mauzy, pp. 20, 22, 66, etc.)

Jacob Kisling Mauzy, and wife Rebecca, had issue— Frances Catherine, b. August 29, 1848, d. July 27 1895, unmarried, and Joseph Huffman, first named, b. April 12, 1851.

Joseph Mauzy and Emma have generously maintained the Mauzy tradition of hospitality, which, being handed down through the old tavern days, has been interpreted to include for those in need, a goodly proportion of charity.

In the operation of his farm, Mr. Mauzy is now ably aided by his son, to whom, since his arrival at maturity, the details of the management have largely been delegated.

With the family, following her husband's death (Thomas Calvin Brubaker, b. December 23, 1838, m. January 28, 1864, d. March 4, 1908), resided Mrs. Phoebe Brubaker, the sister of Mr. Mauzy's mother.

Joseph Mauzy, and wife Emma (125922), had issue—

(1259221) a daughter—b. and d. Nov. 20, 1898.
(1259222) JACOB KISLING—b. Jan. 21, 1900;; m. Dec. 29, 1928, Irene Funkhouser, dau. of Joseph D. N., of Pleasant Valley (above Harrisonburg), and wife Laura C., nee Pence. Resides at the home of his father.

(125923) NANCY GORDON HARRISON (1860), the daughter of John Harrison (12591), and wife Barbara Katherine, married, October 14, 1891, Joseph C. Byrd (1258723), the son of William P. Byrd. See Clan of John Harrison, 1. Line of Capt. Reuben Harrison, 2. Line of Thomas Warren, 3. Line of Joseph Burkholder, 4. Line of William P. Byrd. (Seventh Generation.)

---

3. LINE OF NATHANIEL HARRISON

(125921) REUBEN W. HARRISON (1830-1913), the son of Nathaniel Harrison (12592), and wife Mary, married, November 26, 1850, Hannah Sellers, (1832-1900), the daughter of Michael Sellers, of Rockingham.

Reuben Harrison and wife resided at Melrose, on the Valley Pike, about midway between Harrisonburg and Lacey Spring. He was the owner of a farm, and engaged somewhat in cabinet making, having in his younger days actively devoted his time to the industry, establishing a splendid trade. During the War-between-the-States, he served for a time in the Confederate Army, as a soldier, but was shortly detailed to the supervising and making of caskets, at his shop at home. He is referred to, in *The Annals of Augusta County*, as "the present Reuben Harrison of Rockingham."

Issue—

(1259211) NATHANIEL GREEN—b. Sept. 2, 1851; d. Mar. 19, 1857.
(1258212) FRANCES DIANA—b. Nov. 13, 1852; d. 1925; m. 1880, Edward Neck, from England.
See further record.
(1259213) DAVID WARREN—b. Oct. 3, 1854; d. 1925 c; m. Katherine Anderson. Resided at Front Royal, Va.; Issue—
1. Charles Frederick—d. —— unmarried.
(1259214) REUBEN MOORE—b. Aug. 24, 1856; d. May 4, 1930; m. Elizabeth Hasler. (decd.) Resided at Island Ford, in Rockingham. No issue.
(1259215) MARY ELIZABETH—b. Sept. 10, 1858; m. Thomas O'Neill, Supt. of Schools, Memphis, Tenn.
See further record.
(1259216) WILLIAM L. YANCEY—b. Mar. 28, 1861; d. Nov. 5, 1934; m. Virginia McLaughlin.
See further record.

(1259217) NANCY GORDON—b. Aug. 6, 1863; m. 1st, Apr. 1885, A. DUNCAN RINGHAM (d. ——), m. 2nd, Feb. 13, 1902, John Robinson. Issue by first marriage—
1. Pearl—b. Sept. 4, 1886; d. Dec. 19, 1906.

(1259218) MARTHA VIRGINIA—b. Apr. 21, 1866; d. ——; m. 1890, FRANKLIN HUTCHINS. Issue—
1. Verner O.—

(1259219) MICHAEL HOWARD—b. Sept. 14, 1868; m. Emily W. Wood, b. Feb. 16, 1870, dau. of Capt. John I. Wood.
See further record.

(1259220) JOHN HANCOCK—b. Jan. 27, 1871; d. aged about three days.

(1259221) SAMUEL ADAMS—b. twin of John Hancock; d. aged about 3 days.

(1259222) JASPER NEWTON—b. Mar. 6, 1872; m. Frances Burrows, of Canada.
See further record.

(1259223) HENRY HIGH—b. Sept. 18, 1874; m. 1st, Mannie White; m. 2nd, Virginia Bane.
See further record.

(D. H. S. MSS., etc.)

(125923) JACOB COWAN HARRISON (1832-1912), the son of Nathinael Harrison (12592), and wife Mary, married, November 14, 1854, Elizabeth Helen Hayne (Von Hayne), (1832-1898), the daughter of Jacob Hayne, and wife Eliza Burnley Duke (the latter from Hanover County), of Rockingham. She was a sister of the second wife of Daniel Harrison (12594), his uncle. Jacob Harrison, and wife, resided near Trinity Church on the Keezletown Road, to the north of Harrisonburg, where he owned a valuable farm. During the War-between-the-States he served in the Confederate Army, in the 7th Virginia Cavalry, Gen. Rosser's Brigade. Issue—

(1259231) ALICE IDA—b. Sept. 9, 1855; d. Sept. 25, 1878, unmarried.

(1259232) ADA LILLIAN—b. Aug. 15, 1857; Resides at Falls Church, Va., unm.

(1259233) MINNIE ELTON—b. Aug. 25, 1859; d. Feb. 26, 1931; m. Jan. 19, 1912, Franklin James Lee, b. Apr. 30, 1868, near Notre Dame, Ind. Resided at Idlewood, Va.. No issue.

(1259234) NATHANIEL HAYNE—b. Nov. 8, 1861; d. Sept. 6, 1931; m. Feb. 8, 1888, Sarah Anne Frances, b. Oct. 20, 1864. Resided near Calverton, Va. Mrs. Harrison now resides near Auburn, Va.

(1259235) NINA LEE—b. Mar. 28, 1864; d. Oct. 21, 1907, unmarried.

(1259236) MARY STEVENS—b. June 27, 1866; m. Feb. 5, 1890, William Cornelius Florence, b. Oct. 19, 1861. Resides in Columbus, O.
See further record.

(1259237) ANNIE LAURIE—b. Nov. 19, 1868; m. Nov. 18, 1891, Robert Franklin Fletcher, b. May 9, 1864.
See further record.

(1259238) EDWARD LEE—b. Oct. 3, 1870; m. Sept. 4, 1919, in Chicago, Ill., Olive Gertrude Hubbard, b. Oct. 10, 1898, in Chicago. Resides in Chicago, Ill. No issue.

(1259239) HARRIETT GRAEME—b. June 11, 1872; m. Sept. 5, 1911, Harry A. Pope, b. July 16, 1873, Maquoeta, Iowa, d. Feb. 12, 1917. (Member of Columbia Lodge No. 30, AF&AM, Columbus, Ohio.) No issue. She resides at Falls Church, Va.

(1259240) Burnley Duke (Rev.)—b. May 23, 1874; d. June 14, 1924; m. 1st, Aug. 26, 1902, Crete Mattox, b. at Williamsburg, Va., dau. of Prof. Marion Mattox, of Wm. and Mary College, and wife, Virginia Webster; m. 2nd, June 10, 1922, Dessa Belle Slagle, b. Toledo, Ohio, Mar. 18, 1896, now resident of Detroit, Mich.

(1259241) Ernest Paul—b. Oct. 29, 1883; m. Sept. 14, 1910, Betty Keith Swetnam.
See further record.

P/460

3. LINE OF DANIEL HARRISON

(125941) JOHN HARRISON (1835-1921), the son of Daniel Harrison (12594), and (first) wife Rhoda, nee Brown, removed with his father to Tennessee, in which State he married, December 21, 1865, Mary Emily Rankin, born December 23, 1836, died March 9, 1919. They resided near Dandridge in Jefferson County, Tennessee, on the French Broad River, where he was a well to do farmer. Issue— P/460

(1259411) Arrobell—b. Nov. 5, 1866. Resides at the old homestead. (unm.)
(1259412) Nancy Cordelia—b. Mar. 15, 1868; d. Oct. 2, 1868.
(1259413) Sarah Ellen—b. July 26, 1869. Resides at the old homestead. (unm.)
(1259414) Thomas Daniel—b. Nov. 19, 1870; d. Oct. 1, 1874.
(1259415) Ida Adaline—b. Nov. 22, 1872; m. Aug. 10, 1892, William Blackburn.
See further record.
(1259416) Lydia Olie—b. Dec. 10, 1874; m. Oct. 6, 1904, Joseph Walker Moore.
See further record.
(1259417) Arthur Early—b. June 20, 1877. Resides at the old homestead.
(1259418) John Marshall—b. Apr. 10, 1879; d. Feb. 23, 1899.
(1259419) Marion Emmett—b. Apr. 23, 1882; m. Dec 20, 1920, Myrtle Holbert.
See further record.

All except the 2nd, 4th, and 8th, residing in Tenn., 1929.

HINKLE

(125943) MARY HARRISON (1839-1907), the daughter of Daniel Harrison (12594), and wife Rhoda, nee Brown, born in Rockingham, married in Tennessee, May 19, 1859, George Hinkle, and removed with him by way of Missouri, to Ft. Collins, Colorado, where she died. Issue—

(1259431) John M.—b. Feb. 12, 1860; d. Jan. 24, 1887.
(1259432) Julia M.—b. Nov. 22, 1861; d. Nov. 11, 1925; m. Nov. 9, 1881, Chester Blunt.
See further record.
(1259433) Hannah Elizabeth—b. Mar. 14, 1863; m. May 19, 1888, L. H. Harding.
See further record.
(1259434) Nannie Josephine—b. Nov. 27, 1864; d. Jan. 23, 1903, unmarried.
(1259435) Mary W.—b. Feb. 3, 1867; d. Dec. 15, 1923; m. Feb. 22, 1893, Alexander Chisholm.
See further record.

(1259436) Emma Rhoda—b. June 9, 1868; m. Oct. 26, 1892, Frank L. Blunt, brother of Chester, above.
See further record.
(1259437) Lydia Willie—b. May 20, 1870. (unmarried.)
(1259438) Charles Edward—b. Nov. 1, 1871, (unmarried.)
(1259439) Alice Magnolia—b. May 3, 1873, (unmarried.)
(1259440) Henry—b. May 17, 1875; d. Mar. 16, 1902.
(1259441) Ella—b. Mar. 22, 1877; m. July 1, 1896, Frank Hiedelberger.
See further record.
(1259442) Minnie Irene—b. June 12, 1882; d. Sept. 8, 1890.

(125944) JOSEPH HARRISON (1840-1911), the son of Daniel Harrison (12594), and wife Rhoda, nee Brown, migrated with his father from Virginia to Tennessee. He married, October 24, 1872, Susan Slaton, born in Stokes County, North Carolina, July 31, 1846. She died Aug. 4, 1920. Joseph Harrison and wife resided in Jefferson County, Tennessee, where he was a well to do farmer. Issue—

(1259441) Mary Frances—b. Aug. 22, 1873; d. July 4, 1894, unmarried.
(1259442) Rhoda Rebecca—b. Nov. 1, 1874; m. Nov. 13, 1892, John Wesley Solomon.
See further record.
(1259443) Nancy Virginia—b. Apr. 4, 1876; m. Oct. 24, 1897, W. H. Bryan, who d. Dec. 15, 1915.
See further record.
(1259444) John David—b. Nov. 9, 1877; m. Feb. 14, 1903, Lillie May Moore.
See further record.
(1259445) Lydia Catherine—b. Oct. 15, 1879; d. Feb. 22, 1921; m. Aug. 22, 1906, William Allen.
See further record.
(1259446) Thomas Slaton—b. Nov. 1, 1881; m. Feb. 21, 1913, Annie Fry.
Issue—
1. Nathan Dennis—b. Sept. 25, 1914.
(1259447) Daniel—(twin of Thomas); m. Aug. 25, 1906, Ethel Cox.
See further record.
(1259448) William Alexander—b. Mar. 29, 1884, (unmarried.)
(1259449) Harriett—b. Aug. 22, 1886; m. Aug. 24, 1902, John Robert Moore.
See further record.
(1259450) Pressley George—b. Oct. 13, 1889; m. Jan. 15, 1920, Ruth Morie. Volunteered in the World War, July 4, 1917, served 'till close of war, wounded in action. Issue—
1. Joseph Alexander—b. Oct. 20, 1920.

All except the first and fifth residing in Tenn. 1929.

TARWATER

(125946) NANCY MARIA BROWN HARRISON, (1843-1892), the daughter of Daniel Harrison, (12594), and wife Rhoda, nee Brown, following her father's removal from Rockingham to Tennessee, spent some years in the home of John Moore, (123433) of Rockingham, who married her aunt, Elizabeth Ann (Betsy Ann) Harrison. She married in Tennessee, February 1869, upon the eve of her father's removal to the West, John Tarwater, with whom, on her honeymoon, she accompained her father to Missouri. In 1892, while moving with her husband, and family, to Texas, she died on the way, in Indian Territory, leaving four or more children, whose names are not known.

(125948) JACOB HAYNE HARRISON (1851-1922), the son of Daniel Harrison (12594), and (second) wife Huldah, nee Hayne, born in Rockingham County, Virginia, removed with his parents to Tennessee, thence to Missouri, from which State he migrated to Texas, settling in San Antonio, where he died.

"Jake" Harrison was a gifted poet, and author. A brief sketch of him appears in the *Texas Literature Reader*, a State text book, used in the sixth and seventh grades. (1928). His poems, and other literary works, have been extensively published throughout the states; selections appear in a book of Texas writers prepared by Dr. Egerton, of the University of Texas, and in the *Library of Southern Literature*. See introduction to this Chapter. In early life he was a teacher, justice of the peace, newspaperman, and civil engineer. For many years he was connected as an officer with a large financial firm of Dallas, Texas.

He married, first, at Hubbord, Texas, September 19, 1878, Theodocia C. Powell, daughter of W. L. Powell, a prominent farmer of Hubbord. He married, second, Lillian Kendrick Byrn, of San Antonio. He died January 25, 1922.

Issue by first marriage—

(1259481) CLAUDE NORVELL—b. June 11, 1879; m. Aug. 2, 1903, Ollie May Womack, dau. of J. M. Womack, of Hutto, Texas. Issue—

1. Edith—b. Dec. 6, 1904; m. May 16, 1926 Oscar G. Eckhardt, Jr.
2. Claude Newton—b. Jan. 3, 1908.
3. Jake H.—b. May 3, 1912.
4. Mary Mae—b. Jan. 14, 1918.
5. Hal—b. June 26, 1922.

(1259482) DIXIE—b. ——.

(1259483) JUSTIN—b. Aug. 15, 1882; m. Sept. 1906, at Corsicana, Texas, Mary Robinson.

CROPP

(125950), LYDIA VIRGINIA HARRISON (1853-1879), the daughter of Daniel Harrison (12594), and wife Hulda, nee Hayne, married in Missouri, Dr. Septimus Cropp, resident of Carroll County, that State. Issue—

(1259501) LILLIAN—m. —— Widmyer, (decd.) of Texas. (six children.)

(1259502) NOEL—m. ——. Resides in Texas.

(Both spent some time as children, following their mother"s decease, in Virginia, with their aunts, Maria and Kate Hayne.)

BECK

(125951) HARRIETT GRAHAM HARRISON (1855-1934), the daughter of Daniel Harrison (12594), and second wife, Huldah, married, at Bosworth, Missouri,

December 31, 1880, Albert W. Beck (d. February 12, 1931), of Carroll County, this State. They resided for many years near Hale, where Mr. Beck owned a valuable farm. In 1929, he retired from farming and became a resident of Hale. Mrs. Beck's death occurred August 3, 1934. She was a charter member of the old Hurricane Baptist Church. As a child, she accompained her father in his boat as he journeyed with his family down the French Broad, Tennessee, and Ohio Rivers, to the Mississippi, thence to St. Louis, where they boarded a steamer for Miami Station. Says the *Hale Leader*, in regard to her passing: "It is lives such as the one brought to a sudden close that give us our best citizens and a heritage of honor and integrity of which we may well be proud."

Issue—

(1259511) Lula—b. Oct. 9, 1881; m. Oct. 16, 1911, W. C. Steward, of Minneapolis, Minn.

(1259512) Johnse—b. Aug. 25, 1891; m. June 1, 1922, Carrie Grant. Resides in Indianapolis, Ind.

(125955) ANDREW JOHNSON HARRISON (1862), the son of Daniel Harrison (12594), and wife Huldah, nee Hayne, born in Green County, Tennessee, moved as a child with his parents to Carroll County, Missouri. From Missouri in February, 1890, he removed to Texas, in which State he now resides at Goldthwaite, where he has long been postmaster. He was first appointed to the office by President McKinley, in 1897, and resigned, July 1, 1913. Following President Harding's inauguration, he was reappointed, in 1923, and has since continued in the office. (1932.)

A. Johnson Harrison married, first, Oct. 1, 1889, in Missouri, Elizabeth E. Crose, born in Moberly County, Missouri, February 11, 1867. Her death occurred in Texas, January 22, 1897. Her grandfather, A. M. Stringfield, of Bloomington, Illinois, was a widely known farmer, and horse raiser, of that State. A number of his descendants, in and about Bloomington, are prominent in business affairs there.

Mr. Harrison married, second, May 18, 1898, Myra M. Gardner, born in Travis County, Texas, February 19, 1877. She died June 22, 1918. Her paternal grandparents were born and reared near Petersburg, Virginia. Her mother's parents removed from Tennessee, to Texas, before the War-between-the-States. Their name was Morris.

Andrew Johnson Harrison had issue—

By wife Elizabeth, nee Crose,

(1259551) Myrtle O.—b. July 20, 1890; m. ——; Resides in Denison, Texas.

(1259552) Daniel Hayne—b. Feb. 11, 1893, (Cashier of First National Bank of Goldthwaite.)

(1259553) Myra Lois—b. Oct. 12, 1895; d. Oct. 12, 1907.

By wife Myra, nee Gardner,

(1259554) Anna Joyce—b. Mar. 13, 1899; m. 1st, Barrett Buck, of Virginia. He died in 1929. At the beginning of the World War, he joined the Canadian forces, with which he served two years. He resigned upon the U. S. entering the war, and enlisted in the U. S. Army, A. E. F. At the close of the war he was a Lieutenant. During his services in France he was gassed, which is believed to have contributed largely to his early death. No issue. Mrs. Buck m. 2nd, John D. Watt. Residence, Shanghai, China.

(1259555) HANNAH FAY—b. June 11, 1901; d. Jan. 19, 1902.
(1259556) GLADYS NEWTON—b. Jan. 13, 1902; m. 1925, Wallace Gerald Brown, of Kenedy, Texas. (now connected with Sou. Pac. RR.)
(1259557) EMMA DELL—b. Feb. 20, 1904; d. Dec. 9, 1918.
(1259558) DOROTHY CAROLINE—b. Aug. 11, 1906, (engaged in teaching.)
(1259559) JACOB HENRY—b. May 25, 1908.
(1259560) MORRIS MOORE—b. Oct. 11, 1911; d. June 8, 1913.
(1259561) MAX WELDON—b. Aug. 26, 1913.

(125957) GILBERT NEWTON HARRISON (1866-1927), the son of Daniel Harrison (12594), and wife Huldah, nee Hayne, was born in Green County, Tennessee, and reared in Carroll County, Missouri. He died a noted lawyer, and financier, of Texas.

After completing the normal course at the University of Missouri, G. Newton Harrison was for three years superintendent of schools of Bosworth, of the same State, during which interval he began the study of law under the tuition of James L. Minnis, of Carrollton. He completed his legal education at the University of Michigan, where he obtained his L. L. B. degree, in 1893. The same year he began the practice of law in Goldthwaite, Texas, with Judge J. L. Lewis, under the firm name of Lewis and Harrison. Three years later, he settled at Brownwood, Texas, where he continued to reside until his death. His firm represented the Santa Fe Railroad, many important oil companies, and other large corporations. He was vice president of the First National Bank, of Brownwood, from 1923 until his death. In 1924, he organized the West Texas Telephone Company, of which he was president, also until his death.

A Republican in politics, Mr. Harrison was a leader in the affairs of his party, in the State, and on various occasions the party's nominee for state office, including Chief Justice of the Supreme Court, and Attorney General. In 1904, 1908, and 1924, he was a delegate to the Republican National Convention. He was a member of the American Bar Association, was an authority on constitutional law, and frequently delivered addresses on this subject before various organizations.

"In numerous ways he left the imprint of his stainless character and noble example upon the record of his generation." (See, *The National Cyclopaedia of American Biography, Vol. XXI*, 1931, p. 131, wherein his protrait also appears.)

Gilbert Newton Harrison married, February 15, 1905, at Brownwood Texas, Belle Grinnan, daughter of William Welch Grinnan, merchant, of Tyler, Texas.

Issue—

(1259571) HULDAH—b. Dec. 1, 1905; m. June 1, 1927, WILLIAM FRANKLIN JONES, Attorney at law, of Marshall, Texas. Issue—
1. Jerene—b. Nov. 1, 1928.
2. William Franklin (Jr.),—b. Apr. 27, 1931.

(1259572) GILBERT NEWTON—b. Dec. 25, 1909. Attorney at law, of Brownwood.
(1259573) ANNA BELLE—b. May 24, 1914.

---

3. LINE OF REUBEN N. HARRISON

(125961) JOHN THOMAS HARRISON (1843-1915), the son of Reuben N. Harrison (12596), and wife Catharine, married, January 16, 1873, Emma White, of

Cincinnati, Ohio, the daughter of Joseph and Cynthia White. They removed, about 1879, to near Hardin, Ray County, Missouri, where he purchased a farm, and continued to reside until his death. Issue—

(1259611) CATHERINE—b. Oct. 19, 1875; m. James B. McGuire, b. Apr. 2, 1873.
See further record.
(1259612) REUBEN N.—b. Feb. 13, 1877; m. 1st, Lillian T. Sinclair, d. 1905; m. 2nd, Zatella Faulkner.
See further record.
(1259613) LAURA SANTEE—b. Sept. 10, 1879. (unmarried.)
(1259614) BESSE LEE—b. Sept. 19, 1881. (unmarried.)
(1259615) DONALD THOMAS—b. Mar. 23, 1888; m. Dec. 25, 1913, Mary Shackelford Fraizer, b. Nov. 17, 1889. Resides in California.
See further record.

(125963) DANIEL SMITH HARRISON (1845-1919), the son of Reuben N. Harrison (12596), and wife Catharine, resided in Harrisonburg with his brother Charles, at whose home he died, unmarried, April 26, 1919. He was the owner of a valuable tract of land near town, and was for many years associated with the city's administration. Regarding his demise, *The Daily News-Record,* of Harrisonburg (April 28, 1919). in a more lengthy tribute to his memory remarks—

"During a large part of his life he was a consistent member of the Presbyterian church and he stood high in Masonic circles, an order to which he was particularly attached. At the age of seventeen he entered the army of the Confederacy during the war between the states and was a lieutenant under Major George Chrisman, who was in charge of a company of seventeen year old boys. His later life proved him to be a splendid citizen of the state, which he upheld, and during the latter years of his life he was connected with the city's treasury department."

He was one of the kindliest of men, a faithful Christian, and a true friend, and endeared to all associated with him. He was the author of what has been herein referred to as the "D. S. H. MSS.", a skeleton outline of the genealogy of many branches of the Harrison family of Rockingham. This he began compiling in his later years. He was accurate and painstaking, and greatly interested in the history of the family. He was widely acquainted, conducted much local research, and was an authority thoroughly to be relied on. It is much to be regretted that he did not live to finish his work.

(125966) CHARLES DeWITT HARRISON, (1851-1933), the son of Reuben N. Harrison, (12596), and wife Catharine, married, June 3, 1891, Anna M. H. Hank, (1864-1901), of Baltimore, Maryland, daughter of Dr. John William Fletcher Hank, and wife Anna Keener, the sister of Bishop Keener, of the Baltimore Conference, M. E. Church, South.

Charles Harrison, and wife, settled in Harrisonburg, where he was a prominent attorney at law. He was educated at New Market Polytechnic Institute, and at the University of Virginia. From 1883 to 1889, and from 1912 to 1916, he was Commonwealth Attorney of Rockingham. He was a member of the Presbyterian Church, of Harrisonburg, and was long associated with public affairs of the town, and county. (See, *Daily News-Record,* April 22, and 24, 1933.)

Issue—

(1259661) Catharine—b. Mar. 24, 1892; m. June 28, 1922, Alfred Lawrence Leigh, of Fairfax County, Virginia.
See further record.

(1259662) Anna Keener—b. Nov. 3, 1893, (unmarried)

(1259663) Alice Strother—b. Apr. 17, 1896. (unmarried.)

The last two reside at their father's home in Harrisonburg.

3. LINE OF ANDREW HENTON

(125991) JOHN HENTON (1846-1908), the son of Andrew Henton, and wife Barbara (12599), nee Harrison, married, May 9, 1882, Florence Alberta West, of Rockingham, daughter of Wallace West, and wife Elizabeth, the daughter of John Cowan. John Henton and wife resided at Melrose, to the north of Harisonburg, where his widow continues to reside. Issue—

(1259911) Elsiee Eliza Catherine—b. Nov. 1, 1883; d. Sept. 4, 1884.

(1259912) Ella Maud Alberta—b. Jan. 21, 1885; d. Apr. 15, 1885.

(1259913) William Andrew—b. Feb. 27, 1886; d. Jan. 20, 1897.

(1259914) George Harrison—b. Nov. 16, 1887; m. Mable Neck, dau. of Edward, and wife Frances, (1259212). Resides at Dayton, Va.

(1259915) Ethel Florence—b. May 16, 1890; (unmarried) Resides in Washington, D. C.

(1259916) Arthur Woodley (Rev.)—b. Mar. 11, 1897; m. June 2, 1926, at Free Union, Va., Rosamont Ruth Proffitt, dau. of Rice Proffitt. Resides at Minnehaha Springs, W. Va. (1931.)

(1259917) John Edward—b. June 28, 1900; (unmarried). Resides in Philadelphia, Pa.

(1259918) Lida Mary—b. July 7, 1903; (unmarried.) Resides in Washington, D. C.

(D. S. H. MSS.,etc.)

NEFF

(125993) MARY ELIZABETH HENTON (1850-1914), the daughter of Andrew Henton, and wife Barbara (12599), nee Harrison, married, May 30, 1871, William H. Neff, of Lacey Spring, Virginia. Issue—

(1259931) Mary Cammie—b. Dec. 28, 1872; (unmarried) Resides in Ohio.

(1259932) Lida Catherine—b. Nov. 9, 1874; Resides in Staunton, Va.

(1259933) Louis Cameron—b. Nov. 9, 1876; m. Vivien Higgs, resides near Lacey Spring.

(1259934) Franklin—b. Jan. 26, 1879; m. Sallie Arey, of Chicago, Ill. Resides in Chicago.

(1259935) Lula Gordon—b. Sept. 2, 1882; m. Charles Fletcher, Resides in Chicago, Ill.

(1259936) Margaret May—b. Dec. 2, 1883; (unmarried) Resides with father at Lacey.

(1259937) Ella Henton—b. Nov. 29, 1885; d. Mar. 30, 1900.

(1259938) Hugh—b. Aug. 28, 1890; (unmarried.)

(D. S. H. MSS.)

2. LINE OF JOHN CHRISMAN

3. LINE OF JOSEPH CHRISMAN

(126011) JOHN CHRISMAN (   ), the son of Joseph Chrisman (12601), and (first) wife Elizabeth, nee Lincoln, is fondly mentioned by Herring Chrisman, in his *Memoirs of Lincoln*... "Through all the days of our early years," says the author, "Jack was my double. We slept in the same bed, studied the same books and were exactly of the same size, tastes and dispositions. We attended the same college and Jack became a very elegant and accomplished writer." . . . "He married a beautiful and accomplished lady. He was an honorable, scholarly man and as free from the love of money as his great cousin. He died recently of simple old age, county treasurer at Bozeman, Montana, and his daughter Bettie, the most beautiful of women, is county superintendent of schools in that county.." (*Memoirs of Lincoln*, written in 1900, p. 53.)

Issue—

(1260111) BELLE—Resides in Montana.
(1260112) BETTIE—(unmarried) Resides at Kolin, Montana.
(1260113) JO ANDY—Resides in Montana.
(1260114) PAUL—Resides in Montana.
(1260115) SALLIE—d. ——; m. —— DEAN.

Issue—a son,

1. Howell.

She died when her son was "quite small."

(W. H. C. papers.)

(126014) JOSEPH MARCUS CHRISMAN (1831-1911), the son of Joseph Chrisman (12601), and wife Jane, nee Chrisman, born in Rockingham County, Virginia, died at Broken Bow, Nebraska. He migrated with his father from Virginia to Missouri, in 1837, and, in 1882, settled in Chester County, Nebraska, where he went through many hardships as a pioneer.

Joseph M. Chrisman married, first, October 31, 1854, Lucy Isabell Richardson, of Front Royal, Virginia, daughter of Marcus Richardson, and wife Harriett Chrisman, a sister of his (Joseph's) mother. She died in 1889. He married, second, 1894, Mrs. Mary Deerisling, of Front Royal, who now (1931) resides with his daughter, Harriett, and the latter's husband, at Broken Bow.

Issue by first marriage—

(1260141) SAMUEL HENRY—d. in infancy.
(1260142) ELIZABETH DE CALMESE—m. R. B. SARGENT.

Issue—

1. Glen Joseph.
2. Charles Harrison.
3. Irene Spalding.
4. Kennith Chrisman.

All of whom are married and have children.

(1260143) ALBERT RICHARDSON—m. Emma Tooley.

Issue—

1. Raymond.
2. Allen.
3. Lucy Belle
4. Mary Dean.
5. Joseph

(1260144) MARCUS JOSEPH—d. Oct. 1929; m. Lillian Beattie.
Issue—
1. Lee.
2. Lloyd.
3. Albert.
4. Alice.

(1260145) LUCIE BELLE—m. GEORGE SWEENEY.
Issue—
1. Lucie—d. "aged about 18."
2. Rita.
3. Ruth.
4. Malcolm George.

(1260146) HENRY EUGENE—m. Bernice Hunter.
Issue—
1. Estelle.
2. Esper
3. Hugh.
4. Harry Eugene.

(1260147) HARRIETT—m. CHARLES SAMUEL TOOLEY.
Issue—
1. Ruth Catherine Brooks—d. at birth.

(1260148) JENNIE RUTH—Resides with her sister Hattie, at Broken Bow.

(W. H. C. papers.)

(126016) CHARLES CHRISMAN (-1924 c), the son of Joseph Chrisman (12601), and wife Jane, nee Chrisman, married Bettie Brooks, whose death occurred in 1927, several years following his. Like his brothers John and Joseph, he migrated from Missouri to the northwest.

In 1864, Charles Chrisman and his brother, Henry, visited the home of their cousin, Herring Chrisman, at St. Augustine, Knox County, Illinois, on which occasion a band of men "came up from the village," and threatened to mob them, "because they were from the South, as they called it." It so happened that Mr. Nathaniel Ervin, of Burlington, Iowa, a former deputy sheriff of Rockingham,—under Herring Chrisman's father—was stopping at the Chrisman home for the night, and sizing up the situation, met them at the front gate, where, after keeping about a half dozen of the leaders at bay, he "finally persuaded them to go home and leave without doing any harm."

Charles Chrisman and wife, Bettie, had issue—

(1260161) SALLIE—d. young.
(1260162) TAYLOR—d. young.
(1260163) CLEVE—
(1260164) LEWIS—
(1260165) IRENE—m. —— Waite.
(1260166) J[OHN?]—Resides in, or near, Broken Bow, Neb.
(W. H. C. papers.)

3. LINE OF GEORGE HARRISON CHRISMAN

(126021) HERRING CHRISMAN (1823-1911), the son of George Harrison Chrisman (12602), and wife Martha, born in Rockingham County, Virginia, married, September 25, 1854, Emma Hunt Berry, of Sharon, Connecticut. He was the author of the *Memoirs of Lincoln*, frequently referred to herein.

Herring Chrisman was educated in law, at Washington University, now Washington and Lee, (Lexington, Va.), and from 1847, to 1852, was Commonwealth Attorney of Rockingham.

In 1854, he migrated to Illinois, where he became a member of the Chicago Bar during the city's boom days. In Chicago, he dealt to a considerable extent in city real estate, backed by friends in Virginia. From Chicago, he moved to Knox County, Illinois, in which county he took up a homestead, purchased 1,000 acres of adjoining land, and fattened cattle for the Union Army. During this interval, he lived on his farm a part of the time, and practiced law at Galesburg, and Monmouth, in Knox, and Warren, counties.

He next followed his eldest son to Pottawattamie County, Iowa, where the family purchased 1040 acres of prairie land. From Pottawattamie County, he rode on horse back to Monona County, the same State, where, within a short time, he bought 7,000 acres of land, near Mapleton. Backed by his partners, he proceeded to fence, and improve, these lands, in the meantime moving his family to Mapleton, from Abington, Illinois.

At Mapleton, he divided his activities between his land and cattle interests, and law practice. He was elected County Attorney of Monona by a land-slide of votes, and was many times elected president of the Monona County Bar Association. He died at Mapleton, Iowa, at the ripe old age of eighty-seven.

Issue

(1260211) Nathaniel Berry—b. Oct. 13, 1855; d. Nov. 4, 1934, in Iowa; m. Genette Parmer.

(1260212) William Herring—b. Sept. 15, 1858; m. Jan. 1, 1895, Charlotte C. Downs, of Omaha, Nebraska. Residence, Mapleton, Iowa. Issue—
- 1. Roswell Herring—b. Sept. 15, 1900. (Junior member of Chrisman & Chrisman, law firm, Mapleton, Iowa. Residence Chicago, Ill. With Continental Ill. National Bank.) m. Oct. 2, 1926, Virginia Haynes, of Boston, Mass. Issue—
  - 1. Barbara Lee—b. Aug. 17, 1928, at Boston.
  - 2. William Herring—b. June 23, 1932.

(1260213) George—b. Nov. 11, 1860; d. Oct. 5, 1861.

(1250214) Virginia—b. Sept. 1, 1863.

(1260215) Charles Edward—b. June 26, 1869; m. ———, Resides at Ortonville, Minn. (two sons.)

(126022) BURKE CHRISMAN (1827-1895), the son of George Harrison Chrisman (12602), and wife Martha, setttled shortly before the War of 1861-65, in Philadelphia, Pennsylvania, where he was a practicing physican. He was at one time a Major in the Virginia State Volunteer Militia. (See, *Wayland,* p. 135.) Dr. Chrisman married Henrietta Warder, the daughter of John H., and Abigail Hoskins Warder, of Philadelphia. Issue—

(1260221) George Warder—b. July 3, 1858; d. Aug. 24, 1879.
(All interred in New Erection Churchyard.)

BUCKLEY-WILLIAMS

(126023) MARGARET ANN CHRISMAN (1829-1915), the daughter of George Harrison Chrisman (12602), and wife, Martha, married, first, Chancellor Benjamin Buckley, of Mississippi. He commanded the second Mississippi Regiment in the Mexican War. She married, second, as his third wife, Dr. William Williams, of Harrisonburg, Virginia, whom she survived some years. Issue by first marriage—

(1260231) NANNIE—

(126024) GEORGE CHRISMAN (1832-1915), the son of George Harrison Chrisman (12602), and wife Martha, married, Nov. 13, 1867, Lucy Gilmer Grattan, of Rockingham, born August 9, 1835, died March 8, 1923. They resided in the Edom neighborhood of Rockingham, at the old homestead of his father.

George Chrisman, during the War-between-the-States, served as an officer in the Confederate Army. He was Captain of Chrisman's Infantry, 1861, a company organized in Rockingham, at the beginning of the war, and in 1864, was the Captain of the "Boy Company" of Cavalry, an organization of seventeen year old boys. (See page 524, Also *Wayland*, pp. 318 and 370.) He was known widely as Major Chrisman, and as observed elsewhere, has been quoted by various authors, in the latter years of his life, regarding his disclosure that President Lincoln's grandmother, Bathsheba, was originally a Herring.

Following the war, Major Chrisman became interested in the raising of pure bred stock, and for forty years, or more, was a leader in the county in pointing out and introducing the best strains. He was first to introduce Poland-China hogs into Rockingham. These he brought in from Illinois. His thoroughbred cattle were awarded many premiums at various fairs from 1877 to 1885, and from the latter year, to 1896, he contributed numerous articles to the Rockingham Register, regarding stock raising, Percheron horses, farming, etc.

Major Chrisman, and wife, had issue an only child, viz—

(1260241) MARTHA GRATTAN—b. July 27, 1873; d. Aug. 11, 1874.

(All interred in New Erection Churchyard.)

(126025) WILLIAM JOSEPH CHRISMAN (1834-1912), the son of George Harrison Chrisman (12602), and wife Martha, married, first, May 28, 1865, Jane Giles, of Nelson County, Virginia, who died in 1873. He married, second, Jan. 13, 1875, Virginia Gay, of Rockingham, or Shenandoah. (b. Jan. 13, 1847, d. Sept. 2, 1880 ?).

William Chrisman resided near Hopkin's Mill, to the north west of Mt. Clinton, in Rockingham, where he was a prominent farmer. Early in the War of 1861-65, as disclosed by his brother Herring's memoirs, he was in charge of buying live stock for the Confederate Army.

Issue—

By wife Jane, nee Giles.

(1260251) MARY GAY—b. Feb. 16, 1866; m. June 1906, William Fallis.

(1260252) MARTHA H.—b. Apr. 20, 1867; d. Apr. 29, 1931, at Harrisonburg, unm.

(1260253) MARGARET ANN—b. July 4, 1868; m. Sept. 10, 1896, Dr. CARY NELSON DUNLAP, of Middlebrook, Augusta Co., Va.; Issue—
1. Margaret—
2. Frances—
(1260254) OLIVE—b. Mar. 31, 1870; m. May 1912, Virgil Kirkman.
(1260255) HENRIETTA—b. Feb. 5, 1871; d. Aug. 8, 1872. (Interred at New Erection.)

By wife Virginia, nee Gay.
(1260256) EMMA NEAL—b. Sept. 9, 1876; m. Apr. 20, 1899, CHARLES MICHAEL FRANK; Issue—
1. Chrisman—b. 1901.
2. Virginia—b. 1903.
3. William—b. 1906.
4. Genevive—b. 1908.
5. Robert E. Lee—b. 1910.
(1260257) WILLIAM GEORGE (Dr.)—b. Apr. 22, 1878; m. Rachel Eastham, of Charlottesville, Va. Issue—
1. George—Resides at Blacksburg, Va.
(D. S. H. MSS., etc.)

---

2. LINE OF CHARLES C. SPEARS

GLASGOW

(126031) ELIZABETH SPEARS (   ), the daughter of Charles C. Spears, and wife Margaret M. (12603), nee Chrisman, married William Glasgow, of Fincastle, Botetourt County, Virginia. Issue—

(1260311) FRANKLIN—
(1260312) JOSEPH—
(1260313) MARGARET—m. Dr. Armstrong.

(126034) REBECCA SPEARS (   ), the daughter of Charles C. Spears, and wife Margaret M. (12603), nee Chrisman, married Willam Rice Warren, (12851), of Harrisonburg, Virginia, the son of Jehu Warren. (See 2. Line of Thomas Warren, 3. Line of Jehu Warren, page 506.)

---

2. LINE OF SAMUEL HARRISON

3. LINE OF JOHN CAMPBELL

(126141), ISAAC CAMPBELL (   ), the son of John Campbell, and wife Mary (12614), nee Harrison, married Eliza C. Lockridge, now deceased. Rev. Campbell and wife resided at "The Grottoes," in Rockingham, where he continues to reside. Issue—
(1261411) FRANCES H.—
(1261412) MARY C.—m. W. A. Roan.
(1261413) HARRISON L.—m. Jane Henlin. Resides in Staunton, Va. Issue—
1. Wilson—b. Feb. 1914.
2. James—b. 1922.

(1261414) Sarah Frances—m. Jasper Grove.
(1261415) Kate Ann—(unmarried, 1930.) Resides with her father.
(D. S. H. MSS., etc.)

(126143) HOWARD S. CAMPBELL (   ), the son of John Campbell, and wife Mary (12614), nee Harrison, married, first, Jennie Whitmore. Following her death, he married, second, Margaret Taylor. Issue—

By wife Jennie, nee Whitmore.

(1261431) Frances—
(1261432) Alice—

By wife Margaret, nee Taylor.

(1261433) Emma—m. Thomas Lucas.
(1261434) Raymond—
(1261435) Elmore—
(D. S. H. MSS., etc.)

CHAPTER XXIV

Many Being Settlers of Other States

SIXTH GENERATION—CONTINUED

ALSO THE SEVENTH AND EIGHTH, OF THE LINES HEREIN

"He leaves the loved soil of Virginia behind,
Where the dust of his fathers is fitly enshrined."
—J. R. THOMPSON.

WITH THE PASSING of more recent years, the numerous lines of ancestral descent from the early Valley of Virginia pioneers have ever continued to diverge, until today, representatives of these lines may be found in most every State in the Union. In the instance of the Harrisons, their descendants are known to be scattered, at large, across the continent, from Virginia to California, and from New York to Texas. Over half of the States of the nation, in the course of this work alone, are named, in locating their homes; yet, other descendants there are, whose States are unknown, owing to the necessary dropping of some of the lines of descent, in want of further trace regarding them. In Thomas Harrison's Clan particularly, several lines, as late as the fifth and sixth generations, have thus been discontinued.

Not alone, have the early lines in the West continued to spread, but others too there are, that have of later years, gone out from the region of the Shenandoah. Such is the process of time. Of these later lines, many a forefather of the individuals involved, sleeps beneath the green sod of Old Rockingham. On the gentle slopes of beautiful Woodbine, in Harrisonburg, and at the other hallowed spots about the county, their markers may be found; ever guarded by some sturdy oak, or other friendly tree, under whose shade the generations, in reverence, have tarried.

In this, and the past Chapter, something of over 700 immediate descendants of the sixth generation, ie., members of the seventh, are named, together with over 350 of the eighth, and a few of the ninth generation. With the sixth and seventh generations, the record largely passes, as will have been observed regarding John Harrison's Clan, from those who have gone before to those now living. In the following pages, various lines of Capt. Daniel Harrison, Thomas Harrison, and of Capt. Robert Cravens, are continued, as far as information is at hand, to the present. Several of the lines of descent from the first two, are, today, yet to be found represented in Rockingham; although under other family names. These are thought to be given fairly complete, as traced. In the case of Capt. Robert Cravens, none of his descendants of today are known to be in the county; certainly none of the name. The last is believed to have departed from Rockingham, in the person of Dr. Joseph Cravens. But their valued contributions to the upbuilding of the communities with which they have chosen to identify themselves elsewhere, have continued; furnishing an interesting illustration, of the inspiration of a splendid heritage, from "the days of yester-year."

CLAN OF CAPT. DANIEL HARRISON

1. LINE OF JESSE HARRISON, SR.

2. LINE OF DANIEL HARRISON

3. LINE OF PATTON D. HARRISON

WILLIAMS

(163231) ANN PATTON HARRISON (1823-1844), the daughter of Patton Douglas Harrison (16323), and wife Polly, nee Elgin, married, May 19, 1842, John Stuart Williams, of Kentucky, son of Gen. Samuel, and grandson of Raleigh Williams, of Virginia. Issue— an only daughter—

(1632311) Molly Elliot—b. July 21, 1843; residing 1927, at "The Pines," the homestead of her father, which she inherited from him. (See page 467); m. Col. JAMES H. HOLLOWAY, (decd.) Issue—a daughter—

1. Mary—m. THOMAS LEWIS VAN METER. Resides at "The Pines." Issue—

    1. Amelia—now Mrs. Amelia Van Meter Rogers. Resident at "The Pines."

(See also, Benjamin F. Van Meter's *Genealogies and Biographical Sketches of Old Families of Virginia and Kentucky.)*

* * * * * *

A CONTEMPORARY LINE

Byron Patton Harrison, United States Senator from, and native of, Mississippi, is of Virginia descent; his grandfather, Benjamin Harrison, having "moved from Virginia to Mississippi in the 19th century, and settled at Crystal Springs." The latter, relates a Mississippi authority, belonged "to the Southern branch of the Harrison family of New England." His wife was Hettie Bryant. Robert Harrison, his son, served as a volunteer in the Confederate Army. Robert married Mary Ann Patton. Byron Patton Harrison, the son of Robert and Mary Ann, was born at Cyrstal Springs, Copiah County, Mississippi, August 29, 1881. He married, January 19, 1905, Mary Edwina McInnis, the daughter of Hugh McInnis, and wife Matilda, of Leaksville, Miss. Three children—Byron Patton, Jr.; Catherine; and Mary Anne. Home, Gulfport, Miss. (See, *National Cyclopaedia of American Biography,* Current Volume, 1926, p. 173; also, *The Official and Statistical Register of the State of Miss.,* 1917, by D. Rowland, p. 600; and *Who's Who in the South,* 1927.)

---

2. LINE OF BENJAMIN HARRISON

3. LINE OF REV. MICHAEL DECKER

(163442) WILLIAM PORTER BASCOM DECKER (1838-1899), the son of Rev. Michael Decker, and wife Eliza Jane (16344), nee Harrison, was born at La Porte, Indiana, and died at Colfax, Washington. He married, and left two children, viz:

(1634421) William H.—m. ——; Resides at Page, Nebraska.

A daughter—

1. M. Margaret—m. —— Morrow. Resides at Lincoln, Neb.

(1634422) Cora—m. Louis R. Miller, of Pullman, Washington.

3. LINE OF WILLIAM M. HARRISON

AXE

(163471) ELLA W. HARRISON (1851-1881), the daughter of William M. Harrison (16347), and wife Eliza, married, 1875, Frank M. Axe, of Indiana. He died December 14, 1906. Issue—

(1634711) GRACE L.—b. May 10, 1877; m. Mar. 7, 1907, Charles O. Wiltfong, of Chesteron, Indiana.

(1634712) ROSS HARRISON—b. Mar. 16, 1880; m. Mar. 7, 1907, Nell M. Gidley. Resides at Chesterton, Ind.

(Dates from the Bible record before referred to. See page 390.)

---

1. LINE OF COL. DANIEL SMITH
2. LINE OF JOHN SMITH
3. LINE OF JUDGE DANIEL SMITH

CRAIG—EFFINGER

(165121) MARGARET DAVIS SMITH (1810-), the daughter of Judge Daniel Smith, of Rockingham (16512), and wife Frances, early in life became the "center of a brilliant cultured company which gathered in her father's hospitable home, 'Waverly,' and during her long life was at all times considered one of the most brilliant and facinating women of the state, a strong and accurate mind, combined with great kindness of heart, dignity and character." She married, first, in 1834, John Craig, who died prior to 1845. In 1845, she married, second, M. Harvey Effinger, a banker of Harrisonburg, Virginia. In June 1898, as a resident of Staunton, Virginia, she "revisited Harrisonburg at the age of 89." (*Wayland*, p. 242.)

Issue—

Of JOHN CRAIG, and wife Margaret, nee Smith

(1651211) ROBERT—d. 1889, unmarried.

Of M. HARVEY EFFINGER, and wife Margaret, nee Smith

(1651212) J. FRED—b. May 13, 1846; m. Nov. 27, 1886, Frances Strother Smith b. Mar. 17, 1861, dau. of John Williams Green Smith, (165126), Issue—

1. J. Fred—b. Aug. 4, 1887; d. 1888.
2. Margaret Smith—b. Jan. 1, 1889; d. 1889.
3. Robert Craig—b. May 24, 1890.
4. Frances Smith—b. Apr. 4, 1892.
5. Catherine Taylor—b. Aug. 16, 1896.

(D. S. H. MSS., etc.)

SCOTT

(165122) ELIZABETH STROTHER SMITH (1814-), the daughter of Judge Daniel Smith (16512), and wife Frances, married, August 2, 1832, Judge Christopher Columbus Scott (1807-1859), of Arkansas, at whose decease she was left a widow. Issue—

(1651221) DANIEL—b. June 4, 1833; d. May 20, 1857, unmarried.

(1651222) FRANK T.—b. 1835; m. 1869, L. McMahon.

Issue—

1. Francis T.
2. Jane—
3. Christopher C.—
4. Frances T.—
5. Mary—

(1651223) Mary Frances—b. June 14, 1837; m. July 18, 1854, JOHN W. TOBIN, of New Orleans, La. Issue—
1. Mary H.—b. Feb. 4, 1856; d. 1859.
2. Daniel G.—b. Feb. 25, 1858; d. 1859.
3. Mary—b. Nov. 16, 1859; m. CHARLES P. McCANN. Issue—
    1. Kate—b. 1882.
    2. Fannie Tobin—b. 1883.
    3. David C.—b. 1884.
    4. Charles—b. 1887.
4. Fanny—b. July 10, 1863; m. Capt. T. H. UNDERWOOD, U. S. A. Issue—
    1. Tobin—b. 1897.
5. Maude—b. July 30, 1867; m. LEON C. GILBERT. Issue—
    1. Gustavus—b. 1893.
6. Ellen—b. July 24, 1869; m. A. S. J. WHITE. Issue—
    1. Maude—b. 1898.
    2. Ellen—b. 1899.
7. John Francis—b. June 17, 1871.

(1651224) Christopher C.—b. 1839; m. Jane Toney.
Issue—
1. Elizabeth—m. Bleecker Luce, of Ft. Smith, Ark. She is now a resident of Washington, D. C.
2. Birdie—m. Dr. Sharpe, of St. Louis, Mo.
3. Nellie—b. 1883.

(1651225) Elizabeth—b. 1841; m. LEVI GILLIARD.
Issue—
1. Scott—
2. Lillie—m. CHARLES URQUHART, of New Orleans, La. Issue—
    1. Alice—b. 1892.
    2. Lillian—b. 1894.
    3. Wilkins—b. 1897.

(1651226) Robert—b. 1844; d. Aug. 1848.

(1651227) Catherine—b. 1846; d. 1864, unmarried.

(1651228) Julia—b. 1848; m. J. W. CARHART.
Issue—
1. Whitefield—b. 1876.
2. Lucy—d. in infancy.

(1651229) Nellie—b. 1852; m. Dr. A. A. TUFTS.
Issue—
1. Maude Shippen—b. 1873; d. 1876.

(D. S. H. MSS., etc.)

BEIRNE

(165124), FRANCES EVELYN SMITH (1819-), the daughter of Judge Daniel Smith (16512), and wife Frances, married, July 2, 1839, Andrew Plunkett Beirne. Issue—

(1651241) Mary Frances—b. June 15, 1840; m. July 9, 1861, JOHN MARSHALL KINNEY. Issue—

1. Nettie—b. Apr. 12, 1863; m. Edward Hartman.
2. Cabell—b. Apr. 3, 1866; m. 1892, Anette Trowbridge.
3. Evelyn—b. Aug. 12, 1872; m. John A. Renalhan.
4. Beirne—b. Apr. 17, 1875.

(1651242) Andrew Plunkett—b. Apr. 6, 1842; joined the Confederate Navy, 1861, captured at Mobile, 1865; m. Dec. 19, 1867, Elizabeth Caperton. Issue—

1. Lewis Caperton—b. Oct. 1, 1868; m. 1902, Rhoda Beatty.
2. Elizabeth—b. Oct. 20, 1870.
3. Mary—b. Dec. 17, 1872.
4. Andrew—b. Sept. 14, 1874.
5. Frances—b. Nov. 25, 1876.
6. Alice Beulah—b. Aug. 21, 1880.

(D. S. H. MSS., etc.)

TAMS

(165125) MARIE ANTIONETTE SMITH, (1827-1902), the daughter of Judge Daniel Smith (16512), and wife Frances, married, Apr. 29, 1847, at "Waverly," Rockingham County, Virginia, the home of her father, William Henry Tams, (1824-1873), of Staunton, Virginia, native of Fayetteville, North Carolina, and son of William Tams from England. William Henry Tams died at Raleigh Springs, in Rockingham. Issue—

(1651251) Mary Purviance—b. July 14, 1848; d. June 10, 1849.
(1651252) Fannie Smith—b. May 28, 1850.
(1651253) William Purviance—b. Mar. 11, 1852; (Cashier Augusta National Bank of Staunton, 1880), m. Nov. 17 1880, Sue Lewis Fraizer, b. May 19, 1859, dau. of Hon. William and Susan Fraizer, of Staunton. Issue—

1. William Fraizer—b. Mar. 17, 1882.
2. William Purviance—b. May 19, 1883.

(1651254) Margaret—b. July 18, 1854; d. June 4, 1856.
(1651255) Marie Antionette—b. July 8, 1856.
(1651256) Mary Caroline—b. Aug. 2, 1858; d. June 25, 1875.
(1651257) Rosalie Beirne—b. Mar. 21, 1860; m. Dec. 9, 1880, CONWAY McNEECE WHITTLE, son of Commodore William C. Whittle. Issue—

1. William Tams—d. in infancy.
2. Rosalie Beirne—
3. Mary Conway—d. in infancy.

(1651258) Brisco Donaghe—b. Feb. 28, 1862; d. Jan. 14, 1889, unmarried.
(1651259) Florence Brownlow—b. Sept. 22, 1864; d. July 14, 1865.
(1651260) Weightman Henson—b. Aug. 20, 1867; m. Alice Beamer.

(D. S. H. MSS., etc.)

(165126) JOHN WILLIAMS GREEN SMITH (1829-), the son of Judge Daniel Smith (16512), and wife Frances, married, first, November 30, 1853, Catherine M. Taylor, who died January 18, 1873. He married, second, March 13, 1875, Sarah McKeldon. Issue—

By wife Catherine, nee Taylor

(1651261) MARIE ANTIONETTE—b. Nov. 28, 1855; d. Oct. 9, 1868.

(1651262) ANNIE TAYLOR—b. Sept. 29, 1857; m. 1st, Mar. 4, 1878, WILLIAM SHANDS. He died, October 12, 1880. Issue—

1. William—b. May 5, 1879.

m., 2nd, Feb. 4, 1891, Walter Newman Peale. He d. Feb. 6, 1894. No issue—

(1651263) FRANCES STROTHER—b. Mar. 17, 1861; m. J. Fred Effinger, (1651212), son of M. Harvey Effenger.

(1651264) CATHERINE TAYLOR—b. Jan. 10, 1864; m. Feb. 27, 1889, BENJAMIN GAUSE GREEG. Issue—

1. Benjamin Gause—b. Nov. 21, 1889.
2. Lucius Smith—b. May 11, 1892.
3. Jessie Chestnut—b. Aug. 22, 1896.

(1651265) LUCIUS GREEN—b. Nov. 3, 1871; m. June 30, 1896, Jessie Bright Dent, descendant of an early Maryland family. Issue—

1. Garrard Dent—b. June 27, 1897.

By wife Sarah, nee McKeldon.

(1651266) HERBERT MCKELDON—b. Apr. 10, 1876; m. Feb. 1, 1898, Ida Morgan Glover.

(D. S. H. MSS., etc.)

---

2. LINE OF BENJAMIN SMITH

3. LINE OF JOHN SMITH

NOYES

(165613) ELIZABETH FRANCES SMITH (1819-), the daughter of John Smith (165161), and wife Adamena, married, William Noyes, of Charleston, present West Virginia. Issue—

(1656131) ADELBERT—
(1656132) CHARLES—
(1656133) WRIGHT—
(1656134) JOHN SMITH—m. Mary McKay. Residence, Louisville, Ky.

(First three residents of W. Va., 1903.)
(D.S.H. MSS., etc.)

(165614) JOHN BENJAMIN SMITH (1822-1887), the son of John Smith (16561), and wife Adamena, married, July 18, 1844, Caroline Amelia Welsh, of Virginia, daughter of Levi Welsh, and wife, Catherine G., nee Slaughter. After passing part of his early life with his grandmother, Elizabeth Cravens Smith, at Lancaster, Ohio, John Smith returned to Charleston, now West Virginia. In 1854, he removed with his family to Louisville, Kentucky, where he rapidly rose to prominence as a merchant and financier. He retired from active business in 1857, but later engaged in banking, and was the founder of the Bank of Commerce, at Louisville, of which he was president for many years. Issue—

(1656141) Levi Welsh—b. 1845; d. 1848.
(1656142) Mary Cornelia—b. Feb. 9, 1848; m. 1st, June 14, 1871, H. D. NEWCOMB, of Louisville, Kentucky. He d. Aug. 10, 1874. Issue—
1. Warren Smith—b. Aug. 10, 1872; d. Jan. 16, 1895.
2. H. Dalton—b. Nov. 24, 1873. (grad. of Yale, 1896.)
m. 2nd, May 1878, RICHARD TENBROECK. He d. Aug. 1, 1892. Issue—
1. Richard—b. Sept. 13, 1879.
(1656143) Kate Welsh—b. Sept. 13, 1850.
(1656144) Amelia—b. 1852; d. young.
(1656145) Rogers Morris—b. Mar. 20, 1858, (grad. U. of Va.) Resident of Jefferson Co., Kentucky; m. June 8, 1881, Jane McKay Hamilton, b. Aug. 21, 1860, dau. of Samuel S. Hamilton, of Maryland. Issue—
1. Elizabeth H.—b. June 6, 1883. Residing St. Matthews, Ky., 1903.
(D. S. H. MSS., etc.)

3. LINE OF MAJOR JOSEPH BROWN

(165621) BENJAMIN SMITH BROWN, ( ), the son of Major Joseph Brown, of Rockingham, and wife Ann, (Nancy) (16562), nee Smith, married, Catherine Thomas. Issue—

(1656211) Joseph—
(1656212) Jesse Burgess—
(1656213) Richard—
(1656214) Catherine—m. John James
(D. S. H. MSS.)

KNOWLTON

(165624) ELIZA BROWN, ( ), the daghter of Major Joseph Brown, and wife Nancy, (16562), nee Smith, married ——— Knowlton. Issue—

(1656241) Benjamin—
(1656242) Julia—
(D. S. H. MSS.)

MEACHAM

(165625) OPHELIA BROWN (1816-1883), the daughter of Major Joseph Brown, and wife Nancy (16562), nee Smith, married, March 20, 1839, Worthy Paul Meacham, (1802-1853). They resided in Ohio, where he died. She died in Ross Valley, California. Issue—

(1656251) Benjamina Catherine—b. Mar. 15, 1841; d. Nov. 26, 1882, at San Francisco, Cal.; m. at San Francisco, Apr. 3, 1866, WILLIAM HARNEY. Issue—

1. Annie Ralston—b. Jan. 25, 1867; m. Dec. 8, 1885, at Fern Hill, Ross Valley, Cal., EVAN C. EVANS, an Englishman. Issue—
    1. Evan—C. b. Sept 21, 1886.
    2. Henry L.—b. Mar. 3, 1888.
    3. Arthor C.—b. Dec. 8, 1890, Residing in England, 1903.

(1656252) Anna Roxalina—b. Jan. 31, 1844; m. July 11, 1867, at San Francisco, Cal., ALBERT DIBBLEE, b. Feb. 18, 1821, at White Plains, N. Y., d. Dec. 6, 1895, Ross Valley, Cal. Issue—

1. Albert James—b. Feb. 25, 1870; m. Apr. 21, 1899, Ethel Rogers, of Columbus, O. Residing San Francisco, Cal., 1903.
2. Anita Lavina—b. Feb. 8, 1871.
3. Harrison—b. Apr. 30, 1874, m., Jan 11, 1899, Adelia Halliday Davidson, at San Rafael, Cal.
4. Benjamin Harrison—b. July 8, 1876.

(1656253) Adeliade Ellen—b. June 19, 1846; d. Oct. 12, 1881, Shanghai, China; m. 1st, Mar. 1, 1866, A. D. ELWELL, d. Dec. 3, 1874. Issue—

1. Frank—b. Nov. 27, 1866; m. ————. Issue—
    1. Frank—
    2. George—
    3. Adelaide—
    4. Burnadine—

m. 2nd, Dec. 8, 1876, Dr. HENRY W. BOONE, of South Carolina.

(D. S. H. MSS., etc.)

---

3. LINE OF ROBERT SMITH

(165634) JAMES SMITH (1841-), the son of Robert Smith, (16563), of near Lancaster, Ohio, and wife Phoebe, married, Rebecca McLeary. Issue—

(1656341) William C.—
(1656342) Robert Mc Leary—

RUTTER

(165635) FRANCES SMITH (1844-), the daughter of Robert Smith (16563), and wife Phoebe, married, June 2, 1870, Samuel Rutter. Issue—

(1656351) Robert Smith—b. Mar. 14, 1871.
(1656352) Elizabeth—b. Aug. 1875.

(D. S. H. MSS.)

---

3. LINE OF JOHN CREED

(165652) GEORGE CREED (1814-1845), the son of John Creed, and wife Margaret (16565), nee Smith, of near Lancaster, Ohio, married, October 25, 1836, Elizabeth A. Clement. They resided in or near Lancaster, Ohio. Issue—

(1656521) George—b. July 19, 1838; m. Dec. 6, 1864, Alice Peters.

Issue—
1. Mary Low—b. Sept. 1865; d. Dec. 1865.
2. Frank P.—b. Sept. 2, 1867; m. Mar. 1894, Ida Mitchell. Issue—
1. Frederick—b. 1894.
2. Garrett—b. 1896.
3. Ann Maria—b. July 19, 1898.
4. Cornelia—b. Oct. 1899.
3. Ann Peters—b. Nov. 15, 1871; m. Mar. 1895, Dr. W. H. SILBAUGH. Issue—
1. George Creed—b. 1896.
2. Harold—b. 1898.
4. Fannie—b. Jan 5, 1875; m. Mar. 1897, CHARLES W. GRIFFITH. Issue—
1. Paul Winters—b. Oct. 1897.

(1656522) Mary Livering—b. Jan. 17, 1840; m. 1858, FREDERICK F. LOW. Issue—
1. Flora—b. Dec. 4, 1858, Maysville, Cal.

(1656523) John Marshall—b. Apr. 30, 1842; m. 1872, Mary Sullivan. Issue—
1. Joseph—b. Nov. 1, 1872, San Francisco, Cal.
2. George Dominick—b. Aug. 11, 1874.
3. Ellen Elizabeth—b. Oct. 30, 1876.
4. Mary Agnes—b. Jan. 22, 1878; d. Dec. 31, 1878.
5. Elizabeth Ann—b. July 5, 1879.
6. Charles B.—b. Mar. 11, 1881.

(1656524) Charles Hopkins—b. May 20, 1844; m. Louise Withoff. Issue—
1. Celia Withoff—b. Oct. 29, 1868, near Lancaster, Ohio.
2. Mary Low—b. June 10, 1870.
3. Elizabeth Clement—b. Jan. 27, 1873.
4. Anna Withoff—b. Oct. 22, 1874.
5. Flora Low—b. Sept. 22, 1876.
6. Louise Withoff—b. Oct. 15, 1878.
7. George—b. Aug. 13, 1880; d. Feb. 14, 1883.
8. Jeannie Collette—b. Sept. 26, 1882.
9. Charles Henry—b. Apr. 4, 1885.

RITCHIE

(165653) MARY CREED (1816-), the daughter of John Creed, and wife Margaret (16565), nee Smith, married William A. Ritchie. Issue—

(1656531) Creed—d. 1877; m. ——, left 3 children.
(1656532) Henry—d.—killed in the War-between-the-States
(1656533) Alexander—d.—killed in the War-between-the-States.
(1656534) Catherine—m. CHARLES SIMPKINS, of San Francisco, Cal. Issue—

1. Alice—m. ROBERT COLEMAN. Issue—
   1. Robert—
   2. Caroline—
2. Henry—

(1656535) MARGARET—m. William Walbridge. No Issue.
(1656536) JAMES—m. Phoebe Boerstler.
Issue—
1. Elizabeth—
2. Margaret—

(1656537) WILLIAM—
(D. S. H. MSS., etc.)

PARKS

(165655) MARGARET DAVIS CREED (1820-1866), the daughter of John Creed and wife Margaret (16565), nee Smith, married Major Andrew Parks, a lawyer of Charleston, now West Virginia. He died in 1864. Issue—

(1656551) CREED—killed in the War-between-the-States.
(1656552) BUSHROD WASHINGTON—m. ——; d. 1875.
(1656553) HARRIOT WASHINGTON—m. June 26, 1867, T. W. TALLMADGE, of Washington, D. C. Issue—
1. Flora—b. Oct. 1, 1868; d. Feb. 1900.
2. Andrew Parks—b. Jan. 16, 1870, Washington, D. C.

(1656554) ANDREW PARKS—Resident of West Virginia, (1903).
(D. S. H. MSS., etc.)

FALL

(165656) JANE HARRISON CREED (1822-1859),the daughter of John Creed, and wife Margaret (16565), nee Smith, married John C. Fall, of California. Issue—

(1656561) KATE—d. in infancy.
(1656562) SALLIE—m. Commodore ROGERS, of the U. S. Navy.
Issue—
1. Ralph Fall—

(D. S. H. MSS.)

---

3. LINE OF BENJAMIN HARRISON SMITH

BROOKS

(165671) CYNTHIA ELIZABETH SMITH (1827-), the daughter of Benjamin Harrison Smith (16567), of Charleston, West Virginia, and wife Roxalana, married Fred F. Brooks. Issue—

(1656711), LILLY RAND—b. 1852; m. 1874, WILLIAM BURLINGHAM.
Issue—
1. Frederick Harrison—b. Jan. 18, 1877.
2. William—b. Oct. 15, 1879.
3. Prentis—b. Oct. 14, 1881.

(1656712) MORRIS ODEN—b. 1862.
(D. S. H. MSS., etc.)

(165672), ISAAC NOYES SMITH (1831-), the son of Benjamin Harrison Smith (16567), and wife Roxalana, married, Caroline Shrewsbury Quarrier. He graduated at Washington and Lee University, Lexington, Virginia, (B. A.), studied law, and in 1859, and 1860, represented Kanawah County, now West Virginia, in the legislature. During the War-between-the-States, he was a Major of the 22nd Virginia Regiment, C. S. A. Issue—

(1656721) BENJAMIN HARRISON—b. Mar. 20, 1862; d. May 18, 1887.
(1656722) ALEXANDER QUARRIER—b. Mar. 24, 1864; m. June 2, 1891, Ethelind Parker Appleton, b. June 28, 1867. Issue—
1. Benjamin Harrison—b. July 16, 1893.
2. Elsie—b. Mar. 25, 1898.
3. Everard Appleton—b. April 1, 1900.
(1656723) HARRISON BROOKS—b. Sept. 7, 1866; m. May 12, 1896, Katherine Dana Bowne, b. June 8, 1872. Issue—
1. Harrison Bowne—b. Mar. 2, 1898.
2. Helen Dana—b. Mar. 2, 1900.
(1656724) ELSIE QUARRIER—b. Apr. 4, 1869; m. Nov. 29, 1892, FREDERICK M. STAUNTON, b. May 17, 1866. Issue—
1. Caroline Quarrier—b. May 6, 1894.
(1656725) ISAAC NOYES—b. Dec. 21, 1876; m. Oct. 25, 1890, Elizabeth Adelaide Dana, b. Oct. 24, 1876.
(1656726) CHRISTOPHER TOMPKINS—b. Feb. 16, 1879.
(1656727) WINSTON SHREWSBERRY—b. Dec. 23, 1880; d. Oct. 10, 1882.
(D. S. H. MSS., etc.)

JONES

(165673) ROXALANA EMELINE SMITH (1841-), the daughter of Benjamin Harrison Smith (16567), and wife Roxalana, married, Col. Amos Balfour Jones. Issue—
(1656731) LENA—b. 1865; m. 1st, WILLIAM B. DIXON.
Issue—
1. William Boulton—
m. 2nd, D. L. Laine.
(D. S. H. MSS., etc.)

3. LINE OF JAMES HARRISON SMITH

LATTA

(165681) ELIZABETH TRACY SMITH (1829-), the daughter of James Harrison Smith (165681), of Lancaster, Ohio, and wife Elizabeth, married, December 10, 1850, William Latta. He died November 13, 1874. Issue—

(1656811) JOHN—m. 1885, Mary E. Smith.
Issue—
1. Harrison Smith—b. 1886.
(1656812) JAMES—d. unmarried.
(1656813) WILLIAM—m. 1st, Sarah Bennett.

Issue—
1. James—b. Dec. 1, 1880.
m. 2nd, Ellen M. Stewart. Issue—
1. Alice—b. July 8, 1888.
(1656814) CATHERINE—m. 1st, S. G. GRISWOLD.
Issue—
1. Latta—b. 1876.
m. 2nd, Horace S. Wade, of Orange, New Jersey.
(1656815) ELIZABETH—m. Dr. L. H. LAIDLEY, of St. Louis, Mo.
Issue—
1. Latta—d. in infancy.
2. Paul—b. 1882.
3. Edward—b. 1886.
(1656816) MORTON BRASEE—b. Sept. 11, 1868; d. July 16, 1896.
(D. S. H. MSS., etc.)

---

2. LINE OF WILLIAM SMITH

3. LINE OF COL. WILLIAM B. YANCEY

CONRAD

(166141) DIANA SMITH YANCEY (1831-1895), the daughter of Col. William B. Yancey, and wife Mary (16614), nee Smith, born September 15, 1831, married George Oliver Conrad, of Harrisonburg, born June 29, 1823. She died September 8, 1895. His death occurred January 23, 1907.

George O. Conrad, was for a time before the War of 1861-65, mayor of Harrisonburg. He became a resident of the town in 1836, and for many years was engaged in the jewelry business. During the war he served in the Confererate Army as a member of the 14th Regt. of Va. Cavalry, McCausland's Brigade. His family had long been settled in the present Elkton region, and on his mother's side he was a descendant of Adam Miller of the early Massanutten colony, elsewhere noticed. Stephen Conrad is named on the Augusta records in 1758. On August 30, 1763 he patented land on Boone's Run, "between Piked Mountain and Shenandore River," to which he later added by purchase. He died in 1767, leaving a widow Catherine, and at least, sons George and Stephen. A Stephen Conrad qualified Capt. of the Rockingham militia Apr. 23, 1781.

George O. Conrad, and wife, Diana, had issue—

(1661411) THOMAS WILLIAM—b. July 28, 1851; d. Jan. 24, 1908; m. 1st, Minnie Palmer; m. 2nd, Lucy Jeffries.
(1661412) EDWARD SMITH—b. 1853; d. 1916; m. Jennie Irick.
Issue—
1. Charles E.—(M. D.), of Harrisonburg, Va.; m. Ann Gilliam, of Lynchburg, Va. Issue—
1. Gilliam—
2. Virginia—
2. Laird—m. Margaret Davis.
3. Mary Margaret—d. in infancy.
4. Evelyn—
(1661413) MARY LYNN—(unmarried.) Resides in Harrisonburg.

(1661414) FANNIE KYLE—m. Dr. THOMAS OLIN JONES, of Harrisonburg, b. Oct. 25, 1851; d. Nov. 22, 1914; son of Rev. John C. Jones, of Baltimore Conference, M. E. Church, South. Issue—
1. Olin Conrad—b. Feb. 4, 1887; d. Nov. 28, 1913.
2. Corin—b. Aug. 28, 1893; d. Jan. 20, 1919; m. Michael Fletcher, of Harrisonburg.

(1661415) MARGARET ELIZABETH—m. 1st, JOHN L. LOGAN, (decd.) Issue—
1. Conrad—Prof. of English, State Teachers College, Harrisonburg, m. Mary Jarmin.
2. Margaret—m. William Royal Smithey, Prof. of Sociology, Univ. of Va.

m. 2nd, Judge TALFOURD N. HAAS, of Harrisonburg. Issue—
3. Elizabeth—m. Albert Kemper, now of Bluefield, W. Va.
4. Hamilton—Attorney at law, Harrisonburg, Va.

(1661416) GEORGE NEWTON—m. Emily Pasco, dau. of Senator Pasco, of Florida. Resides in Harrisonburg, where he is a prominent member of the Bar. Commonwealth Attorney, 1899-1912, of Rockingham, and later served his county in the State Senate. Issue—
1. Jessie—m. Howard Gibbons, of Harrisonburg.
2. Mary Pasco—m. James Stevenson, Prof., Davidson College.
3. George—(unmarried.)
4. Samuel—(unmarried.)
5. John—(unmarried.)

(Dates from markers in Woodbine Cemetery, in Harrisonburg.)

(166142) THOMAS LAYTON YANCEY (1833-1862), the son of Col. William B. Yancey, and wife Mary (16614), nee Smith, born February 23, 1833, died February 11, 1862, married Margaret Newman, born April 14, 1836, died September 23, 1911, the daughter fo Dr. A. M. Newman, (1810-1900), and wife Rebecca (1817-1896). Thomas L. Yancey served as a Captain in the Confederate Army. He and wife resided in Rockingham. Following his death, his widow married Lieut. L. C. Myers, (C. S. A.), of Harrisonburg, born June 30, 1840, died January 8, 1929.

Thomas Layton Yancey, and wife, had issue—

(1661421) MARY REBECCA—b. Dec. 7, 1856; d. Jan. 19, 1886; m. GEORGE E. SIPE, of Harrisonburg, (as his 1st wife), Issue—
1. Reba—m. Dr. Byrd Willis, of Rockymount, North Carolina,
2. Mary Dorsey—m. ——. Resides in the Phillipine Islands.

(1661422) WILLIAM—b. July 17, 1859; d. Jan 22, 1891; m. Sallie Yancey.

(Dates from markers in Woodbine Cemetery, in Harrisonburg.)

(166143) WILLIAM B. YANCEY (1836-), the son of Col. William B. Yancey, and wife Mary (16614), nee Smith, born December 15, 1836, married February 15, 1860, Julia Victoria Winsboro, born September 5, 1838, the daughter of Capt. William Winsboro, and wife Lucy, (1808-1893), daughter of Col. Joseph Mauzy. (See page 516.) William B. Yancey served as a Captain in the Confederate Army. He was permanently disabled by a severe wound in battle, May 12, 1864. (See, *Wayland*, p. 139.) He and wife resided near McGaheysville, in Rockingham, where he was a prominent farmer. Issue—

(1661431) William L.—b. Nov. 24, 1860; d. July 31, 1901; m. Oct. 27, 1885, Mary A. Gibbons. Issue—

1. Kemper—m. Edith Stafford, of Texas. Resides in Washington, D. C.
2. Mary V.—m. Dr. Noland M. Canter, of Harrisonburg, Va.
3. William M.—m.———.
4. Ruth—b. Feb. 27, 1899; d. July 27, 1899.
5. Lois—(unmarried)
6. Robert—m. ———; Resides, Raleigh, N. C.
7. Charlotte—m. Hilliard Boyce, of Harrisonburg.
8. Mildred—b. Apr. 28, 1900; d. Sept. 10, 1921, unmarried.

mary A. mauzy
Mauzy

(1661432) Thomas Layton—b. Jan. 15, 1863; m. Nov. 16, 1887, Mary A. Mauzy, dau. of George Whitfield Mauzy, (and wife Frances R., dau. of John Rush), and granddaughter of Col. Joseph Mauzy. Issue—

1. Christine—m. Howard Leap.
2. Arthur—
3. Hettie—m. ——— Gilliam, of Charlottesville, Va.
4. Whitfield—m. Christine Funkhouser.
5. Lelia—
6. Thomas—

(1661433) Stuart Mauzy—b. Apr. 3, 1865; m. 1st, June 11, 1889, Janie Mumma. She d. July 11, 1889. m. 2nd, Apr. 25, 1895, Bessie Nicholas. Issue—

1. Malcomb—
2. Elizabeth—Resides in Plant City, Florida.

(1661434) Emma Virginia—b. Sept. 11, 1867; m. Nov. 10, 1892, CHARLES GIBBONS, son of Robert A. He d. Feb. 1897. Issue—

1. Hunter—
2. Mary—m. Robert Snapp, of Elkton, Va.

(1661435) Laura Belle—b. Apr. 10, 1870; d. Mar. 24, 1873.

(1661436) Albert Smith—b. May 15, 1873; m. June 23, 1894, Bettie Shipp. Resides in Charlottesville, Va. Issue—

1. Anna V.—
2. Lucretia—
3. Samuel P.—

(1661437) Joe Richard—b. July 20, 1875; d. July 29, 1875.

(1661438) Nettie Irene—b. Dec. 20, 1876; m. May 9, 1900, WHITFIELD LIGGETT MAUZY, b. Apr. 5, 1873, son of Thomas G., and wife Anna Belle Liggett, and grandson of Albert Gallatin Mauzy. (see below), Issue—

1. Whitfield Yancey—
2. Raleigh Armentrout—
3. William Franklin—
4. Charlotte Julia—
5. Emma Irene—
6. Margaret—

7. Thomas Albert—
8. Virginia—

Of McGaheysville.

(1661439) MARY JULIA—b. Aug. 8, 1878; m. Starke Estes, of Orange County, Virginia.

(1661440) FRANKLIN WINSBORO—b. Sept. 2, 1882; m. Sept. 2, 1908, Louise Miller Yancey, dau. of Dr. Layton B. Yancey. Issue—

1. Louise Miller—

(Mauzy records, and others. William L. and dau. Mildred, interred in Woodbine Cemetery, in Harrisonburg. Dates from markers.)

(166144) EDWARD STUART YANCEY (1838-1855), the son of Col. William B. Yancey, and wife Mary (16614), nee Smith, born February 6, 1838, died August 13, 1885, married, August 3, 1858, Frances Virginia Mauzy, born July 31, 1838, died January 21, 1899. She was the daughter of Albert Gallatin Mauzy, and wife Julia (m. October 13, 1836), the daughter of John Nicholas, and granddaughter of Col. Joseph Mauzy. (See page 516.) Edward S. Yancey and wife resided in Rockingham, in or near Harrisonburg. Issue—

(1661441) MARY JULIA—b. Dec. 28, 1859; d. Jan. 8, 1860.

(1661442) CHARLES ALBERT—b. Mar. 13, 1861; m. Sept. 13, 1884; at New Windsor, Colorado, Flora M. Davis. Issue—

1. William Edward—b. Aug. 17, 1885.
2. Frank Lupton—b. June 23, 1887; m. Aug. 11, 1907, Gene McLain. Issue—
    1. Margaret Albert—b. Nov. 8, 1908.
3. Harry Revillo—b. Sept. 23, 1888; d. Aug. 11, 1889.
4. Lula Laura—b. Aug. 3, 1890; d. May 18, 1893.
5. Lena Belle—b. Aug. 13, 1891; d. Apr. 30, 1892.
6. Charles Layton—b. Apr. 13, 1893.
7. Thomas Moffett—b. Oct. 4, 1898.

(1661443) JOSEPH WILLIAM—b. Oct. 3, 1864; m. Aug. 21, 1894, at Ft. Collins, Col. Mattie Hankins. Issue—

1. Fannie Virginia—b. June 22, 1895.
2. Zenith Belle—b. July 19, 1897.
3. Esther—b. Oct. 1, 1903; d. Feb. 24, 1905.
4. Rebecca Pearl—b. Oct. 12, 1905.

(1661444) MAGGIE BELLE—b. Nov. 6, 1866; m. Nov. 14, 1899, at New Windsor, Col. ROBERT REID. Issue—

1. Lyle James—b. Nov. 3, 1890.
2. Joseph William—b. Sept. 18, 1892.
3. Robert Alexander—b. Dec. 1, 1894.
4. Reville Loveland—b. Apr. 1, 1898.
5. Bessie Virginia—b. Jan. 14, 1900.

(1661445) EMMA FLORENCE—b. Dec. 5,1868; d. Sept. 11, 1887.

(166145) CHARLES ALBERT YANCEY ( ), the son of Col. William B. Yancey, and wife Mary (16614), nee Smith, married Julia Morrison. They resided in Harrisonburg, Virginia. Issue—

(1661451) Lottie—
(1661452) Lula—(unmarried) Resides with sister, Nannie, below.
(1661453) Burbridge—m. Minnie Reid. Resides at Univ. of Virginia.
(1661454) Nannie—m. —— McFall. Resides in Arlington Co., Va.

MAUZY

(166147) MARGARET JANE YANCEY (1844-1895), the daughter of Col. William B. Yancey, and wife Mary (16614), nee Smith, born December 31, 1844, died April 4, 1895, married, October 27, 1865, Joseph Nicholas Mauzy, born March 21, 1845, died December 6, 1910, the son of Albert Gallatin Mauzy, and grandson of Col. Joseph Mauzy. (See above.) Joseph Nicholas Mauzy and wife resided at McGaheysville, in Rockingham. Issue—

(1661471) William Albert—b. Sept. 1, 1866; d. Oct. 11, 1879.

(1661472) Thomas Edward—b. May 14, 1868; m. Nov. 27, 1899, Byrd Courtney Roller. Resides at Winston Salem, N. C. Issue—
1. Courtney Roller—

(1661473) Mary Julia—b. May 20, 1870; m. Oct. 26, 1906, EDGAR BROWN SELLERS, son of Dr. T. N. Sellers. Issue—
1. Brown—
2. Edgar—

(1661474) Frances Belle—b. Dec. 30, 1871; m. May 9, 1900, PRENTISS RUSSELL WEAVER, (decd.) son of James Madison Weaver. She resides at Winston Salem, N. C.; Issue—
1. Russell—
2. James—

(1661475) Joseph Layton—b. Feb. 2, 1873; m. Dec. 11, 1900, Eleanor Cameron Harmon, dau. of A. W. Harmon, of Rockbridge Co. Issue—
1. George Watts—
2. Eugene Harmon—
3. Eleanor Cameron—
4. Joseph Layton—
5. Margaret—

(1661476) Nannie Strother—b. Aug. 6, 1875; d. Nov. 13, 1878.

(1661477) Charles Hampton—b. Nov. 27, 1877; m. Mar. 30, 1904, Charlotte Henrietta Richardson. Resides in Harrisonburg, Va. Issue—
1. Charles Hampton—
2. Royal—
3. Charlotte—

(1661478) Diana Lynn—b. Apr. 13, 1880; m. June 15, 1904, JAMES BALLARD DYER. (decd.), of Winston Salem, N. C. Issue—
1. James Ballard—

(1661479) Emma Virginia—b. Nov. 7, 1881; m. May 26, 1909, HOWARD Le ROY HOPKINS. Issue—
1. Howard—
2. Margaret Christiana—m. ——— Funkhouser.

(1661480) Harry Crockett—b. Dec. 23, 1883.

(1661481) MARGARET CHRISTIANA—b. Oct. 4, 1887; m. Roy Gilliam, of Charlottesville, Va.,
(Mauzy records, and others.)

Through the marriage of Lieut Layton Yancey, father of Col. Wm. B., to Frances Lewis, dau. of Thomas Lewis, and wife Jane Strother, the descendants of Col. Wm. B. Yancey are also descendants of John Lewis, the early pioneer of Augusta. (See Chapter XVIII.)

---

2. LINE OF REV. JAMES SMITH

3. LINE OF COL. CHARLES SAGAR

(166214) MARCUS SMITH SAGAR (1831-1897), the son of Col. Charles Sagar, of Oakland, Ohio, and wife Jane Harrison (16621), nee Smith, married December 31, 1858, Eleanor McMaster. They resided in Chicago, Illinois, where he died. Issue—

(1662141) EMMA—d. in infancy.
(1662142) HENRY—m. ———, no issue.
(1662143) ADOLPH—(residing unmarried with mother in Chicago, 1903.)
(D. S. H. MSS.)

(166215) CHARLES HENRY SAGAR (1838-), the son of Col. Charles Sagar, and wife Jane Harrison (16621), nee Smith, married, March 3, 1859, Amelia W. Starkel. They resided at Washington Court House, Ohio, and later in Lebanon, Illinois. Issue—

(1662151) CHARLES EMIL—b. Jan. 15, 1860, (Washington C. H., Ohio); m. at Lebanon, Ill., Sept. 21, 1881, Addie V. Moore. Issue—
1. a daughter—d. Dec. 11, 1882.
2. Charles Le Roy—b. Mar. 6, 1884.
3. Chauncey M.—b. July 20, 1890.

(1662152) FRANCES S.—d. in infancy.
(1662153) EDGAR GRANT—b. Oct. 30, 1864; m. Oct. 16, 1889, Sarah Louise Gleishbrin. Issue—
1. Martha May—b. Nov. 9, 1890.
2. Helen Luella—b. Sept. 5, 1894.
3. Edgar Charles—b. Jan. 8, 1898.

(1662154) JAMES RICHARD, (Rev.)—b. Oct. 5, 1871, (Lebanon, Ill.); m. Feb. 21, 1893, in St. Louis, Mo., Bertha A. Smith. Residence, Hardine, Ill. Issue—
1. Dorothy Bess—b. Nov. 7, 1893.
2. Mildred Mae—b. July 5, 1895. (decd.)
3. Elsie Louise—b. July 27, 1896.
4. James Donald—b. July 22, 1898.
5. Alice Margurite—b. Sept. 2, 1899.

(1662155) JESSE B.—
(D. S. H. MSS., etc.)

ECKERT

(166216) FRANCES HENRIETTA SAGAR (1844-), the daughter of Col.

Charles Sagar, and wife Jane Harrison (16621), nee Smith, married, November 19, 1861, John H. Eckert. Issue—

(1662161) IONA MAY—d. Dec. 1894; m. GEORGE NUNNELLY.
Issue—
1. Ethel—
(1662162) HARRY—d. in infancy.
(1662163) FRANCES A.—m. HENRY JAMES, (decd.) She residing, 1903, Arkansas City, Kansas, with daughter—
1. Frances—
(D. S. H. MSS.)

---

3. LINE OF BENJAMIN F. SMITH

(166233) JOHN STILLY SMITH (1834-), the son of Benjamin F. Smith (16623), of Mankato, Minnesota, and wife Julia, married Mary Dayton. Issue—

(1662331) BENJAMIN DAYTON—m. ——. (Issue.)
(1662332) MINNIE LOUISE—d. 1886.
(1662333) ADA LENA—m. Harvey Williams. (Issue.)
(D. S. H. MSS.)

DUNN

(166234) DIANA JANE SMITH (1836-), the daughter of Benjamin F. Smith (16623), and wife Julia, married Andrew C. Dunn. Issue—

(1662341) MARY TILLINGHAST—m. Francis A. Molyneaux.
(1662342) GERTRUDE—d. in infancy.
(1662343) ELLEN—d. in infancy.
(1662344) EDWARD GANO—d. in infancy.
(1662345) ALICE HOPE—m. William H. Hodgman.
(1662346) ETHEL—d. in infancy.
(1662347) ANDREW PAUL—
(D. S. H. MSS.)

BIXBY

(166235) SARAH SMITH (1837-), the daughter of Benjamin F. Smith (16623), and wife Julia, married Nahum Bixby. Issue—

(1662351) JULIA—m. ———Evans. (decd.)
(1662352) JESSIE—d. ——
(1662353) JAMES—d.——
(D. S. H. MSS.)

PARROT

(166236) MARY HENRIETTA SMITH (1839-), the daughter of Benjamin F. Smith (16623), and wife Julia, married George Parrot. Issue—

(1662361) RUTH—
(1662362) WINNIE—
(1662363) BERNICE—d. ——.
(D. S. H. MSS.)

BROWN

(166237) ELIZA ANN SMITH, (1840-), the daughter of Benjamin F. Smith, (16623), and wife Julia, married C. Brown. Issue—

(1662371) Gertrude—m. Eugene Chamberlain, (Issue.)
(1662372) Effie—m. William (Willie) Chamberlain, (Issue.)
(D. S. H. MSS.)

(166243) HENRY WARDEN BURR SMITH (1850-), the son of Benjamin F. Smith (16623), and wife Julia, married ———, nee Ralph. Issue—

(1662431) Ralph—
(1662432) Roy—
(1662433) Walter—
(1662434) Bessie—
(1662435) Hazel—
(D. S. H. MSS.)

---

3. LINE OF DR. VESPASIAN SMITH

McCORMICK

(166252) LOUISE ELEANOR SMITH (1848-), the daughter of Dr. Vespasian Smith (16625), of Duluth, Minnesota, and wife Charlotte, married 1871, Dr. McCormick. Issue—

(1662521) William Smith—b. 1874.
(1662522) Clinton Priestly—b. 1875.
(D. S. H. MSS.)

(166253) FRANK BRANDEN SMITH (1852-), the son of Dr. Vespasian Smith (16625), and wife Charlotte, married, 1878, Isabel F. Eysten. She died in 1894. Issue—

(1662531) Vespasian—b. 1881; d. 1898.
(1662532) Pauline—b. 1883.
(1662533) Margaret Eysten—b. 1894.
(D. S. H. MSS.)

---

3. LINE OF REV. A. A. DAVIS

MOORE

(166263) ELIZABETH REBECCA DAVIS (1853-), the daughter of Rev. A. A. Davis, of Sunbury, Ohio, and wife Adeline T. (16626), nee Smith, married at Sunbury, Ohio, December 8. 1881, Theodore Moore. Issue—

(1662631) Forrest Benson—b. Oct. 22, 1882.
(1662632) Ernest Smith—b. May 24, 1884.
(D. S. H. MSS.)

---

3. LINE OF CHARLES LYBRAND

SWARTZ

(166271) CHARLESETTE LYBRAND, (1847-1880), the daughter of Charles

Lybrand, and wife Henrietta, (16627), nee Smith, of Mt. Vernon, Ohio, married, November 27, 1867, William Swartz. She died June 1880. Issue—

(1662711) Mary Ella—b. Aug. 26, 1868.
(1662712) Addie Elizabeth—b. Mar. 13, 1871.
(1662713) Daisy—b. Dec. 5, 1873.
(1662714) Henry Ferdinand—b. Sept. 9, 1875.
(1662715) James Benjamin—b. July 26, 1877.
(1662716) George Charles—b. May 27, 1879.
(D. S. H. MSS.)

* * * * * *

END OF SMITH RECORD

The Smith lines included in the D. S. H. MSS. are based on data furnished by Mr. Rogers Morris Smith (1656145), of St. Matthew's, Kentucky, to the late Daniel Smith Harrison, under date of July 20, 1914, with accompaning letter, kindly granting, "perfect liberty to take and use any part of this manuscript you may desire." See also *Boogher*, p. 372.

---

1. LINE OF COL. BENJAMIN HARRISON
2. LINE OF DANIEL HARRISON
3. LINE OF WILLIAM HOPPER

COLEMAN

(167241) BARBARA ANN HOPPER (1819-1855), the daughter of William Hopper, and wife Edith McWilliams (16724), nee Harrison, married, 1835, at Hopkinsville, Kentucky, Hardin Coleman, of Kentucky. Issue—

(1672411) Mary—m. William Wood.
(1672412) Lewis Harrison—m. Jennie Logan, dau. of Judge Stephen Logan, Lincoln's law partner. Issue—
1. Logan—
(1672413) James Owens—Prof. of History, Medvale, Pa.; m. Christopher Bush. (Issue 2 children.)
(1672414) Stephen O.—m. ———. (no issue.)
(1672415) William—m. ———.
Issue—
1. Mary—m. Dr. Morrison, of Springfield, Ill.
(E. O. M. papers.)

(167242) ELIJAH HARRISON HOPPER (1821-1888), the son of William Hopper, and wife Edith McWilliams (16724), nee Harrison, married, 1847, Harriet Bryan. Issue—

(1672421) Caroline—
(1672422) Harrison—m. ———, nee Dillard. (Issue 2 children.)
(1672423) Edith—m. ——— Scales.
(1672424) Susan—m. ———. (no issue.)
(1672425) Bryan—
(1672426) Bettie—
(1672427) Hattie—

(1672428) WILLIAM—
(E. O. M. papers.)

OWENS

(167243) FRANCES MARIA HOPPER (1824-1891), the daughter of William Hopper, and wife, Edith McWilliams (16724), nee Harrison, married, 1842, in Illinois, John M. Owens, a native of Cincinnati, Ohio. Issue—

(1672431) EDITH HARRISON—m. Gessner Hill..
(1672432) THEODOCIA—m. Henry Murdock.
(1672433) ELLA—m. 1st; CHARLES GRAY.
Issue—
1. Owen—
m., 2nd; Major (Dr.) HENRY F. HOYT.
Issue—
2. Terrell—
(1672434) LAURA—m. WILLIAM HACKNEY.
Issue—
1. Frances—
(E. O. M. papers.)

(167245) WILLIAM LOGAN HOPPER (1830-1894), the son of William Hopper, and wife Edith McWilliams (16724), nee Harrison, married, 1852, Lettia Jane Clendenning, of Pennsylvania. Issue—

(1672451) EVA—m. Joseph Shepherd.
(1672452) HARRISON—m. Anne Suddeth,
Issue—
1. Florence—
(1672453) BELLE—m. ——— (no issue.)
(1672454) WILLIAM—d. in infancy.
(1672455) CHARLES LOGAN—m. ——— (no issue.)
(1672456) FRANK—m. ———.
Issue—
1. a son—Dr. of Chemistry, Univ. of Pasadena, California.
(E. O. M. papers.)

OWENS

(167246) MARY THOMPSON HOPPER (1834-1907), the daughter of William Hopper, and wife Edith McWilliams (16724), nee Harrison, married James F. Owens (1829-1901), native of Cincinnati, Ohio, and brother of John M. Owens above. James F. and Mary Owens resided at "Thorndale," the old homestead of William Hopper, in Warren County, Illinois. (See page 475.) Issue—

(1672461) MARIA FRANKS—m. H. M. CHAMBERLAIN
Issue—
1. Inna—
2. William—
(1672462) ANNA BARBARA—m. A. M. Hinckley. (no issue.)
(1672463) MARY EUNICE—b. ——; d. 1930; m. 1889, LAFAYETTE MARKS, of

Newell, W. Va. Resided at Springdale, Arkansas, where he is a prominent orchardist. She owned a silver cream ladle of her great-grandfather, Daniel Harrison's, marked "D. H.". Issue—

1. James Alfred—b. 1891,(unmarried.) U. S. Agr. Dept. fruit expert.
2. Harriet Edith—b. Nov. 10, 1893, teacher, Univ. of Chicago.
3. Margaret Owens—b. Jan. 2, 1897; Sec. to Dean of Agr. Univ. of Chicago.
4. Charles Lewis—b. Sept. 25, 1900. (At home.)

(1672464) CHARLES—m. ——— (no issue.)
(1672465) MARGARET—d. 1896, (unmarried.)
(1672466) EDITH—m. J. B. RANKIN.
Issue—

1. Lois—
2. J. O.—Prof., College of Agriculture, Lincoln, Nebraska.
3. Mary—b. ——, m. ———.

(one other.)

(E. O. M. papers, 1930.)

---

2. LINE OF EZEKIEL LOGAN

3. LINE OF BENJAMIN HARRISON LOGAN

(167714) TIFFIN PEACHY LOGAN ( ), the son of Benjamin Harrison Logan (16771), and wife Catherine, married ————. Issue—

(1677141) EDGAR—
(1677142) PEACHY—

---

3. LINE OF JOHN WILLIAMS

CHRISTIAN

(167773) ELIZA MARIA WILLIAMS ( ), the daughter of John Williams, and wife Angelina (16777), nee Logan, married Joseph Christian. Issue—

(1677731) BERTHA—m. LAWRENCE ALLISON.
Issue—

1. Brook—

(1677732) JESSIE—m. DEMARCUS BROWN.
Issue—

1. Philip—

(1677733) ALICE—

---

3. LINE OF FRANCIS ASBURY LOGAN

(167781) MELVIN CASE LOGAN (1844), the son of Francis Asbury Logan (16778), and wife Elizabeth, married December 4, 1873, Ellen J. Anderson. Issue, one child—

(1677811) OLIVE AGNES—b. July 22, 1874; m. JOHN BRUNDAGE.
Issue—

1. Raymond—
2. Eleanor—

WILSON

(167782) MARGARET VIRGINIA LOGAN (1847), the daughter of Francis Asbury Logan (16778), and wife Elizabeth, married, November 16, 1865, William Henry Wilson. Issue—

(1677821) MAY—
(1677822) HARRY W.,—m. Carrie Doak.
(1677823) MINNIE—m. WILLIAM DOIG.
Issue—
1. Wilson—
(1677824) CARRIE—
(1677825) ELIZABETH—d. ——.
(1677826) BERTHA—
(1677827) JOHN—d. ——.

GRIFFEY

(167783) MARY ELIZA LOGAN (1849), the daughter of Francis Asbury Logan, (16778), and wife Elizabeth, married, October 8, 1868, Levi Griffey. Issue—

(1677831) WALTER—
(1677832) DORA—m. Charles Griffey.

LOGAN

(167784) SARAH PAUL LOGAN (1851), the daughter of Francis Asbury Logan (16778), and wife Elizabeth, married ——— Logan. Issue—

(1677841) WALTER SCOTT—

RENFRO

(167786) LAURA LOGAN (1860), the daughter of Francis Asbury Logan (16778), and wife Elizabeth, married, September 19, 1888, John C. Renfro, of the Hanover, Indiana, vicinity. Issue—

(1677861) HARRIETT E.—(unmarried) Resides near Madison, Ind.
(1677862) CORA—(unmarried)

DEPUTY

(167787) ANNIE ELIZABETH LOGAN (1865), the daughter of Francis Asbury Logan (16778), and wife Elizabeth, married, March 6, 1889, Luther Deputy. Issue—

(1677871) ETHEL—m. John Robey.
(1677872) FLORENCE—
(1677873) FRANK—
(1677874) FRED—
(1677875) ROBERT—
(H. E. R. to D. S. H., 2-2-1914.)

2. LINE OF DR. PEACHY HARRISON

3. LINE OF DR. GESSNER HARRISON

BROADUS

(167921) MARIA CARTER HARRISON (1831-1857), the daughter of Dr. Gessner Harrison (16792), and wife Eliza Carter, married, November 14, 1849, Rev. John A. Broadus, (1827-1895), an eminent Baptist divine.

John A Broadus was born in Culpeper County, Virginia, January 27, 1827, the youngest son of Major Edmund Broadus. In 1843, he joined the Baptist denomination, and three years later entered the University of Virginia, from which he graduated in 1850. (M. A.) For a time he was assistant professor of classic languages, under Dr. Gessner Harrison, his father-in-law. During this interval, he became pastor of the Baptist Church at Charlottesville, Virginia. He resigned from the University in 1853, to devote all of his time to the church. From 1855 to 1857, he served as Chaplain of the University. In 1859, he removed to Greenville, South Carolina, where the Southern Theological Seminary was opened the same year, on October 1st, and from this time on, "the remainder of his life was devoted to the cause and interest of that institution." Following the War of 1861-65, the school was finally established on a secure foundation at Louisville, Kentucky. Many of his sermons and addresses have been published, among the latter an interesting memorial of Dr. Gessner Harrison, delivered July 2, 1873, as may be found in *The Library of Southern Literature.* (Vol. II, page 507.)

Rev. John A. Broadus, and wife Maria (167921), had issue—

(1679211) Eliza Somerville—
(1679212) Anna Harrison—
(1679213) Maria Louise—
(See, *Library of Southern Literature,* Vol. II, p. 503.)

SMITH

(167922) MARY STUART HARRISON (1834-1917), the daughter of Dr. Gessner Harrison (16792), and wife Eliza Carter, married, July 31, 1853, Francis H. Smith, LL. D., professor of natural philosophy, of the University of Virginia. She died December 8, 1917. Dr. Smith and wife resided on West Lawn, at the University, where he died July 5, 1928, in his 99th year.

Francis H. Smith, was the son of Daniel Grove Smith, of Leesburg, Virginia, and wife Eleanor Buckley, of Frederick, Maryland. He was born at Leesburg, October 4, 1829, and was educated at Wesleyn College, Connecticut, and at the University of Virginia, graduating from the latter in 1851. For fifty three years he devoted his energies to the University, and was greatly respected, admired, and beloved, by the host of students who were privileged to attend his lectures. He has been aptly described as "a true type of Southern Chivalry," and as remarked by Prof. C. S. Mitchell, of Richmond College, in his sketch of him, he was "alike the priest of nature and the child-like servant of the church." At the outbreak of the War-between-the-States, he was elected by the Confederate Congress commissioner of weights and measures, in association with Commodore Matthew Maury. He was the author of *The Outlines of Physics,* and was a brilliant conversationalist, and an eloquent lecturer.

Dr. Francis H., and Mary Harrison Smith, had issue—

(1679221) Eliza Lewis Carter—d. Sept. 2, 1880; m. William W. Walker, of Westmoreland County, Virginia.

(1679222) ELEANOR ANNABEL—m. 1st, FIELDING MILES, of Blacksburg, Va. Issue—
1. Elsie—
m. 2nd, Dr. CHARLES W. KENT (decd.), Prof of English Literature, University of Va.; Editor of *The Library of Southern Literature.* Issue—
2. Eleanor—
(1679223) FRANCIS ALBERT—d. in infancy.
(1679224) MARIA d. in infancy.
(1679225) LELIA MARIA—d. ——; m. LUCIEN COCKE, of Roanoke, Va., President of Hollins College. Issue—
1. Francis—
2. Mary Stuart—
3. Lucien—
4. Janie—
(1679226) GESSNER HARRISON—d. Feb. 18, 1892. Grad. of law. Settled in Kansas City, Mo.
(1679227) SUMMERFIELD—d. in infancy.
(1679228) GEORGE TUCKER (M. D.)—Rear Admiral in U. S. Navy.
(1679229) MARY STUART—d. Oct. 15, 1900.
(1679230) ROSALIE—m. Jan. 24, 1899, Dr. ISAAC CARRINGTON HARRISON, of Danville, Va., descendant of the James River family. Issue—
1. Francis Henry (Rev.)—b. June 20, 1900.
2. Mary Stuart—b. Apr. 9, 1902.
3. Anne Carrington—b. July 18, 1904.
4. John Hartwell—b. Feb. 16, 1909.
5. Carrington—b. May 28, 1912.
(1679231) COURTNEY—d. in infancy.
(1679232) JAMES DUNCAN—b. 1879; d. Nov. 8, 1934; a noted painter, New York City.
(Dr. Smith, and wife, interred in University of Va. Cemetery. Splendid portrait of him in Cork & Curls, U. of Va., 1906. Obituary in *Charlottesville Progress,* July 6, 1928; also *Washington Post,* same date.)

(167923) GEORGE TUCKER HARRISON (1835-), the son of Dr. Gessner Harrison (16792), and wife Eliza Carter, married, October 18, 1865, Lelia Bell, daughter of William Bell, of Richmond, Virginia.

George T. Harrison studied civil engineering at the University of Virginia, and graduated therefrom in 1854. Two years later, he graduated from the same institution in medicine. He practiced for a time in St. Louis, Missouri, but returned to Virginia shortly before the War-between-the-States, and was among the first to offer his services to the Confederacy. He was appointed Assistant Surgeon, and afterwards Surgeon, serving to the close of the war. In 1868, he removed to New York City, and for fifteen years served on the staff of the Woman's Hospital as assistant surgeon. He then began a general practice of medicine in the city. He was president of the New York County Medical Association in 1890, and of the New York Obstetrical Society in 1892. In the noted work of Kelly and Burrage, he is described as "an eminent gynacologist, boon companion, raconteur, and wit."

Issue—
(1679231) GESSNER—Physican, New York City.
(1679232) LELIA BELL—
(1679233) ELIZABETH MITCHELL—m. June 15, 1897, WILLIAM HOLDING ECHOLS, Professor of Mathematics, University of Virginia, b. 1860, d. Sept. 25, 1934. Issue—

1. Lilly—
2. Marion Patton—(Lieut.) of West Point.
3. Gessner Harrison—of Freeport, Texas.
4. Robert Lewis—of Princeton, N. J.

(See, *National Cyclopeadia of American Biography,* Vol. 12, p. 136; also *Dictionary of American Medical Biography,* by Drs. Kelly and Burrage, 1928, p. 534; *Boogher,* p. 377; *Washington Post,* Sept. 27, 1934.)

(167925) PEACHY GESSNER HARRISON (1839-), the son of Dr. Gessner Harrison (16792), and wife Eliza Carter, married Julia Riddick. They settled in Richmond, Virginia, where he engaged in business, and in 1902 was holding a Federal position. Issue—

(1679251) EDWARD—
(1679252) GESSNER—
(1679253) LEWIS—(student, Univ. of Va., 1903.)
(1679254) JULIA PEACHY—b. ——.
(All born in Richmond.)

THORNTON

(167928) ELEANOR ROSALIE HARRISON (1847-1920), the daughter of Dr. Gessner Harrison (16792), and wife Eliza Carter, married, December 22, 1874, William Mynn Thornton, (LL. D.), who, the following year, entered upon his brilliant career, as Professor of Applied Mathematics at the University of Virginia—for fifty years; the last twenty-one of which he was Dean of the Engineering Department. He and his wife resided on Monroe Hill, at the University, where he continues to reside.

William Mynn Thornton was born in Cumberland County, Virginia, October 28, 1851, the son of Col. John Thurston Thornton, (C. S. A.). He graduated from Hampden-Sidney College, in 1868 (A. B.), and from the University of Virginia, in 1870. From 1871 to 1873, he pursued special engineering studies at Virginia. He was professor at Davidson College, N. C., from 1874 to 1875, and in the latter year joined the faculty of the University of Virginia. From 1888 to 1896, he was chairman of the faculty. In 1900, he was United States Commissioner to the International Exposition at Paris, France, and in 1904, was a member of the Jury of Awards, Civil Engineering, at the St. Louis Exposition. For several years he was the editor of the *Annals of Mathematics.* He is a member of the American Society of Mechanical Engineers, and a LL.D. of Hampden-Sydney. He married, second, July 30, 1921, Gertrude Waller Massie, of Charlottesville, Virginia.

Dr. William M. and wife Eleanor Rosalie Thornton, had issue—

(1679281)—JOHN T.—Physician, Wheeling, West Virginia.
(1679282) ELIZA CARTER—m. Prof. Thurman, of the Univ. of Va.
(1679283) ELEANOR ROSALIE—Resident of Boston, Mass.

(1679284) Janet—Resident of Boston, Mass.

(1679285) William Mynn, Jr.—(class of 1908, Univ. of Va.), Resident of Syracuse (?), New York.

(1679286) Charles Edward—Resident of South America.

(Locations of 3rd, 4th, and 6th, 1920.)

(See, *Who's Who in America*, Vol. 15, 1928-29; also obituary of Mrs. Thornton in *Charlottesville Progress*, Apr. 8, 1920.)

---

3. LINE OF DR. PEACHY RUSH HARRISON

WILLIAMSON

(167981) MINNIE LYNN HARRISON (1850-1923), the daughter of Dr. Peachy Rush Harrison (16798), and wife Mary Rhodes, married, November 2, 1874, Matthew White Williamson, the eldest son of Major J. D. Williamson, of Rockingham, and wife Martha, nee White. They resided in New Market, Shenandoah County, Virginia, in the residence formerly occupied by her mother. The property is immediately on "The Long Grey Trail."

Upon the death of Dr. Peachy Rush Harrison, of Harrisonburg, his widow took their two daughters to the home of her father, William Rhodes, of "Midway," Albemarle County, Virginia, where the children grew up. Minnie Lynn early showed promise of intellectual gifts, and during the last year of the War-between-the-States was sent to a private school in Farmville, Virginia. Here, the last tides of the war, in surging around the village, left indelible impressions upon her memory. Many of her experiences of the time, she later included in her sketches and stories. In the lean years following the war, the professors of the University of Virginia supplemented their salaries by tutoring, thus it came about that Minnie Lynn Harrison was received as a student in the home of Dr. Francis H. Smith, who had married her cousin. (See above.) She delighted in recalling in after years her "attendance at the University," then a strictly men's school. Truly, "she had her Latin and French and mathematics under great teachers." During this time, she was confirmed in the Episcopal Church, departing somewhat from the Methodist traditions of her family.

In 1867, her mother settled with her, and her sister, in New Market. After a year of apprentice teaching in the village seminary, she attended the famous Powell school in Richmond, from which she returned to New Market, to pursue the profession of teaching. From this time on, the remainder of her life was spent as a resident of the town. She was a true instructor of youth, "and stood worthily in the line of teachers from which she came." Following her marriage, she continued at intervals her profession, but about 1890, turned in her spare time to writing.

Under her pen name of Mary L. Williamson, she published the *Life of Gen. Robert E. Lee for Children*, and within the next twelve years followed this with the lives of Stonewall Jackson, and J. E. B. Stuart, and finally a life of George Washington. Her vivid historical portraits belong among the classics for children, and their widespread use as texts attests the value of her contribution to education. She was a faithful leader in the "Women's Memorial Society of the Lost Cause," and served as its president for more than thirty years.

Her death occurred February 6, 1923. Says the *Shenandoah Valley* of February 15th, 1923. "In Memoriam," "her richly stored mind, her tender sympathies, the freshness of her interest in everything, from home concerns to world politics, and her unselfish devotions made her a rare companion in all the walks of life. She will long be remembered in the light of her social circle . . . As a teacher and historian of the Confederacy, and friend of all, Mrs. Williamson belongs to the community she so faithfully served."

M. White Williamson, was born April 24, 1845, at the old Williamson homestead, "Hardscrabble," on the Valley Pike, a short distance south of New Market. His father was of Huguenot ancestry. The first of the name to settle in the Valley, came in from New Jersey. M. White, or "Squire Williamson," as he was affectionately called in his later life, was for many years mayor of New Market—finally refusing to run for office longer. He frequently served as auctioneer, and was a widely known and successful farmer. He was educated at Virginia Military Institute, Lexington, Virginia, from which he resigned in his second year, at the age of seventeen, to enter the Confederate Army. He was a member of Company F., First Virginia Cavalry, under J. E. B. Stuart's command, and served with Lee at Gettysburg, and at Appomattox. Following the war, he spent several years in Texas before settling in New Market. He was a confirmed member of the Episcopal Church, and for the last eight years of his life was Commander of Neff-Rice Camp of Confederate Veterans. He died at his home in New Market, September 13, 1930.

Matthew White Williamson, and wife Minnie Lynn, had issue—

(1679811) Mary—b. Aug. 15, 1876; (unmarried,) Dean of Hollins College, Hollins, Virginia.

(1679812) Rush Harrison—b. Mar. 30, 1878; d. July 13, 1932; m. Ruth Edwards, of Providence, R. I., May 16, 1916. Resided in Washington, D. C. Asst. to Attorney Gen. U. S., under Pres. Wilson.

(1679813) Martha White—b. Jan. 23, 1880; (unmarried), Resides in New Market, in the former home of her parents.

(1679814) Isabel Hereford—b. June 2, 1888; m. 1909, Keyser Price, son of Capt. Berryman Z. Price, of near New Market. Resides a short distance west of town. Issue—

1. William Keyser, Jr.—b. Jan. 20, 1911. Resides in Waynesboro, Va.

---

2. LINE OF FIELDING HARRISON

3. LINE OF PEYTON L. HARRISON

ELY

(168013) SARAH M. HARRISON ( ), the daughter of Peyton L. Harrison (16801), and wife Elizabeth, married Amos Ely, a native of Philadelphia, Pennsylvania. They resided in Chicago, where both were living in 1873. Issue—

(1680131) Harry—d. aged about 6 years.

(1680132) Albert—

probably others.

(168014) P. QUINN HARRISON (1837-), the son of Peyton L. Harrison (16801), and wife Elizabeth, married, June 4, 1867 Emeline. L. Lamothe, of Alton, Illinois. They resided two miles east of Pleasant Plains, in Sangamon County, Illinois. Issue—

(1680141) Luella—

probably others.

(168016) PETER L. HARRISON ( ), the son of Peyton L. Harrison (16801), and wife Elizabeth, married Elizabeth F. Cartwright, of Sangamon County, Illinois, a kinswoman of his mother. They resided near Pleasant Plains in Sangamon, and had issue two or more children, of whom no further record.

BERRY

(168017) EMILY W. HARRISON ( ), the daughter of Peyton L. Harrison (16801), and wife Elizabeth, married Benjamin Berry, of Morgan County, Illinois. They resided at Pleasant Plains in Sangamon. Issue—

(1680171) Eva May—
probably others.

---

3. LINE OF SIMEON Q. HARRISON

CASSELL

(168053) JENNIE E. HARRISON (1850), the daughter of Simeon Q. Harrison (16805), and wife Mary, married, December 24, 1868, Frank Cassell, a practicing attorney-at-law of Peoria, Illinois. Issue—

(1680531) S. Quinn—
probably others.

HOPPER

(168055) IDA V. HARRISON ( ), the daughter of Simeon Q. Harrison, (16805), and wife Mary, married Andrew Hopper, of Illinois, now deceased. Issue—

(1680551) Harrison—
(1680552) Mary—

---

2. LINE OF WILLIAM HARRISON

3. LINE OF JAMES HARRISON

VAN VORHEES

(168131) VIRGINIA HARRISON (1838-), the daughter of James Harison (16813), and wife Martha Jane, married Edward Ludlow Van Vorhees, a native of New York. Their surviving children in 1914 were—

(1681311) James (M. D.)—m. Clara Graves. Residence, Los Angeles, Cal.
Issue—
1. Lewis—
(1681312) Cornelia—m. Daniel A. Kreamer. (no issue.)
(1681313) Belle—m. DANIEL WALSH, of California.
Issue—
1. Virginia—
2. Norman—
3. Ivan—

(J. B. to D. S. H., 3-30, 1914.)

END OF RECORD OF CLAN OF CAPT. DANIEL HARRISON

CLAN OF THOMAS HARRISON

1. LINE OF EZEKIEL HARRISON

2. LINE OF JESSE HARRISON

3. LINE OF REV. ANDREW MONROE

DENNIS

(177111) MARGARET MONROE ( ), the daughter of Rev. Andrew Monroe, and wife Emily (17711), nee Harrison, married Edward H. Dennis, resident of Howard County, Missouri. Issue—

(1771111) SUSAN (M. D.)—m. Louis H. Hicks (decd.)
(See page 482.)

---

2. LINE OF REUBEN HARRISON

3. LINE OF GEORGE M. HARRISON

ELLIOTT

(177221) ANNA AMANTHA HARRISON (1841-), the daughter of Dr. George M. Harrison (17722), and wife Maria, (17842), nee Houston, married, June 7, 1866, in Virginia, Frank W. Elliott. They resided in Cartwright township, Sangamon County, Illinois, where both were living in 1873. They later removed to Chicago, Ill. Issue—

(1772211) GEORGE— d. ——
(1772212) IRENE H.—
(1772213) CHARLES E.—
(1772214) WILLIAM H.—

HODGEN

(177224) EMMA E. HARRISON (1849-), the daughter of Dr. George M. Harrison (17722), and wife Mary, married, March 28, 1872, Philip Oscar Hodgen, native of Iowa, (see page 483), and resident of Petersburg, Menard County, Illinois. Issue—

(1772241) WILLIAM O.—
(1772242) CLARA M.—
probably others.

BEEKMAN

(177225) M. JENNIE HARRISON (1850-), the daughter of Dr. George M. Harrison (17722), and wife Mary, married, December 26, 1872, George S. Beekman, resident of Tallula, Menard County, Illinois. Issue—

(1772251) HARRY J.—b. 1874, c.
probably others.

BEEKMAN

(177226) JULIA S. HARRISON (1852 c.-1875), the daughter of Dr. George

M. Harrison (17722), and wife Mary, married, January 1, 1874, in Sangamon County, Illinois, William E. Beekman, of Sangamon. Issue—

(1772261) EDWARD J.—b. 1875.

---

1. LINE OF REUBEN HARRISON
2. LINE OF REV. WILLIAM HOUSTON
3. LINE OF THEODORE N. JORDAN

McCREARY

(178431) BELLE J. JORDAN (1846-1931), the daughter of Theodore N. Jordan, and wife Amantha (17843), nee Houston, married, first, about 1865, John (Jack) C. McCreary, of Harrisonburg, Virginia, born March 28, 1839. For a brief time following their marriage, they resided at Smithland, the home of her aunt, where she had spent a part of her girlhood years, and where they were living in November 1873. Mr. McCreary later returned to Harrisonburg, and subsequently he and his wife removed to California, she first. Somewhat late in life they were legally seperated. He returned to Virginia, and died at Harrisonburg, April 9, 1919. She married, second, in September 1907, James B. Wyatt, of Escondido, California, in which city she died, July 21, 1931, subsequent to Mr. Wyatt's death.

John C. McCreary, and wife Belle Jordan, had issue—

(1784311) STUART DOUGLAS—m. in Texas, Johnnie Clyde Fike. Resides in Chico, California. Issue—
1. Stuart Douglas, Jr.—
2. Harold Wyatt—

(1784312) THEODORE—d. in infancy.

(Dates of John C. McCreary's birth and death, from marker in Woodbine Cemetery, Harrisonburg, Va. He was a former Confederate soldier.)

(178432) THEODORE AUGUSTUS HOUSTON JORDAN (1852-1919), the son of Theodore N. Jordan, and wife Amantha (17843), nee Houston, married Claddie Wilson, the daughter of William Miller Wilson (b. May 18, 1828, d. Nov. 16, 1885), and wife, Catherine Hanger (b. Jan. 11, 1829, d. Dec. 16, 1898), the great-granddaughter of Rev. William Wilson, the second pastor of Old Stone Church, (1780-1810), of Fort Defiance, Augusta County, Virginia.

Theodore Jordan was a prominent farmer and business man of Augusta County. For a time, as a young man, he was manager of the Smithland estate. (See page 411.) He and his wife resided at "Mt. Airy," the homestead of her ancestors, at Ft. Defiance, where she died, November 26, 1932. The property, a valuable farm, and handsome brick residence, is located on the eastern or opposite side of "The Long Grey Trail" from the church. The land borders the highway for a distance. The old log house built by Rev. Wilson stood about on the spot of the present residence, and was burned in 1877. Thomas Poage Wilson, the son of Rev. William, was the second of the line to reside there, and was in turn followed by his son, William Miller Wilson, above.

It was Rev. Norvell Wilson, a double first cousin of Thomas Poage Wilson, and nephew of Rev. William Wilson, from whom Theodore Norvell Jordan, the father of Theodore A. H. Jordan, took his middle name. (See page 484.)

Theodore A. H. Jordan, and wife Claddie, nee Wilson, had issue—

(1684321) EDNA WILSON—b. Mar. 13, 1879; d. Aug. 30, 1879.

(1784322) BRUCE—b. Aug. 6, 1883; d. Mar. 10, 1897.
(1784323) BERNICE—(twin of Bruce) resides at Mt. Airy, as above.
(1784324) THEODORE MILLER—b. Feb. 1889; d. aged seven months.
(1784325) CLAUDE WILSON—b. Aug. 22, 1891; m. Oct. 1, 1917, Violet Watson, dau. of Charles Summerville and Dora Effie Hall Watson, of Mt. Sidney. Resides at "Mt. Airy." Issue—

1. Catherine Augustus—b. Sept. 25, 1919.
2. Claude Wilson, (Jr.)—b. Oct. 7, 1921.
3. Charles Watson—b. Oct. 10, 1923.

---

3. LINE OF SAMUEL BOWMAN

(178441) JOHN ROBERT KYLE BOWMAN (1849-), the son of Samuel Bowman, and wife Alscinda (17844), nee Houston, married, first, Nancy E. S. Harrison (1211247), the daughter of Abraham Harrison, and wife Delilah. (See page 497.) They resided in Salem, Virginia, where she died March 4, 1900. He married, second, Lottie ——— (now Mrs. Strickler), who survives him.

Issue—

By first wife, Nancy, nee Harrison—

(1784411) JENNINGS—(decd.)
(1784412) CHARLOTTE—d. Sept. 25, 1907, unmarried.
(1784413) DOROTHY (Dot)—d. ——, (prior to Charlotte's decease.)
(1784414) GEORGE—m. 1st, Lila——. She d. Oct. 25, 1914.

Issue—

1. Clifford—
2. Irene—

m. 2nd, Lucy ———. Issue—

1. George, Jr.—
2. Merle—(a daughter.)
3. Robert—

(1784415) HELLER—(unmarried.)

By second wife, Lottie,

(1784416) ROBERT—
(1784417) BRUCE—
(1784418) MARY—
(Last five residents of Salem, Virginia.)

(178443) WILLOUGHBY N. T. BOWMAN (1854-1930), the son of Samuel Bowman, and wife Alscinda (17844), nee Houston, born in Rockingham County, Virginia, removed to Denver, Colorado, where he died July 6, 1930. He married, following his settlement in Colorado, Jennie Woodward. Issue—

(1784431) ORA—m. Judge JULIAN MOORE, of Denver.

Issue—

1. Martha Lee—
2. Margery—

(1784432) BRUCE—m. Clee Hickman, of Denver. He died July, 1934.
(1784433) CLAUDE—
(1784434) (a son)—

3. LINE OF JOHN W. C. HOUSTON

HUFFMAN

(178451) MARY MATTHEWS HOUSTON (1854-1913), the daughter of John W. C. Houston (17845), and wife Rachel, married, October 29, 1885, in Rockingham County, Virginia, at the home of her sister, Mrs. David W. Harrison, William D. Huffman, of Page County, Virginia, born on February 19, 1861, the son of Joseph Huffman, (b. June 8, 1813, d. June 8, 1872), and wife Mary Ann Hershberger, (b. Nov. 14, 1819 d. July 4, 1914.)

William D. Huffman is a widely connected and well to do farmer, of the Hawksbill neighborhood, to the south of Luray. His father was a descendant of Frederick Huffman, before named. (See page 485.)

Mary Houston Huffman died January 11, 1913. From childhood she was a member of the Methodist church; the faith of her mother. "She led a beautiful Christian life," says a more extended account of her decease, in the *Page Valley Courier*, "and her many virtues and amiable qualities won her the love and esteem of a wide circle."

On March 10, 1915, Mr. Huffman married, second, Mary Ellen Varner, his former wife's first cousin, the daughter of Ambrose B. Varner, (1817-1872), and wife Mary Jane, (1830-1907), nee Huffman. Ambrose and Mary had children a son Edgar, (1863-1930), and two daughters, the other daughter being Elizabeth, the wife of Edgar Huffman, a relative of William D., also resident of Page.

William D. Huffman, and wife Mary Houston, had issue—

(1784511) Zola Estell—b. Sept. 22, 1887; m. Apr. 18, 1923, Charles Weldon Wampler, of Rockingham, the son of John Wampler, (as his 2nd wife.) Residence, near Dayton, Va. Mr. Wampler is a prominent farmer and business man of Harisonburg, and was formerly Farm Demonstrator for the county of Rockingham. Issue—

1. Zola—b. Jan. 19, 1926.
2. William David—b. Apr. 9, 1928.
3. Donald Houston—b. Jan. 12, 1930.

(1784512) Mary Catherine—b. Sept. 6, 1888; d. Sept. 27, 1888.
(1784513) Joseph Clark—b. Nov. 20, 1889; d. June 10, 1890.
(1784514) Edna Blanch—b. Apr. 9, 1894; d. July 5, 1894.
(1784515) Guy William—b. Mar. 23, 1896; d. Oct. 24, 1918, unmarried.
(1784516) Benton Houston—b. July 13, 1899; d. June 4, 1933, unmarried. Killed in automobile accident, Washington, D. C.

(Mrs. Mary Huffman, and the last five above named children, interred in the Huffman family cemetery, on the Hawksbill.)

(178452) ANNA AMANTHA HOUSTON (1856-1921), the daughter of John W. C. Houston (17845), and wife Rachel, married David W. Harrison (125915), the son of John Harrison. See Clan of John Harrison, 1. Line of Capt. Reuben Harrison, 2. Line of David Harrison, 3. Line of John Harrison. (Page 512.)

ROWLES

(178454) JULIA JANETTA HOUSTON (1861-1924), the daughter of John W. C. Houston (17845), and wife Rachel, married Isaac E. Rowles, of Fairfield County, Ohio. They resided for a time near North Berne, where he owned a valuable farm, and later moved to Ada, the seat of Ohio Northern University, in order to better educate their children. While a student at the University, the daughter, a talented musican, died, after which they removed to near Vallery, Colorado, where first the son, and a short time later the husband, died. Upon the latter's death, the broken hearted widow returned to Virginia. She died at the home of Mr. William D. Huffman, above named, in November, 1924.

Isaac E. Rowles, and wife Julia Houston, had issue—

(1784541) Lola C.—b. Apr. 6, 1887; d. Jan. 26, 1908, unmarried.

(1784542) Houston—b. June 6, 1891, at Pleasantville, O.; d. Mar. 22, 1910.

(All interred in the family plot in Forest Rose Cemetery, Lancaster, Ohio.)

Grove

GROVE

(178456) NANCY CLARK A. C. HOUSTON (1868-1905), the daughter of John W. C. Houston (17845), and wife Rachel, married, in Fairfield County, Ohio, September 16, 1891, Frank Green Grove, (b. Oct. 10, 1867, d. Jan. 19, 1932), of Page County, Virginia, a prominent resident of Luray, son of the late John Pendleton Grove, and wife Rebecca Varner, daughter of Ambrose Varner, Sr.

The Groves, as also the Varners and Huffmans, have long been numerous and influential in Page, and are descended from early settlers there. Their ancestral lands are found scattered along the fertile region of the Hawksbill, where many of the present day descendants continue to reside, in the main faithful adherents to the Baptist traditions of their forefathers.

Frank G. Grove was for more than forty years, a leading business man of Luray, and was one of the most popular citizens of Page. He was educated at Richmond College, and early joined his father in the coal, grain, and feed business. He handled a large part of the wheat of the county, and sold a major part of the farming and threshing machinery disposed of in Page, He was a pioneer distributor of oils and gasoline. He was a Knight Templar, and for a time served on the town council of Luray.

Clark Grove, as she was familiarily known to her intimates, was a woman of charming personality, and was much beloved by a large circle of friends. She was a devoted wife and mother, and as her sisters, was from girlhood a member of the Methodist Church; she Mary, and Anna, of the M. E. Church, South.

With her and her husband resided Mrs. Murphy, her sister, during the greater part of the latter's widowhood, and until her marriage to Rev. Kitchen.

Frank G. Grove, and wife, Clark Houston, had issue—

(1784561) Earl Green—b. July 21, 1892; m. Oct. 20, 1914, Blanche Rebecca Bell, of Luray, dau. of Solon Bell. Resides in Luray. Issue—

1. Dorothy Earl—b. June 15, 1917; m. Nov. 16, 1934, Richard Berryman Newman, son of Edgar W. Newman of Woodstock, Virginia. (See Chapter XXV.)

(1784562) Vivien Catherine—b. Sept. 21, 1897; m. Sept. 1, 1934, David Clodfelter, of Washington, D. C.

END OF RECORD OF CLAN OF THOMAS HARRISON

CLAN OF CAPT ROBERT CRAVENS

1. LINE OF JOHN CRAVENS
2. LINE OF REV. WILLIAM CRAVENS
3. LINE OF JOHN CRAVENS

(141421) JAMES ADDISON CRAVENS (1818-1893), the son of John Cravens (14142), and wife Ann, born in Rockingham County, Virginia, was elected a Democrat to the Thirty-seventh and Thirty-eighth Congresses of the United States, from Indiana, serving from March 4, 1861 to March 3, 1865; throughout the period of the War-between-the-States. (See introduction to Chapter XXII.)

In 1820, as a child, James A. Cravens moved with his parents from Rockingham, to Madison Township, Washington County, Indiana, where he attended the public schools. He settled near Hardinsburg, and engaged in agricultural pursuits and stock raising. During the war with Mexico he served as a Major of the Second Indiana Volunteers, in 1846 and 1847. He was a member of the State house of representatives in 1848 and 1849, and of the State senate 1850-1853. In 1854 he was commissioned Brigadier General of the militia. Following his second term in Congress, he was not a candidate for renomination. He was a delegate, in 1866, to the Union National Convention of Conservatives at Philadelphia, and two years thereafter, to the Democratic National Convention at New York. On retirement from public life he resumed farming pursuits. He died in Hardinsburg, June 20, 1893, and was interred in Hardin Cemetery.

About 1843, James A. Cravens married Susan Hardin, the daughter of Aaron and Sarah (Letherman) Hardin. Aaron Hardin was a wealthy landowner, and sponsor of the Methodist Church in the Hardinsburg community. He was from North Carolina.

James A. Cravens, and wife Susan, nee Hardin, had issue—

(1414211) AARON ASBURY—b. July 26, 1844; d. Nov. 26, 1926; m. Aug. 30, 1873, Rebecca Ella Schwartz.—"when his father went to Congress Aaron went to College, 'till 1864—Bloomington College; studied law, and edited a paper." Issue—

1. Frank—b. 1874; d. 1905.
2. James Addison—b. 1876, resides at North Henderson, Illinois.
3. Harry B.—b. 1878, resides in Pe Ell, Washington.
4. Anna—b. 1879, m. Mahlon Coombs. She, a widow, resides in New Albany, Indiana.
5. Martha—b. 1881, resides at Indiana Central College, Indianapolis.
6. Virginia—b. 1884, Dean of Women, Indiana Central College.
7. George—b. 1886, resides at Hammond, Ind.

(1414212) BENJAMIN HARRISON—b. 1846; m. 1st, Susan McIntosh; m. 2nd, Parthenia Harvey Cravens, widow of Frank Cravens; no issue. Resides in Hardinsburg, Indiana.

(1414213) MARGARET ELLEN—d. in infancy.

(1414214) VIRGINIA E.—m. WILLIAM DAVIS. She, a widow resides in Hardinsburg, Ind. Issue—

1. Susie—m. Dr. W. E. Patton, of Orleans, Ind.
2. Elizabeth—m. Fred Summers, of Hardinsburg, Ind.

3. Harriett—m. Claude Radcliffe, of Hardinsburg.
4. Nelle—m. Reare Phillipps, of New Albany, Ind.
5. Frances—m. Alvin Hancock, of Hardinsburg.

(1414215) ANNA—d. in young womanhood.

(1414216) JOHN ROBERT—m. 1st, Matilda McIntosh, (three children, all died in infancy), m., 2nd, Macey Henry. Resides in Hardinsburg, Ind.

(1414217) SUSAN—m. JOHN WILLIAM LAPPING, of Hardinsburg, Ind. Issue—

1. Ray—m. Alice Bullington, resides in Paoli, Ind.
2. Edward—m. Verle Lewelling, resides in Mitchell, Ind.
3. Helen—m. Victor Davis, of Hammond, Ind.
4. Mildred—m. Raymond Burgess, of Paoli, Ind.

(1414218) ELLA—b. 1861; m. 1st, Dr. H. C. Foutz; m. 2nd, T. L. Hammond, of Salem, Ind., no children.

---

2. LINE OF DR. JOSEPH CRAVENS

3. LINE OF DR. ROBERT CRAVENS

(141521) JOHN ROBERT CRAVENS (1819-1899), the son of Dr. Robert Cravens (14152), and wife Sarah, nee Paul and the grandson of the founder of Madison, Indiana, was born in Madison, November 22, 1819. He died at his hill top residence, "Fairmount," in the suburbs of the city, March 22, 1899, a distinguished Indianian, and for many years one of Madison's foremost citizens. As State Senator during the incumbency of Gov. Harry S. Lane, when the latter was elected to the U. S. Senate, 1861, leaving his office to be filled by Lieut. Governor Morton, Senator Cravens thereupon became acting Lieut. Governor. He served until 1863, in which year he entered the Union Army as disbursing officer with the rank of Major. After the war he was again reelected to the State senate, and following his retirement in 1870, was appointed judge of the Jefferson Circuit Court.

As a youth, John R. Cravens attended the State University, graduating at the age of nineteen. He read law in Madison in the office of Joseph G. Marshall. For some years he was associated with W. W. Page, Sr., in milling, but their property burned to the ground. About this time he was elected president of the Madison & Indianapolis Railway Company and of the Shelbyville & Columbus Railway, continuing in office until the reorganization of the properties, when he voluntarily resigned to become editor and proprietor of the Madison Banner, an organ of the Whigs. He was a brilliant and versatile writer, but finding the vexations of journalistic life not to his liking soon retired. Upon the slavery question becoming an issue, he took a bold and aggressive position, and was an outspoken free-soiler. As a natural born orator, of superb voice and fine scholarship, he had no superior on the stump. He was an irresistable campaigner, and as one of the organizers of the Republican party, became a leader.

He was a member of the State senate, 1856-7, 1860, and 1866-70, "and," remarks an authority, "his influence was paramount." During the Horace Greely movement, he became a Liberal Republican, and was placed on the ticket as a Democratic candidate for Lieut. Governor. The year thereafter, he was appointed to the Bench, serving an unexpired term. A memorial, adopted by the Madison Bar, 11th April, 1899, in marking his passing, testifies eloquently, that "he possessed the confidence of the entire Bar, and his decisions and opinions were characterized by that moderation, honesty, practical common sense, justice and wisdom with which he discharged every public office duty. He was a just Judge." He served his city as school trustee for a number of years, and was trustee of the State University, and of Hanover College. In 1858 he became a member of the Presbyterian Church. "He was a gentleman of the old school," says a more extended account of his decease, "and in him was mirrored the stately courtesy, the quiet dignity and the cordial hospitality of the olden-time Virginian."

Judge Cravens married, in 1844, Drusilla Lanier, the daughter of James F. D. Lanier, and (first) wife. She was one of the belles and beauties of Madison, and retained her beauty to the hour of her death, which occurred a few years following that of her husband, as she neared the age of eighty.

LANIER

James Franklin Doughty Lanier, (b. 1800, d. Aug. 29, 1881), a native of Washington, Beauford County, North Carolina, was a prominent banker of Madison, and later one of the leading financiers of the country. He moved to Madison at the age of seventeen with his father, who in the War of 1812 was Major of "Lanier's Independent Battalion Ohio Militia." The family was originally a Virginia one, the immigrant, John Lanier, having settled in Virginia some time prior to 1676, when his name appears on the records. Two of his sons, Sampson and Robert, married Elizabeth and Priscilla, the daughters of Richard Washington. James Lanier, Sr., the great-grandfather of James F. D., served in the Colonial wars and was a member of the Provincial legislature of North Carolina. Becoming interested in raidroad financing, James F. D. Lanier settled in 1848 in New York City, where with Richard H. Winslow, in 1849, he founded the well known Wall Street banking firm of Winslow Lanier & Co. It was he, who, during the War-between-the-States, did so much in sustaining Gov. Morton of Indiana, with money and influence, in holding the State true to the Union cause. His old home at Madison, designed and built for him, by the architect Francis Costigan, 1843-4, one of the finest residences of its day, in the West, and now known as "The James F. D. Lanier Home," has been recently acquired by the State of Indiana, restored, and set apart as a memorial to him.

* * * * * *

Of a gentle, unassuming and truly charitable disposition, Drusilla Lanier Cravens was ever ready to assist in any undertaking that would relieve suffering, or help the needy. In her death Madison lost one of its most charitable and beloved ladies. She was the first president and organizer of the Drusilla Home for old and infirm ladies, at Madison, an institution christened in her honor a short time before her death, and was a liberal patron of the King's Daughters Hospital, also of Madison, the building of which she donated.

Judge John R., and Drusilla Lanier Cravens, had issue—

(1415211) John Paul—d. (prior to 1899.)
(1415212) Robert—d. (after 1899, and prior to his mother's death.)
(1415213) James Lainer—(decd.)
(1415214) Alexander—(decd.)
(1415215) William Jackson—resides in Madison.
(1415216) Elizabeth Gardner—m. W. R. DAVIDSON, (both deceased.)
Issue—
1. William—b. 1928, ("Billiy," now a ward of Miss Drusilla Cravens, below.)

(1415217) Charles L.—resides in Madison.
(1415218) Joseph Marshall—resides in Madison—see below.
(1415219) Mary Louise—m. John Sage, (both deceased.)
(1415220) Drusilla Lanier—resides in Madison—see below.
(1415221) Franklin—(decd.)
(1415222) Margaret—d. in infancy.
(All but the first two, and the last two, surviving children at the time of their mother's death.)

* * * * * *

Of the above—

JOSEPH MARSHALL CRAVENS, in 1902 was elected to the house of representatives of Indiana, and, aside from two intermissions, remained constantly a member of the legislature from then until his recent retirement, in 1930, as State Senator. In 1907, he did not run, and in 1915, he was defeated. He entered the Senate in 1919. Says the *Madison Courier,* of March 29, 1930, in quoting the *Indianapolis News,* regarding his retirement—"Joseph M. Cravens, or Uncle Joe, as he is familiarily known, is definitely out of the active participation in politics for the first time in more than thirty years. Although the veteran legislator from Madison has sung his "swan-song" on other occasions he insists that this time he means it and has rejected all efforts to induce him to become the democratic candidate for state senator from Ohio, Switzerland, Jefferson, and Clark counties, a district he represented for years in the state senate . . . Uncle Joe, on a visit to Indianapolis, Wednesday, explained that his retirement was permanent and that he intended to spend his days on his farm in the hills above Madison. 'What is the use of being a legislator any longer?' he said, 'All the legislative power has been delegated to boards and commissions."

* * * * * *

Cravens Lanier

DRUSILLA LANIER CRAVENS, worthily named for her mother, through her generosity made possible the taking over by Indiana of her grandfather's home, at Madison, as a State Memorial. When James F. D. Lanier ceased to be a resident of the city, his unmarried children continued to occupy his home for a time, after which his eldest son, Alexander C. Lanier, succeeded to it by deed of gift, November 18, 1861. The latter resided there until his death, October 11, 1895. His widow died a few years later. There being no children, and his death removing the last male representative of his family from the State, the property gradually lapsed from its former magnificence, and more than once narrowly escaped being razed. The place however was retained by the heirs, and in 1918, Mr. Charles Lanier, the last surviving son of the original owner, acquired it, and presented it outright to the Jefferson County Historical Society, with the proviso, that should the society fail to maintain it for historical purposes, "it would revert to his niece, Drusilla Cravens." It proved too large a holding for the society to keep up. Definite steps were then taken by the Society of Indiana Pioneers, and other historical agencies, in the direction of State aid, with the concurrence of the Jefferson County society and Miss Cravens, who announced their willingness to surrender their respective interests in the title.

"Justice and courtesy demands," says Geo. S. Cottman, in his splendidly illustrated booklet descriptive of the memorial, "the acknowledgement in this brocure of the debt that is due to Miss Drusilla Lanier Cravens, granddaughter of J. F. D. Lanier. In the rehabilition of the place as a Memorial Home the nice task of finding, choosing and securing the furnishings, and of their arrangement within the house has been left to her. She, far beyond any one else, was the logical person to undertake it, by reason of her expert judgement in such matters, her unflagging zeal and her natural interest as a scion of the family. Unwittingly the result is also a memorial to her taste. In addition to her services as above she has given outright to the collection many treasured family possessions. Last, but not least, she made the gift to the place possible by freely surrendering all right and title to a valuable piece of property to which she had claim under the conditions . . . . stated." (See, *James F. D. Lanier Home, An Indiana Memorial*, pub. by the Dept. of Conservation, of Ind.)

Both Miss Cravens and her sister, Mrs. Elizabeth G. Davidson, contributed liberally to the furnishings of the home, two interesting details, in this connection, occurring in the halls—not to mention other rooms—one being a linen coverlet, furnished by the former, for the small day-bed in the alcove of the upper hall, the other being a tall grandfather's clock, furnished by the latter, for the lower hall. The coverlet was woven of flax spun by Miss Cravens' own hands on the small German wheel in the northwest bed-room. The clock was brought to this country from England by a Lanier, and has been in the family for generations.

Miss Cravens is versatile and highly talented. She is a prominent and much esteemed resident of Madison, where she and several of her elder bachelor brothers make their home together on the hill top overlooking the beautiful Ohio. She is an enthusiastic historian, and antiquarian, and has conducted much research in connection with the history of her country and of its early families, regarding which she is a discriminating authority, with a true instinct for accuracy and thoroughness. Her data includes many valuable records also touching on the history of her own family.

---

3. LINE OF DR. JOHN CRAVENS

WIRT

(141431) MARY ELIZABETH CRAVENS (1822-1868), the daughter of Dr. John Cravens (14153), and wife Ruhama, married, April 23, 1842, at Gallatin, Missouri, Philip Richard Wirt (1815-1866), a merchant of Gallatin, and native of Kentucky, son of John Wirt and wife Mary Simms, married in Kentucky. They resided in Gallatin, where she died, March 1, 1868.

Phillip Richard Wirt, and wife Mary Cravens, had issue—

(1415311) Mary Ruhama—b. April 24, 1843; m. Sept. 3, 1862, THOMAS JOHNSON BROWN, b. Sept. 3, 1832, d. Jan. 14, 1886. Resident of Gallatin, Missouri. Issue—

1. Maggie—b. June 10, 1864; m. June 10, 1890, THOMAS J. RAY, b. Jan. 23, 1864. Issue—
    1. Mildred—b. Apr. 14, 1891; d. Jan. 1893.
    2. Rowena—b. Oct. 24, 1893.
2. Bessie—b. June 20, 1867.
3. Corrinne—b. Jan. 25, 1870.
4. Ethel—b. Mar. 21, 1872.
5. Winnifred—b. Sept. 9, 1877.
6. Benjamin Wirt—b. Oct. 5, 1879.
7. Roe—b. Sept. 12, 1884.

(1415312) William Edward—b. Sept. 8, 1847; m. Jan 8, 1873, Ella Marie Stark, b. Sept. 17, 1853, Hiram, Ohio, d. Apr. 1, 1889, dau. of J. Carroll and Emily M. (Burdick) Stark. Residing at Horton, Kansas, 1891, where his wife died. Issue—

1. Edna Marie—b. Nov. 12, 1873, Allenville, Missouri.
2. Richard Carroll—b. Oct. 22, 1875, d. Sept. 16, 1876.
3. Frederick Cravens—b. Aug. 15, 1878.
4. Edith Elizabeth—b. July 7, 1881.
5. William Edward—b. Aug. 5, 1883.
6. Robert Leroy—b. Mar. 28, 1886.

(Last four born at Gallatin, Mo.)

(1415313) SAMUEL ANDREW RINGO—b. June 15, 1862; d. Aug. 7, 1875; drowned by accident in Grand River.

LEOPARD

(141532) SUSAN CAROLINE CRAVENS (1824-), the daughter of Dr. John Cravens (14153), and wife Ruhama, married, September 19, 1854, in Daviess County, Missouri, John A. Leopard, native of Morgan County, present West Virginia, son of Jacob Leopard, of Virginia, and wife Delilah Dowden, from Ireland. They resided in Gallatin, Missouri, where both were yet living in 1891.

John A. Leopard, and wife Susan Caroline Cravens, had issue—

(1415321) JACOB OSCAR—b. Aug. 10, 1855; m. Apr. 17, 1877, at Springfield, Mo., Belle Buckner. Issue—

1. Mattie Cravens—b. Nov. 23, 1878, Gallatin, Mo.
2. Augusta Eunice—b, Sept. 15, 1880.
3. Lula—b. Jan. 29, 1880.
4. Ethel Frankie—b. Jan ——, 1888.

(Last three born at Boliver, Mo.)

(1415322) CHARLES WILLIAM—b. Aug. 29, 1857. Residing near Gallatin, Mo., unmarried, 1891.

(1415323) FRANK BIDDLE—b. Mar. 4, 1859; m. Nov. 14, 1888, at Kansas City, Mary Merideth. Residing at Kansas City, 1890.

(1415324) JOHN CHAPLINE—b. July 20, 1861, Lawyer of Pattsonburg, Mo., 1890, unmarried.

(1415325) HOLMES DOWDEN—b. Apr. 20, 1863, (unmarried, 1890.)

(141533) ROBERT OSCAR CRAVENS (1827-), the son of Dr. John Cravens (14153), and wife Ruhama, born near Harrisonburg, Virginia, removed, as a child with his parents, to Franklin, Virginia, now West Virgina, thence to Gallatin, Missouri. In 1850, he "went across the plains," to Georgetown, Eldorado County, California, where for two years he was a placer miner. He was elected justice of the peace in 1853, and continued in office through several terms. In 1865, he began the practice of law. He removed to Sacramento, and in 1871, was elected State Librarian, which office he held twelve years. During Cleveland's administration, he was appointed Internal Revenue Collector. In 1890, he was elected police judge of Sacramento. He was a vestryman of the Protestant Episcopal Church—1897, and thereafter.

In a letter of February 22, 1904, dated at Sacramento, California, addressed to a member of the Ft. Smith, Arkansas, branch of the family, he mentions his great grandfather, John Cravens, his grandfather Dr. Joseph Cravens of Harrisonburg, Virginia, his father, Dr. John Cravens, "who died at Gallatin, Missouri, in 1882," and his brother Jerre C. Cravens.

Judge Robert O. Cravens married, March 4, 1865, at Auburn, California, Mary Jane Robinson, a native of Wayne County, New York, the only daughter of Marion Minor Robinson (1820-1863), and wife Almira Van De Car (b. 1820, m. 1840), of New York. Issue—

(1415331) FANNIE ELIZABETH—b. Sept. 23, 1870; d. July 23, 1892.
(1415332) MARY RUHAMA—b. July 19, 1880.
(Both born in Sacramento, Cal.)

DARNELL—McDONALD

(141535) SARAH AMANDA CRAVENS (1832-), the daughter of Dr. John Cravens (14153), and wife Ruhama, born at Franklin, now West Virginia, married, first, February 3, 1848, James Henry Darnell, a native of Woodford County, Kentucky, who died about 1852. She married second, October 12, 1858, at Gallatin, Missouri, William Douglas McDonald, a native of Ross County, Ohio, the son of William McDonald, from Virginia, (d. 1832, in Ohio), and wife Mary Willis, from Maryland, (d. Dec. 1880, in Ohio.) Mrs. McDonald was residing at Jameson, Missouri, 1891. Issue—

Of JAMES HENRY DARNELL, and wife Sarah Cravens,

(1415351) MARY ELLA—b. Oct. 24, 1850, at Gallatin, Mo.; m. Sept. 26, 1871, JOHN NELSON HOWE, b. Feb. 6, 1847, Kirksville, Mo., son of Thompson Boyd Howe, and wife Zipporah Jane Thatcher. Issue—
1. Russel Boyd—b. Nov. 1, 1872, Macon City, Missouri.
2. Robert Cravens—b. July 16, 1875, Sacramento, Cal.
3. Frederick Nelson—b. May 19, 1881.

Of WILLIAM D. McDONALD, and wife Sarah Cravens,

(1415352) JOHN CRAVENS—b. Aug. 24, 1859.
(1415353) EFFIE—b. Apr. 7, 1861; d. Oct. 15, 1862.
(1415354) WILLIAM DOUGLAS—b. Dec. 25, 1862, residing 1890, Jamesport, Mo.; m. Aug. 29, 1888, in Grundy Co., Mo., Hattie Janet Etter, b. Mar. 9, 1866, Will Co., Ill., dau. of Jacob and Delpha Jane (Furguson) Etter. Issue—
1. Effie Delpha Jane—b. Oct. 9, 1889, Daviess County, Mo.
(1415355) AMANDA—b. Jan. 1, 1864.
(1415356) RUHAMA—b. Oct. 6, 1866.
(1415357) ELIZABETH—b. Feb. 26, 1868.
(1415358) JULIA—b. Mar. 7, 1871.
(Last seven born in Daviess Co., Mo.)

(141536) WILLIAM JAMES CRAVENS (1833-1883), the son of Dr. John Cravens (14153), and wife Ruhama, married in 1855, at Gallatin, Missouri, Mary Rebecca Bryan. They resided at Springfield, Missouri, where he died Aug. 10, 1883. Issue—

(1415361) MARY RUHAMA—m. J. H. Hyatt.

(141538) JEREMIAH CHAPLINE CRAVENS (1838-), the son of Dr. John Cravens (14153), and wife Ruhama, born in Saline County, Missouri, married, August 11, 1864, Annie Desloge Smith, born in Lawrence County, Arkansas, Sept. 16, 1843, the daughter of Robert Smith, a native of Georgetown, (Washington), D. C., (b. 1800), and wife Susan Harde McIlvaine, native of Potosi, Missouri. (b. Aug. 1818.)

Jeremiah Cravens attended the University of Missouri, graduating therefrom, July 4, 1860, as a B. A. and M. A. In 1861, he enlisted in the Confederate Army as a private. He served as aide de camp to Gen. Greene, and October 1864, was promoted to Lieut. Colonel. Following the war he began the study of law at Batesville, Arkansas,—1865. He returned to Missouri about 1868, and became a distinguished lawyer there. He settled at Springfield, where he was residing in 1891.

Col. Jeremiah C. Cravens, and wife Annie Smith, had issue—

(1415381) Susan—b. Mar. 13, 1866, resident of Springfield, Mo.; m. Oct. 11, 1887, William Edward Bowden (lawyer), b. Sept. 22, 1851, Henry Co., Tenn, d. Dec. 7, 1889, Thomasville, Ga. (no issue.)

(1415382) Mary Belle—b. May 13, 1867; m. Oct. 11, 1888, Henry Clay Crow, b. Apr. 17, 1860, Pike Co., Mo. Resident of Springfield, Mo.

(1415383) Elizabeth Wirt—b. Aug. 29, 1870.

(1415384) Irene Lee—b. Aug. 2, 1872.

(1415385) Robert Oscar—b. Feb. 4, 1874.

(1415386) Jeremiah Desloge—b. Jan. 19, 1876.

(1415387) Zoe Louise—b. June 15, 1879.

(First two born at Batesville, Arkansas, last five at Springfield, Mo.)

(141539) EDGAR HOLMES CRAVENS (1840-), the son of Dr. John Cravens (14153), and wife Ruhama, born in Daviess County, Missouri, married, 1873, Love Keene, a native of Kentucky. They resided near Gallatin, Missouri, where in 1891, he was engaged in farming. Issue—

(1415391) Effie—

(1415392) John Marshall—

(1415393) Roberta—

(1415394) Corrine—

(1415395) Dean Douglas—

---

3. LINE OF JAMES HARRISON CRAVENS

(141551) JAMES WILLIAM CRAVENS (1827-1876), the son of James Harrison Cravens (14155), and wife Sophia Capito, married, in Indiana, Mary F. Short. He served a year in the Mexican War, in the 3rd Regt. Indiana Volunteers, under Col. James Lane, following which he studied medicine at Ann Arbor, Michigan, and Cincinnati, Ohio, and became a practicing physician.

(141553) JOHN OSCAR CRAVENS (1834-1914), the son of James Harrison Cravens (14155), and wife Sophia Capito, married, in Indiana, 1862, Margaret Hite. She was a granddaughter of Abraham Hite of Harrisonburg, Virginia, and wife Sallie, nee Cravens. (See page 415; also *My Recollections of Rocktown*, by Maria G. Carr,

Abraham Hite
Joist Hite

p. 13.) Abraham Hite was a descendant of Joist Hite, the famous pioneer of the lower Valley. (See pages 117, and 382.)

John Oscar Cravens was a lawyer and banker of much ability and success in Indiana. He served throughout the War-between-the-States, in the 9th Indiana Volunteers, as a private, master sergeant, 2nd Lieut., and A. A. general, with the rank of Major, on Maj. Gen. Milory's staff. In 1888, he was elected a Presidential Elector of Indiana, his district including Versailles, his home city. He died at Versailles in 1914 Issue, six children two of whom lived to reach maturity, viz:

(1415531) George Junius—b. 1869.
(1415532) Thomas Smith—b. 1872. (deceased.)

(141554) JOHN KENNEY CRAVENS (1838-1892), the son of James Harrison Cravens (14155), and wife Sophia Capito, born in Ripley County, Indiana, married April 1861, at Gallatin, Missouri, Fannie Catlett Frame, a descendant of two Virginia families of the said names, resident of Clark and Augusta Counties.

John Kenney Cravens was a distinguished lawyer of Kansas City, Missouri, "Out Where the West Begins." He was admitted to the Bar at Vernon, Indiana, when twenty-one years of age. He then removed to Gallatin, Missouri, and in 1865 settled in Kansas City. He achieved marked success in his profession, and was a prominent and influential man in all social and civic enterprises there. His death occurred in November 1892. Issue—

(1415541) James Harrison—b. 1865; d. Apr. 21, 1931. Attorney at law of professional and social distinction of Kansas City,—graduate of Williams College, (A. B.), and of Columbia University, (M. A.); m. ————. Issue—

1. John Kenney—(decd.)
2. Elizabeth—b. 1915.
3. James Harrison— b. 1918.

(1415542) Lanier—b. 1869; d. Oct. 24, 1917; m. Agnes ————. He served as 1st Lieut. of Artillery in the regular Army of the U. S., and resigned in 1909 for civil life in Canada. At the outbreak of the World War he enlisted with Haig's Canadians, and was killed in action near Ypres, France. Issue—

1. Frances Fairfax—b. 1905.

(1415543) John Smith—b. 1871; m. Dec. 1893, Mildred Mary Myers, dau. of George S. Myers, of St. Louis, Mo. Has resided since his marriage at Pasadena, California, where he is prominent in business and social life.

(1415544) Frances Catlett—b. 1878; m. Oct. 1899, PAGE FRANCIS CARTER. Issue—

1. Marion Catlett—b. 1913.

EWING

(141555) AMANDA MEDORA CRAVENS (1841-1870), the daughter of James Harrison Cravens (14155), and wife Sophia Capito, married, 1860, John Henry Ewing, of Indiana. Issue—

(1415551) Mary Cravens—

(141556) JUNIUS EDWARD CRAVENS (1844-1920), the son of James Harrison Cravens (14155), and wife Sophia Capito, married in 1871, at Indianapolis, Indiana, Emilie S. Stewart. She and her parents were former residents of Maryland.

Junius Edward Cravens was a scientific dental surgeon of international fame, having practiced for several years in Paris. He settled in New York City, where his widow now resides (Riverside Drive) with the son first named below. During the War-between-the-States, he served as a Captain in the 83rd Volunteer Infantry of Indiana. Issue—

(1415561) GEORGE W.—b. 1872, Civil Engineer, New York City.
(1415562) EDWARD—b. 1874, (decd.)
(1415563) JUNIUS E.—artist, San Francisco, Cal.

---

3. LINE OF JACOB KENNERLY

WOODARD

(141562) VIRGINIA ANN KENNERLY (1824-1874), the daughter of Major Jacob Kennerly, and wife Amanda Fitzallen (14156), nee Cravens, married John Woodard, of Indiana. About 1869, they removed to Illinois.

John Woodard, and wife Virginia Kennerly, had issue—

(1415621) CHARLES CRAVENS—b. 1850; d. Oct. 1929.
(1415622) AMANDA—d. aged about 1 yr.
(1415623) KENNERLY—d. aged about 10 yrs.
(1415624) JULIA BELLE—d. aged about 1 yr.
(1415625) OLIVE—resides in Illinois.
(1415626) CATHERINE (Kate)— (unmarried) resides at Shelbyville, Ind. (with family of James Kennerly,—see below.)
(1415627) JOSEPH ROBERT—d. 1916, c, aged 54 years; m. ————.
Issue—
1. a daughter—m. Rev. Jesse Bradberry, of Olney, Ill.

(141563) JAMES THOMAS KENNERLY (1833-1906), the son of Jacob Kennerly, and wife Amanda Fitzallen (14156), nee Cravens, married, 1864, Susan Virginia Syrcle (1842-1923), of Augusta County, Virginia. They resided in Shelbyville, Indiana, in which city their three surviving children now make their home as one family.

James T. Kennerly, and wife Susan Virginia, nee Syrcle, had issue—

Shelbyville, Ind.

(1415631) IRENE—b. 1865; d. 1929, unmarried.
(1415632) MARY B.—(unmarried.)
(1415633) JOSEPH ROBERT—b. 1869; d. 1927, unmarried.
(1415634) AMANDA MAY—
(1415635) MABEL—d. 1876, aged 7 mo.
(1415636) DALLAS E.—(unmarried.)

---

2. LINE OF JAMES CRAVENS
3. LINE OF ROBERT CRAVENS

McMILLIN

(141631) NANCY CRAVENS (1832-), the daughter of Robert Cravens

(14163), and wife Catherine, married J. P. McMillin, of Chattanooga, Tenn. Issue—

(1416311) JAMES—d. 1888; m. Elizabeth Armstrong, (d. 1895), of Knoxville, Tenn.

(1416312) DAVID—m. Minnie Newman, of Crystal Springs, Miss.
Issue—
1. Douglas—Capt., U. S. Army.
2. David—d. 1893.

(1416313) ANN—m. Atwell Thompson, Civil Engr. (both deceased).

LYLE

(141632) ELIZABETH CRAVENS (1834-1885), the daughter of Robert Cravens (14163), and wife Catherine, nee Roddy, married, 1854, George W. Lyle, of Tennessee, born 1828, died 1861.

George W. Lyle and wife Elizabeth Cravens, had issue, a daughter —

(1416321) KATE—b. 1860; m. 1889, Dr. GEORGE R. WEST, of Chattanooga, Tenn., b. 1858. Issue—
1. Lyle B. (M. D.)—b. Feb. 6, 1894; d. Feb. 24, 1930; m. Feb. 6, 1927, Henrietta Adams, of Pine Bluff, Arkansas.
2. George R., Jr.—b. Jan. 20, 1896; m. Nov. 21, 1922, Marian Daniels, of Cincinnati, O. Resides in Chattanooga, Tenn.

(Two infants, Thomas, and George, d. in infancy.)

* * * * * *

Of the above—

KATE LYLE WEST, and her husband, Dr. George R. West, are prominently identified in the cultural and social life of Chattanooga, where he is a widely known physician and surgeon. They reside on the Missionary Ridge—the historic heights to the east of the city, named for the early French missionaries, and the scene of the battle of 1863. Dr. West is a native of Green County, Tennessee, and a graduate of the University of Pennsylvania, 1883.

LYLE BATTEY WEST (1894-1930), was a most promising young physician, and surgeon, of Chattanooga, the medical director of Chattanooga Hospital, and the associate of his father. He was fatally injured in an airplane accident, as he was flying to Florida with a friend on a professional visit to the latter's wife, who had been injured in an automobile accident. He was a graduate of the University of Pennsylvania, class of 1921, and was a man of splendid part.

(141633) JAMES R. CRAVENS (1836-), the son of Robert Cravens (14163), and wife Catherine, married, first, Harriet Rogers. Following her death he married, second, Drucilla Lyle.

In a letter, dated at Ringgold, Georgia, January 25, 1889, and addressed to a member of the Arkansas branch of the family, he states that he was of the family of Robert Cravens, of Chattanooga, and mentions meeting James A. Cravens, of Indiana, a descendant of William Cravens, the brother of his (the writer's) paternal grandfather, whose name was James Cravens. He identifies William as having been a Methodist preacher, and further states that another brother of his grandfather was Joseph Cravens, a physican.

James R. Cravens had issue—

By first wife, Harriet, nee Rogers,

(1416331) ROBERT SPENCER—d. 1884, c; m. Evelyn Gordon.
Issue—
1. Harriet Ophelia—

(1416332) MARY—b. 1865; m. WILLIAM J. SAWYER, of Chattanooga.
Issue—
1. Robert Cravens—m. Rosalie Cunningham. Resides in Denver, Col.

By second wife, Drucilla, nee Lyle

(1416333) HENRY—m. Evelyn Matthews. Resides in Chattanooga.
(1416334) RUTH— (unmarried.) Resident of Chattanooga.
(1416335) JESSE—(unmarried.) Resident of Chattanooga.
(1416336) JAMES—Resident of Houston, Texas.
(1416337) MARVIN—Resident of Texas.
(1416338) LUCY—(unmarried.) Resident of Chattanooga.

ANDERSON

(141634) LYDIA CRAVENS (-1866), the daughter of Robert Cravens (14163), and wife Catherine, married William W. Anderson. Issue, a son—

(1416341) CHARLES CRAVENS—(decd.) m. Margaret Backman. Resided in Chattanooga. Issue—
1. John—Capt., U. S. Army.
2. William D. (M. D.)—m. Rosalie Slaughter. Residence Chattanooga.
3. Margaret—m. Charles Coffey. Residence, Chattanooga.

(141635) JESSE RODDY CRAVENS ( ), the son of Robert Cravens (14163), and wife Catherine, nee Roddy, married, first, Mary Ellen Brown, who died some years thereafter. He married, second, Ida Miller. Issue—

By first wife Mary Ellen, nee Brown,

(1416351) JAMES—
(1416352) CATHERINE—(unmarried.)
(1416353) TROWER—m. ————. Resident of Buford, S. C.
(1416354) ROY—m. ————. Resident of Atlanta, Ga.

By second wife, Ida, nee Miller,

(1416355) MARY—
(1416356) ROBERT—
(1416357) NANCY—
Last three residents of Buford, S. C.

---

1. LINE OF MAJOR ROBERT CRAVENS
2. LINE OF WILLIAM CRAVENS
3. LINE OF JEREMIAH CRAVENS

(148355) WILLIAM MURPHY CRAVENS (1833-1919), the son of Jeremiah Cravens (14835), and wife Kiturah Murphy, born at Fredericktown, Missouri, married, at "Glenwood," Ft. Smith, Arkansas, April 8, 1862, Mary Eloise Rutherford, (b. 1840), the daughter of Col. Samuel Morton Rutherford, a former Virginian, and wife Mary Eloise Beall, daughter of Asa Beall, and wife Jane Edwards. The last named was a daughter of John Edwards, Gent., and wife Susanna Wroe, of Burbon County, Kentucky. John Edwards was a descendant of Willam Edwards, Jr., of Virginia, who, in 1678, married Ann Harrison, said to have been the daughter of Benjamin Harrison, III, of the James River family. (See page 109.)

William Murphy Cravens was one of the outstanding lawyers of the Southwest, where he achieved unusual distinction through a practice of his profession for over sixty years. He was widely known in Arkansas, Missouri, Oklahoma, Indian Territory, and Texas, and practiced before the Supreme Court in Washington, D. C. He was tendered the nomination to Congress, which was equivalent to election, but declined. He enjoyed marked educational advantages in his youth; received his B. A. degree from what is now the University of Arkansas, and was carefully trained in the law. He served in the Confederate Army, 1861-65, attaining the grade of Captain. (In later life he was known by the old Southern courtesy title "Colonel.") He and his wife resided at Ft. Smith, Arkansas. His death occurred at Ft. Smith, January 2, 1919. Mrs. Cravens died in March, 1932.

Col. William Murphy, and Mary Eloise Cravens, had issue—

(1483551) MARGARET RUTHERFORD—b. Jan. 20, 1863; d. Feb. 14, 1863.

(1483552) ELOISE KITURAH—b. Oct. 5, 1864; d. Oct. 21, 1865.

(1483553) JERE MORTON—b. Oct. 25, 1866; m. at Ft. Smith, Ark., Oct. 5, 1892, Emma Sue Tippett. Resides at Ft. Smith. Issue—

1. Mary Agnes—b. Oct. 10, 1894; d. Oct. 20, 1900.
2. Jeremiah Morton—b. Oct. 2, 1901; d. Jan. 11, 1902.
3. Margaret Tippett—b. July 25, 1905.
4. William Tippett—b. Feb. 24, 1914.

(1483554) RICHARD KERR (Col.)—b. Mar. 16, 1869; m. at Ft. Smith, Ark., Nov. 16, 1891, Margaret May. Served in 1st, Army, A. E. F., as Adjutant Gen., Army Artillery, in France. Lieut Col. U. S. Army, 1923, stationed at Manila. Issue—

1. William M., (Maj.)—b. Nov. 22, 1892, at Houston, Texas, m. Nov. 17, 1923, at Grantwood, N. J., Alice Russell Thayer. Stationed at Ft. Leavenworth, Kansas, Feb. 1930. Major, U. S. Army. Issue—
   1. Alyn Thayer—b. July 22, 1930.

(1483555) WILLIAM BEN (Congressman)—b. Jan. 17, 1872; m. at Ft. Smith, Ark., Dec. 19, 1894, Carolyn Dyal. (see below.) Issue—

1. William F.—b. Feb. 15, 1899; m. at Ft. Smith, Ark., Feb. 16, 1926, Elizabeth Bliss Echols. Issue—
   1. William F.— b. Jan. 28, 1929.
2. Nancy Ellen—b. Aug. 12, 1900, m. at Ft. Smith, Ark., Jan. 1, 1921, WILLIAM MARTIN EADS. Issue—
   1. Nancy Cravens—b. Jan. 4, 1922.
   2. William M.—b. Dec. 19, 1926.

(1483556) DU VAL GARLAND (Col.)—b. Apr. 20, 1875; m. at Bristol, Va.-Tenn., June 21, 1905, Florence Iileen Fain. Supt. of Sewanee Military Academy, Sewanee, Tenn. (1923.) Issue—

1. Du Val Garland—b. Aug. 17, 1906.

Col. Samuel Morton Rutherford

Bristol, Tn.

2. William Murphy—b. Aug 27, 1908.
3. John Fain—b. Feb. 10, 1912.
4. Mary Virginia—b. Mar. 12, 1914.
5. Thomas Rutherford—b. Feb. 4, 1918.
(first two b. at Bristol, Tenn., third at Murfreesboro, Tenn.)

(1483557) DAISY RUTHERFORD—b. Apr. 20, 1875, (unmarried.) Resides at Ft. Smith, Arkansas.

(1483558) RUTHERFORD RECTOR—b. Apr. 20, 1875; m. 1st, at Claremore, Okla., Mar. 26, 1901, Nancy Gordon Garrison, of Clarksville, Texas. She d. Sept. 16, 1920, at St. Louis, Mo. He m. 2nd, July 15, 1922, Kathryn Cochrane, of San Angelo, Texas. Residing at St. Louis, Mo., 1923.

Of Whom—

WILLIAM BEN CRAVENS, was elected a Democratic Representative from Arkansas to the Sixtieth, Sixty-first, and Sixty-second Congresses of the United States, serving from March 4, 1907 to March 3, 1913. He attended the Louisville, Kentucky, Military Academy, the Staunton, Virginia, Military Academy, and was graduated from the law department of the University of Missouri, at Columbia, in 1893, in which year he was admitted to the Bar and began the practice of his profession at Ft. Smith, Arkansas. He was the partner of his father, and from 1898 to 1902, the city attorney of Ft. Smith. From 1902 to 1907, he was the prosecuting attorney for the twelfth judical district of his State. Following his election to the Sixty-second Congress, he was not a candidate for re-election in 1912, and at the end of the term resumed his practice of law, as a resident of Ft. Smith. (See, *Biographical Directory of the American Congresses*, 1774-1927, p. 858; also *Who's Who in American*, 1916-1917; and introduction to Chapter XXII, herein.)

---

3. LINE OF NEHEMIAH CHAVENS

(148384) JORDAN EDGAR CRAVENS (1830-1914), the son of Nehemiah Cravens (14838), and wife Sophia, nee Thompson, was the third descendant of Capt. Robert Cravens, the Augusta County, Virginia, pioneer, of the Cravens name, to be elected to Congress. His cousin William Ben Cravens, above, was the fourth; a record belived to be unique, and certainly extraordinary, among the annals of the country.

Jordan Edgar Cravens was a native of Fredericktown, Madison County, Missouri. The year after his birth, he moved with his father to Arkansas. He graduated from Cane Hill Academy, at Boonsboro, now Canehill, Washington County, Arkansas, in 1850, then studied law, and was admitted to the Bar in 1854, beginning his practice in Clarksville, Arkansas. He was a member of the State house of representatives, in 1860. He enlisted in the Confederate Army in 1861, as a private, and was promoted to Colonel the next year, and continued in the service until the close of the war, when he returned to Clarksville. He was prosecuting attorney of Johnson County, 1865, and 1866. From 1866 to 1868, he represented his district as a member of the State senate. In 1872, he was presidential elector on the Democratic ticket of Greely and Brown. He was a Democratic Representative from Arkansas to the Forty-fifth, Forty-sixth, and Fourthy-seventh Congresses, March 4, 1877, to March 3, 1883. In

1882, he was a candidate for re-election, but was defeated. He resumed his practice of law at Clarksville. From 1890 to 1894, he was judge of the circuit court. He died at Ft. Smith, Arkansas, April 8, 1914, and was interred in Oakland Cemetery, at Clarksville. (See, *Biographical Director of American Congresses*, 1774-1927, p. 858.)

Judge Cravens married Emma Batson, daughter of Judge Felix Batson, member of the Confederate Congress, and wife Jean Charnelsie Bettis. Issue—

(1483841) Jean—m. Frederick B. Hallenberg, of Little Rock, Ark.
(1483842) Sophy—m. John Walton Howell, of Hot Springs, Ark.
(1483843) Jessie Edgar—m. J. Smith Ownby, of Dallas, Texas.
(1483844) Batson—m. John W. Gulick, of Ft. Smith, Ark.
(1483845) Louise—d. in infancy.

END OF RECORD OF CLAN OF CAPT. ROBERT CRAVENS

FURTHER RECORD

RESIDENCE OF THE LATE NEWTON GORDON MOORE
By The Long Grey Trail
See page 596.

CHAPTER XXV

Further Descendants of Late and Present Rockingham Lines

SEVENTH TO TENTH GENERATIONS

"And he who gives a child a treat
Makes joy-bells ring in Heaven's street,
And he who gives a child a home
Builds palaces in Kingdom come,
And she who gives a baby birth
Brings Savior Christ again to earth."

—MASEFIELD—*The Everlasting Mercy.*

THE DAUGHTERS OF ISAIAH, through the generations, have ever been wonderful mothers. Truly, they have been much sought as wives, and have been abundantly blessed in their inheritance of a positive genius for happy alliances.

Some of the most interesting studies in tracing the various lines of descent from the early Oyster Bay immigrant, is in following the brilliant achievements of many of the children of these mothers. One such a mother, was amply rewarded for her devotion, in the distinguished careers of her sons, two of whom dedicated their lives to the alleviation of the suffering of mankind. The youngest of the two was born on the first day of the year, 1853.

"JOE PRICE"—MASTER SURGEON

Joseph Price, M. D. LLD., (1853-1911), of Philadelphia, one of the foremost figures in the development of abdominal surgery in America, was born on Smiths Creek in Rockingham County, Virginia. The site of his birthplace was on the land, which, in his grandfather's day, was a part of the Moreland Hall plantation, and which, by this same grandfather's bequest, had been devised to the latter's daughter, Price's mother. Within a short distance of the home, and on the banks of the same creek, most likely on an adjoining tract of land, there had dwelt as a lad in Colonial times, an earlier pioneer in another field, John Sevier, the hero of Tennessee. (See page 146; also, *Kind Words*, by M. Liston Lewis.)

Of Price, it is written, in the annals of medicine—"He stripped from surgery all complicated paraphernalia, and made its technic simple and thorough. Every prominent surgeon in this country today demonstrates in his methods the impress of this master-surgeon. His great vigor of constitution permitted him to travel over the entire country, giving object lessons to an eager profession. He was the greatest exponent of the local hospital and no one dedicated more of these institutions throughout the land. It is impossible to estimate the great good he did the profession and laity by his constant labor to establish this local institution and place within its walls competent operators. To the hour of his death he remained the greatest advocate the country had of the so-called pathalogical era in abdominal surgery. His earnest pleas for early work followed by radical toilets and ever removal of the distal infecting source will stamp his work immortal." *(American Journal of Obstetrics and Diseases of Women and Children,* Vol. LXV, No. 1, 1912.)

"He found", says another eminent authority, "gynecology and abdominal surgery twin babies in swaddling clothes and left them, after a life of extraordinary activity, full grown specialties. Price's personality reached the hearts, while his writings and clinical teachings in some degree moulded the activities of every surgeon in this country and in Canada. To few men has it been given to so impress their personality and their sturdy convictions on their fellows. The secret of his success lay in his fixed purpose of life, his active restless mind, his piercing vision and his long, deft, trained fingers which were at once the envy and despair of other surgeons. Joseph Price easily led abdominal surgery on women in this county for nearly two decades . . . . Price never had any regular collegiate teaching position, and yet he taught more men to do abdominal and pelvic operations and had more grateful followers than any other man in America." *(Dictionary of American Medical Biography,* by Drs. H. A. Kelly and W. L. Burrage, 1928, p. 993.)

"Joe Price," as his friends all called him, never forgot the love he bore for his mother, and his mother's people. It was his delight in later years, to steal away from his busy labors in the great city, when occasion would permit, and with a party of his happy youngsters spend a week or more of their vacation time at Moreland Hall, with its genial host and hostess, Mr. and Mrs. George Harrison, renewing old friendships amongst his relatives and acquaintances of the neighborhood. And such a time these youngsters had riding with him about the country, climbing the old Massanutten, and delving with him into some half-forgotten lore of his childhood days!

* * * * * *

In the following pages, upwards of 450 further descendants of John Harrison, the pioneer, are traced, including over 225 members of the eighth generation, over 200 of the ninth, and several of the tenth; most of whom are living. A goodly number of these, it may be observed, are also descended from the pioneer's grandson, David Harrison, (1259). In a sense, this Chapter is a continuation of Chapter XXIII, wherein some of the John Harrison lines have already been traced as far as the eighth and ninth generations. Owing to John's Clan being the oldest, so to speak, of the various Clans considered, many of the lines of descent from him to the present contain, on the whole, an extra generation, as compared to the average lines of the other Clans.

Instances of this nature occur particularly in the Moore, Walton, and Warren families; all of which involve the older John Harirson lines. In the case of the Moore and Walton families, due to the marriages of three daughters of David Harrison, above named, to members of families a generation further removed than themselves from John Harrison, his descendants, as traced through these daughters, are of a generation less from the immigrant than as traced through their corresponding husbands. Thus, several of the Moore and Walton heads of families, hereinafter named (in capitals), were, through their mother, first cousins of the various Harrison heads named in Chapter XXIII, and their families, while properly listed in the present Chapter are correspondingly contemporaneous with those of Chapter XXIII.

CLAN OF JOHN HARRISON

1. LINE OF ZEBULON HARRISON
2. LINE OF JOHN HARRISON
3. LINE OF ZEBULON A. HARRISON
4. LINE OF ABRAHAM HARRISON

(1211242) ROBERT ALLEN HARRISON (1839-1912), the son of Abraham Harrison (121124), and wife Delilah Rhodes, married, September 12, 1867, Mary Frances Long, the daughter of Adam Long, of Rockingham, and sister of the late Erasmus Long, of near Tenth Legion, in the said county. Robert Harrison and wife resided in Rockingham on their farm at the "Cross Roads", to the south of Keezletown. Issue—

1. Dora—b. Aug. 5, 1868; m. Dec 28, 1886, Henry Lee Pickering, son of Abraham, of Tenth Legion. (See page 379.)
2. Luther Byrd—b. July 8, 1874; d. Oct. 26, 1888.
3. Adam Lewis—b. Aug. 31, 1878; m. Apr. 7, 1901, Effie Carman. Resides near Harrisonburg. Issue—
    1. Lewis Scott—b. Feb. 12, 1902.
    2. Alline—b. Sept. 10, 1903.
    3. Grace Margaret—b. 1905.
    4. Owen—b. Apr. 13, 1906.
    5. Clara Frances—b. Oct. 18, 1908.
4. Harvey Scott—b. July 2, 1880.
5. Rosie May—b. May 13, 1887.

(D. S. H. papers.)

FLOOK

(1211246) MINERVA JANE HARRISON (1848-1917), the daughter of Abraham Harrison (121124), and wife Delilah Rhodes, married, about 1871, William Christian (Christopher) Flook, of Rockingham. They resided on the Keezletown Road near Trinity Church to the north of Harrisonburg, where he owned a farm. Their home was about two miles north of Flook's Spring, (the old Daniel Flook farm), a head water of the eastern branch of the Dry Fork; the scene of the early residence of John Harrison, Jr., son of John, the Pioneer. (See page 164.)

William Christian Flook, and wife Minerva Jane, had issue—

1. David Oscar—b. June 1, 1873; m. about 1905, Addie Lausson. No issue—
2. Ludevius—b. Aug. 25, 1874; d. in infancy.
3. Lydia May—b. July 8, 1875; m. Apr. 21, 1898, John A. Zigler. No issue.
4. Effie Gertrude—b. Sept. 28, 1877; m. Nov. 6, 1909, D. Frank Zigler. No issue.
5. Minnie E. E.—b. Oct. 5, 1879; m. 1905, ROBERT ARMENTROUT. Issue—
    1. Lydia Gertrude Virginia—b. Jan. 19, 1907.
    2. Franklin Flook—b. 1908 c.
    3. Layton Orville—b. 1910.
6. Gracie Lee—b. June 24, 1883; m. about May 1904, CHARLES W. WISE,

Issue—
1. Virginia Ruth—b. Aug. 1907.
7. WILLIE R. H.—b. Aug. 25, 1885; m. Oct. 19, 1910, Edward Armentrout, no issue.
8. ABRAHAM OTIS—b. Jan. 20, 1888; d. Feb. 13, 1906.
9. NANNIE VIRGINIA—b. Dec. 25, 1890.
10. SAM JONES—b. Apr. 26, 1892.
(D. S. H. papers.)

(1211247) NANCY E. S. HARRISON (1851-1900), the daughter of Abraham Harrison (121124), and wife Delilah Rhodes, married John Robert Kyle Bowman, (178441), the son of Samuel Bowman. See Clan of Thomas Harrison, 1. Line of Reuben Harrison, 2. Line of Rev. William Houston, 3. Line of Samuel Bowman. Page 563.

---

1. LINE OF THOMAS MOORE
2. LINE OF CAPT. REUBEN MOORE
3. LINE OF MOSES WALTON, JR.
4. LINE OF REUBEN WALTON

(1234111) MOSES WALTON (1826-1883), the son of Reuben Walton (123411), and wife Mary (12593), nee Harrison, married February 5, 1851, Emily Maria Lauck, the daughter of Morgan Lauck, of Page County, Virginia, (b. July 7, 1796, m. 1824), and wife Ann Maria Ott, (b. Feb. 10, 1804), the daughter of Jacob and Ann Maria Ott. Morgan A. Lauck was the son of Peyton and Amelia Lauck, and a grandson of Col. Peter Lauck. Following his (Morgan's) death, his widow, Ann Maria, married, second, (1833 ?), Samuel Anderson.

Moses Walton and wife were residents of Woodstock, Shenandoah County, Virginia. He represented his county in the State Legislature, 1863-65, and was a member of the Constitutional Convention of 1876-8. He was founder of the well known law firm of Walton and Walton, of Woodstock, which has continued in existance over fifty years.

Issue—
1. ANNIE ELIZABETH—b. Nov. 23, 1851; d. Feb. 14, 1931; m. Oct. 24, 1872, ISAAC SINGLETON HENDRY, b. Dec. 1845, near Frederick, Md.; d. May 27, 1915. Resided in Washington, D. C. Issue—
    1. Annie Moselle—b. Jan. 27, 1874; d. Nov. 27, 1874.
    2. Alma L.—b. Nov. 24, 1875. Resides in Washington, D. C.
    3. Moses Walton—b. Feb. 13, 1879; m. Dec. 19, 1921, Mary E. England. Attorney at Law, Washington, D. C.
    4. Ernest Singleton, (M. D.)—b. Aug. 24, 1881; m. 1918, Isabell Breckinridge. Physician and Surgeon, Washington, D. C.
    5. Morgan Leland—b. Apr. 15, 1888; m. Mar. 15, 1922, Nellye R. Brookes. Attorney at Law, Washington, D. C. Issue—
        1. M. Leland, (Jr.)—b. Nov. 20, 1926.
        2. Sarah Ellen—b. Nov. 27, 1932.
    6. Reginald—b. Jan. 4, 1895; d. Mar. 17, 1895.
2. MORGAN LAUCK—b. Oct. 13, 1853; m. Jan. 25, 1876, Mollie A. March, dau. of Rev. James H. March, and wife Laura A., of Winchester, Va. (She of

Charleston, W. Va.) Resides in Woodstock, Va., where he has long been a prominent member of the Bar. He represented his county and Page in the Virginia Senate 1891-95, and was author of *The Walton Law.* Grad of Randolph Macon College, 1872, and of U. of Va. 1875. Past grand chancellor of the Knights of Pythias, of Va. Issue—

1. Moses O.—b. Nov. 7, 1876; m. Lucie Williams. Resides in Hamilton, Ontario.
2. Laura Lauck—b. July 9, 1879; m. June 17, 1903, JOHN DULIN. He d. Aug 12, 1905. Issue—
    1. Mary Elizabeth—b. Mar. 24, 1905.
3. Clyde Eby—b. July 23, 1881; m. June 29, 1905, Maude A. Johnson. Resides in Woodstock. Issue—
    1. Madolin J.—b. Apr. 14, 1907; m. Dulaney Ward.
    2. Mary Lauck—b. Jan. 6, 1910.
4. Mabel L.—b. Mar. 22, 1884 (unmarried.) Resides in Woodstock.
5. Mary Beall—b. Sept. 20, 1888, (unmarried.) Resides in Woodstock.
6. Emily A.—b. May 4, 1890; m. CHESTER C. HOLLOWAY, of Snow Hill, Md. Issue—
    1. Mary Hastings—(of Woodstock.)
    2. Chester C., Jr.—of Clermont, Fla.
7. Morgan Lauck, Jr.—b. Jan 30, 1892; m. Frances Allen, dau. of Tiphen W. Allen, Jr., and wife Laura Ripley. Attorney at Law, of Woodstock, Va. Issue—
    1. Frances Allen—
    2. Morgan Lauck, III—
    3. Moses (VI)—

3. MARY OTT—b. Mar. 20, 1855; m. Dec. 20, 1877, Judge EDGAR D. NEWMAN, of Woodstock, Virginia, where she resides. He d. Sept. 21, 1927. See below. Issue—
    1. Wilber Lauck—b. Nov. 26, 1880; m. Apr. 18, 1906, Ruth Koontz. He d. Dec. 20, 1928 Issue—
        1. Elizabeth—
        2. Josephine—
        3. Wilber—
        4. Jane—
        5. Ruth—
    2. Edgar Walton—b. Mar. 20, 1884; m. June 12, 1911, Marguerite Helena Price, dau. of Capt. Berryman Z. Price, (see p. 559.) Resides in Woodstock, Va., where he is engaged in banking. Issue—
        1. Edgar Walton, Jr.—(decd.)
        2. Richard Berryman—m. Nov. 16, 1934, Dorothy Earl Grove, dau. of Earl G. Grove (1784561).
        3. Marguerite Price—
        4. Mary Virginia—
        5. Rebecca Keyser—
    3. Helen—b. May 8, 1886; m. June 14, 1910, Dr. W. B. SAGAR, of Danville, Va. Issue—
        1. Edgar Douglas—

2. Frederick Newman—
3. Mary Walton—
4. Harold—
5. William Baird—
6. Donald—
7. Samuel Ott—

4. Harold Hastings, (M. D.)—b. Nov. 17, 1889; m. Oct. 3, 1914, Eleanor Maynard. Issue—
1. Maynard O.—
2. Eleanor Walton—
3. Harold Hastings, Jr.—

5. Houston Hickman—b. Apr. 14, 1892; m. Jan. 6, 1914, Edna F. Jones. Mayor of Edinburg, Va., where he is engaged in banking. Issue—
1. Virginia Flavelle—
2. Craig Walton—

6. Douglas Cook—b. Nov. 25, 1896; m. Dec. 15, 1917, Elizabeth H. Brown. Issue—
1. Wallace Brown—

4. Emma Maria—b. July 13, 1857; d. Jan. 8, 1887 (?); m. Dec. 28, 1884, John S. Keller, of Oklahoma, (at time of his death.) Issue—
1. Emily—m. EDWARD C. McCRAW.
Issue—
1. Charlotte—
2. Richard—
3. Emily—(decd.)

5. Samuel A.—b. Sept. 6, 1858; d. 1919; m. Dec. 15, 1886, Kattie Forrer. Resided in Luray, Virginia, Issue—
1. Mariam—b. Sept. 15, 1887.
2. Lynn—b. Dec. 17, 1890.

6. Maggie Sue—b. July 5, 1860.
7. Alice Haiskell—b. May 25, 1862; m. Dec. 17, 1890, Charles Haslet. (Issue.)
8. David Harrison—b. Aug. 11, 1865; m. Rose Shaw.
Issue—
1. Virginia—

9. Archie Campbell—b. July 17, 1870

(D. S. H. and A. E. M. papers; dates from Walton family Bible. See also Wayland's *History of Shenandoah Co., Va.*, pp. 552, and 571.)

* * * * * *

Judge Edgar Douglas Newman, for years president of the board of trustees of the Randolph Macon system of colleges, and a prominent banker of Shenandoah County, resident of Woodstock, was born March 26, 1854. His father, Benjamin P. Newman, b. January 24, 1823, married May 6, 1851, Elizabeth Hickman. Benjamin P. and Elizabeth Newman had issue—Walter Hickman, b. July 17, 1852, m. June 9, 1890, Sallie Byrd Stephenson; Edgar Douglas, as above; and Caroline Mary, b. July 25, 1862, m. Oct. 18, 1883, Mark B. Wunder.

Samuel Newman and wife Martha, and Mary Newman, the wife of Jonathan Newman were among the founders and early members of the Smiths and Linville's Creek Baptist Church of later Rockingham. They were from Pennsylvania. Samuel and Jonathan were probably descendants of the Oyster Bay Newmans. (See pages 11, 15, and 186.)

On the 15th February, 1748, Samuel Newman, with Jacob Woodley, was named as surety in the qualification of John Dobkin and William James as executors of Rudel Brock's will. Jonathan Newman died in Old Augusta prior to the establishment of the Smiths and Linville's Creek Church. His estate settlement by Samuel Newman was recorded 28th February, 1750. (Will Book 1, pp. 93, and 319.) Samuel Newman, farmer, and wife Martha, the 12th July, 1750, conveyed to Thomas Moore, farmer, 200 acres of land on Smiths Creek, whereon Newman then lived, and originally patented "from Fairfax." (Deed Book 3, p. 253.) This tract was apparently the same that Moore returned to Newman in 1753. (See page 145.) On the 29th August, 1757, Newman patented 175 acres of land on Smiths Creek. He and his wife, Martha, as residents of Frederick County, 20th December, 1762, deeded 105 acres of this land to Mathias Celser (Selzer), also of Frederick. Samuel Newman, Jr., signed as one of the witnesses. (Deed Book 11, p. 233.) The last Saturday of September, 1763, the Smiths and Linville's Creek Church met at Samuel Newman's home. Samuel and Martha petitioned the church for a letter of dismissal, 20th April, 1765, at which time they were preparing to move to "some parts of North or South Carolina." (See pages 181 and 186.)

John Newman, according to Boogher, in his *Gleanings of Virginia History,* emigrated to Virginia in 1635, in the ship "Globe," at the age of twenty four. He settled in James City County, where he patented land in 1644. Between the years 1652 and 1667, he acquired by patents and deeds about 4,000 acres of land in present Lancaster and Richmond counties. His home was at Tarpley's Point, known as Moratico, or Newman's Neck. About 1655, he married, in Rappahannock County, probably the daughter of Paul Woodbridge. His wife died prior to 1677. His will, proven at Tappahannock Court House, (Rappahannock Co.), 1677, names sons, Alexander, Samuel, and John; the first as the eldest, and the others as minors. Samuel, born about 1658, was granted 559 acres of land in 1687, and 200 acres in 1690, in Henrico County. He married, and had sons, Samuel and Jonathan. The latter, Boogher identifies as the Augusta County settler, whose wife was Mary. Jonathan died before Feb. 20, 1748 and left children, John and Walter. Walter Newman, following his father's death, removed with his mother, and uncle Samuel, to present Shenandoah County. He was a soldier in Dunmore's War and a large planter. He married Catherine ———, and had issue ten children, of whom Walter, Jr., married in 1822, and had four children, among them Benjamin P. Newman above. (See *Boogher,* p. 246.)

OTT

(1234112) ELIZABETH HARRISON WALTON (1829- 1893), the daughter of Reuben Walton (123411), and wife Mary (12593), nee Harrison, born March 7, 1829, died March 4, 1893, married, December 17, 1850, John William Ott, born May 3, 1826, died June 30, 1914. They resided in Wodstock, Virginia, for some time, where he was a widely known and successful merchant, and served his county as sheriff. He later moved to Greenville, near Mt. Clinton, in Rockingham, and engaged in farming.

John W., and Elizabeth Walton Ott, had issue—

1. WILLIAM WALTON—b. Dec. 29, 1851; m. Aug. 4, 1901, Mary Bertha Markham, b. June 14, 1869, dau. of Jesse Solomon and Eleanor Markham, of Botetourt County, Virginia. Resides at Munford, Virginia, (1913). Issue—
    1. John Boyd—b. Apr. 28, 1904; d. July 27, 1904.

2. Reuben Walton—b. July 3, 1905.
3. Mary Margaret—b. May 9, 1908.
4. William Worth—b. Sept. 25, 1909; d. Nov. 3, 1909.
5. Elizabeth Catherine—b. Aug. 17, 1912.

2. CHARLES FRANCIS MERCER—b. Feb. 20, 1854; d. Jan. 28, 1872.
3. MARY WALTON—b. July 18, 1856. (unmarried.) Resides near New Erection Church.
4. CATHERINE—b. Aug. 8, 1858; d. Aug. 13, 1858.
5. ANNIE VIRGINIA—b. Aug. 21, 1859; m. ——— Hunter, resides near Greenville, Rockingham County.
6. ELIZABETH MOORE (Lilly)—b. Jan. 3, 1862; m. Nov. 22, 1888, JOHN TALIAFERRO b. 1856, d. Apr. 18, 1934, prominent jeweler of Harrisonburg. Issue—
    1. Frank Ott—b. Sept. 2, 1889; m. Edna Simmers. Resides in Harrisonburg. Issue—
        1. Jack—
        2. June—(twins.)
    2. John Walton—b. Mar. 5, 1891; m. Myra Hervia Potter. Manager of Warren Hotel, Harrisonburg.
    3. Ralph—b. Apr. 27, 1894. (unmarried.)
    4. George—b. July 20, 1895; m. Merna Potts.
    5. Julian Haupe—b. Apr. 8, 1897. (unmarried.)
    6. Anna Champion—b. Sept. 3, 1899; m. Kenneth Livingstone. Resides in Arlington Co., Va.
    7. Charles Heisten—b. July 29, 1904; m. Ruth Firebaugh of Harrisonburg. In the U. S. Consular service, Yucatan, Central America. (1931.)
7. a daughter—b. twin of Lilly; d. day of birth.
8. SAMUELA WARREN—b. Apr. 27, 1864; m. ——— Reed. Resides in Philadelphia, Pa.
9. FRANK CAMPBELL—b. July 6, 1866; m. Nov. 12, 1885, Mary Boyd, b. Oct. 11, 1870. She d. Dec. 14, 1904 Resides in Harrisonburg. Issue—
    1. Charles Walker—b. July 20, 1896.
    2. Elizabeth Rockwell—b. Aug. 10, 1897.
    3. Edmonia Y.—b. Dec. 24, 1898.
    4. Morgan Beard—b. Apr. 23, 1900.
    5. Thomas Reed—b. July 21, 1901.
10. GRACE HEISTEN—b. Apr. 25, 1868; m. ——— Beard, of Augusta County, Virginia.
11. BOYD PEARCE—b. Mar. 26, 1870.
12. JOHN MORGAN—b. Mar. 20, 1872; d. unmarried.

(D. S. H. papers.)

---

3. LINE OF REUBEN MOORE

4. LINE OF MADISON MOORE

(1234311) DAVID HARRISON MOORE (1840-1926), the son of Madison Moore (123431), and wife, Lydia (12595), nee Harrison, married January 15, 1861,

Rebecca C. Sellers (1842-1868), daughter of Reuben and Catherine Sellers, of Rockingham, and sister of the late Jacob Sellers, of Mauzy, in said county.

David Moore was for many years a member of the Board of Supervisors of Rockingham County. He served in this capacity during the erection of the present courthouse at Harrisonburg, 1896-7, as attested by a tablet now affixed to the entrance hall of the building. During the War-between-the-States, he served as a soldier in the Confederate Army. He was the owner of a valuable farm, bordering on the east of the Valley Pike, a short distance south of Virginia Caverns. The land was formerly a part of his father's estate. He and his wife resided there during her lifetime, and in later years he made his home with his daughter, an only child, and her husband, in Harrisonburg; viz—

1. ALICE M.—b. June 17, 1867; m. Dr. John A. Myers, b. Nov. 14, 1856, d. July 8, 1930. She resides in Harrisonburg. No issue—

(Obituary of David Moore in *Shenandoah Valley*, Dec. 2, 1926.)

(1234312) REUBEN WALTON MOORE (1841-1911), the son of Madison Moore (123431), and wife Lydia (12595), nee Harrison, married, May 1, 1866, Fannie E. Chrisman, the daughter of Jack Chrisman, and wife Eleanor Ralston, of Rockingham. (See page 454.)

Reuben Moore was a prosperous farmer. He and his wife resided at the old homestead of his father at Virginia Caverns, the former homeplace of David Harrison, his grandfather. (See page 378.) The residence stands to the west of the Valley Pike, the lawn and farm bordering the highway. The cavern grounds are located on the estate, a few hundred yards west of the home, and in sight of the same.

Reuben Walton, and Fannie Chrisman Moore, had issue—

1. THOMAS A.—b. Sept. 18, 1867; d. Sept. 3, 1924; m. July 7, 1896, Elizabeth H. Allebaugh, b. Dec., 1869, d. Apr. 12, 1927, daughter of Samuel R., and Elizabeth Allebaugh, and sister of Martha, the wife of Samuel Bowman. (See page 484.) They resided at the homestead above; where he was a successful farmer and stockman. Issue—an only daughter;
    1. Frances Elizabeth—b. Nov. 21, 1898; m. June 8, 1922, Thomas Harrison, (1259173), son of George H. Harrison. See later.
2. ELEANOR C.—b. Apr. 18, 1871; d. 1919; m. OWEN BROCK, of Harrisonburg. Issue—
    1. Charles—m. Maggie Lee Walker, of Texas, a neice of Mrs. Newton Harrison. (See p. 523.)
    2. Thomas—m. Virginia Zirkle, dau. of Luther Zirkle, of Harrisonburg.
    3. John—d. Mar. 10, 1928, unmarried.

    First two residents of Harrisonburg.

JENNINGS

(1234313) MARTHA VIRGINIA MOORE (1843-1916), the daughter of Madison Moore (123431), and wife Lydia, (12595), nee Harrison, married, Nov. 21, 1871, Dr. William Thomas Jennings, (1837-1896), of Rockingham. They resided in Lacey Spring, where he was a prosperous family physician of the old school, and enjoyed a wide practice in the county.

Dr. William T. Jennings, and wife Martha Moore, had issue—

Robt L. Yancey

1. Mamie S.—b. Nov. 3, 1873; m. Dec. 24, 1895, ROBERT LAYTON YANCEY, b. May 8, 1873, son of Robert Layton Yancey and wife Amanda Brock. They reside on the Valley Pike where he owns a valuable farm, opposite the late Thomas A. Moore's place. Issue—
    1. William T. Jennings—b. Mar. 27, 1897; d. young, while in school at Front Royal. (Randolph Macon.)
    2. Helen Louise—b. Apr. 16, 1900.
    3. Robert Leonard—b. Nov. 25, 1901.
    4. Martha Moore—b. Sept. 2, 1903.
    5. Lillian Amanda—b. Sept. 11, 1911.
2. Fannie Henry—b. June 20, 1876; d. Dec. 20, 1905; m. Aug. 12, 1897, DERRICK ARCHIBALD BROCK, b. May 1876, brother of Owen, above. He resides at Lacey Spring. (m. 2nd, Florence Koontz.) Issue—
    1. Rosalie T.—b. Dec. 3, 1898; m. June 28, 1930, John H. Byrd, son of Joseph C. Byrd, (1258723.) See later.
    2. William Archibald—b. Feb. 24, 1900; m. Arline Koontz, dau. of Philip, of Rockingham, and sister of Florence, above.
    3. Samuel Bertram—b. Mar. 10, 1901; d. 1918.
    4. Julian Henry—b. Apr. 15, 1902, (unmarried.)

Koontz

    5. Irene Virginia—b. Oct. 8, 1903; married EARL KOONTZ, of near Elkton, Virginia. Resides in Martinsburg, West Virginia. Issue—
        1. James Jennings—
        2. Linwood—
    6. Frances Moore—b. Nov. 8, 1904; m. Aug. 12, 1930, JOHN EDGAR WILLIAMS, of Broadway, Virginia. Issue—
        Eleanor—
3. Elton Moore—b. Oct. 12, 1879; m. Feb. 1, 1906, CLYDE W. KOONTZ, son of Abraham Koontz, of Rockingham, descendant of Col. John Koontz. (See page 365.) Resides in Washington, D. C. Issue—
    1. Maxine Jennings—b. Apr. 15, 1908.
    2. Ivan Moore—b. Aug. 3, 1911.
    3. Nell—b. ——.
    4. Rush—b. —— (twin of Nell.)

(Dates prior to 1930 from D. S. H. papers.)

(1234314) JOHN GORDON MOORE (1846-1909), the son of Madison Moore (123431), and wife Lydia (12595), nee Harrison, married, November, 1872, Alice M. Lewin, (1853-1905), of Rockingham.

John Moore was the owner of a valuable farm on the Valley Pike, adjoining his brother Reuben. He and his brothers lived near neighbors of each other—his land being on the west side of the Pike, to the north of Reuben, and opposite his brother David on the east; the three farms with that of Mr. (Robert) Yancey's, comprising the region between Melrose and Virginia Caverns, as traversed by The Long Grey Trail. The properties were carved out of the Madison Moore estate, which, as before indicated, was earlier a part of his father-in-law's land.

John G., and Alice Lewin Moore, had issue—

1. Lydia Harrison—b. Nov. 23, 1873; m. Oct. 9, 1894, SAMUEL ARCHIBALD WHITE, of Rockingham. Resides in Washington, D. C. Issue—

1. Pauline Moore—b. Aug. 15, 1895; m. Wirt Wise. Resides in Florida.
2. Mabel Lewin—b. Apr. 8, 1897; m. Millard Heatwell. Resides near Washington, D. C.
3. James Henry—b. May 31, 1899; m. Emily Bloom.
4. Carrie Lee—b. May 29, 1903; m. Patrick Dwyer.
5. Alice Virginia—b. Apr. 9, 1908; m. ——— Polita.

(Last three residents of Washington, D. C.)

2. Emily Frances—b. July 2, 1875; d. Feb. 7, 1910; m. Dec. 2, 1908, St. Andrew Myers, of Harrisonburg. Removed to Texas. No issue.
3. Bernice Lewin—b. Jan. 11, 1884; m. Aug. 11, 1909, William F. Nicholas, b. June 10, 1882, son of Charles Nicholas, of Rockingham. Resides at the John G. Moore homestead. No issue.

(D. S. H. papers.)

---

4. LINE OF JOSHUA C. PRICE

(1234321) REUBEN MOORE PRICE (1839-1918), the son of Joshua C. Price, and wife Phoebe (123432), nee Moore, was a prominent attorney of New Hope, Bucks County, Pennsylvania. As a youth he attended Eaton Academy, Kennett Square, Pennsylvania. He reached his majority in 1860, the year of the notable Lincoln and Douglas campaign, and cast his first vote for President Lincoln. He removed with his parents from Rockingham County, Virginia, to Ellendale, Maryland, in the spring of 1861, and in 1863 joined the Northern Army.

Following the war, he settled for a time in Martinsburg, West Virginia, where he edited a paper, the *Berkeley Union*, and practiced law. He was an able writer and orator, and a leader in the Republican party. For a time he was Internal Revenue Collector at Martinsburg. He later removed to New Hope, Pennsylvania and engaged in farming along with his legal pursuits. His death occurred October 4, 1918, at New Hope. He was known as the Mark Twain of Bucks County.

About 1873, he married Miss Caroline Cooper Paxion, who survived him four years. Their children were:

1. Carrol Barnard—b. Dec. 18, 1875; m. June 17, 1908, Edith Michener, b. Dec. 12, 1878. Issue—
    1. Joseph Moore—b. Sept. 29, 1913; d. Apr. 28, 1933.
    2. Carrol Barnard—b. June 11, 1915.
    3. Celia Rogers—b. Oct. 30, 1917.
2. M. Elizabeth—b. Mar. 1, 1877.
3. Reuben Moore—b. Jan. 11, 1879; m. Elizabeth Gest Freedley.
4. Frederick Newlin—b. Jan. 25, 1883.
5. Alice Rachel—b. Jan. 25, 1883; m., ROE SLOAN BREDIN, b. Sept. 9, 1881, d. June 17, 1933. Issue—
    1. Jean Elizabeth—b. May 1, 1915.
    2. Barbara Alice—b. June 28, 1916.
    3. Stephen Price—b. Sept. 17, 1922.

HUGHS

(1234322) CHARITY ANN PRICE (1841-1873), the daughter of Joshua C. Price, and wife Phoebe (123432), nee Moore, married, June 12, 1865, John Thomas

Hughs (1827-1890.) They resided in Baltimore, Maryland, where Mr. Hughs was engaged in merchandising.

John Thomas Hughs, and wife Charity Ann, nee Price, had issue—

1. George Maurice—b. April 4, 1868; m. Oct. 11, 1905, Mary Caroline Babb, b. Aug. 6, 1877. Issue—
    1. Sarah Babb—b. Nov. 6, 1906; m. JOHN BAKER ROACH LONG, b. Nov. 9, 1906. Issue—
        1. Sarah Hughs—b. July 2, 1930.

(1234323) MORDECAI PRICE, M. D. (1844-1904), the son of Joshua C. Price, and wife Phoebe (123432), nee Moore; born in Rockingham County, Virginia moved with his parents as a boy to Maryland, and following their deaths settled, as a youth, in Philadelphia, where he became one of the most eminent abdominal surgeons and gynecologists of the city. (See, *Dictionary of American Medical Biography*, by Drs. Kelly and Burrage, p. 995.)

When fourteen years of age, his leg was caught in a threshing machine which necessitated its amputation. He was in bed for nine months recovering from the accident, but undaunted by the shock and the handicap, he attended Ft. Edward Institute, at Ft. Edward, New York, and in 1869, graduated in medicine from the University of Pennsylvania. He early began specializing in his chosen field, and gradually built up the largest practice of the kind in the country.

He was the associate of his brother,Dr. Joseph Price, in conducting in Philadelphia a private hospital which attained a world-wide reputation for successful operations. Says the biographer of his brother, in the volume before referred to; "as great pioneers such men as he (Joseph) and his brother Mordecai often accomplish more for humanity than many who have poured forth much wisdom from the laboratory."

Mordecai Price died October 28, 1904. He married, September 22, 1871, Frances Fell Remington, who died in 1884. Issue—

1. Annie—b. July 27, 1873; d. ——; m. Oct. 26, 1901, Dr. EDWARD ADAMS SHUMWAY, of Marion, Pa., b. Sept. 3, 1870. Issue—
    1. Edward Adams—b. Feb. 22, 1903.
    2. Norman Price—b. Jan. 23, 1906.
2. Elizabeth Fell—b. May 14,1876; m. Nov. 16, 1901, Dr. JOHN COLTON DEAL, of Philadelphia. Issue—
    1. Margaret Price—b. Oct. 27, 1902; m. Jan. 5, 1925, F. MARCELLUS McDOWELL HEPPE. Issue—
        1. Price Deal—b. Apr. 4, 1927.
        2. Francis Colton—b. Dec. 23, 1932.
    2. Katherine Thomas—b. Aug. 10, 1904; m. June 18, 1927, A. BALFOUR BREHMAN, Jr. Issue—
        1. A. Balfour—b. Jan. 4, 1931.
    3. Frances Remington—b. Apr. 22, 1911; m. Aug. 2, 1933, Humbert Barton Powell, Jr.
3. Frances Edith—b. Aug. 19, 1877; d. May 14, 1894.
4. Louise Remington—b. March 14, 1880; m. June 16, 1908, Dr. MYRON B. PALMER, Jr., of Schenectady, N. Y. Issue—
    1. Myron B.—b. Mar. 3, 1909.

(1234324) ISAIAH BENJAMIN PRICE (1846-1884), the son of Joshua C. Price, and wife Phoebe (123432), nee Moore, was appointed Professor of Mathematics, of Union College, Schenectady, New York, in 1877, a chair which he filled with remarkable success until the time of his death, December 10, 1884.

"His childhood," says his friend, James C. Bell, in his interesting sketch of him, "was one of the happiest: the children were permitted to live a wild free life; care being taken only to foster those traits of character which would tend to make them strong and upright in principle, just and true in every detail of life."

"His love and reverence for his mother," continues the writer, "was beautiful in the extreme; and she was often heard to say: 'Isaiah is my great comfort; he has never given me an uneasy thought'."

In after years (1870), when on a visit to the West, he stopped in Dayton, Ohio, solely to see a family of colored people residing near there who had been given to his mother (by her father, at the time of her marriage), in order to hear them speak of her and the sunny days in Old Virginia. She had attempted to free them before the war, but was thwarted in her plans by her father, who, suspecting her intentions, withheld the legal formality of a deed of gift.

Young Price attended Eaton Academy with his brothers, in 1860, and following his parents' removal from Rockingham County, to Maryland, and their decease a few years later, the responsibility of managing the farm fell upon him. When the Southern Army invaded Maryland, he joined the Union forces.

With his brothers, Mordecai, Joseph, and Thomas, he entered Ft. Edward Institute in the fall of 1867. He later taught there for a time, and then occupied a position at the Friends' High School, of West Chester, Pennsylvania. He next entered Union College, at Schenectady, New York, and in 1872 was appointed tutor. He attended Edinburg University, Scotland, in 1874, and studied under Profs. Kelland and Tate. He returned home the same year, and at the request of his dying sister, Elizabeth, resumed his college work at Union, as Adjunct Professor of Physics, and Tutor of Mathematics, from which position he was later appointed Professor of Mathematics, at the death of Dr. Jackson. (See, *Proceedings of a Meeting of the Theta Chapter of Psi Upsilon in Memory of Professors Isaiah B. Price, and James C. Bell, Jr. held February 21, 1885, at Schenectady, N. Y.;* Printed for the Chapter.)

Isaiah Price married, July, 1878, Ellen Margaret Morton, of Schenectady, by whom he had—

1. MORTON MOORE—b. May 26, 1879; m. Catherine Nisbet Olmsted, b. July 1, 1877. Residence, Germantown, Pa. Issue—
    1. Robert Morton—b. June 30, 1915.
    2. William Olmsted—b. Jan. 26, 1917.
2. ELLEN MARGARET—b. Mar. 17, 1881; m. SAMUEL FERGUSON, of Hartford, Conn., b. Nov. 19, 1874. Issue—
    1. Samuel—b. Oct. 16, 1904.
    2. Margaret—b. Sept. 8, 1907.
    3. Elizabeth Day—b. June 21, 1910; m. THOMAS McCANCE. Issue—
        1. Thomas—b. Nov. 16, 1933.
    4. Mary—b. June 1, 1914.

(1234326) JOSEPH PRICE, M. D. (1853-1911), the son of Joshua C. Price, and wife Phoebe (123432), nee Moore; an outstanding personality in the history of American medicine, and one of the country's greatest surgeons, (of whom some account has been given at the beginning of this Chapter) removed in childhood, with his parents, from Rockingham County, Virginia, to the vicinity of Baltimore. After receiving his early schooling at Ft. Edward, New York, he attended Union College from 1871 to 1872, and in the latter year left college to join the engineering corps of the New York Central Railroad. He graduated in medicine from the University of Pennsylvania in 1877, and for a short time thereafter served as a surgeon on a transatlantic passenger steamer, plying between Philadelphia, Antwerp, and Liverpool, making in all three voyages. The same year he began his life work at the Philadelphia Dispensary. He early became in charge of the obstetrical department, and was the organizer of the gynecological department of the institution, and under his leadership these departments came to be one the most conspicuous and largest clinics of the country.

Most of his work, while associated with the Dispensary, was done in the slums of the city in the midst of squalor and filth. The period was at the dawn of aseptic surgery and the principles of Lister, as based on the researches of Pasteur, were accepted by only a few unreservedly. The older surgeons in authority either rejected the new surgery entirely, or viewed it as an experiment only, and the body of the profession was disposed to adhere to conservative methods, in contrast to what seemed most radical. Price became a militant advocate of the new surgery. "With the courage of a Spartan, and with matchless skill and judgement as an operator, he forged to the front." says Dr. Kennedy, *In Memoriam,* "and completely dominated his unsurgical surroundings by the most brilliant results of any age."

His record with the Dispensary led to his appointment as head of the Preston Retreat, a large endowed obstetrical home, which position he filled from 1887 to 1894. During the entire time he had charge of the Retreat, there was not a death from sepsis. In the interval, with W. O. Penrose, he founded the Philadelphia Gynecean Hospital, (incorporated 1888.)

His admiration for Lawson Tate, "England's pioneer surgical genius," induced him to visit Europe about 1887, and brought him in contact with Tate. He subsequently made a second visit to Birmingham and the two corresponded until the latter's death. Owing to his dexterity as an operator, Price was often spoken of as "The American Tate." He was also a devoted admirer of Marion Sims, an American authority, and friend and ardent follower of Thomas Addis Emmet, of New York.

In 1891, Dr. Price opened his private hospital, at 241 North Eighteenth Street, Philadelphia, in which he was associated with his brother Dr. Mordecai Price (see above) until the latter's death, and with Dr. W. Kennedy until his own death. His masterful work in this institution was world-wide in reputation, and under his leadership it became the largest private hospital in this country for abdominal surgery.

He constantly taught by and through his operations, and so definite was his touch, that most of his work was done with the skill of a juggler. While never making any attempt at speed, he made no useless moves, and his manipulations were such that his work was done with the greatest dispatch. "His capacity for work was unlimited," relates the journal earlier referred to, "and it is doubtful if any operator has done so much difficult abdominal surgery; he never picked his cases and never refused to give any patient the last chance on account of his own mortality." He has been termed by Dr. William Mayo, "the father of abdominal surgery in America."

He was a faithful attendent upon medical societies, and discussed the surgical problems of his day before the county, State, and national organizations in almost every State of the Union, and in Canada. In 1895 he was President of the American Association of Obstetricians and Gynecologists.

A most forceful speaker, with a wit as keen as his surgeons knife, and a spicy humor, when he was known to be in attendance at a meeting, his audience thronged into the room, until even the aisles were crowded, to enjoy his vigorous discussions. He was bitter and unrelenting as a foe, and caustically flayed his opponents. He greatly abhorred commercialism in his profession, and abominated ostentation, or any display of elaborate equipment; "fuss, feathers, and foolishness" he termed it. His instruments and other apparatus of the operating room were of the simplest sort for the work in hand, and his professional charity had no equal. His private hospital was as accessible to the poor as any public institution in America.

Joseph Price married, April 20, 1887, Miss Louisa ("Lou") Troth, of Philadelphia. They were married on the eve of his appointment as head of the Preston Retreat. The position having become vacant, his name came up for consideration by the directors. The salary was large and in addition with it went a big comfortable house and grounds, but the holder of the position was required to be a married man. "Price's candidacy," says his biographer, "was settled in the happiest manner." Having been for some years engaged to Miss Troth, he and his betrothed were immediately married. She survived him twenty-two years.

His death occurred June 8, 1911. A month before his decease, he received his LL. D. degree from Union College. He was an excellent rifle shot, and won the championship at the Philadelphia Centennial. A good likeness of him appears in the January, 1912, number of the obstetrical journal before referred to. (See also, *Surgery, Gynecology and Obstetrics*, Dec. 1932, Vol LV, pp. 788-791.) His residence was at Whitford, Pennsylvania.

Dr. Joseph Price, and wife Louisa, nee Troth, had issue—

1. Marian—b. Jan. 30, 1888. (unmarried.)
2. Phoebe Ann Moore—b. Nov. 16, 1889; m. (1st), April 24, 1913, Dr. FRANCIS BRINTON JACOBS, of West Chester, Pa., b. Sept. 22, 1874, d. Feb. 11, 1932. Issue—
    1. Francis—b. July 7, 1915.
    2. Phoebe Ann—b. Jan. 8, 1922.

    Mrs. Jacobs m. (2nd) Daniel Cornwell.
3. Joseph—b. May 16, 1890; m. Frances Eulalia Baker.
4. Louisa Troth—b. Dec. 2, 1892; m. Sept. 9, 1913, WILLIAM HOLLINGSWORTH WHYTE. Issue—
    1. William Hollingsworth—b. Oct. 1, 1917.
    2. Robert—b. Oct. 26, 1922.
5. Anne—b. July 22, 1894; m. Aug. 11, 1917, JOHN MICKLE HEMPHILL, b. Sept. 6, 1891. Issue—
    1. Alexander—b. May 22, 1921.
    2. Dallett—b. Jan. 13, 1924.
    3. Dolly—b. Aug. 26, 1928.
6. Henry Troth—b. Dec. 8, 1897. (unmarried.) Residence, West Chester, Pa. Served during the World War, in U. S. Navy, (Marine Engr. on Government Transport.)

7. Richard Preston—b. June 13, 1902; m. June 29, 1927, Susan Brewster Cleveland, b. June 15, 1904. Issue—
   1. Richard Preston—b. Aug. 25, 1929.
   2. William Brewster—b. May 3, 1932.

BACHUS

(1234329) CORNELIA (CORRIE) W. PRICE (1857-1911), the daughter of Joshua C. Price, and wife Phoebe (123432), nee Moore, married, March 29, 1877, Bayard Bachus, an attorney at law, of Schenectady, New York. Issue—

1. Elizabeth Chester—b. Jan. 10, 1878; d. Nov. 12, 1922; m. Jan. 7, 1902, WALTER T. PECK, (of the U. S. Diplomatic Service.) Issue—
   1. Elizabeth C.—b. Jan. 7, 1903.
   2. Samuel—b. Jan. 15, 1904.

---

4. LINE OF JOHN MOORE

(1234333) NEWTON GORDON MOORE (1851-1914), the son of John Moore (123433), and wife Elizabeth Ann, (12598), nee Harrison, married, September 27, 1876, Josephine Augusta Henkel, daughter of Dr. Solon Paul Charles Henkel, of New Market Virginia, and wife Maria, nee Miller.

Newton G. Moore was a prominent and well to do farmer of Rockingham. He was a man of marked ability, widely known throughout the Valley, and engaged to a large extent in stock raising. He was the owner of a valuable tract of land on which he and his wife resided, and where she, as his widow, continues to reside, located on the Valley Pike about a mile and a half north of the village of Tenth Legion. The property borders Smiths Creek on the east, and the Court Manor land on the north, and was formerly a part of the Moreland Hall estate, and later the homestead of his father. The residence, a substantial and commodious brick building, erected by the late owner, stands a few hundred yards east of the Pike, and about on the spot of his birthplace. It was on the same farm, nearer the creek, that Thomas Moore, the founder of the family, is said to have settled, and the land has been continually in the posession of the family since.

As a youth, Mr. Moore attended school in Woodstock, and in New Market, in Shenandoah County, and was a pupil of Prof. Joseph Salyards, one of Virginia's noted teachers of the day. He later attended Roanoke College, at Salem, Virginia. He lived to send all of his sons (except an infant who died) to the same institution (from which all but the eldest graduated.) A firm believer in the value of higher education, he also sent all of his daughters to college. His convictions in this respect can be the better appreciated when the number of his children are considered. He was a member of Emmanuel Lutheran Church, (ofttimes locally called the Henkel, or Upper Lutheran Church), of New Market, to which his mother had belonged, and of which his widow has been a communicant since girlhood.

HENKEL

Dr. Solon P. C. Henkel, (b. 1818, d. May 14, 1882), the father of Mrs. Josephine Moore, was sprung from a noted line of Lutheran clergymen. The immigrant, Rev.

Anthony Jacob Henkel, (Hinckel), native of Germany, settled in Pennsylvania about 1717, in what is now Montgomery County. He died in 1728. His great-grandson Rev. Paul Henkel (son of Jacob, son of John Justice, son of the immigrant), a Lutheran missionary, came to New Market in 1783. Of Rev. Paul Henkel's five sons, viz: Solomon, David, Andrew, Ambrose, and Philip, the last four were Lutheran ministers. Rev. Ambrose Henkel, soon after the founding of the Republic, established in New Market a printing business which has continued among his descendants to today, and is now known as the Henkel Press (publishers of the *Shanendoah Valley.)* Schuricht, in his *History of the German Element in Virginia,* (Vol. II, p. 9), relates that Rev. Henkel built the first press with his own hands, and undertook the publication of "German school books and religious works." In 1806, the office was in possesion of Solomon Henkel, son of Rev. Ambrose, and an "A B C book . . . probably the first school book printed in Virginia, was published with lines of poetry and illustrations for each letter of the alphabet, cut in wood by Rev. Henkel himself." A second edition of the book appeared in 1819.

Dr. Solomon Henkel, the only son of Rev. Paul Henkel not to become a minister of the Gospel, married Maria Rebecca Miller, of Winchester, Virginia, and was the founder of a distinguished line of physicians. Two of his sons, Drs. Samuel Godfrey Henkel, and Solon P. C. Henkel, were members of the profession, of whom the latter married, in 1847, Anna Maria Miller, of Winchester, Virginia, and had four sons, Miller A., Solomon, Frederick Lewis and Alfred David, who became physicians. During the War-between-the-States, at the battle of New Market, Dr. Solon P. C. Henkel minstered to the wounded soldiers of both the Northern and Southern armies. His near kinsman, the late Dr. Casper C. Henkel, of New Market, (son of Samuel Godfrey), served as acting surgeon on Stonewall Jackson's medical staff.

* * * * * *

To Newton G. Moore, and wife Josephine, were born an interesting family of children. In all, there were fifteen in number, fourteen of whom lived to reach maturity, and thirteen are today living, as listed below—

1. Annie Elizabeth Harrison—b. Aug. 7, 1877; m. July 21, 1926, Charles Benton Wornom, of Dare, York County, Virginia, (his 2nd wife.)
2. Solon Henkel—b. Nov. 21, 1878; m. Fannie Bell McGlaughlin, of Marlington, W. Va. Resides at Monterey, Virginia. No issue
3. Maria Miller—b. Jan. 3, 1880, (unmarried) at home.
4. John Newton—b. Apr. 22, 1881; m. Oct. 25, 1905, Emma L. Cook, of Washington State, b. Jan. 9, 1885. Removed to Washington in 1901. Resides at Sunny Side, Washington. Issue—
    1. Josephine Catherine—b. Sept. 30, 1906; m. July 14, 1928, HAROLD CRAFT. Issue—
        1. Rose Marie—b. Dec. 7, 1929.
    2. Mary Inez—b. Feb. 1, 1908; m. Nov. 25, 1927, GEORGE A. DAVIS. Issue—
        1. Louisa May—b. Oct. 9, 1928.
    3. Ernest Newton—b. June 30, 1909.
    4. Reuben Gordon—b. Dec. 5, 1910.
    5. Thomas Ira—b. Mar. 8, 1912.
    6. Benjamin Cook—b. Sept. 27, 1913.

7. Hershel Henkel—b. May 20, 1915.
8. Edith Myra—b. Sept 2, 1917.
9. Elizabeth Irene—b. Oct. 17, 1919
10. Harry William—b. Nov. 17, 1921.

5. MARY VIRGINIA—b. Sept. 28, 1882; m. May 8, 1907, HARRY CELSUS COINER, of near Waynesboro, Virginia, farmer, b. Dec. 13, 1878. Issue—
1. Elijah Moore—b. June 18, 1908.
2. Josephine Elizabeth—b. May 6, 1910.
3. Harry Gordon—b. Nov. 27, 1912.
4. twin of last named b. and d. same date.
5. Edgar Reed—b. Jan 10, 1916.
6. Lewis Miller—b. Aug. 10, 1919.
7. Ida Henkel—b. Feb. 10, 1923; d. Mar. 14, 1926.

6. REUBEN WALTON—b. Apr. 21, 1884; m., Jan. 6, 1914, Mildred Worthington Morehead, dau. of Dr. Presley William Morehead, of New Market, Virginia, (later of Clarendon, Va., where he d. 1929.) Resides near Staunton, Virginia. See later. Issue—
1. John Morehead—b. Aug. 15, 1915.
2. Presley William—b. June 1, 1917.
3. Elizabeth Ann—b. Sept. 15, 1923.

7. THOMAS—b. May 15, 1886; m. Feb. 12, 1916, Rita Catherine Harrison, (1259153), dau. of David W. Harrison. See later. Issue—
1. David Warren—b. Dec. 12, 1916.
2. John Newton—b. Feb. 1, 1919.
3. Julia Bruce—b. Dec. 15, 1920.
4. Anna Harrison—b. May 31, 1923.
5. Thomas Henkel—b. Nov. 15, 1931.

8. EMILY FISHER—b. Dec. 24, 1887, (unmarreid), at home.

9. JULIA GERTRUDE—b. Sept. 21, 1889; m. Oct. 27, 1920, BENJAMIN WADE FONTAINE, (farmer) of Wytheville, Virginia. Issue—
1. Mary Moore—b. Aug. 29, 1921.
2. John Wade—b. Jan. 14, 1926.

10. JOSEPHINE—b. Aug. 7, 1891, (unmarried), at home; connected with office of County Supt. of Schools, Harrisonburg, Va.

11. FANNIE CHRISMAN—b. Mar. 2, 1893; m. Aug. 25, 1920, Arthur Allen Austin, of Staunton, Va. (No issue.)

12. JOSEPH PRICE—b. Dec. 4, 1894; m. Sept. 2, 1920, at Cincinnati, O., Myra Alixis Winkler, dau. of Prof. John George Winkler, of Salem, Va. Resides at Remlik, Virginia. Issue—
1. Joseph Price—b. July 8, 1921.
2. Richard Myron—b. Feb. 2, 1923.
3. John George—b. Nov. 22, 1926.
4. Muriel Millicent—b. Aug. 26, 1931.
5. Madeline Enid Pamelia—b. Aug. 1, 1933.

13. a son, anonymus—b. Dec. 17, 1896; d. Feb. 9, 1897.

14. ABRAHAM SCHULTZ—b. Nov. 18, 1897; d. Feb. 12, 1934; m. June 8, 1927, at Mt. Vernon, South Dakota, Cora Theresa Ostrus, dau. of Martin Ostrus. Served for a number of years on faculty of Augustana College, Sioux Falls,

S. D., as head of chemistry department. Returned to Virginia in 1927, and settled in New Market, where he was proprietor of a department store, and an active civic leader. Issue—

1. Helen Virginia—b. Apr. 22, 1928.

15. MARTHA KATHERINE—b. Apr. 26, 1899, (unmarried), engaged in teaching.

(John Moore's grandchildren, it may be observed, are of the 10th generation from Isaiah Harrison, the immigrant.)

* * * * * *

Of the above—

REUBEN WALTON MOORE, after attending Roanoke College, engaged for a time in contracting and railroad construction in western Canada. About the year following his marriage, he was appointed Road Supervisor of Augusta County, Virginia, and removed to Staunton, this county. He served the county for a number of years in this capacity, and then entered the field of general road contracting. He is the builder of a number of important links in Virginia's modern highways. As a resident of Staunton, he purchased the valuable old Lewis farm, a short distance north of the city, on which he and his wife now reside. Mrs. Moore is a native of Rappahannock County, Virginia. Her father, the late Dr. P. W. Morehead, was for many years a leading physican of New Market.

* * * * * *

THOMAS MOORE, son of Newton G., and sole surviving male Moore descendant of Thomas Moore, founder of the family, now resident in Rockingham, (barring his own sons), is a worthy representative of the name long prominent in the county. He is one of Rockingham's widely known farmers, and resides on the ancestral acres. The site of his home affords one of the finest views in the Valley of Virginia. He is the manager of three highly valuable farms; his own, his late father's, and the former David W. Harrison farm, owned by himself and his mother. He resides on the first named tract, which he acquired from his father a short time prior to the latter's death, and which embraces that part of his father's land lying to the west of the Valley Pike, between the Court Manor estate on the north and the David Harrison land on the south. His own two farms border for a mile or more the historic highway. The homestead land lies directly east of his own, and on the opposite side of the Pike from him. The three properties approximate a square mile in area.

Following his graduation from college, in 1907, Thomas Moore resided for a year or so near Williston, North Dakota, where he bought a farm and taught a term of school. He returned to Virginia a short time prior to his marriage. His wife was born and reared on the farm he now jointly owns with his mother. She was educated at Kee Mar College, Hagerstown, Maryland, and at Randolph Macon Womens College, Lynchburg, Virginia. Two of Mr. Moore's sisters, Emily and Julia, are her former Kee Mar classmates, and several of his older sisters also attended the same school.

---

4. LINE OF JOSEPH MOORE

ALLEN

(1234372) MARGARET FRANCES MOORE (1849-1873), the daughter of Joseph Moore, of Shenandoah County, and wife, Virginia (123437), nee Moore, married, November 21, 1870, Linden Allen (1850-1912), of Shenandoah County. They resided a short distance north of Mt. Jackson, on the Valley Pike, where he owned a valuable farm.

Linden and Margaret Frances Allen had issue an only daughter—

1. HATTIE VIRGINIA—b. Nov. 12, 1871; m. about 1894, ALLEN SNYDER, of Mt. Jackson, Virginia. Issue—
    1. Margaret Frances—b. 1896; m. 1st, Comfort Watkins, of Richmond, Virginia.
    2. Beverley Allen—b. 1908; d. 1933.

(D. S. H. papers.)

MILLER

(1234373) SARAH MOORE (1851-1916), the daughter of Joseph Moore, and wife Virginia (123437), nee Moore, married, December 12, 1871, John William Miller (1846-1911), of Shenandoah County, Virginia. They resided on his farm a short distance north of Mt. Jackson. Following his death her last years were spent in the town.

J. William Miller, and wife Sarah, nee Moore, had issue—

1. MABEL MOORE—b. Nov. 21, 1872; d. young.
2. EDITH PRICE—b. about 1885; d. Aug. 31, 1909.

(D. S. H. papers.)

NEFF

(1234374) MARTHA VIRGINIA MOORE (1853-1921), the daughter of Joseph Moore, and wife Virginia (123437), nee Moore, married, September 26, 1880, Milton Neff (1855-1921), a successful banker of Mt. Jackson, Virginia, brother of the late Dr. John Neff, of Harrisonburg, Virginia.

Milton Neff and wife, Martha Virginia, nee Moore had issue—

1. KATIE—b. Oct. 28, 1881. (unmarried.)
2. ROBERTA BEVERLY—b. Oct. 3, 1884. (unmarried.)

Both reside in Mt. Jackson.

(D. S. H. papers.)

(1234377) JOSEPHINE (JO) MOORE (1862), the daughter of Joseph Moore, and wife Virginia (123437), nee Moore, married George H. Harrison (125917), of Rockingham County, Virginia, son of John Harrison. See Clan of John Harrison, 1. Line of Capt. Reuben Harrison, 2. Line of David Harrison, 3. Line of John Harrison, (page 514.)

---

4. LINE OF REUBEN MOORE

HENKEL

(1234381) MARGARET FRANCES MOORE (1852-1886), the daughter of Reuben Moore (123438), and wife, Annis Beaver, married, Apr. 15, 1874, at Moreland Hall, Dr. Miller A. Henkel, born Oct. 25, 1848, eldest son of Dr. Solon P. C. Henkel, of New Market, Virginia, and brother of Mrs. Josephine Moore, widow of Newton G. Moore. (See page 596.) Dr. Henkel and wife for about ten years following their marriage resided in Winchester, Virginia, where he practiced medicine. They Later removed to Florida, in which State both died, she first. (He married 2nd, Aug. 24, 1887, Carrie Hale, of St. Johnsburg, Vermont.) His death occurred in Winter Park, Florida, in 1911.

Dr. Miller A., and Margaret Frances Henkel, had issue—

1. MARY—d. in infancy, in Winchester, Va.
2. ANNIE MARIA—d. in Florida; m. GEORGE FETZER, of Moorefield, West Virginia, where they resided. He is now a merchant of Harrisonburg, Virginia. Issue—
   1. George Miller—d. age 15, at Front Royal, Va., while student at Randolph Macon Academy.
3. MILLER A.—b. Dec. 19, 1878; d. Jan. 29, 1890, in Florida.
4. THOMAS MOORE—m. 1st, Mary E. Biedler, of Pennsylvania; m. 2nd, ———. Resides in Winter Park, Florida. Issue, by first marriage—
   1. Mary—
   2. Miller—
5. FRANCES—m. BAXTER SMITH, of Demorest, Georgia, where they reside. Issue—
   1. Virginia—
   2. William Henkel—

(1234382) MARY C. MOORE (1853-1883), the daughter of Reuben Moore (123438), and wife Annis Beaver, married, May 24, 1878, George H. Harrison (125917), of Rockingham County, Virginia, son of John Harrison. (See page 514.)

(1234383) OSCAR FITZ ALLEN MOORE (1855-1879), the son of Reuben Moore (123438), and wife Annis Beaver, married Mary Alice Henkel, born Oct. 24, 1856, daughter of Solomon Henkel of New Market, Virginia. The name Oscar Fitz Allen was that of a hero in a story, *Children of the Abbey,* and the mother of Oscar Fitz Allen Moore in admiration of the character gave the name to her son. It also occurs among the Cravens.

Oscar F. A. Moore, and wife, resided at Moreland Hall, until about six months prior to his death, when they removed to New Market, Virginia. His widow married, second, Solon Henkel, descendant of Solomon Henkel, the early publisher. She died in New Market, May 17, 1884.

Oscar Fitz Allen Moore, and wife Mary Alice, nee Henkel, had issue—

1. CHARLES H.—b. Apr. 2, 1876; m., 1909, Meta Burke, dau. of John and Margaret Fennimore Burke, of New Market, Virginia. They reside in New Market, where he has long been engaged in merchandising. Issue—
   1. Maran Margaret— (graduate of Wm. & Mary, 1931.)
   2. Charles H., Jr.—(Student, Uni. of Va.)
2. JOHN—b. Apr. 15, 1878; m., Ethel Daniels, (cousin of Dr. Daniels, of Charlottesville, Virginia.) Resided in St. Louis, Missouri, where he was an attorney at at law. d. ——. Issue—
   1. Rodger Daniels—m. Vera ———. (decd.)

2. Esther Virginia—m. Louis Untemyer. Resides near Charlottesville, Virginia. (She is the author of a book of poems.)
3. Randolph—(unmarried.) Lawyer, St. Louis Mo..
4. Nancy Herberta—m. Sidney Kelsey.

---

4. LINE OF WILLIAM F. GAINES

ZIRKLE

(1234402) LUCY GAINES (1863), the daughter of William F. Gaines, and wife, Mary Catherine (123440), nee Moore, married Bradford B. Zirkle, of Rockingham County Virginia, born October 28, 1854, died Feb. 5, 1935, the son of Reuben Zirkle. Mr. Zirkle and wife resided at the old homestead of her father to the east of Smiths Creek, and opposite the Newton G. Moore estate, where he was a prosperous farmer, and where his widow continues to reside.

Bradford B. Zirkle, and wife Lucy, nee Gaines, had issue an only son, viz:

1. Hunter—b. Nov. 1887; m. June, 1911, Julia Price, daughter of Capt. Berriman Z. Price, (decd.) of near New Market, Virginia, (and sister of Keyser Price—see page 559.) Resides at Progress, Pennsylvania. Issue—
    1. Louise Virginia—b. May 29, 1912.

---

1. LINE OF CAPT. REUBEN HARRISON
2. LINE OF NATHANIEL HARRISON
3. LINE OF MIFFORD HANNAH
4. LINE OF NATHANIEL HANNAH

KEEZELL

(1252844) MARY CATHERINE HANNAH (1858-1902), the daughter of Nathaniel Hannah (125284), and wife Belle, nee Rhodes, married, 1886, George B. Keezell (1854-1931), of Rockingham. Her death occurred October 11, 1902.

* * * * * *

Keezletown

George Bernard Keezell was for many years a State senator of Virginia and served in this capacity longer than any man of his generation. He died June 22, 1931. At the time of his death he was the treasurer of Rockingham, and had long been one of the county's leading farmers. He was a native of the county, having been born near Keezletown, July 20th, 1854, the only child of George Keezell, and wife Amanda Fitzallen Peale. His father died in 1862. The latter was a soldier in the War of 1812, and was the son of George Keezell, founder of Keezletown. (See page 240.) Mr. Keezell was educated at Stuart Hall, in Baltimore, and at the age of sixteen took up farming at the old home of his grandfather, (built in 1794), where his mother resided. In 1883 he was elected to the State senate, and was reelected four successive terms from 1895 to 1911. He was a member of the Virginia constitutional convention in 1901, and was a presidential elector in 1904. During his service in the senate he was for a number of years chairman of the Finance Committee. He was especially influential in establishing the State Normal and Industrial School at Harrisonburg, and later served as chairman of the Board of Trustees. A Democrat in politics, he was for twenty-five years chairman of the party's organization in Rockingham. (See, Wayland's *History of Rockingham Co.*, 1912, p. 361.)

On Dec. 10th, 1903 Senator Keezell married, second, Belle C. Hannah (1252841), the only sister of his first wife, and a prominent Rockingham teacher. He resided at the old homestead, where his widow continues to reside.

Senator George B., and Mary Catherine, (Kate M.) Keezell, had issue—

1. George F. A.—b. ——; d. in infancy.
2. Walter B.— b. Sept. 7, 1888; m. Mary Berry, of Madison Co., Virginia.
3. Catherine A.—b. Aug. 2, 1890; m. April 15, 1911, CLAUDE V. SMITH, of Harrisonburg, (head of the Rockingham Farm Bureau.) Issue—
    1. George Bernard—b. Nov. 10, 1912.
    2. Martha—b. Aug. 22, 1915.
    3. Claude V. Jr.—b. Apr. 24, 1917.
    4. Edward—b. June 2, 1919.
4. Rembrandt P. (Capt.)—b. Apr. 10, 1892; m. Meta Echard, resided at Keezletown. Served as Capt. in the A. E. F. during the World War. He died Jan. 18, 1935.
5. Florence A.—b. Sept. 16, 1894; m. J. Fred Simms, of Rockingham.
6. George Orville—b. July 20, 1896; d. Oct. 5, 1906.
7. Nathaniel Harrison—b. June 25, 1898; m. a Miss Carper. Resides at the old home.

(D. S. H. papers, etc.)

---

2. LINE OF THOMAS WARREN

3. LINE OF JOSEPH BURKHOLDER

4. LINE OF WILLIAM P. BYRD

(1258723) JOSEPH C. BYRD (1860), the son of William P. Byrd, and wife Catherine (125872), nee Burkholder, married October 14, 1891, Nancy Gordon Harrison (125923), daughter of John Harrison, and wife Barbara Katherine, nee Hollingsworth.

Joseph Clinton Byrd was born at Mt. Crawford, on the Valley Pike, and moved in childhood with his parents to near Greenmount, a short distance west of Harrisonburg, where he was reared on his father's farm. For some years following his marriage he engaged in merchandising at Mt. Clinton. From there, he removed with his family to Harrisonburg, in which city he has continued to reside for the greater part of the time since, and now resides. About 1920, he retired from merchandising and for several years engaged in farming at the old Harrison homestead, near Mauzy. Upon the recent conversion of the property into a dairy farm by his sons, Mr. Byrd and wife returned to Harrisonburg.

Like Annie of Tharaw and her spouse of old, the "threads of the two lives" of Joseph and Nannie Byrd run truly as one. A devoted couple they are worthy exponents of the olden time Virginia hospitality. She belongs to that winsome band of eight sisters, of whom but three remain, the daughters of John Harrison, all noted hostesses.

Joseph C., and Nancy Harrison Byrd, are the parents of four children,—viz:

1. William Harrison—b. Nov. 10, 1892; m. Nov. 8, 1919, Clyde Prince Sebrell, dau. of Thomas Edwin Sebrell, of Courtland, Virginia. Resides in Harrisonburg. (V. P. and Cashier of the First National Bank.) Served in Battery B., 60th Regt. Coast Artillery Corps, A. E. F., in the World War. (no issue.)

2. EMMA ELIZABETH—b. Apr. 25, 1894, (unmarried), at home.
3. JOHN HOLLINGSWORTH—b. Apr. 28, 1897; m. June 28, 1930, Rosalie T. Brock, dau. of Archibald Brock, and wife Fannie, nee Jennings, and granddaughter of Dr. William T. Jennings, and wife Martha Virginia Moore, (1234313). Resides in Harrisonburg. (With Rockingham National Bank.) Served in U. S. Army, at Camp Lee, during the World War. Issue—
   1. John Hollingsworth—b. 29th Nov., 1932.
4. CATHERINE—b. May 3, 1902; m., June 25, 1932, FRANK OWENS BARKLEY, Jr., of Maysville, Kentucky. Resides in Maysville. Issue—
   1. William Byrd—b. Dec. 16, 1933.

---

2. LINE OF DAVID HARRISON
3. LINE OF JOHN HARRISON
4. LINE OF MICHAEL J. MARTZ

(1259122) HIRAM HARRISON MARTZ (1870), the son of Michael J. Martz, and wife Barbara Katherine, (Kate) (125912), nee Harrison, married in Tennessee, Aug. 1, 1906, Lena May Peters, the daughter of George Peters, and wife Martha Miller, of Tennessee.

Hiram (Harry) Martz is a prosperous and widely known farmer of Shenandoah County, Virginia. He and his wife reside a short distance north of New Market, where he owns a valuable farm. He is a graduate of Washington and Lee University, in Civil Engineering, and for a number of years followed his profession, specializing in railroad construction. During this time, he was resident engineer on various important projects, among them the extension of the C. C. & O. Railroad into the Tennessee coal fields, involving much tunneling. Since his settlement in Shenandoah, he has served his county as a member of the Board of Supervisors, and in other capacities. Upon the recent opening of Virginia Caverns, or old Harrison Cave, to the public, he was the engineer in charge of the surveys and construction work connected therewith.

Hiram Harrison, and Lena Peters Martz, have children—

1. GEORGE MICHAEL—b. Apr. 8, 1907, (died in infancy.)
2. HIRAM WARD—b. May 26, 1908.
3. MARGARET MAE—b. Nov. 9, 1910.
4. MARTHA KATHERINE—b. Aug. 19, 1912.
5. ROBERT GORDON—b. Mar. 15, 1915.
6. VIRGINIA LEE—b. Oct. 30, 1916; d. Jan. 26, 1925.
7. NANCY HARRISON—b. Dec. 13, 1918.
8. SARAH FRANCES—b. Aug. 22, 1921.

---

4. LINE OF DAVID W. HARRISON

(1259152) JOHN HOUSTON HARRISON (1887), the son of David W. Harrison (125915), and wife Anna A. (178452), nee Houston, married, at Charlottesville, Virginia, June 4, 1912, Berta Steptoe Watson, daughter of A. Sidney Watson, deceased, and wife Mary Louise, nee Wheeler, of Charlottesville.

J. Houston Harrison was born and reared on his father's farm in Rockingham, and after attending Ohio Northern University, at Ada, Ohio, one session, pursued mechanical and electrical engineering courses at the University of Virginia, 1905-10, specializing in the degree of mechanical engineer. Following his marriage, he settled in Washington, D. C., having in the meantime entered the service of the Southern Railway Company, in mechanical engineering, with which company he has been connected ever since. From 1914 to 1920, he resided in Charlottesville, Virginia, during which interval he was engaged in locomotive testing on the road in charge of a dynamometer car. In 1920, he returned to Washington, as an assistant superintendent, and the following year established his home in Alexandria, Virginia. (Rosemont.) In 1928, upon the transfer of various offices of the company to Atlanta, Georgia, he moved with his family to Decatur, where he resided until 1931, when he was recalled to Washington, as mechanical engineer of valuation, and other cost studies, and thereupon resumed his residence in Alexandria. (He is a member of the American Society of Mechanical Engineers, the Virginia Historical Society, and is a Royal Arch Mason. Both he and his wife are members of the M. E. Church, South; and she of the Nat. Soc. D. A. R., and of the United Daughters of the Confederacy.)

WATSON

Algernon Sidney Watson, b. February 11, 1838, d. April 6, 1905, was a prosperous farmer and orchardist of Covesville, Albemarle County, Virginia. He was born at "Cove Lawn," where he resided, and was the son of Daniel Edward Watson, (d. 1882), and wife Mary Woods Harris, of "Cove Lawn," and the grandson of Wilkins Watson, of Amherst County, Virginia, and wife Polly, nee Tucker, of Lexington, Virginia. While a student at the University of Virginia, he resigned to enter the Confederate Army, and served throughout the war, eleven months as Stonewall Jackson's courier, and was with the latter at Chancellorsville. As a memento of his services on one occasion, the noted leader presented him with his own sword.

Dr. Daniel Edward Watson was a widely practiced county physician of Covesville. His father, Wilkins Watson, was the son of Edward Watson, b. October 14, 1746, d. November 20, 1839, and wife Annie, nee Noble, b. June 14, 1746, d. April 12, 1812. Edward Watson and wife were married July 9, 1772, and had children—William, b. August 25, 1773, Annie b. February 9, 1775, Alexander, b. December 9, 1776, d. June 7, 1815, John, b. December 6, 1778, Lucy, b. Feb. 13, 1781, d. May 1809, Lilley, b. December 30, 1782, and Wilkins, b. September 13, 1785, m. 1st, December 12, 1809, Polly H. Tucker, b. August 17, 1794, d. August 20, 1838, m. 2nd, March 23, 1843, Elizabeth Ann Henley.

Wilkins and Polly Watson had issue—Daniel Edward, as above, b. October 30, 1810, m. 1st, May 15, 1834, Mary Woods Harris, b. 1811, d. July 23, 1871, m. 2nd, January 22, 1873, Martha Jane Hart; Alberta, b. April 1, 1813, d. November 19, 1813; William Henry, b. May 18, 1815, m. June 7, 1838, Susan C. Dunnington; Ann Eliza, b. July 28, 1817, d. December 25, 1859, m., May 31, 1836, James E. Horner; Judith H., b. December 6, 1819, m., October 19, 1841, Matthew F. Harris; John James, b. April 5, 1822, m., November 11, 1847, Louisa H. Williams; Mary Wilkins, b. April 13, 1824, d. October 30, 1832; George Alexander b. December 31, 1827; Mariah Louisa, b. August 6, 1830, m., November 23, 1848, Lafayette Steptoe; and Lucy Jane, b. September 28, 1832. Wilkins and Elizabeth Watson had issue—Wilkins, b. May 22, 1845, Edwin, b. May 2, 1847, and Lillie Virginia, b. December 31, 1848. Wilkins Watson d. Oct. 4, 1856. (See Watson family Bible.)

Mary Wood Harris, the wife of Dr. Daniel Edward Watson, was the daughter

Mary Woods Harris

of Henry Tate Harris, b. 1787, d. March 8, 1845, and wife Mary Woods Harris, b. August 24, 1788, m., April 16, 1811, d. March, 1874, the daughter of Capt. Benjamin Harris, b. January 30, 1754, d. March 25, 1834, and wife Mary Woods, b. February 20, 1767, m., September 27, 1785, d. August 15, 1844. Benjamin Harris served in the Revolutionary War, first as a private, then as a corporal, in the Virginia Continental Line, and from 1779 to 1782 was a Captain. He joined Lafayette's forces in 1781, and was at the seige of Yorktown. Capt. Harris was the son of William Harris, b. 1706, d. September 25, 1788, and wife Mary Netherland, b. 1719, d. May 20, 1799, and the grandson of Matthew Harris, b. 1687, d. 1727, and wife Elizabeth Lee, m., 1716, d. 1784. (D. A. R. Lineage—National No. 235343.)

Dr. Daniel Edward Watson, and wife Mary's children were—Mary W., b. April 5, 1835, d. March 29, 1873, m. 1st, November 9, 1853, William M. Harris, m. 2nd, Stephen Rodgers; Henrietta V., b. August 8, 1836, d. March 22, 1862, m., December 6, 1855, James N. Anderson; Algernon Sidney, as above, m. May 21, 1873, Mary Louise Wheeler, b. at Lynchburg, Virginia, (1856), dau. of John Vernon and Missouri (Pettijohn) Wheeler; and Ann Eliza, b. January 18, 1841, d. June 16, 1897, m., January 28, 1863, Dr. Hawes N. Coleman, d. July 21, 1877. (Watson family Bible.)

A. Sidney Watson and wife Mary Louise had issue—D. Edward, resident of Crozet, Virginia, m. Elizabeth Garnett, of Charlottesville; Pearl, m. Dr. Montie L. Rea, of Charlottesville; Robert A., b. October 29, 1877, resident of Charlottesville, (V. P. and Trust Officer, Peoples National Bank), m. Sadie R. Baggarly, of Rappahannock Co., Carrie Lee, m. Arthur V. Greenway, of New York City, native of England; Florence Ethel, m. Rev. George W. Taylor, of Va. Conference, M. E. Church, South; Sidney Dunnington, d. 1910, unmarried; Nellie Cleveland, m. M. Daunis McBryde, of Louisiana, now resident of Richmond, Virginia; Berta Steptoe, as above; and Frederick Lewis, ex-Mayor of Charlottesville, m. Mary Waddell, of Charlottesville, (See, *History of Virginia*, pub. by American Historical Society, Vol. IV, pp. 49, and 283.)

* * * * * *

J. Houston Harrison and wife Berta, nee Watson, have issue—

1. ANNA LOUISE—b. Aug. 1, 1913.
2. PEARL ELIZABETH— b. Jan. 21, 1917.
3. JOHN HOUSTON, (JR.)—b. Sept. 30, 1918.
4. DAVID WARREN—b. Nov. 30, 1920.
5. DANIEL EDWARD—b. Mar. 27, 1923.
6. NANCY BYRD—b. Jan. 26, 1926.

(First four born at Charlottesville, Virginia, last two at Alexandria, Virginia.)

(1259153) RITA CATHERINE HARRISON the daughter of David W. Harrison (125915), and wife Anna A. (178452), nee Houston, married, at her father's home near New Market, Virginia, February 12, 1916, Thomas Moore, of Rockingham County, Virginia, son of Newton G. Moore (1234333), and wife Josephine, nee Henkel. See 1. Line of Thomas Moore, 2. Line of Capt. Reuben Moore, 3. Line of Reuben Moore, 4. Line of John Moore. (page 598.)

---

4. LINE OF GEORGE H. HARRISON

(1259172) REUBEN N. HARRISON (1883-1933), the son of George H.

Harrison, (125917), and wife Mary C. (1234382), nee Moore, was a widely known and much beloved invalid, for several years a patient in Rockingham Memorial Hospital, in Harrisonburg, Virginia. He had long been a cripple from the ravages of rheumatism, and was one of the bravest of the brave whose lot it was to be a shut in. As a youth, in his "prep. school" days, his promising career as a student was cut short by the first development of his relentless affliction, and for over twenty-seven years he was confined to his bed, on the flat of his back, without the use of his lower limbs, and with but to a very limited degree, the use of his arms. A few years before his death, he lost his eyesight, and the day before he died he underwent an operation to restore this; from which, due to his weakened condition, he failed to recover. All that medical science could do, all that the best of nursing, and all that a loving father's tender care could provide, was generously supplied throughout his illness. He had probably more medical attention, and hospital experience, than any one of his generation in Rockingham, and was for a year or more in the private hospital of, and a patient under, that master surgeon, Dr. Joseph Price, of Philadelphia. (1907.)

But let no one imagine that Reuben Harrison did not bear his lot cheerfully. One of the brightest of minds, a keen wit, and withal of a sunny philosophical disposition, he was always the life of any group of visitors to his room, and it was furtherest from his wish to entertain them with any description of his illness, or so much as make the mildest of complaints. He was reared at Moreland Hall, his father's home, and resided there until his father retired from farming. During this period of his confinement he read a great deal, and invented several interesting mechanisms for holding his papers and enabling him to use a typewriter, with which he carried on a considerable correspondence. It is thought that the constant use of his eyes in their unnatural position for reading led to their failing. Through his many friends, and his radio, he kept posted on the events of the day, in which he took a keen interest. He was a member of the Presbyterian Church, of Harrisonburg, and his life was an inspiration in its example of fortitude in the face of affliction. He died January 2, 1933.

(1259173) THOMAS MOORE HARRISON (1899), the son of George H. Harrison (125917), and wife, Josephine (1234377), nee Moore, married, June 8, 1922, Frances Elizabeth Moore, the daughter of Thomas Moore, and wife Elizabeth, nee Allebaugh, and the granddaughter of Reuben W. Moore (1234312), and wife Fannie, nee Chrisman.

Thomas Harrison is one of Rockingham's progressive young farmers, specializing largely in live stock. He was educated at Randolph Macon Academy, at Front Royal, Virginia. He and his wife reside at the late Thomas Moore homestead at Virginia Caverns, six miles north of Harrisonburg, on the Valley Pike, where she was born and reared, formerly the homestead of David Harrison (1259), and later of Madison Moore (123431.) (See pages 378, 499, and 589.) The land, as before stated, embraces the cavern grounds, and it was Mr. Harrison who recently leased the historic cave to Col. Brown, the owner of New Market Endless Caverns.

VIRGINIA CAVERNS

Tradition states that the cave was used by the Colonists in 1754, to hide from the Indian raiders. There is much evidence that the savages used it long before this. Kercheval mentions it, as "Harrison's Cave," in his *History of the Valley*, 1833, (page 378.) On its walls may be seen the names and dates of many of its early visitors, cut in the rock, or else "smoked" on the face thereof, by the aid of pine torches. The earliest date so far discovered is said to be 1793. In Century Hall, dates as far back as 1818 are found, one of the oldest of these having been placed there by William Harrison, son of David. The latter, in 1824, improved the entrance by carving therein a stairway out of the solid rock, affording easy access to visitors. During the War-between-the-States, many soldiers visited the cave, and left their names and dates as a memento of their visit, on its walls and columns. The greater number of these dates are of 1862 and 1864, when Fremont, and Sheridan, respectively, were in the Valley. An Ohio company on one occasion camped near the cave and left in it a considerable roster of names conspicuously displayed. The caverns today are beautifully illuminated by electricity, and owing to a newly opened entrance direct from the hillside facing the Pike, furnishing an easy ingress, on a gentle incline, all steps have been eliminated.

* * * * * *

Thomas M. Harrison, and wife, Frances, nee Moore, have an only daughter—

1. ELIZABETH JOSEPHINE—b. April 7, 1925.

---

4. LINE OF JOHN W. HARRISON

(1259183) FRANK HARRIS HARRISON (1892), the son of John W. Harrison (125918), and wife, Virginia, nee Rosenberger, married, October 23, 1913, Lennie Jane Zirkle, the daughter of Reuben Zirkle, of Rockingham, and wife Virginia, nee Allen.

Frank Harrison is a well known stockman and farmer, of near Tenth Legion, in Rockingham. He and his wife reside on his farm to the east of, and adjoining, his late father's land. For several years Frank, and Thomas Harrison, his cousin (above named), were somewhat associated in their live stock transactions, and are today among the leading buyers and shippers in the county.

Frank H. Harrison, and wife Lennie, nee Zirkle, are the parents of six children, viz—

1. VIRGINIA ALLEN—b. Aug. 6, 1914; m. Oct., 1932, STANLEY LOHR, (farmer) of Rockingham. Issue
    1. James Franklin—b. Feb. 5, 1934.
2. JESSE WALTON—b. Dec. 21, 1915.
3. FRANK HARRIS, (JR.)—b. Sept. 15, 1920.
4. JACOB LYNN—b. Sept. 26, 1922.
5. JULIAN ZIRKLE—b. July 19, 1924.
6. GEORGE WILLIAM—b. Mar. 25, 1929.

---

3. LINE OF NATHANIEL HARRISON

4. LINE OF REUBEN W. HARRISON

NECK

(1259212) FRANCES DIANA HARRISON (1852-1925), the daughter of Reuben W. Harrison (125921), and wife Hannah, nee Sellers, married, 1880, Edward Neck, a native of England. They resided in Palatka, Florida, where she died, April 1, 1925.

Edward Neck, and wife Diana, nee Harrison, had issue—

1. REUBEN E.—b. Sept. 27, 1880; m. 1st, Daisy Reynolds, (no issue.); m. 2nd, May Minton. Resides in Palatka, Florida. Issue—
    1. Reuben Edward, Jr.—
2. MABEL ELLEN—b. about 1883; m. George H. Henton, (1259914), son of John. Resides at Dayton, Va. (See page 525.)
3. MAUDE CONSTANCE—m. ——— Oliver.
4. ERNEST JAMES—m. Ray Tompkins, of Palatka, Florida.
    Issue—
    1. Leland—
    2. Maxine—

(D. S. H. papers.)

O'NEILL

(1259215), MARY ELIZABETH HARRISON (1858), the daughter of Reuben W. Harrison (125921), and wife Hannah, nee Sellers, married Thomas J. O'Neill. They reside in Memphis, Tennessee,, where he is the Superintendent of Schools of the city.

Thomas J. O'Neill and wife Mary Elizabeth, nee Harrison, have an only child—

1. DAVID HENRY HARRISON—m. Emily ————. Resides in Memphis, Tenn. (Issue —two sons.)

(1259216) WILLIAM L. YANCY HARRISON (1861-1934), the son of Reuben W. Harrison (125921), and wife Hannah, nee Sellers, married Virginia McLaughlin of near Richmond, Va. He resided in Highland Park, Illinois. Issue—

1. VIRGINIA MINOR—
2. JAMES WALTON—d. Sept. 25, 1918, unmarried.
3. WARREN ALAN—m. Josephine Inman.
    Issue—
    1. Virginia—
4. WILLIAM LEE—m., June 2, 1917, Norene Gannon. Resides in Highland Park, Ill. (Suburb of Chicago.) Issue—
    1. William Joseph—b. Nov. 18, 1918.
    2. Daniel Warren—b. Oct. 10, 1921.
    3. Norene Ann—b. Aug. 29, 1929.
5. HANNAH—m. LEE SPEILWRIGHT STOKER, of Highland Park, Illinois.
    Issue—
    1. Robert—
6. FRANCES—m. William Schultz.

(1259219), MICHAEL HOWARD HARRISON (1868), the son of Reuben W. Harrison (125921), and wife Hannah, nee Sellers, married, June 20, 1894, Emily W. Wood, daughter of Capt. John. I. Wood, and wife, of Rockingham.

Mr. Harrison is the present County Treasurer of Rockingham, having succeeded the late Senator Keezell, a short time before the latter's death. He and his wife reside at Island Ford, where he owns a valuable farm. Issue—

1. HANNAH ELIZABETH—b. Sept. 29, 1896; m. WILLIAM SIPE, of Island Ford, Issue—

1. William H.—
2. John—
3. Harry—
4. Emily—(twin of Harry.)

2. Michael H., (Jr.)—b. Nov. 22, 1902; m. Virginia Yancey, dau. of Tally Yancey, of Rockingham. With Rockingham National Bank of Harrisonburg. Issue—
   1. Elizabeth Ann—
   2. Virginia—
3. Russell M.—b. May 25, 1905; m. Lucile Richards, of Rockingham. Residence, Lacey Spring. Issue—
   1. Warren R.—
   2. Russell Dabney—b. Mar. 29, 1931.

(D. S. H. papers, etc.)

(1259222) JASPER NEWTON HARRISON (1872), the son of Reuben W. Harrison (125921), and wife Hannah, nee Sellers, married, June 6, 1894, Frances Burrows, (b. June 27, 1868) native of the Province of Ontario, Canada, daughter of George Burrows, and wife Maria Mc. Llwaine, from Scotland, and Ireland. They reside in Brunswick, Maryland. Issue—

1. Irene Winifred—b. Apr. 4, 1895; m. Oct. 2, 1914, WILLIAM LeROY BENJAMIN CARE, b. May 5, 1892, son of George Benjamin, and Ida LaVenia Care. Issue—
   1. George Benjamin Newton—b. Nov. 7, 1915.
   2. Frances Lavinia—b. Nov. 29, 1917.
   3. Margaret Marie—b. June 26, 1922.
2. Mabel Frances—b. Oct. 29, 1898.
3. Stanley Wood—b. Oct. 5, 1900.
4. Hannah Sellers—b. June 11, 1902.
5. Reuben Walton—b. May 6, 1904; m. Dec. 22, 1929, Margaret Jane Null, b. Apr. 9, 1910, dau. of James Calvin and Cora May Null, of Brunswick, Md. Issue—
   1. Wanda Jane—b. Aug. 28, 1930.
6. Paul Gordon—b. Feb. 28, 1906.
7. Mary Katherine—b. Aug. 24, 1909.
8. Margaret Pearl—b. Aug. 24, 1909, (twin of Mary Katherine.)
9. Nina Lee Elizabeth—b. June 24, 1911.

(First two born in Chicago, Ill., third in Harrisonburg, Va., remaining six in Brunswick, Md.)

(1259223) HENRY HIGH HARRISON (1874), the son of Reuben W. Harrison (125921), and wife Hannah, nee Sellers, married, first, Mannie Lee White, daughter of Charles White and wife, of near Lacey Spring, Rockingham County. She was born September 21, 1874, and died May 2, 1905

Mr. Harrison married as his second wife Miss Virginia Bane. They reside in Thomas, West Virginia.

Henry High Harrison's children are—

By wife Mannie, nee White,

1. Josephine Louise—m. John Columbus Justus, of Onancock, Va.

By wife Virginia, nee Bane,

2. Frederick Walton—
3. Henry High, (Jr.)—(Student at Shenandoah College.)
4. Virginia Vandiver—(Student of Marshall College, Huntington, W. Va.)

(D. S. H. papers—Dates of Mannie Lee Harrison from tombstone in Lacey Spring Cemetery.)

---

4. LINE OF JOCAB COWAN HARRISON

FLORENCE

(1259236) MAY STEVENS HARRISON (1866), the daughter of Jacob Cowan Harrison (125923), and wife Elizabeth, nee Hayne, married, February 5, 1890, William Cornelius Florence. They reside in Columbus, Ohio.

William C. Florence and wife May Stevens, nee Harrison, have issue—

1. John Rolph—b. Dec. 26, 1890; m. Grace ———. Residing in Columbus, Ohio.
2. Mary Harrison—b. Nov. 22, 1892; d. in infancy.
3. Robert Lee—b. May 23, 1894, (unmarried, 1928.)
4. Burnley Duke—b. Aug. 10, 1896; m. Mildred ———. Residing in Indianapolis, Indiana. (1928.)
5. Thomas Jackson—b. June 8, 1900.

FLETCHER

(1259237) ANNIE LAURIE HARRISON (1868), the daughter of Jacob Cowan Harrison (125923), and wife Elizabeth, nee Hayne, married, November 18, 1891, Robert Franklin Fletcher. They reside near Warrenton, Virginia, where he is engaged in farming.

Robert Franklin Fletcher, and wife Annie Laurie, nee Harrison, have issue—

1. Lillian Harrison—b. Nov. 1, 1892; m. June 5, 1915, Rev. ALBERT EDWARD DeMILLER, b. July 29, 1889, at Mobile, Ala., son of Walter Francis, and Julia Kieneke DeMiller. Reside at Biloxi, Miss. Issue—
    1. Edward Albert—b. May 6, 1916.
    2. Lillian Harrison—b. Apr. 20, 1924.
    3. Ann Catherine—b. Feb. 17, 1926.
2. Annie Laurie—b. Mar. 27, 1895; (unmarried.)
3. Franklin Cowan—b. July 30, 1905.

(1259241) ERNEST PAUL HARRISON (1883), the son of Jacob Cowan Harrison (125923),and wife Elizabeth, nee Hayne, married September 14, 1910, Betty Keith Swetnam, daughter of Charles Fleming and Jennie (Simpson) Swetnam, of Burke, Fairfax County, Virginia. Charles Fleming Swetnam was born in Stafford County, the son of John Alexander Swetnam, of Scotch descent, and wife, Elizabeth Keith Ford. His wife, Jennie Simpson, the daughter of William Henry Simpson, and wife, Annie Catherine Stone, was born near Fairfax Court House, in Fairfax County.

Ernest P. Harrison and wife reside in Falls Church, Virginia. Mr. Harrison is a reviewer and conferee in the income tax unit of the Internal Revenue Department, Washington, D. C. Issue—

1. Betty Keith—b. Sept. 14, 1911, at home, (grad. of Mary Baldwin College, 1934.)
2. Ann Franklin—b. Apr. 21, 1915. (Student at Mary Baldwin College.)

Dandridge Tenn.

3. LINE OF DANIEL HARRISON

4. LINE OF JOHN HARRISON

BLACKBURN

(1259415) IDA ADALINE HARRISON (1872), the daughter of John Harrison (125941), of near Dandridge, Jefferson County, Tennessee, and wife, Mary Emily, nee Rankin, married, August 10, 1892, William Blackburn, of Tennessee, now deceased. They resided near Dandridge.

William and Ida Harrison Blackburn had issue—

1. Thomas McSpadden—b. July 22, 1893; m. June 10, 1919, Casandria Moore Saffell, Issue—
   1. Thomas McSpadden, Jr.—b. June 25, 1920.
   2. Hugh Saffell—b. Aug. 16, 1922.
2. Hugh Harrison—b. Sept. 25, 1895; d. Nov. 9, 1915.
3. Hurley Wert—b. Nov. 1, 1897; m. Oct. 17, 1918, Lois Grace Viola Ellege Issue—
   1. Hillis Eloise—b. Apr. 25, 1920.
   2. Elda Augusta—b. Oct. 18, 1922.
   3. William Lester—b. July 1, 1925.
   4. Elizabeth Lois—b. Jan. 20, 1929.
4. William Ernest—b. Aug. 12, 1899; m. Mar. 28, 1928, Mary Lucile Douglass.
5. Benjamin Alvah—b. Sept. 4, 1901.
6. Odie Roy—b. July 3, 1903.
7. Mabel Ellen—b. Mar. 30, 1905.
8. Elbert Arthur—b. Feb. 22, 1907.
9. John Kenneth—b. Apr. 1, 1910.
10. Anna Louise—b. Mar. 26, 1912.
11. Harriet Grace—b. Oct. 30, 1915.

MOORE

(1259416) LYDIA OLIE HARRISON (1874), the daughter of John Harrison (125941), and wife Mary Emily, nee Rankin, married, October 6, 1904, Joseph Walker Moore, of Tennessee. They reside near Shady Grove, Tenn.

Joseph W. Moore, and wife, Lydia Olie, nee Harrison, have issue—

1. Mary Rebecca—b. July 31, 1905.
2. Troy Rozelle—b. Feb. 7, 1907.
3. Joseph Leonard—b. Mar. 17, 1911.

(1259419) MARION EMMETT HARRISON (1882), of Tennessee, the son of John Harrison (125941), and wife, Mary Emily, nee Rankin, married, December

20, 1920, Myrtle Holbert. They reside at the old homestead of his father on the French Broad River, near Dandridge, Tennessee. Issue—

1. Roger Wayne—b. June 19, 1922.
2. Jewel Dean—b. Dec. 19, 1928.

---

4. LINE OF GEORGE HINKLE

BLUNT

(1259432) JULIA M. HINKLE, (1861-1925), the daughter of George Hinkle, of Fort Collins, Colorado, and wife Mary, (125943), nee Harrison, married, November 9, 1881, Chester Blunt.

Chester and Julia Hinkle Blunt, had issue—

1. Carrie Edna—b. July 31, 1883; d. Mar. 15, 1924; m. Mar. 19, 1913, B. C. Rienks. (no issue).
2. Eunice—b. Sept. 15, 1884; m. July 7, 1920, A. W. Ward. (no issue.)
3. Lephe—b. June 18, 1887, (unmarried.)

(All but first named reside in Colorado.)

HARDING

(1259433) HANNAH ELIZABETH HINKLE (1863), the daughter of George Hinkle, and wife Mary (125943), nee Harrison, married, May 19, 1880, L. H. Harding, of Colorado.

L. H. Harding, and wife, Hannah Elizabeth, nee Harrison, have issue—

1. Ansel—b. Dec. 19, 1881; m. June 2, 1917, Blanche Courtright. Issue—
    1. Dorothy—b. Oct. 21, 1924.
2. Addie—b. Oct. 2, 1883; m. Sept. 24, 1904, ARTHUR SEAMANS. Issue—
    1. James L.—b. Aug. 5, 1905; m. Sept. 11, 1927, Elnora Bachelor. Issue—
        1. Ruth Adele—b. Dec. 21, 1928.
    2. Alice—b. Dec. 6, 1909, (unmarried.)
3. George A.—b. Mar. 20, 1888; m., Aug. 23, 1913, Prudence Blanche Landers, b. June 8, 1889. Resides in Van Nuys, California. Issue—
    1. Prudence Georgean—b. Mar. 2, 1926.
    2. Edward Lamotte—b. Oct. 7, 1927.
4. Charles Edward—b. Sept. 8, 1895; d. Nov. 12, 1923; m. June 1, 1920, Hazel Landers, b. July 11, 1895. Issue—
    1. Elizabeth Nadean—b. Feb. 21, 1922.
    2. Martha Jean—b. Apr. 7, 1924.

Nos. 3 and 4 connected with the Los Angeles City School administration.

CHISHOLM

(1259435) MARY W. HINKLE (1867-1923), the daughter of George Hinkle, and wife Mary (125943), nee Harrison, married, February 22, 1893, Alexander Chisholm.

Alexander and Mary Hinkle Chisholm had issue—

1. James Alexander—b. Dec. 31, 1893; m., Apr. 20, 1926, Maud Dedrick. (no issue.)
2. John William—b. Jan. 12, 1897; m. May 2, 1925, Winifred Agness Lyons. Issue—
    1. John William, Jr.—b. July 2, 1926.
    2. Mary Patricia—b. Dec. 17, 1927.

BLUNT

(1259436) EMMA RHODA HINKLE (1868), the daughter of George Hinkle, and wife Mary (125943), nee Harrison, married, October 26, 1892, Frank L. Blunt, the brother of Chester Blunt, who married her (Emma Rhoda's) sister.

Frank L. Blunt, and wife Emma Rhoda, nee Hinkle, had issue—

1. Nathan Franklin—b. Jan. 12, 1894; d. Feb. 5, 1924; m. Jan. 30, 1921, Verda Lackore. Issue—
    1. La Vern—b. Sept. 23, 1921.
2. Chester Henry—b. Mar. 22, 1904; d. Sept. 30, 1904.

HEIDELBERGER

(1259441) ELLA HINKLE (1877), the daughter of George Hinkle, and wife Mary (125943), nee Harrison, married, July 1, 1896, Frank Heidelberger.

Following his decease Mrs. Heidelberger married, second, December 15, 1920, Dr. P. S. Noe.

Frank, and Ella Hinkle Heidelberger, had issue—

1. Mary Pauline—b. Aug. 18, 1897; m. 1st. Mar. 1, 1920, ARCHIE NICHOL. Issue—
    1. Delora Alice—b. Dec. 6, 1920.
    2. Paul William—b. May 28, 1922.
    3. George Arthur—b. Mar. 6, 1924.

   m., 2nd, Oct. 20, 1928, Edward McVall.
2. Alice Willie Anne—b. July 23, 1903; m. Sept. 15, 1923, PAUL E. WELLS. Issue—
    1. Robert Eugene—b. 1924.
    2. William Richard—b. Jan. 7, 1926.

(No issue of Ella Hinkle by second marriage.)

---

4. LINE OF JOSEPH HARRISON

SOLOMON

(1259442) RHODA REBECCA HARRISON (1874), the daughter of Joseph Harrison (125944), of Jefferson County, Tennessee, and wife, Susan, nee Slaton, married, November 13, 1892, John Wesley Solomon of Tennessee.

John W. Solomon, and wife Rhoda Rebecca, nee Harrison have—

1. Artie May—b. Sept. 19, 1893; m. May 4, 1920, BRYAN MORIE . Issue—
    1. Wilma Beatrice—b. Jan. 20, 1921; d. Nov. 27, 1927.

Solomon Dandridge, Tenn

2. Ernest Floyd—b. Mar. 9, 1923.
3. Robert Earl—b. Sept. 14, 1925.
4. Dorothy Rebecca—b. Jan. 4, 1928.

2. Lester Floyd—b. Mar. 16, 1895; d. May 6, 1907, (accidently shot and killed by a playmate.)
3. Lettie Myrtle—b. Nov. 19, 1896; m. Apr. 23, 1922, RALPH QUARLES. Issue—
    1. Dorothy Elaine—b. Apr. 11, 1923; d. Feb. 18, 1824.
    2. Ralph Clemis—b. Apr. 29, 1925.
    3. Hal Benton—b. ——.
4. Lydia Bethel—b. Oct. 18, 1898; m. Oct. 18, 1919, ALLIE CATE. Issue—
    1. John William—b. Aug. 6, 1920.
    2. Leon—b. Apr. 30, 1922.
    3. Luella Maxine—b. Nov. 1, 1923.
    4. Royal Paxton—b. Aug. 3, 1925.
    5. Bernice—b. May 4, 1928.

BRYAN

(1259443) NANCY VIRGINIA HARRISON (1876), the daughter of Joseph Harrison (125944), and wife, Susan, nee Slaton, married, October 24, 1897, William Hurley Bryan, of Tennessee. He died December 15, 1915.

William H. Bryan, and wife Nancy Virginia, nee Harrison, had issue—

1. Emmett Oral—b. Nov. 1, 1898; m. 1st, Apr. 9, 1921, Ruby Cox. She d. Aug. 9, 1925. Issue—
    1. William Jackson—b. Jan. 29, 1922.
    2. Lena Maude—b. Oct. 27, 1923.
    3. Robert Elmer—b. July 23, 1925.

   m., 2nd, Nov. 26, 1927, Ella Kate Nottingham.
2. Lydia Ethel—b. Feb. 25, 1902; m. Aug. 10, 1919, ELMER COX. Issue—
    1. Clara Kathleen—b. Oct. 26, 1920.
3. Edna Omega—b. Dec. 8, 1908.
4. Nellie Josephine—b. Sept. 26, 1910.

(1259444) JOHN DAVID HARRISON (1877), of Tennessee, the son of Joseph Harrison (125944), and wife Susan, nee Slaton, married, February 14, 1903, Lillie May Moore. Issue—

1. Laura Susan—b. Dec. 18, 1903; m. Sept. 13, 1925, PRESTON PATTERSON. Issue—
    1. Jack Alton—b. June 16, 1926.
    2. Edith Mae—b. Oct. 14, 1928.
2. Jacob William—b. Sept. 13, 1905.
3. George Walker—b. Oct. 29, 1907; d. Dec. 26, 1907.

ALLEN

(1259445) LYDIA CATHERINE HARRISON (1879-1921), the daughter of Joseph Harrison (125944), and wife, Susan, nee Slaton, married, Aug. 22, 1906, William Allen, of Tennessee.

William Allen, and wife Lydia Catherine, nee Harrison, had issue—

1. MARY EUNICE—b. Mar. 22, 1908; m. May 23, 1925, ROBERT ELLIS.
   Issue—
   1. Phyliss Louise—b. Feb. 22, 1926.

(1259447) DANIEL HARRISON (1881), of Tennessee, the son of Joseph Harrison (125944), and wife, Susan, nee Slaton, married, Aug. 25, 1906, Ethel Cox. Issue—

1. AMES RUDOLPH—b. Mar. 28, 1909.
2. GEORGE THOMAS—b. Jan. 7, 1911.
3. JOSEPH TURNER—b. Oct. 7, 1913.
4. CLARCIA LUCILE—b. Mar. 14, 1915.
5. JOHN FRANKLIN—b. Oct. 24, 1917.
6. CORA LEE—b. Oct. 24, 1917. (twin of John Franklin.)
7. RUBY HELEN—b. Sept. 13, 1920.
8. MARGARET CLANDINE—b. Apr. 5, 1925.

MOORE

(1259449) HARRIETT HARRISON (1886), the daughter of Joseph Harrison (125944), and wife, Susan, nee Slaton, married, Aug. 24, 1902, John Robert Moore, of Tennessee.

John Robert and Harriett Harrison Moore had issue—

1. ESTHER HARRISON—b. June 19, 1903.
2. JAMES WALKER—b. Dec. 26, 1904.
3. HASSIE PAULINE—b. Dec. 13, 1907; m. Nov. 6, 1927, Paul Chambers,
4. MARY SUSAN—b. Feb. 17, 1909.
5. TOM WATSON—b. Feb. 25, 1911.
6. REBECCA ISADORA—b. Nov. 3, 1912.
7. JOHN HENRY—b. June 11, 1914.
8. ERSIE LUCILE—b. Aug. 30, 1916.
9. HARRY FOCH—b. Aug. 16, 1918.
10. ROBERT HARREL—b. Sept. 20, 1920.
11. LYDIA MAE—b. Sept. 29, 1922.
12. VIRGINIA MAUD—b. Sept. 14, 1924.
13. FRANK—b. July 29, 1926.

---

3 LINE OF REUBEN N. HARRISON.

4. LINE OF JOHN THOMAS HARRISON

McGUIRE

(1259611) CATHERINE HARRISON, (1875), the daughter of John Thomas

Harrison, (125961), of Hardin, Missouri, and wife Emma, nee White, married, September 7, 1898, James Berry McGuire of Missouri.

James B., and Catherine Harrison McGuire, have issue—

1. Lula Gladys—b. June 9, 1899; m. June 5, 1926, Henry A. Wurtzel.
2. Samuel Hubert—b. Aug. 28, 1900; m., Dec. 23, 1926, Hester E. Oxley.
   Issue—
   1. Samuel Hubert, Jr.—b. Dec. 11, 1928.
3. Mary Emily—b. Nov. 12, 1902; m., Oct. 8, 1921, EVERETT J. FOSTER.
   Issue—
   1. Everett J. Jr.—b. Dec. 17, 1922.
   2. James McGuire—b. Sept. 6, 1925.
   3. Gene Edward—b. Sept. 20, 1927.
   4. Edwin Wayne—b. Mar. 6, 1929.
4. Beulah Frances—b. Nov. 12, 1902; m., May 1, 1923, JAMES SWAFFORD.
   Issue—
   1. Robert Edward—b. Sept. 15, 1928.
5. Catherine Harrison—b. Nov. 20, 1914. (unmarried.)

(1259612) REUBEN N. HARRISON (1877), of Missouri, the son of John Thomas Harrison (125961), and wife, Emma, nee White, married, Sept. 18, 1901, Lillian T. Sinclair. She was born August 12, 1880 and died April 30, 1905. Ruben N. Harrison married, second, January 28, 1924, Zatella Faulkner.

Reuben N., and Lillian Sinclair Harrison, had issue—

1. Zelma Marguerite—b. Oct. 25, 1902; m. May 12, 1923, JETT D. Mc. CANN.
   Issue—
   1. Harrison Neal—
   2. Gerald Eugene—

Reuben N., and Zatella Faulkner Harrison, have issue—

2. Betty Josephine—
3. Bertha Catherine—

(1259615) DONALD THOMAS HARRISON (1888), of Colorado, the son of John Thomas Harrison (125961), and wife Emma, nee White, married, December 25, 1913, Mary Shackleford Frazier. Donald Thomas Harrison was named John Thomas Harrison at birth, but after he came of age had his name changed by law to Donald Thomas Harrison. Issue—

1. Thomas—b. Sept. 27, 1914.

---

4. LINE OF CHARLES D. HARRISON

LEIGH

(1259661) CATHARINE HARRISON (1892), the daughter of Charles D. Harrison (125966), of Harrisonburg, and wife Anna, nee Hank, married, June 28, 1922, Alfred Lawrence Leigh, son of Lewis Cass Leigh and wife, of Fairfax County, Virginia. They reside near Andrews Chapel in Fairfax, on the Leesburg Pike, where he is the owner of a modern dairy farm. Mrs. Leigh is a graduate of the State Teachers

College of Harrisonburg, and prior to her marriage was engaged for a time in teaching in Fairfax.

A. Lawrence and Catharine Harrison Leigh, have children—

1. CHARLES MARMADUKE—b. May 9, 1923.
2. JAMES MERCER—b. Dec. 27, 1925.
3. ANNA ELIZABETH—b. Feb. 16, 1927.
4. WENDELL HARRISON—b. Sept. 1, 1928.

IN CONCLUSION

With this, and the preceeding Chapter, the "See further record" references of this volume close. While many such references, no doubt, have been written in the past, of which this writer is unaware, today, in the active life of the busy living, ever new references are being entered by the descendants of Isaiah Harrison on the fresh pages of time. Sayeth the Scriptures: "A good name is rather to be chosen than great riches;" surely, by this standard, the English immigrant left his descendants a goodly heritage. His honored name, and qualities of birth, handed down through the generations, we may all be proud of, and will, we trust, be maintained—

"Until the stars grow old
And the earth grows cold
And the books of the Judgement Day unfold."

Ever an active family, up and doing, and a living force for progress in its chosen walks of life; the charm of its genealogy lies not only in tracing the connecting links with the numerous biographies of those who have made its history, but that we—like its pioneers of old, who by their struggles in "this lonesome wilderness part of the world," labored that we and others might the better live—may gather inspiration from our heritage, to ever press bravely on, facing our own difficulties; and lead like them the fuller life.

"We thought they slept, the men who kept
The names of noble sires,
And slumbered, while the darkness crept
Around their virgil fires!
But aye! the golden horse-shoe Knights
Their Old Dominion keep,
Whose foes have found enchanted ground
But not a Knight asleep."

—TICKNOR—*The Virginians of the Valley.*

THE END

Bibliography

1. HISTORICAL AND GENEALOGICAL

ENGLAND

ANDREWS, CHARLES M.: History of England, 1903.
BAKER, GEORGE: History and Antiquities of the County of Northampton. London, 1822.
BRIDGES, JOHN: History and Antiquities of Northampton. London, 1891. Vol. I.
BURKE JOHN: General Armory. London, 1851.
CALAMY, EDMUND: An Account of the Ejected Ministers. London, 1702. (2nd ed. 1718.) 2 vols.
THE CHETHAM SOCIETY: Remains Historical and Literary connected with the counties of Lancaster and Chester. Vol. 84.
CLAY, J. W.; editor: Dugdale's Visitation of Yorkshire, Vol. III, London, 1917.
DURHAM AND NORTHUMBERLAND PARISH REGISTER SOCIETY:
Registers of Berwick-upon-Tweed, Northumberland, Vol. I.
Registers of Bishop Middleham, County Durham.
DUGDALE, SIR WM.: The Baronage of England, London, 1675.
EARWAKER, J. E.: History of the Ancient Parish of Sandbach, (Chester.)
EARWAKER, J. E., ed.: Index to Wills and Inventories now preserved in the Court of Probate, Chester. The Record Society, Vols. 12, 14, 18, 20, and 51.
ENGLAND: State Papers of:
Calendar of State Papers, England, Domestic Series; 1653-4; 1660-61; 1664-5; 1671; 1672; 1690-91.
FOSTER, JOSEPH; ed: London Marriage Licenses, 1521-1869.
FOSTER, WM.: Durham Visitation Pedigrees, 1575; 1615, and 1666. London, 1887.
GLAZEBROOK, H. SYDNEY; ed.:
Visitation of Straffordshire, by Sir Henry St. George, 1616, and by Sir Wm. Dugdale, 1663-64. London, 1885.
HARLEIAN SOCIETY PUBLICATIONS:
Grantees of Arms to the end of the 17th Century. Joseph Foster, ed. by Harry Rylands. Vol. LXVI (Harleian Soc.) 1915.
Registers of St. Margaret's, Durham.
The Visitation of Essex. Ed. by Walter C. Metcalf, London, 1875. Harleian Society Vol. XIII.
Visitations of London: 1633-35; Harleian Society Vol. XV. London, 1880.
Middlesex Pedigrees: Harleian Soc. Vol. LXV, London, 1914.
Staffordshire Pedigrees, based on Visitation of Sir. Wm. Dugdale, 1663-4. Harleian Society Vol. 63, London, 1912.
The Visitation of Yorkshire, 1584-5; 1612. Ed. by Joseph Foster. Harleian Society Vol. London, 1875.
HELSBY, THOMAS: History of Chester. Vols. 1 and 2.
HUTCHINSON, WM.: History and Antiquities of County Palatine of Durham, Vols. I-III.
METCALF, WALTER C. ed: Visitations of Northamptonshire, 1564, 1618-19. London, 1887.
INDERWICK, F. A.: Side Lights on the Stuarts.
MURRAY'S Handbook of London. 1876.
PARISH REGISTER SOCIETY:
Marriages and Baptisms of the Parish of the Holy and Undivided Trinity, Chester.
Marriages and Baptisms. Records of the Cathedral, Chester.
NORTHAMPTON, city of: Records of the Borough of Northampton. Pub. by the city. Vol. II. 1898.
SHEHAN, J. J.: History of Kingston-upon-Hull. 1864.
SURTEES, ROBERT: History and Antiquities of the County Palatine of Durham. Vols. I-IV. London, 1816
SURTEES SOCIETY: The Visitation of York. Wm. Dugdale. Surtees Society Vol. XXXVI. London, 1859.
TICKHALL, REV. JOHN: History of Kingston-upon-Hull. 1796.
WINDLE, BERTRAM C. A.: Chester. A Historical and Topographical Account of the City. London, 1903.
THE YORKSHIRE ARCHAELOGICAL SOCIETY RECORD SERIES. Vol. LXIII. Yorkshire Deeds. Edited by Wm. Brown.
YORKE, JAMES: The Union of Honor, by James Yorke, Black-Smith, London, 1640.

SCOTLAND

STODDARD, ROBERT: Scottish Arms. 2 vols. Edinburg, 1881.

IRELAND

CHART, D. A.: The Story of Dublin. London, 1907.
CORPORATION OF DUBLIN: A Book of Dublin. Official Handbook, 1929.
THE DUBLIN PARISH REGISTER SOCIETY:
Parish Registers of Dublin. 12 volumes.
DEPUTY KEEPER OF PUBLIC RECORDS OF IRELAND:
13th Report of. Faints—Elizabeth.
16th Report of.
26th Report of. Index to the Act or Grant Books and to Originial Wills of the Diocese of Dublin to the year 1800.
FITZPATRICK, SAMUEL A. O.:
Dublin. A Historical and Topographical Account of the City, London, 1907.
SEYMOUR, REV. ST. JOHN D.:
Puritans in Ireland, 1647-1661. Oxford Historical and Literary Studies. Vol. XII.
URWICK, WM.: Early History of Trinity College, Dublin.
VICAR, SIR ARTHUR EDWARD: Index to Perogative Wills of Ireland.

NEW ENGLAND

NEW ENGLAND HISTORICAL AND GENEALOGICAL REGESTER. Annually from 1847. Vols. 2, 6, 12, 20, and 22.
SAMUEL SEWALL'S DIARY.

MASSACHUSETTS

BOSTON. Report of the Record Commissioners of the city of.
Document 46.
Volume 9. Births, Baptisms, Marriages, and Deaths, 1630-1699. 1883. Document 130.
Document 44. Book of Possessions.
Document 100. Early History of Boston.
Document 92. Tax Lists of Boston, 1674-1695.
MASS. Printed by the Legislature of—
Massachusetts Bay Colony Records. Vol. I.
BOSTON RECORDS: Suffolk County. Deeds. Libers XI, XII, and XIII.

MAINE

MAINE HISTORICAL SOCIETY: York County Deeds. Vol. I, 1642-1666. In set of 18 vols. 1887-1910.

CONNECTICUT

ATWATER, E. E.: History of the Colony of New Haven. 2 vols. 1881.
HINMAN, H. R.: Catalogue of the first Puritan settlers of the Colony of New Haven. 1846.
MEAD, S. P.: Ye Historie of Ye town of Greenwich. 1911.

RHODE ISLAND

ARNOLD, JAMES N.: Vital Records of Rhode Island, 1636-1850. Births, Marriages, and Deaths. 21 vols.

NEW YORK

BOLTON, ROBERT: History of Weschester County. 2 vols. 1910.
MORGAN, CHRISTOPHER: Documentary History of New York.
NEW YORK HISTORICAL SOCIETY:
Abstracts of Wills on file in the Surrogate's Office, City of New York. 1665-1800. 17 vols. 1892-1908.
NEW YORK GENEALOGICIAL AND BIOGRAPHICAL REGISTER: Annually from 1870. Vols. 4 and 42.

LONG ISLAND, NEW YORK

COX, JOHN, JR.: Annotated and Indexed by:
Oyster Bay Town Records. Vols. 1 and 2. (1653-1704), 1916, 1924. Pub. by the town.
EARDLEY, WM. A.: Flushing Friends Monthly Meeting. Marriage Intentions. (Typewritten copy, Library of Congress.)
FLINT, MARTHA BACKEE: Early History of Long Island. A Colonial Study.
FROST, JOSEPHINE C.; edited by:
Records of the Town of Jamaica, Long Island. Vols. I and II. Long Island Historical Society. 1915.

HEMPSTEAD: Records of North and South Hempstead, Vols. 1 to 8. Pub. by the town, 1896-1903.
HUNTINGTON: Huntington Town Records, including Babylon. Vols. 1 to 3, Pub. by the town, 1887-1889.
MANDEVILLE, REV. G. HENRY:
Flushing, Past and Present. 1860.
NEW YORK HISTORICAL SOCIETY. Vol. LIX, 1926:
Papers of the Lloyd Family of the Manor of Queens Village, Lloyd's Neck, Long Island, N. Y., 1654-1826. Vol. I. Ed. by Dorothy C. Barck.
PELLETREAU, WM. S.: Smithtown, Long Island. Records of the town of, with notes and introduction by Wm. S. Pelletreau. 1898.
PELLETREAU, WM. S.: Long Island Wills. Early Wills of Suffolk County, 1691-1703, with genealogical notes. 1897.
RIKER, JAMES: Annals of Newton. 1852.
SCUDDER, MOSES L.: printed for:
Records of the First Church of Huntington, Long Island, 1723-1779.
THOMPSON, BENJAMIN F.: History of Long Island. Vols. I-IV. 1918.
WOOD, SILAS: A Sketch of the First Settlement of the Several Towns on Long Island. 1824.

NEW JERSEY

DALLY, REV. JOSEPH W.: Woodbridge and Vicinity.
ELLIS, FRANKLIN: History of Monmouth County.
HATFIELD, REV. E. F.: History of Elizabeth, New Jersey. 1868.
JONES, W. A.: History of St. Peter's Church, Elizabeth, N. J.
MESSLER, REV. A.: Centennial History of Somerset County.
MILBURN, THOMAS: An Abstract or Abbreviation of some Few of the Many Testimonys from the Inhabitants of New Jersey. London, 1681.
MORRISTOWN, FIRST PRESBYTERIAN CHURCH OF:
History of the First Presbyterian Church of Morristown, N. J. The Combined Registers. Pub. by the church.
NELSON, WM. (editor): Calendar of New Jersey Wills, Vols. I-III. (Abstracts of wills) Documents Relating to the Colonial History of the State of New Jersey; in N. J. Archive series.
NEW JERSEY: Index of Wills, Inventories, etc. in the Office of the Secretary of State, prior to 1901. N. J. Archive series, 3 vols.
NEW JERSEY: Unrecorded Wills in the Office of Sec. of State, Trenton, N. J. New Jersey Archive series, vols. 9 to 10.
NEW JERSEY HISTORICAL SOCIETY, Collections of:
Proceedings Commemorative of the Settlement of Newark. Vol. II.
SNELL, JAMES P.: History of Essex and Hunterdon Counties. Vol. 1.
SNELL, JAMES P.: History of Hunterdon and Somerset Counties.
SOMERSET COUNTY HISTORICAL SOCIETY. Somerset Quarterly, Vol. 6.
WHITEHEAD, WM. A.; editor of;
Archives of the State of New Jersey, Vols. IV, XXI, and XXII. (Vol. IV. N. Y. Colonial Documents.)
WHITEHEAD, WM. A.: Contributions to the Early History of Perth Amboy and Adjoining Counties.
WHITTEMORE, HENRY: The Founders and Builders of the Oranges. Vols. I and II.
WOODWARD, E. M., AND JOHN F. HAGEMAN: History of Burlington and Mercer Counties.

PENNSYLVANIA

DAVIS, WM. W. H.: History of Bucks County. 1876.
ELY, WARREN. S.: The American Ararat. The South not the Ancestor of the West.
FACKENTHAL, B. F.: Bucks County Pennsylvania Historical Society, Vol. III, Old Pennypack Baptist Church, etc. A Collection of Papers read before the Bucks Co. Historical Society.
HISTORICAL SOCIETY OF MONTGOMERY COUNTY, PENNSYLVANIA:
Historical Sketches. Vol. I.
MYERS, A. C.: Immigration of the Irish Quakers into Pennsylvania. 1902.
PENNSYLVANIA ARCHIVES, Vol. IX
Records of Pa. Marriages prior to 1810 (in Pa. Archive series.)
PENNSYLVANIA HISTORICAL SOCIETY. Pennsylvania Magazine of History and Biography, Vol. 13.
RUPP, I. D.: Thirty Thousand Names of Foreign Emigrants in Pennsylvania (1727-1776). 1898.

DELAWARE

HITCHCOCK, F. H.: Calendar of Delaware Wills, 1682-1800. New Castle County. (pub. by Colonial Dames of America.) 1911.
TURNER, C. H. B.: Rodney's Diary and Other Deleware Records. 1911.
TURNER, C. H. B.: Some Records of Sussex County. 1909.
CONRAD, HENRY C.: History of Delaware, from the earliest settlements to the year 1907. 3 vols. 1908.

MARYLAND

BALDWIN, JANE: Maryland Calendar of Wills, Vols. 1-6, (1635-1732.) 1904-1920.
MARYLAND, ARCHIVES OF: Vols. I, III, and VIII. (Vols. 1-25, pub. 1883-1905.)
MARYLAND HISTORICAL SOCIETY: Maryland Historical Magazine, Vol. I.
NEILL, REV. EDWARD D.: The Founders of Maryland. 1876.

VIRGINIA

AMERICAN HISTORICAL SOCIETY: History of Virginia, ed. by Philip A. Bruce, and others. 6 vols.
BRUCE, PHILIP A: Institutional History of Virginia in the 17th Century, Vol. I, 1910.
BRUCE, PHILIP A.: Social Life in Virginia in the 17th Century. 1909.
BURGESS, LOUIS A.: Virginia Soldiers of 1776. Vol. I.
CAMPBELL, CHARLESS: History of Virginia. 1860.
CARR, MARIA G.: My Recollections of Rocktown, now known as Harrisonburg, from 1817-1820.
CARTMELL, T. K.: Shenandoah Valley Pioneers. 1909.
CHALKLEY, LYMAN: Extracts from the Records of Augusta County, 3 vols. 1912. Pub. by Mary S. Lockwood, Natl. Soc. D. A. R.
COOKE, JOHN ESTEN: Virginia. A History of the People.
CROZIER, WM. A.: Virginia Country Records. Colonial Militia. Vol. I, 1905.
DRAPER, LYMAN C.: Draper MSS. Collection in Wisconsin Historical Society. The Preston Papers, etc.
GREER, GEO. CABELL: Early Virginia Immigrants. 1912.
HENING, WALLER: The Statutes at Large of Virginia, Vols. 1-13, 1823. Samuel Shepherd's Continuation, 3 additional vols. Vols. 7, 9, 10, and 15.
HOTTEN, JOHN CAMDEN: Lists of Emigrants to Virginia. London, 1874.
JOHNSTON, D. E.: Middle River Settlements.
KERCHEVAL, SAMUEL: History of the Valley of Virginia. 3rd edition, 1902.
MC. ALLISTER, J. T.: Virginia Militia in the Revolutionary War. 1913.
MORTON, O. F.: History of Rockbridge County. 1920.
NEILL, EDWARD D.: The Virginia Carolorum.
NORRIS, J. E.: edited by; History of the Lower Shenandoah Valley. 1890
PEYTON, JOHN LEWIS: History of Augusta County. 1882.
PRESBYTERIAN CHURCH OF HARRISONBURG: Year Book of, 1928, pub. by the church.
SCHURICHT, HERRMANN: History of the German Element in Virginia.
SHENANDOAH PUBLISHING HOUSE, INC.
Virginia Highway Historical Markers. 1931.
SMITH, A. D., & Co.; edited by:
Southwest Virginia and the Valley. 1893.
STANARD, W. G.: Some Emigrants to Virginia.
STICKLER, HARRY M.: Massanutten. 1924.
STICKLER, HARRY M.: Rockingham County Marriages. 1928.
SUMMERS, LEWIS PRESTON: History of Southwest Virginia.
UNITED STATES: First Census of, 1790. Heads of Families. Virginia. 1908.
VIRGINIA HISTORICAL SOCIETY:
Virginia Magazine of History and Biography, Vols. 10, 12, 17, 32, 33, and 34.
VIRGINIA STATE COMMISSION OF CONSERVATION AND DEVELOPMENT.
Key to Inscriptions on Virginia Highway Markers. 3rd edition, 1932.
WADDELL, JOSEPH A. Annals of Augusta County, Virginia. 1902.
WAYLAND, JOHN W.: The Fairfax Line. Thomas Lewis' Journal, edited by John W. Wayland. 1925.
WAYLAND, JOHN W.: History of Rockingham County, Virginia. 1912.
WAYLAND, JOHN W.: History of Shenandoah County, Virginia. 1927.
WAYLAND, JOHN W.: Scenic and Historical Guide to the Shenandoah Valley. 1923.
WAYLAND, JOHN W.: Virginia Valley Records, 1930.
WOODS, REV. EDGAR: History of Albemarle County, Virginia. 1901.
LONG, C. M.: Virginia County Names.

WEST VIRGINIA

DANDRIDGE, DANSKE: Historic Shepherdstown. 1910.
MORTON, O. F.: History of Pendleton County. 1910.

KENTUCKY

COLLINS, R. H.: History of Kentucky.
WILSON, SAMUEL: Catalogue of Revolutionary Soldiers and Sailors of the Commonwealth of Virginia from Official Records in the Kentucky State Land Office. Year Book of Society of Sons of the Revolution in Kentucky, 1894- 1913. 1913.

NORTH CAROLINA

NORTH CAROLINA HISTORICAL AND GENEALOGICAL REGISTER.

ILLINOIS

POWER, JOHN C.: History of the Early Settlers of Sangamon County. 1876.
————————: History of Iroquois County.

INDIANA

COTTMAN, GEO. S.: The James F. D. Lanier Home. An Indiana Memorial. Pub. by the Dept. of Conservation of Ind. 1928.

MISSISSIPPI

ROWLAND, D.: The Official and Statistical Register of the State of Miss. 1917.

GENERAL

BANCROFT, GEORGE: History of the United States. Vol. VIII. 1876.
DOUGLAS, EDWARD M.: Boundaries, Areas, Geographical Centers and Altitudes, of the United States. Bulletin 689, U. S. Dept. of Interior, 1923.
DAUGHTERS OF THE AMERICAN REVOLUTION: Magazine. Vol. 61.
HEITMAN, B. F.: Historical Register of Officers of the Continental Army. 1893.
JOURNAL OF AMERICAN HISTORY. Vol. XII, No. 2.
LIBRARY OF SOUTHERN LITERATURE. 16 vols. 1909. Edward A. Alderman, Joel Chandler Harris, and Charles W. Kent, editors. (Vols. II, and XIV.)

BAPTIST

ASPLUND, JOHN: The annual Register of the Baptist Denomination in America, by John Asplund, a Swede. 1790.
BACKUS, ISAAC: History of New England, with particular Reference to the Denomination of Christians called Baptists. 3 vols. Boston, 1777. Printed by Edward Draper.
BENEDICT, DAVID: A General History of the Baptist Denomination in America. 2 vols. Boston, 1813.
HISTORICAL SOCIETY OF DELAWARE; published by:
Records of the Welsh Tract Baptist Meetings, 1701-1828. (Part II, Vol. IV.)
MOSLEY, ISAAC W.,: Henry Sator, 1690-1754. The recital of the life and character of an early adventurer to Virginia, and subsequently a settler of Maryland under Lord Baltimore. (Chestnut Ridge, Md. Baptist Church history.)
KETOCKTON BAPTIST ASSOCIATION OF VIRGINIA:
Minutes of the Ketockton Baptist Association held at Frying Pan, Loudoun County, Virginia, August 1797. 1797. (Library of Congress.)
SEMPLE', ROBERT: History of the Rise and Progress of the Baptists in Virginia. Richmond, 1810.
WRIGHTMAN, C. S.: History of the Baptist Church of Oyster Bay, Long Island.

METHODIST

ARMSTRONG, J. E.: History of the Old Baltimore Conference. 1907.
BANGS, N. AND T. MASON: pub. by:
Journal of Rev. Francis Asbury. (Vols. II and III.) 1821

2. GENEALOGICAL

AMERICAN ANCESTRY: Volume III.
ARMSTRONG, ZELLA: Notable Southern Families, Vol. IV, The Sevier Family.
BARTON, WM. E.: The Lineage of Lincoln. 1929.

BOOGHER, WM. F.: Gleanings of Virginia History. 1903.
BOOKSTOVER, J. E.: The Willet Genealogy.
BRYAN, WM. S., AND ROBERT ROSE: History of the Pioneer Families of Missouri.
BUNKER, MARY POWELL: Long Island Genealogies.
CHRISMAN, HERRING: Memiors of Lincoln. 1930.
CLEMENT, JOHN: Sketches of the First Emigrant Settlers in Newton Township, Old Gloucster County, West Jersey.
CORBIN, MRS. FRANCIS HARRISON: Five Generations of Connecticut Harrisons.
CORNELL, REV. JOHN: Genealogy of the Cornell Family. (N. Y.)
CRAVENS, JOHN W., AND OSCAR H.: Genealogy of the Craven and Barker Families. 1913.
DAUGHTERS OF THE AMERICAN REVOLUTION, National Society of:
Lineage Book, No. 65.
EWING, E. W. R.: Clan Ewing of Scotland.
EWING, PRESLEY KITTEREDGE, AND MARY ELLEN: The Ewing Genealogy.
GENEALOGICAL SOCIETY OF PENNSYLVANIA, Collections of:
Quaker Records, Salem, N. J., Monthly Meetings, Mens Minutes. Vol. IV. 1687-1740. (Pa. Historical Society Library.)
GREEN, RALEIGH TRAVERS: Genealogical & Historical Notes on Culpeper Co. Va., 1900.
HARRISON, ELLA W.: A Chapter of Hopkins Genealogy. 1905
HARRISON, FAIRFAX, edited by: Aris Sonis Focisque. The Harrisons of Skimino. 1910.
HARRISON, HENRY TAZEWELL: A Brief History of the First Harrisons of Virginia. 1915.
HARRISON, WM.: A Partial History of the Harrison Family.
HAYDEN, H. E.: Virginia Genealogies.
HOLLINGSWORTH, W. D.: Hollingsworth Genealogical Memoranda. 1884.
HOUSTON, FLORENCE WILSON: Maxwell History and Genealogy. 1916.
HOUSTON, REV. SAMUEL RUTHERFORD: The Houston Family. 1882. (Cinn.)
HOYT, DAVID, W.: Old Families of Salisbury and Amesbury (Mass.) 3 vols. 1897-1916.
KEITH, CHARLES P.: Ancestry of President Benjamin Harrison. 1893.
KEYSER, CHARLES E.: The Keyser Family.
LAWRENCE, JOHN: Genealogical Memoir of the family of John Lawrence. 1847.
LAWRENCE, THOMAS: Historical Genealogy of the Lawrence Family.
LEA. J. HENRY, AND J. R. HUTCHINSON: Ancestry of Abraham Lincoln. 1926.
LEARNED, MARION DEXTER: Abraham Lincoln. An American Migration.
LEE, F. B.: Genealogical and Personal Memoirs of Mercer Co., N. J. Vol. I. (Lewis Pub. Co.)
LEWIS, M. LISTON: Kind Words.
LEWIS PUB. CO.: Genealogical and Family History of the State of Conn. Vols. I-IV. Compiled under the supervision of Wm. R. Cutter. 1911
LEWIS PUB. CO.: Genealogical and Biographical Record of Preble Co., Ohio. Compendum of National Biography.
LINCOLN, WALDO: History of the Lincoln Family. 1923.
LYLE, MARIA CATHERINE: James Nourse and his Descendants. 1897.
MCCLURE, JAMES A.: The McClure Family. 1914.
MAUZY, RICHARD: Genealogical Record of the Descendants of Henry Mauzy. 1911.
MEADE, (Bishop): Old Churches Ministers and Families of Virginia. 2 vols., 1910. (Index by J. C. Wise, separate.)
MICKLE, ISAAC: Reminiscenses of Old Gloucester (N. J.). 1845.
NELSON, WM.: Biographical and Genealogical Notes from the Volumes of the New Jersey Archives. N. J. Historical Soc. Coll. Vol. IX. 1916.
PELLETREAU, WM. S.: Wills of the Smith Families of New York and Long Island.
PERRINE, HOWLAND DELANO: The Wright Family of Oyster Bay (L. I.) 1923.
POPE, C. H.: The Pioneers of Massachusetts. 1900.
SALEM, NEW JERSEY, HISTORICAL SOCIETY: Our early Settlers.
SAVAGE, JAMES: Genealogical Dictionary of the First Settlers of New England. 4 vols. 1860-1862. (Vol. II.)
SHARPE, RICHARD; Salem New Jersey Historical Society: Cravens Choyce.
SHOURDS, THOMAS: History and Genealogy of Fenwick's Colony (N. J.) 1876.
SMITH, ELEANOR JONES (Mrs.): Mementos of the Golden Wedding at Longwood. (L. I.)
SMYTH, S. GORDON: Bucks County Pioneers in the Valley of Virginia. Paper read at the Friends Meeting House, Wrightstown, Pa., 1923.
STAPLETON, REV. A.: Memorials of the Huguenots in America.
STEWART, J. ADGER: Descendants of Valentine Hollingsworth, Sr. 1925.

STRICKLER, HARRY M.: Forerunners.
TOWNSEND, W. A.: A Memorial of John, Henry, and Richard Townsend. (R. I. and N. Y.) 1865.
TYLER, LYON G.: Tyler's Quarterly Historical and Genealogical Magazine, Vol. IX.
VAN METER, BENJAMIN F.: Genealogies and sketches of the old families of Virginia and Kentucky. 1901.
WILLITS, A. C.: Ancestors and Descendants of James and Ann Willits, of Little Egg Harbor, New Jersey.
WOODRUFF, GEO. C.: Genealogical Register of the Inhabitants of the town of Litchfield, Conn. 1900.

ENGLISH

THE GENEALOGIST: edited by Geo. W. Marshall, New Series, Vol. XVIII, London, 1901.
HOWARD, J. J.: Miscellanea Genealogica et Heraldica, Val. II. London, 1882.
HARLEIAN SOCIETY: Le Neve's Pedigrees of the Knights. Harleian Soc. Vol. XIII.

3. BIOGRAPHICAL

ABBOTT, WILLIS: Carter Henry Harrison. A Memoir.
BEVERIDGE, ALBERT: Abraham Lincoln. 3 vols.
BIOGRAPHICAL DICTIONARY OF THE AMERICAN CONGRESSES, 1774-1927.
DICTIONARY OF AMERICAN MEDICAL BIOGRAPHY, by Drs. Howard A. Kelly and Walter L. Burrage.
BUTT, DR. A. P., in, Surgery Gynecology and Obstetrics, Vol. LV Dec. 1932.
JOHNSON, FREDERICK: Memorials of Old Virginia Clerks. 1888.
KENNEDY, DR. W., in American Journal of Obstetrics and Diseases of Women and Children. Vol. LXV, No. 1, 1912.
THE NATIONAL CYCLOPAEDIA OF AMERICAN BIOGRAPHY: Vols. XII, XXI, and Current Volume, 1926.
PSI UPSILON, THETA CHAPTER, Proceedings of a Meeting of, in Memory of Profs. Isaiah B. Price and James C. Bell. Schenectady, N. Y., Feb. 21, 1885.
TARBELL, IDA: The Life of Abraham Lincoln. Vol. I.
TAYLOR, JAMES B.: Lives of Virginia Baptist Ministers. 1837.
TYLER, LYON G.: Encyclopaedia of Virginia Biography. Vol. I, 1915.
UNIVERSITY OF VIRGINIA ANNUAL: Corks and Curls 1906.
WEEMS, MASON, (Parson): Life of Washington. (Reprint) 1927.
WHITTEMORE, THOMAS: Life of Hosea Ballou, 4 vols. 1854-1865
WHO'S WHO IN AMERICA: 1916-1917, 1928-1929.
WHO'S WHO IN THE SOUTH: 1927.

ENGLISH

BURTCHCALL AND SADLER: Alumini Dublinenses.
DALTON, SIR CORNELIUS NEAL: The Real Capt. Kidd. A Vindication. 1911.
DICTIONARY OF NATIONAL BIOGRAPHY: Vols. IX, XVII, XIX, and XXXIV.
FIRTH, CHARLES H.: Memoir of Major Gen. Thomas Harrison. Proceedings of the American Antiquarian Society, Vol. VIII.
SIMPKINSON, C. H.: Thomas Harrison, Regicide and Major General, London, 1905.

4. NEWSPAPERS

BALTIMORE SUN: March 3, 1848; Nov. 20, 1904; Jan. 24, 1907.
CHARLOTTESVILLE PROGRESS: April 8, 1820. July 6, 1928.
HEARST'S SUNDAY AMERICAN, Atlanta, Ga.: May 18, 1930.
MADISON, (Ind.) COURIER: Mar. 29, 1930.
PAGE VALLEY COURIER: Jan. 12, 1913.
TIMES DISPATCH: old file, New Albany, Ind.
VIRGINIA STANDARD, Richmond: Nos. 24 and 41.
TIMES DISPATCH, Richmond Virginia: Mar. 2, 1924.
ROCKINGHAM NEWS-RECORD: Feb. 21, 1921; Sept. 28, 1929; Jan. 23, 1933.
SHENANDOAH HERALD: April 8, 1822.
SHENANDOAH VALLEY: Feb. 15, 1923; Aug. 13, 1925; Mar. 10, 1932.
WASHINGTON POST: July 6, 1928.

Acknowledgments

In a study of this nature with the sources of genealogical material so widely scattered any lightening of the burden of research is most welcome. It is with a sense of deep gratitude therefore, that acknowledgement is here made to all who in any way have aided me in furnishing material.

I recall with pleasure the many happy contacts made, and the personal interviews and correspondence conducted over so many years with numerous kind assistants. Some, I am sorry to say, are no longer among the living, but my hope is that this book may help to preserve their memory, and in some small measure repay the others for their time and trouble. The task has been greater, and the scope has been extended beyond what was first contemplated. For each delay valuable new material tracing additional lines has been added, necessitating the postponement of publication.

Among the first to proffer his assistance in the task of quarrying out the line of descent from John Harrison, the early Augusta County pioneer, was the late Daniel Smith Harrison, of Harrisonburg. For several years prior to his death we worked together. At his decease he left in manuscript form a genealogical outline of many of the John Harrison lines, and some of the Capt. Daniel Harrison and Thomas Harrison lines, together with various notes on other lines as he had record of, and which he contemplated adding to his manuscript. These papers were kindly handed me by his brother, my cousin, after Mr. Harrison's death. The brother, too, is now deceased, but to both I owe a debt of gratitude for their generous assistance, and the use of this material. It almost wholly consists of names and dates, gathered at much pains, largely among Rockingham families. Probably no one in the county was as familiar with Harrison data on the records at Harrisonburg, and had conducted as wide a correspondence with enquirers from other States as Mr. Harrison. He was truly a final authority.

It was he who first called my attention to the existance of the old water bottle, and suggested that enquiry be made regarding it. For its history, I am much indebted to Miss Lucy Barbour Ewing, and to her sister , Mrs. David F. Ward, of Washington, D. C., from whom I also received kind assistance regarding Ewing lines.

For the loan of the valuable record book of the early Smiths and Linville's Creek Baptist Church, I am indebted to the late Mr. Charles H. Urner, of Richmond, Va., to my cousin, the late Reuben N. Harrison, of Harrisonburg, and to the late Mr. Amos Estep, of Cootes Store, Va. I am also indebted to Mr. Urner for early records of the New Market Baptist Church, and to Mr. Henry W. Scarborough, of Philadelphia, for material in regard to Silas Hart, one of the early Baptists of Rockingham, and senior member of the first court.

For much of the early Davison material I have to thank Mr. Arthur H. Davison, of Des Moines, Iowa, also my cousin, Mrs. Charles B. Wornom, of Dare, Va. To the latter I am indebted, too, for notes regarding the Walton, Newman, and Ott families, and to her and her sister, Miss Maria Moore, of Rockingham, for Moore and Henkel data. Valuable information in regard to the Price lines was generously furnished me by Mr. Henry T. Price, of West Chester, Pennsylvania.

To Miss Sarah Ellen Harrison, of Dandridge, Tenn., I am under obligation in regard to materials touching on the Tennesssee, Missouri, and Colorado descendants of Daniel Harrison, great-grandson of John, the pioneer, and in the realm of the Texas branch of the family, to Mr. Andrew Johnson Harrison, of Goldthwaite, and to Mrs.

Gilbert Newton Harrison, of Brownwood, Texas. For similar material regarding the descendants of Daniel's brother Nathaniel, my thanks are due Miss Ada L. Harrison, of Falls Church, Va.

Touching on the numerous western descendants of Capt. Daniel Harrison, Augusta County pioneer, I am indebted to Mrs. LaFayette Marks, deceased, of Springdale, Arkansas, for the loan of her collection of papers, including many pertinent abstracts of the records at Harrisonburg. Kind aid in regard to the early branches of this family was also received from the late Mrs. Minnie Lynn Williamson, of New Market, Va., and from Mrs. Amelia Van Meter Rogers, of Lexington, Ky.

Among the Cravens lines I have drawn heavily on the highly valuable collection of papers generously loaned me by Miss Drusilla Lanier Cravens, of Madison, Indiana, to whom I am much obligated for both Cravens and Harrison information. I desire also to express my appreciation to Mrs. George R. West, of Chattanooga, Tenn., and to Miss Daisy Rutherford Cravens, of Ft. Smith, Arkansas, for their kind aid in connection with the Tennessee, Missouri, and Arkansas branches of this family.

To Mr. William H. Chrisman, of Mapleton, Iowa, I am indebted for the use of his valuable papers in regard to the Herring, Hite, Chrisman, and Lincoln families. Mr. Chrisman recently published his father's *Memoirs of Lincoln,* in which are included some notes I was glad to supply, the basis for which may be found in this present volume.

I am indebted to the late Mr. J. F. Blackburn, Clerk of the Circuit of Rockingham, for his kind assistance in supplying many pertinent records.

For the many courtesies and generous aid in furnishing much general information in regard to tracing many past and present Valley families, I desire to express again my appreciation to my aunt, Miss Fannie Harrison, of Harrisonburg. Also in this connection I am much indebted to my cousin, Miss Emma E. Bryd, of Harrisonburg, both of whom have generously contributed of their time in assisting me in my quest for local material.

To the many others who have assisted me in my researches in connection with specific families, whose names are too numerous to include in this list, I wish to express my sincere thanks.

Index

"Index-learning turns no student pale,
Yet holds the eel of science by the tail."

—A—

—B—

—C—

—I—

—J—

—N—

—O—

—S—

—U—

—V—

—W—

—X—

—Y—

—Z—

CORRIGENDA

Page 4,	2nd paragraph, 1st line; Tom's Brook should read Thom's Brook.
Page 21,	the signer of the deed, John Whight, should read John Wright.
Page 37,	last paragraph, 2nd line; the first "of" should be ommitted.
Page 39,	last line of the verse should read, "And be a friend to man."
Page 69,	4th paragraph, 5th line; state should read states.
Page 80,	3rd paragraph, 3rd line; Fritz-Geffry should read Fitz-Geffrey.
Page 83,	2nd paragraph, 2nd and 3rd lines, Aukland should read Auckland.
Page 91,	1st paragraph, 2nd line; Benjamin II should read Benjamin III.
Page 91,	1st paragraph following the verse; 4th line; emmigration should read emigration.
Page 92,	4th paragraph, 8th line; count should read account.
Page 94,	3rd paragraph, 8th line; puishment should read punishment.
Page 99,	1st line; threating should read threatening.
Page 104,	2nd line; Raphe should read Rafe.
Page 126,	12th line from bottom; Pendelton should read Pendleton.
Page 131,	4th paragraph, 1st line; warrents should read warrants.
Page 172,	1st paragraph, 10th line; the Dispensation should read that Dispensation.
Page 174,	6th paragraph, 1st line; weaker should read weak.
Page 180,	3rd paragraph, 3rd line; propiretors should read proprietors.
Page 207,	13th line; Pendelton should read Pendleton.
Page 217,	last line; 1755 should read 1775.
Page 241,	last paragraph, 7th line, the word "the" before "North" should be omitted.
Page 249,	9th line from bottom; Dec. 22, 1790, should read Dec. 29, 1790.
Page 317,	2nd paragraph, 2nd line; before Michael should appear the word, likely.
Page 321,	5th line from bottom; if should read of.
Page 323,	17th line from bottom; 1788 should read 1778.
Page 389,	10th line from bottom; Alimo should read Alamo.
Page 411,	5th paragraph, 2nd line; 1749 should read 1794.
Page 441,	5th paragraph, 3rd line; Sept., 1805, should read Sept.7, 1805.
Page 445	2nd parapraph, 4th line; Rose should read Ross.
Page 455,	4th paragraph under "Line of David Harrison," 3rd line; north should read south.
Page 462,	2nd paragraph under Henton, 4th line (a duplicate) should be omitted.
Page 464,	2nd line from bottom; (12851) should read (125851).
Page 482,	3rd line from bottom; Sailsbury should read Salisbury.
Page 532,	2nd paragraph, 5th line; the first "the" should be omitted.
Page 535,	18th line; Leon C. Gilbert should read Leon G. Gilbert.
Page 536,	last line, Henson should read Hanson.
Page 540,	9th line from bottom; Jeannie should read Jennie.
Page 542,	23rd line; Shrewsberry should read Shrewsbury.
Page 549,	10th line from bottom; Jessie should read Jesse.
Page 572,	12th line; 1832 should read 1831.
Page 604,	5th line; the word Rockingham should be omitted.